Microsoft®
Exchange Server Training Kit

PUBLISHED BY
Microsoft Press
A Division of Microsoft Corporation
One Microsoft Way
Redmond, Washington 98052-6399

Library of Congress Cataloging-in-Publication Data
Unkroth, Kay.
    Microsoft Exchange Server Training Kit / Kay Unkroth.
        p.   cm.
    Includes index.
    ISBN 1-57231-709-4
    1. Electronic data processing personnel--Certification.
    2. Microsoft software--Examinations--Study guides.   3. Microsoft
Exchange server. I. Title.
    QA76.3.U55 1998
    005.7'13769--dc21   98-3872
                                                  CIP

Printed and bound in the United States of America.

2 3 4 5 6 7 8 9 WCWC   3 2 1 0 9 8

Distributed in Canada by ITP Nelson, a division of Thomson Canada Limited.

A CIP catalogue record for this book is available from the British Library.

Microsoft Press books are available through booksellers and distributors worldwide. For further information about international editions, contact your local Microsoft Corporation office or contact Microsoft Press International directly at fax (425) 936-7329. Visit our Web site at mspress.microsoft.com.

Macintosh and TrueType fonts are registered trademarks of Apple Computer, Inc. BackOffice, Microsoft, the Microsoft Internet Explorer logo, Microsoft Press, MS, MS-DOS, Visual Basic, Windows, and Windows NT are registered trademarks and MSN, Outlook, and Visual InterDev are trademarks of Microsoft Corporation. Other product and company names mentioned herein may be the trademarks of their respective owners.

Acquisitions Editor: David Clark
Program Manager: Jeff Madden
Project Editor: Wendy Zucker
Technical Editors: Helmut Krüger, Tim Upton, Nick Cavalancia
Manuscript Editors: Ina Chang, Wendy Zucker

Contents

Foreword

In the following pages you will find the work of many people, both Exchange experts and non-Exchange experts. It took us more than a year to produce Microsoft Exchange Server Training Kit because we wanted to provide a work that covers all the important aspects of Exchange Server 5.5. As the page count of this book makes clear, Exchange Server 5.5 is an extremely complex messaging system that has many features to offer.

The main purpose of this book is to help you prepare for the Exchange Server 5.5 MCP exam to become a Microsoft Certified Professional (MCP), but this book is also meant as a technical guide for daily business. In other words, this book will fulfill its purpose if you can read it with pleasure, if it helps you to pass the MCP exam successfully, and if it becomes your personal assistant in accomplishing design and administration tasks and in solving messaging-related issues in your company.

One foundation for this book is the Microsoft Official Curriculum (MOC) training material for Exchange Server, and therefore I want to thank the entire MOC team before anybody else. The great work of this team influenced the organization and content of this book.

I want to thank my technical editors: Helmut Krüger, Tim Upton, and Nick Cavalancia. They worked very hard to correct all my technical mistakes and misinterpretations. I gladly share the success of this work with them. Should you still find any mistakes on the following pages, these are mine only.

Helmut worked with me from the very beginning, while Tim and Nick came to our team later as additional resources. Especially at the beginning, Helmut worked hard with me on the text and his feedback caused me to constantly rewrite each chapter until we finally reached an acceptable standard. (Helmi, I never told you before, that often I could hardly stand to read your rigorous feedback.) We worked together in the same Microsoft Support team for many years until I left in 1996 to become an independent system consultant, trainer, and author. Back in 1992 Helmut was my mentor, helping me learn the depths of Windows 3.1 when I began my career as a support engineer. One year later we both switched over to supporting messaging networks of small and large Microsoft customers in Central Europe; at that time the product was MS Mail 3.0. When Exchange Server 4.0 went beta, we began supporting this new messaging platform. Today, Helmi troubleshoots small environments as well as networks containing up to tens of thousands workstations, which is a self-explanatory certification of his technical skills.

Tim and Nick are also experienced networking experts who have specialized in local area networks and wide area networks since the late 1980s. Both feel at home in very large computer networks. Nick is a certified networking engineer for Microsoft and for Novell NetWare environments. He has worked with messaging systems for more then five years and with Exchange Server since it became available in its first beta version. Tim's experience in messaging solutions, dates back to an age when Microsoft Mail was still called Network Courier and was owned by a Canadian company in Vancouver. He came into contact with Exchange Server early on, when version 4.0 was still not even a beta. Tim and Nick are experienced technical trainers and I'm sure there is not one version of an Exchange Server MOC training that they haven't taught.

Surrounded by so much technical know-how, you would think I could have slept soundly. But apart from ensuring technical correctness, I wanted to be especially sure that the practical exercises of this book are easy to understand. My good friend, Claus Herbert, and my 16-year old stepson, Scott Kincaid, helped me in this endeavor. Claus worked carefully through the exercises, while Scott checked them one more time, updated them, and then produced all the screenshots you see in this book. In order to accomplish their tasks they had to click through every step. My hidden "test" was to see whether they could accomplish this task without further assistance and they did so with excellence. Yes, it's true: almost my entire family participated in the preparation this book. My wife Jean read through all the chapters to correct my language wherever it was difficult to understand. She actually doesn't like computers at all and she is far from becoming an Exchange administrator, so she must love me very much to put up with all this technical stuff. Thank you, my wonderful Lady Buggy.

The member list of our team is not yet complete because my wife was not the only person who worked on the language. Of course, a professional book requires professional copy editing and I don't want to miss the chance to thank Wendy Zucker and her editing team, because they worked extremely hard to bring everything into the shape that you, the reader, have every right to expect.

I don't want to forget the production team that certainly worked hard and with precision to get everything, especially the figures, done the way we wanted it.

There are two names left to mention. Without them, this entire project would not have come to fruition. Thomas Pohlmann promoted me at Microsoft Press in Germany and David Clark is the person who listened to him. Both gave me the chance to write this book and I can only hope that I met their expectations.

And this leads me to the last part of this foreword where I want to thank you, dear reader, for your interest in Exchange Server 5.5 and for holding this book in your hands—because without you, this book would be meaningless.

About This Book

Welcome to Microsoft Exchange Server 5.5 Training. This book explains in detail how to implement Exchange Server 5.5 successfully in your enterprise. Exchange Server 5.5 contains new features and provides better performance than Exchange Server 5.0, but the features of the previous version are still available. This book provides you with self-study material to prepare for the following exams of the Microsoft Certified Professional Program:

- Exam 70-076, *Implementing and Supporting Microsoft Exchange Server 5.0*

- Exam 70-081, *Implementing and Supporting Microsoft Exchange Server 5.5*

Note For more information on becoming a Microsoft Certified Systems Engineer, see the section titled "The Microsoft Certified Professional Program," later in this chapter.

Each chapter in this book is divided into lessons. Most lessons include hands-on procedures that allow you to practice or demonstrate a particular concept or skill. Each chapter ends with a short summary of all chapter lessons in the form of review questions to test your knowledge of the chapter material.

The "Getting Started" section of this chapter provides important setup instructions that describe the hardware and software requirements in order to complete the procedures in this course. The section also provides information about the networking configuration necessary to complete some of the hands-on procedures. Read through this section thoroughly before you start the lessons.

Intended Audience

This book was developed for information system (IS) professionals who need to design, plan, implement, and support Microsoft Exchange Server 5.5 or who plan to take the related Microsoft Certified Professional program exams 70-076 or 70-081. Prerequisites include:

- A solid understanding of networking concepts, principles, and practices, such as those presented in Microsoft's Networking Essentials Self-Paced Training

- Working knowledge of the Microsoft Windows 95 interface or the Windows NT Server 4.0 interface

- Successful completion of either of the following courses:

    Supporting Microsoft Windows NT Server version 4.0

    Supporting Microsoft Windows NT Core Technologies

Reference Materials

You might find the following reference materials useful:

- Microsoft Exchange in Business

- Microsoft Exchange Connectivity Guide

- Microsoft BackOffice Resource Kit: Part One; Microsoft Exchange Server Resource Guide

- Microsoft BackOffice Resource Kit: Part Two; Microsoft Exchange Server Resource Guide, Supplement One

- Microsoft Exchange Server 5.5 Product Documentation

About The CD-ROMs

The Supplemental Course Material compact discs contain a variety of informational aids that may be used with this book. These aids might include multimedia presentations, sample data, demonstrations, and files used in hands-on exercises.

The multimedia presentations supplement some of the key concepts covered in the book. You should view these presentations when suggested, and then use them as a review tool while you work through the material. A complete version of this book is also available on line with a variety of viewing options.

For information about using the online book, see the section, "About the Online Book," later in this introduction.

The Supplemental Course Material compact disc also contains files required to perform the hands-on procedures, and information designed to supplement the lesson material. These files can be used directly from the CD-ROM or can be copied onto your hard disk by using the Setup program. The files may include demonstrations of key concepts, practice files for the exercises, and additional articles about related concepts.

Many of the demonstrations and supplemental articles require an HTML browser. If Microsoft Internet Explorer is installed on your system (as described in the "Getting Started" section), simply double-click on any of these files to view them. The remaining demonstrations are stored as AVI files. If your machine has standard multimedia support, you can view these demonstrations by double-clicking on them.

Features of This Book

Each chapter opens with an "Overview" section, which describes the key issues that will be elaborated upon. Each lesson also provide its own short overview, which specifically outlines the covered topics. Whenever possible, lessons contain practical exercises that give you an opportunity to use the skills being presented or explore the part of the application being described. All procedures are identified with a bullet symbol.

The "Review" section at the end of each chapter allows you to test what you have learned in the lesson.

The "Questions and Answers" section contains all of the book's review questions and corresponding answers.

Notes

Notes appear throughout the lessons.

- Notes marked **Important** contain information that is essential to completing a task.
- Notes marked **Note** contain supplemental information.
- Notes marked **Caution** contain warnings about possible loss of data.

Conventions

- Hands-on exercises that you are to follow are presented in numbered lists of steps (1, 2, and so on).

- The words *select* or *highlight* are used for highlighting folders, file names, text boxes, menu bars, and option buttons, and for selecting options in a dialog box.

- The word *click* is used for carrying out a command from a menu or dialog box.

Notational Conventions

- Characters or commands that you type appear in *italic* type.

- *Italic* in syntax statements indicates placeholders for variable information. *Italic* is used to introduce new terminology. *Italic* is also used for book titles.

- Names of files and folders appear in *italic*. Unless otherwise indicated, you can use all lowercase letters when you type a file name in a dialog box or at a command prompt.

- Names of folders appear in *italic* and initial caps. Unless otherwise indicated, you can use all lowercase letters when you type a folder name in a dialog box or at a command prompt.

- Dialog boxes, containers, menu items, buttons, and other elements appear in **bold**, except when you are to type them directly.

- Acronyms appear in all UPPERCASE.

- Monospace type represents code samples, examples of screen text, or entries that you might type at a command prompt or in initialization files.

- Square brackets [ ] are used in syntax statements to enclose optional items. For example, [*filename*] in command syntax indicates that you can choose to type a file name with the command. Type only the information within the brackets, not the brackets themselves.

Keyboard Conventions

- A plus sign (+) between two key names means that you must press those keys at the same time. For example, "Press ALT+TAB" means that you hold down ALT while you press TAB.

- You can choose menu commands with the keyboard. Press the Alt key to activate the menu bar, and then sequentially press the keys that correspond to the highlighted or underlined letter of the menu name and the command name. For some commands, you can also press a key combination listed in the menu.

- You can select or clear check boxes or option buttons in dialog boxes with the keyboard. Press the Alt key, and then press the key that corresponds to the underlined letter of the option name. Or you can press Tab until the option is highlighted, and then press the spacebar to select or clear the check box or option button.

- You can cancel the display of a dialog box by pressing the Esc key.

Chapter and Appendix Overview

This self-paced training course combines notes, hands-on procedures, multimedia presentations, and review questions to teach you how to implement and support Microsoft Exchange Server 5.5. This training course is designed to be completed from beginning to end, but you can choose a customized track and complete only the sections that interest you. (See the next section, "Finding the Best Starting Point for You," for more information.) If you choose the customized track option, see the "Overview" section in each chapter. Any hands-on procedures that require preliminary work from preceding chapters refer to the appropriate chapters.

The book is divided into the following chapters:

- The "About This Book" section contains a self-paced training overview and introduces the components of this training. Read this section thoroughly to get the most educational value from this self-paced training and to plan which lessons you will complete.

- Chapter 1, "Introduction to Microsoft Exchange," explores the basic features and characteristics of Exchange Server 5.5. This chapter emphasizes the client/server–based communication model and compares it to previous messaging systems that relied on shared-file and directory structures. You can also read about the Exchange Server architecture and the elementary features that make the Exchange messaging system a leader in the industry.

- Chapter 2, "Installing Microsoft Exchange Server," covers the available methods for the installation of Exchange Server 5.5 and its optimization. You can learn how to create new sites, join existing sites with an additional server, and upgrade existing servers to Exchange Server 5.5.

- Chapter 3, "Microsoft Exchange Server Architecture," discusses the architecture of Exchange Server 5.5, emphasizing its core components and its optional components. You can also read about the communication paths among the various core components that are required in order to accomplish the essential tasks of a messaging system.

- Chapter 4, "Communication in an Exchange Server Environment," explains the server-to-server communication specifically within sites, which is also known as *intrasite communication*. This chapter explains the various types of data that are transferred between servers. You can also read about the active server components that generate, transfer, and receive these data types.

- Chapter 5, "Creating and Managing Recipients," introduces the management of recipient objects as they are supported in an Exchange Server organization, and discusses the possible recipient objects that can be used to address e-mail messages. You can learn about the purpose and configuration of mailboxes, custom recipients, distribution lists, and public folder objects.

- Chapter 6, "Microsoft Exchange Client Architecture and Installation," introduces the program family of the Microsoft Exchange Client and the Microsoft Outlook applications. Both client systems exploit the powerful features of Exchange Server in a similar way, so they are discussed together. This chapter also covers the features of the MAPI subsystem, which is the foundation for both client systems.

- Chapter 7, "Configuring the Microsoft Exchange Client," leads you through the creation and configuration of messaging profiles as well as the configuration of messaging-related options of the Exchange Client and Outlook. This chapter also explains the default MAPI information services that come with the products.

- Chapter 8, "Managing Server Configuration," deals with the standard Windows NT utilities and the Exchange Administrator program, which are the tools you use to control the Exchange Server organization. This chapter features the most important configuration objects of the Exchange Administrator program and the various management levels of an Exchange Server organization.

- Chapter 9, "Introduction to Intersite Connectors," thoroughly explains the installation and configuration of the messaging connectors that are powerful enough to bind sites together directly. You can read about message routing and the purpose of the Gateway Address Routing Table (GWART), and you can read about the directory replication connector, which allows you to replicate site configuration information across the organization.

- Chapter 10, "Internet Mail Service," deals with connecting an organization to the Internet using the Internet Mail Service (IMS). Following a discussion of SMTP (Simple Mail Transfer Protocol) and other relevant Internet standards is a detailed explanation of the architecture, installation, and configuration of the IMS. For example, you can read about a method of "hacking" the IMS, which allows you to examine its message queues.

- Chapter 11, "Internet Protocols," explains Exchange Server support for the Post Office Protocol version 3 (POP3), Internet Message Access Protocol version 4 (IMAP4), Lightweight Directory Access Protocol (LDAP), Network News Transport Protocol (NNTP), and the Hypertext Transfer Protocol (HTTP). These protocols are implemented in Exchange Server 5.5 as a response to the growing demand for Internet connectivity.

- Chapter 12, "Creating and Managing Public Folders," examines the management of public folders as they reside on single Exchange Server computers. You can read how to manage public folders at the site level and the server level as well as about how to provide access to individual public folders across site boundaries. This chapter also discusses public folder strategies and the advantages and disadvantages of single and multiple public folder instances.

- Chapter 13, "Public Folder Replication," continues the discussion about public folders by introducing various public folder replication scenarios. This chapter deals with the actual folder replication process and explains the replication model, transport mechanism, and the purpose of the Public Folder Replication Agent (PFRA). You can also read about solutions for public folder rehoming conflicts in Exchange Server 5.5.

- Chapter 14, "Implementing Advanced Security," explains the technology and methods of message encryption as they are integrated in Exchange Server 5.5. After reading a brief overview of Advanced Security, you can read about the architecture of the Key Management Server, its components, their interaction, and their administration in single sites and multiple site organizations. This chapter also covers the two stages of enabling Advanced Security and the processes of message signing and message sealing.

- Chapter 15, "Maintaining Servers," discusses the most important server maintenance issues. The emphasis of this chapter is the maintenance of Exchange Server databases, including available backup strategies and corresponding restore operations. Also introduced are various important maintenance utilities, such as the Message Tracking Center.

- Chapter 16, "The Exchange Server Forms Environment," deals with the development, installation, and use of electronic forms and workgroup applications as they are supported within Exchange Server. You can learn how to use both the Electronic Forms Designer and the Outlook Forms Designer, and you can learn how to maintain electronic forms libraries in your organization. Valuable sample applications show you what can be done based on electronic forms.

- Chapter 17, "Exchange Clients in a NetWare Environment," outlines the integration of Exchange Server 5.5 into Novell NetWare networks. As you will read, native Novell NetWare workstations can access Exchange Server resources without the need for reconfiguring the existing network. This chapter also briefly discusses the components that can simplify the Windows NT Server–Novell NetWare integration.

- Chapter 18, "Connecting to Microsoft Mail and Schedule+," emphasizes the Microsoft Mail Connector, Directory Synchronization with MS Mail, and the Microsoft Schedule+ Free/Busy Connector. You can read about the architecture of these components as well as how to use them to seamlessly integrate MS Mail environments with Exchange Server organizations.

- Chapter 19, "Connector for Lotus cc:Mail," introduces you to the connecting component of Exchange Server to Lotus cc:Mail. This chapter provides an overview about the Connector for Lotus cc:Mail architecture, its components, its administration, and Windows NT Registry Keys. You will also learn about issues regarding critical configuration aspects.

- Chapter 20, "Connector for Lotus Notes," explains how to connect Exchange Server 5.5 to Lotus Notes networks. You can read about the features and characteristics of the Connector for Lotus Notes and about its architecture. This chapter also discusses in detail how connector components interact with each other to transfer messages and synchronize directory information and how you can test the connection behavior after installation and configuration.

- Appendix A, "Questions and Answers," lists all the review questions from the book. Each question shows the page number where the question appears and provides the best answer.

Finding the Best Starting Point for You

Because this book is self-paced, you can skip some lessons and revisit them later. But note that you must complete the procedures in Chapter 2, "Installing Microsoft Exchange Server," before you can perform procedures in the other chapters. Use the following table to find the best starting point for you.

If you	Follow this learning path
Are preparing to take the Microsoft Certified Professional exam 70-076, "Implementing and Supporting Microsoft Exchange Server 5.0" or Microsoft Certified Professional exam 70-081, "Implementing and Supporting Microsoft Exchange Server 5.5"	Read the "Getting Started" section. Work through Chapters 1 through 10, and then work through the remaining chapters in any order.
Are specifically interested in the installation and configuration of the Microsoft Exchange Client 5.0 or Microsoft Outlook 8.03	Read Chapter 1 and then read Chapters 6 and 7.
Want to learn about the administration of Microsoft Exchange Server in single-site environments	Read Chapters 1 through 5 and Chapter 7.
Want to learn about the configuration of multiple sites	Read Chapters 1–5 and then Chapters 9 and 10.
Want to find information about the support of Internet protocols	Read Chapters 10 and 11.
Are searching for information regarding public folder administration, including public folder replication across multiple sites and support of electronic forms	Read Chapters 1–5, Chapters 9 and 10, and then work through Chapters 12 and 13; for information about electronic forms, read Chapter 16.
Considering the implementation of Advanced Security features in your Exchange Server organization	Read Chapter 14.
Are looking for tips on how to maintain an Exchange Server	Read Chapters 1–5, Chapter 8, and then Chapter 15.
Interested in learning how to connect Exchange Server 5.5 to foreign messaging systems	Read Chapters 1–4, Chapters 9 and 10, and then Chapters 18–20.
Want to review information about specific topics from the exam	Use the "Where to Find Specific Skills in This Book" section that follows this table.

Where to Find Specific Skills in This Book

The following tables provide a list of the skills measured on certification exam 70-081, *Implementing and Supporting Microsoft® Exchange Server 5.5.* The tables lists the skill and where in this book you will find the lesson relating to that skill.

Note Exam skills are subject to change without prior notice and at the sole discretion of Microsoft.

Skill Being Measured	Location in Book
Planning	
Choose an implementation strategy for Exchange Server	Chapters 9 and 12
Develop the configuration of an Exchange Server computer	Chapters 1–4
Identify strategies for migration from previous versions of Exchange Server to Exchange Server 5.5	Chapter 2
Develop a long-term coexistence strategy based on IMAP4 and LDAP	Chapter 11
Develop an infrastructure for Exchange Server	Chapters 1–4 and 8–16
Choose installation and integration strategies for Exchange Server client applications	Chapters 6, 7, 16, and 18
Develop long-term administration strategies	Chapter 15
Develop security strategies	Chapter 14
Develop server-side scripting strategies	Chapter 16
Installation and Configuration	
Install an Exchange Server computer	Chapter 2
Configure Exchange Server for message recipients	Chapter 5
Configure connectivity to a mail system other than Exchange Server	Chapters 9 and 18–20
Configure synchronization of directory information between Exchange Server and other mail systems	Chapters 18–20
Configure directory replication	Chapters 9 and 10
Install and configure Exchange Server client computers	Chapters 6, 7, and 17
Import directory, message, and scheduling data from existing mail systems	Chapter 7

Skill Being Measured	Location in Book
Installation and Configuration	
Configure address lists and accounts by using the Administrator program	Chapter 5
Configure the MTA within a site	Chapter 8
Configure the MTA among sites	Chapter 9
Configure Internet protocols and services	Chapters 10 and 11
Configure message tracking	Chapter 15
Configure server locations	Chapter 12
Configure Advanced Security	Chapter 14
Configuring and Managing Resource Access	
Manage site security	Chapters 2–5 and 7
Manage users	Chapter 5
Manage distribution lists	Chapter 5
Manage the directory	Chapters 2–5, 8, and 9
Manage public IS databases	Chapters 12, 13, and 15
Manage private IS databases	Chapter 15
Back up and restore the Exchange Server organization	Chapter 15
Manage connectivity	Chapters 9–11 and 18–20
Monitoring and Optimization	
Configure a Link Monitor and a Server Monitor	Chapter 15
Optimize Exchange Server	Chapter 2
Optimize foreign connections and site-to-site connections	Chapters 9, 10, and 18–20
Monitor and optimize the messaging environment	Chapter 15
Monitor server performance by using SNMP and MADMAN MIB	Chapter 15

continues

continued

Skill Being Measured	Location in Book
Troubleshooting	
Diagnose and resolve upgrade problems	Chapters 2 and 15
Diagnose and resolve server installation problems	Chapters 2 and 15
Diagnose and resolve migration problems	Chapters 2, 7, 15, and 18–20
Diagnose and resolve connectivity problems	Chapters 9, 10, and 18–20
Diagnose and resolve problems with client application connectivity	Chapters 6, 7, and 15
Diagnose and resolve IS problems	Chapters 3, 5, 8, 12, 13, and 15
Diagnose and resolve server directory problems	Chapters 3, 4, 8, 9, and 15
Diagnose and resolve server resource problems	Chapters 2, 8, and 15
Diagnose and resolve message delivery problems	Chapters 3, 4, 8, 9, and 15
Diagnose and resolve backup problems and restore problems	Chapter 15
Diagnose organization security problems	Chapter 14

The following tables provide a list of the skills measured on certification exam 70-076, *Implementing and Supporting Microsoft® Exchange Server 5.0.*

Skill Being Measured	Location in Book
Planning	
Plan the implementation of Exchange Server 5.5	Chapters 1 and 2
Plan the configuration of an Exchange Server computer	Chapters 2, 3, 4, 8
Plan migration to Exchange	Chapters 2, 18, and 19
Plan a long-term coexistence strategy	Chapters 9, 10, 11, 18, and 19
Plan an infrastructure for Exchange	Chapters 1–4, 8–13, and 18–19
Plan Exchange Client installation and integration	Chapters 6 and 7
Plan long-term administration	Chapter 15
Plan licensing	Chapter 2

Skill Being Measured	**Location in Book**
Installation and Configuration	
Install an Exchange Server computer	Chapter 2
Configure Exchange Server for message recipients	Chapter 5
Configure connectivity to a foreign system	Chapters 18 and 19
Configure directory synchronization between Exchange and other mail systems	Chapters 18 and 19
Configure directory replication	Chapters 9 and 10
Import directory, message, and scheduling data from existing systems	Chapter 7
Install and configure Exchange Server clients	Chapters 6 and 7
Configure address lists and accounts using the Exchange Administrator program	Chapter 5
Configure the MTA	Chapters 8 and 9
Configure messaging connectivity between sites	Chapters 9 and 10
Configure Internet protocols and services	Chapter 11
Configure message tracking	Chapter 15
Managing Resources	
Manage site security	Chapters 2, 5, and 14
Manage users	Chapter 5
Manage distribution lists	Chapter 5
Manage the directory	Chapter 3, 4, 8, and 9
Manage Public Information Stores	Chapters 12 and 13
Manage Private Information Stores	Chapters 5 and 15
Back up and restore the Exchange organization	Chapter 15
Manage connectivity	Chapters 9–11, 18, and 19
Monitoring and Optimization	
Configure a Link Monitor and a Server Monitor	Chapter 15
Optimize Exchange Server	Chapter 2
Optimize foreign connections and site-to-site connections	Chapters 9–11, 18, and 19
Monitor and optimize the messaging environment	Chapter 15

continues

continued

Skill Being Measured	Location in Book
Troubleshooting	
Diagnose and resolve upgrade problems	Chapters 2 and 15
Diagnose and resolve server and client installation problems	Chapters 2 and 6
Diagnose and resolve migration problems	Chapters 2, 6, 15, 18, and 19
Diagnose and resolve connectivity problems	Chapters 9, 10, 15, 18, and 19
Diagnose and resolve problems with client connectivity	Chapters 6, 7, 15, and 17
Diagnose and resolve information store problems	Chapter 15
Diagnose and resolve Exchange Server directory problems	Chapters 9 and 15
Diagnose and resolve resource problems	Chapters 2 and 15
Diagnose and resolve message delivery problems	Chapters 4, 8, 9, and 15
Diagnose and resolve backup and restore problems	Chapter 15

Getting Started

This self-paced training course contains hands-on procedures to help you learn about Microsoft Exchange Server 5.5.

To complete some of these procedures, you must have two networked computers or be connected to a larger network. Both computers must be capable of running Microsoft Windows NT Server 4.0. It is also necessary to install Windows NT Service Pack 3 or higher, Microsoft Internet Information Server 3.0, and Active Server Pages on the test computers.

Caution Several exercises may require you to make changes to your servers. This may have undesirable results if you are connected to a larger network. Check with your network administrator before attempting these exercises.

Hardware Requirements

Each computer must have the following minimum configuration. All hardware should be on the Microsoft Windows NT Hardware Compatibility List.

- Intel Pentium 133 MHz or higher
- 32 MB RAM (64 MB is ideal)
- 500 MB IDE hard disk (more than 1 GB is ideal)
- CD-ROM drive
- Network Adapter

Software Requirements

The following software is required to complete the procedures in this course. A 120-day evaluation copy of Exchange Server 5.5 is included on the CD-ROMs in this kit.

- Windows NT Server 4.0 plus 3 Windows NT installation floppy disks
- Service Pack 3 for Windows NT Server 4.0 (with IIS 3.0 and ASPs)
- Microsoft Exchange Server 5.5 Enterprise Edition
- Microsoft Outlook 97 version 8.03

Note The 120-day evaluation edition provided with this training are not the full retail product and are provided only for the purposes of training and evaluation. Microsoft Technical Support does not support this evaluation edition. For additional support information regarding this book and the CD-ROMs (including answers to commonly asked questions about installation and use), visit the Microsoft Press Technical Support web site at *mspress.microsoft.com/mspress/support/.* You can also e-mail *tkinput@microsoft.com*, or send a letter to Microsoft Press, Attn: Microsoft Press Technical Support, One Microsoft Way, Redmond, WA 98052-6399.

Setup Instructions

Set up your computer according to the manufacturer's instructions.

Most exercises require networked computers. You must make sure the computers can communicate with each other. The first computer will be configured as a primary domain controller (PDC), and will be assigned the computer account name NEWYORK-1 and the domain name STOCKSDATA. This computer will act as a domain controller running Internet Information Server 3.0 with Active Server Pages in STOCKSDATA.

The second computer will first act as a backup domain controller (BDC), and will be assigned the computer account name NEWYORK-2 and the domain name STOCKSDATA. For the exercises starting with Chapter 10, install the second computer as a PDC and assign the computer account name LONDON-1 and the domain name ENGLAND. In both cases, this computer runs Internet Information Server 3.0 with Active Server Pages as well.

Caution If your computers are part of a larger network, you *must* verify with your network administrator that the computer names, domain name, and other information used in setting up Microsoft Exchange Server 5.5 as described in Chapter 2 do not conflict with network operations. If they do conflict, ask your network administrator to provide alternative values and use those values throughout all of the exercises in this book.

Windows NT 4.0 Server Installation

Follow these steps to install the Windows NT Server software on your computer. Three Windows NT server setup disks, which come with the Windows NT Server 4.0 CD-ROM, are required. You can also create the setup disks manually using the **winnt /ox** or **winnt32 /ox** command.

To install Windows NT 4.0 Server:

1. Insert the floppy disk labeled Setup Disk 1 (which is also known as the Setup Boot Disk) into drive **A:**.

2. Switch on your computer.

3. During the boot process, insert the Microsoft Windows NT server compact disc into the CD-ROM drive.

4. When prompted, insert the Windows NT Server Setup Disk 2 into drive **A:** and press the Enter key.

5. A **Welcome to Setup** screen appears. Press Enter.

6. A screen appears, asking if Windows NT Server Setup should attempt to detect mass storage devices in your computer. Press Enter.

7. When prompted, insert the Windows NT Server Setup Disk 3 and press Enter.

8. A Windows NT Server Setup screen appears, listing recognized devices. If necessary, press *S* to specify additional devices.

9. After all devices have been specified and recognized, press the Enter key to continue the installation.

10. A screen appears, displaying the **Windows NT Licensing Agreement**. Read the licensing agreement and use the page down key to scroll down.

11. At the end of the licensing agreement, press the F8 key to agree and to continue setup.

12. Setup might inform you that Windows NT has been found on your computer, in which case you must press *N* to install a new version of Windows NT. (You will delete any existing version later during setup.)

13. A hardware and software components screen appears. Ensure that the displayed configuration matches your computer. If necessary, select any incorrect components and press Enter to change the device setting.

14. Highlight the option labeled **The Above List Matches My Computer** and press Enter to continue.

15. A screen appears, displaying the current partitioning scheme of your hard disk. Select the **C:** partition and press the *D* key. If no partitions exist, continue with step 19.

16. If a screen appears informing you that you are deleting a system partition, press Enter to continue the deletion.

17. A warning is displayed, informing you that all data on the partition will be lost. Press the *L* key to delete the partition.

18. A screen appears, displaying the current partitioning scheme. If a partition exists, continue with step 16.

19. Highlight the **Unpartitioned Space** and press the *C* key.

20. A screen appears, prompting for the size of the new partition. The maximum size of the hard disk is suggested by default. If the capacity of the hard disk is not larger than 1 GB, accept the default. Otherwise, delete the default value and type *1024* in the **Create Partition Of Size (In MB)** box. Press Enter to create the partition.

21. A screen appears, listing the new unformatted partition. Highlight the **Unpartitioned Space** and press the *C* key. If **Unpartitioned Space** is not listed, continue with step 23.

22. A screen appears, prompting for the size of the new partition. Press Enter to accept the default and to continue the installation.

23. Ensure that **C:** is selected and then press Enter.

24. A screen appears, asking if you want to have the current partition formatted as FAT or NTFS. Select **Format The Partition Using the NTFS File System** and press Enter.

25. Setup formats the hard disk.

26. A screen appears, prompting you for the installation directory for Windows NT. Accept the default directory, which is **\Winnt**, and press Enter to continue.

27. A screen appears, asking if you want Windows NT Server Setup to examine your hard disk for corruption. Press Enter to continue with an examination of the hard disk(s).

28. Setup copies a miniature version of Windows NT server to your hard disk. After that, a screen appears, stating that this portion of setup has been completed. Remove the floppy disk from drive **A:** and press Enter to restart your computer and continue with setup.

29. Once the computer has rebooted, Setup converts the FAT partition into an NTFS partition without any interaction. The computer automatically reboots a second time.

30. Once the computer has rebooted, a **Windows NT Server Setup** dialog box appears. Click **Next**.

31. Another **Windows NT Server Setup** dialog box will appear. In the **Name** box, type *Administrator*. In the **Organization** box, type *STOCKSDATA*. Click **Next**.

32. A **Windows NT Server Setup** dialog box appears, asking you for the 10-digit CD Key. Enter the valid CD key of your Windows NT server copy and then click **Next**.

33. A **Windows NT Server Setup** dialog box appears, displaying available Licensing Modes. Select **Per Seat** and then click **Next**.

34. A **Windows NT Server Setup** dialog box appears, prompting for a computer name. In the **Name** box, type *NEWYORK-1* and then click **Next**.

Note If you are installing the second computer, type *NEWYORK-2* or *LONDON-1* instead of *NEWYORK-1*.

35. In the next **Windows NT Server Setup** dialog box, ensure that **Primary Domain Controller** is selected and then click **Next**.

Note If you are installing NEWYORK-2, select **Backup Domain Controller** and then click **Next**.

36. If you are installing a PDC, a **Windows NT Server Setup** dialog box appears, asking for a password of the Administrator account. In the **Password** box and again in the **Confirm Password** box, type *password* and then click **Next**.

37. A **Windows NT Server Setup** dialog box appears, prompting you to create an Emergency Repair Disk. Select **No, Do Not Create An Emergency Repair Disk** and then click **Next**.

38. A **Windows NT Server Setup** dialog box appears, listing various components you can install. Accept the default settings and click **Next**.

39. A **Windows NT Server Setup** dialog box appears, informing you that Setup is now ready to guide you through the installation of Windows NT Networking. Click the **Next** button to continue.

40. A **Windows NT Server Setup** dialog box appears, asking whether you are connected to a network through a modem or a network adapter. Ensure that **Wired To The Network** is selected and then click **Next**.

41. A **Windows NT Server Setup** dialog box appears, asking if you want to install Microsoft Internet Information Server. Ensure that the corresponding check box is selected and then click **Next**.

42. A **Windows NT Server Setup** dialog box appears, allowing you to search for network adapters or select them from a list. Click **Start Search**.

43. Verify that the installed network adapter was detected or click the **Select From List** button and choose your adapter manually. Click **Next** once the driver for your network adapter is listed.

44. A **Windows NT Server Setup** dialog box appears, listing available network protocols. Deselect **NWLink IPX/SPX Compatible Transport** and ensure that NetBEUI is also not selected. Click **Next**.

45. A **Windows NT Server Setup** dialog box appears, showing **Network Services**. Click **Next**.

46. A **Windows NT Server Setup** dialog box appears, stating that Windows NT is ready to install the networking components. Click **Next**.

47. If network adapter specific dialog boxes appear, specify required configuration settings as appropriate and then click **OK** or **Continue** as required.

48. A **TCP/IP Setup** dialog box appears, asking if you wish to use DHCP. Click **No.**

49. A **Microsoft TCP/IP Properties** dialog box appears. In the **IP Address** box, type an appropriate IP address (for example, *166.16.1.1*) and in the **Subnet Mask** box, type an appropriate subnet mask (for example, *255.255.255.0*). Click **OK**.

> **Note** If you install a second computer, specify an IP address of 166.16.1.2, but use the same subnet mask. IP addresses must be unique in your network.

50. A **Windows NT Server Setup** dialog box appears, showing network bindings. Click **Next**.

51. A **Windows NT Server Setup** dialog box appears, stating that Windows NT is ready to start the network. Click **Next** to start the network.

52. A **Windows NT Server Setup** dialog box appears, asking you for the domain name. In the **Domain** box, type *STOCKSDATA*. Click **Next**.

> **Note** If you are installing NEWYORK-2 (as a BDC), a dialog box appears, asking you for the **Domain Name, Administrator Name**, and **Administrator Password** at step 51. In the **Domain** box, type *STOCKSDATA,* in the **Administrator Name** box, type *Administrator*, and in the **Administrator Password** box, type *password*. Ensure that the PDC (NEWYORK-1) is available in the network when you click **Next**. If you are installing LONDON-1 (as a PDC), type *ENGLAND* in the **Domain** box and then click **Next**.

53. A **Windows NT Server Setup** dialog box appears. Click **Finish**.

54. A dialog box appears, showing the options and services of Windows NT. Deselect the **Gopher Service** and then click **OK**.

55. A **Microsoft Internet Information Server 2.0 Setup** dialog box appears, stating that the \Inetsrv directory does not exist and asking if Setup should create it. Click **Yes**.

56. A **Publishing Directories** dialog box appears, showing default directories for different services. Click **OK** to accept the default directories.

57. A **Microsoft Internet Information Server 2.0 Setup** dialog box appears, asking if you want to create the new directories. Click **Yes**.

58. An **Install Drivers** dialog box appears, displaying **Available ODBC Drivers**. In the **Available ODBC Drivers** box select **SQL Server** and then click **OK**.

59. A **Date/Time Properties** dialog box appears. Select your **Time Zone** and then click **Close**.

60. A **Detected Display** dialog box appears, stating that the system has found a video adapter in your machine. Click **OK**.

61. In the **Desktop Area** box, select **800 by 600 pixels** and then click **Test**.

62. A **Testing Mode** dialog box appears, stating that the new mode will be tested for approximately five seconds. Click **OK**.

63. After five seconds, a **Testing Mode** dialog box appears, asking if you have seen the test bitmap properly. If so, click **Yes**.

64. A **Display Settings** dialog box appears, stating that if you want to save your settings you must click OK in the **Display Properties** dialog box. Click **OK**.

65. In the **Display Properties** dialog box, click **OK**.

66. A **Windows NT Setup** dialog box appears, stating that Windows NT 4.0 Server has been installed successfully. Click **Restart Computer**.

To prepare Windows NT 4.0 Server and to install Service Pack 3

1. After the server has rebooted, press CTRL+ALT+DEL to display the **Logon Information** dialog box. In the **Password** box, type *password* and then click **OK**.

2. A **Welcome** dialog box appears. Click **Close**.

3. Click the **Start** button, point to **Programs**, point to **Administrative Tools (Common)**, and then click the **Disk Administrator** shortcut.

4. A **Disk Administrator** dialog box appears, stating that this is the first time you have started Disk Administrator. Click **OK**.

5. A **Disk Administrator** program window appears. Right-click **D:** and then click **Format**.

6. A **Format D:** dialog box appears. Under **File System**, select **NTFS** and under **Format Options**, select **Quick Format**.

7. Click **Start**.

8. A **Format D:** dialog box appears, stating that formatting will erase all data on this disk. Click **OK** to continue.

9. A **Formatting D:** dialog box appears, stating that the format is complete. Click **OK**.

10. Click **Close**.

11. Close the **Disk Administrator** program window.

12. Insert the **Microsoft Windows NT Service Pack 3** compact disc in the CD-ROM drive and close any applications that might appear automatically (such as Microsoft Internet Explorer).

13. Click the **Start** button, point to **Programs**, and then click **Windows NT Explorer**.

14. Switch to the root directory of the CD-ROM and then double-click the **Spsetup** (Spsetup.bat) file to install the Service Pack.

15. A **Welcome** dialog box appears. Click **Next**.

16. The **Software Licensing Agreement** dialog box appears. Read the agreement and click **Yes** if you agree to the terms.

17. A **Service Pack Setup** dialog box appears, asking you to select what type of installation is desired. Make sure that **Install the Service Pack** is selected and then click **Next**.

18. A **Service Pack Setup** dialog box appears, asking if you would like to create an uninstall directory. Ensure that **Yes, I Want To Create An Uninstall Directory** is selected and then click **Next**.

19. A **Service Pack Setup** dialog box appears, stating that the setup program is ready to complete. Click **Finish** to complete the installation.

20. A **Windows NT Service Pack Setup** dialog box appears, stating that the installation has been completed. Remove any disks from the **A:** drive and click **OK** to reboot the computer.

To install Active Server Pages

1. After the server has rebooted, press CTRL+ALT+DEL to display the **Logon Information** dialog box. In the **Password** box, type *password* and then click **OK**.

2. A **Welcome** dialog box appears. Clear the check box **Show This Welcome Screen Next Time You Start Windows NT** and then click **Close**.

3. Ensure that the **Microsoft Windows NT Service Pack 3** compact disc is in the CD-ROM drive and then start or switch to the Windows NT Explorer.

4. Open the \IIS30\Asp directory on the CD-ROM and double-click the **Aspsetup** (Aspsetup.bat) file.

5. The **Microsoft Active Server Pages Setup** window and a **License Agreement** dialog box appear. In the dialog box click **I Agree** to continue.

6. Click **Next**.

7. A **Stop Internet Information Services** dialog box appears, asking if you want to stop the services of the Internet Information Server. Click **Yes**.

8. A **Select Options** dialog box appears. Accept the default selection and then click **Next**.

9. In the **Select Path** dialog box, accept the installation path (C:\Inetpub\ASPSamp) and then click **Next**.

10. Setup copies the ASP files to your hard disk.

11. A **Setup Is Complete** dialog box appears. Click **OK**.

12. An **Information** dialog box appears, informing you that an icon named **Active Server Pages Roadmap** has been added to your **Microsoft Internet Server (Common)** program group. Click **OK**.

13. A **Start Internet Information Server** dialog box appears. Click **Yes** to restart the IIS.

14. Close all windows on the desktop and shut down the Windows NT server computer.

About The Online Book

The CD-ROMs also include an online version of the book that you can use to launch demonstrations, link to all the referenced articles, and view lessons on screen as you work through the exercises.

To install the online version of the book, do the following:

1. Insert the Supplemental Course Materials CD-ROM into your CD-ROM drive.

2. On the Windows taskbar, click **Start**.

3. Select **Run** from the **Start** menu.

4. Type *d:\ebook\setup* (where *d* is your CD-ROM drive letter).

5. Click **OK**.

6. Follow the setup instructions that appear.

7. The Setup program for the online book installs a desktop icon and a program item identified with the title of the book. If it does not already exist, the Setup program creates a Microsoft Press program group for the program item. To view the online book, you can either select the program item or double-click the desktop item.

The Microsoft Certified Professional Program

The Microsoft Certified Professional (MCP) program provides the best method to prove your command of current Microsoft products and technologies. Microsoft, an industry leader in certification, is on the forefront of testing methodology. Our exams and corresponding certifications are developed to validate your mastery of critical competencies as you design and develop, or implement and support, solutions with Microsoft products and technologies. Computer professionals who become Microsoft certified are recognized as experts and are sought after industry-wide.

The Microsoft Certified Professional program offers six certifications, based on specific areas of technical expertise:

- *Microsoft Certified Professional (MCP).* MCPs demonstrate in-depth knowledge of at least one Microsoft operating system. Candidates may pass additional Microsoft certification exams to further qualify their skills with Microsoft BackOffice products, development tools, or desktop programs.

- *Microsoft Certified Professional + Internet.* MCPs with a specialty in the Internet are qualified to plan security, install and configure server products, manage server resources, extend servers to run CGI scripts or ISAPI scripts, monitor and analyze performance, and troubleshoot problems.

- *Microsoft Certified Systems Engineer (MCSE).* MCSEs are qualified to effectively plan, implement, maintain, and support information systems in a wide range of computing environments with Microsoft Windows 95, Microsoft Windows NT, and the Microsoft BackOffice integrated family of server software.

- *Microsoft Certified Systems Engineer + Internet (MCSE + Internet).* These MCSEs have advanced qualification to enhance, deploy and manage sophisticated intranet and Internet solutions that include a browser, proxy server, host servers, database, and messaging and commerce components. In addition, an MCSE+Internet–certified professional can manage and analyze Web sites.

- *Microsoft Certified Solution Developer (MCSD).* MCSDs are qualified to design and develop custom business solutions with Microsoft development tools, technologies, and platforms, including Microsoft Office and Microsoft BackOffice.

- *Microsoft Certified Trainer (MCT).* MCTs are instructionally and technically qualified to deliver Microsoft Official Curriculum (MOC) through a Microsoft Authorized Technical Education Center (ATEC).

Microsoft Certification Benefits

Microsoft certification, one of the most comprehensive certification programs available for assessing and maintaining software-related skills, is a valuable measure of an individual's knowledge and expertise. Microsoft certification is awarded to individuals who have successfully demonstrated their ability to perform specific tasks and implement solutions with Microsoft products. Not only does this provide an objective measure for employers to consider, it also provides guidance for what an individual should know to be proficient. And as with any skills-assessment and benchmarking measure, certification brings a variety of benefits: to the individual, and to employers and organizations.

Microsoft Certification Benefits for Individuals

As a Microsoft Certified Professional, you receive many benefits:

- Industry recognition of your knowledge and proficiency with Microsoft products and technologies

- Access to technical and product information directly from Microsoft through a secured area of the MCP Web Site

- Logos to enable you to identify your Microsoft Certified Professional status to colleagues or clients

- Invitations to Microsoft conferences, technical training sessions, and special events

- A Microsoft Certified Professional certificate

- A subscription to Microsoft Certified Professional Magazine (North America only), a career and professional development magazine

Additional benefits, depending on your certification and geography, include:

- A complimentary one-year subscription to the Microsoft TechNet Technical Information Network, providing valuable information on monthly CD-ROMs

- A one-year subscription to the Microsoft Beta Evaluation program, which provides you with up to 12 free monthly CD-ROMs containing beta software (English only) for many of Microsoft's newest software products

Microsoft Certification Benefits for Employers and Organizations

Through certification, computer professionals can maximize the return on investment in Microsoft technology. Research shows that Microsoft certification provides organizations with:

- Excellent return on training and certification investments by providing a standard method of determining training needs and measuring results

- Increased customer satisfaction and decreased support costs through improved service, increased productivity and greater technical self-sufficiency

- Reliable benchmark for hiring, promoting and career planning

- Recognition and rewards for productive employees by validating their expertise

- Retraining options for existing employees so that they can work effectively with new technologies

- Assurance of quality when outsourcing computer services

To learn more about how certification can help your company, see the backgrounders, white papers, and case studies available at *www.microsoft.com/train_cert/cert/bus_bene.htm*:

- The Microsoft® Certified Professional Program Corporate Backgrounder (mcpback.exe 50K)

- A white paper (mcsdwp.doc 158K) that evaluates the Microsoft Certified Solution Developer certification

- A white paper (mcsestud.doc 161K) that evaluates the Microsoft Certified Systems Engineer certification

- Jackson Hole High School Case Study (jhhs.doc 180K)

- Lyondel Case Study (lyondel.doc 21K)

- Stellcom Case Study (stellcom.doc 132K)

Requirements for Becoming a Microsoft Certified Professional

The certification requirements differ for each certification and are specific to the products and job functions addressed by the certification.

To become an MCP, you must pass rigorous certification exams that provide a valid and reliable measure of technical proficiency and expertise. These exams are designed to test your expertise and ability to perform a role or task with a product, and are developed with the input of professionals in the industry. Questions in the exams reflect how Microsoft products are used in actual organizations, giving them "real world" relevance.

Microsoft Certified Product Specialists are required to pass one operating system exam. Candidates may pass additional Microsoft certification exams to further qualify their skills with Microsoft BackOffice products, development tools, or desktop applications.

MCPs - Specialist: Internet are required to pass the prescribed Microsoft Windows NT Server 4.0, TCP/IP, and Microsoft Internet Information System exam series.

MCSEs are required to pass a series of core Microsoft Windows operating system and networking exams, and BackOffice technology elective exams.

MCSDs are required to pass two core Microsoft Windows operating system technology exams and two BackOffice technology elective exams.

MCTs are required to meet instructional and technical requirements specific to each MOC course they are certified to deliver. In the United States and Canada, call Microsoft at (800) 636-7544 for more information on becoming an MCT. Outside the United States and Canada, contact your local Microsoft subsidiary.

Technical Training for Computer Professionals

Technical training is available in a variety of methods, with instructor-led classes, online instruction, or self-paced training available at thousands of locations worldwide.

Self-Paced Training

For motivated learners who are ready for the challenge, self-paced instruction is the most flexible, cost-effective way to increase knowledge and skills.

A full line of self-paced print and computer-based training materials are available direct from the source—Microsoft Press. MOC courseware kits for advanced computer system professionals are available from Microsoft Press and the Microsoft Developer Division. Self-paced training kits from Microsoft Press feature print-based instructional materials, along with CD-ROM–based product software, multimedia presentations, lab exercises, and practice files. The Mastering Series provides in-depth, interactive training on CD-ROM for experienced developers. These are both great ways to prepare for MCP exams.

Online Training

For a more flexible alternative to instructor-led classes, turn to online instruction. It's as close as the Internet and it's ready whenever you are. Learn at your own pace and on your own schedule in a virtual classroom, often with easy access to an online instructor. Without ever leaving your desk, you can gain the expertise you need. Online instruction covers a variety of Microsoft products and technologies. It includes options ranging from MOC to choices available nowhere else. Online training is training on demand, with access to learning resources 24 hours a day.

Online training is available through Microsoft Authorized Technical Education Centers.

Authorized Technical Education Centers

Authorized Technical Education Centers (ATECs) are the best source for instructor-led training that can help you prepare to become an MCP. The Microsoft ATEC program is a worldwide network of qualified technical training organizations that provide authorized delivery of MOC courses by MCTs to computer professionals.

For a listing of ATEC locations in the United States and Canada, call the Microsoft fax service at (800) 727-3351. Outside the United States and Canada, call the fax service at (206) 635-2233.

Technical Support

Every effort has been made to ensure the accuracy of this book and the contents of the companion disc. If you have comments, questions, or ideas regarding this book or the companion compact disc, please send them to Microsoft Press using either of the following methods:

E-mail:
tkinput@microsoft.com

Postal Mail:
Microsoft Press
Attn: Microsoft Exchange Server Training Editor
One Microsoft Way
Redmond, WA 98052-6399

Microsoft Press provides corrections for books through the World Wide Web at *mspress.microsoft.com/support/*.

Please note that product support is not offered through the above mail addresses. For further information regarding Microsoft software support options, please connect to *www.microsoft.com/support/* or call Microsoft Support Network Sales at (800) 936-3500.

Evaluation Edition Software Support

The evaluation edition of Microsoft Exchange Server 5.5 included with this book is unsupported by both Microsoft and Microsoft Press, and should not be used on a primary work computer. For online support information relating to the full version of Microsoft Exchange Server 5.5 that might also apply to the evaluation edition, you can connect to *support.microsoft.com/*.

For information about ordering the full version of any Microsoft software, please call Microsoft Sales at (800) 426-9400 or visit *www.microsoft.com*. Information about any issues relating to the use of this evaluation edition with this training kit are posted to the Support section of the Microsoft Press Web site (*mspress.microsoft.com/support/*).

C H A P T E R   1

Introduction to Microsoft Exchange

This chapter explores the basic features and characteristics of Microsoft Exchange Server 5.5. The client/server–based communication model will be presented and compared to earlier messaging systems that relied on shared-file and directory structures.

Overview

E-mail messaging was born in the seventies, back when mainframes dominated the computer industry and users ran their applications on these centralized informational storage sites. Originally, e-mail was just a mainframe "hack" that allowed one user write information into a specific section of another user's storage area. Interpersonal communication became possible this way. Over the years, more complicated e-mail systems have been developed, but the idea behind these newer systems remains the same. If you take a closer look, you can find this principle at work in all Exchange Server versions as well—the mailboxes embody the concept of exposing a section of each user's storage area to other users.

Lesson 1 introduces the basic features of the Exchange Server 5.5 messaging platform. The shared-file principle and the client/server technology are compared to emphasize the preferable characteristics of a modern messaging system. The organization of Exchange Server computers in a Microsoft Windows NT Server network are also discussed.

Lesson 2 briefly discusses the available messaging clients that can be used to access an Exchange Server, including the Exchange Client family and Microsoft Outlook. Examples of supported clients relying on Internet mail access protocols are also listed.

Lesson 3 examines the Exchange Server infrastructure. Core components— the essential server services that always have to run—are discussed, as are the optional components, which can add valuable features to the messaging network. Important administrative tasks and tools are also outlined.

In the following lessons, you will be introduced to:

- A comparison of shared-file and client/server messaging systems
- The support provided by Exchange Server for industry messaging standards
- The hierarchical object model used by Exchange Server
- General Exchange Server implementation issues concerning security aspects at the Windows NT level

Lesson 1: Introduction to Microsoft Exchange Server

This book is primarily a self-study training manual for Exchange Server 5.5, but it is also, to a certain degree, the story of a fictitious company called STOCKSDATA. The company's administrators are thinking about implementing a messaging system, but they're not sure which one to use. What are the arguments to convince them to use Exchange Server? To say that Exchange Server is a client/server messaging system is probably not the most illustrative statement. Maybe it's more convincing to point out that Exchange Server 5.5 is a Microsoft product. In fact, this is not the least reason to use it.

This lesson introduces the Exchange Server platform. As promised, you can read about the features of shared-file and client/server systems, their advantages, and their disadvantages. This lesson continues with a listing of messaging protocols and industry standards supported by Exchange Server. The most important internal hierarchical structures and their influence in an Exchange Server network will also be highlighted. This lesson concludes with an introduction to the security features of Microsoft Windows NT and how they affect the implementation of the Exchange Server.

At the end of this section, you will be able to:

- Identify the most important Exchange Server features
- Describe the differences between a shared-file and a client/server messaging system
- Explore the Exchange Server hierarchy
- Name the results of Windows NT security integration

Estimated time to complete this section: 20 minutes

Microsoft Exchange Server Features

Exchange Server 5.5 is a modern messaging and workgroup-computing platform. It has been developed based on the client/server model—a development concept of the nineties, one might say. It provides secure access to mailboxes, public folders, address books, and other components. In addition to normal e-mail messaging, this platform provides scheduling capabilities across an organization. You can also use this system for efficiently sharing information based on public folders, electronic forms, and custom applications. (See Figure 1-1.)

Multiple Client Platform Support

Exchange Server 5.5 does not force its users to adhere to a particular operating system for it to run their messaging clients. It supports a variety of client platforms, including MS-DOS, Windows 3.1, Windows for Workgroups 3.11, OS/2, Windows 95, Windows NT, and Apple Macintosh System 7.x. UNIX-based messaging clients can also be utilized to access resources on an Exchange Server; they will typically rely on common Internet standards.

Exchange Server Core Components

An Exchange Server is a collection of server-based processes running on a Windows NT Server computer. It is a complex system of four or more Windows NT services and three or more databases. The four most important services are the Directory Service (DS), the Information Store (IS), the Message Transfer Agent (MTA), and the System Attendant (SA). These services must run on every server. The core databases contain the directory, the mailboxes, and the public folder data. The directory provides information about the hierarchy of the Exchange system and the objects within the hierarchy, such as the address lists. The mailbox is the repository of private messages. The public folders, as their name implies, maintain messages and other items for public access. The core and optional server components are covered in more detail in Chapter 3, "Microsoft Exchange Server Architecture."

The Exchange Server administrator has the responsibility to configure, manage, and monitor the server components. Constant maintenance can ensure that a server remains functional and at the users' disposal.

Hierarchy

The basic terms for the description of the hierarchy of every Exchange Server are *organization*, *site*, and *server*, and every messaging network consists of at least one of each. The organization provides the common context for all resources in the entire messaging network. Sites, on the other hand, allow you to group multiple servers together to simplify their administration. The server, finally, maintains the private mailboxes, the public folders, and other resources.

Single Sites

You can group multiple servers together in a single site to increase the efficiency of the server-to-server communication and to simplify administration. Servers within the same site will communicate directly with each other. The good news about this configuration is that you don't need to control this communication—in fact, a direct controlling mechanism is not even provided. Site-level configuration settings are distributed to all servers automatically, which is the foundation of easy administration. The server-to-server communication within a single site is explained in more detail in Chapter 4, "Communication in an Exchange Server Environment."

Multiple Sites

If an administrator has reasonable objections against a huge single site, he or she can implement multiple sites to gain complete control over the communication between servers. The transfer of messages between sites relies on messaging connectors. By adjusting the connector parameters and attributes, an administrator can optimize the communication, which is especially desirable if the communication generates transmission costs. You can read more about the configuration of intersite connections in Chapter 9, "Introduction to Intersite Connectors."

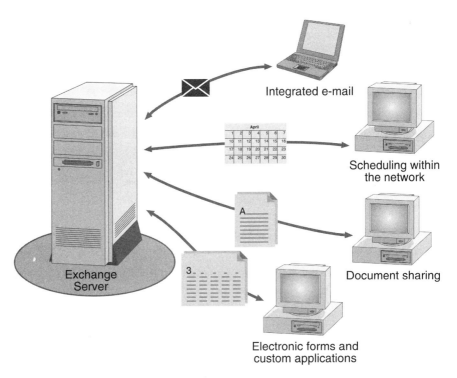

Figure 1-1. Microsoft Exchange features.

The characteristics of Exchange are as follows:

- Utilization of the client/server model

- E-mail, scheduling, document sharing, electronic forms, and custom applications

- Support for clients on MS-DOS, Windows 3.1, Windows for Workgroups 3.11, Windows 95, Windows NT, OS/2, and Apple Macintosh version 7.x

- Support for UNIX-based clients via the Hypertext Transfer Protocol (HTTP), the Lightweight Directory Access Protocol (LDAP), the Post Office Protocol version 3 (POP3), the Internet Message Access Protocol version 4 (IMAP4), the Simple Mail Transfer Protocol (SMTP), and the Network News Transferring Protocol (NNTP)

- Reliance on four core Windows NT services (DS, IS, MTA, and SA)

- Structure based on organization, site, and server configuration

Shared-File Messaging Systems

In the eighties and early nineties, PC networks were basically constructed to share files and printers throughout the computer network. File and print servers such as Novell NetWare or Microsoft LanManager systems provided access to their servers' shared resources in a rather passive way. The user working on a client computer had to log on to a particular network server before being able to use its shared directories in the same way that he or she could use any local hard disk or printer.

Shared-File Messaging Process

Shared-file messaging systems depend on the file-sharing capabilities of a network server. They maintain a structure of directories and files at a centralized location. These centralized structures are often called *post offices*. Every user who wants to participate in e-mail messaging needs to access a mailbox within a post office. In other words, the post office serves as the mailbox repository for multiple users. Typical messaging systems that use shared-file post offices are Microsoft Mail for PC networks and Lotus cc:Mail.

Client Sending and Polling

To send messages, users must write their data into the directories, or mailboxes, of the post office. The users on the receiving end, on the other hand, recognize the written data as incoming messages. The post office itself is a passive file structure, meaning that the client programs must perform all processing of sending and receiving. To check for new messages, clients must poll the post office at regular intervals. (See Figure 1-2 on page 9.)

All message processing is accomplished through the client programs. Even system processes, such as message transfer agents, which transfer messages between post offices, can be seen completely as clients. Consequently, shared-file systems do not require a powerful server machine. Powerful client machines are preferred instead. Furthermore, the network traffic is usually high due to client polling. A fast computer network can help to avoid bottle-necks when numerous messaging clients access the same post office at the same time to poll for new messages.

As shown in Figure 1-2, the shared-file message flow follows this route :

1. The user creates and sends a message.

2. The client places the message in the post office on the server.

3. The message is stored in the recipient's storage area in the post office.

4. The recipient's client polls the post office to determine whether there are any new messages.

5. The recipient receives (downloads) new messages from the post office.

Evaluation of Shared-File Messaging

Every shared-file–based messaging system depends on a passive post office that resides on a network server. These messaging systems are independent of the underlying network operating system so long as read/write access to the post office is guaranteed. For instance, it is possible to use Microsoft Mail 3.x in combination with Novell NetWare environments, LanManager for UNIX, Windows NT Server, IBM LanServer, DEC PathWorks, and other network operating systems.

Server Resources

As mentioned, an advantage of a shared-file–based e-mail system is the fact that it doesn't need a very powerful machine on the server side.

Security

Shared-file–based e-mail systems are easy to install, which is another advantage. The configuration of the network server is also quickly accomplished. Once the post office has been installed, the administrator must grant read/write access for the post office-data structure to all users—that's it. Of course, the administrator must still set up the mailboxes for each user, but they can be configured in a straightforward manner using the messaging system's administrative utilities. Every user who has a mailbox can send and receive e-mail messages immediately through the appropriate messaging client software.

On the other hand, the direct read/write access to and within the post office is one of the critical disadvantages of the shared-file messaging concept because it basically allows all users to delete files. Users can potentially damage the internal structures of a post office by deleting files either inadvertently or intentionally. Furthermore, read/write access allows users to utilize the post office location as a sort of hard disk extension to store private data. The administrator has no efficient way to prevent this misuse. As a result, the shared-file messaging system provides only a limited amount of security.

Polling

Clients have to poll their passive post offices for new messages—there's no way around it. All the work it takes to download messages must also be done solely by the clients, which generates a high volume of network traffic. To make matters worse, polling will always happen at regular intervals, even if there are no new messages to retrieve. The user cannot easily prevent message polling because clients need to detect new incoming messages in the post office. (See Figure 1-2.)

Server-Based Rules

The passive character of the post office is a disadvantage when users want to activate automatic rules for incoming messages. Let's say you want to automatically inform other users about your absence from the office. Out-of-office notifications could cover this task perfectly. They would be sent back to the sender automatically as new e-mails arrive in your mailbox. An out-of-office rule would determine the text of the message, whether you want the automatic reply sent only once to each sender, and so on.

To be most efficient, this rule should also fire while the client is not running. But the post office is passive and does not perform any actions. So what should play the active role? As a matter of fact, you would need to keep your client computer running during your entire time out of the office. To put it plainly, client-based mailbox rules are often useless.

Scalability

Another disadvantage of the post office is its limited scalability. Microsoft Mail postoffices, for instance, are limited to 500 users. This limit is hardcoded. But even if it were not implemented that way it wouldn't be advisable to create more than 500 mailboxes on one server because each polling client is a drain on system resources. The more clients that are polling for new files at a given moment (which implies the execution of costly file input/output operations within each polling event), the busier—and slower—the server will be.

Imagine that 500 client programs are using several common files in a post office for sending and receiving e-mail messages at the same time. When one client opens common files for writing, these files must be locked to prevent accidents. In other words, all other clients must wait until one client has completed its write operation. The more clients that access the same post office, the more often these common files will be locked and the more often all other clients will have to wait. The effect of having to wait can be worsened if the underlying network operating system is not optimized for fast input/output operations.

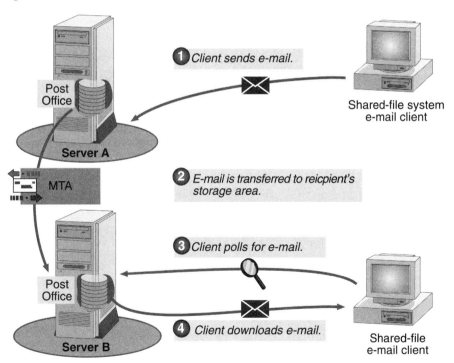

Figure 1-2. Shared-file messaging systems.

The advantages of shared-file systems include:

- Low requirements for server hardware
- Independence of the network operating system
- Ease of maintenance in homogenous environments

The disadvantages of shared-file systems include:

- Limited security due to the fact that every user needs read/write access to the post office
- High network traffic because of client polling for new messages
- Client load while processing messages at the local computer
- Reduced scalabiliy

Client/Server Messaging Systems

Windows NT supports client/server applications based on Remote Procedure Calls (RPC) according to the Distributed Computing Environment (DCE) specification of the Open Software Foundation (OSF). Consequently, Windows NT–based client/server messaging systems, such as Exchange Server, can use RPCs to implement a method for accessing the central repository of personal e-mail messages and public data, which differs from the shared file approach.

Active Windows NT services will be running on the same server that is communicating with the client programs, making the limits of the passive post office structure a thing of the past. The client/server concept allows distribution of the workload between the server and the client. Within an Exchange Server system, the client program needs only to request the data and the server will process the requests to return the results.

Client/Server Messaging Process

Exchange Server 5.5 is indeed a good example of a client/server messaging system. An Exchange client can send its requests to the server using RPCs. The server will also use RPCs to return the results of the processing back to the client. Likewise, the server can contact the client using RPCs. For example, the active server will notify the client when any new messages arrive.

The active core components that run permanently on the Windows NT server are the Information Store (IS), Directory Service (DS), Message Transfer Agent (MTA), and System Attendant (SA) services. The Information Store is the Windows NT service that assists the clients in sending and receiving messages and in accessing public folders.

Messages will flow as follows when using Microsoft Outlook (or Exchange Client 5.0), as shown in Figure 1-3:

1. The client delivers the message to the server.

2. The server processes the message, determines the home server of the recipient, and sends the message to that server.

3. The receiving server determines the appropriate message storage location and places the message in the messaging database.

4. The server notifies the recipient's client of the message's arrival.

5. The recipient's client connects to the server and requests to receive the message.

Evaluation of Client/Server Messaging

A client sending a message to an active server doesn't need access to a shared-file post office. The client communicates solely with the active server services in order to deliver the message. The server services, in turn, are the actual components that write messages into and read messages from the server's messaging databases. No other components require direct read/write access. This is a significant advantage of the client/server system, because the lack of need for components requiring read/write access allows a much higher security level for server-based resources than does a shared-file post office. The good news for the administrator is that users can no longer misuse the central e-mail message storage location.

A second advantage of the client/server messaging system is the server's ability to inform clients about the arrival of new messages. This mechanism avoids the need for client polling and helps to reduce network traffic significantly. Client programs contact the server only when the user explicitly specifies that messages should be accessed and downloaded.

Server Platform

A client/server messaging system is more scalable than a shared-file system. Because clients do not poll the active messaging server and files will not be opened directly by any messaging client, more clients can connect to the server at the same time. Furthermore, it is possible to design the client hardware more specifically. The distributed computing mechanism allows the more extensive processing to be moved to the server instead of having the clients do all the work.

From the point of view of the server machine, central processing is a disadvantage. Even servers don't like having to do the work of others. When numerous clients send their requests to the server and wait for the returned results, the server can become very busy. Consequently, you should equip the server computer with powerful hardware resources, such as multiple processors and as much RAM as possible. In this case, the rule of thumb simply is: the more, the better.

Note Unlike a file and print server, the active server of a client/server messaging system requires powerful and often more expensive hardware resources.

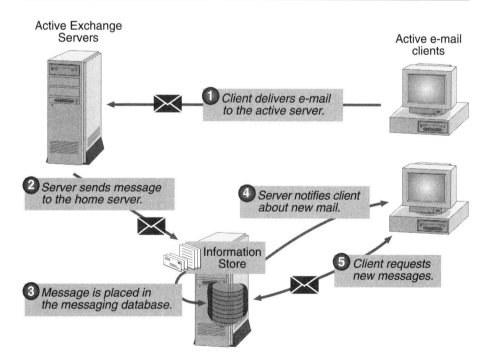

Active Exchange
Servers

Active e-mail
clients

1 Client delivers e-mail
to the active server.

2 Server sends message
to the home server.

4 Server notifies client
about new mail.

Information
Store

5 Client requests
new messages.

3 Message is placed in
the messaging database.

Figure 1-3. Client/server messaging systems.

Some advantages of client/server messaging systems include:

- Higher security, because the client doesn't need read/write permission in the post office

- Reduced network traffic, because the active server can inform the client about the arrival of new messages (making polling unnecessary)

- Scalability, which makes client/server messaging systems suitable for the needs of small and large organizations

The disadvantage of client/server messaging systems is:

- The need for powerful server hardware, which is required due to the amount of processing performed by the server

Microsoft Exchange Server Compatibility

Messaging systems are typical computer network applications. They don't make much sense if they are used as a stand-alone application on a single computer. The bigger the computer network, the more heterogeneous the installed system base will be. The Internet, for instance, combines all kinds of computer systems. For this reason, protocol standards have been developed to allow different computer systems to communicate with each other. Exchange Server 5.5 supports the relevant messaging standards, making it a tremendously flexible platform. (See Figure 1-4 on page 18.)

Support of Messaging Standards

Exchange Server 5.5 is designed to work in complex messaging networks where more than one system exists. The MTA of the Exchange Server, for instance, is a component that has been developed based on the CCITT (ITU) X.400 Standard (1988). Consequently, it is possible to implement an Exchange Server natively in any X.400 backbone. Because of the backward compatibility of the X.400 standard, you can use the Exchange Server to connect to older 1984-X.400 as well as to newer 1992-X.400 systems. In theory, the connection to a 1992-X.400 system is not problematic, because the 1992-X.400 system would have to be 1988-X.400 backward compatible as well. You can read more about the X.400 features of Exchange in Chapter 9.

Internet Support

The X.400 standard was most popular during the time of the Exchange Server 4.0 development phase. Today, the Internet, which continues its exponential growth, is the single most important messaging network. One of the Internet's most significant advantages is its reduced cost factor. Transmission costs are lower than for public X.400 networks. Furthermore, Internet messaging protocols are easy to configure and Internet addresses are far more convenient to use than their complex X.400 pendants. If you happen to disagree, you might change your mind once you have completed Chapter 9, "Introduction to Intersite Connectors," and Chapter 10, "Internet Mail Service."

Exchange Server 5.5 addresses the increased demand for Internet connectivity. Using this version, you can connect your messaging network to SMTP and Enhanced SMTP (ESMTP) hosts to send and receive messages to and from the Internet. You'll read more about this topic in Chapter 10.

In addition, you can connect an Exchange Server to the USENET via NNTP, which allows the reception and distribution of information from and to newsgroups. Several other Internet standards and protocols, such as Multi-purpose Internet Mail Extensions (MIME), LDAP, POP3, IMAP4, and HTTP are likewise supported. These protocols are covered in further detail in Chapter 11, "Internet Protocols."

Post Office Protocol Version 3

If you want to program a successful application, you should write it for the most common operating systems that can be found on PCs today—Windows 95 and Windows NT. If you want to develop a successful messaging system, it's a good idea to support the most common Internet client protocols, one of which is POP3. Exchange Server 5.5 already supports POP3 clients, as did version 5.0. In other words, you can use POP3 client software regardless of your operating system to download messages from an Exchange Server. In fact, the POP3 client doesn't know that it is communicating to a host that is specifically an Exchange Server.

Note POP3 is a read-only protocol, which allows you to read messages from your server-based Inbox. Access to other message folders, such as **Sent Items**, is not possible because folder operations are not defined within this protocol.

Internet Message Access Protocol Version 4

IMAP4 , like POP3, is an Internet Client Access protocol, but IMAP4 is more powerful, more flexible, and more complex than POP3. It allows you to access all kinds of server-based messaging folders, to search folders for specific messages, and to download messages completely or partially (attachments only). Therefore, it's not surprising that modern Internet Mail clients such as Microsoft Outlook Express and Netscape Communicator support this protocol to allow more flexible access to messaging resources. The popularity of the IMAP4 protocol is on the rise throughout the Internet today.

Note The support of the IMAP4 protocol is a new Exchange Server feature introduced in version 5.5. It allows you to access messaging folders using any IMAP4rev1-compliant client software.

Hypertext Transfer Protocol

The implementation of HTTP support into Exchange Server 5.x offers interesting opportunities. Like IMAP4 clients, Internet browsers can access all kinds of server-based resources. So you can work with your mailbox and public folders and query the Global Address List just as you would using Outlook. In order to be able to make use of these possibilities your Internet browser has to support Java script and frames—Internet Explorer version 3.x and 4.0 or Netscape Navigator are good examples of browsers that do so.

Besides being able to validate connections, you can allow anonymous access to public folders. This is exciting because it allows Internet publishing in a convenient form. Let's say the fictitious company STOCKSDATA plans a survey about public opinion regarding the chance to make money with international oil stocks. They can invite the whole world to join the discussion if they design a public folder, create a Web-based workgroup application, associate the workgroup application with the public folder, and publish the contents of the public folder on the Internet. Employees of STOCKSDATA and its affiliates will be able to access this discussion forum using their Exchange Clients or Outlook. Users around the world can join the discussion using any supported Internet browser software. The development of discussion forums and workgroup applications is covered in Chapter 16, "The Microsoft Exchange Server Forms Environment."

Messaging Application Programming Interface

Another industry standard, the Messaging Application Programming Interface (MAPI), is also supported by Exchange Server. Actually, it was Exchange Server 4.0 that made MAPI a powerful messaging standard. MAPI is more than a single protocol; it's a description of a messaging client architecture. It defines the interfaces for both the client and the underlying messaging system. Native Exchange clients and Outlook rely on MAPI as well as several additional server components, such as the Internet Mail Service (IMS). Many different vendors of messaging systems now provide MAPI drivers for standardizing the access to their messaging servers. More information about MAPI, its components, and its configuration is provided in Chapter 7, "Configuring the Microsoft Exchange Client."

Industry messaging standards supported by Exchange include:

- CCITT X.400 recommendations—1984 and 1988 certified
- Internet standards such as SMTP, POP3, IMAP4, MIME, LDAP, HTTP, and NNTP
- MAPI

Coexistence

Messaging did not start with Exchange Server. You might already use another e-mail system in your enterprise. In this situation, it would be desirable to integrate the new platform seamlessly into the existing network in order to allow all users to communicate with each other through e-mail. Exchange Server supports direct connections to Microsoft Mail using the MS Mail Connector and to Lotus cc:Mail using the Connector for Lotus cc:Mail. These connecting components are covered in Chapter 18, "Connecting to Microsoft Mail and Schedule+ 1.0," and Chapter 19, "Connector for Lotus cc:Mail."

In addition, Exchange Server 5.5 supports direct connections to Lotus Notes through the Connector for Lotus Notes, to Professional Office Systems (PROFS) through the PROFS/OV connector, and to System Network Architecture Distributed Systems (SNADS) via the SNADS connector. The Connector for Lotus Notes will be explained in Chapter 20, "Connector for Lotus Notes." The Connector for OfficeVision/VM(PROFS) and the Connector for SNADS are not covered in this book. Neither connector is as widely used as the Connector for Lotus Notes, for instance, and the explanation regarding the connectivity between PC networks and SNA networks is beyond the scope of this book.

You will definitely come across foreign messaging systems if you plan to connect to other institutions, departments, and companies—not everybody has discovered the advantages of Exchange Server 5.5 just yet. A common messaging standard, such as X.400 or SMTP, allows you to build the e-mail bridge. First you have to contact the remote administrator to determine which standard to utilize, and then you can configure the connection accordingly. Exchange Server 5.5 supports the most important standards (X.400 and SMTP) and can connect to any other system that supports these messaging standards as well.

Third-party gateways can provide additional connectivity to DEC ALL-IN-1, MEMO, fax, voice mail, or MHS.

Heterogeneous Computer Networks

The task of integrating an Exchange Server into a heterogeneous environment can be accomplished quickly. UNIX machines, for instance, can easily connect to a computer running Windows NT Server along with Exchange Server using Transmission Control Protocol/Internet Protocol (TCP/IP). Possible UNIX clients are POP3 or IMAP4 programs and any Internet browser that supports Java script and frames. UNIX-based newsreader applications can also be considered possible clients.

Exchange Server 5.5 can benefit from the powerful capabilities of Windows NT Server if you want to integrate this system into a Novell NetWare network. The NWLink IPX/SPX compatible transport, Gateway Services for NetWare, and the SAP Agent must be installed on the Windows NT Server computer to make this possible. Messaging clients running on native Novell NetWare workstations will then be able to access the Exchange Server resources using the IPX/SPX protocol. More information about integration with a Novell NetWare environment is provided in Chapter 17, "Microsoft Exchange Clients in a NetWare Environment."

Windows NT Server further provides connectivity to Systems Network Architecture (SNA) through the DLC protocol and to AppleTalk networks by means of the Services for Macintosh, which come with Windows NT. Hence, it is possible to access Exchange Server resources from those networks as well. Users working on Apple Macintosh workstations, for example, could connect to their mailboxes using either the Exchange Client for Macintosh or the newer Outlook client. SNA connectivity is required for the PROFS and SNADS connector.

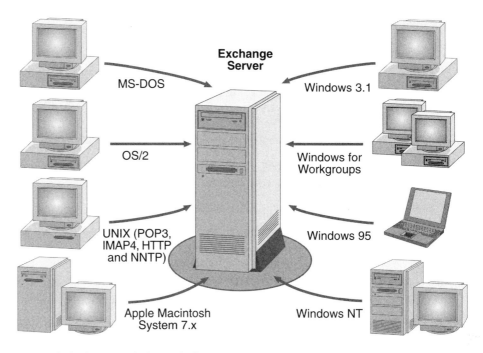

Figure 1-4. Supported client platforms.

Client platforms supported by Exchange Server include:

- MS-DOS
- Windows 3.1
- Windows for Workgroups 3.11
- Windows NT
- Windows 95
- Apple Macintosh System 7.x
- OS/2
- UNIX through POP3, IMAP4, HTTP, and NNTP protocols

The Microsoft Exchange Hierarchy

Exchange Server is designed to operate in small, medium, large, and very large computer networks. To illustrate, in some large companies there exist operational Exchange Server networks with more than 25,000 client computers. Smaller networks are easier to configure and to implement. Larger configurations typically have a complex and heterogeneous structure. Yet the organization of Exchange Server resources—their hierarchical composition—remains the same regardless of the network's complexity.

Organization

Every Exchange Server messaging network is a single organization. This is the largest administrative unit. Within the hierarchy, the organization forms the highest level, and therefore the common context, for all objects that belong to lower hierarchical levels. The most important ones are sites and Exchange Server computers. Servers outside this context cannot take part in the organization's operations. To put it more plainly, Exchange does not support multiple-organization configurations.

Note Servers of different organizations cannot share their configuration information or their address books with each other.

It is important that you make your final decision about the name of your organization at the time of the first server installation. Figure 1-5 shows that you need to enter the same case-sensitive organization name during the setup of additional Exchange Server computers later on if you want to build a common hierarchical context.

Note The organization name is case sensitive, can be up to 64 characters long, and cannot be changed without reinstalling all servers.

Site

Within the organization hierarchy, Exchange Server computers are grouped together in smaller units called sites. Sites represent the second important hierarchical context. Generally, a site consists of one or more server computers. Multiple servers need a Local Area Network (LAN) or a high-bandwidth permanent Wide Area Network (WAN) that can be used just as a LAN to contact each other. The intrasite communication relies on RPCs. Servers will communicate directly with one another to transfer messages and to synchronize their configuration and directory information.

Every Exchange organization consists of one or more sites. This simplifies the administration because the sites allow you to configure and manage multiple servers as single units utilizing sitewide configuration parameters. You must make your final decision about the name of your first site while installing the first Exchange Server computer. Additional servers might join this site at a later time. On the other hand, if you want to group servers in multiple sites, you can specify additional site names manually during the server installation. (See Figure 1-5.) You can read more about the installation of Exchange Server in Chapter 2, "Installing Microsoft Exchange Server."

Note Site names are case sensitive, can be up to 64 characters long, and cannot be changed without reinstalling all servers belonging to the site.

Server

Servers maintain mailboxes, public folders, address books, and other information. They will be represented as single objects within the Servers container under the site to which they belong. The name of a particular server object will always be identical to the server's computer name. It will be obtained automatically during the server installation and written to the Exchange Server directory.

Note You cannot rename a Windows NT Server once an Exchange Server has been installed on top of it. Otherwise, you will lose the directory information.

Each server object allows you to administer the corresponding Exchange Server computer separately, regardless of common default settings that have been specified at the site level. This might be necessary if you want to delegate specific server roles to selected Exchange Server computers. For instance, you might want to configure a server that contains only public folders. The configuration of a dedicated public folder server is covered in Chapter 12, "Creating and Managing Public Folders."

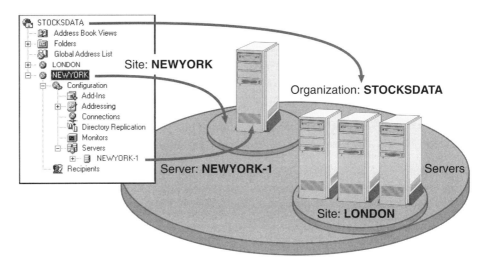

Figure 1-5. Microsoft Exchange hierarchy.

The three most important levels of the Exchange hierarchy are:

- Organization, which provides the common context for all Exchange Server computers

- Site, which simplifies Exchange administration and allows you to specify site-level default settings for all servers in a site

- Server objects level under the Servers container, which allows configuring of specific server settings independently of predefined site-level settings

Windows NT Security Integration

Exchange Server 5.5 is a Microsoft BackOffice product that runs only on Windows NT Server 4.0 (with SP3). It is specifically designed to utilize the Windows NT domain security mechanisms. This security model provides secure single logon, individual access control, and auditing.

Secure Single Logon

A particular Windows NT domain is a group of Windows NT computers that shares a common user account database for centralized administration. The Primary Domain Controller (PDC) maintains this database. Backup Domain Controllers (BDCs) might also exist. BDCs hold a copy of the PDC's user account database. The user account database will be used to validate users across the network.

Only a single logon to a Windows NT domain is necessary to obtain access to all its resources. You must supply a valid user name plus a password. The PDC or one of the BDCs will validate your access based on the specified credentials. Once you are logged on, you are known within the entire domain. You will be able to connect to the desired resources on all servers of the domain if you have the required permission.

If you install an Exchange Server on top of a Windows NT Server, you will have to maintain mailboxes, public folders, and configuration objects on this server as well. In other words, you will create additional server-based resources. Of course, these resources must be protected from unauthorized access; otherwise, every user could read all other users' messages. All access to server-based resources must be validated. Consequently, every mailbox maintains a primary Windows NT account attribute. You must log on to the Windows NT Domain using this account to open a particular mailbox. The Exchange Client and Outlook will display an error message instead of presenting you with the contents of the wanted mailbox if you logged on using a different account. In this situation, access to the intended mailbox will be denied.

Note Exchange Server is fully integrated into the Windows NT Server architecture and benefits from the Windows NT security mechanisms. Users must log on to and be validated by a Windows NT Domain before they can access server-based resources. An explicit logon to a mailbox is not necessary.

Individual Access Control

During every logon process, Windows NT Server assigns a security token to the user. This token determines the security context, which is the access to system services and resources. The token works similarly to a normal house key, but the account uses the security token to open computer resources. Every time you access objects in a domain, your security token will be checked and access permissions will be granted accordingly. (See Figure 1-6.)

Note Every time you connect to an Exchange Server, the server checks your security token (your key) in order to grant or deny access to mailboxes, public folders, and any other resources.

Exchange Server will recognize you as soon as you access its resources. It's possible to specify in detail what kind of access level you can receive for a particular object, such as a mailbox. Obviously, an administrator has a different level of access privileges than does a regular user. Several individual rights and predefined roles, consisting of specific arrangements of rights, can be granted to each account for every object within the Exchange hierarchy.

Because Exchange Server objects exist independently of Windows NT Server, user permissions must be specified separately using the Exchange Administrator program. More information regarding security issues is provided in Chapter 8, "Managing Server Configuration."

Note Permissions to administer Windows NT Server do not automatically grant equal permissions to administer an Exchange Server. Exchange Server administrators must be explicitly designated, and are usually privileged Windows NT administrators.

Auditing

Auditing refers to a system's manner of recording the access to its resources and the use of user privileges—such as logon activities—to detect breaches in security. Auditing is an important Windows NT Server feature that you need to understand if you want to keep track of user activities on your server. The desired information can be examined through the Security Event Log using the Event Viewer program.

Exchange Server utilizes the auditing capabilities of Windows NT to write its own security information to the Security Event Log. You can configure an Exchange Server computer to audit changes to the configuration of services and directory objects. Based on the security information, you will be able to identify the type of configuration activities and the Windows NT user account that has performed a specific action.

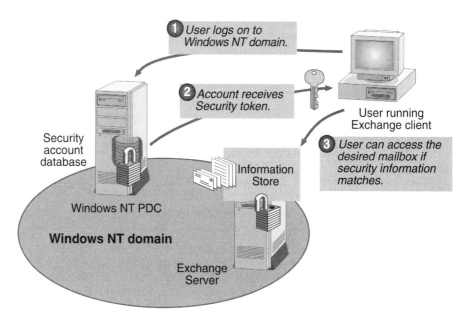

Figure 1-6. Accessing a mailbox on an Exchange Server.

The advantages of Windows NT Server integration include:

- Individual access control, which allows the administrator to specify different levels of access to selected user accounts

- Auditing, in which Exchange writes security events of interest, such as logon activities and changes to the configuration of Exchange objects to the Windows NT Security Event Log

- Single logon, in which the user needs to log on to Windows NT only once to get access to all resources in the network, including a mailbox on a Microsoft Exchange Server

Lesson 2: Microsoft Exchange Clients

Exchange Server 5.5 supports a wide variety of messaging clients because of its implementation of popular messaging standards. You should determine if your users want all the available features at their disposal (as in the Exchange Client or Outlook), if they're able to manage with only some of the features (such as in the Internet Browser or an IMAP4rev1-compliant client), or if they can get along with just the basics (as provided by a POP3 client). Depending on the actual needs, hardware may be exchanged, operating systems may be upgraded, and network structures may be redesigned.

This lesson deals with possible client programs that can be used to access personal and public messaging information that is stored on an Exchange Server 5.5. The Exchange Client family deserves to be mentioned first, although Outlook could replace this family entirely. Microsoft Outlook is an interesting alternative to Exchange, so its description follows immediately thereafter. A listing of alternative clients based on Internet standards concludes this lesson.

At the end of this lesson, you will be able to:

- List the Exchange Client programs and their basic features

- Describe the way Outlook uses the Exchange Server

- List the other clients

Estimated time to complete this lesson: 35 minutes

Microsoft Exchange Client Family

The Exchange Client is still one of the best choices if you want to use the features of an Exchange Server. This client allows you to work with messages from your personal mailbox as well as with items stored in public folders. Likewise, you can maintain schedule and calendar information, although this functionality is not implemented into the Exchange Client directly. Rather, it's available separately in Schedule+ 7.5. Furthermore, the Exchange Client can support advanced features such as electronic forms and other extensions, which allow users to adapt the client to their specific needs. You can use electronic forms within the Exchange Client, but you have to start a second program (Microsoft Electronic Forms Designer) to create and design them. For this reason, it's accurate to refer to the Exchange Client as a program family. (See Figure 1-7 on page 28.) In the following sections, the members of this program family will be introduced separately.

Microsoft Exchange Client

The beginning of a new application development project is usually a process of investigation. You must figure out what the needs of your customers are in order to program a successful piece of software. If you were asked to name your needs and expectations of any modern messaging client, you'd certainly include in your list a messaging client that supports Exchange Server, MS Mail, Internet Mail, CompuServe, The Microsoft Network (MSN), Lotus cc:Mail, and so on. You'd also want the messaging client to support all this at the same time and in a single session.

The Exchange Client is the messaging application that fulfills this wish. This client has been developed based on the MAPI industry standard, which makes it a universal viewer, allowing you to access, share, and organize messaging-related information in a platform-independent manner. Users of the Exchange Client will usually work with Exchange Server resources, but Exchange Server is only one possible messaging repository. The features of the Exchange Client are explained in more detail in Chapter 6, "Microsoft Exchange Client Architecture and Installation."

Personal Information

Obviously, connecting to many different messaging systems at the same time requires a flexible client. It doesn't matter which system delivers the messages; the client stores the items and groups the information in one place known as the universal inbox. Your inbox is not restricted to e-mail messages—it can group word processing documents, graphs, voice mail, faxes, spreadsheets, presentation graphics, meeting requests, and other data.

Collaborative Data

A client has access to public folders and their content, in addition to personal mailboxes, when connecting to an Exchange Server. Public folders allow you to distribute common material conveniently across your organization. Like private message folders, public folders can store e-mail messages, word processing documents, and other data. You might also use electronic forms in conjunction with public folders. Using all the features of public folders simultaneously, you can configure a document library, a sales tracking application, a social discussion media for child support, or a forum for beer drinkers. The extensive support of interactive one-to-many or many-to-many communication—where users can place information into and read information out of a public folder using a workgroup application— is one of the more powerful features of the Exchange Server messaging platform. The development of workgroup applications is discussed in Chapter 16.

Exchange Server 5.x provides moderated public folders, which are the monitored versions of regular public folders. If you are the moderator of a set of public folders, you can check the information before it's posted in the folder and becomes available to the public. New items will be sent to you for review. If you accept a new item, it will be placed in the public folder and thusly distributed across the organization. You can read more about public folders and their configuration in Chapter 12.

Microsoft Schedule+

Schedule+ 7.x is an integrated schedule, calendar, and personal information manager. It can be used primarily to manage your own schedule, but it is also a workgroup application—a group scheduler, so to speak. If you use it in conjunction with an Exchange Server, you can efficiently plan meetings and projects for a whole group of users.

Let's say you want to plan a meeting on Monday morning, which ten employees must attend. Because you have access to the Global Address List of the organization, you can easily select the desired attendees by using Schedule+. But what if one or many of the attendees have other arrangements made for this time? How do you find an available time to schedule the meeting in this case? Based on the scheduling information of attendees you have selected, you can check Free/Busy times so that you can see at a glance whether all attendees are available. More information about Free/Busy times is provided in Chapter 18.

Exchange Server maintains Free/Busy information based on a hidden public folder for every user who utilizes Schedule+. The personal calendar information, on the other hand, is stored in a hidden folder in your mailbox. It is also possible to configure a local calendar file in addition to the existing calendar. The local file is especially crucial when working off line. The scheduling information will be automatically synchronized between the server and the local file the next time you work on line.

Schedule+ items and their uses are as follows:

- Appointments, which are scheduled for a specified time period, can be private, tentative, and/or recurring
- Tasks, which will keep the user apprised of the current status of the task
- Projects, which group tasks together
- Events, which are appointments that don't occupy a specific amount of time during the day
- Alarms, which set up times when a reminder message should appear
- Contacts, which store addresses, phone numbers, and general notes

Electronic Forms Designer

The Electronic Forms Designer is a tool that allows for easy development of workgroup applications. This is done using electronic forms and without needing to know a programming language. In other words, everyone can create basic electronic forms to save and replace paper forms. Electronic forms are easier to handle because users can conveniently send them through the messaging network. Forms can also be assigned to public folders if you want to post the information into a dedicated repository that can be replicated across the organization rather than send them to specific recipients. Public folder replication is covered in Chapter 13, "Public Folder Replication."

If more sophisticated forms are needed, the Electronic Forms Designer can be used as a starting point for your own development projects. You can create the basic form using the Electronic Forms Designer and enhance the form using the 16-bit version of Microsoft Visual Basic 4.0. As a matter of fact, the Electronic Forms Designer can create only 16-bit applications. Electronic forms and sample applications are outlined in Chapter 16.

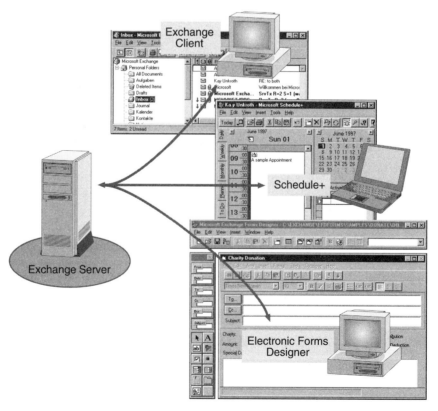

Figure 1-7. Microsoft Exchange Client family.

Some features of the Exchange Client are:

- Electronic Forms Designer, which can be used to create electronic forms without needing to know a programming language

- Exchange Client, which is the universal inbox that groups e-mail messages from various messaging systems, word processing documents, graphs, voice mail, faxes, spreadsheets, presentation graphics, and other information in a single place

- Schedule+, which is a task manager and task reminder, a calendar, a group scheduler, and a personal information manager

Microsoft Outlook Client

Outlook 97 integrates Microsoft Office 97 applications with e-mail, personal organization, and workgroup software, and enables organizations to develop and deploy workgroup applications based on Office. This client will be your best choice if you want to work seamlessly with a messaging client and the installed Office applications. In fact, Outlook 97 is the primary messaging client for Exchange Server 5.5, and its version 8.03 ships with the server product.

Outlook 97 enables you to upgrade from Exchange Client 5.0 directly. The migration process will result in a complete replacement of the prior client. Outlook users are able to use all the messaging functions that are available in the Exchange Client, plus scheduling, Electronic Forms Designer, and some new features like the Windows Explorer (from within the same application). A concise listing of the most important Outlook features is listed below.

Special Folders

Like the Exchange Client, the Windows-based Outlook is a MAPI-compliant application, so Outlook can act as your universal inbox. Fortunately, you don't need to reconfigure your mailbox on the Exchange Server when you migrate from the Exchange Client to Outlook. Using Outlook, the special **Contacts**, **Calendar**, **Tasks**, **Journal**, and **Notes** folders in your mailbox are automatically created the first time you log on through the existing messaging profile. Although your mailbox will store new items in special folders, the old folders can still be accessed as usual. (See Figure 1-8.) The configuration of messaging profiles for Outlook is covered in Chapter 7.

Forms

Outlook comes with new forms capabilities that are provided on the 32-bit Windows platforms. These forms are generally smaller and faster than their counterparts of the previous version of the Electronic Forms Designer because they don't need to be compiled. Interpreted at run time, however, they are available only within Outlook. This is a critical aspect of Outlook forms in mixed environments—the native Exchange Client 5.0 is not able to load and display them without having Outlook installed on the same computer. Also, the 16-bit and the Macintosh versions of Outlook are not able to handle Outlook forms. Outlook, on the other hand, can start the older 16-bit forms in any situation. Moreover, Outlook 97 version 8.03 supports HTML forms that have been created using Microsoft Visual InterDev. Regardless of the client platform (Macintosh, 16-bit, or 32-bit), Outlook can launch these forms in your default Internet browser. The electronic forms development platforms are explored in more detail in Chapter 16.

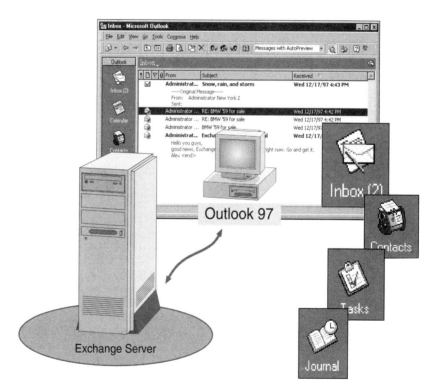

Figure 1-8. Microsoft Outlook client.

Messaging-related features of the Outlook client include:

- Seamless Office integration, in which Outlook mirrors the interface and the commands of Office 97

- E-mail enhancements, such as AutoNameCheck, message tracking, message recall, and hyperlinks

- Calendar and scheduling enhancements, such as meeting request processing, attendee tracking, and appointment duration

- General enhancements, such as one-click access to personal folders, ActiveViews, multilevel sorting, and creation of custom forms for any Outlook data type

- Task management enhancements, such as task requests and tracking, status reports, categories as projects, and Outlook Journal

- Outlook Forms, from which users can create custom workgroup and workflow applications

Other Clients

Exchange Server 5.5 is also referred to as the Internet edition of Exchange Server. It offers even more extended connectivity to the Internet than does version 5.0, but connections to the Internet can still be problematic. For example, if you are planning to allow your users to access an Exchange Server from the Internet using POP3 software, an IMAP4-compliant client, an Internet browser, or newsreader programs (as shown in Figure 1-9), you should take care not to open the network of the entire company for everyone's access. Otherwise, you might be "visited" someday by guests who are anything but welcome. Dedicated security equipment, which is not part of the Exchange Server product, will be necessary in this case. Within an intranet, however, such equipment is usually not required.

POP3 Clients

A POP3 client is a client program that relies on the Post Office Protocol version 3, such as Microsoft Internet Mail, Outlook Express, Netscape Navigator Mail, and Eudora. Exchange Server 5.5 supports all of these. Of course, since POP3 is an open Internet standard, other POP3 e-mail programs can also be used to connect to the server.

A POP3 client is able to read messages from a particular user's inbox only. Messages within other folders cannot be accessed. A POP3 client is not able to encrypt messages or to browse the Global Address List. Querying the address list is possible only if your POP3 client additionally supports LDAP as Directory Access protocol. You can read more about the POP3-based and LDAP-based features in Chapter 11.

IMAP4 Clients

Modern Internet Mail clients such as Outlook Express and Netscape Communicator utilize the Internet Mail Access Protocol version 4 for accessing server-based resources. IMAP4 is far more flexible and powerful than POP3 and will more than likely replace POP3 programs in the future. For instance, you can decide whether to use a server-based repository of e-mail messages or a local message store when using Outlook Express 4.0. IMAP4-based access to public folders on an Exchange Server 5.5 is also possible, which implies that you can participate in discussion forums directly.

IMAP4 is a complex protocol that allows you to specify, in detail, which portion of a particular message you want to download. It is not, however, a protocol for sending messages. IMAP4 clients utilize SMTP to accomplish this task. So if you want to support IMAP4 clients completely, you need to install and start the IMS on one of the Exchange Server computers in your organization. The implementation of IMAP4 within Exchange Server 5.5 is covered in Chapter 11.

Internet Browser

You can use any Internet browser to access the Exchange Server through HTTP. Registered users can log on to their personal mailboxes in order to read and send e-mail messages. Both validated and anonymous users are able to access public folders and the Global Address List. Of course, it's at the administrator's discretion that anonymous users are allowed access, which can be done separately for both public folder access as well as access to the Global Address List.

With HTTP, messaging becomes independent of the application being used. The user can access the Exchange Server resources based on a Uniform Resource Locator (URL), and the data is represented just as any other HTML document. To be able to display the documents, the Web browser needs to support Java script and Frame components. The configuration of Web-based access to an Exchange Server is covered in Chapter 11.

Newsreader

POP3 and IMAP4 clients and Internet browsers are not the only Internet clients supported by Exchange Server—the NNTP is supported as well. Newsreader clients can access the data in public folders, which have been published on the Internet in the form of newsgroups. Microsoft Internet News is one example of a dedicated newsreader program. Outlook Express can also be used to access newsgroups through NNTP. Users working with these clients are not limited to read-only access; they can also post new items if they have the appropriate permissions as specified through public folder properties. The configuration of NNTP will be covered in Chapter 11.

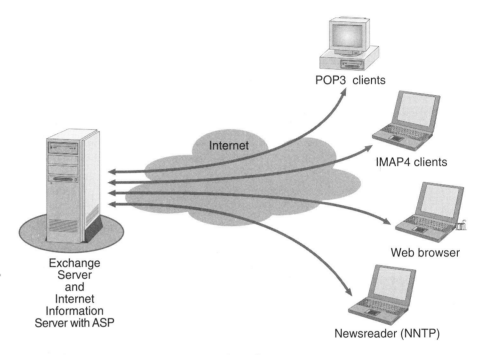

Figure 1-9.   Client access to Exchange from the Internet.

Some examples of Internet messaging clients are:

- Eudora (POP3)
- MAPI Internet Mail Transport Provider (POP3)
- Internet Explorer 3.x and 4.0 (HTTP)
- Internet Mail (POP3)
- Internet News 3.0 (NNTP)
- Microsoft Outlook Express (POP3 and IMAP4)
- Netscape Navigator 2.0 Plus or higher (HTTP)
- Netscape Communicator (POP3 and IMAP4)
- Netscape Navigator Mail (POP3)

Lesson 3: Exchange Server Messaging Infrastructure

Maintaining an Exchange Server organization is sometimes hard work, but you can make it interesting for yourself. To successfully maintain a server, constant monitoring of its components is essential. Exchange Server assists you with this task. Nevertheless, there are so many server components that you'll need to know which tools to use for which kind of components and monitoring.

This lesson covers the composition of an Exchange Server computer by introducing its essential and optional components. A brief description will reveal the purpose of each element, and the new components of Exchange Server 5.5 will be more fully described. In addition, several important maintenance tools are introduced to demonstrate what can be done to keep an Exchange Server permanently available on the network. Various Windows NT tools, as listed at the end of this section, might assist you in the task of managing the installed Exchange Server computers within your messaging organization.

At the end of this lesson, you will be able to:

- Identify Exchange Server core components
- List optional server components
- Plan the usage of Server and Link Monitors
- Name the relevant Windows NT tools for Exchange Server administration

Estimated time to complete this lesson: 30 minutes

Exchange Server Core Components

Only an administrator who is able to ensure that the core services of his or her Exchange Server computers are running can sleep soundly. These Windows NT services are required to accomplish essential server tasks, such as validating user access to server-based resources, processing address queries, sending and delivering messages, maintaining data in private and public folders, and replicating information for other servers.

Note If one of the core services (as shown in Figure 1-10) stops due to a critical state, the system must be considered nonfunctioning.

Directory Service

The DS is the brain of an Exchange Server. It stores the configuration information about the messaging infrastructure of your organization. This component keeps track of sites, servers, mailboxes, public folders, and other objects within the Exchange hierarchy. It stores this information in a database called Dir.edb. The server would lose its memory if you replaced the Dir.edb with a fresh, empty file.

Whenever you change the configuration of an Exchange Server, for example when creating a new mailbox or a messaging connector, the DS will distribute the configuration changes to all other servers across the organization. This can be accomplished through direct RPC communication within a site or by e-mail messages between sites. The directory replication within a site is covered in Chapter 4 and between sites in Chapter 9.

Message Transfer Agent

The MTA is the heart of the server. It is a pump that keeps the e-mail messages running through the veins and arteries of the messaging network. It is a native X.400 system based on the standards of the 1988 conformance year. The MTA is also responsible for message routing and address resolution. The tasks of the MTA are covered in Chapter 4 and in Chapter 9.

Information Store

The IS is the structured repository for all server-based user information, such as messages, Word documents, multimedia objects, and electronic forms. This service is also responsible for maintaining mailboxes and public folders. Mailboxes are stored in the Priv.edb database; public folders are kept in a database file called Pub.edb. The mailbox management is explained in Chapter 5, "Creating and Managing Recipients," while public folders are the main topic of Chapter 12.

Both databases—Priv.edb and Pub.edb—can grow rapidly, since they maintain all the user information (messages, documents, and so forth). Unfortunately, these databases were limited to 16 GB each in Exchange 5.0 and in earlier versions. You might think that 16 GB is a huge repository, but any limit is still a limit. Exchange Server 5.5 eliminates the 16-GB limit for all those administrators who need and appreciate really big servers.

Note Exchange Server 5.5 databases are not limited to 16 GB. In other words, only the hard disk capabilities of the server computer will determine the maximum capacity of the IS.

The time seems to be ripe for huge servers. The backup performance has been improved (up to 25 GB of throughput per hour) and Exchange Server 5.5 supports the cluster server technology. Microsoft Cluster Server can be configured using the Enterprise Edition of Windows NT Server, which provides single-node failover in case of emergencies. However, a cautious administrator will still avoid gigantic servers with huge Information Store databases for several reasons that will be discussed in Chapter 15, "Maintaining Servers."

System Attendant

The SA regularly checks the server to make sure everything is running smoothly and services the maintenance routines of the Exchange Server, such as the online defragmentation of the messaging databases. It is also responsible for the routing table recalculation. If you stop this service, all other Exchange Server services will also be stopped in order to prevent any uncontrolled behavior in the system.

Note You can shut down an entire Exchange Server by stopping the System Attendant service.

The SA will be involved if you are monitoring servers through Server Monitors. Furthermore, it allows you to check the state of messaging connectors and paths automatically by using Link Monitors. You can read more about Server and Link Monitors in Chapter 15.

The core services of the Exchange Server are:

- DS, which maintains information that describes the Exchange Server organization, including mailboxes, distribution lists, servers, sites and their configuration, and more

- MTA, which provides routing functions to deliver messages between servers and sites

- IS, which contains public and private stores (databases) that maintain user messages and public folder contents

- SA, which provides diagnostic and logging capabilities for connectors and services, launches the Exchange Server maintenance routines, and recalculates routing tables

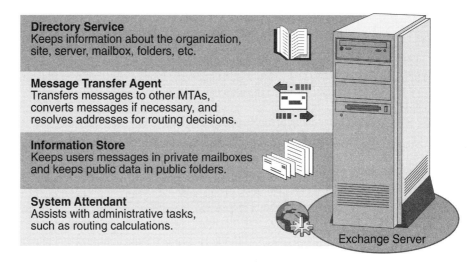

Directory Service
Keeps information about the organization, site, server, mailbox, folders, etc.

Message Transfer Agent
Transfers messages to other MTAs, converts messages if necessary, and resolves addresses for routing decisions.

Information Store
Keeps users messages in private mailboxes and keeps public data in public folders.

System Attendant
Assists with administrative tasks, such as routing calculations.

Exchange Server

Figure 1-10. Exchange Server core components.

Optional Components

Optional server components can extend the standard functionality of your Exchange Server. The optional components mainly provide connectivity to foreign messaging systems such as SMTP-based hosts in the Internet. Valuable optional services such as the Advanced Security are also features of additional components.

Depending on the situation, components can be more or less important for a particular organization. This will become clear when you are introduced to the topology of the STOCKSDATA corporation in later chapters. Their network will rely heavily on Internet connections. If the Internet mail connections of this organization are not working reliably, the functionality of the whole system will be seriously—and negatively—impacted.

Internet Mail Service

The IMS can be considered an additional component. It is implemented as a separate Windows NT service that provides connectivity to SMTP hosts over the Internet or an intranet. Basically, only one IMS is necessary to connect the entire organization to the Internet. It is also possible to connect multiple sites together through IMS links. To maintain a Global Address List for an organization consisting of multiple sites, directory replication can be performed through IMS links as well. The IMS is explained in more detail in Chapter 10.

Internet News Service

The INS is an optional component that allows you to configure newsfeeds for USENET newsgroups. Using the INS, you can transfer information from USENET newsgroups to public folders and vice versa. The data is exchanged using NNTP. The INS is covered in Chapter 11.

Outlook Web Access Components

Another element, the Outlook Web Access components, allows you to publish Exchange Server information over the World Wide Web to users running appropriate Internet browsers. In addition to the Exchange Server and the Outlook Web Access components, Microsoft Internet Information Server (IIS) 3.0 or higher must be running within your network. As an enhancement to Exchange Server 5.5, access to calendar objects is now possible using an Internet browser. The components that provide HTTP-based access to the Exchange Server are covered in Chapter 11.

Microsoft Mail Connector

You will use the Microsoft Mail Connector to integrate your Exchange Server seamlessly into an existing MS Mail network. Large organizations might want to use Exchange Server and Mail 3.x in tandem at least during the time of a migration from one system to another. Connectivity between both systems is therefore an essential criterion if the e-mail communication between users cannot be interrupted. The Mail Connector and other issues concerning Mail are covered in Chapter 18.

Directory Synchronization Agent

The Mail Connector is also the basis of the Mail Directory Synchronization. (See Figure 1-11.) The active service that processes the DirSync messages is the Directory Synchronization Agent (DXA). Once synchronized, Exchange users will be able to select Mail addresses from their Global Address List. Likewise, Mail users will be able to select Exchange recipients from their post office address lists—and if enabled, from their Global Address List as well. The configuration of the Mail Directory Synchronization is covered in Chapter 18.

Schedule+ Free/Busy Connector

If you connect an Exchange Server to an MS Mail network through the Mail Connector, Schedule+ Free/Busy information can also be exchanged between both systems. To accomplish this task, you need to configure the Schedule+ Free/Busy Connector in order to exchange the information. You can read more about the Schedule+ Free/Busy Connector in Chapter 18.

Connector for Lotus cc:Mail

If you plan to integrate Exchange Server 5.5 with a Lotus cc:Mail messaging network, the Connector for Lotus cc:Mail should be taken into consideration. (See Figure 1-11.) This connector allows for the transferring of messages between both systems. This connector can also be used to perform Directory Synchronization between Exchange and Lotus cc:Mail—no additional component is required to synchronize the addresses between these two systems. The Connector for Lotus cc:Mail is the topic of Chapter 19.

Connector for Lotus Notes

Lotus Notes and Exchange Server are some of the most widely used messaging and workgroup computing platforms today. Exchange 5.5 offers extensive connectivity to Lotus Notes, which allows you to integrate the Exchange platform into an existing Lotus Notes network. This new connector supports not only the exchange of e-mail messages but also the synchronization of directory information between both systems. The Connector for Lotus Notes is covered in more detail in Chapter 20.

PROFS and SNADS Connectors

Exchange Server 5.5 offers connectivity to PROFS and SNADS systems in addition to the Connector for Lotus Notes. The PROFS connector, as its name implies, allows you to connect to PROFS, which is a messaging system on IBM mainframe computers. Several newer messaging systems, such as IBM OfficeVision/VM, provide backward compatibility to PROFS on mainframe computers. If you want to exchange messages with other users through the SNA Distribution Services (SNADS), you will find the SNADS connector very useful. Examples of SNADS-compliant systems are IBM OfficeVision/ VM, IBM OfficeVision/400, SoftSwitch Central, and Verimation Memo. The PROFS connector is the topic of Chapter 21, and the SNADS connector is covered in Chapter 22.

Key Management Server

Another optional component, the Key Management Server (KMS), in contrast to all the other components that have been introduced so far, does not provide any messaging connectivity. Instead, it allows users to encrypt messages or to sign them digitally for originator approval. This service maintains its own database to store X.509 certificates and public encryption keys for users. It is the basis of the Advanced Security features implemented in Exchange Server. The KMS components are explained in Chapter 14, " Implementing Advanced Security.

Microsoft Exchange Chat Service

Exchange Server 5.5 supports real-time communication between users through its Exchange Chat Service. This service enables users running any Internet Relay Chat (IRC) software or extended IRC client to establish a session with the Exchange Server. In other words, Exchange Server 5.5 allows you to create a chat server network for real-time one-to-one, one-to-many, and many-to-many conversations.

If you're a conservative messaging administrator, you might have strong objections against the implementation of the Chat Service into Exchange Server 5.5. Chat supports real-time communication, which means all participants have to be on line, while messaging and workgroup computing uses the idea of storing and forwarding information independently of any recipient's online or offline state. However, chatting represents another form of interactive communication, which can be considered a useful add-on to the general fuctionality of a messaging network based on Exchange Server.

Microsoft Exchange Event Service

The Event Service is the service that supports server-side Exchange Scripting Agents. These agents allow you to create and activate event-driven script–based routines for personal and public folders. Simple workflow and collaboration automation becomes possible using these agents. You can read more about server-side scripts and the Event Service in Chapter 16.

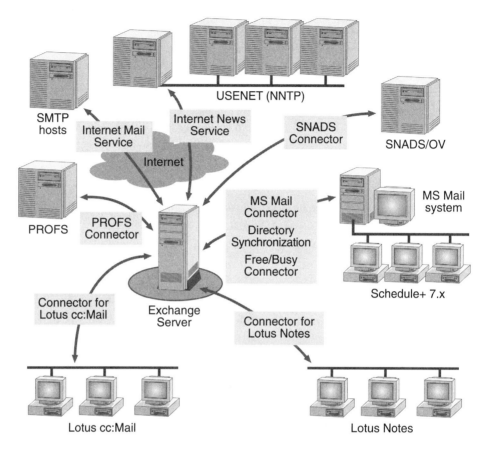

Figure 1-11. Connectivity provided by additional components.

The following are the optional components of Exchange Server:

- Outlook Web Access components, which permit access to Web-based e-mail, address books, and public folders

- Connector for Lotus cc:Mail, which provides message transfer and Directory Synchronization between Exchange Server sites and Lotus cc:Mail post offices

- Connector for Lotus Notes, which provides message transfer and Directory Synchronization between Exchange Server sites and Lotus Notes

- IMS, which provides interoperability between Exchange Server and SMTP-based mail systems

- INS, which allows USENET newsgroups to be exposed as public folders and public folders to be exposed as USENET newsgroups

- KMS, which provides the encryption and digital signature service

- Exchange Chat Service, which allows users to communicate with each other using an IRC or extended IRC client

- Exchange Event Service, which supports server-side scripting agents for simple workflow and collaboration automation

- MS Mail Connector, which provides interoperability between Exchange Server and MS Mail 3.x systems

- DXA, which provides a mechanism to exchange e-mail addresses between Exchange Server and MS Mail 3.x systems

- Schedule+ Free/Busy Connector, which allows sharing Free/Busy times between Exchange Server and MS Mail

- PROFS Connector, which allows Exchange users to exchange messages with PROFS users

- SNADS Connector, which can be used to transfer messages back and forth between Exchange Server and SNADS systems such as IBM OfficeVision400

Reliability of Exchange Server

So long as users have no reason to complain—and there should be no complaints when an administrator is faster in solving critical states than users are in discovering problems—administrators will be regarded with respect. Exchange Server provides several tools that allow you to be always one step ahead of your users in discovering critical situations.

Important Tasks

It's easy to describe the most important task of a messaging system—it has to transfer messages from point A to point B. As the Exchange Server administrator, you have to guarantee that this will always work as expected. Nothing destroys users' confidence in a backbone more than a system that loses or delays messages somewhere. In fact, in a homogeneous Exchange Server organization, you can realize message delivery times in the range of 2 minutes, provided that Site Connectors in a LAN are used and that your users are not sending an inordinate number of messages.

Fortunately, Exchange Server allows you to configure more than one messaging connector between point A and point B, with the advantage that messages are still able to travel to their destination if one messaging connector is not available for some time. The MTA is sophisticated enough to discover this state and will use the alternate route. This concept of "security through redundancy" can be enhanced, if necessary, by installing different connectors on different servers and, if the underlying infrastructure allows, by selecting different physical links and network protocols for them.

Load balancing between all connectors is another advantage. It's even possible to route a message to another site first (point C) to transfer the item to point B. Intersite replication will ensure that all connectors—and therefore all available messaging paths—of an organization are well known in all locations. The message handling between sites is covered in more detail in Chapter 9.

Server Monitoring

As mentioned, the DS, MTA, IS, SA, and possibly other components need to be running on an Exchange Server in order to provide messaging features to users. The most important services should be monitored constantly just to make sure that they are running. Either you do all the work manually or you let the system accomplish the task automatically. Instead of manually examining the services using the **Services** applet of the Control Panel, it's much more convenient to employ Server Monitors, which are active components that check the state of specified services on remote servers. (See Figure 1-12.)

Server Monitors are features of the Exchange Administrator program. One Server Monitor can monitor multiple servers and multiple Server Monitors can be launched using one Administrator program. If one of the monitored components shuts down for any reason, a Server Monitor can accomplish different tasks, depending on how it is configured: it can try to restart the service, it might reboot the whole server automatically, and it will certainly notify you about the critical state. A carefully configured Server Monitor will always keep you well informed of the server's status. Plus, it can be a valuable tool to prevent temporary problems from turning into critical situations. It is therefore a key component of reliable Exchange Server maintenance. More information about Server Monitors is provided in Chapter 15.

Link Monitoring

Running Exchange Server services is one of the two most important criteria to guarantee that a message can travel from point A to point B. A broken messaging connector, however, cannot be detected using a Server Monitor. For this reason, Exchange Server provides Link Monitors to measure the transmission speed. The most important configuration parameter of a Link Monitor is the message transfer time limit for a round trip from point A to point B and back to point A. (See Figure 1-12.)

The Link Monitor is an active component, that can be configured for every logical messaging link to another site or foreign system. The monitor itself—with support from the SA—will send test messages to remote systems (point B) awaiting their returned replies. A functioning connector will transport the test messages to the target system and back, keeping the specified time limit. By receiving the response, the link will be considered in good working order. On the other hand, if a test message cannot be received within the specified limit, the link will be considered broken. In this case, the Link Monitor will inform you about the broken state. This way you can correct configuration problems immediately and message delays can be kept to a minimum. Link Monitors are explained in Chapter 15.

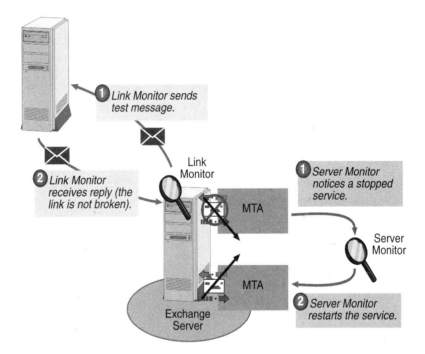

Figure 1-12. Server and Link Monitors.

Exchange provides reliability through the following features:

- Intelligent rerouting of messages, so that if one connection fails, Exchange Server automatically reroutes messages through other connections that point to the same recipient

- Link Monitor, which checks that test messages sent to other sites or to foreign systems can make a round trip within a specified length of time

- Server Monitor, which checks the services running on servers that are reachable through RPC for the server on which a Server Monitor is running, allows services to be restarted automatically, and even reboots the whole server without manual intervention

Leveraging of Windows NT Features

Exchange Server enables several administrative Windows NT tools to handle and monitor Exchange Server resources properly. (See Figure 1-13.) Most of the extensions are installed during the setup of the Exchange Administrator program. More information about Windows NT tools is provided in Chapter 8.

Control Panel and Server Manager

The Services applet of the Control Panel can be used to start and stop the Exchange Server services. The Control Panel is also useful if you want to check the status of Windows NT services. The startup type and the service account information can be counterchecked. Likewise, if you want to administer the services of a remote computer, you can use the Server Manager instead. The **Services** command under the **Computer** menu will display the **Services On Computer** dialog box, where you can accomplish the administrative tasks remotely just as you would locally using the Control Panel.

Event Viewer

The Event Viewer is a helpful tool if you want to analyze the status of services to identify possible problems through the Application Event Log. The level of detail for the available information depends on the diagnostics logging level, which can be set for a large number of categories that each service provides individually. In the event of a problem the logging level can be increased to obtain more detailed information. Once a critical situation has been clarified, it is advisable to decrease the logging level.

Note Warnings and errors are always written to the Application Event Log, independently of the current diagnostics logging settings.

User Manager for Domains

The User Manager for Domains will be typically used to create, modify, and delete Windows NT user accounts. The Exchange Server Setup extends this program in order to add Exchange functionality. A clear indicator of the extension is the **Exchange** menu. The extension allows you to create a corresponding mailbox at the same time you create a new Windows NT account. On the other hand, this extension can delete a user's mailbox if you delete the account again. The creation of user mailboxes is covered in Chapter 5.

Windows NT Backup

The Exchange Server Setup replaces the existing Windows NT Backup program completely. The enhanced Exchange Server version includes the standard file and directory backup functionality as well as the ability to back up and restore Exchange directories and information store databases while the Exchange Server services are running (online backup). While the directory and the information store databases can be backed up separately, a discrete backup of the public and private information store databases is not possible. To the regret of most administrators, a separate backup or restoration of mailboxes is also not possible. However, Exchange Server 5.5 introduces a feature called "Deleted Items Recovery," which allows users of Outlook version 8.03 to recover deleted messages or folders without the need for administrative intervention. The various backup types are covered in Chapter 15.

Note The backup performance has been improved significantly with Exchange Server 5.5. Now it is possible to achieve backup rates of approximately 25 GB per hour.

Performance Monitor

The Performance Monitor allows you to create reports about resource consumption on a server based on monitor counters. These reports can be used to track resource usage for billing and future capacity planning.

Specific Exchange Server objects and performance counters will be added to the Performance Monitor during the Exchange Server installation. Likewise, the Exchange Server Setup places several preconfigured Performance Monitor files in the Microsoft Exchange program group. You can use the files immediately to measure the workload of the server, to identify how many messages are awaiting delivery in message queues, and how many users are currently connected to an Exchange Server. Performance Monitor counters are also discussed in Chapter 2.

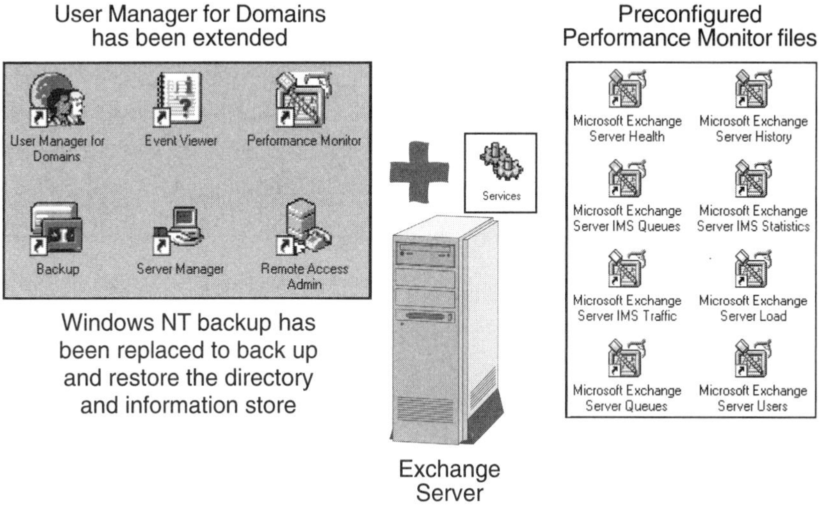

User Manager for Domains
has been extended

Preconfigured
Performance Monitor files

Windows NT backup has
been replaced to back up
and restore the directory
and information store

Exchange
Server

Figure 1-13. Windows NT tools used to administer an Exchange Server.

The most important administrative Windows NT tools are as follows:

- Control Panel, to start and stop local Exchange services
- Event Viewer, to view events logged by Exchange Server services
- Performance Monitor, to monitor the workload of the Exchange Server for capacity planning and to create other reports
- Server Manager, to start and stop local and remote Exchange services
- User Manager for Domains extended with Mailumx.dll, to create mailboxes right at the time of the Windows NT account creation
- Windows NT Backup, to back up and restore the Exchange directory and information store

Review

1. A company is planning to implement Exchange Server. As an administrator, you need to determine the possible client platforms. What platforms are supported?

   _____

   _____

   _____

   _____

2. What are the disadvantages of a shared-file messaging system?

   _____

   _____

   _____

3. Why would you prefer a client/server over a shared-file messaging system?

   _____

   _____

   _____

4. What are the most important levels of the Exchange Server hierarchy?

   _____

   _____

   _____

5. Exchange Server has been implemented tightly into the Windows NT domain security. What are the advantages?

   _____

   _____

   _____

6. An organization has installed Exchange Server 5.5. Now it's time to send and receive messages, but the users also want to be able to manage scheduling information. Furthermore, users want to create and design electronic forms, and discussion forums based on public folders and they don't use Office 97. What clients would you suggest?

_____

_____

_____

7. You want to migrate from Exchange Client to Outlook. What has to be reconfigured?

_____

_____

8. The Exchange Server supports a variety of Internet protocols. What clients can be used to access information on the server?

_____

_____

_____

_____

9. What are the most important Exchange Server services that need to be running on every server? What tasks must they be able to handle?

_____

_____

_____

10. What additional connector components come with Exchange Server 5.5?

_____

_____

_____

_____

_____

_____

11. You plan to connect the Exchange organization to the Internet. Users need to be able to send and receive messages to and from SMTP-based systems. Also, relevant newsgroups must be distributed within the organization. Which additional components would you install?

_____

_____

_____

_____

12. You are planning to implement a dedicated Exchange Server that will maintain newsgroup information for your organization on a very large scale. What is the largest size your information store databases can grow to?

_____

_____

_____

_____

13. What components would you configure to automatically check the status of important services and connections to other sites?

_____

_____

_____

C H A P T E R   2

Installing Microsoft Exchange Server

This chapter explores the available methods for the installation of Microsoft Exchange Server 5.5 and its optimization. The Exchange Server setup program allows the administrator to create new organizations and sites, join existing sites with additional servers, and upgrade existing servers from previous versions to Exchange Server 5.5.

Overview

The installation of a single Exchange Server computer is not a very complex task. It just takes a few mouse clicks and some configuration parameters, and the first server has been installed. But you're doing more than just installing a server; you're also launching a new messaging network. Several irreversible decisions regarding the network configuration will be made at this point. This becomes especially clear as you add new resources to the messaging network, since you will need to install them in a context that has been predefined by that time. In other words, if you need to change the fundamental parameters of your messaging network at a later date, you will have to reinstall one or many existing servers. Consequently, it is recommended that you design the implementation plan carefully before you install the first server. This forethought can help avoid unnecessary work during the rollout.

Lesson 1 explains the prerequisites for Exchange Server 5.5. You'll read about the hardware and software requirements that are necessary to complete an installation successfully. The three different installation types (**Minimum**, **Typical**, and **Complete/Custom**) will be introduced as well.

In Lesson 2 you'll learn how to create a new site. You will also learn how to add a new server to an existing site or upgrade an existing server to version 5.5.

Two special modes of the setup program and one specific setup scenario are the topic of Lesson 3. The first special setup mode is the maintenance mode, which is useful if you want to add additional components to an Exchange Server once the server has been installed. The second mode is the unattended Setup mode, which allows you to predefine installation options in detail in an initialization file and to install an Exchange Server computer without manual interaction. The specific setup scenario, in turn, describes the installation of an Exchange Server 5.5 in a clustered environment.

Post-installation considerations will be discussed in Lesson 4. You'll read about the optimization of an Exchange Server computer as well as about existing methods to improve the security of its resources. The separate installation of the Exchange Administrator program is also covered.

Lesson 5 concludes the installation considerations by presenting possible installation problems and the appropriate methods to avoid and, if necessary, to resolve them. This lesson provides, for instance, a detailed description about why and how NetBEUI can cause the setup procedure to crash.

Four practical exercises complete this chapter. They further clarify the theoretical explanations given throughout the chapter by guiding you through the steps of creating a new site, adding a server to an existing site, and optimizing the server installation.

In the following lessons, you will be introduced to:

- The hardware and software requirements for installing Exchange Server
- Installation types (**Mininum, Complete/Custom, and Typical**)
- Creating a new site
- Adding a server to an existing site
- Upgrading existing servers to version 5.5 and what you must do during an upgrade
- Adding server components to an existing server
- Running the Exchange Server Setup program unattended
- Installing Exchange Server 5.5 in a clustered enviroment
- Optimizing the server and analyzing file locations and default permissions
- Resolving common installation problems

Lesson 1: Preparing for a Microsoft Exchange Installation

Mr. Fred Pumpkin, one of the administrators at STOCKSDATA, was certain that the Exchange Server setup would be piece of cake. But after he installed a Windows NT server, inserted the Microsoft Exchange Server 5.5 CD-ROM, and launched the setup program, he was greeted with this message: "This version of Microsoft Exchange Server requires Windows NT Server version 4.0 (Build 1381: Service Pack 3) or later." After clicking the **OK** button twice, his installation attempt was finished, but unsuccessful.

This lesson will explain the system requirements that must be met in order for you to avoid getting the same message Mr. Pumpkin received, and to successfully install an Exchange Server computer with all the desired options. This lesson will also direct your attention toward the several points that are important for you to keep in mind when designing an implementation plan. For instance, you'll read about Windows NT dependencies, which must be taken into consideration before you can launch the setup program. This lesson concludes with an introduction to the available installation types.

One practical exercise is included, which will guide you through the steps of creating Windows NT accounts as well as local and global groups. It is a prerequisite for completing the exercises in the lessons that follow.

At the end of this lesson, you will be able to:

- Describe the installation requirements for Exchange Server 5.5
- Name the software requirements for a successful installation
- Plan hardware requirements
- Describe Windows NT security dependencies
- Assign Exchange Server permissions to additional administrator accounts
- Use the various installation types to set up the desired components on the server

Estimated time to complete this lesson: 35 minutes

System Requirements

The system requirements for a successful server installation will vary depending on the situation. The setup of the first server in an organization is the installation of an Exchange Server in a new site. This implies that the following tasks must be accomplished: organization and site names must be defined, a service account must be specified, and several other requirements—such as hardware and software dependencies—must be met. The installation of additional servers, on the other hand, introduces new questions, so you must decide whether to create a new site or to add the server to a site that already exists. In the case of multiple sites, you will need to install connecting components, which might introduce further dependencies.

Hardware Requirements

Exchange Server 5.5 needs powerful hardware, as shown in Figure 2-1 on page 59. This is hardly surprising, since this messaging platform is a client/ server system, which usually requires a strong server computer. The actual hardware requirements, however, are difficult to ascertain. While minimum requirements can be determined quickly, they're seldom sufficient for a server that is supposed to cope with real-world demands. Nevertheless, if you check the official documentation, you will not find much discussion about detailed sample configurations—the flexibility of this system is simply too enormous to calculate the actual hardware requirements without exact testing. Therefore, this chapter cannot present a general formula for detailed configurations; instead, it encourages the usage of the Load Simulator (Loadsim.exe).

The Load Simulator is a tool that can simulate multiple users on an Exchange Server computer. It can be found in the BackOffice Resource Kit 2.0 and can run on Windows NT 3.51 or 4.0. The Load Simulator can simulate any number of users sending and receiving messages distributed over a user-defined time frame. According to the specified settings, this tool will automatically create mailboxes and public folders in order to send messages between them using one or many server computers. Hence, it provides a way to measure the expected load of work that your users might generate. In addition, you can use the Performance Monitor to create reports for detailed analyses about average delivery times, resource usage, and so on. You can create a draft about the necessary hardware requirements for your organization based on the reports and the test installation.

Although not all users read and send the same number of e-mail messages in a given time frame, it's to your advantage to determine the average volume of e-mail, per user, sent and received per user in your organization. This can help you to design the server hardware to better accommodate your users' needs. The Load Simulator, for instance, classifies users in three categories, as listed on the following page. Although your users might have different demands, these categories can help design a reliable test scenario for your organization:

Type	Messages sent/day	Messages read/day	Max. Inbox size (in messages)
Light	7	20	20
Medium	20	56	125
Heavy	39	119	250

Fortunately, Windows NT—and therefore Exchange Server—is widely scalable. If you discover that additional hardware, such as more memory (RAM) or more processors, is required, you have the option to add these components at any time. Exchange Server takes advantage of powerful and sophisticated hardware configurations such as multiprocessor computers and caching disk array controllers.

Software Requirements

Exchange Server 5.5 can be installed on Windows NT Server 4.0 only, and you must also apply Service Packs (SP) to your server installation. A Service Pack is a collection of solutions for known problems that arose after a major version of the main product (Windows NT 4.0 in this case) was released. Generally, the newer the SP, the better. You will not be able to install Exchange Server 5.5 on a Windows NT 4.0 platform without SP3 (remember Fred Pumpkin's attempt, earlier in this chapter).

Note It is advisable to apply the newest Service Packs for Windows NT Server and Exchange as soon as they become available. The most current Service Pack versions can always be found at *www.microsoft.com*.

Exchange Server 5.5 supports clustering. If you want to benefit from such a configuration, however, you need to install the Enterprise Edition of Windows NT Server 4.0. The steps required to install an Exchange Server in a clustered environment will be discussed later in this chapter.

Domain Dependencies

The underlying domain structure and the planned site topology of your organization must be determined prior to the installation. This is important for the following two reasons:

1. You must have administrative permissions on the computer onto which you'll install Exchange Server 5.5. In other words, the computer needs to be located in your own domain or in a domain that trusts your domain. If this is not the case—if you cannot access the computer using your account—you will not be able to install or manage the Exchange Server computer.

2. Windows NT domain dependencies also exist in respect to the Site Services Account. A common account must be used for all servers that will be grouped together in a single site. It might, however, be the case that a common service account is impossible, perhaps because of the existing Windows NT domain structure. In this situation, you will be forced to implement a multiple site organization. The features of Windows NT security are also covered in the section, "Windows NT Dependencies," later in this lesson.

Server-to-Server Communication

In order to allow direct communication between Exchange Server computers in a site, Remote Procedure Calls (RPC) must be supported. RPCs are always built on top of LAN protocols; however, server RPCs cannot utilize every LAN protocol. Only TCP/IP and the SPX/IPX-compatible protocol called NWLink provide the required connectivity. WAN protocols, such as X.25, are not supported as platforms for RPCs at all; they require messaging connectors, which automatically result in multiple site configurations.

Note Although NetBEUI is a true LAN protocol, it is not supported for server-to-server communication.

RPCs are communication methods that consume a lot of network bandwidth (transmission capacity of your network) and should therefore not be used if the net available bandwidth between servers is low (for example, a 28.8 Kbps dial-up connection). Servers connected through high-bandwidth networks can be grouped together in a single site, while servers connected through slow links should be installed in different sites, because RPCs will not necessarily be used for intersite communication. If you are not sure if the net available capacity of your network connection allows single-site implementation, you can measure the network traffic patterns using network-monitoring software (such as Microsoft Network Monitor), or the Windows NT Performance Monitor before you start the actual rollout. Important factors (measured in packets per second) are as follows:

- Total network capacity minus consumed capacity of network links
- Total bandwidth minus consumed bandwidth of bridges and routers
- Available bandwidth during network peak hours

Note The server-to-server and client-to-server response time will become unpredictable if network traffic exceeds the effectively available network bandwidth.

Internet Mail Service

The IMS is the Exchange Server component that provides connectivity to SMTP-based and ESMTP-based systems. The IMS also allows you to use existing Internet connections instead of dedicated network lines to connect sites. This might be advantageous if your company is spread over a large geographic area (as is our sample company, STOCKSDATA). Because SMTP is an Internet protocol, the IMS depends on TCP/IP. You should install TCP/IP if you want communication with the Internet.

Internet News Service

Like the IMS, the INS relies on TCP/IP for network communication. The INS allows an Exchange Server to participate as a newsgroup host in the USENET, and provides the ability to replicate public folders between organizations through newsfeeds. However, additional system resources, such as disk space and RAM, must be provided for your newsfeeds service. For instance, it is appropriate to assume that a large newsfeed to the USENET requires approximately 2 GB of data per day.

Outlook Web Access

To allow HTTP-based access to the server using an Internet browser, you must install TCP/IP and IIS 3.0 or higher with Active Server Pages. This preparation can be done automatically if you update an existing Windows NT Server 4.0 with IIS 2.0 to Windows NT 4.0 SP3. The installation point for the Active Server Pages can be found on the Windows NT Server SP3 CD in the \IIS30 directory.

Note Exchange Server 5.5 provides HTTP-based access to server-based resources through its Outlook Web Access component, which relies on IIS 3.0 extended with Active Server Pages or the IIS 4.0.

You don't need to install IIS 3.0 with Active Server Pages or IIS 4.0 and Outlook Web Access locally on every Exchange Server computer. If the RPC communication between the IIS and all Exchange Servers within the organization is working, it's sufficient to configure only one IIS in your entire network. In this case, users can access the server-based resources arbitrarily on every Exchange Server using an appropriate Internet browser.

Apple Macintosh Support

If you need to support users on Apple Macintosh platforms using the Exchange Client or Outlook for Macintosh, you'll need to install the Windows NT Services for Macintosh on the Exchange Server computer that hosts the mailboxes of these users. These services are also required if you want to exchange messages between a StarNine Mail for AppleTalk network (formerly known as MS Mail for AppleTalk) and your Exchange organization.

Connectivity to PROFS and SNADS

PROFS and SNADS are services available in SNA networks. PC networks, on the other hand, are not explicitly designed to access SNA network resources directly. You will typically have to install an SNA gateway—such as Microsoft SNA Server—in your PC network to provide convenient connectivity between the PC network and the SNA network. In addition to installing Microsoft SNA Server, you will need to install the SNA client on the Exchange Server that runs the PROFS or the SNADS connector.

Licensing

Licensing is an important issue, but Microsoft's licensing agreements are not always easy to understand. If you have any doubts, go to *www.microsoft.com.* and search on the word "License" for the product you're looking for.

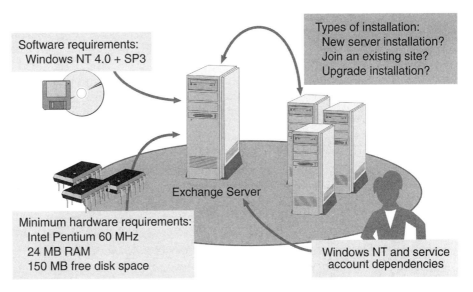

Figure 2-1. Considerations for installation of an Exchange Server.

The following software must be installed prior to installing Exchange Server:

- Windows NT Server version 4.0 (SP3 or later)

- Windows NT Services for Apple Macintosh, if you are installing the MS Mail Connector to exchange mail with StarNine/MS Mail (AppleTalk) or to support users running the Exchange Client or Outlook on Macintosh platforms

- TCP/IP for Windows NT, if you're installing the IMS or INS or you want to provide connectivity to server-based resources through common Internet Access Protocols

- Microsoft SNA Server and SNA client software, if you need to connect your Exchange organization to PROFS or SNADS systems

Microsoft Exchange Server Responsibilities

So long as your entire organization consists of one Exchange Server computer, the server's responsibilities are well defined. The server will simply be responsible for all kinds of server tasks, such as the maintenance of mailboxes, public folders, and messaging connectors to foreign systems, and the delivery of messages between users. Several other tasks, such as directory replication or public folder replication, need not be performed. However, the situation changes immediately if you add a second computer to the site. All of a sudden, directory replication processes have to be launched, the public folder hierarchy has to be replicated, and the MTA has to transfer interpersonal messages between servers. Furthermore, it is possible to configure dedicated servers, which can add more complexity—and efficiency—to your messaging network. It's to your advantage to know the specific tasks a particular server might need to accomplish. This will certainly help you design the hardware platform as accurately as possible.

Mailboxes

One of the primary Exchange Server tasks is the maintenance of storage space for mailboxes, as they are the main repositories of users' incoming messages and other personal items. Although you cannot determine exactly how many messages the users of an Exchange Server computer might store on the server or how much space they'll consume, you should make a reasonable estimate in order to reserve an appropriate amount of disk space. Storage limits can help to keep disk space consumption for the storage of private information under control. In this way, a maximum limit of available space per mailbox can be defined.

With the Enterprise Edition of Exchange Server 5.5 the Private Information Store can handle data beyond the previous limit of 16 GB. Mailboxes reside in the Priv.edb database file. Nevertheless, the data repository consists of two components, the actual database file and associated transaction log files. All these files are located in the \Exchsrvr\Mdbdata directory. You need to consider transaction log files in addition to the database itself when planning the capacity of your server. More information about Exchange Server databases and the log files associated with them is provided in Chapter 15, "Maintaining Servers."

Validating the access permissions of each user as he or she accesses a mailbox will also consume server resources. Futhermore, the more mailboxes that reside on a server the busier the Information Store will be in delivering messages to and from them. As you begin to create numerous mailboxes on a server, it is advisable to have more RAM than originally available and maybe a second processor.

Public Folders

E-mail messages and other objects can be stored in public folders. These types of folders enable you to share information across the entire organization, but, they will consume hard disk space on the server. If you plan to maintain many public folders, you need to reserve enough disk space for both the public folder database and its associated transaction log files. Exchange Server 5.5 eliminates the 16-GB limitation for the Public Information Store just as it does for the Private Information Store. The database file for the Public Information Store is called Pub.edb and can be found in the \Exchsrvr\Mdbdata directory. There are transaction log files for temporary storage of information as well. The Exchange Optimizer can separate the transaction log files from the Pub.edb, the same way it does for the Private Information Store and the Directory databases to improve the reliability of the server configuration. More information about good reasons to separate these files is provided in Chapter 15.

Public folders and their content can be copied to other servers within the same site or to different sites. Public folder replication and the resolution of possible public folder conflicts will also consume hardware resources. Validating user access to public folders needs to be taken into consideration as well. Issues concerning public folders are covered in Chapter 12, "Creating and Managing Public Folders."

Scripting Agents

Exchange Server 5.5 supports simple workflow and event-driven processing of messages in mailboxes and public folders through the Microsoft Exchange Event Service. Based on simple scripts that have been associated with a particular folder, this Windows NT Service will initiate *scripting agents* to perform predefined actions when a new message is posted to the folder, when an existing message is modified or deleted, or when a scheduled event occurs. Only the Exchange Server Scripting Agent is provided with Exchange Server 5.5. In contrast, the actual scripts (executed by the scripting agent) are called *Folder Agents*, which can be written in VBScript or JScript. The development of folder agents based on the Event Service and the Exchange Server Scripting Agent is covered in more detail in Chapter 16, "The Microsoft Exchange Server Forms Environment."

Because they rely on the server-based Event Service, scripting agents will consume resources on your Exchange Server computer. (See Figure 2-2 on page 65.)

Directory Replication

Directory replication between Exchange Server computers allows the Exchange organization to operate as an entire unit. Within a site and between sites, replication ensures that the organization's configuration data is consistent and kept up to date. Within sites, the directory replication is done using RPCs. This communication method is powerful but consumes network resources. Between sites, on the other hand, the Exchange Directory Replication Agent (DRA) handles the exchange of configuration information based on e-mail messages. The DRA is an additional component of the DS, which also consumes hardware resources on the server.

If you plan to add a new server to an existing site, it might be necessary to verify the available disk space of the new computer beforehand. You should be aware that you'll automatically import the site's directory through the directory replication during setup. The directory is implemented in a database file named Dir.edb. Check the size of the Dir.edb file in the Exchsrvr\Dsadata directory of an existing server to get an idea how much disk storage you'll need to reserve for a copy of the site's directory. This file will usually be several megabytes large and might even grow to more than than a gigabyte if your organization is large enough. The new server needs to have enough free hard disk space to receive a complete copy of the directory database. (See Figure 2-3 on page 71.)

Directory replication within sites is covered in Chapter 4, "Communication in a Microsoft Exchange Server Environment." The intersite replication is explained in Chapter 9, "Introduction to Intersite Connectors."

Message Transfer Agent

The MTA transfers messages that are intended for recipients on other servers, sites, or foreign messaging systems. The MTA communicates with other servers in the same site directly through RPC. To transfer information between sites, the MTA uses messaging connectors. All messaging connectors—with the exception of the Site Connector and the Dynamic RAS Connector—require converting messages into formats that the connector or the remote system is able to interpret. The conversion of messages and the MTA-to-MTA communication are, again, processes that require hardware resources. The work of the MTA is highlighted in Chapter 4. The purpose and configuration of messaging connectors is covered in detail in Chapter 9.

Internet Protocols

Data available in private mailboxes, public folders, or in the directory database can be provided to users over Internet or intranet connections. Several protocols, such as HTTP, IMAP4, LDAP, NNTP, POP3, and SMTP, are available for this purpose. If you want to connect your server to the USENET through NNTP, you must plan for enough disk space, because the amount of data that a newsfeed sends to your server can be huge (several gigabytes). Consequently, an Exchange Server, which is supposed to provide access to and from the Internet, requires additional hardware, depending on its concrete tasks. Strong security considerations, especially in respect to Internet connectivity, might lead to additional investments.

Gateways

An Exchange Server might also be responsible for delivering messages to or from foreign messaging systems through gateways or additional messaging components. The Exchange Server Enterprise Edition, for instance, includes messaging connectors to connect an Exchange organization to MS Mail, Lotus cc:Mail, Lotus Notes, PROFS, and SNADS systems. Other gateways and components from third party vendors, such as a fax gateway, can also be installed. Typically, these components are implemented in one or more separate Windows NT services, consuming your expensive server hardware yet again.

The conversion and transportation of interpersonal messages and the exchange of e-mail addresses (known as Directory Synchronization) are the primary tasks these services will have to handle.

Server and Link Monitors

Additional processes can run on your server that may assist the administrator in the tasks of permanent server maintenance. Server Monitors will check the status of Windows NT services, and Link Monitors will ensure that the messaging connections are functioning. Server Monitors can automatically perform predefined actions should a critical situation occur. A Link Monitor, in turn, generates frequent test messages, sends them, and is responsible for receiving the automatic responses. As a result, monitors consume hardware resources on the Exchange Server. You should not do without Server and Link Monitors, but the potential need for a few more bytes of RAM should be taken into consideration.

Microsoft BackOffice Systems

Other components that have nothing to do with Exchange at all, such as additional BackOffice servers, can also be installed on the Exchange Server computer. For example, you might be planning to install Microsoft Systems Management Server on the same server, in which case you must also install SQL Server. A configuration with Exchange Server plus SQL Server plus Systems Management Server requires an extraordinary hardware platform. You can configure a Windows NT PDC computer with an IIS 3.0, Active Server Pages, Outlook Web Access, and the regular Exchange Server installation to provide access to server-based resources using Internet browser applications. The collection of these Windows NT services requires a very powerful hardware platform as well.

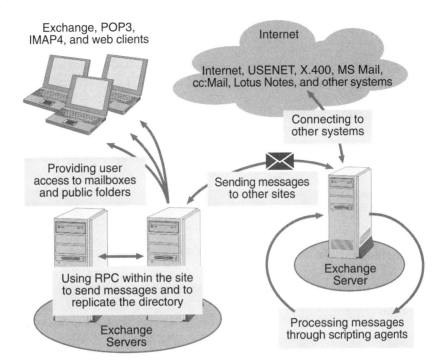

Figure 2-2. Responsibilities of an Exchange Server.

The following lists the minimal hardware necessary for installing an Exchange Server:

Microprocessor	Disk space	RAM
Pentium 60 MHz or higher, or a supported RISC-based micro- processor, such as the Digital Alpha AXP or the IBM PowerPC.	At least 150 MB of available disk space for Exchange Server after Windows NT Server has been installed. Adequate free disk space for the Windows NT Server pagefile (50 MB plus the amount of physical RAM).	At least 24 MB (32 MB for RISC- based systems).

To provide an acceptable platform for Exchange Server testing, the following hardware is recommended:

Microprocessor	Disk space	RAM
Intel Pentium 133 MHz or faster.	Sufficient disk space for your users' e-mail and public folder physical drives. Adequate information. Multiple free disk space for the Windows NT Server pagefile (100 MB plus the amount of physical RAM).	At least 32 MB.

Windows NT Dependencies

The better you understand the security mechanisms of Windows NT domains, the easier the installation and administration of an Exchange Server or a whole organization will be. In fact, the design of an Exchange Server organization according to the already existing Windows NT domain topology is a key factor in successful implementation.

Windows NT Permissions

When you install an Exchange Server on a Windows NT Server computer, you apply many changes to the computer's configuration. New components, such as the DS, IS, MTA, and SA, must be registered in the Windows NT Registry. Consequently, you must log on to the Windows NT Server computer with administrative privileges in order to install the server successfully. If you start the setup program without having the necessary permissions, you will be informed that your account needs to be a member of the Windows NT Server's Administrator group. The setup program will terminate immediately after that information is displayed.

Microsoft Exchange Server Permissions

Every user wanting to connect to an Exchange Server computer to access mailboxes, public folders, address books, or other resources must log on using an account that has been granted the appropriate permissions. In general, every occurrence of access to the server-based resources will be validated— and it will be denied if incorrect or insufficient security information has been supplied. For example, you will not be able to open another user's mailbox without explicit permissions.

Main Administrator

Explicit administrative permissions are also necessary if you want to manage the resources in a site. Although an Exchange Server administrator is typically a Windows NT administrator, the reverse is not necessarily true. By default, only the administrator who has installed the first server in a site receives administrative privileges at the Exchange level. This account is known as the main administrator account. Permissions for additional administrators must be granted manually to selected Windows NT accounts. As soon as this has happened, these accounts can start the Exchange Administrator program to perform configuration tasks in the site.

Default Permissions

By default, the main administrator account and the Site Services Account will receive full rights on a newly installed Exchange Server. The main administrator account receives **Permission Admin** privileges while the service account becomes a **Service Account Admin**. The difference is that the **Service Account Admin** role also includes the **Replication** right.

Displaying Security Information

You can use the **Options** command on the **Tools** menu within the **Admin.exe** to display detailed security information. On the **Permissions** property page within the **Options** dialog box, enable the check boxes **Show Permissions Page For All Objects** and **Display Rights For Roles On Permissions Page** to get the maximum available security information for each object. Corresponding controls will then appear at each object's **Permissions** property page. The security information allows you to examine the set of permissions for predefined roles and to grant detailed permissions to administrators and other users of your organization, thus creating custom roles.

The predefined roles are:

- **Admin**, which is sufficient for all administrative tasks except permission modification

- **Permissions Admin**, which is similar to the **Admin** role but includes permission modification

- **Service Account Admin**, which connects to and exchanges data as a service—all available rights are granted

- **Send As**, which allows the user to send messages as a mailbox (not available at the organization level)

- **User**, which contains the **Send As** privilege, the **Modify User Attributes**, and **Mailbox Owner** rights (not available at the organization level)

- **View Only Admin**, which allows analyzing the configuration within a site—no changes are allowed (available only at the site level)
- **Search**, allows viewing the contents of the selected container

Minimum Rights to Display the Configuration

Every user is able to start the Exchange Administrator program, but simply starting it is not enough. The user needs to log on to the server that he or she wants to examine. Access will be granted or denied based on the supplied security information. The Administrator program automatically sends the user's Windows NT credentials (consisting of the domain name, user name, and password) to the specified Exchange Server. If the user does not have sufficient privileges, a warning message about insufficient privileges will be displayed instead of the server's configuration.

Note To grant a user read-only access to the configuration information of a site, the user's Windows NT account needs the rights of a **View Only Admin** at the site level.

Granting View Only Permissions

Using the Exchange Administrator program, select the <Site> object, open the **File** menu, and then choose the **Properties** command to designate a View Only Administrator. In the dialog box that appears, switch to the **Permissions** property page and then click the **Add** button. Once you have added the desired account to the list of **Windows NT Accounts With Permissions**, open the combo-box labeled **Roles** in order to select **View Only Admin**. When you apply the configuration changes, the user will be able to connect to the Exchange Server through the Administrator program to examine configuration settings, but without having the ability to change them.

Security Levels

If you examine the Directory Information Tree (DIT) of an organization using the Administrator program, you'll find three main containers that form the nodes for various other objects. These nodes are the <Organization>, <Site>, and **Configuration** container, and they maintain three independent security contexts. In other words, permissions must be assigned explicitly at each container if you want to allow an user to manage an organization completely.

Lower levels will not inherit rights assigned at the organization level. Rights assigned at the site level will not be inherited to the context of the configuration. Only the objects within the **Configuration** container will inherit the permissions you have specified on the configuration level.

Note If you want to designate additional Exchange Server administrators and to vest them with full privileges, you must assign the role of a **Permissions Admin** to their Windows NT accounts at the <Organization>, <Site>, and **Configuration** container.

The levels of administrative permissions are:

- Organization, which provides security at the root level; rights will not be inherited

- Site, which maintains administrative security for each existing site; rights will not be inherited

- Configuration, which represents the configuration of all servers in a particular site; all objects within the Configuration container will inherit security information assigned to this object

Site Services Account

One of the most important accounts within a site is the Site Services Account, also known as the *service account*. The MTA, DS, IS, and other Exchange Server services use this account to access their associated data and to identify each other within a site. The Site Services Account must have all possible rights within the local site, and all services within a site must use the same account. On the other hand, the Site Services Account does not require administrative Windows NT permissions because Registry settings will not be modified as services communicate with each other.

Note It is important that all servers within a site use the same service account. Otherwise, intrasite communication cannot take place. (See Figure 2-3 on page 71.)

Creating a must Site Services Account

It is strongly recommended that you create a separate service account for use by all Exchange Server services. This account must be a member of the **Domain Users** group and needs the additional Windows NT rights **Logon As A Service**, **Restore Files And Directories**, and **Act As Part Of The Operating System**. The password of the Service Account should be configured as **Password Never Expires**.

When you run Setup to create a new site, you will be asked for the Site Services Account and the corresponding password. You might discover you've missed the opportunity to create this account before starting the setup program. Fortunately, it isn't necessary to cancel the current setup to rectify this problem. Instead, you can switch to the Program Manager or Windows NT Explorer to start the User Manager for Domains. After creating the missing Site Services Account, you can switch back to the Exchange Server setup. At this point, you can select the new account in order to continue the installation. If the desired account was not provided with the additional Windows NT rights mentioned above at the time of the installation, the setup program grants them automatically. A message box will inform you about this process.

Site Services Account Permissions

If you examine the Exchange Server permissions of the Site Services Account after the successful installation of the server, you'll notice that no predefined role has been assigned at the organization level. All existing rights, except for the Search privilege, have been granted directly instead, resulting in a Custom role. At the site and configuration level, however, the predefined role **Service Account Admin** has been specified. This role grants the service account full access to all resources, since all lower levels will inherit the permission settings of the configuration level.

Note The Site Services Account must have full permissions for all existing objects of an Exchange Server computer, but it does not need to have administrative permissions under Windows NT. The Site Services Account requires the rights **Logon As A Service**, **Restore Files And Directories**, and **Act As Part Of The Operating System,** in addition to the ordinary **Domain Users** privileges.

Advantages of a Dedicated Site Services Account

When creating a new site during setup, the Site Services Account will default to the installing user who is currently logged on. It's a good idea, however, to change this account to separate the Exchange Server services from any user context. This practice brings about different advantages. For example, password handling becomes easier because the password of the Site Services Account requires special treatment. If the password needs to be changed for some reason, it must be done from within the Exchange Administrator program through the **Service Account Password** property page of the site's **Configuration** container object. The detailed steps necessary to change the service account password are outlined in Chapter 15.

Site Services Account and Multiple Sites

Multiple sites require a more complex configuration and administration because messaging connectors must be used to connect the sites with each other. The Site Connector, for instance, requires information about the accounts of both sites if they are not identical (which might be the case if both sites belong to the same or trusted NT Domains). This connector needs to access the servers in the context of the correct account. (See Figure 2-3.) If the Site Connector uses invalid security information, the transfer of messages will fail. It is advisable to use one common service account wherever possible and for all sites, so long as the Windows NT domain topology permits this configuration.

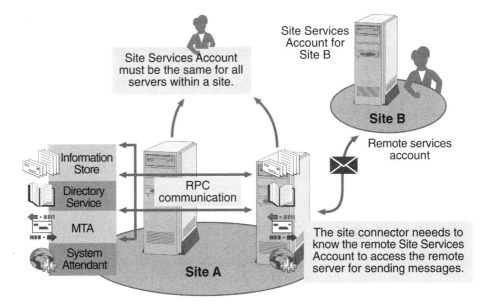

Figure 2-3. The Exchange Service Account.

The following list contains the dependencies between the Site Services Account and Exchange Servers within a site:

- A new Exchange Server cannot join an existing site if the existing Site Services Account is not available to it.

- One Site Services Account can be used for all sites in single or trusted Windows NT domain environments.

- Membership of the Windows NT Domain Users group is sufficient.

- A Site Services Account doesn't need to be a member of the Windows NT Domain Admins group.

- The Site Services Account must be the same for all Exchange servers in a site.

- The Site Services Account is used to validate local and remote Exchange Server services before access to local data storages or RPC communication can take place.

- The Site Services Account needs the rights **Logon As A Service**, **Restore Files And Directories**, and **Act As Part Of The Operating System** in addition to the ordinary Domain Users privileges.

Exercise 1: Creating Accounts for Exchange Administration

Windows NT security and user account relationships are essential for Exchange Server administration. For example, you will use Windows NT accounts and groups to assign your users access permissions to Exchange objects (mailboxes, public folders, and so on).

Estimated time to complete this exercise: 15 minutes

Description

In this exercise, you will create a Windows NT user account, a global group, and a local group. The Windows NT account will be used later to administer a test Exchange Server computer. In order to exactly follow the steps outlined in this and all the following exercises, your server should have the name *NEWYORK-1* and should be installed as a Primary Domain Controller (PDC).

Although this exercise is not directly related to any topic of this chapter, the preparation of Windows NT accounts and groups is an essential task of Exchange Server administration. Detailed information about the account management under Windows NT is provided through the Help file of the User Manager and additional Windows NT literature.

Note The User Manager for Domains allows you to create Exchange Server mailboxes if the Exchange Administrator program has already been installed. If this is the case, the dialog box to create new mailboxes will appear as you follow this exercise (in Task 1a after step 9). You can cancel the dialog to bypass the mailbox creation. At this point, it is assumed that no Exchange Server has been installed. Mailboxes will be created in Exercise 6.

- Task 1a describes the steps for creating a Windows NT user account that will be used for the administration of Exchange Server systems.

- Task 1b describes the steps for creating a Windows NT global group.

- Task 1c describes the steps for creating a Windows NT local group.

Prerequisites

- Windows NT Server 4.0 with SP3 should be installed as a Primary Domain Controller (PDC), which is the recommended method, a Backup Domain Controller (BDC), or a member server in a domain environment.

- The server should have the name *NEWYORK-1*.

- The PDC must to be available in the network.

- Log on to Windows NT with administrative privileges (for example, with the Administrator account, which is automatically created when a new NT Server is installed).

- The exercises in this book assume that you are performing all steps directly at the test server.

Task 1a: Creating an Administrative User Account

1. Click the **Start** button, point to **Programs**, point to **Administrative Tools (Common)**, and then select **User Manager For Domains**.

2. Select **New User** on the **User** menu.

3. Use the following information to create a new user:

In this box	You supply
Username	*Admin-NY1*
Full Name	*Administrator New York-1*
Description	*Microsoft Exchange Server Administrator*
Password	*password*
Confirm Password	*password*

4. Clear the **User Must Change Password At Next Logon** check box.

5. Select the **Password Never Expires** check box.

6. Select **Groups**.

7. In the **Not Member Of** box, select **Domain Admins** and then click **Add**.

8. Click **OK**.

9. In the **New User** dialog box, click **Add**.

10. Click **Close**.

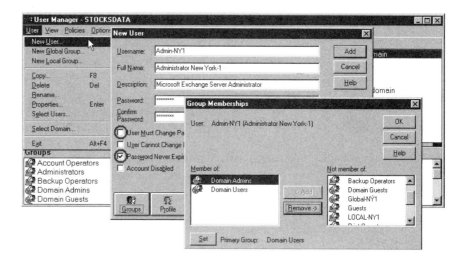

Task 1b: Creating a Global Group

1. In the **User Manager For Domains**, select **Admin-NY1**.

2. On the **User** menu, select **New Global Group** to display the **New Global Group** dialog box.

3. In the **Group Name** box, type *Global-NY1*.

4. In the **Description** box, type *Exchange Global Admins Group*.

5. Click **OK**.

6. The global group **Global-NY1** appears in the Groups window of the User Manager and is marked with the icon for Global Groups on the left side.

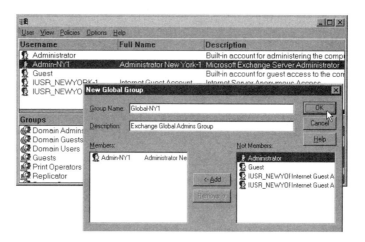

Task 1c: Creating a Local Group

1. In the **Groups** box of the User Manager, select **Global-NY1**.

2. On the **User** menu, select **New Local Group**.

3. In the **Group Name** box, type *Local-NY1*.

4. In the **Description** box, type *Exchange Local Admins Group*.

5. Click **Add** to display the **Add Users And Groups** dialog box.

6. In the **Names** box, select **Global-NY1** and then click **Add**.

7. Click **OK**.

8. Within the **New Local Group** dialog box, click **OK**.

9. On the **User** menu, click **Exit**.

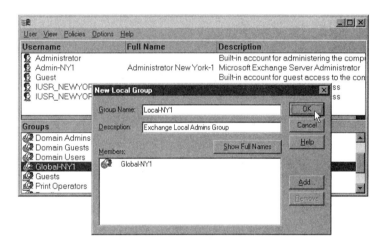

Review

You can create Windows NT user accounts as well as local and global groups in a Windows NT domain using the User Manager for Domains. At the time of creation you can assign a user name, a full name, a description, and a password to the new account. It is also possible to add the new account to existing Windows NT user groups. Windows NT groups can facilitate the administration because they allow permissions to be granted and withdrawn from multiple users in one step. A global group can contain user accounts, while a local group can contain user accounts and global user groups.

Types of Installation

The setup program offers three options for installing Exchange Server 5.5 on a Windows NT Server computer where no Exchange Server exists yet. These options are **Typical**, **Complete/Custom**, and **Minimum**. Select the option that best meets your implementation plan. (See Figure 2-4.)

> **Note** In the context of this book, the term *Installation Type* stands for a *Typical*, *Minimum*, or *Complete/Custom* installation, which can be chosen according to available installation options. In contrast, the term *Installation Method* means the difference between *creating a new site* and *adding a server to an existing site*, as explained later in this chapter in Lesson 2, "Organizational Contexts for Installation."

Typical Installation

With the exception of the Event Service, only the Exchange Server core components and the Administrator program will be installed when choosing the **Typical** option. Setup will not copy any additional components to the computer's hard disk. This type of installation is most useful if no connections to other sites or foreign systems are necessary.

> **Note** In rare circumstances, Setup might not provide the **Typical** option. This will happen if not enough free disk space is available to perform a **Typical** installation.

The components installed during a **Typical** installation are:

- DS, MTA, IS, and SA components (core components)
- Extensions to the Windows NT User Manager for Domains
- Exchange Administrator program
- Exchange Server databases
- Modified Windows NT Backup
- Performance Monitor Counters
- Performance Wizard
- Event Service

Minimum Installation

The **Minimum** installation type installs only the Exchange Server core components and the Event Service. The Administrator program or additional messaging connectors will not be installed. This type of installation should not be used for the first server in a new site because the Exchange Administrator program will be missing. This program is necessary to control the new server. On the other hand, a **Minimum** installation might be the best choice if the Exchange Administrator program has already been installed on a different computer and local administration is not required.

The components installed during a **Minimum** installation are:

- DS, MTA, IS, and SA components (core components)
- Exchange Server databases
- Event Service
- Performance Wizard

Not installed are:

- *Extensions to User Manager for Domains*
- *Exchange Admin program*
- *Modified NT Backup*
- *Performance Monitor Counters*

Complete/Custom Installation

The **Complete/Custom** installation provides the most flexible control over the setup process. You can select additional components directly and independently of each other. All available components, including all additional messaging connectors, can be selectively installed. Additional components include the MS Mail Connector, Lotus cc:Mail Connector, X.400 Connector, Exchange Event Service, Key Management Server, and the Outlook Web Access components. It is also possible to copy the Exchange Server documentation (**Books Online** option) separately to the computer's hard disk. For this reason, you might prefer the **Complete/Custom** installation type most of the time. The core and additional components are covered in Chapter 3, "Microsoft Exchange Server Architecture."

The **Complete/Custom** installation is also the best choice if you don't want to install any server components at all. This will be the case if you want to install only the Administrator program separately on a computer running Windows NT Server or Windows NT Workstation. A separate Administrator program can be used to manage the organization remotely from your desk. However, it's important to note that the Exchange Administrator cannot be installed under Microsoft Windows 95. The Exchange Administrator program is covered in Chapter 8, "Managing Server Configuration."

The following components can be installed selectively with the **Complete/Custom** installation option:

- **Books Online**, which provides online documentation about Exchange Server
- **Connector for Lotus cc:Mail**, which provides connections to Lotus cc:Mail post offices

- **Key Management Server**, which provides Advanced Security features such as message signing and encryption

- **Microsoft Exchange Administrator program**, which installs all administration tools and modifies existing Windows NT Programs, such as the User Manager for Domains and the Windows NT Backup, and adds Exchange-specific counters to the Performance Monitor

- **Microsoft Exchange Event Service**, which supports server-side event-driven scripting agents for simple workflow

- **Microsoft Exchange Server software,** which includes all core components

- **Microsoft Mail Connector**, which permits connections to MS Mail 3.x postoffices and StarNine/MS Mail for AppleTalk servers

- **Outlook Web Access**, which provides Web clients access to Exchange Server services through IIS 3.0 and IIS 4.0 (Active Server Pages must be available on the IIS prior to the Outlook Web Acess installation)

- **X.400 Connector**, which connects and transfers data to other Exchange Server computers and foreign X.400 systems based on the X.400 standards

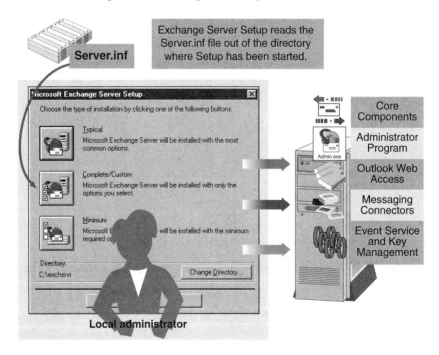

Figure 2-4. Setup options during new server installation.

Lesson 2: Organizational Contexts for Installation

The number of sites an organization needs depends on several factors, and fewer is not always better. Single site organizations can be realized if LAN or high-bandwidth WAN connections between all involved servers can be assumed. Furthermore, the Site Services Account needs to be available to all servers. In other words, you will need to implement multiple sites if your network connections do not support RPC due to low available network bandwith, prevent a common service account, or generate transmission costs. Political and geographical considerations can also come into play. Nevertheless, multiple sites add complexity to the organization and increase the demand for administration and maintenance.

This lesson discusses the issues associated with the general Exchange Server 5.5 installation methods. You'll read about the important parameters for creating new sites as well as about considerations for joining existing sites. You'll also find a brief discussion regarding the upgrade to Exchange Server 5.5.

Two practical exercises conclude this lesson. They'll guide you through the steps of installing Exchange Server 5.5 on a new site and joining the newly created site with a second server later on.

At the end of this lesson, you will be able to:

- Create a new site

- Install a server within an existing site

- Upgrade an existing Exchange Server to version 5.5

Estimated time to complete this lesson: 45 minutes

Creating a New Site

Sites represent delimited administrative precincts within an organization. As you create new sites, you need to designate new administrators for them. Depending on the Windows NT domain structure, these administrators can be the same people who manage existing sites. It's also possible to designate completely different user accounts. Multiple sites are therefore ideal for distributed administration. However, all administrators should be aware that their sites are part of an organization. Centralized coordination of management activities is highly recommended even if the actual administrative tasks are distributed among different accounts, since configuration changes will be replicated to all sites and servers. Moreover, there exist a few administrative measures that can directly affect remote sites.

Organization, Site, and Server Names

Organization and site names should be carefully planned prior to the installation of the first server because these names cannot be changed without reinstalling all affected Exchange Servers. Thus, at the time of the first Exchange Server installation, keep in mind that you will be making some irreversible decisions.

The display names for the organization and the site are changeable using the Administrator program, but this is just a cosmetic change since the old names will remain in the directory. The directory names are the truly important parameters for intersite and intrasite communication.

Organization

The name of the organization can be up to 64 characters long and should represent the entire company. The organization name is case sensitive and must match exactly for all sites. Sites with different organization names will not be able to replicate their directory information with each other. In other words, different names would prevent consistent organization.

Site

Site names can be up to 64 characters long as well and are also case sensitive. Typically, site names refer to locations of company branches, but any naming convention can be appropriate. A site name must be unique within the organization because it will be used for message routing decisions.

Server

The name of the Windows NT Server computer on top of which an Exchange Server is going to be installed is important also because it will be written to the directory database during the installation. As with the organization and site names, the name of the computer cannot be changed once the Exchange Server setup has been completed successfully without putting the server into a nonfunctional state. If the server name has been changed accidentally, resetting it to the original name (using the **Network** applet of the Control Panel) brings the Exchange Server installation back to life.

Note There is no direct way to rename an Exchange Server. Renaming will lead to lost configuration information and therefore to a nonfunctional server.

If you rename a server, you will lose:

- All connector/Directory Synchronization Agent configurations on the server

- All configuration information that is not directly related to mailboxes on the server

- All profiles for users who connect to the server

For these reasons, it is advisable to include the computer name into the naming scheme considerations for your organization as well. Server names can be up to 15 characters long and follow the Windows NT naming conventions.

The Exchange Server naming conventions are as follows:

- The Organization name can be up to 64 characters long and is case sensitive.

- The Site name can be up to 64 characters long and is case sensitive.

- The Server name can be up to 15 characters long and follows the Windows NT naming conventions.

Name of the Directory for Installation

When you install an Exchange Server 5.5 with default settings, you will place the server files in various directories under C:\Exchsrvr. Setup creates several subdirectories named \Add-Ins, \Address, \Bin, \Ccmcdata, \Connect, \Docs, \Dsadata, \Dxadata, \Imcdata, \Insdata, \Kmsdata, \Mdbdata, \Mtadata, \Res, \Tracking.log, \Webdata, and \Webtemp. These subdirectories make up a complete Exchange Server installation.

You might also find an \Exchsrvr directory on every other hard disk drive in your computer. This will be the case if you have launched the Exchange Performance Optimizer at the end of the server setup. The Optimizer places the files across all drives in order to increase the server performance and reliability. You can read more about reliable server configurations in Chapter 15.

If you want, you can change the server directory during the installation. You need to click the **Change Directory** button on the dialog box that asks you to select the installation type. It is also possible to enter a nonexistent directory name to have Setup automatically create this directory for you. After that, you can continue with a **Typical**, **Complete/Custom,** or **Minimum** installation as usual. (See Figure 2-5.)

CD Key

During the setup process, a dialog box will appear, asking you for a valid CD Key or product ID (PID), as shown in Figure 2-5. The CD Key is a unique 10-digit number, which can be found on your compact disc jewel case. Each packaged product contains its own CD Key or serial number. You must enter the correct numbers in order to continue installation. If you contact Microsoft

Product Support Services concerning your Exchange Server installation, you will probably be asked for this information as well. As setup continues, you must agree to the licensing issues before you can specify the name of the organization and new site.

Service Account

The Site Services Account and its password must also be provided. This account will be used to initialize the new server directory accordingly. Also, all Exchange Server components that are selected for installation will be configured to start under the context of the service account. (See Figure 2-5.)

Setup grants the additional Windows NT rights **Logon As A Service**, **Restore Files And Directories**, and **Act As Part Of The Operating System** to the Site Services Account if they are missing at the time of installation. A dialog box will inform you about the Windows NT permission changes.

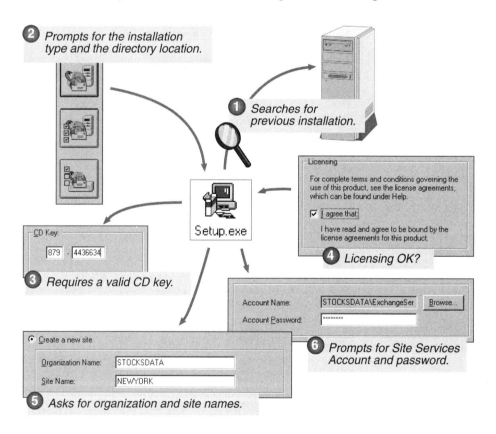

Figure 2-5. Information gathered during new server installation.

The functions completed by Setup during installation in a new site are as follows:

1. Display the Licensing Agreement, which you will need to accept in order to continue

2. Search for a previous Exchange Server installation

3. Provide the option to select the installation type and to change the Exchange Server directory path

4. Ask the administrator to enter a valid CD Key

5. Provide Per Seat Licensing Mode only

6. Ask for organization and site names

7. Prompt for information about the Site Services Account and password

8. Verify the account information and grant additional Windows NT rights, if necessary

9. Copy the necessary files and directories to the local hard disk

10. Update the Windows NT Registry

11. Share directories, such as Connect$, for network access

12. Start the System Attendant and Directory Service

13. Initialize the Directory and the Directory Information Tree

14. Start the IS and MTA

15. Create the Exchange program group

16. Install optional components and write their entries to the Windows NT Registry

17. Suggest Performance Optimizer when setup completes successfully

Exercise 2: Installing a Microsoft Exchange Server

A minimum hardware platform will be sufficient to install an Exchange Server in a test environment. It's recommended, however, that you use a computer with an Intel Pentium processor, 32 MB RAM, and 250 MB free hard disk space, if possible.

Estimated time to complete this exercise: 25 minutes

Description

In this exercise, you will create a new site. You need to configure the Site Services Account as a member of the Domain Users group, but you don't need to grant any additional Windows NT rights manually. Setup will assign the required rights **Logon As A Service**, **Restore Files And Directories**, and **Act As Part Of The Operating System** automatically. The **Complete/ Custom** installation mode is suggested in this exercise because it provides the maximum flexibility. The names of the organization and site will be used for all subsequent exercises in this book. If you would rather use your own names, you will need to replace the example names during later exercises as appropriate.

This exercise relies on a Windows NT Server named NEWYORK-1, which resides in a domain called STOCKSDATA. You can use another computer or domain name, but you make sure that you're replacing the names used in this book with your own names throughout all subsequent exercises. NEWYORK-1 has been installed as a PDC.

Note This exercise outlines the installation steps that are required when using the Microsoft Exchange Server Enterprise Edition CD. The setup procedure may vary slightly if you are using a different installation media.

- Task 2a describes the steps for creating a dedicated Windows NT user account to be used by the Exchange Server services.
- Task 2b describes the steps for installing Exchange Server.
- Task 2c describes the initial steps for creating a new site.
- Task 2d describes the steps for finishing the installation of Exchange Server.
- Task 2e describes the steps for having the Exchange Optimizer configure your Exchange Server system for optimum performance at the end of the installation procedure.

Prerequisites

- Windows NT Server 4.0 with SP3
- IIS 3.0 or 4.0 with Active Server Pages if you want to install Exchange Server with all components
- The server must be a member of a Windows NT domain; it can be a PDC, BDC, or a member server
- The minimum size of the Windows NT pagefile should be no smaller than 100 MB plus the amount of physical RAM installed in the server

- Log on as Admin-NY1 to NEWYORK-1 in order to complete this exercise

Task 2a: Creating the Exchange Service Account

1. Click **Start**, point to **Programs**, point to **Administrative Tools (Common)**, and then click on **User Manager For Domains**.

2. On the User Manager's **User** menu, select **New User**.

3. Create a new user using the following information:

In this box	You supply
Username	*ExchangeService*
Full Name	*Exchange Service Account*
Description	*Exchange Service Account for NEWYORK*
Password	*password*
Confirm Password	*password*

4. Clear the **User Must Change Password At Next Logon** check box.

5. Select the **Password Never Expires** check box.

6. Click **Add**.

7. Click **Close**.

8. On the **User** menu, click **Exit** to close the User Manager.

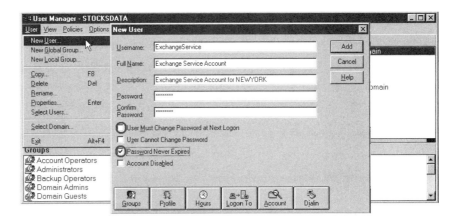

Task 2b: Installing Exchange Server

1. Insert the Exchange Server CD-ROM.

2. Click **Start**, point to **Settings**, click **Control Panel**, click **Add/Remove Programs**, and then click **Install**.

3. Click **Next**, type the letter of your CD-ROM, and then type *\SERVER\SETUP\I386\Setup.exe*. Alternatively you can search for the location of the Setup.exe using the **Browse** button.

4. Click **Finish**.

5. In the **Microsoft Exchange Server Setup** dialog box, read the License Agreement and click **Accept**.

6. Click **Complete/Custom** to launch the **Microsoft Exchange Server Setup - Complete/Custom** dialog box.

7. Accept all default options and click **Continue**.

8. The **Microsoft Exchange Server Setup** dialog box appears, stating that the IIS service will be stopped temporarily. Click **OK**.

9. In the **CD Key** box, enter the valid CD key of your Exchange Server copy and then click **OK**.

10. The **Microsoft Exchange Server Setup** dialog box appears, displaying the entered CD key; click **OK**.

11. In the **Licensing** dialog box, select the **I Agree That** check box, and then click **OK**.

12. The **Organization and Site** dialog box appears.

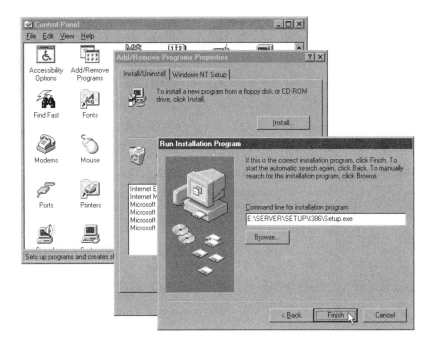

Task 2c: Creating a New Site

1. Within the **Organization And Site** dialog box, verify that **Create A New Site** is selected.

2. Enter the following information to identify your Exchange site:

In this box	You supply
Organization Name	*STOCKSDATA*
Site Name	*NEWYORK*

3. Click **OK**.

4. In the **Microsoft Exchange Server Setup** dialog box prompting you to confirm the creation of a new site, click **Yes**.

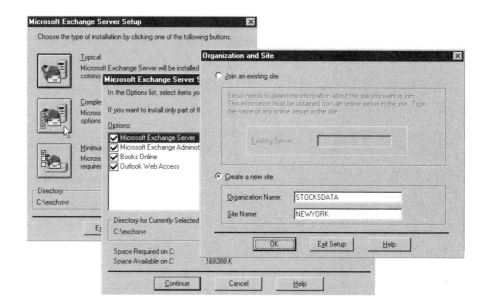

Task 2d: Assigning the Site Services Account

1. In the **Site Services Account** dialog box, click **Browse** to display the **Add User Or Group** dialog box.

2. In the **Names** box, click **ExchangeService** and then click **Add**.

3. Click **OK**.

4. In the **Account Password** box, type *password* and then click **OK**.

5. A **Microsoft Exchange Server Setup** message box appears, indicating that the STOCKSDATA\ExchangeService account has been granted the **Log On As A Service**, **Restore Files And Directories**, and **Act As Part Of The Operating System** rights.

6. Click **OK**.

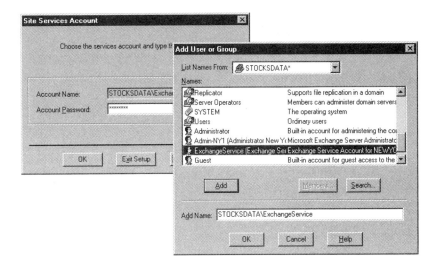

Task 2e: Running the Exchange Optimizer

1. In the **Microsoft Exchange Server Setup** dialog box, click **Run Optimizer**.

2. In the **Microsoft Exchange Performance Optimizer** dialog box, click **Next**. The Exchange Server services will be stopped.

3. Click **Next** to accept the defaults.

4. The **Microsoft Exchange Optimizer** analyzes your hard disk drives and then displays a message indicating that it has completed disk analysis. Click **Next**.

> **Note** The Performance Optimizer will display a warning message if only one hard disk is available on the server computer. As a result, the optimization procedure will skip steps 5 and 6.

5. The **Microsoft Exchange Optimizer** displays suggestions for storing the Exchange Server files. Click **Next**.

6. The **Microsoft Exchange Performance Optimizer** dialog box appears, indicating that some files will be moved. Click **Next**.

7. The **Microsoft Exchange Performance Optimizer** dialog box appears, indicating that it has completed its task. Click **Finish**. The Exchange Server services that were stopped in step 2 will be started again.

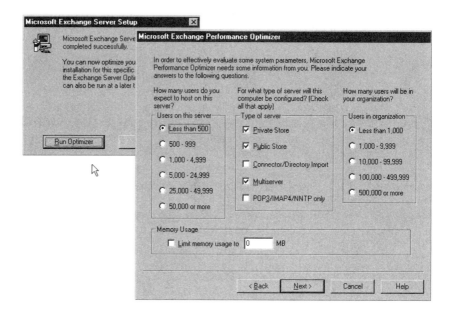

Review

The Site Services Account must be created using the User Manager for Domains. It is recommended—but not necessary—that you create this account before the actual Exchange Server installation begins. The account does not need to be a member of the Domain Admins or Administrators group; Domain Users group membership is sufficient. However, it is highly recommended that you clear the check box **User Must Change Password At Next Logon** while creating the account within the User Manager for Domains to avoid password-related problems during setup. It is also a good idea to check the **Password Never Expires** option to avoid password-related problems at a later time.

An Exchange program group will be created during the setup process. This group will contain the following icons:

- Exchange Administrator
- Exchange Migration Wizard
- Exchange Optimizer
- Exchange Server Health
- Exchange Server History
- Exchange Server IMS Queues

- Exchange Server IMS Statistics

- Exchange Server IMS Traffic

- Exchange Server Load

- Exchange Server Queues

- Exchange Server Users

- Books Online

At the end of the setup process, it is a good idea to run the Performance Optimizer. The Optimizer configures the Exchange Server to use the existing hardware platform in an efficient way. It optimizes the configuration according to parameters such as the number of users, whether the server will host public folders, or bridgehead tasks. If you don't run the Performance Optimizer right at the end of setup it is also possible to run Setup without a final optimization. In this case, click the **Exit Setup** button at the end of the setup sequence. You can start the Performance Optimizer any time you want at a later date. The Performance Optimizer is covered in more detail later in this chapter, under "Post-Installation Considerations."

Adding a Server to an Existing Site

From an administrator's point of view, the process of joining an existing site seems to be easier than the creation of a new site. But a complex process—the directory replication—performs the join behind the scenes, so you do need the rights of a Permissions Admin within the site that you want to join. Furthermore, you need administrative Windows NT permissions. With Windows NT 4.0, the default security has changed, so only members of the local Windows NT Administrators group can access the Registry of a Windows NT computer over the network. The setup program will have to read the Registry entries from the remote server you'll specify during the setup procedure. It will do this under the security context of the user who launched it.

Advantages of Joining an Existing Site

It is preferable to install large sites, because they simplify the administration of multiple servers. Site-level parameters allow you to configure default settings for all of the servers. Any new configuration settings will be distributed automatically to all other servers through the intrasite directory replication mechanism.

Direct MTA-to-MTA Communication

The MTA is responsible for the message transfer between servers. Within a site, this can be accomplished directly and without a messaging connector. You do not need to configure the server-to-server communication under normal circumstances.

Dedicated Servers

A site containing only one server doesn't provide much flexibility because the single server must fulfill all imaginable tasks. Multiple servers, however, allow you to distribute the work between them if you create dedicated servers. A dedicated server can be a public folder server, a private mail server, or a communication server. A public folder server, for example, does not contain any mailboxes and can be designed specifically to provide fast public folder access. Alternatively, a private mail server manages mailboxes only and can be fine-tuned to offer the shortest response time for client access. A communication server or messaging bridgehead, in turn, would be responsible for the message transfer to other sites. Such a server would maintain the IMS, X.400 Connector, and other connector types. The bridgehead concept is covered in more detail in Chapter 9.

Moving Mailboxes Between Different Servers

Multiple servers in a single site allow the administrator to distribute mailboxes efficiently. Obviously, the more users you have to support, the more servers you should install in your site. Less obvious are the advantages of the Move Mailbox feature, which becomes available as soon as more than one server exists in a site. This feature might be one of the most valuable of the Administrator program in emergency cases.

Let's say you are experiencing serious server problems that force you to reckon with a complete server crash sooner or later. What should you do with the hundreds of mailboxes that reside on the server? One possibility would be to perform a full backup to ensure that no messages will be lost in case the server finally crashes and has to be replaced. Or, more conveniently and more securely, you could simply move all the mailboxes to another computer in the same site, which ensures that the user data always remains available. Once you have replaced the old computer, you can move the mailboxes back to the newly installed server. If the mailboxes are moved carefully, users will not be at all aware of the manipulation. In fact, it's possible to replace all servers in a site, step by step, without having users realize that something has changed in the backbone. Moving mailboxes between sites, however, is not supported directly.

Existing Server

To join an existing site, you must specify an existing server instead of the organization and site name. Setup will automatically connect to the specified remote server to gather the required configuration information. If the server cannot be found, Setup notifies you and prompts you for another server. It doesn't matter which of the existing Exchange Server computers in the target site you specify, because they all keep a complete copy of the site's directory information. (See Figure 2-6.)

Site Services Account Password

If you want to join an existing site with a new computer, the Setup program needs to access the Registry of an existing server to obtain the Site Services Account information. To initialize the replication process successfully, the password of the Site Services Account must be entered.

You don't need to enter the service account name since the name of the Site Services Account will be determined from the existing server. This mechanism prevents you from entering wrong service account information.

First Directory Replication

Once you have entered the correct password, the directory replication can be initiated, but the actual replication process will be postponed until all local configuration information has been written to the new Exchange Server directory. The replication will be launched at the end of the setup process, when the initialization of the local directory is complete.

Setup will directly access the directory of the specified remote server in order to add its own entry to the remote server's directory. The new entry informs the remote server about the joining server. In this situation, the remote server starts the directory replication process. The complete directory information will be replicated to the new server as soon as the new server asks for the changes (which happens, as mentioned above, at the end of the installation).

The replicated directory contains all available information about other servers and the current site configurations. Using this information, it is possible to initiate the directory replication with all remaining servers within the site, and eventually the whole site will be synchronized. Each of the Exchange Server computers will contain a complete copy of each other's directory. More information about the communication between Exchange Server computers in a site is provided in Chapter 4.

Protocol Dependencies

The RPC communication between all servers in a site must work perfectly. In other words, either TCP/IP or NWLink (IPX/SPX) must be installed and configured. These two are the only classic Windows NT network protocols supported for Exchange Server-to-Server communication—provided that protocols for Banyan Vines or AppleTalk networks are not used primarily to connect Windows NT servers together. The third typical Windows NT LAN protocol, NetBEUI, is not a supported option for this task. You can read more about problems with this protocol in "The NetBEUI Trap," later in this chapter.

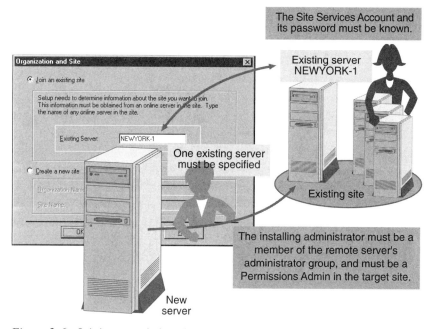

Figure 2-6. Joining an existing site.

To join an existing site, you must:

- Specify the name of an existing Exchange Server computer in the target site. The setup program will attempt to contact the existing server via an RPC and, when found, will query the directory for the name of the organization and the site to which it belongs

- Know the Site Services Account password for the existing site

- Be granted the Permissions Admin role for the site's Organization, Site, and Configuration objects

- Be a Windows NT administrator on the local and remote computer

Exercise 3:
Adding a Microsoft Exchange Server to a Site

A minimum hardware platform of a computer with an Intel Pentium processor, 32 MB RAM, and 250 MB hard disk space is recommended if you want to join an existing site. Depending on the size of the directory in the existing site, more disk space might be required. The directory replication will fill the new server's Dir.edb database file at the end of the setup process.

Estimated time to complete this exercise: 25 minutes

Description

In this exercise, you will start Setup.exe to add an Exchange Server to an existing site. The **Complete/Custom** installation mode is recommended because it provides you with the maximum possible flexibility. Once you have elected to join an existing site, Setup prompts you to specify an existing Exchange Server computer. The names of the organization and site will be obtained from there. This server must be up and running at installation time.

- Task 3a describes the steps for creating a dedicated Windows NT user account to be used by the Exchange Server administrator to join an existing site.

- Task 3b describes the steps for assigning the new Windows NT account administrative permission in a site.

- Task 3c describes the initial steps for joining a site.

- Task 3d describes the steps necessary to finishing the installation of Exchange Server.

- Task 3e describes the steps for running the Exchange Optimizer in order to configure your Exchange Server system for optimum performance.

Prerequisites

- The PDC of the domain STOCKSDATA, which should be called NEWYORK-1, must be available and the Exchange Server services must be running

- A second computer with the name NEWYORK-2 should be installed as a BDC in the same domain

- You must know the password of the Site Services Account

- Permissions Admin status must be assigned to user Admin-NY1 at the <Organization>, <Site>, and **Configuration** container objects of the existing site (which is called NEWYORK and consists of server NEWYORK-1 so far)

- Either TCP/IP or NWLink must be installed on both servers, NEWYORK-1 and NEWYORK-2

Task 3a: Windows NT Preparations

1. Log on as Admin-NY1 to NEWYORK-2.

2. On NEWYORK-2, start the **User Manager For Domains**.

3. On the **User** menu, click **New User**.

4. Create the new user using the following information:

In this box	You supply
Username	*Admin-NY2*
Full Name	*Administrator New York-2*
Description	*The second administrator in New York*
Password	*password*
Confirm Password	*password*

5. Clear the **User Must Change Password At Next Logon** check box.

6. Select the **Password Never Expires** check box.

7. Click **Groups** to display the **Group Memberships** dialog box.

8. Select **Domain Admins**, and then click **Add**.

9. Select **Global-NY1,** and then click **Add**.

10. Click **OK**.

11. Click **Add**.

12. Click **Close**.

13. On the **User** menu, click **Exit** to close the User Manager.

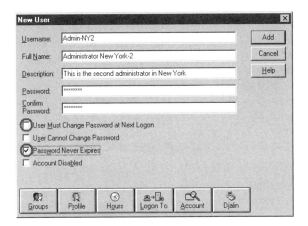

Task 3b: Microsoft Exchange Preparation

1. On server NEWYORK-1 click **Start**, point to **Programs**, point to **Microsoft Exchange**, and then click **Microsoft Exchange Administrator**. In case the **Connect to Server** dialog box appears, type *NEWYORK-1* or search for server **NEWYORK-1** using the **Browse** button, and then click **OK**.

2. Select the Organization object **STOCKSDATA**.

3. Open the **File** menu and select **Properties**.

4. In the **Properties** dialog box, select the **Permissions** tab.

5. Click **Add** and select the account **Admin-NY2** in the **Names** list, click **Add**, and then click **OK**.

6. In the **STOCKSDATA Properties** dialog box, open the **Roles** list and select **Permissions Admin.**

7. Click **OK**.

8. Select the object for the site **NEWYORK**.

9. Open the **File** menu and select **Properties**.

10. In the **Properties** dialog box, select **Permissions**.

11. Click **Add** and select the Account **Admin-NY2**, click **Add**, and then click **OK**.

12. Select **Permissions Admin** under **Roles** and then click **OK**.

13. Select the **Configuration** object under the site **NEWYORK**.

14. Open the **File** menu and click **Properties**.

15. In the **Properties** dialog box, select **Permissions**.

16. Click **Add** and select the account **Admin-NY2**.

17. Click **Add** and then click **OK**.

18. Select **Permissions Admin** under **Roles** and click **OK**.

19. Exit the **Microsoft Exchange Administrator** program.

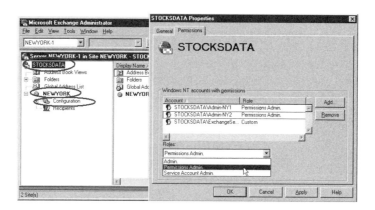

Task 3c: Installing Microsoft Exchange Server

1. On server NEWYORK-2, log on as Admin-NY2.

2. Insert the Exchange Server CD-ROM.

3. Click **Start**, point to **Settings**, click **Control Panel**, double-click **Add/Remove Programs**, and then click **Install**.

4. Click the **Next** button, type the letter of your CD-ROM drive, and then type \SERVER\SETUP\I386\Setup.exe. Alternatively, you can search for the location of the Setup.exe using the **Browse** button.

5. Click **Finish**.

6. In the **Microsoft Exchange Server Setup** dialog box displaying the Licensing Agreement, click **Accept.**

7. In the dialog box displaying the installation options, click **Complete/Custom**.

8. Accept all default options and then click **Continue**.

9. A **Microsoft Exchange Server Setup** dialog box appears stating that the Internet Information Server services will be stopped temporarily. Click **OK**.

10. In the **Microsoft Exchange Server Setup** dialog box, enter the CD Key of your Exchange Server CD and then click **OK** twice.

11. The **Licensing** dialog box appears. Select **I Agree That**, and then click **OK**.

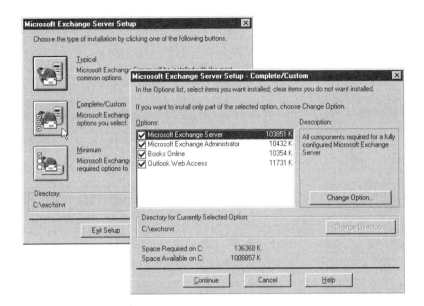

Task 3d: Joining an Existing Microsoft Exchange Site

1. Within the **Organization And Site** dialog box, click **Join An Existing Site**.

2. Enter the name of the existing server, for example **NEWYORK-1**, into the **Existing Server** box.

3. Click **OK** to continue.

> **Note** If you are joining a server and its version number is older than 5.0, a message box will appear with this statement: **Setup will update the directory information in <Organization> and then restart the Microsoft Exchange services on <Old Server> for changes to take effect. No users on <Old Server> will be able to read and send mail while the services are being restarted. Do you wish to continue?** In this message box, click **OK**. A second message box will be displayed with this message: **Setup needs to upgrade this site's directory schema to the 5.5 version. To install additional version 4.0 servers into an upgraded site, follow the instructions in the README file.** In this message box, click **OK**.

4. The **Confirm Exchange Site And Organization** dialog box appears. Verify that the **Server**, **Organization**, and **Exchange Site** information is correct and then click **Yes**.

5. The **Site Services Account** dialog box appears. Notice that the **Browse** button is not available when the server is joining an existing site.

6. In the **Account Password** box, type *password* and then click **OK**.

7. After the local installation steps have been completed successfully, an Exchange Server Setup dialog box appears, indicating that the directory replication has been initiated. Click **OK**.

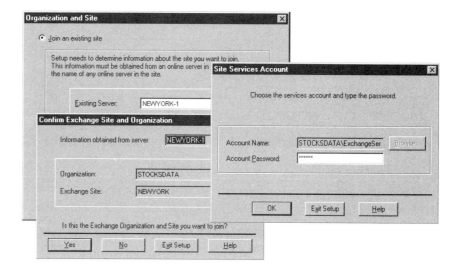

Task 3e: Running the Exchange Optimizer

1. In the **Microsoft Exchange Server Setup** dialog box, click **Run Optimizer**.

2. The **Microsoft Exchange Performance Optimizer** dialog box appears. Click **Next**.

3. Click **Next** to accept the defaults.

4. The Optimizer analyzes your hard disk drives and then displays a message indicating that it has completed disk analysis. Click **Next**.

5. The Optimizer displays suggestions for storing the Exchange Server files. Click **Next**.

6. The **Microsoft Exchange Performance Optimizer** dialog box appears, indicating that some files will be moved. Click **Next**. (This message box appears only if more than one hard disk drive is available.)

7. The **Microsoft Exchange Performance Optimizer** dialog box appears, indicating that it has completed its task. Click **Finish**.

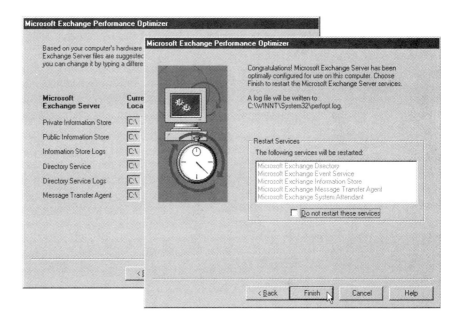

Review

When the option **Join Existing Site** is selected, the Exchange Server setup receives the site's configuration from the server that you specify during installation, so you'll need to specify the password of the Site Services Account only during the installation. This password is necessary to start the server-to-server communication later on. Setup copies all necessary files to the local hard disks and starts the core services of the new Exchange Server computer. After that, all selected additional components will be installed. When Setup has finished this process, directory replication will be started automatically and the new server will retrieve the complete directory of its site.

When Setup is successfully completed, it suggests running the Performance Optimizer. The Optimizer allows the Exchange Server to use the existing hardware platform in the most efficient way according to the desired server configuration (number of users, public folders, bridgehead, and so on). The Performance Optimizer is covered in more detail later in this chapter in Lesson 4, "Post-Installation Considerations."

Upgrade a Server Within a Site

Exchange Server 5.5 offers several enhancements that are not available in Exchange Server 5.0 or earlier. The support of the IMAP4 protocol, Advanced Security changes, the Connector for Lotus Notes, and other enhanced features such as the Exchange Event Service make it easy for you to implement the new version into an existing organization.

Many changes have been made to the DS and IS between versions 4.0 and 5.0 and some changes also exist between 5.0 and 5.5. The upgrade procedure varies slightly depending on whether you're upgrading Exchange Server version 4.0 or 5.0. To upgrade verson 4.0 DS and IS databases, Setup will convert them to version 5.0 first before converting them into the 5.5 format. Of course, Exchange Server 5.0 databases are converted to version 5.5 in only one cycle.

Note An administrator wanting to launch the Setup program on an existing Exchange Server computer needs to be a Permissions Admin in the site as well as a Windows NT Administrator.

Upgrade Mode

Setup will detect the existence of an older Exchange Server version, and the version number will be read from the server's directory. Exchange Server Setup also checks the language. When detecting an older server version, Setup switches to the Upgrade mode and displays the **Upgrade** button. Clicking this button starts the replacement of all local Exchange Server files on the computer. Although all server files will be replaced, Setup will not change the existing configuration during the upgrade; only the databases will be updated.

Upgrade Strategies

Exchange Server 5.5 allows you to upgrade servers within a site in any order. A specific upgrade strategy is not required, although care needs to be taken in multiple-site environments.

Multiple-Site Strategy

It is recommended that you start the upgrade procedure with the replication bridgehead servers within your organization. Bridgehead servers must be upgraded first because they are responsible for all the directory replication to other sites in your organization.

All existing bridgehead servers should be upgraded in one step. Depending on site size and message traffic, it's possible that the version information for newly upgraded servers might be delayed in replication. Administrators are encouraged to allow replication to complete itself before upgrading other Exchange Server computers. Once the replication has finished, other servers can be upgraded in any order. (See Figure 2-7.)

Upgrade Security Issues

The Site Services Account of Exchange Server version 4.0 needed only the Windows NT rights to **Logon As A Service** and **Restore Files And Directories** in addition to its **Domain User** role. This has been changed with Exchange Server version 5.0; the additional right **Act As A Part Of The Operating System** is also required. This right is specifically used for the POP3 support. It allows the server to impersonate connecting users for mail service. If the Site Services Account does not have the **Act As A Part Of The Operating System** right, POP3 mail users will not be able to access their inboxes. Because support for POP3 is still part of Exchange Server 5.5, the Site Services Account needs the same set of rights as in version 5.0.

During the upgrade of Exchange Server 4.0, you will be asked where to upgrade the databases—in place or at a different location. However, the different location cannot be a network resource. If you choose the **Upgrade To A Different Location** option for a fault-tolerant upgrade, sufficient disk space must be available on the different location for both the current and the new databases. The reason behind the need for 100 percent additional free disk space is the fact that the fault-tolerant upgrade creates a copy of the databases first, which it upgrades afterwards. If an error occurs during upgrade, the whole process can be quickly rolled back. The in-place upgrade procedure, on the other hand, upgrades the original database files and needs less free disk space. It requires additional disk space that is approximately 15 percent of the size of the current databases. In the case of an upgrade error, however, a restore from backup is often required to bring the server back to a consistent state.

Key Management Server Databases

KM Server databases did not change between Exchange Server 4.0 and 5.0, but changes have been implemented in version 5.5. Therefore, an existing KM Server database will be upgraded to Exchange Server 5.5 if Setup detects a KM Server installation. It is important to note that not every Exchange administrator can upgrade an existing KM Server—only a KM administrator can complete the upgrade successfully. As a KM administrator, you must supply the KM Server password during the upgrade, because this password is used to decrypt the database.

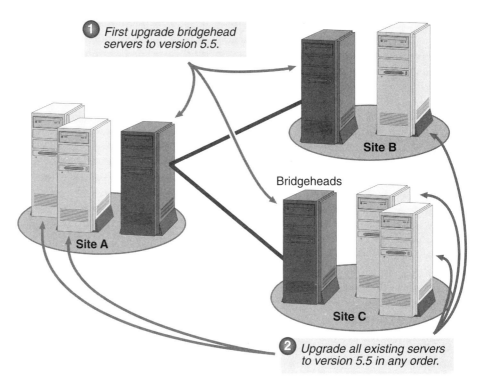

Figure 2-7. Upgrading to Exchange Server 5.5.

The recommended strategy for upgrading multiple sites to Exchange Server 5.5 is as follows:

1. First upgrade directory bridgehead servers from Exchange 4.0 or 5.0 to version 5.5

2. Then upgrade other nondirectory bridgehead servers to Exchange 5.5 in any order

Lesson 3: Maintenance Mode and Unattended Setup

The Exchange Server Setup program provides options to further manage the server installation after the initial setup has been completed. You can add or remove additional server components at any time by running the setup program in maintenance mode. Of course, you can't remove core components without removing the entire server, since these components must always be active on every Exchange Server computer. The Setup program's unattended mode, on the other hand, offers interesting options for advanced server installation. As you'll see, the unattended mode provides you with more control over the setup procedure than does a manual installation. The Exchange Server 5.5 Setup program is also able to identify Microsoft Cluster environments, and can therefore offer installation options that will allow you to configure the server for proper cluster support. At the end of this lesson, you'll find a description of issues regarding the setup on a Cluster Server, including the advantages of such a configuration and respective Exchange Server limitations.

At the end of this lesson, you will be able to:

- Use the Setup Maintenance Mode to install and remove Exchange Server components
- Run Exchange Server Setup unattended
- Install Exchange Server 5.5 on a Microsoft Cluster Server

Estimated time to complete this lesson: 35 minutes

Setup Maintenance Mode

The Exchange Server Setup program can be started at any time. If you run it on a computer that already has Exchange Server 5.5 installed, it will switch into the maintenance mode. Using this mode, you have the ability to add and remove components (**Add/Remove** option) or to reinstall the entire Exchange Server (**Reinstall** option). It's also possible to completely remove the server installation (**Remove All** option). (See Figure 2-8.)

Setup will detect the presence of any Exchange Server installation by reading the following Registry key:

```
HKEY_LOCAL_MACHINE
    \SOFTWARE
        \Microsoft
            \Exchange
                \Setup
```

Maintenance Mode Information

As you select new components to add, Setup will read the corresponding installation files (.INS) to obtain installation-related information about the component files that will be copied to the computer. The .INS files also contain a description of necessary configuration entries, which have to be written to the Windows NT Registry.

A component can be removed by deselecting its entry in maintenance mode. Setup will read the appropriate uninstallation file (.UNS) to remove the corresponding files, services, and Registry entries.

Reinstalling an Exchange Server

It might be a good idea to reinstall an Exchange Server if you suspect important files have been corrupted. The reinstallation can replace these files, thereby repairing any server components. Setup will check the current version of the installed software before it overwrites the server files. Files with newer version numbers than on the installation CD will not automatically be replaced. To replace those files with files of the appropriate version, you must also reinstall the previously installed SP. Besides refreshing directories and files, Setup also renews Windows NT Registry settings of installed Exchange Server components.

The database files and template information will not be overwritten. This means that the reinstallation of an Exchange Server is not really risky, but often useful, when Windows NT Registry entries must be updated or when files are corrupted and finding out what exactly is broken looks like an inordinately time-consuming job.

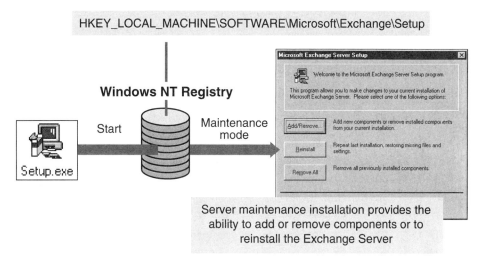

Figure 2-8. Launching the maintenance mode.

The maintenance installation is useful for:

- Adding or removing optional Exchange Server components

- Repeating the entire Exchange Server installation without losing directory and configuration information

- Removing the Exchange Server

Unattended Setup Mode

It is possible to customize the Exchange Server setup process by using a file typically named Setup.ini—although you can use a different name if you prefer. This file can supply all the information needed for an automatic installation of Exchange Server. No additional user input is necessary, and Setup can run unattended. When you use the unattended mode, multiple installations on different computers can run at the same time. However, you should keep in mind that the directory replication will be launched during the installation if you specify that newly installed servers will join existing sites. This process of directory replication will allocate considerable network bandwidth. Therefore, not too many servers should be installed at the same time within the same site and network segment. If too many new directories are created almost at the same time, this might have an adverse effect on the network performance until all server directories have replicated all changes with each other. (See Figure 2-9 on page 111.)

Primary Domain Controller

Before running Setup in unattended mode, you should verify that the PDC is available. The unattended mode must validate the Site Services Account with the PDC. A BDC is not sufficient.

Command Line Options

You can start setup in unattended mode by using the following command line:

```
Setup /Q [path to this file]\SETUP.INI
```

For example, you will start Setup /Q C:\Info\SETUP.INI to install an Exchange Server based on a Setup.ini file from the C:\Info directory. Other Command line options are:

- **/R** installs a new Exchange Server and prepare it for restoration of a database backup
- **/U** reinstalls or upgrades the Exchange Server

Setup.ini Options

Several sample Setup.ini files and instructions for using Setup /Q can be found on the Exchange Server CD. They reside in the \Server\Support\ Batsetup\Setup directory. The following list contains all available entries for a Setup.ini:

Option	Description
[Product ID]	
cdkey=	Your product ID, formatted as: xxx-xxxxxxx
[Paths]	
ServerDest=	Where the server will be installed
AdminDest=	Where Admin will be installed if selected
[Components]	
Services=	Whether to install the server services
Administrator=	Whether to install Administrator program
MSMailConnector=	Whether to install MS Mail Connector
cc:Mail=	Whether to install the Connector for cc:Mail
X400=	Whether to install the X.400 Connector

(continues)

(continued)

Option	Description
[Components]	
Active Server Components=	Whether to install the Outlook Web Access Components
Sample Applications=	Whether to install the sample applications
Books Online=	Whether to install online documentation
Event Service=	Whether to install the Event Service
[Site]	
SiteName=	Name of new site if no ExistingServerName is provided
SiteProxyName=	Proxy Name of site if new site is created
ExistingServerName=	If the server is joining an existing site, server in that site
[Organization]	
OrganizationName=	Organization name if a new site is being created
OrganizationProxyName=	Organization Proxy name, if a new site is being created
[ServiceAccount]	
AccountName=	Service account name if creating a new site
AccountPassword=	Service account password
[Licensing]	
PerSeat=	Whether to set up licensing on a Per Seat basis
[SitePermissions]	
Account1=	Account to which Site Administrative permission is to be given (0-4 accounts can be given this permission)
Account2=	Account to which Site Administrative permission is to be given
Account3=	Account to which Site Administrative permission is to be given
Account4=	Account to which Site Administrative permission is to be given

(continues)

(continued)

Option	Description
[X400]	
Country=	X.400 Country name if creating a new site
AdminManDomName=	X.400 ADMD name if creating a new site
PrivManDomName=	X.400 PRMD name if creating a new site
Organization=	X.400 Organization name if creating a new site
OrgUnit1=	X.400 OU1 name if creating a new site
OrgUnit2=	X.400 OU2 name if creating a new site
OrgUnit3=	X.400 OU3 name if creating a new site
OrgUnit4=	X.400 OU4 name if creating a new site

As you can see, it's possible to specify all options in the Setup.ini that you can determine during a manual setup as well. Some additional information, such as proxy names for the site and organization as well as X.400 parameters, provide even more control over the installation process. To create the Setup.ini file you can use Notepad or any word processing program such as Microsoft Word. But you'll have to save the Setup.ini as an ASCII file.

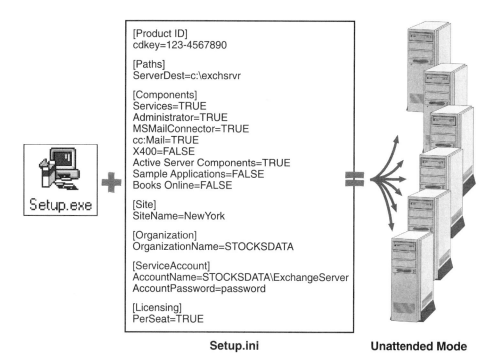

```
[Product ID]
cdkey=123-4567890

[Paths]
ServerDest=c:\exchsrvr

[Components]
Services=TRUE
Administrator=TRUE
MSMailConnector=TRUE
cc:Mail=TRUE
X400=FALSE
Active Server Components=TRUE
Sample Applications=FALSE
Books Online=FALSE

[Site]
SiteName=NewYork

[Organization]
OrganizationName=STOCKSDATA

[ServiceAccount]
AccountName=STOCKSDATA\ExchangeServer
AccountPassword=password

[Licensing]
PerSeat=TRUE
```

Setup.ini   **Unattended Mode**

Figure 2-9. Running multiple setup instances in batch mode.

The requirements to run setup in unattended mode are as follows:

- All necessary information must be supplied in a Setup.ini file

- The Setup.ini file is an ASCII file

- The PDC must be running and accessible for Site Services Account validation

- The command line switch /Q [path to this file]\SETUP.INI allows you to run the unattended mode

Installing Exchange Server in a Clustered Environment

The Enterprise Edition of Windows NT Server 4.0 supports the cluster technology, which can be used to bind multiple servers so tightly together that they will act as one logical unit. Clustering is a method that provides reliability through complex hardware redundancy. Servers within a cluster interact with each other to provide failover support in the case of emergencies. If a particular process fails on one server, another server takes over, thus continuously providing server-based resources to the network. In other words, clustering can significantly improve the reliability of your server-based applications, such as Microsoft SQL Server or Exchange Server. However, Cluster Server currently supports only two nodes (computers) per cluster.

Configuration Requirements

The purpose of a cluster is to provide multiple servers to the network as one virtual server. Hence, a cluster requires a LAN-like connection for client access, and the protocol used in the LAN must be TCP/IP. You must bind the two nodes of a Cluster Server using a separate, isolated LAN. Both nodes must share a common SCSI bus to access a central SCSI hard disk system, which must also be shared between the cluster nodes. This shared disk system becomes the storage media for the cluster-aware applications. Both nodes can then get access to the cluster resources, as shown in Figure 2-10 on page 115. In addition, each node requires a local (not shared) hard disk, which will host the operating system and the Exchange Server software.

Note It is recommended that you use identical hardware platforms and configurations for both nodes of a particular Cluster Server. Furthermore, you must install the hot fixes available from *ftp://ftp.microsoft.com/bussys/winnt/ winnt-public/fixes/usa/nt40/hotfixes-postsp3/roll-up/* before you install Exchange Server.

A dedicated service—the Cluster Service—is the heart of every Cluster Server. It maintains the physical and logical resources such as shared directories, Windows NT services, and the common cluster configuration information (IP address, network name, and so on). Resources can be defined using the Cluster Administrator program on one of the nodes.

Note Services such as the IS can run only on one node at a given time.

Installing Supported Exchange Server Services

Applications or services that are cluster aware can be installed conveniently in a clustered environment. Within Exchange Server 5.5, the DS, IS, MTA, SA, IMS, and Event Service are cluster-aware components, but if you want to install one of the remaining components (such as the INS or the Connector for Lotus cc:Mail) in a clustered environment additional configuration steps must be taken using the Cluster Administrator program.

The following Exchange Server components are not supported in a cluster environment:

- Dynamic RAS Connector
- Internet Mail Service using Dial-Up connections
- Internet News Service using Dial-Up connections
- Outlook Web Access
- StarNine Mail for AppleTalk Networks
- Exchange Connector for Lotus Notes
- Exchange Connector for SNADS
- X.400 Connector using X.25
- X.400 Connector using TP4
- Exchange Connector for IBM OfficeVision OV/VM (PROFS)
- Third-party connectors and gateways

Exchange Server 5.5 must be installed on the first and the second node of the Cluster Server. The Setup program is run on the first node to install the server on the shared SCSI hard disk system. Setup will detect that it is running on a Cluster Server and will display a dialog box, notifying you that you are installing the Exchange Server in a clustered environment. Once you have verified that this is the desired form of installation, Setup will copy files to the primary node's Windows NT System32 directory, copies files to the clustered drive, and creates resources in the Exchange Server cluster resource group. Setup will then add the cluster-aware Exchange Server services as resources to the Cluster Group, which must be defined prior to the installation using the Cluster Administrator program. The Setup program is then run on the second node to complete the installation. For this purpose, you must choose the **Update Node** option, which copies the Exchange Server files to the second node's Windows NT System32 directory and creates and registers the Exchange Server services.

Note Whenever additional components—for example, IMS, INS, MS Mail Connector, Exchange Connector for Lotus cc:Mail, Exchange Scripting Service, or KM server—are added or removed from the primary node, the secondary node must be updated using the **Upgrade Node** option of the Exchange Server Setup.

Cluster Operation and Viability

The nodes of a Cluster Server must communicate with each other and work as a single unit to provide automatic recovery from service failures. The nodes' Resource/Failover Managers are the components responsible for monitoring the viability of the resources. These managers have the ability either to restart unavailable services or to take those services and their dependent resources over to the other node, depending on the number of failures that have occurred in a specified period. The default threshold is three failures detected within 900 seconds.

Let's say you have installed Exchange Server 5.5 in a clustered environment. The cluster-aware services (DS, IS, MTA, SA, IMS, and Event Service) are now running on the first node. At this point the second node is not executing the Exchange Server services at all, so clients will access the first node through the commonly defined network name and IP address of the Cluster Server. The second node, however, can run other processes, such as SQL Server or IIS 4.0. Both servers are operating independently of each other, but now let's imagine that a server failure has been detected in one of the Exchange Server services. It is the responsibility of the Resource/Failover Manager on node A to detect the failure and to enumerate all dependent services and resources to move them over to node B. The steps to do this are as follows:

1. All failed resources, including resources dependent upon the failed services and the resources upon which the failed resources depend, are enumerated.

2. The Resource/Failover Manager on node A takes off line all resources in the dependency tree. Those without further dependencies are taken off line first.

3. The Resource/Failover Manager on node A notifies the Resource/Failover Manager on node B to take over the failed resources.

4. The Resource/Failover Manager on node B brings the resources on line in reverse dependency order. In other words, resources with the most dependencies are brought on line first.

The Exchange Server services will be running on node B once this procedure has been completed. Clients will now access the second node through the commonly defined network name and IP address of the Cluster Server. The resources of a Cluster Server are tested periodically to ensure that the failover procedure will work in case of an emergency.

Note The Clustering Technology provides fault tolerance only if the reason for the failure is located somewhere outside the Exchange Server databases and message queues. If the MTA service crashes due to a corrupted message placed in a message queue, failover will not work, since the MTA service—which is started automatically on node B—will crash for the same reason.

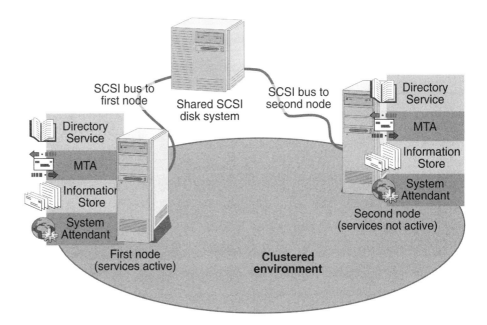

Figure 2-10. Microsoft Cluster Server configuration.

The hardware requirements for Cluster Server configuration are as follows:

- Central SCSI hard disk system, which is shared between the nodes
- Common SCSI bus, which provides access to the shared SCSI storage media for both nodes
- Dedicated and isolated LAN link between the nodes
- LAN-like connection and TCP/IP support between cluster and clients
- Local hard disk on each node for Windows NT Server 4.0 Enterprise Edition

The required resource definitions are as follows:

- Cluster Server's IP address
- Cluster Server's network name

Lesson 4: Post-Installation Considerations

A typical all-purpose Exchange Server must be able to handle mailboxes, public folders, messaging connectors, and several other resources. You can, however, also configure servers that are solely responsible for mailboxes or public folders or messaging connectors, or other individual tasks if you want to distribute these tasks over multiple servers. The implication here is that all these servers must be optimized differently. A server maintaining mailboxes must respond to messaging clients as quickly as possible. Another server maintaining public folders only should do this as well, but it might also have to replicate the data to other servers in the organization. A messaging bridge-head, finally, does not need to respond to messaging clients at all. Its primary purpose is to transfer messages to remote sites and foreign messaging systems as quickly as possible.

This lesson presents the tasks an administrator must take into consideration once a server has been installed. This includes the optimization of a server installation for specific tasks. This optimization will allow the server components to use the existing hardware in the most efficient way possible. Various aspects concerning the security of server files and directories are also covered in this lesson.

This lesson concludes with a practical exercise, which verifies that the test installation that was done in the previous exercises of this chapter was successful.

At the end of this lesson, you will be able to:

- Optimize the Exchange Server configuration

- Specify default and minimum network access permissions on server share points

- Install the Exchange Administrator program on a Windows NT Workstation

Estimated time to complete this lesson: 30 minutes

Optimizing the Server

It is highly recommended that you optimize the server installation once the setup is complete. Fortunately, you don't have to optimize the server manually. A separate tool—the Performance Optimizer—is able to configure the most important server components according to several parameters, such as the number of mailboxes, the number of public folders, and so on. The Performance Optimizer will be installed along with the Exchange Server.

Starting the Optimizer

You can click the **Run Optimizer** button at the end of the setup procedure to start the optimization process for the first time immediately after the server has been installed. The Performance Optimizer is also available through an icon in the **Microsoft Exchange** program group, so you can start it any time you want later on. In fact, it should be launched whenever the server hardware has been modified or the number of users on a server or within the organization has changed significantly. It is also a good idea to optimize the server again if you have installed optional server components. Information about specific server tasks such as a messaging bridgehead configuration should be taken into consideration during the optimization process as well.

Note   The Performance Optimizer is an application that must run locally on the server that will be optimized.

File Locations

The Optimizer does not only optimize the various server components, it can also improve the reliability of your installation by improving the components' recoverability in cases where a hard disk is inaccessible. It does so by placing the Exchange Server directories on all available local hard disks. An intensive hardware analysis will be performed beforehand in order to gather necessary performance data, which allow the Optimizer to determine the best places for databases and their transaction log files. Once the files have been moved, the Optimizer modifies the Windows NT Registry settings accordingly. Reliable server installations are covered in Chapter 15.

Adjusting Performance Settings

You can customize the Optimizer settings manually at run time by supplying a special command line switch at the command prompt. First you need to switch to the \Exchsrvr\bin directory and then run **Perfwiz -V**. The Performance Optimizer will provide additional pages that allow you to control system parameters directly. For instance, you can adjust the number of database buffers needed for the IS. Normally, the number of IS buffers depends on the number of Exchange Clients that connect to the server. They will be allocated in 4KB blocks. (See Figure 2-11.)

Core Service Optimization

Another system parameter the Performance Optimizer can set is the maximum number of threads for all active Exchange Server components. A thread is the smallest executable unit of a Windows NT program. The more threads a component can start, the better its response time will be, but the more hardware resources it will consume. You can control the minimum and maximum number of IS threads as well as the number of threads that will be created for the DS. In addition, you can specify the maximum number of read threads, which the MTA will use to obtain information from the DS.

Client Performance Optimization

You can affect client performance through the manipulation of server parameters. The maximum number of categorizations and restrictions stored on the server computer, for instance, has a direct influence. When users choose the **Group By** command on the Exchange Client's **View** menu to arrange message items in their server-based mailboxes and in public folders, categorizations will be stored on the server. Categorizations provide the information about how to group items. Restrictions, in turn, are sets of data generated during a Find or Filter operation. Restrictions will also be stored on the server so that the client does not need to reorder the items every time a folder is opened. The higher the number of stored categorizations and restrictions, the better the client performance is in these respects. However, more server disk space might be necessary if the maximum number of cached categorizations and restrictions is increased.

Server Optimization in Unattended Mode

You can run the Performance Optimizer in silent mode to optimize the server configuration without manual interaction. This option is especially useful when installing Exchange Server 5.5 in unattended mode using a Setup.ini file. In silent mode, the Performance Optimizer relies on a text file named Perfopt.inf, which contains the desired parameters. This file must reside in the same directory as the Performance Optimizer executable file (Perfwiz.exe), otherwise you have to specify the desired file using the -F option (for example, Perfwiz -F C:\Optimize.inf). If you don't use the -F option, which leads implicitly to the silent mode, you can launch the silent mode using the optional parameter -S (Perfwiz -S).

Perfopt.inf File Format

The structure of the Perfopt.inf file is relatively simple and straightforward. It is a ASCII file that must contain one section labeled **[Perfwiz]** and six configuration entries. A sample file might contain the following parameters:

```
[Perfwiz]
Users=1
Org Users=1
Server Type=8
Don't Restart=FALSE
Analyze Disks=TRUE
Move Files=TRUE
```

Note The unattended Setup of Exchange Server can also initiate the Performance Optimizer in silent mode when the section and entries of the Perfopt.inf to the Setup.ini file are added. In this case, the Performance Optimizer can run automatically at the end of the installation because the unattended Setup creates a text file named Perfopt.inf using the settings of the [Perfwiz] section as specified in Setup.ini. The Perfopt.inf is placed in the same directory as the perfwiz.exe file.

Perfopt.inf Options

The Perfopt.inf options and their purposes are as follows:

Option	Purpose
Users	Number of users on this server
	0 = less than 500; 1 = 500 – 999; 2 = 1,000 – 4,999; 3 = 5,000 – 24,999; 4 = 25,000 – 49,999; 5 = more than 50,000
Org Users	Number of users in the organization
	0 = less than 1,000; 1 = 1,000 – 9,999; 2 = 10,000 – 99,999; 3 = 100,000 – 499,999; 4 = more than 500,000
Server Type	Role of the server within the site
	1 = Private Server; 2 = Public Server; 4 = Connector; 8 = Multi Server; 16 = POP3 /IMAP4/NNTP Server
Don't Restart	Determines whether the services should be restarted once the optimization is complete.
	TRUE or FALSE
Analyze Disks	Determines whether the computer's hard disk configuration should be analyzed prior to the optimization.
	TRUE or FALSE
Move Files	Determines whether files should be moved to their optimal locations.
	TRUE or FALSE

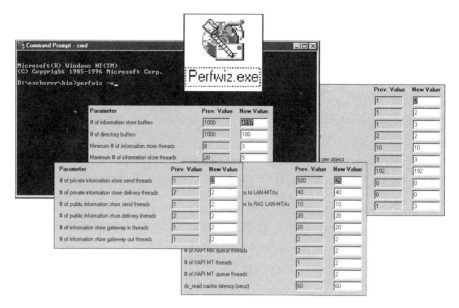

Figure 2-11. Customization of Performance Optimizer settings.

The Performance Optimizer configures the file location for the following components:

- Directory database files
- IS database files (Private and Public IS separately, if appropriate)
- MTA queues
- Transaction log files (DS and IS separately, if appropriate)

Default File Locations and Structure

During the installation, Setup creates the directory structure to host the Exchange Server files. If you accept the default settings, they will be placed under the C:\Exchsrvr directory. You might find an additional Exchsrvr directory on each of your hard disk drives. This will be the case if you have started the Performance Optimizer by clicking the **Run Optimizer** button at the end of the setup procedure. The Performance Optimizer spreads the files across the existing local disk drives to achieve maximum performance and reliability for the Exchange Server computer. (See Figure 2-12.)

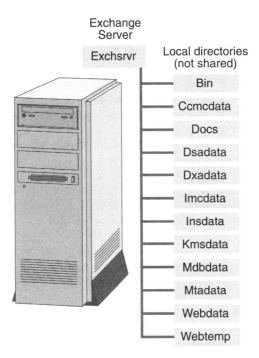

Figure 2-12. Non-shared file locations of Exchange Server.

Exchange Server Setup creates the following directories on the
server computer:

Folder name	This directory contains
Add-ins (shared as Add-ins)	Extensions for the Exchange server. By default, this directory has subdirectories for the MS Mail Connector (\MS), Schedule+ Free/Busy Connector (\MSFB), the IMS (\SMTP), and the INS (\INS) extensions.
Address (shared as Address)	E-mail Proxy DLLs that are necessary for address generation in Exchange Server. By default, MS Mail, SMTP, CCMAIL, and X.400 Proxy DLLs can be found.
Bin	Important Exchange Server program binaries. For example, the Exchange Administrator Program and the Performance Optimizer are copied to this directory.
Ccmcdata	Directory and temporary storage location for the Lotus cc:Mail Connector.

(continues)

(continued)

Folder name	This directory contains
Connect (hidden share, shared as Connect$)	Exchange Connector Components. Default components for the MS Mail Connector, Internet Mail Service, the Connector for Lotus cc:Mail, and Schedule+ Free/Busy Connector will be copied into this directory.
Connect\Msmcon\ Mail data (hidden share, shared as Maildat$)	MS Mail Connector post office.
Docs	Exchange Server documentation in HTML format.
Dsadata	Directory Service Database.
Dxadata	Database for the Directory Synchronization with MS Mail.
Imcdata	The working directory for the IMS.
Insdata	The working directory for the INS.
Kmsdata	Key Management database and corresponding log files.
Mdbdata	Private and public IS and associated transaction log files.
Mtadata	The directory for the MTA. Contains log files and configuration information as well as messages that are currently processed and MTA queues.
Res (shared as Resources)	Msg. DLLs for the IMS, MTA, and other components.
Tracking.log (shared as tracking.log)	Log files used for message tracking of the Exchange Server.
Webdata	Files for Outlook Web Access.
Webtemp	Temporary directory for Outlook Web Access.

Share Point Permissions

The Setup program automatically shares specific directories of the server for network access. It's a good idea to restrict access to these share points in order to increase the security of the server-based resources. Knowing the share point permissions and the processes that need access to them helps to secure the Exchange Server appropriately. (See Figure 2-13 on page 124.)

Add-ins

The Add-ins directory contains extensions for the Exchange Administrator program. The Administrator program is designed to be the universal tool for most of the Exchange administration tasks. Third-party gateways and other components can extend the Administrator program when extension files are placed into this directory.

Address

The Address directory is the place for proxy address generation DLLs. A proxy address generator is typically responsible for the automatic generation of default e-mail addresses. Each address generator corresponds to a specific e-mail address type. Examples are SMTP, X.400, MS Mail, and Lotus cc:Mail. Addresses of these types will be generated by default for every mailbox, but it is also possible to install additional proxy address generators along with third-party messaging connectors.

Connect$ and Maildat$

The Connect$ share is a hidden share that provides a network share point for messaging connectors. Files for the cc:Mail Connector (\Ccmail), the IMS (\Mseximc), the Schedule+ Free/Busy Connector (\Msfbconn), and the MS Mail Connector (\Msmcon) reside there. Several .TRN files used for character translation of IA5 message text reside in the \Trn directory. The \Maildata subdirectory can be found in the \Msmcon directory. It represents the MS Mail Connector postoffice. Although it is possible to connect to this postoffice through the Connect directory, it is explicitly shared again as Maildat$. (See Figure 2-13.) The architecture of the MS Mail Connector is covered in Chapter 18.

Resources

Resource files are used for Windows NT event logging. They are shared as the Resources network share point. Event logging features are explained along with each Exchange Server component throughout this book.

Tracking.log

The Message Tracking Center relies on log files, which can be found in the Tracking.log network share if message tracking has been enabled. The MTA, IS, and messaging connectors will record information about messages that have been transferred or delivered. Using the Message Tracking Center, you can connect to each of the available share points within your organization to examine the path a particular message has taken. The message tracking capabilities of Exchange Server are covered in Chapter 15.

Increasing Security

By default, all shared directories are accessible for every user in the domain. This is certainly not a secure configuration, but it guarantees a properly functioning system. You can, however, remove the **Everyone** group from the list of accounts with permissions in order to restrict access to the shared directories. After that, you have to grant the appropriate rights to specific accounts. At the minimum, the Site Services Account and the local administrators group must have full access to the directories.

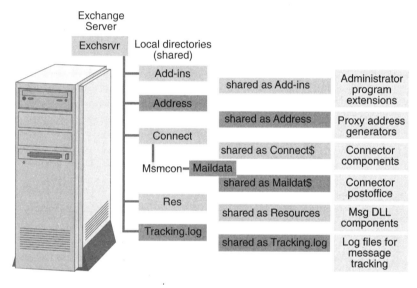

Figure 2-13. Shared directories of an Exchange Server.

Characteristics of shared Exchange Server directories are as follows:

Directory	Shared as	Permissions
C:\Exchsrvr\Add-ins	Add-ins	Administrators and Exchange service account: Full Control
		Everyone: Read
C:\Exchsrvr\Address	Address	Administrators and Exchange service account: Full Control
		Everyone: Read
C:\Exchsrvr\Connect	Connect$	Administrators and Exchange service account: Full Control
		Everyone: Read

(continues)

(continued)

Directory	Shared as	Permissions
C:\Exchsrvr\Connect\ Msmcon\Maildata	Maildat$	Administrators and Exchange service account: Full Control
		Everyone: Full Control
C:\Exchsrvr\Res	Resources	Administrators and Exchange service account: Full Control
		Everyone: Read
C:\Exchsrvr\Tracking.log	Tracking.log	Administrators and Exchange service account: Full Control
		Everyone: Read

Installing the Exchange Administrator Program

The Exchange Administrator program can run on any Windows NT computer. Exchange Server setup copies this application to the computer during a **Typical** or **Complete/Custom** installation. Its executable file, labeled Admin.exe, can be found in the Exchsrvr\Bin directory if you have accepted the default installation directory.

Note You cannot run the Administrator program from a Windows 95 computer.

Windows NT Tools Extensions

As Setup installs the Administrator program, the User Manager for Domains will also become extended (with functionality provided by Mailumx.dll). A new menu called **Exchange** is a clear sign of the User Manager extension. Furthermore, Setup replaces the original Windows NT Backup program with a Microsoft Exchange Server version. The new backup program allows you to perform online backups of the Microsoft Exchange Server databases.

Installation Using the Maintenance Mode

You have the option to add the Administrator program to an existing Exchange Server installation at any time using the maintenance mode of the Setup program. This might be required if you have installed a server without the Administrator program using the **Minimum** installation. The Setup program will switch into the maintenance mode automatically, since the Exchange Server has been already installed, thus providing the ability to add the Administrator program to the current installation. (See Figure 2-14.)

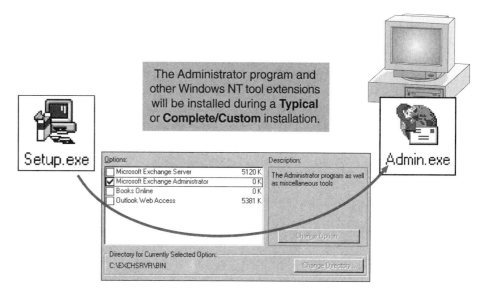

Figure 2-14. Installing the Exchange Administrator program.

Site-Level Administration Feature

The Exchange Administrator program supports the centralized administration of sites and servers. In other words, if all Exchange Server computers are connected over network links that support the RPC communication, you can configure them remotely using a single Administrator program from the desktop of a Windows NT computer.

Remote administration is not possible over links that don't support the RPC mechanism. Therefore, it might be necessary to install multiple copies of the Administrator program in networks with multiple network segments. You can use the RPCPing utility to test the RPC communication between computers. If RPCPing works fine, the Administrator program will work as well. RPCPing will be discussed in Chapter 15.

Configuring Site Defaults

Using the Administrator program, you can configure the servers in a site most efficiently through site-level default parameters. The parameters reside in the directory and will be automatically updated on all servers through directory replication. For instance, when you change the default site addressing for a particular address type such as SMTP, the changes will be replicated to all other servers. Once replicated, all servers will use the new addressing format to generate proxy e-mail addresses for new mailboxes and other recipient objects. Site-level administration is covered in detail in Chapter 8, while information about the server-to-server communication in a site is explained in Chapter 4.

Server-Specific Settings

Some configuration changes will be written to the local Windows NT Registry instead of the server's directory. For example, you can adjust the Diagnostics Logging settings of a service or a messaging connector, or specify display names for directory objects. These changes, written to the Registry, will not be replicated and will not affect the other Exchange Servers in the site.

The site-level changes that are updated through directory replication include:

- Connector settings
- Core component settings
- Distribution lists
- Mailbox configuration changes
- Modifications of rights
- Site-level Internet protocol settings

Exercise 4: Verifying the Installation

You can use the Services applet of the Control Panel to verify that the Exchange Server services you've installed in the previous exercises have been started. You can also use the Server Manager if you want to check a remote Windows NT computer.

Estimated time to complete this exercise: 10 minutes

Description

In this exercise, you will use the Control Panel to verify that all the core services of your Exchange Server have been started.

- Task 4 describes the steps for verifying that the core Exchange Server services were successfully started.

Prerequisites

- Log on as Admin-NY1 to NEWYORK-1 to complete this exercise.

Task 4: Verifying the Installation

1. Start the Control Panel.

2. Double click the **Services** icon.

3. Verify that the following services are started:

   - Exchange DS
   - Exchange Event Service
   - Exchange IS
   - Exchange MTA
   - Exchange SA
   - Remote Procedure Call Locator
   - Remote Procedure Call Service

4. Close the **Services** dialog box.

5. Exit the Control Panel.

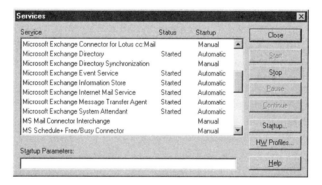

Review

The Control Panel is one of the central administration tools that allows you to start and stop the entire Exchange Server or parts of it without rebooting the machine. Stopping and restarting a service might be necessary from time to time. For example, restarting the MTA forces this service to start immediately transferring messages destined for other sites.

Lesson 5: Common Installation Problems

The list of ordinary installation problems is short. Problems related to permissions and forgotten account passwords are the main issues that cause trouble. Other difficulties might be NetBEUI-related issues stemming from joining an existing site.

This lesson introduces the most common installation problems as they might occur while you run Exchange Server Setup program. In addition to the discussion of account permissions and password-related problems, you'll find valuable information regarding the NetBEUI trap as well as dependencies of the various server services.

At the end of this lesson, you will be able to:

- Address permissions-related installation problems

- Identify unfavorable network configurations

- Verify dependencies between Exchange Server services

Estimated time to complete this lesson: 20 minutes

Troubleshooting Installation Problems

Missing Windows NT permissions or improper permissions at an existing Exchange site that you want to join will cause harmless installation problems. The solution is relatively simple—you need to log on using an appropriate installation account.

Windows NT Administrator Group

If you don't have the permissions of an administrator on the Windows NT Server computer onto which you want to install an Exchange Server, a dialog box will appear immediately after you have started the Setup program. This dialog box informs you that your Windows NT account needs to be a member of the **Administrators** group. You will not be able to run Setup successfully without the appropriate Windows NT permissions. (See Figure 2-15.)

Permissions Admin

If you want to join an existing site, two permissions-related problems can occur. One possible problem is caused by missing permissions on the Windows NT Server computer, and the other problem is caused by missing permissions within the site you want to join. These problems will prevent a successful installation. In order to add a new Exchange Server computer to a site, you must have been granted the **Permissions Admin** role on the target site's Organization, Site, and Configuration container objects. Otherwise, Setup will not be able to read the necessary configuration information from the remote servers directory and will therefore fail. (See Figure 2-15.)

Service Account Password

When you join an existing site, Setup will read the required configuration information from the specified server when you have specified the correct Windows NT and Exchange Server permissions. Setup reads the security information from the remote server's Registry and prompts you for the password of the Site Services Account. However, this query for the service account password can pose difficulties. If the given password is incorrect, the installation will report a failure. It will then give you another chance to enter the correct password. If you still can't remember the correct password, you will not be able to complete the join.

There exists a solution to prevent the cancellation of the current setup program if you have forgotten just the Site Services Account password but can log on with an NT account with appropriate Exchange permissions. You need to use the Exchange Administrator program to administer an Exchange Server that already exists in the site you want to join. At the **Configuration** container object below the <Site> object, you can use the **Service Account Password** property page to change the password of the Site Services Account to a new, known value. However, care must be taken if you have installed Exchange Server in a clustered environment—in this case you need to manually change the passwords for the Exchange services on the second node via the Services applet of the Control Panel. To match the password at the Windows NT level, you must also change the account password within the User Manager for Domains. You will then switch back to Exchange Server Setup where you can enter the new service account password. The service account will be validated, and Setup can continue to install the new Exchange Server in the existing site.

Mapi32.dll

During an Exchange Server installation, all MAPI-related files will be replaced. If a MAPI-based client or custom application is running at the time of Exchange Server setup, an error message will appear notifying you that the Mapi32.dll file is in use. Before you go on with Setup, you should close all MAPI programs. When you switch back to Exchange Server Setup, you can click the **Retry** button to continue the installation.

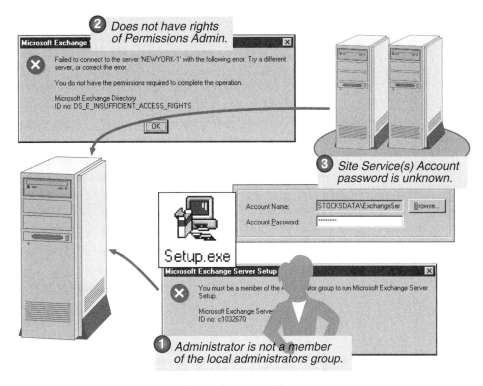

Figure 2-15. Permission-related installation problems.

Possible installation problems and their solutions are as follows:

- Improper Exchange Server permissions; you must have the Permissions Admin role on the target site's <Organization>, <Site>, and **Configuration** containers if you want to join an existing site

- Improper Windows NT permissions; you must be a member of the local Administrators group of the local and remote Windows NT Server computer

- Incorrect password for the Site Services Account; the installation will report a failure and will give you another chance to enter the correct password

- Mapi32.dll in use; close all MAPI programs and stop all MAPI-aware services and then click the **Retry** button after switching back to Setup

The NetBEUI Trap

The NetBEUI protocol is not a supported protocol for the server-to-server communication. Therefore, you should not install NetBEUI on a computer that is supposed to join an existing site if the selected server in the target site is running NetBEUI as well. The existence of NetBEUI can lead to installation problems because the directory replication cannot be performed over this protocol.

Let's say TCP/IP and NetBEUI are installed on the same Windows NT Server computer. In this situation, all it takes is a small TCP/IP configuration problem (for example, a wrong subnet mask on one machine) and the communication between the servers will switch over to the NetBEUI protocol. If the network communication is performed without routers in between, everything seems to work fine. Network access to shared directories works without any problems. In other words, the TCP/IP configuration problem is perfectly hidden so long as routers are not involved. Otherwise, the TCP/IP problem becomes obvious since NetBEUI is not routable.

Launching Setup

Exchange Server Setup will start normally, and you can join the existing site as usual. You will be asked for the name of the existing server in the site. If you have correct permissions, the configuration information can be read and Setup installs nearly everything on the new Exchange Server computer. However, at the end of the setup process, the new directory must be initialized. The first directory replication should happen.

The Problem

Directory replication relies on RPC communication, but RPC between Exchange Servers is not supported through NetBEUI. At this point, the TCP/IP problem mentioned above will lead to the error message as shown in Figure 2-16.

Missing Directory Database

Do not follow the suggestions of the error message shown. The message suggests restarting the DS, but the directory (Dir.edb) has not been initialized yet. If you try to start this service, the system will crash, usually with a GPF in User32.exe. Exchange Server cannot operate without a directory, however. You must not restart the computer because the Exchange Server services have been configured already and will start automatically during the next system start. The automatic startup of the DS can lead to a crash as well.

As long as the true reason for the noninitialized directory—the TCP/IP communication problem—has not been solved, simply restarting the Exchange Server Setup will not help.

Removing an Incomplete Installation

It is impossible to remove the crashed installation using the maintenance mode of the Setup program. A second setup does not launch the maintenance mode if the first setup has not been completed successfully. This makes it difficult to remove the incomplete installation. To remove the incomplete Exchange server installation, the following steps must be executed:

1. The Windows NT Registry entries for the Exchange Server services can be cleaned manually. The location of these Windows NT Registry settings is listed in the section "Exchange Server Service Dependencies" later in this lesson. Alternatively, the Exchange Server services should be configured for the **Manual** startup type. Follow Exercise 4, "Verifying the Installation," if you need assistance to find the relevant services.

2. The TCP/IP configuration should be examined and corrected. If possible, the NetBEUI protocol should be removed altogether. If necessary, the computer should be restarted to make the network configuration changes take effect.

3. The existing \Exchsrvr directory on your local hard disk needs to be deleted once the server has been rebooted. It is also advisable to test the TCP/IP communication using the TCP/IP Ping or—even better—the RPCPing utility. If Ping/RPCPing finds the desired remote server, Setup can be started and will complete successfully. For example, if server NEWYORK-2 joins the site NEWYORK, an administrator can use the command **Ping NEWYORK-1** in order to ensure that the remote server is available through TCP/IP. The RPCPing utility is explained in Chapter 15.

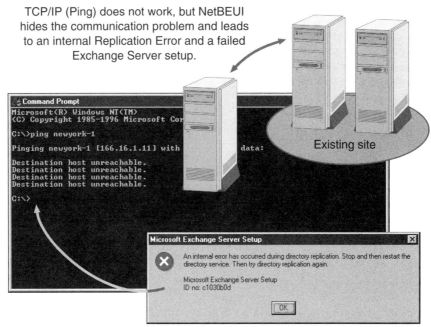

Figure 2-16. Directory replication crashes over NetBEUI.

It should be noted that NetBEUI on Exchange Server computers:

- Is not supported for server-to-server communication
- May hide network communication problems in other protocols
- Leads to configuration problems after Setup has failed
- Adds unnecessary protocol overhead to the local network configuration

Exchange Server Service Dependencies

Exchange Server Setup will initialize all server services, such as the MTA, IS, DS, and SA. It does so by writing entries for these services and other components to the Windows NT Registry. As shown in Figure 2-17, settings for Exchange Server services will be stored under:

```
HKEY_LOCAL_MACHINE
    \SYSTEM
        \CurrentControlSet
            \Services
```

This key will provide subkeys for all the Exchange services that have been installed. For example, the information about interservice dependencies of the MTA service can be found through the value MSExchangeMTA\ DependOnService.

Some other settings that have been written to the Windows NT Registry affect the behavior of the Exchange Administrator program and—if installed —of an Exchange client. These settings can be found in the SOFTWARE\ Microsoft\Exchange subkey under HKEY_LOCAL_MACHINE.

Whenever possible you should avoid directly changing any of the displayed values using the Registry Editor. This is necessary only in rare cases and requires in-depth knowledge about the meaning of the value in question and the effect of changing it. In most cases, it is better to use the Exchange Administrator program instead to control the server. This program provides a more secure way to adjust values and directory entries and should be used whenever possible.

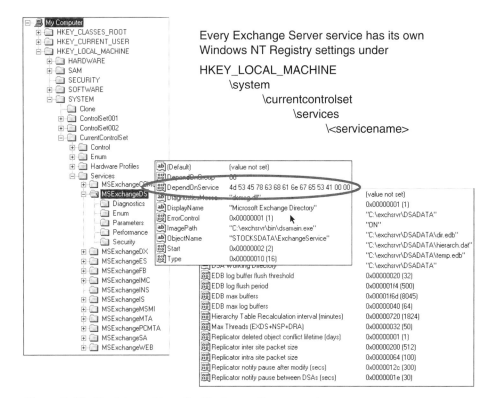

Every Exchange Server service has its own Windows NT Registry settings under

HKEY_LOCAL_MACHINE
    \system
        \currentcontrolset
            \services
                \<servicename>

Figure 2-17. Registry settings for Exchange Server services.

Dependencies of core and additional Exchange Server components are as follows:

Microsoft Exchange service and Registry key	Dependencies
Connector for Lotus cc:Mail	Exchange DS
(MSExchangeCCMC)	Exchange IS Event Log
DS (MSExchangeDS)	Exchange SA
Directory Synchronization (MSExchangeDX)	Exchange MTA
Event Service (MSExchangeES)	Exchange IS
IS (MSExchangeIS)	Exchange DS
IMS (MSExchangeIMC)	Exchange IS Exchange MTA TCP\IP Services

(continues)

(continued)

Microsoft Exchange service and Registry key	Dependencies
INS (MSExchangeINS)	Exchange IS TCP/IP Services
MS Mail Connector Interchange (MSExchangeMSMI)	Exchange DS Exchange MTA Event Log
Schedule+ Free/Busy Connector (MSExchangeFB)	Exchange DS Exchange IS Event Log
MTA (MSExchangeMTA)	Exchange DS
SA	Windows NT Event Log
(MSExchangeSA)	NtLmSsp (Windows NT/LAN Manager security support provider) RPCLOCATOR RPCSS (RPC service) Workstation Server
Key Management Server (MSExchangeKMS)	Exchange IS

Review

1. You're the administrator of a company and you plan to install Exchange Server 5.5 as your messaging system. Users want to send and receive e-mail messages via the Internet. In addition, you want to allow some users access from the Internet to messages stored in mailboxes and public folders. Which Exchange Server components would you need to install to satisfy the users' needs? Which software requirements must be met to run all the necessary components?

_____

_____

_____

_____

_____

2. Exchange Server 5.5 requires powerful hardware, but you decide to test this system on a smaller machine prior to the actual implementation. What is the minimum hardware equipment you should use for a test computer? What are the recommended hardware requirements?

_____

_____

_____

_____

3. What are the required Windows NT permissions for the Site Services Account?

_____

_____

_____

4. To save disk space, you have used the **Minimum** installation option during setup of the first server. Now you want to create mailboxes. Why can't you manage the Exchange Server? What type of installation could you use to install all required components? How can you add the components to the server that was installed with **Minimum** installation type?

_____

_____

_____

_____

5. You want to designate additional administrators in a site. The additional accounts will be responsible for mailbox creation and extended configuration tasks. What are the three security levels you need to configure for new administrators? What minimum permission is required to display the site's configuration information?

_____

_____

_____

_____

6. As an administrator, you need to install an Exchange Server in a new site. While Setup is completing successfully, you realize that you have misspelled the organization name. What do you need to do to correct the organization name?

_____

_____

_____

7. What important names are required to initialize the directory of a new Exchange Server installation during setup?

_____

_____

_____

_____

_____

8. What are the names of the hard disk directories that Setup creates during the server installation?

_____

_____

_____

_____

_____

9. The number of users wanting to send e-mail messages has increased, so you have decided to install an additional Exchange Server computer. You will add the new server to the existing site. What are the advantages of a single site organization?

_____

_____

_____

_____

10. You start the installation of a new Exchange Server. This server should join an existing site. During setup, you are informed that you don't have the required permissions to install the server, so the setup process terminates. What are the required Windows NT permissions you must have on the local computer? What permissions must your account possess at the Exchange level to join an existing site?

_____

_____

_____

_____

_____

11. You are planning to install a new Exchange Server that will be added to an existing site. The server maintains user home directories and will be responsible for messaging tasks in the future. The Windows NT home directories already exist. Users access their directories using NetBEUI, and the network operates without problems. Why do you need to change the server configuration anyway?

_____

_____

_____

_____

_____

12. You are using Exchange Server version 4.0 in a complex environment. Because of the extended Internet features implemented in version 5.5, you decide to upgrade the messaging network. What upgrade strategy should you use?

_____

_____

_____

_____

13. Another administrator has previously installed an Exchange Client on a
    server computer, which is an unsupported configuration. To clean up the
    unsupported configuration, you have decided to remove the client with
    all its components. You then find that the IMS no longer works properly
    because the MAPI32.dll is missing. How can you fix this problem?

    _____

    _____

    _____

    _____

    _____

14. You plan to install 10 Exchange Server computers. All of them should be
    added to an existing site. The server installation should be performed
    unattended in order to run setup simultaneously on more than one
    computer. Where do you specify setup information? Why shouldn't you
    add all 10 new servers at the same time to the existing site?

    _____

    _____

    _____

    _____

    _____

15. Why should you start the Performance Optimizer at the end of a new
    Exchange Server installation?

    _____

    _____

    _____

    _____

16. You have doubled the amount of RAM on a server computer. You have also added a disk array for better input/output performance. How can you configure the Exchange Server to access the new hardware resources efficiently?

_____

_____

_____

_____

17. Some Exchange Server directories such as Add-ins or Tracking.log will be shared for network access during the installation. You don't want regular users to access the existing network shares. How can you secure the Exchange Server installation?

_____

_____

_____

_____

18. The messaging network of your company consists of one single site. Five server computers exist within this site. You want to administer all these computers from a Windows NT Workstation in your office. What needs to be installed on the Windows NT Workstation? How do you install the additional components?

_____

_____

_____

19. During the join of an existing site, setup prompts for the password of the Site Services Account, but none of the available administrators can remember the valid password. What has to be done to successfully add the new server to the site?

_____

_____

_____

_____

_____

20. Which network protocols are supported for server-to-server communication? Which protocol should not be used if a server is joining an existing site?

_____

_____

_____

21. The Windows NT Server can't start the Workstation service because another computer with the same name has been detected in the network. How does this problem affect the Exchange Server?

_____

_____

_____

22. Which Exchange Server 5.5 components can be installed in a clustered environment?

_____

_____

_____

23. During the installation of an additional computer in an existing site you receive the following error message: "Failed to connect to server <Server Name> with the following error. Try a different server or correct the error. You do not have the permissions required to complete the operation." What is most likely the cause of that error?

_____

_____

_____

CHAPTER 3

Microsoft Exchange Server Architecture

This chapter examines the architecture of the Microsoft Exchange Server, its core components, and its optional components. Each component has its own specific functions to fulfill, but all components must interact to function as a physical unit.

Overview

Exchange Server 5.5 is a complex component-based system that can be extended to meet your needs exactly, but the basic functionality of a messaging and workgroup platform will exist no matter how you configure it. By default, users can send e-mail messages and share information through public folders. If additional features, such as extensive connectivity to the Internet, are required, you can add the necessary components to the running server at any time. You should therefore be familiar with the available server components, their features, and their interaction with each other to maintain the Exchange organization in accordance with the needs of your users.

Lesson 1 of this chapter provides a listing and concise description of the essential and additional Exchange Server elements. You'll read about their purpose and functionality.

Lesson 2 describes the communication paths among the various core components that are required to accomplish the essential tasks of a messaging system. A description of the message flow through a single server, within a single site, and across the entire organization will illustrate the theoretical explanations.

In the following lessons, you will be introduced to:

- The various core and optional components of Exchange Server 5.5
- The communication paths of the Administrator program and MAPI-based clients
- The communication partners of each core component
- The communication partners of optional Exchange Server components
- The flow of messages on a single server
- The flow of messages between servers

Lesson 1: Microsoft Exchange Server Components

The administrator of an organization should be able to identify and describe the different modules that make up an Exchange Server computer. A general understanding of the core components (DS, IS, MTA, and SA) and their interaction is absolutely necessary, since they provide the basic messaging capabilities. Optional components should also be understood, as they provide alternative connectivity and add valuable functionality to the standard server. Without an awareness of the various components, you will not be able to properly address configuration or troubleshooting issues.

This lesson provides a brief yet complete overview of the elements of the Enterprise Edition of the Exchange Server 5.5 platform.

At the end of this lesson, you will be able to:

- Describe the parts of the IS
- Describe the tasks of the DS
- Identify the responsibilities of the MTA
- Name the tasks of the SA and use it to shut down the entire Exchange Server
- List the various optional components and describe their features

Estimated time to complete this lesson: 30 minutes

Exchange Server Core Components

Core components are required for the proper operation of every Exchange Server computer. They are generally implemented as Windows NT services. Exchange Server 5.5 cannot perform the tasks of a functioning messaging platform if you stop one of these services, which are responsible for message routing and delivery, maintenance of e-mail information, and implementation of the directory services. They will be installed and started automatically regardless of the selected Setup type (**Minimum**, **Typical**, or **Complete/Custom**).

Directory Service

The importance of the DS is quickly demonstrated. Just open the **Services** applet of the Control Panel, select the **Microsoft Exchange Directory Service**, and then click **Stop**. You will notice that the other Exchange Server services—with the exception of the SA—are dependent on a working DS and must be stopped as well.

Responsibilities of the Directory Service

The DS maintains the configuration information of the server, the existing sites, and the structure of the organization. This information must be synchronized between all servers. To accomplish this task, the DSs running on all servers must communicate with each other through a process known as *directory replication*. The directory replication within a site is explained in detail in Chapter 4, "Communication in an Exchange Server Environment."

All other components must contact the DS to obtain the current configuration data. The IS, for instance, must obtain security information from the Directory as users log on to mailboxes or access public folders. In addition to maintaining the security information, the mailbox configuration, and the public folder design, the DS maintains information about the directory replication, existing message routing paths, and the server-based address books in its directory database. Note that this list is not exhaustive, however.

Responsibilities of the DS include:

- Retaining addresses, distribution lists, and configuration information about mailboxes, public folders, sites, and services

- Maintaining directory information and automatically replicating this information to all servers in a site

Directory Database

The directory database named Dir.edb resides in the \Exchsrvr\Dsadata directory and stores all the relevant configuration information of the organization. Its design is based on the X.500 standard, although it contains some non-X.500 characteristics as well. The only component that has direct access to this database is the DS itself. All remaining server components must contact the DS using local RPCs to obtain configuration, security, or structure information.

Note The DS is the only service that has direct access to the directory database (Dir.edb). All other elements must contact this service to obtain directory information.

Accessing the Directory

Most server components access the Directory using local RPCs, but they are not the only components that use RPCs to do so. "Ordinary" users also contact the DS to access the server-based address books using the Exchange Client, Outlook, or an appropriate Internet browser. RPCs perform the client-server communication. In addition, access to the Directory through the Lightweight Directory Access Protocol (LDAP) is possible with Exchange Server 5.5. The LDAP implementation is covered in Chapter 11, "Internet Protocols."

Message Transfer Agent

The MTA is a real X.400 system that conforms to the 1984 and 1988 CCITT (ITU) X.400 standards. As its name implies, this service is primarily responsible for the message transfer to other servers in the same site, to other sites, and to foreign messaging systems. The message transfer within the same site is accomplished using RPCs. If a message must be transmitted to another site or to a foreign messaging system, messaging connectors are used in conjunction with the MTA.

MTA Tasks

In addition to transmitting messages, the MTA is responsible for message routing decisions and, if necessary, the message conversion between the Exchange Server format and the native X.400 format. Furthermore, the MTA is responsible for expanding server-based distribution lists. Distribution lists contain the actual recipient addresses, so they must be expanded to determine the best possible routing path to every recipient. Distribution lists and other recipient objects are covered in Chapter 5, "Creating and Managing Recipients."

Responsibilities of the MTA include:

- Expanding distribution lists for mapping and routing messages

- Mapping and routing messages and converting documents as needed from native Exchange format Microsoft Database Exchange Format (MDBEF) to native X.400 and vice versa

- Submitting messages to the message queues of the IMS, the MS Mail Connector, the Connector for Lotus cc:Mail, the Connector for Lotus Notes, the PROFS Connector, the SNADS Connector, and other Exchange Development Kit (EDK) Connectors developed by Independent Software Vendors (ISVs)

- Submitting, delivering, and routing messages to other Exchange MTAs and foreign X.400 MTAs

Verifying the MTA Responsibilities

You can determine the value of the MTA by stopping its service through the **Services** applet of the Control Panel. Once this service has been stopped, you need to start the Exchange Client or Outlook to test the server behavior. The value of the MTA can be illustrated by sending three test messages in this situation. Address the first message to a recipient on your home server, the second message to a recipient on another server within your site, and the third message to a distribution list. You'll see that only the message destined for a recipient on your home server will leave the Outbox of your client. The other two messages must remain there until you restart the MTA. Only the MTA can deliver the second message to the recipient's home server and expand the distribution list of the third message. (See Figure 3-1 on page 151.) The detailed message flow within a site is covered under "Core Component Communication," later in this chapter.

Information Store

The IS and its databases are considered to be the most important server components, as seen from the perspective of a user, because they are the structured repository of all server-based user data, such as e-mail messages and public folder items. From the standpoint of an administrator, however, the IS is only one of four server components that must be maintained permanently. Users access the IS using the Exchange Client, Outlook, an appropriate Internet browser, a POP3 client, or an IMAP4-compliant application. It is also possible to access public folders through NNTP.

Two Repositories

The IS divides user data into two categories: private and public. Private messages are maintained in private mailboxes, while public data can be shared among users through public folders. You can split the IS into the Private IS and the Public IS. Both maintain their own database file, and these databases together form the complete server store. The private message store database is named Priv.edb; the public message store is named Pub.edb. Both database files reside in the \Exchsrvr\Mdbdata directory.

Note Only the IS service has direct access to the database files Priv.edb and Pub.edb. All other components, such as the MTA, messaging connectors, newsfeeds, or messaging clients of users, must contact the IS to place their information on the server.

The two types of IS are:

- Public information store, which maintains information stored in public folders

- Private information store, which maintains all messages sent to an individual or a selected group of addresses in private folders

Dedicated Server Configurations

A private server is one that maintains a private message store. A public server is one that contains a public message store. In a default configuration, an Exchange Server will be both a private and a public server. It's possible to delete one of the message stores from the server to create a dedicated private server or a dedicated public server. It is also possible to configure a server that has neither a private nor a public message store. These servers usually assume the role of messaging and replication bridgehead servers. Such configurations have advantages and disadvantages as outlined in Chapter 12, "Creating and Managing Public Folders," and in Chapter 13, "Public Folder Replication."

System Attendant

The SA is also implemented as a Windows NT service. This component performs regular maintenance tasks, such as recalculating the routing table and starting the defragmentation routines of the Directory and the IS.

Note The SA must be running before any other Exchange Server service can start.

The responsibilities of the SA include:

- Building the routing tables in a site
- Generating e-mail addresses for new recipients as they are created in the directory
- Maintaining the message tracking log
- Launching maintenance routines to defragment Exchange Server databases
- Supporting additional components, such as the Key Management Server
- Supporting Link Monitors for permanent testing of the availability of message paths
- Supporting Server Monitors for permanent testing of the status of remote Exchange Servers

Shutting Down the Entire Server

The SA can assist you in the task of shutting down an entire server, which might be necessary if you want to perform an offline backup or accomplish other maintenance tasks. To shut down all core services and optional components, you need only to launch the **Services** applet of the Control Panel, select the **Microsoft Exchange System Attendant**, and then click **Stop**.

Starting the Entire Server

You can't start the server services the same way you stopped them. You need either to reboot the Windows NT Server computer or to start every component manually through the **Services** applet of the Control Panel, as explained in Chapter 2, "Installing the Microsoft Exchange Server."

Fortunately, an easier way to restart all the services is to write a small batch file. For example, you can use the following batch file to restart all core services of an Exchange Server using a single command (EMSSTART.BAT).

```
REM ******************************************
REM This Batch starts only the core services
REM of the Microsoft Exchange Server
REM EMSSTART.BAT
REM ******************************************
net start MSExchangeSA
net start MSExchangeDS
net start MSExchangeIS
net start MSExchangeMTA
REM *********** server activated ***********
```

If you want to start optional components, such as the Event Service, you need to enhance this batch file accordingly.

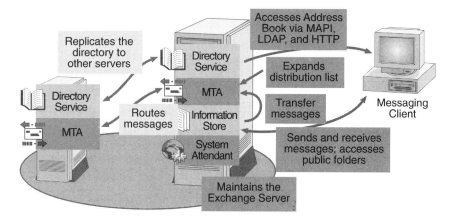

Figure 3-1. Responsibilities of the core components.

The core components and their responsibilities are listed below:

- DS; stores all relevant information about the structure of the organization and the properties of its objects; replicates the information automatically to all other server(s) in the same site

- MTA; routes messages and expands distribution list; sends messages directly to other servers in the same site and to other sites and foreign systems through messaging connectors; communicates with the IS to get messages written into folder-based message queues and to receive them from there

- IS; structured repository of all server-based user information. Personal e-mail messages are kept in the private message store, while public folder data is kept in the public message store

- SA; assists the administrator in carrying out tasks such as keeping the routing table updated and performing database maintenance; can be used to shut down the entire Exchange Server

Optional Exchange Server Components

Optional components can enhance the connectivity and functionality of the basic Exchange Server. They can be used to connect sites, to connect an organization to foreign mail systems, or to implement extra features such as Advanced Security. These components don't usually need to be running on every Exchange Server computer within an organization. The Key Management Server, in fact, must not be running on more than one server in your organization. Optional components are shown in Figure 3-2 on page 158.

Internet Mail Service

The IMS connects the Exchange organization to messaging systems that use SMTP to exchange data. As a new feature in Exchange Server 5.x, the IMS also supports Enhanced SMTP (ESMTP). ESMTP allows users to request delivery status notification about their sent messages. Although ESMTP is relatively new, it is becoming the preferred message transfer protocol for Internet systems. For instance, ESMTP allows the IMS to retrieve information about message sizes before the actual message delivery starts, which is useful if you have restricted the maximum acceptable size of messages coming from the Internet. The IMS of Exchange Server 5.5 can request queued messages from remote ESMTP hosts. Conversely, remote ESMTP hosts can request queued messages from the IMS on a per-domain basis.

Intersite Connections

The IMS has been implemented directly into the Exchange Server architecture to improve its performance, and it can be used to connect sites into one homogenous organization. Connected sites can replicate their directories with each other so that all configuration and address information is known across the whole organization. The distribution of directory replication information between sites is based upon system messages. The IMS can transport these replication messages. Once the directory replication has been completed, public folder replication can also be configured over the IMS.

POP3 and IMAP4 Client Support

POP3 and IMAP4 themselves are read-only protocols, so their clients will use SMTP to send messages. Consequently, POP3 and IMAP4 clients require an active SMTP counterpart in the organization that can be reached through TCP/IP. The IMS can act as such a SMTP component, which accepts the incoming messages to route them further across the Internet or the organization. The configuration of the IMS is covered in Chapter 11.

Internet News Service

Exchange Server 5.x versions contain the INS, which allows for the replication of information in public folders with USENET newsgroups. Usenet news hubs support NNTP and can therefore replicate their newsgroups with an Exchange Server through newsfeeds. Depending on the INS configuration, pull feeds or push feeds transfer discussion articles between newsgroups and public folders. In this way, it's also possible to use the INS to replicate the contents of public folders with Exchange Server computers in other organizations.

Outlook Web Access Components

Outlook Web Access components allow you to publish Exchange information over the World Wide Web to users running an appropriate Internet browser. The browser client uses HTTP to access the Exchange Server via IIS 3.0 or 4.0 using a Uniform Resource Locator (URL). You must configure the IIS plus Active Server Pages before you can install the Outlook Web Access components through the Exchange Server Setup.

HTML-MAPI Translation

The active components of Outlook Web Access that have been installed on the IIS receive the incoming browser request. They then translate HTTP on the browser side into MAPI-based RPCs on the server side, making access to server-based resources possible.

Server-Based Resources

Using an Internet browser that supports Java script and frames, you can access private messages from your mailbox, collaborative data from public folders, and recipient information from the Global Address List. In fact, messaging becomes independent of the application (Internet browser) being used. You can access the server-based resources just as you can access any other Web document in HTML format. This doesn't mean that the actual message objects have been converted into HTML documents, however. A translation between MAPI and HTML is performed dynamically by Outlook Web Access running on the IIS instead. Outlook Web Access will be discussed in detail in Chapter 11.

MS Mail Connector

The MS Mail Connector provides connectivity to MS Mail postoffices as well as to StarNine/MS Mail (AppleTalk) servers. The MS Mail Connector itself basically consists of the MS Mail Connector Interchange component, one or more MS Mail MTA services, and a MS Mail Connector Postoffice. The Connector Postoffice provides the native MS Mail interface for the MS Mail messaging network. To transfer messages back and forth into MS Mail systems, the MS Mail Connector must communicate with the MTA on the Exchange Server side. On the other hand, the MS Mail Connector can connect to one or more MS Mail postoffices on the MS Mail side. Its architecture and configuration will be explained in detail in Chapter 18, "Connecting to Microsoft Mail and Schedule+ 1.0."

Directory Synchronization with MS Mail

The DXA is the active component that exchanges address information between Exchange Server and MS Mail by using the MS Mail DirSync protocol. During a DirSync cycle, address list changes will be sent from the MS Mail postoffices and the Exchange Servers to a DirSync Server. This server collects and processes all the changes it receives during the cycle and returns the updated master address list to the requesting postoffices and Exchange servers. Once an entire DirSync cycle has been completed, all postoffices and Exchange Servers are synchronized with each other, and each will contain a complete Global Address List.

DirSync Requestor

The DXA can act as a DirSync Requestor. In this configuration, the Exchange Server computer sends its address updates to the DirSync Server and also receives the updated master list from there. Once the current master address list has been received the DXA imports the MS Mail addresses as custom recipients into the Exchange Server directory. Within a site, more than one DirSync Requestor is supported to distribute the Exchange addresses to multiple MS Mail networks, and vice versa.

DirSync Server

The DXA can also be configured as a DirSync Server. In this configuration, it receives and processes the address updates from MS Mail postoffices. It then sends the address updates (the master list) back to the DirSync Requestors. The MS Mail addresses are maintained as custom recipients on the Exchange Server computer as usual. It is not, however, possible to configure more than one DXA Server in a site, although you can have as many DXA Servers as you have sites in your organization. More information regarding the configuration of the DXA is provided in Chapter 18.

Schedule+ Free/Busy Connector

When you connect your organization to an MS Mail network using the MS Mail Connector, you might also want to exchange Schedule+ Free/Busy information between both systems. To do this, configure the Schedule+ Free/Busy Connector, which exchanges calendar free and busy information between Schedule+ users working on Exchange Servers and Schedule+ users working on MS Mail postoffices. The Schedule+ Free/Busy Connector configuration is covered in Chapter 18.

Connector for Lotus cc:Mail

If you plan to integrate Exchange Server 5.5 in a Lotus cc:Mail messaging network, use the Connector for Lotus cc:Mail. This connector allows you to send messages between both systems, but the Connector for Lotus cc:Mail can connect to only one cc:Mail post office directly. Messages destined for other Lotus cc:Mail post offices must be routed within the Lotus cc:Mail messaging network.

Directory Synchronization

The Connector for Lotus cc:Mail supports Directory Synchronization between Exchange Server and the Lotus cc:Mail post office so that you can import and export e-mail addresses directly. The connector performs the Directory Synchronization based on the Lotus Import/Export programs. In fact, the process of exchanging addresses is less complex than the MS Mail Directory Synchronization. The configuration and usage of the Connector for Lotus cc:Mail is explained in Chapter 19, "Connector for Lotus cc:Mail."

Connector for Lotus Notes

The Connector for Lotus Notes is part of the Exchange Server 5.5 Enterprise Edition. It provides connectivity to a Lotus Notes network by means of message transfer and directory synchronization. This connector relies on Lotus Notes client software and this software must be installed on the server that will run the connector service. The installation, configuration, and usage of the Connector for Lotus Notes are covered in Chapter 20, "Connector for Lotus Notes."

Key Management Server

The KM Server offers Advanced Security features, such as encryption and digital signatures, for e-mail messages. The KM Server maintains its own database within the \Kmsdata directory of the Exchange Server installation for storage of the users' X.509 certificates and encryption keys.

Signing and Sealing Messages

Once the KM Server has been installed in your organization you can allow your users to sign and seal messages. A signed message lets you verify whether someone has tampered with this message on its way to the destination mailbox. A sealed message, on the other hand, is completely encrypted and prevents unauthorized persons from reading the information. A user who has been enabled with Advanced Security features can send secured messages to other users who have also been enabled. In other words, it's impossible to send signed or sealed messages to users who are not enabled with Advanced Security.

Additional Gateways and Connectors

Connectors and gateways can convert, transfer, and deliver messages from Exchange Server to foreign systems, and vice versa. For example, one gateway may enable users to send messages as faxes or to exchange messages with a third-party messaging system such as PROFS. The Enterprise Edition of Exchange Server 5.5 provides specific connectivity to PROFS and SNADS "out of the box," but additional gateways must be purchased and installed on your server if you want to extend the communication paths of your organization even further (such as fax, voice mail, and the like).

Event Service

The Event Service of Exchange Server 5.5 allows you to develop server-based scripting agents, which can process message items and other data in public folders on an event-driven basis (valid events in this respect are new message creation, message deletion, and so forth). Simple workflow and script-based automation becomes possible. The Event Service and scripting agents are covered in Chapter 16, "The Microsoft Exchange Server Forms Environment."

Optional components and their functions are as follows:

- Connector for Lotus cc:Mail; to support message transfer and Directory Synchronization between Exchange Server sites and Lotus cc:Mail systems
- Connector for Lotus Notes; to support message transfer and Directory Synchronization between Exchange Server and Lotus Notes
- Directory Synchronization with MS Mail; to support the synchronization of address information between Exchange Server and MS Mail 3.x systems
- EDK Gateways and Connectors from third-party vendors
- Event Service; to provide a programmatic way to enhance collaboration, workflow, and automation features through scripting agents
- IMS; to provide interoperability between Exchange Server and SMTP-based mail systems

- INS; to allow you to replicate USENET newsgroups with public folders

- KM Server; to offer Advanced Security features such as encryption and digital signature

- MS Mail Connector; to provide interoperability between Exchange Server and MS Mail 3.x systems

- Outlook Web Access components; to provide Web-based access to e-mail, the Global Address List, and public folders

- Schedule+ Free/Busy Connector; to allow the sharing of free/busy data between Schedule+ users working on Exchange and MS Mail networks

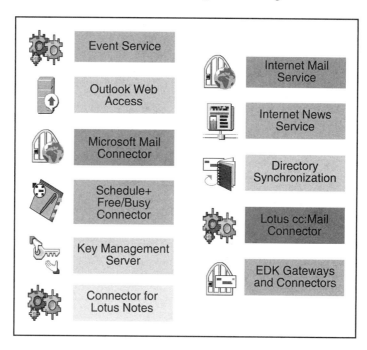

Figure 3-2. Optional components for Exchange Server.

Lesson 2: Exchange Component Communication

Each Exchange Server component owns and manages specific information. The DS, for instance, maintains the directory database, the IS is responsible for the private and public message store, and the MTA relies on its messages queues. Components such as the DXA and the KM Server provide additional data repositories. Following the object-oriented programming model, only that particular component has direct access to a repository that is responsible for its maintenance. All remaining server elements must communicate with this repository service through RPCs to obtain the desired information. For example, the MTA cannot access the directory database (Dir.edb) directly, so it must contact the DS to obtain address information. Well-defined communication paths have been implemented, and knowledge of these paths can help you understand the functionality of the Exchange Server system.

This lesson introduces the various communication paths between the core components themselves as well as the paths between the core components and the Exchange Client and Administrator program. The communication between optional components and the core components is also discussed. At the end of this lesson, you can read about the flow of messages through a single server and through multiple servers.

At the end of this lesson, you will be able to:

- Describe the communication between Exchange Client and Server components
- Describe the communication between the Exchange Administrator program and Server components
- Describe the communication between the various core components
- Describe the communication between core and optional components
- List the transmission phases of the message flow in a single-server environment
- List the transmission phases of the message flow in a multiple-server environment

Estimated time to complete this lesson: 45 minutes

Core Component Communication

Each of the core components has its specific purpose, and only the interaction of all the core services makes for a complete Exchange Server. However, not every component needs to communicate with every other component. This is simply not necessary for a well-organized messaging system like Exchange. (See Figure 3-3.)

Communication Mechanisms

As one server component shares information with another server component, communication is accomplished through Local Procedure Calls (LPCs). LPCs are the local version of RPCs, and are used between the IS, DS, MTA, and SA in a single-server environment. Regular RPCs, on the other hand, are used when the components of one server need to communicate with their counterparts on another server in the same site, such as with DS-to-DS and MTA-to-MTA communication.

Exchange Administrator Program

You can start the Administrator program whenever you want to change or inspect the configuration of Exchange Server components. You can also use the Administrator program to create new mailboxes, custom recipients, or distribution lists. In other words, this program provides the capability to manage most aspects of the server configuration, so the Administrator program must communicate with all core server components. If you're running this application directly on the server computer, the communication takes place through LRPCs; otherwise, the communication takes place through RPCs.

Exchange Clients

Neither Exchange Client nor Outlook needs to establish a communication link to all available server components: only communication to the IS and the DS is required. Clients must communicate with the IS to access mailboxes and public folder data. RPC communication with the DS is necessary to log on to Exchange Server as well as to browse the Global Address List and other server-based address book views. Bear in mind that the installation of an Exchange Client or of Outlook directly onto an Exchange Server computer is not recommended by Microsoft because client files might replace important server fixes (for example, Mapi32.dll).

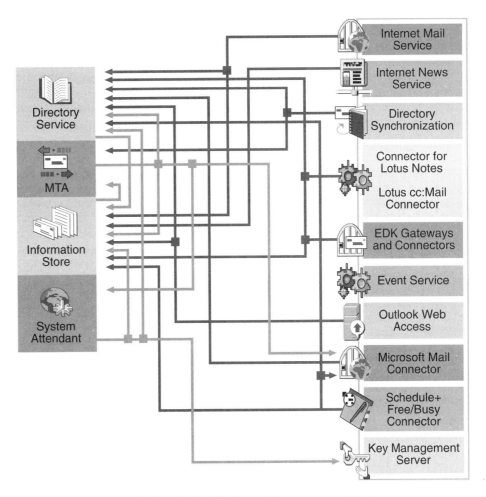

Figure 3-3. An example of confusing Exchange Server communication.

The following list describes the basic level of Exchange Server functionality:

- Administrator program controls the configuration of all core and additional server components

- Client program provides access to the private information store to send and receive messages, and to the public information store for public folder access; the DS is contacted for address information retrieval

- DS, MTA, IS, and SA are the four components required to run on the server to provide basic messaging services; they communicate with each other through LRPCs when they're running on the same server or through RPCs when they're running on different servers but are within the same site

Clients and Administrator Program Component Communication

Communication will always take place through RPCs so long as you are using the Exchange Client, Outlook, or the Exchange Administrator program on the client side. The client sends requests to the server and the server returns the result of the processed requests back to the client.

Administrator Program Communication

The Administrator program allows you to administer every Exchange Server computer that is accessible through RPCs. The Administrator program must be able to communicate with all core components. In other words, if a service is not running, the associated component cannot be administered. You would instead be notified that the communication with the desired component has failed.

MTA

If you try to view messages awaiting delivery in MTA message queues before the MTA service has been started, the RPC communication to the MTA will fail and you won't be able to view the content of the queues. Start the MTA service and switch back to the Exchange Administrator program to display the message queue information. The purpose of message queues is explained in detail in Chapter 15, "Maintaining Servers."

Directory Service

The Exchange Administrator program must communicate with the DS in order to manage address book entries and other objects, such as monitors and messaging connectors. When you change the configuration of any objects within the directory, these modifications are replicated automatically to all existing directories in your site. The Directory is responsible for replicating the changes, which allows you to specify settings that have a sitewide validity just by configuring these site default settings in a single server.

Information Store

The IS is the Administrator program's communication partner when you change public folder settings. Using the Administrator program, you can specify which public folders your server will maintain. You can also configure the Exchange Server to become a dedicated public or private server in your site. The configuration of the IS is covered in more detail in Chapter 12 and in Chapter 13.

System Attendant

The SA is contacted in the event that a Link Monitor or Server Monitor needs initializing. A Link Monitor allows you to check the status of messaging paths to other sites and foreign systems. A Server Monitor checks the status of selected Windows NT services on the local and selected remote servers. If a critical situation occurs, the Server Monitor can perform predefined actions, such as restarting a service or rebooting the server. To activate a configured monitor, use the **Start Monitor** command under the Administrator program's **Tools** menu, which initiates the RPC communication with the SA. Server and Link Monitors are covered in Chapter 15.

Key Management Server

The Exchange Administrator program can also access optional components. Communication with the KM Server is necessary, for instance, if you want to enable users with Advanced Security features. Note that the KM service must be accessible through RPCs if you want to create security tokens or designate additional security administrators. The administration of KM Server is covered in detail in Chapter 14, "Implementing Advanced Security."

Client Communication

The Exchange Client and Outlook gain access to the resources of an Exchange Server computer through RPCs. The IS and the DS are the two core components that are engaged to accomplish the necessary tasks of a messaging client. (See Figure 3-4.) Exchange Clients will be explored in detail in Chapter 6, "Exchange Client Architecture and Installation," and Chapter 7, "Configuring the Exchange Client."

Directory Service

Clients can initiate communication with the DS to display the Global Address List and other server-based address lists and address book views, modify server-based distribution lists, or resolve e-mail addresses. In general, whenever a user selects an existing Exchange Server recipient from the Global Address List or another server-based address book (for example, to address a message or to specify access permissions for a mailbox), RPC communication with the DS will take place. RPC communication with the DS will also take place when a user logs on to an Exchange server.

Information Store

MAPI-based clients must initiate communication with the IS service to send e-mail messages, to manipulate folder data, and to change private and public folder properties. Therefore, you will work primarily with the IS, and most of the time the client starts the communication.

If you have not configured a local Personal Folder Store file (.PST file), all message items will be stored on the Exchange Server computer in the private message store, which sends messages to and receives messages from other users. New folders created in your mailbox will be stored in the Private Information Store as well. If you send a message, the message item is placed in your Outbox folder on the server and marked for delivery.

The IS itself initiates the communication for only one purpose: to notify the client that new mail has arrived. This mechanism allows the clients to dispense with the polling algorithm of shared-file system clients.

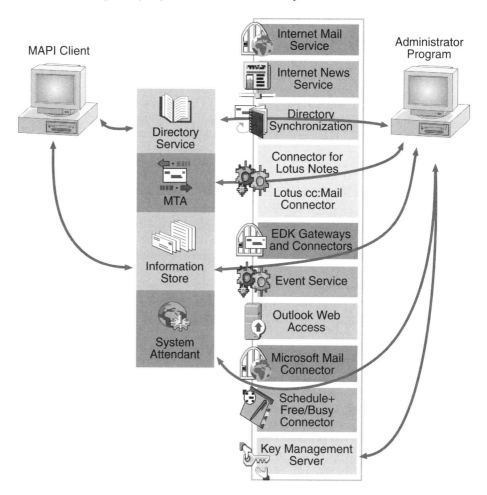

Figure 3-4. Communication between the administrator/client and Exchange Server.

The Exchange Administrator program communicates with the following Exchange Server components:

- DS; to display, create, modify, and delete recipient objects, and to iterate through the Directory Information Tree (DIT), as well as to view mailbox properties, distribution lists members, and other directory objects

- IS; to configure mailboxes and folders, move user mailboxes to other servers, view statistics, control public folder replication, and obtain information about user connections

- KM Server; to create security tokens for use by clients when setting up advanced security, revoke advanced security for users, and designate additional KM administrators

- MTA; to manipulate messages in queues and control the MTA behavior

- SA; to configure Server and Link Monitors, and generate and maintain the routing table

System Attendant

The SA is the service that all other Exchange Server services rely on, and this service helps the administrator to perform necessary maintenance tasks. This component communicates primarily with the DS and the IS, but it also communicates with the KM Server—if this component has been installed. (See Figure 3-5.)

Directory Service

The SA must communicate with the DS to build routing tables and to check the consistency of the directory replication information. In addition, the SA works with the DS to generate proxy e-mail addresses for newly created recipient objects.

Information Store

The SA also contacts the IS whenever you activate a Link Monitor. The SA communicates with the IS to place the monitor messages in its hidden Outbox. The IS notifies the SA about test messages and replies coming in from other SAs.

Key Management Server

The SA performs important tasks in the background if the KM Server has been installed in your organization. The SA receives the requests of users in the form of e-mail messages from the IS to enable the Advanced Security that the administrator has configured for them. First the SA has to "unwrap" the e-mail messages to retrieve the requests. Next it communicates with the Exchange KM Server service to take over the users' security keys and X.509 certificates. The KM Server is covered in Chapter 14.

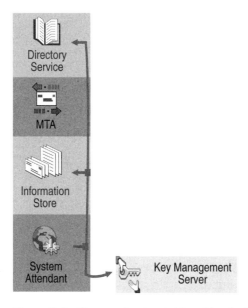

Figure 3-5. Communication initiated by the System Attendant.

The SA communicates with the following components:

- DS; to build and rebuild the routing table, to generate proxy e-mail addresses for new recipients and other directory objects, and to check directory replication information
- IS; to send and receive Link Monitor notifications
- KM Server; to store and manage security signature and encryption information during the configuration of Advanced Security for a user

Directory Service

The DS is contacted by most of the other Exchange Server components, but it initiates the communication to only a few of them. (See Figure 3-6.)

Information Store

The DS starts the communication with the IS whenever directory replication between sites must be performed, because the directory replication information must be carried out by means of e-mail-messages, which are handled by the IS and the MTA. The DS generates, receives, and processes these messages. The intersite directory replication is covered in detail in Chapter 9, "Introduction to Intersite Connectors."

Remote Directory Services

Within a single site, the directory replication is performed without the participation of the IS or the MTA. Instead, the local DS contacts the remote DS directly through RPCs. Once the directory replication has been accomplished successfully, each server in a site maintains a complete copy of every other server's directory. .

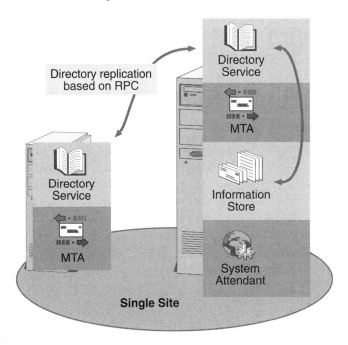

Figure 3-6. Communication initiated by the DS.

The DS communicates with the following components:

- Local IS; to establish the e-mail–based directory replication between sites
- Remote DS within the same site; to establish the RPC-based directory replication in a site

Message Transfer Agent

The MTA transfers only those messages that are destined for a remote system. This remote system can be any server in the same site, a remote site, a remote organization, or a foreign X.400 component. If other messaging connectors have been installed, the MTA uses their services by means of message queues to route the messages successfully. The configuration of the MTA is explained in Chapter 8, "Managing Server Configuration" and routing methods used by the MTA are covered in Chapter 9.

Directory Service, Remote MTAs, and the Information Store

The MTA must have access to appropriate routing information; otherwise, it cannot transfer a message to its destination. The MTA therefore initiates the communication with the local DS to determine the location of recipient's mailbox. If the home server attribute of a recipient points to a remote server within the same site, the MTA can establish a direct communication with the remote MTA through RPCs to transmit the message. If, on the other hand, the MTA receives an inbound message in which the home server attribute points to the local server, it communicates with the local IS to deliver the message to the recipient's mailbox. (See Figure 3-7.)

Messaging Connectors

If a message is sent to a remote site or to a foreign X.400 system, the MTA uses a messaging connector to transfer the message. The MTA can establish a direct connection using the Site Connector, X.400 Connector, Dynamic RAS Connector. The Site Connector and the Dynamic RAS Connector can connect only different sites together, but the X.400 Connector is also capable of connecting an Exchange Server organization to a foreign X.400 system based on the 1984 or 1988 conformance year. All EDK-based messaging connectors will not be accessed by the MTA, because they communicate directly with the IS.

MS Mail Connector

The MTA can also initiate the communication with the MS Mail Connector if messages are transferred between MS Mail and your organization. The MS Mail Connector Interchange service, a component of the MS Mail Connector, interacts with the MTA in this case.

System Attendant

The MTA contacts the SA to keep tracking log files up to date if the message tracking feature has been enabled. In this situation, you can verify the detailed path that a message has taken on its way through the organization, which is a convenient way to identify bottlenecks or the sources of delivery problems.

You can use the message tracking center of the Exchange Administrator program to search the tracking log files for information concerning selected messages. Message tracking will be explained in detail in Chapter 15.

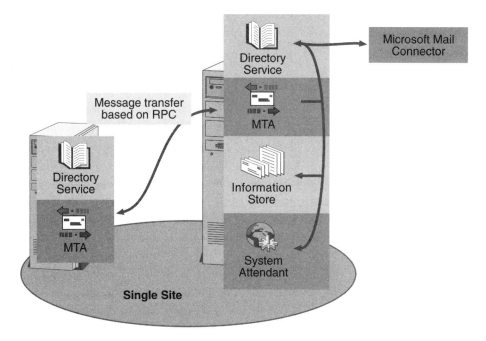

Figure 3-7.   Communication initiated by the MTA.

The MTA communicates with the following components:

- DS; to resolve e-mail addresses in order to accomplish routing decisions
- IS; to deliver and retrieve messages
- MS Mail Connector; to exchange mail with MS Mail and StarNine/MS Mail (AppleTalk) users
- Other Exchange MTAs in the same site; to transfer messages through RPCs
- Site, X.400, and Dynamic RAS Connectors; to send messages to other sites and foreign X.400 systems
- SA; to request the creation of and provide the information for log file entries

Information Store

The IS works primarily with the messaging clients. Other components, such as the SA, the MTA, and the DS, are contacted as messages are delivered within an organization. (See Figure 3-8.)

Messaging Clients

Usually it is the client that initiates the communication, with one exception—the IS initiates the communication itself to notify the Exchange Client or Outlook when new mail has arrived.

Directory and the MTA

The IS is also involved if users exchange messages with one another. Let's say you send one particular message to three recipients. Two recipients reside on your home server and one recipient exists on a remote server somewhere in your site. The client places the message in its Outbox and marks it for delivery. In other words, the client must contact the IS to indicate that a message is awaiting delivery. The IS, in turn, communicates with the DS to learn that two of the three recipients reside on the local Exchange Server computer. The IS delivers the message immediately to them. The IS then starts communication with the MTA because it must initiate the message transfer to the third recipient on the remote server.

Additional Messaging Connectors and Gateways

When you address and send a message to a recipient who exists in a foreign mail system, the IS might also be involved. This is because the IS maintains the message queues for the IMS, the Connector for Lotus cc:Mail, and any other gateways you might have installed on your Exchange Server. These message queues are hidden private folders, which are named MTS-IN and MTS-OUT. The MTA places outgoing messages into the connector's MTS-OUT folder and the IS announces the presence of new mail awaiting delivery to the messaging connector. MTS-IN is used in the reverse manner. The respective messaging connector or gateway places inbound messages into its MTS-IN folder and notifies the IS, which then—if necessary—informs the MTA that a new message is waiting for its attention. In this situation, the MTA retrieves the message from the IS to route it to the destination server.

System Attendant

The IS provides delivery-related data to the SA, which is necessary if you want to maintain tracking log information. If you enable the tracking log feature for the IS, the message tracking center can be used to verify whether and when a particular message has arrived at its destination mailbox. This feature is similar to the MTA tracking log functionality.

MAPI client

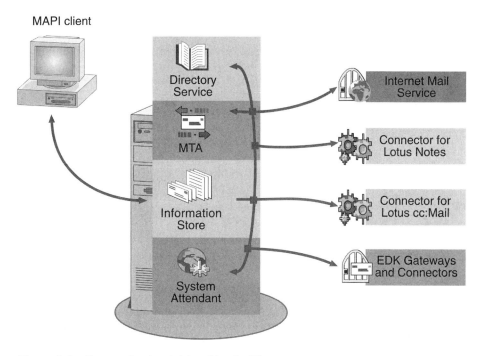

Figure 3-8. Communication initiated by the IS.

The IS communicates with the following components:

- Clients; to notify them that new mail messages have arrived
- Connectors for Lotus cc:Mail and for Lotus Notes; to announce the presence of new mail awaiting transfer
- DS; to resolve user addresses and to retrieve information about recipients
- IMS; to announce the presence of new mail awaiting transfer
- MTA; to submit messages for delivery by the MTA to remote servers, either directly or via a connector; MTA also expands distribution lists to perform routing for every recipient
- SA; to request the creation of and provide information for tracking log files to be used by the message tracking center
- Third-party gateways and connectors; to announce the presence of new mail awaiting transfer

Optional Component Communication

Optional Exchange Server components initiate communication with core components to provide their functionality to the messaging network. The most important
service, which is used by nearly every additional component, is the IS. Another
important communication partner is the DS. (See Figure 3-9 on page 177.)

Internet Mail Service

The IMS has been implemented as a separate Windows NT service. It communicates only with the DS and the IS. The IMS is explained thoroughly in
Chapter 10, "Internet Mail Service."

MTS-OUT and MTS-IN

The IMS maintains one message queue for incoming messages and one for
outgoing messages within the IS. You can picture these message queues as
folders in a mailbox. The only specific characteristics about them are their
names and their folder structures. Instead of an Inbox, the IMS uses a folder
named MTS-OUT to receive all e-mail messages that are awaiting delivery to
remote SMTP systems. Just as a user reads messages from the Inbox, the IMS
reads the messages from its MTS-OUT folder. The folder named MTS-IN, on
the other hand, can be compared to a user's Outbox. Using this folder, the
IMS places those messages on the server that should be sent into the Exchange organization.

Message and Address Formats

The IMS is a messaging connector that allows you to establish connections
between an Exchange Server computer and remote SMTP and ESMTP
systems. Therefore, it has the responsibility to convert Exchange Server
messages into valid SMTP formats (such as plain text, UUENCODE, and
MIME). The originator and recipient addresses of outgoing messages must
also be converted into SMTP addresses, because all other formats will cause
delivery problems. To convert an Exchange address into an SMTP address,
the IMS uses the services of the directory. It needs to pass the Exchange
address to the DS to receive the corresponding SMTP address. The SMTP
address is then placed into the outgoing message.

Active Server Components

The ASCs—in conjunction with Outlook Web Access—perform the translation between HTML and MAPI on an IIS. Because of this translation, Internet
browsers can view server-based resources as normal HTML documents when
accessing an Exchange Server. Outlook Web Access actually accesses the
Exchange Server on behalf of the browser.

Information Store

The IS is involved in the process of accessing mailboxes and public folders through Outlook Web Access. Depending on the users' logon credentials, the IS may grant more or fewer permissions to them. A validated user can work with his or her mailbox and also with the public folders if appropriate permissions have been granted. An anonymous user, however, can work only with a specified subset of public folders, known as *published public folders*. You can read more about published public folders in Chapter 11.

Directory Service

Outlook Web Access also allows you to browse the Global Address List using an Internet browser. To retrieve the address information, a communication link to the DS must be established. Outlook Web Access uses MAPI through RPCs to get the address information, and then translates it into an HTML document before sending it to the browser.

Internet News Service

Exchange Server supports the distribution of public folders as newsgroups. The INS can retrieve information from external USENET newsgroups to provide this information to Exchange users as messages in public folders.

Information Store

The INS is responsible for maintaining newsfeeds, which can transfer information from USENET to public folders, or vice versa. An outgoing newsfeed checks the content of public folders for new items. An incoming feed places new items from USENET into public folders through NTTP. As a result, communication between the INS and the IS is necessary.

Microsoft Mail Connector

The MS Mail Connector is a messaging connector that consists of three components: the MS Mail Connector Interchange, the MS Mail Connector Postoffice, and the MS Mail MTA service. Only the MS Mail Connector Interchange, however, communicates with other Exchange Server services. The MS Mail Connector Postoffice is a passive shared-file structure, and the MS Mail MTA transfers messages only within the MS Mail network (a number of MS Mail postoffices including the MS Mail Connector Postoffice), as does any other native MS Mail MTA process.

Directory Service

The MS Mail Connector Interchange communicates with the DS to perform address conversions. It must convert addresses from the Exchange Server format to the MS Mail format before it places outbound messages into the MS Mail Connector Postoffice.

MTA

To transfer e-mails from MS Mail and StarNine/MS Mail (AppleTalk) systems into Exchange Server, the MS Mail Connector Interchange service must communicate directly with the MTA. The MTA starts communication with the MS Mail Connector Interchange if messages are sent to the MS Mail messaging network.

Directory Synchronization

The Directory Synchronization with MS Mail uses a complex protocol that is implemented by MS Mail. The protocol was introduced with MS Mail version 3.0. Special system e-mail messages carry the address update information between the directory synchronization server (DirSync server) and Requestor postoffices. When a DirSync cycle has been completed, the Requestors' address lists are up to date. This protocol will be explained in more detail in Chapter 18.

DXA, DS, and MTA

The DXA is the Directory Synchronization component of Exchange Server, which operates according to the MS Mail DirSync protocol to synchronize address list changes with MS Mail postoffices. DXA maintains the MS Mail addresses as custom recipients in the directory and sends those Exchange addresses to the MS Mail postoffices that have been included in the DirSync configuration. The DXA must communicate with the DS. The DXA also must communicate with the MTA because address information must be wrapped in MS Mail DirSync messages, which are sent to the MS Mail postoffices. This process works the other way as well: incoming MS Mail address list updates are received from the MTA.

Schedule+ Free/Busy Connector

The Schedule+ Free/Busy Connector is responsible for exchanging Free/Busy information with Schedule+ users who reside on MS Mail postoffices. The distribution of Free/Busy times is based on e-mail messages, so the Schedule+ Free/Busy Connector relies on the MS Mail Connector in order to transfer Free/Busy messages to and from the MS Mail postoffices.

Information Store

Schedule+ Free/Busy information is kept in a hidden public folder on the Exchange Server computer, so the Schedule+ Free/Busy Connector communicates with the IS. The connector retrieves the Free/Busy times of Exchange users from the IS and places them in e-mail messages to be sent by MS Mail postoffices. Information received from MS Mail is handed over to the IS.

Directory Service

The Schedule+ Free/Busy Connector needs to know which user belongs to which site; it must therefore communicate with the DS to retrieve this information. If you activate the option to send updates for the local site only (**Send Updates For This Site Only** option of the Free/Busy Connector), the connector must check the site information of each user to include only those in the information exchange who reside in the connector's site.

Connector for Lotus cc:Mail

The Connector for Lotus cc:Mail is a messaging connector that has been developed based on the EDK.

Information Store

The Connector for Lotus cc:Mail uses its own MTS-IN and MTS-OUT system folders to maintain its message queues, as does the IMS. The Connector contacts the IS to retrieve messages from MTS-OUT once the connector has been notified by the IS. It also communicates with the IS to place inbound messages in MTS-IN. These queues used in conjunction with the connector store—the Exchsrvr\Ccmcdata directory—send outbound messages and retrieve inbound messages.

Directory Service

The Connector for Lotus cc:Mail converts addresses from the Exchange Server into a valid Lotus cc:Mail format and vice versa. But the addresses themselves—Exchange Server as well as proxy addresses in the cc:Mail format for Exchange mailboxes, custom recipients and distribution lists—are maintained by the DS. As a result, the Connector contacts the DS on the Exchange Server to obtain the required information. Likewise, the Connector for Lotus cc:Mail contacts the DS to perform the Directory Synchronization with Lotus cc:Mail.

Exchange Development Kit Gateways

The EDK is the basis of many third-party gateways. It defines a common environment for all these messaging components, all of which behave in a similar way. The Connector for Lotus Notes, the PROFS connector, and the SNADS connector are good examples.

Information Store

Every EDK connector maintains message queues named MTS-IN and MTS-OUT and other optional folders in the IS. The EDK connector uses a temporary MAPI profile to communicate with the server's core services, which will be stored under the Registry keys for the Site Services Account. The temporary MAPI profile is required to access the desired server resources, such as the IS and the DS. MAPI profiles are covered in Chapter 7.

Directory Service

The DS will assist the gateways in converting addresses from the Exchange Server into the required third-party formats, and vice versa. Several connectors, such as the Connector for Lotus Notes, can also synchronize directory information between Exchange and the third-party messaging systems to which they provide connectivity.

Event Service

The Event Service is responsible for executing installed scripts (also called *folder agents*) through scripting agents in case a specific event (for example, message creation) occurs for a given messaging folder. Folder agents are installed in a system public folder on the server. Consequently, a scripting agent, which is launched by the Event Service, communicates with the IS to retrieve the scripts it fires, and it communicates with the IS to access and process the actual data.

Key Management Component

The Key Management component does not initiate any communication to other Exchange components. The configuration of this component is covered in Chapter 14.

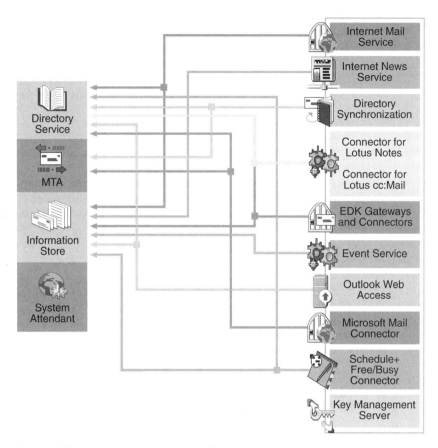

Figure 3-9. Communication initiated by optional components.

The following optional components initiate communication with the other components listed below them:

Outlook Web Access

- DS; to resolve address information and check user privileges

- IS; to process messages in mailboxes and public folders

Connector for Lotus cc:Mail

- IS; to process messages from and to Lotus cc:Mail post offices

- DS; to process Address Book information and perform Directory Synchronization

(continues)

(continued)

Connector for Lotus Notes

- IS; to process messages from and to Lotus Notes
- DS; to process Address Book information and perform Directory Synchronization

Directory Synchronization

- DS; to create, modify, or delete user definitions from remote systems; to check for modifications in the Exchange address list that need to be distributed to foreign systems
- MTA; to receive and submit DirSync-related messages from and to foreign systems

Event Service

- IS; to track and process events and data

Internet Mail Service

- DS; to look up Internet addresses
- IS; to process messages for SMTP users as well as incoming messages

Internet News Service

- IS; to process messages in public folders

Key Management Server

- Does not initiate any communication with Exchange core components

MS Mail Connector

- DS; to resolve recipient addresses and convert them into Exchange Server or MS Mail formats, respectively
- MTA; to transfer mail from and to MS Mail and StarNine/MS Mail (AppleTalk)

PROFS Connector, SNADS Connector, and other EDK Gateways

- IS; to deliver messages from foreign systems to Exchange and vice versa
- DS; to resolve recipient addresses and to obtain foreign mail address information for Exchange Server addresses, and vice versa

(continues)

(continued)

Schedule+ Free/Busy Connector

- IS; to receive and store schedule information from MS Mail postoffices and to send schedule information from Exchange Server to MS Mail

- DS; to retrieve Address Book information

Single-Server Message Flow

Message flow describes the component-by-component movement of a message within a system. Usually the message flow begins when a user sends a message, and ends when the message has been delivered to the recipient's mailbox. The moment the recipient actually reads the message, however, there is no longer any message flow. This is because a recipient does not necessarily need to be on line to allow for message delivery.

Server Components

The core components determine the route of a message by comparing the attributes of the recipient's address with attributes for the local site and address spaces, which are defined in the routing table. Depending on the route a message has to take, one or more components are involved in the message transmission.

Local Delivery

Only the messaging client, the IS, and the DS are involved in the local delivery, which is also known as *single-server message flow*. Let's say you've sent a message to another user on the same Exchange Server. In this situation, the IS delivers the message directly. First the client places the message in the Outbox and marks it for delivery. Then the IS requests address information about the recipient from the DS. The DS informs the IS that the recipient resides on the local computer. With this information, the IS is able to deliver the message directly into the recipient's Inbox. In addition, the IS notifies the client about the arrival of the new message if the recipient is currently on line. The recipient's client displays the new message immediately in its Inbox. (See Figure 3-10.)

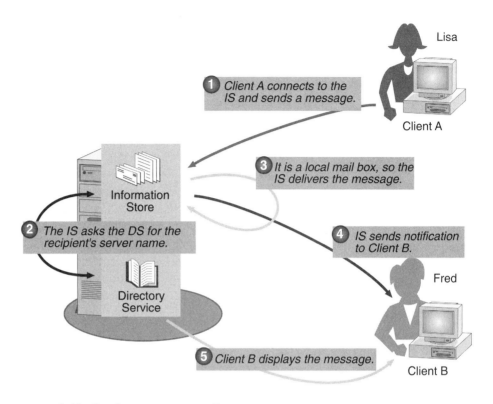

Figure 3-10. Single-server message flow.

The message flow within a single server is as follows:

1. A user starts a MAPI-based client to connect to the Private Information Store and submits a message destined for a recipient.

2. The IS asks the DS for the recipient's home server name.

3. The IS finds that the recipient's mailbox resides on the local server (recipient's home server name equals the IS local server name) and delivers the message.

4. If the recipient is currently logged on, the IS sends a notification to the recipient's client. Otherwise, notification is postponed until the recipient logs on.

Multiple-Server Message Flow

In a more complex scenario a message can be sent to a recipient on another computer either in the same site or in another site. Just as in the single-server example, the Exchange Client delivers the message to the IS. The IS asks the

DS for the name of the server where the mailbox resides. Because the recipient's home server is not the local server, the message must be transmitted to the MTA. The MTA contacts the DS to analyze the recipient's site name. The MTA determines whether the recipient resides in the local site or somewhere else.

Intrasite Message Flow

If the recipient's site name equals the name of the local site, the MTA asks the DS for the recipient's home server attribute. The MTA must determine this attribute to establish a direct RPC connection to the MTA on the recipient's home server. Once the communication path has been established, the message can be transferred.

The remote MTA receives the message and queries its local DS again for the recipient's site name. This name still equals the local site name, so the MTA retrieves the home server attribute. This time the attribute points to the server on which the MTA is running, so the MTA discovers that the message must be transferred to the local IS. Finally, the IS places the message in the recipient's Inbox. You can read more about the MTA communication within a site in Chapter 4.

Intersite Message Flow

If the recipient's site name does not match the name of the local site, the message must be delivered across the site boundary. In this case, a direct RPC connection between the involved MTA services is not possible. You must use a messaging connector to establish a connection to the remote site, but first you must determine which connector is best for sending the message. This process is known as *message routing*. The MTA compares the recipient address with the entries in the Gateway Address Routing Table (GWART) to find an appropriate messaging connector to the remote site. The message is then placed in this connector's message queue. (See Figure 3-11.) The purpose of the messaging connector is to transfer the message to the remote site where the recipient's mailbox resides.

At the remote site, the MTA queries its DS to figure out whether the message requires further routing. It's possible that the recipient resides in still another site or on another server in the same site, or that it has a local mailbox. If the recipient has a local mailbox, the message is delivered to the local IS for delivery. If the recipient is located on another server in the target site, the MTA uses a direct RPC connection to the destination MTA, as described in the section, "Intrasite Message Flow." If further routing through additional sites or foreign systems is necessary, the message is placed in a connector message queue so that the message can be sent to the next MTA, where the routing process starts again.

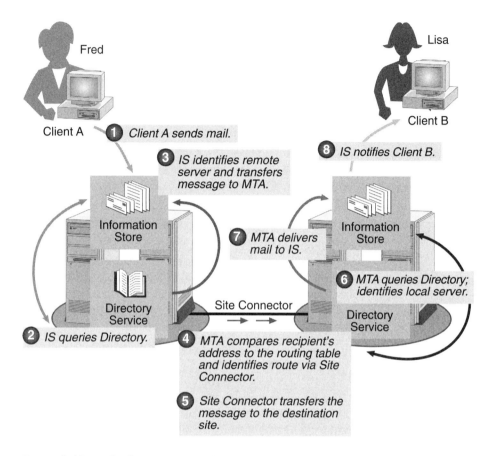

Figure 3-11. Multiple-site message flow.

Between multiple sites the message flow is as follows:

1. A user utilizes a MAPI-based client to connect to the Private Information Store and submits a message destined for a recipient in another site.

2. The IS asks the DS for the name of the server on which the recipient's mailbox resides.

3. The IS compares the response of the DS to the current IS name, and, because they are different, the IS sends the message to the MTA for further routing and transmission.

4. The MTA asks the DS for the recipient's local site name. Because this is not the local site name, the MTA compares the e-mail address with the routing table and finds a messaging connector that can transfer the message.

5. The MTA transfers the message to the message queue of the appropriate messaging connector. The messaging connector transfers the message to its peer at the remote site, where the message is finally passed to the remote MTA.

6. The remote MTA asks its local DS for the site and then the home server of the recipient. The MTA learns that the local server is the recipient's home server.

7. The MTA delivers the message to the IS.

8. The IS delivers the message to the recipient's Inbox and sends the client a notification that a new message has arrived.

Review

1. What are the Exchange Server core components?

_____

_____

2. In order to perform an offline backup, you want to shut down the Exchange Server without rebooting the Windows NT Server computer. Which of the core components must be stopped directly in order to stop all other server components as well?

_____

3. As an administrator of your organization, you want to allow users to work with MAPI-based and POP3-based messaging clients. You need to configure POP3 support to allow POP3 clients to send and receive messages. Which additional components must be configured?

_____

4. In order to provide HTTP-based access to public folders, mailboxes, and the Global Address List, you want to install the Outlook Web Access components. How do you add this component to your Exchange Server? What is required to install Outlook Web Access?

_____

_____

_____

5. In order to improve the security in your organization you have decided to implement Advanced Security features. What two relevant features does the Key Management Server (KM Server) provide?

6. You have stopped the MTA service. How does this affect the behavior of connected Exchange Clients?

7. As an administrator you have stopped the IS service. How does this affect Exchange Clients?

8. In order to satisfy growing messaging demand, you decide to install a second Exchange Server computer. You will add this server to the existing site to make administration easier. Which two components communicate directly with each other between both servers?

9. List the core components with which the IS communicates.

10. As a user you can send messages successfully to other users who reside on the same home server. However, messages destined to recipients on other servers within the same site remain in your Outbox. What is the likely source of the problem?

11. As a user you can send messages successfully to other users who reside in the same site. Messages destined to recipients in other sites cannot be delivered and result in Non-Delivery Reports (NDRs). What is the likely source of the problem?

C H A P T E R   4

Communication in an Exchange Server Environment

This chapter covers the general aspects of server-to-server communication before focusing on the communication between servers in sites, which is also known as *intrasite communication*. As discussed in Chapter 3, servers within a single site use RPCs to transfer data between each other.

Overview

Sites are organizational units that group together multiple servers. These servers act as a complete and integral system, which simplifies their administration and configuration. The configuration information at the site level must be shared among all servers and any configuration changes that have been applied to one server must be distributed to all other servers. Furthermore, e-mail messages must be transferred between servers as users residing on different servers exchange interpersonal information. Exchange does all of this automatically once you have properly configured your Exchange Servers.

Lesson 1 provides an overview of the server-to-server communication within and between sites. The various types of data that are transferred between servers are discussed. You can also read about the active server components that generate and receive these data types.

Lesson 2 explores the characteristics of intrasite communication in more detail. You'll read about the common communication methods and the directory replication protocol as implemented in Exchange Server 5.5.

Lesson 3 discusses the role of the MTA within single sites. The MTA transfers most of the information between servers, and this lesson explains its communication methods and other tasks, such as the address name resolution for message routing decisions.

In the following lessons, you will be introduced to:

- The types of data transferred between components via server-to-server communication
- The methods by which the DS communicates in an intrasite environment
- The methods by which the MTA communicates in an intrasite environment
- The process the MTA uses to route messages between servers

Lesson 1: Server-to-Server Communication

The servers of an organization transfer various kinds of information to one another in addition to transferring regular user messages. Several forms of data are exchanged between the server core components on different servers; only the method of server-to-server communication within a site differs significantly from the communication between sites.

This lesson lists and explains the data types that can be transferred between the servers of an organization. The differences between intrasite and intersite communication are highlighted. You'll learn about the server components that are engaged in server-to-server communication.

At the end of this lesson, you will be able to:

- List the information types transferred between Exchange Server components
- Name the core components that transfer information between servers in a site

Estimated time to complete this lesson: 20 minutes

Types of Data Transferred Between Components

If Exchange Server computers are grouped together in a site, they must be able to exchange data directly with each other using RPCs. If an Exchange organization consists of more than one site, however, the communication between sites always takes place through messaging connectors. (See Figure 4-1 on page 190.)

Interpersonal Messages

The main purpose of a messaging system is to transfer e-mail messages from one user to another. Users create messages, address them, and then send them using their messaging client. Users also employ their messaging client to read messages they've received in their mailbox. It is the responsibility of the messaging backbone to transfer the messages to the recipients' mailboxes. Messages sent directly between users are known as *interpersonal messages*.

Directory Replication Information

While intrasite directory replication always relies on direct RPC communication, intersite directory replication cannot assume that RPCs are supported. Between sites, directory information is distributed via of e-mail messages. These messages are also called directory replication messages, and they carry information about configuration changes from one site to other sites within your organization. A special component of the DS, the Directory Replication Agent (DRA), generates and receives these messages. You must configure explicit replication links if you want to enable intersite directory replication. The directory replication between sites is covered in Chapter 9, "Introduction to Intersite Connectors."

Directory replication within a site, also called *intrasite replication*, is performed automatically using RPCs. The DS of one server contacts all other DSs within its site to notify them about local directory changes. The communication of the DS within sites is covered in Lesson 2, "Intrasite Server Communication," later in this chapter.

Note Between sites, the DS sends its directory changes as system e-mail messages through the MTA. Within sites, the DSs of each server communicate directly with each other using RPCs.

Information Store Messages

The IS maintains the public folders and their hierarchy, among other things. Using e-mail messages, the public folder hierarchy is replicated automatically to all other servers that own a Public Information Store. The replication of the hierarchy allows all users to skim through the list of the existing folders using the Microsoft Exchange Client, Microsoft Outlook, or an appropriate Internet browser. More information about public folder access is provided in Chapter 12, "Creating and Managing Public Folders."

If you want to access the contents of a public folder, an RPC connection must be established to the server maintaining the folder content. But the RPC communication method is not always supported, such as on WAN connections between sites. In such cases, you'll need to create a new instance of the public folder locally to provide RPC connectivity. The content of a public folder can be replicated to the local site through e-mail messages. Public folder replication is explained in detail in Chapter 13, "Public Folder Replication."

Both the automatic replication of the public folder hierarchy and the optional replication of public folder contents are wrapped in replication messages. These messages can be sent over the messaging network the same way as interpersonal messages.

Link Monitor Test Messages

Link Monitors allow you to test the condition of a particular connection path on a regular basis, and are especially useful for testing messaging connectors and gateways across site boundaries. A Link Monitor can generate test messages in well-defined intervals, and it can address these test messages to remote servers, to regular users, or to custom recipients. The test messages are sent to determine whether a reply is received within a given time span. If so, the connection is considered operational. More information about Link Monitors is provided in Chapter 15, "Maintaining Servers."

Note Link Monitor test messages are another class of system messages that the MTA must handle.

Other Information Types

Several other types of e-mail messages can also be transferred through your messaging network. For example, Directory Synchronization messages can transfer address information between the Exchange Server organization and an MS Mail network. Complete address lists are efficiently updated in this manner. The Directory Synchronization with MS Mail is covered in Chapter 18, "Connecting to Microsoft Mail and Schedule+ 1.0."

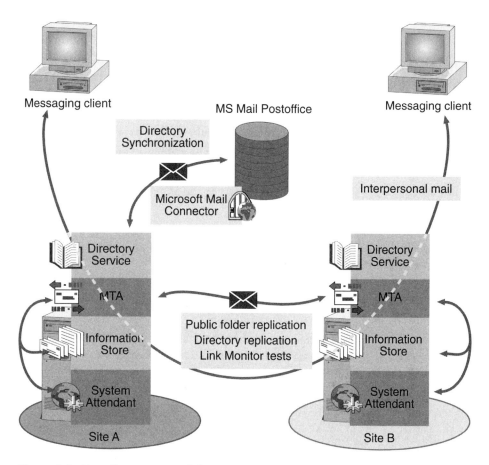

Figure 4-1. E-mail messages and their purpose.

Exchange Server transfers these types of messages:

- Directory Synchronization messages (MS Mail DirSync protocol)
- Interpersonal e-mail messages
- Link Monitor messages
- Messages for public folder hierarchy and public folder content replication
- Replication messages for directory changes

Components of Server-to-Server Communication

The two core components that manage the entire information transfer between Exchange Server computers within a site are the MTA and the DS. The level to which the DS is involved in the exchange of information depends upon whether the information is transferred between Exchange Server computers in a single-site environment or in a multiple-site organization.

Directory Service

Exchange Server computers normally contains a complete copy of the organization's directory, and it is the duty of the DS to maintain this copy and keep it up to date. The DS of the computer NEWYORK-1, for instance, can contact the DS of the server NEWYORK-2 directly, as shown in Figure 4-2. This is possible because NEWYORK-1 and NEWYORK-2 reside in the same site named NEWYORK. Within the same site, it is assumed that there is enough available network bandwidth to support RPC communication. A common Site Services Account is used to validate the RPC communication request. Consequently, RPCs are the ideal communication method for transferring new configuration changes across the site efficiently. Directory replication within a site is explained in the Lesson 2, "Intrasite Server Communication," later in this chapter.

Direct DS-to-DS communication over RPCs is not supported between sites because LAN connectivity cannot be assumed and a common service account is not guaranteed in this case. Consequently, the DSs must use the e-mail message transport instead. A special component, a Directory Replication Connector, must be configured to send and receive directory updates in the form of e-mail messages between servers of separate sites. The directory replication mechanism remains the same in all other aspects as it does for the intrasite replication.

Message Transfer Agent

The MTA is responsible for transferring messages to other servers, sites, and foreign X.400 systems. The MTA is also responsible for placing outbound messages in corresponding message queues if additional messaging connectors have been installed. Messages awaiting further routing in inbound message queues are also being processed by the MTA. The transfer of messages between sites is covered in Chapter 9.

The MTA handles all types of messages, regardless of whether the messages are interpersonal or a result of directory replication, public folder replication, Directory Synchronization, or Link Monitors. In order for the MTA to handle these messages, they must occur in one of two messaging data formats: the Exchange Server format, called Message Database Encoding Format

(MDBEF) and the X.400 interpersonal messages (IPM) format. The conversion between these formats is handled by the MTA itself, while the conversion to other formats, such as MS Mail or Lotus cc:Mail, is performed by messaging connectors and gateways.

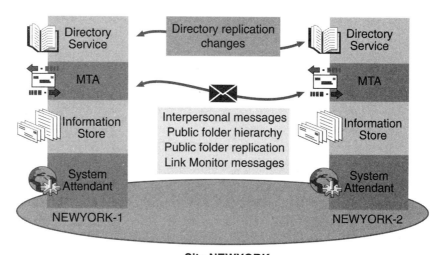

Figure 4-2. Intrasite server-to-server communication.

Core components and the type of information they transfer within a site are as follows:

- DS; which replicates directory changes to all other servers within a site through RPCs

- MTA; which transfers interpersonal messages, intersite directory replication messages, messages of public folder content and public folder hierarchy replication, and Link Monitor test messages

Lesson 2: Intrasite Server Communication

Exchange Server computers automatically transfer various kinds of information to each other within a single site, with or without your intervention. They must do this to operate as an organizational unit. Users residing on different servers within a site can communicate with each other without the need for explicit configuration of messaging paths. Likewise, access to public folders is always guaranteed regardless of whether the corresponding content is maintained by the local server or a remote server within a site. These features are possible because a large amount of network bandwidth is assumed within a site, which allows for the utilization of a bandwidth-consuming but powerful network communication method.

This lesson explores the unique features and characteristics of intrasite communication. You'll read in detail about the RPC communication mechanism as well as about the various aspects of intrasite directory replication.

At the end of this lesson, you will be able to:

- Explain the RPC communication method

- Describe DS communication within a single site

- Address issues related to intrasite security and the Site Services Account

Estimated time to complete this lesson: 25 minutes

Server Communication Within Site Boundaries

The process of data transfer and information distribution within a site is also known as *intrasite communication*. This form of server-to-server interaction is generally performed through RPCs. Exchange Server can use RPCs to transfer data back and forth because the required available network capacity within sites allows the use of bandwidth-consuming protocols. Furthermore, all servers within a site use the same Sites Services Account, which allows for efficient access validation of server services accessing resources on a remote server. As explained in the previous lesson, the DS and the MTA are the two server components that communicate directly with remote servers through RPC.

RPC-Client

RPC communication always takes place between an RPC-client and an RPC-server. Applied to intrasite communication, this means that the role of the RPC-client is assumed by the requesting Exchange Server computer, while the role of the RPC-server is assumed by the responding Exchange Server. Although it might sound confusing, the requesting Exchange Server is indeed the RPC-client. The architecture of RPC hides the complex network functionality from the RPC-client and the RPC-server modules. Both the RPC-server and the RPC-client programs assume that they are calling local program routines. Instead of calling the real function, however, the call of the RPC-client is directed to what is known as the client stub code. The client stub takes the function call and translates the received parameters into data packets for network transmission. The client stub uses the RPC run-time library functions to transfer the data to the RPC-server. (See Figure 4-3.)

RPC-Server

The RPC-server has an RPC run-time library at its disposal as well. The RPC-server run-time functions can take the network request in order to transfer the data to the server stub code. The server stub translates the data and hands the information over to the actual server procedures also known as *remote procedures*. A remote procedure processes the request and then returns the resulting data back to the server stub. The rest of the data flow is symmetrical to the first part of the procedure. (See Figure 4-3.)

RPC Run-Time Library

The RPC run-time library for Windows NT has been implemented in a file named Rpcrt4.dll. The run-time library provides its functions to both the RPC-server and the RPC-client procedures. Important functions that are part of the RPC run-time library start with "RPCBinding."

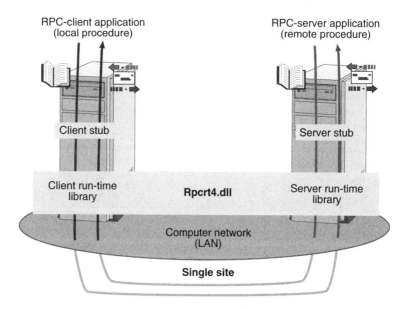

Figure 4-3. Intrasite communication based on RPCs.

The intrasite communication mechanism flows as follows:

1. The RPC-client calls the client stub code.

2. The client stub translates the parameters into a data packet for transmission over the network.

3. RPC-client run-time library functions transfer the data (via the network transport) to the RPC-server.

4. RPC-server run-time functions receive the network request.

5. RPC run-time library functions transfer the data to the server stub code.

6. The server stub translates the data and passes it to the actual server procedures.

7. The remote procedure returns the result to the server stub.

8. The server stub transmits the results to the RPC-client using a procedure that is symmetrical to the one described in steps 2 through 6.

Directory Service Communication in an Intrasite Environment

The directory replication, as implemented in Exchange Server, follows the principles of a multimaster model. This model allows you to manage all the directory information without the need for a central storage place. In other words, the directory is distributed between all Exchange Server computers within a single site. Each server is a directory master and each maintains an entire copy of the site's directory. The directories of all servers in a site are basically identical.

Directory Replication Delay

The multimaster model allows you to change the site configuration at any server in your site. Configuration changes applied to one directory are replicated to all other directories to keep them synchronized, but the directory replication doesn't happen immediately. After a delay of five minutes, called *replication latency*, the local DS sends a notification to the other DSs that changes have occurred. The local DS maintains a cached list of all those servers that will receive a notification. The five-minute delay that occurs after the last change has been implemented to maximize the efficiency of the replication cycle. This makes it possible to collect multiple configuration changes for batch replication. At the end of the replication latency time span, the local DS notifies the first remote DS. It then pauses for 30 seconds to allow the notified server to retrieve the changes. If the contacted server does not request any changes within this timeframe, the next server on the list will be notified.

Universal Sequence Numbers

Figure 4-4 on page 198 shows that the directory replication mechanism is always a pull mechanism. This means that the initiating server cannot push directory information arbitrarily to other servers. Instead, it is the duty of the remote servers to specify the exact information they want to obtain from the initiating server.

Tracking Configuration Changes

The DSs keep track of configuration changes that have already been received in order to avoid requesting the same data or transactions twice. The server on which a modification has occurred will send a replication notification to all the servers that receive its directory changes. Remote servers can then request the server-specific USN from the local server, which is used to identify configuration changes. In fact, it is up to the remote server to compare the received USN against the formerly known USN of the notifying server to determine which modifications have to be requested.

Note Directory replication is always a pull and never a push.

Requesting Configuration Changes

Whenever you change the configuration of a server, you are creating or modifying directory objects. Modifications must be marked to allow remote servers to detect and request them. For this purpose, the **USN-Changed** attribute is used, which is contained in each directory object. Let's say you are committing the modification of a mailbox object to the directory database. At this point, the mailbox object's **USN-Changed** attribute receives the server's updated USN. Every server maintains its own internal USN that is increased every time an object within the server's directory is modified.

Once the modified mailbox object has been assigned the increased USN value, remote servers must be notified about the configuration alteration. All remote servers that have their modifications replicated by the local server are contained in a list called REPS_TO. The remote servers will receive a replication notification from the local server in sequence.

REPS_TO is not the only list an Exchange Server maintains. REPS_FROM is its counterpart, and it contains a list of all the servers from which a particular DS accepts replication information. Along with the actual reference, a server-specific USN is stored and associated with each known server. As a DS receives replication notification from a server that is contained in REPS_FROM, it requests that server's current USN value. This server returns its current USN to the requesting DS, which can then compare the received USN with the former USN. Both numbers might match, in which case the requesting server assumes that it is up to date and does not request any directory updates from the remote server.

If the incoming USN is higher than the former number, the DS requests all directory objects from the remote server that show a **USN-Changed** value greater than the former USN. As the server returns the requested objects, the requesting DS includes the changes in its directory and updates the stored USN value for the remote server. Its directory is up to date upon completion.

Sometimes the incoming USN is smaller than the stored USN. This is typically the case when the remote server has been restored from a backup. In such a scenario, directory replication ensures that the remote server is brought up to date. In other words, the local DS notifies the remote server that it should ask itself for directory replication changes. Then, as the remote server requests and retrieves missing directory objects, it becomes synchronized with the current state of the site configuration again. This process is also known as *backfilling*.

Intrasite and Intersite Replication

The replication mechanism based on USNs remains the same regardless of whether intrasite or intersite replication has to be performed. Only the communication mechanism will change from direct RPCs to e-mail messages between sites, but this does not affect the mechanism that keeps track of changes.

Service Account and Intrasite Security

Every attempt to access an Exchange Server computer must be validated to prevent unauthorized access to server-based resources. Validation must also occur for the directory replication based on RPCs. Therefore, a DS must use the Site Services Account information to validate the RPC connection to remote services.

Simplified Validation

Because all Exchange Server services within the same site need to run under the context of the same service account, the validation of security information is relatively simple within sites. In other words, the security information is available to all directory services because all servers use the same Site Services Account. A server using the wrong account information for any reason cannot contact other servers in the site.

Changing the Service Account

Microsoft Product Support Services recommends that you do not change the Site Services Account unless absolutely necessary (for instance, because the Site Services Account's password has been compromised). If you do so anyway you should be aware that it will take some time until all servers within the site are updated with the new account information. Meanwhile, this delay leads to communication problems between servers with old account information and servers with new account information.

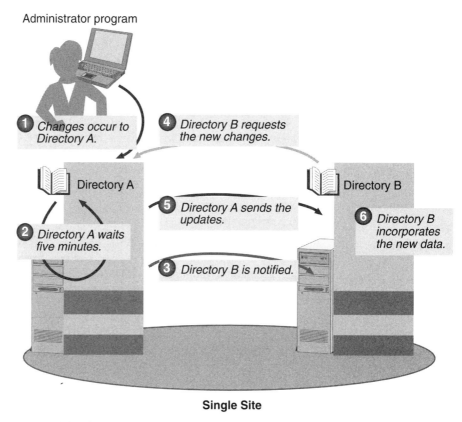

Single Site

Figure 4-4. The intrasite directory replication mechanism.

Exchange Server replicates directory changes as follows:

1. Changes occur at the local directory.

2. The local DS waits five minutes after the last change before sending the notification to the other servers.

3. All available remote directories are notified one after the other.

4. Each notified DS requests the changes that have not been retrieved yet.

5. The local DS responds with the updates.

6. Each requesting DS can then incorporate the data into its directory.

Lesson 3: The MTA in an Intrasite Environment

The MTA is the main component responsible for the server-to-server communication in an organization, so it deserves its own separate section. The MTA transfers all possible types of information via e-mail messages between Exchange Server computers, with the exception of intrasite directory replication. Several steps are necessary to transfer a message successfully, however. Recipient addresses must be analyzed, a valid route must be detected, and the message must be transmitted physically. As always, significant differences exist between the intrasite and intersite message transfer.

The main focus of this lesson is the MTA communication within a single site; the role of the MTA between sites is explained in more detail in Chapter 9. This lesson presents the processes that are launched to transmit a message successfully to its destination. The address resolution and the resulting determination of the message route are also explained.

At the end of this lesson, you will be able to:

- Describe the communication between MTAs in an intrasite environment
- Identify the responsibilities of the MTA with respect to message routing and address resolution
- Determine the parameters that influence the route a message can take in a single site

Estimated time to complete this lesson: 35 minutes

MTA Communication in an Intrasite Environment

The MTA is the central component for all kinds of message transfer between servers. Within a site, this transfer is accomplished by using RPCs. Between sites, the MTA uses messaging connectors.

MTA-to-MTA Interaction

The two different types of communication between Exchange Servers within a site are the directory replication and the MTA-to-MTA interaction. The directory replication was explained in Lesson 2, "Intrasite Server Communication," earlier in this chapter. As mentioned in that section, directory replication distributes configuration information between the servers of a site. The MTA-to-MTA interaction, on the other hand, is responsible for the message transfer between Exchange Server computers. The transfer of a message within a single site is shown in Figure 4-5 on page 201.

All other server components, such as the IS and the SA, cannot communicate directly with each other—they must use the services of the MTA instead. These other components must wrap their information in e-mail messages and address them to their appropriate components running on remote servers. Once delivered, the receiving component unwraps the information and processes it, thereby maintaining updated resources.

Note   RPC connections between MTAs are secured by the fact that they must be established based on the Site Services Account. Only a validated MTA can transfer messages to any other MTA.

Message Routing

The process of sending and receiving e-mail messages involves various MTA actions. First the MTA resolves the recipients' e-mail addresses. It checks the home server attribute of each particular recipient to determine whether to perform message routing based on the GWART. If the home server attribute points to a server in the local site, the message can be transferred to that server directly by means of intrasite MTA-to-MTA communication. However, if the home server attribute points to a location outside the local side, the MTA must locate a valid routing path to the actual destination. To do this the MTA must compare all relevant recipient addresses to the GWART. Based on the GWART, the MTA can determine which connector to use for message transfer. The GWART is explained in more detail in Chapter 9.

If you send a message to a distribution list, the MTA is responsible for the list's expansion. It expands the list by requesting the needed information from the DS. Once each member of a distribution list has been obtained from the DS, message routing will be performed as for single recipients.

MTA Protocol Configuration

As soon as the local MTA has determined an appropriate remote MTA in the local site, an RPC connection can be established between the two MTAs to transfer the message. To transmit an item successfully, however, a communication protocol must be used between them. It is important to ensure that the protocol parameters of each communication partner are matched.

You don't need to worry about matching protocol parameters because they are site-level settings. In other words, as you modify the MTA protocol settings on one server using the **MTA Site Configuration** object in the **Configuration** container of the Administrator program, you automatically modify these settings for all other MTAs in your site. The intrasite directory replication distributes the new parameter changes, guaranteeing that the configurations match one another across your site. The MTA configuration is covered in Chapter 8, "Managing Server Configuration."

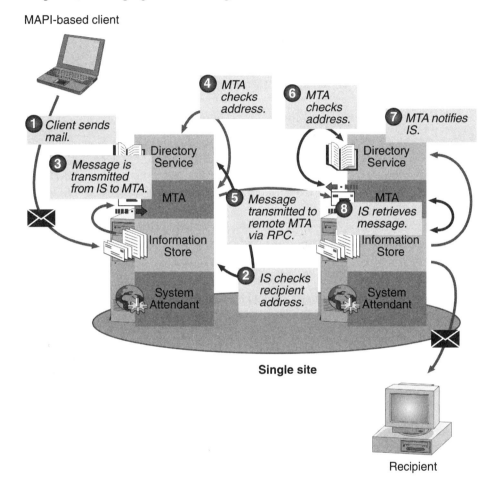

Figure 4-5. MTA intrasite communication.

The tasks of the MTA within a site are as follows:

- Expanding distribution lists
- Resolving e-mail addresses of recipients
- Connecting to remote MTAs to transfer messages
- Receiving messages from other MTAs

Resolving the E-Mail Address

Recipient addresses are the foundation of efficient MTA message routing. Several address types exist within an Exchange Server system, such as addresses in the Exchange Server format or foreign addresses known as proxy e-mail addresses. The Exchange Server format represents server-based recipient objects such as mailboxes, distribution lists, custom recipients, and public folders. An example of a foreign address is the SMTP address of a recipient that allows access from and to the Internet.

Exchange Server Formats

The DS generates an X.500 Distinguished Name (DN) for every object in the directory when the object is created. The DN is the internal Exchange Server e-mail address that is used to route messages within the organization. Another supported format is the X.400 Originator/Recipient (O/R) Name, but the DN is preferred.

X.500 Implementation

The Exchange Directory resembles the X.500 directory standard. For instance, the X.500 Directory System Agent (DSA) corresponds to the DS running on every Exchange Server computer. X.500 is a CCITT (ITU) recommendation that defines precisely how the names of directory objects should be created.

Note Every object in the directory owns a DN, which follows the X.500-standard as one of its attributes.

The Exchange Directory is not a real X.500 directory in every respect. For example, a few objects such as the <Organization> container differ from their counterparts in the X.500 specification. Other concepts, such as the utilization of DNs, however, are applied as described in the specification.

Distinguished Names

A DN actually serves as a pointer to the location of an object within the DIT. The Exchange Server–specific top-level object is always the name of the organization, for example, STOCKSDATA in Figure 4-6 on page 204. Consequently, the DN for the organization is /o=STOCKSDATA. The second element of a DN usually describes the site, such as /ou=NEWYORK. Further information can be provided through unique pointers to an actual item. A DN always proceeds from general elements to more specific elements when it is read from left to right. This means that the parent object of each element is always found at the left side of the element. For example, the DN of Fred Pumpkin's mailbox could be /o=STOCKSDATA/ou=NEWYORK/cn=Recipients/cn=FredP. (See Figure 4-6.)

DNs and Relative DNs

In addition to using complete X.500 DNs, Exchange Server uses relative DNs. A relative DN refers to the last part of a DN, shown as FredP in Figure 4-6. The last part of the DN is relative to its parent.

Message Routing Based on DNs

If you peruse the DN of Fred Pumpkin, you can follow the path to the **Recipients** container, where the mailbox actually resides. You can easily verify that the mailbox labeled FredP is located in a site called NEWYORK. The MTA can locate a recipient's home site the same way. Therefore, the MTA routes any messages for FredP to NEWYORK. Once a particular message has reached Fred's local site, the relative DN can be processed further. The DS resolves the relative DN to Fred's mailbox object that possesses a home server attribute. The home server attribute, in turn, allows his home server to be determined. If the home server is not the local server, the MTA establishes a direct RPC connection to the destination, and then delivers the message.

Note Within a single site, the message transfer must always be direct—only a *hop count* of one is permitted. The hop count is the number of servers a message passes before it reaches its final destination.

Proxy E-Mail Addresses

Every messaging system maintains its own e-mail address format. For example, the old MS Mail system uses a 10x10x10 address for its network, postoffice, and mailbox names, while PROFS systems employ a format of 8x8 to specify the user name and node name. SMTP expects the user to specify the address in the format of *User@FullyQualifiedDomainName*. Other systems can use different formats.

Depending on which components have been installed, more or fewer e-mail addresses in different formats might be required for Exchange objects. In other words, your users need the same number of foreign addresses as foreign messaging systems that have been connected to the Exchange organization. To make things easier for the administrator, the most common foreign addresses are created automatically, regardless of whether the foreign messaging systems are actually connected to the organization at the present time. For instance, if you have installed the Exchange Server 5.5 Enterprise Edition as outlined in Chapter 2, mailboxes are supplied with proxy addresses for Lotus cc:Mail, MS Mail, and SMTP in addition to X.400 and its native DNs. If third-party gateways have been installed, proxy addresses in other formats might also be generated.

Note Because the MTA is a native X.400 (88) message transfer agent, recipient objects always have an X.400 proxy e-mail address. You cannot disable the X.400 address type.

Exchange Server uses the DNs for its own purposes. Proxy addresses are required only when a message is to be sent to or received from a foreign mail system. The gateway or messaging connector replaces your DN with the required proxy address if necessary. On the other hand, if inbound messages are delivered to your mailbox, the MTA substitutes the specified proxy address with your DN before the message routing is performed.

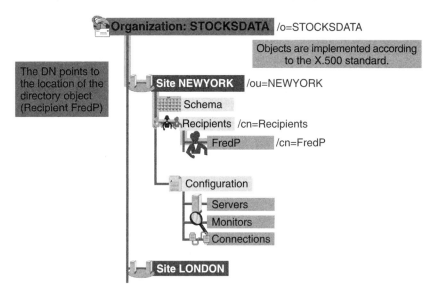

Figure 4-6. The Directory Information Tree and Distinguished Names.

Below is a list of Exchange Directory features that do not conform to the X.500 specification:

- The Exchange top-level object is called Organization. The corresponding X.500 object is called World.

- The Exchange container named Global Address List exists directly below the top-level object. No corresponding object is defined in the X.500 specification.

Determining the Message Route

Message routes can be either restricted to a single site or can span many sites and even different messaging systems. The difference has a deep influence on the methods that are used to route messages to their final destination. This lesson investigates the message routing between sites and to foreign systems as well as the methods of message routing within a single site.

Routing Between Sites and to Foreign Systems

In general, routing begins as soon as a message has been delivered to the MTA. The local MTA can receive messages from the local IS, from remote MTAs in the local site, and from messaging connectors. The MTA uses the GWART to determine logical delivery routes to remote sites and to foreign e-mail systems. The GWART relies on e-mail address spaces, which are tables that contain entries that are associated with specific messaging connectors. A messaging connector, in turn, can handle messages sent to a particular e-mail address, which belongs to one of the connector's address spaces. For instance, a recipient residing on the Internet might be reachable through an IMS. Consequently, you can associate an SMTP address space with this particular connector, which causes the MTA to place all messages destined for the Internet recipient into the outbound message queue of the IMS.

Existent Recipient Objects

Once the MTA has received a particular message, it must query the DS for the DN of all message recipients. DNs are returned if the information can be found in the directory database, which the MTA uses to determine the recipient's destination site. The MTA must compare each recipient's site name to the local site name and—if the names don't match—must route the message according to the GWART routing information. In the case of mismatched names, the MTA places the message in the outbound message queue of an appropriate messaging connector. The messaging connector will then transfer the message to the remote site.

Nonexistent Recipient Objects

Not every recipient must necessarily exist in the directory. Users can also specify recipient addresses manually or use Personal Address Book references. In these cases, the MTA uses the recipient's X.400 O/R Name to determine the best route to the recipient. The MTA checks the validity of the O/R Name first, since only valid addresses can be handled.

Note A Non-Delivery Report will be generated immediately if a user forgets to specify the Country (C), Administration Management Domain (ADMD), or Private Management Domain (PRMD) in an X.400 O/R address.

If the address is valid, the MTA can determine which messaging connector to use based on the GWART. As a result, the MTA places the message into the most suitable outbound message queue for delivery to the destination.

Routing to Foreign Systems

The MTA detects the address type of a recipient address. If, for instance, an MS Mail, Lotus cc:Mail, or SMTP address has been specified, a corresponding address space entry must exist in the GWART. Based on this entry, the MTA can determine and route the message.

Non-Delivery Reports

If the MTA cannot determine a valid routing path for a specific recipient address, an NDR will be generated and sent back to the originator, which indicates that a particular recipient address was unknown. The NDR typically contains the recipient's address so that the originator can use it for reference. Once the address has been corrected, the message can be re-sent.

Routing Within the Local Site

If a message is sent to a recipient in the same site as where the originator resides or if a message reaches the recipient's home site through a messaging connector, the MTA must determine whether the message has reached its destination site. To check this information, the MTA examines the recipient's DN or X.400 O/R address as described earlier in this section. (See Figure 4-7.)

Mailboxes

If a message has been addressed to mailboxes residing on the local computer, the MTA passes that message to the local IS, which then delivers the message. Conversely, the MTA transmits a message to its destination MTAs through intrasite communication if the recipients reside on other servers within the same site. The remote MTAs will then transfer the messages to their local ISs for delivery.

Custom Recipients

Custom recipients reside in the directory as do other recipient objects, but they do not maintain a local message repository. Instead, custom recipients reference a foreign address somewhere outside the Exchange organization. If a message has been sent to a custom recipient, the MTA queries the DS for the underlying foreign recipient address. Once this address has been received, the routing process can start again and the message will be delivered to the appropriate messaging connector or gateway. The creation and management of custom recipients is covered in Chapter 5, "Creating and Managing Recipients."

Distribution Lists

If a message is sent to an e-mail address that represents a distribution list, the MTA expands the list to contain all recipients from the directory. The routing process is then restarted separately for each member. If more than one route is required in order to reach all recipients, multiple copies of the message are created before the MTA routes the message to the appropriate message queues. For example, the MTA creates two copies if some recipients reside in a remote site that is accessible through a Site Connector and other recipients are located on the Internet, which is accessible through an IMS. The purpose of distribution lists is covered in more detail in Chapter 5.

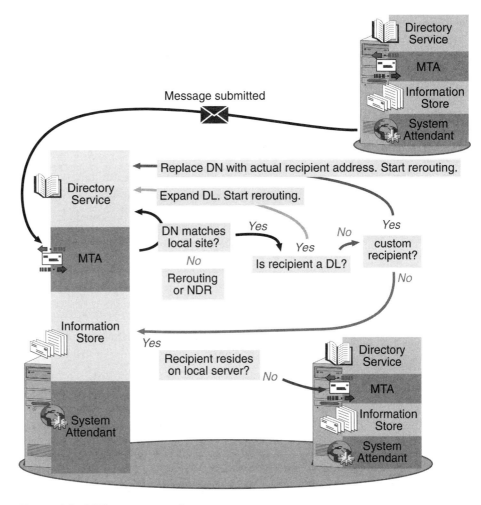

Figure 4-7. MTA message routing.

The MTA routing algorithm is as follows (as shown in Figure 4-7, on the previous page):

1. If the recipient is specified by a DN, the recipient's home site can be found as part of the DN.

2. The MTA compares the site name from the DN to the local site. If the two site names don't match, the message must be routed to its destination site.

3. If the part of the destination address that is interpreted as the site name matches the local site and the address refers to a custom recipient, the MTA retrieves the recipient's underlying address from the directory and restarts the routing process using the new address. In many cases, this involves routing to foreign messaging systems.

4. If the part of the destination address that is interpreted as the site name matches the local site and the recipient is a mailbox on the local Exchange Server computer, the MTA passes the message to the local IS for delivery to the recipient's mailbox.

5. If the part of the destination address that is interpreted as the site name matches the local site and the recipient is a mailbox on another computer in the same site, the MTA sends the message to the recipient's home MTA for delivery through RPCs.

6. If the recipient is specified by an O/R Name instead of a DN and the part of the O/R Name that is interpreted as the site name does not match the name of the local site, the MTA checks whether the address is in a valid X.400 format. The message will then be routed according to the GWART.

7. If the O/R Name is not valid, the message is returned to the sender as an NDR.

Review

1. Which server component is responsible for the exchange of information between Exchange Server computers in different sites?

   _____

   _____

2. What communication method is used between DSs within a single site?

   _____

3. Which message types are transferred by the MTA?

   _____

   _____

4. What is the advantage of the multimaster replication model?

_____

_____

_____

5. You have changed the configuration of a site, but the directory replication has not started immediately. How long will the DS wait before it notifies the other DSs in the site? What is the advantage of this delay?

_____

_____

_____

6. What is the purpose of Universal Sequence Numbers (USNs)?

_____

_____

7. What is the advantage of a common Site Services Account?

_____

_____

8. You are creating new mailboxes on a specific server. You want to send test messages to the new users, but your own mailbox resides on another server within the same site. How long will you have to wait until the new mailboxes appear in the address lists of your server?

_____

_____

_____

_____

9. Why do you need to use the same Site Services Account for all servers within a site?

_____

_____

_____

_____

10. Which Exchange Server components rely on the MTA to exchange information within a single site?

_____

_____

_____

11. You send an e-mail to a user on another server within your site. How does the MTA locate the final destination of the message?

_____

_____

_____

_____

12. What are the parts of a recipient's DN within an Exchange Server organization?

_____

_____

C H A P T E R   5

Creating and Managing Recipients

This chapter discusses the various kinds of recipient objects that can be found in an Exchange Server organization. All types of recipient objects commonly are grouped together in recipients containers that in turn are used to structure the server-based address lists of your organization.

Overview

Maintaining recipient objects is an essential part of the Exchange Server administration because recipient objects are the basic elements of address lists. Although a personal address book can also be used, users typically work with server-based address information (for example, the Global Address List) to specify the desired recipients of messages conveniently. Exchange Server uses recipient information such as the home server attribute of a mailbox not only to address interpersonal messages but also to deliver messages successfully. The DS maintains recipient objects and server-based address lists.

Lesson 1 of this chapter discusses the various recipient objects within an Exchange organization, that can be used to address e-mail messages. Also covered are mailboxes, custom recipients, distribution lists, and public folder objects.

Lesson 2 discusses creating and managing mailboxes, which usually are the most important recipient objects in an organization. You'll learn how they are created using the User Manager for Domains as well as the Microsoft Exchange Administrator program. You can also read about a valuable feature of the Administrator program, which assists in the task of creating multiple mailboxes in one step.

Lesson 3 of this chapter provides an introduction to distribution list management. You can read about the creation of distribution lists and how to configure them using the Administrator program.

Custom recipients are the topics of Lesson 4. These are useful if you want to maintain information about users that do not exist within your organization. The various types and properties of the custom recipients are discussed in this lesson.

Lesson 5 concludes this chapter with a discussion about the properties that all recipient objects have in common. In addition, you'll find answers to issues such as how to use templates for efficient mailbox creation, how to clean a mailbox administratively, and how to move a mailbox to another server.

This chapter includes seven practical exercises, which clarify the theoretical explanations about mailbox management and the creation of recipient containers, distribution lists, and custom recipients.

In the following lessons, you will be introduced to:

- Different types of Exchange Server recipients
- Creation and configuration of mailboxes
- Creation and configuration of distribution lists
- Creation and configuration of custom recipients
- Properties that recipient objects have in common
- Management of mailboxes, custom recipients, and distribution lists

Lesson 1: Types of Recipient Objects

Every resource that can receive e-mail messages must be referenced through a corresponding recipient object. The resource itself might reside physically either in your messaging network or outside the organization. The corresponding recipient objects, however, are always created on an Exchange Server to maintain a reference to the actual destination in the directory. Consequently, recipient objects are the elements used to build the server-based address lists.

This lesson introduces the different recipient objects as they can be used in an Exchange Server organization to create server-based address lists. (See Figure 5-1 on page 217.) Mailboxes, distribution lists, custom recipients, and public folders are the four classes of recipient objects at your disposal. A brief description of each recipient object is provided in this lesson, while more details are covered throughout this chapter. Maintaining public folders is also the topic of Chapter 12, "Creating and Managing Public Folders."

At the end of this lesson, you will be able to:

- Describe the differences between mailbox, custom recipient, distribution list, and public folder recipient objects

Estimated time to complete this lesson: 25 minutes

Considerations About Recipient Objects

A main task of an Exchange Server system is to maintain private and public user data. Private data such as personal e-mail messages are kept in mailboxes. Shared data, such as Microsoft Word documents of public interest, on the other hand, can be placed in public folders. Mailboxes and public folders are resources that can receive e-mail messages, Word documents, and other items, but because they are maintained by the IS, they are not, strictly speaking, recipient objects. As a matter of fact, recipient objects that correspond to mailboxes and public folders reside in the server's directory rather than in the IS.

Note A recipient object is a *reference* to a message repository, but it is not the repository itself.

Mailboxes

A messaging network such as an Exchange Server organization illustrates the concept of *asynchronous communication*. In contrast to synchronous communication, where people interact in real time (for example, on the telephone or in a chat session), asynchronous connections do not require the other person to be on line. You don't have to worry about whether a recipient has his or her messaging client running when you send an e-mail message to his or her address.

Server-based information repositories (also known as mailboxes in Exchange Server) are necessary to support asynchronous communication. When using your messaging client to send an e-mail message to another user, you are placing this message indirectly—by means of the services of Exchange Server—into that user's mailbox. In turn, recipients obtain the messages directly from their mailboxes using a messaging client as well. A recipient can read and download messages at any time, independent of the sending process.

Whenever you create a mailbox for a user of your organization, you create a corresponding mailbox recipient object as well. The mailbox itself resides in the Private Information Store on one computer only, but the DS will replicate the corresponding recipient object to all servers in your organization. This way, all servers in your organization will "learn" that a new mailbox exists somewhere. The fact that a particular mailbox object appears in the directories of all servers does not mean its content also resides on all servers.

By default, mailbox recipient objects appear in the server-based address lists of your users' messaging clients and in the Exchange Administrator program, although it is possible to hide them. However, if a mailbox recipient object is visible, it provides users with useful information about the recipient to whom the actual mailbox belongs. The maintenance of the mailbox recipient objects is also the maintenance of detailed Exchange user information.

It is difficult to distinguish between mailboxes and their corresponding recipient objects. You actually use the recipient object as it appears in the Administrator program to control the settings of its corresponding mailbox resource. It's acceptable to refer to both items as the mailbox and to think of them as a logical unit. For an illustration of this process, run this experiment: stop the IS service on NEWYORK-1, start the Exchange Administrator program, and then try to create a mailbox. As you know, the IS (stopped) maintains mailboxes while the DS (running) takes care of the mailboxes' recipient objects. You might find it hard to believe that you can create mailboxes when the IS isn't running, but this experiment proves that you have created a mailbox recipient object only. The mailbox itself, in turn, will be initialized in the IS the first time you log on using a messaging client.

Note Using the Administrator program, you will work primarily with mailbox recipient objects. Using the Microsoft Exchange Client or Microsoft Outlook, you can log on to the actual mailbox resource.

Distribution Lists

Distribution lists can be used to reference one or many recipients, but usually they represent a group of recipient objects. In fact, a distribution list can contain mailboxes, custom recipients, public folders, and encapsulated distribution lists. Instead of having you always address each recipient separately and directly, distribution lists allow you to conveniently send messages to any number of users at one time: simply select one address book entry instead of however many individuals are on your list. It is the task of the Exchange Server—the MTA to be exact—to resolve the distribution lists to deliver the messages to each recipient. The distribution list expansion mechanism is covered in Chapter 4.

Custom Recipients

Custom recipients can reference mailboxes that don't exist within your own messaging network, which means that they are not part of the Private or Public Information Store of an Exchange Server. Custom recipients are useful for connecting the organization to a foreign messaging system, such as MS Mail, Lotus cc:Mail, or Lotus Notes. The Directory Synchronization with these particular systems, for example, will automatically create a custom recipient object for each MS Mail, Lotus cc:Mail, or Lotus Notes user within the Exchange system. The MS Mail Directory Synchronization is explained in Chapter 18, "Connecting to Microsoft Mail and Schedule+ 1.0." Directory Synchronization with Lotus cc:Mail is discussed in Chapter 19, "Connector for Lotus cc:Mail," and Directory Synchronization with Lotus Notes is covered in Chapter 20, "Connector for Lotus Notes."

The Internet is another example of a foreign messaging system, and you will probably communicate often with others through an Internet connection. Using custom recipients, you can create a dedicated server-based address list for those businesses with whom your company communicates most often. Users in your organization will then be able to select partner references from the dedicated address list just as they would from any other address book using their Exchange Client or Outlook.

Public Folders

Public folders maintain messaging-related items just as do mailboxes, but they are available to all users in an organization (unless the administrator has limited the access to them). Using the Exchange Client or Outlook, users will typically post new information into a public folder. However, users can send messages to public folders as well because every public folder contains associated e-mail addresses.

The fact that public folders can be reached via e-mail has several advantages. For example, you can include these in distribution lists to maintain a filing system for e-mail communication. The addresses of public folders may also be useful if you want to receive messages from Internet list servers. Instead of subscribing to the list server with the e-mail address of your private mailbox, which might then become overloaded with messages of lesser importance, you can subscribe using the address of a public folder. All messages from the list server will then be delivered to the public folder where you can organize, group, or filter the information as appropriate. You can also specify age limits for public folder items to keep received information up to date and to keep the size of the public folder under control.

By default, all public folders are hidden from the Global Address List. To make them visible, launch the folder's property pages using the Administrator program. You can then switch to the **Advanced** property tab where the **Hide From Address Book** check box is provided. Clearing this check box enables users to select the public folder from the server-based address book as they would do for any other recipient object. Public folders are covered in detail in Chapter 12.

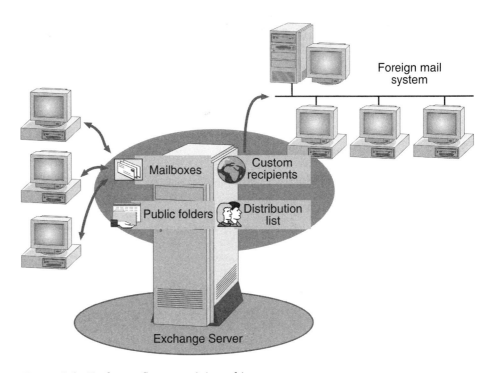

Figure 5-1. Exchange Server recipient objects.

The different types of Exchange recipients and their functions are as follows:

- Custom recipients, to point to a foreign address outside the organization
- Distribution lists, for convenient addressing of recipients; all kinds of recipient objects can be members of distribution lists
- Mailboxes, to provide mail delivery and e-mail repositories for Exchange users
- Public folders, to provide a data repository for public access (it's possible to send data to public folders as well as post information in the folders)

Lesson 2: Creating and Configuring Mailboxes

Mailboxes are a key feature of every messaging system. Every Exchange user, for example, must have a mailbox to send and receive messages. Therefore, the creation and configuration of mailboxes is one of the main duties of an Exchange Server administrator. This task is made easier with the tools and extensions that come with the Exchange Administrator program.

This lesson covers the creation and management of mailbox objects using the User Manager for Domains, the Exchange Administrator program, and additional tools that allow you to create multiple mailboxes at one time. Mailbox-specific configuration tasks are also explained.

Five practical exercises are included in this lesson to clarify the theoretical, explanations. The exercises will guide you through the mailbox management steps, such as the assignment of permissions, the creation of mailboxes using the User Manager or the Administrator program, and the application of Import features.

At the end of this lesson, you will be able to:

- Create mailboxes using the User Manager for Domains
- Create and configure mailboxes within the Exchange Administrator program
- Identify mailbox-related administration tasks

Estimated time to complete this lesson: 45 minutes

Creating Mailboxes Using the Microsoft Windows NT User Manager for Domains

The User Manager for Domains is the primary tool used to create and manage user accounts in a Microsoft Windows NT domain. Every user must have a Windows NT domain account in order to log on and access network resources. If a user is to participate in an Exchange Server organization he or she also needs a mailbox, so it is desirable to create both the domain account and the mailbox for a user at the same time.

User Manager for Domains Extension

The User Manager for Domains is a good place to create simultaneously both the domain account and the mailbox, but it needs a corresponding extension to support the creation of mailbox objects. This extension, plugged in during the installation of the Exchange Administrator program, can be found in a file named Mailumx.dll. This extension allows you to create a new mailbox at the same time that you create a Windows NT domain account by employing a user interface that is the same one displayed in the Administrator program. (See Figure 5-2.) The extension provides the link between the User Manager for Domains and the mailbox property pages. In addition, a new User Manager for Domains menu labeled **Exchange** offers several configuration options, such as settings for the default Exchange Server and a default Recipients container.

To implement the DLL, the Exchange Server Setup program creates a reference in the Registry. The relevant entry can be found under:

```
HKEY_LOCAL_MACHINE
    \SOFTWARE
        \Microsoft
            \Windows NT
                \CurrentVersion
                    \Network
                        \UMAddOns
```

The User Manager for Domain extension will also remove a corresponding mailbox at the same time you delete a Windows NT account.

Windows NT Domain Management

Any Windows NT administrator can manage the security account database of a domain, but that doesn't necessarily mean that he or she will also be able to configure mailboxes. As mentioned in Chapter 1, not every Windows NT administrator is necessarily an Exchange Server administrator. To create new mailboxes and Windows NT accounts using the extended User Manager for Domains, the administrator must have the rights of a Permissions Admin within the Exchange Server organization in addition to the regular administrative Windows NT permissions. The steps to designate new Exchange Server administrators are outlined in Exercise 5, "Assigning Exchange Administrator Permissions."

A mailbox is associated with the corresponding Windows NT account through its **Primary Windows NT Account** attribute. This attribute can be determined automatically, as can the **Alias** name and the **Display** name. The **Alias** name refers to the Windows NT user name. The **Display** name is derived from the full name of the Windows NT account. The administrative **Notes** attribute displays the user account description. You can also specify manually all available additional properties for mailboxes, such as delivery restrictions, delivery options, message sizes, and storage limits.

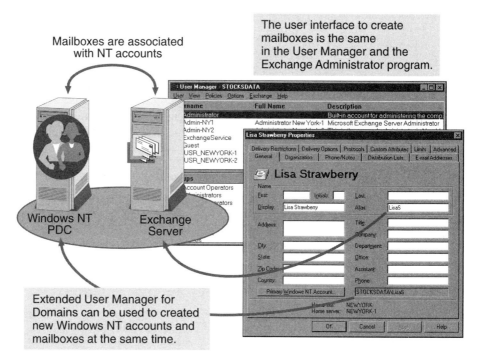

Figure 5-2. Mailbox creation using the User Manager for Domains.

The rights required to administer Windows NT and Exchange Server at the same time are as follows:

- Membership in the Windows NT **Domain Admins** group, to create and delete Windows NT domain accounts

- **Permissions Admin** for the <Organization>, <Site>, and **Configuration** objects, to create and delete mailboxes

Exercise 5: Assigning Exchange Administrator Permissions

An administrator who wants to add new mailboxes to a site must have the privileges associated with the role of a Permissions Admin for the <Organization>, the <Site>, and the **Configuration** containers at the Exchange level. Additionally, administrative rights for the Windows NT domain are required to configure the Windows NT accounts.

Estimated time to complete this exercise: 15 minutes

Description

In this exercise, you will designate additional Exchange Server administrator accounts. It is suggested that you configure a local Windows NT group as a container for Exchange administrators to simplify the management of administrator accounts.

- Task 5a describes the steps for configuring the Exchange Administrator program to display the available roles and rights for Exchange Server objects.

- Task 5b describes the steps for allowing all members of a Windows NT local group to administer organization-level properties of an Exchange Server organization.

- Task 5c describes the steps for allowing all members of a Windows NT local group to administer site-level properties of an Exchange Server organization.

- Task 5d describes the steps for allowing all members of a Windows NT local group to administer Configuration container-level properties of a site within an Exchange Server organization.

Prerequisites

- Ensure that at least one Exchange Server is running in your site.

- The Exchange Administrator program must be installed locally.

- You must be logged on to the Windows NT domain as the Exchange Server's main administrator (the person who installed the Exchange Server). If you have performed Exercises 1 through 4 as described in Chapter 2, this will be the account Admin-NY1 of the Domain STOCKSDATA.

Task 5a: Showing Permission Roles

1. Start the **Microsoft Exchange Administrator** program from the **Microsoft Exchange** program group.

2. Enter the name of your server (*NEWYORK-1*) in the **Connect To Server** dialog box or select the server using the **Browse** button.

3. Select the **Set As Default** check box, and then click **OK**.

Note If you have already started the Exchange Administrator program and have connected to your server prior to this point, you might be connected to your server automatically without executing step 2 and step 3.

---

4. On the **Tools** menu, click **Options**.

5. In the **Options** dialog box, select the **Permissions** tab.

6. Select the **Display Rights For Roles On Permissions Page** check box.

7. Click **OK**.

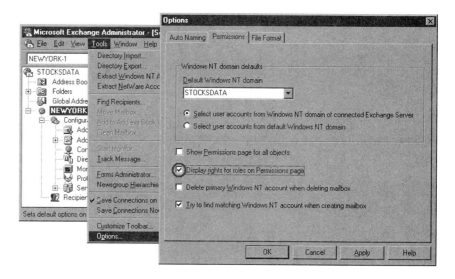

Task 5b: Configuring Organization Permissions

1. In the Administrator program, select the <Organization> object (**STOCKSDATA**), open the **File** menu, and click the **Properties** command.

2. In the **Properties** dialog box for the object **STOCKSDATA**, select the **Permissions** tab.

3. Click **Add** to launch the **Add Users And Groups** dialog box.

4. In the **Names** box, click the local group **Local-NY1**, and then click **Add**.

5. Click **OK**.

6. A **Microsoft Exchange Administrator** dialog box appears indicating that local groups can be used only in the domain where they are created, so members of this group will not be able to administer this resource from other domains. Click **OK**.

7. Notice that **STOCKSDATA\Local-NY1** has been added with the role of **Admin**.

8. In the **Windows NT Accounts With Permissions** box, verify that **STOCKSDATA\Local-NY1** is selected.

9. In the **Roles** list, select **Permissions Admin**.

10. Click **OK**.

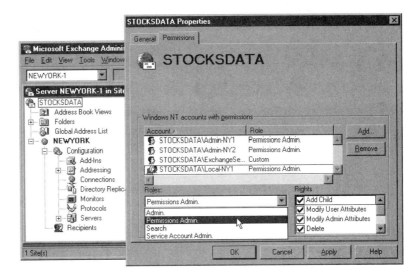

Task 5c: Configuring Site Permissions

1. In the Administrator program, select the <Site> object (**NEWYORK**), open the **File** menu, and click the **Properties** command.

2. Select the **Permissions** tab in the **NEWYORK Properties** dialog box.

3. Click **Add** to launch the **Add Users And Groups** dialog box.

4. In the **Names** box, click **Local-NY1**, and then click **Add**.

5. Click **OK**.

6. A **Microsoft Exchange Administrator** dialog box appears, stating that local groups can be used only in the domain where they are created, so members of this group will not be able to administer this resource from other domains. Click **OK**.

7. Notice that **STOCKSDATA\Local-NY1** has been added with the role of **Admin**.

8. In the **Windows NT Accounts With Permissions** box, verify that **Local-NY1** is selected, and then, in the **Roles** list, click **Permissions Admin**.

9. Click **OK**.

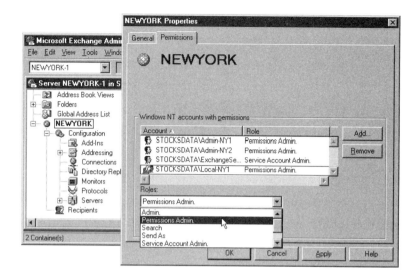

Task 5d: Configuring Configuration Container Permissions

1. Expand the <Site> object **NEWYORK** if necessary.

2. Highlight the **Configuration** object, open the **File** menu, and then click **Properties**.

3. The **Configuration Properties** dialog box appears. Select the **Permissions** tab.

4. Click **Add** to launch the **Add Users And Groups** dialog box.

5. In the **Names** box, click **Local-NY1**, and then click **Add**.

6. Click **OK**.

7. A **Microsoft Exchange Administrator** dialog box appears, stating that local groups can be used only in the domain where they are created, so members of this group will not be able to administer this resource from other domains. Click **OK**.

8. Notice that **STOCKSDATA\Local-NY1** has been added with the role of **Admin**.

9. In the **Windows NT Accounts With Permissions** box, verify that **STOCKSDATA\Local-NY1** is selected, and then, in the **Roles** list, click **Permissions Admin**.

10. Click **OK**.

11. On the **File** menu, click **Exit**.

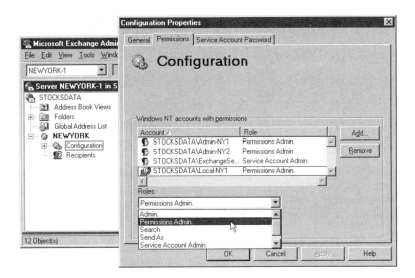

Review

To display permissions and roles for Exchange Server objects, open the associated **Permissions** property page. The check boxes that allow you to configure the way **Permissions** property pages are displayed in general can be found using the **Options** command under the **Tools** menu and by clicking the displayed **Permissions** tab.

Administrative privileges within the organization can be granted to single Windows NT users as well as to user groups. Using a local Exchange Administrator group simplifies the management of administrator accounts. Instead of configuring Exchange privileges at organization, site, and configuration levels for each administrator separately, it is sufficient to add and remove Windows NT accounts to and from the local group to grant and withdraw administrative privileges. A local group, however, is bound to the domain where it has been created.

Exercise 6: Creating a Microsoft Exchange Mailbox Using User Manager for Domains

For this exercise it is assumed that the Exchange Administrator program has been installed on the local computer, which implies that the User Manager for Domains has been extended through the Mailumx.dll. This extension allows you to create and administer a Windows NT account and its associated mailbox at the same time.

Estimated time to complete this exercise: 15 minutes

Description

In this exercise, you will use the User Manager for Domains to create both a Windows NT account and its associated mailbox at the same time. The new user account can be used as a template for other accounts that will later be added to the Exchange Server. You will use this account as a template in Exercise 9, "Creating New Mailboxes Using Directory Import," later in this chapter.

- Task 6 describes the steps for creating a template account that contains common information. This account can later be used to create other accounts within the organization. Because this account is meant to be a template only, it will be disabled at the Windows NT level so that it cannot be used to log on to Windows NT.

Prerequisites

- Log on as Admin-NY1 to NEWYORK-1 to complete this exercise.

- Extend the User Manager for Domains with the Mailumx.dll. In other words, the Exchange Administrator program must have been installed locally.

Task 6: Creating a Windows NT User Account

1. Click the **Start** button, point to **Programs**, point to **Administrative Tools (Common)**, and then click **User Manager For Domains**.

2. On the **User** menu, click **New User**.

3. Complete the **New User** dialog box using the following information:

In this box	You supply
Username	*LisaS*
Full Name	*Lisa Strawberry*

In this box	You supply
Password	*lisas*
Confirm Password	*lisas*

4. Clear the **User Must Change Password At Next Logon** check box.

5. Select the **Password Never Expires** check box.

6. Select the **Account Disabled** check box, and then click **Add**.

7. A dialog box to create a new mailbox for the user appears. Notice the **Display** name, **Alias** name, **Primary Windows NT Account**, **Home Site**, and **Home Server** information.

Note It's possible that a **Connect To Server** dialog box will appear before you are able to create the new mailbox. In this case, enter the server name *NEWYORK-1* and then click **OK** to complete step 7.

8. Select the **Phone/Notes** tab.

9. In the **Business** box, type *See HR for number*.

10. In the **Fax** box, type *1-800-555-1212*, and then click **OK**.

11. A blank **New User** dialog box appears.

12. Click **Close**.

13. Exit the **User Manager for Domains**.

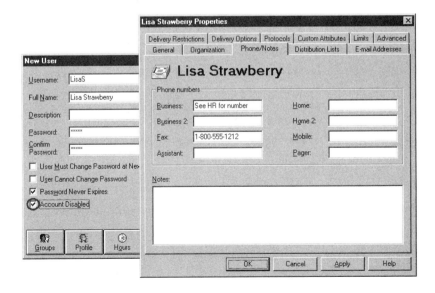

Review

The original User Manager for Domains can be used to create Windows NT accounts. It will be extended during the installation of the Exchange Administrator program to allow you to create both Windows NT accounts and associated Exchange mailboxes at the same time.

The user interface of the User Manager for Domains displays the mailbox properties exactly as the Exchange Administrator program does, which makes it possible to specify all the desired mailbox properties within the extended User Manager for Domains. You must have the rights of a Permissions Admin within a particular site (<Organization>, <Site>, and **Configuration** containers) to successfully add mailboxes to an Exchange Server.

Creating and Configuring Mailboxes Using the Administrator Program

The Exchange Administrator program is the most important tool for configuring and maintaining the organization, sites, and servers. For example, you'll use it to create mailboxes, custom recipients, and distribution lists. The Exchange Administrator program is a true Windows NT program that cannot be installed on other platforms like Microsoft Windows 95. You'll find more information about the Exchange Administrator program in Chapter 8, "Managing Server Configuration."

Mailbox Creation

You can create a new mailbox through the **File** menu of the Administrator program by selecting the **New Mailbox** command to display the **Properties** dialog box of the new mailbox. Using this dialog box, you can specify all available mailbox properties, including the **Alias** name and the **Display** name. An alternative to the **New Mailbox** command on the **File** menu is the **New Mailbox** button on the Administrator program's toolbar. You can also create mailboxes using the Import tool, which is discussed in the section, "Extract and Import Features," later in this lesson.

Mailbox Configuration

To configure a mailbox successfully, some—but fortunately not all—mailbox properties must be specified. However, additional attributes can be useful: it's simply more convenient for the users if they are provided with phone numbers, locations, and custom attributes for each recipient throughout the address book. The additional attributes might be helpful in distinguishing recipients with identical display names. Other property pages refer to the mailbox maintenance, which is covered in the section, "Mailbox Maintenance Tasks," later in this lesson.

Essential Configuration Parameters

The most important parameters—the **Alias** name and the **Display** name—can be controlled through the **General** property page of each mailbox object. The **Primary Windows NT Account** must also be specified on this property page. Although it's possible to create items that do not have a **Primary Windows NT Account**, all three properties are mandatory if a user wants to use a mailbox. If the intended Windows NT account does not exist at the time of the mailbox creation, it can be created using the Administrator program. (See Figure 5-3.)

Optional Parameters

The remaining attributes are not essential for the creation of a mailbox, but they can be useful for documenting the structure of your company through the server-based address book. You can specify the recipient's address, title, office location, assistant, and other information on the **General** page. By using the **Organization** property page, you can record information about the manager and the direct reports of a mailbox owner.

In addition to the telephone number you entered on the **General** page, you can also specify several telephone numbers and added notes using the **Phone/Notes** property page. If all this information is still not sufficient to meet your needs, you can define custom attributes using the **DS Site Configuration** object in the site's **Configuration** container. These attributes can be set through the **Custom Attributes** property page of each recipient object. You will define a custom attribute in Exercise 22, "Setting a Custom Attribute for Several Recipients," in Chapter 8.

Further information regarding the mailbox configuration is provided in the section, "Mailbox Creation Tasks," later in this lesson.

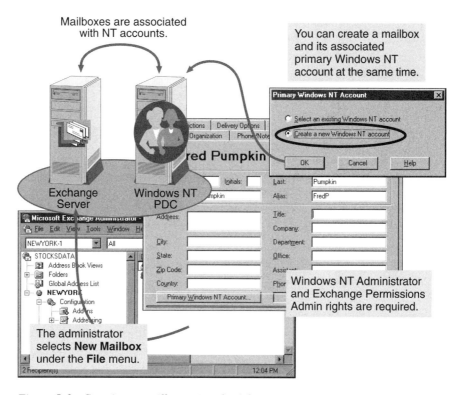

Figure 5-3. Creating a mailbox using the Administrator program.

Mailbox property pages that allow you to specify detailed recipient information are as follows:

- **General**; to define **Alias** name, **Display** name, **Primary Windows NT Account** and other user-specific information

- **Organization**; to enter information about managers and direct reports

- **Phone/Notes**; to provide information about private and business telephone numbers as well as short notes about the recipient

- **Custom Attributes**; to specify additional custom information

Exercise 7: Creating an Exchange Mailbox Using Exchange Administrator

The Exchange Administrator program is the main application for administering an Exchange Server organization, but not every Exchange Server setup option necessarily installs the Administrator program. By default, only the

Complete/Custom and **Typical** installation types copy the required files to the computer's hard disk. Fortunately, Setup enables you to add the Exchange Administrator program to the current installation at any time. In other words, the maintenance mode can be used later to install the Exchange Administrator program. Once it has been installed, its binary file (Admin.exe) can be found in the Exchsrvr\Bin directory. Chapter 2 provides more information about the various available installation options.

Estimated time to complete this exercise: 15 minutes

Description

In this exercise, you will use the Exchange Administrator program to create a new mailbox for an already existing Windows NT account. You can use the **General** property page of the new recipient to select an already existing Primary Windows NT Account. Alternatively, you can create new Windows NT accounts at the same time you add new mailboxes to an Exchange Server. In order to configure the mailboxes successfully, you must have the permissions of a Windows NT domain administrator. (See Figure 5-3.)

- Task 7 describes the steps for creating a mailbox for an existing Windows NT account using the Exchange Administrator program.

Prerequisites

- The PDC and the home Exchange Server for the new mailbox must be available.

- Log on as Admin-NY1 to NEWYORK-1 to complete this exercise.

Task 7: Create a Mailbox Using Microsoft Exchange Administrator

1. Click the **Start** button, point to **Programs**, point to **Microsoft Exchange**, and then click **Microsoft Exchange Administrator**.

   Note If you have already completed Exercise 5, the administrator program will display the administrative window of the server **NEWYORK-1** automatically after startup.

2. On the **File** menu, click **New Mailbox**.

3. If a **Microsoft Exchange Administrator** dialog box appears indicating that recipients cannot be created in the selected container, click **OK** to switch to the **Recipients** container of site NEWYORK.

4. The **Properties** dialog box appears.

5. On the **General** property page, type the following information:

In this box	You supply
First	*Fred*
Last	*Pumpkin*
Display	*Fred Pumpkin* (filled in automatically)
Alias	*FredP* (filled in automatically)

6. Click **Primary Windows NT Account**.

7. Make sure that **Select An Existing Windows NT Account** is activated, and then click **OK** to display the **Add User Or Group** dialog box.

8. In the **Names** box, click the account **Admin-NY1**.

9. Click **Add**.

10. Click **OK**.

11. Click **OK** again.

12. On the **File** menu of the Administrator program, click **Exit**.

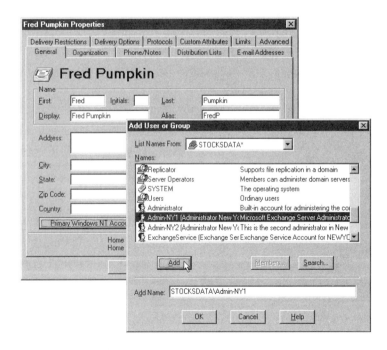

Review

The Exchange Administrator program is the main tool for adding new recipient objects to a site. It can be used to configure new objects or to change the properties of already existing objects. One of the most important properties of every mailbox is the **Primary Windows NT Account**. The intended user will not be able to log on to the mailbox if his or her Windows NT account has not been specified as the primary account. To successfully create a mailbox the administrator is required to define the **Alias** name and the **Display** name as well. Additional information can be entered at the time of the mailbox creation, but is not mandatory and can be supplied at a later time.

Extract, Export, and Import Features

Creating multiple mailboxes using the **New Mailbox** command of the Administrator program's **File** menu can be an arduous task. Creating mailboxes for a few users may be acceptable, but it's not a good use of time to create mailboxes manually for 20, 50, 100, or more users. The creation of many mailboxes at the same time typically will be an issue if you are implementing Exchange Server 5.5 into an existing computer network (for example, Windows NT or Novell NetWare), where configured user accounts exist. Fortunately, the Administrator program provides import and extract capabilities that can help significantly with the task of mailbox creation.

Extracting Account Lists

The extraction utility of the Administrator program allows you to gain information from the user account databases of Novell NetWare servers, Microsoft LAN Manager systems, and Windows NT domain controllers. This information is written to a Comma-Separated-Values file (.CSV) that can then be used to import the accounts into the Exchange Server. In other words, once you have created an import file, you can create mailboxes for each existing networking user in one step.

The account information can be extracted using either the **Extract Windows NT Account List** or the **Extract NetWare Account List** command. Both commands are located on the Administrator program's **Tools** menu.

Windows NT and LAN Manager Accounts

You will use the **Extract Windows NT Account List** command to extract user account information from available Windows NT domain controllers. You must be logged on to the Windows NT domain—Domain User privileges are sufficient in this case—from where you want to extract the user account information. The **Extract Windows NT Account List** command also allows you to extract user account information from LAN Manager servers.

Novell NetWare Accounts

The **Extract NetWare Account List** can be used to retrieve user account information from existing Novell NetWare 2.x, 3.x, or 4.x servers. Novell NetWare 4.x servers must run with the bindery emulation enabled because the extraction tool cannot work directly with NetWare Directory Services (NDS) information. You must be logged on with supervisor rights to the Novell NetWare server from where you want to get the user information. The configuration of an Exchange Server computer in a Novell NetWare environment is covered in Chapter 17, "Microsoft Exchange Clients in a NetWare Environment."

The Directory Import Command

One you have extracted the desired account information into a .CSV file, you can launch the Import tool of the Administrator program to complete the mailbox creation task. You will need to open the **Tools** menu again, but this time you will select **Directory Import**. You can then specify the desired import file (.CSV) through the **Directory Import** dialog box to automatically create the mailboxes for all users listed in that file.

Creating Windows NT Accounts

Because you have the option to create Windows NT user accounts along with their mailboxes, you can manually specify mailboxes in an import file for which no associated Windows NT user account exists so far and import the information using the Directory Import feature. The required Windows NT accounts and their corresponding mailboxes will be conveniently and automatically created in this manner at the same time.

Note To create Windows NT accounts, you must have Domain Administrator privileges at the Windows NT level.

Modifying Mailbox Properties

If you further examine the **Tools** menu, you'll find the **Directory Export** command, which allows you to export existing mailboxes, custom recipients, and distribution lists into a .CSV file based on their recipients container. For example, you may select the Global Address List under **Container** in the **Directory Export** dialog box to export all existing mailboxes within your organization. You can then modify the specified .CSV file using any text editor or spreadsheet application, such as Microsoft Excel. This allows you to adjust attributes easily for multiple recipient objects. Once you have saved the modifications, you can reimport the modified .CSV file to update all mailboxes. In other words, the combination of the **Directory Export** and the **Directory Import** command enables multiple recipient objects at one time.

Import Header Tool

The Import Header tool is an additional utility that allows you to create .CSV file templates. These import file templates will specify the attributes you want to export using the **Directory Export** command. Mailbox attributes and the attributes of distribution lists and custom recipients can then be modified and reimported using the **Directory Import** option. The Import Header tool is included in the Microsoft BackOffice Resource Kit and is named Header.exe.

Note The DS must be running before you start the Import Header tool. This utility communicates with the Directory to obtain information about available object attributes.

Exporting Attributes

The Administrator program's **Directory Export** feature does not automatically export all available attributes of a recipient object. Instead, only a subset of common properties is exported without further configuration. If you want to obtain a specific attribute that is not exported by default, such as the **Secondary-Proxy-Addresses** attribute, you must first create an import header file using the Import Header tool. Import header files are simply empty .CSV files, but they already contain the first line that specifies the properties you want to receive. For example:

```
Object-Class,Display Name,E-mail Addresses,Secondary-
Proxy-Addresses
```

The Import Header tool will list all available attributes that you can select by a click of the mouse.

Once you have created a .CSV file that contains all the desired attributes, you can begin to export the recipient objects. Within the **Directory Export** dialog box, click the **Export File** button and then select the created import header file. The Administrator program will read this file to receive the list of specified attributes before it launches the export process. All specified attributes will be exported using this file. They can then be modified and reimported as usual. (See Figure 5-4.)

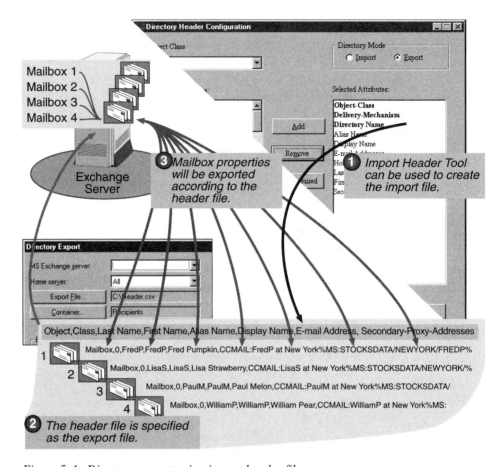

Figure 5-4. Directory export using import header files.

The advantages of Directory Import, Export, and Extract capabilities are that they:

- Allow for the extraction of all properties of an object within the Exchange directory using import header files

- Allow you to extract existing user accounts from Novell NetWare, LAN Manager, and Windows NT networks

- Allow the simultaneous modification of multiple mailboxes

- Can be used to create many mailboxes in a single step

- Allow easy and partially-automatic property adjustment through Excel

Exercise 8: Creating a New Recipients Container

Recipients containers allow you to group recipient objects together within the directory. They have the advantage of providing a structured view within the address book of a site. In other words, you can use the recipients containers to create more sophisticated address book structures. Unfortunately, a mailbox cannot be moved to another recipients container once it has been created within a container.

Estimated time to complete this exercise: 15 minutes

Description

In this exercise, you will create a recipients container using the Exchange Administrator program. The new container will later be used to import mailboxes to group them together.

- Task 8 describes the steps for creating a new recipients container.

Prerequisites

- Log on as Admin-NY1 to NEWYORK-1 to complete this exercise.

Task 8: Creating a New Recipients Container

1. Start the Exchange Administrator program and make sure that it connects the server **NEWYORK-1**.

2. Select the site object (**NEWYORK**).

3. On the **File** menu, point to **New Other**, and then select **Recipients Container**.

4. Complete the **Properties** dialog box using the following information:

In this box	You supply
Display name	*NEWYORK-1 Accounts*
Directory name	*Accounts on NEWYORK-1*

5. Click **OK**.

6. Notice that the **NEWYORK-1 Accounts** container appears in the left pane of the administration window under the site object, at the same level as the two default containers **Configuration** and **Recipients**.

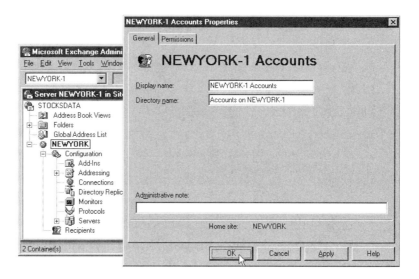

Review

Recipients containers can be added to the directory using the Administrator program. New containers can be placed at the same level as the original **Recipients** container of the site or under an existing recipients container. These allow you to structure the address book by grouping related recipients together.

Exercise 9: Creating New Mailboxes Using Directory Import

The **Directory Import** feature of the Exchange Administrator program offers a comfortable way to create multiple mailboxes, custom recipients, and distribution lists and allows you to modify existing ones. The bases of the directory import are import files, which contain the information to create or modify the recipient objects. These import files can be created manually or through the Extraction and Export features of the Administrator program.

Estimated time to complete this exercise: 25 minutes

Description

In this exercise, you will create new mailboxes for existing Windows NT accounts using the directory extract and import features of the Administrator program. It is recommended that you create several Windows NT accounts individually in your test environment before you begin this exercise.

- Task 9a describes the steps for extracting the Windows NT accounts into a .CSV file for editing and importing.

- Task 9b describes the steps for editing the resulting .CSV file. Specifically, you'll remove accounts that are already associated with mailboxes or that do not need a mailbox.

- Task 9c describes the steps for automatically creating mailboxes based on the information derived from the .CSV file.

Prerequisites

- Log on as Admin-NY1 to NEWYORK-1 to complete this exercise. In order to import—and therefore create—new mailboxes you require the rights of an Exchange Permissions Admin.

- Make sure the PDC is available.

Task 9a: Extracting Windows NT Accounts

1. Start the **Microsoft Exchange Administrator** program and verify that you are connected to server **NEWYORK-1**.

2. On the **Tools** menu, click **Extract Windows NT Account List**.

3. In the **Windows NT User Extraction** dialog box, verify that the Windows NT domain is **STOCKSDATA** and that the domain controller is **NEWYORK-1**.

4. Click **Browse**.

5. In the **File Name** box, type *NTIMPORT* and then click **Save** to specify a file named Ntimport.csv in the Exchsrvr\Bin directory (default directory), which will be created in the following step.

6. On the **Windows NT User Extraction** dialog box, click **OK**.

7. A message box appears, stating that the extraction of Windows NT user account information was completed without errors.

8. Click **OK**.

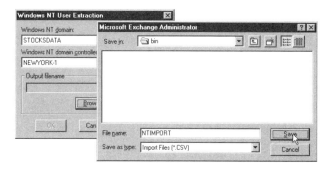

Task 9b: Preparing the Ntimport.csv File for Directory Import

1. Click the **Start** button, and then click **Run**.

2. In the **Open** box, type *notepad c:\EXCHSRVR\BIN\NTIMPORT.CSV*.

3. Check the content and make modifications as necessary (for example, delete the references to **ExchangeService**, **Guest**, **IUSR_NEWYORK-1**, **IUSR_NEWYORK-2**, and **LisaS**).

4. Save the changes to the file, and then exit **Notepad**.

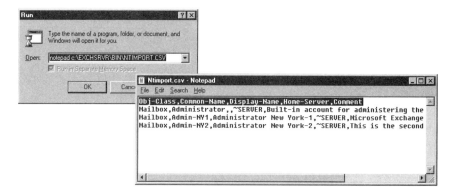

Task 9c: Using Directory Import to Add New Recipients

1. In the **Microsoft Exchange Administrator** program, on the **Tools** menu, click the **Directory Import** command.

2. In the **Directory Import** dialog box, verify that the **Windows NT Domain** is **STOCKSDATA** and that the **MS Exchange Server** is **NEWYORK-1**.

3. Click **Container** to launch the **Directory Import Container** dialog box.

4. Select **NEWYORK-1 Accounts**, and then click **OK**.

5. Select the **Always Use Selected Container** option button.

6. Click **Recipient Template**, and then click **Lisa Strawberry**.

7. Click **OK**.

8. Click **Import File**.

9. Select the file NTIMPORT.CSV that was created in Task 9a, and then click **Open**.

10. In the **Directory Import** dialog box click **Import**.

11. A message box appears stating that the directory import was completed without errors.

12. Click **OK**.

13. In the Exchange Administrator program click the recipients container **NEWYORK-1 Accounts** to view all imported recipients.

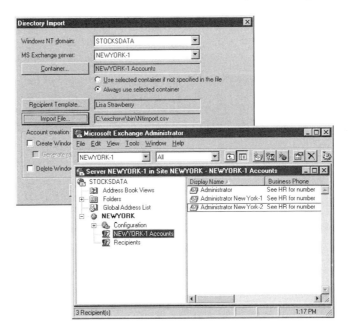

Review

The import file provides an easy way to adjust settings and properties for multiple recipient objects at virtually the same time. Once all the necessary information has been specified, the Administrator program can be used to import mailboxes, custom recipients, and other objects directly from the file into the Exchange directory. Recipients can be created in any existing recipients container such as the one you created in Exercise 8.

Mailbox Maintenance Tasks

As mentioned earlier in the section, "Creating and Configuring Mailboxes Using the Administrator Program," the **Alias** name, **Display** name, and **Primary Windows NT Account** are the essential mailbox parameters, although the **Primary Windows NT Account** is not absolutely necessary for mailbox creation. These parameters are displayed on the **General** property page along with other settings that can be used to provide detailed recipient information via the address lists of an organization. You can also use the **Organization**, **Phone/Notes**, and **Custom Attributes** property pages to maintain valuable information about users. While many mailbox attributes serve only to provide information, others have a more administrative function. You will work primarily with the property pages labeled **Distribution Lists**, **E-Mail Addresses**, **Delivery Restrictions**, **Delivery Options**, **Permissions**, **Protocols**, **Limits**, and the **Advanced** property page to manage mailbox resources within the Administrator program. All types of recipient objects have the **Distribution Lists**, **E-Mail Addresses**, **Delivery Restrictions**, and **Permissions** pages in common; their functions are covered in Lesson 5, "Recipient Object Management," later in this chapter.

Hiding a Mailbox and Other Advanced Properties

Exchange Server supports hidden mailboxes that do not appear in any address lists. You can, for example, hide administrative gateway accounts or any other mailbox that you might have created for a specific purpose. To do this, use the **Advanced** property page to select the **Hide From Address Book** option.

Note You can send e-mail messages to a hidden mailbox if you know the e-mail address, although a reference does not appear in any server-based address book.

If you examine the **Advanced** property page, you will find several other important configuration settings, so you'll be able to specify a simple display name, determine trust levels, define online listings information for the Microsoft Internet Locator Service (ILS), and determine an Outlook Web

Access server name. The Outlook Web Access server name, for example, allows you to specify an Outlook Web Access server that will be accessed to launch custom forms and meeting requests. This is necessary if users want to open meeting requests and custom forms messages using a POP3 or IMAP4 client, since these clients use Outlook Web Access to support extended forms. POP3 and IMAP4 clients display forms items as messages containing an URL that points to the Outlook Web Access server.

Changing the Home Server

A user's home server is the Exchange Server computer that maintains his or her mailbox. The home server attribute can be determined on the **Advanced** property page. (See Figure 5-5.) It can be changed in order to move a particular mailbox to another server in the same site. The process of moving a mailbox is covered in detail in Lesson 5, "Recipient Object Management," later in this chapter.

Delegating Access

The **Delivery Options** property page allows you to configure **Send On Behalf Of** permissions and alternate recipients. The owner of a mailbox listed with the **Give Send On Behalf Of Permission To** option will be able to send messages in place of the actual user. This option is useful, for instance, if an assistant needs to send messages on behalf of a manager. Likewise, you can use the **Delivery Options** property page to define an **Alternate Recipient**, who receives the messages that have been sent to the selected mailbox. The **Deliver Messages To Both Recipient And Alternate Recipient** option allows you to fine-tune the **Alternate Recipient** setting.

Internet Protocols

Exchange Server offers flexible access to its resources through the HTTP, LDAP, NNTP, POP3, and IMAP4 Internet messaging protocols. By default, all supported Internet protocols are enabled. To disable the protocols selectively or to specify configuration settings on a per-mailbox basis, you can switch to the **Protocols** property page. The Internet protocol support of Exchange Server 5.5 is covered in Chapter 11, "Internet Protocols."

Mailbox Quotas

Exchange Server 5.5 extends the options to set mailbox storage and message size limits, so it's logical that version 5.5 also introduces a new property page labeled **Limits** to allow you to set quotas independently of the IS defaults on a per-mailbox basis. (Exchange Server 5.0 provided several quota options on the **Advanced** property page.)

Previous versions of Exchange Server have included the options to set maximum values for outgoing and incoming message sizes for mailboxes. The same is true for the IS storage limits **Issue Warning (K)** and **Prohibit Send (K)**. The **Issue Warning (K)** setting determines at which mailbox size (in KB) a user will receive automatic warning messages that indicate the mailbox has exceeded its permitted size. The **Prohibit Send (K)** option, in turn, allows you to set a second limit, which prohibits the user from sending messages until he or she deletes or downloads messages from the server in an effort to decrease the sever-based mailbox size. Exchange Server 5.5 also features the **Prohibit Send And Receive (K)** option, which restricts the mailbox user even more than does the **Prohibit Send (K)** option. A user would not be allowed to participate in e-mail messaging until the mailbox size is decreased. It is advisable to set storage limits according to the following formula: **Issue Warning (K) < Prohibit Send (K) < Prohibit Send And Receive (K)**.

Deleted Items Recovery

Another interesting option that has been included in Exchange Server 5.5 is the **Deleted Items Retention Time** option. This setting specifies the number of days deleted items are held in a mailbox until they are deleted permanently. This setting also makes it possible to prevent permanent deletion until the IS has been backed up. By default, general Private Information Store settings will be applied, but you can override these settings on a per-mailbox basis on the **Limits** property page if you want. As long as the number of days of the retention time is not exceeded, deleted messages are not permanently removed. To put it plainly, a user running Outlook version 8.03 can recover those deleted items without the need of administrative intervention, as they will not yet have been permanently deleted.

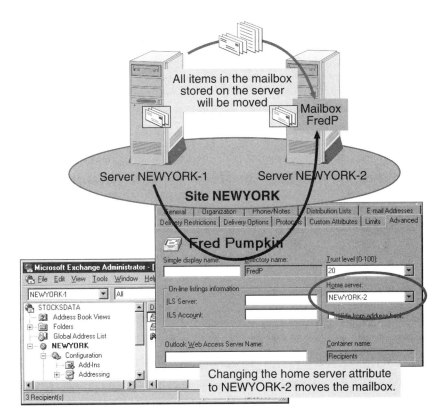

Figure 5-5. Changing the home server attribute.

The most important additional mailbox property pages and their functions are as follows:

- **Advanced**; to define a simple display name, hide the recipient from the address book, determine the home server, set the trust level, and provide several other options

- **Delivery Options**; to designate a mailbox delegate and to configure an alternate recipient

- **Limits**; to set mailbox limits independently of the IS defaults

- **Protocols**; to configure HTTP, LDAP, NNTP, IMAP4, and POP3 settings on a per-mailbox basis

Lesson 3: Creating and Configuring Distribution Lists

In addition to providing a convenient way to address multiple users at one time, distribution lists can also provide a way to reflect to some degree the structure of a company in terms of its departments and project groups. A nice feature of distribution lists is that you can transfer the responsibilities of their management to each particular team: your valuable time doesn't have to be consumed by this task. The administrator might be responsible only for the creation of the distribution lists. A designated distribution list owner—a team member—can be designated to manage the distribution list membership throughout its existence.

This lesson introduces you to distribution list creation and configuration using the Exchange Administrator program. This lesson discusses the features that are unique to distribution lists while other features, which can be applied to all recipient objects, are covered in Lesson 5, "Recipient Object Management," later in this chapter.

A practical exercise will outline the steps that are necessary to create a distribution list.

At the end of this lesson, you will be able to:

- List the advantages of distribution lists
- Create and configure distribution lists

Estimated time to complete this lesson: 20 minutes

Distribution List Configuration

To configure a distribution list means to specify a number of properties. The most important attribute is, of course, its member list: distribution list members will receive all messages that are sent to the distribution list. Other important properties are the **Display** name, **Alias** name, distribution list **Owner**, and the **Expansion Server** for the distribution list. All these properties can be controlled within the Administrator program using the **General** property page that each distribution list object provides.

Specifying a Distribution List Owner

Distribution lists typically refer to project teams, workgroups, or departments, although it's seldom the case that an Exchange Server administrator has detailed insight into all the existing team structures and their changes over time. Therefore, it makes sense to move the responsibilities of the distribution list management to the team itself. (Team members will know who belongs—

at least, they should.) To specify a user who will control the member list of a certain distribution list, you need to designate a distribution list owner. The owner can modify the member list using an Exchange Client or Outlook. He or she doesn't need to have any administrative rights on the Exchange Server itself, which helps to distribute group-specific administrative tasks to ordinary users (as opposed to administrative users).

Note Specifying a distribution list owner relieves the administrator of work.

Designating an Expansion Server

When a user sends a message to a distribution list, the Exchange Server must resolve the distribution list into the addresses of all recipients. If not all members of the distribution list reside on the sender's home server, routing decisions need to be made as well, once all member addresses of the distribution list are retrieved. The MTA is responsible for both expanding the list and routing the message.

By default, every server's MTA expands distribution lists, which implies that the home server of the sender performs the expansion. Every distribution list expansion means additional workload for a server, so it might be a good idea to concentrate the workload for distribution list expansion onto specially designated servers. For each distribution list a server can be designated that is always responsible for expanding that distribution list using the **Expansion Server** setting on the **General** property page. It also makes sense to move the expansion of the larger distribution lists from less powerful to more powerful servers within a site. Such a configuration is also helpful if the local server is already busy with other tasks while another server within the site tends to be idle. (See Figure 5-6.)

Note You cannot specify an expansion server that resides outside the local site.

Choosing Advanced Settings

Like other recipient objects, a distribution list provides an **Advanced** property page, which contains additional configuration parameters. Using the **Message Size** parameter, for example, you can limit the maximum size of incoming messages the distribution list accepts. Messages with a size exceeding this limit are simply rejected. It is recommended that you limit the message sizes for large distribution lists to help prevent critical backbone problems. Users often want to share certain attachments—such as true-color bitmaps or funny programs—with their friends and fellow employees, and these large attachments often present a maintenance problem for the messaging administrator. Not every user is aware that a computer network has limited bandwidth for sending large attachments to large distribution lists.

Hidden Membership

By default, every Exchange user can examine the members of each distribution list using the client's address book, but this is not always desirable for a variety of sensitivity or security reasons. To hide the members of a special distribution list, select the **Hide Membership From Address Book** check box on the **Advanced** property page.

Out-of-Office Messages

Out-of-Office (OOF) messages are a useful feature. Processed by the server, these messages are automatic replies that are generated when originators send a message to a recipient who has the OOF function enabled. OOF notifications inform all originators about why the recipient is unavailable and when he or she will be available again.

By default, OOF notifications are not generated for messages sent to distribution lists. This helps to avoid potential floods of OOF replies if a user sends messages to a large list where many members are out of the office. But sometimes it might be better to enable this feature, especially if the number of members in a group is small. You can select the **Allow Out Of Office Messages To Originator** check box on the **Advanced** property page to enable this option.

Other Distribution List Settings

If you further examine the **Advanced** property page, you'll find several additional distribution list options. They are **Report To Distribution List Owner**, **Report To Message Originator**, and **Hide From Address Book**. The **Report To Distribution List Owner** option, for instance, allows the distribution list owner to request and receive delivery reports for messages sent to the distribution list. A delivery report can be requested for each message and allows you to determine whether all members of a distribution list can be reached. The **Report To Message Originator** option has the same effect, but it allows each message originator to request and receive delivery reports. This option is enabled by default. If the options **Report To Distribution List Owner** or **Report To Message Originator** have been disabled, originators will still receive notifications, but these will be generated from the distribution list directly instead of from every member.

Another parameter—the **Trust Level**—allows you to include the distribution list in the Directory Synchronization with MS Mail, Lotus cc:Mail, Lotus Notes, and other systems.

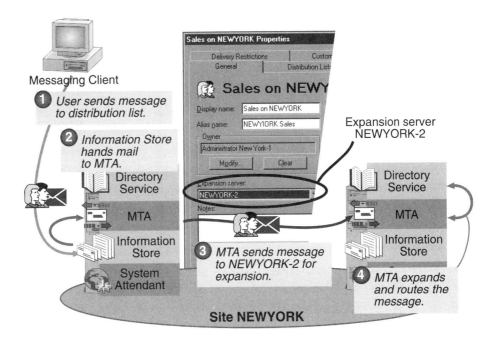

Figure 5-6. Distribution list expansion.

The advanced settings and their functions are as follows:

- **Allow Out Of Office Messages To Originator**; sends OOF notifications to the originator of a message even if the recipient, who is currently OOF, received the message only because he or she is a member of a distribution list

- **Hide From Address Book**; prevents the distribution list from appearing in the server-based address lists

- **Hide Membership From Address Book**; prevents the members of a distribution list from being displayed in the server-based address lists

- **Message Size**; limits the size of messages accepted by the distribution list

- **Report To Distribution List Owner**; allows the owner of a distribution list to request detailed delivery reports and NDRs

- **Report To Message Originator**; allows the originator of a message to request delivery reports and NDRs directly from the members of the distribution list rather than from the distribution list itself

- **Trust Level**; determines whether the distribution list is a subject of the Directory Synchronization with other e-mail systems

Exercise 10: Creating a Distribution List

As mentioned earlier, distribution lists offer a convenient way to reach multiple recipients through a single address book entry. All recipient objects—mailboxes, custom recipients, public folders and other distribution lists—can be members of a distribution list.

Estimated time to complete this exercise: 10 minutes

Description

In this exercise, you will use the Exchange Administrator program to create a distribution list. You will add members to the list and you will specify a distribution list owner using the property pages of the new object.

- Task 10 describes the steps for creating a distribution list that can be used as an addressee for messages that are to be sent to a group of recipients.

Prerequisites

- Log on as Admin-NY1 to NEWYORK-1.

Task 10: Creating a Distribution List

1. Start the **Microsoft Exchange Administrator** program and verify that you are connected to server **NEWYORK-1**.

2. Expand the container **NEWYORK**, if necessary, and then click **Recipients**.

3. On the **File** menu, click the **New Distribution List** command.

4. Complete the **Properties** dialog box using the following information:

In this box	You supply
Display name	*Sales on NEWYORK*
Alias name	*NEWYORK Sales*

5. Under **Owner**, click **Modify**.

6. In the **Distribution List** dialog box select **Administrator NewYork-1**, and then click **OK**.

7. Under **Members**, click **Modify**.

8. Select the users shown here (press the Ctrl key during the selection):

   - Administrator New York-1

   - Administrator New York-2

   - Fred Pumpkin

   - Lisa Strawberry

9. Click **Add**.

10. Click **OK**.

11. In the **Sales on NEWYORK Properties** dialog box click **OK**.

12. Notice that the distribution list **Sales on NEWYORK** is displayed in the **Recipients** container as new recipient with a group icon on the left side.

13. Exit the Exchange Administrator program.

Review

The most important properties of a distribution list are the **Alias** name, **Display** name, **Members** list, and the **Owner** account. Users can send messages to a group of recipients by addressing them to the distribution list. They use the list's display name in order to do so. A message sent to a distribution list will be sent to all its members. To accomplish this, the list must be expanded by the MTA, which will obtain the e-mail addresses for all member accounts from the directory. Once the e-mail addresses have been resolved, the message can be routed to its destinations according to the routing rules described in Chapter 4.

Lesson 4: Creating and Configuring Custom Recipients

The basic purpose of a custom recipient is to provide a way to include a foreign e-mail address into the address books of an Exchange Server organization. Let's say Mr. John Apple, a STOCKSDATA partner, has the SMTP address *JohnA@sombrero.com*. His address can be included in the Global Address List of the STOCKSDATA company. Ms. Lisa Strawberry, the Director of Customer Services and Business Relations, will then be able to address messages to Mr. Apple just as she does for any other recipient in the organization (for example, Mr. Fred Pumpkin).

This lesson will cover the specific aspects of the custom recipient creation and configuration. You'll read about the various types of custom recipients as well as advanced configuration issues.

A practical exercise is included in this lesson to outline the steps necessary to create a custom recipient object.

At the end of this lesson, you will be able to:

- Describe the purpose of custom recipients
- Create and configure custom recipient objects

Estimated time to complete this lesson: 20 minutes

Custom Recipients

Unlike a mailbox, a custom recipient doesn't have a repository for messages on an Exchange Server computer. The custom recipient is usually a representation for a recipient that exists outside the organization's own messaging network. In fact, it is impossible to create a custom recipient that references a mailbox within its own organization; custom recipients are used when connecting to MS Mail, Lotus cc:Mail, or Lotus Notes and are often created automatically by the Directory Synchronization processes with these messaging systems. It is, however, also possible to create them manually to maintain server-based references to partners, customers, and other users that reside somewhere outside the organization (on the Internet, for example).

Creating a Custom Recipient

Using the Exchange Administrator program, you can create a custom recipient manually through the **New Custom Recipient** command, which can be found on the **File** menu. The directory import feature of the Administrator program provides a second way to create these objects. In fact, the import feature is valuable if you connect your organization to a system that does not support the Directory Synchronization features of Exchange Server 5.5. If you connect to MS Mail, Lotus cc:Mail, or Lotus Notes, however, you can create custom recipients automatically through the Directory Synchronization. (See Figure 5-7.) This procedure is explained in Chapter 18, Chapter 19, and Chapter 20.

Specifying the Type of Recipient

Custom recipients can be seen as a sort of interface between an Exchange address and a foreign e-mail address. Since Exchange Server can handle several foreign e-mail address types, several types of custom recipients can exist as well. Consequently, you need to specify the type of underlying e-mail address when creating a new custom recipient. You can select between MS Mail, MacMail, Lotus cc:Mail, Internet, and X.400 address formats directly. For any other type of address, a generic **Other Address** type is available. Once you have made you choice, you can enter the e-mail address information in the *<Address Type>* **Address Properties** dialog box.

Custom Recipient Display Names

The display name of a custom recipient is independent of its underlying e-mail address and can be defined by the administrator at will. For example, the address book entry **Partner J. Apple From Los Angeles** might reference the address *JohnA@sombrero.com*. In this case, Lisa Strawberry would simply select **Partner J. Apple From Los Angeles** from the Global Address List and the message to John would be addressed correctly.

The independence of the display name is helpful if an e-mail address is cumbersome or hard to remember. Alphanumeric e-mail addresses, for instance, are not very user friendly. With an address such as *934938421-0001@offline.edu* it would take only a small typo and a wrong recipient might receive confidential information. Unfortunately, several messaging administrators seem still to believe that such e-mail addresses are acceptable, but you can compensate for the inadequacy of e-mail addresses by using custom recipients in your own organization. You need only to define a user-friendly display name. The address *934938421-0001@offline.edu*, for instance, can be buried in a custom recipient object, which provides a user-friendly display name such as *Prof. H. P. Leek-Straw*. Addressing e-mail messages to Ms. Leek-Straw becomes much easier because users would select only the corres-ponding custom recipient object from the Global Address List.

Custom Recipients and Message Routing

Let's say Lisa Strawberry selects a custom recipient entry from the Global Address List to send a message to Mrs. Prof. Leek-Straw. Lisa Strawberry's messaging client transfers the item to the IS as usual. At this point, the IS recognizes that it is not responsible for attending to this particular recipient and passes the message to the MTA. The MTA, in turn, must communicate with the DS to replace the Exchange address of the custom recipient *Prof. H. P. Leek-Straw* with the actual e-mail address *934938421-0001@offline.edu*. Offline.edu is part of the address space of a specific messaging connector—preferably an IMS—and the MTA will route the message appropriately. MTA message routing is explained in Chapter 9, "Introduction to Intersite Connectors."

Configuring Advanced Settings

The Exchange Server directory handles custom recipients in a manner similar to the way it handles mailboxes so that you can, for example, specify a size limit for messages sent to a particular custom recipient. You can also hide the recipient from the organization's server-based address lists. If the actual recipient's messaging system is not capable of handling rich text information, such as bold and color text formatting or positioned attachments within the text, you can deselect the **Allow Rich Text In Messages** option on a per-recipient basis using its **Advanced** property page. Messages sent to a recipient who has been disabled with the **Allow Rich Text In Messages** option will contain plain text only because the rich text information will be discarded.

The most important options you can select on the **Advanced** property page are as follows:

- **Message Size**; to limit the size of messages accepted by a particular custom recipient

- **Allow Rich Text In Messages**; to allow for rich text formats such as bold and colored text (rich text also allows the positioning of attachments)

- **Hide From Address Book**; to prevent the custom recipient from appearing in server-based address lists

- **Primary Windows NT Account**; to allow a user to send messages as a custom recipient (this option can be compared to **Send As** permissions)

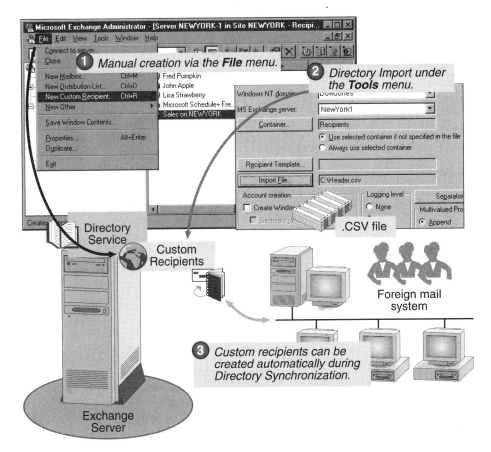

Figure 5-7. Methods for creating custom recipients.

Exercise 11: Creating a Custom Recipient

A custom recipient is a directory object similar to a mailbox, but unlike a mailbox, the custom recipient does not maintain an e-mail repository in the Private Information Store. Instead, it references an e-mail address that points to a recipient outside the organization. Therefore, custom recipients are useful for adding references to foreign recipients in the Global Address List. The underlying e-mail address can be of any type such as SMTP, MS Mail, Lotus cc:Mail, X.400, or others.

Estimated time to complete this exercise: 10 minutes

Description

In this exercise, you will use the Administrator program to create a custom recipient. The suggested e-mail address type for the custom recipient is Internet (an SMTP address), but you can use any address type you want. You will place the new custom recipient into the **Recipients** container of the site **NEWYORK**.

- Task 11 describes the steps for adding a custom recipient with an underlying SMTP address to the directory of the Exchange organization.

Prerequisites

- Log on as Admin-NY1 to NEWYORK-1 to complete this exercise.

Task 11: Creating a Custom Recipient

1. Make sure the **Microsoft Exchange Administrator** program is started and that you are connected to server **NEWYORK-1**.

2. On the **File** menu, select **New Custom Recipient** to launch the **New E-Mail Address** dialog box.

3. Click **Internet Address**, and then click **OK**.

4. In the **Internet Address Properties** dialog box, enter *JohnA@sombrero.com* under **E-Mail Address**.

5. Click **OK**.

6. In the **Properties** dialog box enter the following information:

In this box	You supply
First	*John*
Last	*Apple*
Alias	*JohnA* (will be filled automatically)

7. Click **OK**.

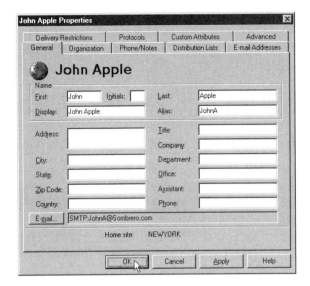

Review

When creating a custom recipient, you must specify the underlying e-mail address first. The underlying e-mail address usually points to a recipient in a foreign messaging system or another Exchange Server organization. The custom recipient allows you to place a reference to a foreign recipient into the directory of your own organization. Once the custom recipient object is created you can specify recipient information for the object in a similar way as you would for mailboxes. Likewise, custom recipients can exist in the same **Recipients** container as mailbox objects and distribution lists. Alternatively, you can place the custom recipients into a designated container, which might have been created for custom recipients of a specific type to keep them visually apart from internal mailbox objects.

Lesson 5: Recipient Object Management

All the different types of recipient objects reside in the directory databases of every Exchange Server computer. All recipient objects are elements that form address lists, provide detailed address information, and can be used to address e-mail messages. It makes sense, then, that all recipient objects have several properties in common besides various object specific attributes. These common properties allow the administrator to maintain mailboxes, distribution lists, custom recipients, and public folders in a uniform way. The maintenance of mailbox objects, however, is the most important management task.

This lesson discusses the management of those aspects that can be applied to all recipient objects. Common tasks such as specifying secondary proxy e-mail addresses or delivery restrictions are covered. However, you can also read about how to clean and move a mailbox, which is not appropriate for distribution lists, custom recipients, or public folders.

At the end of this lesson, you will be able to:

- Describe settings that mailboxes, custom recipients, distribution lists, and public folders have in common

- Configure common properties of recipient objects

- Use templates for efficient mailbox creation

- Search for recipients within the Administrator program

- Clean a mailbox

- Move mailboxes between servers in a site

Estimated time to complete this lesson: 15 minutes

Common Properties

The property pages that mailboxes, distribution lists, custom recipients, and public folders have completely in common are **Distribution Lists**, **E-Mail Addresses**, and **Custom Attributes**. (See Figure 5-8 on page 261.) This is also true for the **Permissions** property page, although its usage is common to all directory items, not just recipient objects.

Another property page, **Delivery Restrictions**, is also common to most of these recipient objects, with the exception of public folder objects. This is because public folders are configured separately using the Exchange Client or Outlook. You can read more about the public folder configuration in Chapter 12.

Several other common properties can be found on the specific property pages of each recipient object type. For example, all recipient objects have a display name, which appears in the client's address book and in the Exchange Administrator program.

Distribution List Membership

Using the **Distribution Lists** property page, you can control the distribution list membership of each particular recipient object. Each recipient object can be a member of one or more lists, and the lists to which an object belongs can be found under **Distribution List Membership**. To add or remove a particular object to or from existing lists, click the **Modify** button. The other way to control the membership is to configure a particular distribution list object directly. As mentioned, this is not only available to administrators but also to the owner of a distribution list who may be an ordinary mailbox user.

Secondary E-Mail Addresses

By default, every Exchange user has four proxy e-mail addresses, one for each of the following types: *CCMAIL*, *MS* (MS Mail), *SMTP*, and *X.400*. These addresses will be determined automatically based on several configuration parameters, such as the organization and site names. They will be used to reach the Exchange recipient from foreign messaging networks. As with mailboxes, all other recipient types have proxy e-mail addresses. Consequently, an Internet user can specify your SMTP address to send messages to your mailbox or the SMTP address of a distribution list by specifying the e-mail address of a distribution list (for example, *NEWYORKSales@newyork.stocksdata.com*) to reach multiple recipients.

It is possible to enhance the list of proxy e-mail addresses by defining more than one e-mail address for a particular recipient object. This is especially useful if your Exchange system coexists with another messaging system, for example during the time of migration from the other system to Exchange Server. Let's say you have integrated an Exchange Server into an MS Mail network. The MS Mail network is connected to the Internet and a particular user has the SMTP address *user@company.com*. In this situation, if the user is migrated to the Exchange Server organization, a new SMTP address will be generated. The new format might be *user@site.organization.com*. Obviously, both addresses are not the same, but Internet users can still use the old address to send messages to the user. You should associate the new mailbox with the old address to route all incoming messages to the correct location.

The old address, or *secondary e-mail address*, can be defined through the **E-Mail Addresses** property page. Click the **New** button, select the desired type from the **New E-Mail Address** dialog box, click **OK**, and then enter the address as appropriate. Once specified, secondary addresses will be displayed in the **E-Mail Addresses** list. To be more easily distinguished, they are displayed in a smaller font than the primary e-mail addresses.

Note Exchange Server uses the primary e-mail address information for outgoing messages. Incoming messages can be sent to all configured proxy e-mail addresses of a mailbox, distribution list, custom recipient, or public folder.

Delivery Restrictions

Exchange allows you to configure delivery restrictions on a per-recipient basis, which affects incoming messages. You can configure the **Accept Messages From** list on the **Delivery Restrictions** property page to specify all senders from which a selected recipient is to accept messages. Once this selection becomes effective, Exchange Server will reject messages from other senders. You will typically use this list if the number of accepted senders is small. By default, all senders are accepted.

On the other hand, the **Reject Messages From** list contains all senders from whom messages will be rejected, while messages from all other senders will be accepted. You can use this list if you want to prohibit a specific user or a small group of senders from sending messages to the configured recipient. By default, no messages are rejected.

Note The **Delivery Restrictions** property page is not available for public folders.

Custom Attributes

Property pages contain many predefined attributes that can be selected by the administrator to provide information about every recipient. For example, mailboxes and custom recipients provide attributes such as a **Display** name, **Address**, **City**, **State**, and **Zip Code**. Nevertheless, these predefined attributes might not be sufficient for your organization. For this reason, Exchange Server offers ten additional custom attributes per site, which can be defined using the **DS Site Configuration** object's **Custom Attributes** property page. The **DS Site Configuration** object can be found in the **Configuration** container of each site. Its configuration is explained in detail in Chapter 8.

For example, you can change the **Custom Attribute 1** to *Year Employed* through the **DS Site Configuration** object to record employment-related information within the Global Address List. To enter the "Year Employed" information for a particular recipient, display its properties and switch to the **Custom Attributes** property page. You'll notice that the entry for **Custom Attribute 1 (1)** has been replaced by **Year Employed (1)**. In the field associated with this label you can enter whatever information is useful for your organization. Custom attributes can carry any kind of information, and they may apply the information to all recipient objects within a site. Exercise 22, "Setting a Custom Attribute for Several Recipients," (in Chapter 8) describes the steps necessary to define the **Year Employed** custom attribute.

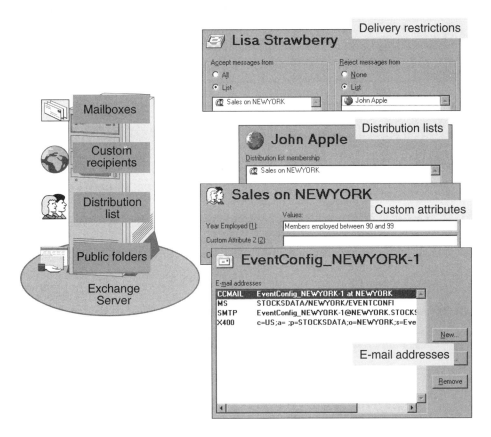

Figure 5-8. Common recipient information.

The common property pages for all recipient objects are:

- **Custom Attributes**; to enter useful additional information that is not covered by predefined attributes

- **Delivery Restrictions**; to specify who can or cannot send messages to the recipient (this property page is not available for public folders)

- **Distribution Lists**; to define list membership and to add and remove the recipient to and from distribution lists

- **E-mail Addresses**; to add, edit, or remove proxy e-mail addresses

Managing Recipient Objects

The management of recipient objects entails adjusting recipient object properties to provide useful information through server-based address lists. You can set object properties recipient individually or through template information. In addition, you should be familiar with several advanced maintenance aspects, such as the tasks of cleaning and moving mailboxes. Cleaning might be necessary if a mailbox seems to occupy too great a portion of server resources regardless of specified quotas. You can move a mailbox as an option to protect the users' private data in cases of emergency.

Using Templates for Mailbox Creation

A template is basically a recipient object that can be used as a model for new items. With the exception of public folders, every recipient object can act as a template object. Templates allow you to specify common settings as default values for all new recipient items. For example, if you use a template based on a recipient object that is a member of a particular distribution list, all recipient objects derived from this template will become members of the same distribution list automatically.

You can use templates in two ways, either by clicking the **Duplicate** command on the **File** menu or by specifying the object as a **Recipient Template** in the **Directory Import** property page of the **Tools** menu.

Finding a Recipient

It might become difficult to find a particular mailbox just by searching a recipients container if the number of existing recipient objects is large. To find a particular recipient in the shortest time possible, use the **Find Recipients** command under the **Tools** menu of the Administrator program. You can search for recipients anywhere in the organization based on a variety of criteria, such as first name, last name, and so on.

You can also filter recipient objects that will be displayed in the Administrator program. Using the Administrator program's **View** menu, you can specify whether to display mailboxes, custom recipients, distribution lists or public folders only, or all the objects. The **Hidden Recipients** command is available on the same menu, which allows you to display the hidden recipients. Note that all non-hidden recipients become invisible when you select this option.

Cleaning a Mailbox

Just as a person's home might be his or her castle, a mailbox is his or her private domain. Hence, an administrator should not directly access any user's mailbox to perform maintenance or any other task. In cases where a mailbox seems to grow unexpectedly large and unwieldy, however, you have the option to step in. You can reduce the contents of a mailbox administratively according to specific criteria. This process is usually called *cleaning a mailbox*, but it should probably be called *using the last possible method*. Be aware that you intrude upon the privacy of a user when cleaning his or her mailbox, possibly causing that user to lose trust in the security of the messaging system.

The Hard Way

If there is no way around cleaning out a mailbox, select the desired mailbox and choose the **Clean Mailbox** command under the **Tools** menu. You then need to select the cleanup criteria within the **Clean Mailbox** dialog box. You can either delete the selected items directly or move them to the user's **Deleted Items** folder. Moving items to the **Deleted Items** folder allows the user to recover important information before it is deleted permanently.

The Smart Way

Instead of cleaning a mailbox, you can indirectly control the usage of the mailbox resources through quotas known as mailbox size limits, as described earlier in this chapter. Quotas can be set for each mailbox individually, either by using its **Limits** property page or at the server level by using the **General** property page of the **Private Information Store** object. This way, you're able to control the server-based resources without touching the user's castle. The configuration of the server's **Private Information Store** object is covered in detail in Chapter 8.

Moving a Mailbox

You can move a mailbox to another server within a site in two ways. You can either change the **Home Server** attribute on the **Advanced** property page of the mailbox or you can select the mailbox in the contents pane of the Administrator program, and then choose the **Move Mailbox** command from the **Tools** menu. (See Figure 5-9.)

Note   You cannot move mailboxes between sites.

The Emergency Solution

Mailboxes are located on one server only and their contents will not be replicated. This implies that the server must be running to allow its users access to their private data and to the messaging network. In other words, if you needed to reinstall an Exchange Server completely—let's say a Windows NT component is not functioning correctly for some reason—all users residing on this computer would be affected. The more users that are affected, the worse the situation.

A perfect solution for such a problem is the "mailbox parade" to another server in the local site. Select all recipients from the **Server Recipients** container in the affected server, click the **Move Mailbox** command, and select the new home server. Multiple mailboxes, even in chunks of several hundreds, can be moved in this manner to their new home. Mailboxes can even be moved regardless of whether their clients are currently on line.

Updating the Client Profile

As part of a client/server system, Exchange Clients and Outlook communicate with the server using RPCs. This is not a permanent connection in the form of a directory mapping, so you can move a mailbox to a new server even while the client is on line. In any case, it's wise to keep the old server running until all clients have been started again. The old server will inform the clients at their next startup about the new home server and the clients will update their corresponding messaging profiles appropriately. Once the profile has been updated, it points to the correct server again. The moving of a mailbox is invisible to all users.

Under rare circumstances, a manual adjustment of the server name might be necessary once the mailbox has been moved. This would be the case if the client was off line while you moved the mailbox and the old server is no longer available when the client tries to log in again. The configuration of messaging profiles is covered in Chapter 7, "Configuring the Microsoft Exchange Client."

Mailbox Sizes

Exchange Server stores messages as *single-instance items*, which are objects that exist only one time in the IS, but can be referenced by more than one recipient. For example, a 1-MB message referenced by ten recipients on the same server will consume only 1 MB of disk space. If one recipient deletes the message from his mailbox, only his pointer (reference) to the message will be removed. If the last recipient deletes the message, the system erases the object from the IS. Only if a user reads and modifies the object will it be copied as a private instance to his or her mailbox.

As you move mailboxes, the space required to store their contents might increase on the destination server. This happens because the process of moving a mailbox needs to include all the user's server-based messages. If moved mailboxes contain messages that are not available on the target server, these messages must be created in the Private Information Store of the destination server. Consequently, moving mailboxes can result in an increased demand for storage space on the target server.

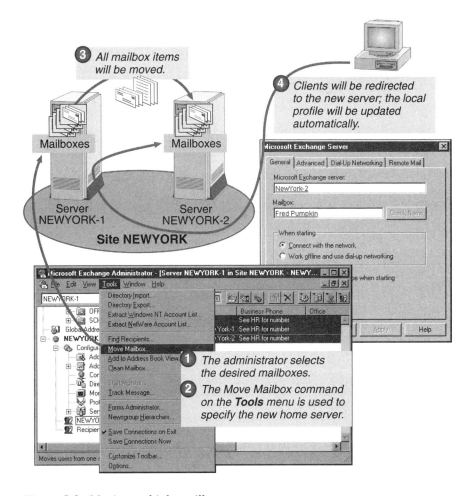

Figure 5-9. Moving multiple mailboxes.

The advanced mailbox configuration features of the Administrator program are:

- **Move Mailbox**; to move multiple mailboxes simultaneously to a new home server

- **Clean Mailbox**; to remove messages from mailboxes administratively and in accordance with specific criteria

- **Find Recipients**; to find particular recipients quickly by means of certain search criteria

- **Duplicate** from the **File** menu; to use an existing recipient object as a template for new recipients (the template information will be used to specify default properties)

Review

1. What is a custom recipient?

   _____

   _____

   _____

   _____

2. What is an Exchange Server mailbox?

   _____

   _____

   _____

   _____

3. What is a distribution list?

   _____

   _____

   _____

   _____

4. What must be configured in order to handle public folders as you would any other recipient?

   _____

   _____

   _____

   _____

5. Which set of permissions is required to create a Windows NT account and the associated mailbox within the User Manager for Domains?

   _____

   _____

   _____

6. You are the administrator of an existing Novell NetWare 4.x network and have installed an Exchange Server to provide extended messaging capabilities. The Windows NT Server, Gateway Services for NetWare, and the Exchange Server are operating perfectly. Now you want to configure mailboxes for all existing users. What steps must be performed to create the mailboxes as efficiently as possible?

7. The export and import features of the Exchange Administrator program can be used to assign additional proxy addresses to mailboxes. These features allow all existing mailboxes to be exported into a file. Additional addresses can then be assigned by editing the file using Excel or any word processing program. The changes need to be reimported into the Exchange Server for the new proxy addresses to take effect. What are the particular steps you need to perform in order to accomplish this task?

8. How do you hide a particular mailbox from the address book?

9. How do you move a single mailbox to another server in the same site?

10. Recipient containers can be used to group recipients to organize the server-based address books. How can you move a particular recipient from one container to another?

_____

_____

_____

_____

11. The company STOCKSDATA has 157 employees, and every employee has a mailbox. A distribution list called All Stockers contains all the mail-boxes. Recently William Pear sent a 12-MB message to this distribution list to distribute scanned pictures. Fred Pumpkin, one of the administra-tors, assumes that this will probably happen again and wants to prevent it. What would you recommend?

_____

_____

_____

_____

_____

_____

12. You have created a temporary distribution list for a specific and confiden-tial project. You don't want to allow users to explore the list membership. What do you need to configure?

_____

_____

_____

_____

13. How can you accomplish the transfer of distribution list management responsibilities to a regular user?

_____

_____

_____

14. How do you configure a distribution list to send Out-of-Office notifications to originators of messages that have been sent to the distribution list?

_____

_____

_____

15. Your Exchange Server is a very busy server. Another server in another site has fewer tasks to perform so you decide to designate this computer as an expansion server. How do you accomplish the configuration?

_____

_____

_____

16. You recently connected your Exchange Server organization to an MS Mail network and a Lotus cc:Mail post office. Now you want to exchange address information between all three systems. How do you accomplish this task?

_____

_____

_____

_____

_____

_____

17. What types of custom recipients can exist?

_____

_____

_____

_____

18. You want to configure an Exchange Server to act as a backbone for an MS Mail system. The MS Mail system should be connected to the Internet through the Exchange Server. MS Mail recipients must be able to send and receive messages to and from the Internet. What do you need to configure on the Exchange Server in order to accomplish this task?

_____

_____

_____

_____

_____

_____

_____

19. You are planning to create multiple mailboxes by using the Directory Import feature of the Administrator program. However, many properties, such as distribution list memberships, are exactly the same for all mailboxes. How would you preconfigure common mailbox properties most efficiently?

_____

_____

_____

_____

_____

_____

C H A P T E R   6

Microsoft Exchange Client Architecture and Installation

This chapter introduces the program family of the Microsoft Exchange Client and Microsoft Outlook applications. Both client systems exploit the powerful features of Microsoft Exchange Server in a similar way.

Overview

Because both Exchange Client and Outlook provide access to all client-relevant features of Exchange Server, it might be difficult to decide which program would best fit your needs. To help you choose, Lesson 1 of this chapter covers the most important messaging features of both client systems.

Lesson 2 explains the Messaging Application Programming Interface (MAPI) subsystem, which is the foundation of all the messaging features in the Exchange Client and Outlook. A general understanding of its architecture, information services, and messaging profiles is therefore essential, regardless of which client you eventually choose.

Lesson 3 discusses the actual client installation and the tools an administrator has available to simplify the task of the client configuration. For example, the Setup Editor can be used in conjunction with a shared network installation point to set Exchange Client configuration parameters prior to the installation. Configuration options that Outlook provides are also explained.

Two practical exercises outline the steps required to install the Exchange Client and Outlook on a Windows NT computer.

In the following lessons, you will be introduced to:

- The different Exchange Client platforms
- The various Exchange Client features
- The supported platforms for Outlook
- Available Outlook features as provided by the particular client platform
- Installation requirements for Exchange Client and Outlook
- The various methods available to install the Exchange Client
- The various methods available to install Outlook

Lesson 1: Microsoft Exchange Clients

An Exchange client is a messaging application that communicates directly with an Exchange Server using RPCs. Such a client provides access to server-based resources in their native Exchange Server format. By this definition, Outlook is nothing but an Exchange client. Client examples are Outlook for Windows 3.x, Windows 95, Windows NT, and Outlook for Macintosh. Exchange Server 5.5 also provides backward compatibility to the Exchange Client 5.0 family, which is available for MS-DOS, Windows 3.x, Windows 95, Windows NT, and Apple Macintosh.

At the end of this lesson, you will be able to:

- Describe the significant functions of the Exchange Client
- Explain the client interface of Outlook
- Identify features of the Exchange Macintosh client
- List the features of Outlook for Windows 3.x
- Name the features of Outlook for Macintosh

Estimated time to complete this lesson: 30 minutes

Client Interface Overview

The Exchange Client 5.0, Microsoft Schedule+, and the Electronic Forms Designer form the actual native client family for Exchange Server. However, Outlook 97 version 8.03 is the primary client for Exchange Server 5.5. During the release of Exchange Server 5.0, Outlook 97 became available as part of the Microsoft Office 97 package. Outlook 97 provides more functionality than Exchange Client 5.0 and was meant to replace the entire Exchange Client family. Outlook 97 and its successor Outlook 98 are also native clients for the Exchange messaging platform.

The Exchange Client family provides the user interfaces to exploit all the Exchange Server capabilities. You use the Exchange Client to send, receive, store, and view messages; Schedule+ to create and maintain appointments and meetings; and the Electronic Forms Designer to design new 16-bit electronic forms.

On the other hand, Outlook is a substitute for the entire Exchange Client family because it provides all the essential messaging features in one application. Using Outlook, you can work with e-mail messages, maintain contact information, store scheduling data, and design electronic forms using the Outlook Forms Designer, which is part of this application on the 32-bit platforms.

General Client Interface Features

The term *general client interface features* refers to the functionality that both the Exchange Client and Outlook have in common. Both applications provide similar features for composing, viewing, and storing e-mail–related information. When you compose a new message, you can format the content using colored text and other rich text features. While you're composing you don't need to worry about the recipient's client being able to read the rich text information since both the Exchange Client and Outlook are able to display it properly when the message is read. Another feature both clients have in common is that they always store messages in message folders.

A user who is familiar with the Exchange Client will quickly learn to work with Outlook. Both programs have the same architectural features based on the MAPI subsystem. Therefore, the migration from the Exchange Client can be easily managed. (See Figure 6-1 on page 277.)

Information Repository

Both the Exchange Client and Outlook use the concept of message folders to maintain e-mail messages, word processing documents, spreadsheets, voice mail files, electronic forms, and other items in a structured way. According to their purpose, these folders are named *Public*, *Private*, *Offline* and *Personal Folders*. Public folders are used to store collaborative information that is intended to be available to many users in an organization. Private folders refer to those folders that reside on a user's server-based mailbox and are typically available to only one user. They can be synchronized with offline folders, which are nothing more than direct copies of the server-based information placed in a local file with an .OST extension. Offline folders provide access to the information stored in private folders even when the server is unavailable. Messages are also stored locally in personal folders, but personal folders are not synchronized with a server-based mailbox. They are typically used in conjunction with the client's Remote Mail option, which provides the ability to upload and download specific messages to and from the server at certain times. Personal folders reside in local .PST files.

Public Folders

Public folders are special message folders because they can be made available to all users in an organization, unlike the other folders. In other words, as soon as you create a public folder, all other users may have access to it. These folders constitute the foundation of public forums and Exchange workgroup applications. Let's say you want to design a discussion forum about the National Football League. First you need to create an appropriate electronic form, and then you'll need to install this form in the desired public folder. Users who want to participate in the discussion will launch the form and use it to post their discussion contributions. When a user reads items in the discussion public folder, the form is used again to display the information. Electronic forms are covered in more detail in Chapter 16, "The Microsoft Exchange Server Forms Environment."

Public folders are maintained by the IS service of Exchange Server. Only minor differences exist in managing them via the Exchange Client or Outlook. Using either client program, you can create new public folders, grant access permission to specific users, and define custom views in a similar way. The public folder management is treated in more detail in Chapter 12, "Creating and Managing Public Folders."

Custom Views

A *view* is a set of instructions that determines the way the content of a public, private, or personal folder is displayed within the Exchange Client or Outlook. The **Normal** view of the Exchange Client arranges the messages stored in a folder according to the times they are received. The columns display the following message attributes: **Importance**, **Item Type**, **Attachment**, **From**, **Subject**, **Received**, and **Size**. The **Normal** view is the default view within the Exchange Client. Outlook, in contrast, uses the **Messages With AutoPreview** view as the default view which displays the message's **Importance**, **Icon**, **Flag Status**, **Attachment**, **From**, **Subject**, and **Received** columns.

A **Normal** view of the folder's content is adequate under most circumstances. Other predefined personal views, however, might be more useful if you want to group the information in a folder. The other predefined personal views can be selected through the Exchange Client's **Personal Views** option on the **View** menu. For example, you can select **Group By Subject** and reorder messages according to their subject lines. This way, all messages that are about a particular topic are grouped together regardless of when they were received.

You might want to define your own custom views if none of the predefined views provide the desired functionality. A custom view can be used to display, order, and filter items according to the **Conversation Topic**, the **Subject**, the **Sender**, and other criteria. To design a view within the Exchange Client or Outlook, click the **Define Views** command on the **View** menu. This displays a **Define Views** dialog box, in which you click the **New** button. Before continuing, you must define a name in the **View Name** box. You will then use the four buttons named **Columns**, **Group By**, **Sort**, and **Filter** in Exchange Client to design the view. Furthermore, you must decide whether the new custom view is bound to a specific folder (folder view) or is generally available for all your folders (personal view). If you are working in Outlook, however, you must specify the **Type Of View** (for example, **Table**, **Timeline**, **Card**, **Day/Week/Month**, or **Icon**) at the **Create A New View** dialog box before you can click **OK**. You will then come to the **View Summary** dialog box, where you will find five buttons labeled **Fields**, **Group By**, **Sort**, **Filter**, and **Format,** which allow you to specify how messages should be ordered and displayed.

If you're defining a custom folder view for a public folder, be aware that available Outlook view types such as **Timeline**, **Card**, **Day/Week/Month**, **Icon**, and **Table** cannot be displayed using Exchange Client 5.0. In general, the Exchange Client is able to handle only its own view type, so if both client programs are deployed in your organization, it's best to define public folder views using the Exchange Client. Folder views that have been defined using the Exchange Client will be displayed and can be used as **Exchange 4.0** view types within Outlook.

Server-Based Rules

Server-based rules are sets of instructions that determine the automatic processing of incoming messages. Both the Exchange Client and Outlook support the definition of server-based rules and their management through the Inbox Assistant, the Out of Office Assistant, or the Folder Assistant on public folders. Because Exchange Server 5.5 is a client/server system, neither of these clients is required to execute the rules. The client can disconnect completely, but the server still continues to reply to messages, move them to desired folders, delete them, or perform any other actions you specify based on message properties.

For example, let's say you are a member of the **Microsoft Exchange Server Admins** distribution list, which is used to send configuration requests to all administrators. You have created a private folder in your mailbox called **Admin Requests** to personally keep track of requests sent to this distribution list. Instead of manually moving all relevant messages to this folder, you can let the server do this work for you by defining a server-based rule. To define this rule, open the **Tools** menu and choose the **Inbox Assistant** command. Within the **Inbox Assistant** dialog box, click the **Add Rule** button. This displays the **Edit Rule** dialog box. To apply the rule to all incoming messages sent to the distribution list, **Microsoft Exchange Server Admins** must be entered in the **Sent To** box. Then check the **Move To** box, and click the **Folder** button. To finish the rule definition, select the **Admin Requests** folder, and then click **OK** three times. All incoming messages sent to the **Microsoft Exchange Server Admins** distribution list will be moved immediately to your **Admin Requests** folder regardless of whether the client is active.

Server-Based Rules and Deferred Action Messages

In some situations server-based rules cannot provide the desired results without direct support of the Exchange Client or Outlook. Let's say the server-based rule mentioned previously must move the messages to a Personal

Folder residing in a .PST file, in which case the server cannot accomplish this task because the .PST file is available only to the client. Instead of moving the messages directly, the server creates specific messages known as *Deferred Action Messages (DAM)*, which contain instructions for the client to move the messages according to the rule. The next time the user logs on, those DAMs are sent to his or her client and the client program moves the affected messages before displaying the content of the Inbox. Typically the user is not aware that it is the client that moves the messages to the .PST file.

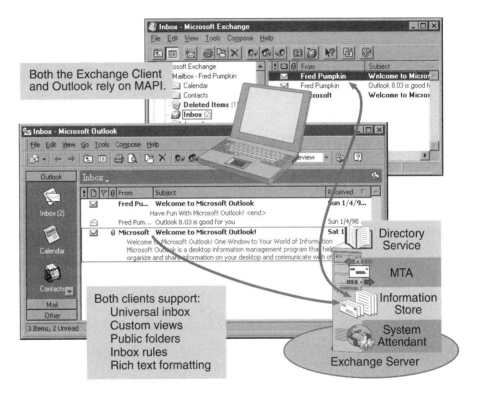

Figure 6-1. Common Exchange Client and Outlook features.

Features common to Exchange Client and Outlook and their functions are as follows:

- Custom views of the Exchange 4.0 type; to sort the contents of a folder by author, date, keywords, and other information

- Inbox Assistant/Out of Office Assistant; to create rules to automatically process incoming messages

- Public folders; to store collaborative data accessed by multiple users using different clients

- Rich text formatting; to format message contents using colored and bold text as well as other formatting structures that are preserved across most client platforms

- Universal Inbox; to access various messaging systems (that provide MAPI information services) in a single session and to handle messages of all types, including documents, pictures, graphics, or faxes from a single location

Microsoft Outlook Client

The Outlook client integrates Microsoft Office 97 applications with messaging, scheduling, and workgroup capabilities. Therefore, it can be treated as a complete replacement of the entire Exchange Client family on Windows 3.x, Windows 95, Windows NT, and Apple Macintosh computers. Its major components are the actual files of the Outlook program itself plus the several additional modules that extend the basic functionality, such as the Exchange Server Components, Visuals for Forms Design, Electronic Forms and Templates, and utilities for importing existing user information. Outlook can also work with Schedule+, provided that Schedule+ has been installed on the same computer.

Architecture

The Windows-based versions of Outlook rely on the MAPI subsystem to access messaging backbones through information services such as Exchange Server, Microsoft Mail, or Internet Mail. This application supports all kinds of message folders, the definition of views, server-based rules, and more, thus acting as a universal Inbox. In addition, Outlook can access regular files stored within file directories on the user's hard disk, similar to Windows Explorer.

Outlook Address Book

Outlook introduces a new MAPI Address Book service labeled *Outlook Address Book*, which displays the items of the Outlook Contacts folder in the address book. Through the MAPI subsystem, the contact information can be used in every MAPI-aware application, such as Microsoft Word, the Exchange Client, Schedule+, and others. In other words, the Outlook Address Book allows you to maintain all your contact information in a single location.

Even within Outlook, the Outlook Address Book adds valuable features, so you can use the contact information to address new messages more conveniently. For example, to keep track of a particular customer, you need to create a corresponding item in your **Contacts** folder. Select the **Contacts** folder, and then click **New Contact** on the **Contacts** menu. Once you have entered all the available customer information (including a valid e-mail address), click the

Save And Close button on the toolbar. If you want to send an e-mail message to this customer, simply compose a new message as usual, click the **To** button, select **Contacts** in the **Show Names From The** drop-down list box, and specify the customer reference as a message recipient. The message will be sent to the customer using the e-mail address you entered for the Contacts item. The configuration of the Outlook Address Book service is covered in more detail in Chapter 7, "Configuring the Microsoft Exchange Client."

Migration

Outlook has been designed to integrate fully with Office 97 and to completely replace the Exchange Client family. With Outlook you can use all existing message folders, custom views, electronic forms, and some existing client extensions. (See Figure 6-2 on page 285.)

Outlook can use the same MAPI profile that might already have been created for the Exchange Client, which simplifies the migration process significantly. Only the Outlook Address Book will be added during setup. This happens automatically, so additional profile configuration is not necessary. The configuration of messaging profiles is explained in Chapter 7.

E-Mail Features

Outlook contains all the same e-mail features that are available with the Exchange Client. For example, Outlook can place hyperlinks to the Internet (*www.microsoft.com*), hyperlinks to e-mail addresses (*userX@domain.com*) and hyperlinks to regular files (*file:\\computer\share\folder\file.txt*) in e-mail messages. In addition, Outlook offers several improvements regarding e-mail–related information.

Message Tracking

Message tracking provides a convenient method to gather per-message status information about requested delivery or read receipts. A *delivery receipt* is a message that is automatically sent back to the originator when the e-mail arrives in the recipient's Inbox. A *read receipt* is an automatic e-mail reply that is generated as soon as the recipient actually reads the message. In other words, if you receive a delivery receipt you know that the original message has been received, and if you receive a read receipt you know that the original message has actually been opened.

You can check the status of read receipt requests any time you want, which is useful if you're tracking the receipts from a large number of users. To do this, open your copy of the original message, which is in your **Sent Items** folder. When you glance over the opened message window you'll notice the **Tracking** property page. When you switch to this page, a table of the status of all read and delivery receipts is displayed.

Note The **Tracking** tab is not displayed if no tracking information exists. In other words, the **Tracking** tab is not available so long as no receipt has been received.

Voting

Voting is the gathering of short responses about individual topics based on Outlook's message tracking capabilities. This feature works not unlike a read receipt request, but in this case you request a receipt about the recipient's opinion via e-mail. These responses are gathered and maintained on a per-message basis by Outlook. To gain a quick overview of the votes at any time, just open your copy of the original message from the **Sent Items** folder.

For example, you might want to ask your colleagues whether the Outlook startup times are acceptable. To do this, compose a new message, type *Is the Microsoft Outlook startup time OK?* in the **Subject** box, and address it to all pertinent employees. Then click the **Options** tab in the message window and select the **Use Voting Buttons** check box. From the list box next to the check box select **Yes; No**. The message is now ready to be sent. The recipients will receive the message, read it, and express their opinions about the topic using the **Yes** or **No** button. The responses are then sent back to you automatically, and are collected and applied to your copy of the original message, which resides in the **Sent Items** folder. To determine whether you need to improve the hardware platforms of your colleagues, open your copy of the original message, and then click the **Tracking** tab, which is provided within the message window as soon as status information exists. A table will be displayed listing all the received responses.

Note Users can receive and respond to voting messages using Outlook for Windows 3.x or Outlook for Macintosh. However, it is not possible to create voting messages using these clients.

Recalling Messages

Outlook makes it possible to recall messages that have already been sent. *Recalling* messages refers to either the deletion of an original message out of the recipients' mailboxes or its replacement with another message. This request will be sent to the recipients as a regular e-mail message, but is processed only if the original message has not yet been read or moved from the recipient's Inbox. Because message recalling is not always guaranteed, you will receive a status report, which allows you to check whether a recall request has been processed successfully.

Let's say you want to invite a friend for dinner, and since this friend is another user in your Exchange Server organization, you simply send the invitation using e-mail. Just as you click the **Send** button, you realize that you specified the wrong time, but the message has already been sent, so it's too late to correct the text of the original message. You now have the option to call your friend, but this would hardly be high tech. Taking the modern approach, you use Outlook again. Using your copy of the original message, which resides in your **Sent Items** folder, you create a recall request. In this case, you would request replacing the original message with a corrected version that states the revised time. You send this recall message to your friend, and when it arrives and is processed, it replaces the former, incorrect invitation. The message can be replaced automatically at the time of its arrival if your friend has enabled the option **Process Delivery, Read, And Recall Receipts On Arrival** at the **E-Mail** property page of Outlook's **Options** dialog box, which can be displayed through the **Options** command on the **Tools** menu. Nevertheless, your friend can disable this preference, in which case the original message will be replaced only when he or she opens the recall message. A status report is automatically sent back to you indicating the success of the operation. If your friend has already read the incorrect version, however, or has moved it out of the Inbox, the status report will indicate the failure of the replacement.

Note Outlook for Windows 95 and Windows NT—as well as for Windows 3.x and Macintosh—support recall messages.

Recovering Messages

Although Outlook moves deleted messages to the **Deleted Items** folder before expunging them permanently, users sometimes accidentally delete objects from their message repository. In Exchange Server 5.0 and earlier versions this meant the administrator had to restore the entire Private Information Store. The bigger the information store, the more time-consuming the restore operation and so the more important your messages need to be to warrant recovery.

Exchange Server 5.5 addresses this issue with the *deleted items retention* feature. So long as the retention time is not exceeded, items will not be removed permanently from the IS. In other words, by using Outlook version 8.03, users can recover deleted items without the administrator's assistance within the retention time interval that has been specified for the user's mailbox. The user simply selects the **Deleted Items** folder before opening the **Tools** menu. The **Recover Deleted Items** command will be available, which launches the **Recover Deleted Items From – Deleted Items** dialog box, where all available messages will be listed. The user can select the desired object for recovery, and can do so without having the administrator restore the IS.

Note If you install Outlook version 8.03 on a computer that already has Exchange Client 5.0, then the Exchange Client is extended to provide the **Recover Deleted Items** command on its **Tools** menu as well.

Microsoft Outlook and Schedule+

Outlook contains all the existing Schedule+ information, such as Appointments and Notes, but it also has new features that are not available in Schedule+ 7.x. Outlook supports Journal items, Calendar views, and views for Contact and Task information. Differences also exist in the way Outlook stores the items: while Schedule+ uses a hidden folder on the server-based mailbox and a synchronized local calendar file (.SCD), Outlook maintains the information using the **Calendar**, **Contacts**, **Tasks**, **Journal**, and **Notes** folders in the user's mailbox. Existing Schedule+ information needs to be imported explicitly if you want to use it with Outlook.

Outlook imports Schedule+ information based only on .SCD files, so any Schedule+ information stored on the Exchange Server is inaccessible. Therefore, if you want to import the server-based information, you need to create a local .SCD file, synchronize it, and use it to import information. To start a particular import cycle, open the **File** menu within Outlook and click the **Import And Export** command. In the **Import And Export Wizard** choose the **Import From Schedule+ Or Another Program Or File** option and select the appropriate .SCD file. At this point you'll have three choices regarding how duplicated entries should be treated. You can ignore duplicate entries, replace existing ones, or create a separate entry for each instance of a duplicate item so that both will exist later within Outlook. Once the scheduling information has been imported, Schedule+ can be removed from the computer.

You don't have to remove Schedule+ when you install Outlook, since both applications can coexist quite well. If you don't want to remove Outlook right away, you need only inform Outlook which program to use as the primary calendar application. This is the program that creates and edits appointments, meetings, and other scheduling items. You won't be able to take advantage of the Outlook features if you specify Schedule+ as the primary calendar application during the Outlook setup. If at a later time you want to use Outlook as the primary scheduling application, however, just deselect the **Use Microsoft Schedule+ As My Primary Calendar** option on the **Calendar** tab of the **Options** command on the **Tools** menu. The corresponding Registry setting can be found under:

```
HKEY_LOCAL_MACHINE
   \Software
      \Microsoft
         \Office
            \8.0
               \Outlook
                  \SchedPlusOption
                     \UseSchedPlus
```

A value of 0 means that Outlook is used to perform scheduling tasks.

Note Outlook for Windows 3.x and Outlook for Macintosh provide the same features as Schedule+ 7.x. In addition, Windows 3.x users can display the Calendar details, Tasks, and Contacts in a separate window. Outlook for Macintosh users, however, cannot view Calendar details of those using Outlook for Windows 95 and Windows NT.

Views

Like the Exchange Client, Outlook provides a set of default views, which can be used to arrange messages in a folder. If the default views are not sufficient, you can create new views or modify the existing ones with the **Define View** and **Format View** commands on the **View** menu. Outlook provides additional view types compared to the table views available in the Exchange Client. The additional view types include **Card**, which displays items as in a card file; **Icon**, which represents files with individual icons; **Table**, which arranges the information in rows and columns; **Timeline**, which indicates chronology and duration for a folder; and **Day/Week /Month**, which displays the information in the form of a calendar page.

To arrange the columns of an existing view, you can use the client's drag-and-drop capabilities. For example, if you drag a column out of the client area and drop it, the column will be deleted. The column order can also be changed using drag-and-drop.

Groupware Capabilities

Outlook 97 relies on public folders to take full advantage of its groupware capabilities. To create a typical workgroup application, you will design an electronic form, associate it with a public folder, and define a folder view to arrange the folder content in an organized manner. For this purpose, Outlook provides its own forms development tool that replaces the former Electronic Forms Designer. You can find it using the **Design Outlook Form** command on the **Tools** menu of most of the existing Outlook forms. Unlike the Electronic Forms Designer, which requires forms to be compiled before their use, the Outlook Forms Designer creates 32-bit forms that are usually available immediately. They can be extended using Visual Basic Script.

Once you have created the electronic form, you must associate the form with a public folder or a forms library to complete the workgroup application. To do this, open the **File** menu within the Outlook Forms designer and click the **Publish Form As** command. Define the form's name that you are currently installing in the **Publish Form As** dialog box. This dialog box also contains the **Publish In** button, which gives you the option to select whether to install the new form in an existing forms library or in a folder. For example, if you want to create a workgroup application associated with a public folder, you should select the desired folder at this time. Click the **Publish** button to complete the installation.

If you use Outlook forms, be aware that Exchange Clients, Outlook for Windows 3.x, or Outlook for Macintosh are unable to launch them. More information about electronic forms and their use in mixed Exchange Client/ Outlook environments is provided in Chapter 16.

Document Explorer

You'll see that the Outlook bar contains several shortcuts, such as **My Desktop**, which allow you to access Windows Explorer features for browsing and finding Office documents. You can also create your own shortcuts to directories of your hard disk on the Outlook bar and associate customized folder views with them. For example, you can associate a view of the Timeline view type with the Windows directory, thus displaying all files and folders according to their **Modified** attribute.

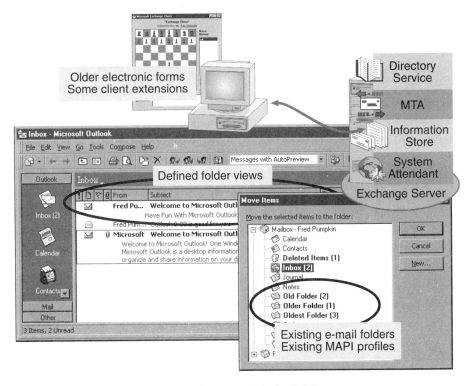

Figure 6-2. Backward-compatible features of Outlook 97.

The design goals of Outlook are:

- Integration with Office applications, which allows you to develop workgroup applications that combine Office documents with messaging features

- Combination of messaging and scheduling clients, which provides e-mail and scheduling features through one user interface and which stores the information in one location

- Creation of a client for personal and shared information, which allows users to store private information in private message folders and maintain collaborative data in public folders

- Simple upgrade capabilities, which allows migration to Outlook without the need to reconfigure the messaging profiles and support for the coexistence of the Exchange Client family and Outlook in one organization

- New class of information sharing, which provides new folder view types and form features that can be used in conjunction with public folders on an Exchange Server

Macintosh Clients

Windows NT Server systems are accessible for Apple Macintosh computers provided the Services for Macintosh have been installed. Because Exchange Server is based upon Windows NT Server functionality, it benefits from this connectivity and offers Macintosh clients access to server-based resources. Therefore, an Exchange Client, Schedule+, and Outlook for Apple Macintosh computers is available. (See Figure 6-3 on page 289.)

The user interface of the Exchange Client for Macintosh is similar in design to the Windows-based clients, and the functionality of both client types, except advanced features, is also similar. The primary difference is that the Macintosh client doesn't rely on MAPI, because the MAPI subsystem is not implemented on Apple Macintosh platforms. Therefore, some features such as electronic forms of the Electronic Forms Designer are not available.

Exchange Client Applications and Controls

Four main applications form the entire Exchange Client for the Macintosh. They are the Setup program, the Exchange Settings application, the actual Microsoft Exchange and Schedule+ programs, and the Inbox Repair Tool.

Start the client Setup to install the required program files and to create the associated items on the Macintosh. The user interface of the Setup program client is similar to its Windows counterpart in that it provides a familiar installation environment. Just as its Windows-based equivalent, the Setup for the Macintosh client does not configure the client.

The second main program is the Exchange Settings application, which is installed during setup. You use this program to create and manage the actual client profiles. To provide you with a familiar user interface, this program is similar to the **Mail And Fax** applet of the Control Panel on Windows95 and Windows NT. You can also apply the steps outlined in Chapter 7 to create valid client profiles on the Macintosh.

The actual client program is the third main application, which is in the form of Exchange and Schedule+, and which provides the integrated e-mail client and scheduling application. The e-mail client was introduced with the Service Pack 2 (SP2) for Exchange Server 4.0, also known as Microsoft Exchange 4.0a. The Schedule+ application first came with Exchange Server 5.0. Both versions have a similar user interface to the clients for the Windows platforms.

To complete the similarities with the Windows-based platforms, Setup installs the Inbox Repair Tool for Macintosh computers. This is the fourth main application, which you can use to fix file corruption on your Personal Folder Store file. A Help file is also copied to the hard disk and contains further information on how to use this tool. The Windows-based Inbox Repair Tool is covered in Chapter 15, "Maintaining Servers."

Architecture

The Exchange and Schedule+ application forms a proprietary application that does not rely on a MAPI subsystem—its operation requires some common Macintosh storage locations, which are used to maintain preferences and supporting files in addition to specific folder structures. The two folders are named *Preferences* and *Exchange Temp Items*. The standard Preferences folder, which is located in the **System** folder, is used as the default Preferences folder. It stores most of the supporting files that make up the Exchange and Schedule+ application. The Exchange Temp Items folder, on the other hand, stores temporary files created by the client during a particular session. The client creates temporary items when you open a message attachment. The temporary file is deleted when you close the application.

Outlook for Macintosh

The Outlook for Macintosh client offers a look and feel similar to the 32-bit Outlook version and includes an Outlook bar and a Folder Banner. The Outlook bar can be customized, and the Folder Banner allows you to group message items as you want. Likewise, the arrangement of menu and toolbar options is similar to the 32-bit version. As mentioned, Outlook for Macintosh supports calendar and group scheduling features and can replace the Exchange Client for Macintosh family.

Functional Differences

Because of the architectural differences between the Macintosh and the Windows operating systems, not all Windows-based client features are supported on the Macintosh platform. For example, electronic forms can't be launched because MAPI doesn't exist. You also can't use any of the MAPI information services. You can connect to an Exchange Server computer only if you're using a Macintosh client. Integrated Remote Mail functionality is also not available, so you'll need to ensure that LAN connections exist between the Macintosh Clients and the Exchange Server computer. LAN connections are supported for AppleTalk and TCP/IP.

Although the user interfaces of the Macintosh and Windows-based Exchange and Outlook clients are similar and an Inbox Repair Tool is provided for both platforms, the format of the Personal Folder Store (.PST) files is different. They are not compatible with each other, and you cannot interchange them.

The person-to-person key security feature that allows users of Windows-based clients to exchange their Advanced Security information with users in other organizations is also not supported. Consequently, you cannot rely on Advanced Security features of Exchange Server to send encrypted messages to users in foreign Exchange Server organizations using the Macintosh client. Sending signed and sealed messages to users in your own organization, however, is supported. Message encryption is covered in more detail in Chapter 14, "Implementing Advanced Security."

The features and functions not available on Macintosh clients are:

- Exchange and complex Outlook forms cannot be launched.
- Information services to messaging platforms other than Exchange Server are not supported.
- MAPI programmability does not exist on Macintosh platforms.
- Outlook Calendar details cannot be displayed.
- Person-to-person key security cannot be used.
- Remote Mail functionality does not exist.

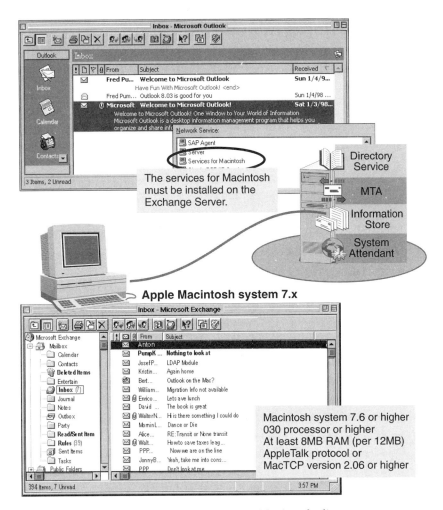

Figure 6-3. Connecting to Exchange using a Macintosh client.

Lesson 2: Client Architecture

Exchange Server supports a variety of messaging clients, so it's necessary to separate them into several groups. Certainly the clearest distinction can be made between Internet and Exchange clients. Internet clients are easy to distinguish if you take their supported communication protocol into consideration. A definition of Exchange client program types, however, is not that easy. Nevertheless, it is possible to divide the existing Exchange client programs into two groups, the non-Windows–based applications and the Windows-based applications, since significant differences exist between them. Non-Windows–based clients cannot benefit from the MAPI subsystem, while Windows-based clients take full advantage of its capabilities. This is because MAPI is implemented neither in MS-DOS nor on the Macintosh platform, but it is available on Windows 3.x, Windows 95, and Windows NT.

Because MAPI is a specification that defines interfaces regardless of the operating system, the architecture of the Windows 3.x, Windows 95, and Windows NT clients is basically the same. Even Outlook shows hardly any difference in this respect and can therefore be treated the same way as all other Windows-based clients.

If you take a closer look at the MAPI architecture you'll notice that the client is actually not communicating directly with the underlying messaging backbone. Information services, which have been configured in a messaging profile, are utilized instead. Information services and all other components of the MAPI subsystem are introduced in this lesson.

At the end of this lesson, you will be able to:

- Describe the MAPI subsystem

- Identify MAPI components, such as information services

- Identify available client and service provider interfaces

- Plan client message store configurations

Estimated time to complete this lesson: 35 minutes

MAPI Subsystem

MAPI is part of the Windows Open Services Architecture (WOSA), and exists only on Windows platforms. MAPI defines interfaces at two layers, which allows the creation of client applications as well as the development of information services. The client-side specification is called the *client interface* and the system-side specification is known as the *service provider interface*.

MAPI and WOSA

The seamless implementation of MAPI into the Windows operating system was a strategic decision by Microsoft Corporation, because with MAPI the operating system finally offers a standardized and vendor-independent messaging subsystem for all possible backbones. Because of this subsystem, client developers no longer need to write dedicated extra program code to support multiple messaging platforms. Instead, client developers can access information services provided by manufacturers who want to make their messaging platforms available via MAPI.

Industry Standard

MAPI is the result of an effort among Microsoft and more than a hundred independent software vendors (ISVs), messaging system providers, corporate developers, and messaging consultants. They all had the goal to develop a messaging programming interface that met the needs of vendors while providing flexibility for future messaging and workgroup computing applications. Since MAPI allows programmers to focus on their specific development tasks rather than on messaging programming, MAPI is a widely adopted standard. Today a broad variety of MAPI-based applications exists and you can get MAPI information services for most of the important messaging backbones. Even the 32-bit Lotus cc:Mail release 8 has a MAPI client. The Lotus cc:Mail information service can even be used in Outlook to access the cc:Mail post office.

Advantages

MAPI provides many advantages over system-specific interfaces because it frees the developer from the task of learning how to program different messaging systems separately. In other words, no matter which backbone and information services you use, MAPI stays the same. The Windows-based client, which utilizes the MAPI interface, is therefore backbone-independent and can run without any change against a variety of messaging systems.

Let's say you are a developer who needs to write a messaging application. As soon as you decide to develop this application based on MAPI, you become completely backbone-independent. You can install a transport driver for MS Mail and your messaging application will be an MS Mail client. You can install the Exchange Server transport and your program turns into an Exchange client, although you didn't change anything on the client program itself. Your program can also become a Microsoft Network (MSN) client if you use it in conjunction with the MSN driver on Windows 95, or you can configure the Internet E-mail Transport if you would rather use it as a POP3/SMTP client application. And last but not least, your application can even be a client for all these and more backbones at the same time. (See Figure 6-4 on page 294.)

The following are the advantages of MAPI:

- Client can run MAPI against multiple messaging systems, even simultaneously
- MAPI is built in into Windows
- Separation of messaging backbone and client
- Vendor-independent API

Disadvantages

MAPI is only a specification and not a messaging system in and of itself. It provides only a common way to access messaging backbones. You always need to have a MAPI information service available for your existing messaging backbone before you are able to use any MAPI-based client in conjunction with it. (See Figure 6-4.)

MAPI Subsets

MAPI is a powerful specification that defines both the client and the service provider interface, but a powerful specification also typically requires a powerful (and expensive) programmer. Extensive MAPI programming, however, is not always appropriate. If you develop a database application that needs to use only the messaging system as its transport media, forcing you to switch to C++ programming might be a bit much in this case. To simplify messaging programming, the MAPI client interface has been broken down into several subsets. Available subsets are Simple MAPI, Common Messaging Calls (CMC), and Collaborative Data Objects (CDO). (CDO was formerly known as Active Messaging.) The entire client interface is sometimes called Extended MAPI.

Simple MAPI and CMC provide the basic functionality for sending and receiving messages. More complex operations, such as copying messages from the Inbox to other folders, are not available. If you require these features, you can use CDO instead, which also allows for the creation of calendar and scheduling applications. It can be used, for instance, in conjunction with script languages to create active Web pages that are messaging-, scheduling-, and workgroup-computing–aware. Extended MAPI goes beyond every other set of interfaces and provides the most flexible control over all programmable MAPI objects. This API, therefore, would be the right choice if you were considering developing an application similar to the Exchange Client or Outlook. (See Figure 6-4.)

The Exchange Client interfaces and their features are:

- CDO; powerful and easy to use

- CMC; basic messaging functions are implemented for sending and receiving messages as well as for accessing MAPI address book

- Extended MAPI; provides full access to Messaging API functions

- Simple MAPI; basic messaging functions are implemented for sending and receiving messages as well as for accessing MAPI address book

Messaging Client Application Categories

To emphasize the complexity of MAPI dependencies, a distinction has been made between messaging applications. Basically three types exist: *messaging-aware applications*, *messaging-enabled applications*, and *messaging-based workgroup applications*.

Messaging-Aware Applications

Messaging-aware applications do not depend on the existence of the MAPI subsystem because they make use of only the basic e-mail functions to perform operations that are not part of their core functionality, such as sending messages. Consequently, messaging features can be treated as an add-on to messaging-aware applications. For example, Word can send documents as e-mail messages but it can also be used when no messaging system exists. In this case, only the e-mail feature is unavailable.

Messaging-Enabled Applications

Messaging-enabled applications cannot exist without the underlying messaging subsystem. Electronic forms (16-bit) are good examples of such programs because they are simply unable to start without the existence of a valid MAPI configuration.

Messaging-Based Workgroup Applications

Messaging-based workgroup applications represent the most complex messaging program category. They make full use of all the capabilities of the MAPI subsystem and its information services. These programs are messaging clients such as the Exchange Client, Schedule+, and Outlook. (See Figure 6-4.)

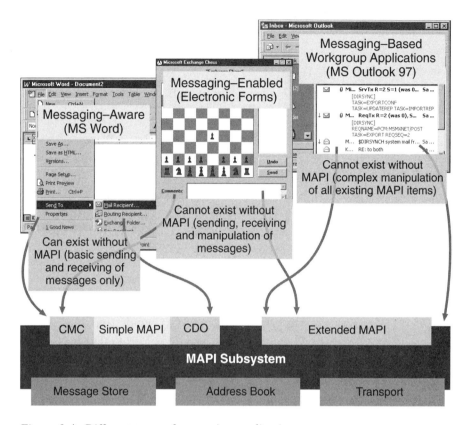

Figure 6-4. Different types of messaging applications.

The types of messaging applications and their most useful APIs are as follows:

- Messaging-aware applications: Simple MAPI, CMC, or CDO
- Messaging-enabled applications: CDO or Extended MAPI
- Messaging-based workgroup applications: Extended MAPI

Information Services

Information services are separated into transport services, address books, and message stores, and the Windows-based messaging client uses them as appropriate whenever it needs to access messaging resources. The client uses transport services to access the various messaging backbones, regardless of their data formats or their mechanisms of sending and receiving messages. Furthermore, the client uses message store services to maintain messages in public, private, or personal folders, and it uses address book services to resolve recipient addresses.

Address Book Provider

An address book provider maintains and provides information about recipient objects to the client. The address book provider is an essential component of the MAPI subsystem because without available recipient objects, it would be impossible to send newly-composed messages.

For example, you compose a new message and enter the name of the desired recipient in the **To** box. At this point, the recipient is nothing but a string, which means the recipient name still needs to be resolved to become a unique recipient object. Otherwise, the messaging backbone will not know how to deliver the message. The address will be resolved automatically when the message is sent. If you want, you can also resolve the addresses manually by using the **Check Names** command on the **Tools** menu of the **New Message** window. To resolve the address, the client communicates with the MAPI address book service—for example, the Exchange Server address book. If the address resolution succeeds, the display name of the recipient becomes underlined.

Server-Based Address Books

The server-based address book contains the recipient objects that exist within the Exchange Server organization. The Emsabp32.dll maintains this service, which is part of the MAPI driver for Exchange Server.

As mentioned in Chapter 5, the possible recipient objects on Exchange Servers are mailboxes, distribution lists, public folders, and custom recipients. They are organized in Recipient containers, which are also used to display the server-based address list in a structured way within the address book of the Exchange Client and Outlook. To create alternate views of the recipients, you can define address book views using the Exchange Administrator program. Despite all the possible address book views that you might have created on the server, the addresses of all possible recipients in the organization are also grouped together within the Global Address List. Because the Global Address List contains all recipients, it is used by default for address resolution.

Offline Address Book

The Offline Address Book—also maintained by the MAPI service for Exchange Server (Emsabp32.dll)—contains a local copy of the server-based Global Address List. Once downloaded, it will be used in all situations where the server-based address book is unavailable during offline operation. To download the address information from the server, open the client's **Tools** menu, point to the **Synchronize** option, and then click **Download Address Book**. You can read more about the offline address book configuration in Chapter 7.

Personal Address Book

The Personal Address Book is maintained within a local .PAB file by the Mspst32.dll, which represents the Personal Address Book and the Personal Folder Store service. It is used as the repository for all kinds of personal addresses, especially those that do not exist within the organization. For example, you can create a personal address book entry for a customer who resides in a foreign mail system that can be reached through the Internet. Once created, you can use the new entry to address messages to the customer just as you would to any other recipient who resides within your own Exchange Server organization. The configuration of address books is covered in detail in Chapter 7.

Message Store Provider

A Message Store Provider maintains the user's e-mail messages in message folders. Whenever you open a message, save it, copy it to another folder, or delete it, your client communicates with a message store service by using the MAPI subsystem. The Emsmdb32.dll is involved so long as you are working with items stored on an Exchange Server. The Emsmdb32.dll is part of the MAPI service for Exchange Server and provides the services required for accessing public folders as well as the private folders of your mailbox. The Emsmdb32.dll is also involved if you are working with an Offline Folder Store.

You can also configure a Personal Folder Store within a local .PST file, which allows you to create an additional repository for folders to download messages from the server. In other words, a .PST file can be used to keep the size of the server-based mailbox small. The Personal Folder Store service has been implemented in a file called Mspst32.dll. The configuration of the Personal Folder Store as well as the Exchange Server service is covered in more detail in Chapter 7.

Message Transport Provider

A Message Transport Provider is responsible for physical message delivery. This service takes outgoing messages from the MAPI subsystem to transfer them to the underlying messaging backbone to which it corresponds. The Message Transport Provider then hands received messages over to the MAPI subsystem for delivery to the client.

The Exchange Client and Outlook Setup programs provide the option to install the Exchange Server and the MS Mail Transport. Examples of other available transport services are the Internet E-mail Transport, which communicates with a POP3/SMTP host, and the MSN Transport, which allows you to download messages from the Microsoft Online Network. (See Figure 6-5.)

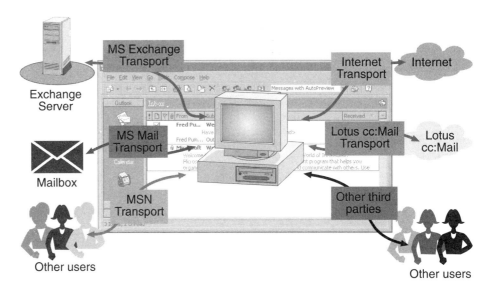

Figure 6-5. The universal Inbox.

MAPI service providers and their functions are as follows:

- Internet E-mail Transport provider; to send and receive messages using SMTP and POP3

- Exchange Server Transport and Store provider; to send and receive messages and to store them in server-based mailboxes or in .OST files

- Microsoft Fax Transport provider (Windows 95); to send faxes

- MSN Transport provider (Windows 95); to download messages from the Microsoft Network

- MS Mail Transport provider; to send and receive messages to and from MS Mail

- Outlook Address Book provider; to provide the contents of Contacts folders to client address books

- Personal Address Book provider; to store personal addresses

- Personal Folder Store provider; to store messages locally in a .PST file

- Other providers for additional messaging systems such as Lotus cc:Mail are also available and are provided by ISVs

Messaging Profiles

One of the primary goals of the MAPI subsystem is to extend easily to provide access to various messaging systems either simultaneously or in separate sessions. To meet this goal, messaging profiles are used. A messaging profile, sometimes also called a MAPI profile, is the set of those information services that should be activated during a particular session. All required configuration settings are stored in the messaging profile. Consequently, at least one messaging profile needs to exist to successfully start a MAPI-based messaging client. (See Figure 6-6.) The configuration of messaging profiles is covered in more detail in Chapter 7.

Profile Wizard

The Profile Wizard, also called *Microsoft Outlook Setup Wizard* (formerly known as Inbox Setup Wizard), guides you through the process of configuring a messaging profile, and can be launched in a variety of ways. For example, you can use the **Mail** applet (it might also be called **Mail And Fax**) of the **Control Panel** to display existing messaging profiles and their configurations. If you add a new profile, the wizard is automatically launched. The Profile Wizard also appears if no profile exists when you start the Exchange Client or Outlook. The client is simply unable to operate without a valid profile, so the wizard prompts for all the required information to create a valid messaging profile before the actual client is started.

Note The Exchange Client 5.0 will launch the **Microsoft Outlook Setup Wizard** if Outlook version 8.03 has been installed on the same machine. It will launch the **Inbox Setup Wizard** if Outlook 8.03 is not installed. The **Microsoft Outlook Setup Wizard** and the **Inbox Setup Wizard** provide almost the same functionality.

Multiple Profiles

The MAPI subsystem is able to use only one profile at a time; however, more than one profile can be created on the same computer. While completing the exercises in this book, you might have already configured multiple profiles on the test server NEWYORK-1. One profile might connect you to the mailbox Fred Pumpkin, another to Administrator New York-1, but only one profile will be activated at any particular time. You can choose the desired profile at client startup according to its name in order to connect to the desired mailbox.

The Exchange Client and Outlook use the default profile automatically if more than one profile exists. Nevertheless, it is possible to configure the clients to prompt you for the profile name at every session startup. To do this, enable the **Prompt For A Profile To Be Used** option on the **General** property page of the client's **Options** dialog box, which can be found using the **Options** command on the **Tools** menu of the Exchange Client and Outlook.

Multiple Users

Windows NT and Windows 95 provide support for multiple users who share a single computer, because these operating systems can maintain messaging profiles on a per-user basis. This means that the profile settings of one user do not affect the configuration of any other. Profiles for the user currently logged on are stored in the Registry under:

```
HKEY_CURRENT_USER
    \Software
        \Microsoft
            \Windows Messaging Subsystem
                \Profiles
```

Subkeys exist that correspond to every profile a user has created.

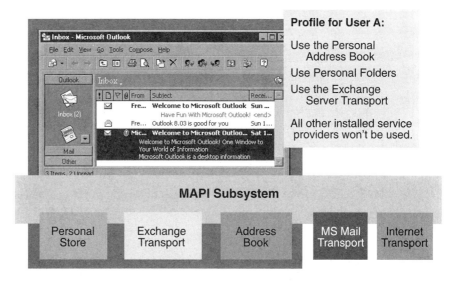

Figure 6-6. Transport provider configuration via messaging profiles.

The functions of messaging profiles are to:

- Configure service providers according to the client needs
- Provide easy-to-select working environments for messaging applications
- Specify service providers to be used in a client session

Client Message Store Options

Two information services—the Exchange Server service and the Personal Folder Store service—maintain messages in message folders on a server or in a message folder file. Three message stores can be configured using these two services. The Exchange Server service allows you to access all server-based folders and also gives you the Offline Message Store (.OST files), which is a synchronized copy of the server-based folders that are kept available when working off line. The third message store is maintained by the Personal Folder Store (.PST files). Personal folders are useful if you want to download messages from the server to reduce the size of the server-based mailbox or to use the Remote Mail features of the Exchange Client and Outlook. (See Figure 6-7 on page 302.)

Server-Based Message Storage

The server-based message store is usually the primary location for message storage because it provides many valuable features. For example, local hard disk space is not consumed for message storage and user messages are automatically included in the regular server backup process. Server-based message folders can also be shared between users to distribute information more efficiently. Therefore, the server-based message store is divided into two different types, the public and the private store. The Public Information Store maintains the public folders, which are used to share information with other users in the organization. The Private Information Store, in turn, maintains the server-based mailboxes for all users that reside on a particular Exchange Server. Mailboxes are typically not shared with many other users. Both stores, however, are accessed only through the Exchange Server IS service.

Client-Based Message Storage

You can work with an Offline Folder Store or a Personal Folder Store because both keep messages locally on the computer's hard disk. This can be helpful if, for example, you want to work without being connected to the network.

.PST Files

The Personal Folder Store is implemented as a separate information service (Mspst32.dll). It maintains a local .PST file, which contains the personal folders and their messages. Like the server-based folders, personal folders can contain data types such as e-mail messages, documents, spreadsheets, multimedia files, as well as others. To protect the .PST files against unauthorized access, you can set up a .PST file password.

A Personal Folder Store maintains messages independently of an Exchange Server. You can add this message store to your messaging profile, create a personal folder file, start the client, and then move your messages from the server-based store to the folder file. This reduces the size of the server-based mailbox since the downloaded messages no longer exist on the server. Down-loaded messages are subsequently available regardless of an active server connection. (See Figure 6-7.)

A Personal Folder Store is necessary if you want to move a mailbox to another site. First you need to download all messages to personal folders; and then you can disconnect from the old home server. The server-based mailbox can then be deleted safely since the messages no longer exist on the server. You must create the desired mailbox on the new home server within the other site, and then you'll connect to this server to upload all the messages from the .PST file again. All messages will become available and will be included in the backup cycles of the server. The process to move mailboxes within a single site has been explained in Chapter 5.

Personal Folders also allow you to use the remote mail function of the Exchange Client and Outlook. You can establish a connection to the server using Dial-Up Networking to download header files. The header files will list all available message items that currently reside in your server-based Inbox. Thus, you can specify which server-based messages to download, which to delete immediately without downloading, and which to copy to your local .PST file. Unfortunately, it's not possible to access any folders other than the Inbox while in Remote Mail mode.

Note A .PST file can grow up to a size of 2 GB and can contain a maximum of 64,000 items.

.OST Files

The Offline Folder Store must be chosen if you want to maintain messages primarily on the Exchange Server computer, and you also need the messages to be available locally for offline operation. As soon as you configure an offline folder file, system folders such as the **Inbox**, **Outbox**, **Sent Items**, and **Deleted Items** are synchronized. If you're using Outlook, the **Calendar**, **Contacts**, **Journal**, **Notes**, and **Tasks** folders are also included. Additional folders can be selected, but you should keep in mind that synchronized offline folders are copies of server-based folders, which means you actually keep each message in two locations.

One of the most significant advantages of the offline folder store is that you can include public folders in offline operations. First you need to add the desired public folder to your **Favorites** lists while working on line, which are in the **Public Folder** container. Then right-click the folder and select **Proper-ties** from the context menu. Within the **Properties** dialog box switch to the **Synchronize** property page where you can select the folder to be available both on line and off line. It is important to note, however, that you download a copy of the entire folder content to your local .OST file when you synchronize the folder. You can add new items to the folder, or modify and delete existing ones, even during offline operation. When you log on to the server again, any changes made to the offline copy will be uploaded and the modifications will appear in the online folder.

Using off line folders can become a disadvantage when connecting to a server with slow dial-up links, because it might take a long time to synchronize large folders. Keep in mind that you must always synchronize all the changes to a folder, which means you can't selectively synchronize single messages or messages that meet certain criteria. (See Figure 6-7.)

Note The offline message store has been implemented directly into the **Microsoft Exchange Server** transport provider, which is listed under "Information Services" as a MAPI service provider. Therefore, you cannot work with offline folders if you are connecting to a different messaging system.

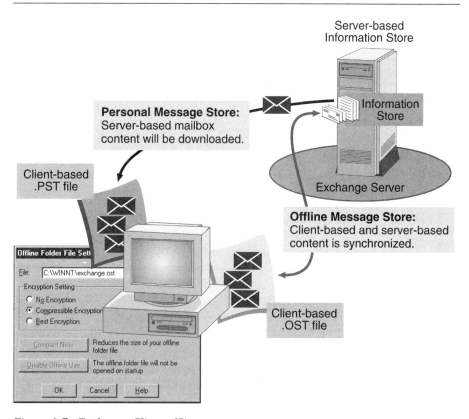

Figure 6-7. Exchange Client offline support.

Basic configuration issues to consider before working while disconnected from the server are as follows:

- The client must be configured to start and work off line if no permanent connection to the server is available (Select the **Work Offline And Use Dial-Up Networking** option on the **General** property page of the **Microsoft Exchange Server** transport provider).

- An Offline Address Book or a Personal Address Book should exist.

- Offline Folders allow you to keep a local copy of server folders (local replication).

- Offline Folders allow you to work with public folders off line through synchronized public folder shortcuts.

- The server-based mailbox will be synchronized automatically with the contents of the Offline Folders when an online connection is established again.

- In Personal Folders, Mail header files can be retrieved separately from the message contents to reduce the time necessary for downloading messages through telephone links.

- Personal Folders and the Remote Mail mode allow you to specify which server-based messages should be downloaded through Dial-Up Networking, which should be deleted on the server without downloading, and which should be downloaded while a copy is kept still at the server.

- Personal Folders don't provide a way to work with public folder contents while off line.

Lesson 3: Client Installation

Exchange Server implementation also involves the preparation of the client rollout. This preparation can include one of two different approaches, depending on the client operating system and hardware platform. Both approaches exclude each other: either you decide to use a particular messaging client and consider upgrading the installed computer base where necessary to meet the expectations of that client, or you leave it to the installed base and choose the client accordingly. For example, you will first need to upgrade existing Windows 3.x workstations to Windows 95, or Windows NT, before you can install the 32-bit version of Outlook. On the other hand, if you are unable to upgrade the operating system, you are forced to use Outlook for Windows 3.x with its reduced functionality. No matter which method you use, hardware requirements of the various clients must be determined before making a decision.

Once you have chosen a particular messaging client, you typically start the installation rollout. As expected, the client installation offers you a broad variety of setup options. The different options, when to choose them, and what kind of tools to use adjust the client setup process to meet users' specific needs is covered in this lesson.

At the end of this lesson, you will be able to:

- List the hardware requirements for each existing Exchange Client and Outlook

- Perform a local installation

- Install a client using a shared network installation point

- Use installation tools to configure client parameters prior to setup

Estimated time to complete this lesson: 45 minutes

Client Installation Requirements

The installation requirements for each of the available clients vary based on the operating system. Disk space and memory (RAM) requirements range between 2 and 46 MB and 1 and 16 MB, respectively. As a rule of thumb, you can install any of the available clients if a computer has an Intel 486 processor or higher, 16 MB of RAM, and 50 MB of free disk space.

MS-DOS–Based Exchange Client

The MS-DOS–based client requires between 2 and 3 MB of disk space for installation and at least 1 MB of RAM to operate. It uses TCP/IP, IPX/SPX, or NetBEUI to communicate with the Exchange Server computer via RPC.

When you start the Exchange Client in monitor mode by supplying the parameter -M to the command line, you can work with other MS-DOS programs in the foreground. You will be notified as new e-mail arrives, but the Client offers only the basic messaging features since MAPI is not available on MS-DOS. For example, Schedule+ or support for electronic forms are not implemented.

Note Although Outlook is the primary client for Exchange Server 5.5, an MS-DOS–based Outlook client does not exist.

Unlike Windows-based clients, MS-DOS–based clients cannot:

- Import mail message files (.MMF) and Personal Address Book (.PAB) files
- Support Exchange Forms Designer and Outlook forms
- Allow more than one **AutoSignature** entry
- Implement special remote configurations such as Download Headers Only

Windows 3.x–Based Clients

The Windows 3.x–based Outlook client requires between 12 and 22 MB of disk space, while the 16-bit Exchange Client needs between 12 and 20 MB of disk space. Both clients require a minimum 8 MB of RAM to operate properly, 12MB if electronic forms will be used. They can communicate with the Exchange Server via RPC over IPX/SPX and NetBEUI, and, if Windows Sockets are installed, via TCP/IP as well.

The Exchange Client for Windows 3.x is a full MAPI-based client, which means it supports all messaging features, including Schedule+, electronic forms, and personal folder stores. Outlook for Windows 3.x, in turn, supports all features of the 32-bit Outlook version except Outlook forms, Microsoft Visual Basic Script, and the Client Object Model. Remote Mail functionality exists for Exchange and Outlook, but it is implemented in a separate component called ShivaRemote. The ShivaRemote configuration is covered in Chapter 7.

Windows 95–Based Exchange Client

The Exchange Client for Windows 95 is an upgrade to the Windows Messaging Client, which comes with Windows 95. It requires between 12 MB and 22 MB of disk space, depending on the selected installation option, and at least 8 MB of RAM to operate properly. The Windows 95–based client can use RPC via TCP/IP, IPX/SPX, or NetBEUI to communicate with the Exchange Server.

Windows NT–Based Exchange Client

Like the Windows 95 Exchange Client, the Exchange Client for Windows NT communicates with the Exchange Server computer using TCP/IP, IPX/SPX, or NetBEUI. This client needs between 12 MB and 22 MB of disk space and at least 16 MB of RAM for proper operation.

Outlook for Windows 95 and Windows NT

Outlook, which represents the other full-featured Microsoft messaging client, is supposed to replace the former Exchange and Schedule+ applications. Its 32-bit version is available for Windows 95 and Windows NT. This application requires 8 MB of RAM on Windows 95 and a minimum 16 MB of RAM on Windows NT. To get reasonable performance, however, you should consider doubling the minimum requirements. Depending on the selected installation options, between 26 and 46 MB of disk space are required.

Macintosh-Based Client Considerations

The Macintosh clients require a minimum of an 030 processor and at least 8 MB of RAM to operate. In order to run all Outlook features, including the Calendar, 12 MB are required. For a minimum installation, you will need 12 MB of disk space, while 16 MB disk space is necessary if you want to install the client (either Exchange or Outlook) with all options.

Note You should use Macintosh operating system version 7.6 or higher. It is further recommended that you activate the virtual memory and set its size to a minimum of 1 MB plus the installed physical memory (for example, 17 MB if you have 16 MB of RAM).

Both the Exchange Client and Outlook communicate with the Exchange Server using the AppleTalk protocol or TCP/IP. If you use TCP/IP, MacTCP 2.06 or higher must be used on the Macintosh. Windows NT Services for Macintosh must be installed on the Windows NT Server that is running Exchange Server; otherwise, the communication between the Macintosh client and Windows NT Server computer cannot take place. (See Figure 6-8.)

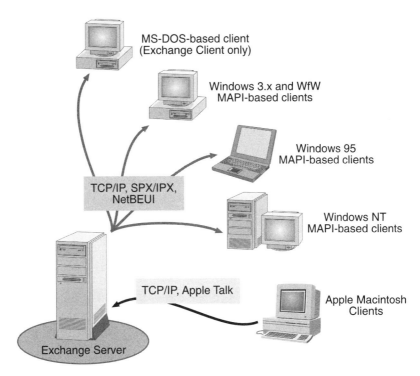

Figure 6-8. Supported Exchange Client platforms.

The installation requirements for each client are listed below:

Microsoft Exchange Client	Protocols required	Disk space: minimum/maximum	Minimum RAM required
MS-DOS–based Client	RPC via TCP/IP, IPX/SPX, or NetBEUI	2 MB/3 MB	1 MB
Windows 3.x–based Exchange Client	RPC via TCP/IP (with Windows sockets support), IPX/SPX, or NetBEUI	12 MB/20 MB	8 MB
Windows 3.x–based Outlook Client	RPC via TCP/IP (with Windows sockets support), IPX/SPX, or NetBEUI	12 MB/22 MB	8 MB
Windows 95–based Exchange Client	RPC via TCP/IP, IPX/SPX, or NetBEUI	12 MB/22 MB	8 MB
Windows NT–based Exchange Client	RPC via TCP/IP, IPX/SPX (NWLink), or NetBEUI	12 MB/22 MB	16 MB

(continues)

(continued)

Microsoft Exchange Client	Protocols required	Disk space: minimum/maximum	Minimum RAM required
Outlook Client for Windows 95 and Windows NT	RPC via TCP/IP, IPX/ SPX (NWLink), or NetBEUI	26 MB/46 MB	8 MB on Windows 95 and 16 MB on Windows NT
Macintosh Exchange Client	AppleTalk File Protocol or TCP/IP 2.06	14 MB	8 MB
Macintosh Outlook Client	AppleTalk File Protocol or TCP/IP 2.06	12 MB/16 MB	8 - 12 MB

Performing a Local Installation

A local installation refers to the method of installing all client files on the computer's local hard disk. The Exchange Client, for instance, offers three different local installation options: **Typical**, **Custom**, and **Laptop**. Outlook has only two options—**Typical** and **Custom**. Depending on whether you install a client from CD-ROM or a shared network installation point, installation options can vary. For example, the **Workstation** or **Run From Network Server** option is not available when installing the Exchange Client or Outlook from CD-ROM. (See Figure 6-9 on page 311.) The options to install clients from the network are covered in more detail in "Performing a Shared Installation," later in this lesson.

Installing the Exchange Client

When you start the Exchange Client Setup program, you will be met with several installation options to select the components you want to install. The **Typical**, **Custom**, and **Laptop** options are always available when installing an Exchange Client from CD-ROM. They are also usually available when you start Setup from a shared network installation point, but they might be suppressed if you use the Setup Editor. Using the Setup Editor in conjunction with a shared network installation point is explained later in this section under "Installation Tools."

The **Typical** installation copies the necessary Exchange and Schedule+ client files to the local computer, but to save disk space, it does not install the transport service for MS Mail. The **Custom** option, on the other hand, offers you the most flexible control over the setup process. This option can be used, for example, to copy all components of the Exchange Client to the computer's hard disk or to add and remove components to and from an existing installation. If you want to save as much disk space as possible, however, you will need to select the **Laptop** option because it includes only the Exchange and the Schedule+ application files. Spell checker, online Help, and Schedule+ import/export files are omitted to save your valuable disk space for other applications.

Installing Outlook

Like the Exchange Client, Outlook offers local installation options that can help specify in detail which client components to install. The **Typical** installation option installs all the components that are usually required by the average user. However, if you need complete control over the setup process and the selection of Outlook components, you can choose the **Custom** option.

Setup.lst

The Exchange Client and Outlook Setup programs read their Setup.lst file from the installation point to determine what must be accomplished for a successful client installation. For example, temporary and hidden directories, which are necessary to decompress the client's compressed cabinet files (.CAB), will be created based on the Setup.lst information. Likewise, the text of several warning messages is defined here, but it is not recommended that you modify this file manually.

Exchng.stf and Outlook.stf

The Exchng.stf file (Exchange Client) and the Outlook.stf file (Outlook) contain the necessary information to successfully launch the Setup procedure. The extension .STF stands for Setup Table File. If you install the client from CD-ROM, the source files will be copied to a temporary installation directory (as defined in Setup.stf) before the actual setup process begins. In general, .STF files are used to provide you with information about available options during setup and to control the setup process according to your decisions. For example, if you select the **Custom** installation option, client components can be selected individually. The Exchng.stf and Outlook.stf files will determine which options are available and which components are listed as you click the **Change Option** button during setup to determine, in detail, which components to install.

Once the client files have been installed on the local hard disk, the Exchng.stf file will be copied to the Exchange Client directory. The Outlook.stf file, in turn, will be placed by default in the \Program Files\Microsoft Office\Office\ Setup directory. Setup will then edit the Win.ini file on Windows 3.x computers, or the Registry on Windows 95 and Windows NT, to define a reference path to that file. This is necessary to register the installed software with the operating system. For example, you can remove a client installation using the

Add/Remove Programs applet of the Control Panel because the Exchng.stf has been registered in the exchng32.exe@<version number> value under following key:

```
HKEY_LOCAL_MACHINE
  \SOFTWARE
    \Microsoft
      \MS Setup (ACME)
        \Table Files
```

The Outlook.stf will be registered in the Microsoft Outlook@<version number> value under the same key.

Default.prf and Outlook.prf

The Default.prf and Outlook.prf files contain preconfigured settings, which can be used to generate a messaging profile after client installation. The extension .PRF stands for Profile Descriptor File. By default, no Default.prf exists for the Exchange Client, but it can be created using the Setup Editor. Outlook, on the other hand, uses the Outlook.prf file, which follows the same file format specification as the Default.prf. An Outlook.prf file that contains settings to connect to an Exchange Server can be found on the installation CD under \Outlook.w32\Office. If a Default.prf or Outlook.prf file exists in the client installation point, Setup copies this file to the local Windows directory. The Automatic Profile Generator (Newprof.exe) can then be used to generate the user profile accordingly. The purpose of .PRF files and the Automatic Profile Generator is explained in more detail later in this lesson.

Maintenance

Whenever you start the Exchange Client or Outlook Setup program, it checks whether the client has already been installed on the local computer. It does so by verifying the existence of the Exchng.stf/Outlook.stf file according to the Win.ini or Registry settings. If an existing client installation is detected, Setup checks whether a MAPI-based client is running at the moment. If so, it will pause in order to avoid conflicts with open files, and will ask you to close these programs. Setup continues and launches the **Maintenance** mode, which gives you the option to add or remove client components based on the Exchng.stf/Outlook.stf file. You can select the components you want to add to your installation, or you can deselect those you want to remove. If you elect to remove components and continue with the Maintenance mode, Setup deletes the deselected component references from the system entirely.

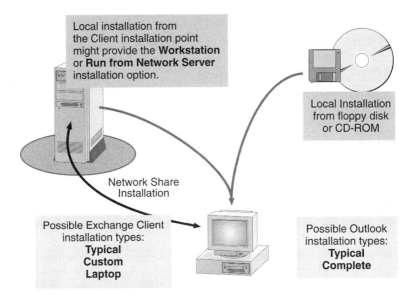

Figure 6-9. Client installation modes.

The different installation modes are:

- **Custom**; to gain most flexible control over the setup process

- **Laptops** (Exchange Client only); to install the application files only; no additional files are copied

- **Run From Network Server** (Outlook Client); to create an Outlook installation, which runs from a network share

- **Typical**; to install the files required by the average user

- **Workstation** (Exchange Client); to create an Exchange Client installation that runs from a network share; only configuration files are copied to the local hard disk

Exercise 12: Installing Exchange and Outlook Clients

Although the setup information required to install Outlook differs from installation of the Exchange Client, most of the relevant information about messaging is the same. This exercise focuses on Outlook as the newest and primary Windows-based messaging client; however, the Exchange Client will also be installed.

Estimated time to complete this exercise: 45 minutes

Description

In this exercise, you will install the Exchange Client and the Outlook client. After Setup has been completed successfully, you will create a messaging profile to allow Outlook to connect to the Exchange Server. Finally, you will start Outlook to view newly created items.

Note Although this exercise suggests installing the Exchange Client and Outlook on an Exchange Server computer, this is not a supported configuration. It is suggested only to spare you an additional computer for testing. To install the clients, it is highly recommended that you stop the server services beforehand (otherwise, Setup may hang or produce error messages). If, at a later time, the client is removed from the server, do not remove common files, since this will cause the Exchange Server to malfunction. Do NOT install a client on a "real" server.

- Task 12a describes the steps for installing Exchange.

- Task 12b describes the steps for installing Outlook 97.

- Task 12c describes the steps for creating a profile and for configuring information services in an Exchange profile.

Prerequisites

- Have the Microsoft Exchange Client 5.0 installation CD available (comes with Exchange Server 5.0).

- Have the Microsoft Outlook version 8.03 installation CD available (comes with Exchange Server 5.5).

- Make sure that Exchange Server services are stopped during client installation. The services must be restarted manually through the **Services** applet of the Control Panel once the client installation is complete (rebooting the server will also restart the services).

- Complete this exercise while logged on as Admin-NY1 on NEWYORK-1.

Task 12a: Installing Exchange Clients

1. Insert the Microsoft Exchange 5.0 Client CD-ROM.

2. Click **Start**, **Settings**, **Control Panel**, **Add/Remove Programs**, and then click **Install**.

3. Click **Next** and then click **Browse**.

4. Switch to the folder <CD-ROM drive>\ENG\WINNT\i386.

5. Select the **Setup** object.

6. Click **Open**, and then click **Finish**.

7. A **Microsoft Exchange Setup** dialog box appears. Click **Continue**.

8. The **Name And Organization Information** dialog box appears, prompting for registration information.

9. In the **Name** box, type *Admin-NY1*.

10. In the **Organization** box, type *STOCKSDATA* and then click **OK**.

11. Click **OK** again.

12. In the **Microsoft Exchange Setup** dialog box displaying the default directory path, click **OK**.

13. Click **Custom** to launch the **Microsoft Exchange – Custom** dialog box.

14. Click **Continue**.

15. Files are copied to the local hard disk.

16. A message box appears, indicating that Setup was completed successfully.

17. Click **OK**.

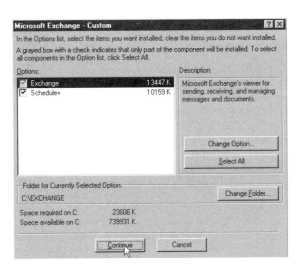

Task 12b: Installing Outlook Version 8.03

1. Insert the Microsoft Outlook version 8.03 CD-ROM.

2. Click **Start**, **Settings**, **Control Panel**, **Add/Remove Programs**, and then click **Install**.

3. Click **Next** and then click **Browse**.

4. Select the **Setup** program from the <CD ROM drive>:
   \Outlook.W32 directory.

5. Click **Open**, and then click **Finish**.

6. A **Microsoft Outlook 97 Setup** dialog box appears: click **Continue**.

7. The **Name And Organization Information** dialog box appears, prompting for registration information.

8. In the **Name** box, verify the information or enter *Admin-NY1*.

9. In the **Organization** box, verify the information or enter *STOCKSDATA*, and then click **OK**.

10. A **Confirm Name And Organization Information** dialog box appears: click **OK**.

11. A **Microsoft Outlook Setup** dialog box appears. Enter the CD Key of your installation CD-ROM and then click **OK**.

12. Click **OK** to confirm the Product ID.

13. A **Microsoft Outlook Setup** dialog box appears, displaying the default directory path. Accept the defaults and click **OK**.

14. Click **Custom** to launch the **Microsoft Outlook Setup – Custom** dialog box.

15. Click **Select All**, and then click **Continue** to copy the program files to the local hard disk.

16. If Setup detects Schedule+ on your computer (because you performed Task 12a earlier), a message box appears, asking whether to use Schedule+ as your primary calendar instead of Microsoft Outlook. Click **No**.

17. A **Microsoft Outlook Setup** message box appears, indicating that Setup completed successfully.

18. Click **OK**.

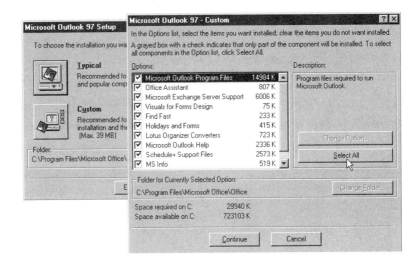

Task 12c: Creating a Messaging Profile

1. Verify that the Exchange Server services are running (reboot the server if necessary and log on as Admin-NY1 again).

2. On the **Desktop**, double-click the **Inbox** icon.

3. A **Microsoft Outlook Setup Wizard** dialog box appears.

4. Clear the **Microsoft Mail** and **Internet E-Mail** check boxes (which might not exist if you have not installed the client with all options) and then click **Next**.

5. A **Microsoft Outlook Setup Wizard** dialog box appears, prompting for your Exchange Server computer and mailbox name. Under **Microsoft Exchange Server**, type *NEWYORK-1*. Under mailbox, type *Fred Pumpkin*.

6. Click **Next**.

7. A **Microsoft Outlook Setup Wizard** dialog box appears, asking if you travel with this computer. Verify that **No** is selected, and then click **Next**.

8. A **Microsoft Outlook Setup Wizard** dialog box appears, asking for the path to your Personal Address Book. In the edit box, enter the path to your personal Address Book (for example, *[Drive]:\EXCHANGE\ ADMIN-NY1.PAB*), and then click **Next**.

9. A **Microsoft Outlook Setup Wizard** dialog box appears, asking if you want to run Outlook automatically every time you start Windows. Verify that **Do Not Add Outlook To The Startup Group** is selected, and then click **Next**.

10. Click **Finish**.

11. The Microsoft Exchange Client appears.

12. On the **File** menu, click **Exit And Log Off**.

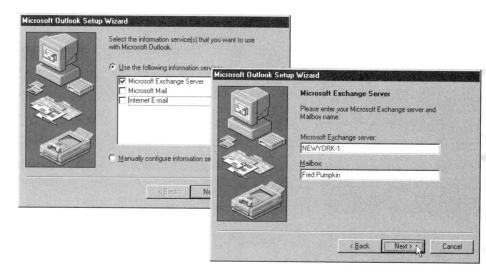

Review

During the installation process you have a choice between several installation types. The **Custom** option provides the most flexible control because you can select specific components you want to install. After clicking **Continue,** files will be copied and Setup completes successfully.

Before you can use any MAPI-based client, a messaging profile must be created. You can select the information services you want to use from the list of installed drivers to configure the messaging profile. Even if you start the Exchange Client (without an existing profile), the **Microsoft Outlook Setup Wizard** is launched and will prompt you for the required information.

To connect to an Exchange Server, you must include the **Microsoft Exchange Server** transport in your profile. You can add other information services, such as a Personal Address Book or a Personal Folder Store, to the configuration to extend your Exchange Client or Outlook session. Once the profile has been generated, but not before, the Exchange Client and Outlook can start.

Performing a Shared Installation

A shared client installation refers to a configuration where the majority of the client files are kept on a file server within the network. Only essential configuration files will be copied to the local computer to save as much hard disk space as possible for other applications. (See Figure 6-10 on page 318.)

Differences in Client Installation Points

Two different types of client network installation points can be created that differ in terms of available setup options. The first type of installation point does not provide the option to install a client in the network at all. In other words, such an installation point can be compared to a 1:1 copy of the installation CD-ROM that has been created only on a network share. To build an installation point of this type for Exchange Client 5.0, you need to execute the Setup program that is located in the CD-ROM's root directory for your client language. In contrast, Outlook provides a file called UCSetup.exe, which can be found in the installation CD-ROM's root directory for your Outlook client language. This lesson does not consider this type of installation point because it offers the local installation options only.

The second type of network installation point (also called shared network installation point) is more interesting because it is the actual access point for a network installation. Such an installation point must be created explicitly for each client version (Windows 3.x, Windows 95, Windows NT, and so on) by running the corresponding Setup program with the **/A** option. (See Figure 6-10 on page 318.)

The **Workstation** installation option (Exchange Client) or **Run From Network Server** option (Outlook) becomes available only when you execute the corresponding client's Setup program from a shared network installation point. By choosing the **Workstation** option, you leave most of the client files on the network server, in contrast to the local installation, where you copy all files to the workstation's local hard disk. Furthermore, a network installation won't create the temporary setup directories on the local hard disk, which saves as much local disk space as possible even during the time of the client installation.

Note The advantages of a shared installation, such as saved local disk space, can also become disadvantages. For instance, most of the files must be loaded from the file server during client startup, which increases network traffic and typically slows down the client startup process. Likewise, if the network server is temporarily down or not available for any reason, you won't be able to start the Exchange Client or Outlook at all.

Creating a Shared Installation Point

All Windows-based Exchange and Outlook clients allow you start the Setup program by supplying the **/A** command line parameter (**Setup /A**). The MS DOS–based client, on the other hand, offers a **Shared** option within its setup procedure. The Macintosh clients do not support the opportunity to install a sharing point or a shared instance.

MS-DOS–Based Client

As mentioned, it is possible to create a shared installation point for the MS-DOS–based Exchange client, but there is no separate command line option to accomplish this. To copy all relevant client files to an install point for shared mail, the administrator starts the Setup as usual and then selects the **Shared** option.

Windows-Based Clients and Shared Windows Installations

If your users are running their Windows operating systems from a shared network installation, you will need to create the shared network installation point from a workstation that uses the same shared Windows installation as your users. Likewise, you—but not the users—will need write permission on both the shared installation point and the shared Windows directory because **Setup /A** will copy the system files of the MAPI subsystem to the Windows directory rather than to the shared installation point. Consequently, if write permissions are missing, the MAPI files cannot be copied and **Setup /A** will fail. The fact that a part of the client installation files is copied into the shared Windows directory means that if your users are loading their operating systems from different network locations, you will have to perform **Setup /A** separately for each shared Windows installation.

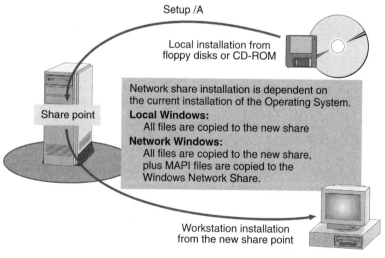

Figure 6-10. Creating a shared network installation point.

The steps required for a shared network installation of a Windows-based Exchange Client are as follows:

1. Create the shared network installation point using **Setup /A**.

2. Run the Exchange Client or Outlook Setup from the shared network installation point.

3. Select **Workstation** (Exchange Client) or **Run From Network Server** (Outlook) during setup.

Installation Tools

The Setup Editor and the Automatic Profile Generator are the most powerful installation tools at the administrator's disposal. These tools can be used in conjunction with a shared network installation point to adjust the behavior of the Exchange Client setup procedure as well as the configuration of the Windows-based Exchange Client. For example, you can use the Setup Editor to suppress the local installation options, such as **Laptop**, **Typical**, and **Custom**. The Setup Editor can also preconfigure a Windows 3.x Outlook client installation point. On the other hand, you can use the Automatic Profile Generator in conjunction with a profile descriptor file to create messaging profiles for all Windows-based clients.

Setup Editor

The Exchange Setup Editor offers the convenience of modifying important configuration files on a shared network installation point. Those files are the Setup.stf, Exchng.stf, and the Default.prf file. Modifications applied to them will affect the client setup process and, as a result, the client configuration.

The Setup Editor is available only on Windows platforms; a version for MS-DOS does not exist. This utility can be found on the Exchange Client CD in the \Stfedit directory and on the Outlook client CD in the \Support\Stfedit directory. You'll notice that two executables are provided, Stfedt16.exe and Stfedtr.exe. You must use the Stfedt16.exe to adjust settings at the Windows 3.x platform, but you'll need the Stfedtr.exe program if you want to control the behavior of the Setup program for clients on Windows 95 or Windows NT. Be careful not to interchange the Setup Editor versions, because you'll experience possible installation problems if you are using Stfedt16.exe to modify the configuration files on a shared installation point for Windows 95 or Windows NT clients.

You also need to pay attention to the client language, because configuration files such as Exchng.stf and Setup.stf are typically localized and are therefore language dependent. In other words, you'll need to use the English Setup

Editor to configure the English client and the French version to adjust the settings for the French client. If the languages of the editor and the client do not match, you will experience configuration problems as well.

Note The Setup Editor does not support the modification of files for a shared network installation of the 32-bit Outlook client.

Making Modifications with the Setup Editor

The Setup Editor can be used to adjust the Setup process itself, the client configuration, and the configuration of a default user profile. Important settings will be applied to the Exchng.stf and the Default.prf file. For example, the RPC Binding Order will be determined based on the Exchng.stf file. The configuration of the RPC Binding Order is treated in more detail in Chapter 7.

User Profile Settings

User profile settings are configured using only the Default.prf or an Outlook.prf file. However, the Setup Editor does not create an Outlook.prf as would be required for an automatic user profile configuration when running the Windows 95–based and Windows NT–based Outlook clients. You must manually configure the Outlook.prf file within the corresponding client installation points.

When you examine the shared network installation point for the Exchange Client at the moment it has been created, you'll notice that a Default.prf does not exist—only a Template.prf is provided. When it first starts up, the Setup Editor creates a copy of the Template.prf named Default.prf. The Default.prf is later used for the basic configuration of common user settings. For example, using the Setup Editor you can specify which information services to install and include in a default user profile. To configure advanced settings, however, or to configure user settings in conjunction with Outlook, you will need to edit manually the Default.prf/Outlook.prf using a text editor. The format of the .PRF files is explained later in this lesson under "Default Profile Generation."

The Template.prf has an easy-to-use reset mechanism. As soon as you delete the Default.prf from the shared network installation point, you reset all existing user profile customizations. This is because the Template.prf file is used again to generate a fresh Default.prf the next time you start the Setup Editor, which returns it to the starting point. On the other hand, the Setup Editor itself also provides a mechanism to undo the most recent changes, because it creates backup copies of the Exchng.stf and Default.prf files in the BAK directory of the shared client installation point. You simply need to restore the files from there and the most recent changes will be undone.

Automatic Profile Generator

The Automatic Profile Generator (Newprof.exe) is the actual installation tool that uses the Default.prf or Outlook.prf to create the MAPI profile for the user. The Exchange Client Setup launches this application in the background if it detects the Default.prf file on the shared network installation point after copying this file to the Windows directory. Outlook Setup checks for the Outlook.prf. The Automatic Profile Generator itself, however, can also be started manually at any time to create additional profiles or to modify existing ones. By default, it will be installed in the Exchange Client directory. Outlook will replace the original program with a newer version. You can run this tool by specifying the following options:

```
NEWPROF [-P <Path to .PRF file>] [-S] [-X] [-Z]
```

-P   References the complete path to the .PRF descriptor file.

-S   Provides a user interface to select the .PRF file, and to display status and error messages.

-Z   Displays MAPI status codes in case any errors are encountered. Can only be used in conjunction with the -S switch.

-X   Executes NEWPROF.EXE **-S** automatically without user interaction. Requires the **-P***<Path to the .PRF file>* switch.

Outlook Default Profiles

Outlook 97 uses the **Microsoft Outlook Setup Wizard** to create a default messaging profile. As mentioned earlier in this chapter, this utility is launched when Outlook is started without a valid messaging profile. This wizard also appears if you add a new profile to the existing ones using the **Mail and Fax** applet from the Control Panel.

It is also possible to automatically create a default profile for every user who wants to use Outlook on a particular computer. Only the Outlook.prf file within the Windows directory needs to be edited. Settings can be applied prior to the actual client installation when creating the desired Outlook.prf file in the client installation point. Setup will then detect and automatically copy this file to your Windows directory at installation time.

Note   To enable the automatic profile generation, the HomeServer= setting must be set correctly in the Outlook.prf file. The listed server can be any server in your organization that can be reached through direct RPC communication. However, a default profile will be generated only the first time a user starts Outlook on a particular computer. It is also important to note that the Windows NT account name must match the user's mailbox alias, otherwise the profile must be adjusted manually before Outlook can be used.

Two sample .PRF files, the Exchange.prf and the None.prf, are available if you have installed the Microsoft Office 97 Resource Kit. For the settings to take effect, copy one of them from the \Program Files\ORK97\Outlook\Profiles directory to the shared network installation point, and rename it as *Outlook.prf*. The None.prf file can be especially useful if you want to launch the Outlook Setup Wizard to access the options for configuring a new profile during the client startup.

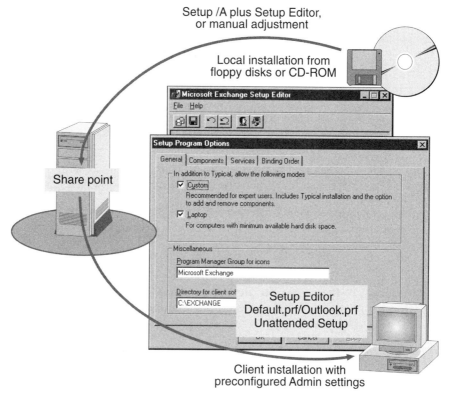

Figure 6-11. Customizing the installation process.

To modify the Exchange Client Setup, follow these steps:

1. Use the Setup Editor to modify default Setup options.

2. Edit the resulting Default.prf file to specify further Client Profile settings.

3. Use the automatic profile generator (NEWPROF.EXE) to configure the client profiles automatically.

To modify Outlook for Windows 95 and Windows NT Setup, follow these steps:

1. Edit the Outlook.prf file in the client installation point manually.

2. Use the automatic profile generator (NEWPROF.EXE) to configure the client profiles.

Default Profile Generation

The Exchange Client's Default.prf and Outlook's Outlook.prf offer several options to specify default profile settings and to configure information services. Basic configuration settings for the Default.prf can be specified using the Setup Editor; however, the Outlook.prf and several advanced Exchange settings can be adjusted only if you edit the .PRF file using a text editor.

Let's say that Fred Pumpkin, our STOCKSDATA administrator, wants to customize his profile. The profile should reflect his given name and surname and should point to his home server. He edits the Outlook.prf to modify the line **ProfileName=Microsoft Outlook** in the **[General]** section. The result is as follows: **ProfileName=***Fred Pumpkin*. Furthermore, he needs to set the **HomeServer** line, which can be found in the **[Service2]** section, to *NEWYORK-1*. To ensure that the current profile will be overwritten, Fred still has to verify that the option **OverwriteProfile** is set to *Yes* in the **[General]** section. Then he can execute the Automatic Profile Generator (Newprof.exe) to specify the modified .PRF file. Newprof.exe will create a fresh profile and name it Fred Pumpkin, as shown in Figure 6-12 on page 325.

The **[General]** section of a Profile Descriptor File contains the default settings, which are related to the user profile but not to a specific information service. The following entries can be adjusted:

`Custom=1`	Indicates that this is a customized PRF.
`DefaultProfile=[Yes/No]`	The profile being created will be set as the default profile if this is set to YES.
`DefaultStore=<Service ID>`	By default, the value is set to Service2, which corresponds to the Exchange Server Service. The **[Service List]** section determines this relationship.
`OverwriteProfile=[Yes/No]`	If set to Yes, existing profiles with the same name will be overwritten. If set to No and a profile with the same name already exists, the new profile will not be created.
`ProfileName=` `<Name of the Profile>`	Specifies the name used for the profile to be created.

The **[Service List]** section lists all the services that will be included in the default profile. The following entries are examples (default list):

- Service1 = Microsoft Exchange Client or Microsoft Outlook Client
- Service2 = Microsoft Exchange Server
- Service3 = Personal Address Book

You can adjust the settings for each of the services in their corresponding sections, **[Service1]**, **[Service2]**, and **[Service3]**. For example, the following settings, which can be set under the [Service2] section, affect the Exchange Server transport:

`MailboxName=`	Name of the Exchange Server mailbox for a user.
`HomeServer=`	Name of the Server computer where the mailbox exists.
`OfflineFolderPath=`	Location of the offline folder file (.OST).
`OfflineAddressBookPath`	The directory of the offline address book.
`ExchangeConfigFlags`	To specify how to connect to the Exchange Server. 4 = Normal 6 = Ask whether to connect or work off line at startup. 12 = Allow clients to be authenticated via the Internet. 14 = Combination of 6 and 12.
`ConversionProhibited`	TRUE = NEWPROF will copy the mailbox name to the profile without resolving it. FALSE = NEWPROF will check the server and mailbox name and copy them to the profile only if they are correct.

Sections for the Exchange Client, Outlook, and other MAPI components exist as well, and each section contains a listing of the supported configuration settings. For this reason, these settings are not explicitly listed here.

Limitations

Although you have extensive control over the customization of information services, some configuration settings cannot be specified. For example, it is impossible to configure Inbox rules or Out of Office rules using the Automatic Profile Generator. Some other settings such as the AutoSignature or any Schedule+ options are also not adjustable through profile descriptor files.

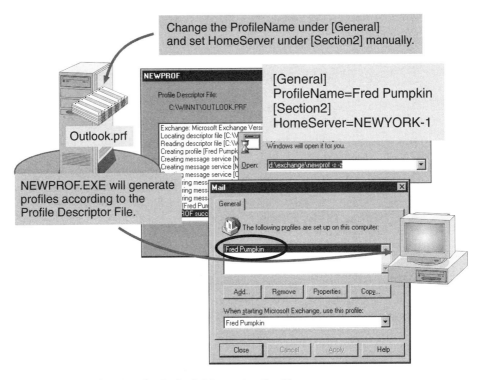

Change the ProfileName under [General]
and set HomeServer under [Section2] manually.

[General]
ProfileName=Fred Pumpkin
[Section2]
HomeServer=NEWYORK-1

Outlook.prf

NEWPROF.EXE will generate
profiles according to the
Profile Descriptor File.

Figure 6-12. Adjusting the Default Messaging Profile.

The unsupported configuration settings are as follows:

- Auto Signature
- Change columns, sort order, filters, and views
- Disable displaying the BCC box
- Disable displaying the From box
- Inbox assistant rules
- Out of Office configuration
- Public folders favorites configuration
- Schedule+ options
- Toggle folders, view/hide toolbar, and view/hide status bar
- Toolbar customization

Unattended Client Installation

The unattended Setup mode, which is launched using the **/Q** command line parameter, is the basis for automatically installing the Exchange Client or Outlook on numerous workstations simultaneously. You can distribute the clients by running **Setup /Q** with Login Scripts, or by using Microsoft Systems Management Server (SMS). If you want to use SMS to distribute the client software, you must use SMS packages files (.PDF). The Exchange Client software and Outlook provide the necessary .PDF files for Windows 3.x, Windows 95, and Windows NT. (See Figure 6-13.)

Several additional command-line parameters such as **/R**, **/U**, and **/Y** are also available. They can be used to specify an unattended maintenance installation. For example, use the **/R** option to reinstall the client, which is helpful if files become corrupted or have been accidentally deleted. Use the **/Y** option if you want to rewrite the client's Registry settings and to recreate its icons without actually reinstalling the client software. Specify the **/U** command if the client should be removed completely from a workstation computer. Another interesting option is the **/G** parameter, which creates a log file of all files that are copied to the local hard disk during setup, plus Registry entries that will be written (for example, Setup /Q /G C:\LogFile.log).

Some command line parameters can't be used together. For example, the reinstallation mode (**/R**) cannot be used with the removal option (**/U**) because they exclude each other.

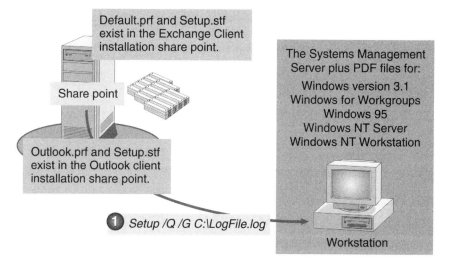

Figure 6-13. Running the Client Setup unattended.

The Setup command-line parameters and their functions are as follows:

- **Setup /A**, to launch the administrative mode to create a shared installation point
- **Setup /G** *"filename,"* to list the files installed and registry settings made during setup (Windows 95 and Windows NT only)
- **Setup /Q[0|1|T]**, to run the setup unattended (not for MS-DOS)—0 shows exit button, 1 hides Exit button, T hides all display
- **Setup /QN[1|T]**, to run the setup unattended and suppress the reboot process—available on Windows 95 only
- **Setup /R**, to reinstall the client
- **Setup /S**, to specify a valid source directory
- **Setup /T**, to specify a valid table file such as Outlook.stf
- **Setup /U[A]**, to remove client components but leave shared components, or with /UA option to remove all components
- **Setup /X** *"filename,"* to set network location for tracking active Outlook installation processes in a log file
- **Setup /Y**, to restore the default settings
- **Setup /N** *"user name,"* to set the name of the registered user of the software
- **Setup /O** *"organization name,"* to set the name of registered user's organization
- **Setup /K** *"1234567890,"* to set the CD key of your program package

Exercise 13: Creating, Sending, Receiving, and Reading a Message

The main purpose of this exercise is to verify that Outlook is working properly. This short exercise demonstrates how to create messages, and how to send and receive them using Outlook. This exercise emphasizes the commands on the **Compose** menu and the features of the **Microsoft Outlook Inbox**.

Estimated time to complete this exercise: 10 minutes

Description

In this exercise, you will compose and send a message. You can address the message to your own account to receive the new mail immediately, which proves that Outlook has been installed properly and that the configuration settings of your messaging profile are correct.

- Task 13 describes the steps for verifying that Outlook 97 is working.

Prerequisites

- Complete Exercise 12, "Installing Exchange and Outlook Clients."
- Complete this exercise logged on as Admin-NY1 on NEWYORK-1.

Task 13: Creating, Sending, and Reading a Message

1. Double-click the **Microsoft Outlook** shortcut on the desktop.

2. The Office Assistant appears, displaying the **Welcome to Microsoft Outlook!** dialog box. Deselect the **Show These Choices At Startup** check box and then click **OK**.

3. On the **Compose** menu, click **New Mail Message**.

4. The **Untitled - Message** dialog box appears, displaying a blank message form. Click the **To** button.

5. In the **Select Names** dialog box, select *Fred Pumpkin* from the default address list displayed on the left side and click **To**.

6. Click **OK**.

7. In the **Subject** box, type *Welcome to Microsoft Outlook*.

8. Type a short message.

9. On the **File** menu, click **Send**.

10. When a message arrives, double-click to open it.

11. A **Message** window is displayed showing the contents of the message.

12. On the **File** menu, click **Close**.

13. The focus is set back to the **Microsoft Outlook** window, displaying the **Inbox**.

14. On the **File** menu, click **Exit And Log Off**.

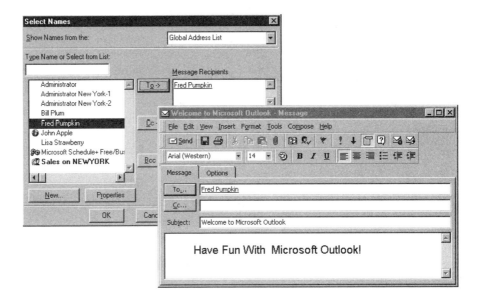

Review

To test the client configuration, it is sufficient to send a message to your own mailbox. Once the message is listed in your Inbox, you will have verified that the messaging client has been installed correctly. That you have received the test message proves that the messaging profile has been configured properly.

Review

1. Which programs are parts of the Microsoft Exchange Client family?

_____

_____

2. Because of the integrated messaging, calendar, and scheduling capabilities of Outlook, you want to migrate to the new program from your Exchange Client. What needs to be reconfigured once the installation has been completed?

_____

_____

_____

_____

3. A user has continued using Schedule+ as the primary calendar application, although Outlook is currently used as the messaging client. Now the user wants to remove the Exchange Client and Schedule+ from the computer. How can you switch to Outlook as the primary calendar application?

_____

_____

_____

_____

4. Some users in your organization work on Macintosh computers, so you've installed Outlook for Macintosh. Which features of the Windows-based clients are not available to Macintosh users?

_____

_____

_____

_____

5. What types of messaging applications exist and what are their characteristics?

_____

_____

_____

_____

_____

_____

_____

6. Which information services can be installed using the Exchange Client Setup?

_____

_____

_____

7. Which information services can be installed using the Outlook Setup?

_____

_____

_____

8. What is a messaging profile?

_____

_____

_____

_____

9. Where in Windows 95 are the messaging profiles of the currently logged-on user stored?

_____

_____

_____

10. Which two message stores can be configured to keep messages available off line?

_____

_____

_____

_____

11. How many entries can a .PST file contain and what is its size limit?

_____

_____

12. What are the requirements for installing the Exchange Client on Windows 95?

_____

_____

_____

_____

13. What are the installation requirements of the Exchange Client for Windows NT?

_____

_____

_____

14. What are the installation requirements to install the Windows 95 and Windows NT versions of Outlook 97?

_____

_____

_____

_____

15. You want to install the Exchange Client on your portable computer, which has limited hard disk capacity. Which installation option would you select to save the greatest amount of disk space?

_____

_____

_____

_____

16. What process must be completed before installing Outlook using the **Run From Network Server** mode?

_____

_____

_____

17. Some users in your company need to install the Exchange Client, and you want to assist them with a preconfigured client configuration. (For example, you want to provide the name of the Exchange Server computer.) What process must be completed before automatically creating a default profile during the client installation?

_____

_____

_____

_____

_____

18. You want to specify messaging profile settings for Outlook so that the client environment is configured automatically. How can you achieve this?

_____

_____

_____

_____

19. You want to install the Outlook for Macintosh client on a Macintosh computer with 64 MB RAM. How should you configure the virtual memory?

_____

_____

C H A P T E R   7

Configuring the Microsoft Exchange Client

This chapter covers the creation and configuration of messaging profiles as well as the messaging-related options of the Microsoft Exchange Client and Microsoft Outlook. The default MAPI information services are discussed.

Overview

The Exchange Client and Outlook can work with a wide variety of messaging systems simultaneously because they rely on the MAPI subsystem. MAPI defines several types of information services, such as address book providers, message stores, and transport services, which are configured by means of messaging profiles. A messaging profile can include the Microsoft Exchange Server transport, a Personal Folder Store, and the Outlook Address Book. However, a configuration that includes only the Exchange Server transport might be sufficient. The tremendous flexibility of the MAPI subsystem is one of its most important features. Its main disadvantage is that you must configure the required information services on the client side.

Lesson 1 of this chapter covers the basic aspects of messaging profiles. You will read about their creation as well as their configuration. The default information services that come with the Exchange Client will also be discussed.

Lesson 2 deals primarily with the Personal Folder Store. Its configuration and critical security aspects will be outlined. You will also learn about the configuration of the main message delivery location.

Lesson 3 discusses the advantages and disadvantages of the Offline Folder Store. Examples of when to use local replication will be given.

Lesson 4 covers the support of roving users, which are users who work frequently with messaging clients on different computers. Several issues regarding the profile configuration for multiple computers will be explained.

Lesson 5 outlines the configuration tasks concerning the support of remote users. The Remote Mail option and the use of an Offline Folder Store will be discussed. You'll also read about ShivaRemote, which is a component required for remote users on MS-DOS and Windows 3.x computers.

Lesson 6 explains the various configuration options of Outlook. This lesson also highlights the default configuration settings.

Lesson 7 concludes this chapter with an examination of the Exchange Server transport. This service is certainly the most important component when working with Exchange or Outlook in an Exchange Server organization. You'll read about its optimization as well as about the configuration of delegate access to your mailbox.

Six practical exercises are included in this chapter that cover the profile creation, Offline Folder Store configuration, and other topics, such as the optimization of the RPC binding order.

In the following lessons, you will be introduced to:

- The creation of user profiles
- The configuration of offline folders
- Methods for supporting roving users
- Methods to support the needs of remote users
- The configuration of Outlook messaging options
- The configuration of the Exchange transport provider

Lesson 1: Creating Profiles

The installation of an Exchange Client or Outlook is performed in two stages. In the first stage the Setup program copies the client files to the local hard disk. It also configures relevant Registry settings, such as entries for the WordMail feature, which allow you to use Microsoft Word as your primary editor for new messages. Microsoft Schedule+ and other client extensions are configured. When Setup exits, the first stage is completed successfully, but you still can't start the client. The second stage—the creation of a messaging profile—must also be completed. Messaging profiles describe the set of MAPI information services that users can employ in a particular client session. Messaging profiles can include several transport drivers, Personal Folder Stores, a Personal Address Book, the Outlook Address Book, and other optional components.

This lesson introduces the creation of messaging profiles and explains them in respect to the Exchange Client as well as Outlook. Options for modifying profiles will also be outlined. The default services that come with the Exchange Client and Outlook will be listed.

A practical exercise leads you through the creation of a new profile to allow a user to connect to an Exchange Server using either the Exchange Client or Outlook.

At the end of this lesson, you will be able to:

- Describe the purpose of messaging profile
- List available information services

Estimated time to complete this lesson: 15 minutes

Messaging Profiles

Messaging profiles describe the user's working environment: they are therefore considered user-specific configuration sets. A profile of Fred Pumpkin, for example, will not interfere with any profile settings that Lisa Strawberry has configured for her own purposes on the same computer. Generally speaking, each user must possess a profile containing the required information services, such as an Exchange Server, Internet E-Mail, or MS Mail, for accessing the desired messaging systems during a particular session.

Operating System Dependencies

Windows 95 and Windows NT messaging profiles are stored in the Registry in the context of the user who is currently logged on. For Windows 95 those profiles can be found under:

```
HKEY_CURRENT_USER
    \Software
        \Microsoft
            \Windows Messaging Subsystem
                \Profiles
```

Windows NT provides a slightly different path to locate the profiles:

```
HKEY_CURRENT_USER
    \Software
        \Microsoft
            \Windows NT
                \CurrentVersion
                    \Windows Messaging Subsystem
                        \Profiles
```

In other words, Windows 95 and Windows NT support multiple users working alternately on a single computer. Each time a particular user logs on, his or her personal settings will be activated, because the settings are part of the user profile.

The messaging profile for Windows 3.x–based clients are stored in a file called Exchange.ini, while the MS-DOS–based client assumes the existence of a file called Exchange.pro.

Creating a Messaging Profile

It is impossible to start the Exchange Client or Outlook without having a MAPI profile. A MAPI profile can be configured through the **Mail** or **Mail And Fax** applet of the Control Panel, which will launch the Microsoft Outlook Setup Wizard—formerly known as the Microsoft Exchange Setup Wizard or the Inbox Setup Wizard. The Setup Wizard is a tool that simplifies the creation and configuration of messaging profiles. The Setup Wizard guides you through a series of wizard pages to collect the required information as described in Chapter 6.

You can launch the Setup Wizard during the startup of the Exchange Client or Outlook by selecting **New** from the **Choose Profile** dialog box. However, this dialog box will be displayed only if you have selected the **Prompt For A Profile To Be Used** radio button on the client's **General** property page in the **Options** dialog box. This dialog box can be launched through the **Options** command under the **Tools** menu.

The Setup Wizard can also be launched automatically. This will usually be the case the first time you start a newly installed Exchange Client because a profile will not yet have been created. Of course, you also have the option to delete all existing profiles to cause the Setup Wizard to be launched the next time you start your client. To delete the existing profiles, you need to open the **Mail** or **Mail And Fax** applet of the Control Panel and then click the **Show Profiles** button. A list of all existing profiles will appear on the **General** property page. They can be deleted using the **Remove** button. Deleting the existing profiles is especially useful for troubleshooting user connection problems. A new profile is easily generated with the assistance of the wizard. (See Figure 7-1.)

Interaction with the user is not usually necessary for creating an Outlook profile, because this application will create a default profile automatically if a file labeled Outlook.prf has been placed in the Windows directory beforehand. But the profile-generation feature will be activated only when a user starts Outlook for the first time. On subsequent startups, Outlook will not create a profile, but will launch the Setup Wizard instead. So it is possible to force the Setup Wizard to start by deleting all existing profiles and restarting Outlook. This method will be used in Exercise 14, "Creating a New Profile."

In order to suppress the Setup Wizard when starting Outlook for the first time, an Outlook.prf file is automatically copied to your Windows directory during the installation of Outlook, using the installation CD-ROM or a network installation point that contains an Outlook.prf file. Outlook version 8.03 generates a profile that contains the Exchange Server transport service and the Outlook Address Book. However, the version of Outlook that shipped with Office 97 (which is also known as version 8.0), provides an Outlook.prf file that, by default, creates a profile using a .PST file as the default delivery location for messages. Exchange Server users who implement this release might find their inboxes empty as messages are moved to a .PST file that they did not notice was automatically created for them. To resolve this problem, those users need to adjust the primary mail delivery location manually, as explained in the section, "Assigning a Location for Incoming Mail" in Lesson 2, "Personal Folder Store."

Multiple Profiles

It is possible to create more than one profile for a single user. To create a new profile, open the Control Panel and double-click the **Mail** or **Mail And Fax** icon. Alternatively—if the Exchange Client has been installed—right-click the **Inbox** icon on your Desktop, and then choose **Properties** from the context menu. In the resulting dialog box, click the **Show Profiles** button to switch to the **General** property page that shows a list of all existing profiles. Clicking the **Add** button on this property page will launch the Setup Wizard again, allowing you to create a new profile.

If multiple profiles exist, you must define which profile you want to use when you start the client. The default profile can be selected on the list box labeled **When Starting Microsoft Exchange, Use This Profile** on the **General** property page after selecting **Show Profiles** from the **Mail** or **Mail And Fax** applet of the Control Panel. This profile will then be used automatically when you start the Exchange Client or Outlook. You can also manually select a profile during each client startup if the option **Prompt For A Profile To Be Used** has been activated as mentioned previously. In this configuration, the client will prompt you for the desired profile.

Modifying an Existing Profile

You can modify the current profile from within the client using the **Services** command on the **Tools** menu, which displays the **Services** dialog box. A similar dialog box can be reached through the **Mail** or **Mail And Fax** applet of the Control Panel or the **Properties** command of the desktop's **Inbox** icon. The **Services** dialog box contains the **Add** and **Remove** buttons, which permit you to add and remove information services from the current profile. The **Properties** button, again, can be used to configure the settings of the currently selected service.

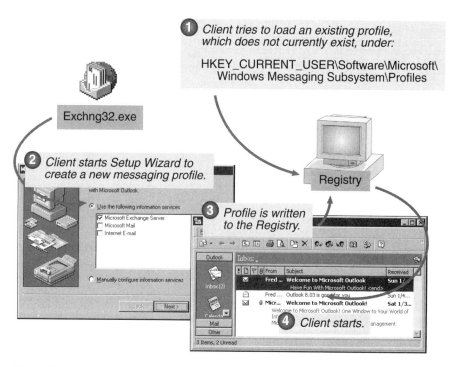

Figure 7-1. Launching the Setup Wizard for profile creation.

The default profile services for the Exchange Client and their functions are:

- A Personal Address Book (.PAB) file; to store personal addresses that do not exist in the server-based address books

- The Microsoft Exchange Server transport; to connect to the home server where the user's mailbox resides

The default profile services for Outlook 97 version 8.03 and their functions are:

- The Microsoft Exchange Server transport; to connect to the home server where the user's mailbox resides

- The Outlook Address Book service; to display the content of the Contacts folder in the Address Book

Exercise 14: Creating a New Profile

A messaging profile describes the information services that a user accesses by means of his or her MAPI-based messaging client. The profile also stores the configuration settings for the included services, such as the user's display name and the home server name if the Exchange Server transport has been configured.

Estimated time to complete this exercise: 15 minutes

Description

In this exercise, you will create a messaging profile using the Setup Wizard. The purpose of this exercise is to demonstrate the automatic startup of this wizard in case no messaging profile exists. Outlook, however, will try to outwit you by creating a default profile the first time it starts. This is actually a smart feature, but not desired in this particular exercise. Therefore, you need to delete the default profile manually once Outlook has been started.

Note If a new default profile is created automatically every time you start Outlook (for example, instead of step 30 in Task 14a), it might be necessary to ensure that a local copy of the file Outlook.prf does not exist in your Windows subdirectory.

- Task 14a describes the steps for starting the Setup Wizard and to configure information services in a messaging profile.

- Task 14b describes the steps for verifying that Outlook 97 is working properly with the newly created profile.

Prerequisites

- Outlook 97 version 8.03 must be installed on the test computer.

- Exchange Server must be running on NEWYORK-1.

Task 14a: Creating an Exchange Profile

1. Log on as Admin-NY1 to the domain STOCKSDATA.

2. Click the **Start** button, point to **Programs**, point to **Administrative Tools (Common)**, and then click **User Manager For Domains**.

3. On the **User** menu, click **New User**.

4. Complete the **New User** dialog box using the following information:

In this box	You supply
Username	*BillP*
Full Name	*Bill Plum*
Description	*User Account with Admin Permissions*
Password	*Billp*
Confirm Password	*Billp*

5. Clear the **User Must Change Password At Next Logon** check box.

6. Select the **Password Never Expires** check box.

7. Click the **Groups** button.

8. Under **Not Member Of** select **Domain Admins**, click **Add**, and then click **OK**.

9. Click **Add**, which adds the user to the Window NT accounts database and then activates the Exchange extension of the **User Manager For Domains**. (It might be necessary to connect to NEWYORK-1, which is the Exchange Server.)

10. The **Bill Plum Properties** dialog box appears.

11. Notice that the **Display** name, **Alias** name, **Primary Windows NT Account**, **Home Site**, and **Home Server** information is automatically added.

12. Click **OK** to close the dialog box of the Exchange extension.

13. A blank **New User** dialog box appears.

14. Click **Close**.

15. Exit the **User Manager** and log off from Windows NT.

16. Log on to Windows NT as BillP.

17. Click **Start**, and then point to **Settings**. Start the **Control Panel**.

18. Double-click the **Mail** icon.

19. Make sure that Exchange Server is selected, and then click **Properties**.

20. Under **Microsoft Exchange Server**, enter *NEWYORK-1*.

21. Click **Check Name** to resolve the mailbox name to Bill Plum.

22. Click **OK** twice and then close the **Control Panel**.

23. On the **Desktop**, double-click the **Microsoft Outlook** shortcut.

24. Microsoft Outlook starts, presenting the **Welcome To Microsoft Outlook** dialog box. Clear the **Show These Choices At Startup** check box, and then click **OK**.

25. On the **File** menu, click **Exit And Log Off**.

26. On the Desktop right click the **Inbox** icon, and then click **Properties**. (If you haven't installed the Exchange Client, use the **Mail** applet from the Control Panel instead.)

27. The **Microsoft Outlook Properties** dialog box appears. Click **Show Profiles**.

28. Click **Remove**, and then in the subsequent message box click **Yes**.

29. Click **Close,** and then close the Control Panel.

30. On the **Desktop**, double-click the **Microsoft Outlook** shortcut.

31. A **Microsoft Outlook Setup Wizard** dialog box appears. Clear all check boxes except **Microsoft Exchange Server**, and then click **Next**.

32. A **Microsoft Outlook Setup Wizard** dialog box appears prompting for your Exchange Server and Mailbox name.

33. Enter *NEWYORK-1* under **Microsoft Exchange Server** and *BillP* under **Mailbox**.

34. Click **Next**.

35. A **Microsoft Outlook Setup Wizard** dialog box appears, asking if you travel with this computer. Verify that **No** is selected, and then click **Next**.

36. A **Microsoft Outlook Setup Wizard** dialog box appears, prompting for the personal Address Book file name.

37. In the **Path** box, type *C:\EXCHANGE\BILLPLUM.PAB*.

38. Click **Next**.

39. A **Microsoft Outlook Setup Wizard** dialog box appears, asking whether to add Outlook to the Startup group. Verify that **Do Not Add Outlook To The Startup Group** is selected, and then click **Next**.

40. A **Microsoft Outlook Setup Wizard** dialog box appears, telling you what information services are set up in the newly created profile. Click **Finish**.

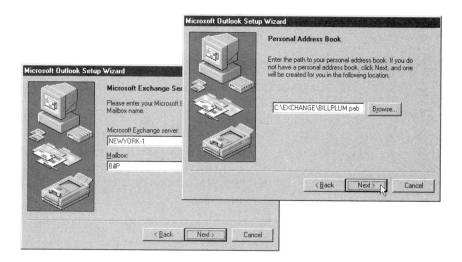

Task 14b: Creating and Sending a Message

1. On the **Compose** menu, click **New Mail Message**.

2. Click **To**.

3. The **Select Names** dialog box appears. Select **Bill Plum**.

4. Click **To**.

5. Select **Bill Plum**, and then click the **To** button.

6. Click **OK**.

7. In the **Subject** box, type *A short message*.

8. In the message text area, type whatever text you want (in this example, *Have fun with Microsoft Outlook*).

9. On the toolbar, click **Send**.

10. Verify that the message is delivered to your Inbox.

11. Open and read the message, and then on the client's **File** menu, click **Exit And Log Off**.

12. Log off Windows NT.

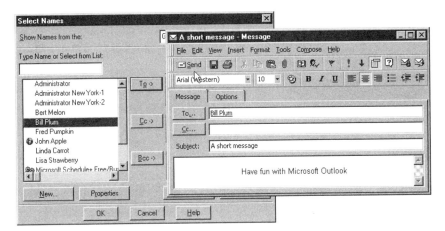

Review

You can use various methods to create messaging profiles using the Outlook Setup Wizard. The wizard launches automatically when you start the Exchange Client or Outlook and you haven't configured a messaging profile. (The exception is that you start Outlook for the first time in conjunction with an Outlook.prf file.) The wizard gathers all the required configuration information from you to create a default profile, after which the client can start successfully.

Note Unlike the automatic profile generation feature of Outlook 97, the Setup Wizard does not include the Outlook Address Book in your messaging profile by default. You need to add this service manually to your messaging profile if you want this feature.

Information Services

The MAPI subsystem provides a segmented architecture. The MAPI-based messaging client, such as the Exchange Client or Outlook, resides on the top of the architecture. On the bottom, you can find the information services, which provide access to specific components and messaging systems. For instance, the Exchange Server information service allows your client to connect to an Exchange Server, while the Personal Address Book service maintains a local address book file as a repository for your personal e-mail contact information.

As mentioned previously, your client will access available information services when specified through a messaging profile. Each messaging profile is basically a subset—a selection—of all information services that have been installed on your computer. So you might connect only to an Exchange Server even though the information service for MS Mail exists on the computer as well. Nevertheless, a messaging profile can include multiple information services. In other words, you can include the Exchange Server transport with a Personal Folder Store, Outlook Address Book, and a Personal Address Book in a single profile. If you want, your messaging profile can contain extra services, such as Internet E-Mail, MSN (Microsoft Network), or MS Mail.

Available Information Services

When you configure messaging profiles using the Setup Wizard, you check implicitly for available information services. The wizard displays them in a dialog box to allow you to select those you want to include. Each information service must be registered in a file called Mapisvc.inf, which can be found in the Windows\System(32) directory. You can look at the Mapisvc.inf file in further detail using any text editor, such as Notepad.exe.

The Setup Wizard offers only those services that are referenced in the Mapisvc.inf. For example, the MSN transport driver is not supported on Windows NT and therefore not included in Mapisvc.inf, and as a result, the wizard will not list it as an available information service for a Windows NT messaging profile. The Mapisvc.inf file will also be read when you create or modify profiles manually using the **Mail** or **Mail And Fax** applet of the Control Panel. Try this test: Open the **Mail** or **Mail And Fax** applet and click the **Add** button. The **Add Service To Profile** dialog box is displayed listing all the installed services under **Available Information Services**, such as those displayed in Figure 7-2 on page 350.

Personal Folder Store

The Personal Folders information service maintains a local file with a default .PST extension. The .PST file, which can be placed on the computer's hard disk or on a file server, offers one option for working disconnected (off line) from the Exchange Server. This local storage mechanism is used by the Exchange Client and Outlook to provide their Remote Mail functionality. The various Remote Mail options are covered later in this chapter in Lesson 5, "Remote Users." Details on configuring Personal Folders are also covered later in this chapter.

Personal Address Book

The Personal Address Book has been implemented in the Mspst32.dll file in conjunction with the Personal Folder Store, but the Personal Address Book does not store messages. Instead, it is responsible for maintaining the e-mail addresses of your private contacts. It can serve these addresses just as a server-based address book does. The Personal Address Book is especially useful if you want to maintain addresses that do not exist in your organization's Global Address List. The Personal Address Book stores recipient addresses in a file with a .PAB extension.

Outlook Address Book

The Outlook Address Book is a new information service that is added to your computer during the Outlook installation. It is implemented in a dynamic link library named Contab32.dll. The purpose of this information service is to display the items in the Outlook Contacts folder as an address book.

Not many configuration parameters exist for this service. The only option you have is to remove a Contacts folder from the address book using the **Remove** button. New Contacts folders cannot be added using the **Outlook Address Book** property page. To add a Contacts folder as an address book, right-click the desired folder itself. Then select the **Properties** command from the Context menu. The **Outlook Address Book** property page will be available—if the selected folder has been defined as an Outlook Contacts type—where you can select or deselect the **Show This Folder As An E-Mail Address Book** option. The Outlook Address Book, in conjunction with public folders, offers an interesting feature: a public folder of the Contacts type allows you to configure a shared address book for individual contacts of a team, department, or enterprise.

Let's say Fred Pumpkin wants to create a central Contacts folder for the customers of the STOCKSDATA company. This Contacts folder will be used as a central phone book, so he needs to create a new Contacts public folder using Outlook. He opens the **File** menu and points to the **Folder** option. He then selects the **Create Subfolder** command. In the **Name** box he types *Central STOCKSDATA Address Book* and in the **Folder Contains** box he selects **Contact Items**. Under **Make This Folder A Subfolder Of** he chooses **All Public Folders**, and then clicks **OK**. A new icon is created on his Outlook bar, which he can right-click to select the **Properties** command. Fred then switches to the **Outlook Address Book** property page, where he must enable the **Show This Folder As An E-Mail Address Book** option to ensure that the new Contacts folder can be displayed as an address book. Now he can simply fill the new public folder with contact information about all customers and the central phone book has become a reality. More information about the creation and management of message folders is provided in Chapter 12, "Creating and Managing Public Folders."

Microsoft Mail

The MS Mail information service is implemented in a file called Msfs32.dll. Using the Exchange Client or Outlook in conjunction with this driver, you can connect to a Workgroup or MS Mail 3.x postoffice on line or in remote mail mode. The most important MS Mail transport properties are the path to the postoffice, the mailbox name, and the password. The mailbox name and password can be configured on the service's **Logon** property page. You can have the client automatically enter your MS Mail postoffice password by enabling the **When Logging On Automatically Enter Password** option on the **Logon** property page.

Internet E-Mail

Outlook supports Internet standards such as POP3 and SMTP if the Internet E-mail transport service has been installed and configured. When this information service is included in your profile, a new **Internet E-Mail** property page will be available in the **Options** dialog box, which can be reached through the **Options** command on the **Tools** menu. You can define the send and reply e-mail formatting for Internet messages on this page.

The Internet E-mail service has been implemented in two separate DLLs; the Inetab32.dll and Minet32.dll files. The Inetab32.dll file is the portion of the Internet E-Mail transport that handles recipient addresses when sending messages to Internet recipients. The Minet32.dll file represents the actual implementation of the transport service. This component is used when sending messages to SMTP hosts (such as an IMS) via SMTP and when downloading messages through the POP3 protocol from a POP3 host, which might also be an Exchange Server. Therefore, the SMTP server and the POP3 server names, along with the account name and the password, must be specified in this information service. Other important parameters refer to your personal information, such as your e-mail address and reply address.

Exchange Server

The Exchange Server information service is certainly the most important component for those working within an organization that uses Exchange Server for messaging. This transport provider is implemented in three dynamic link libraries called Emsabp32.dll, Emsmdb32.dll, and Emsui32.dll. As their names imply, they communicate with the DS to display the server-based address books (Emsabp32.dll) and with the IS service to send and receive messages (Emsmdb32.dll). The Emsui32.dll is responsible for providing the property pages and dialog boxes that allow you to configure this service. Only in rare cases must you use the Registry Editor instead of the Emsui32.dll. This scenario will be described in the section, "Configuring the Transport," later in this chapter.

Other Information Services

Other transport drivers offer connectivity to additional messaging systems as well as the default services. For example, the MSN transport provider can be used to send and receive messages using this online network in Windows 95. Other information services are available from third-party manufacturers as well, such as the CompuServe transport or the Lotus cc:Mail transport driver.

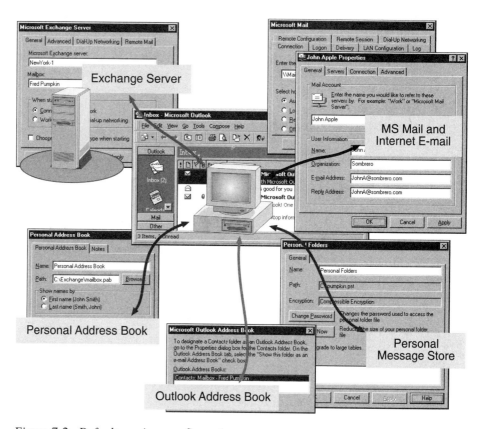

Figure 7-2. Default services configuration.

The most important information services and their functions are:

- Internet E-Mail transport; to send and receive messages to and from the Internet via SMTP and POP3

- Exchange Server transport; to access all resources on an Exchange Server

- Outlook Address Book; to display the content of Contacts folders as address books

- MS Mail transport; to send and receive messages within an MS Mail network

- Personal Address Book; to store personal addresses

- Personal Folder Store; to store messages locally in a .PST file

Lesson 2: Personal Folder Store

Within an Exchange Server organization, users typically maintain e-mail–related information in their server-based mailboxes. Other repositories of e-mail messages are public folders, which also reside on the server. However, it might be useful to keep messages locally on the workstation's hard disk as well, if for instance you have exceeded the maximum mailbox size on your server-based mailbox. It might also be necessary to maintain e-mail messages locally if you want to work off line.

This lesson covers the Personal Folder Store, which introduces a local message repository that can be used to download e-mail messages from an Exchange Server. A Personal Folder Store is also the basis for working with the Remote Mail options of the Exchange Client and Outlook. Furthermore, you can use this repository to archive messages.

A practical exercise will guide you through the steps for adding a Personal Folder Store to your current messaging profile.

At the end of this lesson, you will be able to:

- Configure the Personal Folder Store
- Assign a location for incoming messages

Estimated time to complete this lesson: 30 minutes

Working with Personal Folders

A Personal Folder Store maintains messages and other items in a .PST file, which can be accessed using the Exchange Client or Outlook. The Personal Folder Store information service is responsible for displaying the folder hierarchy in the client's folders pane, and the contents of the personal folders in the contents pane. In other words, the Personal Folder Store allows you to work with personal folders in the same way you work with private or public folders on an Exchange Server. This implies that you can define personal folder views and associate electronic forms as usual.

Another valuable use of Personal Folders Stores is message archiving. Older messages can be copied to a .PST file and deleted from the Exchange Server. Users can then back up their .PST files individually. In fact, each user who uses one or more .PST files stored on the local workstation's hard disk is individually responsible for correct backups, because messages are no longer kept on the Exchange Server where regular backup occurs. (See Figure 7-3.)

Creating a Personal Folder Store

A .PST file can be located on the computer's local hard disk or on a file server within the network, but you must add the Personal Folders information service to your messaging profile before you can use any .PST file. You can do this through the **Services** command on the client's **Tools** menu, which displays the **Services** dialog box. This dialog box provides the **Add** button that leads to the **Add Service To Profile** dialog box. Select the **Personal Folders** option from the list of **Available Information Services**. Select **Personal Folders**, and then click **OK**. The **Create/Open Personal Folders File** dialog box will be launched, which allows you to create a new .PST file or to select an existing one. When creating a new repository, the **Create Microsoft Personal Folders** dialog box appears and permits you to configure the properties of the new store in detail.

Configuration Parameters

The path to the .PST file is the most important configuration parameter you'll specify for a Personal Folder Store. This path will be determined automatically when you create a new Personal Folder Store, but it can be changed later if you want to move a .PST file to another directory. However, the path to the .PST file cannot be modified through the property pages, so you'll need to move the desired file to the new directory first using the Windows Explorer. You can then display the properties of the Personal Folder Store within your messaging profile to adjust the .PST file path through the **Create/Open Personal Folders File** dialog box. This dialog box will also appear if you try to open the root folder of the Personal Folder Store within the messaging client once the .PST file has been moved.

To test the adjustment of the .PST file path, first exit your messaging client before opening the **Mail** or **Mail And Fax** applet of the Control Panel. At this point you can include a new .PST file in your profile (for example, *C:\Move.pst*). Close the **Mail** or **Mail And Fax** applet and the Control Panel, switch to Windows Explorer, and then move the *Move.pst* file to a different location (for example, *C:\Temp*). Now you can launch the Exchange Client (or Outlook) and the client will start without any problems. After a short delay, which can be shortened even further if you open the new personal folders container by means of a mouse click, a message box will appear, notifying you that the file **C:\Move.pst** cannot be found. When you click **OK**, the **Create/Open Personal Folders File** dialog box appears, enabling you to correct the path. Take care not to click **Cancel**, or subsequent attempts to open the folder will result in a message box informing you that the **C:\Move.pst** file cannot be found, rather than displaying the **Create/Open Personal Folders File** dialog box. In this scenario you either would adjust the file path through the properties of the Personal Folder Store within your messaging profile (**Services** command on the **Tools** menu), or you would restart the client to launch the **Create/Open Personal Folders File** dialog box automatically.

For your convenience, the Personal Folder Store properties offer several additional configuration options, so you can, for example, define a user-friendly display name to be used by the Exchange Client or Outlook. The display name identifies the corresponding root folder in the client's folder pane. The default name is **Personal Folders**. You should change the display name if you plan to configure more than one Personal Folder Store file for a single messaging profile, so you can easily distinguish between the different folder stores within your client.

As you explore the Personal Folder Store properties further you'll discover that it's possible to specify an encryption algorithm. Depending on the security level you need, you can select the options **No Encryption**, **Compressible Encryption**, and **Best Encryption**. Although the format of a .PST file is rather confusing, a user can open such a file to read message texts using a text editor if **No Encryption** has been selected.

Personal Folder Security

It is prudent to protect Personal Folder Store files using an encryption algorithm and a password, since .PST files contain your personal messages. You can optionally save the .PST password within your messaging profile.

If you define a password, however, there is one possible catch. The password itself will be stored within the .PST file to protect it from unauthorized access, so you must provide the password on every client startup to open the .PST file. For the sake of convenience, you can save the password in your current messaging profile so the client can read the password from the profile without having to prompt you for it. You will simply be able to start your client and access your personal folders immediately.

You might end up forgetting your password as time passes and you are no longer prompted for it. Even so, you'll still be able to use the .PST file, since the password is saved in the messaging profile. You will, however, have a problem if you need to create a new profile, which must always include the old .PST file. As soon as you try to include the existing .PST file, a dialog box will pop up asking you for the password. If you have forgotten the password, there is no way to recover it. If you have deleted the old profile (which stored the password), the data in the .PST file is lost. If you still have access to the old profile, however, you can log on to the Personal Folder Store again—since the password is available in the old profile—to move all messages to a new .PST file.

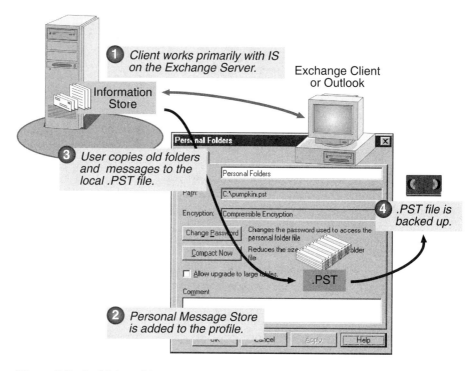

Figure 7-3. Archiving old messages.

The functions of Personal Folder Store files are to:

- Archive old messages
- Download folders and messages from the messaging server to reduce the size of the mailbox on the server
- Keep messages locally on a portable computer for working off line (without connection to the messaging server)
- Maintain a message repository for Remote Mail clients

Exercise 15: Adding a .PST File to Your Profile

A Personal Folder Store allows you to keep messages locally. You can create personal folders to download messages from your server-based mailbox. The downloaded information is placed in a .PST file.

Estimated time to complete this exercise: 10 minutes

Description

In this exercise, you will add a .PST file to a messaging profile. The configuration parameters, such as the path to the .PST file, will be examined.

- Task 15 describes the steps necessary to add a Personal Folder Store service to a messaging profile.

Prerequisites

- Log on as Admin-NY1 to NEWYORK-1.
- Have a floppy disk available to store a copy of the .PST file.

Task 15: Adding a .PST File to a Profile

1. Start **Microsoft Outlook**.
2. On the **Tools** menu, click **Services**.
3. The **Services** dialog box appears. Click **Add**.
4. In the **Add Service To Profile** dialog box, click **Personal Folders**, and then click **OK**.
5. The **Create/Open Personal Folders File** dialog box appears.
6. In the **Look In** list, select **(C:)**.
7. In the **File Name** box type *Pumpkin*, and then click **Open**.
8. The Personal Folders dialog box appears, displaying general information regarding the new folder. Click **OK**.
9. The **Services** dialog box appears, displaying profile information that includes **Personal Folders**.
10. Click **OK**.
11. On the **View** menu, click **Folder List**.

12. Notice that the **Personal Folders** container has been added to the folder list.

13. Insert a formatted disk into the floppy disk drive. Start the **Windows NT Explorer** from the **Programs** group and copy the .PST file created in step 8 to the floppy disk.

14. Close Explorer.

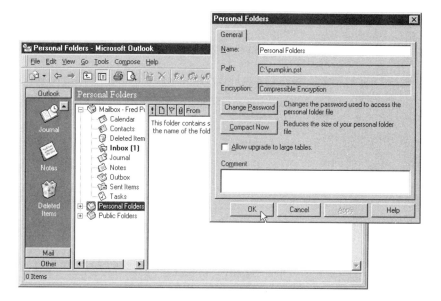

Review

A Personal Folder Store can be added to the current profile while the client is running. It is not required that you restart the client to work with the new set of personal folders. During the creation of a new Personal Folder Store the user is required to define information about the path to the .PST file and the desired encryption algorithm. A password may also be defined.

Assigning a Location for Incoming Mail

The MAPI subsystem has been designed to work as a module and to allow the Exchange Client to work as the universal Inbox for all kinds of messaging systems. Outlook is also a MAPI-based application, which can adopt the role of the Universal Inbox by replacing the former Exchange Client.

If more than one messaging system exists, users can combine multiple information services in one profile to connect to them at the same time. Let's say you have a POP3 account on the Internet, a message account on MSN, and a mailbox account on an Exchange Server. Accordingly, you can install the Internet E-Mail service and the MSN transport plus a Personal Folder Store to download messages from your POP3 host and from MSN. The Personal Folder Store is required because neither the Internet E-Mail service nor the MSN transport provides any message folders. You also must configure the Exchange Server transport to connect to your server-based mailbox. For this reason, you will see only three top-level folder objects representing the Personal Folder Store, your Exchange Server mailbox, and the Public Folders.

Two potential personal mail repositories exist within this configuration: the Personal Folder Store and your server-based Exchange mailbox. The client needs to know where to deliver incoming messages. Using the **Services** command on the **Tools** menu, you can configure the message delivery. Switch to the **Delivery** property tab to select the primary Inbox under **Deliver New Mail To The Following Location**. For instance, if you specify the Personal Folder Store, all incoming messages will be delivered to the Inbox in the .PST file. In this case, messages delivered to the Inbox on the Exchange Server will be downloaded automatically and placed as incoming messages into your personal store. (See Figure 7-4.)

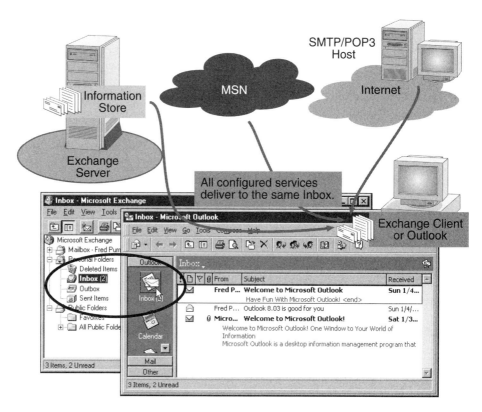

Figure 7-4. Configuring the primary Inbox.

Follow these steps to assign the primary Inbox:

1. Open the **Tools** menu.
2. Select the **Services** command.
3. Switch to the **Delivery** property tab.
4. Select the desired message store under **Deliver New Mail To The Following Location.**
5. Notice that the client downloads all messages from the server-based mailbox to the Inbox of the selected store.

Lesson 3: Configuring Offline Folders

Users ordinarily work on line, connected to their messaging network, where they have access to their server-based mailboxes and public folders. Sometimes a permanent connection to an Exchange Server is impossible—if for example, a user wants to read and write e-mail messages while traveling in an airplane. Obviously, the server-based repositories are unavailable in this situation, so a local repository of e-mail messages is required. A Personal Folder Store is one solution, which can be included in the messaging profile. An Offline Folder Store, which is similar to Personal Folders but can be synchronized with the Exchange Server and be used off line, is another solution.

This lesson introduces the features and configuration of the Offline Folder Store as it is provided through the Exchange Server transport. Advantages and disadvantages of the Offline Folder Store will be discussed.

This lesson contains a practical exercise that outlines the configuration of Offline Folders using Outlook. It will guide you through the basic configuration steps as well as through the task of synchronizing the local and server-based folder replicas.

At the end of this lesson, you will be able to:

- Explain the purpose of Offline Folders
- Describe the configuration of Offline Folders

Estimated time to complete this lesson: 20 minutes

Working with Offline Folders and Offline Address Books

Offline Folders are the basis of a process known as *local replication*. The folders are local copies of server-based message folders. Hence, the Offline Folder Store can be used in conjunction only with an Exchange Server. The Offline Address Book is a local copy of the server-based recipient information, which provides required addresses while working off line.

Note The Offline Folder Store and the Offline Address Book—as implemented in the Exchange Server transport service—allow you to work while disconnected from the server.

Local Replication Example

Instead of downloading messages from an Exchange Server, you can use an Offline Folder Store to replicate a copy of your folders, along with their messages, to your workstation. In other words, server-based folders and the client-based offline store are synchronized containing the same information when enabling the local replication. In this situation, you will be able to access either the server-based folders on line or the local replicas off line.

Let's say Fred Pumpkin has configured an Offline Folder Store to synchronize his server-based folders **Calendar**, **Contacts**, **Deleted Items**, **Inbox**, **Journal**, **Notes**, **Outbox**, **Sent Items**, and **Tasks**. While he is working on his laptop at home, he can read and delete messages from the **Inbox**. He can also reply to particular messages. In this situation, he is working with his offline folders. Any messages that he has sent will remain in his local **Outbox** replica. Fred inserts his laptop into his docking station the next morning when working in his office. He starts the client and a connection is established with the server. At this point, the new information residing in the offline store will be replicated to Fred's server-based mailbox. Items that Fred has deleted the evening before while working with his offline **Inbox** will now be deleted from the server-based **Inbox** as well. Likewise, the messages in the offline **Outbox** are replicated to the server-based **Outbox**, where the IS service of the Exchange Server can retrieve them for delivery. (See Figure 7-5 on page 364.)

Configuring Offline Folders

As mentioned, the Offline Folder Store has been implemented into the Exchange Server transport. Consequently, it can be configured through the transport service's property pages within a messaging profile. You can display these property pages through the **Services** command on the client's **Tools** menu. On the **Services** property page, select **Microsoft Exchange Server**, and then click **Properties**. By activating the option **Choose The Connection Type When Starting** on the **General** property page you can conveniently select the connection type (on line or off line) at every client startup. To configure an Offline Folder file, however, switch to the **Advanced** property page. Here you will find the **Offline Folder File Settings** button, which launches the **Offline Folder File Settings** dialog box. This dialog box looks similar to the configuration dialog box for a new .PST file. You must define a name for and a path to the new .OST file. Another important setting determines which encryption algorithm should be used for the storage file.

Note An .OST file (by default, \<Windir>\Outlook.ost) might already exist if you answered **Yes** to the question **Do You Travel With This Computer?** during the profile creation within the Setup Wizard. An .OST file is associated with a profile. If you create a new profile, you will need to create and synchronize a new .OST file before it can be used with the new profile.

Configuring Message Folders to be Available Off Line

The system folders **Inbox, Outbox, Deleted Items**, and **Sent Items** are replicated automatically as soon as you enable the offline folders using an Exchange Client 5.0. When using Outlook, the Outlook-specific folders **Calendar, Contacts, Journal, Notes**, and **Tasks** are also synchronized. The other server-based private and public folders can be configured for local replication as well.

Additional folders are not included in local replication by default when offline folders are created. If you would like another folder synchronized, you must explicitly enable synchronization using the property pages of the folder. In this scenario you must right-click the desired folder to select the **Properties** command. On the **Synchronization** property page, which is available only after you have created offline folders, you can select **When Offline Or Online** under **This Folder Is Available**. The selected folder can be synchronized from then on.

Note If you want to configure a public folder for local replication you must first drag the folder to the **Favorites** container. You can then configure it the same way you configure private folders.

Synchronization Capabilities

It is recommended that you force the synchronization between the server-based folders and the local replica of folders once they have been included in the local replication. This will ensure that the offline store contains the current data. Selecting the **Synchronize** option on the **Tools** menu, you can select either **This Folder**, which will synchronize the currently highlighted folder only, or **All Folders**, which will synchronize all folders that are members of the local replication.

If you want information about the current status of the synchronization between the server-based folder and the offline replica, open the **Synchronization** property page of the desired folder again (right-click the folder and then select the **Properties** command). You'll be able to determine the date and time of the last synchronization event, along with the current number of items in both the server-based folder and offline folder.

> **Note** When you reconnect to the Exchange Server, the automatic synchronization permits you to upload only the changes you made while working off line. With the Exchange Client, you must use the **All Folders** command under the **Synchronize** option of the **Tools** menu to force the download of any changes from the server to your offline folders. Outlook, in contrast, allows you to download messages automatically upon exiting this application. To enable this option, select the **Options** command on the **Tools** menu. Select **When Online Synchronize All Folders Upon Exiting** on the **General** property page.

Offline Address Book

While working off line, server-based address books are generally unavailable, which means that you cannot address new messages to recipients in your organization. Only replies to messages, which have been received and synchronized, are possible. To keep the address information available while working off line, you must download the Offline Address Book from the server while working on line.

To download the Offline Address Book from the server, access the **Download Address Book** command from the **Synchronize** option on the **Tools** menu. To reduce the size of the address book downloaded to your machine and therefore to reduce transmission time, you can choose to download the address book without details, which are not required for message creation and addressing. Likewise you can specify the option to download address book changes that have occurred since the last synchronization only. The corresponding **Download Changes Since Last Synchronization** option is activated by default (in the **Download Address Book** dialog box), which will reduce the time required to synchronize the Offline Address Book even further.

> **Note** The function that makes it possible to download address book changes has just been introduced in Exchange Server 5.5. Hence, the **Download Changes Since Last Synchronization** option cannot be used in conjunction with earlier Exchange Server versions.

Offline Address Book Files

The Offline Address Book (.OAB) files are usually stored in the current Windows directory. At a minimum, four .OAB files are always downloaded, but a fifth file is available for downloading if you have specified the retrieval of address details as well. The Anrdex.oab file provides indexes for Ambiguous Name Resolution. The Rndex.oab file helps to manage e-mail addresses. Address book templates are copied to Tmplts.oab. Address details are kept in the Details.oab and Browse.oab files. The Details.oab file is usually the largest file because it keeps all the detailed information about the users of your organization. You should not delete this file manually if it becomes too large—use the Exchange Client or Outlook to remove the Details.oab file instead. You then need to download the Offline Address Book one more time, but this time without detailed information.

Note The **Download Changes Since Last Synchronization** option must be deselected if you want to ensure that the Details.oab file will be deleted. Selecting only the **No Details** option from the **Download Offline Address Book** is not sufficient.

Disadvantages of Offline Folders

When you examine the synchronization capabilities of the local replication in more detail, you can determine that there is no option to selectively download messages that meet certain criteria. Offline Folders always receive all new items from their corresponding server-based folders, and vice versa. This can be a disadvantage on slow dial-up connections, since it might take a long time to synchronize all new messages that arrived while you were off line. For this reason, the concept of the local replication is a preferred solution for users who often access their server through a LAN connection with sufficient network bandwidth. A Personal Folder Store used in conjunction with Remote Mail features might be a better solution for users who usually work over slow dial-up connections.

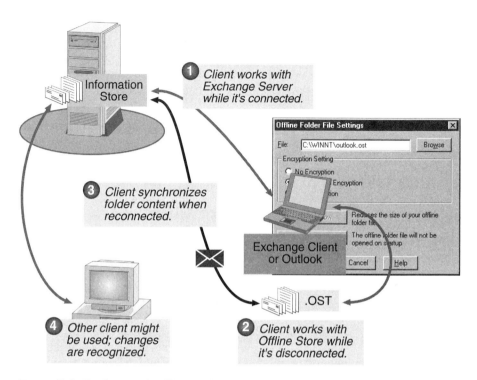

Figure 7-5. Working with offline folders.

The system folders that are always members of local replication are:

- Exchange Client: **Deleted Items**, **Inbox**, **Outbox**, **Sent Items**
- Outlook: **Calendar**, **Contacts**, **Deleted Items**, **Inbox**, **Journal**, **Notes**, **Outbox**, **Sent Items**, **Tasks**

Exercise 16: Configuring Outlook to Use Offline Folders

Offline folders are the best choice for users who occasionally work disconnected from their Exchange Server. The offline folder file maintains a local replica of server-based folders and their contents. They are a perfect choice for working off line with public folders.

Estimated time to complete this exercise: 25 minutes

Description

In this exercise, you will configure an Offline Folder Store file using the properties of the Exchange Server transport service. You will place the .OST file on your local hard disk. Once you have done this, you can start Outlook to specify which folders to include in the local replication. You will then check the Synchronization statistics of selected folders through the folder's **Synchronization** property page.

- Task 16a describes the steps for configuring Outlook to prompt for the selection of a connection type when starting, either on line or off line.

- Task 16b describes the steps for verifying the synchronization status of a folder and to synchronize all folders.

- Task 16c describes the steps for testing the use of offline folders.

Prerequisites

- Complete Exercise 14.

- Make sure there is at least one message in your Inbox.

Task 16a: Configuring Offline Folders

1. Log on to the STOCKSDATA domain at NEWYORK-1 as **BillP**, and then start **Microsoft Outlook**.

2. On the **Tools** menu, click **Services**.

3. The **Services** dialog box appears. Select **Microsoft Exchange Server**.

4. Click **Properties**.

5. In the **Microsoft Exchange Server** dialog box, select the **Choose The Connection Type When Starting** check box.

6. Click the **Advanced** tab.

7. Click **Offline Folder File Settings** to display the **Offline Folder File Settings** dialog box.

8. In the **File** box, type *C:\EXCHANGE\BILLP.OST*.

9. Click **OK**.

10. A message appears, asking you if you would like to create the new .OST file. Click **Yes**. (Your **Calendar**, **Contacts**, **Deleted Items**, **Inbox**, **Journal**, **Notes**, **Outbox**, **Sent Items**, and **Tasks** folders are now configured for off line use.)

11. Click **OK** twice.

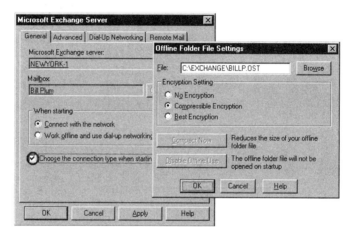

Task 16b: Synchronizing Offline Folders

1. In Outlook, right-click the **Inbox** on the Outlook bar, and then click **Properties** to display the **Inbox Properties** dialog box.

2. Click the **Synchronization** tab. Notice that this folder is marked as being available when off line or on line. The statistics for this folder indicate that it has not yet been synchronized.

3. Click **OK**.

4. On the **Tools** menu, highlight **Synchronize** and then click **All Folders**.

5. Right-click the **Inbox** again, and verify on the **Synchronization** property page that it has been synchronized. Verify synchronization for the **Calendar**, **Contacts**, **Deleted Items**, **Journal**, **Notes**, **Outbox**, **Sent Items**, and **Tasks** folder also.

6. Click **OK**.

7. On the **File** menu, click **Exit And Log Off**.

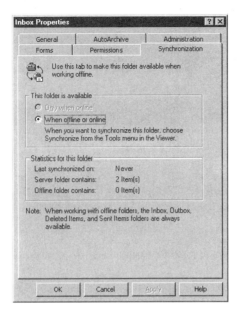

Task 16c: Testing Offline Folders

1. On the **Desktop**, double-click the **Microsoft Outlook** shortcut icon.

2. A **Microsoft Exchange Server** dialog box appears, prompting you to select a connection type. Click **Work Offline**.

3. **Microsoft Outlook** appears.

4. In your **Inbox**, open a message. You have access to your **Inbox** while working off line because you synchronized your local .OST file with your server-based Inbox in Task 16b.

5. Modify the message labeled "A short message" in your **Inbox** with new text: *This is a modification.*

6. Close the message.

7. A **Microsoft Outlook** dialog box appears, asking you if you want to save the changes in your message. Click **Yes**.

8. Exit and exit **Microsoft Outlook**.

9. Start **Microsoft Outlook** again.

10. A **Microsoft Exchange Server** dialog box appears, prompting you to select a connection type. Click **Connect**.

11. **Microsoft Outlook** appears.

12. Open the message in your **Inbox** that you modified while working off line. Notice that the changes are synchronized with your server-based copy of the message. This happened because the synchronization of offline changes occurs automatically when you reconnect.

13. Close the message.

14. On the **Tools** menu, click **Services**.

15. The **Services** dialog box appears. Click **Microsoft Exchange Server**.

16. Click **Properties**.

17. The **Microsoft Exchange Server** dialog box appears. Clear the **Choose The Connection Type When Starting** check box.

18. Click **OK**.

19. The **Services** dialog box appears.

20. Click **OK**.

21. In the **File** menu, click **Exit And Log Off**.

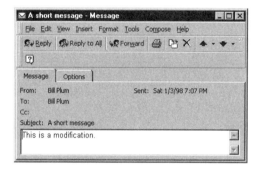

Review

Offline folder file creation can be accomplished through the Exchange Server transport properties. In the **Offline Folder File Settings** dialog box you define the name and the directory in which you want to store the .OST file. You will use the **Synchronization** property page to specify which folders to synchronize.

Lesson 4: Roving Users

Roving users are users who work with multiple computers or multiple messaging clients. Multiple clients usually require the configuration of multiple profiles, but the creation of centralized messaging profiles can simplify the configuration task. The mechanism to implement centralized messaging profiles, however, depends on the operating system that has been installed on the client computers.

This lesson discusses the support of roving users by explaining the creation and configuration of centralized profiles. You'll find information regarding the support of users working on computers based on MS-DOS, Windows 3.x, Windows 95, and Windows NT. In addition, some points to consider regarding the configuration of Personal Folder Stores will be discussed.

At the end of this lesson, you will be able to:

- Support roving user configurations for MS-DOS–based and Windows 3.x–based clients

- Support roving user configurations for Windows 95–based and Windows NT–based clients

Estimated time to complete this lesson: 10 minutes

Roving User Configuration Issues

To simplify the task of creating messaging profiles for roving users, you can implement server-based profiles. The server-based profiles will be copied to every workstation a roving user logs on to, automatically providing the same messaging environment to the user. Since messaging profile information is stored differently on different client operating systems, you must consider the requirements of each client platform. For example, if a roving user works on machines with MS-DOS, Windows 3.x, and Windows 95, you must create one profile for each platform separately. Fortunately, no significant differences exist between Windows 95 and Windows NT clients.

MS-DOS–Based Exchange Client

The MS-DOS–based Exchange Client stores its messaging profile in a file called Exchange.pro. You can find this file in the Exchange Client directory on the workstation's local hard disk. This file can be copied to a file server, perhaps into the home directory of the roving user. To use the server-based Exchange.pro file instead of the local version, start Exchange using the **-p** command line switch to specify to the profile location on the server drive. This switch can be used to specify both the path and the name of the profile, as in the command line **Exchange -pM:\Exchange.pro**.

Windows 3.x–Based Clients

Windows 3.x–based clients store their messaging configuration in a file named Exchange.ini. This file is placed in the Exchange Client directory and can be copied or moved into another directory on a server. In this case, you must reference the location of the Exchange.ini file within the [MAPI] section of the Win.ini file, where there exists a parameter called ProfileDirectory16 that points to the valid Exchange.ini. The following example demonstrates how to modify the Win.ini to get this configuration to work:

```
[MAPI]
ProfileDirectory16=<path to the user's home directory>
\Exchange.ini
```

If Windows 3.x has been configured as a shared network installation, you can store the modified Win.ini file in the user's home directory. For convenience, you also can place the corresponding Exchange.ini in the user's home directory. In fact, this is the most convenient method for supporting roving Windows 3.x users.

Windows NT–Based and Windows 95–Based Clients

Both Windows NT and Windows 95 provide built-in support for roving users because Exchange Clients and Outlook on both platforms store messaging profiles within the user's context in the workstation Registry. Of course, the user profile can be stored as a server-based profile. A server-based Windows NT profile can be assigned to each account using the User Manager for Domains. Once the account of the roving user has been associated with a server-based profile, its settings are copied to the local configuration each time the roving user logs on to the domain. The same settings, including the messaging profile, are thus available on every Windows 95 or Windows NT computer.

Note Windows NT Server supports the concept of mandatory user profiles, which implies that the user cannot change the server-based profile settings. Configuration changes (for example, a new MAPI profile) applied during one session will be lost when the user logs off Windows NT. Mandatory profiles must contain a valid messaging profile to support the Exchange Client or Outlook. In other words, the user needs to configure his or her messaging environment before the administrator converts the server-based profile to become mandatory. Otherwise, users would have to create a new profile during each session.

Personal Folder Store Considerations

Roving users typically want to have access to all their messages from within any messaging client they are using. If they have stored some of their messages in one or more Personal Folder Stores, precautions must be taken to make sure the associated .PST files are available all over the network. Therefore, .PST files should be placed on a file server that can be accessed using every client machine. In other words, if a common file server is not available, a roving user should refrain from using Personal Folder Stores. He or she can instead use only the server-based mailbox as the repository for messages.

Outlook Web Access

The HTTP-based access to server-based mailboxes is an alternative to all other roving user options. By using a regular Web browser that supports Java Script and Frames (such as Internet Explorer 4.0), users can gain access to their mailbox through Outlook Web Access running on an Active Server (such as IIS 3.0 with ASPs or IIS 4.0). However, roving users should be aware of security risks when using browser applications. Browser programs view the messaging items in HTML pages, which might be cached temporarily on the workstation. If a roving user does not delete those cached pages manually after a session, other users can simply open them later to read personal information. More information about Outlook Web Access is provided in Chapter 11, "Internet Protocols."

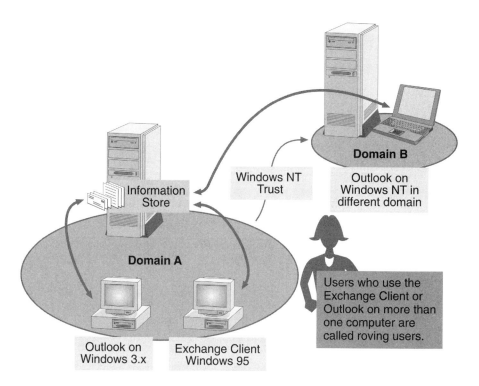

Figure 7-6. Characteristics of a roving user.

The different platform-dependent profile locations are as follows:

- MS-DOS–based Exchange Client; which stores the messaging profile in the file Exchange.pro

- Windows 3.x–based client; which stores its settings in the Exchange.ini file

- Windows 95–based and Windows NT–based clients; which use the Registry to store the messaging configuration

Lesson 5: Remote Users

Remote users work off line using a modem or Integrated Services Digital Network (ISDN) card to establish connections to their Exchange Server for sending and downloading messages. The Remote Mail features of the Exchange Client and Outlook allow you to download messages selectively. Used with a Personal Folder Store, Remote Mail might be the best choice if you need to work over slow links.

This lesson explains the features that allow you to support remote users. Remote Mail options of the Exchange Client or Outlook allow remote users to participate in the organization's operation. Remote Mail features are available for clients based on MS-DOS, Windows 3.x, Windows 95, and Windows NT. Macintosh-based clients don't offer support for Remote Mail.

At the end of this lesson, you will be able to:

- Describe the support of remote users by means of the Exchange Server transport

- Identify important configuration issues and dependencies

Estimated time to complete this lesson: 25 minutes

Remote User Support

Users who work via modem or ISDN lines usually don't work on line permanently. They compose new messages and read downloaded messages while disconnected from the server. In other words, they connect to the server only to send and download new messages, which helps to reduce the amount of time spent dialed in, thus reducing communications costs. For this reason, downloaded messages are maintained in a local repository, which can be created by means of a Personal Folder Store.

Note You cannot use the Remote Mail features of either the Exchange Client or Outlook if an Offline Message Store has been configured. In this situation you must disable the Offline Message Store prior to using Remote Mail.

Remote Mail in Windows 95 and Windows NT

Windows 95–based and Windows NT–based clients allow you to configure remote mail connections through the property pages of the Exchange Server transport service. Both clients rely completely on the Dial-Up Networking capabilities of their respective operating system platforms.

Starting Off Line

You might want to start the Exchange Client or Outlook off line: this saves startup time, since the client won't try to connect to a server. Starting off line suppresses the dialog box that would otherwise inform you that a connection to the server could not be established. To be sure your Exchange Client or Outlook always starts off line, activate the **Work Offline And Use Dial-Up Networking** option on the **General** property page of the Exchange Server transport within your messaging profile. An alternative is to select the **Choose The Connection Type When Starting** check box. This allows you to select whether to work off line or on line at every startup.

Specifying the Dial-Up Connection

The **Dial-Up Networking** property page of the Exchange Server transport gives you the option to select the dial-up connection that may have been configured using Dial-Up Networking. The account information used to establish a connection with the remote dial-up server can be specified under **User Name**, **Password**, and **Domain**. This account does not necessarily need to be the same account that you use to connect to your server-based mailbox.

Remote Mail Connections

You can establish remote mail connections through the **Remote Mail** command on the client's **Tools** menu. This command launches the **Microsoft Exchange Server - Remote Mail** window if you are working with the Exchange Client. Outlook displays a submenu and an additional toolbar labeled **Remote**. The submenu, in turn, allows you to launch the **Remote Connection Wizard** through the **Connect** command and to display the **Remote Tools**. (See Figure 7-7 on page 378.)

A connection to the Exchange Server is established when you click **Connect**. While this connection is up and running the headers of messages in your server-based mailbox are downloaded and the messages composed off line are uploaded. Header information is displayed either in the **Microsoft Exchange Server - Remote Mail** window (Exchange Client) or in Outlook's regular Inbox as an envelope icon with a little telephone. You can then disconnect manually from the server using the **Disconnect** command, or automatically by using the **Disconnect After Connection Is Finished** check box, found on the **Remote Mail** property page of the Exchange Server transport service.

Based on the retrieved header information, you can select which messages to be downloaded or deleted without downloading the next time you connect. For this purpose, three options are available in the **Microsoft Exchange Server - Remote Mail** window and in Outlook. You can mark a message for retrieval, which will move the message to your local store the next time you connect. You can retrieve a copy, which also moves the message to your local store but leaves a copy on the server, or you can mark a message for deletion, which will delete the message from the server without first downloading it the next time you work on line. Because you can select each message individually, Remote Mail is perfectly suitable for downloading only the messages you want over slow dial-up connections.

Scheduled Connections

If you want to automate the process of establishing a connection and of processing marked items, you can configure scheduled connections through the **Remote Mail** property page of the Exchange Server transport. Once scheduled connections have been defined, the client establishes connections to the server automatically based on the specified schedule. During these connections the client behaves the same way as during remote mail connections that have been started manually. (See Figure 7-7 on page 378.)

When connecting to the server through scheduled connections, you might also want to automate the retrieval of messages. For this purpose, you can configure *filters*, which affect the download of messages. So long as no filter criterion has been defined, all messages will be downloaded.

The **Remote Mail** property page provides the required controls to set the desired filters. Filters can be specified for manual connections under the **Remote Mail Connection** category and for scheduled connections under **Scheduled Connections**. The **Filter** button becomes available if you activate the corresponding **Retrieve Items That Meet The Following Conditions** option. Click the **Filter** button to display the **Filter** dialog box, where you can define your criteria for the message retrieval. All messages that do not meet your criteria will remain on the server.

Using ShivaRemote

Dial-Up Networking is not available for MS-DOS and Windows 3.x platforms. As a result, you must use ShivaRemote to access an Exchange Server remotely. ShivaRemote is a Point-to-Point Protocol (PPP) client that supports IPX/SPX, TCP/IP, and NetBEUI.

Installing ShivaRemote

The Exchange Client and Outlook CD-ROMs include two versions of ShivaRemote, one for the MS-DOS–based client and one for the Windows 3.x–based client. These provide different setup procedures, as described in the following section.

MS-DOS–Based Clients

The MS-DOS version of ShivaRemote doesn't have a separate Setup program. Instead, you can install ShivaRemote during the setup of the MS-DOS–based Exchange client. All the ShivaRemote files will be copied into the client directory. You can also start the client's Setup program at any time to copy the ShivaRemote files at a later time.

Windows 3.x–Based Clients

During a **Typical** installation of the Windows 3.x–based client, an icon for setting up ShivaRemote will be placed in the **Microsoft Exchange** program group. You must run this Setup program separately in order to install the ShivaRemote software. This Setup program will modify the Autoexec.bat, Win.ini, and System.ini files. The original files will be backed up with a .000 extension and placed in the ShivaRemote directory. ShivaRemote Setup copies all its relevant files into this directory, except for Vnb.386 and Ctl3d.dll. These files will be copied to the \Windows\System directory.

ShivaRemote with the MS-DOS–Based Client

To work remotely using an MS-DOS–based client, you must first run the Connect.exe from the client directory. This establishes the ShivaRemote connection to the RAS server. Then you can start the Exchange Client. The MS-DOS–based client doesn't have any built-in remote functionality, so you cannot download message headers. In other words, you'll work with the client as though a permanent network connection exists.

ShivaRemote with Windows 3.x–Based Clients

The ShivaRemote Setup program inserts only the references for the Dial.386 driver into the System.ini and modifies the MS-DOS search path to include the ShivaRemote directory. Any further configuration steps are not performed. To work with ShivaRemote, the configuration must be completed manually.

Two different network drivers can be used within Windows or Windows for Workgroups: the real mode and the protected mode drivers. The configuration of ShivaRemote varies depending on which driver has been selected.

Real Mode Network Configuration

In order to use ShivaRemote, you must modify the Config.sys, Autoexec.bat, and System.ini. In a real mode network configuration, the **net start** command must be added to the Autoexec.bat. In addition, the following entries must be added to Config.sys:

```
device=c:\Windir\Protman.dos /i:c:\windir
device=c:\Shiva_dir\Dialndis.exe
```

The System.ini must be modified if you are using Windows for Workgroups, which entails setting the LoadRMDrivers= Yes entry within the [network drivers] section.

Protected Mode Configurations

Windows for Workgroups can also be configured to use ShivaRemote in protected mode. Start the **Network** application in the **Network** program group and add a new network adapter. Select **Unlisted** and then type the path to the Shiva files to install the protected mode Shiva dial-in driver. The driver then must be configured in respect to the appropriate network protocols. Restart the computer to finish the installation.

Once ShivaRemote has been configured properly, it can be used in conjunction with the Remote Mail options of the Windows 3.x–based Exchange Client and Outlook for Windows 3.x.

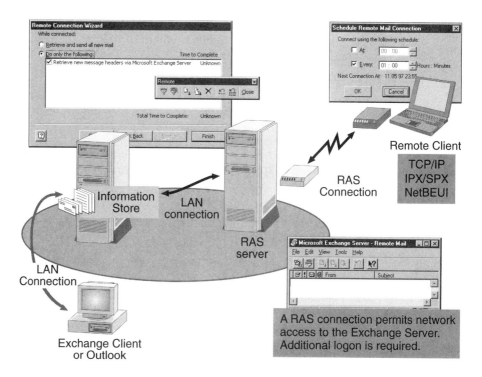

Figure 7-7. Remote client connections.

The platform-dependent remote configurations are as follows:

- MS-DOS–based client; ShivaRemote support via Connect.exe
- Windows 3.x and Windows for Workgroups; ShivaRemote real mode or protected mode drivers
- Windows 95–based and Windows NT–based clients; via Dial-Up Networking and the Exchange Server transport service
- Macintosh-based clients; no direct support of Remote Mail functionality

Lesson 6: Outlook Configuration Options

Most of the e-mail–related configuration settings for Outlook are identical or at least comparable to the settings in the Exchange Client. Even the menu options have been placed in the same position to provide a similar method of configuration. For instance, the **Options** command can be found in the **Tools** menu of both clients, which displays the **Options** dialog box that allows you to adjust the general client behavior to your personal needs.

This lesson covers several configuration options that affect the behavior of your messaging client, namely Outlook. A brief explanation of client extensions is presented. You can read about options that affect new message composition as well as rules that can manipulate received items. Spell checker settings and parameters concerning your primary calendar application are also introduced.

An exercise has been included in this lesson to guide you through the steps of configuring the e-mail–related Outlook options. You'll configure parameters that affect how you compose and read e-mail messages.

At the end of this lesson, you will be able to:

- List the Outlook configuration parameters
- Configure basic Outlook settings

Estimated time to complete this lesson: 30 minutes

Outlook Settings Related to E-Mail

Outlook is a powerful program that provides many more features than just the ability to send e-mail messages: it is also a combined scheduling and work-group application. Outlook offers a wide variety of configuration options that can be launched through the **Options** command on the **Tools** menu. However, the entire configuration of Outlook is not the topic of this section. Only the options that affect the e-mail functions will be explored.

Configuring the Startup Mode

Typically, Outlook starts without asking which messaging profile it should use. This is the default behavior, but if multiple profiles have been configured, you might want to select the desired profile when the client starts. To do this, open the **Tools** menu in Outlook, select the **Options** command, switch to the **General** property page, and activate the **Prompt For A Profile To Be Used** option under **Startup Settings**. A **Choose Profile** dialog box will appear every time you start the client, offering available profiles that you have defined for different messaging configurations.

Outlook Extensions

The Inbox Assistant and Out of Office Assistant are good examples of Outlook extensions that stretch the basic client functionality. The Inbox Assistant, for instance, allows you to specify rules for automatic message processing, while the Out of Office Assistant can be used to generate out-of-office notifications, which inform the originators of e-mail messages that you are currently unavailable. Both assistants are launched through the **Tools** menu, where you'll find the **Inbox Assistant** and **Out of Office Assistant** commands if you have already opened your **Inbox** folder.

Try removing both assistants from Outlook to better understand the maintenance of client extensions. First open the **Options** command on the **Tools** menu, switch to the **General** property page, and click the **Add-In Manager** button. A dialog box appears with the **Exchange Extensions** check box. Once you have cleared this check box, click **OK** twice to accept the configuration changes and to close the **Options** dialog box. When you open the **Tools** menu, you'll find that the **Inbox Assistant** and **Out of Office Assistant** commands are missing. Outlook is still the same application, but its functionality has been reduced. To restore the assistants, enable the **Exchange Extensions** check box again. Client extensions are an example of Outlook's flexibility.

E-Mail Processing

Outlook can perform several actions on e-mail messages automatically as they arrive in your Inbox. You can select an action such as playing a sound, changing the cursor, or displaying a message box. The message box offers the option to read the message immediately. The message box will be activated by enabling the **Display A Notification Message** option of the **E-Mail** property page within the **Options** dialog box. (See Figure 7-8 on page 382.)

Other settings that can be found on the **E-Mail** property page affect the Settings for the automatic processing of e-mail messages. Available options are **Process Delivery, Read, and Recall Receipts On Arrival**, **Process Requests And Responses On Arrival**, and **Delete Receipts And Blank Responses After Processing**. If Microsoft Word has been installed on your computer, you can also activate the **Use Microsoft Word As The E-Mail Editor** option to use Word for composing new messages.

Default Settings for New Messages

The **Sending** property page of the **Options** dialog box provides control over the default parameters for new messages. These parameters are enabled by default, so you don't need to set them for each message specifically. The available settings include the font you want to use, the default importance and sensitivity of messages, and whether to allow a comma as an address separator. Furthermore, you can enable the new **Automatic Name Checking** feature of Outlook, which performs address resolutions as you type a recipient address into a new message's **To, CC,** or **BCC** line.

Other available options on the **Sending** property page relate to tracking sent messages and saving copies of what you send. You can request an automatic delivery receipt on all messages by enabling **Tell Me When All Messages Have Been Delivered**, or request a read receipt with **Tell Me When All Messages Have Been Read.** By default, a copy of each message you send is kept in the **Sent Items** folder. If you don't want to keep copies of your messages, disable **Save Copies Of Messages In Sent Items Folder.** If you reply to messages in folders other than your in **Inbox,** replies can be saved in the same folder as the message by enabling **In Folders Other Than The Inbox Save Replies With The Original Message.** Forwarded messages are also saved by default, but this can be disabled using the **Save Forwarded Messages** option.

Configuring Read Options

Read options affect the behavior of the client when scrolling through the list of e-mail messages that have been stored in a particular message folder. For instance, these options determine what should be displayed after deleting or moving an item. You can open another message above or below the removed one, or return to Outlook's Inbox. You also can include and indent the original text when replying to or forwarding messages. All these settings can be specified through the **Reading** property page of the **Options** dialog box.

Spell Checker Options

Outlook can check your e-mail messages for typos and other spelling errors. You will be informed if a word has been spelled incorrectly, and you have the opportunity to correct the text before you send your message. This feature is comparable to the spell checker function of Word.

The configuration of the Outlook spell checker is set through the **Spelling** property page of the Options dialog box. The five options are **Always Suggest Replacements For Misspelled Words, Always Check Spelling Before Sending, Ignore Words In UPPERCASE, Ignore Words With Numbers,** and **Ignore Original Message Text In Reply Or Forward**.

Defining Delegates

On the **Delegates** property page, you can designate an assistant or configure delegate permissions regarding the Outlook folders of your mailbox. A delegate can send messages on your behalf and modify calendar and task items. Use the **Permissions** button to define permissions for a particular user. Delegate access to a mailbox is explained in the section, "Delegate Access," later in this chapter.

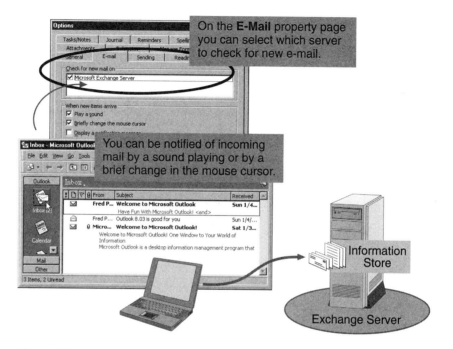

Figure 7-8. Checking new e-mail with Outlook.

The Outlook options that apply to message items specifically are as follows:

- **AutoArchive**; determines when and where to automatically archive Outlook information

- **Delegates**; designates delegates who can send mail on your behalf and receive messages that have been addressed to you

- **E-Mail**; defines actions to be performed when new messages arrive

- **General**; specifies deletion settings, prompts for an existing profile upon startup, sets dial options such as settings for dialing and phone numbers, and uses the **Add-In Manager** button to install client extensions

- **Journal**; configures journal items and contacts

- **Manage Forms**; manages and install forms

- **Reading**; defines how Outlook continues after an open message is moved or deleted

- **Reminders**; configures particular actions to perform when a reminder comes due

- **Security**; sets up advanced security

- **Sending**; sets specifications for formatting text and mail properties for new messages when sending

- **Spelling**; suggests replacements for misspelled words and can opt to always check spelling before sending

- **Tasks/Note**; specifies task defaults, task color options, and task working hours

Exercise 17: Configuring Options for Processing Messages

Message options defined at the client level allow you to specify default settings that affect the overall handling of messages. For example, the spell checker configuration influences how the text of all composed messages will be checked.

Estimated time to complete this exercise: 10 minutes

Description

In this exercise, you will define several Outlook options that are related to sending, spelling, and delivering messages. You will also verify various settings regarding the configuration of information services. You will check the folder that will be used for incoming messages, as well as the address list that will be displayed first when opening the Address Book.

- Task 17a describes the steps for configuring some of the options that are related to reading a message.

- Task 17b describes the steps for configuring some of the options that are related to sending a message.

- Task 17c describes the steps for configuring some of the options that are related to checking the spelling in a message.

- Task 17d describes the steps for setting some of the options that are related to configuring a delivery location for all incoming mail and defining the address list you want to use as a default.

Prerequisites

- Outlook must be started.

Task 17a: Configuring Read Options

1. On the **Tools** menu, click **Options**.

2. The **Options** dialog box appears. Click the **Reading** tab.

3. In the **After Moving Or Deleting An Open Item** list, click **Return To The Inbox**.

4. In the **When Replying To Message** dialog box, click **Font**.

5. The **Font** dialog box appears. Choose the font settings you want for the reply text.

6. Click **OK**.

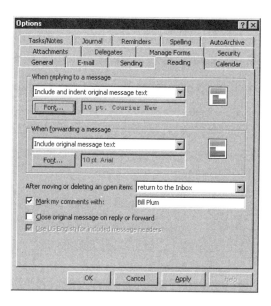

Task 17b: Configuring Send Options

1. Click the **Sending** tab.

2. Click **Font**.

3. The **Font** dialog box appears. Choose the font settings you want to use when sending a message.

4. Click **OK**.

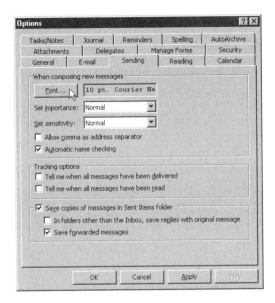

Task 17c: Configuring Spelling Options

1. Click the **Spelling** tab.

2. Verify that the **Always Suggest Replacements For Misspelled Words** check box has been selected.

3. Select the **Always Check Spelling Before Sending** check box.

4. Verify that the **Ignore Original Message Text In Reply Or Forward** check box has been selected.

5. Click **OK**.

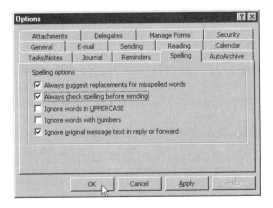

Task 17d: Viewing Addressing and Delivery Options

1. On the **Tools** menu, click **Services**.

2. The **Services** dialog box appears. Click the **Addressing** tab.

3. Click the **Show This Address List First** list.

4. Notice the various address list containers that can be selected in addition to your Personal Address Book.

5. Verify that **Global Address List** is selected.

6. Click the **Delivery** tab.

Note Using this tab, you can change the delivery location of incoming e-mail messages. You can also configure the priority order of your mail transports. For instance, if you have two transports that support SMTP mail, the first transport listed will process outbound SMTP messages.

---

7. Click **OK**.

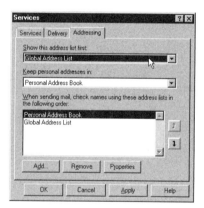

Review

The **Options** dialog box offers several configuration parameters. Those that affect the behavior of Outlook regarding reading, editing, and sending of messages are grouped on the **Reading**, **Spelling**, and **Sending** property pages. Furthermore, the **Delivery** property page of the **Services** dialog box provides default settings regarding the installed information services. You can configure, for example, the delivery location for incoming messages on this page. You can also change the priority order of the messaging services that deliver messages. This option is especially useful if you have more than one transport service included in your messaging profile. With the **Addressing** property page of the **Services** dialog box you can specify which address list to display first when opening the Address Book.

Lesson 7: Configuring the Transport

The Exchange Server transport is the most important MAPI component that both the Exchange Client and Outlook must use to connect to an Exchange Server, so you will configure this transport independently of the actual client being used. Important configuration parameters, which can be set through the property pages of the Exchange transport service, are the mailbox and home server names. However, several other parameters can also be specified, such as the Offline Folder Store configuration and Remote Mail options. It might be necessary to optimize the transport by means of direct manipulation of Registry entries.

This lesson covers the configuration and optimization of the Exchange Server transport service. The optimization is primarily a task of reordering the RPC communication mechanisms. A brief discussion about importing existing data will outline the steps to retrieve information from older Mail Message Files (.MMF) and .PAB files. You can also read about the configuration of delegate access to mailbox resources, as it might be required to designate assistants and coworkers as custodians of your messages.

This lesson contains two practical exercises. The first exercise identifies the Registry entries that can be modified to optimize the startup process of the Exchange Client or Outlook. The second exercise guides you through the steps necessary to grant **Send On Behalf** permissions to another user.

At the end of this lesson, you will be able to:

- Optimize the RPC communication between the Exchange Server and the client

- Import existing .MMF and .PAB information

- Describe the various levels and configure the delegate access for your mailbox

Estimated time to complete this lesson: 30 minutes

Exchange Server Transport

The Exchange Server transport uses RPCs for client-server communication. RPCs are used any time the client interacts with the server, including when setting up the Exchange Server transport service itself. Let's say that you are configuring the transport service through the **Mail** or **Mail And Fax** applet of the Control Panel. Using the **General** property page of the **Microsoft Exchange Server** dialog box, you enter the name of the home server under

Microsoft Exchange Server and the display name of your mailbox under **Mailbox**. You can then check immediately to see whether the connection to the server is functioning by clicking the **Check Name** button. This procedure resolves the mailbox name, while RPCs are working under the surface to accomplish this task. If both server name and mailbox name can be resolved as indicated by an underline, the RPC communication was successful. At this point you have good reason to assume that the client-server communication can take place without any problems. (See Figure 7-9.)

RPC Methods

RPCs are a high-level mechanism for interprocess communication (Application layer of the OSI network model). Software components that communicate using RPCs can build their connection upon a vast variety of network protocols including Local RPCs, TCP/IP, SPX/IPX, Banyan Vines IP, Named Pipes, and NetBIOS. Some client computers will have multiple protocols installed and therefore will have multiple ways to establish an RPC connection. Exchange will attempt to communicate over the available protocols in a sequential order until a connection can be established or until all options have been tried without success.

Let's use the example of a Windows NT Workstation in a Novell NetWare server environment to describe the establishment of the RPC connection. An NT workstation will have TCP/IP installed by default as well as SPX/IPX to connect to NetWare servers. When you start Outlook using the default configuration, the client will try to locate the Exchange Server on the local computer first. Because the server does not reside on the local machine, this connection attempt will fail. The client will then try to communicate through TCP/IP, but if network routers or the Exchange Server are not set up to support TCP/IP, the attempt to establish communication fails again. It could take several minutes for the TCP/IP connection to fail, as name resolution requests are sent to DNS servers (if a DNS server is defined on the client) and these queries will not time-out for two or three minutes in most environments. By default, the third connection attempt will be performed over SPX/IPX, and voilà! Finally the server can be reached, so it answers the incoming request and communicates with the client. The RPC connection has been established, but not before two time-consuming and unsuccessful attempts were made. Hence, you probably want to optimize the RPC connect order for Workstations in a Novell NetWare environment.

This optimization will be described in "Client Connection Order," later in this lesson. Further server and client configuration regarding a native Novell NetWare network are covered in Chapter 17, "Microsoft Exchange Clients in a NetWare Environment."

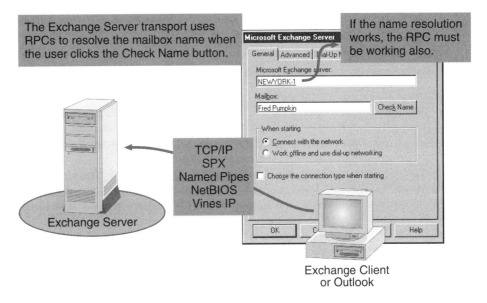

Figure 7-9. Resolving the mailbox name through RPCs.

The supported RPC communication methods between MAPI-based clients
and an Exchange Server are:

- Banyan Vines IP; integrates Exchange Server in Banyan Vines
  networks—available on Windows NT, Windows 95, and Windows
  for Workgroups 3.11 only

- Local RPCs; used when the client and server are installed on the
  same machine

- Named Pipes; connects to the server using the built-in Windows NT
  security

- NetBIOS; connects to the server using NetBIOS over NetBEUI, SPX/IPX,
  or TCP/IP

- SPX/IPX; supports native Novell NetWare workstations via SPX/IPX
  over Windows Sockets

- TCP/IP; uses Windows Sockets or TCP/IP

Client Connection Order

The client will attempt to connect to the server using all available communication methods in a sequential order until it can either connect successfully or
until all methods have failed. The default connect order for clients based on

Windows 95 and Windows NT–based clients is Local RPC, TCP/IP, SPX/IPX, Named Pipes, NetBIOS, and Banyan Vines IP. Windows 3.x–based clients will use Named Pipes first, then SPX/IPX, TCP/IP, NetBIOS, and finally Banyan Vines IP.

Modifying the Connection Order

You can modify the client connection order prior to the actual client installation via the Exchange Client Setup Editor in conjunction with a shared installation point. Unfortunately, this option is not available for the 32-bit Outlook client. To modify the binding order for the Exchange Client, select the **Modify Setup Program Options** command on the Setup Editor's **Tools** menu. Then click the **Binding Order** tab to set the adjustment.

When adjusting the client connect order using the Setup Editor, you are actually changing Exchng.stf file entries within the shared installation point. These entries are dependent upon the operating system. For instance, you can find the following entry for Windows 95 and Windows NT if you have specified TCP/IP first, and then SPX/IPX, followed by Named Pipes:

```
61 AddRegData """LOCAL""",
"""Software\Microsoft\Exchange\Exchange Provider""",
"""Rpc_Binding_Order""", """ncacn_ip_tcp,ncacn_spx,ncacn_np,"""
```

And for Windows 3.x–based clients:

```
62 AddIniLine """exchng.ini""", """Exchange Provider""",
"Rpc_Binding_Order""", """ncacn_ip_tcp,ncacn_spx,ncacn_np"""
```

Modifying the Connect Order on Windows 95 and Windows NT

Once the Windows 95–based or Windows NT–based client has been installed, you can use the Registry Editor to change the Rpc_Binding_Order value (as shown in Figure 7-10). This configuration method is available for both the Exchange Client and Outlook 97. The Rpc_Binding_Order value can be found under:

```
HKEY_LOCAL_MACHINE
  \SOFTWARE
    \Microsoft
      \Exchange
        \Exchange Provider
```

The list of communication methods must be separated by commas. If you want, you can rearrange or delete entries to speed up the client startup process. For workstations in a Novell NetWare environment, to complete our example, you would place the **ncacn_spx** synonym on the first position. With this modification, the client will try to communicate through RPCs over SPX first. Because

SPX is the common protocol to the client and Exchange Server, the client connects to the server on its first attempt, thus avoiding time-consuming, unsuccessful connection attempts via Local RPC and TCP/IP. For your reference, you'll find a complete list of protocol synonyms below Figure 7-10.

Modifying the Connect Order on Windows 3.x and Windows for Workgroups

You can also change the connect order for Windows 3.x clients. A corresponding entry will be placed in the Exchange.ini file, since the Windows 3.x–based clients don't store configuration settings in a Registry. To change the order, you simply adjust the Rpc_Binding_Order entry. The protocol synonyms are the same as for Windows 95 and Windows NT.

Modifying the Connect Order on MS-DOS

In some cases you might also need to change the binding order for the MS-DOS–based Exchange Client. As with Windows-based clients, the connection order can be changed before or after the installation. To change the connection order before installation, you must edit the Mlsetup.ini file within a shared installation point. You would have to modify the following line:

```
RPC_BINDING_ORDER=ncalrpc,ncacn_np,ncacn_spx,ncacn_ip_tcp,netbios
```

On the other hand, if you want to modify the connection order for a client that has already been installed, you need to change the RPC_BINDING_ORDER environment variable that is set in the Autoexec.bat file.

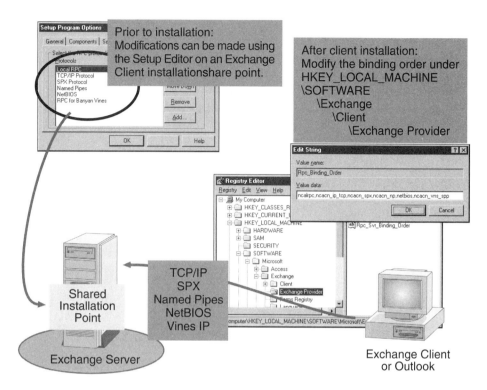

Figure 7-10. Modifying the binding order on Windows 95.

The RPC communication methods are listed below:

- Local RPC: **ncalrpc**
- RPC over Named Pipes: **ncacn_np**
- RPC over NetBIOS: **netbios**
- RPC over SPX: **ncacn_spx**
- RPC over TCP/IP: **ncacn_ip_tcp**
- RPC over Vines IP: **ncacn_vns_spp**

Exercise 18: Viewing the Client RPC Connection Order in the Registry

The Exchange Client and Outlook can connect to an Exchange Server using a variety of RPC communication methods. To establish a connection, clients try all the methods in sequential order until one method works or the list has been exhausted. Depending on the local configuration and available network protocols, it might be advisable to modify the connection order.

Estimated time to complete this exercise: 15 minutes

Description

In this exercise, you will use the Windows NT Registry Editor to examine the Rpc_Binding_Order value. If desired, you can modify the connect order to optimize the startup process of your client.

- Task 18 describes the steps for viewing, and possibly changing, the RPC connect order in the Windows NT Registry.

Prerequisites

- Log on as Admin-NY1 to NEWYORK-1.

Task 18: Viewing the Client RPC Connection Order in the Registry

1. Click the **Start** button, and then click **Run**.

2. In the Open box, type *REGEDT32* and then click **OK**.

3. Switch to the **HKEY_LOCAL_MACHINE On Local Machine** child window.

4. Open **SOFTWARE**, **Microsoft, Exchange**, and then **Exchange Provider**.

5. View the **Rpc_Binding_Order** value.

   Note Notice the default binding order for Exchange clients. First is a Local RPC, followed by TCP/IP (Sockets), followed by SPX (Sockets), Named Pipes, NetBIOS, and Banyan Vines.

6. Exit the **Registry Editor**.

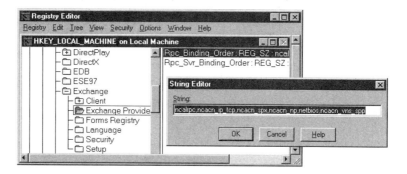

Review

The RPC_Binding_Order value can be examined and modified using the Registry Editor (for Windows 95 and Windows NT). The relevant setting is located under:

```
HKEY_LOCAL_MACHINE
  \SOFTWARE
    \Microsoft
      \Exchange
        \Exchange Provider
```

By default the binding order specifies RPC, followed by TCP/IP (Sockets), SPX, Named Pipes, NetBIOS, and Banyan Vines IP.

The order will vary if the client has been installed from a shared installation point where an administrator used the Setup Editor to adjust the connect order.

Importing a .MMF or a .PAB File

MS Mail is the predecessor to Exchange Server. In MS Mail networks, users typically work with Windows-based MS Mail 3.x clients, which store messages in Mail Message Files (.MMF). The .MMF files can be seen as a sort of predecessor to .PST files. Depending on the configuration, .MMF files are kept either locally or within an MS Mail postoffice.

As an administrator you can use the Migration Wizard to migrate existing MS Mail mailboxes to Exchange Server. This is a convenient way to configure an Exchange mailbox for every existing MS Mail user. You can also import existing messages from .MMF files into the newly created mailbox—so long as the .MMF files are stored in the postoffice.

The Migration Wizard does not provide the option to migrate .MMF files that have been kept locally on client machines. For this reason, .MMF import features have been implemented into the Exchange Client and Outlook, so users can use the **Import** command on the Exchange Client's **File** menu to import their existing messages manually. Outlook offers the **Import And Export** command on the **File** menu for the same purpose. (See Figure 7-11.)

Note Using the **Import** or **Import And Export** command you can import e-mail messages from .MMF files as well as personal addresses from existing (.PAB) files.

Importing an .MMF

Windows-based MS Mail clients store messages and the Personal Address Book in .MMF files, so you have the option to import messages, personal addresses, or both. The MS Mail client uses a security mechanism based on a password to prevent unauthorized access to messages stored in an .MMF file. For this reason, you must provide this password when importing an .MMF file.

Messages can be imported into the server-based mailbox or into a .PST file. When messages are imported into a .PST file, the Personal Folder Store can be created during the import cycle. Messages will be copied to the newly created store, and once they have been copied, you can work with them as with any other messages. The Import procedure is a one-way street: messages cannot be moved back into an .MMF file. But the Import doesn't change the source file, which means that the messages will remain untouched in the original .MMF file.

Note The **Import** command is implemented in the Windows-based Exchange clients only.

Importing a .PAB

Addresses in .MMF files can be imported using the **Import Personal Address Book Entries** option, which is also accessible through the **Import** command.

Exchange Clients store personal addresses in .PAB files. You might want to import from existing .PAB files as well. To do so, select the **Import** command on the Exchange Client's **File** menu to import the addresses. Then select the .PAB file through the **Specify File To Import** dialog box. When you click **OK**, the addresses will be added to your current Personal Address Book. A status message about the duration of the import process and any errors will be displayed at the end of the import routine.

Microsoft Outlook

Outlook also supports the import of .MMF files and .PAB files. It provides the **Import And Export** command on the **File** menu to launch the **Import And Export Wizard**. In contrast to the Exchange Client, where you can select the .MMF or .PAB file directly, you must specify the **Import From A Microsoft Mail File (.MMF)** option to import the same information using Outlook. Even if you want to import a .PAB file, select **Import From A Microsoft Mail File (.MMF)** first. Then click **Next** and select the desired .PAB file instead of an .MMF file. Although the method is different, the result of the import action will be the same as with the Exchange Client.

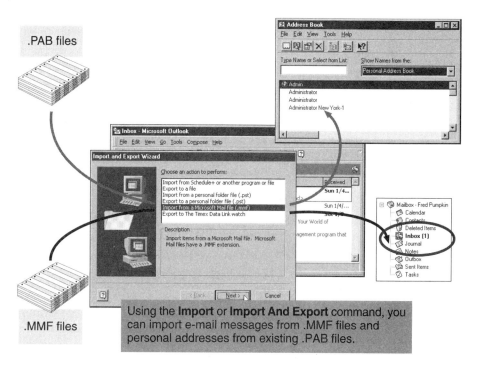

Figure 7-11. Importing information in Outlook.

The characteristics of imported information in both Exchange and Outlook clients are as follows:

- Messages from .MMF files can be imported into either .PST files or into the mailbox on the Exchange Server

- Personal addresses from .MMF files can be imported into a .PAB file

- Personal addresses from .PAB files can be imported into another .PAB file

Delegate Access

Delegate access refers to a configuration where one user is able to read and send messages on behalf of another user. Such a configuration is especially desirable for people in management positions who want to have their assistants handle the daily correspondence.

Granting Access Permissions to Private Folders

At minimum, read access to your **Inbox** is required if an assistant will be reading your incoming messages. Access rights can also be granted to other folders, such as **Contacts** and **Calendar**. It's possible to grant access permissions to all existing message folders of your mailbox and the mailbox object itself.

To assign an assistant the appropriate level of access, select the **Options** command on Outlook's **Tools** menu. Click the **Add** button on the **Delegates** page to select the assistant from the Global Address List. You are then prompted to specify access permissions for each Outlook system folder (**Calendar**, **Contacts**, **Inbox**, and so forth). If you want to grant permissions for other private folders, display the appropriate folder's properties by right-clicking the mouse. Then switch to the **Permissions** property page where you can specify user permissions as for a public folder. This is also the procedure that Exchange Client users employ if they want to assign access permissions on their mailbox.

Granting Send-On-Behalf-Of Delegate Access

You must grant your assistant permission to send messages on your behalf if you want the delegate to compose or reply to certain messages, such as meeting requests. Depending on the level of access that has been granted to a delegate, the delegate's name will appear in messages that have been sent on your behalf. Anyone with delegate access to your mailbox is granted **Send On Behalf Of** permissions, which means that they can use the **From** button to add your name to the **From** field when composing messages. Recipients of the message will see your name under **Sent On Behalf Of** beside your assistant's name in the **From** field. The Exchange Client provides the **Exchange Server** tab, where you can add the assistant's mailbox through the **Add** button.

You might want your assistant to send messages on your behalf but without being able to read your messages. In this case, you must not grant read permission to your mailbox, Inbox, or any other folder. The **Send On Behalf Of** rights will not be affected by folder privileges. You will typically grant the assistant at least read permission for your mailbox and Inbox folder, however, in order to allow him or her to reply to your incoming messages.

Send-As Delegate Access

The assistant's name won't appear in messages sent on your behalf if you grant the assistant the **Send As** permission through the **Permissions** property page within the Exchange Administrator program. On your mailbox **Permissions** property page, you can add the desired Windows NT account to the list of **Windows NT Accounts With Permissions** and then grant the **Send As** right explicitly. In this case, a message sent on your behalf will look exactly as if you had sent the item yourself, and recipients have no way to know that a coworker was the actual originator. (See Figure 7-12.)

It might be necessary to enable the **Permissions** property page first, because it is not displayed by default. It can be enabled through the **Show Permissions Page For All Objects** check box that can be found on the **Permissions** property page of the **Options** dialog box. This dialog box can be launched through the **Options** command on the Administrator program's **Tools** menu. The **Display Rights For Roles On Permissions Page** check box must also be selected, otherwise the **Send As** right is not available on the **Permissions** page.

Note The **Send As** right does not allow the delegate to open your folders or messages. You must grant the assistant read permission for your mailbox and Inbox if you want to allow him or her to read your incoming messages.

Using Delegate Access

The Exchange Server transport permits a user to work with more than one mailbox in a single session. A delegate can add your mailbox to his or her profile using the **Advanced** property page of the transport service. The additional mailbox will then appear in the folder list of the client's folder pane.

The assistant needs at least the read permission for the mailbox and subfolder to open any additional mailbox and its subfolders, such as the **Inbox**. Once the read permission has been granted, he or she can use the **Advanced** property page of the Exchange Server transport to include your mailbox into his or her messaging profile (as outlined in Exercise 19). However, permissions at the mailbox level are not required if your assistant opens your message folders using the **Open Special Folder** command on Outlook's **File** menu. The Exchange Client does not provide this feature.

Sending Messages on Behalf of Another User

A delegate who wants to send a message on your behalf must select the **From Box** command on the standard send form's **View** menu in the Exchange Client. This command is named **From Field** if you have installed Outlook, which is the same as the Exchange Client's **From Box**. Selecting this command enables a **From** button on the send form. Clicking this button launches a dialog box, which allows the delegate to specify your display name as the name of the actual originator. Before sending the message, the client will verify that the sender has the appropriate permissions. If the assistant does not have the necessary privileges, a corresponding message box will be displayed and the client returns to the composed message. In this case, the message cannot be sent.

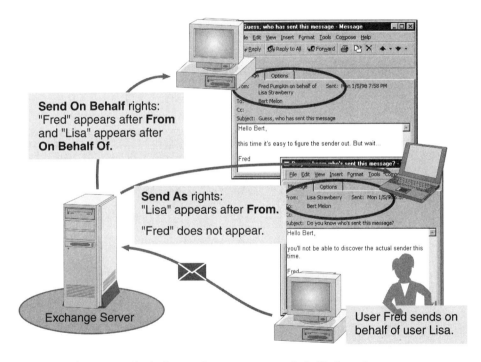

Figure 7-12. Two methods for sending messages on behalf of another user.

The delegate access permissions and their results are:

- **Send On Behalf Of**; delegate's name appears on the **From** line and the user's name appears on the **On Behalf Of** line of messages

- **Send As**; delegate's name is hidden from recipients; the name of the mailbox owner appears on the **From** line instead

Exercise 19: Configuring and Using Send-On-Behalf-Of Delegate Access

A delegate is a person who can send messages on your behalf and can be given the permission to read messages from your **Inbox** and other folders. Two different levels of delegate permissions exist: the **Send On Behalf Of** and **Send As** permissions, which determine whether the delegate's name appears in messages that have been sent on behalf of another user.

Estimated time to complete these exercises: 15 minutes

Description

In this exercise, you will use Outlook to change your Inbox permissions. You will assign a user the privilege to read messages in your Inbox and to use the **Options** dialog box to assign delegate permissions to send messages on behalf of another user.

- Task 19a describes the steps for granting another user **Reviewer** access for your mailbox. This allows your delegate to view the hierarchy of your private folders. Unless you grant additional permissions, your delegate will not be able to view the contents of any subfolder.

- Task 19b describes the steps for granting your delegate permission to send items on your behalf, and also for granting permission to view the contents of your Inbox.

- Task 19c describes the steps for sending a message on behalf of another user and demonstrates the effect on the Outlook message header.

Prerequisites

- Log on as the user BillP first and later as Admin-NY1 to NEWYORK-1.

- A messaging profile for each user account is required.

Task 19a: Modifying Permissions on a Mailbox

1. Log on as BillP to NEWYORK-1, and double-click the **Microsoft Outlook** shortcut on the Desktop.

2. Within Outlook, verify that the **Folder List** is selected on the **View** menu.

3. Right-click **Mailbox - Bill Plum**, and then click **Properties For "Mailbox - Bill Plum."**

4. The **Mailbox - Bill Plum Properties** dialog box appears. Click the **Permissions** tab.

5. Notice that the default permissions prevent anyone else from gaining access to the mailbox. Click **Add**.

6. The **Add Users** dialog box appears. Click the appropriate user to be your delegate, and then select **Administrator New York-1**.

7. Click **Add**, and then click **OK**.

8. The **Mailbox - Bill Plum Properties** dialog box appears. In the **Name** box, click **Administrator New York-1**, and then in the **Roles** list, select **Reviewer**. Notice the permissions that are associated with the status of a **Reviewer**.

9. Click **OK**.

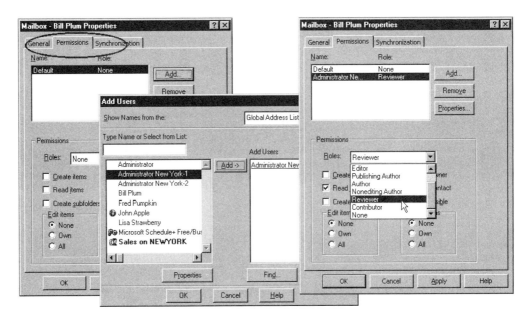

Task 19b: Granting Send-On-Behalf-Of Permissions and Modifying Permissions in the Inbox

1. On the **Tools** menu, click **Options**.

2. The **Options** dialog box appears. Click the **Delegates** tab.

3. Notice that the **Delegates** box is empty. Click **Add**.

4. The **Add Users** dialog box appears. Click your delegate user, and then select **Administrator NewYork-1**.

5. Click **Add**, and then click **OK**.

6. The **Delegate Permissions: Administrator NewYork-1** dialog box appears. In the **Inbox** list box, click **Reviewer (Can Read Items)**, and then click **OK**.

7. The **Options** dialog box appears. Notice that the delegate is now listed.

8. Click **OK**.

9. Select **Exit And Log Off** from the file menu.

10. Log off from Windows NT.

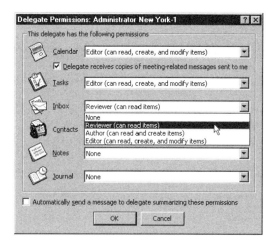

Task 19c: Opening a Mailbox with Granted Delegate Access

1. Log on as Admin-NY1 to NEWYORK-1.

2. Open the **Control Panel** and double-click the **Mail** icon.

3. The **Admin-NY1 Properties** dialog box appears. Click the **Show Profiles** button.

4. Click **Copy**.

5. Enter *Delegate Profile* under **New Profile Name**, and then click **OK**.

6. Under **When Starting Microsoft Exchange, Use This Profile** select **Delegate Profile**.

7. Verify that **Delegate Profile** is selected, and then click **Properties**.

8. Verify that **Microsoft Exchange Server** is selected, and then click **Properties**.

9. Enter **Admin-NY1** under **Mailbox** and then click **Check Name** to resolve the mailbox name to **Administrator New York-1**.

10. Click **OK** twice and then click **Close** to close the **Mail** dialog box.

11. Close the **Control Panel**, and then double-click the **Microsoft Outlook** shortcut.

12. On the **Tools** menu, click **Services**.

13. The **Services** dialog box appears. Click **Microsoft Exchange Server**, and then click **Properties**.

14. The **Microsoft Exchange Server** dialog box appears. Click the **Advanced** tab.

15. Click **Add**.

16. In the **Add Mailbox** box, type the name of the appropriate user (*Bill Plum*).

17. Click **OK**.

18. The **Microsoft Exchange Server** dialog box appears. Notice that the new mailbox has been added to the mailboxes list under the **Open These Additional Mailboxes** header in the **Mailboxes** field.

19. Click **OK**.

20. The **Services** dialog box appears. Click **OK**.

21. Notice that the mailbox to which you have been granted delegate access appears. Attempt to open the mailbox. Verify that you can open **Calendar**, **Inbox**, and **Tasks**. Notice that the folders to which you have not been granted access do not appear.

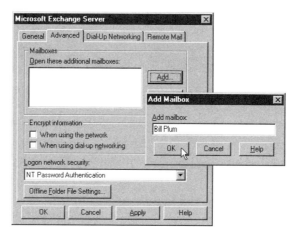

Task 19d: Sending a Message on Behalf of a Mailbox Owner

1. On the **Compose** menu, click **New Mail Message**.

2. The **Untitled - Message** dialog box appears.

3. If no **From** button is displayed, open the **View** menu, and then click **From Field**.

4. A **From** button is added to the message header. Click **From**.

5. The **Choose Sender** dialog box appears. Select **Bill Plum**.

6. Click **OK**. The **From** line displays the selected user.

7. Click **To**.

8. In the **Select Names** dialog box select **Administrator NewYork-1**, and then click **To**.

9. Click **OK**.

10. Type a subject and a short message, and then on the toolbar click **Send**.

11. When the new message arrives, open the new message.

12. Notice that the **From** field indicates that the message is from you on behalf of the user for whom you are a delegate.

13. Close the message.

14. On the **File** menu, click **Exit And Log Off**.

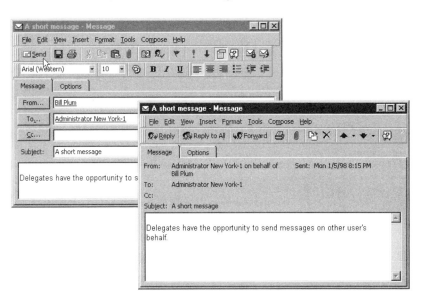

Review

You can designate assistants or delegates using the Exchange Client or Outlook. An assistant can be granted the right to read your messages by assigning the read permission on your mailbox and the desired folders. The default permissions, however, prevent anyone but the mailbox owner from accessing a mailbox.

You can also designate the delegate to send messages on your behalf. To do this, select the **Options** command under the **Tools** menu to display the **Options** dialog box. Switch to the **Exchange Server** property page (Exchange Client) or the **Delegates** property page (Outlook), where you can specify the desired account as a delegate.

Review

1. What are messaging profiles?

   _____

   _____

   _____

   _____

   _____

2. Where are messaging profiles stored?

   _____

   _____

   _____

3. Which tool assists you with creating messaging profiles?

   _____

   _____

4. How do you launch the Setup Wizard?

   _____

   _____

   _____

   _____

5. How do you create a profile automatically without the assistance of the Setup Wizard?

   _____

   _____

   _____

   _____

6. What are the MAPI services that come with Outlook?

   _____

   _____

   _____

   _____

7. What is the purpose of a Personal Folder Store?

_____

_____

_____

_____

_____

8. How do you change the path to a .PST file?

_____

_____

_____

_____

_____

9. You have configured a Personal Folder Store and the Exchange Server transport. How do you define the Personal Folder Store as the location for incoming messages?

_____

_____

_____

_____

_____

10. What elements must be configured in order to enable local replication?

_____

_____

11. Which folders are automatically configured to be available off line and on line when using the native Exchange Client?

_____

_____

12. Which folders are automatically configured to be available off line and on line when using Outlook?

_____

_____

13. What is the disadvantage of the Offline Folder Store?

_____

_____

_____

14. What is the most significant advantage of the Offline Folder Store?

_____

_____

_____

15. Which Exchange executable command line option must you use to specify the location and name of the messaging profile for MS-DOS–based clients?

_____

16. Where can you specify the location of messaging profiles for Windows 3.x–based clients?

_____

_____

_____

_____

17. How do you assign centralized messaging profiles to roving users who work on Windows 95 and Windows NT computers?

_____

_____

_____

_____

_____

18. Which e-mail repository must be configured to use the Remote Mail features of the Exchange Client or Outlook?

_____

19. Which e-mail repository must not be configured if you want to use the Synchronize features of the Exchange Client or Outlook?

_____

20. Where can you configure scheduled remote connections?

_____

21. What are the advantages of the Remote Mail features?

_____

_____

_____

22. Which component must be installed to support Remote Mail connections for Windows 3.1–based clients?

_____

23. Several users in your company work on Macintosh computers running the Macintosh–based Microsoft clients. How can you support remote connections for these users?

_____

_____

_____

_____

24. What are two extensions of Outlook?

_____

25. You want to display a message box providing the option to read new messages immediately when they arrive in your Inbox. How do you configure Outlook so you can do this?

_____

_____

26. During the setup of Outlook you have selected Schedule+ as your primary calendar application. Now you want to switch entirely to Outlook calendar. How do you configure Outlook to act as your primary calendar application?

_____

_____

_____

27. As an administrator, you want to designate an assistant for your Inbox. Where can you grant the desired permission?

28. Where can you optimize the RPC connection order for Windows 95–based and Windows NT–based clients?

29. What is the default order to connect to a server using Windows 95–based and Windows NT–based clients?

30. How do you adjust the binding order prior to the installation of the Windows 95–based and Windows NT–based Exchange Client?

31. You want to migrate MS Mail 3.x users from a postoffice into Exchange Server. All .MMF files reside in the postoffice. Which tool can you use to import the existing e-mail messages?

32. You want to migrate MS Mail 3.x users from a postoffice into Exchange Server. All .MMF files reside outside the postoffice. Which tool can you use to import the existing e-mail messages?

33. You have configured several .PAB files that contain different personal contact information. Now you want to create a .PAB file that contains the information in all of them. How can you accomplish this task?

34. Which permissions must be granted to allow an assistant to answer your incoming correspondence?

_____

_____

35. A delegate is sending messages on your behalf, but you don't want the delegate's name to appear on the **From** line of the message header. What kind of permission must be granted to the assistant in order to achieve this?

_____

_____

CHAPTER 8

Managing Server Configuration

This chapter deals with the standard Microsoft Windows NT utilities that play important roles in the administration of Exchange, as well as the Microsoft Exchange Administrator program. These are the tools that the administrator typically uses to control the Exchange Server configuration.

Overview

The utilities that manage an Exchange Server installation can be divided into two groups: standard Windows NT utilities and Exchange Server tools. Windows NT utilities are the User Manager for Domains, Server Manager, Control Panel, and other applications, such as the Performance Monitor, Task Manager, Event Viewer, Registry Editor, and the Backup program. The

Exchange Administrator program and the Performance Optimizer represent the most important Exchange Server tools. Lesson 1 of this chapter explains briefly when each of these utilities should be used.

Lesson 2 focuses on the Exchange Administrator program, which is the most important management tool. This program is designed to cover most, if not all, important configuration tasks at the site level and at the server level. Its user interface, customization options, and the procedure to assign users permissions within the hierarchy of an Exchange organization are described.

Once you are familiar with the Exchange Administrator program, you can start managing an Exchange Server organization. The most important configuration objects at the site level and the server level and their property pages are covered in Lesson 3 and Lesson 4.

To complete this chapter, five practical exercises are provided to guide you through some basic configuration steps using the Exchange Administrator program.

In the following lessons, you will be introduced to:

- The Windows NT Server tools used to manage Exchange Server computers

- The function, user interface, and configuration options of the Exchange Administrator program

- The management of site configurations

- The configuration of server level objects, which enable you to manage servers independently of site level defaults

Lesson 1: Server Management Tools

Exchange Server components are integrated tightly into the operating system. Therefore, Windows NT utilities can be used to accomplish management tasks. This lesson will help you understand when to use which specific Windows NT tool to maintain an Exchange Server installation.

Exchange Server tools, such as the Administrator program and the Performance Optimizer, are also explained briefly in this lesson. The Administrator program generally is used to control the configuration of an Exchange Server, while the Performance Optimizer is more specialized in server optimization tasks. It can be said that the Exchange Administrator program is the universal utility that allows you to configure all the important Exchange Server components.

At the end of this lesson, you will be able to:

- Identify the Windows NT utilities useful for the administration of Exchange Server computers

- List the management tasks that can be accomplished using the Administrator program

- Describe the scenarios that require the use of the Performance Optimizer

Estimated time to complete this lesson: 25 minutes

Windows NT Server Maintenance Tools

All active Exchange Server components run as services on a Windows NT Server computer. Therefore, you can use existing Windows NT tools to manage Exchange Server computers. (See Figure 8-1 on page 420.)

Control Panel

The **Services** applet of the Control Panel is the Windows NT utility that is probably accessed most often in connection with Exchange Server administration. In fact, this utility is so important that many administrators create a shortcut to the **Services** applet on their desktop in order to launch it more conveniently. It can be used to stop and restart local Windows NT services and it allows you to verify whether the Site Services Account information has been specified correctly. In general, the **Services** applet is the best choice whenever you want to manage the Exchange Server services on a local Windows NT Server computer.

Let's say you want to stop an entire Exchange Server to perform an offline backup. To do this, simply open the Control Panel and double-click the **Services** icon. This displays the **Services** dialog box, where you can select **Microsoft Exchange System Attendant** from the list of installed services, and then click the **Stop** button. Notice that not only is the SA stopped, but the **Microsoft Exchange Message Transfer Agent**, **Microsoft Exchange Directory**, **Microsoft Exchange Information Store**, and all other Exchange Server services are stopped also. These services all depend on the SA, so the entire Exchange Server is shut down.

Server Manager

The Server Manager is a powerful Windows NT tool that allows you to manage essentially all Windows NT Server computers within a system of trusted domains. So you can view information about resource usage on the local and remote servers, determine the role of a domain controller (PDC or BDC), or start and stop services.

The fact that you can control local and remote Windows NT Services brings the Server Manager into the position to replace the **Services** applet of the Control Panel. Start this program, select the desired server, and then click **Services** on the **Computer** menu. This displays a dialog box that lists all installed services and can be used in exactly the same way as the **Services** applet.

On local and remote servers, the Server Manager can be used to:

- Check the Services configuration on a selected server
- Configure Server properties, such as accessed shared directories and resources in use
- Determine the roles of domain controllers for managing domains
- Remotely start and stop services
- Send messages to connected users

Event Viewer

In general, all Exchange Server services write their status information into the Application Event Log. This log file is a permanent repository that allows you to examine the health of a server using the Windows NT Event Viewer at any time. Since the Event Viewer can also connect to remote Windows NT Server computers, you can check the status of multiple servers from a single Windows NT workstation.

Exchange Server services typically place numerous entries into the Application Event Log file, so you should increase its size. To do this, open the Event Viewer's **Log** menu, and then click the **Log Settings** command. A dialog box appears, providing the required controls to set the new log file size. You can also specify that the old log entries be deleted automatically.

Note Bear in mind that the number of entries in the Application Log can become overwhelming if you set the Diagnostics Logging level for one or more Exchange Server components to **Maximum**, because the most detailed status information will then be retrieved.

User Manager for Domains

The User Manager for Domains is typically used to create and manage user accounts in a Windows NT Server domain. The Exchange Administrator program is the primary tool used to create new mailboxes and associate them with existing Windows NT accounts. It seems that the separation of these tasks means that you must work with two administrative programs whenever you want to create a new account plus an associated mailbox.

Creating new Windows NT accounts and their associated mailboxes using only the User Manager sounds reasonable enough and would certainly simplify their administration. Fortunately, this option is available, but the User Manager must first be extended. For this purpose, Exchange Server supplies a DLL called Mailumx.dll, which is installed during the setup of the Exchange Administrator program. The DLL adds the **Exchange** menu to the User Manager and allows the creation of mailboxes by displaying the same user interface that is used within the Exchange Administrator program.

Performance Monitor

The Windows NT Performance Monitor is a valuable tool that can be used to analyze the workload of the local and of remote Exchange Server computers. It gathers the information based on performance counters. Using this tool, you can create diagrams and reports to analyze the usage of computer resources, which can help determine potential hardware bottlenecks.

To add and remove Performance Monitor objects and counters, the Exchange Server Setup uses two Windows NT utilities: Lodctr.exe and Unlodctr.exe. The Lodctr.exe installs performance counters, while the Unlodctr.exe removes them again at the command prompt. Usually you don't need to execute these utilities manually. If you detect at any time that a performance counter is missing, you can start the Exchange Server Setup instead, which is launched in maintenance mode because it detects the existing Exchange Server installation and which offers the **Reinstall** option. By choosing **Reinstall**, you can replace corrupted files and missing Registry entries, including the missing performance counter.

The Performance Monitor can also be used if you just want to check the current state of a server. For example you can monitor the number of messages awaiting delivery in message queues by double-clicking the **Microsoft Exchange Server Queues** icon in the **Microsoft Exchange** program group. **Queues** and other preconfigured Performance Monitor Workspace (.PMW) files are installed during the Exchange Server setup. These workspaces are good examples of the Performance Monitor's usefulness and can be adjusted to meet your specific needs.

The preconfigured .PMW files are:

- **Health**; displays the amount of processor time and pagefile-related operations the Exchange Server services are consuming

- **Load**; shows the throughput of the server, including the rate of messages submitted and delivered, processed RPC packets, and performed directory replication activities

- **History**; displays the number of currently logged-on users, MTA work queue length, and memory paging

- **Users**; displays a histogram of the number of users currently logged on, and provides a quick thermometer-like view of how many clients are being served

- **Queues**; exhibits the send-and-receive queues of the Public and Private Information Stores as well as the work queue of the MTA

- **IMS Queues**, **IMS Statistics** and **IMS Traffic**; display activities and the workload of the IMS

Registry Editor

The Registry Editor can be used to inspect and modify the configuration parameters of all Exchange Server services because their settings are maintained entirely within the Windows NT Registry. But take care when modifying parameters directly, since modifications are usually written to the Registry immediately without activating an explicit Save command. In addition, no security mechanism exists to prevent you from entering invalid parameters and values. Either by accident or on purpose, an Exchange Server installation can be seriously damaged due to invalid configuration settings.

On the other hand, some configuration parameters cannot be specified using any other administration tool. For example, you must use the Registry Editor to activate the Text Event Logging feature of the MTA. This is necessary if you want to create text log files in addition to the Application Event Log. To enable the Text Event Logging feature, set the Text Event Log value to 1. This value can be found under:

```
HKEY_LOCAL_MACHINE
    \SYSTEM
        \CurrentControlSet
            \Services
                \MSExchangeMTA
                    \Parameters
```

The text event log files, which are then found in the Exchsrvr\Mtadata directory, can be useful for analyzing problems of Exchange Server services. Text event log files are called Evx.log (where x is a number), with Ev0.log containing the most recent entries. You could use them, for instance, to document a critical service state in case you need to contact Microsoft Product Support Services.

Task Manager

The Task Manager allows you to monitor, control, start, and terminate programs and processes that are running on a Windows NT computer. In Windows NT 4.0 you can launch this tool by right-clicking the clock on the Windows toolbar and selecting **Task Manager** from the context menu that appears. When you look at the program window of the **Task Manager**, you'll notice the **Processes** tab and the **Performance** tab. The **Processes** property page provides information about the resources being consumed by each currently running process, while the **Performance** property page provides a dynamic overview about CPU and memory usage.

Sometimes you might get the impression that an Exchange Server service stops responding and hangs for no apparent reason. Let's say the shutdown of the MTA service takes a long time, but a shutdown that takes longer than a few hours does not necessarily mean that the server hangs or is malfunctioning. So it is not advisable to simply "kill" the process by switching off the computer or terminating the MTA process in the **Task Manager**. Rather, you should examine the MTA service and check whether it occupies the CPU at 100 percent capacity. If it does not, the service is most likely operating properly and should not be terminated. On the other hand, if the MTA is using the CPU at close to 100 percent capacity, you can assume that there's a problem with the MTA. Only in this case is it advisable to terminate the process directly using the **Task Manager**.

More detailed information about the usage of the Task Manager in conjunction with Exchange Server 5.5 is provided in Chapter 15, "Maintaining Servers."

Windows NT Backup

The Windows NT Backup program provides the basic utilities for backing up a Windows NT Server computer. This program will be replaced with an enhanced version during the Exchange Server setup, since the standard version is not able to back up the DS and IS databases while the services are running. Without replacing the Windows NT Backup, only an *offline backup* can be performed, which means that the Exchange Server-specific sub-directories are backed up along with the Registry. A disadvantage of an offline backup is that all Exchange Server services must be stopped before-hand. In other words, Exchange Server resources are unavailable during the time of the backup operation. The replaced version, in turn, allows you to create *online backups* while all services are running. When creating an online backup, you have the option to save the DS and the IS databases separately. Unfortunately, it is impossible to perform backup and restore operations at the mailbox level. The Windows NT Backup and the various online backup types are covered in more detail in Chapter 15, "Maintaining Servers."

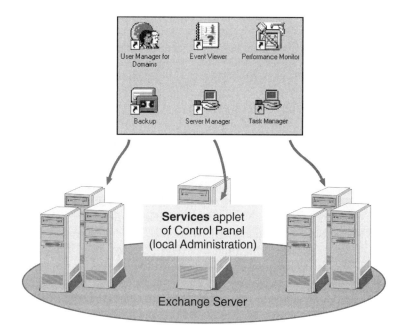

Figure 8-1. Windows NT tools for administering an Exchange Server.

The most important administrative Windows NT tools are:

- Services applet of the Control Panel; to start and stop local Exchange Server services

- Server Manager; to control services on the local and remote computers

- Event Viewer; to view events logged by Exchange Server services

- User Manager for Domains plus Mailumx.dll; to create and delete mailboxes at the time of the Windows NT account creation or deletion

- Performance Monitor; to collect statistics about the Exchange Server and to view resource consumption

- Registry Editor; to specify configuration settings, such as the Text Event Log value, which cannot be specified interactively

- Task Manager; to control Windows NT processes and to provide dynamic system information

Exchange Server Tools

The two main Exchange Server tools are the Administrator program and the Performance Optimizer, as shown in Figure 8-2. Both tools are installed during the Exchange Server setup and can then be launched using the corresponding icons in the **Microsoft Exchange** program group.

Exchange Administrator Program

The Administrator program is simply the most important utility for managing an Exchange organization interactively. You can use this application to accomplish all kinds of management tasks regarding the site and server configuration. As outlined in Chapter 3, this program communicates with all core components through RPCs. Configuration changes are written either to the directory database or to the Windows NT Registry. If you change mailbox properties, for instance, you modify entries in the directory database. If you set the Diagnostics Logging level for certain categories of a particular messaging connector, you write changes to the server's Windows NT Registry. For this reason you must be an administrator of both the domain and the site to use all the available features of the Administrator program.

The Administrator program can be installed on any Windows NT computer, including Windows NT Workstation. In fact, when the Setup program detects that it is launched on Windows NT Workstation 4.0, it will provide only the option to install the Administrator program. This program is not available, however, on Windows 95.

Theoretically, every Exchange Server computer that can be reached through RPCs can be configured using a single Administrator program instance. This configuration allows you to set up a dedicated computer for administration. Multiple Administrator program installations on different machines are necessary to manage all existing servers if the RPC communication mechanism is not supported because of the existing network topology.

Performance Optimizer

As its name implies, the Performance Optimizer assists you in the optimization of server installations. It determines the best configuration of core components based on the available hardware to enable Exchange Server services to use the existing resources most efficiently. The Performance Optimizer is also the right tool for determining the optimal location of the DS and IS databases and their transaction log files.

Whenever the hardware or software configuration of an Exchange Server computer changes, it's a good idea to launch the Performance Optimizer. Because the optimizer analyzes the existing hardware platform and reconfigures the services accordingly, you will gain the best possible performance. If you do not run the Performance Optimizer after the hardware or software configuration has changed considerably, the server will operate less efficiently than is possible. It's also advisable to start the Performance Optimizer when the number of users, public folders, or messaging connectors has been changed significantly. (See Figure 8-2.)

The Administrator program enables you to:

- Configure messaging connectors and directory replication
- Configure the organization, including all sites and services
- Migrate existing user accounts from Windows NT or Novell NetWare account lists based on import files
- Monitor server services and connections
- Perform all administrative tasks on a single workstation
- Set user permissions

The Performance Optimizer enables you to:

- Determine the best location of the DS and IS databases and their transaction log files
- Optimize the Exchange Server components to use the existing hardware in the most efficient way
- Optimize the server components regarding the number of users, the number of public folders, and specific server tasks

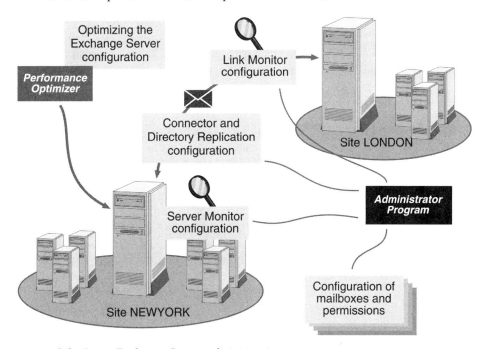

Figure 8-2. Basic Exchange Server administration.

Lesson 2: Fundamentals of the Administrator Program

The Exchange Administrator program is a Windows NT application that displays the entire Exchange Server organization in a tree-like structure known as the Directory Information Tree (DIT). The DIT, its site and server level configuration objects, and the user interface of the Administrator program itself must be understood in order to manage the organization efficiently. Moreover, an understanding of the different security levels is necessary if you want to designate additional administrators.

in order to provide a comprehensive overview of the Administrator program, this lesson first introduces the most relevant aspects of its user interface, followed by an introduction to customization options. The organizational structure of the DIT is discussed. At the end of the lesson, the most powerful mode of the Administrator program, the Raw mode, is examined.

At the end of this lesson, you will be able to:

- Investigate the Administration Window of the Exchange Administrator program
- Customize the Administrator program
- Maneuver through the hierarchy of an organization
- Start the program in Raw mode
- Describe the inheritance of permissions within the DIT

Estimated time to complete this lesson: 35 minutes

Viewing the Administration Window

An *Administration window* is a child window of the Administrator program. In its two panes, it displays the directory information of the selected server using the DIT, which represents the hierarchy of an organization. You will maneuver through the DIT to carry out your configuration tasks.

Administration Window

The Administration window uses two panes to display the entire configuration of the organization. The left pane is known as the *container pane,* since it displays only container objects. The right pane is called the *contents pane,* since it displays the contents of a selected container. The contents of a container object usually consists of leaf objects (objects that don't contain any other objects themselves) and sublevel containers. (See Figure 8-3.)

The Administrator program is capable of displaying multiple Administration windows at the same time when you select additional servers through either the Server button (which can be added to the toolbar as described in "Customizing the Administrator Program" later in this lesson), the Server list box on the toolbar, or the **Connect To Server** command on the **File** menu. Typically you connect to more than one server to compare their configuration settings. To distinguish between different windows, the server and site names are displayed in the title bar.

Types of Objects

Configuration items are divided into two groups: container objects and leaf objects. While container objects might contain leaf objects and sub-level containers, leaf objects do not contain other items. Container objects provide access to other items and form the hierarchy of the organization within the container pane of the Administration window. In addition, container objects can be configured by means of property pages. Leaf objects, in turn, provide only configuration properties but no embedded objects. Since you access both types of objects in a similar manner to perform management tasks, they are displayed together in the contents pane.

You can distinguish a container object from a leaf object by determining which pane it appears in. Container objects appear in both the container pane and the contents pane. Leaf objects appear only in the contents pane. Also, you can figure out whether the selected object is a container by double-clicking it in the contents pane. If it is a container object, its contents will open in the contents pane. If it is a leaf object, its property pages will be displayed instead. If you want to display the property pages of a container item, use the **Properties** command on the **File** menu, the **Properties** button on the toolbar, or simply use the ALT+ENTER key combination.

When you look at the DIT of your organization, you'll find that the **Configuration** object of a site contains, for example, the **Connections** and **Site Addressing** items. The **Configuration** object appears in the left pane and is a container object. The **Connections** element is a sub-level container since it maintains leaf objects for configured messaging connectors. Because the **Connections** element is a container, it appears in both the left pane and the right pane of the Administration window. Unlike **Configuration** and **Connections**, the **Site Addressing** item is not displayed in the left pane. It is a leaf object that appears only in the right pane and does not contain any other elements. (See Figure 8-3.)

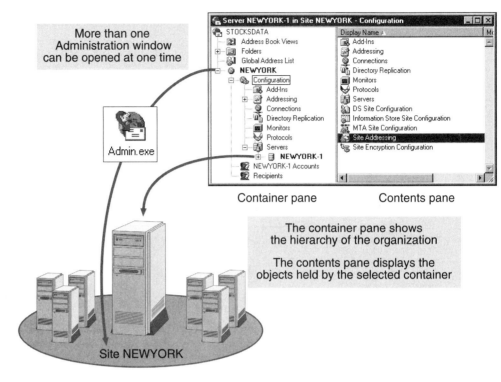

Figure 8-3. The Administration window.

The main components of the Administration window and their functions are:

- Container pane; the left pane that displays the container objects
- Contents pane; the right pane that displays all the objects contained within the currently selected container object
- Container objects; can contain other objects for grouping purposes
- Leaf objects; don't contain other objects but represent the actual messaging entity, such as a mailbox or a connector

Customizing the Administrator Program

As an Exchange Server administrator, you will work with the Administrator program on a regular basis, since it covers most management tasks. Sooner or later, the Administrator program will become a personal tool for you and you'll want to customize it in accordance with your preferences. Fortunately, it is possible to modify its views, columns, and toolbar on a per-user basis, which means that your adjustments will not change the settings of any other administrator who may be working on the same workstation. Settings and parameters for views and configured columns are stored in the Windows NT Registry under:

```
HKEY_CURRENT_USER
    \Software
        \Microsoft
            \Exchange
                \MSExchangeAdmin
                    \Desktop
```

Customizing the Toolbar

The toolbar is a feature of the Exchange Administrator program that was introduced with Exchange Server version 5.0. The toolbar provides convenient access to container objects and to commands that are used frequently. Rather than navigating through various container objects in the DIT, you can simply switch to the **Configuration**, **Recipients**, **Connections**, or **Servers** container by clicking the corresponding button. Also, the toolbar can be used to provide shortcuts to commands such as **Connect To Server** or **Directory Import**.

To modify the toolbar, open the **Tools** menu and click the **Customize Toolbar** command, or double-click anywhere in the toolbar outside an actual button. Then add and remove whichever buttons you want. Since the settings are stored on a per-user basis, they won't interfere with the settings of other administrators.

Custom Options

Custom options determine how configuration items, such as mailbox and custom recipient objects, are displayed within the Administrator program. Some of these settings are maintained on a per-administrator basis, while other settings are universal in scope. Per-administrator settings determine how items are sorted and filtered within the Administration window's contents pane. The settings affect the way objects are displayed but not the objects themselves. Universal options, on the other hand, are related to the creation of recipient objects and have direct influence on some properties of newly created objects.

View Menu

The Administrator program's **View** menu provides all the necessary options to sort and filter items. The **View** menu allows you to arrange mailboxes either according to their display name or by the date when they were last modified. On the **View** menu, point to **Sort By** and click the **Display Name** or **Last Modified Date** command as appropriate. Furthermore, the **View** menu offers other various filter commands, such as **Mailbox**, **Custom Recipients**, **Distribution Lists**, **Public Folders**, and **Hidden Recipients**. These commands allow you to restrict the display to specific object types. For example, you would activate the **Hidden Recipients** option to display recipients that are hidden from the address book.

Tools/Options

To specify universal client options, open the **Tools** menu and click the **Options** command. This displays the **Options** dialog box, which provides three property pages: **Auto Naming**, **Permissions**, and **File Format**. On the **Auto Naming** property page you can adjust the automatic naming scheme that affects the mailbox name creation, while on the **Permissions** property page you can specify settings regarding Windows NT security. Available settings are shown in Figure 8-4.

For instance, the Auto Naming scheme describes how the alias name of new recipient objects is constructed automatically. The default setting determines **First Name And Last Initial (JohnS)**, which means that as soon as you create a new mailbox and enter a given name in the **First** box, this name becomes part of the mailbox name. When you enter the surname in the **Last** box, the Administrator program automatically takes the first letter of the surname to complete the mailbox name creation. For example, you created a mailbox for Fred Pumpkin in Chapter 5. As you typed *Fred* in the **First** box and *Pumpkin* in the **Last** box, the suggested mailbox name became *FredP*.

Once you have finished entering the required mailbox information, a primary Windows NT account should be specified or created. The default Windows NT domain, which is used to display existing account information or to create a new Windows NT account, can be specified on the **Permissions** property page. The most important option, however, is the **Show Permissions Page For All Objects** check box, which allows you to display the **Permissions** tab for all configuration objects, as shown in Figure 8-4.

Address Book Views

An Address Book View allows you to arrange mailboxes, custom recipients, public folders, and distribution lists in additional containers, although the actual member objects of an Address Book View might reside in different places within the organization. In other words, Address Book Views are virtual container objects that group recipients together based on attributes they have in common. This grouping makes it possible to create a detailed view of the structures of your company through the address book window of the Exchange Client and Outlook.

Some views, however, have the sole purpose of simplifying Exchange Server management. For example, you can group all the recipients together that reside on the same home server to make them easily accessible using the Administrator program. Select the **Address Book View** command under **New Other** on the **File** menu, enter a desired **Directory Name** and **Display Name**, switch to the **Group By** property page, and then select the **Home Server** entry in the **Group Items By** list box. Click the **OK** button twice, once to close the **Properties** dialog box and once to confirm that a process has been started to create the Address Book View. Administrative views must not appear in client address books. To hide such a view, simply clear the **Show This View In The Client Address Book** check box on the view's **Advanced** property page. The view's property pages can be displayed again when you select the view object and press ALT+ENTER. Alternatively, you can use the **Properties** command on the **File** menu. Address book views have a universal character and will be available to all Exchange Server administrators.

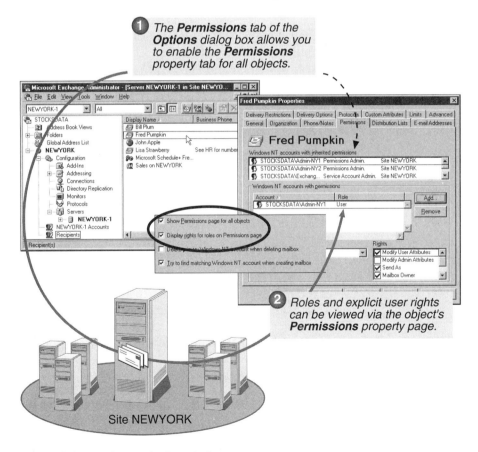

Figure 8-4. Displaying the Permissions property page.

The customization options in the Administrator program and their functions are as follows:

- Address Book Views; to group recipients together based on common directory attributes

- Auto Naming; to specify how display names and alias names are automatically generated when a new mailbox is created

- Columns; to specify which columns to display and in what order

- Permissions Settings; to specify settings for viewing permission information

- Toolbar; to provide shortcuts to frequently used commands or container objects

- Views; to select which type of recipient objects to view (mailboxes, distribution lists, custom recipients, public folders, and hidden recipients)

- Windows NT Domain default settings; to specify which Windows NT domain will be selected when working with Windows NT account information (for example, to add a user account to the list of users with permissions on a directory object)

Hierarchy of an Organization

When you want to create and manage a complex Exchange Server organization, you cannot accomplish the entire task in just one step. Your best course of action is to split complex configuration projects into smaller, more manageable tasks based on configuration objects, which are arranged to form the hierarchy of an organization.

Top Level

The <Organization> object is located at the top level. It builds the common context for all resources that belong to a particular Exchange Server messaging network. Exchange Server computers that have been installed in the same organization can potentially exchange all kinds of data, including interpersonal messages and directory information.

Site Level

More containers—one for each site—are found at the site level, located under the <Organization> object. These <Site> objects contain two sublevel objects: the **Recipients** and the **Configuration** containers. The **Recipients** container provides quick access to all recipient objects of a site, while the **Configuration** container holds the site level configuration items of the IS, DS, MTA,

SA, and other components. Changes applied to the objects under the **Configuration** container will affect all servers in a site because these servers replicate their directory changes automatically to each other. (See Figure 8-5.)

Server Level

When you examine the contents of the **Configuration** container, you'll find, among other things, the **Servers** sublevel container. <Server> objects are kept therein, each representing one server within the selected site. Together they form the server level configuration context, which has a higher priority than the site level. This means that configuration parameters specified at this level will override the site-level default settings. By using the server-level configuration objects for the Private or Public Information Store, the DS, or the MTA, you can configure dedicated servers. Examples of dedicated servers within a site are messaging bridgeheads or public servers. The configuration of a dedicated public server is covered in Chapter 12, "Creating and Managing Public Folders."

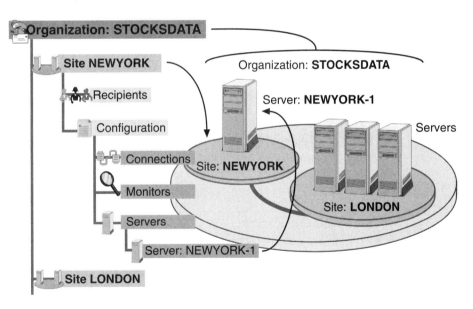

Figure 8-5. The DIT within the Administrator program.

Important hierarchical objects within the DIT are as follows:

- <Organization> object; the root of the hierarchy, represents the common context for all configuration information related to the organization

- <Site> object; holds the **Configuration** and **Recipients** container

- **Recipients** container; provides quick access to mailboxes, custom recipients, distribution lists, and public folders maintained within the site

- **Configuration** container; contains all site-level configuration objects; any configuration changes made at this level affect all servers in a site

- <Server> objects within the **Servers** container; provide configuration objects for server-level configuration; changes affect a particular server only

Permission Contexts and Permission Flow

Theoretically, every user has the ability to start the Administrator program, but a successful connection to an Exchange Server depends on the effective permissions of the user. The server validates each user and grants access to its resources only to users who have the required permissions in the selected site. All other users trying to connect will receive an error notification, which will be displayed instead of the organization's hierarchy. To designate additional administrators, you must grant them the appropriate permissions on certain configuration objects.

Note If you have completed Exercise 3, "Adding an Exchange Server to a Site," you have already assigned administrative permissions to an account named Admin-NY2 within the site NEWYORK.

Contexts and Permissions Inheritance

A permissions context defines the boundaries of a particular security level. In other words, when user permissions are assigned to objects in a specific context, these permissions will not be passed on to objects in another context.

Note Three independent levels exist that are associated with the <Organization> object, <Site> object, and **Configuration** container object within the DIT.

Permissions inheritance is the mechanism that affects permissions configurations automatically. Permissions assigned on parent containers will be inherited by sub-level containers. However, permissions cannot be inherited between different security levels, so the administrator must be aware of the different security contexts.

To allow a particular user to connect to a Exchange Server using the Administrator program, at a minimum the **View Only Admin** role must be assigned to the user account on the site level. Adding another administrator, however, requires more rights. You must grant the corresponding Windows NT account the **Permissions Admin** role directly to the <Organization>, <Site>, and

Configuration container object because the permissions associated with this role will not be inherited between them. On the other hand, permissions granted within one security context, such as the <Site> container or the **Configuration** container object, will be inherited within their context.

Permissions can be granted to Windows NT user groups, which makes it easier to "hire and fire" Exchange Server administrators. Once you have assigned a Windows NT group administrative permissions within the organization, you can add the Windows NT accounts of designated Exchange Server administrators to this group. As soon as users are members of such a group, they can use the Administrator program to perform management tasks. To revoke administrative permissions, it is sufficient just to remove the desired account from this group using the User Manager for Domains.

The characteristics of the different permissions contexts are as follows:

- Organization; permissions are not inherited by any sub-level containers

- Site; permissions apply to the system public folders, Address Book Views, and to the site's recipients containers

- **Configuration**; permissions are inherited to all objects within this container

Predefined Roles

Predefined roles are sets of user rights that simplify the task of permissions assignment. To illustrate, instead of assigning separately a new administrator the rights **Add Child**, **Modify User Attributes**, **Modify Admin Attributes**, **Delete**, **Logon Rights**, and **Modify Permissions,** you would simply assign the role **Permissions Admin** to the desired account at the three security levels, and the job is done.

Different roles can be assigned to Windows NT accounts on different security levels. It's possible, for instance, to designate, an administrator who can create and manage mailboxes without being able to change configuration settings within the site. Such an administrator needs to possess the **Permissions Admin** role at the organization and site levels, while the **View Only Admin** role would have to be specified at the configuration level.

The predefined roles and their functions are as follows:

- **Admin**; necessary and sufficient for all administrative tasks except permissions modification

- **Permissions Admin**; similar to **Admin** role plus permissions modification

- **Search**; search for directory objects and their attributes

- **Send As**; send messages as a mailbox or instead of another user

- **Service Account Admin**; connect to and exchange data as a service; all available rights are granted

- **User**; log on to a mailbox, send and receive messages, and modify user attributes

- **View Only Admin**; read-only connections within the site, no changes are allowed

Rights for Roles Option

Before you can display the particular rights of a predefined role, the options **Show Permissions Page For All Objects** and **Display Rights For Roles On Permissions Page** must be activated. (See Figure 8-4.) These options are located on the **Permissions** property page of the **Options** dialog of the Administrator program, which you can display by opening the **Tools** menu and clicking the **Options** command. You can then display the desired information using the **Permissions** property page of the selected hierarchy object. If these options are activated, whenever you select a predefined role from the **Roles** box, its associated set of rights will be displayed under **Rights** as shown in Figure 8-4. The set of rights associated with the user of a mailbox, for instance, are shown in Figure 8-6.

From time to time—under rare circumstances—it might be desirable to create custom roles, including sets of user rights that are not covered by a predefined role. In this case, you would probably first assign the desired user account a predefined role and later modify the set of rights. A particular right allows the user to perform a specific task. The following table lists the available rights that you can include in new roles:

Right	Description
Add Child	To create objects below the selected object (i.e., create mailboxes in a recipient's container)
Modify User Attributes	To modify user-level attributes (i.e., modify members of a distribution list)
Modify Admin Attributes	To modify administrator-level attributes (i.e., modify the job title and display name fields in a mailbox)
Delete	To delete objects
Logon	To access the directory (you need this right to use the Administrator program)
Modify Permissions	To modify permissions on existing objects (i.e., modify access permissions on mailboxes)

Right	Description
Replication	To replicate directory information with other servers (required by the service account for intrasite replication)
Mailbox Owner	To read and delete messages in a mailbox
Search	To search for directory objects and attributes
Send As	To send messages with the sender's return address

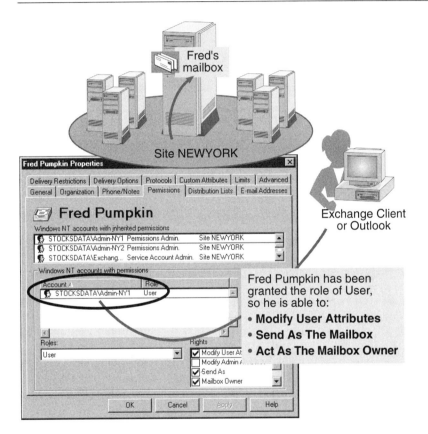

Figure 8-6. The role required to send and receive messages.

The following table lists the associations between rights and default roles:

	Admin	Permissions Admin	Service Account Admin	View Only Admin	User	Send As	Search
Add Child	X	X	X				
Modify User Attribute	X	X	X		X		
Modify Admin Attributes	X	X	X				
Delete	X	X	X				
Logon Rights	X	X	X	X			
Modify Permissions		X	X				
Replication			X				
Mailbox Owner			X		X		
Send As			X		X	X	
Search							X

Exchange Administrator's Raw Mode

The Raw mode is the most powerful operation mode of the Exchange Administrator program because it allows you to view the Exchange Server directory in its plain (raw) form. You can examine the Raw properties of every existing container object or leaf object, and you can set and modify all possible directory attributes that a directory object can have. But be careful if you modify attributes in Raw mode —it's possible to set an Exchange Server configuration in an inoperable mode by entering invalid configuration information. The Administrative windows in Raw mode are shown in Figure 8-7 on page 438.

Command Line Options

To start the Administrator program in Raw mode, supply the command line switch **/R** to the **Admin** command. You can do this using the Windows NT command prompt. Change to the Exchsrvr\Bin directory, type *Admin /R,* and then press the ENTER key. If desired you can also change the **Microsoft Exchange Administrator** shortcut on the **Microsoft Exchange** program group to include the **/R** option, or you can specify a particular value in the Windows NT Registry to always launch Admin.exe in Raw mode.

Registry Value

To run the Exchange Administrator program in Raw mode without supplying the **/R** option, the Registry value RawMode=[0,1] can be specified under:

```
HKEY_CURRENT_USER
    \Software
        \Microsoft
            \Exchange
                \MSExchangeAdmin
                    \Desktop
```

A value of 1 means that the Administrator program will always run in Raw mode.

Mode-Dependent Administrator Program Changes

Additional options become available when the Administrator program has been started in Raw mode, such as the **Raw Directory** command on the **View** menu. When you click this command, a new object named **Schema** appears under the site container. You can select this object in the container pane and, as a result, all the various attributes within the Exchange directory will be displayed in the content pane of the Administrator program window. (See Figure 8-7.)

When you inspect the Raw mode further, you will discover the **Raw Properties** command on the **File** menu. This command is used to display the directory attributes of a particular object, such as a mailbox. When you display the Raw properties of an object, you also have the option to modify them. Such low-level administration, however, is seldom necessary. To avoid directory inconsistencies, it is advisable that you use the regular administration interface wherever possible instead of the Raw mode properties.

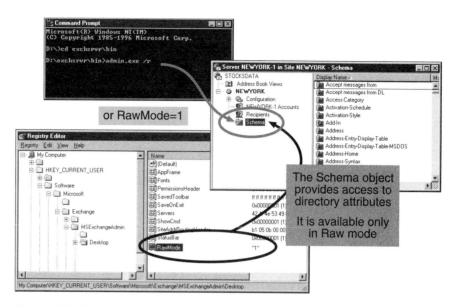

Figure 8-7. The Raw mode of the Exchange Administrator program.

The following Administrator program command line parameters are available:

Command switch	Description
/e	Export Mode; runs the command line export utility
/h or **/?**	Help Mode; displays user help on startup
/i	Import Mode; runs the command line import utility
/m [site/]<Monitor name>/<Server name>	Starts the specified Monitor on startup
/r	Raw Mode; provides access to all attributes of Exchange Objects
/s <Server name>	Connects to the specified server on startup
/t [r|n|nr]	Suspends server monitoring temporarily (r = suspends repairs during maintenance, but sends notifications; n = suspends notifications, but performs repairs; nr = suspends repairs and notifications; no additional option = resets the monitor to normal mode)

Lesson 3: Managing Site Configuration

This lesson introduces the various important configuration objects that can be found within the **Configuration** container. Following a brief introduction, the site level configuration of the DS is explained and illustrated by means of a practical exercise. Also, you'll read about the configuration options provided by the Site Addressing object. An exercise will guide you through the steps of adjusting the SMTP site addressing scheme. This lesson also illustrates how to define custom attributes for recipient objects and how to include them into the search dialog of the client's Address Book. Several practical exercises are included to help you put the theoretical information into practice. Last but not least, you can also find information about the various site level configuration parameters of the MTA.

At the end of this lesson, you will be able to:

- List the site configuration objects and their purpose
- Modify Address and Details Templates
- Configure site-level properties for the Directory
- Configure site-level properties for the Site Addressing
- Configure site-level properties for the MTA

Estimated time to complete this lesson: 60 minutes

Site Configuration Objects

Site configuration objects can be found in the **Configuration** container of each site. Examples are the **MTA Site Configuration** and the **DS Site Configuration** items. Modifications applied to these items will affect all servers in the site. It is not important which member server you actually connect to for site management, because the multimaster model of the DS determines that all servers within the local site have equal rights and replicate their directory modifications with each other. It can be said that the **Configuration** container represents the directory of a site. (See Figure 8-8.)

Site Configuration Properties

Site configuration properties represent default parameters, which are used to manage multiple Exchange Server computers in the most efficient manner. All core components—the DS, IS, MTA, and the SA—can be configured at the site level. Objects representing messaging connectors and other components that are related to the site's configuration are also provided at the site level.

For instance, you can change the password of the Site Services Account through the **Configuration** container's **Service Account Password** property page. Because the password is changed on the site level, directory replication ensures that the new configuration takes effect on all servers. Consequently, it's guaranteed that the service account information is always consistent. As explained in Chapter 1, the service account information must be the same for all Exchange Server computers in a site.

Overview of Site Configuration Objects

Depending on the installed components, various configuration objects can appear in the **Configuration** container. They are **Add-Ins**, **Addressing**, **Connections**, **Directory Replication**, **Monitors**, **Protocols**, **Servers**, **DS Site Configuration**, **Information Store Site Configuration**, **MTA Site Configuration**, **Certification Authority**, **Site Addressing**, and **Site Encryption Configuration**.

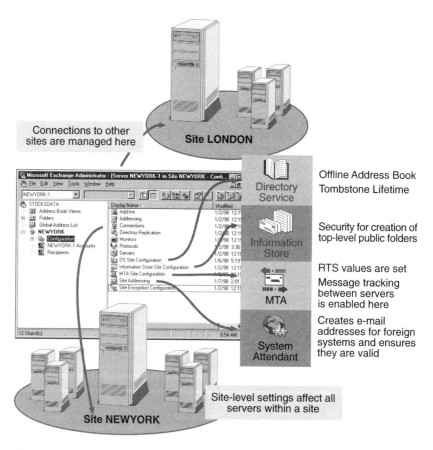

Figure 8-8. Core components and site administration.

Objects that can be used for site-level administration and their purpose are as follows:

- Add-Ins; used for Exchange Server add-in products (for example, Connector for Lotus Notes)
- Addressing; holds containers for templates and proxy generators within a site
- Connections; contains configuration objects regarding connections to other sites and foreign mail systems
- Directory Replication; provides objects for directory replication connectors
- Monitors; holds configured Link Monitors and Server Monitors
- Protocols; provides objects to specify site defaults regarding HTTP, IMAP4, LDAP, NNTP, and POP3
- Servers; holds objects for all the servers within the site
- DS Site Configuration; provides properties for site-level directory configuration
- Information Store Site Configuration; holds information primarily for configuration of public folders, such as Top-Level Folder Creation and Site Affinities
- MTA Site Configuration; provides properties to specify Reliable Transfer Service (RTS) values, such as association parameters, transfer time-outs, connection retry times, and checkpoint sizes
- Site Addressing; provides sitewide addressing configuration defaults
- Site Encryption Configuration; provides configuration parameters related to Advanced Security
- Certification Authority; appears when a KM server has been installed

DS Site Configuration Properties

The **DS Site Configuration** object can be used to manage default settings for the DS. The most important settings affect the maintenance of the directory database, while other settings affect the generation of the Offline Address Book. (See Figure 8-9 on page 444.) Furthermore, you can specify which recipient attributes to include in intersite directory replication. You can also selectively configure which attributes to return to address book queries of validated and anonymous users.

Tombstones

Tombstones are used to mark deleted directory objects. In other words, whenever you delete a directory item, such as a mailbox, you create a tombstone for this object. The object itself still exists, but because of the tombstone, it is now hidden from the Directory. The tombstone is also a directory object, so it is replicated automatically to all other servers within the site. The deleted mailbox object will disappear from all servers as soon as the related tombstone reaches them.

Garbage Collection Interval

The *Garbage Collection Interval* determines the interval at which the directory database defragmentation will occur. As users work with an Exchange Server and administrators carry out configuration tasks such as mailbox creation and deletion, the directory database becomes fragmented. Database fragmentation decreases the performance of the DS. To put it plainly, a directory database that is heavily fragmented can cause DS problems. For this reason, it is recommended that you defragment the directory database on a regular basis.

During garbage collection, the SA checks the directory database for deleted objects. It removes them and their associated tombstones according to the tombstone lifetime. The actual size of the database, however, is not decreased by the deletion of tombstones or other expired objects because the space occupied by deleted items is marked only as available. If you want to compress the database physically, you must perform an offline defragmentation. Offline defragmentation is explained in Chapter 15.

The **Tombstone Lifetime** can be specified at the **DS Site Configuration** object. You should keep in mind that a tombstone must not be removed from the directory before it is replicated to all servers. The lifespan of tombstones should be long enough to guarantee that all servers receive them before they are deleted through garbage collection. Usually the default value of 30 days is sufficient.

Anonymous Directory Access

The **General** tab provides the **Anonymous Account** button, which can be selected to specify an account which should be used for anonymous access to the directory. This account allows the DS to access directory information on behalf of anonymous users. You can select an existing Windows NT account or create a new account.

Note This anonymous account is an internal account used by the DS only. It is not identical to an account you might set on Exchange Server resources, such as for anonymous access to public folders.

Offline Address Book

As outlined in Chapter 7, the Offline Address Book can be downloaded from the server using an Exchange Client or Outlook. This address book is required if you want to compose new messages during offline operation. (See Figure 8-9.)

The Offline Address Book must be generated on the server before clients can download it. This is accomplished by the DS of the first server, which has been installed in a site. The Offline Address Book location can be changed, however, using the **Offline Address Book** property page of the **DS Site Configuration** object. Moving the Offline Address Book to a new location is necessary especially if you want to remove the first server from the site. Moreover, you can specify which recipient container objects to include in the generation process. It is also possible to configure multiple Address Books for offline usage if your address book server is running Exchange Server version 5.5, in which case you'll use the **Add** button on the **Offline Address Book** tab. In this scenario, users will be prompted to select the desired Offline Address Book during address book synchronization using an Exchange Client or Outlook.

Note By default, the Offline Address Book is generated between two and three o'clock every morning. However, if you modify recipients frequently, you might want to generate Offline Address Books more often. In this case, you can use the **Offline Address Book Schedule** property page to specify how often and when you want Offline Address Books to be regenerated.

Directory Attributes

Directory attributes are, so to speak, properties of directory items such as recipient objects. A validated user who uses a MAPI client's Address Book to examine the address details of a recipient is theoretically able to retrieve all available attributes, although his or her client typically requests informative attributes only. On the other hand, it is not desirable to provide all directory information to anonymous users who might access the Directory through LDAP clients.

You can use the **Attributes** property page of the **DS Site Configuration** object to specify which attributes to return during LDAP address book searches based on the access type (validated or anonymous). You can also specify which directory attributes to include into the directory replication between sites. By default, almost all attributes are included, but the set of information can be limited if required.

Custom Attributes Labels

As outlined in Chapter 5, Exchange Server recipient objects provide a variety of predefined properties and attributes that can be specified to provide helpful information to users of an organization through their address books. But sometimes those predefined aren't sufficient. In the event that you need additional attributes, you can define them using the **Custom Attributes** tab of the **DS Site Configuration** object. You can define up to 10 custom attributes that will be applied to all recipient objects within the site. Exercise 20, "Modifying the DS Site Configuration," will guide you through the steps of defining a custom attribute.

Note Custom attribute labels will not be replicated throughout your organization. The contents of the custom attribute fields, however, are replicated. It is therefore necessary to coordinate the naming of custom attributes at the organization level; otherwise, data may be displayed in wrong fields across your organization.

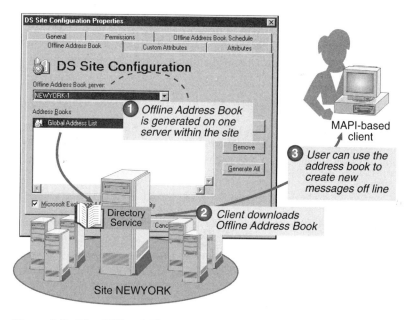

Figure 8-9. The Offline Address Book.

The **DS Site Configuration** property pages and their purpose are as follows:

- **Attributes**; to specify which attributes are available to which requestors, or whether an attribute should be replicated between sites

- **Custom Attributes**; to create particular characteristics associated with a recipient object

- **Offline Address Book Configuration**; to designate the Offline Address Book server, as well as which recipient containers to include in the Offline Address Book

- **Offline Address Book Schedule**; to specify when to regenerate the Offline Address Book

Exercise 20: Modifying the DS Site Configuration

The **DS Site Configuration** object provides access to settings concerning the garbage collection interval, tombstone lifetime, anonymous directory account, and the Offline Address Book generation. In addition, you can define custom attributes to provide additional recipient information to the users of an organization, and you can determine which attributes to include in LDAP address book searches and in intersite directory replication.

Estimated time to complete this exercise: 15 minutes

Description

In this exercise, you will configure the tombstone lifetime and the garbage collection interval. However, you won't be able to measure any immediate differences when altering these parameters, as the steps are outlined for demonstration purposes only. You will also define a custom attribute called *Year Employed*. This attribute is used in a later exercise to create a custom dialog box. Lastly, you will configure the generation of the Offline Address Book.

- Task 20a describes the steps for modifying the number of days a tombstone exists before expiring. You will also set the intervals at which expired tombstones are deleted from the system and the directory is defragmented for maximum efficiency.

- Task 20b describes the steps for defining a custom attribute that is associated with an Exchange recipient object.

- Task 20c describes the steps specifying the recipient container that will be used to generate the Offline Address Book.

Prerequisites

Complete this exercise logged on as Admin-NY1 on NEWYORK-1.

Task 20a: Changing the Tombstone Lifetime and the Garbage Collection Interval

1. Click the **Start** button, point to **Programs**, point to **Microsoft Exchange**, and then click **Microsoft Exchange Administrator**.

2. Expand the site container **NEWYORK**, and then select the **Configuration** container.

3. In the right pane, click the **DS Site Configuration** object, and then on the **File** menu, click **Properties**.

4. The **DS Site Configuration Properties** dialog box appears. In the **Tombstone Lifetime** (Days) box, type *5*.

5. In the **Garbage Collection Interval (Hours)** box, type *18* and then click **Apply**.

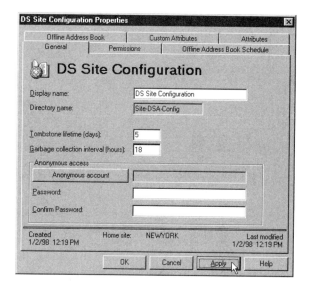

Task 20b: Changing a Custom Attribute

1. Click the **Custom Attributes** tab.

2. In the **Custom Attribute 1** box, type *Year Employed*.

3. Click **Apply**.

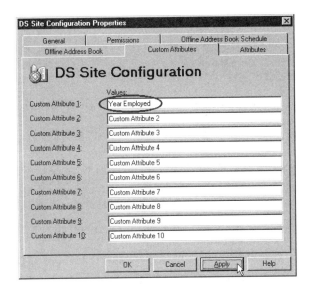

Task 20c: Generating the Offline Address Book

1. Click the **Offline Address Book** tab.

2. Verify that **Recipients** is selected under **Address Books**, click **Remove**, and then click **Add**.

3. The **Offline Address Book Container** dialog box appears. Highlight **Global Address List**, and then click **OK**.

4. In the **DS Site Configuration Properties** dialog box click **Generate All.**

5. A **Microsoft Exchange Administrator** dialog box appears, indicating that all changes to this site object will be saved before the Offline Address Book is generated. Click **OK**.

6. A **Microsoft Exchange Administrator** message box appears, indicating that the generation of the Offline Address Book has been completed successfully. Click **OK**.

7. The **DS Site Configuration Properties** dialog box reappears.

8. Click **OK**.

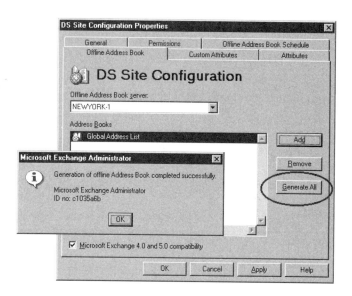

Review

The garbage collection interval and the tombstone lifetime can be adjusted using the **DS Site Configuration** object within the site's **Configuration** container.

You can also define custom attributes, which allow you to specify additional information for recipient objects. By way of illustration, the *Year Employed* attribute has been defined to display additional recipient information about the employment year of the users.

The Offline Address Book can contain all the addresses of the organization. You can also restrict its content by specifying recipient containers explicitly. To force generation of the Offline Address Books, click the **Generate All** button. Offline Address Books also can be generated and updated automatically depending on the **Offline Address Book Schedule** settings.

Site Addressing Properties

Exchange Server is the chameleon of messaging systems. When connected to a foreign X.400 system, it behaves as a native X.400 system. Internet SMTP hosts see an Exchange Server as just another SMTP system. If you've coupled the organization with a Lotus cc:Mail post office, the Exchange Server acts like a huge cc:Mail post office. And guess what Exchange Server 5.5 simulates when you connect to a Lotus Notes network using the Connector for Lotus Notes?

Foreign E-Mail Addresses

Because Exchange Server can connect to foreign messaging systems of various kinds, users must possess e-mail addresses of the corresponding formats. Thus, every user has an X.400, SMTP, Lotus cc:Mail, and MS Mail address by default, in addition to his or her original Exchange address. Users might have other address formats if additional messaging connectors have been installed, such as the Connector for Lotus Notes. Depending on the Site Addressing format, proxy e-mail addresses will be generated automatically during mailbox creation. If you need to correct this format, you can do so through the **Site Addressing** property page of the **Site Addressing** object located in the **Configuration** container. As shown in Figure 8-10, the four default address types are CCMAIL, MS, SMTP, and X400.

The default format of the proxy e-mail addresses depends on the address type itself, although usually the site and organization names are used as elements in conjunction with the user's mailbox name.

The following formats are chosen by default for the four standard proxy addresses:

- SMTP site address follows the format *@Site.Organization.com*
- X.400 addresses are formed using *c=US;a=;p=organization;o=site; s=last name;g=first name* (note that there is a space for 'a=')
- Lotus cc:Mail site address is defined as *at Site*
- MS Mail address is determined by the network and postoffice name of the Connector postoffice, which results in *Organization/Site*

In order to change the format of the X.400 address, the SMTP address, or the Lotus cc:Mail address, double-click the **Site Addressing** object within the **Configurations** container. The **Site Addressing Properties** dialog box is displayed, where you can click the **Site Addressing** tab. On the **Site Addressing** property page the **Edit** button is provided, which allows you to modify, for example, the SMTP site address. The MS Mail address, however, cannot be changed in the **Site Addressing** object; a convenient method to change this address type is covered in Chapter 18, "Connecting to Microsoft Mail and Schedule+ 1.0."

Routing Table Maintenance

The **Routing** property page displays the various existing messaging paths, which the MTA can use to perform routing decisions. Whenever you add a new address space to a messaging connector, the routing information must be updated. This is also true for modifications and the removal of existing address spaces. The routing table update is accomplished during the routing recalculation cycle. This happens daily at three o'clock in the morning (Greenwich Mean Time) by default, but you can change the calculation time by using the **Routing Recalculation Schedule** property page.

If you don't want to wait for the next automatic routing recalculation cycle to happen, click the **Recalculate Routing** button on the **Routing** property page. A short delay might occur until the routing information is updated, but once the table of associations between address spaces and messaging connectors is updated according to your preferences, the MTA can route messages accordingly. Message routing based on address spaces is covered in Chapter 9, "Introduction to Intersite Connectors."

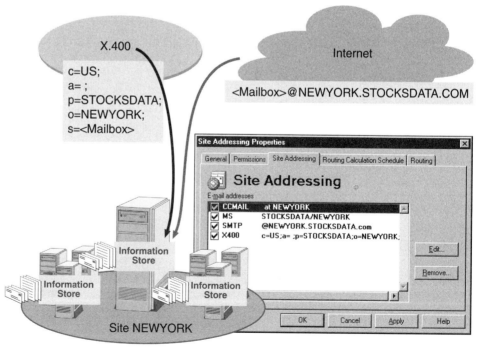

Figure 8-10. Site Addressing defaults.

The **Site Addressing** property pages and their purpose are as follows:

- **General**; to designate a server responsible for routing table calculation

- **Permissions**; to designate NT user accounts for administration

- **Routing Calculation Schedule**; to specify when the routing table is recalculated automatically

- **Routing**; to view the current routing table for the site and to start routing recalculation manually, if necessary

- **Site Addressing**; to enter site-specific addressing information used by various proxy generators

Exercise 21: Changing the Site SMTP Addresses

Besides changing the site addressing scheme for proxy e-mail addresses, which is the actual topic of this exercise, the **Site Addressing** object can also determine the current routing table entries and modify the routing recalculation schedule, as mentioned earlier.

Estimated time to complete this exercise: 10 minutes

Description

In this exercise, you will modify the default SMTP address space for the local site. Using the **Site Addressing** object within the **Configuration** container, you will delete the site name portion from the SMTP site address. Once the changes have been applied, you can regenerate the proxy SMTP address for all existing mailboxes and other recipient objects. You will verify the changes by inspecting the properties of a mailbox. For example, Fred Pumpkin's e-mail address will change from *FredP@NEWYORK.STOCKSDATA.com* to *FredP@STOCKSDATA.com*.

- Task 21 describes the steps for modifying the SMTP address for the site and for all existing recipients.

Prerequisites

- Complete this exercise logged on as Admin-NY1 to NEWYORK-1.

- Ensure that some mailbox objects exist on the Exchange Server.

Task 21: Changing the Site SMTP Addresses

1. Start the **Microsoft Exchange Administrator** program and connect to the server **NEWYORK-1**.

2. Expand the site object **NEWYORK**, and then click the **Configuration** container.

3. In the right pane, click the **Site Addressing** object, and then, on the **File** menu, click **Properties**.

4. In the **Site Addressing Properties** dialog box click the **Site Addressing** tab.

5. Site addressing information appears, displaying e-mail addresses. Click the **SMTP** address, and then click **Edit**.

6. The **SMTP Properties** dialog box appears. In the **Address** box, delete **NEWYORK** from the e-mail address.

7. Click **OK**.

8. The **Site Addressing Properties** window appears, displaying e-mail addresses, including the modified SMTP address. Click **OK**.

9. A **Microsoft Exchange Administrator** dialog box appears, indicating that the site addresses of type(s) [SMTP] have been modified and asking if you want to update recipient e-mail addresses now. Click **Yes**.

10. A **Microsoft Exchange Administrator** message box appears, indicating that a process has been started to update the recipient e-mail addresses. Click **OK**.

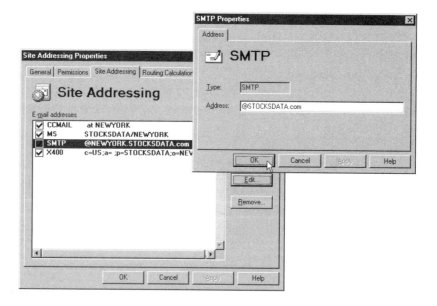

Review

Typically, every mailbox on an Exchange Server has four types of proxy e-mail addresses: SMTP, X400, MSMAIL and CCMAIL. The Site Addressing scheme determines how the common part of these addresses will appear for each mailbox that is created. You can change this addressing scheme using the **Site Addressing** object. To keep all addresses consistent you also have the option to regenerate the existing proxy e-mail addresses for all mailboxes of the site to reflect configuration changes. It is also possible to skip the regeneration. In that case, existing mailboxes will keep their old address formats, while new mailboxes will reflect the new site addressing.

Addressing Container Object

The **Addressing** container object contains various sub-level containers. These containers, in turn, keep **Details Templates**, **One-Off Address Templates** and **E-Mail Address Generators**. You use these objects chiefly to control dialog boxes, which are used to display recipient information within the messaging clients.

Purpose of Templates

Address and details templates are sets of instructions that determine how to display dialog boxes within the Address Book of the Exchange Client and Outlook. The templates themselves are stored on the server, but they are actually used by the messaging clients.

Templates are language dependent. When displaying the details of an address or when searching for a particular recipient, some clients, depending on their language, might not be able to display the required address dialog boxes. Installing the corresponding address details templates on the server can solve these problems. In other words, if different client languages, such as English, French, and German, are being used to connect to an Exchange Server, the English, French, and German templates must be imported into the **Addressing** container of the site. The import file (.CSV) of the Details and One-Off Address templates can be found on the Exchange Client and Outlook installation CD-ROMs.

Details Templates

The details templates are used to display detailed recipient information within the Exchange Client or Outlook. Also, they describe the search dialog box, which allows users to search the server-based address books for a particular address. You can modify these templates to create custom dialog boxes.

One-Off Address Templates

The One-Off Address templates determine the client dialog boxes that prompt the user to enter e-mail address information for user-defined recipients. A one-off address describes a recipient address that does not exist in the server's Global Address List or in any of the user's personal address books. The default template formats usually are sufficient, since one-off information depends on e-mail addresses rather than on any detailed recipient information. If necessary, the default templates can also be modified.

E-Mail Address Generators

E-mail address generators determine how proxy e-mail addresses will be generated (as shown in Figure 8-11). When you install a messaging connector, such as the IMS, the MS Mail Connector, or the Connector for Lotus cc:Mail, all recipients of the entire organization should receive an SMTP, MS Mail, or Lotus cc:Mail address. Obviously the formats of these addresses differ from one another, but because of the corresponding e-mail address generators, the Exchange Administrator program can create the correct proxy addresses in accordance with the address type. By default, Exchange Server 5.5 provides the following proxy generators:

- SMTP proxy generator (INPROXY.DLL); generates Internet proxy e-mail addresses [**SMTP**]

- MS Mail proxy generator (PCPROXY.DLL); generates MS Mail e-mail addresses [**MS**]

- X.400 proxy generator (X400PROX.DLL); generates X.400 e-mail addresses [**X400**]

- Lotus cc:Mail proxy generator (CCMPROXY.DLL); generates Lotus cc:Mail e-mail addresses [**CCMAIL**]

Every additional messaging connector or gateway supplies its own appropriate e-mail address generator. By installing such gateways you implicitly extend the Exchange Administrator program for new e-mail address generators. The Administrator program will then be able to initiate processes to create corresponding proxy e-mail addresses for the recipients of your organization. The actual creation of proxy e-mail addresses, however, is the task of the e-mail address generator.

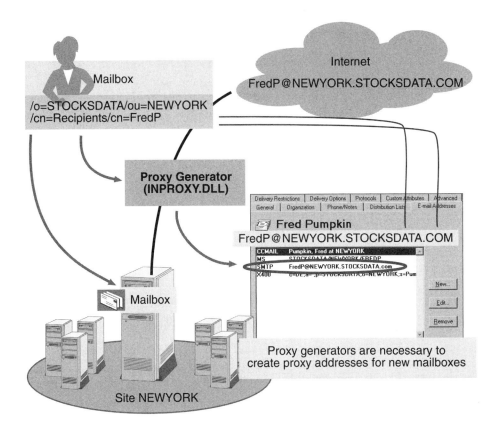

Figure 8-11. Proxy address generation.

The **Addressing** object holds the following containers:

- The **Details Templates** container; holds language-dependent detail templates for various informational and optional dialog boxes, which are displayed on the clients, such as **Custom Recipient**, **Distribution List**, **Mailbox**, **Public Folders**, and **Search Dialog**

- The **E-Mail Address Generators** container; contains generators for automatic creation of proxy e-mail addresses

- The **One-Off Address Templates** container; provides One-Off Address templates in various languages for client dialog boxes that prompt the user for one-off address e-mail information

Exercise 22:
Setting a Custom Attribute for Several Recipients

Custom attributes allow you to specify user information that is not covered by predefined recipient object attributes. They can contain any type of information. To examine their contents, display the address details information within the Exchange Client or Outlook.

Estimated time to complete this exercise: 10 minutes

Description

In this exercise, you will set the *Year Employed* attribute for several recipients. This attribute was created in Exercise 20. The *Year Employed* attribute gives you an attribute that you can use to extend the Search Dialog template in Exercise 23, "Modifying a Details Template."

- Task 22a, Task 22b, and Task 22c describe the steps for assigning a value to the *Year Employed* custom attribute.

Prerequisites

- Details templates should be installed according to the client languages.

- Complete this exercise logged on as Admin-NY1 on NEWYORK-1.

- Exercise 8 and Exercise 20 must already have been completed.

Task 22a: Setting the Year Employed Attribute for a New User

1. Start the **Microsoft Exchange Administrator** program and make sure you are connected to **NEWYORK-1**.

2. Expand the site **NEWYORK**, and then click the **NEWYORK-1 Accounts** container. The **NEWYORK-1 Accounts** container was created in Exercise 8 in Chapter 5.

3. On the **File** menu, click **New Mailbox** to open the **Properties** dialog box of the new mailbox.

4. In the **First** box, type *Bert*.

5. In the **Last** box, type *Melon*.

6. Click **Primary Windows NT Account** to display the **Primary Windows NT Account** dialog box.

7. Click **Create A New Windows NT account**, and then click **OK**.

8. In the **Create Windows NT Account** dialog box, click **OK**.

9. A message box appears, indicating the Windows NT account just created was given a blank password. The user will be required to change the password upon first logon. Click **OK**.

10. Click **OK** again.

11. In the right pane, click **Bert Melon** and then, on the **File** menu, click **Properties**.

12. The **Bert Melon Properties** dialog box appears.

13. Click the **Custom Attributes** tab.

14. In the **Year Employed** box, type *1990* and then click **OK**.

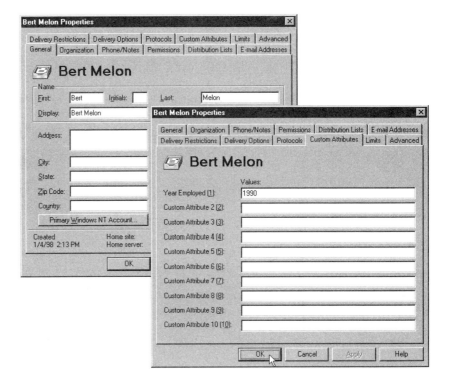

Task 22b: Setting the Year Employed Attribute for a New Second User

1. On the **File** menu, click **New Mailbox**.

2. The **Properties** dialog box appears.

3. In the **First** box, type *Linda*.

4. In the **Last** box, type *Carrot.*

5. Click **Primary Windows NT Account** to display the **Primary Windows NT Account** dialog box.

6. Click **Create A New Windows NT Account**, and then click **OK**.

7. In the **Create Windows NT Account** dialog box, click **OK**.

8. A message box appears, indicating the Windows NT account just created was given a blank password. The user will be required to change the password upon first logon. Click **OK**.

9. Click **OK** again.

10. In the right pane, click **Linda Carrot**, and then on the **File** menu, click **Properties**.

11. In the **Linda Carrot Properties** dialog box that appears click the **Custom Attributes** tab.

12. In the **Year Employed** box, type *1990* and then click **OK**.

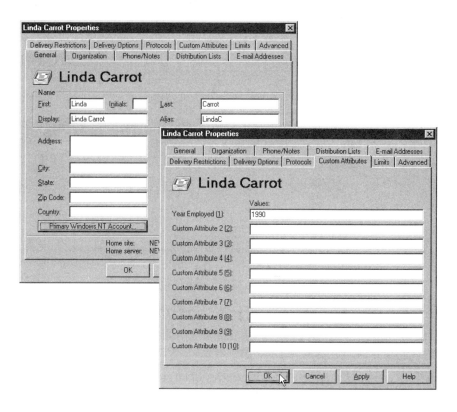

Task 22c: Setting the Year Employed Attribute for a New Third User

1. On the **File** menu, click **New Mailbox**.

2. The **Properties** dialog box appears.

3. In the **First** box, type *William*.

4. In the **Last** box, type *Pear*.

5. Click **Primary Windows NT Account** to display the **Primary Windows NT Account** dialog box.

6. Click **Create A New Windows NT Account**, and then click **OK**.

7. In the **Create Windows NT Account** dialog box, click **OK**.

8. A message box appears, indicating the Windows NT account just created was given a blank password. The user will be required to change the password upon first logon. Click **OK**.

9. In the **William Pear Properties** dialog box click the **Custom Attributes** tab.

10. In the **Year Employed** box, type *1992* and then click **OK**.

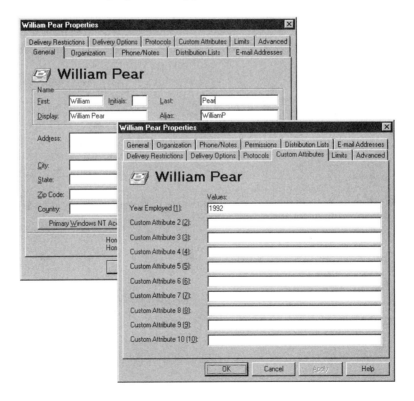

Review

Custom attributes, such as the *Year Employed* value, can be assigned to mailboxes to provide additional recipient information. Each recipient object provides the **Custom Attributes** property page for this purpose. Once you have defined a custom attribute at the site level, its name appears in the position of the former placeholder **Custom Attribute(x)**.

Template Modification

Address and Details templates allow you to customize the look of dialog boxes for MS-DOS–based and Windows-based clients through their sets of properties. When you customize a template, you modify these properties that, again, define the components and their position on the address dialog boxes. (See Figure 8-12.)

Templates Property Page

To add controls or to reposition existing ones, select the desired template within the **Addressing** container to display its properties. Then switch to the **Templates** property page, where you'll find the **New**, **Edit**, **Test**, and **Original** buttons, among others. Click the **New** button to insert new items and click the **Edit** button to redefine existing controls. The **Test** button allows you to preview the dialog box. The **Original** button on the **Templates** property page can be used to undo all template modification and to restore them to their original state.

Language Dependencies

In order to keep the appearance of a client interface consistent and because templates are language dependent, you need to modify each of them separately in case users in a site have multiple client languages in use. For example, if users in your site use the English and the French client versions, you will need to modify the English and the French templates to provide a common customized user interface. Otherwise, if you edit only the English version, changes will appear in the English client only.

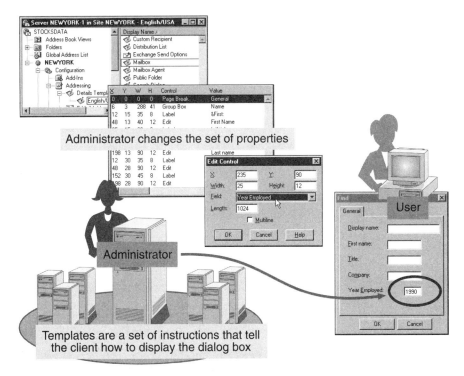

Figure 8-12. Address and details template modification.

The characteristics of templates are as follows:

- Templates are sets of instructions that determine the look of address dialog boxes within the Exchange Client and Outlook.

- Templates can be modified manually to customize the dialog boxes.

- Templates are located in their language-specific sub-level container within the **Addressing** container.

- Changes should be applied to all installed languages to display a common set of dialog boxes across all client versions.

Exercise 23: Modifying a Details Template

The **Addressing** container holds the Address and Details templates, which can be modified to display custom attributes or to achieve other client behavior.

Estimated time to complete this exercise: 15 minutes

Description

In this exercise, you will modify the **Search Dialog** details template to extend the number of available parameters for address book searches. The modified search dialog box will allow users to search for addresses based on a custom attribute. You will test the changes within the Administrator program and within Outlook.

- Task 23a describes the steps for changing the **Search Dialog** details template so that a custom attribute such as *Year Employed* will appear on the form when a client search is run.

- Task 23b describes the steps for verifying the appearance of the *Year Employed* custom attribute in the **Search Dialog** details template.

- Task 23c describes the steps for testing the changes you made to the **Search Dialog** details template by searching for all recipients with a specific year of employment.

Prerequisites

- Complete the exercise logged on as Admin-NY1 on NEWYORK-1.

- Exercise 14 and Exercise 22 must already have been completed.

Task 23a: Adding the Custom Attribute to the Search Dialog Details Template

1. Start the **Microsoft Exchange Administrator** program and ensure that you are connected to the server NEWYORK-1.

2. Expand the site **NEWYORK**, the **Configuration** container, the **Addressing** container, the **Details Templates** container, and then click **English/USA**.

3. In the right pane, click the **Search Dialog** object, and then on the **File** menu, click **Properties**.

4. In the **Search Dialog Properties** dialog box, click on the **Templates** tab. (A **Loading Schema** dialog box appears while the schema is being loaded.)

5. Click **New** to display the **Select Control Type** dialog box.

6. Select **Label**, and then click **OK**.

7. The **Label Control** dialog box appears. For each box listed next, type the following:

In this box	You supply
X:	*175*
Y:	*90*
Width:	*55*
Height:	*12*
Text:	*Year &Employed:*

Note There is no space between the "&" and the "E" in *Employed*.

8. Click **OK**.

9. The **Search Dialog Properties** dialog box appears with *Year &Employed:* added at the top of the list.

10. In the **Value** column of the list box below **Search Dialog**, select *Year &Employed:*, and then click **Move Down**. The *Year &Employed:* label must be listed below **Page Break** in the **Control** column in order for it to be displayed on the search page.

11. Click **New** to display the **Select Control Type** dialog box.

12. Select **Edit**, and then click **OK**.

13. The **Edit Control** dialog box appears. For each box listed next, type the following:

In this box	You supply
X:	*235*
Y:	*90*
Width:	*25*
Height:	*12*

14. In the **Field** list, select **Year Employed**.

15. Click **OK**. The **Search Dialog Properties** dialog box reappears.

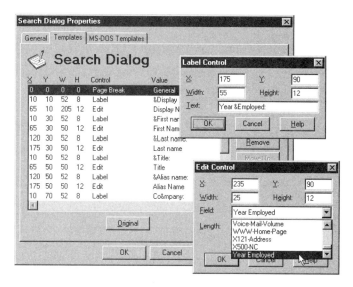

Task 23b: Testing the Modified Search Dialog Details Template

1. Click **Test** to display the **Search Dialog Template Test** dialog box.

2. Verify that the **Year Employed** edit box appears correctly with the "E" in *Employed* underlined.

3. Click **OK** to switch back to the **Search Dialog Properties** dialog box.

4. Click **OK**.

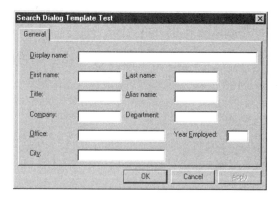

Task 23c: Searching for All Recipients with a Year Employed Attribute of 1990

1. If you are logged on, log off from Windows NT.

2. To log on, press CTRL+ALT+DEL.

3. In the **User Name** box, type *BillP*.

4. In the **Password** box, type *Billp* and then click **OK**.

5. On the **Desktop**, double-click the **Microsoft Outlook** shortcut.

6. On the Outlook toolbar, click **Address Book** to display the **Address Book** dialog box.

7. On the toolbar of the **Address Book** dialog box, click **Find Items**. The **Find** dialog box appears.

8. In the **Year Employed** box, type *1990* and then click **OK**.

9. The **Address Book** dialog box reappears, displaying entries for Bert Melon and Linda Carrot. These users have a **Year Employed** property of **1990**.

10. Close the Address Book.

11. Exit Microsoft Outlook.

12. Log off from Windows NT.

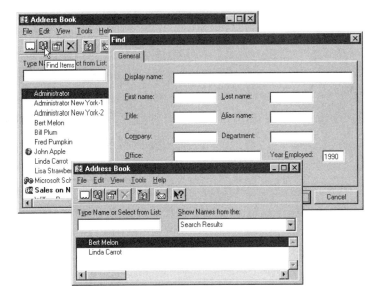

Review

Using the **Search Dialog** details template within the **Details Templates** container, you can modify the search dialog box for Exchange Clients and Outlook. You can associate new controls with any existing directory attributes (in this example you used a custom attribute). If you include a custom attribute, such as *Year Employed*, users can find recipients that meet the specific criteria through address book searches.

MTA Site Configuration Properties

The MTA is the Exchange Server core component responsible for message transfer. The most important configuration parameters, which can be specified using the **MTA Site Configuration** object, refer to protocol parameters and message transfer settings. Changes applied at the site level through the **MTA Site Configuration** property pages affect all servers in the site. In other words, all MTA instances of a site use exactly the same parameters. (See Figure 8-13 on page 469.)

Modifying Reliable Transfer Service Values

Reliable Transfer Service (RTS) values, such as the *checkpoint size*, *recovery timeout*, and *window size* affect the transmission of data between MTAs. RTS values can be controlled using the **Messaging Defaults** property page.

The checkpoint size determines the amount of data that can be sent before a checkpoint must be inserted into the data stream during message transmission. A checkpoint—inserted by the sending MTA and confirmed by the receiving MTA—indicates the amount of data that the remote MTA has securely received. This data doesn't need to be retransmitted if a communication error occurs. To complete a message transfer after a communication error, the sending MTA can restart the communication at the position of the most recent checkpoint. Therefore, a checkpoint keeps the retransmission of messages flowing efficiently.

The default checkpoint size is 30 KB, but you should decrease the checkpoint size if the network is less reliable than the average Ethernet LAN. On the other hand, a small checkpoint size increases the protocol overhead for message transmission, so you can increase the checkpoint size safely in situations where network connections are of high quality. A checkpoint size of zero determines that no checkpoint is set during the transmission.

The recovery timeout specifies the time interval for a broken connection to become reestablished before the MTA deletes the checkpointed information. If this timeout is exceeded, the message transfer must start from the beginning. By default, the MTA keeps checkpointed data for 60 seconds.

The window size allows you to specify the number of *data packages* an MTA can send unacknowledged to a remote MTA. A data package is a block of data (typically 16 KB in size) that can be transmitted to the communication partner in a single unit. Messages larger than the package size will be broken into multiple packages that are then transmitted sequentially to the destination and then rejoined at the receiving end. Using a window size of 1, for instance, the receiving MTA must inform the sender immediately when a unit has been received properly. If a package is corrupted, the receiving end must request that data unit again. This acknowledgement adds protocol overhead to the communication—provided that high-quality network links (for example, Ethernet LAN) are used and data packages seldom become corrupted. In this situation, it is desirable to reduce the amount of acknowledgments by increasing the window size, because the larger the window size, the greater the amount of data that can be transferred in one step. However, if a data package becomes corrupted, this specific package must be retransmitted along with all packages that had already been sent before the error was realized. This means that the larger the window size, the greater the amount of data that potentially must be retransmitted in the case of a corrupted data package. For this reason, it is recommended that you increase the window size only on reliable network connections. You should decrease the size on less reliable connections. The default window size is five packages.

The RTS values are as follows:

- **Checkpoint Size (K)**; the amount of data to be transferred before a checkpoint is inserted

- **Recovery Timeout (sec)**; the amount of time the MTA waits for a reconnection before deleting checkpointed information

- **Window Size**; number of data packets that can go unacknowledged before data transfer is suspended

Modifying Connection Retry Values

Connection retry values determine how many times the MTA can try to establish a connection to transfer a particular message. By default, the MTA tries to connect to a remote MTA 144 times. If it still can't establish a connection after all those attempts, it sends an NDR back to the originator. If an attempt to open a connection has failed, the MTA waits ten minutes before it makes another effort.

Once the connection has been established, the MTA starts to send the data. If a communication error occurs at this point, data must be resent. The Max Transfer Retries value specifies how often the MTA attempts to send a message. By default, the MTA tries to send the message twice before it stops delivery. Moreover, the Transfer Interval value determines the delay before a message will be sent again. By default, the MTA waits two minutes to allow the remote MTA to recover.

The Connection Retry values are as follows:

- **Max Open Retries**; the maximum number of times the system tries to open a connection

- **Max Transfer Retries**; the maximum number of times the system tries to transfer a message across an already open connection

- **Open Interval (sec)**; the amount of time the system waits before attempting to reopen a connection after an error

- **Transfer Interval (sec)**; the amount of time the system waits before resending a message over an already open connection

Modifying Association Parameters

An *association* is a logical connection between two systems that is used to transfer messages. First the originating MTA establishes a physical connection, and then it establishes the logical connection. More than one association can be set on the same physical path. Association parameters determine how long the MTA waits for responses before disconnecting and how long it keeps an association open after having sent a message. It is also possible to specify the number of messages that can be queued up before the MTA opens an additional association over the same physical connection to speed up the message transfer. By default, the MTA establishes an additional association for every 50 messages that are queued.

The association values are as follows:

- **Disconnect (sec)**; the amount of time the system waits for a response before terminating a connection

- **Lifetime (sec)**; the amount of time the system keeps an association open after a message is sent

- **Threshold (msgs)**; the maximum number of queued messages directed to a remote system before the MTA opens another association

Modifying Transfer Timeouts

Exchange Server handles messages according to how priorities have been set. A high priority message requires a higher level of attention than does a low priority message. Even NDRs are generated more quickly if a high priority message cannot be delivered. You can assign different timeout values to different message priorities based on seconds per kilobyte (sec/K). The higher the sec/K value, the longer the MTA attempts to send a message. The default values are 1000 sec/K for urgent, 2000 sec/K for normal priority, and 3000 sec/K for non-urgent e-mail messages.

The transfer timeout values are as follows:

- **Non-Urgent**; the amount of time (in sec/K) that passes before the system sends an NDR for a non-urgent message

- **Normal**; the amount of time (in sec/K) that passes before the system sends an NDR for a normal message

- **Urgent**; the amount of time (in sec/K) that passes before the system sends an NDR for an urgent message

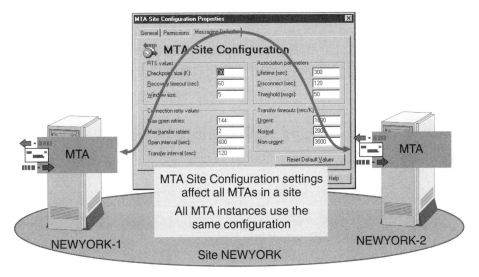

Figure 8-13. MTA Site Configuration.

The non-protocol relevant MTA site configuration parameters are:

- **Directory Name**; the name of the MTA object in the directory (read only)

- **Display Name**; to identify the **MTA Site Configuration** object in the Administration window

- **Enable Message Tracking**; to write information about messages to the tracking.log directory; the message tracking center can access this information to track a message

- **Windows NT Accounts With Permissions** (on the **Permissions** property page); to designate administrators who are able to configure the MTAs at the site level

Lesson 4: Managing Server Configuration

Each server maintains its own set of services, including core and additional components. You can control them by using the site-level default settings, or you can configure them individually at the server level.

The various server-level configuration objects are introduced in this lesson. A practical exercise explains the server-level MTA and IS configuration.

At the end of this lesson, you will be able to:

- Identify server configuration objects

- Modify general server properties

Estimated time to complete this lesson: 35 minutes

Server Configuration Objects

Server configuration objects allow you to configure a particular server individually and independent of site-level default settings. In general, server configuration has a higher priority than the configuration of site defaults.

The server-level configuration objects are the **Private Information Store**, **Public Information Store**, **Protocols**, **Server Recipients**, **Directory Service**, **Directory Synchronization**, **Message Transfer Agent**, and the **System Attendant**. You can find them under each **Server** object (for example, **NEWYORK-1** as shown in Figure 8-14 on page 474). The **Server** object, in turn, is located in the **Servers** container, which is a sub-level container of the **Configuration** object.

Directory Service

The **Directory Service** object's **General** property page features two important buttons, **Update Now** and **Check Now**. Both of these can be used to resolve directory inconsistencies within a site and between sites. Using the **Update Now** button, you can force a directory replication cycle. This is helpful if you want to update the configuration of a site immediately. For example, you might want to propagate the existence of a new messaging connector to all servers as soon as possible in order to make the new connection available to all users. This button is unavailable if only one server exists in a site. The **Check Now** button, in turn, is most useful if you want to update settings regarding the directory replication between sites.

Knowledge Consistency Checker

The Knowledge Consistency Checker (KCC) maintains the replication paths between servers in a site. It also maintains replication links to remote sites using directory replication connector objects. The purpose of the KCC can be demonstrated when you create a replication connector. No significant changes appear in the DIT during its configuration, but if you open the properties of the **Directory Service** object and click the **Check Now** button, a new site object and its **Configuration** container will be displayed in the hierarchy immediately. The KCC carries out the creation of these items. The empty containers are a sign that the logical replication link to the remote site has been established. It is now up to the directory replication to fill the new container objects with the current data.

Replication paths are maintained in two internal directory lists called REPS-TO and REPS-FROM. The REPS-TO list contains those servers to which new changes will be replicated. REPS-FROM is the list of servers from which the local server will accept replication information. Using these lists, the KCC contacts remote servers to verify that they are synchronized with the directory information of the local server. A routine check is performed once a day and whenever you change the local directory. If inconsistencies are detected, the KCC forces a directory replication cycle to correct the problem.

The consistency check is performed on every server and might therefore take a while. You'll experience a measurable replication delay, especially if the site is very large. In other words, changes applied to one server don't appear immediately on all other servers. Although you can force the directory replication using the **Update Now** or **Check Now** buttons, you can't reduce the replication delay. Clicking these buttons several times won't solve the delay, but will increase network traffic unnecessarily.

Note Clicking the **Update Now** or **Check Now** buttons multiple times does not solve any directory replication problems nor does this approach decrease the directory replication delay. Instead, an administrator will only slow down the directory replication further through increased network traffic.

Diagnostics Logging

If you suspect that the DS might malfunction, you can increase the diagnostics level on the **Diagnostics Logging** property page of the **Directory Service** object. You should do this in order to gather detailed information about the service's operation. Several categories are listed, such as **Garbage Collection**, **Internal Processing**, **Knowledge Consistency Checker**, **Replication**, and more. Bear in mind that detailed information is written to the Application Event Log, and that the log file will fill up quickly if you select the **Maximum** level.

A detailed check is advised, for instance, if the directory replication keeps you waiting for an unexpectedly long time. You can use the Event Viewer to analyze the Application Event Log for error messages regarding possible problems.

Message Transfer Agent

The MTA is an X.400 messaging component based on the 1988 conformance year. Its name and password can be defined using the **Local MTA Name** and **Local MTA Password** controls on the **General** property page. Both parameters are required to establish connections and associations to other MTAs or foreign X.400 systems through an X.400 connector. More information about the configuration of the X.400 Connector is provided in Chapter 9.

Setting Up an MTA Password

By default, the **Local MTA Name** reflects the name of the Exchange Server computer. The **Local MTA Password** field is left blank, but you can secure incoming and outgoing connections if you specify a password. The **Local MTA Password** can be up to 64 characters long and both the **Local MTA Name** and the **Local MTA Password** are case sensitive.

Maximum Message Size

A maximum message size can be specified on the **General** property page of the **Message Transfer Agent** object. This size limitation causes the MTA to reject larger messages, which will then be returned to the originator. This way, you have the option to limit the usage of the messaging backbone independently of users or messaging connectors.

Recalculate Routing

The **Recalculate Routing** button is probably the most frequently used control on the **General** property page. Similar to the **Recalculate Routing** button of the **Site Addressing** object at the site level, the **Recalculate Routing** button on the server level updates the GWART of the MTA. It is therefore advisable that you click this button when the local routing information has been changed but the changes are not yet reflected in the routing table. This will force the changes to become effective. More information about the GWART is given in Chapter 9.

Message Queues

The **Queues** property page of the **Message Transfer Agent** object lists the messages that are awaiting delivery. The MTA maintains a message queue for every connector, every server in the local site, the Public Information Store, and the Private Information Store, and places the messages into these queues according to the routing table information. A message queue that is filled with numerous messages can indicate a connector problem or a corrupted message. You can delete critical messages that might block a message queue administratively from within the **Queues** property page. This generates an NDR that informs the originator about the message deletion. The maintenance of message queues is outlined in Chapter 15.

Diagnostics Logging

The Diagnostics Logging feature of the MTA is perhaps one of the best troubleshooting aids to use when experiencing problems in message delivery. The most important diagnostics categories are **X.400 Service**, **APDU**, and **Interoperability**. You can use the Site Connector, X.400 Connector, or Dynamic RAS Connector to gather detailed information about transfer problems in the Application Event Log when you've increased the logging level of these categories. As usual, you will use the Event Viewer to examine the collected information. Another valuable feature you can use to collect information about the MTA's operation is Text Event Logging, which was discussed earlier in this chapter.

Public Information Store

Using the **Public Information Store** object, you can specify the size of the storage space that each public folder can allocate, the replication schedule, age limits, and many other settings that affect all public folders maintained by the local Exchange Server computer.

The **Public Information Store** object is represented as a container object that houses further objects for displaying the most important status information in a convenient way, unlike the **Public Information Store** object in Exchange Server 4.0. These objects are **Folder Replication Status**, **Logons**, **Public Folder Resources**, and **Server Replication Status**. The management and administration of public folders using the **Public Information Store** object is covered in Chapter 12.

Private Information Store

The **Private Information Store** object is used to set general mailbox properties and to examine status information using the **Logons** and **Mailbox Resources** property pages. These pages display detailed information about users who are currently logged on and the total amount of storage space being consumed. Also, leaf objects named **Logons** and **Mailbox Resources** have been implemented since Exchange Server 5.0 under the **Private Information Store** container object. These two leaf objects provide the same mailbox status information as do the property pages.

Storage Limits

Storage limits might be the most important setting in the **Private Information Store** object, because they allow you to manage the size of the Priv.edb database on the server. The quotas that can be set are **Issue Warning**, **Prohibit Send**, and **Prohibit Send And Receive**. **Issue Warning** determines the level at which users will receive warning messages indicating that their mailboxes exceed the permitted size. **Prohibit Send** prevents a user from sending messages. This level is typically applied after **Issue Warning** has been reached. It is important to note, however, that this message store limit does not affect incoming messages, so a mailbox can continue to grow even after the **Prohibit Send** level has been reached. **Prohibit Send And Receive**, in turn, does not allow the user to participate further in any e-mail communication. It is recommended that you set this parameter higher than the **Prohibit Send** parameter. As soon as this level is reached, the user must reduce his or her mailbox size in order to be able to send and receive messages again. By setting this parameter at a high level you can, for instance, prevent a mailbox from growing uncontrolled while the mailbox owner is out of the office for an extended amount of time.

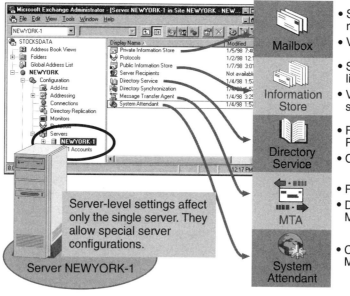

Figure 8-14. Core components at the server level.

System Attendant

The **System Attendant** object allows you to control the maintenance of message tracking log files. For this purpose, it has the **Remove Log Files Older Than ... Days** box on its **General** tab, which can be used to determine when message tracking log files should be deleted. It is also possible to specify that the old log files not be removed at all. By default, tracking files are kept for seven days and are then deleted by the SA service.

Tracking logs are created on a daily basis in the \Exchsrvr\Tracking.log directory. They can contain transmission and delivery information from the MTA, IS, IMS, and additional messaging connector components. Based on this information, you can determine the path a message has taken through your organization by using the Message Tracking Center of the Administrator program. Message Tracking is covered in more detail in Chapter 15.

The administrative server-level configuration objects and their functions are as follows:

- **Directory Service**; to force directory replication and to check directory consistency between servers

- **Directory Synchronization**; to configure parameters regarding directory synchronization with MS Mail 3.x systems (explained in Chapter 18)

- **Message Transfer Agent**; to rebuild the routing table after configuration changes, to determine maximum message sizes, to view and manage message queues, and to determine where to expand the distribution lists

- <MTA Transport Stack> objects (for example, **TCP (NEWYORK-1)**); to define the transport used with an X.400 Connector or a Dynamic RAS Connector (explained in Chapter 9)

- **Private Information Store**; to configure mailbox quotas and to view resource information

- **Protocols**; to hold configuration objects for LDAP, NNTP, POP3, and IMAP4 protocol settings (explained in Chapter 11, "Internet Protocols")

- **Public Information Store**; to provide settings for determining message age limits and issuing warning levels; to display status information about shared resources and logged-on users

- **Server Recipients**; to house the recipients that belong to a particular server

- **System Attendant**; to provide settings for message tracking log files

Exercise 24: Modifying the Server's MTA and Public Information Store Properties

The configuration at the server level affects the server itself but no other servers within the site. This allows you to achieve special server configurations, such as a messaging bridgehead, a public server, or a private server.

Estimated time to complete this exercise: 15 minutes

Description

In this exercise, you will specify a maximum message size for the MTA. If messages later exceed this limit, they will be returned to the sender and it will be indicated that the message was too large. The user then has the option to reduce the message size and resend the e-mail message.

Using the **Public Information Store** object, you will define an age limit for all items stored in public folders. These settings will affect only the public folders that are maintained by the local server. Task 24b serves the purpose of demonstration only, since public folders are covered in more detail in Chapter 12 and in Chapter 13, "Public Folder Replication."

- Task 24a describes the steps for limiting the message size that the local MTA will handle. All messages that exceed this limit will be returned to the originator.

- Task 24b describes the steps for setting age limits for messages stored in public folders. This will determine how long messages can remain in a public folder before they expire and are deleted.

Prerequisites

- Log on to NEWYORK-1 as Admin-NY1 to complete this exercise.

Task 24a: Setting the Maximum Message Size for a Server's MTA

1. Start the **Microsoft Exchange Administrator** program and connect to the server NEWYORK-1.

2. Expand the site **NEWYORK**, expand **Configuration**, and then expand the **Servers** container.

3. Select the server object **NEWYORK-1**.

4. In the right pane, click the **Message Transfer Agent** object, and then on the **File** menu, click **Properties**.

5. The **Message Transfer Agent Properties** dialog box appears.

6. In the edit box under **Message Size**, type *2048*.

7. Click **OK**.

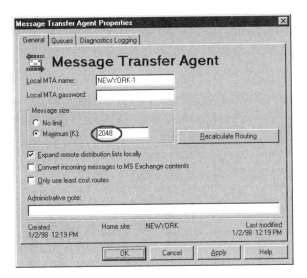

Task 24b: Setting the Age Limit for Data in the Server's Public Information Store

1. In the right pane, highlight the **Public Information Store** object, and then on the **File** menu, click **Properties**. This displays the **Public Information Store Properties** dialog box.

2. Click the **Age Limits** tab.

3. In the **Age Limit For All Folders On This Information Store (Days)** textbox, type *90*.

4. Click **OK**.

5. Exit **Microsoft Exchange Administrator**.

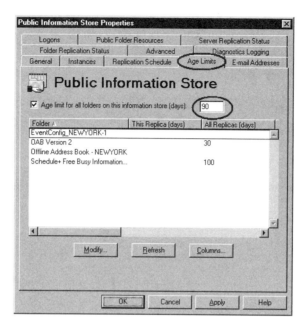

Review

Using the **Message Transfer Agent** object, you can specify a maximum message size on the **General** tab. If a message size limit has been entered, the MTA rejects larger messages and returns them to the originator.

The **Public Information Store** object can be used to configure the default size limit of public folders. It is also possible to set age limits. Public folder administration is covered in Chapter 12.

Modifying Server Properties

The **Server** container itself is another important administrative item, because its properties are related to general and specific server maintenance and configuration tasks. Properties, such as the **Server Location** box on the **General** property page, allow you to manage the server configuration. Server locations, for instance, are logical server groups that provide further control over Address Spaces and public folder access in large sites. They are outlined in more detail in Chapter 12.

Information Store Maintenance

The databases of the IS, Priv.edb and Pub.edb, become fragmented as users send, receive, store, and delete messages or work with public folders. Fragmented databases slow down the server, consume more hard disk space than necessary, and can cause serious problems if the fragmentation exceeds a certain level. To avoid all these negative effects, you can schedule online maintenance routines for Public Information Store and Private Information Store defragmentation using the **IS Maintenance** property page. In a default configuration, maintenance routines are performed between one o'clock and six o'clock every morning (Greenwich Mean Time).

The online maintenance routines do not decrease the size of the database files—they mark recovered space as available only. If you want to compact the databases, however, use the offline maintenance utility Eseutil.exe. First check the actual path to the database files through the **Database Paths** property page. Then stop the server services, since Eseutil.exe is an offline defragmentation tool. Then defragment the databases by running Eseutil.exe from the Windows NT command prompt, supplying the path to the desired database as a command line parameter. Eseutil.exe is covered in detail in Chapter 15.

Online Backup Strategies

In general, three strategies exist to back up an Exchange server online. They are the full, the incremental, and the differential backup. In a default Exchange Server configuration, however, only full backups can be made since transaction logs, the basis of the incremental and differential backup types, are overwritten automatically during normal server operation. If you want to make incremental or differential backups you must disable the automatic deletion of transaction log files first. The corresponding **Circular Logging** check boxes for the **Directory** and the **Information Store** can be found on the server's **Advanced** property page. You can read more about the various backup types and their use in Chapter 15.

On the other hand, if you have restored an Exchange Server from a recent backup, check the consistency between the directory and the IS databases. To correct any inconsistencies, click the **Consistency Adjuster** button on the **Advanced** property page under **Data Consistency**.

Monitored Services

The services a Server Monitor is responsible for can be specified on the **Services** property page. By default, the DS, IS, and MTA are monitored, as shown in Figure 8-15. Other Windows NT services can be selected optionally as well.

A Server Monitor ensures that all monitored services are functioning. If a monitored service is shut down for any reason, the Server Monitor performs predefined actions, such as sending a notification to an administrator, restarting the service automatically, or rebooting the entire server. Server Monitors are covered in detail in Chapter 15.

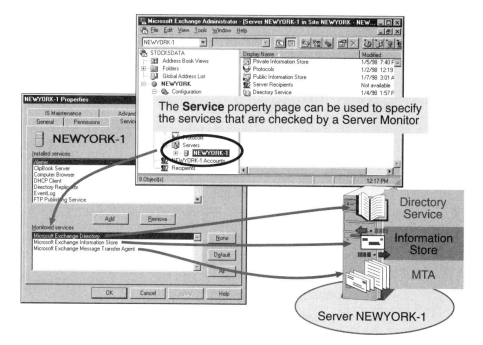

Figure 8-15. Specifying monitored services via the Server Configuration object.

The **Server** object tabs and their purpose are as follows:

- **Advanced**; to disable circular logging and to adjust directory and IS inconsistencies

- **Database Paths**; to display where directory and IS databases reside

- **Diagnostics Logging**; to set diagnostic logging levels for all core components from a centralized location

- **General**; to create server locations for the purpose of controlling public folder access

- **IS Maintenance**; to configure the online maintenance schedule, including defragmentation of ISs

- **Locales**; to determine how date, currency, and time values are displayed depending on the client languages

- **Services**; to specify which services will be checked by a Server Monitor

Review

1. Some users are complaining that they cannot connect to their home server. As their administrator, you want to verify that all servers are functioning. What tool can you use to check the status of the services on the servers from your Windows NT Workstation?

   _____

   _____

   _____

   _____

2. You want to configure an entire Exchange Server organization using the Administrator program on your Windows NT Workstation computer. How do you install this program and which of the existing servers in your organization can be configured?

   _____

   _____

   _____

   _____

   _____

3. You add more RAM to an Exchange Server computer. The server performance has been increased but you want to use the new hardware in the most efficient way. What tool should you use to optimize the server configuration?

   _____

   _____

4. To connect two sites you must first configure a messaging connector. What is the name of the container object that holds the corresponding leaf objects, and where can it be found within the DIT?

   _____

   _____

5. How do you distinguish between container objects and leaf objects?

   _____

   _____

6. You configure a dedicated workstation that will be used for the administration of a site. Other administrators will also use this workstation to perform their site management tasks. While you are working with the Administrator program, you adjust the order of columns within the Administration window. Will the modifications affect the work of other administrators?

_____

7. To provide an easy way to generate alias names for new mailboxes, you have changed the **Auto Naming** scheme using the Administrator program. How does this setting affect the work of other administrators who use the same workstation?

_____

_____

8. The company has hired a new Exchange Server administrator. You, as the main administrator, must assign the new administrator the appropriate role of a **Permissions Admin.** At which three levels must you assign the permissions explicitly?

_____

_____

_____

9. You want to adjust the MTA checkpoint size for all servers within a site. To do this you decide to change the corresponding site-level settings. What object provides the necessary properties for configuration? What object is its parent container?

_____

_____

_____

10. You decide to create a customized Offline Address Book, which should not contain address information of remote sites. Where do you configure the relevant Offline Address Book settings?

_____

_____

_____

_____

_____

11. You have added the IMS to an existing site. Now you want to send
    messages to recipients over the Internet. A message is returned as a
    non-delivery notification that indicates that the recipient was unknown,
    although you assigned the correct SMTP address space to the IMS.
    How do you resolve the routing problem?

    _____

    _____

    _____

    _____

    _____

12. You want to change the look of the mailbox details dialog box within
    Outlook. Where do you configure this dialog?

    _____

    _____

    _____

    _____

13. You discover that one server within a site does not reflect the current site
    information. What would you do to force a directory replication cycle?
    Where can you find detailed information about possible replication
    problems?

    _____

    _____

    _____

    _____

    _____

14. You want to manage the available disk space on the server, so you define storage limits. Lisa Strawberry's mailbox is larger than the **Storage Warning** setting. Bert Melon's mailbox size exceeds the **Prohibit Send** limit. Fred Pumpkin's mailbox size exceeds the **Prohibit Send And Receive** limit. How do the storage limits affect the work of Lisa, Bert, and Fred?

_____

_____

_____

_____

_____

15. A supervisor of one of the departments calls and wants to know whether Fred Pumpkin is working online. You need to view information about currently logged-on users in order to find out. Which object provides the fastest access to the desired information?

_____

_____

_____

_____

16. Your company's backup strategy relies on offline backups. You want to check the database locations to ensure that all database files are included in a backup configuration. Which property page provides information about existing database paths within the Administrator program?

_____

_____

C H A P T E R   9

Introduction to Intersite Connectors

This chapter examines the main messaging connectors and the directory replication connector. Both connector types are necessary to exchange messages and directory information in an organization that has multiple Exchange sites.

Overview

Just as bridges connect islands, messaging connectors connect multiple sites belonging to an organization. Microsoft Exchange Server 5.5 offers several messaging connectors. Lesson 1 of this chapter describes them and explains how they are used. Lessons 2 through 5 discuss the main connectors in detail.

A *messaging connector* moves messages from an Exchange site to another Exchange site or to a foreign mail system. This chapter explains the configuration options and features of each messaging connector that can be used to connect two Exchange sites. Connectors that can be used to bind Exchange sites together to a homogeneous organization are also called *main connectors*. The IMS is discussed only briefly here because it is covered in more detail in Chapter 10, "Internet Mail Service."

This chapter also explains multiple connector configurations. The MTA's use of the GWART to route messages is highlighted. The GWART structure is introduced here, along with how to analyze existing routing paths.

Lesson 6 covers the various aspects of directory replication between sites, also known as *intersite directory replication*. It also covers replication topology, replication bridgeheads, the replication connector configuration, and the methods of forcing intersite replication. You will learn about transient and adjacent sites, how they depend on each other, and the problems that may occur if you ignore their relationship.

This chapter also includes five exercises that will guide you through the steps of configuring and testing messaging and directory replication connections. Exercise 25 is the most complex. It basically repeats all the exercises in the preceding chapters, but its primary purpose is to reduce the number of computers necessary to complete the subsequent exercises in this book.

In the following lessons, you will be introduced to:

- Communication between sites
- Site Connector configuration
- X.400 Connector configuration
- Configuring the Dynamic Remote Access Service (RAS) Connector to establish communication links between remote sites
- Message routing across multiple connectors
- Directory replication bridgeheads and their role in creating replication connections between sites

Lesson 1: Intersite Communication

Intersite communication is the transfer of data between sites using e-mail messages. Intersite communication is accomplished using messaging connectors; all information destined for a remote site is transferred using the MTA in conjunction with a connector.

Before introducing the various messaging connectors, this lesson will discuss the reasons for separating servers in multiple sites and the types of information that can be transferred between sites. You'll also see a list of messaging connectors that come with Exchange Server, followed by an explanation of address spaces and their functions.

Exercise 25 at the end of this chapter will refresh your memory about the subjects covered in earlier chapters. Even more important, it will prepare your second test computer for the later exercises in this book.

At the end of this lesson, you will be able to:

- Design multiple site organizations
- List the available messaging connectors
- Identify the types of data that might have to be transferred using a messaging connector
- Describe the purpose of address spaces
- Remove an Exchange Server from a site

Estimated time to complete this lesson: 90 minutes

Reasons for Having Multiple Sites

A single site makes Exchange Server administration wonderfully easy. But sometimes you might be forced to separate servers in multiple sites. The possible reasons for this were covered in Chapter 1. They include Windows NT security dependencies, network topology restrictions, geographical issues, and political considerations regarding the administration of an organization with multiple departments.

Separated Administration

Many administrative and security settings can be controlled at the site level, allowing all servers in a site to be managed as a unit. Different administrators can be designated for each site. You might consider having multiple independent administration locations, but don't assume that one site configuration will not affect the other sites. With independent administration, a situation might develop in which the left hand doesn't know what the right hand is doing and, as a result of such a situation, design and configuration problems can and will occur. Therefore, you should establish a central board of administrators if you have a complex organization. The board can control configuration activity while the operational tasks themselves can still be performed at multiple locations.

Our fictitious company, STOCKSDATA, which is responsible for worldwide distribution of stock market information, has five locations (as shown in Figure 9-1) and each location is configured as a separate Exchange site. Having multiple sites can ease the impact on the network while providing a convenient administration model. Simple operational tasks such as the creation of mailboxes can be performed independently of the other sites. All STOCKSDATA administrators, however, must discuss topology or configuration changes before applying them because most changes will affect the entire organization.

Communication Control

Because the transfer of information between sites depends on messaging connectors, intersite communication can be controlled. Every connector is represented as a configuration object within the **Connections** container. Using the Administrator program, you can adjust connector parameters using the property pages of the corresponding directory object. Many connectors allow you to specify times for connector activation, set message size limits, control which users can use the connector, and determine which servers will be responsible for intersite communication.

E-mail–based transport via messaging connectors offers several advantages. The data is compressed by an average ratio of 5:1 before it is sent across a connector, which saves on expensive network bandwidth. Likewise, a message with multiple destinations across a single connector will be sent only once. In other words, even if the message must reach multiple servers in a remote site, it will be sent as a single message instance, with each destination listed as a recipient. In this process, known as a *fan out*, the remote MTA will forward the message to additional servers or users. Moreover, the information transfer is independent of the actual network topology, since many different messaging connectors can be used transparently. For instance, a message from PARIS to recipients residing on NEWYORK-1 and NEWYORK-2 needs to be sent to NEWYORK only once, either directly by using the French Internet access point or indirectly by using the connection to FRANKFURT first and the German Internet access point second. (See Figure 9-1.)

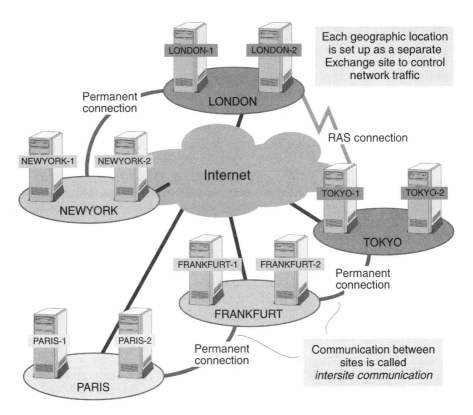

Figure 9-1. A multiple-site organization.

The reasons that you might need to use multiple sites are as follows:

- A common Site Services Account is unavailable
- Inadequate network bandwidth is available between servers
- Political or geographical considerations
- WAN transmission must be optimized to keep costs down

Intersite Messages

Unlike communication within a site where both the DS and the MTA can establish connections to DSs and MTAs running on other servers, all communication between sites is handled by the MTA only. Therefore, all data, including directory replication information, must be wrapped in e-mail messages in order to be sent to a remote site. The MTA becomes the most important core component for intersite communication, upon which all other components such as the DS and IS rely. All core services are mission-critical, of course.

Directory Information

Directory replication between sites is based on e-mail messages because support for direct RPC communication cannot be assumed between sites. Only the MTA handles intersite communication by means of messaging connectors and understands how to move e-mail messages. (See Figure 9-2.) An internal component of the DS, the Directory Replication Agent (DRA), wraps a message cover around the replication data and sends the data to the destination Directory service. The IS and the MTA must handle the actual delivery of the replication message. Once the DRA receives the replication data, it unwraps it and incorporates the changes into its local directory. Although the transport mechanism changes, the directory replication protocol stays the same. Intersite directory replication is covered in more detail in Lesson 6, "Directory Replication," later in this chapter.

Information Store Communication

The transfer of information related to the IS between servers does not change between sites. IS instances always replicate the public folder hierarchy and the public folder content using e-mail messages.

The replication of public folder hierarchy and content is optimized between sites because a particular replication message is addressed to all relevant IS instances. More than one replica can be maintained in a remote site, but only one single replication message needs to be transferred. Once the message is received, it can be split up into multiple instances, one for each destination IS. In other words, IS instances are handled as multiple regular recipients on the **To** line of an interpersonal e-mail message. Public folder replication is covered in more detail in Chapter 13, "Public Folder Replication."

Link Monitor Test Messages

You can use the SA in conjunction with the Administrator program and a configured Link Monitor to automatically check message delivery to each server. The connector check relies on test messages transferred between sites.

The principle of a Link Monitor is simple. It sends a message to a remote recipient such as the System Attendant and waits for a reply. The reply proves that the original test message was received and that the link therefore works. Link Monitor configuration is covered in Chapter 15, "Maintaining Servers."

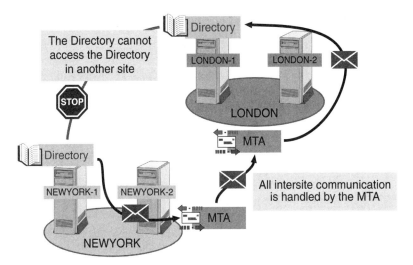

Figure 9-2. Active intersite communication.

Some examples of intersite messages include:

- The DS sends directory replication changes.
- The Private Information Store hands over interpersonal messages to the MTA.
- The Public Information Store sends public folder hierarchy changes.
- The Public Information Store wraps public folder content changes in replication messages.
- The SA (by way of the IS) maintains Link Monitor test messages.

Connector Overview

The family of messaging connectors that comes with Exchange Server 5.5 Enterprise Edition can be divided into two general groups: main connectors and gateway connectors. The main connectors are the Site Connector, X.400 Connector, Dynamic RAS Connector, and the IMS (as shown in Figure 9-3 on page 494). They are more powerful than gateway connectors, such as the MS Mail Connector, the Connector for Lotus cc:Mail, or the Connector for Lotus Notes. Main connectors allow you to connect Exchange sites together. The primary task of gateway connectors is to connect the organization to foreign systems.

Site Connector

The Site Connector is the most powerful and easiest to install of the connectors, but it requires LAN-like connections because RPC connectivity must be established between sites, therefore requiring more available network bandwidth than other connectors. Moreover, you can use it only to connect Exchange sites; you cannot use it to connect to foreign messaging systems. The Site Connector is covered in more detail in Lesson 2, "The Site Connector."

X.400 Connector

The X.400 Connector is the second most powerful connector because the Exchange Server MTA is a native X.400 component. Besides the fact that it can be used to bind sites together, this connector is also the useful choice when you need to connect the organization to foreign X.400 systems. The TCP/IP, TP4, or X.25 transport stacks are supported. More information about the X.400 Connector is provided in Lesson 3, "The X.400 Connector."

Dynamic RAS Connector

The Dynamic RAS Connector uses dial-up connections to transfer messages to other sites. Once a dial-up connection has been established, RPC over TCP/IP, SPX/IPX, or NetBEUI is used to transfer the data.

Dial-up links such as phone lines or ISDN links are usually not as fast as other network connections. For this reason, you should not use the Dynamic RAS Connector as the primary messaging connector unless no other network connectivity is available. On the other hand, this connector is always useful as a redundant connection between sites. The Dynamic RAS Connector is covered in Lesson 4, "Other Main Messaging Connectors," under the section titled "Dynamic RAS Connector."

Internet Mail Service

The IMS allows you to connect sites together through the Internet or an intranet. You can also use it to connect an organization to foreign SMTP systems. Dial-up and permanent connections are supported. The Simple Message Transfer Protocol (SMTP) or the Extended SMTP (ESMTP) protocol is used on top of TCP/IP to transfer messages. The IMS is outlined in detail in Chapter 10, "Internet Mail Service."

MS Mail Connector

As a gateway connector component, the MS Mail Connector provides connectivity to MS Mail networks. The communication can happen through LAN, X.25, and dial-up connections. However, you cannot use this component as a primary connector for intersite communication. The MS Mail Connector is covered in Chapter 18, "Connecting to Microsoft Mail and Schedule+ 1.0."

Lotus cc:Mail Connector

The Connector for Lotus cc:Mail is a gateway connector component that provides connectivity to one Lotus cc:Mail post office per Exchange Server. You cannot use this connector to connect Exchange sites together. More information about this connector is provided in Chapter 19, "Connector for Lotus cc:Mail."

Lotus Notes Connector

If you closely examine Exchange Server 5.5, you will notice the \Exchconn directory on the installation CD-ROM, which contains the Connector for Lotus Notes. This gateway connector provides connectivity to a single Lotus Notes/Domino server through the corresponding Lotus Notes client software. The Lotus Notes/Domino server and the Exchange Server running the connector service act as bridgehead servers. This way, the connector can couple your entire organization with multiple Lotus Notes domains. You can read more about this connector in Chapter 20, "Connector for Lotus Notes."

OfficeVision/VM Connector

The Enterprise Edition also offers connectivity to mainframe messaging systems. The Connector for IBM OfficeVision/VM (PROFS), for instance, is the gateway connector component that provides connectivity to IBM PROFS Version 2 Release 2 Modification Level 2, IBM OfficeVision/VM Release 2 Modification Level 0, and others. The connector requires a Microsoft SNA server in your network and that an SNA client (3270 terminal emulation) be installed on the Exchange Server computer in order to communicate within the SNA network.

SNADS Connector

The Connector for SNADS is also a gateway connector component, and it comes only with the Enterprise Edition of Exchange Server 5.5. It can connect your organization to a variety of messaging systems that rely on SNA Distribution Services or SNADS. Like the Connector for OfficeVision/VM (PROFS), the SNADS Connector uses an SNA server to provide an SNA connection to host-based messaging systems such as IBM OfficeVision/400, Verimation Memo, NB Systems TOSS, and others.

Directory Replication Connector

You cannot use the Directory Replication Connector to connect sites, nor can you use it to connect an organization to a foreign messaging system. This component simply performs directory replication between sites. The Directory Replication Agent uses its configuration information to generate replication messages. You'll find more information about intersite directory replication in Lesson 6 of this chapter, "Directory Replication."

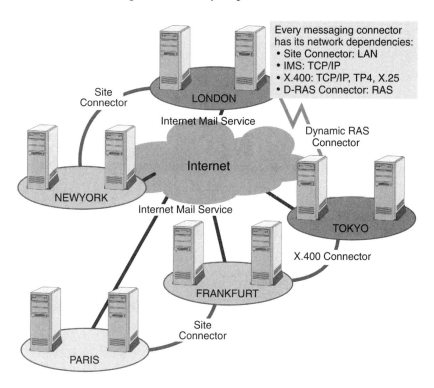

Figure 9-3. Using specific messaging connectors.

The main messaging connectors for connecting sites are:

- The Dynamic RAS Connector, which connects sites using RPC over dial-up connections

- The IMS, which connects sites through the SMTP/ESMTP protocol

- The Site Connector, which connects sites using RPC over TCP/IP, SPX/IPX, and NetBEUI

- The X.400 Connector, which connects sites using X.400 over TCP/IP, TP4 (CLNP) and X.25

Address Space

An address space assigns parts of recipient addresses to messaging connectors in order to perform message routing. You can think of the Exchange Server system in terms of a traditional postal system, in which you provide address spaces and recipient addresses on a letter (e-mail message). The postal address (e-mail address) contains all the required information, such as country (organization), postal code (site), street and house number (home server), and recipient name (mailbox alias). First your letter (e-mail message) is routed based on the country (organization), and then based on the postal code (site name). Once it reaches the desired area (site), it is routed to the correct street and house number (home server). Finally, the recipient name is analyzed to determine the person (mailbox) to whom the letter belongs.

Routing Decisions

To accomplish message routing, the MTA must have address space information available. You define those address spaces on a per-connector basis using the Administrator program. For instance, based on the topology shown in Figure 9-1, you would assign an address space consisting of the organization name STOCKSDATA and the site name LONDON to the IMS in NEWYORK.

Let's say Mr. Fred Pumpkin is a user residing on NEWYORK-1. As soon as Fred sends a message to a user in LONDON, the message is handed over to the MTA. The MTA checks the organization and the site name and discovers that the site name does not match the local site. Now it must find an appropriate connector. It checks the GWART and finds the reference to the site LONDON that points to the IMS. The MTA transfers the message to the IMS for delivery. For more information about message routing and the GWART, see Lesson 5, "Using Multiple Connectors," later in this chapter.

Connections to Foreign Messaging Systems

As soon as you configure a connector to a foreign mail system, users can theoretically send messages to the foreign network. The address format of foreign recipients, however, usually differs from that of Exchange Server. Therefore, you must define new address spaces that correspond to the foreign address type.

If you connect the organization to a foreign X.400 system, you usually have to define X.400 address spaces. SMTP address spaces are most often used in conjunction with the IMS. The MS Mail Connector uses an address space of the MS type to indicate that it connects to an MS Mail postoffice. You usually assign CCMAIL address spaces to messaging connectors if the Connector for

Lotus cc:Mail has been configured to connect the organization to a Lotus cc:Mail post office. This remains the same if you install the Connector for Lotus Notes or any other gateway connector. (See Figure 9-4.)

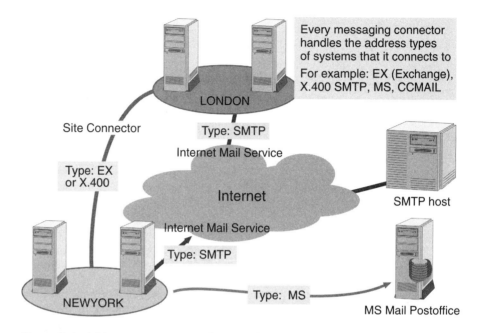

Figure 9-4. Address space types and connections.

Wildcards

You can use wildcards to simplify address space definition. For example, the address space SMTP:* refers to all possible SMTP addresses. An asterisk (*) represents a multi-character wildcard, while a question mark (?) can be used as a single-character wildcard.

Address Space Generation

Address spaces can be configured either manually or automatically. Some connectors, such as the Site Connector, will determine address spaces automatically. Moreover, all connector objects provide the **Address Space** property page so that you can assign additional address spaces to a particular connector manually within the Administrator program. Address spaces can also be replicated between sites during intersite directory replication.

Analyzing Address Spaces

You can view all address space information available to a site within the Administrator program using the **Routing** property page of the **Site Addressing** object. Each connector object provides the **Address Space** property page, which you can use to examine the address spaces of each connector. In addition, a plain text copy of the GWART is kept in the file Gwart0.mta, which can be found in the \Exchsrvr\MMtadata directory.

Here are some Address Space examples:

Address Type (Mail System)	Address Example	Address Space
Lotus cc:Mail	user at postoffice	at postoffice
MS Mail	NETWORK/PO/user	NETWORK/PO
SMTP	*user@stocksdata.com*	stocksdata.com
X.400	c=US;a= ;p=STOCKSDATA; o=NEWYORK;s= Pumpkin;g=Fred	c=US;a= ;p= STOCKSDATA;

Defining the Scope of Address Spaces

You can define local address spaces, like any other address spaces, using the **Address Space** property page, which every messaging connector provides. On this property page, you can click the **New** button to launch the **New Address Space** dialog box. In this dialog box, you must select an address type (**X.400**, **SMTP**, **MS**, or **Other**) and then click the **OK** button. A **Properties** dialog box will appear; on the **General** tab, you enter the desired address space information. Then you can switch to the **Restrictions** property page to specify the scope of the new space. Three levels are provided: **Organization**, **This Site**, and **This Location**. **Organization** is the default setting; it causes the address space to be replicated to servers throughout the organization. **This Site** prevents replication across the local site boundary. **This Location** does not prevent the replication of the new address space in the local site, but the address space-connector association is available only to users who reside on an Exchange Server within the same server location. Server locations are covered in more detail in Chapter 12, "Creating and Managing Public Folders."

Creating Address Space Entries in Remote Sites

Imagine Mr. Fred Pumpkin's situation as an administrator of the STOCKSDATA organization. (See Figure 9-5.) To connect all sites together, he created Internet connections using the IMS. He used local SMTP address spaces at each site so that other sites would not learn about each other's SMTP connection. Therefore, he prevents the creation of complex routing paths, which can lead to inefficient message flow (as shown in Figure 9-5) because the replication of address spaces is avoided. The site PARIS, however, does not yet have an Internet connection at its disposal. Until a direct Internet connection is available, users in PARIS will have to send their Internet messages using the IMS in FRANKFURT. In other words, Internet (SMTP) messages must be routed to FRANKFURT first. Therefore, Fred or one of his French colleagues must assign the SMTP:* address space to the Site Connector between FRANKFURT and PARIS manually. Of course, this address space should only be available in PARIS. The correct address scope is **This Site**.

It is important to note that the address spaces assigned to connectors in remote sites should also be configured as local address spaces. Otherwise, the new address space information will be replicated to all other sites, creating a complex and inefficient routing path. For instance, as soon as you define a regular SMTP address space instead of a local one for the Site Connector between PARIS and FRANKFURT, you replicate this reference to all other sites and introduce the "private" IMS of FRANKFURT to the entire organization.

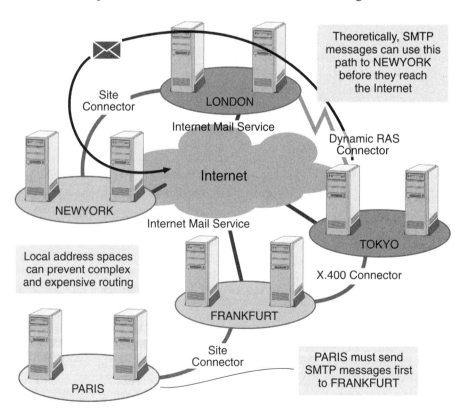

Figure 9-5. Inefficient routing based on replicated address spaces.

Address spaces and their functions are as follows:

- **Organization**; address space is replicated throughout the organization. Each user residing on any server in the organization can send messages of this type through the connector.

- **This Site**; address space is replicated throughout the site only. Each user residing on any server in the site can send messages of this type through the connector. Users in other sites cannot use this address space.

- **This Location**; address space is replicated throughout the site only. Only users residing on a server that belongs to the same server location can send messages of this type through the connector.

Exercise 25: Installing Exchange Server in a New Messaging Site

The implementation of multiple sites in an organization might be the result of several elements: Microsoft Windows NT security dependencies, considerations about the available network bandwidth, transmission costs, geographical reasons, and political reasons can influence the design of an organization's topology.

Estimated time to complete this exercise: 180 minutes

Description

In this exercise, you will remove the existing server NEWYORK-2 from the site NEWYORK. You must then completely reinstall this computer as a new PDC called LONDON-1 (domain: ENGLAND) and configure IIS 3.0, the latest SP, and Microsoft Active Server Pages. You must then use LONDON-1 to install Exchange Server 5.5 in a new site. The new site will be called LONDON. To make the administration of the organization more complex and somewhat more realistic, no trust relationship will be established between the STOCKSDATA and ENGLAND domains. As a result, a second Site Services Account will be required for the new site.

The exercise covers more than the creation of a new site; it also serves as a review of all the preceding exercises. You will install a server in a new site, designate administrators, create mailboxes, install Outlook, and configure messaging profiles. You will also adjust the new site's addressing scheme.

- Task 25a describes the initial steps for removing the old Exchange Server from the messaging site NEWYORK.

- Task 25b describes the steps for completing the removal of the Exchange Server.

- Task 25c describes the steps to create a new Site Services Account for the new Exchange Server.

- Task 25d describes the steps for an initial installation of Exchange Server.

- Task 25e describes the initial steps for creating a new site.

- Task 25f describes the steps for completing the Exchange Server installation.

- Task 25g describes the steps for creating a new administrator account.

- Task 25h describes the steps for verifying that the necessary Exchange Server services have been successfully started.

- Task 25i describes the steps for configuring the Administrator program to display the rights and roles for all Exchange Server objects.

- Task 25j describes the steps for allowing all members of a Windows NT local group to administer site-level properties of an Exchange Server organization.

- Task 25k describes the steps for allowing all members of a Windows NT local group to administer **Configuration** container properties for a site.

- Task 25l describes the steps for modifying the SMTP address for the site and for all existing recipients.

- Task 25m describes the steps for creating new mailboxes on the new Exchange Server for several Windows NT users.

- Task 25n describes the steps for installing Outlook.

- Task 25o describes the steps for creating a profile and configuring information services for Outlook.

Prerequisites

- Make sure that Windows NT Server (at least SP3, Exchange Server, and the Outlook installation media) is available.

- Complete Task 25a logged on as Admin-NY2 on the server NEWYORK-2.

- Complete Task 25b logged on as Admin-NY1 on the server NEWYORK-1.

- Complete Tasks 25c-f as the Administrator on the server LONDON-1.

Task 25a: Removing Exchange Server

1. Insert the Exchange Server installation CD-ROM and exit any application that might be launched automatically.

2. Click the **Start** button, point to **Settings**, click **Control Panel**, double-click the **Add/Remove Programs** applet, and then click the **Install** button.

3. Click the **Next** button, type the letter of your CD-ROM and then *\SERVER\SETUP\i386\SETUP*, and then click **Finish**.

4. A **Microsoft Exchange Server Setup** dialog box appears. Click **Remove All**.

5. A **Microsoft Exchange Server Setup** dialog box appears, asking you to verify that you want to remove Exchange Server. Click **Yes**.

6. A **Microsoft Exchange Server Setup** dialog box appears, stating that the Internet Information Server services will be stopped temporarily. Click **OK**.

7. The **Microsoft Exchange Server Setup** dialog box appears, asking whether you wish to remove shared messaging components. Click **No**.

8. Files are removed as Exchange Server 5.5 is removed. The **Microsoft Exchange Server Setup** message box appears, stating that the Exchange Server Setup has completed the removal of Exchange Server. Click **OK**.

9. Shut down and restart Windows NT.

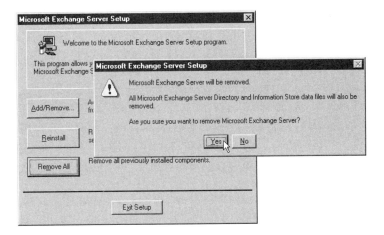

Task 25b: Removing NEWYORK-2 Residual Information from the Directory Store on NEWYORK-1

1. Click the **Start** button, point to **Programs**, point to **Microsoft Exchange**, and then click **Microsoft Exchange Administrator**.

   Note CAUTION: Do not proceed beyond this point until the server NEWYORK-2 has completed its restart process.

2. Expand the site object **NEWYORK**, expand the **Configuration** container, expand the **Servers** container, and then click **NEWYORK-2**.

3. On the **Edit** menu, click **Delete** to display the **Deleting Server NEWYORK-2** dialog box, which verifies that NEWYORK-2 is inaccessible.

4. A **Microsoft Exchange Administrator** dialog box appears, asking if you want to delete server NEWYORK-2 without first moving the mailboxes and gateways. Click **Yes**.

   Note For demonstration purposes, the mailboxes on server NEWYORK-2 were not moved to NEWYORK-1 beforehand. Of course, a cautious administrator would use the **Move Mailbox** command on the **Tools** menu to move all mailbox resources to another server before removing a server.

5. A **Microsoft Exchange Administrator** dialog box appears, stating that all public folder instances on NEWYORK-2 will be deleted and asking if you are sure that you want to delete server NEWYORK-2. Click **Yes**.

6. An **MS Mail Connector** message box appears. Click **OK**.

7. Another **MS Mail Connector** message box appears. Click **OK**.

8. A **Microsoft Exchange Administrator** message box appears, stating that the server NEWYORK-2 has been deleted. Click **OK**.

9. Verify that NEWYORK-2 is no longer visible in **NEWYORK**.

10. Click **NEWYORK-1**. On the **File** menu, click **Properties**.

11. The **NEWYORK-1 Properties** dialog box appears. Click the **Advanced** tab.

12. Click **Consistency Adjuster**.

13. In the **DS/IS Consistency Adjustment** dialog box, select the **All Inconsistencies** option.

14. Click **OK**.

15. A **Microsoft Exchange Administrator** dialog box appears, stating that DS/IS consistency will take ownership and change permissions on all public folders from unknown sites. Click **OK**.

16. A **Microsoft Exchange Administrator** message box appears, stating that DS/IS consistency has been successfully verified. Click **OK**.

17. The **NEWYORK-1 Properties** dialog box reappears. Click **OK**.

18. On the **File** menu, click **Exit**.

19. Log off from Windows NT.

Note Now you must completely format the Windows NT server NEWYORK-2 if you have only two server computers available. The new Windows NT Server computer should be named LONDON-1 and should be installed as a PDC in a domain called ENGLAND. Be sure that the IIS will be installed during Setup. You must also install Windows NT SP3 or higher and install Active Server Pages from the SP CD-ROM.

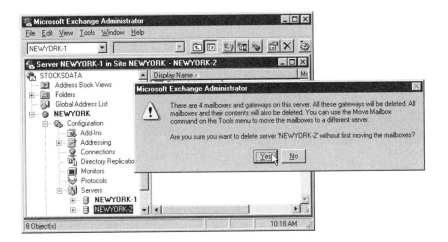

Task 25c: Creating the Site Services Account

1. Press CTRL+ALT+DEL to log on to server LONDON-1, which has just been installed in the domain ENGLAND.

2. The **Logon Information** dialog box appears. In the **User Name** box, type *Administrator*; in the **Password** box, type *password* and then click **OK**.

3. Click the **Start** button, point to **Programs**, point to **Administrative Tools (Common)**, and then click **User Manager For Domains**.

4. On the **User** menu, click **New User**.

5. The **New User** dialog box appears.

6. Create the new user using the following information:

In this box	You supply
User Name	*ServiceExchange* (note that there is no space between Service and Exchange)
Full Name	*Exchange Account*
Description	*Microsoft Exchange Server Service London*
Password	*password*
Confirm Password	*password*

7. Clear the **User Must Change Password At Next Logon** check box.

8. Select the **Password Never Expires** check box.

9. Click **Add**. A blank **New User** dialog box appears.

10. Click **Close**, and then exit User Manager.

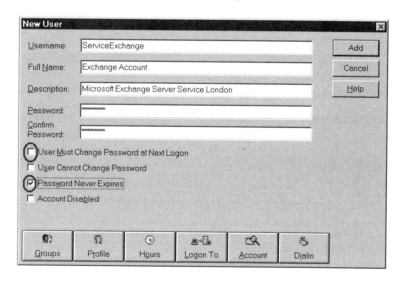

Task 25d: Installing Exchange Server

1. Insert the Exchange Server CD-ROM and exit any application that might be launched automatically.

2. Click the **Start** button, point to **Settings**, click **Control Panel**, double-click **Add/Remove Programs**, and then click **Install**.

3. Click the **Next** Button, type the letter of your CD-ROM drive followed by :*SERVER\SETUP\i386\SETUP*, and then click **Finish.**

4. A **Microsoft Exchange Server Setup** license dialog box appears. Click **Accept**.

5. A **Microsoft Exchange Server Setup** dialog box appears, displaying installation options. Click **Complete/Custom**.

6. The **Microsoft Exchange Server Setup – Complete/Custom** dialog box appears. Verify that the default options are selected, and then click **Continue**.

7. A **Microsoft Exchange Server** dialog box appears, stating that the Internet Information Server services will be stopped temporarily. Click **OK**.

8. A **Microsoft Exchange Server** dialog box appears, asking for your CD Key. Enter the correct ID and click **OK**.

9. A **Microsoft Exchange Server** dialog box appears, displaying your Product ID. Click **OK**.

10. The **Licensing** dialog box appears. Select the **I Agree That** check box, and then click **OK**.

11. The **Organization And Site** dialog box appears.

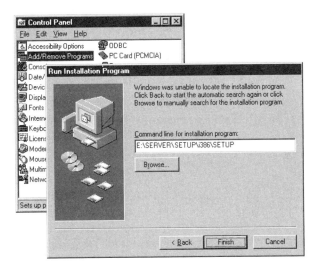

Task 25e: Creating a New Site

1. Verify that **Create A New Site** is selected.

2. Type *STOCKSDATA* for the organization name and *LONDON* for the site name (both in all capital letters) to identify your Exchange Server site. Click **OK**.

3. A Microsoft Exchange Server Setup message appears, prompting you to confirm the creation of a new site. Click **Yes**.

4. The **Site Services Account** dialog box appears, prompting for an account name and password to use.

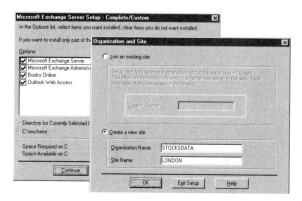

Task 25f: Assigning the Site Services Account

1. In the **Site Services Account** dialog box, click **Browse**.

2. The **Add User Or Group** dialog box appears. In the **Names** list box, select **ServiceExchange**, and then click **Add**. Click **OK**.

3. The **Site Services Account** dialog box reappears, displaying the account name you selected.

4. In the **Account Password** box, type *password* and then click **OK**.

5. A **Microsoft Exchange Server Setup** dialog box appears, listing the additional rights that have been granted to the **ServiceExchange** account. Click **OK**.

6. Exchange Server will be installed. At the end of the setup procedure, a **Microsoft Exchange Server Setup** dialog box will appear. It is a good idea to click the **Run Optimizer** button to optimize the server installation.

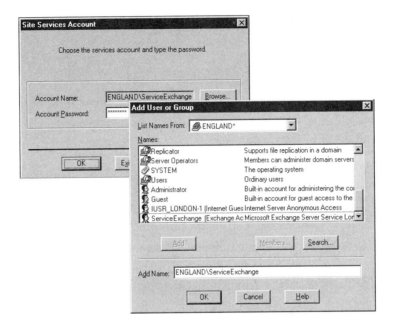

Task 25g: Verifying the Installation

1. Click the **Start** button, point to **Settings**, and then click **Control Panel**.

2. Double-click the **Services** icon, and then verify that the following services have started:

   - Microsoft Exchange Directory

   - Microsoft Exchange Event Service

   - Microsoft Exchange Information Store

   - Microsoft Exchange Message Transfer Agent

   - Microsoft Exchange System Attendant

   - Remote Procedure Call (RPC) Locator

   - Remote Procedure Call (RPC) Service

3. Close **Services**, and then exit the **Control Panel**.

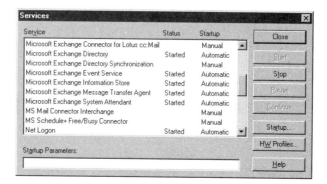

Task 25h: Creating an Administrative User Account

1. Click the **Start** button, point to **Programs**, point to **Administrative Tools (Common)**, and then click **User Manager For Domains**.

2. **User Manager** appears. On the **User** menu, click **New User**.

3. The **New User** dialog box appears.

4. Use the following information to create a new user:

In this box	You supply
Username	*Admin-L1*
Full Name	*Administrator London-1*
Description	*Microsoft Exchange Server Administrator*
Password	*password*
Confirm password	*password*

5. Clear the **User Must Change Password At Next Logon** check box.

6. Select the **Password Never Expires** check box.

7. Click **Groups** to display the **Group Memberships** dialog box.

8. In the **Not Member Of** list box, select **Domain Admins**, and then click **Add**. Click **OK**.

9. The **New User** dialog box appears. Click **Add**.

10. The **Connect To Server** dialog box appears, prompting for a server to connect to.

11. Click **Browse**, verify that **LONDON-1** is selected, and then click **OK**.

12. The **Connect To Server** dialog box appears, displaying **LONDON-1**. Select the **Set As Default** check box, and then click **OK**.

13. The **Administrator London-1 Properties** dialog box appears. Click **Cancel**.

Note You will create a mailbox for this Windows NT account in Task 25m, so you should cancel the mailbox creation at this point.

---

14. A blank **New User** dialog box appears. Click **Close**.

15. Select **Admin-L1**.

16. On the **User** menu, click **New Local Group**.

17. Type *Local-L1* in the **Group Name** box. The **New Local Group** dialog box appears.

18. Type *Exchange Local Admins Group in London* in the **Description** box.

19. Click **OK**.

20. On the **User** menu, click **Exit**.

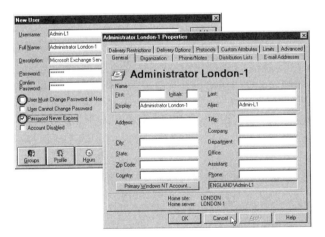

Task 25i: Configuring the Administrator Program to Show Individual Permissions Attributes When Assigning Permissions

1. Click the **Start** button, point to **Programs**, point to **Microsoft Exchange**, and then click **Microsoft Exchange Administrator**.

2. The **Connect To Server** dialog box appears. If the server LONDON-1 is not already displayed, click **Browse**. If it is displayed, skip to step 4.

3. The **Server Browser** dialog box appears. Click **LONDON-1**, and then click **OK**. The **Connect To Server** dialog box reappears.

4. Select the **Set As Default** check box, and then click **OK**.

5. **Microsoft Exchange Administrator** appears. On the **Tools** menu, click **Options**.

6. The **Options** dialog box appears. Click the **Permissions** tab.

7. Select the **Display Rights For Roles On Permissions Page** check box, and then click **OK**.

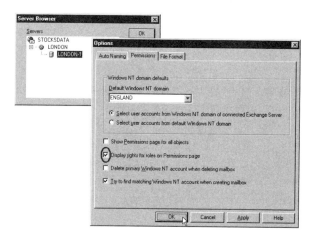

Task 25j: Configuring Site Permissions

1. In the left pane, click the site object **LONDON**. On the **File** menu, click **Properties**.

2. The **LONDON Properties** dialog box appears.

3. Click the **Permissions** tab.

4. Click **Add**.

5. The **Add Users And Groups** dialog box appears. In the **Names** box, click **Local-L1**, and then click **Add**.

6. Click **OK**.

7. A **Microsoft Exchange Administrator** message box appears, notifying you that Local groups can be used only in the domain in which they are created, so members of this group will not be able to administer this resource from other domains. Click **OK.**

8. Notice that **ENGLAND\Local-L1** has been added with the role of **Admin**.

9. In the **Windows NT Accounts With Permissions** box, verify that **ENGLAND\Local-L1** is selected. In the **Roles** list, select **Permissions Admin**.

10. Click **OK**.

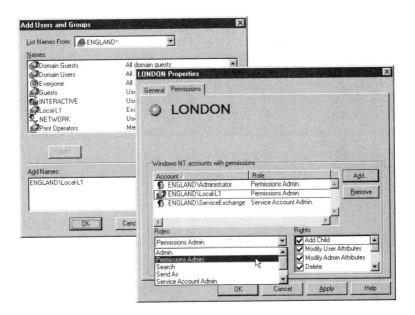

Task 25k: Configuring Permissions for the Configuration Container

1. Expand the site-object **LONDON**, and then select the **Configuration** container.

2. On the **File** menu, click **Properties**.

3. The **Configuration Properties** dialog box appears. Click the **Permissions** tab.

4. Click **Add**.

5. The **Add Users And Groups** dialog box appears. In the **Names** box, click **Local-L1**, and then click **Add**.

6. Click **OK**.

7. A **Microsoft Exchange Administrator** message box appears, notifying you that Local groups can be used only in the domain in which they are created, so members of this group will not be able to administer this resource from other domains. Click **OK**.

8. Notice that **ENGLAND\Local-L1** has been added with the role of **Admin**.

9. In the **Windows NT Accounts With Permissions** box, verify that **ENGLAND\Local-L1** is selected. In the **Roles** list, select **Permissions Admin**.

10. Click **OK**.

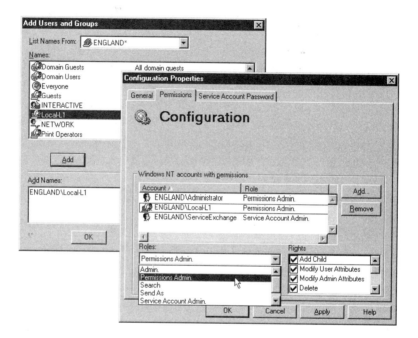

Task 25I: Changing the Site SMTP Address

1. In the right pane, double-click the **Site Addressing** object.

2. The **Site Addressing Properties** dialog box appears. Click the **Site Addressing** tab.

3. Select the **SMTP** address, and then click **Edit**.

4. The **SMTP Properties** dialog box appears. In the **Address** box, delete **LONDON.** from the address. Be sure to remove the period after **LONDON** but leave the @ symbol. Change the top-level domain identifier from *com* to *uk*.

5. Click **OK**.

6. The updated site addressing information appears, displaying e-mail addresses including the new SMTP address. Click **OK**.

7. A **Microsoft Exchange Administrator** dialog box appears, indicating that the SMTP site address has been modified and asking if you want to update recipient e-mail addresses now. Click **Yes**.

8. A **Microsoft Exchange Administrator** message box appears, indicating that the recipient e-mail addresses are being updated.

9. Click **OK**.

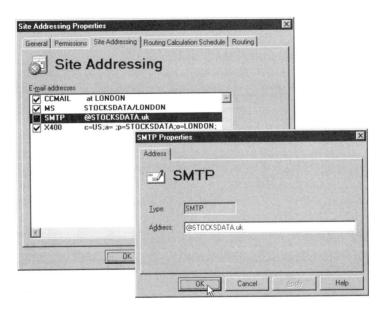

Task 25m: Creating a Mailbox

1. On the **File** menu, click **New Mailbox**.

2. A **Microsoft Exchange Administrator** dialog box appears, prompting you to switch to the **Recipients** container of the site LONDON. Click **OK**.

3. The **Properties** dialog box appears. In the **First** box, type *Admin-L1* and then click **OK**.

4. A **Microsoft Exchange Administrator** dialog box appears, asking if you want to use the Windows NT account **Admin-L1** in domain **ENGLAND** for this mailbox. Click **Yes**.

5. On the **File** menu, click **New Mailbox** to display the **Properties** dialog box again.

6. In the **First** box, type *Robin*. In the **Last** box, type *Sherwood,* then click **OK**.

7. The **Primary Windows NT Account** dialog box appears. Select **Create A New Windows NT Account**, and then click **OK**.

8. The **Create Windows NT Account** dialog box appears, showing the **NT Domain** and the **Account Name**. Click **OK**.

9. A message box appears with the following message: "The Windows NT Account you just created was given a blank password. The user will be required to change the password upon first logon." Click **OK**.

10. On the **File** menu, click **Exit**.

11. Log off Windows NT.

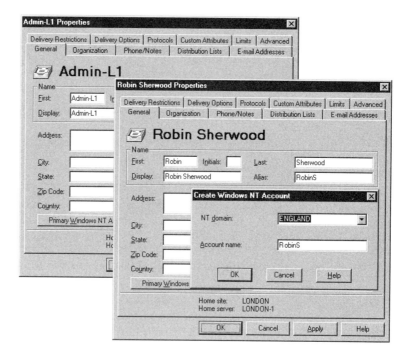

Task 25n: Installing Outlook

1. To log on, press CRTL+ALT+DEL.

2. In the **User Name** box, type *Admin-L1*.

3. In the **Password** box, type *password*, and then click OK.

4. Start the **Services** applet of the Control Panel to stop the **Microsoft Exchange System Attendant** (and all other Exchange Server services). Close the **Services** applet and the **Control Panel**.

5. Insert the Outlook 97 CD into your CD-ROM drive.

6. Click the **Start** button, point to **Settings**, and then click **Control Panel**. The **Control Panel** appears.

7. Double-click **Add/Remove Programs**, and then click **Install**.

8. Click the **Next** button.

9. Click **Browse**.

10. A **Browse** dialog box appears. Double-click on the folder **Outlook.w32**, select the **Setup** file, and click **Open**.

11. Click **Finish**.

12. A **Microsoft Outlook 97 Setup** dialog box appears. Click **Continue**.

13. The **Name And Organization Information** dialog box appears, prompting for registration information.

14. In the **Name** box, type *Admin-L1*.

15. In the **Organization** box, type *STOCKSDATA* and then click **OK**.

16. Click **OK** to confirm the registration information.

17. A **Microsoft Outlook 97 Setup** dialog box appears, prompting you for the CD Key. Enter the CD Key of your Outlook version, then click **OK**.

18. A **Microsoft Outlook 97 Setup** dialog box appears, displaying your Product ID.

19. Click **OK**.

20. A **Microsoft Outlook 97 Setup** dialog box appears, displaying a default directory path. Click **OK**.

21. A **Microsoft Outlook 97 Setup** dialog box appears, displaying installation options. Click **Custom**.

22. The **Microsoft Outlook 97 Setup - Custom** dialog box appears. Click the **Select All** button.

23. Click **Continue**.

24. Files are copied to the local hard disk.

25. A **Microsoft Outlook Client Setup** message box appears, indicating that the setup was completed successfully. Click **OK**.

26. Reboot the Windows NT Server computer.

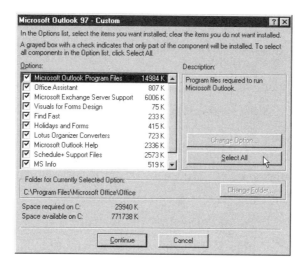

Task 25o: Creating a New Profile for Admin-L1

1. Log on as Admin-L1 to the server LONDON-1.

2. Click the **Start** button, point to **Settings**, and then click **Control Panel**.

3. The **Control Panel** appears.

4. Double-click the **Mail** or **Mail And Fax** icon. The **Mail** dialog box appears. Click **Add**.

5. The **Microsoft Outlook Setup Wizard** dialog box appears.

6. Clear all check boxes except the **Microsoft Exchange Server** check box. Click **Next**.

7. A **Microsoft Outlook Setup Wizard** dialog box appears, prompting for your Exchange Server computer and mailbox name.

8. In the **Microsoft Exchange Server** box, type *LONDON-1*

9. Verify that the **Mailbox** name is **Admin-L1**, and then click **Next**.

10. A **Microsoft Outlook Setup Wizard** dialog box appears, asking if you travel with this computer. Verify that **No** is selected, and then click **Next**.

11. A **Microsoft Outlook Setup Wizard** dialog box appears, prompting for the personal Address Book filename. In the edit box, type *C:\OUTLOOK\Admin-L1.PAB*, and then click **Next**.

12. A **Microsoft Outlook Setup Wizard** dialog box appears, indicating that the configuration is complete. Click **Finish**.

13. The **Mail** or **Mail And Fax** dialog box reappears. Verify that the profile **Admin-L1** is selected, and then click **Properties**.

14. The **Admin-L1 Properties** dialog box appears. Click **Add**.

15. The **Add Service To Profile** dialog box appears. Select **Personal Folders**, and then click **OK.**

16. The **Create/Open Personal Folders File** dialog box appears. Change to the C:\Outlook directory, type *Admin-L1.PST* in the **File Name** field, and then click **Open**.

17. The **Create Microsoft Personal Folders** dialog box appears. Click **OK**.

18. The **Admin-L1 Properties** dialog box reappears. Click **OK**.

19. The **Mail** or **Mail And Fax** dialog box reappears. Click **Close**.

20. Exit the **Control Panel**.

21. On the **Desktop**, double-click the **Microsoft Outlook** shortcut and log on with the profile **Admin-L1**. Notice that Outlook creates sample items for the new mailbox.

22. The **Office Assistant** appears, displaying a **Welcome To Microsoft Outlook!** dialog box. Clear the **Show These Choices At Startup** check box and click **OK**.

23. Exit **Microsoft Outlook**.

24. Log off from Windows NT.

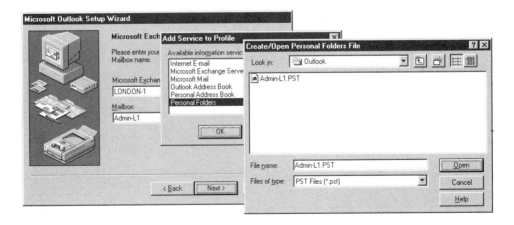

Review

To remove Exchange Server, the administrator must start the Setup program. Three options are provided: **Add/Remove Programs**, **Reinstall**, and **Remove All**. Click the **Remove All** button to start the removal process. In addition to public folders, all mailboxes that reside on the server will be deleted as well. It is therefore advisable to move existing mailboxes to another server in the same site before starting the removal process. Likewise, be careful about public folders, especially the Offline Address Book, messaging connectors, and directory replication connectors.

Once a server has been removed, you must clean out the site directory that will still contain a representation of the former server. Directory objects can be removed using the Administrator program. Within the **Servers** container, select the directory object that references the old server (for example, NEWYORK-2). Then select **Delete** on the **Edit** menu. The Administrator program will verify that Exchange Server no longer exists in the computer network and delete the reference from the directory. To ensure that the removal of a server has not left orphaned objects in the directory, you should run the DS/IS Consistency Checker. You can launch this program by clicking the **Consistency Adjuster** button using the local server object's **Advanced** property page.

To install a new Exchange Server in a new site, you must log on as an administrator. By default, the installing user gets administrator permissions on the new site. Additional administrators can be designated later on. Windows NT groups can simplify this task. Additional administrators need the Admin or Permissions Admin rights on all three security levels: organization, site, and configuration.

If you have installed the Exchange Server on a new Windows NT Server computer, potential clients must use an appropriate profile in order to connect. First, you must create mailboxes on the server and assign the correct Windows NT user permissions. You can then configure clients to connect to the new server. At a minimum, you must specify the desired mailbox and server name using the properties of the Microsoft Exchange Server transport service.

Lesson 2: The Site Connector

The Site Connector provides an efficient, easy to configure message paths between two Exchange sites. Because this connector offers many advantages, it is typically the administrator's first choice when connecting a multiple-site organization.

This lesson introduces the general features of the Site Connector and describes its configuration. It also explains how to select potential target servers in remote sites and how Windows NT security affects Site Connector configuration.

At the end of this lesson, you will be able to:

- Describe the Site Connector features
- Create and configure the Site Connector
- Determine target server costs
- Create a Site Connector in a non-trusted Windows NT domain topology

Estimated time to complete this lesson: 45 minutes

Site Connector Considerations

The Site Connector is easy to configure. It uses RPC as its communication mechanism and therefore requires a LAN-like connection, as shown in Figure 9-6. In some environments, the Site Connector can operate about 20 percent faster than the X.400 Connector.

RPC Encryption

Site Connectors can benefit from secure RPC connections. An exception is the French Exchange Server version, because France prohibits the importation of encryption technology. In all other versions, however, Windows NT uses a 40-bit encryption algorithm to secure data transmission over RPC. In other words, interpersonal and server-to-server messages of any kind are secured when they are transferred through a Site Connector.

Note Server-based RPC encryption is enabled by default. In contrast, client-based RPC encryption (Outlook–Exchange Server communication) is not secured. Nevertheless, you can enable encrypted RPCs for client-based communication on the **Advanced** tab of the Microsoft Exchange Server transport service.

Simplified Creation

When an administrator creates a Site Connector, most of the configuration information is retrieved from the remote site. This simplifies configuration significantly. You can configure the Site Connector in the local site and in the remote site at the same time within the same instance of the Administrator program. To do so, you must be logged on with an account that has Permissions Admin rights in both sites.

Faster Operation

The Site Connector operates faster than other connectors because it doesn't have to convert the Exchange Server data format into another format. It transfers the information directly to the remote site using RPC over TCP/IP, IPX/SPX, or NetBEUI.

Note Server-to-server communication within a site cannot rely on NetBEUI, but the communication between sites on top of this protocol is supported.

Most Reliable Connector

The Site Connector, by default, can contact every server in a remote site in order to transfer messages. All existing servers are potential target servers. If one server is temporarily unavailable, the Site Connector connects to another one and sends the message to the destination site. In other words, the Site Connector is reliable because it does not depend on a particular server in the remote site. The Site Connector maintains a list of all potential target servers. You can read more about target servers and their configuration in the section, "Target Server Cost," later in this lesson.

The following are features of the Site Connector:

- Easy to configure because it reads required configuration data from the remote site's directory

- Can automatically configure both the local and remote sides of the Site Connector

- Requires permanent connection RPC over TCP/IP, IPX/SPX, or NetBEUI

- Uses 40-bit encryption during data transfer

- Is the most efficient connector

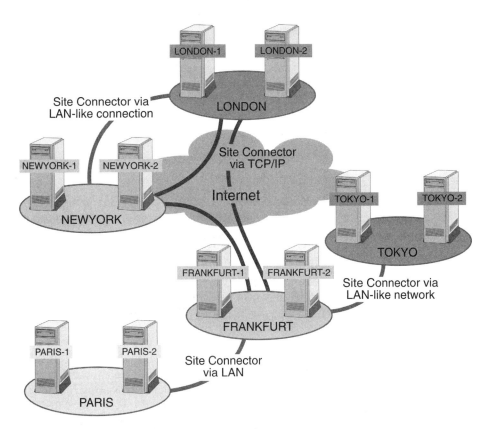

Figure 9-6. Possible Site Connector connections.

Configuring the Site Connector

You can create and configure a Site Connector using the **Site Connector** command under the **New Other** option on the Administrator program's **File** menu. You can then find a corresponding configuration object for each connector within the **Connections** container under the site's configuration object. The **Site Connector** command might be missing if you are not using Exchange Server 5.5 Enterprise Edition. In this case, you must install the connector package first.

Existing Remote Server

As shown in Figure 9-7, the NetBIOS name of one remote server computer is the most important configuration parameter; you must provide it when you create a new Site Connector. This server will be accessed to automatically retrieve the required configuration information about the remote site (such as the list of all existing servers).

Target Servers

Target servers are potential communication partners that a Site Connector can contact if messages need to be transferred. By default, all existing servers in a remote site are listed as target servers. You can assign different cost factors to particular target servers to implement load balancing. You can also exclude specific servers from the list by using the **Target Servers** property page of your Site Connector. Target server configuration issues are covered in "Target Server Cost," later in this lesson.

Messaging Bridgeheads

A messaging bridgehead server is an Exchange Server computer that performs all intersite communication for its local site. With a true messaging bridgehead, one dedicated local server can contact only one dedicated target server. If a server is dedicated to the bridgehead function, it can be optimized specifically for communication tasks. Use of a bridgehead is optional with a Site Connector. Although the bridgehead will relieve other servers in the site from intersite connections, the reliability of the Site Connector is reduced because the bridgehead server must be available to transfer messages to another site.

On the Site Connector's **General** property page, you will see the **Messaging Bridgehead In The Local Site** option. By default, it is set to **Any Server**, which means that all local servers can transfer messages across site boundaries. However, if you want to use a messaging bridgehead, you must select one existing server as a messaging bridgehead for the local site. From there, messages that must be sent to a particular remote site will first be delivered to the messaging bridgehead before they are sent via the Site Connector to reach their destination.

So far, the local messaging bridgehead can still contact any existing remote server. As a result, the target server list must be restricted to only one server in order to implement a true bridgehead. You can achieve this by using the **Target Servers** property page.

As shown in Figure 9-6, you would need to take the following steps to implement a messaging bridgehead configuration between LONDON and NEWYORK:

1. Create the Site Connector between both sites.

2. On the **General** tab of the Site Connector in NEWYORK, specify NEWYORK-1 as the local bridgehead.

3. On the **General** tab of the Site Connector in LONDON, specify LONDON-1 as the local bridgehead.

4. Switch to the **Target Servers** property page of the connector in NEWYORK and remove LONDON-2 from the target service list.

5. Remove NEWYORK-2 from the target server list in LONDON.

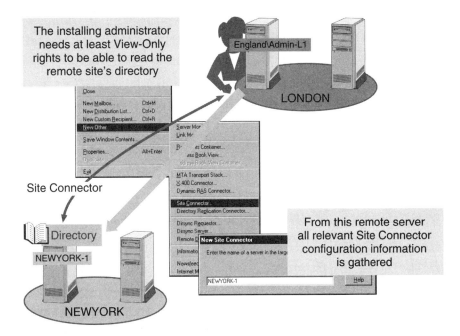

Figure 9-7. Retrieving Site Connector configuration information.

The Site Connector property pages and their functions are as follows:

- **Address Space**; which contains the X.400 address space for the remote site; you can add, edit, or remove further address spaces

- **General**; to identify the target site and set a connection cost; you can also designate a specific local server as a messaging bridgehead

- **Override**; to set up a Site Connector to a site with a different Site Services Account

- **Target Servers**; to specify which servers will receive messages and the costs associated with transmitting to each message

Target Server Cost

The target server cost is used to focus message traffic onto particular servers in the target site. Target server selection is based on the weighted average cost of all target servers available to the site connector. You can assign this value to target servers using the **Target Server** property page of a particular Site Connector.

Cost Factor

The cost factor, assigned on a per-server basis, can vary between 0 and 100. Specifying a value of 0 causes the Site Connector to use only this particular target server. A value of 100 causes the Site Connector to exclude the particular server from the message transfer. A server with a cost value of 100 will be contacted only if all other target servers are unavailable.

Target Server Load Balancing

Target server load balancing means the distribution of messages between servers based on the weighted average of cost factors. For example, a Site Connector with two target servers will transfer approximately two-thirds of the messages to the first server and the other third to the second server if the cost values of the first and second server are 5 and 50. (See Figure 9-8.)

The calculation of the Site Connector workload can be confusing if more than two servers are contacted in the target site. Generally, all assigned cost factors must be taken into consideration. You can determine the probability with which a possible target server will be contacted by using the following formula: Probability [in %] = 100 * {(100 – cost factor of target server) / [(number of target servers * 100) – (sum of all cost factors)]}.

Server	Cost	Difference = 100 - cost	Probability [in %] = 100 * (difference/sum)
Server A	1	99	44.2
Server B	50	50	22.3
Server C	50	50	22.3
Server D	75	25	11.2
Server E	100	0	0
Sum of all cost factors	276		
Sum = (number of target servers*100) – (sum of all cost factors)		224	

Because of the load balancing mechanism, the selected target server might not be the recipient's home server. This is not a problem, however, since the receiving target server can transfer the message to the recipient's home server using a direct RPC connection. The message might also be routed to a third site or to a foreign mail system.

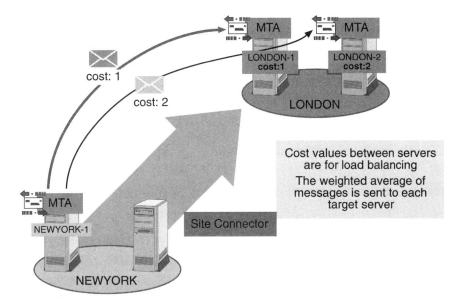

Figure 9-8. Load balancing between target servers.

The characteristics of the default target server are as follows:

- All target servers can be viewed on the **Target Servers** property page
- Each server in the remote site is a potential target server
- Site Connector reads the list of all existing servers from the directory of the specified remote server
- Target server in a remote site need not be the home server of the recipient

Site Connector Security with Windows NT Domains

Windows NT security issues play an important role in Site Connector configuration and operation. Disregarding these issues can lead to message transfer problems. Also, you cannot create a particular Site Connector if you don't have the required permission in both sites.

Required Administrative Permissions

When you create a Site Connector, you must specify an existing remote server that will be contacted in order to retrieve important configuration information. To simplify the process further, you can also create the connector in both sites at the same time. Your Windows NT account must have at least the permissions of a View-Only Admin at the site level and Admin rights on the **Connections** container. Typically, however, you will be a Permissions Admin in the local site and in the remote site if you want to configure both ends of the connector.

Site Connector creation can become difficult if you need to connect two sites that have been implemented in different Windows NT domains without a trust relationship. For instance, an administrator account in NEWYORK cannot have the Permissions Admin rights in LONDON because the account is simply not available. Hence, the remote server cannot be contacted, the required configuration information cannot be retrieved, and the Site Connector cannot be created. Windows NT provides a solution for this problem without requiring the creation of a trust relationship, but you must create two identical administrator accounts, one in NEWYORK and one in LONDON. If the administrator name and password match exactly, you can use this account to create the Site Connector.

Note Windows NT domain controllers validate a user from a nontrusted domain and grant access to local resources if an identical local user account (account name and password) exists. You can use this identical account to grant a remote administrator the rights of a Permissions Admin in the local site. Nonetheless, the target Exchange Server must be installed on a domain controller; otherwise, this validation mechanism will not be available.

Overriding Service Account Information

The Site Connector communicates with the target server using RPC over TCP/IP, IPX/SPX, or NetBEUI. By default, the Site Connector will use the Site Services Account to connect to the remote site . If two sites use the same Site Services Account, access will be granted and messages can be transferred, but different sites might use different Site Services Accounts. In such a case, message transfer is impossible as long as the mismatching account information is not adjusted using the **Override** property page on the Site Connector.

As shown in Figure 9-9, the site NEWYORK uses the service account STOCKSDATA\ExchangeService (STOCKSDATA is the account's Windows NT domain and ExchangeService is the service's username). ENGLAND\ServiceExchange, on the other hand, is the service account for LONDON. Obviously, the account information does not match. Therefore, the Site

Connector between these sites requires further administration. To adjust the required information, use the connector's **Override** property page. Specify the account ENGLAND\ServiceExchange for the connector in NEWYORK, and then specify STOCKSDATA\ExchangeService for the connector in LONDON. Once you do this, the Site Connector in NEWYORK can use ENGLAND\ServiceExchange to establish connections with either LONDON-1 or LONDON-2. The Site Connector in LONDON takes the override information STOCKSDATA\ExchangeService to establish connections with NEWYORK-1 and NEWYORK-2. Messages can then be transferred between the sites.

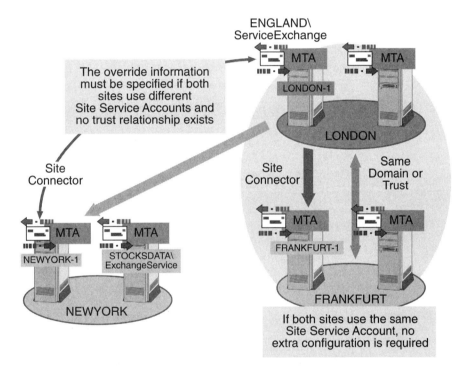

Figure 9-9. Site Connector security dependencies.

The following are important points about managing Site Connector security:

- If both sites use the same service account, no further configuration is required.

- If the service accounts for the sites are different, you can use the **Override** property page to identify the remote service account.

Exercise 26: Configuring the Site Connector

The Site Connector is the most powerful messaging connector. It can operate in LAN-like environments using TCP/IP, the NWLink IPX/SPX-compatible Transport, or NetBEUI. On top of these LAN protocols, the Site Connector uses RPC for communication.

Estimated time to complete this exercise: 25 minutes

Description

In this exercise, you will configure a Site Connector between NEWYORK and LONDON. The computers NEWYORK-1 and LONDON-1 should both be installed as PDCs in their own domains. A trust relationship must not exist between them. Therefore, you must create an identical user account in both Windows NT domains. The accounts must be administrators in their local Exchange sites as mentioned in the section, "Site Connector Security with Windows NT Domains," earlier in this lesson.

Since both sites are configured with different Site Services Accounts, you must enter the service account information for each remote site using the **Override** property page. This enables the Site Connector to contact the remote server on behalf of the correct account.

Note Be careful when specifying Override information. The Site Connector cannot transfer messages if wrong information (such as the wrong account name, password, or domain name) has been entered. In this case, you might see the following error in the Application Event Log: *Event-ID 9318, "An RPC communications error occurred. Unable to bind over RPC. Locality Table (LTAB) index: 3, NT/MTA error code: 5. Comms error5, Bind error 0, Remote Server Name LONDON-1 [MAIN BASE 1 500 %10] (14)."*

- Task 26a describes the steps for creating identical Windows NT accounts in two nontrusted domains.

- Task 26b describes the steps for establishing a Site Connector in both directions between two sites.

- Task 26c describes the steps for testing a Site Connector.

Prerequisites

- You must have two Exchange Server computers in different sites.

- Make sure that the servers are installed in different domains with no trust relationship between them. The servers must therefore use different Site Services Accounts.

- You must log on to both computers using an account that has administrative privileges on the Exchange sites.

- Make sure that either Outlook or the Exchange Client is installed on both test computers.

Task 26a: Creating a Common Installation Account

1. Press CTRL+ALT+DEL to log on to the server LONDON-1.

2. In the **User Name** box, type *Admin-L1*.

3. In the **Password** box, type *password*, and then click **OK**.

4. Click the **Start** button, point to **Programs**, point to **Administrative Tools (Common)** and then click **User Manager For Domains**.

5. In the User Manager, select the **Admin-L1** account and press **F8** to display the **Copy Of Admin-L1** dialog box.

6. In the **Username** box, type *Admin-NY1*.

7. In the **Full Name** box, type *Administrator New York-1*.

8. In the **Description** box, type *Shadow Account for Site Connector Installation*.

9. In the **Password** box, type *password*. Type *password* in the **Confirm Password** box as well.

10. Clear the **User Must Change Password At Next Logon** check box.

11. Select the **Password Never Expires** check box if it is not already selected.

12. Click **Groups** and verify that the new account is a member of the local Exchange Administrators group. If it is not, select **Local-L1** in the **Not Member Of** list box and click the **Add** button.

13. Click **OK**.

14. Click **Add**.

15. The **Connect To Server** dialog box appears. Click **Cancel**.

16. Click **Close**.

17. Exit **User Manager for Domains**.

18. Log off Windows NT.

19. Log onto the server LONDON-1 as *Admin-NY1*.

20. Start the **Exchange Administrator** program and connect to server LONDON-1. Verify that the new account has permission to configure the site LONDON.

21. Right-click the **Network Neighborhood** icon on the **Desktop**.

22. Click **Explore**.

23. Open the **Entire Network** container.

24. Open the **Microsoft Windows Network** container.

25. Open the **STOCKSDATA** container and try to access the computer NEWYORK-1.

26. You will be granted access without being prompted for a password, even though the servers LONDON-1 and NEWYORK-1 exist in two different domains with no trust relationship between them.

27. Switch back to **Exchange Administrator**.

28. Open the **File** menu and click **Connect To Server**.

29. Enter *NEWYORK-1*, and then click **OK**.

30. Verify that Admin-NY1 has permission to configure the site NEWYORK.

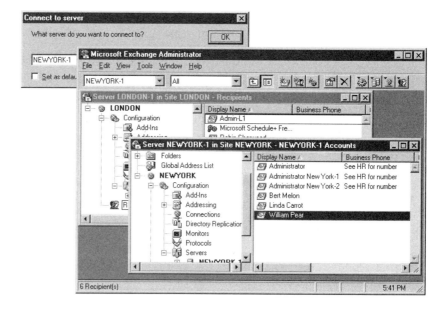

Task 26b: Configuring a Site Connector

1. Close the Administration window of the server NEWYORK-1; the Administration window of the server LONDON-1 should remain open within **Exchange Administrator**.

2. Open the **File** menu, point to **New Other**, and then click **Site Connector**.

3. A message box appears, indicating that you must switch to the **Connections** container of the LONDON site to create a connector. Click **OK**.

4. A **New Site Connector** dialog box appears. Enter *NEWYORK-1* as the server name in the target site and click **OK**.

5. The **Site Connector (NEWYORK) Properties** dialog box appears. Click the **Override** tab.

6. In the **Windows NT Username** box, type *ExchangeService*. (This is the service account name of the site NEWYORK.)

7. In the **Password** box, type *password* (the service account password of the site NEWYORK).

8. In the **Confirm Password** box, type *password*.

9. In the **Windows NT Domain Name** box, type *STOCKSDATA* (the domain name in NEWYORK).

10. Click **OK**.

11. A message box appears, asking if a site connector should be created in the remote site NEWYORK as well. Click **Yes**.

12. Switch to the **Override** property page.

13. In the **Windows NT Username** box, type *ServiceExchange* (the service account name of the site LONDON).

14. In the **Password** box, type *password* (the service account password of the site LONDON).

15. In the **Confirm Password** box, type *password*.

16. In the **Windows NT Domain Name** box, type *ENGLAND* (the domain name in LONDON).

17. Click **OK**.

18. A message box might appear, indicating that the Administrator program was unable to confirm that the service account ENGLAND\ServiceExchange has the required permissions in the site LONDON. Click **OK**.

19. Close **Exchange Administrator**.

Task 26c: Testing a Site Connector

1. Log on to the server NEWYORK-1 using the account Admin-NY1.

2. Log on to the server LONDON-1 using the account Admin-L1.

3. Start **Microsoft Outlook** on both computers. On NEWYORK-1, use a profile that opens the mailbox **Fred Pumpkin**.

4. On NEWYORK-1, open the **Tools** menu and click **Address Book**.

5. Double-click your address (i.e., **Fred Pumpkin**).

6. Switch to the **E-mail Addresses** property page.

7. Write down your X.400 O/R Address (for example, c=us; a= ;p=STOCKSDATA;o=NEWYORK;s=Pumpkin;g=Fred). (Note the space between "a=" and the next semicolon.)

8. Click **OK** and close the **Address Book** dialog box.

9. On the computer LONDON-1, click the **New Mail Message** icon on the toolbar.

10. In the **To** box, type the X.400 O/R Address gathered in step 7 (for example, *[X400:c=us;a= ;p=STOCKSDATA;o=NEWYORK;s=Pumpkin;g=Fred]*. (Note the space between "a=" and the next semicolon).

11. Enter a **Subject** and the following message text: *This is a Test-Message sent to the X.400-address of Fred Pumpkin via the Site Connector between LONDON and NEWYORK.*

12. Click the **Send** button on the toolbar.

13. Verify that the message was delivered to Fred Pumpkin on the server NEWYORK-1.

14. Reply to the message to confirm that message transfer works in both directions.

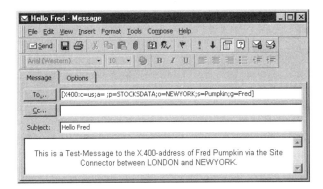

Review

You must have Permissions Admin rights in both sites if you want to configure a Site Connector. If multiple nontrusted Windows NT domains exist, you can create an identical user account for the administrator in both domains. The account names and passwords must be the same to access resources in the remote domain.

Configuring the Site Connector is easy. Essentially, you only have to specify the name of an existing remote server and configure the **Override** page when different Site Services Accounts are in use. On the connector's **Override** page, you must specify the account of the remote site. This allows the Site Connector to contact a remote server on behalf of the remote service account.

If a connection between sites has been configured, you should test the new message link. To address a test message to a recipient in the remote site, you can use the corresponding X.400 O/R Name. This address can be specified directly in the **To** line using the following format: *[X400: c=us; a= ;p=STOCKSDATA; o=NEWYORK; s=Pumpkin; g=Fred]*. The brackets belong to the address. You should send a test message in both directions to confirm that the new message path is working properly.

Lesson 3: The X.400 Connector

The Exchange Server messaging platform is compliant with international X.400 messaging standards. Using its X.400 Connector component, you can connect an organization to foreign messaging systems that also support the X.400 standard. You can also use this connector between Exchange sites. When connecting sites, however, you must keep in mind that you will implicitly implement messaging bridgeheads in your site. Further, the X.400 Connector does not support the concept of multiple target servers (which the Site Connector does).

This lesson covers the X.400 Connector installation and configuration and the three MTA transport stacks that can be used in conjunction with a X.400 Connector. It also includes an exercise on MTA transport stacks. This lesson also covers the configuration of the X.400 Connector object within the Administrator program. Another exercise will guide you through the steps to connect two sites using a X.400 Connector over TCP/IP.

At the end of this lesson, you will be able to:
- Describe the benefits of the X.400 Connector
- Configure the MTA transport stack
- Configure the X.400 Connector

Estimated time to complete this lesson: 45 minutes

X.400 Connector Considerations

The X.400 standard is an international guideline that was developed by an organization called the Comité Consultatif International Télégraphique et Téléphonique (CCITT). This organization no longer exists; a new agency of the United Nations called the International Telecommunications Union (ITU) has taken its place.

X.400 generally describes features for computer-based message handling systems. The standard is based on the Open Systems Interconnection (OSI) reference model and the protocols defined by International Standards Organization (ISO). X.400 allows users to exchange e-mail no matter what computer-based messaging handling system they are using.

X.400 Publication Schedule

The CCITT published updated X.400 recommendations every four years. Each update introduced new features but remained completely compatible with previous versions. The first real X.400 recommendation was published in 1984; it is known as the *Red Book* because of the color of its cover. The 1984 recommendation had several weaknesses in the area of message handling. The 1988 X.400 recommendation introduced more X.400 message body parts and envelope properties. For instance, *Object Identifiers* could be used to describe message attachments precisely so that, for instance, attachment names and other object properties could be preserved. The 1988 X.400 standard is called the *Blue Book*. The next standard, the *White Book*, was published in 1992. It mainly extended the addressing mechanism. It was the last publication of the CCITT. The ITU published another update in 1996—the *Green Book*.

Management Domains

X.400 messaging networks are segmented into several blocks called *management domains*. A management domain is basically a messaging network that is maintained by a single organization. This organization can be a public operating agency (such as a telecom organization) or a private company. Consequently, management domains are divided into *public management domains* and *private management domains*—also known as Administration Management Domains (ADMDs) and Private Management Domains (PRMDs). National and international e-mail messaging backbones are formed based on ADMDs and PRMDs. As recommended by the ITU, PRMDs handle private messages internally, and external messages destined to other PRMDs always go through its ADMD. In theory, PRMDs generally communicate with each other through ADMDs. In other words, they depend on ADMDs. ADMDs represent the highest level of X.400 management. However, in practice many PRMDs communicate directly with each other to reduce the transmission costs of e-mail messaging.

Originator/Recipient Names

X.400 systems use a complex addressing scheme for message routing and delivery. The four types of addresses, which are also called *O/R Names* or *O/R Addresses*, are Mnemonic, Numeric, Terminal, and Postal. A mnemonic address identifies a recipient based on country, ADMD, and PRMD. Further address information (such as surname and given name) is required to form the entire address. If you replace the additional information using a numeric identifier, you create a Numeric address. The Terminal address is formed by means of a network or terminal ID. Postal addresses identify the physical delivery system in which a user resides.

The following table shows O/R Name fields:

Label	Abbreviation	Attribute Type	Syntax
G	Given Name	Given name	G=Fred;
I	Initials	Initials	I=FP;
S	Surname	Surname	S=Pumpkin;
Q	Generation	Generation qualifier	Q=Sr;
CN	Common Name	Common name	CN=Fred Pumpkin;
X.121	X.121	X.121 address	X.121=493098722102
N-ID	N-ID	UA numeric ID	N-ID=208973240
T-TY	T-TY	Terminal type	T-TY=TTY;
T-ID	T-ID	Terminal identifier	T-ID=309;
O	Organization	Organization	O=NEWYORK;
OU1	Org.Unit.1	Organizational unit 1	OU1=Administration;
OU2	Org.Unit.2	Organizational unit 2	OU2=USA;
OU3	Org.Unit.3	Organizational unit 3	OU3=NY;
OU4	Org.Unit.4	Organizational unit 4	OU4=Manhattan;
P	PRMD	PRMD name	P=STOCKSDATA;
A	ADMD	ADMD name	A=MCI;
C	Country	Country	C=US;
DDA	DDA	Domain defined attribute	DDA:type=value (i.e., DDA:SMTP= *JohnA@sombrero.com*)

With the exception of the DDA field, O/R Names are not case sensitive.

Note The fields C, A, and P are mandatory; a valid X.400 address must also contain at least one of the optional fields for unique identification.

Message Types

The X.400 standard distinguishes between two general message types: interpersonal messages (IPMs) and interpersonal notifications (IPNs). IPMs are the actual messages that users send to recipients. IPNs convey status information, such as delivery reports. IPNs are primarily used to transport receipt (RN) or non-receipt (NR) information.

IPMs are the most important message class because they transport the actual user data. X.400, which is strongly influenced by standard business messaging practices, defines two general structures that make up an interpersonal message—the header and the body. The header contains information that is required for transporting the message to its destination, including recipient and originator addresses. It also includes routing information that will be inserted by the message handling system that transfers the message. The body contains the actual message. The message can consist of several body parts, which allows for attachments to be included with e-mail messages.

Let's say you have attached a Word document to an e-mail message. The resulting IPM body contains at least one block for the message text and one block for the Word document. The table below shows the defined body parts and the reference numbers that identify the data structures:

Body Part Number	Body Part
0	IA5 Text
1	Telex (ITA2 5-bit)
2	Voice
3	G3 Facsimile
4	Text Interchange Format (TIFO)
5	Telex (T.61)
6	Videotex
7	Nationally Defined
8	Encrypted
9	Forwarded IP Message
10	Simple Formatable Document (SFD)
11	Text Interchange Format 1 (TIF1)
12	Octet String
13	ISO6937 Text
14	Bilaterally-defined (Binary)
15	Binary File Transfer (first defined in 1988)

Protocol Stacks

The X.400 Connector allows an MTA to use three transport stacks for communication: TCP/IP, TP4/CLNP, and X.25. TCP/IP is used in the Internet and in intranets. Transport Protocol class 4 TP4 is an OSI protocol that uses

Connection-Less Networking Protocol CLNP. X.25 is a WAN protocol that supports packet-switching networks. (See Figure 9-10.) TCP/IP and TP4/CLNP let you connect a site to other X.400 systems and sites over a LAN. In X.25 WAN environments, you can configure the X.400 Connector for X.25 support. In this case, you must install an X.25 EICON card on the Exchange Server computer.

Message Handling

The X.400 Connector converts messages from the proprietary Exchange Server format into the correct X.400 format before they are transferred. The message conversion requires extra processing, which reduces performance. Therefore, this connector is less efficient than the Site Connector.

On the other hand, the X.400 Connector gives you more control over what goes across the messaging link. You can set message size limits, schedule connections, or allow particular users to make use of the connector. Messages that exceed the specified message size limit will not be transferred. This is an especially useful setting when you are connecting two sites through an expensive X.25 WAN connection or if you have limited network bandwidth available. You can also restrict the use of the connector on a per-user basis, and you can set a schedule as to when the connector should be activated.

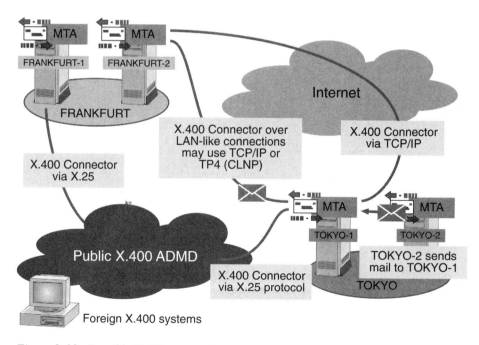

Figure 9-10. Possible X.400 connections.

The X.400 Connector has the following features:

- Allows you to control who can send messages through a particular connector

- Allows you to control when messages are transferred

- Can be used to connect to any X.400 system

- Is less efficient than the Site Connector because of message conversion

- Is more complex than the Site Connector

- Supports restriction of message size transfer

- Supports the TCP/IP, TP4, and X.25 protocols

MTA Transport Configuration

The configuration of an X.400 Connector is divided into two parts: the configuration of the MTA transport stack and the configuration of the X.400 Connector itself. First you must configure the MTA transport stack because this component provides access to the underlying network protocol—TCP/IP, TP4/CLNP, or X.25, as shown in Figure 9-11. The actual protocols must be configured at the Windows NT level. You can then continue the configuration through the X.400 Connector object itself. These configuration steps are covered later in this lesson in the section, "Configuring the X.400 Connector."

TCP/IP

The TCP/IP transport stack lets you establish X.400 connections through the Internet and intranets. To install this stack, you must first install the TCP/IP protocol and configure it within Windows NT. Next, start the Exchange Administrator program, open the **File** menu, point to **New Other**, and click **MTA Transport Stack**. A **New MTA Transport Stack** dialog box appears, in which you can select the **TCP/IP MTA Transport Stack** option. You usually don't have to specify further configuration settings because the local protocol configuration will be determined by the Windows NT Server con-figuration. You can, however, specify a Transport Service Access Point (TSAP), Session Service Access Point (SSAP), or Presentation Service Access Point (PSAP) using the **TCP (<*server name*>) Properties** dialog box. (You enter the TSAP, SSAP, and PSAP in the **T Selector**, **S Selector**, and **P Selector** boxes, respectively.)

TP4/CLNP

The second supported transport, TP4/CLNP (or TP4 for short), is much less common than TCP/IP. Implemented as a streams protocol within Windows NT, it guarantees reliable delivery of data packets because it uses sequence numbers and checksums. Nevertheless, TP4 is less powerful than TCP/IP because it requires the additional Streams environment under Windows NT. You can use TP4 to communicate with foreign X.400 systems or with remote Exchange Server computers. It is most often used to communicate with foreign X.400 systems that are unable to use the TCP/IP protocol (such as MS Mail Gateway to X.400).

You can install TP4 as you would any other Windows NT protocol—by using the **Network** applet in the Control Panel. The required files are on the Windows NT Server CD under Drvlib\Protocol\TP4Setup\i386. You should copy the contents of this directory to a floppy disk and install the protocol from there. During installation, the Service Access Point for the Network layer (NSAP) is configured automatically. By default, the computer name of the Exchange Server will be used. The TP4 NSAP is comparable to an IP address. To modify the address setting at any time, use the **Protocols** property page of the **Network** dialog box. Simply select the TP4/CLNP Protocol entry and click the **Configure** button.

Once you install the TP4 protocol, you can configure the TP4 MTA transport stack using the Administrator program. Open the **File** menu, point to **New Others**, and click **MTA Transport Stack**. Then select **TP4 MTA Transport Stack** and click **OK**. Further configuration is not required because the NSAP information will be retrieved from the Windows NT Server configuration. You can also specify a TSAP, SSAP, and PSAP using the **T Selector**, **S Selector**, and **P Selector** boxes, as mentioned above for the TCP/IP stack.

X.25

You can use the X.25 protocol to communicate with a remote X.400 system using a packet-switching network (such as a public X.400 provider). The X.25 protocol, also called Transport Protocol class 0 (TP0), is OSI-compliant and is designed specifically for WAN connections. A special computer adaptor—an X.25 card—and a synchronous modem are required. Exchange Server supports EICON X.25 cards only.

Before you can install the X.25 MTA transport stack, you must install an EICON card plus its Windows NT protocol drivers. The X.25 configuration is very complex and can be done only using the configuration utilities that come with the EICON X.25 card. The X.121 address is the most important information that must be configured. After that, select the **MTA Transport Stack** command under **New Others** on the Administrator program's **File** menu to select the **EICON X.25 MTA Transport Stack** option. During installation, the local X.121 address will be determined based on the Windows NT configuration. As usual, you can define additional service access points using the **T Selector**, **S Selector**, and **P Selector** boxes; however, these options are not necessarily required for proper X.400 Connector operation.

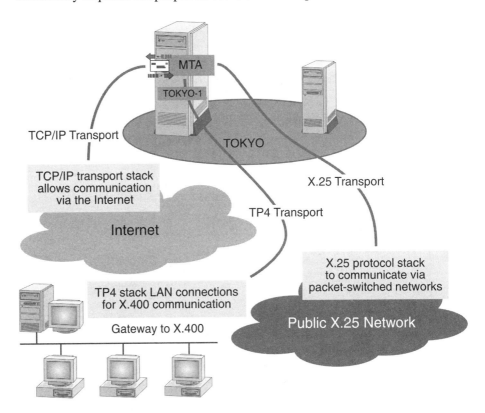

Figure 9-11. X.400 transport stacks.

The transport stacks have the following characteristics:

- TCP/IP stack is the most common and is used in LAN-like environments such as the Internet or intranets
- TP4/CLNP stack is the next fastest and is used in LANs
- X.25 stack is used to communicate through packet-switching networks

Exercise 27: Installing the TCP/IP MTA Transport Stack for Exchange

Configuring an X.400 Connector is a complex task. You must install the appropriate MTA transport stack before you can configure the X.400 Connector. The transport stack provides access to the installed Windows NT protocols and their corresponding configuration. In general, the X.400 Connector can use TCP/IP, TP4/CLNP, or the X.25 protocol.

Estimated time to complete this exercise: 15 minutes

Description

In this exercise, you will install the TCP/IP MTA transport stack and use it to complete the configuration of an X.400 Connector. Since TCP/IP is already installed and configured within Windows NT, only a few installation steps with the Administrator program are required.

- Task 27a describes the steps for configuring a TCP/IP MTA transport stack for use by the X.400 Connector on the server LONDON-1.

- Task 27b describes the steps for configuring a TCP/IP MTA transport stack for use by the X.400 Connector on the server NEWYORK-1.

Prerequisites

- Complete Task 27a logged on as Admin-L1 to LONDON-1.

- Complete Task 27b logged on as Admin-NY1 to NEWYORK-1.

- Make sure that TCP/IP is installed and configured on both Windows NT Server computers.

- Make sure that the communication between the computers through TCP/IP is operating without any problems. You should test the connectivity with **Ping** before performing this exercise.

Task 27a: Installing the TCP/IP MTA Transport Stack on the Exchange Server Computer LONDON-1

1. To log on, press CTRL+ALT+DEL.

2. In the **User name** box, type *Admin-L1*.

3. In the **Password** box, type *password* and then click **OK**.

4. Click the **Start** button, point to **Programs**, point to **Microsoft Exchange**, and then click **Microsoft Exchange Administrator**.

5. On the **File** menu, point to **New Other**, and then click **MTA Transport Stack** to display the **New MTA Transport Stack** dialog box.

6. In the **Type** box, click **TCP/IP MTA Transport Stack**.

7. In the **Server** box, click **LONDON-1**, and then click **OK**.

8. A **TCP (LONDON-1) Properties** dialog box appears. Click **OK**.

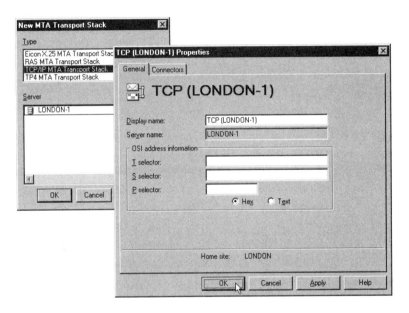

Task 27b: Installing the TCP/IP MTA Transport Stack on the Exchange Server Computer NEWYORK-1

1. To log on, press CTRL+ALT+DEL.

2. In the **User Name** box, type *Admin-NY1*.

3. In the **Password** box, type *password* and then click **OK**.

4. Click the **Start** button, point to **Programs**, point to **Microsoft Exchange**, and then click **Microsoft Exchange Administrator**.

5. On the **File** menu, point to **New Other**, and then click **MTA Transport Stack** to display the **New MTA Transport Stack** dialog box.

6. In the **Type** box, click **TCP/IP MTA Transport Stack**.

7. In the **Server** box, click **NEWYORK-1**, and then click **OK**.

8. A **TCP (NEWYORK-1) Properties** dialog box appears. Click **OK**.

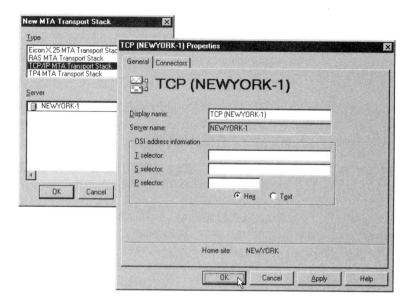

Review

Before you can configure an X.400 Connector, the appropriate transport stack must be installed. The TCP/IP transport stack is one possibility. TP4 and X.25 stacks are also provided. These transport stacks make the underlying configuration of the Windows NT network protocol accessible. Since protocols are configured within Windows NT, not much configuration work is required when you install the TCP/IP transport stack within the Administrator program.

During the MTA transport stack configuration, a protocol stack object is created under the corresponding server object. Using this item, you can adjust the transport stack parameters (such as the PSAP, SSAP, or PSAP) at any time.

Configuring the X.400 Connector

You can configure the X.400 Connector object as soon as an MTA transport stack has been installed. The X.400 Connector configuration can be complex, especially when you are connecting to a foreign X.400 system.

Beginning the Configuration

To begin the configuration, open the **File** menu, point to **New Others**, and select the **X.400 Connector** command. A **New X.400 Connector** dialog box appears, listing all installed MTA transport stacks. Select the one you want and click **OK**. In the next dialog box, you will see eight property pages. Use the **General** property page to specify how the display and directory name of the new connector object will appear in the Directory Information Tree. Also, you can examine whether this X.400 Connector uses the correct MTA transport stack.

Connect Request Information

Every X.400 connection is a secured connection. In other words, an X.400 MTA that wants to contact another MTA will identify itself within its connect request. The identification information includes the name and password of the local MTA and the remote MTA. If this information does not match the configuration of the remote X.400 Connector, the connection request is refused. (Messages will not be transferred.)

You can set the name and password of the local MTA using the **Message Transfer Agent** object at the server level. The default name of the MTA is the name of the server and there is no default password. This information must be presented to the remote administrator so that the remote MTA can be configured properly. You must also retrieve the name and password of the remote MTA from the remote administrator to complete the configuration. Enter the retrieved information in the **Remote MTA Name** and **Password** boxes on the X.400 Connector's **General** property page.

Note The MTA password is case sensitive. If you misspell it, connections will not be established and messages will not be transferred.

Transport Stack Configuration

The transport stack configuration, which you specify on the **Stack** property page, does not refer to the configuration of the local computer. You must specify the configuration of the remote MTA (SSAP, PSAP, and TSAP). You can leave the corresponding fields blank if no additional service access points have been defined. Likewise, you must inform the remote administrator about the transport stack configuration of your X.400 Connector. This information will be set using the corresponding MTA transport stack item at the server level.

Further transport stack configuration depends on the actual protocol used to connect to the remote MTA. The TCP/IP protocol requires the host name or IP address of the remote MTA computer. If the TP4/CLNP protocol is used, you must specify the Network Service Access Point. The X.25 stack requires the X.121 address of the target MTA.

Overriding Local Information

You may want to override the name and password of the local MTA, especially when you are connecting an organization to a public X.400 network. The public X.400 carrier provides only the required MTA name and password. To change the information on a per-connector basis, you can use the **Override** property page. The X.400 Connector will use the information to establish connections with the remote system. The local MTA name and password configured at the server level will be ignored. You can also adjust the various connection parameters on the **Override** property page, which override the MTA site configuration parameters.

Advanced Configuration Issues

Advanced X.400 configuration is typically required when you connect an organization to a foreign X.400 system, because the features of the remote MTA must be identified. The MTA conformance year, for instance, must match the conformance year of the foreign system because significant differences exist between the 1984 and 1988 X.400 standards. If the specified conformance year doesn't match, communication problems will occur. To put it plainly, a connection cannot be established successfully in this situation.

On the **Advanced** property page, you can specify the X.400 features that should be enabled for a particular X.400 connection. Important settings are the MTA conformance mode, X.400 link options, message size limits, and X.400 body parts. Another important setting is the global domain identifier (GDI) of the remote system. It prevents message transfer loops and consists of the country, ADMD, and PRMD attributes. (See Figure 9-12.)

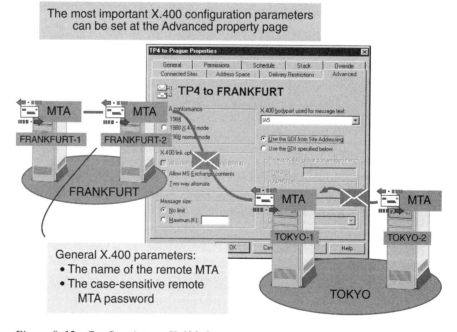

Figure 9-12. Configuring an X.400 Connector over TP4.

The X.400 Connector property pages and their functions are as follows:

- **Address Space**; defines the type and format of routing addresses; cost can be assigned to optimize the routing

- **Advanced**; specifies the X.400 message format and transfer procedures when you send messages to a remote X.400 system or to Exchange Server

- **Connected Sites**; specifies site name and address information about remote Exchange sites that can be reached using a particular connector; this property page must be completed before directory replication can be performed over this connector

- **General**; specifies the **Display Name, Directory Name Remote, MTA Name, Remote MTA Password**, and the **Transport Stack**

- **Override**; overrides default MTA attributes

- **Schedule**; sets the communications schedule; you can specify **Never, Always** (communication occurs when mail arrives that must be delivered), **Selected Times** (up to 15-minute intervals) or **Remote Initiated** (waits for the remote MTA to connect)

- **Stack**; specifies required address information such as IP address or Service Access Points for the remote system

Exercise 28: Configuring the X.400 Connector

The X.400 Connector, which is based on the 1988 conformance year, is a complex and powerful Exchange Server component. You can use it to connect an organization to foreign X.400 systems or to connect sites using the TCP/IP, TP4, or X.25 protocols. As a main connector, it can maintain connected sites information, which is required to enable intersite replication.

Estimated time to complete this exercise: 25 minutes

Description

In this exercise, you will configure the X.400 Connector between two sites. Since the X.400 Connector uses the messaging bridgehead concept, you will configure the connector between servers LONDON-1 and NEWYORK-1 directly in order to connect the sites LONDON and NEWYORK.

Note When you configure the X.400 connector, the optional MTA password is case sensitive.

- Task 28a describes the steps for configuring X.400 Site Addressing for the site LONDON.

- Task 28b describes the steps for configuring the X.400 Connector as a connector in LONDON.

- Task 28c describes the steps for configuring the X.400 Connector as a connector in NEWYORK.

Prerequisites

- You must complete this exercise logged on as Admin-NY1 on NEWYORK-1 and as Admin-L1 on LONDON-1.

- Make sure that the TCP/IP transport stack is installed on both servers (as outlined in Exercise 27).

- If you have configured the Site Connector between LONDON and NEWYORK as described in Task 26, delete the connector object from the **Connections** container of both sites. Otherwise, messages might not be routed to the new X.400 Connector.

Task 28a: Configuring the X.400 Site Addressing in the Site LONDON

1. Log on to **LONDON-1** as *Admin-L1* and start the **Exchange Administrator** program.

2. Expand the site object **LONDON**.

3. Expand the **Configuration** container.

4. In the right pane, double-click **Site Addressing** to display the **Site Addressing Properties** dialog box.

5. Switch to the **Site Addressing** property page.

6. Select the X.400 address **c=US;a= ;p=STOCKSDATA;o=LONDON**.

7. Click **Edit**.

8. In the **Country/Region** list box, select **GB (United Kingdom)**.

9. Click **OK**.

10. A message box appears, indicating that the Site Addresses of type(s) [X400] have been modified. Click **Yes** to update all e-mail addresses to match the new site address.

11. A message box appears, indicating that a process has been started to update the recipient e-mail addresses. Click **OK**.

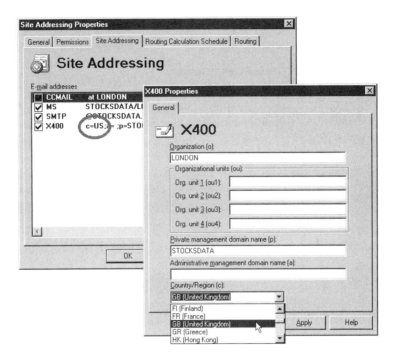

Task 28b: Configuring the X.400 Connector in LONDON

1. On the **File** menu, point to **New Other**, and then click **X.400 Connector**.

2. The **New X.400 Connector** dialog box appears, displaying **TCP/IP X.400 Connector** in the **Type** list box. Click **OK**.

3. Click **OK** when you are prompted to switch to the **Connections** container of the site LONDON.

4. Type the following information:

In this box	You supply
Display Name	*NEWYORK-1 Connector*
Directory Name	*NEWYORK-1 Connector*
Remote MTA Name	*NEWYORK-1*

5. Click the **Schedule** tab, and verify that **Always** is selected.

6. Click the **Address Space** tab, and then click **New**.

7. A **New Address Space** dialog box appears. Select **X400** and click **OK**.

8. Specify the information on the following page:

In this box	You supply
Organization (o):	*NEWYORK* (the name of the other site)
Private Management Domain Name (p):	*STOCKSDATA*
Administration Management Domain Name (a):	Enter only a space. (The space is required because this field must not be left empty.)
Country/Region (c):	**US (United States)**

9. Click **OK**.

10. Click **OK**.

11. Click the **Stack** tab.

12. Verify that **Remote Host Name** is selected. In the **Address** box, type *NEWYORK-1* (the name of the bridgehead computer in the other site).

13. Click the **Connected Sites** tab.

14. Click **New**.

15. In the **Site** box, type *NEWYORK* (the name of the other site).

16. Click the **Routing Address** tab. Select **US (United States)** under **Country/Region**.

17. Click **OK**.

18. Click **OK**.

19. A **Microsoft Exchange Administrator** message box appears, indicating that you must configure both sides of this connection before messages can be sent successfully. Click **OK**.

20. In the left pane, open the **Servers** container.

21. Click **LONDON-1.** In the right pane, double-click **Message Transfer Agent**.

22. The **Message Transfer Agent Properties** dialog box appears. Click **Recalculate Routing**.

23. A **Microsoft Exchange Administrator** message box appears, indicating that the new routing information will take several minutes to replicate across the site. Click **OK**.

24. Click **OK** to close the **Message Transfer Agent Properties** dialog box.

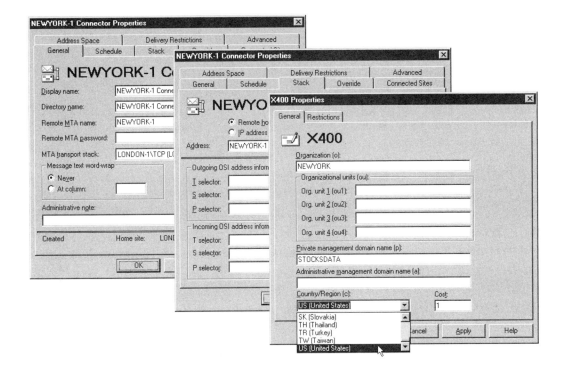

Task 28c: Configuring the X.400 Connector in NEWYORK

1. Be sure that you are logged on to the server NEWYORK-1 as Admin-NY1. Start the **Exchange Administrator** program.

2. On the **File** menu, point to **New Other** and click **X.400 Connector**.

3. The **New X.400 Connector** dialog box appears, displaying **TCP/IP X.400 Connector** in the **Type** list box. Click **OK**.

4. Click **OK** when you are prompted to switch to the **Connections** container.

5. Type the following information:

In this box	You supply
Display Name	*LONDON-1 Connector*
Directory Name	*LONDON-1 Connector*
Remote MTA Name	*LONDON-1*

6. Click the **Schedule** tab, and verify that **Always** is selected.

7. Click the **Address Space** tab, and then click **New**.

8. The **New Address Space** dialog box appears. Select **X400**, and then click **OK**.

9. Specify the following information:

In this box	You supply
Organization(o):	*LONDON*
Private Management (p): Domain Name	*STOCKSDATA*
Administration Management (a): Domain Name	Enter a space.
Country/Region (c):	Select **GB (United Kingdom)**

10. Click the **Restrictions** property page and verify that **Organization** is selected under **Scope**.

11. Click **OK**.

12. Click the **Stack** tab.

13. Verify that **Remote Host Name** is selected. In the **Address** box, type *LONDON-1* (the name of the bridgehead computer in the other site).

14. Click the **Connected Sites** tab.

15. Click **New**.

16. In the **Site** box, type *LONDON* (the name of the other site).

17. Click the **Routing Address** tab, and then select **GB (United Kingdom)** under **Country/Region**.

18. Click **OK**.

19. Click **OK**.

20. A **Microsoft Exchange Administrator** message box appears, indicating that you must configure both sides of this connection before messages can be sent successfully. Click **OK**.

21. In the left pane, expand the **Servers** container.

22. Click **NEWYORK-1**. In the right pane, double-click **Message Transfer Agent**.

23. The **Message Transfer Agent Properties** dialog box appears. Click **Recalculate Routing**.

24. A **Microsoft Exchange Administrator** message box appears, indicating that the new routing information will take several minutes to replicate across the site. Click **OK**.

25. Click **OK** to close the **Message Transfer Agent Properties** dialog box.

26. At this point, you should confirm that messages can be sent between LONDON and NEWYORK as described in Task 26c.

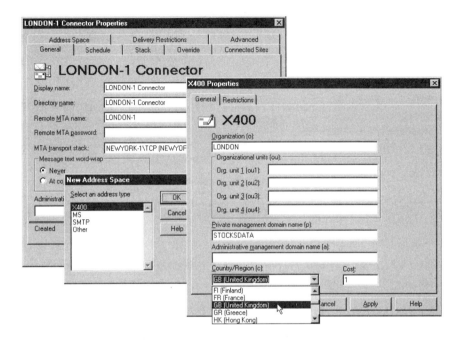

Review

When you install an X.400 Connector, you select the desired MTA transport stack (such as the TCP/IP transport) from a list of all installed stacks on a server in the site. The transport stack makes the underlying network protocol accessible. The most important configuration parameters are the **Remote MTA Name** and the **Remote MTA Password**. You must spell these correctly and remember that they are case sensitive. To allow the MTA to use the new connector for message delivery, you must assign an address space. To include newly defined address spaces in the routing table, you can force the routing recalculation using the **Recalculate Routing** button of the MTA or the Site Addressing object.

To enter network address information about the remote system, use the **Stack** property tab. If you are using the TCP/IP transport stack, you must enter the host name or the IP address of the remote MTA's computer. If you specified additional service access points (SSAP, TSAP, and PSAP) on the remote computer, you must specify them here as well.

Lesson 4: Other Main Messaging Connectors

In addition to the Site Connector and the X.400 Connector, the main messaging connector family includes the IMS and the Dynamic RAS Connector. You can use these to connect multiple Exchange sites within an organization. The IMS provides valuable features when Internet connections exist. If no permanent network connection exists, you can still bridge sites using the IMS or the Dynamic RAS Connector.

This lesson briefly introduces the IMS (which is covered in greater detail in Chapter 10), and then introduces the Dynamic RAS Connector and how to configure it.

At the end of this lesson, you will be able to:

- Describe the intersite features of the IMS

- Design Dynamic RAS Connector links

- Configure the Dynamic RAS Connector

Estimated time to complete this lesson: 25 minutes

Using the Internet Mail Service

The IMS is a connector component that is implemented in Exchange Server as a separate Windows NT service. As shown in Figure 9-13, you can use the IMS to connect sites. You can also use it to connect an organization to foreign SMTP and ESMTP systems (through the Internet or an intranet).

Installation

Exchange Server 5.5 emphasizes Internet connectivity. As a result, the IMS is tightly integrated into the product—you cannot deselect it during the Exchange Server installation. The IMS is created with the Internet Mail Wizard, which simplifies installation significantly, and can be maintained using the Administrator program.

Features

Because of its tight integration into the server's operation, the IMS has remarkable performance. It can route and redirect SMTP messages, and it supports a wide variety of international character sets. Moreover, it supports encrypted messages over SMTP and can use permanent or dial-up connections. You must create a Postmaster account during installation, which will receive status notifications and undeliverable messages. The configuration of the IMS is covered in more detail in Chapter 10.

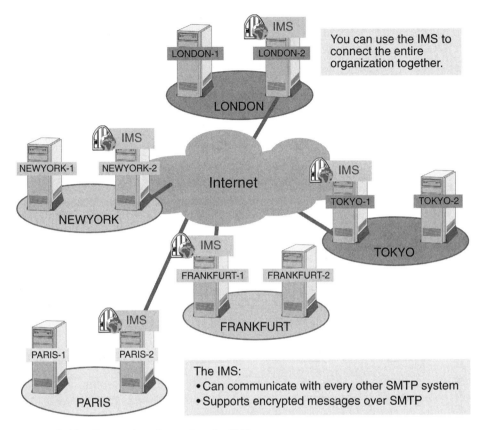

Figure 9-13. Connecting sites using the IMS.

The IMS has the following features:

- Communicates with other SMTP systems
- Has high performance because of native implementation
- Routes SMTP messages to other SMTP servers
- Provides enhanced support for international character sets
- Supports SMTP and ESMTP
- Supports encrypted messages over SMTP
- Internet Mail Wizard makes installation easier

Dynamic RAS Connector

The Dynamic RAS Connector uses the Windows NT Remote Access Service (RAS) to establish a connection for communicating with a remote Exchange Server computer using RPCs. As messages await delivery, it establishes the dial-up connection using a telephone line, ISDN line, or X.25 connection, and then it contacts the remote server. It is similar to the X.400 Connector in that it uses the messaging bridgehead concept.

Dynamic RAS Connector Configuration

The configuration of the Dynamic RAS Connector has three parts: the RAS and Dial-Up Networking configuration, the transport stack configuration, and the actual connector configuration.

Dial-Up Networking

You must set up Windows NT Dial-Up Networking directly on the Exchange Server computer in order to provide access to the remote computer network. The required installation and configuration tool is provided within Windows NT. You can click the **Dial-Up Networking** icon in the **Accessories** program group to begin the installation and configuration. Once you complete the configuration, you should test the connection using the **Dial-Up Networking** tool.

To establish a connection to the remote computer network, you must log on using a privileged Windows NT account. Typically, the remote network administrator will designate a dedicated account for the Exchange Server using the **Remote Access Admin** program in the **Administrative Tools (Common)** program group.

Protocol Support over RAS

Because RAS supports TCP/IP, NetBEUI and NWLink, Exchange Servers can communicate with each other through NetBIOS over all of the protocols or via SPX sockets or TCP/IP sockets. RAS communication over TCP/IP, however, requires extra configuration.

Conflicts can occur when you use RAS in conjunction with Dynamic Host Configuration Protocol (DHCP) and Windows Internet Name Service (WINS). You can generally use DHCP to assign dynamic IP addresses to incoming RAS connections. Even when RAS clients are not connected, the RAS server will lease several IP addresses from the DHCP server, which helps to optimize the process of address assignment. An IP address can be assigned immediately to a connecting client without the need for the RAS server to communicate with the DHCP server, which would slow down the process of address assignment. If you check active leases within the DHCP Manager program, you'll see these cached addresses as active leases. The address assignment works just fine, but the WINS registration will become invalid as soon as DHCP issues a different IP address from an existing RAS connection. In other words, NetBIOS name resolution and registration will fail in this scenario.

Note To avoid DHCP-related and WINS-related configuration problems, assign static IP addresses to RAS adapters that are used by the Dynamic RAS Connector.

You should note that RAS cannot perform proper NetBIOS name resolutions if RAS and WINS are installed on the same computer. In this scenario, RAS will query only the local WINS server even if it needs to query another WINS server in the network to find an association between a NetBIOS name and an IP address. If you ignore this configuration issue, NetBIOS names will not always be resolved properly.

Note Do not install WINS on a RAS server. You will need at least two servers in your network—one for RAS and one for WINS.

When you use TCP/IP over RAS, connections should always be initiated from the same site; otherwise, you might have problems with the WINS registration. It is best to configure the Dynamic RAS Connector in one site as remote-initiated while the remaining partner is responsible for connection establishment on a scheduled basis. You can configure these parameters using the connector's **Schedule** property page. This configuration is a hub scenario, in which one server acts as the central Dynamic RAS Connector hub. Only the central hub initiates the connection to remote sites—one after another—which prevents dial-in congestion. Alternatively, if your remote sites require a long distance call, you can have all calls initiated from the remote sites so that they are responsible for telephone costs. The remote servers dial into the central hub to deliver mail and can pick up any mail that is waiting to be delivered to the remote site.

RAS MTA Transport Stack

Just as the X.400 Connector requires an MTA transport stack to gain access to the underlying transport protocols, the Dynamic RAS Connector requires that an MTA transport stack be installed in order to gain access to the RAS services. RAS services are configured using the **Dial-Up Networking** program.

Installing the RAS MTA Transport Stack

To install the RAS transport stack, start the **Administrator** program, open the **File** menu, point to **New Other**, point to **MTA Transport Stack**, and then select **RAS MTA Transport Stack**. Using the property pages of the RAS MTA transport stack, specify a **Display Name** to identify the object within the Administrator program and (optionally) an **MTA Callback Number**. All other information will already be determined within Windows NT.

MTA Callback

The callback mechanism lets you increase network security because it calls back the originating Exchange Server while the connection is being established. It also transfers telephone costs to the communication partner.

The originating server connects to the RAS server that is supplying the account information and the callback number. It then releases the connection. The remote Windows NT RAS server dials the callback number; the connection is reestablished, and the called Exchange Server can contact the remote server in order to send the queued messages.

Dynamic RAS Connector Configuration

The actual communication is performed by the Dynamic RAS Connector, which uses the configured dial-up connection through the installed RAS MTA transport stack. To create the connector object, you use the Administrator program's **File** menu again: Point to **New Other** and select **Dynamic RAS Connector**.

First you must define a **Display Name** and a **Directory Name** to identify the new Dynamic RAS Connector object. Other important settings on the **General** property page are the **Remote Server Name**, **MTA Transport Stack**, **Phone Book Entry**, and **Message Size**. The **Remote Server Name** box identifies the remote Exchange Server computer. This computer is not necessarily the dialed Windows NT RAS server. (See Figure 9-14.) The dialed Windows NT RAS server is referenced through the **Phone Book Entry**, which you must select. To avoid bottlenecks caused by large messages sent over slow dial-up lines, you should limit the connector's **Message Size**, which can be set between 1 and 9,999,999 KB.

Scheduling Connections

Some telephone companies charge communication costs based on the time of day. It is a good idea to transfer messages during low-cost periods (such as late at night). Using the **Schedule** property page, you can configure specific times or blocks of time during which the connector will be allowed to dial. The shortest activation period is 15 minutes.

RAS Override

The Dynamic RAS Connector must contact the remote Exchange Server computer on behalf of the remote Site Services Account to establish communication. If you do not complete the **RAS Override** parameters, the Dynamic RAS Connector will use the credentials of the local Site Services Account, under which the local MTA operates. The Site Services Account that establishes the connection must have RAS dial-in permissions in the remote site as well as access to the **Configuration** container in the remote Exchange site. In most cases, you may want to use the Site Services Account of the remote site as the override account to avoid permissions problems when connecting. You must enter the required account information on the **RAS Override** property page. Other settings on this page are **MTA Callback Number** and **Overriding Phone Number**. They can be useful if you want to configure multiple RAS Connectors. The **MTA Callback Number** overrides the default number specified at the RAS MTA transport stack for this connector. You can use the **Overriding Phone Number** box to change the number specified in the telephone book.

MTA Override

Dial-up connections usually provide an acceptable transmission rate. But sometimes telephone links are not very reliable. If a particular connection is poor, you can optimize the data transfer by reducing the **Window Size** and **Checkpoint Size** parameters. If you are calling long distance, you might want to change the **Association Lifetime** parameter from the default of 300 seconds to something much shorter, like 30 seconds. Otherwise, the connection will stay up for five minutes (300 seconds) before the call is disconnected. These parameters are on the **MTA Override** property page. For detailed information about MTA protocol parameters, see Chapter 8.

Directory Replication Considerations

You should be cautious when transferring directory replication messages through a Dynamic RAS Connector. Some directories can be many megabytes in size, but telephone links are typically not designed to handle a large amount of data. In addition, you should not configure message size limits if you want to ensure proper intersite directory replication. If you do configure message size limits, directory replication messages might be refused, and this might lead to directory inconsistency between sites. In other words, your flexibility in balancing the Dynamic RAS Connector workload will be reduced if directory replication messages must be transferred. Intersite directory replication is covered later in this chapter in Lesson 6, "Directory Replication."

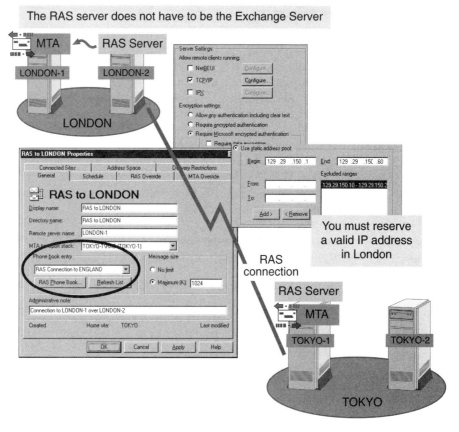

Figure 9-14. Connecting sites via a RAS Connector.

The elements of Dynamic RAS Connector configuration are as follows:

- Specify a RAS telephone book entry
- Configure the Dynamic RAS Connector within the Administrator program
- Configuration of delivery restrictions is possible, but this will not affect incoming messages
- Specify the directory name, display name, remote server name, and a RAS telephone book entry to dial
- Passwords are case sensitive
- Administrator can specify exactly when a component becomes active
- Specify the type and format of address spaces and assign cost factors to them

Lesson 5: Using Multiple Connectors

Many roads lead to Rome. If one road is closed for repair, you can take another. To provide a reliable messaging network, you should implement many messaging connectors. If one doesn't work, messages can take another connector to reach their destination.

This lesson deals with implementing multiple messaging connectors between sites. It discusses the advantages and features of a multi-connector topology, explains how to prevent message loops, and discusses how to retrieve information about the structure and content of the GWART. Finally, it will cover message retransmission and the connector selection process.

At the end of this lesson, you will be able to:

- Configure multiple connectors between two sites
- Assign cost values to connectors
- Explain message routing and the purpose of the GWART
- Read the GWART to determine routing paths

Estimated time to complete this lesson: 35 minutes

Multiple Connectors

To increase security through redundancy in message paths, you can install more than one connector between sites. Additional messaging connectors can transfer messages if the first connector is temporarily or permanently out of order. You can also use multiple messaging connectors to implement load balancing. Instead of having one particular connector transfer all messages, you can place the workload on many connectors.

The MTA and Multiple Connectors

Multiple messaging connectors are configured to connect the same sites, provide load balancing, and reliability for message transfer. Nevertheless, a single message can be routed to its destination using only one connector. The MTA determines the best connector during a process known as selection. Once the best connector is found, the message is placed in the message queue for the selected connector. You'll find more information about the selection process in the section, "Connector Selection," later in this lesson.

Reliable Configurations

For maximum reliability, you should implement different types of connectors using different network communication methods. For example, if a computer network collapses, blocking out the Site Connector, another connector can still transfer messages using a telephone connection.

As shown in Figure 9-15, the Site Connector uses a permanent physical connection to transfer messages to LONDON. A second physical connection exists independently in the form of a dial-up Internet connection using the IMS. Messages to LONDON are usually transferred through the Site Connector because it is has the lowest cost values in this configuration, which is desirable because it is the most powerful connector. If the permanent WAN connection is temporarily unavailable for any reason, messages are rerouted to the IMS, which transfers the messages to LONDON. The communication between both sites still works.

Assigning Cost Values to Connectors

Cost values determine which connector to select for message transfer. As shown in Figure 9-15, the Site Connector is used primarily to transfer messages between LONDON and NEWYORK. This is achieved by assigning the Site Connector the lowest cost value. The cost value can range from 1 to 100; under normal operating conditions, the connector with the lowest cost is selected. Only when messages cannot pass the Site Connector are they rerouted and transferred by the IMS.

If, however, you assign the same cost values to both the Site Connector and the IMS, messages are placed on both connectors equally, thus providing a form of load balancing. Cost values are often assigned based on the actual costs generated on a particular network link.

Preventing Message Loops

In complex organizations, message loops can, theoretically, happen. For example, if you set up an address space called MS:* in NEWYORK that points to LONDON and an address space called MS:* in LONDON that points to NEWYORK, you have a message loop that affects all messages addressed to MS Mail recipients. Loops can also result from the sophisticated rerouting features of the MTA.

As messages travel from site to site through multiple connectors, message loops probably exist if sophisticated MTA rerouting is enabled. Imagine that three sites have been connected with each other in a ring formation. Using X.400 Connectors, let's say that site A is connected to site B and site C, site B is connected to site A and site C, and site C is connected to site A and site B. If a message has been sent from site A to site C, it can now travel through the direct Site Connector (A - C) or through the indirect path via site B (A - B - C). If site C becomes unavailable for any reason, the MTAs in site A reroute messages to site B for further transmission. The MTAs in site B will also be unable to transfer the messages and will reroute them back to site A (site B has two message paths at hand; B - C and B - A - C). If the MTAs in site A were to attempt to reroute the message again over site B (because the path A - C is still not working), they would create a message loop. Message loops are dangerous for a messaging backbone and must be prevented. Exchange Server uses a mechanism based on cost values assigned to each message object to prevent message loops. The cost value of a particular messaging connector is added to a message as soon as the message passes the connector. If the message cost value is higher than the cost value of the connector, the connector must no longer be used. Therefore, if the message, due to complex rerouting, reaches the same site again, it cannot pass the same messaging connector one more time. Only connectors with higher cost values are a concern. If no other connector is available to handle the message, an NDR is generated and sent back to the originator and the message loop is prevented. Furthermore, you can strictly prevent an MTA from performing rerouting if you enable the **Only Use Least Cost Routes** option on the MTA's **General** property page.

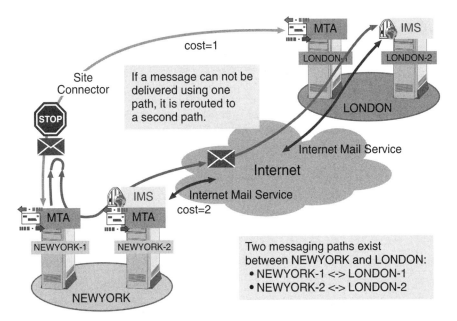

Figure 9-15. Multiple message paths.

For reliable message path configuration:

- Install more than one connector type between two sites
- Multiple X.400 Connectors can be configured between two sites to use different transport stacks
- Third sites can provide alternative paths to the destination site

Message Routing and Selection

Message routing is the process of directing messages to their destinations through message path selection. Message paths can span intersite connections, messaging connectors to foreign systems, or a combination of both. To route messages correctly, you must associate address spaces (possible destinations) with messaging connectors. The MTA compares each recipient address of every message against all address spaces and determines on a per-recipient basis all the connectors that can transfer the message. One connector is selected from among all eligible connectors and the message is placed in the connector's message queue, thereby completing the routing and selection process. The messaging connector transfers the message to the remote server, where the routing process starts again. The message is routed further until it reaches its destination server. Finally, it goes to the IS for delivery to the recipient's mailbox.

Determining the Best Connector

When the MTA receives a message from the IS or another MTA, it retrieves the recipient information from the message. It contacts the DS to check whether each recipient resides in the local site. If a recipient resides in the local site, the message is transferred directly to the recipient's home server using intrasite communication. If the recipient does not reside in the local site, the message is transferred elsewhere using a messaging connector. In the latter case, the MTA contacts the DS again to compare the recipient addresses to the GWART. (The GWART contains all defined address spaces and their association with messaging connectors.) The result is a set of connectors that can be used to transfer the message. If more than one connector can be used (see Figure 9-16), the best connector is determined based on cost values and other criteria. The MTA then places the message in the best connector's message queue. The selection process is covered later in this lesson under "Connector Selection."

If no connector can deliver a particular message, an NDR is generated and sent to the originator. The NDR names the MTA and indicates the reason for the delivery problem.

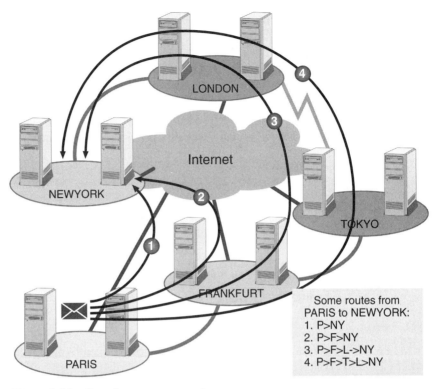

Figure 9-16.   Complex message routing.

The basic message routing mechanism is as follows:

1. The MTA retrieves the recipient's address from the message.

2. It compares the address to all configured address spaces.

3. The connector with the most detailed match wins.

4. If more than one connector is retrieved, the MTA selects the best connector.

5. The MTA places the message in the best connector's message queue.

The Gateway Address Routing Table

The GWART contains the associations of address spaces with messaging connectors and their cost factors. It is stored in the Directory database and is maintained by the SA. The MTA uses the GWART to determine logical routes for message delivery. You can examine the current GWART entries using the **Routing** property page of the **Site Addressing o**bject within the **Configuration** container at any time.

Rebuilding the Routing Table

The SA launches a process known as *routing table recalculation* to incorporate address space changes into the routing table. By default, the recalculation is performed at two o'clock every morning and every time a change is made that affects routing in the site. You can change the schedule using the **Routing Calculation Schedule** property page of the **Site Addressing** object. You can also update the GWART manually by clicking the **Recalculate Routing** button on the **Routing** property page. A manual routing recalculation might be necessary, as there can be some delays in propagating the changes throughout a site and you want to immediately merge a newly defined or recently changed address space into the GWART.

Using the **General** property page of the **Site Addressing** object, you also can specify the **Routing Calculation Server,** which will rebuild the GWART based on the routing calculation schedule. This server recalculates the GWART and replicates the newly created routing table to all other servers.

Reading the GWART

To examine the GWART, you can use the **Routing** property page of the **Site Addressing** object. However, the amount of displayed information is limited and you cannot print the routing table. It's more convenient to use the GWART text dump files, which are written to the Exchsrvr\Mtadata directory, to analyze the routing entries. The text dump file name of the current GWART is Gwart0.mta. The Gwart1.mta maintains a version of the GWART before the most recently changed file. You might find it useful to refer to this file when troubleshooting routing problems and when you want to see what routing changes have occurred most recently.

You can examine the GWART, as you would the MTA, to determine the path a message can take. Scan through Gwart0.mta to find an address space that matches the hypothetical recipient address. Each existing address space appears on a separate line. If multiple address spaces exist that match the destination, select the most detailed match. You can then locate the associated messaging connector and its cost factor on the line of the address space that most closely matches the destination.

Each GWART is divided into three areas, each corresponding to an address type: the X.500-distinguished name (DN), the X.400 O/R address (O/R), and the X.400 Domain Defined Attributes (DDA). DDAs are actually a form of an X.400 O/R address, but they are treated separately within the GWART because they represent all kinds of proxy e-mail addresses, such as SMTP, MS Mail, and cc:MAIL. (See Figure 9-17.)

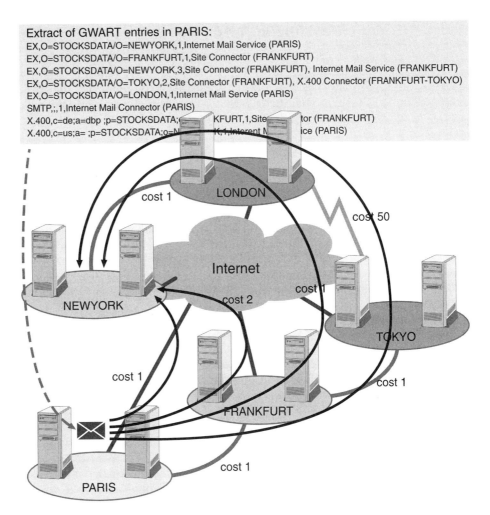

Extract of GWART entries in PARIS:
EX,O=STOCKSDATA/O=NEWYORK,1,Internet Mail Service (PARIS)
EX,O=STOCKSDATA/O=FRANKFURT,1,Site Connector (FRANKFURT)
EX,O=STOCKSDATA/O=NEWYORK,3,Site Connector (FRANKFURT), Internet Mail Service (FRANKFURT)
EX,O=STOCKSDATA/O=TOKYO,2,Site Connector (FRANKFURT), X.400 Connector (FRANKFURT-TOKYO)
EX,O=STOCKSDATA/O=LONDON,1,Internet Mail Service (PARIS)
SMTP,;,1,Internet Mail Connector (PARIS)
X.400,c=de;a=dbp ;p=STOCKSDATA;   KFURT,1,Site   tor (FRANKFURT)
X.400,c=us;a= ;p=STOCKSDATA;o=N   K,1,Internet M   ice (PARIS)

Figure 9-17. An example of a GWART.

The GWART is:

- Part of the Exchange Server Directory
- Used by the MTA to compare recipient addresses against address spaces
- Dumped to a text file called Gwart0.mta; you can conveniently examine the existing routing paths in this file

Transmission Retries

Transmission retry values determine the number of times a messaging connector tries to transfer a message before returning the message to the MTA. The message transfer is usually accomplished in the first attempt, but in some situations, such as when a remote messaging bridgehead is unavailable because of maintenance routines, a delivery attempt might fail.

Configuring Retry Parameters

Using the **Messaging Defaults** property page of the **MTA Site Configuration** object in the **Configuration** container, you can set site-level default parameters for retry values that affect all configured Site, X.400, and Dynamic RAS Connectors. In addition, X.400 Connector and Dynamic RAS Connector objects provide the **MTA Override** property page, which you can use to overwrite the site-level default settings.

Retrying the Transmission

Based on the default retry values, the MTA will attempt to establish a connection to the remote system up to 144 times (**Max Open Retries**). If it cannot establish a connection, it starts a new routing process after 10 minutes to retrieve the next best connector (**Open Interval**). If the 144th attempt in this new process fails, it returns the message to the originator as an NDR.

For example, let's say that the connection to the remote system is established without any problems and the MTA then tries to transfer the message through the messaging connector to the remote MTA. If the first transfer fails for any reason, the MTA waits two minutes (**Transfer Interval**) before attempting to send the message again across the same open connection. By default, it will make two transmission attempts (**Max Transfer Retries**).

Rerouting the Message

If the MTA discovers delivery problems, it will reroute messages using a different messaging connector if possible. Based on the GWART, it will determine the next connector that can transfer the message to its destination within a new routing cycle. If only one connector exists, it will retry this connector. In all other cases, it will try other connectors based on their cost factors and retry counts. The MTA will stamp messages with retry counts and reroute them until they are transferred or until the retry limit is reached. (See Figure 9-18.)

The MTA can perform message rerouting so long as the Site Connector, X.400 Connector, or Dynamic RAS Connector is involved in the message transfer because it uses these connectors directly. However, the MTA cannot determine delivery problems when transferring messages through the IMS, MS Mail Connector, or any other EDK-based gateway connector. These connectors implement their own Windows NT services that do not communicate directly with the MTA. Instead, communication takes place indirectly using message folders that maintain the message queues. As soon as the MTA places a message in the message queue of the IMS, MS Mail Connector, Connector for Lotus cc:Mail, Connector for Lotus Notes, and so on, it considers the message successfully delivered.

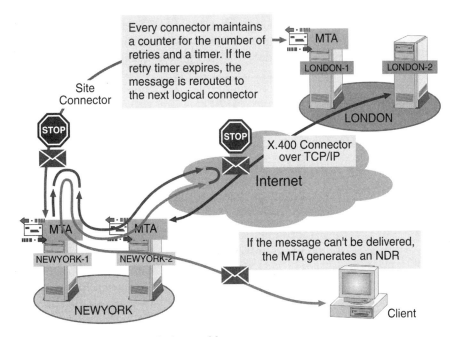

Figure 9-18. Data transmission problems.

The retry mechanism relies on the following mechanisms:

- Each message maintains a number of retries for each particular connector.
- If the maximum number of retries is reached, the MTA generates an NDR.
- The retry mechanism is implemented based on retry values.
- If the Open interval expires, the MTA reroutes the message.

Connector Selection

Complex organizations require a complex selection process to determine the best messaging connector for a particular message. The GWART must be analyzed to retrieve the set of all potential connectors. At this point, it is the task of the final connector selection to reduce the list of all potential connectors to one that will in the end be used to transfer the message. (See Figure 9-19.)

Retry Count Check

The MTA checks the retry count of a particular message because it indicates whether a connector has already been tried. The count reflects the number of unsuccessful delivery attempts per connector. Each connector maintains a maximum retry count. The MTA excludes any connectors whose maximum retry count has been reached. If all connectors have exceeded the maximum number of retries, the MTA sends an NDR to the originator.

Check Delivery Restrictions

If a connector has a delivery restriction that prevents the message from being transferred, that connector is eliminated. If a connector has a message size limit and a message arrives exceeding that limit, the connector rejects the message so as not to waste CPU resources and bandwidth.

Activation Schedule Check

In the next phase, the MTA verifies the activation schedules of all remaining potential messaging connectors. If a connector is active, its state is Active Now. Active connectors are always the MTA's first choice. If a connector is not active but is scheduled to connect at a later time, its state is Will Become Active In The Future. If multiple connectors will become active in the future, the MTA selects the connector that will become active first. The third state is called Remote Initiated, which means that the connector does not initiate any connection but waits for a remote MTA to connect. Remote-initiated connectors are the last choice of the MTA. The fourth state, Never, indicates a disabled connector. You generally set the activation schedule of a particular connector to Never if you want to take care of maintenance routines. In this state, the connector will not initiate or receive connections, so the MTA won't select it for message routing.

Only the X.400 Connector and the Dynamic RAS Connector maintain activation schedules. As a result, the state of other connectors is always active.

Least Retry Count

The next phase begins if multiple connectors still remain. In this case, the MTA checks the per-connector retry counter of the message again and selects the connector with the lowest value count. If multiple connectors show the lowest retry count, the MTA selects the connector that is not currently retrying a connection.

Retry State Check

The open retry timer indicates the time elapsed since the last attempt to establish an association and is used to determine the delay between connection attempts. The open retry timer starts when the connection to a remote MTA fails. A connector attempts to establish the connection again when the open retry timer expires. Each MTA maintains an open retry timer for each local connector; only remote connectors cannot be considered and are therefore excluded from this check. In order to prevent the MTA from routing a message to a connector that failed the last time it tried to establish a connection, any local connector that is not in a retry state should be used.

Let's say that you are using a X.400 Connector over TCP/IP and a Dynamic RAS Connector. A message is routed to the X.400 Connector because of a previous selection, but the X.400 connection has failed, so the message is routed to the Dynamic RAS Connector. New messages are then routed directly to the Dynamic RAS Connector if they arrive at the MTA before the open retry timer of the X.400 Connector expires.

Cost Factor Check

In the next phase of the process, the MTA skips all messaging connectors that show a cost factor lower than the current message cost value. Each message maintains a message cost value in order to prevent message loops. As soon as a message passes a particular messaging connector successfully, the cost factor of the connector is added. If a message is routed back to a previous site for any reason, it cannot pass the same messaging connector again since its cost value is now higher than the cost factor of that connector.

Finally, if multiple connectors remain, the MTS selects the connector with the lowest cost value. If, again, multiple connectors have the same cost value, the MTA prefers connectors installed on the local computer over connectors installed on remote servers. Using local connectors reduces the need for additional routing that the remote MTA must otherwise perform to finally transfer the message to the destination site.

Load Balancing

If, regardless of all preceding selection checks, multiple potential connectors still exist, the MTA performs load balancing. It decides at random which connector to use. On average, the same number of messages will be placed on all potential connectors.

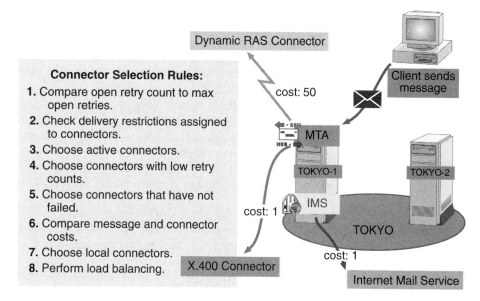

Connector Selection Rules:
1. Compare open retry count to max open retries.
2. Check delivery restrictions assigned to connectors.
3. Choose active connectors.
4. Choose connectors with low retry counts.
5. Choose connectors that have not failed.
6. Compare message and connector costs.
7. Choose local connectors.
8. Perform load balancing.

Figure 9-19. The connector selection.

The process for connector selection is as follows:

1. Compare open retry count to max open retries.

2. Check delivery restrictions assigned to connectors.

3. Choose active connectors.

4. Choose connectors with low retry counts.

5. Choose connectors that have not failed.

6. Compare message and connector costs.

7. Choose local connectors.

8. Perform load balancing.

Lesson 6: Directory Replication

Sites begin as lonely islands in the ocean of the messaging network—until they discover that they are not alone. But only if they receive configuration information about other sites can they be fully aware of other resources in their organization. Configuration information can be replicated across site boundaries, but, unlike intrasite directory replication, intersite directory replication requires manual configuration steps.

This lesson discusses intersite directory replication. You will learn about replication bridgehead servers, transitive and adjacent replication connections, and how to design the replication topology for an organization. You will also learn about configuring the Directory Replication Connector and how to force replication to happen. At the end of the lesson is an exercise on setting up directory replication.

At the end of this lesson, you will be able to:

- Describe the role of a directory replication bridgehead
- Identify transitive connections
- Design a directory replication topology
- Configure directory replication between sites

Estimated time to complete this lesson: 25 minutes

Directory Replication Considerations

Directory replication between sites does not happen directly because support for direct communication between directory services of different sites cannot be guaranteed. Directory replication information must be wrapped in e-mail messages, which the MTA transfers using messaging connectors.

Connected Sites

The Connected Sites information, which can be specified on main connectors, indicates that an Exchange site is available via the connector. The connected sites information is required so that directory replication connectors can be created. As shown in Figure 9-20, directory replication connectors can work over the Site Connector, X.400 Connector, Dynamic RAS Connector, or the IMS. The Site Connector does not require additional configuration because it can be used only to connect sites together, and therefore a connected site is implied. All the other connector objects provide the **Connected Sites** property page, where you can specify the name of the remote site.

Directory Replication Connector

The Directory Replication Connector provides the information required to maintain intersite directory replication messages. An internal component of the Directory, the Directory Replication Agent (DRA), uses each configured replication connector to send and receive replication messages. The actual transfer of replication messages, however, is the task of the MTA and the configured messaging connectors. Consequently, the Directory Replication Connector is dependent on the messaging connector.

However, directory replication messages are not bound to a particular connector. They are addressed to the DRA of an Exchange Server computer in a remote site and are managed in exactly the same way as all other e-mail messages. They can be rerouted or sent across various connections (even foreign mail systems) to reach their destination.

Replication Bridgehead Concept

Intersite directory replication generally uses the bridgehead concept. In other words, replication messages are addressed to only one server in the remote site, and the remote server sends replication messages only to the local replication bridgehead. The servers first merge the configuration changes in their directories and then distribute the changes within the local site using intrasite directory replication. Since replication bridgeheads are central directory replication pivot points, you might consider implementing dedicated servers in large organizations.

Preventing Replication Problems

Intersite directory replication information can be up to several MB in size. The replication schedule can also be set to **Always,** which generates several messages every 15 minutes. In other words, a replication connector can create numerous replication messages in a relatively short time. To avoid MTA problems with message queue backlogs, you should test the configured messaging connectors before you enable directory replication. Otherwise, you might end up with message queues filled with more than 50,000 e-mail messages waiting to be delivered. To verify that messaging connectors are working properly, you can configure a Link Monitor. Link monitors are covered in Chapter 15.

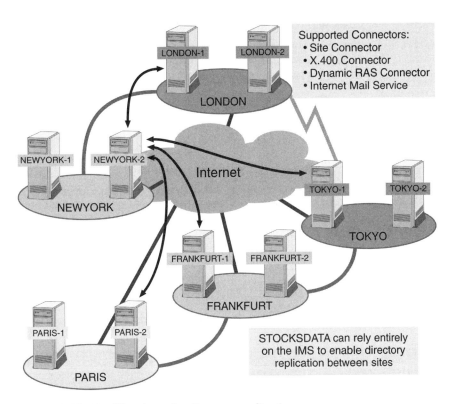

Figure 9-20. Enabling intersite directory replication.

The features of the Directory Replication Connector are as follows:

- Depends on Connected Sites information from messaging connectors that have been configured between two sites
- Only one replication bridgehead can be responsible for a remote site
- Directory replication performed by the DRA, a part of the DS
- Wraps the directory replication in normal messages

Directory Replication Bridgeheads

Within a single site, multiple directory replication bridgeheads can exist, but only one bridgehead can be responsible for a particular remote site. (See Figure 9-21.) The local bridgehead server and the remote bridgehead server are determined when you configure the Directory Replication Connector. You can select both servers using the **Local Bridgehead Server** and **Remote Bridgehead Server** boxes on the replication connector's **General** property page.

Flow of Directory Replication Information

Intersite directory replication uses the pull model—a server generally cannot push its changes into another server's directory. Directory replication bridgeheads always request intersite replication changes.

During each replication cycle, the local replication bridgehead server notifies the remote replication bridgehead that it would like to retrieve a list of changes that have occurred in the remote site. The remote directory replication bridgehead responds with a list of items that have changed. Update Sequence Numbers (USNs) are used to keep track of what items have changed. It is then up to the local bridgehead to request the directory changes from the remote site. The notification and the request are sent in the form of e-mail messages. Once the changes are retrieved, they are incorporated into the local directory. They can then be distributed to all other servers within the same site. The concept of directory replication based on USN values is covered in detail in Chapter 4.

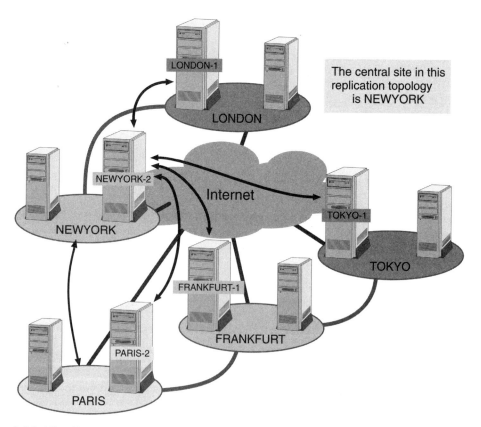

9-21. *The directory replication bridgehead of a fictitious company.*

The features of the directory replication bridgehead are as follows:

- Requests changes; doesn't push them

- Handles intersite replication to one or more sites

- Only one bridgehead can connect to a specific site

- Replication messages can take any possible routing path to the destination DS

Transitive Connections

A transitive replication connection is a virtual link between two sites through a third site. For example, after you set up a Directory Replication Connector between NEWYORK and PARIS, PARIS will also retrieve information about LONDON, FRANKFURT, and TOKYO. (See Figure 9-22.) As a result, the connection to NEWYORK is adjacent, while all others are transient.

Multiple Replication Sources

Exchange Server doesn't allow multiple paths to the same source of information in order to avoid replication of redundant configuration data. As shown in Figure 9-22, this means that as soon as you configure the Directory Replication Connector between NEWYORK and PARIS, you cannot configure an additional connector between PARIS and FRANKFURT. This is disallowed because the adjacent connection to NEWYORK already transfers the configuration information about FRANKFURT to PARIS.

You can actually configure both replication connectors to FRANKFURT and to NEWYORK at the same time. No warning message will be displayed because the transient information has not yet been replicated. You can create both connector objects and replication will begin. This does not mean that you have outwitted intersite directory replication, however. An error notification will be written to the Windows NT Event Log when the replication problem is discovered. The configuration information about FRANKFURT will not appear in PARIS until the redundant replication connector to FRANKFURT is deleted.

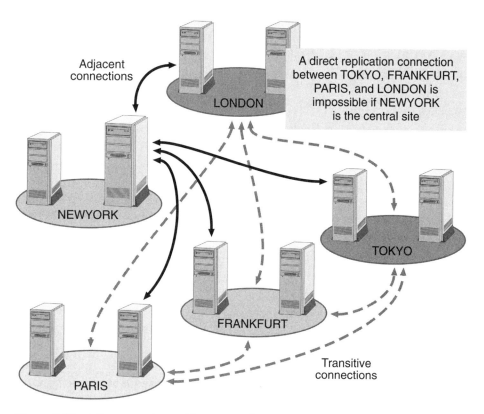

Figure 9-22. Adjacent and transitive connections.

The features of transient and adjacent replication connections are as follows:

- Adjacent connections refer to an actual Directory Replication Connector configured between two sites.

- Transient connections are virtual connections between two sites over a third site. You do not have to set up a Directory Replication Connector in order to retrieve configuration information on transient sites.

Directory Replication Topology

Intersite directory replication is relatively easy to implement in an Exchange Server organization if you can rely on a carefully designed replication topology. The more complex the organization, the closer all administrators must work together. Otherwise, adjacent connections will be created where transient links were designed, and directory replication problems will occur.

Transport Independence

The topology of the directory replication connectors does not have to follow the direct path of messaging connectors. Because replication information is sent as e-mail messages, it matters only that a replication message can get to its destination over any combination of messaging connectors.

Transient Delays

The topology shown in Figure 9-22 represents an optimally designed organization. Replication delays are minimized, and each site can be reached with a maximum of two hops. If the administrator in LONDON modifies the properties of a mailbox, for instance, the changes are first replicated to NEWYORK (one hop) and then to PARIS, FRANKFURT, and TOKYO at basically the same time (two hops).

Note If an organization grows to three or more sites, you can reduce the hop count to two if you implement a star topology.

One important topology is a configuration in which each site is adjacent to another. As shown in Figure 9-23, four hops exist between TOKYO and LONDON. By default, intersite replication is activated every three hours. But for this example, assume that the schedule has been changed to once a day using the **Schedule** property page of each Directory Replication Connector. If directory changes occur on the server TOKYO-2, these changes are first replicated within the local site to TOKYO-1. TOKYO-1 is the local replication bridgehead. Because the activation schedule has been changed in all sites, it can take an entire day to receive the changes in FRANKFURT and another day to receive the modifications in PARIS, NEWYORK, and finally in LONDON. The configuration changes performed in TOKYO will reach LONDON after four days.

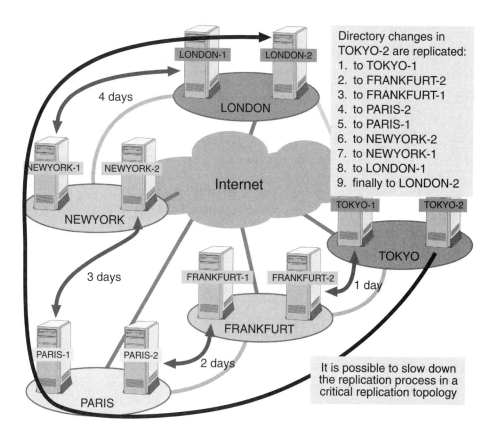

Directory changes in TOKYO-2 are replicated:
1. to TOKYO-1
2. to FRANKFURT-2
3. to FRANKFURT-1
4. to PARIS-2
5. to PARIS-1
6. to NEWYORK-2
7. to NEWYORK-1
8. to LONDON-1
9. finally to LONDON-2

It is possible to slow down the replication process in a critical replication topology

Figure 9-23. A poorly designed directory replication topology.

Some reasons for intersite replication delays are as follows:

- Problems with a messaging connector can delay directory replication messages

- Directory replication occurs only at specified times (by default, every three hours)

- Many replication hops are implemented

Configuring Directory Replication

The configuration of directory replication between sites happens in two stages. First you configure the Connected Sites information using a messaging connector's **Connected Sites** property page, and then you create and configure the Directory Replication Connector.

Creating a Directory Replication Connector

You can create a Directory Replication Connector after you specify the Connected Sites information. Open the Administrator program's **File** menu, point to **New Other,** and click the **Directory Replication Connector** command. The **New Directory Replication Connector** dialog box will appear, providing the option to configure both sites at the same time. You must enter the name of a remote server and then click **OK.** The property pages of the new Directory Replication Connector will appear. You can adjust the local and remote bridgehead server as well as the replication schedule, and then click **OK** again to complete the replication connector configuration.

Forcing Directory Replication

Once you create a Directory Replication Connector, you can immediately start directory replication. Activate the KCC, which creates new directory objects for the adjacent site and its **Configuration** container, by clicking the **Check Now** button on the **General** property page of the server-level **Directory Service** configuration object. (See Figure 9-24.) The **Directory Service** object is covered in detail in Chapter 8.

Once the KCC has created objects for other sites, directory replication information can be pulled from the remote site by selecting the **Request Now** button on the **Sites** property page of the Directory Replication Connector. As shown in Figure 9-23, the administrator in LONDON might want to pull changes from TOKYO. In this case, it is necessary to force the directory replication to occur first in FRANKFURT, and then in PARIS, NEWYORK, and finally LONDON.

Backfilling

Backfilling ensures that a container with old information is filled with all missing or updated directory changes. This is necessary if a server has been restored from a backup. Backfilling is also required if a server has been down for maintenance while directory modifications were being made on another server.

Backfilling occurs automatically when intersite Directory Replication Connectors are first set up. Figure 9-24 shows a Directory Replication Connector that has been configured between LONDON and NEWYORK. To force intersite replication, click the **Check Now** button and launch the KCC, which examines the directory and establishes the new replication link to LONDON. The KCC creates two empty containers: **LONDON** and **Configuration**. At this point, the backfill process is used to request directory information from both sites.

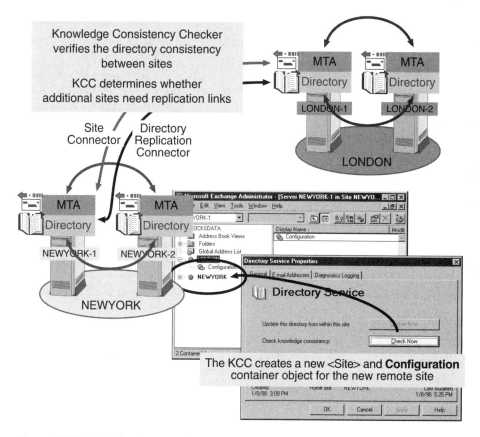

Figure 9-24. Initiating intersite directory replication.

Some important features of Directory Replication Connector configuration are as follows:

- Directory Replication Connectors work over the Site Connector, the X.400 Connector, the Dynamic RAS Connector, and the IMS

- You must run the KCC to force the replication process to start immediately

- Only adjacent sites have to be specified through a Directory Replication Connector

The tasks of the KCC are as follows:

- Reads the local directory to get information about new sites

- Creates the <Site> and **Configuration** containers in the local site to hold configuration information for the remote site

- Verifies directory consistency between servers in the local site and the remote replication bridgeheads

Exercise 29: Performing Directory Replication

If sites are connected together through messaging connectors, you should configure Directory Replication so that a Global Address List of all users in the organization is created. Intersite directory replication also enables MTAs to learn about all possible message routes and connectors in other sites.

Estimated time to complete this exercise: 45 minutes

Description

In this exercise, you will create a directory replication connection between LONDON and NEWYORK using the Administrator program. You must have the rights of a Permissions Admin. This exercise demonstrates the independent configuration of both sites, which makes the Directory Replication Connector configuration more complex. You ordinarily won't need to force directory replication, but in this exercise you will set the replication schedule to **Always** to allow the intersite replication to start immediately. Otherwise, you would have to wait another three hours to see measurable configuration modifications.

- Task 29a describes the steps for configuring a directory replication connector between the sites NEWYORK and LONDON in the site LONDON.

- Task 29b describes the steps for configuring a directory replication connector between the sites NEWYORK and LONDON in the site NEWYORK.

- Task 29c describes the steps for verifying the successful directory replication between the sites.

Prerequisites

- Make sure that a messaging connector (either the Site Connector or the X.400 Connector) exists between the sites NEWYORK and LONDON.

- Make sure that the connector is working properly before you start to configure the directory replication.

- Log on to server LONDON-1 as Admin-L1 to complete Task 29a.

- Log on to server NEWYORK-1 as Admin-NY1 to complete Tasks 29b and 29c.

Task 29a: Configuring a Directory Replication Connector Between Two Sites (LONDON and NEWYORK)

1. Log on to the server LONDON-1 as Admin-L1.

2. Start the **Microsoft Exchange Administrator** program.

3. On the **File** menu, point to **New Other,** and then click **Directory Replication Connector.**

4. Click **OK** when you are prompted to switch to the **Directory Replication** container of the site **LONDON.**

5. A **New Directory Replication Connector** dialog box appears. Select the option **No, Remote Site Is Not Available On This Network.**

6. In the **Server In Remote Site** box, type *NEWYORK-1,* and then click O**K.**

7. The **Directory Replication Connector (NEWYORK) Properties** dialog box appears. Click the **Schedule** tab, and then click **Always.**

8. Click **OK.**

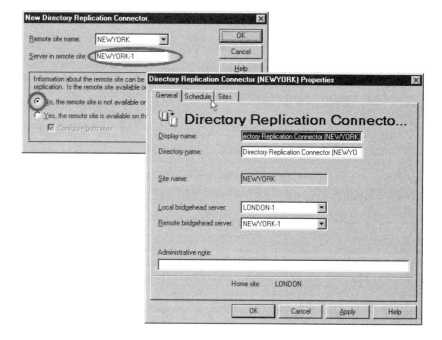

Task 29b: Configuring a Directory Replication Connector Between Two Sites (NEWYORK <-> LONDON)

1. Log on to the server NEWYORK-1 as Admin-NY1 and start the **Microsoft Exchange Administrator** program.

2. On the **File** menu, point to **New Other,** and then click **Directory Replication Connector**.

3. Click **OK** when you are prompted to switch to the **Directory Replication** container of the site NEWYORK.

4. A **New Directory Replication Connector** dialog box appears. Select the option **No, The Remote Site Is Not Available On This Network**.

5. In the **Server In Remote Site** box, type *LONDON-1* and then click **OK**.

6. The **Directory Replication Connector (LONDON) Properties** dialog box appears. Click the **Schedule** tab and then click **Always**.

7. Click **OK**. When the replication is complete, you will see the other site in the hierarchy with the following container objects: **Configuration**, **Add-Ins**, **Addressing**, **Connections**, **Directory Replication**, **Monitors**, **Protocols**, **Servers**, and **Recipients**.

Note The replication process might take up to 20 minutes.

---

8. Verify that the replication is complete by clicking the **Recipients** container of the remote site (LONDON) and then viewing the mailboxes in the site LONDON.

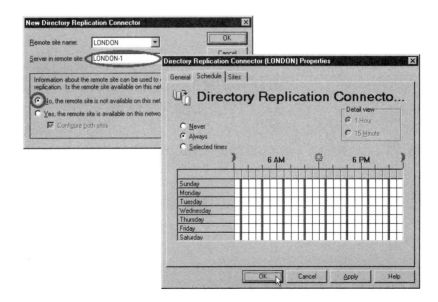

Task 29c: Verifying the Intrasite Directory Replication

1. On NEWYORK-1, double-click the **Microsoft Outlook** icon on the desktop.

2. On the **Tools** menu, click **Address Book.**

3. The **Address Book** window appears. Verify that the **Global Address List** is selected in the **Show Names From The** box.

4. Select **Admin-L1** from the list of possible recipients.

5. On the toolbar, click the **New Message** button.

6. The **Untitled - Message** dialog box appears. In the **Subject** box, type *Hello Admin-L1.*

7. In the message text box, enter some text, such as *Does it always rain in London?*

8. Select the message text. Click the **Center** button on the toolbar, and then click **Font Color.** Select **Maroon** and format the text as bold and size 18.

9. Click **Send** on the toolbar.

10. On LONDON-1, verify that Admin-L1 has received the test message.

11. On both computers, exit all applications and log off Windows NT.

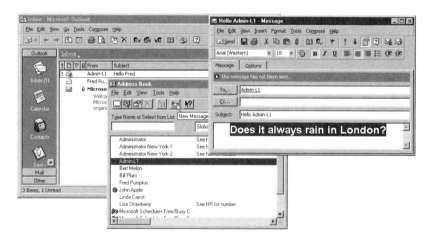

Review

The intersite concept follows the bridgehead principle. During configuration, you will need to identify the remote bridgehead server. The local bridgehead is determined automatically; it is the local computer on which you are installing the Directory Replication Connector. Using the replication connector's **General** property page, you can adjust the bridgehead servers if desired. The activation schedule is another important setting, which may be modified to achieve the desired configuration. By default, new replication connectors become active every three hours. If desired, you can configure the KCC to always be active.

Once the replication connector is configured, the KCC creates a replication link to the remote site. Two empty container objects for the remote site will appear in the Administration window during the initial directory replication. It is up to the backfill process to fill these containers with configuration objects such as recipient items.

Review

1. Your company wants to implement Exchange Server 5.5. The company does not have any subsidiaries, and all of its computers are connected using a LAN. It has two Windows NT domains, one for the human resources department and one for all other employees. Due to security considerations, no trust relationship can exist between the domains. How many sites must be created?

2. A fictitious company named Sombrero has two locations, one in New York and one in Mexico City, with a permanent 1 MB X.25 connection between them. The X.25 data transfer generates transmission costs. Should the administrator implement a single site to make administration easier?

3. What kind of information is wrapped in e-mail messages for intersite communication?

4. What advantages does intersite communication provide?

5. You need to connect two sites, and you want to enable directory replication. No permanent network connection exists between the sites, but dial-up connections are available, which can also be used to connect to the Internet. Which two messaging connectors can you use to connect the sites together?

_____

_____

6. Which three messaging connectors can you use to connect NEWYORK and FRANKFURT? (See Figure 9-3 on page 494.)

_____

_____

_____

_____

7. To connect your organization to the Internet, you installed the IMS. Which address space type should you associate with this connector?

_____

_____

8. To exchange messages with users on a DEC ALL-IN-ONE system, you created an X.400 connection to their DEC MailBus400 MTA. The X.400 system uses the address c=*US;a= ;p=STOCKSDATA;o=Mailbus.* Routing information about this particular X.400 connection cannot be replicated to other sites in the organization, but you want the users to be able to send messages through the connection. How should you assign the address space to the X.400 Connector?

_____

_____

_____

_____

_____

9. The workload of the servers within your local site is high, so you implemented local messaging bridgehead computers to offload the intersite message transfer from other servers. Now you need to connect to a new site that contains only one server. You have decided to implement a Site Connector, but you want to keep the messaging bridgehead concept in the Local site. How do you configure the Site Connector?

_____

_____

_____

_____

_____

10. You need to configure a Site Connector, but the Site Services Accounts in the two sites are different. When you began installing the connector, you received notification that access to the remote server's directory was denied due to missing access rights. You want to configure both sites in a common Windows NT domain. What do you do to configure the Site Connector?

_____

_____

_____

_____

11. You want to balance the messaging load between three servers in your site. Server A should receive approximately double the number of messages as server B. Server C should be accessed only if server A and server B are not available. Which cost values should you assign to servers A, B, and C?

_____

_____

_____

_____

12. You want to create a Site Connector between sites in nontrusted domains. What steps should you take in Windows NT and Exchange Server to install the connector?

_____

_____

_____

_____

_____

_____

13. Your company is using a worldwide X.400 messaging network using various protocols such as TCP/IP and X.25. As an administrator, you have the task of implementing Exchange Server. How can you benefit from the existing messaging network?

_____

_____

_____

_____

14. You connected two sites using an X.400 Connector that uses an X.25 connection. The communication between both sites worked without any problems, but the demand on messaging has increased and the X.400 Connector has become a bottleneck in one site. Intersite messages are queued back on this server and delivery is delayed. What should you do to remove the bottleneck?

_____

_____

_____

_____

15. A company has three sites, all of which are connected using X.400 Connectors. You want to connect the organization to a public X.400 provider. The provider has sent you the required configuration parameters for the X.400 connection, and the required MTA name and password differ from the local MTA name and password. How should you configure the X.400 Connector?

_____

_____

_____

16. To connect your organization to the Internet, you need to install the IMS. What should you install on the server before you begin, and which tool should you use to begin the IMS installation?

_____

_____

_____

17. What are the disadvantages of directory replication over dynamic RAS connections?

_____

_____

_____

_____

18. You have configured two messaging connectors between NEWYORK and LONDON. One connector, the Site Connector, uses TCP/IP for communication, while the X.400 Connector uses the TP4 protocol. What do you do to provide load balancing between the Site Connector and the X.400 Connector?

_____

_____

19. A member of your administration team has changed address spaces. Messages are incorrectly routed because of the new entries. You are in charge of correcting the routing problem. Where do you find information about correct routing table entries?

    _____

    _____

    _____

20. Your company is planning to connect two sites. Directory replication must be performed. Which connector do you use to connect the sites? Which connector makes intersite replication configuration easiest?

    _____

    _____

    _____

21. Your company has three sites that are connected via X.400 Connectors. You are planning to enable intersite replication to share all directory information within the organization. You configured the Connected Sites information and began creating Directory Replication Connectors. Within site A, you created a replication link to site B and site C. You also wanted to configure the replication link between site B and site C, but it didn't work. Why not?

    _____

    _____

    _____

22. You want to configure directory replication connectors between three sites. Sites A and B are connected through a Site Connector, while sites A and C use a X.400 Connector to transfer messages. What will be different when you configure the replication connector between sites A and B and between sites A and C?

    _____

    _____

    _____

    _____

23. Which topology is an optimal directory replication configuration?

_____

_____

24. You created a directory connector between two sites, and, in order to speed up the replication process, you clicked the Check Now button to force replication. The KCC created the replication link, and the new container objects appeared in the Directory Information Tree. But now, after a long time, the container objects are still empty. What should you do to see if a replication problem exists?

_____

_____

C H A P T E R   1 0

Internet Mail Service

This chapter explains how to connect an organization to the Internet using the IMS, which is available in all Microsoft Exchange Server editions.

Overview

E-mail is so much more flexible than paper faxes that it might soon replace faxes altogether. Many companies and home users are connected to the Internet and use e-mail messages to exchange all kinds of information. Users can even encrypt the data to ensure the privacy of their messages. Support for digital signatures is also a common feature.

Lesson 1 of this chapter covers the basics of SMTP and ESMTP and briefly discusses the related Requests for Comments (RFCs). It then takes a close look at the IMS architecture and describes a method of "hacking" the IMS that lets you examine its message queues. Other topics covered include the Domain Name System (DNS) and how to send messages using SMTP.

Lesson 2 covers the installation and use of the IMS and explains planning and security considerations. It also covers how to customize the IMS configuration within the Exchange Administrator program. In addition, Lesson 2 describes settings that you can control in the Registry Editor to optimize the IMS.

This chapter also provides six exercises to guide you through the process of preparing for the IMS installation, configuring the DNS, and actually installing and configuring the IMS. The exercises also show you how to configure SMTP message routing, analyze the IMS operation, and implement intersite directory replication using the IMS.

In the following lessons, you will be introduced to:

- The protocols and services that the IMS uses to transfer messages
- IMS installation
- Configuring and using the IMS
- Optimizing the IMS

Lesson 1: The Internet Mail Service

The IMS is tightly integrated into Exchange Server to provide the best possible performance. It uses SMTP or ESMTP to transfer messages to foreign SMTP hosts on the Internet and intranets. It is a main messaging connector that can also connect multiple sites. Indeed, the IMS can form the backbone of an organization's entire messaging system. (See Figure 10-1.)

This lesson provides an overview of the IMS and the required communication protocols, such as TCP/IP and SMTP. It also lists related RFCs, which are platform-independent industry standards on the Internet. Next, it covers the IMS architecture and introduces a method of accessing the message queues of the IMS directly using the Mdbview utility. Finally, it discusses DNS and various SMTP and ESMTP commands and provides an outline of the IMS address encapsulation feature.

An exercise is provided so you can prepare the test installation for all the following exercises and ensure a proper TCP/IP configuration. You must also clear the existing Exchange Server test configuration.

At the end of this lesson, you will be able to:

- Describe the features of the IMS
- Explain how the IMS transfers messages to SMTP and ESMTP hosts
- Explain the purpose of DNS
- Identify encapsulated addresses

Estimated time to complete this lesson: 45 minutes

Overview of IMS

Exchange Server was originally designed according to the X.400 and X.500 standards, so its native communication methods and message formats are not SMTP-aware. Exchanging messages with SMTP systems requires conversion of the message format and use of SMTP. The IMS accomplishes these tasks. It maintains its own Windows NT service, which is created during installation of the IMS within the Exchange Administrator program.

Internet Mail Wizard

The Internet Mail Wizard is an Administrator program tool for installing and configuring the IMS. It guides you through the basic configuration steps to quickly connect your organization to the Internet. Both permanent and dial-up connections are supported. Once you have installed the IMS, you can use its property pages to perform more complex configuration tasks. The Internet Mail Wizard is covered in detail in the section, "Starting and Configuring the IMS," later in this chapter.

IMS Implementation

The IMS, like the Site, X.400, and Dynamic RAS Connectors, is a main messaging connector. Unlike the other main connectors, however, it does not communicate directly with the MTA. The IMS design is similar to the architecture of a gateway connector; it maintains its own message queues, which reside in the Private Information Store. The IMS communicates primarily with the IS to retrieve outgoing messages from the store and to place incoming messages into the store. In addition, it communicates with the DS because recipient and originator addresses must be converted between the Exchange Server format (Distinguished Name, or DN) and the Internet e-mail format (SMTP).

Simple Mail Transfer Protocol

SMTP is an Internet standard that rules the transfer of e-mail messages between two messaging hosts. It also defines the message formats. ESMTP extends the SMTP features. It allows users to request delivery status notifications on their outgoing messages and to specify a message size limit for incoming ESMTP connections. Both SMTP and ESMTP require TCP/IP as their connection-based transport mechanism.

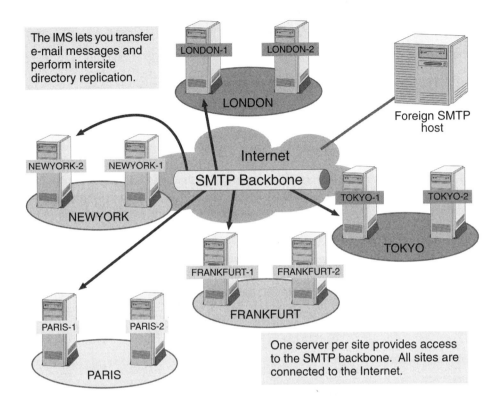

The IMS lets you transfer e-mail messages and perform intersite directory replication.

One server per site provides access to the SMTP backbone. All sites are connected to the Internet.

Figure 10-1. An SMTP backbone.

The features of the IMS are as follows:

- Can communicate with every other SMTP system
- Performance is high because of IS support of Internet message formats
- Provides route redirection for SMTP messages
- Has enhanced support for international character sets
- Supports SMTP and ESMTP
- Supports encrypted messages over SMTP
- Its Internet Mail Wizard eases installation

TCP/IP, SMTP, and RFCs

Data communication is possible only if all communication partners have the same commands and responses at their disposal. TCP/IP defines common commands for establishing reliable network connections. SMTP determines how to transfer messages on top of TCP/IP connections. Both TCP/IP and SMTP, along with many other protocols, are defined in RFCs.

TCP/IP

TCP/IP is a protocol family that was originally designed to create a reliable Wide Area network. In the 1980s, this network became known as the Internet. TCP and IP are actually different protocols. IP is a "connectionless" protocol. Its scope is to identify, route, and deliver datagrams across a computer network. TCP, on the other hand, is "connection-oriented." Its responsibility is to manage the connections with remote hosts to ensure that data packets are received in sequential order and to detect whether data packets have been lost or corrupted on their way across the network. Data sequencing relies on acknowledgements, which the receiver returns to the sender as correct packages are received. Packages are checked for corruption by means of checksums. TCP resides on top of IP. (See Figure 10-2.)

IP Address Information

An IP address is more than a number. It identifies a particular computer—a network adapter in a computer, to be exact—and the network segment to which the computer belongs. Every IP address has two parts: the Host ID and the Network ID. The IP address must be unique within the entire TCP/IP network. This is an especially important issue for Internet connections.

A subnet mask is used to separate the Network ID from the Host ID. Interpreted in binary format, a 1 within the subnet mask identifies a digit, which belongs to the Network ID. A 0 always refers to the HOST ID. For example, a host's IP address is 125.050.120.010 and its subnet mask is 255.255.255.000. Presented in binary format, the address information appears as follows:

IP address:	01111101.00110010.01111000.00001010
Subnet mask:	11111111.11111111.11111111.00000000
Network ID	01111101.00110010.01111000
Host ID	00000000.00000000.00000000.00001010

The IP address 125.050.120.010 refers to a Host with the decimal ID number of 10, which exists in a network with an ID of 125.050.120.

TCP/IP Sockets

Port numbers identify applications, which can be reached through a TCP/IP connection. Each application specifies the unique port number of the desired target process in its open request. To direct the request to the correct remote host, the host's IP address must also be provided. The port number plus the IP address is known as a Socket. Various RFCs define *well-known port numbers* for commonly used applications. SMTP applications, for instance, always expect to contact another SMTP application on port 25 of a remote host. Well-known port numbers are generally platform independent, meaning they are always the same across all platforms. You can check a list of well-known port numbers on any Windows NT Server computer. Use Notepad to open the file called Services, which can be found in \Winnt\System32\Drivers\Etc. This file contains a list of numerous ports, along with a short description.

SMTP and ESMTP

SMTP and ESMTP are application protocols that describe the procedures and formats for transferring e-mail messages between two active systems. To send a message, an SMTP/ESMTP application first connects to port 25 of the remote host. The remote SMTP system (such as the IMS) answers the incoming request. The SMTP communication is established, and e-mail messages can be transferred. (See Figure 10-2.)

RFCs

IP is defined in RFC 791. TCP procedures are specified in RFC 793. SMTP is described in RFC 821, and the format of SMTP messages is detailed in RFC 822. ESMTP features are described in RFC 1869.

The IMS also supports RFC 1521 and RFC 1522. RFC 1521 describes the use of character set labels in messages, and RFC 1522 allows formatting of header information (such as e-mail addresses and subject fields that use extended characters). To put it plainly, RFC 1521 and 1522 together describe nothing but the well-known MIME standard.

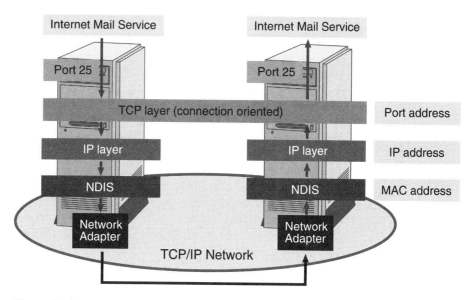

Figure 10-2. An SMTP connection over TCP/IP.

The functions of IP, TCP, and SMTP are as follows:

- SMTP uses port 25 to connect to remote systems via TCP/IP; it describes the connection procedure, information transfer commands, and message formats

- TCP implements connection management, sequencing, and acknowledgments on top of IP to provide a secure communication path; in contrast to IP, TCP is connection-oriented

- IP transmits single datagrams to destination hosts; the datagrams are handled discretely and the protocol is connectionless

Exercise 30: Preparing the Site and the TCP/IP Configuration

The IMS relies on TCP/IP because it uses SMTP and ESMTP to transfer messages. TCP/IP provides a reliable network connection through its connection management, sequencing, and data package acknowledgment.

Estimated time to complete this exercise: 15 minutes

Description

In this exercise, you will verify the TCP/IP configuration at the Windows NT Server level. Proper configuration is required to avoid IMS problems later on. For proper preparation of the test environment, it is also recommended that you remove existing intersite connections that have been created prior to this exercise, such as in Exercise 28 and Exercise 29 of Chapter 9.

- Task 30a describes the steps for checking the TCP/IP configuration of the test environment using the Control Panel, the Ipconfig utility, and Ping. You should check the TCP/IP protocol stack on both NEWYORK-1 and LONDON-1.

- Task 30b describes the steps for removing the X.400 Connector and the Directory Replication Connector between the sites NEWYORK and LONDON. The steps are described for LONDON; you should repeat them for NEWYORK.

Prerequisites

- Log on as Admin-NY1 on the server NEWYORK-1 and as Admin-L1 on the server LONDON-1.

- The TCP/IP transport stack must be installed on both Exchange Server computers.

Task 30a: Verifying a Computer's TCP/IP Configuration

1. On LONDON-1, click the **Start** button, point to **Settings**, click **Control Panel**, and then open the **Network** applet.

2. Switch to the **Protocols** tab and select **TCP/IP Protocol** in the **Network Protocols** list box.

3. Click **Properties**.

4. On the **IP Address** tab, verify that the parameters **IP Address**, **Subnet Mask,** and **Default Gateway** match the required network configuration —in other words, verify that TCP/IP is configured properly to support communication between NEWYORK-1 and LONDON-1. Click **OK**.

5. Click **OK**.

6. Close the **Control Panel**.

7. Click the **Start** button, point to **Programs,** and click **Command Prompt**.

8. In the command prompt window, type *ipconfig/all* and then press Enter. (To see the entire output of this command on screen, you might have to increase the **Window Size** and the **Screen Buffer Size** in the properties of the command prompt.)

9. Verify the displayed TCP/IP configuration.

10. Try to ping the other computer. For example, if you are working on the server LONDON-1, type *ping NEWYORK-1*, and then press Enter. Verify that the other machine replies to the ping.

11. Close the **Command Prompt** window.

12. Repeat steps 1 through 11 on the other machine.

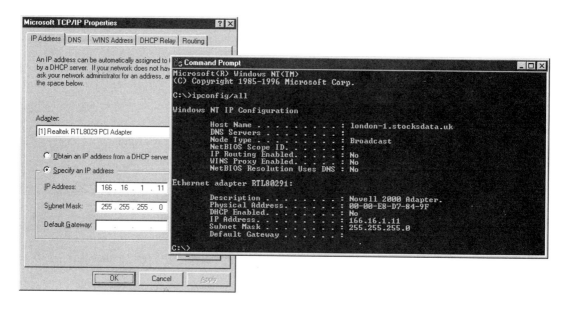

Task 30b: Deleting the Directory Replication Connector and the X.400 Connector

1. Verify that you are logged on to the server LONDON-1 as Admin-L1.

2. Click the **Start** button, select **Programs**, select **Microsoft Exchange**, and then click **Microsoft Exchange Administrator**.

3. In the left pane, double-click the site-object **LONDON** and the **Configuration** container, and then click on the **Directory Replication** container. In the right pane, select the **Directory Replication Connector (NEWYORK)** object.

4. Open the **Edit** menu, and click **Delete**. Or press the Delete key.

5. A **Microsoft Exchange Administrator** dialog box appears, asking if you are sure you want to delete the directory replication connector. Click **Yes**.

6. A **Microsoft Exchange Administrator** dialog box appears, asking if you want the directory replication connector in the remote site NEWYORK be deleted also. Click **No**.

7. A **Microsoft Exchange Administrator** dialog box appears, telling you that the directory replication connector has been deleted from the local site, that you must delete the connector from the remote site NEWYORK as well, and that you must allow up to an hour for replicated data to be completely deleted. Click **OK**.

8. A **Microsoft Exchange Administrator** dialog box appears, displaying the following message:

```
Note If you plan to reconnect to NEWYORK in the future,
any public folders that are modified or deleted in
either site will be replicated to the other site after
the sites are reconnected. Additionally, you should not
run the DS/IS consistency adjuster because public
folder permissions and owners will be changed.

If you never plan to reconnect to NEWYORK, you should run
the DS/IS consistency adjuster to take ownership of all
public folders replicated to this site. Run this from the
Advanced property page of any server in this site.
```

9. Click **OK**.

10. In the left pane, click **Connections**. In the right pane, select **NEWYORK-1 Connector**.

11. Open the **Edit** menu and click **Delete**. Or just press the Delete key.

12. A **Microsoft Exchange Administrator** dialog box appears, asking if you are sure that you want to delete **X.400 TCP/IP Connector NEWYORK-1 Connector**. Click **Yes.** If the Site Connector created in Exercise 25 still exists, perform the remaining steps (13–16).

13. In the right pane, select **Site Connector (NEWYORK)**.

14. Open the **Edit** menu and click **Delete**. Or press the Delete key.

15. A **Microsoft Exchange Administrator** dialog box appears, asking if you are sure that you want to delete **Site Connector (NEWYORK)**. Click **Yes**.

16. Repeat steps 1 through 15 on the server NEWYORK-1 as Admin-NY1, but keep in mind that you will be working with NEWYORK-1, not LONDON-1.

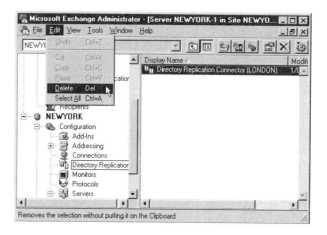

Review

A valid TCP/IP configuration is essential for the IMS to operate. If necessary, you can adjust settings using the **Network** applet of the Control Panel. You can use the Ipconfig utility to quickly verify the current TCP/IP configuration. To display all configured options, use the **/ALL** command line parameter. You can use the Ping utility to test IP connectivity to other hosts.

How the IMS Works

The IMS communicates only with the Directory and the IS. The MTA is not directly involved. Instead, the MTA places outgoing messages in the IMS message queue, where they will be retrieved. The MTA also receives messages from the IMS through the incoming message queue.

Delivering an Outbound Message to the IMS

Let's say that a user residing on the server NEWYORK-2 sends a message to a recipient, such as *JohnA@sombrero.com*, who resides in a foreign SMTP system. (See Figure 10-3.) The IS receives the message and hands it over to the local MTA. The MTA compares John's address with available address spaces in its GWART and discovers a reference to the IMS on NEWYORK-1 because the address space *@sombrero.com* has been assigned this IMS instance. The MTA uses RPC to transmit the message directly to NEWYORK-1. The MTA on NEWYORK-1 again compares the recipient address against the address space entries in its GWART. It finds a matching entry in the GWART that points to the local IMS. As a result, the MTA communicates with the local IS to transfer the message to the outbound message queue of the IMS. A private folder called MTS-OUT represents this message queue. The GWART, address spaces, and the message routing mechanism are covered in Chapter 9.

Retrieving a Message from the Outbound Message Queue

The IMS uses a MAPI profile to communicate with the Private IS and the DS. It is notified as soon as new outbound messages arrive in its MTS-OUT folder. At this point, the IMS retrieves the outbound messages. Since the message format must meet the SMTP requirements, it initiates conversion of the message content and any attachments. Once the content conversion is complete, the message is placed in the data directory \Exchsrvr\Imcdata\Out. (The \Exchsrvr\Imcdata directory structure is the temporary storage location for all inbound and outbound messages.)

The IMS uses the IMAIL features of the IS to issue the message conversion. IMAIL is a component of the IS that can handle objects in regular Internet e-mail formats such as UUENCODE and MIME. (IMAIL improves Exchange Server performance for Internet messaging.)

Converting Address Information

The address information of SMTP messages must also meet SMTP requirements. All non-SMTP address types, regardless of their format, must be converted. To accomplish this task, the IMS contacts the DS to retrieve an SMTP address for each recipient. If no SMTP address can be found for a specific recipient, the IMS encapsulates the information, thus creating a valid address. It then places the SMTP addresses into the converted message. Address encapsulation is explained in the section, "Address Encapsulation," later in this chapter.

Sending the Converted Message

The IMS retrieves the IP address of the remote host based on the Fully Qualified Domain Name (FQDN), such as *sombrero.com*. DNS will most likely be used for name resolution. The local IMS connects to the remote host through TCP/IP port 25. (Port 25 is reserved for incoming SMTP requests.) The message is sent as soon as the connection is established. Once the connection is released, the remote SMTP host delivers the message to the recipient. (See Figure 10-3.)

Receiving a Message

The process of receiving Internet messages is almost exactly the reverse of the process of sending them. The MTS-IN folder of the IMS is used to place incoming messages into the IS, where the MTA can pick them up. Significant differences will exist only if Secure/Multipurpose Internet Mail Extensions (S/MIME) messages have been received. In this case, message conversion cannot take place because the IMS cannot decrypt the message. Of course, only the correct recipient should be able to read an encrypted e-mail. Consequently, content conversion is bypassed and the message is placed as an S/MIME message in the MTS-IN folder.

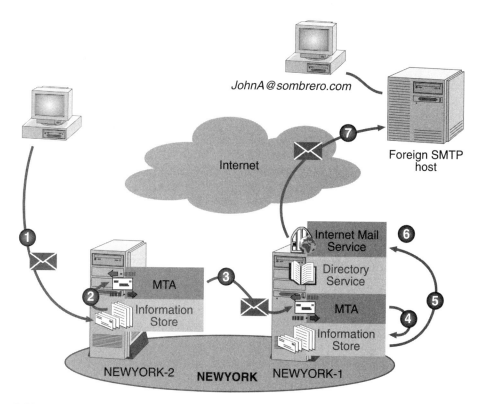

1. Message is sent to JohnA@sombrero.com. 2. IS hands mail to MTA. 3. MTA routes mail to NEWYORK-1. 4. MTA places mail in MTS-OUT. 5. IMS retrieves mail and requests conversion. 6. Addresses are replaced (SMTP). 7. Mail is transferred to remote host.

Figure 10-3. SMTP message flow.

The message handling process for SMTP recipients is as follows:

1. The IS receives the message from Outlook.

2. The IS checks to see whether it is responsible for the recipient and hands the message over to the MTA, if appropriate.

3. The MTA compares the recipient address with the GWART to determine a corresponding message path. The MTA routes the message to an available messaging connector, such as the IMS.

4. The MTA places the message in the IMS's MTS-OUT folder. This folder represents the outbound queue.

5. The IS notifies the IMS about the new message, and the IMS retrieves the message. It then initiates the content conversion through the IMAIL service that is part of the IS.

6. The converted message is placed in Exchsrvr\Imcdata\Out.

7. The IMS contacts the DS to retrieve SMTP addresses for all message recipients.

8. The SMTP address information is applied to the converted message.

9. The IMS uses TCP/IP to connect to the remote host through port 25.

10. The IMS delivers the message using SMTP.

The IMS Messaging Profile

The IMS maintains system folders such as MTS-IN and MTS-OUT within the IS. MTS-IN is the incoming message queue, while MTS-OUT is for outbound messages. To access these folders, the IMS uses MAPI and a messaging profile.

Automatic Profile Generation

The messaging profile of the IMS is created when you start the corresponding Windows NT service. It is deleted during the IMS shutdown. Therefore, if you want to examine the IMS profiles, the IMS must be running.

Profile Location

The IMS operates in the context of the Site Services Account. Accordingly, the IMS messaging profile is stored in the HKEY_USER hive in the Windows NT Registry as a key related to the Site Services Account. You can examine the settings using the Windows NT Registry Editor. To more easily determine the IMS messaging profile location, first log on as the Site Services Account. You might have to grant the service account permission to log on locally to the Windows NT Server computer because the service account is usually a domain user who cannot log on locally to a domain controller by default.

You can find relevant Registry settings under:

```
HKEY_CURRENT_USER
    \Software
        \Microsoft
            \Windows NT
                \CurrentVersion
                    \Windows Messaging Subsystem
                        \Profiles
```

Creating a Spy Profile

You can "steal" the IMS profile and access the message queues on behalf of the IMS using the MDB Viewer utility, which is on the Exchange Server CD in the \Server\Support\Utils\i386 directory. The binary file is called Mdbvu32.exe. With this utility, you can delete corrupted messages and correct other message queue problems.

To access the IMS profile, log on as the Site Services Account. Then start the Registry Editor. You can maneuver down the HKEY_CURRENT_USER hive to find the Profiles key, as mentioned above. If the IMS is running, you can find numerous profiles called **MSExchangeIMC xxxxxxxxxx** (where xxxxxxxx represents a number). Just save the first subkey to your disk.

At this point, you can create a "spy profile." First, manually add a new Registry key under the Profiles key. You can use a descriptive name such as *IMS Spy*. Next, restore the Registry settings, which were saved previously. As you restore the settings into the IMS Spy key, you will create the desired MAPI profile. You can use it to access the message queues using the MDB View program. (See Figure 10-4.)

Examining the Message Queues

Now it's time to break into the private hemisphere of the IMS! For this exercise, first stop the IMS and send some test messages to Internet recipients. The messages will be delivered to the MTS-OUT folder, where they will innocently wait for the IMS to pick them up. This time, you will "be the IMS" by starting the MDB View program and choosing the **IMS Spy** profile to log on. Open the **MDB** menu and select the **OpenMessageStore** command. The **Select Message Store To Open** dialog box will appear. Choose **Internet Mail Connector (NEWYORK-1)**. Click the **Open** command, which will make the **Open Root Folder** option available on the **MDB** menu. Select this command to display the **MAPI_FOLDER - Root** dialog box. In this dialog box, find the IMS system folders (under **Child Folders**). Now you can access these folders.

For example, you can double-click **MTS-OUT** so that exiting messages will be displayed in the **Messages In Folder** pane. To delete a selected message, select the **lpFLD->DeleteMessages()** function from the **Operations Available** box. Note that NDRs are not created in this case. To complete the deletion, click the **Call Function** button and confirm by clicking **OK**. (See Figure 10-4.)

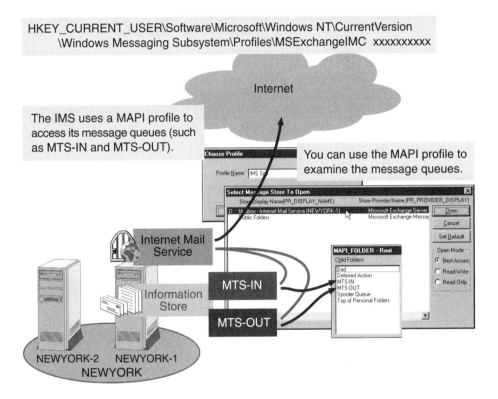

HKEY_CURRENT_USER\Software\Microsoft\Windows NT\CurrentVersion
\Windows Messaging Subsystem\Profiles\MSExchangeIMC xxxxxxxxxx

Figure 10-4. MDBView access to IMS folders.

MAPI profiles are stored in the Registry in the context of the Site Services Account. Follow these steps to access the IMS folders:

1. Log on as the Site Service Account to find the IMS MAPI profiles quickly.

2 Export the IMS MAPI profile and import it again to capture the dynamic IMS settings.

3. You can use MDB View to access the IMS system folders on the IS.

Overview of DNS

In the beginning, there was no DNS. Hosts had to maintain information about all other hosts on the Internet using a file called HOSTS to associate IP addresses with host names. As the number of hosts on the Internet increased, the HOSTS capabilities were exhausted. A new, more dynamic, system was needed to maintain the overwhelming amount of address information. Today, computers on the Internet, such as Exchange Servers running an IMS, typically query DNS servers to retrieve IP addresses for host names. DNS is a distributed database system.

SMTP Addresses

The IMS uses the SMTP address information in e-mail messages to determine which remote host to contact. Once the IP address of the corresponding SMTP host has been retrieved through DNS or the HOSTS list, a connection can be established and the message is sent.

First-Level Domain Names

A server in LONDON has the host name of *london-1.stocksdata.uk*. Below the top-level domain, *uk*, is the first-level domain, *stocksdata*. (*london-1* is the computer name.) The first-level domain includes the names of companies and other institutions and organizations. You must register the first-level domain name of your organization with the Internet Network Information Center (InterNIC) if you plan to connect to the Internet.

Subdomain Names

If you want to implement a hierarchical structure into the naming scheme of your organization, you can add names of subdomains separated by periods (.) to the left of the first-level domain name (for example, *frankfurt.stocksdata.de*). Read from right to left to see the hierarchy of an Internet domain from top to bottom. Most companies do not use subdomains because they want to hide their internal structures from the Internet. Microsoft, for example, uses only the first-level name (and the top-level domain name) in its SMTP name space: *microsoft.com*.

SMTP Address Registration

A complete SMTP address consists of *user name "at" host name*. Every SMTP host can perform message routing based on this information. The host name, or the FQDN, lets you determine the system that a user resides on. You usually use the DNS to retrieve the IP address of the target SMTP host by supplying the host name or FQDN. DNS name resolution is covered in more detail later in this lesson under "DNS Name Resolution."

Remote hosts will contact your IMS if the FQDN of your SMTP address is registered in DNS and points to your organization. To receive Internet messages, you must therefore register the domain name of your organization along with the IP address of your IMS in a DNS server. Otherwise, remote hosts will not be able to retrieve the IP address of your IMS.

SMTP addresses have the following characteristics:

- First-level name is usually registered with the InterNIC
- Hierarchical structure with subdomains might exist
- First-level domain represents company/organization names

Definition of DNS

DNS provides a hierarchical naming system that lets you retrieve IP addresses of hosts by specifying either a host name or a domain name. This system relies on a distributed database maintained by multiple DNS servers. A DNS database known as a *zone* maintains the actual IP address information of an organizational or geographical area. Zones are organized in a tree-like structure, which spans Internet domains. This tree, in turn, reflects the hierarchy of top-level and middle-level domains. Middle-level domains might split into further domains, often called subdomains. (See Figure 10-5 on page 616.)

Domain Name Space

The nodes of the DNS tree structure correspond to *domain name spaces* of various levels. Similar to a file system, in which a folder can contain subfolders, each domain can contain subdomains. A parent domain maintains the domain name space for all subdomains. For instance, a top-level domain such as *.com* maintains the address space for all its first-level domains, such as *sombrero.com* or *microsoft.com*. At the top of the DNS tree, which contains all top-level domains, is the DNS root. (See Figure 10-5.)

DNS Name Resolution

Let's say that an IMS wants to retrieve the IP address of an SMTP host in order to transfer a message to an Internet mail recipient. The IMS uses a TCP/IP component, known as the *Resolver*, to contact the local DNS server that is supplying the recipient's domain name. If the supplied domain name cannot be resolved locally, the local DNS server will query another DNS server on behalf of the Resolver.

Which DNS Server to contact is determined based on the hierarchy of the supplied domain name (*sub-domain.middle-level domain.top-level domain*). The local DNS server examines this name to find the lowest common domain name level between the local and the target domain name. For example, the lowest common domain name level of *sombrero.com* and *stocksdata.com* is the top-level domain *.com*. The lowest common level of *stocksdata.com* and *stocksdata.uk* is the root level. Once the necessary level is reached, the query is passed down the tree until the IP address is found. (See Figure 10-5.)

The query can therefore be passed to many DNS servers before the IP address is finally returned. The IP address is passed back through all involved servers until the local DNS server returns the address information to the Resolver. After that, the IMS receives the IP address, establishes the connection, and transfers the message.

The DNS query mechanism works as follows:

1. The Resolver passes a query to its local name server.

2. The local name server tries to resolve the FQDN; if necessary it queries other name servers on behalf of the Resolver.

3. The query starts at the most common level of the DNS tree and works its way down until it finds the requested data.

4. The requested data is then sent back up the tree until it reaches the Resolver, which had issued the request in the first place.

DNS Mail Exchanger Records

A DNS Mail Exchanger (MX) record points to a computer that can transfer messages using the SMTP protocol. Just as you can implement multiple IMSs in an Exchange Server organization, an Internet domain can contain multiple SMTP hosts. Consequently, more than one MX record can exist per domain. In addition, it is possible to grade the importance of hosts by assigning priorities to MX records. This mechanism is similar to the cost factor for Exchange messaging connectors. Only when the most important hosts (those with lowest preference values assigned to them) are unavailable are less important hosts contacted. This feature can provide fault-tolerance for incoming messaging connections.

You can use the Name Resolution Test utility (Restest.exe) to verify whether an e-mail domain name is registered in a DNS MX record. This utility is on the Exchange Server CD in the \Server\Support\Utils\i386 directory. Its command line is *restest [-debug] domain_name*. For example, the utility might return the following MX records if you query a domain name such as *sombrero.com*:

```
host[0] = '104.81.110.3'
host[1] = '104.81.110.4'
host[2] = '104.81.110.7'
host[3] = '104.81.110.5'
```

Windows NT Name Resolution

The IMS uses Windows NT name resolution whenever it cannot retrieve IP addresses using DNS or the local HOSTS file. If the domain name is not registered in a DNS MX record, the IMS checks the HOSTS file of the Windows NT Server (in the *<Windows NT>*\System32\drivers\etc directory). If the name isn't in the HOSTS file, DNS is searched again for A and CNAME records. If this attempt is still unsuccessful, Windows NT NetBIOS name resolution must deliver the IP address or the message will be returned to the sender in an NDR stating that the host was unknown. NetBIOS names can be associated with IP addresses using either Windows Internet Name Service (WINS) or the LMHOST file. WINS is a Windows NT network service that allows a WINS server to register IP addresses of computers in the network automatically. The LMHOST resides in the same directory as the HOSTS file.

Test Utilities

If you want to test the IP connectivity to a destination, you can use the TCP/IP Ping utility. Ping can take a host name or a domain name as a command line parameter. It resolves the name to the IP address and sends IP datagrams to the destination. To verify the DNS mail exchanger record, you can use the Restest.exe utility. You can also use the TCP/IP utility NSLookup to examine DNS records. NSLookup examines the DNS in more detail, but Restest is easier to use.

To check the MX records for *microsoft.com*, for instance, you would do the following:

1. Open the command prompt window.

2. Type *NSLookup* and press Enter.

3. Type *set type=mx* and press Enter.

4. Type *microsoft.com* and press Enter.

5. Analyze the returned information, and then type *exit* to close NSLookup.

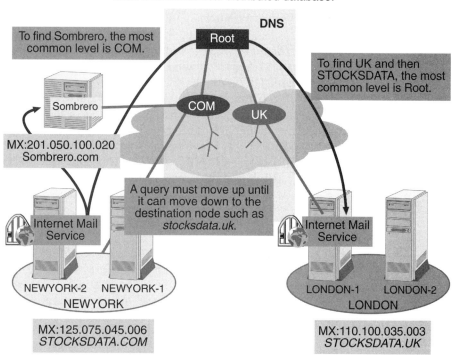

Figure 10-5. DNS name resolution.

The following top-level domains exist:

- ARPA: Temporary ARPANET domain (obsolete)
- COM: Commercial organization
- EDU: Educational institution
- GOV: Government institution
- INT: International organization
- MIL: Military group
- NET: Major network support center
- ORG: Organization other than those above
- <country code>: Individual country (for example, DE for Germany, UK for United Kingdom, and so forth)

Carylen Sungel

SMTP Send Process

SMTP defines the commands and responses at the application layer, which must be used between SMTP systems to transfer messages. For example, you can use these commands to specify sender and recipient information, and to initiate and terminate the transfer of the actual message content.

To initiate an SMTP conversation, the local host must connect to TCP/IP port 25 of the target SMTP host. The remote host, which listens to this port, receives the incoming request and sends back a welcome message such as **220 london-1. stocksdata.uk ESMTP Server (Microsoft Exchange Internet Mail Service 5.5.1960.3) ready**. To start the SMTP session, the local IMS should send the **HELO** command. The remote host accepts the incoming session, and the initiating application can start transferring messages. (See Figure 10-6.)

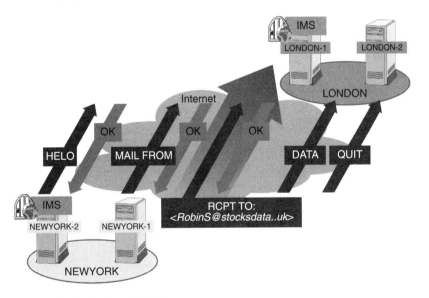

Figure 10-6. Sending SMTP messages.

To send an SMTP message manually, take these steps:

Note To follow the steps below, you need an active SMTP host (such as Exchange Server with IMS running). The IMS installation and configuration are covered in Lesson 3, "Starting and Configuring the IMS."

1. Click the **Start** button, and then select the **Run** command.
2. Type *Telnet* and click **OK** to start the Telnet utility.

3. Click **Preferences** on the **Terminal** menu.

4. In the **Terminal Preferences** dialog box, select **Local Echo**, and then click **OK**.

5. Click **Remote System** on the **Connect** menu.

6. Under **Host Name**, type the name of an IMS server (for example, *LONDON-1*).

7. In the **Port** box, type *25*, and then click **Connect**.

8. A TCP connection is set up to the remote host, and the following response is displayed in the Telnet window: **220 london-1.stocksdata.com ESMTP Server (Microsoft Exchange Internet Mail Service 5.5.1960.3) ready.**

9. Type *HELO* and press Enter.

10. The SMTP host replies with **250 OK**.

11. Type *MAIL FROM: robin.sherwood@stocksdata.uk* and press Enter.

12. The SMTP host replies with **250 OK - mail from <robin.sherwood@stocksdata.uk>**.

13. Type *RCPT TO: fred.pumpkin@stocksdata.com* and press Enter. (You should use an existing address.)

14. The IMS replies with **250 OK - Recipient <fred.pumpkin@stocksdata.com>**.

15. Type *DATA*.

16. The IMS replies with **354 Send data. End with CRLF.CRLF**.

17. Press Enter, and then type some text.

18. Press Enter, and then press Enter.Enter. (The "." between both instances of the word "Enter" is a period.)

19. The IMS replies with **250 OK**.

20. Type *QUIT* to close the connection.

21. The IMS replies with **250 OK closing the connection**.

SMTP Service Extensions

SMTP is a tried-and-true Internet specification. It has been in use for nearly two decades, and it is powerful and easy to implement. But it has some limitations in security and in other areas. In the mid-1990s, when SMTP messaging boomed across the Internet, the need for several protocol extensions became evident. ESMTP answered all of those needs by allowing implementation of additional protocol features without requiring modification of existing SMTP host configurations.

ESMTP enhances SMTP by providing a framework for two basic types of extensions—registered and unregistered. An example of a registered extension is the **DNS** command, which notifies the receiving system that a Delivery Status Notification should be returned to the sending host. Another example is the **SIZE** command, which lets you restrict the size of incoming messages before they are transmitted. Unregistered commands, also known as local verbs, must start with an *X* to indicate that they are not standardized. The **XEXCH50** command, as supported by the IMS, is such a local verb. You use **XEXCH50** to allow a sending IMS to send Exchange Server–specific content in messages.

As shown in Figure 10-7, each ESMTP session begins with the **EHLO** keyword (as opposed to the **HELO** command that initiates an ordinary SMTP session). The syntax is *EHLO <domain name>*. Older SMTP systems that do not support ESMTP reply to **EHLO** with an error response code of 500. After receiving response code 500, the initiating ESMTP system can determine that it is communicating with a standard SMTP host. The initiating host can then establish the session as usual using **HELO**. It can thus guarantee that existing SMTP hosts do not have to be reconfigured. However, RFC 1869 suggests the **HELO** command or the **QUIT** command as a response to error responses. Obviously, ESMTP systems that terminate the communication attempt using **QUIT** cannot communicate with older systems. This is especially critical for Internet communication, in which all kinds of SMTP and ESMTP systems can exist.

Note The IMS is a smart ESMTP component because it responds to error code 500 with the **HELO** command. You can use this component without further configuration in all SMTP and ESMTP environments.

If, on the other hand, a contacted SMTP host supports service extensions, it will answer **EHLO** with answer code 250. The receiving host will then send a list of all its supported ESMTP extensions.

The following table lists several ESTMP verbs supported by the IMS.

Command	Description
XEXCH50	Allows Exchange Server computers to identify each other for transferring Exchange Server–specific content in messages
HELP	Returns a list of commands supported by this server; described in RFC 821

(continues)

(continued)

Command	Description
DSN	Specifies Delivery Status Notification during message transmission to generate delivery failure status to the sending system; described in RFC 1891
SIZE	Determines the size of a message prior to acceptance; described in RFC 1870
AUTH=LOGIN	Lists the mechanism used for Simple Authentication and Security Layer (SASL); Exchange Server 5.5 supports only the LOGIN mechanism
TLS	Transport Layer Security advertises the ability to provide a Secure Sockets Layer connection between the SMTP communication partners; the initiating system must establish the TLS connection

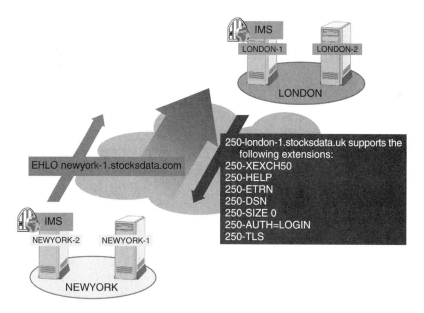

Figure 10-7. Establishing an ESMTP session.

To test the ESMTP features of the IMS, do the following:

1. Click the Telnet utility and verify that the local echo feature is enabled.

2. Click **Remote System** on the **Connect** menu.

3. Under **Host Name**, type the name of an IMS server (for example, *NEWYORK-1*).

4. In the **Port** box, type *25*, and then click **Connect**.

5. A TCP connection is set up to the remote host, and the following response is displayed in the Telnet window: **220 newyork-1.stocksdata.com ESMTP Server (Microsoft Exchange Internet Mail Service 5.5.1960.3) ready**.

6. Type *EHLO* and press Enter.

7. The SMTP host replies with a list of all supported features, as shown in Figure 10-7.

8. Type *HELP* and press Enter.

9. The IMS replies with **214-Commands:**

   214-   HELO   MAIL   RCPT   DATA   RSET
   214-   NOOP   QUIT   HELP   VRFY   ETRN
   214-   XEXCH50 STARTTLS AUTH
   214 End of HELP info

10. You can send a test e-mail message, as described for the SMTP protocol.

11. Type *QUIT* to close the connection.

12. The IMS replies with **250 OK closing the connection**.

SMTP Verify Request

You can use the SMTP **VRFY** command to retrieve recipient information from a remote SMTP host. The answer to **VRFY** will always include the user's full name and SMTP address. (See Figure 10-8.)

By default, this command is disabled for the IMS so that anonymous communication partners cannot query the address information of your organization. In the predecessor of the IMS, the Internet Mail Connector of Exchange Server 4.0, this command was not supported at all.

To enable the **VRFY** command, you must add a new DWORD value called EnableVRFY to the Registry settings of the IMS:

```
HKEY_LOCAL_MACHINE
    \System
        \CurrentControlSet
            \Services
                \MSExchangeIMC
                    \Parameters
```

When this value is set to 1 and the IMS is restarted, the **VRFY** command is supported.

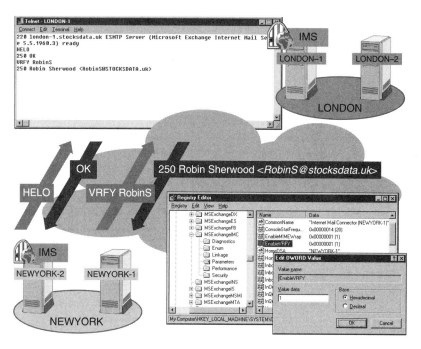

Figure 10-8. Verifying user addresses.

A **VRFY** example:

1. Sent: **VRFY FredP**
2. Received: *250 Fred Pumpkin <FredP@STOCKSDATA.com>*

Address Encapsulation

Address encapsulation is an IMS feature that ensures that all address information in an SMTP message follows the SMTP format. What is valid for recipient information is also valid for the originator—addresses must be converted to meet the SMTP requirements. A general messaging rule determines that a reply to received messages should always be possible.

Reasons for Address Encapsulation

The IMS usually contacts the DS to replace the current recipient information with SMTP proxy addresses for outbound messages. But a proxy SMTP address cannot be retrieved if no recipient information can be found in the directory database (for example, because no custom recipient exists for a given recipient's address). For this reason, the IMS must derive a valid SMTP address from the available address information using address encapsulation.

This situation can occur when you are backboning foreign messaging systems using an Exchange Server organization. For instance, you can connect a Microsoft Mail network to the Internet indirectly. In this case, messages are first passed from MS Mail to Exchange Server using an MS Mail Connector, and then they are routed to the IMS. At this point, the message, including all address information, must be converted to the SMTP format. But if the Directory Synchronization with MS Mail is not enabled, originator information cannot be found in the Directory because the originator actually resides on an MS Mail postoffice. Therefore, the IMS must encapsulate the originator address. The MS Mail Connector and Directory Synchronization are covered in Chapter 18, "Connecting to Microsoft Mail and Schedule +."

Address encapsulation also takes place when you connect two sites using the IMS. The DN is encapsulated if an Exchange user's address must be preserved.

Encapsulating Address Information

The IMS encapsulates foreign addresses using a naming pattern that always begins with IMCEA, which is an abbreviation for Internet Mail Connector Encapsulated Address. (The predecessor of the IMS was called Internet Mail Connector; address encapsulation has been available since the IMC was released with Exchange Server 4.0.) An identifier for the encapsulated address type, such as MS or X400, immediately follows, resulting in a string such as *IMCEAMS* or *IMCEAX400*. Then, following a dash, is the original address information. Invalid characters such as a colon (:) and a slash (/) are replaced with a dash (-) or an underline (_). As usual, the e-mail domain name is added after the @ sign to create a valid SMTP address.

The example above involved an MS Mail user. The MS Mail address of the originator is MS:NET/PO/MAILBOX. The IMS encapsulates this information and, using the encapsulation pattern, generates IMCEAMS-NET_PO_MAILBOX. As for any other users, the domain name (such as *stocksdata.uk*) is appended to create the complete SMTP address (IMCEAMS-NET_PO_MAILBOX@*stocksdata.uk*). The address information is valid, so replies are possible. (See Figure 10-9.)

Replying to Encapsulated Addresses

A reply to an encapsulated address is always possible because the domain name part (for example, *stocksdata.uk*) points to the organization in which the SMTP message is located. Consequently, an IMS receives the message reply. It retrieves the **IMCEA** string, which indicates that the original address information must be retrieved from the remaining address part. The IMS then converts the remaining part (MS-NET_PO_MAILBOX) into the original address (MS:NET/PO/MAILBOX). This original replaces the encapsulated address for inbound messages to allow the MTA further routing. The MTA checks the recipient address (MS:NET/PO/MAILBOX), determines the MS address type (which corresponds to an address space associated with the MS Mail Connector), and transfers the message to the connector's message queue. The MS Mail Connector then delivers the message to the recipient's MS Mail postoffice.

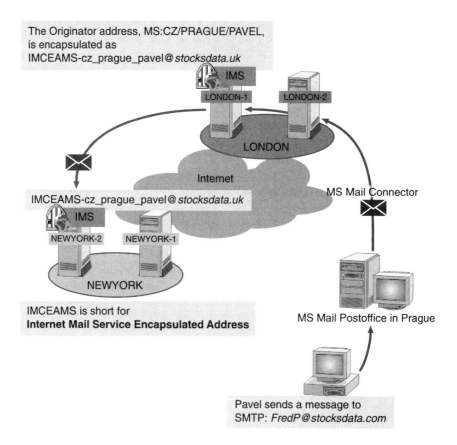

Figure 10-9. Encapsulation of e-mail addresses.

The encapsulation format is as follows:

1. Identifier for the connector: IMC

2. Identifier for encapsulated address: EA

3. Identifier for address type: EX, MS, X400, and so forth

4. A dash (-) followed by the actual e-mail address

Lesson 2: Starting and Configuring the Internet Mail Service

It's great to have a wizard around. You just name your wish, and all of a sudden the wish comes true. And what if your wish is to have a worldwide e-mail network? Meet the Internet Mail Wizard, which you can access via the **Internet Mail Service** command under **New Other** on the Administrator program's **File** menu. After you express your desires using a few buttons and edit boxes—abracadabra! Within 15 minutes your organization is connected to the worldwide Internet.

This lesson deals with the planning, installation, and configuration of the IMS, including installation prerequisites, the Internet Mail Wizard, and how to customize the IMS using two Registry settings that affect user name and reverse name resolution.

The lesson includes five exercises that guide you through a sample IMS configuration, from the DNS verification to the configuration of intersite directory replication on top of IMS connections.

At the end of this lesson, you will be able to:

- Design an organization's access to SMTP hosts
- Use the Internet Mail Wizard to install the IMS
- Start the IMS
- Describe special configuration options for dial-up connections
- Customize the IMS using the Exchange Administrator program and the Windows NT Registry

Estimated time to complete this lesson: 45 minutes

Planning IMS Connections to SMTP Hosts

Using one or many instances of the IMS, you can connect to remote SMTP hosts, including other IMS services, through permanent or dial-up connections. To avoid bottlenecks and inefficient message routing, you should plan these connections carefully. Your considerations should include security issues as well so that you can avoid surprises when you connect to the Internet. The DNS configuration is also important if you ever want to receive SMTP messages via the Internet.

Connecting to Remote Hosts

To support permanent or dial-up SMTP connections through the IMS, you must configure the TCP/IP protocol stack first within Windows NT Server. Permanent connections require only the TCP/IP configuration, while dial-up connections require the configuration of the Windows NT Dial-Up Networking component as well.

Dial-up connections are usually provided by your Internet Service Provider (ISP), but you can also configure a private dial-up computer network that exploits the Windows NT RAS capabilities. In this case, you set the entire dial-up configuration, including support for Point to Point Protocol (PPP), an appropriate phone book entry, and the user account, which is used for dialing in. All kinds of dial-up connections to ISPs, however, require PPP or at least the older Serial Line Internet Protocol (SLIP) for basic connectivity. On top of PPP or SLIP, TCP/IP provides a reliable and connection-oriented link between SMTP systems.

Configuring DNS

DNS configuration is an issue when you connect to the Internet, and possibly when you have an intranet in which DNS servers are configured for internal use. DNS can maintain the IP addresses of all your SMTP hosts. All other hosts can retrieve these IP addresses by supplying the host or domain name to their local DNS server. If you are connecting directly to the Internet, you must register the domain name of your organization with the Internet Activities Board in order to catalog your IP addresses using the global Internet DNS.

Determining Security Issues

On the Internet, every IMS by default accepts incoming connections from any other Internet host. However, this is typically not desirable if the server resides directly in a company network. In a more secure configuration, one server outside the corporate network accepts all incoming SMTP connections and then forwards the messages to the destination IMS. The servers in the background are configured to accept incoming connections from the outside host only.

In this configuration, the relay host is said to be installed in the *Demilitarized Zone (DMZ)*. To restrict incoming connections, use the **Connections** property page of the second IMS. The **Connections** property page contains a field labeled **Accept Connections**. This field contains a **Hosts** button, which launches the **Specify Hosts** dialog box. Click the **Add** button in this dialog box to set the remote host's IP address. After you restart the IMS, only the specified relay host can contact the IMS within your organization. Since the

IMS provides relay host functionality, you can use two Exchange Server computers to create such a configuration. To increase security further, you can implement even more complex configurations with additional hardware and software (such as packet-filtering routers and firewalls).

Here are some other security considerations:

- You can set message size limits, which apply to both incoming and outgoing messages, using the IMS's **General** property page. If an incoming message exceeds the size limit, the IMS stops writing data to disk and discards the remaining information. This ensures that huge messages sent from the Internet to your IMS will not fill the server's hard disk.

- The **Delivery Restrictions** property page allows you to control which users have permission to send mail through the IMS.

- Using the **Advanced Options** button on the **Internet Mail** property page, you can disable the delivery of automatically generated outbound replies (such as out-of-office messages). In this way, you can prevent internal information from being sent to Internet users. You can also set delivery options on a per-domain basis using the **E-Mail Domain** button.

- You can use the **Security** tab to secure outbound connections to other SMTP hosts. You can specify Windows NT Server Challenge/Response, Simple Authentication and Security Layer (SASL), or Secure Sockets Layer (SSL). SASL and SSL can be used in conjunction with any host. Windows NT Server Challenge/Response allows you to encrypt messages that will be transferred between two Exchange Server computers using RSA RC4 40-bit encryption technology.

Planning and Configuring Multiple IMS Connectors

You can install multiple instances of the IMS on different servers within your organization if your organization is large and your Internet mail traffic is heavy, but generally you can install only one IMS per Exchange Server. To balance the workload between servers, you can define appropriate address spaces and cost factors, which will affect outbound messages. Address spaces can also be replicated between sites, which means that the messaging path can span multiple sites and connectors if necessary. (See Figure 10-10.)

If your network has multiple IMS instances, you can define multiple DNS MX records, which affect inbound mail transfer. Remote SMTP hosts will attempt to connect to the IMS using the lowest MX record preference number first. If more than one IMS has the same preference number, one will be selected at random. If a connection cannot be established to either one, another available IMS with a higher number will be contacted.

Using the **Connections** property page of the IMS, you can also define dedicated IMS instances that only can send outbound messages or only receive inbound messages. For example, one server can be responsible for all outbound message traffic, while another server somewhere in the organization can be responsible for all incoming messages.

Binary Attachments

The IMS supports binary attachments of messages in two ways: it allows a message to contain binary data in the form of either UUENCODED 7-bit text strings or MIME.

UUENCODE is the traditional method for attaching binary data. But one disadvantage is that several different implementations exist. MIME, on the other hand, is the modern form of encoding message attachments, and it has been widely adopted across the Internet. It is defined in RFC 1521 and 1522.

MIME provides a way to exchange message text in different languages (character sets) along with binary data. Consequently, you can create and read messages that contain a variety of character sets (other than US-ASCII), and you can transfer RTF structures, images, sounds, video files, and so forth along with the message.

Internet messages can also be encrypted. S/MIME allows messages to be signed and sealed. This specification relies on an X.509-conform public-key encryption method. An S/MIME object contains the message in the form of a MIME body part with the content type *application/x-pkcs7-mime*, which is basically just a binary attachment. However, the IMS must handle S/MIME messages differently than it does MIME items because it cannot decrypt the data. In other words, it cannot issue content conversion using the IMAIL feature of the IS. However, a minimal amount of processing can be performed to provide support for S/MIME signatures to MAPI-based clients.

Let's say that an Internet user has sent you a signed message in S/MIME format but the message has not been sealed. If client support for S/MIME Signatures is enabled for the IMS via the **Clients Support S/MIME Signatures** check box on the **Internet Mail** property page, you will receive signed Internet messages in Microsoft Outlook with an additional attachment containing the digital signature. The name of the attachment will be SMIME.P7S. The message is viewable because it has not been sealed and you can use the SMIME.P7S attachment to verify the message integrity and origin. However, if the client-support for S/MIME is disabled, the message will not contain the digital signature and will simply appear as a standard message in Outlook. To enable or disable the support of S/MIME signatures, use the **Clients Support S/MIME Signatures** check box on the **Internet Mail** property page.

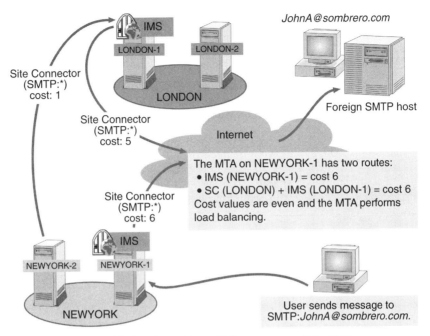

Figure 10-10. Load balancing with multiple instances of the IMS.

The characteristics of IMS are as follows:

- IMS, as a main messaging connector, can be used to connects sites using SMTP connections

- Can act as a relay host

- Makes possible the forwarding of all outgoing mail to a relay host

- One or more instances of the IMS can connect an organization to the Internet; you can configure separate outbound and inbound paths

Exercise 31: Verifying the DNS Configuration

SMTP message routing is performed based on e-mail domain names, which each SMTP address contains. DNS, which is the most popular domain name management system on the Internet today, maintains a hierarchical database of IP address information for host and domain name resolution. SMTP hosts are registered on DNS servers in MX records. The IMS can retrieve the IP address of a target host using DNS to establish a connection for message transfer.

Estimated time to complete this exercise: 15 minutes

Description

In this exercise, you will configure the TCP/IP transport stack for DNS use and prepare the HOSTS file for NEWYORK-1 and LONDON-1 (you will use a HOSTS file instead of a DNS server in the following exercises because DNS is not the main topic of this book). This means that the IMS will retrieve IP addresses from a HOSTS file. The result is the same as with a DNS server; the domain name will be resolved, and a connection can be established.

Note The HOSTS file contains references of host names to IP addresses. Place the IP address in the first column followed by the corresponding host name. Separate both entries in each single line by at least one space. This exercise suggests you use tabs (<tab> key) for structured separation.

- Task 31a describes the steps for verifying and adjusting the domain names of the servers belonging to the Microsoft Exchange organization.

- Task 31b describes the steps for associating the domain *stocksdata.com* with the IP address of the server NEWYORK-1.

- Task 31c describes the steps for associating the domain *stocksdata.uk* with the IP address of the server LONDON-1.

Prerequisites

- Make sure that TCP/IP is installed and configured on both computers.

- Log on to the server NEWYORK-1 as Admin-NY1.

- Log on to the server LONDON-1 as Admin-L1.

Task 31a: Verifying DNS Configuration

1. Log on to the server LONDON-1.

2. Start the **Control Panel**, and open the **Network** applet.

3. Switch to the **Protocols** tab, and select the **TCP/IP Protocol**.

4. Click **Properties**.

5. Switch to the **DNS** property page.

6. Verify the host name in the **Host Name** text box. It should be **london-1**. If not, change it.

7. In the **Domain** text box, type *stocksdata.uk*.

8. Check the existing DNS servers in the **DNS Service Search Order** list (if there are any).

9. Click **OK**.

10. Click **OK** to close the **Network** applet.

11. Click the **Start** button, point to **Programs**, and click **Command Prompt**.

12. Type **Ipconfig /all** and press Enter. If your Command Prompt window happens to be too small, use the **Ipconfig /all |more** command to display the information one page at a time.

13. Verify the **Host Name** in the **Windows NT IP Configuration** section. It should be *london-1.stocksdata.uk*.

14. Log on to the server NEWYORK-1.

15. Start the **Control Panel**, and open the **Network** applet.

16. Switch to the **Protocols** tab, and select the **TCP/IP Protocol**.

17. Click **Properties**.

18. Switch to the **DNS** property page.

19. Verify the host name in the **Host Name** text box. It should be *newyork-1*. If it isn't, change it.

20. In the **Domain** text box, type *stocksdata.com*.

21. Check the existing DNS servers in the **DNS Service Search Order** list (if there are any).

22. Click **OK**.

23. Click **OK** to close the **Network** applet.

24. Click the **Start** button, point to **Programs**, and click **Command Prompt**.

25. Type **Ipconfig /all** and press Enter.

26. Verify the **Host Name** in the **Windows NT IP Configuration** section. It should be *newyork-1.stocksdata.com*.

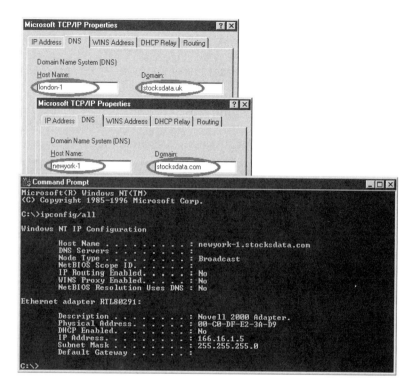

Task 31b: Registering the Domain STOCKSDATA.com

1. Start **Windows NT Explorer** on the server LONDON-1.

2. Move to the directory **<Windir>\system32\drivers\etc**.

3. Find the file named **HOSTS**; note that the filename does not have an extension.

4. Double-click **HOSTS** to display the **Open With** dialog box. Select **NOTEPAD** and click **OK.**

5. Search for the line *127.0.0.1   localhost.*

6. On the next line, type *<IP address of server NEWYORK 1> stocksdata.com* (for example, *166.16.1.5   stocksdata.com*). You will probably have to enter a different IP address for the server NEWYORK-1. If you do not know its IP address, you can find it by typing *ping NEWYORK-1* on a command line. If the server can be pinged, it will reply with its IP address. (Note the tab between the IP address and *stocksdata.com*.)

7. Save the modified file. Verify that the file is saved without a filename extension. (Notepad appends a .TXT extension by default, which you must delete.)

8. Open the **Command Prompt** window, and type *ping stocksdata.com*.

9. Verify that the remote domain has been found.

10. Start Windows NT Explorer on the server NEWYORK-1.

11. Move to the directory **<Windir>\system32\drivers\etc**.

12. Search for the **HOSTS** file.

13. Find the line *127.0.0.1   localhost*.

14. On the next line, type *<IP address of server NEWYORK-1>
stocksdata.com* (for example, *166.16.1.5   stocksdata.com*). You will probably have to enter a different IP address for the server NEWYORK-1. If you do not know its IP address, you can find it by typing *ping NEWYORK-1* on a command line. If the server can be pinged, it will reply with its IP address. (Note the tab between the IP address and *stocksdata.com*.)

15. Save the modification and verify that **HOSTS** does not have a filename extension. (Notepad appends a .TXT extension by default, which you must delete.)

16. Open the **Command Prompt** window, and type *ping stocksdata.com*.

17. Verify that the remote domain has been found.

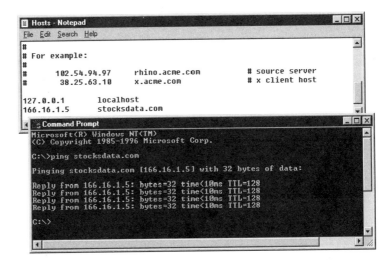

Task 31c: Registering the Domain STOCKSDATA.uk

1. Start Windows NT Explorer on the server LONDON-1.

2. Move to the directory **<Windir>\system32\drivers\etc**.

3. Edit the **HOSTS** file using **Notepad.exe.** Note that **HOSTS** does not have a filename extension.

4. Search for the line you entered in Task 31b (for example, *166.16.1.5 stocksdata.com*).

5. On the next line, type *<IP address of server LONDON-1> stocksdata.uk* (for example, *166.16.1.11   stocksdata.uk*). You'll probably have to enter a different IP address for the server LONDON-1. If you do not know its IP address, you can find it by typing *ping LONDON-1* on a command line. (Note the tab between the IP address and *stocksdata.uk*.)

6. Save the modified file. Verify that it is saved without a filename extension.

7. Open the **Command Prompt** window, and type *ping stocksdata.uk*.

8. Verify that the remote domain has been found.

9. Start **Windows NT Explorer** on the server NEWYORK-1.

10. Move to the directory **<Windir>\System32\drivers\etc**.

11. Edit the **HOSTS** file using **Notepad.exe**.

12. Search for the line you entered in Task 31b (for example, *166.16.1.5 stocksdata.com*).

13. On the next line, type *<IP address of server LONDON-1> stocksdata.uk* (for example, *166.16.1.11   stocksdata.uk*). You'll probably have to enter a different IP address for the server LONDON-1. If you do not know its IP address, you can find it by typing *ping LONDON-1* on a command line. (Note the tab between the IP address and *stocksdata.uk*.)

14. Save the modified file. Verify that it is saved without a filename extension.

15. Open the **Command Prompt** window, and type *ping stocksdata.uk*.

16. Verify that the remote domain has been found.

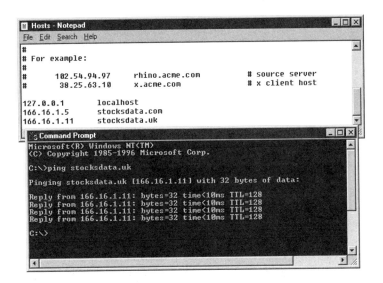

Review

To find the appropriate destination host for an SMTP recipient, the e-mail domain name must be resolved to an IP address. Once the IP address is retrieved, the connection can be established.

To install and use the IMS in a test environment, you can use the HOSTS file to register e-mail domains. For example, you can associate the IP address of LONDON-1 with the e-mail domain *stocksdata.uk*. Once registered, an IMS can transfer SMTP messages to the remote host. You can use the Ping utility to verify that the addresses have been associated correctly.

Using the Internet Mail Wizard

Every Exchange Server edition offers to install the IMS through the Internet Mail Wizard, an Administrator program utility. This wizard simplifies the IMS installation. It guides you through the most important IMS configuration steps, which ensures that you have achieved a minimal but probably correct configuration. Once the basic configuration is done, the wizard starts the IMS automatically to finish the installation.

Using the Internet Mail Wizard

The Exchange Server installation media is not required for installing the IMS. Instead, you can launch the Internet Mail Wizard at any time using the Administrator program's **Internet Mail Service** command on the **File** menu.

Welcome Pages

The first two wizard pages inform you about the steps that you will need to take to complete the installation, including the required configuration of the TCP/IP protocol stack. Read the welcome pages carefully, and then click the **Next** button.

Exchange Server Page

You will be prompted for the name of the Exchange Server computer that will run the IMS. You can specify any server in the local site. Select the **Allow Internet Mail Through A Dial-Up Connection** check box if you are using a dial-up link to the Internet.

Dial-Up Page

If you selected the **Allow Internet Mail Through A Dial-Up Connection** check box on the **Exchange Server** page, select a phone book entry (from the RAS phone book) for the dial-up connection on the **Dial-Up** page. Click the **Next** button to continue the installation.

Connection Page

If the IMS will connect to the Internet directly, select the **Use Domain Name System (DNS) To Send Mail (Typical)** option. If you want to implement a smart host or relay host topology, select **Route All Mail Through A Single Host** and enter an IP address or a host name. All outbound messages will be forwarded to the specified host.

Note The IMS can act as a smart host.

Address Space Page

Every messaging connector, including the IMS, requires at least one address space in order to make the connector available for MTA message routing decisions. To assign an address space of **SMTP:*** to the IMS, which will cover all outbound SMTP messages, select **All Internet Mail Addresses (Typical)**. Or you can select **Only Mail Destined For A Particular Set Of Addresses**. In this case, you must specify the routing information on the IMS's **Address Space** property page explicitly after the installation is complete. Address spaces are covered in detail in Chapter 9.

Site Addressing Page

On this page, you can adjust the site addressing scheme for the local site. If you change the site addressing scheme, all existing SMTP proxy addresses will be affected. By default, Exchange Server suggests a pattern based on the format *site.organization.com*. But you can enter a completely different site address if needed.

You can also adjust the site addressing later using the **Site Addressing** property page of the **Site Addressing** object under the **Configuration** container (as detailed in Chapter 8).

Postmaster Account

On this page, you specify a postmaster mailbox, which will receive undeliverable NDRs, status notifications, and other messages for the IMS administrator. You can either create a new mailbox or select an existing one for this purpose. If you create a new one, your Windows NT account will become its designated **Primary Windows NT Account**.

Site Services Account Page

The IMS runs as a separate Windows NT service. It operates within the context of the Site Services Account so that it can contact the Directory and the IS. For this reason, you must enter the password of the service account in the **Password** box.

Install Page

Use the **Back** button on this page if you need to correct configuration settings. Click the **Finish** button to complete the IMS installation.

Starting the IMS

The Internet Mail Wizard will start the IMS automatically after the configuration parameters are written to the Windows NT Registry. A new Windows NT service called **Microsoft Exchange Internet Mail Service** will appear in the **Services** applet of the Control Panel. You can manually stop and start this service at any time. This is especially important when you need to change the IMS configuration later on, because such changes usually require a restart of the IMS to become effective.

To test the new IMS installation, you can send SMTP messages to another Internet user—such as a test mail account provided by your ISP. The test account will reply to your test message automatically, which will confirm that the service is functioning properly. (See Figure 10-11.)

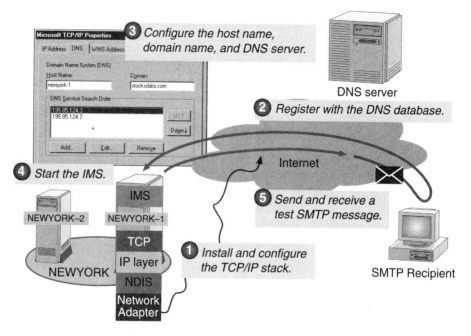

Figure 10-11. Starting the IMS.

The Internet Mail Wizard leads you through the following pages to install and initially configure the IMS:

1. **Welcome**; explains the wizard process and installation requirements

2. **Microsoft Exchange Server**; to select the server and to specify whether a dial-up connection will be used

3. **Dial-Up**; to select the correct connection entry from the RAS phone book

4. **Connection**; to specify whether the IMS will use DNS to send mail or if all messages will be routed to the same foreign host

5. **Address Space**; to specify the default address space of the IMS

6. **Site Addressing**; to specify the site address scheme for generating the proxy SMTP e-mail addresses

7. **Postmaster Account**; to specify the administrator mailbox, which will receive undeliverable NDRs and other system messages

8. **Site Services Account**; to specify the password of the service account

9. **Install**; to start the actual installation or go back to other wizard pages to correct configuration settings

Exercise 32: Installing and Configuring the IMS

The IMS is tightly integrated into Exchange Server 5.5, so you don't have to install it separately using the Exchange Server Setup program. Instead, you use the Internet Mail Wizard.

Estimated time to complete this exercise: 20 minutes

Description

In this exercise, you will install the IMS on NEWYORK-1 and LONDON-1 using the Internet Mail Wizard. Once the IMS is installed, you will test the connection by sending messages between both sites.

- Task 32a describes the steps for installing and starting the IMS on NEWYORK-1 and LONDON-1 using the Internet Mail Wizard.

- Task 32b describes the steps for ensuring that attachments are sent by the IMS using rich text formatting.

- Task 32c describes the steps for verifying that the IMS is configured to accept Internet messages.

- Task 32d describes the steps for enabling the logging of IMS events.

Note Tasks 32a through 32d describe the steps required to configure the IMS on the server LONDON-1 only. To exchange SMTP messages between LONDON-1 and NEWYORK-1 you need to perform the corresponding steps on the server NEWYORK-1 as well.

Prerequisites

- Complete Exercise 31.

- Log on to the server NEWYORK-1 as Admin-NY1.

- Log on to the server LONDON-1 as Admin-L1.

Task 32a: Running the Internet Mail Wizard for the Initial IMS Configuration

1. Click the **Start** button, point to **Programs**, point to **Microsoft Exchange**, and then click **Microsoft Exchange Administrator**.

2. On the **File** menu, point to **New Other**, and then click **Internet Mail Service**. A **Microsoft Exchange Administrator** dialog box might appear, asking if you want to switch to the **Connections** container of the current site. If it appears, click **OK**.

3. An **Internet Mail Wizard** page appears, welcoming you to the Internet Mail Wizard. Click **Next**.

4. An **Internet Mail Wizard** page appears, informing you about tasks that should have been completed already. Read the information carefully, and then click **Next**.

5. An **Internet Mail Wizard** page appears, asking you to select the Exchange Server computer in your site on which you want to install the IMS. Verify that LONDON-1 is selected, and then click **Next**. (The server will be NEWYORK-1 if you are installing the IMS in the site NEWYORK.)

6. An **Internet Mail Wizard** page appears, asking how you want to send mail. Verify that **Use Domain Name System (DNS) To Send Mail. (Typical)** is selected, and then click **Next**.

7. An **Internet Mail Wizard** page appears. Verify that **All Internet Mail Addresses (Typical)** is selected, and then click **Next**.

8. An **Internet Mail Wizard** page appears, asking you to specify the site address for proxy SMTP e-mail addresses for your users. Change the address to @*stocksdata.uk* if necessary. (Verify that the address is @*stocksdata.com* for NEWYORK when you are installing the IMS on NEWYORK-1.)

9. Click **Next**.

10. An **Internet Mail Wizard** page appears, asking you to specify the administrator mailbox that will receive undeliverable NDRs and other messages for the postmaster. Click **Select A Mailbox Or Distribution List**.

11. Click **Select** to display the **Administrator Mailbox** dialog box.

12. Select **Admin-L1**, and then click **OK**. (Select **Fred Pumpkin** for the IMS in NEWYORK.)

13. Click **Next**.

14. An **Internet Mail Wizard** page appears, asking for the password for the service account. In the **Password** box, type *password*. Click **Next**.

15. The last **Internet Mail Wizard** page appears. Click **Finish** to create the IMS.

16. A **Microsoft Exchange Administrator** message box appears, stating that a process has been started to update recipient e-mail addresses. Click **OK**.

17. A **Microsoft Exchange Administrator** message box appears, stating that the IMS has been successfully installed and started. Click **OK**.

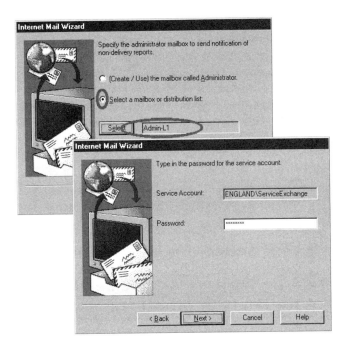

Task 32b: Configuring the IMS Message Content Settings

1. In the left pane of the Administrator program, switch to the **Connections** container of the site LONDON.

2. In the right pane, double-click the **Internet Mail Service (LONDON-1)** object.

3. The **Internet Mail Service (LONDON-1) Properties** dialog box appears. In the **Message Content** field of the **Internet Mail** tab, verify that **MIME** and **Plain Text** are selected under **Attachments (Outbound)**.

4. Click the button **Advanced Options** to display the **Advanced Options** dialog box.

5. In the **Send Microsoft Exchange Rich Text Formatting** list box, select **Always**. (Note that Out-Of-Office responses and other automatic replies are disabled by default.)

6. Click **OK**.

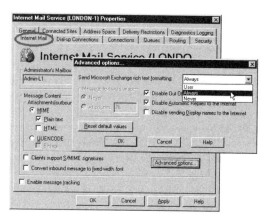

Task 32c: Configuring the IMS Delivery Restrictions Settings

Click the **Delivery Restrictions** tab.

1. The **Delivery Restrictions** information appears. Verify that the IMS is configured to accept messages from all senders and to reject messages from none.

Task 32d: Configuring the IMS Diagnostics Logging Settings

1. Click the **Diagnostics Logging** tab.

2. In the **Category** field, select the categories **Initialization/Termination, Addressing, Message Transfer, SMTP Interface Events, Internal Processing, SMTP Protocol Log,** and **Message Archival.**

3. In the **Logging Level** field, click **Maximum**.

4. Click **OK** to close the **Internet Mail Service (LONDON-1) Properties** dialog box.

5. If this is the first time that you have launched the **Internet Mail Service (LONDON-1) Properties** dialog box, a message box will appear, telling you that you must configure other SMTP hosts to deliver mail to your IMS before it will receive Internet messages. Click **OK**.

Review

The Internet Mail Wizard asks for the basic information required to install and start the IMS. This makes the installation of a working IMS easy for the administrator. You can specify advanced settings (such as rich text formatting) directly on the IMS property pages. The **Internet Mail Service** object resides in the **Connections** container, which exists in the **Configuration** container. Whenever you change the IMS configuration using this object, you must restart the Windows NT service of the IMS. You can control Windows NT services using the **Services** applet of the Control Panel or the Server Manager.

Customizing the IMS

The **Internet Mail Service** configuration object, which is in the **Connections** container, offers many configuration parameters on 11 property pages. Some of these pages, such as **Connected Sites**, **Address Space**, **Delivery Restrictions**, and **Diagnostics Logging**, are common to all messaging connectors. Others, such as **Internet Mail**, **Connections**, **Security**, and **Routing**, are specific to the IMS.

DNS or Relay Host

Depending on the topology and security considerations, you can configure the IMS to connect your organization either directly to the Internet or to a relay host that will deliver outbound messages to and from the Internet. (See Figure 10-12 on page 649.) When the **Use Domain Name Service (DNS)** option on the **Connections** property page of the IMS is enabled, the IMS will use DNS to retrieve IP addresses for e-mail domains. To transfer all messages to a relay host instead, select **Forward All Messages To Host** and then specify the IP address or the name of the relay host.

To define the route to remote e-mail domains in greater detail, use the **E-Mail Domain** button on the same property page. Clicking this button displays the **E-Mail Domains** dialog box, which provides (among other things) the **Add** button. By clicking this button you can specify on an e-mail domain basis whether to use DNS or a relay host. You can also specify a dial-up connection on an e-mail domain basis if you are not permanently connected to the Internet.

Inbound and Outbound Connections

In a large organization, it is best to install multiple IMS instances to implement load balancing across many Exchange Server computers. You can define one set of dedicated IMS services to take care of inbound messages and another to handle outbound traffic. To specify the transfer mode of a particular IMS, you can use the **Connections** property page as well. Within the **Transfer Mode** field four options—**Inbound & Outbound**, **Inbound Only**, **Outbound Only**, and **None (Flush Queues)**—are provided, as well as an **Advanced** button, which you can click if you want to restrict the maximum number of simultaneous connections.

The **None (Flush Queues)** option is especially useful if you plan to delete an IMS. Select it to stop the MTA from delivering messages to the IMS outbound message queue. The IMS will also stop accepting incoming mail. Messages remaining in its message queues, however, will still be delivered. Once the message queues have been emptied, you can delete the IMS object using the **Delete** command on the **Edit** menu of the Administrator program. Pressing the DEL key also does the job.

Restricting IMS Usage

The IMS lets you restrict its availability to users that reside only on the local Exchange Server computer. If you select the **Clients Can Only Submit If Homed On This Server** check box, users residing on other servers can no longer submit messages through this IMS. However, this option requires that you set the **Only From Hosts Using** option to **Authentication** or **Auth And Encrypt** in the **Accept Connections** frame on the **Connections** property page.

You must also set the **Only From Hosts Using** option to **Authentication** or **Auth And Encrypt** if you want to restrict IMS availability to authorized accounts. The corresponding check box, **Clients Can Only Submit If Authentication Account Matches Submission Address**, is under the **Clients Can Only Submit If Homed On This Server** option. It requires that the sender of an e-mail message has **Send As** permissions for the mailbox in order to submit messages through the IMS. The sender can be a mailbox owner or a member of a group that is assigned mailbox ownership. The IMS can determine whether a sender has **Send As** permissions by analyzing the message's **From** box. **Send As** permissions were covered in the context of configuring delegate mailbox access using Outlook in Chapter 7.

Note The **Clients Can Only Submit If Homed On This Server** and **Clients Can Only Submit If Authentication Account Matches Submission Address** options require additional Directory queries, which affect the performance of the Exchange Server.

Message Transfer Quotas

Using message transfer quotas, you can control which inbound and outbound messages the IMS will accept by setting a maximum size in kilobytes. To set a limit, switch to the **General** property page. Enter a value in the **Maximum (K)** text box under **Message Size**. This setting can help you control how much hard disk space the IMS occupies for message delivery. An NDR will be generated for all messages that exceed the maximum allowable size.

Monitoring Message Queues

As a separate messaging connector, the IMS maintains its own message queues within the IS. To monitor these queues, you can use the **Queues** property page. Select the **Inbound Messages Awaiting Conversion** queue if you want to check for inbound messages that must still be converted from an SMTP format into the Exchange Server format. Select the **Inbound Messages Awaiting Delivery** queue to list all messages that have already been converted and are waiting to be picked up by the MTA. Similar message queues are maintained for outbound messages—**Outbound Messages Awaiting Conversion** and **Outbound Messages Awaiting Delivery**. Message queues are discussed further in Chapter 15, "Maintaining Servers."

Note Another convenient way to check IMS message queues is by using the **Microsoft Exchange Server IMS Queues** item in the **Microsoft Exchange** program group. It is a preconfigured .PMW file that launches the Performance Monitor to display all four message queues in chart form.

SMTP Routing

The IMS allows rerouting and forwarding of SMTP messages to other SMTP hosts on the Internet or an intranet. In other words, the IMS can act as a smart host between different Internet mail systems. However, incoming SMTP messages are not rerouted by default. Instead, messages addressed to recipients that cannot be found in the Global Address List of the organization are rejected. The originator receives an NDR.

Enabling SMTP Message Routing

To enable message routing, you must use the **Routing** property page of the IMS. First you must select the **Reroute Incoming SMTP Mail (Required For POP3/IMAP4 Support)** option. As its name implies, this option is needed not only for the rerouting of messages that come from other SMTP hosts, but this option is also required if users within the local Exchange organization run POP3 or IMAP4-compliant messaging clients and want to send messages to users on the Internet. This is because those clients will contact the IMS directly rather than through the IS since they use the SMTP protocol for sending messages. For this reason, those clients appear as foreign SMTP hosts rather than as MAPI clients to the IMS. Support for POP3 and IMAP4 clients is explained in more detail in Chapter 11, "Internet Protocols."

When you select the **Reroute Incoming SMTP Mail (Required For POP3/ IMAP4 Support)** option, no e-mail domain is specified explicitly and all domains are configured as outbound at first. In other words, all messages sent to the IMS are rerouted back to the Internet. Since this is not desirable for your own e-mail domain, you must identify its corresponding domain name as inbound. In addition, you can specify that messages for particular e-mail domains be forwarded to other domains and specific SMTP hosts.

To define more than one e-mail domain as inbound, you can use the **Add** button several times. This is necessary if your organization maintains multiple SMTP domains (for example one for each existing site). It can also be necessary if the organization connects foreign messaging networks (with different e-mail domain names) to the Internet indirectly. On the other hand, you can reference multiple domain names by using a single "inbound" entry because it takes only a detailed match (from the right to the left) to reference domain names. Let's say that *stocksdata.com* has two subdomains, *newyork.stocksdata.com* and *losangeles.stocksdata.com* Both are configured implicitly as inbound once you specify *stocksdata.com* as inbound because both domain names match *moc.atadskcots* (reading from right to left).

Keep in mind that SMTP message rerouting is disabled for any inbound domain. NDRs are generated if recipients, whose domain names were specified as inbound, are not in the Global Address List. This is an important issue when you are connecting a foreign system, such as an MS Mail or a Lotus cc:Mail network, to the Internet indirectly. In this case, you must enable Directory Synchronization, which lets you maintain the complete address list of a foreign system in the Global Address List of the Exchange Server.

The characteristics of message rerouting are as follows:

- Exchange Server 5.5 can act as a smart host
- Rerouting is based on e-mail domains
- The rightmost part of a recipient address must match the rerouting entry
- E-mail domains need not be specified completely
- If no entry is made for a particular domain, the domain is considered as outbound
- SMTP address spaces for Exchange Server recipients must be specified as inbound domains

Configuring Security

SMTP hosts that are exposed to the Internet typically cannot restrict access to their TCP/IP port 25 if they need to accept Internet messages from all kinds of sources. SMTP has no built-in security features. It is recommended that you consider improving the security of your Internet connection through a second IMS and a relay host configuration, as mentioned earlier. To improve security even further, you can secure the connection between the exposed IMS in the DMZ and the second IMS in your intranet through SASL, SSL, or Windows NT Server Challenge/Response Authentication and Encryption mechanisms.

SASL adds authentication features to IMS communication. The command for identifying the IMS is **AUTH**, as discussed in Lesson 1 of this chapter. However, the IMS supports only the LOGIN authentication feature, which is not yet part of a specification. LOGIN uses a 64-bit-encoded user ID and password sequence that can be compared against a Windows NT account. Common SASL mechanisms, however, are KERBEROS version 4, GSSAPI, and SKEY. The IMS does not currently support these mechanisms, but future versions might.

Note Because LOGIN is not a standardized authentication feature, ESMTP systems other than the IMS cannot be contacted using this method.

SSL—also known as Transport Layer Security (TSL)—provides an additional security layer between the transport (TCP) level and the application (SMTP) level. It uses a pair of asymmetric keys (a public/private key pair) to encrypt all data before it is passed to the TCP layer. In other words, all data sent across the network can be sealed.

Note SASL and SSL have not yet been formalized as RFC standards.

To enable secure outbound connections to other Exchange Servers, you can use the **Security** property page. Click the **Add** button to define the authentication and encryption methods on a per-domain basis. In general, you can choose between SASL/SSL and Windows NT Challenge/Response security. You can configure incoming connections on the **Connections** tab. Click the **Hosts** button in the **Accept Connections** frame to open the **Specify Hosts** dialog box. Click the **Add** button to open the **Add** dialog box. There you can enter the remote host's IP address and subnet mask and set the **Only Accept From This Host If It Uses** option (to **Auth And Encrypt**, for example).

Note You can use the **Security** tab and the **Hosts** button on the **Connections** tab to enable security features when you use SMTP connections to other Exchange Server computers. However, messages are encrypted only during transmission, not during processing at the Exchange Server, which means that users receive unencrypted messages although the data transmission itself is secured.

Use the property pages as follows:

- **Address Space**; to assign address spaces for MTA routing

- **Connected Sites**; to prepare directory replication between sites

- **Connections**; to define the transfer mode and host settings

- **Delivery Restrictions**; to restrict the availability of the IMS on a per-user basis

- **Diagnostics Logging**; to determine which IMS categories should be logged at which level in the Event Viewer

- **Dial-Up Connections**; to select and configure RAS connections and to set corresponding logon information

- **General**; to set default message size limits for inbound and outbound messages, as well as an administrative note

- **Internet Mail**; to specify MIME settings, attachment settings, an Administrator's mailbox, and more

- **Queues**; to check status information about IMS message queues

- **Routing**; to define SMTP message reroute information

- **Security**; to enable SASL and SSL security or set Windows NT account information for outbound connections on a per-e-mail domain basis

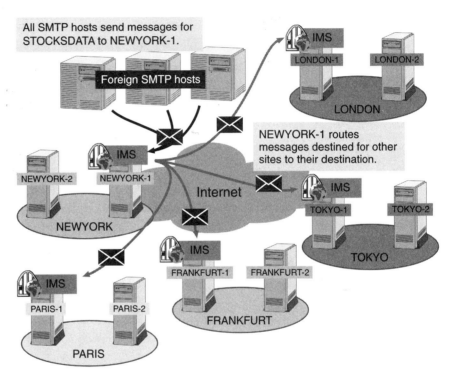

Figure 10-12. A smart host configuration with Exchange Server.

Exercise 33: Configuring Routing

The IMS can route SMTP messages on the Internet or an intranet. Because of this feature, Exchange Server can act as a relay or smart host between SMTP systems.

Estimated time to complete this exercise: 15 minutes

Description

In this exercise, you will configure the routing table of the IMS and examine the IMS routing settings that are required to support POP3 and IMAP4 clients.

- Task 33a describes the steps for configuring SMTP message routing so that POP3 clients can send messages to the IMS and have them routed properly.

- Task 33b describes the steps for forcing the recalculation of the routing table to initialize IMS addresses for use by Exchange Server.

- Task 33c describes the steps for stopping and restarting the IMS so that SMTP rerouting and POP3/IMAP4 support can take effect.

Prerequisites

- Complete Exercise 32.

- Log on to the server NEWYORK-1 as Admin-NY1.

- Log on to the server LONDON-1 as Admin-L1.

Task 33a: Configure Routing

1. Log on as Admin-NY1 on NEWYORK-1 and as Admin-L1 on LONDON-1.

2. Start the **Exchange Administrator** program and display the properties of the installed IMS on both computers.

3. Click **Routing** to display the **Routing** property page.

4. Select **Reroute Incoming SMTP Mail (Required For POP3/IMAP4 Support)**.

5. Note that on both servers, an entry for the local domain is created automatically in the **Routing** list box during IMS setup. NEWYORK-1 already has an entry for the domain *stocksdata.com*, and LONDON-1 has an entry for the domain *stocksdata.uk*.

6. Click **Add** to display the **Edit Routing Table Entry** dialog box.

7. In the **E-Mail Sent To This Domain** box, type the name of the remote e-mail domain. Type *stocksdata.com* for LONDON-1 and *stocksdata.uk* for NEWYORK-1.

8. Verify that **Should Be Accepted As 'Inbound'** is selected, and then click **OK**.

9. The **Routing** dialog box appears again.

10. Click **OK**.

11. An **Internet Mail Service** message box appears, indicating that the IMS must be restarted for the changes to take effect.

12. Click **OK**.

Task 33b: Rebuilding the Routing Table

1. Open the **Configuration** container of the current site.

2. In the right pane, double-click the **Site Addressing** object.

3. The **Site Addressing Properties** dialog box appears. Click the **Routing** tab.

4. Click **Recalculate Routing**.

5. A **Microsoft Exchange Administrator** message box appears, stating that the new routing information will take several minutes to replicate across the site and take effect. Click **OK**.

6. The **Site Addressing Properties** dialog box appears again. Click **OK**.

7. On the **File** menu, click **Exit**.

Task 33c: Stopping and Restarting the IMS

Reminder: Perform these steps on both NEWYORK-1 and LONDON-1.

1. Click the **Start** button, point to **Settings**, and then click **Control Panel**.

2. Double-click the **Services** icon.

3. Select **Microsoft Exchange Internet Mail Service**, and then click **Stop**. A **Services** dialog box appears, asking if you are sure you want to stop the IMS. Click **Yes** and wait until the service stops.

4. Click **Start** to restart the IMS. Wait until the service restarts again.

5. Click **Close**.

6. Exit the Control Panel.

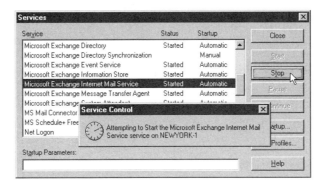

Review

You must use the **Routing** property page of the IMS configuration object to enable message routing. The **Reroute Incoming SMTP Mail (Required For POP3/IMAP4 Support)** option already represents a basic message routing configuration. This setting is required for POP3/IMAP4 client support. So long as no e-mail domain is specified explicitly, all domains are configured as outbound. But to receive messages from the Internet, you must define the local domain names as "inbound." SMTP rerouting is not performed for inbound domains.

E-mail messages can also be rerouted to other SMTP hosts. To configure this option you must define the target SMTP host on a per-domain basis.

Dial-Up Connections

The IMS supports dial-up connections to other SMTP-based systems on the Internet or in an intranet. This is an interesting alternative to the Dynamic RAS Connector.

Configuring the Connection

To support dial-up links to the Internet, you must first configure a Dial-Up Networking connection within Windows NT. After you verify that the Internet connection works, you can specify the corresponding phone book entry during the IMS installation. To change the connection later, you must use the **Dial-Up Connections** property page. You can also use this page to define an SMTP/ESMTP command for retrieving inbound messages and the logon information that is required for establishing the connection to the remote SMTP host.

You might want to activate the IMS only during specific times—for example, when telephone rates are low. On the **Dial-Up Connections** property page, you can schedule the activation on a daily or weekly basis. You can set active periods in the form of intervals or dedicated hours.

Retrieving Inbound Messages

When you are using a dial-up connection to the Internet, incoming messages are usually queued on an SMTP host of your ISP when the IMS is off line. Once your IMS becomes active, it must send a command to the remote SMTP host to retrieve queued messages. The IMS can use the TURN command, ETRN command, or a custom command to initiate mail retrieval.

Retrieving Mail Using TURN

TURN is a fairly old command that you can use to notify a remote SMTP system that the local host is ready for mail retrieval. This command is described in RFC 821. However, not all SMTP hosts support TURN. The IMS, for instance, can retrieve messages by sending TURN out to the other host, but it cannot respond to incoming TURN notifications.

The chief disadvantage of TURN is that it does not provide any security features. No verification of the remote machine is required to retrieve queued messages. Of course, it is unacceptable if every host can retrieve e-mail without providing authentication. Several systems therefore require an authenticated outbound connection before they allow the use of TURN. If your remote server requires a secured connection, you must specify the necessary logon information on the **Security** property page, as described earlier in this chapter.

Retrieving Mail Using ETRN

Modern ESMTP systems use the ETRN command, which provides security through the IP address and host name. ETRN signals a remote ESMTP server to send its queued messages to the local host. The request is based on FQDNs (such as *microsoft.com*). ETRN is defined in RFC 1985 and is widely accepted across the Internet.

The IMS in Exchange Server 5.5 supports the ETRN command completely. That means it can use ETRN to request data from a remote host, and it can answer incoming ETRN requests by sending queued messages to the requesting system. Figure 10-13 shows a scenario in which both the ISP and its customer use the IMS of Exchange Server 5.5 to queue and request data.

To request messages from a remote host, you must configure the ETRN command on a per-domain basis in the **Mail Retrieval** dialog box. Unfortunately, ETRN is supported only for dial-up connections. To hold messages until remote hosts ask for them using ETRN, you must specify the corresponding e-mail domains explicitly. Click the **E-Mail Domain** button on the

Connections property page to display the **E-Mail Domains** dialog box. Then click the **Add** button, enter the desired **E-Mail Domain** name, and select the **Queue Messages For ETRN** check box. (See Figure 10-13.) Then click the **OK** button three times.

Retrieving Mail Using a Custom Command

Some ISPs use SMTP systems that do not support TURN or ETRN. They typically require proprietary methods for retrieving messages. For instance, your ISP might use the sendmail application on its host. This application asks you to log on and retrieve queued messages using a remote shell. The **remote shell** (rsh) command initiates the session once the dial-up connection is established through PPP or SLIP.

For example, the IMS on LONDON-1 can use the following command to launch sendmail through a remote shell on a host at Provider.com: *RSH PROVIDER.COM –L <logon alias> "/user/lib/sendmail –Q –Rstocksdata.com"*. You can define this command using the **Custom Command** option in the **Mail Retrieval** dialog box, which you can open by clicking the **Mail Retrieval** button on the **Dial-Up Connections** tab.

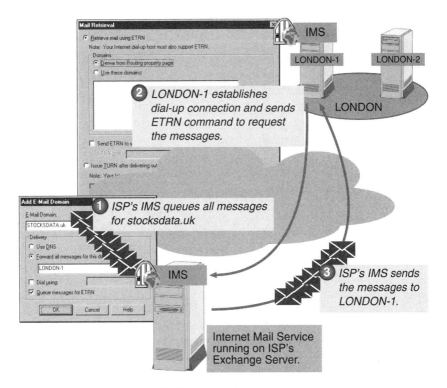

Figure 10-13. Using the ETRN command.

The mail retrieval configuration options are as follows:

- **Custom Command**; to define a command, such as remote shell

- **Do Not Send Retrieval Command**; to configure send-only hosts

- **Issue TURN After Delivering Outbound Mail (Requires Outbound Authentication)**; to request inbound messages from the remote host using TURN

- **Send TURN To Specified Host Instead Of Outbound Mail Host**; to retrieve inbound mail using TURN from a host other than the one that accepts the outbound messages

- **Retrieve Mail Using ETRN**; to request messages from a remote host either for specified domains (**Use These Domains** option) or for all domains in the routing list (**Derive From Routing Property Page** option)

- **Send ETRN To Specified Host Instead Of Outbound Mail Host**; to retrieve inbound mail using ETRN ESMTP from a host other than the one that accepts the outbound messages

User Name and Reverse Name Resolution

When communicating with users across the Internet, you might discover that some messages display originator information in the form of SMTP addresses (for example, *FredP@stocksdata.com*), while others show an originator's friendly name (for example, Fred Pumpkin). The latter are user friendly. Therefore, the IMS places each originator's friendly name in outgoing messages by default. This feature is also known as User Name Resolution.

Reverse Name Resolution, on the other hand, provides information that allows you to examine the path a message has taken through the Internet. To give it a try, launch Outlook and open a message you've received from the Internet. Display the message properties using the **Properties** command on the **File** menu and check the message for SMTP header information. As you can see, each SMTP host usually inserts its own address and time of receipt into the SMTP header of messages it handles, so you can follow a message's path from the originator to the recipient. In fact, SMTP header information can be quite interesting and enlightening.

Nevertheless, User Name Resolution and Reverse Name Resolution consume Exchange Server resources. User Name Resolution, for instance, requires that the IMS contacts the DS, and Reverse Name Resolution introduces additional message processing. To increase server performance, you might therefore want to disable both features. Unfortunately, there is no dedicated tool for accomplishing this task. You must use the Windows NT Registry Editor directly instead. You can create the corresponding values under the following key. (See Figure 10-14.)

```
HKEY_LOCAL_MACHINE
    \System
        \CurrentControlSet
            \Services
                \MSExchangeIMC
                    \Parameters
```

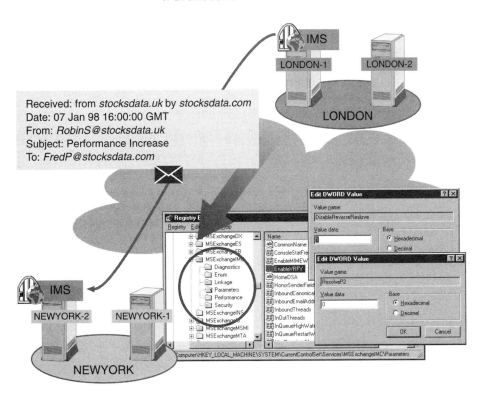

Figure 10-14. Disabling name resolution.

The following values disable name resolution:

- DisableReverseResolve [REG_DWORD] = 1; Disables Reverse Name Resolution

- ResolveP2 [REG_DWORD] = 0; Disables User Name Resolution

Exercise 34: Sending and Receiving SMTP Mail Using Outlook

After the IMS is installed, users can send messages to SMTP recipients. At least one SMTP address space must be associated with the IMS so that the MTA will place the SMTP messages into the IMS's outbound message queue (where they will wait for conversion and delivery). Message conversion cycles and other processes can be logged to the Application Event Log if Diagnostics Logging is enabled.

Estimated time to complete this exercise: 20 minutes

Description

In this exercise, you will use Outlook to send test messages through the IMS to and from another site. To verify message conversion, you will also enable the Diagnostics Logging feature. Later, you can use the Windows NT Event Viewer to examine the Application Event Log for SMTP protocol and SMTP interface events.

- Task 34a describes the steps for sending and receiving SMTP mail using Outlook to verify that the IMS was configured properly.

- Task 34b describes the steps for viewing SMTP events using the Event Viewer.

Prerequisites

- Complete Exercise 33.

- Ensure that Outlook is installed on both LONDON-1 and NEWYORK-1.

- Ensure that valid messaging profiles exist for Exchange mailboxes on both computers.

- Log on to NEWYORK-1 as FredP.

- Log on to LONDON-1 as Admin-L1.

Task 34a: Sending and Receiving SMTP Mail Using Outlook

1. On the **Desktop**, double-click the **Microsoft Outlook** shortcut on both computers.

2. From the server LONDON-1, send a new message to *FredP@stocksdata.com* by typing *FredP@stocksdata.com* in the **TO** box. Format the message text as bold and maroon.

3. Wait for the message from the originator Admin-L1 to arrive in Fred Pumpkin's mailbox on NEWYORK-1, and then reply to it.

4. Wait until Admin-L1 receives the response from Fred Pumpkin.

5. Open the response to verify that it is the correct message.

6. From NEWYORK-1, send a message to *Admin-L1@stocksdata.uk.*

7. Verify that Admin-L1 has received the message.

8. Exit **Outlook** on both machines.

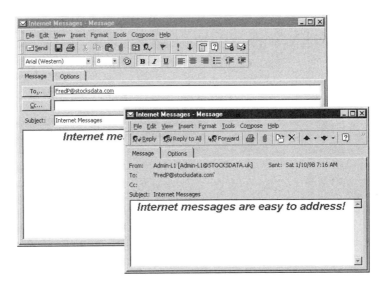

Task 34b: Viewing SMTP Events Using the Event Viewer

1. On LONDON-1, click the **Start** button, point to **Programs**, point to **Administrative Tools (Common),** and then click **Event Viewer**.

2. On the **Log** menu, verify that **Application** is selected.

3. Click **Filter Events** on the **View** menu to display the **Filter** dialog box.

4. In the **Source** box, select **MSExchangeIMC**.

5. In the **Category** box, verify that **All** is selected, and then click **OK**.

6. You will see information about incoming and outgoing SMTP connections as well as inbound and outbound messages.

7. Close the **Event Viewer**.

8. Close the **Event Log** and start Windows NT Explorer.

9. Switch to the \Exchsrvr\IMCData\Log directory.

10. Check that a .LOG file exists, and open it using Notepad. This file contains information on the communication between NEWYORK-1 and LONDON-1.

11. Close Notepad.

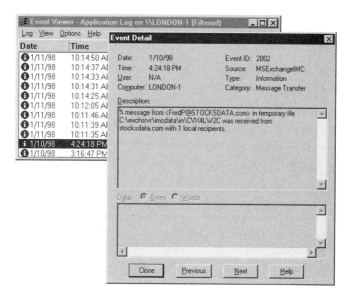

Review

The IMS can record status information about internal processes in the Application Event Log based on Diagnostics Logging settings. You can enable categories such as **Initialization/Termination**, **Addressing**, **Message Transfer**, **SMTP Interface Events**, **Internal Processing**, **SMTP Protocol Log**, and **Message Archival** separately using the **Diagnostics Logging** property page of the IMS.

Exercise 35: Configuring Site Replication Using the IMS

The IMS is a main messaging connector and provides all the features for enabling intersite directory replication. First you must configure the Connected Sites information. Then you can create and configure a Directory Replication Connector.

Description

In this exercise, you will reconfigure directory replication between NEWYORK and LONDON. For this example, no other connector besides the IMS should be configured between the sites. If other connectors remain (that is, still exist, such as the Site Connector or the X.400 Connector from previous exercises), delete them before continuing with this exercise.

- 35a describes the steps for configuring the **Connected Sites** property page of the IMS on LONDON-1.

- Task 35b describes the steps for configuring the **Connected Sites** property page on NEWYORK-1.

- Task 35c describes the steps for creating a Directory Replication Connector between LONDON and NEWYORK on top of the IMS.

- Task 35d describes the steps for creating a Directory Replication Connector between NEWYORK and LONDON on top of the IMS.

Prerequisites

- Log on to NEWYORK-1 as Admin-NY1.

- Log on to LONDON-1 as Admin-L1.

Task 35a: Specifying Connected Sites Information on LONDON-1

1. Click the **Start** button, point to **Programs**, point to **Microsoft Exchange**, and then click **Microsoft Exchange Administrator**.

2. In the left plane, open the site object **LONDON**. Open the **Configuration** container, click on the **Connections** container, and in the right pane double-click **Internet Mail Service (LONDON-1)** to display the **Internet Mail Service (LONDON-1) Properties** dialog box.

3. Click the **Connected Sites** tab, and then click **New**.

4. Type the following information:

In this box	You supply
Organization	*STOCKSDATA*
Site	*NEWYORK*

5. In the same dialog box, switch to the **Routing Address** tab.

6. Type in the information shown in the table below:

In this box	You supply
Type	*SMTP*
Cost	*1*
Address	*STOCKSDATA.com*

7. Click **OK.**

8. The **Internet Mail Service (LONDON-1) Properties** dialog box reappears. Click **OK**.

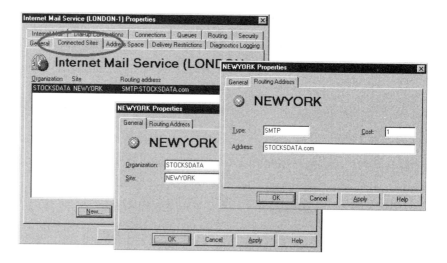

Task 35b: Specifying Connected Sites Information on NEWYORK-1

1. Make sure that you are logged on to NEWYORK-1 as Admin-NY1.

2. Click the **Start** button, point to **Programs**, point to **Microsoft Exchange**, and then click **Microsoft Exchange Administrator**. Make sure that you are connected to NEWYORK-1.

3. In the left pane, open the site object **NEWYORK**, and then open the **Configuration** container. Click the **Connections** container, and in the right pane double-click **Internet Mail Service (NEWYORK-1)** to display the **Internet Mail Service (NEWYORK-1) Properties** dialog box.

4. Click the **Connected Sites** tab, and then click **New**.

5. Type the following information:

In this box	You supply
Organization	*STOCKSDATA*
Site	*LONDON*

6. In the same dialog box, switch to the **Routing Address** tab.

7. Type in the information shown in the table below:

In this box	You supply
Type	*SMTP*
Cost	*1*
Address	*STOCKSDATA.uk*

8. Click **OK.**

9. The **Internet Mail Service (NEWYORK-1) Properties** dialog box reappears. Click **OK**.

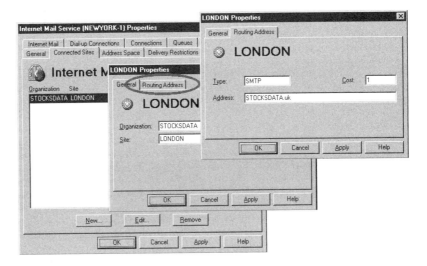

Task 35c: Configuring a Directory Replication Connector Between Two Sites (LONDON and NEWYORK)

1. Make sure that you are logged on to LONDON-1 as Admin-L1 and that the **Exchange Administrator** program is running.

2. On the **File** menu, point to **New Other**, and then click **Directory Replication Connector**.

3. Click **OK** when you are prompted to switch to the **Directory Replication** container of the site LONDON.

4. A **New Directory Replication Connector** dialog box appears. Select the **No, The Remote Site Is Not Available On This Network** option.

5. In the **Server In Remote Site** text box, type *NEWYORK-1*, and then click **OK**.

6. The **Directory Replication Connector (NEWYORK) Properties** dialog box appears. Click the **Schedule** tab, and then click **Always**.

7. Click **OK**.

Task 35d: Configuring a Directory Replication Connector Between Two Sites (NEWYORK and LONDON)

1. Make sure that you are logged on to NEWYORK-1 as Admin-NY1 and that the **Exchange Administrator** program is running.

2. On the **File** menu, point to **New Other**, and then click **Directory Replication Connector**.

3. Click **OK** when you are prompted to switch to the **Directory Replication** container of the site NEWYORK.

4. A **New Directory Replication Connector** dialog box appears. Select the **No, The Remote Site Is Not Available On This Network** option.

5. In the **Server In Remote Site** text box, type *LONDON-1*, and then click **OK**.

6. The **Directory Replication Connector (LONDON) Properties** dialog box appears.

7. Click the **Schedule** tab, and then click **Always**.

8. Click **OK**.

Note Wait until directory replication is complete. When it is complete, you will see the other site in the hierarchy with the following components: Configuration, Add-Ins, Addressing, Connections, Directory Replication, Monitors, Servers, and Recipients. Refresh the view within the Administrator program by pressing the F5 key to verify that the items have been replicated. The replication process should take less than 20 minutes.

---

9. Verify that replication is complete by opening the **Recipients** container from the remote site and viewing its mailboxes. Check that the directory information of NEWYORK is also available in LONDON.

10. Log off Windows NT on NEWYORK-1 and LONDON-1.

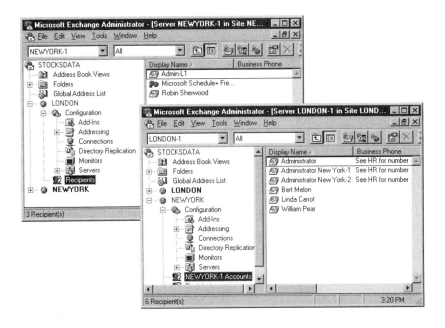

Review

The IMS enables SMTP message transfer and provides the **Connected Sites** property page, which you can use to configure information on remote sites. You must do this if you want to create a Directory Replication Connector on top of the IMS. Once created, the Directory Replication Connector creates and receives and the IMS transfers intersite directory replication messages.

Review

1. As an administrator of an organization, you need to connect two sites. Both locations have permanent network connections to the Internet. Which three messaging connectors can you use? Which one should you prefer? Why?

   _____

   _____

   _____

   _____

   _____

2. Which TCP/IP port is used to connect to a remote SMTP system?

   _____

3. What are the names of the outbound and inbound system folders of the IMS?

   _____

   _____

   _____

4. How does the IMS retrieve the IP address of the destination host?

   _____

   _____

   _____

   _____

5. Which utility can you use to test name resolution and TCP/IP connectivity?

   _____

   _____

6. Your organization has been connected to various foreign mail systems, including MS Mail, and now you are connected to the Internet. A remote administrator calls you because a strange-looking e-mail address has been received from your SMTP domain. The format of the address is *IMCEAMS-cz_prague_pavel@stocksdata.uk*. What kind of address is this and which recipient does it reference?

_____

_____

_____

7. You want to increase the security of a messaging network, so you decide to implement a relay host. The host will forward SMTP messages to and from an Exchange Server organization and the Internet. Can you use an Exchange Server to achieve a relay host configuration?

_____

8. Which command should you select within the Administrator program to start the IMS installation? Which Windows NT and Exchange Server configuration information is required?

_____

_____

_____

_____

_____

_____

_____

9. Two Exchange Server computers exist in one site. One server was installed using the Typical installation option and the other using the Minimum installation option. Now you want to install and configure the IMS on the server that was installed with the Minimum installation. What do you have to do to install the IMS?

_____

_____

_____

_____

10. Since you implemented an IMS, your company has become the target of attacks from the Internet. Large messages have been sent to the company's SMTP entry point to block the IMS. What can you do to reduce the effects of those attacks?

_____

_____

_____

_____

_____

11. You want to provide fault tolerance for incoming Internet messages. Messages should arrive at their destinations even when one IMS is down for maintenance. Which topology is best for an organization with two sites?

_____

_____

_____

_____

_____

_____

_____

_____

12. Which commands can the IMS use to request queued messages from a remote SMTP host?

_____

_____

13. Which command requests queue SMTP messages from an Exchange Server computer?

_____

_____

C H A P T E R   1 1

Internet Protocols

This chapter deals with Microsoft Exchange Server support for POP3, IMAP4, LDAP, NNTP, and HTTP. These protocols are implemented in Exchange Server 5.5 as a response to the growing demand for Internet connectivity.

Overview

In the early nineties, powerful messaging networks were built chiefly using X.400 systems. At the time it seemed that the X.400 standard was the comprehensive solution for worldwide messaging networks, so Microsoft Exchange Server 4.0 relied heavily on powerful X.400 capabilities. Meanwhile, the Internet boomed and began to adopt a non-X.400 messaging network. Exchange Server version 5.0 and version 5.5 are Microsoft's answer to the current trends. Today, Exchange Server is a powerful X.400 messaging system that provides far-reaching support of many Internet protocols. This chapter covers the various Internet protocols that can be used to access Exchange Server resources.

Lesson 1 of this chapter provides a brief overview of the Internet protocols supported by Exchange Server. You can read about the location of configuration objects within the DIT and the various levels of Internet protocol management.

Lesson 2 covers POP3 and IMAP4 in detail. IMAP4 can and will replace POP3 completely because it provides the same functionality and it allows you to work with additional messaging folders (for example, public folders). This lesson provides information about the implementation of these protocols, their operation, and their configuration. The components that must be installed and configured to allow POP3 and IMAP4 clients full operation are explained.

Lesson 3 discusses LDAP implementation. LDAP is a derivation of the X.500 standard, which allows the construction of global directories. This lesson discusses the functions provided by the Exchange Server 5.5 implementation and explains how to configure directory access.

Lesson 4 covers NNTP. Here you can read about the installation and configuration of the INS as well as the creation of newsgroups and newsfeeds. Information about those clients that you can use to access and manage newsgroups is also provided. The aspects of NNTP management and a method to test the NNTP connectivity are also discussed.

The support of Internet browser applications is covered in the last lessons of this chapter. Lesson 5 focuses on the functionality and configuration of HTTP, while Lesson 6 deals with Outlook Web Access, its architecture, and its installation.

Four exercises will guide you through the basic aspects of configuring Internet protocols. You will configure Microsoft Outlook Express as an example of a POP3, IMAP4, and LDAP client, and you will use Microsoft Internet Explorer 4.01 to access mailboxes, public folders, and the Global Address List through HTTP.

In the following lessons, you will be introduced to:

- The implementation of the POP3 protocol at the site, server, and mailbox levels
- The aspects of supporting IMAP4-compliant clients
- The configuration of LDAP
- The configuration of NNTP
- The configuration of the INS
- The basic configuration of HTTP
- The basic configuration of Outlook Web Access

Lesson 1: Overview of Protocol Support

The Internet is an immense information resource. It is so enormous and overwhelming that some people are already beginning to ask themselves whether they really require all the facts, news, data, knowledge, and so on that it provides. The amount of information is still growing and new technology branches, such as merchant systems that can be used to create Internet-based shopping centers, are still reaching across the Internet.

This lesson introduces the protocols that have been implemented into Exchange Server 5.5 to provide seamless integration into the Internet. The location of configuration objects within the DIT will be examined. Furthermore, you can gain information about site- and server-level configuration issues. A discussion of the configuration at the mailbox level completes this lesson.

At the end of this lesson, you will be able to:

- List the supported Internet protocols
- Configure the site default properties of the Internet protocols
- Configure server-level properties for NNTP, LDAP, IMAP4, and POP3
- Configure the Internet protocol support per mailbox

Estimated time to complete this lesson: 20 minutes

Internet Protocols Support

Exchange Server 5.5 supports many common Internet access protocols that increase the flexibility of this system significantly. Users working on UNIX-based workstations, for instance, can connect to Exchange Server resources using any POP3 or IMAP4 client or an Internet browser that supports Java script and Frames. (See Figure 11-1.) LDAP clients can be used to query the Exchange Server Directory to retrieve recipient information. Newsreader applications can download items from public folders through NNTP. In addition, discussion forums on the USENET—also called newsgroups—can be replicated with public folders.

POP3

POP3 is a messaging protocol that defines the commands needed to download messages from a host; it is a read-only protocol. For this reason, you can use POP3 only to download messages from your server-based Inbox. Access to other server-based folders is not possible. The most recent POP3 features are described in RFC 1939 and RFC 1957. More information about the POP3 configuration is provided later in this chapter in Lesson 2, "Internet Message Access Protocols."

IMAP4

IMAP4 is a modern Internet access protocol that allows you to download messages from a host. It further allows you to access all kinds of server-based messaging folders. You are not restricted to Inbox-only access using an IMAP4-compliant client as you are when using a POP3 client. This lack of restriction enables you to maintain all messages entirely at the server. You are not forced to create a local message repository at the workstation. IMAP4 is described in a series of RFCs, most importantly in RFC 2060. IMAP4 is covered in more detail in Lesson 2.

LDAP

LDAP is a derivation of the X.500 directory access protocol. It maintains similar functionality but is less complex. LDAP is, however, still more complex than POP3 or SMTP. This protocol has been defined in RFC 1777.

Exchange Server 5.5 supports the LDAP read and write functions. LDAP clients can look up address strings within the Directory and can also modify properties of directory items. In order to manage client access, you can configure LDAP configuration objects at the site and server levels. LDAP configuration is not necessary for individual mailboxes. You'll find more information about the LDAP implementation in Lesson 3, "Lightweight Directory Access Protocol," later in this chapter.

NNTP

NNTP is a protocol that is commonly used on the USENET to distribute information contained in newsgroups by means of newsfeeds. The USENET is a worldwide discussion system, comparable to a huge Internet bulletin board. Newsgroups, the basic USENET elements, contain information of any kind, which are comparable to public folders. Newsfeeds are the active components that replicate new information from one newsgroup to another by means of NNTP. This protocol is defined in RFC 977.

Within Exchange Server, newsgroups are implemented as public folders. Newsfeeds, on the other hand, can be created using the INS. Newsfeeds are the active components that replicate the information between public folders and newsgroups on the USENET, but they are not the only active component. Incoming newsreader connections are controlled directly by the IS. The configuration of NNTP is covered in more detail later in this chapter in Lesson 4, "Internet News Service and NNTP."

HTTP

HTTP is used to transfer documents formatted in HTML between an Internet host, or Web site, and an Internet browser, or Web browser. Exchange Server supports HTTP, which means that you can use your Web browser to access mailboxes, public folders, and the Global Address Book. The server-based resources are not, however, directly accessible. You must configure instead an IIS 3.0 (or higher) with support for Active Server Pages. This configuration is also known as an *Active Server*. In addition, you must set up Outlook Web Access, which is the component that translates messages from the Exchange Server format into HTML. Users who are logged on can access their entire mailbox just as they would using an Exchange client. They can also work with existing public folders. Anonymous connections are supported, but anonymous users cannot access any mailboxes.

Configuration settings are adjusted only at the site and user levels, but not at the server level. This is because HTTP support has not been implemented directly into Exchange Server 5.5. Instead, a flag is used to signal whether HTTP-based access is allowed. You can read more about the HTTP configuration in Lesson 5, "Hypertext Transfer Protocol," later in this chapter.

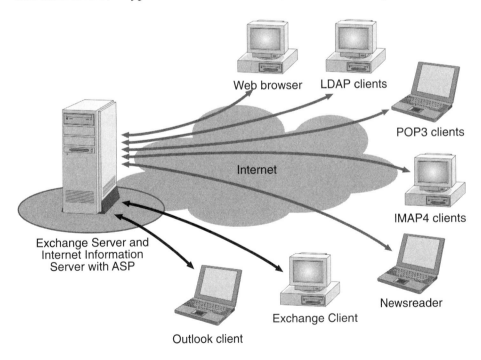

Figure 11-1. Client access to Exchange Server.

The Internet access protocols supported by Exchange Server and their corresponding clients are as follows:

- HTTP; Internet Explorer, or Netscape Navigator
- IMAP4; Outlook Express, or Netscape Communicator
- LDAP; Microsoft Internet Mail 3.01, or Outlook Express
- NNTP; Microsoft Internet News 3.0, or Outlook Express
- POP3; Outlook Express, Netscape Navigator Mail, or Eudora

Protocol Container Objects

All Internet protocols are enabled at the site, server, and mailbox levels by default, and incoming connections are accepted from any workstation. To put it plainly, each user who resides on an Exchange Server can use a POP3/IMAP4 client, an Internet browser, a newsreader application, or LDAP utility running on any computer to access mailboxes, public folders, or the Directory. When connecting to the Internet, however, it is desirable to increase the system security through more restrictive configurations.

Protocols Container

The **Protocols** containers, implemented at the site and server level, not only contain the management objects for POP3, IMAP4, LDAP, NNTP, and HTTP configuration, but are also management object themselves. The **Protocols** containers provide a total of four property pages, while only three—**General**, **Connections**, and **MIME Types**—actually refer to Internet protocol settings. On the **General** property page, for instance, you can define an **Outlook Web Access Server Name**. This name will identify the server in your site that has Outlook Web Access installed. This server is not necessarily an Exchange Server, but it is an Active Server providing Outlook Web Access. More information about Outlook Web Access is provided in Lesson 6, "Outlook Web Access," at the end of this chapter.

Protocol Administration

As mentioned previously, the Internet protocol administration is organized in three levels: site, server, and mailbox. Using the site-level objects, you can specify default settings for LDAP, NNTP, POP3, IMAP4, and HTTP. In contrast, server-level objects allow you to override the site-level defaults to achieve special server configurations using LDAP, NNTP, POP3, and IMAP4. A server-level HTTP object does not exist. The mailbox level, in turn, allows you to set user-specific settings regardless of the site- or server-level configuration.

As shown in Figure 11-2, IMAP4 has been disabled at the site level. This means that IMAP4 clients are not supported in NEWYORK. But Fred Pumpkin, one of the fictitious STOCKSDATA administrators, has enabled IMAP4 support at the server level for NEWYORK-1. All mailboxes that reside on NEWYORK-1 are affected and users residing on this server are able to reconnect. To prevent a particular user, such as Lisa Strawberry, from accessing a mailbox through IMAP4, this protocol needs to be disabled again at the mailbox level.

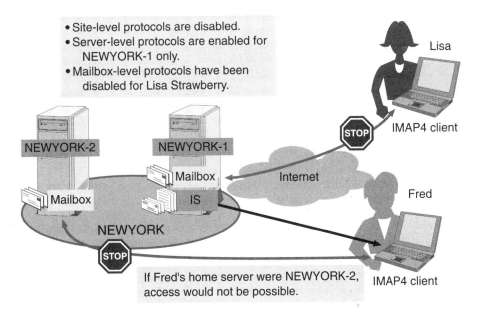

Figure 11-2. Restricting access to server resources.

The basic protocol configurations are as follows:

- Disabled at the site and the server but enabled at a mailbox; access to the server is impossible

- Disabled at the site level and enabled selectively on a server; only the connection to the enabled server is possible

- Enabled at the site and the server but disabled at a mailbox; access to the server is possible only for those users who do not have the protocol disabled for their mailboxes

- Enabled at the site level and disabled on a server; only a connection to the servers that do not have the protocol disabled is possible

Configuring Site and Server Protocol Properties

This section describes the configuration of Internet access using the **Protocols** container objects that can be found on the site and server levels. Both site- and server-level configurations are summarized in this section because their property pages do not differ significantly. The check box **Use Site Defaults For All Properties**, which is on the **General** property page of the **Protocols** container at the server level, illustrates the most significant difference between the two levels.

Restricting Client Access

Client connections to an Exchange Server can be accepted or rejected over Internet protocols based on the client's TCP/IP address. To identify the workstations that are accepted or rejected, select the **Protocols** object and then select **Properties** from the **File** menu to access the **Connections** property page. Select the **Accept/Reject Specified Connections** option, and then click the **New** button to enter the workstations' IP addresses and subnet masks.

Note Address rules with the highest priorities should be placed at the top of the address list.

If you want to secure incoming connections by explicitly listing individually accepted workstations by their IP addresses, specify the IP address of the workstation and a subnet mask of 255.255.255.255. If you want to specify a range of IP addresses, use the IP address and subnet mask. For example, specifying the IP address 24.112.93.0 and a subnet mask of 255.255.255.0 restricts the range to all IP addresses that start with 24.112.93. As shown in Figure 11-3, Fred's workstation has been explicitly granted access to the server, while another user's IP configuration shows an invalid IP address. Consequently, the other user has no chance to connect the server-based resources directly.

Note The settings specified through the **Protocol** container property pages will not affect incoming HTTP connections. HTTP-based access to the server can be restricted using the **Advanced** property page of the server's **WWW** service in the IIS Internet Service Manager.

Registering MIME Types

MIME types are a modern way to encode messages in 7-bit character streams. The primary and sub-MIME types can be defined to identify the encoded message content. Primary types describe the data in general, while the sub-MIME type describes the actual data format. For example, a regular picture stored in a .GIF file can be characterized as an *image* of the format *gif*.

Because both types are specified together and combined with a slash (/), the complete description is *image/gif*. If desired, you can define additional MIME types, such as *application/msexcel* for an .XLS file.

To provide the IS with information about MIME type associations, you can use the **MIME Types** property page of the **Protocols** container object. Several default associations already exist; however, you can define new mappings. Duplicate MIME types and file name entries are allowed for extensions, but only the first occurrence found in the list is used. You must place a higher priority MIME type and file name entry at the top of the list to rank one mapping over another.

Note The IS converts messages between the MAPI-based message format and the Internet formats (MIME and UUENCODE) as messages are requested by Outlook or an Internet mail application. This IS feature is called *IMAIL*.

Non-Protocol–Specific Settings

Non-protocol–specific settings are those settings that are provided for every directory object, usually on the **General** and the **Permissions** property pages. Such settings are the **Display Name**, an **Administrative Note**, and the defined access permissions. The **Display Name** of the **Protocols** container can contain up to 256 alphanumeric characters. The **Administrative Note** can contain up to 1024 characters and is visible in the Administrator program only. While these two settings can be found on the **General** property page, you can manage access permissions on the **Permissions** property page.

The Internet protocol property pages and their functions are as follows:

- **Connections**; to increase security by limiting the group of IP addresses that might contact the Exchange Server using Internet protocols

- **General**; to change the display name, to add an administrative note, and to specify an Outlook Web Access server name

- **MIME types**; to associate file name extensions with MIME types for inbound and outbound conversion

- **Permissions**; to grant permissions to special administrator accounts

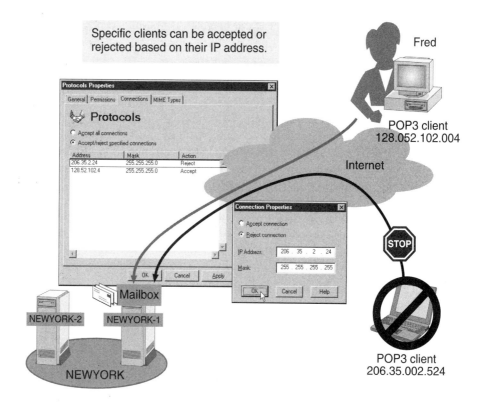

Figure 11-3. Rejecting Internet connections.

Configuring Mailbox Protocols Properties

Every mailbox object provides the **Protocols** property page, which can be used to manage Internet protocols configuration on an individual mailbox basis. While it is possible to enable or disable HTTP only for a particular mailbox, NNTP, IMAP4, and POP3 provide more flexible control. Besides enabling and disabling the protocols, you can also define message formats and MIME type associations as described earlier. Because LDAP is not used to access any mailbox resources, it cannot be managed on a per-mailbox basis.

Mailbox properties have a higher priority than server- or site-level settings, with one exception. (See Figure 11-4.) When disabling an Internet protocol at the server level, this special configuration takes precedence over all other settings. In other words, it is not possible to disable a particular Internet protocol at the server level and then enable it again selectively for a few mailboxes by using the mailbox properties. If you want to enable Internet protocol support for only a few users, you must disable the protocols for all other mailboxes instead.

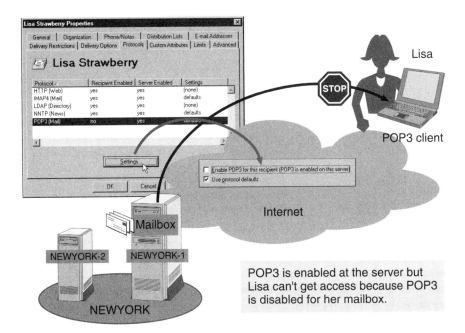

Figure 11-4. Specifying mailbox-level protocol settings.

The protocol-dependent mailbox configuration options are as follows:

- **HTTP (Web)**; to enable and disable HTTP-based access for the recipient
- **IMAP4 (Mail)**; to enable and disable IMAP4 for this recipient and to specify protocol settings such as MIME, UUENCODE, and character sets
- **LDAP (Directory)**; not configurable at the mailbox level
- **NNTP (News)**; to enable and disable NNTP for this recipient and to specify protocol settings such as MIME or UUENCODE
- **POP3 (Mail)**; to enable and disable POP3 for this recipient and to specify protocol settings such as MIME, UUENCODE, and character sets

Lesson 2: Internet Message Access Protocols

First the bad news: You will probably need to invest in hardware upgrades of your workstations if you want to use the most current versions of MAPI-based clients. Powerful applications, such as Outlook, require a powerful hardware platform. But the good news is that you don't need to use the most current MAPI-based clients in order to work in an Exchange Server organization. By using alternative programs, such as POP3 and IMAP4 clients, you can avoid immediate hardware investments.

In this lesson, you will read about the implementation of the POP3 and IMAP4 protocols into Exchange Server 5.5. First the POP3 protocol itself is discussed briefly, followed by an introduction to IMAP4. Then the architecture and operation of the protocols' Exchange Server implementation is explained. This lesson later focuses on configuration options for POP3 and IMAP4 at the server side and at the client side. A typical client configuration using Exchange Server connections will be introduced, followed by a presentation of various options for troubleshooting problems with POP3 and IMAP4 connectivity.

Two exercises are included in this lesson to illustrate the important POP3/IMAP4 configuration issues. Once you have verified the default protocol configuration, you will install Outlook Express along with Internet Explorer 4.01. The configuration of Outlook Express is covered in detail and will be used as an example for a POP3 client as well as an IMAP4 client. In fact, you will configure both access protocols in a single session to learn the functional differences.

At the end of this lesson, you will be able to:

- Describe the features of POP3

- Describe the characteristics of IMAP4

- Explain the operation and architecture of POP3 and IMAP4 in an Exchange Server environment

- Configure POP3 and IMAP4 clients based on typical configuration scenarios

Estimated time to complete this lesson: 55 minutes

POP3 Overview

POP3 is a read-only protocol that is designed to download messages only from a POP3 host. As an Internet standard, it is a platform-independent protocol, so you can use any POP3 client on any platform to connect to any POP3 host system, including Exchange Server 5.5. Examples of POP3 clients are Outlook Express, Eudora, and Netscape Navigator Mail.

Downloading Messages

POP3 has been designed specifically to download messages from a POP3 host. (See Figure 11-5.) This means that you cannot send messages to a host by means of POP3. This lesson will tell you what else you need to configure in order to do so. POP3 has been implemented directly in the IS. This architecture provides the best performance because additional components are not required and further component-to-component communication through local RPCs is not necessary.

Supported RFCs

Exchange Server 5.5 supports POP3 functionality as outlined in several RFCs, most notably RFC 1939 and RFC 1734. RFC 1939 describes the actual POP3 commands that are used to download messages. RFC 1734 standardizes the AUTH command, which comes into play to indicate that an authentication mechanism must be used to access a host.

Limitations

When using a POP3 client in conjunction with Exchange Server, only the Inbox can be accessed to download messages; other folders are inaccessible. Likewise, it is impossible to use any Advanced Security features of Exchange Server 5.5 for signing or sealing messages, so it's impossible to access encrypted messages. Support for server-based Inbox rules, the Out of Office assistant, and MAPI-based electronic forms are not available to POP3 clients.

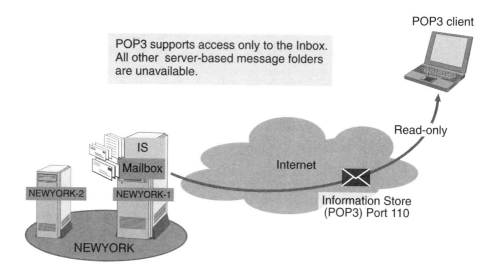

Figure 11-5. Implementation of POP3.

The general characteristics of POP3 are as follows:

- Does not support extensive messaging features
- Is defined in RFC 1939
- Is simple in design and provides support for reading messages only
- Permits AUTH command as described in RFC 1734
- IS implements POP3 support

POP3 Operation

A POP3 session flows as follows:

1. The client connects to the POP3 host's TCP/IP port 110.
2. The user logs on to the host supplying the user name and password.
3. The user checks for new messages.
4. The client downloads the messages and then disconnects from the server.
5. The POP3 host cleans up the server-based message repository.

Authentication Commands

As mentioned earlier, Exchange Server 5.5 relies on the AUTH command to provide an authentication and security mechanism for server-based mailboxes. Although this command is optional, anonymous POP3 access to an Exchange server is not allowed. In order to log on to a mailbox, you must use the Windows NT Challenge/Response mechanism or you must supply a user name and the corresponding password in non-encrypted form. With the latter option, the user name must be specified according to the following format: *Domain name/Windows NT Account/Mailbox Alias*. The POP3 password is your Windows NT domain password.

It is possible to simplify the user name identification by ensuring that the Windows NT Account and Mailbox alias are the same. In this situation, it is sufficient to supply only the user name, because the alias will be assumed to be the same as the NT account.

Note To log on as quickly as possible, always supply the user name in its complete format.

Commands and Responses

POP3 commands are not case sensitive. They consist of a keyword followed by arguments, if necessary. Each keyword is separated from its arguments by a single space. Only printable ASCII characters are allowed. Commands supported by Exchange Server are listed immediately following Figure 11-6.

POP3 responses are a combination of a status indicator and a keyword. Additional information may follow. Again, only printable ASCII characters can be used. The two existing status indicators are the positive (**+OK**) and negative (**-ERR**) response; both appear in uppercase letters. To give an example of a positive indicator, the server's typical response to an incoming connection on port 110 is **+OK Microsoft Exchange POP3 server version 5.5.1960.6 ready**.

POP3 Session States

A POP3 session progresses through three states, called *Authorization*, *Transaction*, and *Update*. The Authorization state is reached when a server's welcome message is received after the client has opened the TCP/IP port 110. In this state, the user account information can be sent to the server. Once the user has been validated, the session enters the Transaction state. Now, the user can read, download, or delete e-mail messages as desired. The session is released by sending the **QUIT** command to the server. At this point, the session enters the Update state, where the POP3 server sends a good-bye message to the client and releases the TCP/IP connection. (See Figure 11-6.) It is important to note that the IS performs the actual message processing on the server during the Update state once the client connection has been released.

Let's say Fred Pumpkin uses a POP3 client to log on to his mailbox on NEWYORK-1 and subsequently downloads all new messages from his Inbox. During download, the messages on the server are marked for deletion but are still available. Then Fred's client sends the **QUIT** command to enter the Update state. The TCP/IP connection will be released, and the marked messages deleted.

Figure 11-6. POP3 session lifetime.

POP3 commands supported by Exchange Server are as follows:

- **AUTH** *mechanism*; specifies the type of authentication
- **DELE** *msg*; deletes the message
- **LIST** *[msg]*; identifies the size of the message number
- **NOOP**; no operation
- **PASS** *string*; password
- **QUIT**; ends the Transaction state and the POP3 session
- **RETR** *msg*; retrieves the message
- **RSET**; cancels message deletion

- **STAT**; provides information about messages (number and size)
- **TOP** *msg n*; displays specific portions of the message header as identified by *n*
- **UIDL** *[msg]*; returns a specific message number
- **USER** *name*; identifies a mailbox

IMAP4 Overview

In contrast to POP3, IMAP4 allows you to download messages from basically every server-based messaging folder, including public folders. (See Figure 11-7 on page 688.) IMAP4 further introduces features that permit the manipulation of messages and message folders directly at the server, eliminating the need for a local message repository. IMAP4 can synchronize a client with a server.

Accessing Server-Based Resources

Running an IMAP4 client allows you to create, delete, rename, and move messaging folders and their content. You can also download messages partially or in their entirety. This last is an interesting feature because it allows you to initiate, for instance, the download of an attachment only. IMAP4 allows you to request specific portions of message text, but this feature is seldom used because it is more difficult to implement into client software. Of greater interest might be the ability to maintain flags along with their messages; this allows a client to indicate whether a message has already been read.

Offline Mode, Online Mode, and Disconnected Mode

IMAP4 has three modes that a client can enter: the offline mode, the online mode, and the disconnected mode. The offline mode illustrates a typical remote client session, in which the client connects to the server occasionally to download all messages to the local workstation. The client then disconnects and the user works with the local message store. The principle of this mode is also found in every POP3 client. POP3 clients, however, do not recognize the online mode or the disconnected mode—these are IMAP4 characteristics only. During online mode operation, you can manipulate messages and folders directly in a server-based repository, such as your Exchange Server mailbox. Typically, a local message store is not maintained when a user works on line continually, so a permanent connection to the server is required and must exist for the entire lifetime of the session. The disconnected mode is a sort of a mix between the offline mode and the online mode. An online message store and an offline message store are both required because your client will download messages selectively from the server during online operation. Working off line, you still have the ability to access your messages. Any changes applied in offline mode will be resynchronized with the server during the next online operation. This mechanism works similarly to the Offline Message Store of the Exchange Server transport as described in Chapter 7.

IMAP4 Authentication Mechanisms

Although RFC 1731 defines the authentication mechanisms to be used with IMAP4, Exchange Server 5.5 supports none of these. RFC 1731 recommends Kerberos version 4, GSSAPI, and S/Key, but Exchange Server uses three different authentication methods to impersonate clients. They are Basic (Clear Text), Windows NT Challenge/Response, and Microsoft Commercial Internet System (MCIS). All three methods can be combined with Secure Sockets Layer (SSL) encryption technology.

If the default Basic (Clear Text) authentication methods have been enabled, clients are not forced to encrypt the user name or password. Instead, they can use the LOGIN command directly to transmit this information to the server in readable text. Users running Internet Mail 3.0, for instance, can use this method to log on.

Windows NT Challenge/Response is more complex and secure than Basic (Clear Text), because it uses the Windows NT network security mechanisms for authentication. To initiate the Windows NT Challenge/Response authentication, the client sends the **AUTH NTLM** command to the host. The server returns a positive response code. At this point, the client sends a negotiation message to the server, which contains random information. This random information is important because the server will use it to create a unique string also known as the *challenge*. The server transmits the challenge to the client. The client must encrypt the challenge using your Windows NT password before it sends the encrypted information back to the server. The encrypted information corresponds to the *response*. The server, of course, knows the user's password and can decrypt the response in order to compare the result against the original challenge. If the response and the challenge match one another, the server sends a notification to the client that the user logged on successfully. Otherwise, the client will receive an "access denied" message.

MCIS uses a Windows NT Challenge/Response mechanism for authentication, but in an optimized form for Internet networking.

Note Exchange Server 5.5 uses the same authentication mechanisms for all Internet protocols.

Supported RFCs

IMAP4-compliant features are defined in several RFCs. They are as follows:

- RFC 1731; describes the IMAP4 authentication mechanisms
- RFC 1732; addresses compatibility issues with IMAP2
- RFC 1733; describes the offline mode, the online mode, and the disconnected electronic mail mode
- RFC 2060; defines the actual IMAP4rev1 protocol
- RFC 2061; outlines compatibility with the IMAP2bis protocol
- RFC 2062; lists IMAP obsolete syntax
- RFC 2086; describes the IMAP4 Access Control List (ACL) extension
- RFC 2087; introduces the IMAP4 QUOTA extension to limit access to server-based resources
- RFC 2088; defines IMAP4 non-synchronizing literals
- RFC 2095; standardizes the IMAP/POP AUTH extension
- RFC 2177; describes the IMAP4 IDLE command
- RFC 2180; defines how to access a mailbox multiple times simultaneously
- RFC 2221; allows one IMAP4 host to redirect clients based on LOGIN and AUTHENTICATE referrals

The most important recommendation is RFC 2060. It describes the features and commands that a messaging client must support in order to be IMAP4 compliant. Outlook Express is an example of such a client.

Non-Synchronizing Literals

Some of the remarkable features of IMAP4 are non-synchronizing literals, as described in RFC 2088. Using these literals, a client can indicate that a line of data continues on the next line through a string formatted as **{XX+}**. XX is a number that indicates how many characters will follow on the next line. An IMAP4 host will not send any response codes to the client if it detects a non-synchronizing literal, so you might find the following line in an IMAP4 protocol log file:

```
* OK Microsoft Exchange IMAP4rev1 server version 5.5.1960.6
(stocksdata.com) ready
A000 LOGIN STOCKSDATA/Admin-NY1/FredP {08+}
password
A000 OK LOGIN completed.
```

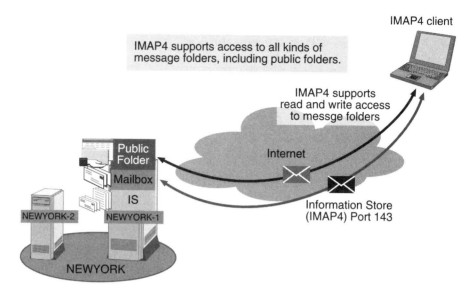

Figure 11-7. Implementation of IMAP4.

The general characteristics of IMAP4 are as follows:

- Does not support Advanced Security features

- Is defined in RFC 1731, 1732, 1733, 2060, 2061, 2086, 2087, 2088, 2095, 2177, and 2180

- Is a complex protocol that provides support for downloading and uploading messages

- Support is implemented in the IS

IMAP4 Operation

IMAP4 is a protocol that contains 24 commands and 15 server responses. This protocol also describes the session states and which client command can be used in which session state. For example, you will receive a negative response if you try to access a mailbox before being logged on (for example, **BAD LIST command received in invalid state**).

IMAP4 Session States

IMAP4 defines four session states: *Non-Authenticated*, *Authenticated*, *Selected*, and *Logout*. (See Figure 11-8 on page 691.) The Non-Authenticated state is entered as soon as an IMAP4 client connects to TCP/IP port 143 at the server. In this state, the client must supply authentication credentials; most commands cannot be used yet. The server greeting *** OK Microsoft Exchange IMAP4rev1 server version 5.5.1960.6 (stocksdata.com) ready** is an example of a response allowed in this state. When the client logs on using the **LOGIN** command, the session enters the Authenticated state. The client must select a mailbox or folder in this state, using the **SELECT** command for this purpose. This mailbox selection allows the client to enter the Selected state, in which most of the IMAP4 commands are available. **STORE** and **FETCH** are good examples of such commands. Users typically work with their IMAP4 clients in Selected state while working with messages. Once work has been finished, the user logs off. The client then transmits the **LOGOUT** command to the server and the connection enters the Logout state. The connection is terminated and the server closes the connection, sending a good-bye notification that includes the server version (for example,*** BYE Microsoft Exchange IMAP4rev1 server version 5.5.1960.6 signing off 0012 OK LOGOUT completed**).

Note Client commands can be used only in their corresponding state. It is a protocol error to use a command outside the appropriate state context.

Anonymous Access

Exchange Server 5.5 supports anonymous access to public folders based on IMAP4. The following configuration steps are required to enable this form of access:

1. Enable anonymous IMAP4 access through the **Anonymous** property page of the corresponding protocol object within the Administrator program.

2. Specify an anonymous account at the same location.

3. Within the Administrator program or using Outlook, define anonymous access permission for particular public folders.

The configuration of public folders is covered in Chapter 12, "Creating and Managing Public Folders."

If anonymous access has been enabled, users connecting anonymously don't need to supply valid user information in order to enter the Authenticated state, but they do need to supply logon credentials. The IS will not perform password verification, but it does record the logged on user in the Application Event Log.

Note Anonymous IMAP4 users can access a mailbox in addition to public folders. This mailbox must have an alias that is the same as the name of the IMAP4 anonymous account.

Commands and Responses

IMAP4 commands are strings (not case sensitive) of printable ASCII characters, which consist of a tag followed by a keyword and its arguments, if necessary. Each keyword is separated from its arguments by a single space. IMAP4 client interactions are ruled by commands transmitted by a client and responses returned by the server. All interactions are kept in the form of lines terminated through a Carriage-Return Line-Feed pair (CRLF). Non-synchronizing literals are the only exception to this convention.

An identifier, known as a *tag*, is a prefix to each client command. These tags are necessary because multiple commands might be in progress simultaneously. As the server responds to a command, it uses the tag to identify the command to which the response belongs. However, data transmitted by the host and status notifications that are not associated with a client command must be prefixed with the token "*". These constructs are called *untagged responses*.

IMAP4 responses are a combination of a client command tag (or the * sign) and the actual response. Additional information may follow. Only printable ASCII characters can be used. The positive is **OK**, while a negative response is indicated through either **BAD** or **NO**. The responses are in uppercase letters. **BAD**, for instance, will indicate that a protocol error has been encountered. **NO**, on the other hand, can be used to indicate a general failure. An example of a server's positive response when opening a mailbox (**0007 SELECT "INBOX"**) is **0007 OK [READ-WRITE] SELECT completed.** A negative example is **LIST BAD Protocol Error: "No space following tag in IMAP command"**, which indicates that the tag was missing (the **LIST** command was mistakenly interpreted as the tag). Important commands supported by Exchange Server are listed immediately following Figure 11-8.

IMAP4 Session Example

The following listing contains an example of an IMAP4 session. It has been prepared using Telnet and may serve as a reference if you want to test IMAP4 connectivity yourself. Commands are marked in boldfaced type.

```
* OK Microsoft Exchange IMAP4rev1 server version 5.5.1960.6
(stocksdata.com) ready
0000 LOGIN STOCKSDATA/Admin-NY1/FredP password
0000 OK LOGIN completed.
0001 SELECT "INBOX"
* 8 EXISTS
* 0 RECENT
* FLAGS (\Seen \Answered \Flagged \Deleted \Draft)
* OK [PERMANENTFLAGS (\Seen \Answered \Flagged \Deleted
\Draft)]
* OK [UNSEEN 1] Is the first unseen message
* OK [UIDVALIDITY 43] UIDVALIDITY value.
```

```
0001 OK [READ-WRITE] SELECT completed.
0002 FETCH 1 ALL
* 1 FETCH (FLAGS () INTERNALDATE " 8-Jan-1998 16:12:27 -
0800" RFC822.SIZE 357 ENVELOPE ("Thu, 8 Jan 1998 16:12:27 -
0800 " "Welcome to Microsoft Outlook" (("Fred Pumpkin" NIL
"FredP" "STOCKSDATA.com"))(("Fred Pumpkin" NIL "FredP"
"STOCKSDATA.com"))(("Fred Pumpkin" NIL "FredP"
"STOCKSDATA.com"))(("Fred Pumpkin" NIL "FredP"
"NEWYORK.STOCKSDATA.com")) NIL NIL
NIL"<71A239C57D88D111A57A00C0DFE23AD90
F4E@stocksdata.com>"))
0002 OK FETCH completed.
0003 STORE 1 flags \Deleted
* 1 FETCH (FLAGS (\Deleted))
0003 OK STORE completed.
0004 EXPUNGE
* 1 EXPUNGE
* 7 EXISTS
0004 OK EXPUNGE completed.
0005 LOGOUT
* BYE Microsoft Exchange IMAP4rev1 server version 5.5.1960.6
signing off
0012 OK LOGOUT completed.
```

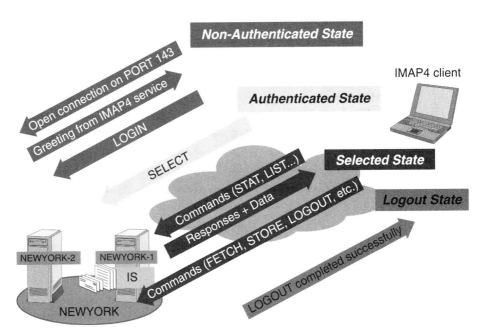

Figure 11-8. IMAP4 session states.

The important IMAP4 commands are listed below:

- **LOGIN** *user password*; identifies the user
- **SELECT** *folder*; selects a folder; messages in the folder can then be accessed
- **FETCH** *message number*; retrieves an entire message
- **CLOSE**; returns to a state where you can select again and remove deleted messages (deleted flag set)
- **EXPUNGE**; removes deleted messages (deleted flag set)
- **STORE** *message* **flags***command*; modifies a message; the **flags** command can specify a number of actions; valid **flags** commands are:

  \Seen; message has been read

  \Answered; message has been answered

  \Flagged; message is marked for urgent/special attention

  \Deleted; message is marked for removal

  \Draft; message has not been completed

- **LIST**; retrieves a list of folders stored in a mailbox
- **SUB** *foldername*; retrieves a list of all folders stored within the specified folder
- **LOGOUT**; closes the connection to the server

Internet Mail Access Architecture

Full-featured POP3/IMAP4 clients provide a complete set of messaging features through POP3/IMAP4 and SMTP. SMTP is necessary because neither POP3 nor IMAP4 provide functions to send messages. Consequently, you must maintain POP3/IMAP4 and SMTP hosts in your organization if you want to support users running POP3 and IMAP4 clients. Every Exchange Server theoretically can support these clients for downloading and sending messages. (See Figure 11-9.)

Active Components

Because of performance reasons, the active POP3/IMAP4 component has been implemented directly into the IS. As mentioned earlier, this feature is also called IMAIL. It accomplishes all required tasks for supporting the Internet protocols, including user access validation and message conversion into appropriate formats (for example, MIME, UUENCODE, and ASCII). You don't need to create an additional Windows NT service for POP3 or IMAP4 support. SMTP, however, is supported by means of the IMS, which represents an additional Windows NT service. It accepts incoming SMTP connections from POP3 and IMAP4 clients just as it does from any remote SMTP host. Inbound SMTP messages can be rerouted to the Internet, or they can be delivered to the Exchange Server organization.

TCP/IP Ports

To download messages, POP3 clients connect to their home server's TCP/IP port 110. IMAP4 clients access port 143. If you send a message, the client connects to port 25 of a server running the IMS. The POP3 or IMAP4 host will always be the computer where your mailbox resides; it is not necessary to install the IMS on each host as well. In fact, you can dedicate an IMS running on any Exchange Server in your organization as the SMTP communication partner for all your Internet mail clients. The only restriction is that this server must be reachable through TCP/IP.

Sending Messages

Let's say Fred, residing on NEWYORK-1, uses his IMAP4 client to send a message to William, who resides on NEWYORK-2. As shown in Figure 11-9, Fred's message is first delivered to the IMS on NEWYORK-1. The IMS receives the incoming message and performs SMTP rerouting based on the recipient address (*WilliamP@stocksdata.com*). Because *stocksdata.com* is defined as an inbound domain, the IMS contacts the IS and delivers the message to the inbound message queue (MTS-IN). The IS hands the incoming message over to the MTA. The MTA is then responsible for routing the message to the intended destination within the organization.

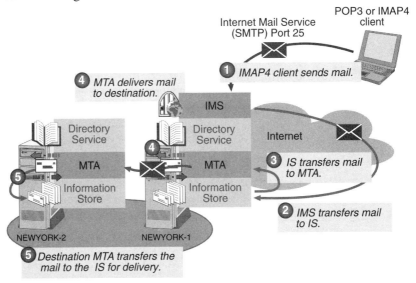

Figure 11-9. Sending messages via POP3/IMAP4 clients.

The message flow when sending messages via POP3/IMAP4 clients is as follows:

1. The POP3/IMAP4 client uses SMTP to send a message to the IMS.

2. The IMS receives the message and places it in the inbound queue.

3. Message rerouting is performed to send the message to the Internet/ Intranet or the Exchange Server organization, depending on the recipient addresses.

4. The IS is contacted in order to place messages in the IMS inbound queue (MTS-IN) if the recipients' e-mail domains are defined as inbound.

5. The IS notifies the MTA.

6. The MTA received the mail and routes it according the GWART and e-mail address spaces.

7. The message is transferred to the destination MTA.

8. The destination MTA again checks the recipient address, ascertains that the local server is the recipient's home server, and transfers the message to the local IS.

9. The IS delivers the message and informs the client.

10. The client displays the received messages in its Inbox.

Configuring Protocol Support

The configurations of POP3 and IMAP4 parameters do not differ significantly, so it is appropriate to cover the configuration of POP3 and IMAP4 connectivity together in the following section. However, it should be pointed out that IMAP4 allows you to configure anonymous access, to include public folders in the folder list for clients, and to enable fast message retrieval. All these options are not available when configuring POP3.

Configuration Objects

POP3/IMAP4 client support is enabled by default, but specific configurations can be set by controlling the corresponding parameters at the site, server, and mailbox levels. The Administrator program provides the required corresponding configuration objects, called **xxxx (Mail) Site Default** at the site level and **xxxx (Mail) Settings** at the server level (xxxx stands for either POP3 or IMAP4). A **Protocols** property page is also implemented for every mailbox object. Because the POP3/IMAP4 clients require SMTP to send messages, configuration of the IMS may also be required to support these clients. (See Figure 11-10.)

Site and Server Protocol Properties

The **xxxx (Mail) Settings** objects at the server level have only two noticeable differences from their **xxxx (Mail) Site Defaults** objects counterparts. They are the **Diagnostics Logging** property page and the check box **Use Site Defaults For All Properties** on the **General** property page. All other controls are the same. The management at both levels is therefore similar.

Server-level settings supersede site-level configuration parameters. But site-level parameters are active and server-level settings are inactive by default. In order to configure POP3/IMAP4 parameters individually for each server, you must first clear the **Use Site Defaults For All Properties** check box on the **General** property page of the **POP3** or **IMAP4 (Mail) Settings** object. You'll see that server-level protocol settings become available. For instance, you can clear the **Enable Protocol** check box on the **General** property page if you want to disable the POP3 or IMAP4 support for a particular server.

Determining User Authentication Methods

Exchange Server can validate user access based on the **Basic (Clear Text)**, **Basic (Clear Text) Using SSL**, **Windows NT Challenge/Response**, and **Windows NT Challenge/Response Using SSL** authentication methods, all of which are enabled by default. You can also use MCIS to validate user access. Corresponding check boxes labeled **MCIS Membership System** and **MCIS Membership System Using SSL** are available and can be selected in addition to the default mechanisms.

It is advisable to disable the **Basic (Clear Text)** method if you want to increase server security. Otherwise, user account names and passwords can be transferred in clear text between the client and the server. You can clear the **Basic (Clear Text)** check box on the **Authentication** property page if all POP3/IMAP4 clients can handle at least the **Basic (Clear Text) Using SSL** option. SSL itself is not an authentication method, but it provides the elements required for data encryption.

Closing Idle Connections

A POP3/IMAP4 client program, which connects to the server and opens a connection, consumes server-based resources. If such a program terminates unexpectedly, the server connection might remain open, consuming server-based resources indefinitely. It is recommended that you check for idle connections and automatically release them after a few minutes.

You can use the **Idle Time-Out** property page to specify how long POP3 and IMAP4 connections can remain idle before they are closed. By default, the IS disconnects all clients that have not been active for 10 minutes.

Mailbox Configuration

The mailbox is the resource from which users can download messages. Usually one particular user will access one particular mailbox (his or her own). You can manage POP3 and IMAP4 on a per-user basis indirectly through the management of mailboxes. The mailbox-level configuration, however, differs from the server- and site-level configurations in that it provides a property page called **Protocols**. On this property page is the **Settings** button, which displays the **Protocol Details** dialog box. Click this button once you have selected either the **POP3(Mail)** or the **IMAP4(Mail)** entry from the list of available Internet protocols. Then you can disable or re-enable POP3 or IMAP4 for a particular user by selecting either the **Enable POP3 For This Recipient** check box or the **Enable IMAP4 For This Recipient** check box. You can also override message format settings (MIME or UUENCODE) by clearing the **Use Protocol Defaults** check box.

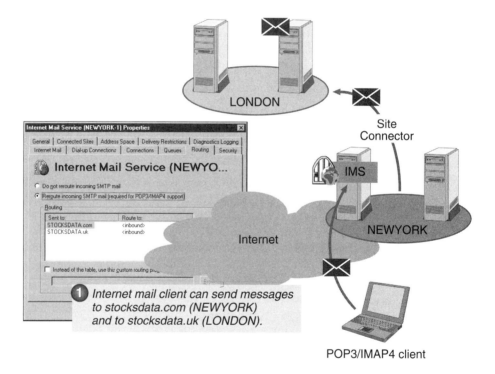

Figure 11-10. Configuring routing for POP3 support.

The configuration property pages that are common to both POP3 and IMAP4 are as follows:

- **Authentication**; to configure supported authentication methods such as **Basic (Clear Text)**, **Basic (Clear Text) Using SSL**, **Windows NT Challenge/Response**, **Windows NT Challenge/Response Using SSL**, **MCIS Membership System**, and **MCIS Membership System Using SSL**

- **Diagnostics Logging**; to enable the logging of events for the **Content Engine**, **Connection**, **Authentication**, **Client Actions**, and **Configuration** categories

- **General**; to change the display name and to enable the protocol

- **Message Format**; to set parameters for MIME, UUENCODE, and Exchange rich-text formatting

- **Idle Time Out**; to close idle connections (timeout default 10 minutes)

- **Anonymous** (an IMAP4-specific configuration property page); to specify an anonymous IMAP4 account that is used primarily for anonymous public folder access

Exercise 36: Configuring Internet Message Access Protocols for the Site

POP3 and IMAP4 protocol settings can be configured at three levels: the site level, the server level, and the mailbox level. Server-level settings are of higher priority than site-level defaults.

Estimated time to complete this exercise: 10 minutes

Description

In this exercise, you will use the Administrator program to configure site-level default settings for the POP3 and IMAP4 protocols. You will verify that access to server-based mailboxes is possible. You have the option to examine other configuration parameters by switching to corresponding property pages.

- Task 36 describes the steps for verifying that the POP3 and IMAP4 protocols are enabled for all servers in a site.

Prerequisites

- Log on either as Admin-NY1 to server NEWYORK-1 or as Admin-L1 to server LONDON-1.

Task 36: Configuring the POP3 Protocol Object

1. Click **Start**, select **Programs**, select **Microsoft Exchange**, and then click **Microsoft Exchange Administrator**.

2. In the left pane expand the site object (**LONDON** or **NEWYORK**), expand the **Configuration** container, and then select the **Protocols** container.

3. In the right pane, double-click the **POP3 (Mail) Site Defaults** object.

4. The **POP3 (Mail) Site Defaults Properties** dialog box appears. Verify that the **Enable Protocol** option is checked. You can switch to the other property tabs, such as **Authentication** and **Message Format**, to inspect the default settings. When you are done, click **OK** to close the dialog box again.

5. In the right pane, double-click the **IMAP4 (Mail) Site Defaults** object.

6. The **IMAP (Mail) Site Defaults Properties** dialog box appears. Verify that the **Enable Protocol** option is checked. You can switch to the other property tabs, such as **Authentication**, **Anonymous**, or **Message Format**, to inspect the default settings. When you are done, click **OK** to close the dialog box again.

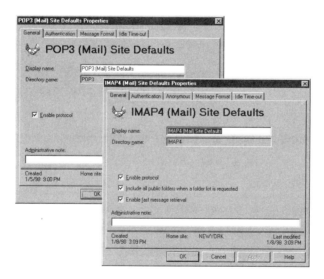

Review

POP3/IMAP4 protocol settings can be adjusted within the Administrator program using the **xxxx (Mail) Site Defaults** object, which are in the **Protocols** container under the **Configuration** container. It is possible to disable or re-enable POP3/IMAP4, to configure supported authentication methods, and to specify message formats such as MIME, UUENCODE, and Exchange Rich Text. In order to disconnect idle connections, you can enter a timeout value in minutes on the **TimeOut** property page (the default is 10 minutes).

Typical POP3/IMAP4 Client Configuration Parameters

Many different POP3 and IMAP4 clients exist and are widely adopted in the Internet. They all have many features and configuration parameters in common because they use well-defined methods to access their hosts. One might say that Internet mail clients are all the same, and if you know one, you know them all.

POP3/IMAP4 Server Name

The POP3/IMAP4 server name is equivalent to the host name of the Exchange Server that maintains the user's mailbox. In other words, this parameter references the user's home server.

SMTP Server Name

The SMTP server name is the name of the server that accepts messages from POP3/IMAP4 clients and further routes them to their destinations. In an Exchange Server organization, the SMTP server is usually a server that maintains the IMS. The SMTP server does not need to be the same computer as the POP3 or IMAP4 host.

E-Mail Address

An e-mail address must be provided during client configuration because it will be used to provide the originator information in outgoing messages. The e-mail address should match the user's proxy SMTP address, although any SMTP address may be specified.

Bear in mind that messaging systems route messages according to e-mail addresses. If a wrong address has been configured, the wrong originator information will be inserted into messages. Therefore, it is not guaranteed that you will receive any replies to POP3 or IMAP4 messages.

Account Name

The account name is used to specify the mailbox you want to access. Exchange Server requires a combination of Windows NT domain name, user name and mailbox name. The format is domain/user/mailbox. Although you can skip the domain name and user name part in cases where the user name matches the mailbox name, the client log on will be faster if all information has been provided. The password is always the user's Windows NT password.

Note If your client supports the Windows NT Challenge/Response authentication method (such as Outlook Express), you can configure your client to use Secure Password Authentication to log on to your mailbox. In this case, you don't need to provide an account name.

Example of POP3 Client Configuration

As shown in Figure 11-11, Fred's mailbox resides on NEWYORK-1. The IMS has also been installed on this computer to provide the required SMTP server to the POP3 client. Fred Pumpkin is a user of the STOCKSDATA domain. His Windows NT account name and the corresponding mailbox alias are FredP. The following options must be provided for Fred's POP3 client:

In this box	You supply
Name	*Fred Pumpkin*
Organization	*STOCKSDATA*
E-mail address	*FredP@stocksdata.com*
Outgoing mail (SMTP) Server	*NEWYORK-1*
Incoming mail (POP3) Server	*NEWYORK-1*
POP3 Account	*STOCKSDATA/Admin-NY1/FredP*
Password	*password*

Example of IMAP4 Client Configuration

If Fred Pumpkin wants to access his mailbox on NEWYORK-1 by means of an IMAP4 client, he must configure the corresponding IMAP4 parameters as shown in the following table. Not surprisingly, these parameters look pretty much the same as Fred's settings for a POP3 client.

In this box	You supply
Name	*Fred Pumpkin*
Organization	*STOCKSDATA*
E-mail address	*FredP@stocksdata.com*
Outgoing mail (SMTP) Server	*NEWYORK-1*

(continues)

(continued)

In this box	You supply
Incoming mail (IMAP4) Server	*NEWYORK-1*
IMAP4 Account	*STOCKSDATA/Admin-NY1/FredP*
Password	*password*

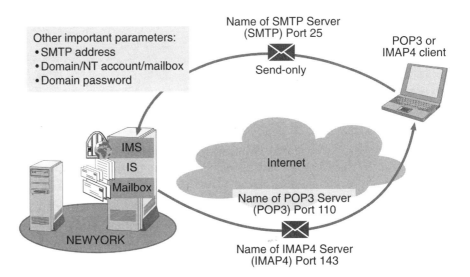

Figure 11-11.   Important POP3/IMAP4 client information.

The POP3/IMAP4 information required for mailbox access is as follows:

- **Password**; the Windows NT domain password for the user

- **Account name**; Windows NT domain/Windows NT account/Exchange mailbox

- **E-mail address**; the user's SMTP proxy address

- **POP3/IMAP4 server name**; the Exchange Server name or its IP address

- **SMTP server name**; the IMS computer name or its IP address

Testing the Connectivity

POP3 and IMAP4 are plain-text application layer protocols. Tools such as the Telnet utility can be used to log on to the server manually, which allows you to check whether POP3/IMAP4 connections are working. The **Basic (Clear**

Text) authentication method, however, must be enabled when using Telnet. Although this is the default configuration, it is advisable to verify the current settings through the **Authentication** property page of the POP3 or IMAP4 configuration object at the site and server levels.

Preparation

Before you begin testing a POP3 or IMAP4 connection, ensure that the **Local Echo** option of the **Terminal Preferences** dialog box has been activated; otherwise, you won't be able to see what you're typing. This dialog box can be displayed through the **Preferences** command on the **Terminal** menu.

Connecting to the Host

In order to connect to a target POP3 host, open the **Connect** menu, select **Remote System**, and enter the Host Name and Port 110. When you click the **Connect** button, you will receive the welcome message from the server: **+OK Microsoft Exchange POP3 server version 5.5.1960.6 ready**.

If you want to connect to the IMAP4 component of your Exchange Server, specify port 143 instead. When you do this, you will receive the following welcome message: *** OK Microsoft Exchange IMAP4rev1 server version 5.5.1960.6 (stocksdata.com) ready**.

Logging On Using POP3

To test whether a POP3 client is able to log on to the server, enter **USER** *<domain_name/nt_account/mailbox>* to provide the desired user information. After you have pressed the ENTER key, a positive response, **+OK**, should be returned from the server. At this point, you can enter the password using the command **PASS** *<password>*. The positive response will be **+OK User successfully logged on**. (See Figure 11-12.)

Reading Messages Using POP3

To display existing messages, enter the **STAT** command. A positive response will include the number of messages residing in the Inbox, such as **+OK 2 645**. To read the first message enter the **RETR** command (**RETR 1**). Other commands, such as **DELE** for deleting messages, are also available.

Disconnecting POP3 Hosts

To release the connection, enter the **QUIT** command. The answer **+OK Microsoft Exchange POP3 server version 5.5.1960.6 signing off** indicates a successful disconnection.

Logging On Using IMAP4

IMAP4 allows you to log on to the server through a single command line. The required command is **LOGIN** as described in the section, "IMAP4 Operation," earlier in this lesson. Using **LOGIN**, enter the account name and the password in one line along with the command and a preceding tag. A **LOGIN** example is: **0000 LOGIN STOCKSDATA/Admin-NY1/FredP password**.

Reading Messages Using IMAP4

Before you can read a message, you must select a message folder. The corresponding command is **SELECT**, which allows you to specify the desired folder on the same line (for example, **0001 SELECT "INBOX"**). A positive response to **SELECT** returns the number of messages that particular folder contains. If the folder contains messages, you can download them using the **FETCH** command. **FETCH** expects you to indicate the desired message through a reference number. Furthermore, you need to indicate which part of the message you want to retrieve (for example, **0002 FETCH 1 ALL**). If the server responds positively, you will receive the referenced message or messages.

Disconnecting IMAP4 Hosts

To release the connection, enter the **LOGOUT** command. The response "*** BYE Microsoft Exchange IMAP4rev1 server version 5.5.1960.6 signing off 0012 OK LOGOUT completed.**" indicates a successful disconnection.

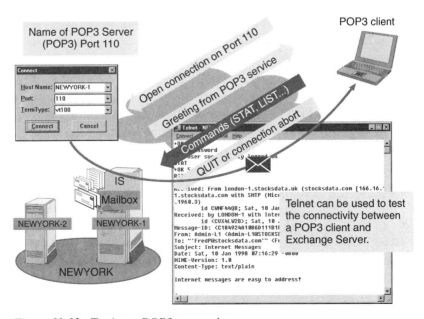

Figure 11-12. Testing a POP3 connection.

The following is a sample POP3 communication with Telnet:

1. Start Telnet and enable **Local Echo** under **Preferences** on the **Terminal** menu.

2. Open the **Connect** menu and choose **Remote System**.

3. Enter the name of the Exchange Server under **Host Name**.

4. Enter *Port 110* in the **Port** box, and then click **Connect**.

5. Note the greeting of the POP3 server (**+OK Microsoft Exchange POP3 server version 5.5.1960.6 ready**).

6. Enter **USER** *<domain/nt_account/mailbox>* (use valid information).

7. Verify the **+OK** response.

8. Enter **PASS** *<password>* (use valid information).

9. Verify the positive response (**+OK User successfully logged on**).

10. Enter **STAT**.

11. Notice the positive response and the number of e-mail messages in the Inbox and the size of all messages (if no messages are present, **+OK 0 0** is returned).

12. If messages exist, enter **RETR 1** to read the first message.

13. Enter **QUIT**.

Protocol Logging

Exchange Server provides POP3/IMAP4 protocol logging features to keep track of the client-server communication. Protocol logging can be especially useful for troubleshooting purposes. It is not difficult to read a POP3 or IMAP4 protocol trace because the conversation is basically a clear text communication. (See Figure 11-13.)

Protocol Logging

By default, logging is not enabled, but you can enable protocol logging if you suspect communication problems between POP3/IMAP4 clients and Exchange Server. Using the Registry Editor, you need to define corresponding values under the following sub-key:

```
HKEY_LOCAL_MACHINE
    \System
        \CurrentControlSet
            \Services
                \MSExchangeIS
                    \ParametersSystem
```

The two important values for POP3 protocol logging are POP3 Protocol LogPath and POP3 Protocol Logging Level. The first value must point to the directory where the POP3 logging files will be created (for example, L0000001.log). The value POP3 Protocol Logging Level, in turn, specifies the logged POP3 protocol details. Values that refer to the IMAP4 protocol can also be used similarly. They are called IMAP4 Protocol LogPath and IMAP4 Protocol Logging Level.

Be aware that whenever you modify these settings directly using the Windows NT Registry Editor, you must restart the IS service in order for the new parameters to take effect.

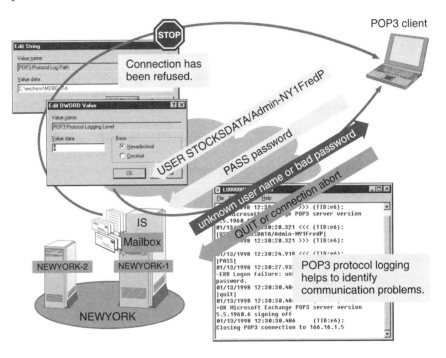

Figure 11-13. Keeping a record of a POP3 conversation.

The POP3 protocol logging levels available via "POP3 Protocol Logging Level" are as follows:

- 0; no logging
- 1; minimum logging
- 4; enables maximum protocol logging
- 5; logs message text along with maximum protocol information
- Other values are invalid

Exercise 37: Installing Outlook Express

Regardless which POP3/IMAP4 client you are using, an account name, the corresponding password, your e-mail address, a POP3/IMAP4 server name, and sometimes a SMTP server name must be specified for all clients.

Estimated time to complete this exercise (without downloading the Internet Explorer 4.01 from the Internet): 35 minutes

Description

In this exercise, you will install Outlook Express. This client comes with Internet Explorer 4.01 and can be used as a native POP3 or IMAP4 client to access an Exchange Server. In addition to providing POP3 and IMAP4 support, this client can also be used as a newsreader application.

- Task 37a describes the steps for downloading and installing Outlook Express along with Internet Explorer 4.01 from the Internet. The entire process might take you more than four hours. Nevertheless, this method will always allow you to install the newest IE4 release available. Alternatively and to save time, you can install IE 4.01 from the companion CD-ROM included with this book.

- Task 37b describes the steps for configuring Outlook Express to send messages through SMTP and to receive them via POP3. This configuration can be used as a sample for other clients as well.

- Task 37c describes the steps for retrieving all messages from an Exchange Server. This task also describes the steps for sending a POP3 message.

- Task 37d describes the steps for configuring Outlook Express to receive mail trough IMAP4. This configuration can be used as a sample for other IMAP4 clients.

- Task 37e describes the steps for uploading messages to Exchange Server via IMAP4.

Prerequisites

- A workstation with Internet connectivity and an installed Web browser is required.

- Log on to server NEWYORK-1 as Admin-NY1.

- Some messages should exist in the mailboxes Admin-NY-1 and Admin-L1.

Task 37a: Installing Internet Explorer and Outlook Express

1. Log on to NEWYORK-1 as Admin-NY1 and connect to the Internet.

2. Double-click the **Internet Explorer** icon on the desktop.

3. Connect to **http://www.microsoft.com/ie/ie40/download/ie4.htm**.

4. Under **Windows 95 & NT 4.0** click **Internet Explorer 4.01 (English)**. (The original Internet Explorer of Windows NT Server 4.0 does not support Frames. Hence, the download option might be displayed differently if you are using a browser that does support Frames and scripts.)

5. Download and save the IE4Setup.exe to your disk.

6. Double-click the downloaded IE4Setup.exe to start the installation of Internet Explorer 4.0/4.01.

7. An **Internet Explorer 4.0 Active Setup** dialog box appears. Click **Next**.

8. An **Internet Explorer 4.0 Active Setup** dialog box appears. Select **I Accept The Agreement** and then click **Next**.

9. An **Internet Explorer 4.0 Active Setup** dialog box appears. Select **Install** and then click **Next**.

10. An **Internet Explorer 4.0 Active Setup** dialog box appears. Select **Standard Installation** and then click **Next**.

11. An **Internet Explorer 4.0 Active Setup** dialog box appears. Select **No** to prevent updating your desktop and then click **Next**.

12. An **Internet Explorer 4.0 Active Setup** dialog box appears, asking you to specify the country and language for active channels. Select **United States** and then click **Next**.

13. An **Internet Explorer 4.0 Active Setup** dialog box appears, prompting for a installation directory. Accept the default path (**C:\Program Files\Plus!\Microsoft Internet**) and then click **Next**.

14. An **Internet Explorer 4.0 Active Setup** dialog box appears, asking you to select a download site. In the **Region** box select **North America** and in the **Download Sites** box select a site near to your location, and then click **Next**.

15. Setup prepares your computer for Internet Explorer installation. The download might take up to four hours.

16. Once Internet Explorer has been downloaded, setup continues automatically. At the end of the setup procedure, an **Internet Explorer 4.0 Active Setup** message box appears, informing you that Setup has finished the installation. Click **OK**.

17. Setup configures the system. Click **OK** to restart the computer.

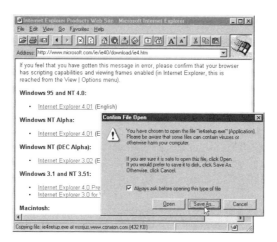

Task 37b: Configuring Internet Mail from NEWYORK-1 to Send and Receive Mail

1. Log on as Admin-NY1 to the server NEWYORK-1. Notice that the **Microsoft Internet 4.0 Setup** has set up several components (such as Internet Explorer, Internet tools, security, and so forth). Other additional personalized settings will be configured.

2. Close the **Welcome – Microsoft Internet Explorer** window and then double-click **Outlook Express** on the desktop.

3. The **Internet Connection Wizard** dialog box appears. Click **Next**.

4. An **Internet Connection Wizard** dialog box appears, asking you to specify an Internet connection option. Select **I Want To Set Up A New Connection On This Computer To My Existing Internet Account Using My Phone Line Or Local Area Network (LAN).** Click **Next**.

5. An **Internet Connection Wizard** dialog box appears, asking you to specify the connection type. Select **Connect Using My Local Area Network (LAN).** Click **Next**.

6. An **Internet Connection Wizard** dialog box appears, asking whether you are using a proxy server. Select **No** and then click **Next**.

7. An **Internet Connection Wizard** dialog box appears, asking whether you want to set up an Internet mail account now. Verify that **Yes** is selected, and then click **Next**.

8. In the **Display Name** box, type *Admin-NY1* and then click **Next**.

9. In the **E-Mail Address** box, type *Admin-NY1@stocksdata.com* and then click **Next**.

10. Verify that **POP3** is selected under **My Incoming Mail Server Is A …
Server**.

11. In the **Incoming Mail (POP3 or IMAP) Server** box, type
NEWYORK-1.STOCKSDATA.com.

12. In the **Outgoing Mail (SMTP) Server** box, type
NEWYORK-1.STOCKSDATA.com.

Note The outgoing mail server (SMTP) is the server on which you
installed the IMS during the exercises of Chapter 10.

---

13. Click **Next**.

14. Verify that **Log On Using** is selected and under **POP Account Name**,
type *STOCKSDATA/Admin-NY1/FredP.*

15. In the **Password** box, type *password.*

16. Click **Next**.

17. Under **Internet Mail Account Name**, type *Fred's POP3 Inbox.*
Click **Next**.

18. An **Internet Connection Wizard** dialog box appears, asking you to
specify an **Internet News Account**. Select **No** and then click **Next**.

19. An **Internet Connection Wizard** dialog box appears, asking you to set
up a Internet directory service account. Select **Yes** and then click **Next**.

20. Under **Internet Directory (LDAP) Server**, type
NEWYORK-1.STOCKSDATA.com.

21. Select **My LDAP Server Requires Me To Log On** and then click **Next**.

22. Select **Log On Using Secure Password Authentication** and then
click **Next**.

23. An **Internet Connection Wizard** dialog box appears, asking whether
you want to check addresses using this directory service. Select **Yes** and
then click **Next**.

24. Under **Internet Directory Service Name**, type *Fred's LDAP service* and
then click **Next**.

25. An **Internet Connection Wizard** dialog box appears, stating that the
installation has been completed. Click **Finish**.

26. A **Browse For Folder** message box appears. Accept the default location
and then click **OK**.

27. **Outlook Express** will be launched. On the **Tools** menu, click **Accounts**.

28. The **Internet Accounts** dialog box will be displayed. Click the **Mail** tab and then click **Properties** to display the **Fred's POP3 Inbox Properties** dialog box.

29. Switch to the **Advanced** tab.

30. Check **Leave A Copy Of Messages On Server** and then click **OK**.

31. Click **Close**.

32. In the left pane of **Outlook Express**, select the **Inbox** folder.

33. An **Outlook Express** dialog box appears, asking whether you want to make Outlook Express your default mail client. Clear the **Always Perform This Check When Starting Outlook Express** check box, and then click **No**.

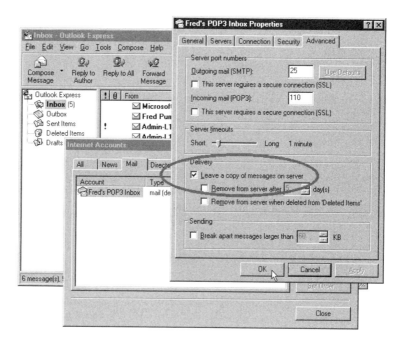

Task 37c: Retrieving and Sending New Messages

1. On the toolbar, click **Compose Message**.

2. On the **To** bar click the **Select Recipient From A List** button.

3. The **Select Recipients** dialog box appears. Click the **Find** button.

4. A **Find People** dialog box appears. Under **Look In** select **Fred's LDAP Service** and then under **Name** type *Admin-L1*.

5. Click **Find Now**.

6. **Admin-L1** will be found. Select this entry and then click the **To** button.

7. Click **OK**.

8. Position your cursor in the **Cc** line and then type *FredP@stocksdata.com*.

9. Position your cursor in the **Subject** field and then type *This is an Outlook Express message*.

10. Click in the message text area and type *Outlook Express supports many Internet protocols and may be used instead of MAPI-based clients to access an Exchange server.* Format the color, size, and style of the text as desired.

11. Click the **Send** button on the toolbar. The **New Message** window will be closed.

12. In **Outlook Express** click **Send And Receive** on the toolbar.

13. Open and read the received message.

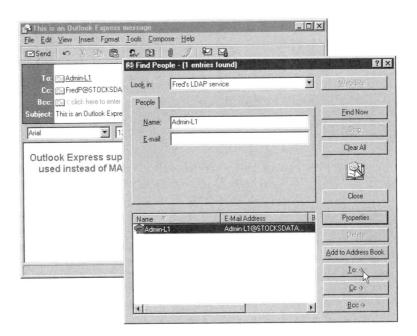

Task 37d: Accessing Exchange Server Through IMAP4

1. On the **Tools** menu, click **Accounts**.

2. Verify that the **Mail** property page is selected, click the **Add** button, and then click **Mail**.

3. Under **Display Name** type **Admin-NY1 Via IMAP4**. Click **Next**.

4. Verify that **Admin-NY1@stocksdata.com** is displayed under **E-Mail Address** and then click **Next**.

5. Verify that **IMAP** is selected under **My Incoming Mail Server Is A ... Server**.

6. In the **Incoming Mail (POP3 or IMAP) Server** box, type *NEWYORK-1.STOCKSDATA.com*.

7. In the **Outgoing Mail (SMTP) Server** box, type *NEWYORK-1.STOCKSDATA.com*.

8. Click **Next**.

9. Verify that **Log On Using** is selected and under **IMAP Account Name** type *STOCKSDATA/Admin-NY1/FredP*.

10. In the **Password** box, type *password*.

11. Click **Next**.

12. Under **Internet Mail Account Name** type *Fred's IMAP Mailbox*. Click **Next**.

13. Verify that **Connect Using My Local Area Network (LAN)** is selected and then click **Next**.

14. Click **Finish**.

15. An **Outlook Express** dialog box appears, asking whether you want to download the folder list for your IMAP account. Click **Yes**.

16. When the download of the folder list is completed, click **Close** to close the Internet Accounts dialog box.

17. Notice that a new mailbox object called **Fred's IMAP Mailbox** appears in the left pane of **Outlook Express**. Select this item.

18. On the **File** menu, select **Folder** and then select **Subscribe All Folders**.

19. An **Outlook Express** dialog box appears, asking if you want to subscribe all folders. Click **Yes** to continue.

20. Notice that all folders of your server-based mailbox have been subscribed. These folders do not yet contain any message items.

21. In **Outlook Express** click **Send And Receive** on the toolbar.

22. Open the **Inbox** under **Fred's IMAP Mailbox** and verify that it contains the test message created in Task 37c. (No other messages exist because they were downloaded previously through POP3.)

23. Double-click the **Microsoft Outlook** shortcut and check that this exact message is contained in Fred's server-based mailbox.

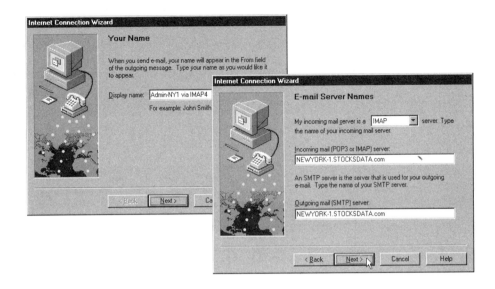

Task 37e: Uploading Messages Through IMAP4

1. In the left pane of **Outlook Express**, open the **Inbox** under the **Outlook Express** container.

2. Multiple messages appear (at the minimum you should find the test message created in Task 37c). Open the **Edit** menu and then click **Select All**.

3. On the **Edit** menu click **Move To Folder**.

4. A **Move** dialog box appears. Open the container **Fred's IMAP Mailbox**, select the **Inbox** under it, and then click **OK**. Note that all messages disappear from the **Inbox** under **Outlook Express**.

5. Switch to the **Inbox** under **Fred's IMAP Mailbox** and verify that all messages have been moved successfully. The test message created in Task 37c will appear twice.

6. Switch to **Microsoft Outlook** and verify that all messages have been uploaded to the Exchange Server. All messages will appear marked as read.

7. Close all applications and log off Windows NT.

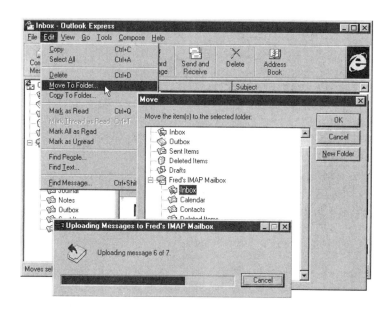

Review

The POP3/IMAP4 account name requires special attention because it is a combination of the user's domain, account, and mailbox names. The pattern is *<Windows NT domain/Windows NT account/Exchange mailbox>*. A password must also be supplied that corresponds to the Windows NT domain password of the user. Alternatively, you can choose the Secure Password Authentication to log on with your Windows NT credentials automatically.

Other important settings concern the actual message handling. The e-mail address should be the user's SMTP proxy address. The POP3 or IMAP4 server name corresponds to the name of the Exchange Server (or its IP address) where the mailbox of a particular user resides. In order to send messages successfully, the SMTP server name must also be specified. In an Exchange Server organization, this parameter refers typically to a computer running the IMS.

Lesson 3: Lightweight Directory Access Protocol

The flood of information coming from the Internet is overwhelming. The expansion of the Internet itself is not the problem, however; the difficulty is in the coordination of the information. No globally and commonly maintained directory exists that provides a catalog of Internet resources. But a directory standard known as LDAP does exist, which Exchange Server supports in order to provide access to its directory.

This lesson covers the basic aspects of the LDAP implementation into Exchange Server 5.5. The first section provides an overview about the LDAP protocol and the sections that follow discuss directory access methods and the LDAP configuration.

At the end of this lesson, you will be able to:

- Describe the LDAP implementation in Exchange Server 5.5
- Configure LDAP site and server properties

Estimated time to complete this lesson: 15 minutes

LDAP Client Support

The LDAP is a derivation of the X.500 Directory Access Protocol (DAP). It was originally developed at the University of Michigan to provide a more efficient way to build and access a hierarchical directory based on object attributes. This industry standard, described in RFC 1777, consists of 16 overall commands and responses.

Features

As designed for the Internet, LDAP uses the TCP/IP transport mechanism for client-server communication. The server "listens" for incoming requests on TCP/IP port 389. To provide security, LDAP uses an encoding scheme called Basic Encoding Rules (BER). The encryption is performed on top of the transport layer (TCP).

LDAP implementations assume support for the X.500 naming model for maximum interoperability between client and server. In other words, systems that reference directory objects through Distinguished Names (for example, Exchange Server) provide an ideal platform for LDAP clients.

Supported Versions

Three LDAP versions currently exist, although the third version has not yet been specified completely. Exchange Server supports all functions of the second version and some of the third LDAP version.

LDAP is enabled by default in Exchange Server 5.5. Any LDAP application, such as Outlook Express, can therefore be used to look up the Exchange Server directory as soon as the server is started. (See Figure 11-14.)

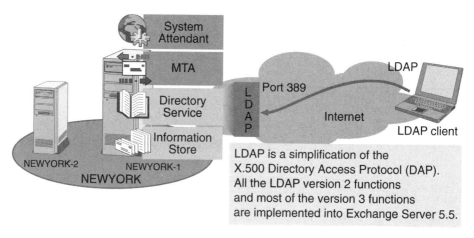

Figure 11-14. Implementation of LDAP in Exchange.

The LDAP commands and responses supported by Exchange are as follows:

- **BindRequest**; initiates a session with the server
- **BindResponse**; allows or denies the bind request
- **UnbindRequest**; terminates a session with the server
- **SearchRequest**; initiates a search for a specific entry in the directory
- **SearchResponse**; sends a search result to the client
- **ModifyRequest**; modifies a directory entry
- **ModifyResponse**; sends the result of a requested modification
- **AddRequest**; adds a directory entry
- **AddResponse**; sends the result of a request to add a directory entry
- **DelRequest**; deletes a directory entry
- **DelResponse**; returns the result of a delete request

The LDAP commands not supported by Exchange 5.5 are as follows:

- **ModifyRDNRequest**; modifies the relative distinguished name (RDN) of a directory object

- **ModifyRDNResponse**; returns the result of a requested RDN modification to the client

- **CompareDNRequest**; compares a string with the DN of a directory object

- **CompareDNResponse**; returns the result of a DN comparison to the client

- **AbandonRequest**; instructs the server to abandon a request that is outstanding

Directory Access Methods

LDAP has been tightly integrated into Exchange Server to provide the best possible performance. According to Figure 11-15, LDAP is part of the DS, so it's possible to search for entries in the Exchange directory with any client that supports LDAP, as well to more traditional clients such as Outlook and the Administrator program.

LDAP, MAPI, and XDS

LDAP provides directory access to LDAP-based clients such as Microsoft Outlook Express. MAPI provides directory access to MAPI-based clients such as the Exchange Client, Outlook, and the Administrator program. A third directory access interface, called XDS, is used exclusively by the Administrator program. Just as the MAPI and XDS functions, LDAP allows for the reading and writing of directory objects and their attributes.

LDAP Access Procedure

Before any LDAP client can access directory information, a session must be established with the server through TCP/IP port 389. If desired, you can change the port number through the **General** property page of the site-level or server-level LDAP configuration objects. The client sends a **BindRequest** command to the server to initiate a session. The server either allows or denies the request, but in either case it informs the client about the current situation using **BindResponse**. Let's say the session is established and the client is now able to query the Directory. To search for a specific directory entry, the client sends a **SearchRequest** to the server, which results in a corresponding **SearchResponse**. Finally, after all queries have been completed and the user quits the LDAP application, an **UnbindRequest** must be sent to the server. Unlike the other requests, the **UnbindRequest** is left unanswered.

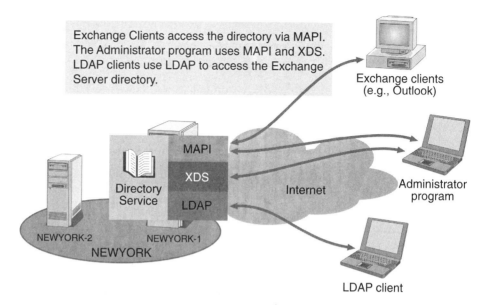

Exchange Clients access the directory via MAPI.
The Administrator program uses MAPI and XDS.
LDAP clients use LDAP to access the Exchange
Server directory.

Figure 11-15. Accessing the Exchange Server directory.

The Directory access interfaces and their related programs are as follows:

- LDAP; all Internet-based LDAP applications
- MAPI; Exchange Client, Outlook, and Administrator program
- XDS; Exchange Administrator program

Configuring LDAP Site and Server Properties

The administration of LDAP can be performed at the site and server levels.
However, unlike any other Internet protocol, no configuration options exist at
the mailbox level.

Configuration Objects

The **LDAP (Directory) Site Defaults** item contains the property pages used
to manage the LDAP default configuration for all servers in a site. The server
level offers the **LDAP (Directory) Settings** configuration object, which can
be used to define settings that apply to a particular server only. Both objects
provide the same configuration options. In order to activate the server level
settings, you need only clear the **Use Site Defaults For All Properties**
checkbox on the **General** tab of the server-level object.

LDAP Directory Access

LDAP supports the same authentication methods as POP3 and IMAP4. The authentication methods you choose to enable can be configured at the server and site levels via the **Authentication** property page of the corresponding LDAP configuration objects.

To allow anonymous access to the directory, select the **Allow Anonymous Access** check box on the **Anonymous** property page. Because this option is enabled by default, each user can access the directory, but by default the information that is returned to an anonymous directory lookup is restricted to fewer fields than are returned by an authenticated user.

Restricting Directory Information

A validated user can usually retrieve all available directory information using a LDAP client. But you can restrict manually the attributes of recipient objects (mailboxes, distribution lists, custom recipients, and public folders). Attributes can be determined on the basis of **Anonymous Requests**, **Authenticated Requests**, and **Intersite Replication** on the **Attributes** property page of the **DS Site Configuration** object. (See Figure 11-16.) The configuration of this object is covered in detail in Chapter 8.

Configuring Searches

Exchange Server allows you to look up the server directory based on substring searches. In other words, you supply a string and LDAP will return all the directory entries that contain the supplied string.

The three types of substring searches are: *initial*, *final*, and *any substring*. *Initial substring searches* will return all objects that match the beginning of the specified directory attribute. For example, a query for "Fr" returns the names "Fred Pumpkin" and "Frank Pea." The *final sub-string search* follows the same principle, except that it checks for matching endings as well. The *any sub-string search* compares the supplied string against any portion of an attribute in the directory. For this reason, a query for "FR" returns "Linda Fritter" in addition to "Fred Pumpkin" and "Frank Pea."

By default, the Directory processes all supplied searches as initial substring searches (**Treat "Any" Substring Searches As "Initial" Substring Searches (Fast)**), but you can change this behavior through the **Search** property page. You can refuse other searches when selecting the **Allow Only "Initial" Substring Searches (Fast)** option. You can also click the **Allow All Substring Searches (Slow)** radio button, which activates the *any search type*. However, this option requires the most processing from the server.

Idle Timeouts

To close idle connections and to recover consumed resources, you can specify a timeout value at the **Idle Time-Out** property page. By default, idle connections will be disconnected after 10 minutes.

Server Referrals

If you compare the configuration options of the LDAP implementation of Exchange Server versions 5.0 and 5.5, you'll discover that the **Referrals** tab is provided only in the later version. Exchange Server 5.5 supports server referrals, which are mechanisms for redirecting LDAP clients to other LDAP servers in case a client request cannot be fulfilled by the local server.

For example, let's say Fred Pumpkin is using Outlook Express. Usually he queries the Directory of his home server for recipient information. This works fine until he creates a search that his server cannot perform. For example, he might ask for the phone number of Jose Pepper, who resides in another organization such as *sombrero.com*. At this point, Fred's home server can return a server referral if the server has been configured through the **Referrals** property page. A referral can point to a server outside STOCKSDATA that contains the desired information. It is up to the client to connect to this server, transmit the query, and display the result. Multiple referral entries might be possible, but the client will always try the **Default Referral** first.

Note Referrals can point only to LDAP servers outside their own organization.

To summarize, the elements of LDAP configuration are as follows:

- Allows anonymous access by default
- Supports Basic (Clear Text), Windows NT Challenge/Response, and MCIS authentication
- Default timeout to close idle connections is 10 minutes
- Enable or disable LDAP on the **General** property pages
- Specifies referrals to other LDAP servers outside the home organization
- Specifies returned Directory attributes based on **DS Site Configuration** settings page
- Configuration options exist at site and server levels

- Server-level properties are inherited from site settings if not explicitly specified

- Site and server levels provide nearly identical user interfaces

- Configures how search requests are handled on the **Searches** property page

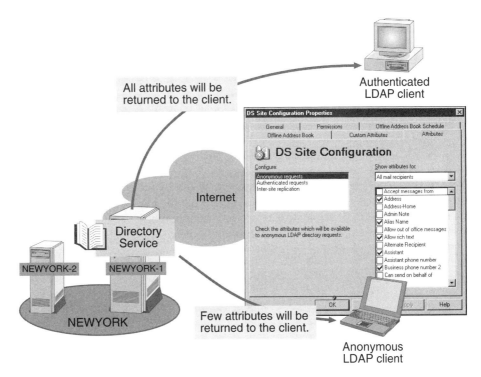

Figure 11-16. Configuring attributes available to authenticated and anonymous LDAP clients.

Lesson 4: Internet News Service and the Network News Transfer Protocol

The USENET is a communication network based on NNTP that relies on distributed discussion forums known as newsgroups. More than 20,000 newsgroups exist, but it can still be difficult to find the information you're seeking. Several Web sites, such as the Alta Vista Search Engine (*altavista.digital.com*) or the Yahoo USENET Web page (*www.yahoo.com/News/Usenet*), can simplify your journey into the USENET network as a *subscriber*. Exchange Server, on the other hand, is a system that allows you to start using the USENET as an *information source*. Using the INS in conjunction with public folders, you have the ability to create your own USENET site and to replicate newsgroups across the USENET.

This lesson provides a brief discussion of the INS, and then explains the USENET architecture and its methods for distributing information. An introduction to the Newsfeed Configuration Wizard, which creates and configures new newsfeeds then follows. You'll read about the manual configuration of newsfeeds and the use of public folders for publishing information. Because the INS depends on NNTP, NNTP management will be discussed. Finally, this lesson provides a method for testing the NNTP communication using the Telnet utility.

At the end of this lesson, you will be able to:

- Describe newsgroups and newsfeed features
- Use the Newsfeeds Configuration Wizard to create newsfeeds and install the INS
- Configure newsfeeds using their property pages
- Specify properties for public folders so that they can be published as newsgroups

Estimated time to complete this lesson: 35 minutes

Introduction to the INS

The USENET consists of newsgroups and newsfeeds. Newsgroups are the actual discussion forums; they maintain articles that are posted as users participate in discussions. Newsfeeds, in turn, replicate articles across the USENET to all instances of a particular newsgroup.

Newsgroups

Newsgroups can be compared to regular public folders of an Exchange Server. Newsgroups can represent the context of discussions, as do public folders. Articles posted in newsgroups represent the bits and pieces of discussions, as do messages in public folders. Last but not least, articles are replicated to all instances of a particular newsgroup across the USENET, just as messages are replicated to all instances of a particular public folder across the organization. Newsgroup replication requires newsfeeds, while public folder replication relies on IS replication links. Is it surprising that Exchange Server relies on public folders to maintain newsgroups?

Some newsgroups are moderated, which means that a new article must first be sent to a moderator for approval before it appears in the actual newsgroup forum. The Exchange INS supports moderated newsgroups because it supports moderated public folders. The management of public folders is covered in Chapter 12.

Newsreaders

A newsreader application is a client program that can be used to read articles of a newsgroup through NNTP. Public folders can also be accessed because Exchange Server supports NNTP. (See Figure 11-17.) In either case, the client must establish a connection to TCP/IP port 119 to communicate with the server.

Like POP3 and IMAP4 clients, the newsreader contacts the IS directly to retrieve the desired messages formatted in UUENCODE or MIME. The IS takes care of the content conversion through its IMAIL feature.

Note Using the IMAIL function, the IS converts MAPI properties of requested messages into MIME or UUENCODE, and vice versa. However, new messages posted using a newsreader application are not converted immediately into the internal Exchange Server format. This mechanism improves the server performance because the conversion into the internal Exchange Server format will take place only if a MAPI-based client, such as Outlook, requests the information.

Internet News Service

To achieve true USENET functionality, the INS must be installed. It is a separate Windows NT service that relies on the NNTP, as defined in RFC 977. Its primary purpose is to maintain newsfeeds that replicate articles between USENET hosts.

Typically, although not necessarily, you will use the INS to exchange newsgroup information with the USENET. Both permanent and dial-up connections are supported. If you establish a connection using telephone lines or ISDN, you first need to configure Dial-Up Networking within Windows NT Server. Once configured, you can specify the dial-up connection during the installation of newsfeeds. You can also schedule dial-up connections at this time.

Planning Newsfeeds

The newsfeed installation has been simplified through the Newsfeed Configuration Wizard, but newsfeed planning remains an important task that should not be taken too lightly. Otherwise, you might experience problems regarding the available disk space as soon as a newsfeed begins to replicate articles. Newsgroups can contain a huge amount of information, with data up to several gigabytes in size.

A gigabyte of data on the USENET, however, should not be considered the same as a gigabyte of data on the Exchange Server. The IS maintains public folder items in its Pub.edb file as well as in its transaction log files, so it's more accurate to assume that you must reserve double the amount of disk space (2 GB) until you delete the transaction log files through a full backup. Transaction log files and backup strategies are covered in Chapter 15, "Maintaining Servers."

Multiple Newsfeeds

You might want to distribute the load of work between multiple Exchange Server computers in your organization, which can reduce the time required to replicate huge numbers of articles. Multiple servers can replicate different newsgroups to and from the USENET. Take care not to include the same newsgroup hierarchy in multiple newsfeed instances. This will cause redundant article transfer, increased network traffic, and wasted disk space on your server.

The hierarchy of USENET newsgroups is as follows:

- **alt**; contains alternative or controversial topics
- **comp**; contains computer topics, information about software and hardware
- **misc**; contains miscellaneous topics (not classified under other hierarchies)
- **news**; contains information and news about USENET
- **rec**; contains discussions about arts, hobbies, and recreational activities
- **sci**; contains topics about sciences and scientific research
- **soc**; contains social discussions
- **talk**; contains information about politics, religion, and other issues

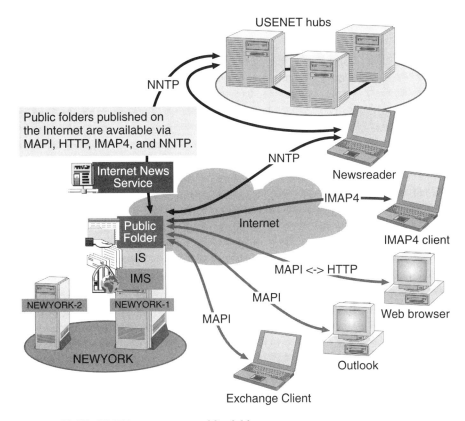

Figure 11-17. NNTP access to a public folder.

Background on Newsfeeds

As a distributed discussion network, the USENET architecture goes beyond the model of simple discussion forums maintained on single servers. The architecture uses newsfeeds to transfer articles between instances of particular newsgroups, which usually reside on multiple servers.

USENET Nodes

The basic elements of the USENET architecture are *hubs* and *leaf nodes*. Hubs are servers that maintain particular newsgroup instances and communicate with other hubs and with leaf nodes. Leaf nodes communicate only with hubs. In other words, if two USENET servers maintain an instance of the same newsgroup, both can initiate and accept NNTP connections to replicate changes that have occurred on one of the replicas. Exchange Server 5.5 can act as either a USENET hub or leaf node. (See Figure 11-18.)

Newsfeed Types

In general, two forms of NNTP data transfer exist: they are the *pull transfer* and the *push transfer*. To imagine a newsfeed you can think of it as a user running a newsreader client. Let's say you want to receive new changes from a remote server, so you first connect to the remote server's port 119. You can then check the remote server for new articles and request those which you have not yet received. In other words, as you pull new articles you are simulating a *pull feed*. On the other hand, you might also want to transfer some new articles. Using the newsreader, you can simply post them to the remote server. You push your information into the host, simulating a *push feed*.

Note A push feed starts the communication to transfer its own information to a remote server. A pull feed contacts a remote node to retrieve new information. Exchange Server supports both push and pull feeds.

Push and pull can also be used to specify which computer initiates the communication:

- Pull feed; Exchange Server computer initiates the connection to the remote server and pulls the information

- Push feed; remote server (such as a provider's host) initiates the connection and pushes the information into the Exchange Server computer

Newsgroup Articles

Articles are generally transferred using NNTP, which is a peer-to-peer command set used for both client-to-server and server-to-server communication. The actual format of USENET articles is defined in RFC 1036; attachments are encoded using either UUENCODE or MIME.

Differences Between Newsfeed Types

The use of NNTP differs slightly between pull and push feeds. While pull feeds need a command set for querying remote servers about available articles, push feeds need a command set for newsgroup creation and article posting. Pull feeds are more flexible than push feeds because they allow you to select the newsgroups that you want to receive. On the other hand, push feeds provide more advantages if the replicated amount of information is very large. When configuring push feeds, you will need the cooperation of your ISP to specify the newsgroups you want to feed into the organization.

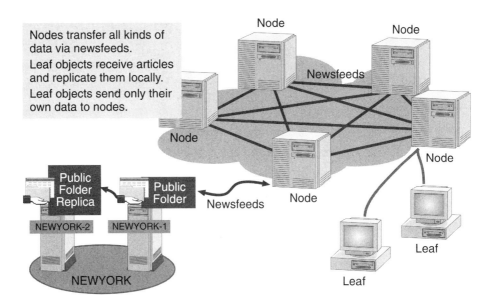

Nodes transfer all kinds of data via newsfeeds.

Leaf objects receive articles and replicate them locally.

Leaf objects send only their own data to nodes.

Figure 11-18. USENET architecture.

The characteristics of the INS are as follows:

- Allows MIME and HTML content
- Supports anonymous access, Basic, Windows NT Challenge/Response and MCIS authentication, and SSL security options
- Acts as a USENET hub and as a leaf node
- Creates and removes newsgroups through USENET control messages
- Allows easy installation through the Newsfeed Configuration Wizard
- Newsgroups provide a public forum for discussions
- Newsreader clients can access public folders
- Creates push and pull feeds
- Push feeds are useful when replicating a large number of articles
- Selects specific newsgroups when configuring pull feeds
- Supports scheduled dial-up connections

Using the Newsfeed Configuration Wizard

The Newsfeed Configuration Wizard simplifies the installation of news-feeds. Integrated into the Administrator program, the wizard can be launched through the **Newsfeed** command under **New Other** on the **File** menu. This wizard creates and starts a new Windows NT service called **Microsoft Exchange Internet News Service**, but this happens only when you configure the first newsfeed on the server.

Welcome Page

The Welcome page is displayed when you launch the Newsfeeds Configuration Wizard. The Welcome page provides general information about required settings. You must have information about your USENET provider, the remote USENET hosts, and required logon credentials at hand in order to install a newsfeed successfully. (See Figure 11-19 on page 731.)

Installed Server

On the second wizard page, select the target server where you want to install the newsfeed and INS. The **USENET Site Name** is also displayed and should correspond to the local site configuration.

Note The default USENET site name will be constructed using the site and organization name. The format is *site.organization.com*. If necessary, you can change the site name on this wizard page.

Types of Newsfeeds

The third wizard page provides you with several options for specifying what kind of newsfeed you want to create. If your ISP has configured a push feed, which transfers new articles to your organization, choose **Accept Incoming Messages (Typical)** under **Inbound Newsfeed Type**. Select **Pull Incoming Messages** if you want to configure an inbound pull feed.

Regardless of the feed type, the communication can be configured either bidirectionally (**Inbound And Outbound (Typical)**) or unidirectionally (**Inbound Only** or **Outbound Only**). If you configure an outbound-only feed, you are forced to configure a push feed. In other words, **Inbound Newsfeed Type** options are unavailable if you configure an outbound-only connection.

Connection Type

The Connection Type wizard page follows, asking whether you want to connect to the remote server through a dial-up connection (**Connect Using Dial-Up Networking** option) or through a permanent link (**Connect Using**

My LAN option). If you're using a dial-up connection, enter the corresponding phone book entry as well as the required account information. In this case, Dial-up Networking (RAS) must be installed and a phone book entry should be created prior to the installation of the newsfeed.

Connection information can be adjusted later through the **Connections** property page of the new newsfeed object. Once the installation has been completed, the newsfeed object can be found in the **Connections** container.

Schedule

The Schedule page allows you to configure the connection interval. You can select a frequency of 15 minutes or 1, 3, 6, 12, or 24 hours. You can also configure the connection interval in more detail later using the **Schedule** property page of the newsfeed object. The smallest interval you can select is 15 minutes.

USENET Site Name

Specify your **Provider's USENET Site Name** on the wizard page that follows. This information is used to access the remote newsfeed computer. Once the newsfeed has been installed, you can change or adjust the **Remote USENET Site Name** through the **Hosts** property page.

Host Computer

In order to allow your newsfeed to contact a remote server, supply either the host name or the IP address of the target system. You can specify more than one remote server. You should contact your ISP if the host names are unknown because at least one name is required for proper newsfeed operation. Besides using the **Remote USENET Site Name**, you can also adjust the host computer information through the **Hosts** property page after installation.

Security

You can set the log on information regarding pull and push feeds on the Security wizard page. A pull feed might be obligated to log on to the remote host using a specific account. The required account information can be entered in the **Log In To Remote Servers As** and **Password** boxes. Push feeds, in turn, can log on to the local Exchange Server computer. In order to be able to identify them, you can assign them a mailbox account using the **Remote Servers Log In As** box. You can modify these settings later through the **Security** property page of the corresponding newsfeed object.

INS Installation Page

This wizard page informs you that the Newsfeeds Configuration Wizard has gathered all the information required to install the INS. Congratulations—this was a thorough interview of eight wizard pages! Click **Next** after you have had a short break and maybe a sip of coffee.

Note When you click **Next** at this point, the Newsfeed Configuration Wizard creates several directory and Registry entries. You will no longer be able to return to previous pages, as you'll find when you try to click the **Back** button.

Service Account

The INS is a separate Windows NT service, so you must supply the password of the Site Services Account if the wizard has not yet created this service during a previous newsfeed installation.

Note When you click the **Next** button, the **Microsoft Exchange Internet News Service** will be created and started. You can see that the service has started through the **Services** applet of the Control Panel.

Administrator Page

This page prompts you for an INS administrator account. This is an account that becomes the owner of all public folders created by this newsfeed. This administrator account will also receive status messages related to the newsfeed operation. Click the **Change** button to display the Global Address List to specify your own mailbox or a mailbox that has been created explicitly for newsfeed administration. The desired mailbox must have been created prior to the installation of the newsfeed, but if you have forgotten this important step during your preparation, you don't need to cancel the installation. Just select your own mailbox temporarily, complete the remaining part of the installation, create the desired mailbox later, and then modify the administrator account through the newsfeed's **General** property page.

Active File

An active file describes the list of all newsgroups a USENET provider has to offer. You will use this file to subscribe your newsfeed to the newsgroups that you want to replicate to your organization. Depending on the ISP, this file can be downloaded using FTP or even NNTP. Contact your ISP for details. If the remote server is an Exchange Server computer, you can download the file directly through the **Download The Active File From My Provider Now** option.

On the other hand, if an active file is not yet available, choose **I'll Configure My Newsfeed Later**. In this case, you will need to provide the active file at a later time through the **Inbound** property page of the corresponding newsfeed. The configuration of this property page is explained later in this lesson in the section, "Advanced Newsfeed Configuration Tasks."

Completing the Installation

The last page of the Newsfeed Configuration Wizard provides a summary about the configuration. This page requires no input. Click the **Finish** button to complete the installation and to create the corresponding configuration object within the **Connections** container (for example, **Newsfeed LONDON.STOCKSDATA.UK (NEWYORK-1)**). You will use this object for further configuration.

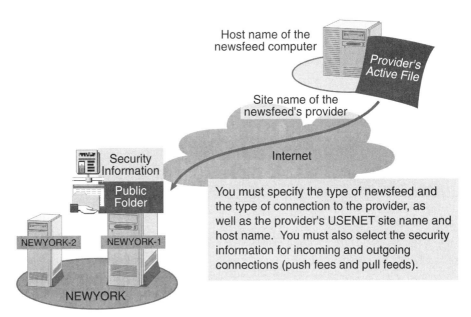

Figure 11-19. Installation of a newsfeed.

The Newsfeed Configuration Wizard dialog boxes and their functions are as follows:

- **Welcome**; to welcome the administrator; requires no input

- **Installed Server**; to select the server on which the newsfeed will be installed

- **Type of Newsfeed**; to select the type of newsfeed
- **Connection Type**; to specify the network connection type to be used when connecting to the USENET host
- **Schedule**; to configure the connection frequency to the USENET host (pull feed only)
- **USENET site name**; to configure the newsfeed provider's site name
- **Host Computer**; to enter the IP address or the host name of the provider's computer
- **Security**; to define security information for pull and push feed (outgoing and incoming connections)
- **Installation**; to inform you that the service is ready to be installed; requires no input
- **Administrator**; to select the INS administrator
- **Active File**; to configure the newsgroups to be included in this newsfeed
- **Finish**; to complete the installation; requires no input

Advanced Newsfeed Configuration Tasks

You can accomplish advanced newsfeed configuration tasks through the property pages that every newsfeed object provides. For instance, it might be necessary to disable a particular newsfeed if you discover that this feed replicates too many articles to your server. In this situation you simply clear the **Enable Newsfeed** check box on the newsfeed's **General** property page. Then you can add new hardware resources to the server before you enable this feed again.

Controlling Inbound Newsgroups

Because Exchange Server maintains newsgroups in the form of public folders, you need to create an associated public folder for each newsgroup that you want to receive. These public folders are also known as *newsgroup folders*.

Creating Newsgroup Folders

You can create public folders for inbound newsgroups using the **Create Newsgroup Folders** dialog box, which can be displayed by clicking the **Create Newsgroup Folders** button on the **Inbound** property page. This dialog box displays all available newsgroups as specified in the provider's active file. Make your choice using the **Include** and **Exclude** buttons. If you want, you can think of this process as subscribing to a newsgroup. When you click **OK**, new public folders will be created in the **Internet Newsgroups** public folder. On the **Inbound** property page, they will appear in the **Select Which Newsgroup Will Accept Messages From This Feed** list.

Creating a newsgroup public folder is not the only configuration step that is required. You must also include the desired newsgroup folder in the newsfeed by clicking the **Accept** button. This extra configuration step is necessary because, although multiple newsfeeds might be able to replicate the same newsgroup to your organization, only one should actually transfer articles of a particular newsgroup from the USENET. Otherwise, you will waste your server's disk space because multiple copies of the same articles will be created. The **Reject** button, which can be found below the **Accept** button, can be useful if you detect that multiple feeds are replicating the same information.

Downloading a New Active File

Sometimes you might want to download a new active file from the USENET provider's host using NNTP, especially if the list of available newsgroups has changed. In this case, click the **New Active List** button on the **Create Newsgroup Folders** dialog box. A **New Active List** dialog box appears, offering the choices **Download From The Newsfeed Provider**, **Via NNTP**, and **Import From A File**. Select the appropriate option and click **OK**. At this point, new information about newsgroups will be received and displayed under **Select Newsgroups You Want To Receive**. You can then create new newsgroup folders as described.

Restricting Message Sizes

The default limit for outgoing messages is 1 MB; an inbound message size limit does not exist. But imposing a message size limit can help to avoid disk space problems, because newsgroups can be huge. In order to set size limits for inbound messages, switch to the **Messages** property page, where you will find both the **Outgoing Message Size** option and the **Incoming Message Size** option.

Controlling Outbound Newsgroups

The USENET is not a one-way street; public folders can also be replicated to the USENET. Of course, you can specify outbound newsgroup folders only for a feed that is configured for outbound use. (See Figure 11-20.)

First you must create a newsgroup hierarchy for a public folder that you want to replicate to the USENET. Then you can include the folder in an outbound newsfeed through the feed's **Outbound** property page. Simply select the desired newsgroup folder, and then click the **Include** button. That's it. The creation of a newsgroup hierarchy is covered in the section, "Setting Properties on Newsgroup Public Folders," later in this lesson.

Bypassing Old Messages

Let's say the server NEWYORK-1 maintained a huge newsgroup that was about 3 GB in size before the server crashed. Fortunately the backup you recently created has been restored, but the newsgroup is now missing approximately 100 MB. In this situation, you have to choose between two options: You can either retrieve the 100 MB of old articles or you can skip them. In the first case, the newsfeed ensures that all articles will automatically be received. In the latter case, you must manipulate the newsfeed so that it does not request the old messages from the remote USENET server again. To accomplish this manipulation, switch to the **Advanced** property page of the affected feed to click the **Mark All As Delivered** button. This single mouse click will prevent the replication of all those articles that were created before you clicked the button.

Checkpoint File

Whenever you click the **Mark All As Delivered** button, you actually update a file called Ics.dat that can be found in the \Exchsrvr\Insdata directory. This file is also known as the INS checkpoint file because it is used to keep track of which messages have already been replicated. Do not delete this file. If you do, you will reset your newsfeeds and greatly increase the amount of data that must be transferred through your network. According to the previous example, your newsfeed would start to replicate all 3 GB of articles even if they have already been replicated!

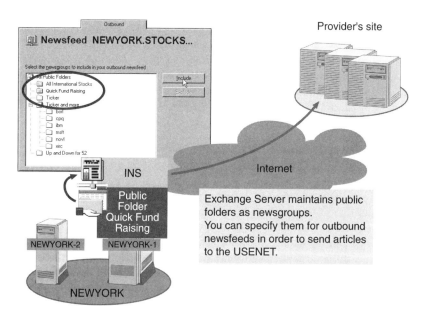

Figure 11-20. Selecting outbound newsgroups.

The newsfeed property pages and their functions are as follows:

- **Advanced**; to mark all newsgroup messages as delivered

- **Connection**; to provide connection information (LAN or RAS)

- **General**; to change the administrator's mailbox, to change the display name, and to disable the newsfeed

- **Hosts**; to enter remote USENET host and site name

- **Inbound**; to select newsgroups (public folders) that will accept newsfeed messages

- **Messages**; to specify message size limits for inbound and outbound messages

- **Outbound**; to select newsgroups (public folders) that will be included in outbound messages

- **Schedule**; to set an activation schedule for the newsfeed

- **Security**; to define the required security to access a newsfeed computer

Setting Properties on Newsgroup Public Folders

The implementation of newsgroups based on public folders provides several advantages. Once the administrator has configured newsgroup hierarchies and newsfeeds, individual users can create and manage newsgroups by creating and configuring public folders. The creation of newsgroups will be covered in the following section. The management of public folders is covered in detail in Chapter 12.

Making Internet Newsgroups Available to NNTP Clients

The **Internet Newsgroups** public folder is the default location for inbound newsgroups replicated to an Exchange Server. This folder represents a hierarchy parent folder. All inbound newsfeeds will maintain their newsgroup folders under the parent folder. You can also use a newsreader client such as Outlook Express to access those public folders through NNTP.

If you want to create additional discussion forums, you need to create manually the associated public folders under a newsgroup hierarchy. However, this is impossible in a default configuration, because you must first modify the client permissions for the **Internet Newsgroups** folder within the Administrator program. To do this, display the **Internet Newsgroups** properties, click the **Client Permissions** button on the **General** property page, and select the desired accounts through the **Add** button. Make sure that not too many accounts have the privilege to create new newsgroups.

Creating New Hierarchies

You can also create new newsgroup hierarchies; in other words, you can define other public folders as hierarchy parents. The parent folders and all sublevel folders under them will then be detected through NNTP. To accomplish this task, switch to the Administrator program, select the **Newsgroup Hierarchy** command on the **Tools** menu, and click the **Add** button within the **Newsgroup Hierarchies** dialog box. A list of all available public folders is displayed, from which you can select the desired folder and click **OK**. The public folder name and the associated newsgroup names are displayed on the list of the **Newsgroup Hierarchies**. To commit to the modifications, click **OK** again.

Note Extended characters and spaces in public folder names will be replaced with dashes in associated newsgroup names. For example, a folder named *Fred's Ideas* will become a newsgroup named *fred-s-ideas*.

Changing Newsgroup Public Folder Properties

When you create a public folder within a newsgroup hierarchy, this folder becomes visible to newsreader applications. As an owner of the public folder, you can prevent NNTP access if you clear the **Publish This Folder To Users Of Newsreader Software** check box on the folder's **Internet News** property page. This property page can be reached by right-clicking the desired public folder in Outlook and selecting **Properties**. When you click **OK** or **Apply**, the public folder loses all its newsgroup properties and becomes just a public folder. Only the selected folder will be affected this way; subfolders are not included. In other words, even if a parent folder is no longer published as a newsgroup, any newsgroup subfolder retains its newsgroup properties.

Other settings, such as a moderator's e-mail address, can also be configured for newsgroup folders. A moderated public folder or newsgroup folder allows a user to forward posted messages to a newsgroup moderator. The moderator reviews the posted information and allows accepted articles to appear in the newsgroup folder. (See Figure 11-21.)

Only one newsgroup folder parameter can be set using the Administrator program—the **Default Character Set,** which is used by the IS to convert messages from the internal Exchange Server format into MIME or UUENCODE. This conversion takes place through IMAIL before articles are sent to newsreader applications. You can adjust this parameter via the **NNTP** property page that every public folder provides.

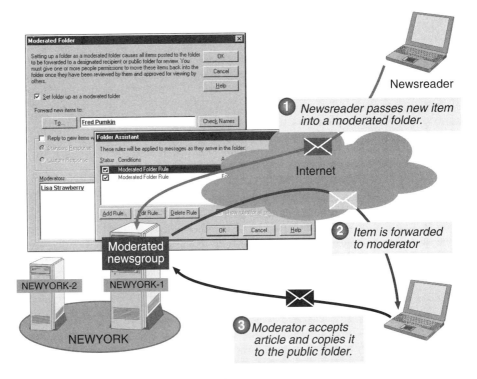

Figure 11-21.   Configuring a moderated newsgroup.

The newsgroup folder management utilities and their functions are as follows:

- Administrator program; to create newsfeeds, newsgroup hierarchies, and to specify NNTP settings

- Exchange Client or Outlook; to create newsgroup folders and to specify permissions, views, and other management tasks

NNTP Management

Managing NNTP at the site and server levels affects all newsfeeds and all clients that want to connect to newsgroups residing on a particular Exchange Server. As usual, site- and server-level settings do not differ heavily and server-level settings override site-level default settings. Several configuration settings affect NNTP the same way as they do for POP3 or IMAP4. The **Idle Timeout** property page, for example, allows you to close inactive connection automatically.

Changing the USENET Site Name

You have the option to adjust the name of your USENET site through the **USENET Site Name** box using the **Newsfeeds** tab. This property page can be found only at the server-level configuration object. Typically, the **USENET Site Name** matches the configuration of your e-mail domain. As mentioned in the section, "Using the Newsfeed Configuration Wizard," the USENET site name will also be displayed on the second wizard page during a newsfeed installation.

Creating an Active File

The **Create Active File** button is located on the **Newsfeeds** property page. This button can be used to save the active list of available newsgroups to a text file. You can send this text file, in turn, to other administrators who want to create newsfeeds to your newsgroups. Users of newsreader programs can also use such an active file to subscribe to newsgroups provided by your Exchange Server.

Control Messages

NNTP control messages perform specific actions on newsgroups, like deleting messages or creating new newsgroups. Remote USENET hosts send control messages, as these hosts want to perform specific actions on the local server. Three types of control messages exist: NEWGROUP, which broadcasts that a new group has been created; RMGROUP, which indicates that an existing group has been deleted; and CANCEL, which sends a request to delete an article that has already been posted to a newsgroup.

Because of security considerations, the NEWGROUP and RMGROUP control messages are not processed automatically. Instead they are queued and can be displayed using the **Control Messages** property page. This page is available only at the site-level configuration object for NNTP. This page lists the message type, the originating host, and when the message was received. If you have received a control message from unknown or suspicious hosts, it is advisable to get rid of the unprocessed messages by clicking the **Delete** button. In typical situations, however, you will click the **Accept** button to apply the changes.

Note Exchange Server does not generate NEWGROUP or RMGROUP control messages. The CANCEL message, however, is generated whenever a user deletes a message in a public folder that acts also as a newsgroup.

Anonymous Access

Exchange Server supports anonymous NNTP-based access to public folders, but anonymous access is disabled by default. To enable this option, select the **Allow Anonymous Access** check box on the **Anonymous** property page. You must grant **Anonymous** account access permissions on a particular public folder through the folder's **Permissions** property page. Usually, the **Anonymous** account has been granted the role **None**, which means anonymous users have no access at all to public folders. You will specify public folder permissions primarily using the Exchange Client or Outlook (as shown in Figure 11-22), although permissions can also be configured within the Administrator program.

Validated Access

Exchange Server provides the same authentication methods to NNTP as it does to other Internet protocols. These authentication methods are Basic (Clear Text), Windows NT Challenge/Response, and MCIS, and all these types can be used in conjunction with SSL.

A validated user will be granted access to newsgroup folders just as if he or she were working with Outlook. The Windows NT account information must be supplied during logon. This can be accomplished automatically through Windows NT Challenge/Response authentication or in the format *Windows NT domain name/account name/mailbox name*. The user password corresponds to the Windows NT password, as described for POP3 and IMAP4.

UUENCODE or MIME Encoding

Most of today's newsreader applications use the UUENCODE scheme to format messages, so this encoding mechanism is enabled by default. If you want, you can enable MIME encoding instead using the **Message Format** property page. You then have the option to provide the message body as plain text, as HTML, or as both. In the latter case, a multi-part alternative MIME body part will be generated. If your newsreader program can handle S/MIME signatures, you can also enable the **Client Support S/MIME Signatures** option. Support for S/MIME is described in more detail in Chapter 10.

The specified settings affect the conversion of outgoing messages from the Exchange Server format into the NNTP newsreader client format. Incoming messages (messages posted using a newsreader client) will not be converted; rather, they will be stored in their native format on the Exchange Server.

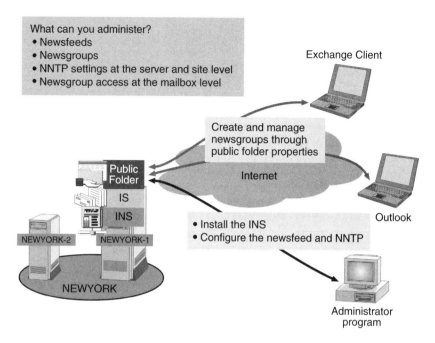

Figure 11-22. Maintaining newsgroups.

The server-level and site-level NNTP property pages and their functions are as follows:

- **Anonymous Access**; to enable anonymous access to newsgroups

- **Authentication**; to specify supported authentication methods such as **Basic (Clear Text)**, **Basic (Clear Text) Using SSL**, **Windows NT Challenge/Response**, **Windows NT Challenge/Response Using SSL**, **MCIS Membership System**, and **MCIS Membership System Using SSL**

- **Control Messages**; to delete or execute control messages from other USENET hosts at the site level

- **Diagnostics Logging**; to keep track of INS status; possible categories for logging are **Content Engine**, **Internet News Service**, **Connections**, **Authentication**, **Client Actions**, **Configuration**, **Replication**, and **NNTP Pull Newsfeeds**

- **General**; to enable NNTP and to allow client access; also, the display name of the configuration object can be changed and an administrative note can be added

- **Idle Timeout**; to disconnect idle newsreaders

- **Message Format**; to select the format of newsgroups messages

- **Newsfeeds**; to examine and configure existing newsfeeds, to set the **USENET Site Name** at the server level, and to create an active file

NNTP Mailbox-Level Administration

The **Protocols** property page displays an **NNTP (News)** entry to determine mailbox-level settings. You can use this option to set specific message content formats such as MIME or UUENCODE or disable NNTP for a particular user. (See Figure 11-23.)

As mentioned in "Configuring Mailbox Protocols Properties," earlier in this chapter, mailbox level settings are a higher priority than site-level or server-level settings, except you cannot re-enable the protocol if it has been disabled at the site or server levels. You will notice a short status indicator under the **Enable NNTP For This Recipient** option, which is there to inform you if the protocol is enabled at the server. Access to newsgroups is possible only with a status of **NNTP Is Enabled On This Server**.

Note You cannot specify support for S/MIME signatures for individual mailboxes. You can enable this feature only at the site and server levels.

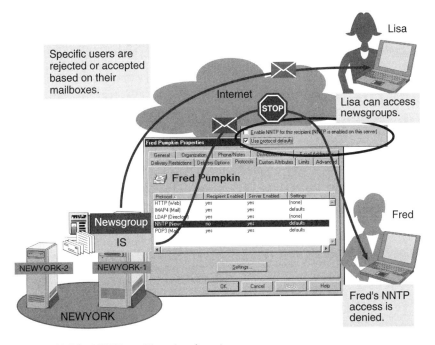

Figure 11-23. NNTP mailbox-level settings.

The two possible NNTP mailbox configuration settings are:

- MIME encoding (plain text/HTML) or UUENCODE
- NNTP enabled or disabled

Troubleshooting NNTP Connectivity

NNTP is an application-layer protocol that can be tested using the Telnet utility. You can establish a test session if Basic (Clear Text) Authentication is enabled on the server. If you know the NNTP commands and responses, you will be able to read messages from available newsgroups.

NNTP Command Format

NNTP commands are not case sensitive. They are represented as keywords followed by arguments, which are separated by a single space. Only printable ASCII characters are valid. When you send a command to the server, you receive a response. Numbers indicate positive or negative responses, accompanied by descriptive text. If you mistype a command, you will be informed in clear text. (See Figure 11-24 on page 745.)

Establishing a Connection

Newsreader applications open TCP/IP port 119 to establish a NNTP session. You connect to this port using Telnet as well, but you should make sure that the **Local Echo** option on the **Terminal Preferences** dialog box has been selected. This dialog box can be launched through the **Preferences** command on the **Terminal** menu. If you don't launch this dialog box, you will not be able to see what you type. Open the **Connect** menu to choose the **Remote System Command.** The **Connect** dialog box appears for you to enter the name of your Exchange Server computer (or its IP address) in the **Host Name** box. Specify the port number **119** using the **Port** box.

An NNTP connection will be established and the server will send this welcome message back to the Telnet client: **201 Microsoft Exchange Internet News Service Version 5.5.1960.6 (posting allowed)**. At this time, enter **MODE READER** to indicate that you are using a newsreader client.

Logging On to the Server

To log on to the server, you must provide valid authentication information using the **AUTHINFO USER** *<domain_name/nt_account/mailbox>* command. A positive response, **381 more authentication required**, should return. Enter the password through the command **AUTHINFO PASS** *<password>*. You should receive a positive response such as **281 authentication accepted**.

Displaying Messages

To display messages, enter the **LISTGROUP** *<NEWSGROUP>* command. A positive response includes the number of e-mails in the newsgroup; for example, **211 list of article numbers follow 4 6 7**. (The sample numbers are actually listed on separate lines.) To read a particular message use the **ARTICLE** *<number>* command. The message and its header information will be received. To quit the connection, use the **QUIT** command; the answer **205 closing connection** indicates the successful operation.

Examining Supported Commands

The **HELP** command is useful if you want to explore the set of supported commands. As you examine the list, you will discover that the **IHAVE** command is available. Exchange Server 5.0 did not provide support for this command, which meant that newsfeeds requiring support for this command were not able to communicate with Exchange Server 5.0. Push feeds typically use **IHAVE** to indicate new articles.

The NNTP commands supported by Exchange Server and listed in the RFCs are:

- **ARTICLE** *message-ID*; to retrieve the article specified by message ID

- **ARTICLE** *nnn*; to retrieve the article specified by the message number (nnn)

- **BODY**; to retrieve the body of a message (used as described for the ARTICLE command)

- **HEAD**; to retrieve only the header lines of the message (used as described for the ARTICLE command)

- **STAT** *{nnn | message-ID}*; no text is returned; if nnn is used, the current article number is set to the value; if a specific message ID is used, the current article number is set to the first article in the group

- **GROUP** *group*; to select a newsgroup

- **HELP**; to display supported commands

- **IHAVE** *message-ID*; to inform a remote host about an article for which the ID is message ID; if the remote host wants a copy of the article, it responds with a command instructing the client to send the article

- **LAST**; to reference the previous article in the current newsgroup

- **LIST**; to return a list of valid newsgroups and associated information

- **NEWSGROUPS** *date time [GMT]*; to list newsgroups since the specified date and time, based on Greenwich Mean Time (GMT)

- **NEWNEWS** *date time [GMT]*; to retrieve a list of message IDs for articles posted or received since the specified date and time based on GMT

- **NEXT**; to move to the next article in the current newsgroup

- **POST**; to indicate that the client is ready to post a message

- **QUIT**; to close the connection

- **SLAVE**; to indicate that this client connection is to a slave server, rather than a user

In addition to the above commands, Exchange supports the following common, non-RFC extensions:

- **AUTHINFO** *[user | password | generic | transact | timple] data*; to authenticate a user

- **DATE**; to determine the current time from the server's perspective; response is in the form: **111 YYYYMMDDhhmmss**

- **MODE READER**; to indicate to the server that the client is a newsreader

- **XHDR** *header [range|, message-ID | article #]*; to retrieve specific headers from a desired article

- **XOVER** *[range]*; to return information from the overview database for the specified article or articles

Protocol Logging

Not only is Exchange Server 5.5 able to keep track of POP3 and IMAP4 communication, it provides protocol logging for NNTP as well. Protocol logging is especially valuable if you suspect communication problems. The corresponding registry keys can be found under:

```
HKEY_LOCAL_MACHINE
    \System
        \CurrentControlSet
            \Services
                \MSExchangeIS
                    \ParametersSystem
```

The value "NNTP Protocol LogPath" must point to the directory where the NNTP logging files (for example, L0000001.log) will be created. "NNTP Protocol Logging Level" specifies the logged NNTP protocol details. By default, this value is set to 0 in order to disable NNTP logging. A value of 1 sets minimal logging, a value of 4 determines maximum logging, and a value of 5 indicates that message text will be logged in addition to maximum protocol information.

Whenever you modify these settings directly using the Windows NT Registry Editor, you will need to restart the IS service for the new parameters to take effect.

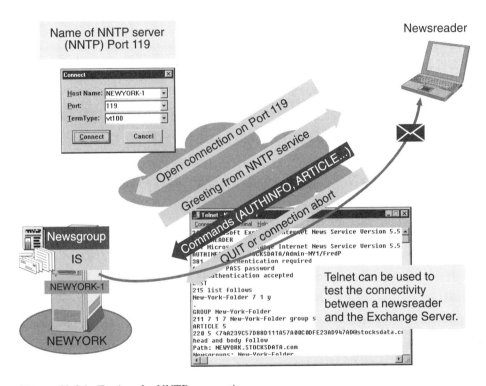

Figure 11-24. Testing the NNTP connection.

The following steps show a sample of NNTP communication with Telnet:

1. Enable **Local Echo** under **Preferences** of the **Terminal** menu.

2. Open the **Connect** menu and choose **Remote System**.

3. Enter the name of the Exchange Server under **Host Name**.

4. Enter the port *119* in the **Port** box, and then click **OK**.

5. Note the greeting of the NNTP server.

6. Enter *MODE READER* to specify that you are a newsreader client.

7. Enter *AUTHINFO USER <domain/nt_account/mailbox>* (use valid information).

8. Verify the **381 more authentication required** response.

9. Enter *AUTHINFO PASS <password>* (use valid information).

10. Verify the positive response and the status information.

11. Enter *LIST* to display a list of newsgroups that this server provides. The list will be empty if public folders have not yet been published as newsgroups on the connected server.

12. If newsgroups are listed, enter *GROUP <folder name>*.

13. Notice the positive response and the number of e-mail messages in the newsgroup (if any exist).

14. If mail exists, enter *ARTICLE <number>* to read a message.

15. Enter *QUIT*.

Lesson 5: Hypertext Transfer Protocol

HTTP is probably the most popular Internet protocol in use today. Its older version 1.0 and its current version 1.1 are both used by Web browser applications to download documents from a Web server and to display the documents to the user. Documents must be formatted using HTML, otherwise Web browsers cannot display their contents. Consequently, implementing HTTP support into Exchange Server means converting MAPI-based resources (for example, messages) into HTML documents, and vice versa.

In the context of this lesson, the term *MAPI-based* refers to *internal Exchange Server format*. MAPI was introduced in Chapter 6.

This lesson covers the management of HTTP using the Exchange Administrator program. Following a brief introduction of the required components, you'll read about the configuration of general and advanced protocol properties as well as *published public folders*. A practical exercise completes this lesson.

At the end of this lesson, you will be able to:

- Describe the HTTP support of Exchange Server
- Configure HTTP within the Administrator program

Estimated time to complete this lesson: 15 minutes

Supporting HTTP-Based Access

Exchange Server 5.5 allows Web browser applications MAPI-based access to mailboxes, public folders, and the Global Address List. At the first glance, this statement seems incorrect because browsers are not aware of MAPI; they communicate instead with Web servers through HTTP displaying HTML documents. However, to an Exchange Server, Web browsers are indeed MAPI-based clients.

To a browser, however, the Exchange Server is a complex Web site. A third, transparent component must be involved that acts as a translator between MAPI and HTML. Neither the Exchange Server nor the browser is aware of the data conversion.

Outlook Web Access Components

Outlook Web Access, also known as a *Web client*, performs all the translation between the Exchange Server and the browser. The Web client relies on CDO, which can be divided into CDO objects and the CDO rendering library. The CDO object library will be used to access items on the Exchange Server in their MAPI-based format. The CDO rendering library is used to convert MAPI-based items into HTML documents before they are sent to the browser. Conversely, HTML documents received from a Web browser will be converted into MAPI items before they are transferred to the Exchange Server.

Java Script and Frames

Outlook Web Access formats HTML documents using Java script and Frames. Your browser must support Java script and Frames if you want to use Outlook Web Access successfully. Internet Explorer 3.0 or higher and Netscape Navigator 2.0 or higher are examples of browser applications that support Java script and Frames.

Active Server

An Active Server is an IIS 3.0 (or higher) that has Active Server Pages (ASP) installed on it. This is the required platform for the Web client. (See Figure 11-25.) It is not necessary, however, to install an Active Server directly on every Exchange Server computer, because Outlook Web Access uses RPCs to access mailboxes. Web browsers will connect to the Active Server when users select the URL that points to Outlook Web Access (for example, *newyork-1.stocksdata.com/exchange*). Outlook Web Access is the actual component that accesses the Exchange Server on behalf of the browser.

Installing the Active Server

Installing an Active Server can be confusing. First you must install IIS 2.0 as included in the Windows NT Server 4.0 package. Then you must install Windows NT SP3 or higher, which updates IIS to version 3.0. At this time you can also install the ASP, which resides on the SP3 CD-ROM in the \iis30\Asp directory. Execute the Aspsetup.bat directly from this directory.

Note If IIS 2.0 has not been installed on the local server, SP3 will create a shortcut on the desktop. Double-clicking this shortcut launches the IIS 3.0 setup. Alternatively, Active Server can be run on IIS 4.0, which is included in the NT 4.0 Option Pack available on CD-ROM or on the Microsoft Web site. IIS 4.0 includes the ASPs and does not require any earlier versions of IIS to be installed, which simplifies the Web server setup considerably.

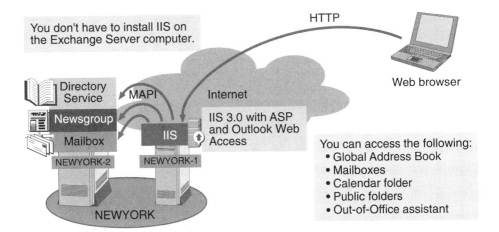

Figure 11-25. Accessing Exchange Server resources via HTTP.

Install these components necessary for supporting browser-based access to Exchange Server:

1. Install IIS 2.0 from the Windows NT Server CD-ROM.

2. Update Windows NT Server to SP3 or higher.

3. Install ASP.

4. Run the Exchange Server Setup to install Outlook Web Access.

Configuring HTTP

Once you have installed IIS 3.0 with ASP and Outlook Web Access, browser-based access to mailboxes, public folders, and the Global Address List becomes possible. Outlook Web Access offers calendar functionality similar to the features that can be found in Outlook 97. This provides a tremendous opportunity to your organization because browsers can now be used as cross-platform clients for messaging on UNIX-based, Macintosh-based, and Windows-based workstations.

Logging On to Exchange Server

To access your server-based mailbox using an Internet browser, you typically enter the URL in the following format: *http://< IIS server name>/Exchange*. When Outlook Web Access receives an incoming request, it sends a Welcome page back to the browser. (See Figure 11-26.) On this page, you have the option to identify yourself or to go on accessing the Exchange Server as an anonymous user. Without further configuration, however, anonymous users don't have much to see. By contrast, a validated user can enjoy almost the same level of access that Outlook provides.

Configuration Objects

The Administrator program can be used to define protocol settings regarding HTTP. A configuration object for HTTP resides in the **Protocols** container at the site level, which is where the configuration objects for IMAP4, LDAP, POP3, and NNTP also reside. This object is called **HTTP (Web) Site Settings** and can be used, for instance, to enable or disable HTTP for the entire site. A server-level configuration object does not exist, which is not the case for the other Internet protocols.

At the mailbox level, you can specify whether to enable HTTP support for a particular user through the **Protocols** property page. Other HTTP settings are not provided.

Note When configuring HTTP, you are configuring only flags in the Exchange Server Directory. The default .ASP files that come with Outlook Web Access check these flags to provide the desired behavior to browser applications.

Publishing Public Folders

A public folder that can be accessed on behalf of the anonymous user account is called a *published folder*. It is theoretically available to all browsers that can access Exchange Server via Active Server, assuming adequate folders have had permissions granted to anonymous users. In other words, when you connect an Active Server to the Internet, all users worldwide can access published folders.

To configure published folders, launch the **HTTP (Web) Site Settings** property pages and click the **Folder Shortcuts** tab. This page allows you to define the list of public folders that anonymous users will see. Click the **New** button, select desired folders below the **New Folder Shortcut** list, and then click **OK**. To adjust folder properties, such as client permissions, select a particular folder shortcut and click the **Properties** button. This will display its property pages. The **Remove** button allows you to remove a public folder from the list of published folders.

You don't need to carry out any further tasks to allow anonymous users access to the Public Information Store in general, because anonymous HTTP-based access to server resources is enabled by default. But you also need to assign the **Anonymous** account client permissions for published folders, which has the default role of **None**. This default setting, in turn, prevents anonymous access to a published folder.

Note If you want to prevent anonymous access in general, clear the check box **Allow Anonymous Users To access The Anonymous Public Folders** on the **General** tab of the **HTTP (Web) Site Settings** object.

Accessing the Global Address List

Exchange Server does not automatically grant anonymous users access to user and address information. By contrast, validated users always have permissions to ask for these address book entries. You can enable anonymous directory lookups through the **Allow Anonymous Users To Browse The Global Address List** option on the **General** property page. You can also determine the number of address book entries that Exchange Server returns to users on the **Advanced** property page. The default setting limits all queries to 50 entries. You can modify this setting by using the **Maximum Number Of Entries** box.

It is not advisable to select the **No Limit** option. Otherwise, it's possible that users unfamiliar with address book searches may effectively download the entire address book through an unfortunate query. This will certainly tie up their clients and it also causes needless network traffic. So long as a limit is defined, queries submitted in more addresses than the allowed number will return a notification to the user asking him or her to refine the search.

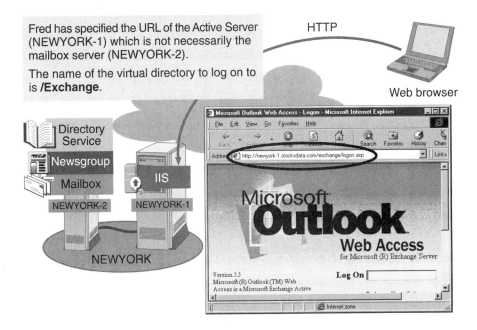

Figure 11-26. The Exchange Server Welcome page.

The public folder property pages and their functions are as follows:

- **Advanced**; to specify the maximum number of returned address book entries

- **Folder Shortcuts**; to define public folders an anonymous user will see

- **General**; to change the display name, add an administrative note, enable HTTP, and to allow anonymous access to published public folders and the Global Address Book

Exercise 38: Configuring HTTP for the Site

An HTTP configuration object called **HTTP (Web) Site Settings** is provided only within the site-level **Protocols** container. Unlike the POP3, IMAP4, LDAP, and NNTP, HTTP cannot be configured at the server level.

Estimated time to complete this exercise: 5 minutes

Description

In this exercise, you will configure HTTP settings for an entire site using the Administrator program.

- Task 38 describes the steps for verifying that HTTP is enabled for all servers in the site, and for allowing anonymous users to browse the Global Address List and have access to the anonymous public folders.

Prerequisites

- Install IIS 3.0 with ASP and Outlook Web Access locally on each test server.

- Log on as Admin-NY1 to NEWYORK-1.

- Optionally, log on as Admin-L1 to LONDON-1 and repeat the steps described in Task 38. Note that subsequent exercises will demonstrate HTTP-based access on NEWYORK-1 only.

Task 38: Configuring the HTTP Object

1. Log on as Admin-NY1 to the server NEWYORK-1, start the **Microsoft Exchange Administrator** program, and make sure it is connected to NEWYORK-1.

2. Open the site level **Protocols** container, and in the right pane double-click the **HTTP (Web) Site Settings** object.

3. The **HTTP (Web) Site Settings Properties** dialog box appears. Verify that HTTP is enabled through the **Enable Protocol** check box.

4. Check **Allow Anonymous Users To Browse The Global Address List**. If desired, switch to another property tab to inspect the default settings. If you are done, click **OK** to close the dialog box again.

5. Exit **Microsoft Exchange Administrator**.

Review

HTTP settings can be configured within the site-level **Protocols** container. Four property pages are provided. On the **General** page you can enable or disable Web browser access. You can also allow or prevent anonymous access to published public folders or to the Global Address Book. On the **Folder Shortcuts** tab, you can select the public folders (also called published folders) an anonymous user will see. On the **Advanced** property page, you can enter the maximum number of returned address book entries. A reasonable limit avoids needless data transfer to clients when clumsy searches are performed.

Lesson 6: Outlook Web Access

Outlook Web Access is a sample application and Microsoft encourages you to modify this application to implement your own Exchange Server/Internet browser interface. To gather valuable information about Web client programming and to download inspiring sample applications, go to this Web page: *www.microsoft.com/ithome/resource/exchange/active/default.htm.*

This lesson explains the Active Server platform and its contents, such as ASPs. It provides a brief overview about CDO. You'll also read about the installation of Outlook Web Access, although this subject was already covered in Chapter 2.

An exercise at the end of this lesson will demonstrate how to use an Internet browser to send and receive messages.

At the end of this lesson, you will be able to:

- Identify the technologies of the ActiveX platform

- Describe the Outlook Web Access architecture

- Work with ASPs

- Explain HTML rendering of MAPI items

Estimated time to complete this lesson: 35 minutes

The Active Platform

Exchange Server capabilities can be extended to the World Wide Web using several components and technologies provided through ActiveX and the Active Server.

ActiveX

ActiveX is a technology that allows you to control one application from within another program. For example, you can write a utility that starts Microsoft Word (which creates a Word object) and inserts the text *ActiveX is a piece of cake* into a Word document (which controls the Word object).

The controlling application is the *Controller*, while the controlled application is the *Server*. The Server offers programmable objects through an object library that typically comes with the product. Based on the object library, the Controller creates and uses the objects that implicitly provide control over the Server.

Let's say you want to develop an application that uses ActiveX to connect to an Exchange Server. In this case, your program becomes the Controller while the MAPI subsystem is the Server. It is the responsibility of the MAPI subsystem (in other words, the Exchange Client or Outlook) to provide the required object library. This library is called CDO and will be installed along with Outlook 97 version 8.03 and with Outlook Web Access. Based on items that the CDO object library provides, you can create programmable items such as a session object within your Controller application. The session object will be used to perform actions such as logging on to Exchange Server.

ActiveX Server Framework

The ActiveX Server framework is the foundation for development platforms based on the IIS, which allows you to create HTML documents, script components, and other HTTP-related services. The ActiveX Server framework supports ActiveX controls that help you develop Internet applications. Examples of ActiveX components are the WinSock Control, HTML Control, or the Shockwave and RealAudio controls that process the multimedia elements in Web documents.

The ActiveX Server framework provides cross-platform interoperability because it allows you to develop distributed network applications based on HTTP. It doesn't matter which operating system your Web browser requires—HTML documents are HTML documents, and they will always be transferred to your browser through HTTP.

Let's say you use the Active Server platform to write a program that resides in an HTML page. Browser applications can then communicate with your program. In other words, your program can gather user input through HTTP. If your Active Server program uses CDO to communicate with an Exchange Server according to HTTP-based user input, you have already created a Web client for Exchange Server. (See Figure 11-27.)

Active Desktop

The Active Desktop is a technology that allows you to browse the hard disks and files on your desktop just as you browse Web sites on the Internet. Using this technology, you can display the content from the Internet (for example, HTML pages, Java documents, graphics, and so forth) in addition to all the objects on your desktop (such as My Computer, Network Neighborhood, and so forth).

Two layers comprise the Active Desktop. They are the *Icon layer* and the *HTML layer*. The Icon layer is responsible for displaying the user interface (icons and shortcuts) to the documents that are maintained by the HTML layer.

Active Server

As mentioned previously, an Active Server is an IIS 3.0 with ASP installed or an IIS 4.0. The Active Server is the foundation of Web server applications because it supports the server-side and script-based programming model. ASPs use the Active Server scripting engine to convert text-based scripts dynamically into application code as needed. You don't need to compile Active Server scripts using a proprietary application or site management system. In other words, scripts are interpreted automatically when you access an HTML document, so you don't need to compile the .ASP files of your Web client. Applications developed for Active Server are accessed through a virtual directory. The virtual directory called /Exchange, for instance, launches the Web client (Outlook Web Access). Because Active Server resides on Windows NT Server, messages and user account information can be secured using SSL encryption. Likewise, the Windows NT Challenge/Response authentication mechanism can be used as a more secure alternative to conventional Basic (Clear Text) authentication.

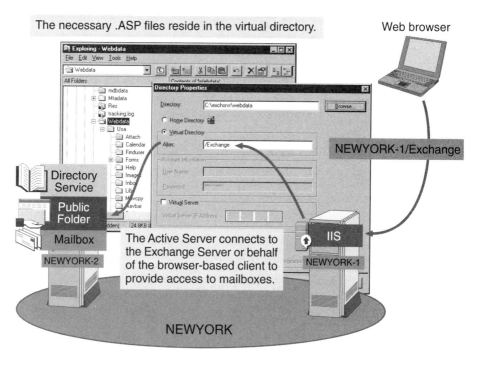

Figure 11-27. Extending IIS 3.0 using ASPs.

The features of Outlook Web Access are as follows:

- Allows access to mailboxes, public folders, and the Global Address List
- Changes interface by modifying the ASP pages
- Accesses messaging resources over the Web
- Supports all browsers with Java script and Frames
- Some access is possible for anonymous users
- Uses SSL encryption for secured authentication
- Supports Windows NT Challenge/Response authentication and Basic (Clear Text)

Outlook Web Access Architecture

Outlook Web Access architecture can provide a secure environment for your messaging network because it relies on Windows NT and the Active Server platform. The architecture can be a perfect solution for users on UNIX systems who must use an Outlook client with integrated e-mail, calendar, and collaboration functions.

File Locations and ASP Files

Outlook Web Access, including its ASPs and the CDO library, must be installed directly on the Active Server. By default, .ASP files are placed in a subdirectory under \Exchsrvr\Webdata according to their language, while the CDO library (olemsg32.dll) usually resides in the \Winnt\System32 directory. The .ASP files represent the actual Web client, which provides the functionality and user interface for opening the server-based resources. You can customize these .ASP files to meet the specific needs of your organization.

Accessing Resources

All access to Exchange Server–based resources is validated, including anonymous access. Although you have the option to log on to Exchange Server as an anonymous user, this does not mean you are unknown. Exchange Server knows you very well as Mr. or Mrs. **Anonymous**, as mentioned earlier. By referencing the Exchange system account **Anonymous**, you can grant access permissions or specify which information to return to those users that do not supply explicit logon credentials.

Outlook Web Access receives your account information through the client-server HTTP connection when you type the name of your mailbox in **Mailbox Name** on the Welcome page and select **Click Here** to log on. This account information is used to access the Exchange Server on your behalf via the CDO library. (See Figure 11-28.)

Validated users can work with their mailbox and public folders and can search the Global Address Book. Generally speaking, they have permissions just as if they were logged on directly using an Exchange Client or Outlook 97.

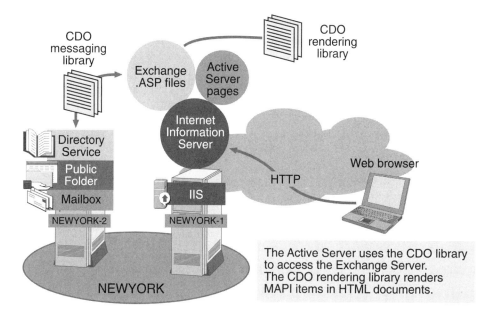

Figure 11-28. Active Server components architecture.

Some of directories that Outlook Web Access uses are as follows:

- \Anon; HTML interface for anonymous public folder access
- \Attach; HTML interface for rendering attachments
- \Finduser; HTML interface for locating a user
- \Forms; specific message and notification forms
- \Help; HTML interface for help
- \Inbox; HTML interface for displaying the Inbox
- \Lib; libraries for script code provided through other .ASP files
- \Movcpy; HTML interface for moving and copying folders
- \Navbar; HTML interface for displaying the navigation bar

- \Options; HTML interface for displaying the Options dialog box (for instance, Out-of-Office options)

- \Calendar; scripts and Java code for the calendar applet

- \Images; .GIF files

Overview of Active Server Pages

ASPs are HTML documents containing Java script and Frame elements. Your browser must support these elements if you want to use it to work with Exchange Server–based resources.

ASP Content

The .ASP files are interlaced with ActiveX script code to call ActiveX controls. These ActiveX controls, in turn, access documents and other items to place them into Web pages. For example, you place MAPI-based items such as regular messages into Web pages when using the Outlook Web Access .ASP files. (See Figure 11-29.)

Modifying ASP Files

You can use an HTML editor to customize existing ASPs which can simplify the start of your development project. For example, you can open the Logon.asp file to replace the text of the Welcome page with your own information. You must save the changes to take the new interface in effect. Start your Internet browser, connect to *<server name>/Exchange*, and verify the new results.

To submit your logon credentials, the browser will be redirected to the Logon.asp file as determined in the Default.htm page. Another important .ASP file is the Logonfrm.asp, which passes your mailbox name to the Exchange Server to retrieve the user's home server attribute. The CDO object library is then called to connect directly to the home server.

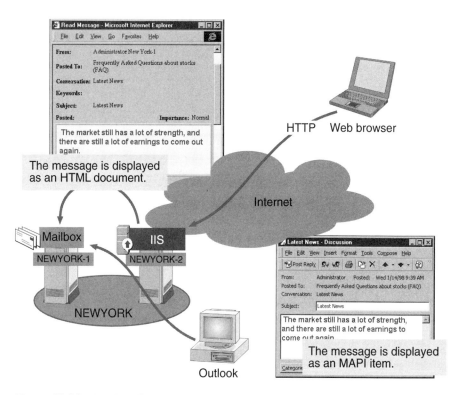

Figure 11-29. A MAPI document and an HTML e-mail document.

The benefits of ASPs are as follows:

- Developers can use their own proprietary authoring environment or any authoring tool.

- Server-side scripts can detect and optimize output for any type of browser.

- Any programming language, such as C++, Microsoft Visual Basic, and Java, can be used to build server components based on ActiveX.

- Developers can use many scripting languages, including VBScript and JavaScript.

Overview of Collaboration Data Objects

CDO components are installed as part of Outlook Web Access. They are the foundation for all kinds of interactive Web-based applications that must access an Exchange Server.

CDO Components

The CDO components are divided into two parts: the CDO object library (olemsg32.dll) and the CDO rendering library (amhtml.dll). Olemsg32.dll is required for accessing resources on the actual Exchange Server computer. The amhtml.dll, in turn, is required to support the translation of MAPI items, such as messages, into HTML documents.

The CDO object library provides the objects that are required to log on to Exchange, to access private and public folders, to read and send messages, to maintain your calendar, to browse the Global Address List, and more. Using this library, you can perform standard messaging functions. In other words, you can work as if you are connected to the Exchange Server computer using a MAPI-based client such as Outlook 97.

The CDO rendering library performs all the conversion between MAPI-based items and HTML documents. The rendering library provides a quick method to render any view without the need for HTML coding because the integrated rendering methods shield you from having to create complex HTML codes. You can use this library if you want to extend the views of your customized Web clients. These views include columns, grouping, sorting, filtering, and conversation threading on folders and messages.

CDO and IIS 3.0

IIS 3.0 includes core objects and basic components, that you might want to use to extend the features of your Web-based clients for Exchange Server. IIS 3.0 provides database access, forms processing, dynamic billboards, file access, browser capability determination, state management, and a content-linking component. For example, the content-linking component allows you to maintain links between separate HTML pages without touching the HTML code, which is similar to the previous/next navigation within Exchange Client.

ASP Applications

ASP applications offer a tremendous resource for workgroup applications. Items stored in public folders can be shared between both MAPI-based clients and Web-based clients, since the objects are always available in their native Exchange Server format. By publishing public folders and creating Web-based forms, you have the ability to create worldwide discussions forums, service applications, and so forth. An interesting example of such a discussion forum comes with the Exchange Server 5.5 CD-ROM. (See Figure 11-30.) The example can be found under the \Server\Support\Collab\Sampler\Culcorn directory. More information about discussion forums is provided in Chapter 16, "The Microsoft Exchange Server Forms Environment."

ASP applications provide a mechanism for combining Exchange Server capabilities with other Microsoft BackOffice platforms. With little or no coding involved, interactive Web sites can be created that provide messaging and groupware functionality. Because Web-browser applications exist independently for all available computer platforms, Web-based workgroup applications are platform-independent as well.

When developing ASP applications, you can choose between creating Web forms instead of electronic forms, or you can create both. In the latter case, users running browsers and users running Outlook can easily share collaborative data. You can also configure the public folder replication if you went to distribute the items of a public folder across the organization, and you can configure newsfeeds if you want to replicate the information even further across the USENET. Public folder replication is covered in Chapter 13, "Public Folder Replication."

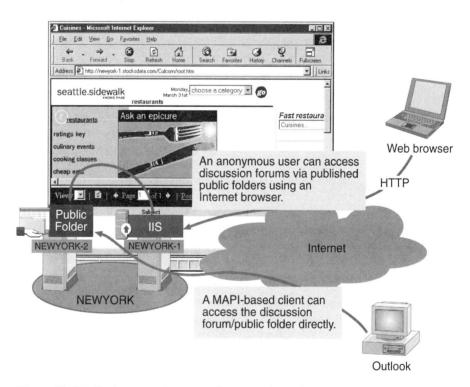

Figure 11-30. Setting up a discussion forum on the Web.

The components of ASPs and their functions are as follows:

- CDO library; provides access to the mailbox and public folders
- CDO rendering library; enables views to be rendered without HTML encoding
- IIS 3.0; maintains links between pages

Outlook Web Access Installation

Outlook Web Access is an optional Exchange Server component. Before you can begin the installation, you must configure an Active Server on the local Windows NT Server computer.

Installation

Select Outlook Web Access using the **Complete/Custom** mode of the Exchange Server Setup program. If the server has been installed already, Setup will launch the maintenance mode. In this case, click the **Add/Remove** button to select **Outlook Web Access**. The installation modes are covered in detail in Chapter 2.

Note Exchange Server Setup prevents the installation of Outlook Web Access if the local server is not running IIS 3.0 (or higher) with ASPs.

Installing Outlook Web Access and Exchange Server on Different Computers

RPC communication must be possible between the Active Server and the Exchange Server computer if you plan to separate the server platforms. The Exchange Server Setup program can detect that you are installing the Web client on a non-Exchange Server computer and will prompt for the name of one particular Exchange Server in your organization. This name is required because Outlook Web Access must have access to directory information. The Directory of the specified server will always be contacted to retrieve the home server attribute of users who try to log on. Using this attribute, the Web client can establish a RPC connection to this server where the user's mailbox resides.

Note When Outlook Web Access and Exchange Server are installed on the same computer, the local Directory is contacted to determine the home server. As a result, you will not be asked for a server name during the Outlook Web Access installation.

The Virtual Directory

The Active Server uses a virtual directory called **/Exchange** to publish Outlook Web Access components. If a browser wants to access the Exchange Server over the Web, the Active Server must specify this directory. You will notice that this virtual directory, which the Internet Service Manager administers, references the location of all active messaging components such as the .ASP files. The default directory for the Web client is C:\Exchsrvr\Webdata. If desired, you can change the location of the .ASP files as well as the name of the virtual directory within the Internet Service Manager program. (See Figure 11-31.)

Note Outlook Web Access will be installed in subdirectories of \Exchsrvr\Webdata according to its language. An IIS 3.0 filter, Exchfilt.dll, determines the language of a browser when a user logs on. The filter appends the language automatically to the URL, creating a valid reference such as \Exchsrvr\Webdata\Usa.

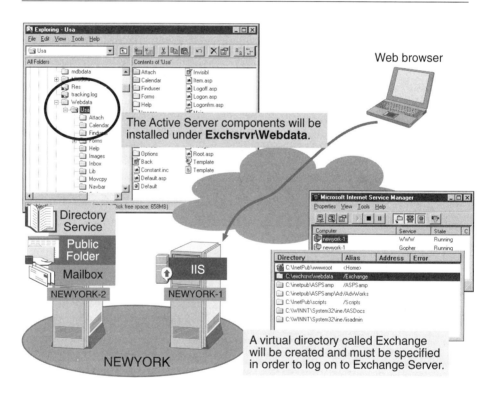

Figure 11-31. Installing Active Server components.

The following summarizes the installation of ASPs:

- Installs through the Exchange Server Setup
- Installs in the Exchsrvr\Webdata directory
- Requires IIS and Active Server
- Publishes as the virtual directory **/Exchange**

Exercise 39: Sending and Receiving Mail Using the Exchange Web Client

Exchange Server 5.5 allows HTTP-based client access to mailboxes, public folders, and the Global Address List through Outlook Web Access. Users can access their private messages using an Internet browser that supports Java script and Frames. Exchange Server presents messages just like any other HTML document.

Estimated time to complete this exercise: 45 minutes

Description

In this exercise, you will access the Exchange Server using an Internet browser such as the Internet Explorer 4.01. The Internet browser will be used to send and receive messages as well as to search recipient addresses within the Global Address List.

- Task 39a describes the steps for sending and receiving mail using Internet Explorer and Exchange Server.
- Task 39b describes the steps for using Internet Explorer to search for names and folders on an Exchange Server.

Prerequisites

- Install IIS 3.0 with ASPs as well as the Outlook Web Access components of Exchange Server 5.5 locally on the test server.
- Start the Windows NT Web service on NEWYORK-1 and/or LONDON-1.
- Log on as Admin-NY1 to NEWYORK-1.

Task 39a: Using Internet Explorer to Send and Receive Mail

1. Click the **Start** button, and then click **Run**.

2. In the **Open** box, type *http://newyork-1.stocksdata.com/exchange*.

3. Click **OK** to display the **Microsoft Outlook Web Access** logon page.

4. In the **Log On** box, type *FredP* and then press the Enter key.

5. If a **Security Alert** dialog box appears, click **Yes**.

6. If an **Enter Network Password** dialog box appears, type *Admin-NY1* in the **User name** textbox and *password* in the **Password** box.

> **Note** Your Windows NT account must be the **Primary Windows NT Account**—or an account with **User** permissions—for the mailbox you want to open; otherwise, the attempt to access the mailbox will always fail and will result in a reappearing **Authentication** dialog box.

7. Click **OK**. (It might happen that an **Internet Redirection** dialog box appears, indicating that you are about to be redirected to a new Internet site. In this case, click **Yes**.)

8. The **Microsoft Outlook Web Access – Microsoft Internet Explorer** window appears. Open a message in your inbox, such the test message created using Outlook Express in Task 37c.

9. Click the **Close** button to close the test message.

10. In the **Microsoft Outlook Web Access – Microsoft Internet Explorer** window, click the **Compose New Mail Message** button on the toolbar.

11. A **New Message – Microsoft Internet Explorer** window appears. Position your cursor in the **To** line and type *FredP@STOCKSDATA.com*.

12. Position your cursor in the **Subject** line and type *Outlook Web Access Test Message*.

13. Click in the message text area and type *Outlook Web Access may be used instead of other messaging clients in order to access an Exchange server.*

14. On the toolbar click **Send** to send the message.

15. Start Outlook, log on to the mailbox of Fred Pumpkin (who is the recipient of the test message sent in step 14) and verify that Fred has received the reply message.

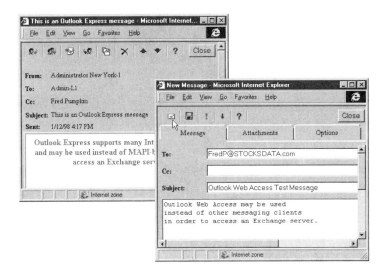

Task 39b: Using Outlook Web Access to Search for Exchange Names and Folders

1. In the **Microsoft Outlook Web Access – Microsoft Internet Explorer** window, click **Find Names** on the Outlook toolbar to display the **Find Names - Microsoft Internet Explorer** window.

2. In the **Display Name** box, type *Fred Pumpkin* and then click **Find**. The search result appears in the lower pane.

3. In the lower pane, click **Fred Pumpkin**.

4. The **Detailed Information - Microsoft Internet Explorer** window appears for Fred Pumpkin. Make a note of the address details and then close this window.

5. Click **Close** to close the **Find Names** dialog box.

6. On the Outlook toolbar, click **Log Off.**

7. On the **File** menu of the Internet Explorer, click **Close**.

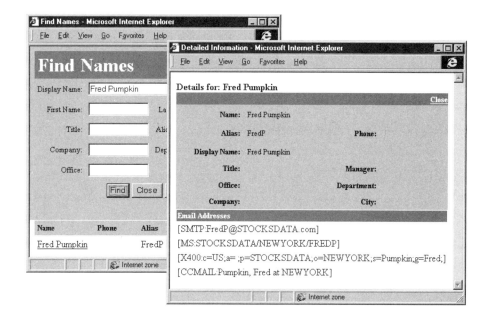

Review

Outlook Web Access is a sample application that works in conjunction with IIS 3.0 (or higher) and the ActiveX framework. The Active Server performs the required translation between MAPI and HTTP. Therefore, you can access Exchange Server resources using an Internet browser that supports Java script and Frames. When Outlook Web Access is installed, users can access mailboxes, public folders, calendar and scheduling items, and address information. Both Anonymous access and validated access are possible.

Review

1. As an administrator of STOCKSDATA, you have connected the organization to the Internet through the IMS. Now you want to support common Internet clients as well. Which Internet protocols does Exchange Server 5.5 support?

   _____

2. Name six client types that you can use to connect to resources located on an Exchange Server.

   _____

   _____

   _____

3. Fred's mailbox resides on NEWYORK-1. He is the assistant for Lisa and Paul, both of whom have granted delegate permission to Fred. Lisa's mailbox resides on NEWYORK-1 while Paul's home server is NEWYORK-2. Lisa must not access her mailbox using POP3. How do you configure the site to allow Fred access to all three mailboxes using a POP3 client?

   _____

   _____

   _____

   _____

4. You want to increase the access security for Exchange Server resources. How do you limit the group of workstations that can access existing servers in your site through Internet protocols?

   _____

   _____

   _____

5. What are the features of a POP3 client?

   _____

   _____

   _____

6. What are the three possible states of a POP3 session?

7. What are the states an IMAP4 client will enter during an entire session?

8. Using a POP3 client, you delete messages out of your Inbox and then you switch to Outlook. You discover that the messages have not been deleted. Why not?

9. Which authentication methods can you use to support all possible POP3/IMAP4 clients?

10. Paul complains that his IMAP4 client program is unable to send messages, but he can download new messages from the Exchange Server. What is the most likely cause of the send problem?

11. A particular IMAP4 client has problems connecting to an Exchange Server. You test the connection using Telnet and are able to log on. How can you determine the source of the connection problem?

_____

_____

_____

_____

_____

_____

12. You recently connected your organization to the Internet and now you want to provide access to server-based directory information using LDAP clients. What must you do to the Exchange Server to allow LDAP clients access to the Directory?

_____

_____

13. Which directory attributes are returned to validated users by default?

_____

_____

14. The STOCKSDATA company has five sites called NEWYORK, LONDON, PARIS, FRANKFURT, and TOKYO. In this organization, Fred Pumpkin wants to configure server referrals so that LDAP clients can be redirected to LONDON-1 in case a search on NEWYORK-1 cannot be fulfilled. What must he do to achieve the desired configuration?

_____

_____

_____

15. What is a USENET hub node?

_____

_____

_____

_____

16. What is a USENET leaf node?

_____

_____

17. What is a push feed?

_____

_____

_____

18. What is a pull feed?

_____

_____

_____

19. What is an active file?

_____

_____

_____

20. What must you configure in order to provide a public folder as an outbound newsgroup to the USENET?

_____

_____

_____

_____

21. Because of a disk crash, an Exchange Server needs to be restored. This server is responsible for maintaining newsgroups and the most recent backup is several days old. What should you do in order to avoid having old articles transferred back to the server once the backup has been restored?

_____

_____

_____

22. A public folder named *Ticker And More* exists in the Internet newsgroups folder. Several subfolders have been created and they all are published to the USENET. You want to stop newsreader access to the *Ticker And More* public folder. How can you do this without affecting the subfolders?

_____

_____

_____

_____

23. Which NNTP setting of a public folder can be modified within the Administrator program?

_____

_____

24. Can you allow anonymous access to newsgroups?

_____

_____

_____

_____

25. How can you test the NNTP service?

_____

_____

_____

26. What is an Active Server?

_____

_____

_____

27. List the three core components of the Active Server platform.

_____

_____

_____

28. Which features must a browser support to get access to an Exchange Server computer over the Web?

   _____

   _____

   _____

29. You want to create your own Web client to achieve special functionality. Which scripting language do you need to use?

   _____

30. What are the main parts of Outlook Web Access?

   _____

   _____

   _____

   _____

31. What is the default directory of the .ASP files for Exchange Server?

   _____

32. How do you access an Exchange Server using a browser?

   _____

   _____

   _____

   _____

C H A P T E R   1 2

Creating and Managing Public Folders

This chapter covers the management of public folders that reside on a single Exchange Server computer. Public folders are useful for sharing information between users across an organization and across the Internet.

Overview

Exchange Server is an efficient electronic communication system. It allows users to communicate with each other using e-mail messages, and it maintains public folders, which are an effective means of sharing information among multiple users. Imagine a discussion forum, implemented through a public folder and published across the Internet, in which your customers can share ideas with each other and with potential customers around the world.

Lesson 1 of this chapter covers the basics of public folders, including their various components and how they are maintained in Exchange Server 5.5. It also discusses the relationship between the core components and why public folders sometimes appear in client address books even though they are not in the public folder hierarchy.

Lesson 2 covers public folder administration via the IS configuration. It discusses site-level and server-level management and provides valuable hints about restricting who can create top-level public folders. It also explains how to access the contents of a public folder even if it is in a remote site.

Lesson 3 covers public folder creation using the Microsoft Exchange Client and Microsoft Outlook, as well as the property pages that you can use to control public folder configuration.

Lesson 4 discusses public folder strategies, including the advantages and disadvantages of using single versus multiple public folders. It also covers the configuration of dedicated public servers and the critical aspects of such configurations.

This chapter includes four exercises, beginning with the creation of a public folder using the Exchange Client and Outlook. The exercises will guide you through the configuration of the IS and the management of public folder properties.

In the following lessons, you will be introduced to:

- The differences between the public folder hierarchy and public folder contents
- Affinity settings and their effect on client connections to other sites in an organization
- Public folder creation
- How to set public folder properties in the Exchange Client or in Outlook
- The advantages and disadvantages of storing a public folder on one server versus on multiple replicas

Lesson 1: Introduction to Public Folders

Public folders are similar to network directories on a Windows NT Server. Multiple users can access the centralized storage location over the computer network and thus share files, programs, and other resources. But public folders provide several advantages over shared directories, which make them ideal for discussion forums and workgroup computing. You can install electronic forms in public folders, send messages to them, and process incoming messages using folder rules. Last but not least, you can replicate them.

This lesson provides a brief overview of public folders, including an introduction to their architecture and information on the relationship between public folders and the Directory.

Two exercises are included. They explain how to create public folders and how to send messages to them.

At the end of this lesson, you will be able to:

- Describe the purpose of public folders
- List the various parts of a public folder
- Create a public folder
- Configure the Directory to provide public folder addresses to users
- Send messages to public folders

Estimated time to complete this lesson: 35 minutes

Public Folder Considerations

Exchange Server 5.5 manages private and collaborative data differently. Mailboxes are storage areas in the Private Information Store. Public folders are maintained in the Public Information Store. An item in a private folder is typically available to one user only. An item in a public folder, however, is immediately available to all users in a site, assuming all users are granted permission to view the item. Additional configuration steps are needed only if you want to provide access across site boundaries.

Information Handling

Public folders are repositories for all kinds of information. They can contain regular e-mail messages as well as multimedia clips, text documents, spreadsheets, and other data. A variety of messaging clients can access these items. The Exchange Client, Outlook, and (to a certain degree) Web browsers can access them using MAPI. Newsreader clients and newsfeeds can use NNTP to get access. Finally, you can use an IMAP4 client to work with server-based folders, including public folders. (See Figure 12-1.)

Electronic Forms

Public folders are the basis of workgroup applications for Exchange Server. You can associate them with electronic forms, which improves applications such as bulletin boards, discussion forums, and customer tracking systems. Imagine a bulletin board that employees can use to buy and sell cars. Of course, they could simply place articles on this bulletin board, but information handling is much easier if a common form gathers the essential information (such as the car type, price, and owner's phone number) from each seller. Electronic forms can also display the information in a structured way. For more information about the development and use of electronic forms, see Chapter 16, "The Microsoft Exchange Server Forms Environment."

Databases

The IS maintains public folders in a database file called Pub.edb in the \Exchsrvr\Mdbdata directory. If you ran the Exchange Optimizer at the end of the Exchange Server Setup or at any later time, a separate \Exchsrvr\Mdbdata directory might have been placed on other hard disk drives. Pub.edb, however, will reside in only one of them.

You can check the location of Pub.edb in the Administrator program by opening the **Database Paths** property page of the local server object (for example, **NEWYORK-1**). The path to the database of the Public Information Store will be listed beside several other entries. More information about the Exchange Server databases is provided in Chapter 15, "Maintaining Servers."

Dedicated Servers

An Exchange Server with a Private Information Store is called a *private server*, and a server with a Public Information Store is a *public server*. Every Exchange Server is both private and public by default, but dedicated configurations are possible. An Exchange Server that maintains only a Private Information Stores is called a *dedicated private server*, while a server that maintains only a Public Information Store is a *dedicated public server*.

Note To create dedicated servers, you must delete either the Private Information Store or the Public Information Store. You can do this at the server level by deleting either the **Private Information Store** or the **Public Information Store** object.

Public Folder Configuration

A user who creates a public folder becomes the folder's owner, but additional owners can be defined. The owner of a public folder can manage permissions and can associate electronic forms, public folder views, and folder rules using the Exchange Client or Outlook. Other configuration settings, such as the public folder replication, can be controlled only using the Administrator program. Of course, you need administrative permissions in your site if you want to control configuration settings in the Administrator program.

Public Folder Replication

Public folder replication ensures consistency of multiple instances of a public folder on different Exchange Server computers. The public folder replication mechanism distributes information only within one organization, however. Public folder replication is covered in Chapter 13, "Public Folder Replication."

Affinities

By default, a newly created top-level public folder is not replicated to any other server. Replication requires an explicit administrative step. But replication is not always necessary because all users in your organization can theoretically have direct access to public folders. Within a site, users can always access the public folder, but users from other sites cannot if *site affinities* have not been defined. Using site affinities, you can allow the Exchange Client and Outlook to check remote sites for the desired public folder contents. Public folder affinities and their uses are covered in Lesson 2, "Information Store Configuration."

The characteristics of the basic public folder features are as follows:

- All public objects are stored in a database called Pub.edb

- Any data—such as e-mail messages, text documents, spreadsheets, multimedia objects, and database files—can be kept in a public folder

- Information sharing among all users in an organization is possible

- Internet publishing is supported

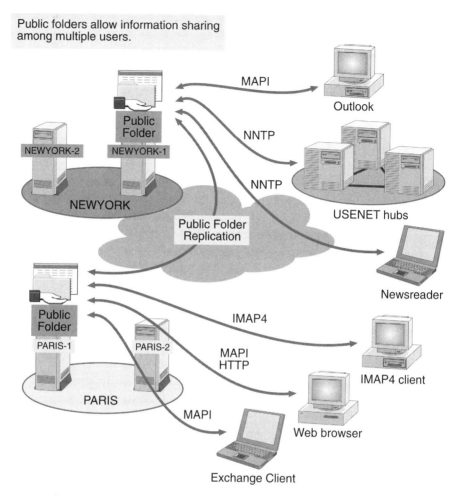

Figure 12-1. Information sharing based on public folders.

Parts of a Public Folder

Every public folder has two parts: the hierarchy and the content. The hierarchy shows a public folder within the public folder tree. The contents consists of the actual items (such as messages and attachments) stored in the public folder.

Public Folder Hierarchy

The public folder hierarchy is a structured tree that develops when multiple folders are created. Top-level folders contain subfolders, and those can contain other subfolders. By navigating through this tree, users running the Exchange Client, Outlook, and Web browsers can locate information. In an

Exchange Client, the public folder hierarchy typically appears in the left pane, also called the *folder pane*. Outlook usually replaces the folder pane with its Outlook bar, but you can display the folder hierarchy by selecting the **Folder List** command on the **View** menu.

The hierarchy is always replicated to all public servers across the organization. Therefore, every user can examine the list of existing folders; however, the contents might not be accessible.

Public Folder Contents

The public folder contents are the actual items in a public folder. To work with the contents, you must open the folder by selecting it in the client's folder pane and displaying the items in the righthand pane, also called the *contents pane*.

When you open a public folder, your client program will send an open request to your home server. If the server has the contents, you will get access. If the server doesn't have the contents, the client must locate the correct server within the site or in another site. If it finds the right server, the client communicates with it directly using RPC and the contents become accessible. If it cannot find the right server or if the target server is inaccessible for some reason, you will receive the following error message: "Unable to display the folder. The contents of this public folder are currently unavailable. Either the Microsoft Exchange Server computer servicing this public folder is down or the public folder has not been replicated to this site. See your administrator."

As shown in Figure 12-2, Jacques Blanc, a French administrator of STOCKSDATA, owns a mailbox that resides on PARIS-2. Because of a default configuration, this is also his public folder server. Whenever Jacques navigates through the public folder hierarchy, his client communicates with PARIS-2. Let's say that Jacques opens a folder that resides on PARIS-1 instead of his home server. PARIS-2 will inform the client that the contents are not available locally and the client will then try PARIS-1. Voilà—the client will find the desired contents and display them. Jacques will not be aware of the redirection because the location of the public folders contents is hidden from the end user.

Public Folder Server

Users work primarily with the public folder server for the Private Information Store in which their mailboxes reside. By default, this is their home server, but the configuration can be changed. You can do this through the **Private Information Store** object at the server level, which provides the **Public Folder Server** box on its **General** property page. To specify a different public folder server, select any server in your site that maintains a Public Information Store. Typically, you must specify a remote public server for dedicated private servers because these servers do not maintain the public folder hierarchy.

Note Dedicated private servers do not maintain the information of any public folder.

Public Folder Location

Top-level folders reside at the top of the hierarchy, directly under the **All Public Folders** container. They are always created on the client's public folder server. As mentioned above, this is most likely the home server associated with the mailbox.

The location of the top-level folder determines the location of all its subfolders, regardless of the creating user's home server. To continue with the previous example, if Monsieur Blanc creates a subfolder under a top-level folder that resides on PARIS-1, he creates this subfolder on PARIS-1 also. His client already communicates with PARIS-1, where the subfolder will be created transparently.

It actually doesn't matter where the data is stored as long as the client has access to the contents over RPC. Network traffic can be decreased, however, if the contents of the public folder are kept locally. You might for this reason, consider multiple replicas, even though they will consume hard disk space. Public folder replication is covered in depth in Chapter 13.

Hierarchy Replication Interval

Every public server maintains a replica of the organization's public folder hierarchy. To keep this hierarchy consistent, public folder hierarchy is replicated between all public servers of an organization in the form of e-mail messages. As soon as a change occurs—for example, if you create a new public folder—a new replication cycle will propagate those changes. By default, hierarchy replication takes place every 60 seconds if modifications have occurred.

The Administrator program does not provide control over the time interval of the hierarchy replication, but you can add a value called *Replication Send Folder Tree* to the Registry settings of the IS under:

```
HKEY_LOCAL_MACHINE
   \SYSTEM
      \CurrentControlSet
         \Services
            \MSExchangeIS
               \ParametersPublic
```

This value represents the interval of the hierarchy replication in seconds.

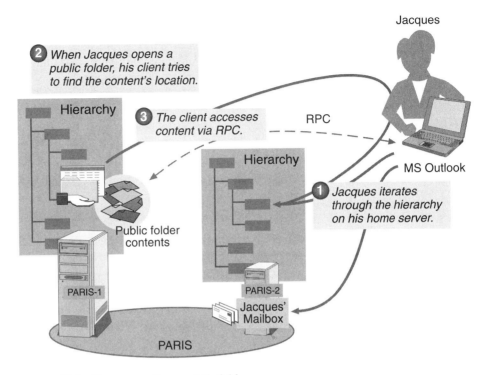

Figure 12-2. Two parts of one public folder.

Replicated parts of a public folder have these characteristics:

- Public folder contents are not replicated to other servers unless explicit replication settings have been specified

- Public folder hierarchy is always replicated to all servers in an organization that maintainS a Public Information Store

Exercise 40: Creating a Public Folder

The Public Information Store maintains the hierarchy information and the public folder contents separately. Top-level folders are created on the client's public folder server. However, the parent folder determines the location of subfolders.

Estimated time to complete this exercise: 10 minutes

Description

In this exercise, you will create a top-level folder using Outlook. You can also use the Exchange Client, but some commands and dialog boxes might differ. You will use this public folder in later exercises.

- Task 40 describes the steps for creating a top-level public folder on an Exchange Server computer.

Prerequisites

- Outlook must be installed and a valid messaging profile must exist.

- The test server LONDON-1 must be available.

Task 40: Creating a Public Folder

1. Log on to the server LONDON-1 by pressing **CTRL+ALT+DEL**.

2. In the **Name** box, type *Admin-L1*. In the **Password** box, type *password* and then click **OK**.

3. On the desktop, double-click the **Microsoft Outlook** shortcut.

4. In the **Folder** list, expand **Public Folders** and then select **All Public Folders**.

5. On the **File** menu, point to **Folder** and then click **Create Subfolder**.

6. The **Create New Folder** dialog box appears. In the **Name** box, type *Admin-L1 Folder*. (You can type *Admin-NY1 Folder* if you are working on NEWYORK-1.)

7. Click **OK** to return to Outlook. An **Add Shortcut To Outlook Bar** dialog box appears. Select the **Don't Prompt Me About This Again** check box and then click **Yes**.

8. The new folder will be displayed as a member object of the **All Public Folders** container.

9. On the **File** menu, click **Exit And Log Off**.

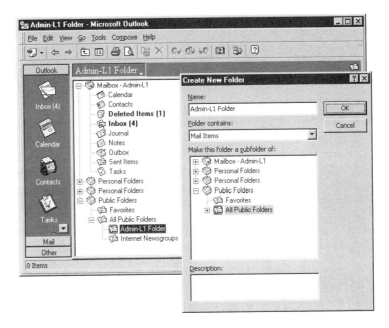

Review

To create a new public folder using Outlook, you can select the **Create Subfolder** command under the **Folder** option on the **File** menu. The **Create New Folder** dialog box will appear, prompting you for the folder name and the type of folder that you want to create. To create a top-level folder, you must select the **All Public Folders** root object under **Make This Folder A Subfolder**. If you want to create a subfolder instead of a top-level folder, select the desired parent folder from the list of public folders.

Public Folders Within the Directory

As explained in Chapter 5, public folders are recipient objects even though they are hidden from the Global Address List by default. You can make them visible by deselecting the **Hide From Address Book** check box on the **Advanced** property page of a public folder object in the Administrator program.

Public Folder Configuration Objects

Every configurable Exchange Server item is maintained in the directory, as are public folders. You can find a configuration object for each public folder in the Administrator program under the **Folders** container at the organization level. Public folder types are divided into **Public Folders** and **System Folders**, but users typically see public folders only.

You can also find the configuration objects for public folders in the **Recipients** container, although you might have to select the **Hidden Recipients** command on the **View** menu first. This command becomes available after you select the appropriate container. Configuration objects in the **Recipients** container are the same as the objects in the **Folders** container.

Note To change the **Recipients** container for all new public folders, you can specify a **Public Folder** container on the **General** property page of the site-level **Information Store Site Configuration** object. A new location will not affect existing public folders. You cannot move any existing recipient objects between **Recipients** containers.

Advantages of Public Folders

Public folders that are treated as potential recipients offer interesting advantages. A database application, for instance, can easily send status information to a public folder. Public folders can also be included in distribution lists, which allows you to keep track of discussions in teams, workgroups, and so forth. This frees team members from having to maintain personal discussion folders for the distribution lists in their mailboxes. In addition, you can revoke permission to delete items from all members and implicitly create an authentic tracking system.

Note Users must have the right to create items in a public folder if they want to send messages to it. Otherwise, an NDR will inform the sender about the missing permissions.

Figure 12-3 shows another useful scenario for public folders. It shows the general steps for subscribing a public folder to a list server on the Internet. List servers automatically distribute e-mail messages that have been sent to a particular address to all members of the list. The message volume can be large, filling your inbox unnecessarily. If this situation sounds familiar to you, you might want to subscribe a public folder instead of your personal mailbox to the list. The e-mail addresses of public folders are listed on the **E-Mail Addresses** tab of the public folder's properties, available in the Administrator program. You provide the address to the list server, and the list server sends all messages to the corresponding public folder. You can view and filter them there. Old items can also be deleted automatically based on age limits.

Some list servers can prevent nonmembers from sending messages to their lists. In other words, since it is the public folder's e-mail address and not your e-mail address that is registered on the list server, you cannot directly send messages as a user of your mail mailbox. In this case, you must grant your Windows NT account **Send As** permission for the public folder. You can then send messages on behalf of your public folder. It might be a good idea to display the public folder in the address book for easy **From** address selection through your client address book. More information about sending messages on behalf of another user is provided in Chapter 7.

Directory Store Latency Issues

The Directory and the Public Information Store maintain information about public folders in different ways. The IS is responsible for the hierarchy and contents, while the Directory cares about directory-related issues.

Different Replication Mechanism

The hierarchy is replicated to all existing public servers of an organization using e-mail messages. If public folder replication has been configured, the contents are also replicated using e-mail messages. Directory replication, however, is performed directly using RPC within the site and using e-mail messages between sites. To put it plainly, two independent processes replicate information about a single object. Depending on which process is completed first, the public folder will first become visible to all other servers in either the directory (address book) or the public folder list (public folder hierarchy).

Hierarchy Replication Completes First

If the replication of the public folder hierarchy is completed before directory replication, public folders become available in the client's public folder list under the **All Public Folders** container. You can also see the configuration object of a particular public folder in the Administrator program when you expand the **Folders** container at the organization level. The public folder object is still missing from the **Recipients** container.

Directory Replication Completes First

To verify the directory replication from within Outlook, you must first make the desired public folder visible in the address book. Once directory replication has been completed, the public folder appears in the Global Address Lists of other servers. Administrators see the corresponding object in the **Recipients** container, while clients can select the public folder from their address book.

If hierarchy replication has not been completed, you might see public folders that are in the address book but are not available under the **All Public Folders** container. As time goes by, this situation will disappear, but it might create some confusion in the meantime.

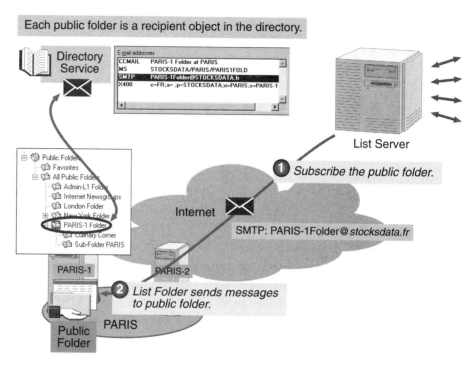

Figure 12-3. Subscribing public folders to list servers.

The features of public folder address book entries are as follows:

- Clearing the **Hide From Address Book** check box allows public folders to be selected just like any other recipients.

- Messages can be sent to public folders.

- Public folders are hidden from the address book by default.

- Public folder replication and directory replication are independent processes that can be completed at different times.

Exercise 41: Sending Mail to a Public Folder

Each public folder must exist in the Public Information Store as well as in the Directory. The IS maintains the hierarchy and content data, while the Directory takes care of the configuration objects. Public folders can be treated as recipient objects.

Estimated time to complete this exercise: 15 minutes

Description

In this exercise, you will configure a public folder to appear in the organization's address book. You will then use Outlook to send messages to the public folder.

- Task 41a describes the steps for making a public folder visible in the Global Address List.

- Task 41b describes the steps for sending messages to a public folder.

Prerequisites

- Complete Exercise 40. Alternatively, you can use any other existing public folder.

- Complete this exercise logged on as Admin-L1 on the server LONDON-1.

Task 41a: Configuring Public Folders

1. Click the **Start** button, point to **Programs**, point to **Microsoft Exchange**, and then click **Microsoft Exchange Administrator**.

2. Expand the **Folders** container under the organization object (for example, **STOCKSDATA**), expand the **Public Folders** container, and then select the **Admin-L1 Folder**.

3. Select **Properties** from the **File** menu.

4. Click the **Advanced** tab.

5. Clear the **Hide From Address Book** check box.

6. Click **OK**.

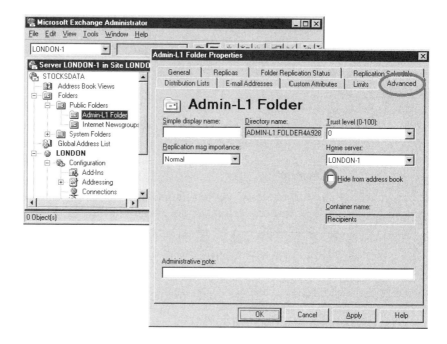

Task 41b: Sending Mail Messages to a Public Folder

1. On the **Desktop**, double-click the **Microsoft Outlook** shortcut. If necessary, select a profile that connects you to the mailbox of Admin-L1.

2. On the **Compose** menu, click the **New Mail Message** button. An **Untitled - Message** form appears.

3. Click **To**. The **Select Names** dialog box appears.

4. In the **Global Address List**, select **Admin-L1 Folder** and then click **To**.

5. Click **OK**.

6. In the **Subject** box, type *Test message to public folder "Admin-L1 Folder."*

7. Type *This is a message from the mailbox of Admin-L1 to the public folder Admin-L1 Folder* and then click **Send**.

8. Open the public folder **Admin-L1 Folder**.

9. Double-click your test message and read it.

10. On the **File** menu, click **Close** to exit Outlook.

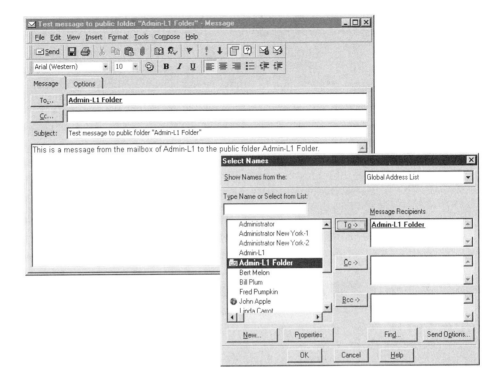

Review

Public folders can appear in the Global Address List. By default, however, they are hidden. To make a public folder visible, start the Administrator program, display the folder's properties, switch to the **Advanced** property page, and deselect the **Hide From Address Book** check box. Once a public folder is visible, you can send e-mail messages to it in the same way that you do to regular users, custom recipients, and distribution lists.

Lesson 2: Information Store Configuration

The IS holds the Public Information Store, which contains the database called Pub.edb. Pub.edb contains the public folders, the public folders store the messages, and the messages store the actual information (the message header, text, attachments, and so forth). This lesson deals primarily with the upper two configurable components: the IS and the Public Information Store.

The first part of this lesson briefly covers the configuration of the IS and important site-level issues. You'll learn about site affinities and how to locate public folder content within a site and across site boundaries. This lesson also provides information about the organization of server resources within very large sites, and it covers the Public Information Store configuration.

An exercise will show you how to configure the IS at the site level for controlling top-level folder creation.

At the end of this lesson, you will be able to:

- Configure the IS at the site level
- Specify public folder affinities
- Describe how clients locate contents
- Configure the Directory to provide public folder addresses to Exchange users
- Group and organize servers in a single site for public folder access
- Configure the Public Information Store at the server level

Estimated time to complete this lesson: 45 minutes

IS Configuration

A default server installation in a typical site does not require any special configuration. All resources are available to all users immediately. However, advanced configurations can be useful if you want to optimize network use and site and server resources. Settings that are made to the **Information Store Site Configuration** properties apply to all ISs in the site.

Top-Level Folder Creation

Top-level folders are at the top of the **All Public Folders** tree. By default, all users can create them. They are placed on the user's public folder server—typically his or her home server. However, top-level folders are special because they determine the location of all subfolders regardless of the user who created them.

Centralizing Public Folders

If you want to centralize the location of all existing public folders, you must ensure that top-level folders are created on only one server in your site. You have two options: You can modify the public folder server attribute of all Private Information Stores in your site to point to only one common server. Or you can restrict permission to create top-level folders to a small group of users (thereby ensuring that top-level folders will be created only on the desired server). Top-level folders ensure that subfolders are created on the same computer. However, the server must be the public folder server of all the users who can create top-level folders—in other words, it should be their home server.

The first option relies too heavily on a single server. The public server names of all Private Information Stores point to the same Public Information Store. Users cannot browse the public folder hierarchy when this Public Information Store is temporarily unavailable (for example, when the server is down for maintenance). The second option is the better one because it achieves the desired result by controlling who can create exposed folders at the top of your public folder hierarchy. (See Figure 12-4.)

Further Reasons to Limit Permissions for Top-Level Folder Creation

It is good practice to limit the permissions for creating top-level folders to a few privileged users because too many users might create too many top-level folders, resulting in a complex or unorganized directory tree. A centralized group can determine the top-level public folders in order to make the public folders more intuitively navigable and to locate information. The centralized group can then grant permissions to other groups to manage the creation, content, and permissions of subfolders.

Restricting Top-Level Folder Creation

Using the Administrator program, you can control who can create top-level folders. The **Top-Level Folder Creation** property page of the **Information Store Site Configuration** object, which is located in the **Configuration** container, provides the required controls. You can grant or restrict permissions to create top-level folders on a per-user basis or you can simply assign the appropriate permissions to distribution lists instead of single mailboxes.

Storage Limitations

The 16-GB size limit of Exchange Server databases has been eliminated in version 5.5. Exchange Server 5.5 databases are restricted only by the capacity of the server's local disk space. Nevertheless, it might be helpful to limit the storage space that public folders can occupy if your server's hard disks don't offer much capacity.

On the **General** property page of the server-level **Public Information Store** object, you can set the public folder storage limit for a particular server. You can also specify storage limits on a per-folder basis using the **Limits** property page of the corresponding public folder object.

Warning Messages

If a folder exceeds the storage limit, the owner will receive a notification message requesting that items be removed. Such messages are sent once a day at 8 o'clock in the evening, referring to the time zone in which the Exchange Server computer is located. If you prefer another time or frequency, you can adjust the settings on the **Storage Warnings** property page of the **Information Store Site Configuration** object.

Storage warnings are also sent to mailbox owners if their mailboxes exceed the limits of the Private Information Store or the specified quotas of the mailbox itself. More information about mailbox limits is provided in Chapter 5.

Message Tracking

Message tracking allows you to examine the path a message has taken through the organization. You enable message tracking by selecting the **Enable Message Tracking** check box on the **General** property page of the **Information Store Site Configuration** object. Information about message delivery is kept in tracking log files. Message tracking is covered in detail in Chapter 15.

The site-level **Information Store Site Configuration** property pages and their uses are as follows:

- **General**; to change the display name, specify a public folder container, and enable message tracking

- **Permissions**; to grant users permission for the **Information Store Site Configuration** object

- **Public Folder Affinity**; to enter remote sites where the public folder contents can also be accessed

- **Storage Warnings**; to set times at which warning messages are sent to a public folder contact or to a mailbox owner if the resource exceeds the specified limits

- **Top-Level Folder Creation**; to control which users can create top-level public folders

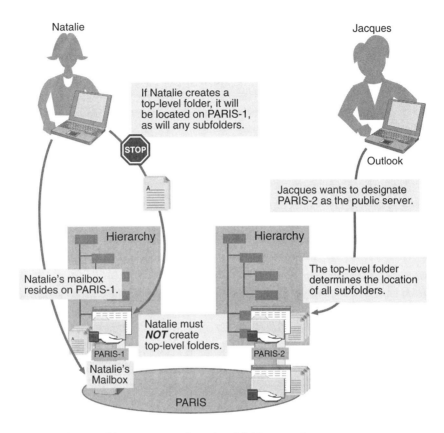

Figure 12-4. Public servers and top-level folder creation.

Public Folder Site Affinity

The term *affinity* can mean *a relationship* or *a natural liking*. You might say, "By default, different sites don't like each other," or "sites do not permit their users access to servers in other sites unless a relationship between the sites has been established." In Exchange Server, affinities are relationships between sites. Clients cannot locate the contents of public folders in remote sites if affinity values have not been set.

Public Folder Content Location

By default, when you open a public folder the client will look for the contents on your home server, any other server in the same server location, and every remaining server in the local site. If one of these computers has the contents, the client will connect immediately. Servers in remote sites will not be contacted because affinities are not specified in a default configuration.

Configuring Public Folder Site Affinity

You can set affinity values only between sites, not between servers. Consequently, you assign affinities at the site level using the **Public Folder Affinity** property page of the **Information Store Site Configuration** object. Public folder affinities are one-way streets. You must specify them for each site independently and assign a cost value; the lowest affinity cost determines the most preferred site.

Values defined in PARIS do not affect the site configuration in NEWYORK. Jacques Blanc, the administrator in PARIS, has defined the values shown in Figure 12-5 to allow clients in PARIS to contact public servers in FRANKFURT, NEWYORK, and LONDON. Fred Pumpkin, the administrator in NEWYORK, has not specified any affinity values, so clients in NEWYORK cannot contact any public servers other than in NEWYORK.

Remote Sites and Public Folder Content

As shown in Figure 12-5, the server PARIS-2 can return a list of three sites to clients that try to open public folders that cannot be found locally. If none of the public servers in its own site has the contents, the client will look in remote sites. It establishes a connection through RPCs and provides access to the public folder. At this point, you work with a public server elsewhere in the organization. For instance, clients in PARIS can connect to servers in FRANKFURT but cannot contact any public server in TOKYO.

Specifying the Contact Order

The site affinity value determines the attractiveness of remote sites. Sites with the lowest affinity values are contacted first. As shown in Figure 12-5, clients in PARIS will contact remote sites in the following order until they locate the content or the open attempt fails:

1. FRANKFURT
2. NEWYORK
3. LONDON

If multiple sites have the same value, they are pooled and then contacted in a random order.

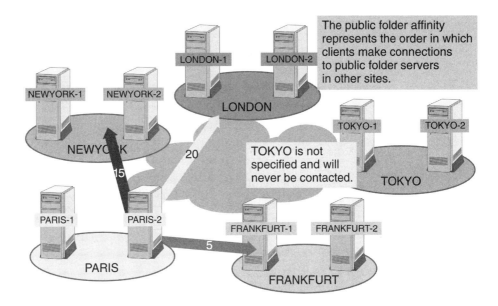

The public folder affinity represents the order in which clients make connections to public folder servers in other sites.

TOKYO is not specified and will never be contacted.

Figure 12-5. Public folder affinities in PARIS.

Public folder affinity values have these characteristics:

- Can be defined for sites, not for single servers
- Determine which remote sites the client will contact if the public folder contents are not in the local site
- Specify the order in which remote sites are contacted (similar to connector cost values)
- Site with the lowest public folder affinity value is tried first
- Affinity values are one way; each site must maintain its own

Client Connection Example

The Exchange Client and Outlook use RPCs to communicate with public servers. Any server in any site can be contacted if affinities have been specified and the RPC communication works.

Let's say that a TCP/IP link exists between PARIS and FRANKFURT and between PARIS and NEWYORK. This means that clients can theoretically contact any server in these three sites using RPC. Monsieur Blanc wants to open a public folder that resides on NEWYORK-1. He browses through the hierarchy of all public folders within his client and selects **New York Folder**. (See Figure 12-6.)

First the client sends an open request to the local public server, PARIS-2. This server does not maintain the contents, so the client tries PARIS-1 because it resides in the same site. The contents do not exist on PARIS-1 either. At this point, it contacts servers in remote sites based on their affinity values. FRANKFURT has a public folder affinity value of 5. The client contacts public servers in this site in any order. But the contents aren't there either. The client then checks for another available remote site based on affinity values. NEWYORK has the next lowest value. The client contacts any public server there, finds the content, and establishes the client-server connection—if Jacques has proper access permissions. Finally the contents are displayed in the client's contents pane.

Windows NT Security and Client Connections

The public server NEWYORK-1 will validate Jacques' open request using his Windows NT domain account. An RPC connection can be established only if Jacques' account is known and has the required permissions to open **New York Folder.**

Security dependencies will prevent a successful connection if domains are nontrusted. Let's say that the servers in PARIS exist in a single domain called FRANCE. The servers in NEWYORK are in a domain called STOCKSDATA. If STOCKSDATA does not trust FRANCE, clients from PARIS cannot access servers in NEWYORK. Jacques' client will not be able to display the contents of **New York Folder** even if it can locate it. To solve this problem, Jacques' must establish a relationship between STOCKSDATA and FRANCE and explicitly grant access rights to Jacques' Windows NT account.

Affinity Problems

You can assign affinities only to sites that permit access to their resources over RPCs. Clients will stop trying to locate the contents if they encounter a problem. Let's say that a Windows NT trust relationship exists between PARIS and NEWYORK but not between PARIS and FRANKFURT. A public folder has been created on NEWYORK-1 and replicated to FRANKFURT-1. A French user, Madame Natalie de Noir, tries to open this folder in PARIS. Her client is redirected to FRANKFURT (after unsuccessful attempts in PARIS). Access permissions are missing in FRANKFURT, so Natalie's client stops looking for the public folder even though she might have had access to the instance in NEWYORK.

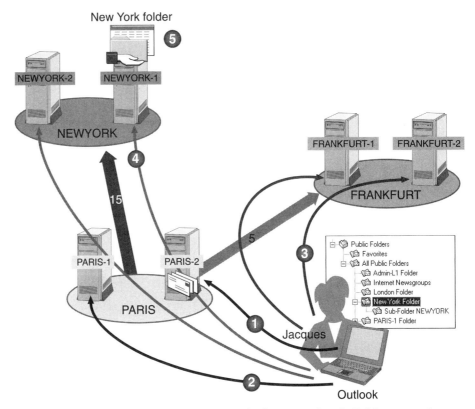

1. Local Public Server.   2. Public server in the same site.   3. Public servers in FRANKFURT.   4. Public servers in NEWYORK.   5. The desired public folder has been found in NEWYORK-1. Jacques' client accesses the public folder via RPC.

Figure 12-6.   Client connection order.

The order in which a client searches for servers that contain public folder contents is as follows:

1. The client checks the local public server.

2. The client checks servers in the same server location as their home server.

3. The client checks all servers that have the location set to *.

4. If the client has an open RPC connection to a potential server, it is checked next.

5. Any remaining servers in the site are checked in random order.

6. The client checks other sites based on their affinity values, beginning with the lowest value.

7. Servers in sites with the same affinity value are pooled and contacted in a random order.

8. The client contacts the site with the next highest affinity value if it hasn't found the contents. This continues until the contents are found or until all servers in all sites that have affinity values have been checked.

Server Location

Large sites make the administration of multiple servers wonderfully easy, but servers require further organization. *Server locations*—the subsites of sites—help in this task.

Local Server Grouping

Let's say that Jacques must install 10 Exchange Server computers in PARIS. He wants to simplify administration, so he implements a single site for all servers. The computer network is powerful enough, but differences exist in the network topology. Some servers are accessible through a fast 100 Mbps link, while others can connect only using an older 4 Mbps segment. (See Figure 12-7.)

In a default configuration, client access to public servers in PARIS is not controlled. If the client cannot find the public folder content on the local public folder server, it checks other public servers at random. A neighbor connected through the 100 Mbps link might be available, but perhaps a 4 Mbps connection is being used. As shown in Figure 12-7, Jacques might end up accessing the server PARIS-X instead of PARIS-1. It would be better to offload the 4 Mbps network segment. To achieve this, the servers within a site must be grouped together with the **Server Locations** property.

Server Locations

With server locations, this grouping can be accomplished. Use the **Server Location** box on the **General** property page of each server object in the Administrator program.

In the Administrator program, Jacques selects **PARIS-2** and presses **ALT+ENTER** to display the properties. He might type *100MBIT* in the **Server Location** box on the **General** property page. As shown in Figure 12-7, PARIS-1 will also be grouped there. He then displays the properties of PARIS-X and types *4MBIT* in the **Server Location** box. He selects all other servers of interest and adds them to the **4MBIT** server location. From here, Jacques' client will try to locate the content of a public folder in the **100MBIT** segment before it contacts any other server in the site.

No Location, Any Location

Jacques might want to place PARIS-2 in the **100MBIT** segment. From the standpoint of a user residing on a server of the **4MBIT** server location, it might be better to place PARIS-2 there also—if this server contains important public folders. To place a server in multiple locations, you must specify an asterisk (*) in the **Server Location** box. Such a server will belong to all defined locations of the site. You can configure servers that should not belong to any subsite using the **<None>** name—the default for all servers in a site. Actually, **<None>** can be considered just another server location.

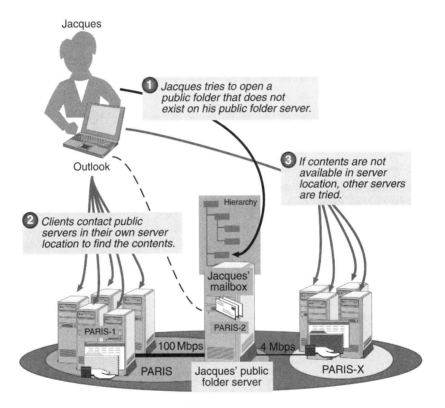

Figure 12-7. Grouping local public servers.

The characteristics of server locations are as follows:

- Allow further grouping of servers within a site
- Can specify them on the server object's **General** property page
- Clients contact servers in the local server location first
- RPC communication can be focused on powerful network segments

Public Information Store Configuration

In a default server-level configuration, the **Public Information Store** object resides under the **Server** container, but you can delete it to achieve a dedicated private server configuration. (See Figure 12-8.)

Specifying Age Limits

Age limits determine how long a public folder keeps items before deleting them automatically. This mechanism can ensure that old information in a public folder will not remain there indefinitely.

Age Limits per Public Information Store

To set an age limit for all public folders on your server, use the **Age Limits** property page of the **Public Information Store** object. Select the **Age Limit For All Folders On This Information Store (Days)** check box to specify the lifetime of items in days.

Age Limits per Public Folder

You can use the **All Replicas (Days)** and **This Replica (Days)** options to configure age limits for public folders. Both are in the **Modify Age Limits** dialog box, which you can display by clicking the **Modify** button after selecting a folder on the **Age Limits** property page.

The value specified under **All Replicas (Days)** affects all instances of a public folder within the organization. **This Replica (Days)** determines the age of public folder items on a single-instance basis. **This Replica (Days)** takes precedence over **All Replicas (Days)**, and both have a higher priority than the **Age Limit For All Folders On This Information Store (Days)** setting for the entire Public Information Store.

Item Recovery

Exchange Server 5.5 allows you to configure a deleted item retention time for public folders. The default is 0 days, which means that items are deleted from the IS immediately. However, if you enter a number larger than 0 or if you select the **Don't Permanently Delete Items Until The Store Has Been Backed Up** option on the **General** property page, the server retains deleted messages in the database as specified. Within the defined time span, users can select the **Recover Deleted Items** command from Outlook's **Tools** menu to restore deleted messages. In this way, the administrator is freed from having to restore an entire server if important messages have been deleted accidentally. A retained item will be removed permanently after the specified period elapses.

Maintaining Public Folder Instances

Not every public server must maintain the contents of all public folders. To determine which folders a particular server should take care of, you must configure the Public Information Store. On the **Instances** property page, specify the replicas that a server will contain. When you add a new instance, its contents will be sent to your server by means of public folder replication. Public folder replication is explained in Chapter 13.

You can also remove any instance from a server except the last public folder instance in the organization. If you try to remove the last instance, when you click the **Remove** button a message box will tell you that you cannot remove the folder because it is the only instance in the site.

Obtaining Public Folder Status Information

The configuration of public folders is one aspect of Public Information Store management. The constant verification of the public folder state is another. Status information can indicate bottlenecks and critical situations.

Public Folder Resources

Using either the **Public Folder Resources** object (which is under the **Public Information Store** container object) or the **Public Folder Resources** property page, you can display status information about the public folder resources on a particular server.

You can view the following information:

- Disk space used in a given public folder
- Last access time for a public folder
- Number of contacts for a public folder
- Number of messages in a public folder
- Number of owners of a public folder
- Path to a public folder in the public folder hierarchy

Logons

The **Public Information Store** container provides the **Logons** object as well as the **Logons** property page. Both can display status information about users who are currently connected, but the **Logons** object is often more convenient to use. You can determine what information to display by clicking the **Columns** button on the **Logons** property page or by selecting the **Columns** command on the **View** menu for the **Logons** object.

Standard status information includes:

- Client version
- Last access time
- Logon time
- User name
- Windows NT account

Folder Replication Status

You can get a quick overview of the replication status of each public folder through the **Folder Replication Status** object and the **Folder Replication Status** property page. If items have been changed locally, the status is **Local Modified**. If the changes have been replicated to all other instances, the status is **In Sync**. Public folder replication is covered in Chapter 13.

Server Replication Status

The **Server Replication Status** object and the **Server Replication Status** property page provide status information on a per-server basis. Each remote server that receives replication messages from the local server is listed. The status of a particular server can be either **Local Modified** or **In Sync**. **Local Modified** means that a local replica has been modified but the changes have not been sent to the replica on a remote server. **In Sync** means that the information has been sent. It does not necessarily mean that the remote server has received and incorporated the changes.

The **Public Information Store** property pages and their functions are as follows:

- **Advanced**; to specify further replication-related settings such as replication interval and replication message sizes
- **Age Limits**; to set a time limit for how long information remains in public folders before it expires and is automatically deleted
- **Diagnostics Logging**; to enable event logging for IS categories
- **E-mail Addresses**; to verify or edit the e-mail addresses of the Public Information Store
- **Folder Replication Status**; to check the replication status of each public folder
- **General**; to set a limit on the size of the folder; if the limit is exceeded, the public folder contact will be warned

- **Instances**; to specify which public folders a server contains

- **Logons**; to display a list of users who are currently connected

- **Public Folder Resources**; to check resource consumption by public folders

- **Replication Schedule**; to configure the public folder replication time

- **Server Replication Status**; to verify the replication status of the selected server with all other servers

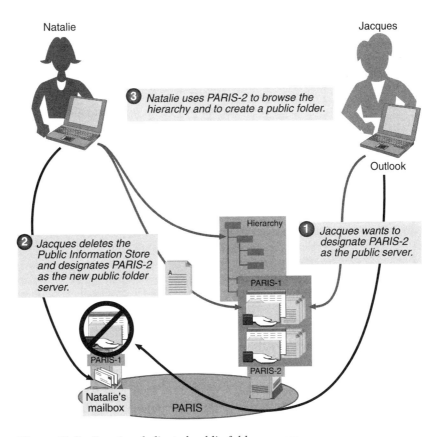

Figure 12-8. Creating dedicated public folder servers.

Exercise 42: Changing Top-Level Public Folder Creation Permissions

Top-level folders appear directly under the **All Public Folders** tree and determine the locations of all subfolders. It is good practice to limit the users who can create top-level folders.

Estimated time to complete this exercise: 25 minutes

Description

In this exercise, you will restrict the permissions to create top-level folders to the group of Exchange administrators. You will also define an affinity value for remote sites in your test environment. If you want to test the effect of site affinities, you should establish a complete trust relationship between STOCKSDATA and ENGLAND. Otherwise, users in NEWYORK and LONDON will not be able to access resources in the other location.

- Task 42a describes the steps for establishing a trust relationship between the Windows NT domains STOCKSDATA (for the server NEWYORK-1) and ENGLAND (for the server LONDON-1).

- Task 42b describes the steps for restricting the ability of users to create top-level public folders on the server LONDON-1.

- Task 42c describes the steps for demonstrating that a user cannot open a public folder in another messaging site without further configuration.

- Task 42d describes the steps for configuring public folder affinity between two Exchange messaging sites.

- Task 42e describes the steps for verifying public folder affinity.

- Task 42f describes the steps for removing public folder affinity between two Exchange messaging sites. Public folder replication and conflict resolution are demonstrated in Exercise 13 of Chapter 6.

Prerequisites

- NEWYORK and LONDON must exist in nontrusted domains (STOCKSDATA and ENGLAND).

- Log on to the server NEWYORK-1 as Admin-NY1.

- Log on to the server LONDON-1 as Admin-L1.

Task 42a: Configuring a Trust Relationship Between STOCKSDATA (NEWYORK) and ENGLAND (LONDON)

1. Log on to the server LONDON-1 by pressing **CTRL+ALT+DEL**.

2. In the **Name** box, type *Admin-L1*.

3. In the **Password** box, type *password* and then click **OK**.

4. Click the **Start** button, point to **Programs**, point to **Administrative Tools (Common)**, and click **User Manager For Domains**.

5. The **User Manager - ENGLAND** dialog box appears. Open the **Policies** menu and click **Trust Relationships**.

6. The **Trust Relationships** dialog box appears. Click the **Add** button under the **Trusting Domains** list box. The **Add Trusting Domains** dialog box appears.

7. Enter the following information:

In this box	You supply
Trusting Domain	*STOCKSDATA*
Initial Password	*password*
Confirm Password	*password*

8. Click **OK**.

9. Click the **Add** button under the **Trusted Domains** list box. The **Add Trusted Domains** dialog box appears.

10. Enter the following information:

In this box	You supply
Trusted Domains	*STOCKSDATA*
Password	*password*

11. Click **OK**.

12. A **User Manager for Domains** message box appears, informing you that the trust relationship cannot be verified. Click **OK**.

13. Click **Close**.

14. Log on to the server NEWYORK-1 by pressing **CTRL+ALT+DEL**.

15. In the **Name** box, type *Admin-NY1*.

16. In the **Password** box, type *password* and then click **OK**.

17. Click the **Start** button, point to **Programs**, point to **Administrative Tools (Common)**, and click **User Manager For Domains**.

18. The dialog box **User Manager - NEWYORK** appears. Open the **Policies** menu and click **Trust Relationships.**

19. The **Trust Relationships** dialog box appears. Click **Add** (to the right of the **Trusting Domains** box). The **Add Trusting Domains** dialog box appears.

20. Enter the following information:

In this box	You supply
Trusting Domain	*ENGLAND*
Initial Password	*password*
Confirm Password	*password*

21. Click the **Add** button under the **Trusted Domains** list box. The **Add Trusted Domains** dialog box appears.

22. Enter the following information:

In this box	You supply
Domain:	*ENGLAND*
Password:	*password*

23. Click **OK**.

24. After several seconds, a **User Manager For Domains** message box appears, telling you that the trust relationship with ENGLAND has been successfully established. Click **OK**.

25. Click **Close** to close the **Trust Relationships** dialog box.

26. On the **User** menu, click **Exit**.

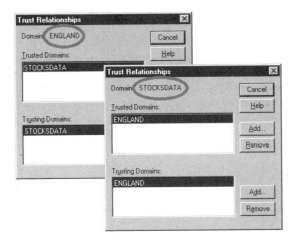

Task 42b: Changing Top-Level Public Folder Creation Permissions

1. Switch to the server LONDON-1 and verify that the **Exchange Administrator** program is running.

2. Expand the site-object **LONDON**, and then click the **Configuration** container.

3. In the right pane, double-click the **Information Store Site Configuration** object.

4. The **Information Store Site Configuration Properties** dialog box appears. Click the **Top Level Folder Creation** tab.

5. In the **Allowed To Create Top Level Folders** box, select **List**.

6. In the **Allowed To Create Top Level Folders** box, click **Modify**.

7. The **Information Store Site Configuration** dialog box appears. Select **Admin-L1** and **Administrator NewYork-1** in the left list box by clicking them while pressing the **CTRL** key, and then click **Add**. Note that the selected names are copied over to the **Allowed To Create Top Level Folders** list box.

8. Click **OK**. The **Information Store Site Configuration Properties** dialog box gets the focus again.

9. Click **OK**.

10. Exit **Exchange Administrator**.

Task 42c: Testing Folder Affinity

1. The way in which you completed Exercise 40 will determine which server and account are the correct ones for you. If you created a public folder in the site LONDON, you must log on as Admin-NY1; otherwise, log on as Admin-L1. Start Outlook.

2. Open the **View** menu and select the **Folder List** command.

3. Expand **All Public Folders**.

4. Try to open the public folder that you created in Exercise 40. A **Microsoft Outlook** message box appears, stating that Outlook is unable to display the folder.

5. Click **OK** to close the message.

6. On the **File** menu, click **Exit And Log Off**.

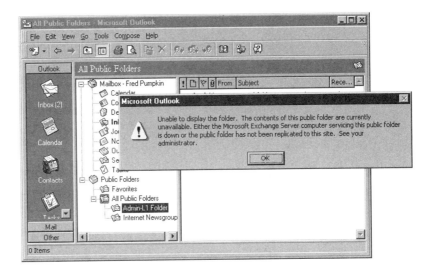

Task 42d: Configuring Public Folder Affinity Between Sites

1. If you are working as Admin-NY1, follow the steps of this exercise exactly. If you are working as Admin-L1, replace **NEWYORK** with **LONDON**.

2. Click the **Start** button, point to **Programs**, point to **Microsoft Exchange**, and then click **Microsoft Exchange Administrator**.

3. Expand the site container **NEWYORK** and then click the **Configuration** container.

4. In the right pane, double-click **Information Store Site Configuration**.

5. The **Information Store Site Configuration Properties** dialog box appears.

6. Click the **Public Folder Affinity** tab.

7. In the **Sites** box, select **LONDON** and then click **Add**.

8. Click **OK**.

9. On the **File** menu, click **Exit**.

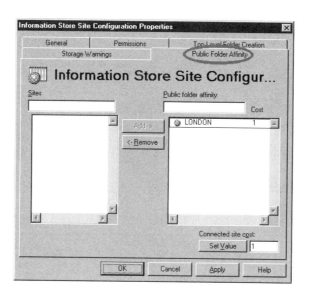

Task 42e: Testing Public Folder Access

1. Make sure that you are logged on with the same account as in Task 42c. Start Outlook.

2. Expand the **Public Folders** container and then **All Public Folders**.

3. Open the public folder that you created in Exercise 40 (for example, **Admin-L1 Folder**).

4. Open a message in the folder.

5. Close the message.

6. On the **File** menu, click **Exit And Log Off**.

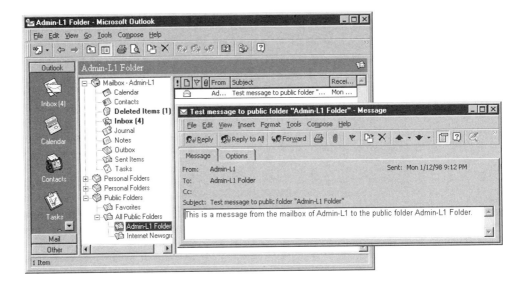

Task 42f: Removing Public Folder Affinity Between Sites

1. Click the **Start** button, point to **Programs**, point to **Microsoft Exchange**, and then click **Microsoft Exchange Administrator**.

2. Expand the appropriate site object and then click the **Configuration** container.

3. In the right pane, double-click **Information Store Site Configuration**.

4. The **Information Store Site Configuration Properties** dialog box appears.

5. Click the **Public Folder Affinity** tab.

6. In the **Public Folder Affinity** box, select the remote site object, and then click **Remove**.

7. Click **OK**.

8. On the **File** menu, click **Exit**.

Review

The **Information Store Site Configuration** object in the **Configuration** container provides the **Top Level Folder Creation** property page. On this page, you can designate who can create top-level folders. To simplify the task, you can assign appropriate permissions to distribution lists instead of single user mailboxes.

On the **Public Folder Affinity** property page, you can associate affinities with remote sites. They will be contacted if the contents of particular public folder are not in the local site. Once it locates the contents, a client will try to access the resources in the remote site to display the items. (Client access must be validated.) If different Windows NT domains exist, you must establish trust relationships. Otherwise, access to the contents might be denied because the user is unknown.

Lesson 3: Creating and Managing Public Folders

Exchange Server 5.5 provides valuable features for configuring public folders, but not all of the administrative interfaces are available in the Administrator program. They are scattered among a variety of clients, property pages, and dialog boxes. Perhaps the next version of Exchange Server will introduce centralized public folder management. For now, however, to create and administer a public folder you must work with at least two programs, the Administrator program and Outlook.

This lesson focuses on the client side of public folder management. You will learn about public folder creation using the Exchange Client and Outlook, as well as about user aids. Then you will learn about managing public folders using the public folder property pages. An exercise will round off the lesson.

At the end of this lesson, you will be able to:

- Create public folders
- Manage public folders within the Exchange Client and Outlook

Estimated time to complete this lesson: 25 minutes

Creating a Public Folder

The idea behind public folders is that users can easily share information. For this reason, users must able to create public folders. The Exchange Client, Outlook, and some other MAPI-based clients such as Outlook Web Access let you create public folders. (See Figure 12-9.) To the regret of many administrators, the Administrator program does not provide a convenient way to create public folders.

Creating a Public Folder Using the Exchange Client

To create a new public folder using the Exchange Client, you select the parent public folder, open the **File** menu, and click the **New Folder** command. Specify the **Folder Name** in the **New Folder** dialog box, and then click **OK**. To create a top-level folder, first select the **All Public Folders** container. Note that the **New Folder** command is available only if you have the required permissions to create subfolders. For example, if you select the **Internet Newsgroups** folder in a default configuration, the **New Folder** command will be unavailable.

You can also use the **New Discussion Folder** command on the **File** menu to create public folders. This command creates new discussion forums efficiently because it predefines some folder properties (such as an **Unread By Conversation** view). However, you must enter the **Folder Name** and an optional **Description** in the **New Discussion Folder** dialog box. This dialog box also offers the **Add This Folder To My Favorites** and **Place A Shortcut To This Folder On My Desktop** options, which add further convenience.

Creating a Public Folder Using Outlook

Like the Exchange Client, Outlook is a MAPI-based application. They share several similarities in the area of public folder creation, but the command names and dialog boxes are slightly different. One way to create public folders in Outlook is by using the **Create Subfolder** command under the **Folder** option on the **File** menu. Another way is to use the **Folder** command under the **New** option the **File** menu. Both commands display the **Create New Folder** dialog box, which asks you for a folder name and the folder type (**Appointment**, **Mail**, **Contact**, **Journal**, **Task**, or **Note Items**). Outlook will assign special properties to the new public folder. You select the parent folder in the **Make This Folder A Subfolder Of** box. Finally, you click **OK** to complete the creation.

Folder Design Cue Cards

Folder Design Cue Cards can provide valuable assistance when users who are unfamiliar with the required configuration and design steps want to create public folders using the Exchange Client. Cue cards are a help system; they explain all of the possible design properties and provide assistance with public folder design tests.

Note Folder Design Cue Cards are not available in Outlook.

To launch the cue cards, select the **Folder Design Cue Cards** command under the **Application Design** option on the **Tools** menu. A window will open, displaying an informational welcome page. Click **Next** to learn about folder creation, forms installation, and others topics.

The cue cards explain the following topics:

Assignment of access permissions

- Creation of folder rules
- Design of folder views
- Installation of electronic forms for a folder
- Selection of other properties

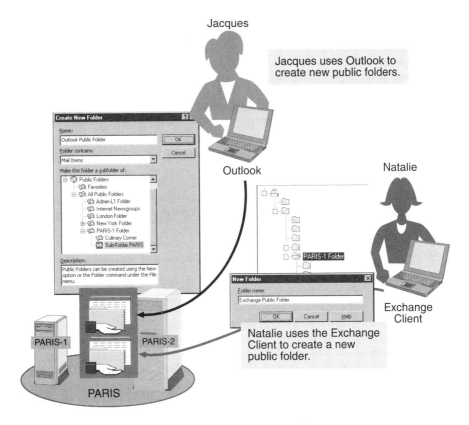

Figure 12-9. User interfaces for creating a public folder.

Managing Public Folder Properties

Every user who creates a public folder automatically becomes its owner. The owner is responsible for the folder's design, which can include access permissions, views, public folder rules, and electronic forms.

Setting Access Permissions

Setting access permissions is one of the most important configuration tasks. You set the permissions using the public folder's **Permissions** property page.

By default, three accounts have access permissions:

- **Anonymous** users' permissions are set to **None**

- The **Default** user is granted **Author** permissions

- The user who created the public folder is granted the **Owner** role

Users who are not explicitly listed receive the permissions granted to the **Default** account. You can treat anonymous users (such as nonvalidated users connecting through an Internet browser) separately using the **Anonymous** entry. The user who created the public folder is listed explicitly because every public folder must have at least one owner. You cannot delete any of these three accounts, but you can designate an additional owner account to delete the original entry.

Custom Roles

You can define custom roles by granting access permissions explicitly. For example, you can select the **Default** account and clear the **Folder Visible** option to hide a public folder from all users who are not listed. **Custom** will be displayed in the **Roles** box. To make the folder visible to specific users, you must add each one to the account list by clicking the **Add** button.

The permissions allow a user to do the following:

- **Create Items**; to create items in the folder
- **Create Subfolder**; to create subfolders in the folder
- **Delete Items**; to delete items
- **Edit Items**; to edit items
- **Folder Contact**; to receive replication conflict notifications, folder design conflict notifications, and quota notifications
- **Folder Owner**; all permissions are granted; the name of the last owner is never removed from the **Names** list
- **Folder Visible**; to view the folder in the **All Public Folders** list
- **Read Items**; to read any items in the folder

Predefined Roles

Predefined roles are a convenient way to assign access permissions to user accounts. They can serve as templates for custom roles.

You can choose from the following roles:

Role	Permissions included in the role
None	Edit Items (none) and Delete Items (none)
Contributor	Create Items, Edit Items (none), and Delete Items (none)

(continues)

(continued)

Role	Permissions included in the role
Reviewer	Read Items, Edit Items (none), and Delete Items (none)
Nonediting Author	Read Items, Create Items, Edit Items (none), and Delete Items (own)
Author	Read Items, Create Items, Edit Items (own), and Delete Items (own)
Publishing Author	Read Items, Create Items, Create Subfolder, Edit Items (own), and Delete Items (own)
Editor	Read Items, Create Items, Edit Items (all), and Delete Items (all)
Publishing Editor	Read Items, Create Items, Create Subfolder, Edit Items (all), and Delete Items (all)
Owner	Read Items, Create Items, Create Subfolder, Folder Owner, Folder Contact, Edit Items (all), and Delete Items (all)

Bypassing Assigned Permissions

When you assign permissions to a parent folder, those permissions are inherited by subfolders when the subfolder is created. Changes in permissions to the parent folder are not automatically propagated to child folders. Be aware of this, because it can lead to a security hole.

The Exchange Client and Outlook display a **Favorites** list next to **All Public Folders**, which provides an easy way to reach popular public folders. Favorites are links that are similar to shortcuts in Windows NT 4.0; they open the desired public folder without having to navigate all its parent folders first. **Favorites** can bypass permissions set on parent folders. (See Figure 12-10 on page 822.)

The following example demonstrates this:

1. Start the Exchange Client or Outlook.
2. Create a new top-level folder called **BackDoor**.
3. Create a subfolder under **BackDoor** called **Sub-BackDoor**.
4. Drag the folder **Sub-BackDoor** to the **Favorites** folder.
5. Verify that a reference to the public folder **Sub-BackDoor** has been created in the **Favorites** folder.

6. Right-click the folder **BackDoor** and then select **Properties**.

7. Switch to the **Permissions** tab.

8. Deselect the **Read Items** permission for your account and then click **OK**.

9. Select **All Public Folders**, and then click the public folder **BackDoor** again to open it. A message box appears, stating that the folder cannot be opened.

10. Open the **Favorites** folder and then select the **Sub-BackDoor** folder.

11. Note that you can open the folder and, if desired, copy items to it.

Note To prevent this way of bypassing permissions, you can change the permissions for subfolders to those that apply to the parent folder. You must use the Administrator program to do this. Select the **Propagate These Properties To All Subfolders** option on the parent folder's **General** property page.

---

12. Start the Exchange Administrator program.

13. Open the **Folders** container under the organization object and then expand the **Public Folders** container.

14. Select the **BackDoor** public folder object and then press **ALT+ENTER** to display its properties.

15. Select **Propagate These Properties To All Subfolders** and then click **OK**.

16. The **Subfolder Properties** dialog box appears. Select **Client Permissions** and click **OK** twice.

17. Switch back to the Exchange Client or Outlook and try to open the public folder **Sub-BackDoor** from within **Favorites**. Access will be denied.

18. The propagation feature of the Administrator program lets you ensure that only users who have permissions at the parent folder level can access the information.

Defining Folder Rules

Folder rules are instructions that cause Exchange Server to perform specified actions on incoming messages (such as sending a standard reply). Folder rules are similar to Inbox rules, which were described in Chapter 7.

To create public folder rules, click the **Folder Assistant** button on the folder's **Administration** property page. In the **Folder Assistant** dialog box, click the **Add Rule** button and then define the desired rules. Because rules are stored and executed on an Exchange Server computer, the **Folder Assistant** button is unavailable when a user is working off line.

Moderated Folders

Moderated folders are the censored version of Exchange Server public folders. They let you review posted items before they appear. Exchange Server forwards all posted messages without modifications to a moderator. The moderator places accepted items in the destination folder. Moderated folders are especially useful when you are setting up discussions across the Internet and USENET because they provide control over the tone, style, and topic of communication.

To configure a moderated folder, click the **Moderated Folder** button on the folder's **Administration** property page. In the **Moderated Folder** dialog box, select the **Set Folder Up As Moderated Folder** check box. In the **Forward New Items To** box, specify the mailbox or public folder to which incoming messages should be forwarded. Specifying a public folder is especially useful if you want to designate more than one moderator. All moderators must be designated under **Moderators** because they must be able to paste approved items into the moderated folder without having them forwarded again to a moderator. You can also configure a standard response that will be returned to users as they post or send new items to the moderated public folder.

The Exchange Client public folder property pages and their functions are as follows:

- **Administration**; to define the initial view, folder rules, and folder type (moderated folder) and restrict the availability of the folder

- **Forms**; to associate electronic forms with folders; more information about electronic forms is provided in Chapter 16

- **General**; to change the display name or the description of a public folder

- **Internet News**; to publish the folder to the Internet (as covered in Chapter 11)

- **Permissions**; to assign roles and permissions to users

- **Views**; to define personal views and folder views

- **Agents**; to provide scripts for server-based folder processing via the Event Service (as discussed in Chapter 16)—this property page appears only if you have the required permissions to create server-based scripts and if Outlook 97 version 8.03 has been installed on the Exchange Client computer

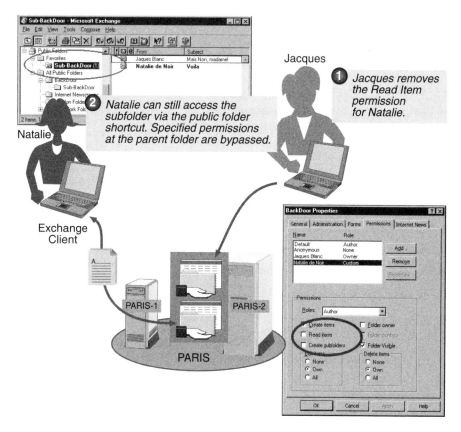

Figure 12-10. Bypassing public folder permissions.

Exercise 43: Managing Exchange Public Folder Permissions

You can create public folders using Outlook or the Exchange Client, and you can design and configure them almost entirely within the same program. You can rename public folders or place them in the list of public folder favorites. Moderated public folders let you screen new items before they are placed in a public folder.

Estimated time to complete this exercise: 30 minutes

Description

In this exercise, you will use Outlook to create a top-level public folder and modify the user permissions. Then you will analyze the inheritance of public folder permissions.

- Task 43a describes the steps for creating a new top-level public folder.

- Task 43b describes the steps for assigning permission levels to users and groups.

- Task 43c describes the steps for demonstrating the difference between group permissions and individual user permissions.

- Task 43d describes the steps for removing the direct permissions to USERs so that group-level permissions apply.

- Task 43e describes the steps for completing the demonstration of the difference between group permissions and individual user permissions.

- Task 43f describes the steps for demonstrating inheritance of top-level public folder permissions when a subfolder is created.

- Task 43g describes the steps for modifying permissions on a top-level public folder in order to set up a test for subfolder inheritance of permissions changes.

- Task 43h describes the steps for demonstrating that permissions are inherited when a folder is created. Subsequent changes to upper-level folder permissions do not automatically flow to subfolders.

- Task 43i describes the steps for demonstrating that you must use the Administrator program to specify that changes in permissions for an upper-level public folder propagate to subfolders.

Prerequisites

- Complete this exercise simultaneously on the server NEWYORK-1 as Admin-NY1 and on the server LONDON-1 as Admin-L1.

Task 43a: Creating a New Top-Level Folder

Note You must perform all steps of this task on both computers.

1. On the **Desktop**, double-click the **Microsoft Outlook** shortcut. Verify that you are connected to the appropriate mailboxes (such as Admin-L1 and Fred Pumpkin).

2. In Outlook, if necessary, click the **Folder List** icon on the toolbar or select the **Folder List** command on the **View** menu.

3. In the **Folder List** pane, expand **Public Folders** and then select **All Public Folders**.

4. On the **File** menu, point to **New** and then click **Folder**.

5. In the **Name** box in the **Create New Folder** dialog box on NEWYORK-1, type *New York Folder*. On LONDON-1 type *London Folder*.

6. Click **OK**.

7. If an **Add Shortcut To Outlook Bar** message box appears, click **No** to avoid the creation of a shortcut to this folder on the Outlook bar.

Task 43b: Modifying Permissions for a Public Folder

1. In the left pane, right-click **London Folder** on LONDON-1, and then right-click **New York Folder** on NEWYORK-1. Click **Properties** to display the **Folder Properties** dialog box.

2. Click the **Permissions** tab.

3. Notice that the default permissions are Author, that the Owner is Admin-L1/Fred Pumpkin, and that Anonymous has no permissions.

4. Click **Add**. The **Add Users** dialog box appears.

5. Click the appropriate user as noted in the following list:

   Admin-L1 on LONDON-1 selects **Robin Sherwood**.

   Admin-NY1 on NEWYORK-1 selects **Administrator New York-1** and **Sales On NEWYORK** by holding down the **CTRL** key while selecting each name.

6. Click **Add**.

7. Click **OK**. The **London Folder Properties** or the **New York Folder Properties** dialog box appears.

8. In the **Name** box on LONDON-1 click **Robin Sherwood**. On NEWYORK-1 click **Sales On NEWYORK**. In the **Roles** list, click **Publishing Author**.

9. On NEWYORK-1 only, select **Administrator New York-1**, and then in the **Roles** list click **Reviewer**.

10. Under **Name**, click **Default**. In the **Roles** list, click **Reviewer**.

11. Click **OK**.

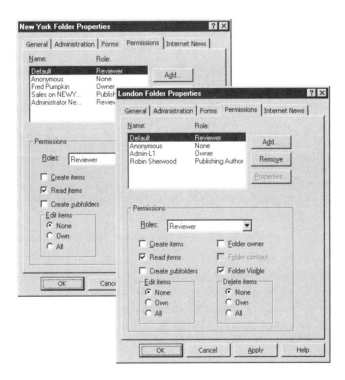

Task 43c: Trying to Create a Subfolder

1. Working as Admin-NY1 on NEWYORK-1 only, close Outlook.

2. Open the Control Panel and double-click the **Mail** icon or the **Mail And Fax** icon.

3. A **Microsoft Outlook Properties** dialog box appears. Click the **Show Profiles** button.

4. The window title changes to **Mail**. Select the existing profile (which connects Outlook to the mailbox of Fred Pumpkin) and then click **Copy**.

5. Under **New Profile Name**, type *Administrator* and then click **OK**.

6. Under **When Starting Microsoft Exchange Use This Profile**, select **Administrator**.

7. In the list of available MAPI profiles, verify that **Administrator** is selected and then click **Properties**.

8. In the list of available information services, verify that **Microsoft Exchange Server** is selected and then click **Properties**.

9. Under **Mailbox**, type *Administrator NewYork-1* and then click the **Check Name** button. Verify that the name is resolved as indicated by the underlined server and mailbox names.

10. Click **OK** twice, and then click **Close**.

11. Close the Control Panel and on the desktop double-click the **Microsoft Outlook** shortcut.

12. Open the **Tools** menu and then click **Options**.

13. Switch to the **General** tab and then select **Prompt For A Profile To Be Used**.

14. Click **OK**.

15. Expand the **Public Folders** container and then **All Public Folders**. Select **New York Folder**.

16. On the **File** menu, point to **New**, and then point to **Folder**.

17. Notice that the **Folder** menu option is not available. This is because the Administrator NewYork-1 account does not have Create Items permission as Reviewer. Although Administrator New York-1 belongs to a group that has Create Items permission as Publishing Author, the permissions granted directly to USERs are more restrictive. Individual user permissions override group permissions.

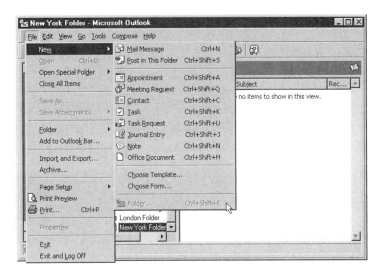

Task 43d: Modifying Permissions for a Top-Level Public Folder

1. As Admin-NY1 on NEWYORK-1, close Outlook and then start it again.

2. A **Choose Profile** dialog box appears, asking you for a profile name. Select the profile that connects you to the mailbox Fred Pumpkin (which is not the profile created in Task 43c), and then click **OK**.

3. Expand the **Public Folders** container and then **All Public Folders**.

4. Right-click the **New York Folder** and then select **Properties**.

5. A **New York Folder Properties** dialog box appears. Switch to the **Permissions** tab.

6. In the **Name** list, select **Administrator New York-1**.

7. Click **Remove**.

8. Click **OK**.

9. Close Outlook and then restart it.

10. A **Choose Profile** dialog box appears, asking you for a profile name. Select the **Administrator** profile (the profile created in Task 43c), and then click **OK**.

11. Expand the **Public Folders** container and then **All Public Folders**. Select **New York Folder**.

12. Open the **File** menu, point to **New**, and verify that the **Folder** command is available. It is available because Administrator New York-1 belongs to a group that has Create Items permission as Publishing Author.

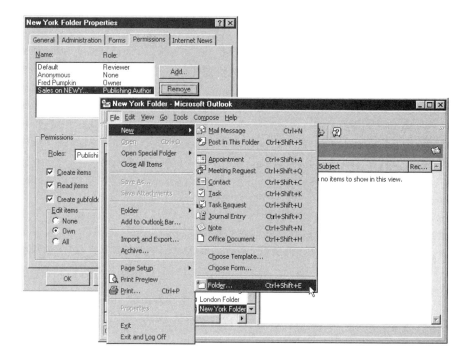

Task 43e: Creating a Subfolder

1. As Admin-NY1 on NEWYORK-1, verify that **New York Folder** is selected.

2. On the **File** menu, point to **New** and then click **Folder**.

3. The **Create New Folder** dialog box appears.

4. In the **Name** box, type *Sub-Folder NEWYORK*.

5. Click **OK**.

6. If an **Add Shortcut To Outlook Bar** dialog box appears, click **No**.

7. Select **Sub-Folder NEWYORK**.

8. On the toolbar, click the **New Post In This Folder** button.

9. In the **Subject** box, type *Posted Information*.

10. Click in the message text area, and then type *With Outlook it is possible to send and post messages.*

11. Format the text as desired. On the toolbar of the **Posted Information - Discussion** window, click **Post**.

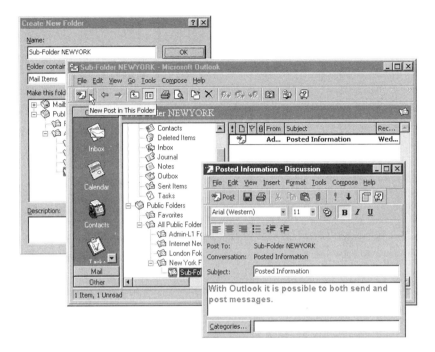

Task 43f: Verifying Inherited Top-Level Public Folder Permissions

1. In the left pane, right-click **Sub-Folder NEWYORK** and then click **Properties**.

2. The **Sub-Folder NEWYORK Properties** dialog box appears. Click the **Permissions** tab.

3. Verify that **Sales On NEWYORK** has the permissions of a **Publishing Author**, that **Fred Pumpkin** and **Administrator NewYork-1** have the permissions of an **Owner**, that the **Default** user is a **Reviewer**, and that **Anonymous** has no permissions.

4. Click **OK**.

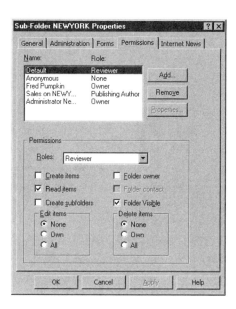

Task 43g: Modifying Permissions for the Top-Level Public Folder

1. As Admin-NY1 on NEWYORK, close Outlook and then restart it.

2. A **Choose Profile** dialog box appears, asking you for a profile name. Select the profile that connects you to the mailbox Fred Pumpkin (which is not the profile created in Task 43c), and then click **OK**.

3. Open the **Tools** menu and then click the **Options** command.

4. Switch to the **General** tab, select **Always Use This Profile**, and then select the profile that connects you to the mailbox Fred Pumpkin. Click **OK**.

5. Expand the **Public Folders** container and then **All Public Folders**.

6. Right-click **New York Folder** and then click **Properties**.

7. The **New York Folder Properties** dialog box appears. Click the **Permissions** tab.

8. Click **Add** to display the **Add Users** dialog box.

9. For the folder, select **Admin-L1** and **Robin Sherwood** while holding down the **CTRL** key. Click **Add**.

10. Click **OK**.

11. The **New York Folder Properties** dialog box appears.

12. Click **OK**.

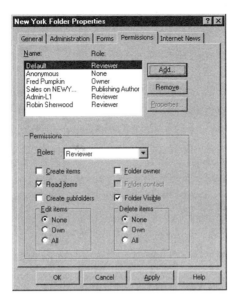

Task 43h: Verifying that Permissions for the Subfolder Have Not Changed

1. On NEWYORK-1, expand the folder **New York Folder**.

2. In the left pane, right-click **Sub-Folder NEWYORK** and then click **Properties**.

3. The **Sub-Folder NEWYORK Properties** dialog box appears. Click the **Permissions** tab.

4. Verify that the permissions for **Sub-Folder NEWYORK** are the same as those listed in Task 43f.

5. Click **OK**.

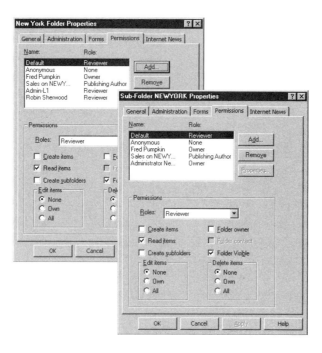

Task 43i: Propagating the Properties of a Top-Level Public Folder to All Subfolders

1. On NEWYORK-1, click the **Start** button, point to **Programs**, point to **Microsoft Exchange**, and then click **Microsoft Exchange Administrator.** Make sure that you are connected to the server NEWYORK-1.

2. In the left pane, expand **Folders**, expand **Public Folders**, and then click the folder **New York Folder**.

3. On the **File** menu, click **Properties** to display the **New York Folder Properties** dialog box.

4. Select the **Propagate These Properties To All Subfolders** check box and then click **OK**.

5. The **Subfolder Properties** dialog box appears.

6. Select the **Client Permissions** check box and then click **OK**.

7. A **Microsoft Exchange Administrator** dialog box appears. Click **OK**.

8. Close the Exchange Administrator program.

9. Switch to Outlook.

10. In the left pane, right-click **Sub-Folder NEWYORK**, and then click **Properties**.

11. The **Sub-Folder NEWYORK Properties** dialog box appears. Click the **Permissions** tab.

12. Verify that permissions for **Sub-Folder NEWYORK** match the changed permissions for the parent public folder.

13. Click **OK**.

14. Exit Outlook.

15. Log off Windows NT.

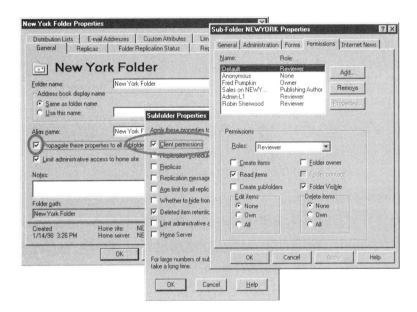

Review

Every user must be validated before gaining access to public folders. The system grants access only to users who have the appropriate permissions. To set permissions, select the desired folder and display its properties. Then specify individually or through user groups who can create, read, modify or delete items in the folder. You can also add and remove users from the access list or change permissions if you have **Owner** permissions.

If you create a top-level folder and assign permissions to it, all subfolders inherit these settings at the time of their creation. If the properties of a parent folder change, however, the new configuration settings are not propagated to the subfolders. Using the propagation feature of the Administrator program, you can specify that permission changes and other modifications affect all existing subfolders.

Lesson 4: Public Folder Strategies

The Administrator program icon is a globe circled by a red arrow combined with an envelope. This icon indicates what Exchange Server is designed for. An equally good Exchange Server icon could be made out of three golden Ps—for Planning, Planning, Planning. The better you plan the topology of your organization, including your public folder strategy, the easier administration will be. This lesson covers the major aspects of public folder strategies.

This lesson points out the various advantages and disadvantages of single and multiple public folder instances and discusses how to implement dedicated public servers.

At the end of this lesson, you will be able to:

- Describe the advantages and disadvantages of single public folder copies
- Describe the advantages and disadvantages of one or more replicas
- Create dedicated public folder servers

Estimated time to complete this lesson: 25 minutes

Single Copy of a Public Folder

Single copies of public folders may or may not be ideal for your purposes. They are, however, the default configuration. In other words, public folders are not replicated to other servers without administrative intervention.

Advantages of Single Public Folders

A single public folder consumes fewer resources because it uses disk space on one server only. Users connect to the central server using RPCs to work with the public folder. The single public folder model works best in small organizations that use only LAN connections.

The centralized location of the public folder simplifies administration. Basically, no intervention is required when users configure their folders using the Exchange Client or Outlook. Because there is no replication delay, changes to the public folder take effect immediately and public folder replication conflicts are impossible. Replication conflicts are covered in Chapter 13.

Disadvantages of Single Public Folders

A single public folder is not always suitable. It does not provide fault tolerance, for example. If the public server shuts down for any reason, the contents of its public folders become unavailable. To implement fault tolerance, you must create redundant public folder instances.

Furthermore, it is impossible to provide load balancing for a single public folder. All users of an organization access one server to open a particular public folder, so this server can become a very busy machine. (See Figure 12-11.)

Clients that want to connect to a remote public server communicate using RPCs. RPCs rely on the underlying network topology. In other words, users can access public folders only if LAN-like connections exist. If a WAN connection connects sites, access to single public folder instances in remote sites might be slow. An open request to a public folder can also fail when Windows NT security does not allow access to remote server resources. The remote server must be able to authenticate users connecting to remote public folder servers.

The features of the single public folder model are as follows:

- Public folder management is centralized in Exchange Server or Outlook
- Relies on the underlying network and Windows NT topology
- No additional disk space required
- No overhead or latency required in public folder replication
- Bottlenecks in public folder access can occur if public server is overloaded
- Public folder is not available during server maintenance

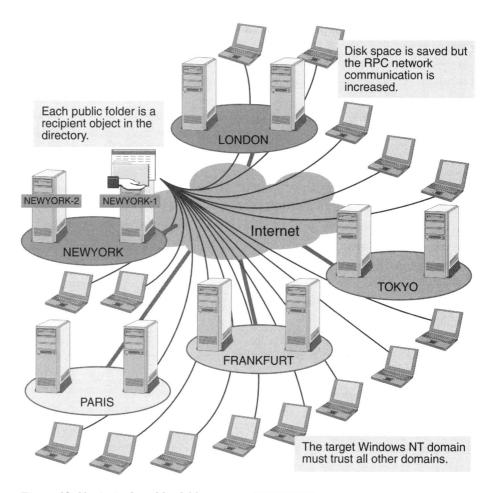

Figure 12-11. A single public folder copy in NEWYORK.

One or More Replicas of a Public Folder

Public folders are easy to clone. You can have the same public folder on any of your Exchange Server computers, even though this is not desirable because it would consume a lot of disk space. Public folder replication ensures that the content of all instances of the same public folder is up to date. This mechanism is covered in more detail in Chapter 13.

Advantages of One or More Replicas

Mission-critical information should not be maintained on only one server in one place. You should clone the information and place it on a second server. If one of the servers becomes unavailable, you can still access the contents. In other words, multiple instances of one public folder provide fault tolerance.

Even if both servers are available, multiple instances provide load balancing because users can work with both replicas at the same time. It also lets you address network topology dependencies. If RPC communication is not supported or if Windows NT security dependencies prevent direct access, you can create a second replica in an accessible location. (See Figure 12-12.)

To reduce traffic on WAN links, you can replicate at least one instance of each public folder to the remote side, even if a LAN-like protocol is in use. This means that users don't have to rely on the WAN connection for public folder access. Instead of having multiple users accessing the same information, the information is transferred once using public folder replication messages. You can also schedule public folder replication and configure other messaging parameters using messaging connectors.

Disadvantages of One or More Replicas

Nothing is completely black and white. That includes multiple public folder replicas. On the one hand, they can reduce network traffic on WAN connections. On the other hand, they can generate unnecessary network traffic if too many instances exist.

E-mail–based public folder replication also causes replication delays. As changes occur in one replica, they are not immediately propagated to all other locations. This can lead to a replication conflict—that is, one public folder might be modified in two locations at the same time, resulting in two different most recent items. Public folder replication conflicts are covered in Chapter 13.

The features of the multiple public folder model are as follows:

- Can provide load balancing
- Changes made to the contents of one public folder instance are not propagated immediately to all other replicas
- Can control network bandwidth use using messaging connector parameters and replication schedules
- Replication can generate messaging and network overhead

- Provides fault tolerance; when one public folder server is down for maintenance, clients can still access the content on another server
- Public folder replication conflicts are possible
- Redundant information requires additional disk space

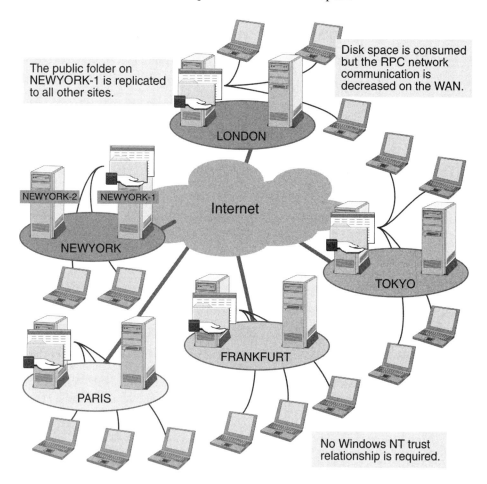

The public folder on NEWYORK-1 is replicated to all other sites.

Disk space is consumed but the RPC network communication is decreased on the WAN.

No Windows NT trust relationship is required.

Figure 12-12. Multiple copies of a public folder.

Dedicating a Public or Private Folder Server

If you plan to connect to USENET through NNTP to download newsgroups, the amount of information you receive might be enormous. If you implement numerous public folders in your organization anyway, you should be aware that extensive public folder access can slow down the server for mailbox access. Specific fault-tolerant implementations and load balancing can improve reliability and server response times significantly.

Dedicated Public Server

A dedicated public server contains only a Public Information Store. The Private Information Store has been removed. This means that a dedicated public server cannot maintain mailboxes. It only serves incoming open requests for public folder contents and provides information about the public folder hierarchy.

Dedicated Private Server

A dedicated private server is the counterpart of a dedicated public server. It does not contain a Public Information Store. This store has been deleted; only the private store remains. Therefore, a private server can maintain mailboxes, but neither the public folder hierarchy nor the content can be kept on a dedicated private server.

Advantages of Dedicated Servers

The separation of server tasks allows you to design hardware resources explicitly and therefore more precisely. All users in the organization can potentially access a public server. The hardware should be optimized for fast network Input/Output, and the layout of the server's hard disk system should be transaction oriented (a RAID array).

A dedicated private server does not typically maintain the mailboxes of all users in the organization. Mailboxes can be distributed across numerous servers and users will connect only to their home server to work with their mailboxes. For this reason, you do not have to optimize the server's hardware in the same way that you do for a dedicated public server. Less powerful machines might be sufficient, provided that you keep the number of mailboxes per private server at a reasonable level.

Because a dedicated public server can take over responsibility of all existing public folders of a site, the response time of remaining private servers will increase with a reduced load. The servers can then focus on mailbox maintenance, and users can benefit from the structured topology of the site.

Additional Advice on Configuring a Dedicated Server

Before you can create a dedicated public server, you must remove the Private Information Store. Likewise, when you create a dedicated private server, you must remove the Public Information Store. You must also be careful in either case to avoid deleting any mailboxes or public folders unintentionally. Before you delete one of these important parts of the IS, you should ensure that they no longer hold data. In other words, you should move either the mailboxes or the local public folder instances to another server within the site prior to the deletion.

Let's say that Jacques wants to configure PARIS-2 as a dedicated public server and PARIS-1 as a dedicated private server. He must move all existing mailboxes from PARIS-2 to PARIS-1 and all public folders from PARIS-1 to PARIS-2. He can do this using the **Move Mailbox** command on the Administrator program's **Tools** menu and the **Replicas** property page of each relevant public folder object. Then he must specify PARIS-2 as the **Public Folder Server** using the **General** property page of the **Private Information Store** object on PARIS-1 (the private server). From here, top-level public folders can be created only on PARIS-2. At this point, he can delete both the Private Information Store on PARIS-2 and the Public Information Store on PARIS-1. He can simply select the desired objects at the server level within the Administrator program and click the **Delete** command on the **Edit** menu. Once the objects are removed, the dedicated public server configuration is complete.

All clients will contact PARIS-2 to display the public folder hierarchy and content. Theoretically, if all Public Information Store instances within a site are deleted, no public folder can be seen because the hierarchy is gone. But Exchange Server guarantees that at least one Public Information Store still exists somewhere in the site. (See Figure 12-13.)

To create public servers:

1. Move all the public folders to the public servers.

2. Configure a Private Information Store on each private server. The **Public Folder Server** attribute must point to the dedicated public server to ensure that future top-level public folders are created on the new public servers.

3. Remove the Private Information Store from the public servers by deleting the **Private Information Store** object from the **Servers** container within the Administrator program.

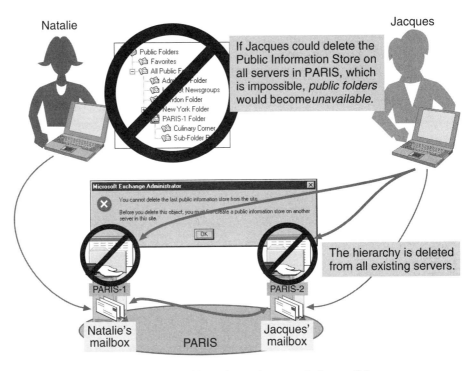

Figure 12-13. A site without a public information store is impossible.

Review

1. What is a public server?

   _____

2. What is a dedicated public server?

   _____

   _____

3. Which communication method is used to access the public folder content of a public server?

   _____

   _____

4. You have configured a dedicated public server in your site. All public folders are placed there, but you did not create any other special server configuration. A user working with Outlook creates a new top-level folder. Where will the new public folder be stored?

---

5. You have configured a dedicated public server in your site. All public folders are placed there, but you did not create any other special server configuration. A user working with the Exchange Client creates a new subfolder. Where will it be stored?

---

6. You want to allow users to send e-mail messages conveniently to a particular public folder by selecting it from the Global Address List (GAL). What must you do to accomplish this?

---

7. Lisa complains that some users can't see her new public folder in their public folder trees, but users on the local server can in fact work with the new folder. What is most likely the cause of the problem?

---

8. You have configured a **Recipients** container for all public folders. However, older public folders remain in the **Recipients** container of your site. Can you move these public folder references to the new container?

---

9. Users of your site must work with a public folder called Sales Tracking. This folder is not kept in the local site, and you don't want to create a local replica of it. RPC communication works between your site and the site where the folder exists. What should you do in Exchange to allow your users access to the public folder content?

10. Clients access the content of a public folder through RPC. As the administrator of a large site, you want to focus this RPC communication within local network segments to offload bandwidth consumption from the backbone. How can you configure the site so that clients will try to locate a public folder's content on servers in their local segment first?

11. You want to ensure that items older than five days are deleted from all public folder replicas in your organization. How can you do this?

12. Can you use the Administrator program to create public folders? If not, which programs can you use?

13. You want to create a new public folder within Outlook. Which command should you choose?

14. You want to prevent a user from viewing the contents of a public folder. Which permissions should you revoke?

_____

15. Which predefined roles can you use to assign public folder permissions?

_____

_____

16. You have configured permissions on a public folder. You also want to include all subfolders. What must you do to change the permissions for all subfolders through the parent folder?

_____

_____

_____

_____

17. What are the disadvantages of single public folder instances within an organization?

_____

_____

_____

_____

18. What are the advantages of multiple replicas of a particular public folder?

_____

_____

_____

_____

19. What are the advantages of a dedicated public server configuration?

_____

_____

_____

C H A P T E R   1 3

Public Folder Replication

This chapter covers the various aspects of different public folder replication scenarios. The public folder hierarchy is always replicated to all public servers in an organization, but the contents is of the folder is not.

Overview

Public folders are the bedrock of distributed Exchange Server conferencing systems, discussion forums, and other workgroup applications. If you compare Figure 12-11 and Figure 12-12 of Chapter 12, you'll find that distributed conferencing systems can optimize communication over a messaging network. Instead of having all users access a single instance "somewhere," you can provide a public folder replica locally for faster and more reliable client access. Public folder replication enables synchronization of the contents of all existing replicas across your organization.

Lesson 1 of this chapter introduces several aspects of public folder replication, showing you its advantages, granularity, and configuration. As you will notice, no user interface is provided to adjust hierarchy replication parameters, but you can read about adjusting the parameters by using the Microsoft Windows NT Registry Editor. The various methods of collecting and delivering public folder instances from and to other public servers are also discussed here.

Lesson 2 explains the actual folder replication process, including discussions of the replication model, the transport mechanism, and the purpose of the Public Folder Replication Agent (PFRA). You can read about the mechanism to keep track of the replication, the propagation of new messages, and the deletion of needless items from all public folders across the organization. This lesson also illustrates the distribution of content modifications and the backfill process. You will also learn about public folder rehoming as well as how to resolve replication conflicts.

Two practical exercises guide you through the various steps for configuring and testing public folder replication and for resolving public folder replication conflicts.

In the following lessons, you will be introduced to:

- The configuration of public folder content replication at the folder level and at the IS level
- The public folder replication process

Lesson 1: Introduction to Public Folder Replication

It is amazing that users can simply place new discussion items in a public folder on a particular server and all of a sudden the information also appears on several other servers in an organization. Public folder replication is the process that makes this remarkable effect possible.

This lesson explains the public folder replication process, beginning with a discussion about replication advantages and emphasizing public folder content replication. You are also introduced to the management of the public folder hierarchy replication and the configuration of the replication process per public folder and per IS.

One practical exercise demonstrates how to configure and test public folder replication by using the Administrator program and Outlook.

At the end of this lesson, you will be able to:

- List the advantages of public folder replication
- Configure the hierarchy replication interval
- Decide when to configure replication per public folder
- Determine when to configure public folder replication through the IS

Estimated time to complete this lesson: 60 minutes

Advantages of Public Folder Replication

The public folder hierarchy has been separated from the public folder contents to distribute the information about the public folder existence to all servers across the organization even if they do not maintain a particular content replica.

Multi-Master Model

The public folder replication process follows the multi-master model. You can change the public folder hierarchy as well as the public folder contents from any location. Each particular replica of the public folder tree and each replica of the public folder contents are essentially a master copy. In fact, you can't distinguish a copy from the original. Public folder replication guarantees that changes made on one instance overwrite the earlier information in other instances to ensure the uniformity of the information.

Note The multi-master model allows you to distribute the workload of public servers because users can work on multiple servers, post new information to their local replica, and have the new information replicated to each other.

For example, Monsieur Jacques Blanc in Paris can configure a replica of a particular public folder on two servers: PARIS-1 and PARIS-2. Some users then work with the content on PARIS-1, while others access the public folder on PARIS-2. Neither PARIS-1 nor PARIS-2 must handle all the client communication. (See Figure 13-2 on page 851.)

In addition, if either PARIS-1 or PARIS-2 temporarily shuts down, the content is still available to all users. They can work directly with either server until the second server comes back again. In this way multiple replicas can increase the reliability of a public folder significantly.

Network Topology Independence

The replication of both the hierarchy and the contents are always performed using e-mail messages. Even within a single site, the IS of the local server does not contact any IS service running on other servers directly.

The e-mail transport provides several advantages because it is a transport media independent of the underlying network topology. So long as you are able to send a regular e-mail message to a destination server, you can create public folder replicas on that server. In other words, you can create a replica on any Exchange Server computer within your organization if you are able to send e-mail messages to each of them. The communication mechanism between sites is discussed in Chapter 9.

Bypassing RPC and Windows NT Limitations

Public folder replication allows you to avoid client connection dependencies by implementing local content replicas in network segments where RPC communication between the client and the server is supported and where Windows NT domain authentication is available. RPC and Windows NT security considerations are not a matter of controversy for public folder replication configurations because the replication transport media is the e-mail message.

As shown in Figure 13-1, Jacques wants to provide employees in TOKYO with access to a public folder called **Japanese Companies in France** that currently resides on the servers in Paris. But only a dial-up WAN connection over the Internet exists between PARIS and TOKYO, so Jacques decides to maintain a copy of the desired folder on the TOKYO-1 server. The content replication ensures that the instances in PARIS and in TOKYO are kept synchronized. Regular SMTP messages transport the updated information between both sites while users in TOKYO work with their local copy. This does not affect the work of users in PARIS in any way.

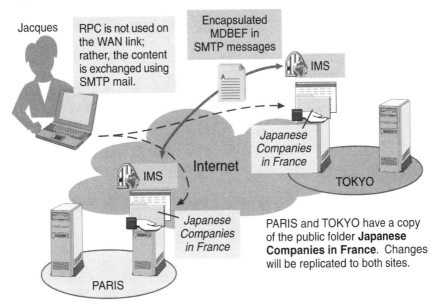

Figure 13-1. Public folder replication using SMTP messages.

The advantages of public folder replication are as follows:

- Distribution of processing load between public servers
- Improvement of response time for local users
- Reliability of information for users when their primary server is unavailable
- Reduction of RPC-based wide area network (WAN) traffic

Public Folder Contents Replication

Before you begin to create replicas, you should carefully plan the public folder replication topology. Too many replicas can increase network traffic unnecessarily, while too few copies affect the network bandwidth because users access the content elsewhere across your computer network.

Granularity of Replication

Granularity of replication refers to the smallest unit that public folder replication is able to transport, which is the e-mail message. As soon as a user modifies an object in one replica, the entire modification must be sent to all other replicas via e-mail. The new object replaces the older version everywhere, accurately updating all copies.

In other words, the IS handles changes at the document level. If a particular public folder contains only one big document, the whole document is replicated whenever a change occurs. If you look at Figure 13-2 you'll see that this fact can impact the Internet access points of PARIS and TOKYO. In this case, the replication mechanism is not very efficient and introduces negative side effects. Thus, public folders are most suitable if the number of items is large and the item size is small. If a public folder contains thousands of documents and you change one document, only this document is replicated.

Granularity of Configuration

Granularity of configuration also refers to the lowest level of public folder management, which occurs at the public folder level. Public folder configuration affects the entire content of the folder, but you cannot apply replication settings directly to single messages in the folder.

Replication Inheritance

When you configure the content replication for a public folder, existing subfolders are not affected. To affect all subfolders, select the **Propagate These Properties To All Subfolders** option on the public folder's **General** property page within the Administrator program. When you click **OK**, you can propagate the settings for top-level **Replicas**, **Replication Schedule**, **Replication Message Importance**, **Client Permissions**, **Age Limit On All Replicas**, **Whether To Hide From The Address Book**, **Deleted Item Retention Time**, **Limit Administrative Access To Home Site**, and **Home Server**.

Subfolders created in replicated public folders, however, inherit the existing replication configuration. But this doesn't mean you cannot configure them independently of their parent folder. If you want to place a top-level folder on PARIS-1 and its subfolders on PARIS-2, you can. The configuration of content replication per public folder within the Administrator program is covered later in this lesson in the section, "Public Folder Replication Configuration."

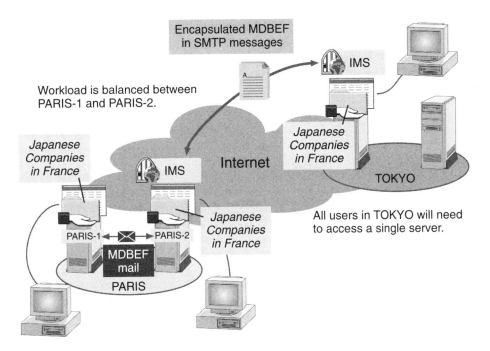

Encapsulated MDBEF
in SMTP messages

IMS

Workload is balanced between
PARIS-1 and PARIS-2.

Japanese
Companies
in France

Japanese
Companies
in France

IMS   Internet

TOKYO

Japanese
Companies
in France

PARIS-1 ◄──►⋈──► PARIS-2

MDBEF
mail

All users in TOKYO will need
to access a single server.

PARIS

Figure 13-2. Load balancing between and within sites.

The basic issues associated with public folder content replication are as
follows:

- Clients that cannot establish RPC connections to a particular public
  folder copy can have access to otherwise inaccessible information.

- Each item within a folder replica can be copied to all other servers
  maintaining a replica.

- Public folder replication can be scheduled.

- Public folder replication must be configured manually, yet new
  subfolders can inherit the settings of their parents.

Public Folder Hierarchy Replication

Each public server always replicates the hierarchy of public folders to all
other known servers. (See Figure 13-3.) Thus it is ensured that clients, such as
the Exchange Client or Outlook, display consistent information within their
folder panes (the public folder tree) no matter what server they connect to.

Modifying the Hierarchy Replication Interval

The Administrator program does not provide features for adjusting the hierarchy replication interval. You need to use the Windows NT Registry Editor to do this. You can modify the Replication Send Folder Tree value (in seconds) under:

```
HKEY_LOCAL_MACHINE
    \SYSTEM
        \CurrentControlSet
            \Services
                \MSExchangeIS
                    \ParametersPublic
```

By default, changes applied to the public folder hierarchy are replicated to all other servers within 60 seconds. Most likely this interval setting is sufficient; however, you can increase the replication interval. This would allow the Public Information Store to collect more changes before it generates a particular replication message.

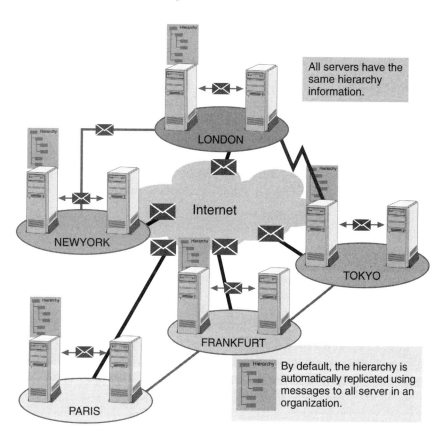

Figure 13-3. Public folder hierarchy replication.

The primary features of public folder hierarchy replication are as follows:

- Ability to set a replication interval using the Windows NT Registry Editor
- Inability to schedule replication intervals within the Administrator program
- Changes are replicated to all public folder servers in the organization
- Replication occurs automatically

Public Folder Replication Configuration

The configuration of the content replication can be accomplished individually through the property pages of each particular public folder object as displayed within the Administrator program. This approach allows you to push replicas of a particular public folder into specified servers in your site or in other sites across the organization.

Creating Replicas

Let's say that Jacques wants to create a replica of the Japanese Companies in the France public folder on TOKYO-1. (See Figure 13-4.) Using the Administrator program, he displays the properties of the **Japanese Companies In France** folder object and switches to the **Replicas** property page. At this point, he can specify TOKYO-1 as a server that needs to maintain a new replica. To do so, Jacques must select the site **TOKYO** within the **Site** box, and then he can add **TOKYO-1** to the list labeled **Replicate Folders To** by using the **Add** button.

Configuring the Replication Schedule

The public folder replication schedule allows replication messages to be generated during those times when most users are not working. Therefore, messaging connections can focus on interpersonal messages during the daytime, while they can transfer replication information at night.

You can configure the replication schedule at two levels: the **Public Information Store** and the public folder object itself. Both object types provide the **Replication Schedule** property page. Typically you want to set a common schedule for all public folder replicas at the server level through the **Public Information Store** object. However, if you have special needs, you can override the settings for each individual public folder.

By default, content replication is set as **Use Information Store Schedule**, which means that modifications on replicas are replicated to other servers based on the schedule set on the IS **Replication Schedule** property page.

You can change the replication interval explicitly for a public folder if you select the **Selected Times** option **Always** or if you select **Never** to disable the replication. The **Selected Times** option allows you to set explicit times when you want the folder to be replicated. **Always** runs replication every 15 minutes. If you don't want a delay of 15 minutes, you can change the **Always** replication interval through the **Advanced** property page of the **Public Information Store** object.

Checking the Replication Status

Just as you can create a replication schedule for all public folders or for an individual public folder, you can also examine the replication status of all replicas or an individual replica. To check the status of all replicas that your server maintains, use the **Folder Replication Status** object under the **Public Information Store** container. This container also provides the same information on its **Folder Replication Status** property page. You can use the **Folder Replication Status** property page of each public folder object if you are interested only in a particular replica's state. All servers that maintain a replica are listed on this page.

The **Status** category provides the most relevant information because it displays the state of the public folder replication. The **In Sync** status indicates that the local replica has not been modified since changes were last sent. If a user has modified the contents of a replica and the changes have not yet been sent to the other servers, the **Local Modified** category is displayed. All servers are placed in the **In Sync** category again as soon as the next replication cycle is complete.

Another interesting category is **Last Received Time**, which provides information about the most recently received updates from a selected server. The **Average Transmission Time** category gives you a hint about the average time that it takes to send updates to a selected server, and **Last Transmission Time (Sec)** indicates when the last transmission to a selected server has occurred.

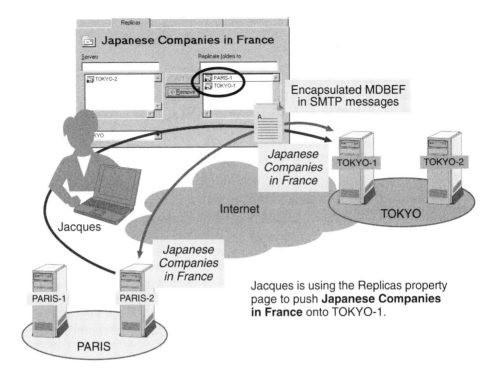

Figure 13-4. Pushing a public folder into a server.

The public folder property pages within the Administrator program that are relevant to replication are as follows:

- **Folder Replication Status**; to display status information for a replicated public folder

- **Replicas**; to specify servers to contain replicas

- **Replication Schedule**; to set the times at which this public folder is to be replicated

IS Public Folder Replication Configuration

Instead of configuring the replication for each public folder individually, you have the option to configure the public folder replication commonly at the server level. This can be compared to a situation where you pull public folder instances from other servers into your server. Most important in this scenario are the **Instances** and **Advanced** property pages of the **Public Information Store** object.

Collecting Public Folder Instances

As shown in Figure 13-5, the French administrator Jacques Blanc decides to create a local copy of the folder called **New York Folder** on PARIS-2. He accomplishes this task by displaying the **Instances** property page of the **Public Information Store** object, selecting **New York Folder** from the list of available **Public Folders** in **NEWYORK**, and then clicking the **Add** button to move this folder to the **Folders On This Information Store** list. At this point, he can click **OK** to create the desired replica on PARIS-2, if administrative access to this folder has not been limited to the local site NEWYORK only.

Restricting Replica Requests

Pulling replicas into a server introduces a critical aspect because it potentially allows an administrator of any site to create an instance of any public folder on his or her servers. This is not always desirable—or do you allow every neighbor to pick flowers from your front yard? Therefore, administrative access to public folders is restricted to the local site by default. If you do want to allow every administrator in your organization this freedom of choice, clear the **Limit Administrative Access To The Home Site** check box on the **General** property page for each public folder. A server-level default setting for this purpose does not exist.

Determining Replication Message Sizes

For illustrative purposes, let's assume that the MTA on NEWYORK-1 has been assigned a maximum message size of 200 KB. Further, imagine that the public **New York Folder** contains an item that is 500 KB. A problem occurs if the 500 KB item is placed in a 500 KB replication message because the MTA on NEWYORK-2 cannot accept such a large message. Consequently, the IS running on NEWYORK-1 must segment the 500 KB item into several small messages and none of them can be larger than 200 KB. Fortunately Fred Pumpkin can determine the maximum message size of replication messages using the **Advanced** property page of the **Public Information Store** object. The IS then fills a message up to the specified limit before it creates another one. The default message size limit is 300 KB.

Not only can the IS segment large objects into multiple replication messages, it can also combine multiple small items into a larger message. For instance, if you modify two 100 KB items in a public folder, both items can be placed into one single replication message (assuming the default size limit is larger than 200 KB). This single message then can be transferred to other servers maintaining a replica of the same public folder. In other words, messaging overhead can be reduced.

Note It is not advisable to reduce the message size limit as long as LAN-like connections exist. However, if you are transferring messages over dial-up connections, reduced message sizes may optimize communication.

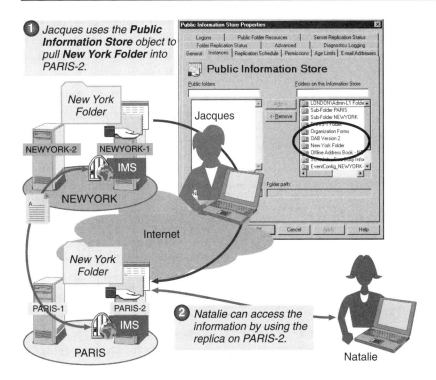

Figure 13-5. Pulling a public folder into a server.

The **Public Information Store** property pages related to public folder replication are as follows:

- **Advanced**; to set the **Replicate Always** interval and the maximum size of replication messages

- **Folder Replication Status**; to display status about the public folders being replicated

- **Instances**; to pull replicas of a specified public folder

- **Public Folder Resources**; to quickly view the amount of space being used by various public folders

- **Replication Schedule**; to set the replication schedule

- **Server Replication Status**; to display replication information for all the relevant servers in the organization

Exercise 44: Configuring and Testing Public Folder Replication

Public folders consist of two parts: the hierarchy and the contents. The hierarchy is always replicated to all servers in an organization, but the contents are not. To replicate the contents of a public folder to another server, you must configure replicas at the Public Information Store level or at the public folder level. Both have their advantages, depending on whether you are pushing or pulling a new replica into a server.

Estimated time to complete this exercise: 45 minutes

Description

In this exercise, you will configure an existing public folder (created in Exercise 40 in Chapter 12) for public folder replication between NEWYORK and LONDON. Public folder replication is possible because the directory replication has been enabled between both sites in Exercise 35 in Chapter 10.

To test the replication, log on as a regular user and send or post messages to the replica of a public folder. New items will appear in all other replicas, too, once the next replication is complete. By default, a replication cycle happens every 15 minutes, so it may take a little while before you can verify the public folder replication.

- Task 44a describes the steps for configuring automatic deletion from a public folder of all messages that are more than 60 days old.

- Task 44b describes the steps for configuring public folder replication of a particular folder within your organization.

- Task 44c describes the steps for testing public folder replication by sending a message to a public folder and then viewing the message in the replica of the public folder.

Prerequisites

- Make sure you have configured two sites (NEWYORK and LONDON) that are connected through the IMS and that you have configured directory replication configured between these two sites.

- Make sure that public folders exist in both sites.

Task 44a: Configuring General Public Folder Options

1. To log on, press **CTRL+ALT+DEL**.

2. In the **User Name** box, type *Admin-L1*.

3. In the **Password** box, type *password* and then click **OK**.

4. Click the **Start** button, point to **Programs**, point to **Microsoft Exchange**, click **Microsoft Exchange Administrator**, and then connect to the server LONDON-1.

5. Expand the **Folders** container that can be found under **Address Book Views**.

6. Expand **Public Folders** and then select the **Admin-L1** folder.

7. On the **File** menu, click **Properties**. The **Admin-L1 Folder Properties** dialog box appears.

8. Click the **Limits** tab.

9. Under **Information Store Storage Limits** verify that **Use Information Store Defaults** is not selected.

10. In the **Age Limit For Replicas (Days)** box, type *60*. This configures the number of days beyond which messages in all replicas of this public folder expire and are automatically deleted.

11. Click the **Replication Schedule** tab. Verify that **Use Information Store Schedule** is selected.

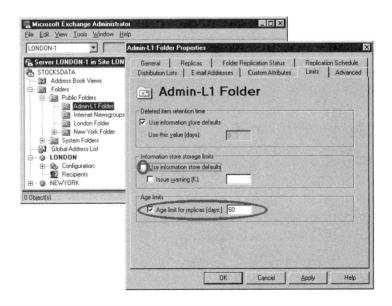

Task 44b: Configuring the Replicas Folder Options

1. Click the **Replicas** tab.

2. In the **Site** list, select **NEWYORK**.

3. In the **Servers box**, click **NEWYORK-1**.

4. Click **Add** and then click **OK**.

5. Expand the **Configuration** container for the site **LONDON**, expand the **Servers** container, and then click **LONDON-1**.

6. In the right pane click **Public Information Store**.

7. On the **File** menu, click **Properties** to display the **Public Information Store Properties** dialog box.

8. Click the **Advanced tab**.

9. In the **Replicate Always Interval** box, type *1*. This will cause public folder replication to occur every minute.

10. Click **OK**.

11. On the **File** menu, click **Exit**.

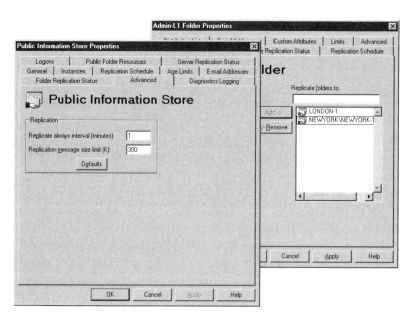

Task 44c: Testing Public Folder Replication

1. On LONDON-1, double-click the **Microsoft Outlook** shortcut on the Desktop.

2. On the toolbar, click **New Mail Message**.

3. Click **To**. The **Select Names** dialog box appears.

4. Select **Admin-L1 Folder**.

5. Click **To**.

6. Click **OK**.

7. In the **Subject** box, type *Testing public folder replication.*

8. In the message text area type, *Public folder replication can only be tested if multiple replicas exist.* Format the message text as desired.

9. Click **Send** and then wait two minutes to allow for replication to occur before proceeding.

10. Open the public folder **Admin-L1** on both LONDON-1 and NEWYORK-1.

11. Notice the message with the subject **Testing Public Folder Replication**. It appears in both replicas.

12. Close **Outlook**.

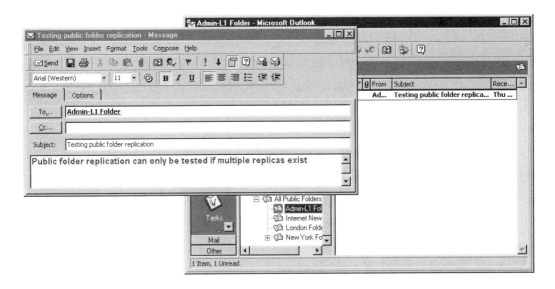

Review

Using the Administrator program, you can configure public folder replication at the Public Information Store level and at the public folder level. To pull messages to your server, use the **Instances** property page of the **Public Information Store** object. Each public folder object allows you to push replicas into remote servers by using the **Replicas** property page.

Lesson 2: Public Folder Replication Process

Whoever sees a wizard performing his art is eager to know the secrets of the magic, but seldom are the secrets revealed. The IS lets items "magically" appear or disappear in public folders because public folder replication is usually a hidden process. All you need to know is that public folder replication uses e-mail messages to transfer information between servers that maintain replicas. Nevertheless, let's take a look behind the scenes to see how the magic works.

This lesson explains the public folder replication process in depth. You'll learn about the PFRA and its methods for monitoring replication changes. Once the replication of modifications is covered, you'll read about the replication and deletion of newly created items. The following section illustrates the backfill process as it is used to resynchronize "out-of-sync" folders. Discussion about public folder replication conflicts, reasons for the conflicts, and their resolution completes this lesson. A practical exercise then follows.

At the end of this lesson, you will be able to:

- Describe the public folder replication process
- Identify the IS components involved in the replication procedure
- Explain the purpose and mechanism of public folder backfilling
- Add and delete public folder replicas
- Determine causes of and solutions for replication conflicts

Estimated time to complete this lesson: 45 minutes

Introduction to the Replication Process

Public folder replication is an information distribution mechanism that allows you to provide copies of public folders for local access and synchronize them between all those servers that maintain a replica. You are forced to implement multiple replicas in networks where direct access to a single copy is not always guaranteed.

Public Folder Replication Transport Mechanism

As mentioned many times, public folder content changes are replicated using e-mail messages. But the replication information must be secured because foreign messaging systems such as SMTP-based hosts on the Internet might be involved in the message transfer. (See Figure 13-6.) The slightest information alteration can cause the replication to malfunction.

IS Responsibilities

The IS is not responsible for ensuring integrity during message transfer. Its task is to maintain a server list per replica that is used to address replication messages to the required remote IS services. The initiating IS must generate replication messages, address them properly, and send them—that's all.

By addressing more than one remote IS within a single replication message, the use of WAN connections and any other e-mail paths is optimized. Similar to an interpersonal message sent to multiple users, the MTA transfers only one message across messaging links. The MTA splits replication messages into multiple instances at the very last point when separate paths must be used.

Message Encapsulation

E-mail–based transport allows you to implement public folder replication independently of the actual network topology. LAN and WAN connections can be used to transfer information to the destination. It is the responsibility of the MTA and the messaging connectors involved to guarantee message integrity until the message reaches its destination (the target IS). A binary attachment in MDBEF provides the required protection mechanism even in cases where the message must travel through foreign systems.

As shown in Figure 13-6, public folder replication messages must be sent over the Internet between NEWYORK and PARIS. At the entry point in PARIS, the IMS obtains MDBEF objects from outbound messages. An MDBEF item contains the original message as a binary file. This binary file encapsulates the message properties and is placed as an ordinary attachment into the SMTP message. At a later time, an IMS in NEWYORK receives the SMTP replication message, extracts the MDBEF attachment, and rebuilds the original message as it was initially sent. Modifications that have been applied to the SMTP message during its way across the Internet are meaningless and cannot cause replication problems.

Public Folder Replication Agent

The PFRA is an internal IS component that handles the generation and evaluation of public folder replication messages. This internal component monitors changes in content and creates replication messages according to the replication interval settings. It is responsible for the integrity of the public folder replication itself, but not for the integrity of public folder replication messages as they are transferred through the messaging network.

Let's say Natalie edits and saves an item in a public folder that is replicated in NEWYORK. (See Figure 13-6.) The PFRA on PARIS-2 monitors this folder and notices that a change has occurred. Consequently, the public folder status switches to **Local Modified**. Honoring the replication schedule, a replication message, which contains the modified item, is generated. The PFRA addresses the e-mail message to all ISs that maintain a replica of the New York Folder (for example, NEWYORK-1), and the message is then sent to its destination through the MTA and the IMS. The PFRA on NEWYORK-1 receives the replication message, checks whether the modified item is more recent than its own, and replaces the older copy. Thus, the replicas in PARIS and NEWYORK are synchronized again. PFRA monitoring is covered in more detail in the section, "Monitoring Message State Information," later in this lesson.

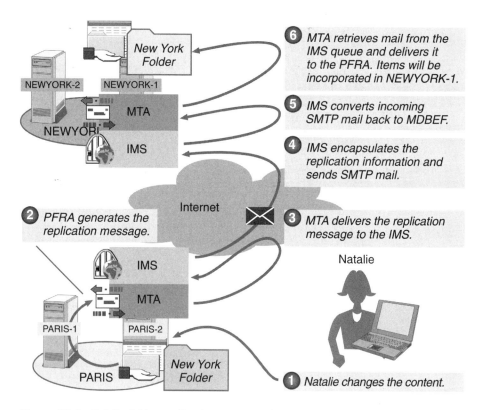

Figure 13-6. Public folder replication across a foreign system.

The responsibilities of the PFRA are as follows:

- Addresses replication messages as determined by the public folder replication configuration
- Creates replication messages

- Monitors changes, additions, and deletions as they occur on replicas of public folders

- Receives replication messages and incorporates the changes into local replicas of public folders

Monitoring Message State Information

Message state information describes the collection of change numbers, time stamps, and predecessor change lists, which allows the PFRA to determine most recent items as they are replicated between public folder instances. For example, the PRFA on NEWYORK-1 must be able to detect that the message stored on NEWYORK-1 needs to be replaced with Natalie's item. (See Figure 13-6.) Every public folder item provides message state information.

Change Number

Change numbers identify public folder and content modifications. They are created using a globally unique information store identifier and a server-specific change counter. The globally unique identifier is a constant, which allows associating changes of an object with a particular IS. The server-specific change counter, in turn, identifies the most recent alteration. It increases whenever modifications are applied.

The server-specific change counter reflects the sequential changes of all objects within the Public Information Store. In other words, whenever users create new public folders, change the design of existing ones, modify the contents of a replica, or perform other Public Information Store–related actions, the server-specific change counter is increased by one. The increased value is then assigned to the modified object to mark it as the most recent.

Predecessor Change List

The predecessor change list permits the PFRA to detect folder replication conflicts. It maintains a list of all ISs that have ever made changes to an object and their server-specific change counters.

Public Folder Replication Conflicts

Public folder replication conflicts occur whenever multiple users modify the same object on two different locations at the same time. As long as the most recent changes have not been replicated to all other replicas, a chance for a replication conflict exists.

Let's say that Natalie works with the New York Folder content on PARIS-2, while Fred does the same using his local replica on NEWYORK-1. Both users work with the same message item x. According to Figure 13-7, item x contains an entry for NEWYORK-1 in its predecessor change list. For simplification, let's say the IS ID is 999 (note that a real ID has far more digits), and the server-specific change counter is 2000. Because item x has so far never changed in PARIS, an entry for PARIS-2 is not yet present.

When both Natalie and Fred save their changes at the same time, the predecessor change list is modified on both locations. The PRFA running on NEWYORK-1 replaces its own entry with the current server-specific change counter—let's say 3000. The predecessor change list of item x on NEWYORK-1 is updated to 999-3000, while item x on PARIS-2 still maintains only the entry 999-2000 because the replication has not yet occurred. A new entry for PARIS-2 is inserted into the predecessor change list—let's say 555-88888.

At this moment, two different copies of one particular message object exist and both are the most recent copy. The most recent server-specific change number of NEWYORK-1 cannot be found in the predecessor change list of item x on PARIS-2. Conversely, the server-specific change number of PARIS-2 is not present in the predecessor change list of item x on NEWYORK-1. This is an indicator that a public folder replication conflict has been created. Public folder replication conflicts and their resolution are covered later in this lesson in the section, "Content Modification and Conflict Resolution."

Time Stamp

The time stamp provides information about when a particular item was last modified. It is used in conjunction with the change number to determine the when an object was replicated most recently. Time stamps never decrease but always increase. In other words, if you modify a message within a public folder and the time stamp of the item is more recent than your computer time, the more recent time stamp is kept, meaning that the time stamp will not be changed. A decrease of the time stamp would be dangerous since it could lead to old information overwriting new changes.

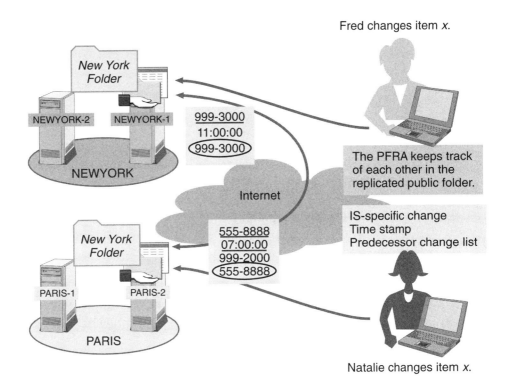

Fred changes item *x*.

New York Folder

NEWYORK-2   NEWYORK-1

NEWYORK

999-3000
11:00:00
999-3000

Internet

The PFRA keeps track of each other in the replicated public folder.

IS-specific change
Time stamp
Predecessor change list

New York Folder

PARIS-1   PARIS-2

PARIS

555-8888
07:00:00
999-2000
555-8888

Natalie changes item *x*.

Figure 13-7.   Monitoring replicated changes.

The components of message state information and their functions are as follows:

- Change numbers; to reflect the sequential modifications for all items of an IS

- Predecessor change list; to allow the detection of replication conflicts

- Time stamp; to identify the most recent changes

Replicating Created and Deleted Messages

Whenever you create a new item in a particular public folder replica, this object must be created in all other existing replicas. Likewise, whenever you delete an object from a public folder, this object must disappear in all other locations. (See Figure 13-8.)

Message Creations

New items receive the current change number, time stamp, and predecessor change list at the time of their creation. The PFRA handles the new object just like any other existing item, wrapping the new object in a replication message and sending it to all other existing instances. The new object appears in all public folder replicas as soon as the replication cycle has been completed.

Message Deletions

Unlike the replication of new or modified items, the replication of message deletions is performed by using IS notification messages. The object to be deleted is indicated through its global unique MAPI identifier. Every IS that receives the notification message independently deletes the object from its public folder replica as well.

Message Expirations

Message expiration refers to the automatic deletion of public folder items through defined age limits. In this case, IS notification messages aren't generated or sent to any other replica. This permits the implementation of a different age limit for every public folder instance. In other words, each IS is responsible for managing its own message expirations. (See Figure 13-8.) The configuration of age limits is covered in Chapter 12.

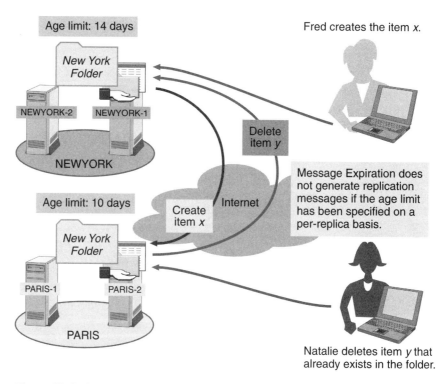

Age limit: 14 days

Fred creates the item *x*.

New York Folder

NEWYORK-2   NEWYORK-1

NEWYORK

Delete item *y*

Age limit: 10 days

Internet

Create item *x*

New York Folder

PARIS-1   PARIS-2

PARIS

Message Expiration does not generate replication messages if the age limit has been specified on a per-replica basis.

Natalie deletes item *y* that already exists in the folder.

Figure 13-8. Item creation, deletion, and expiration.

The various mechanisms that create and delete items in replicated public folders are defined as follows:

- Item creation; a new item is created automatically because of public folder replication in all replicas

- Item deletion; an item is deleted automatically because of public folder replication in all replicas

- Item expiration; a replication message is not sent and every IS maintains its own expiration settings

Replicating Message Modifications

Public folder replication allows you to create a public folder replica for each server that exists in your organization. All replicas exchange their modifications directly with each other. It is therefore possible that a particular replica receives old replication information, and in this case, existing items are not replaced.

Initiating Public Folder Replication

Whenever a user modifies an item in a replicated public folder, a new change number is added to the modified item, its time stamp is updated, the predecessor change list is refreshed, and, finally, public folder replication is initiated.

The PFRA places the message state information (change number, time stamp, and predecessor change list) together with the modified item itself in a replication message. The message is addressed to all servers, which are specified through the **Replicate Folder To** list on the public folder's **Replicas** property page, and, soon afterward, taken over to the MTA for delivery.

Completing Public Folder Replication

As soon as the MTA delivers a message to the destination IS, the replication information (the message state information and the modified item) is extracted to finish the replication cycle. But the PFRA must not simply take the received item as the most recent object. Instead, it must double check the affected items by using the message state information that has been received. An item is replaced only if the change number of the local instance is included in the predecessor change list of the update message. In other words, the most recent changes of the local item are "old stuff" for the update message. (See Figure 13-9.)

In the reverse order, the local item must not be replaced if its change number cannot be found in the update message's predecessor change list. In this case, it's possible that either the local item is more recent than the update message or that a replication conflict has occurred. If the update message's current change number is present in the local item's predecessor change list, the local item is more recent and is not replaced. On the other hand, if the local item's current change number cannot be found in the update message's predecessor change list, a replication conflict has been detected. Replication conflicts are covered later in this lesson in the section, "Content Modification and Conflict Resolution."

For example, Jacques modifies an item in **Japanese Companies In France** on PARIS-2. (See Figure 13-9.) The message receives a new change number (for example, 555-99999) and is replicated to TOKYO-1. The PRFA on TOKYO-1 compares the update message with the local message, checking the predecessor change list of the updated message to find the local message's current change number. Because the current change number is included in this list, it is guaranteed that the new modification was made against a replica of the local item or any later version. Hence, the PFRA on TOKYO-1 replaces the local item with the object of the updated message.

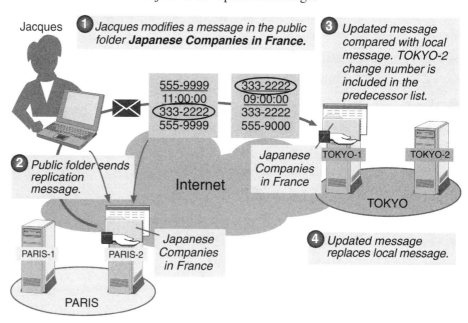

Figure 13-9. Message modification replication.

The process of message modification replication is as follows:

1. A message is modified in a replicated public folder.

2. The originating PFRA assigns a new change number to the object and updates the predecessor list and time stamp.

3. The modified item plus its message state information are sent in the form of an e-mail message to all other public folder replicas.

4. The receiving PFRA compares the update with the local message by using message state information.

5. Depending on the result of the PFRA check, the local item is replaced, the update message is ignored, or a replication conflict is detected.

Out-of-Sync Public Folders and Backfill

As you'll read in Chapter 15, "Maintaining Servers," it's possible to delete public folder replication messages from the message queues of the MTA by using the MTA Check utility (command line **MTACheck /RP**). Even if you delete these messages, the public folder replication ensures that all public folder replicas are synchronized.

No Message Acknowledgment

It is important to note that delivery confirmations are not exchanged between PFRAs because the e-mail–based transport is not suitable for sequencing and data acknowledgments. Only an NDR generated by an MTA might be a hint that a replication message has been lost, but if you wiped out the MTA message queues using the **MTACheck /RP**, even that would not be the case. Consequently, the originating PFRA cannot determine whether a replication message has been received. In fact, as soon as the replication message has been sent, the local PRFA assumes that the replicas are synchronized. When a replication message is sent to its destination, the public folder status switches to **In Sync.** Therefore, a fair chance exists that the folders are not synchronized, although their status tells you differently.

Status Messages

Status messages allow the PFRAs to determine the real status of their replicas by comparing the message state information of the public folder instances themselves. Every public folder maintains a change number, time stamp, and predecessor change list, as do the items of its contents.

Even if the contents of a particular replica have not been changed, status notifications are generated frequently to announce its state to all other instances. The public folder's message state information is included in these messages, and the receiving PRFA extracts this information and checks whether the remote change number is present in its own predecessor list. If it is, the replicas are synchronized. If it is not, the remote PRFA must update its replica. In this case, it sends a *backfill request* back to the other PFRA to receive all the changes that have not yet been incorporated. Backfill responses do not differ from regular replication messages.

Status messages are exchanged periodically, at least once a day. But every replication message carries the status about the affected public folder as well.

Backfill

Backfilling is the process that allows the PFRA components to synchronize any public folder replicas that are out of sync. As shown in Figure 13-10, TOKYO-1 sends its status message on a regular basis to all servers that maintain replicas of the **New York Folder** public folder. The PFRA on NEWYORK-1 receives the status message, compares the message state information of both replicas, and determines that the current change number of the replica on TOKYO-1 is not included in its own predecessor change list. In other words, TOKYO-1 contains more modifications than NEWYORK-1. This is because the replication message from PARIS-2 to NEWYORK-1 has been lost, but the replication between PARIS-2 and TOKYO-1 has been successful. Consequently, NEWYORK-1 returns a backfill request to TOKYO-1, including the old server-specific change number for TOKYO-1. The PFRA on TOKYO-1 then sends all those changes that have a higher change number than indicated in the backfill request (including the modifications once made on PARIS-2) to NEWYORK-1. As soon as NEWYORK-1 receives these modifications, all replicas are synchronized again.

The following situations require a backfill request:

- A public server has been restored from a backup.
- A public server was down while changes occurred.
- A replication message has been lost.

Restoring from a Backup

The backfill process also is launched to recover a server that has been restored from a backup. Otherwise, modifications made since the last backup was prepared would be lost. As usual, the PFRA exchanges its status information and discovers the difference. The missing changes are requested by using the regular backfill process from any other existing replica. Once the backfill process is completed, all replicas are synchronized again. The various backup strategies are discussed in Chapter 15.

Accidental Deletion, Backfill, and a Workaround

Imagine that a user has accidentally deleted all items in a replicated public folder, so you decide to restore the server from a recent backup. The messages are outdated again, but not for long. The backfill process ensures that the public folder replica is brought up to date from the restored backup version. The most recent changes (in this case, the accidental message deletions) are replicated back into the restored Exchange Server and the items once again disappear.

To work around this problem, you can restore the backup to a test machine that is not physically connected to the computer network. Then you can log on using a temporary Exchange Client and download the messages from the public folder into a .PST. You will include this .PST file in your actual messaging profile to copy the items back into the actual replica. As you copy the items from your personal folder back into the actual public folder, you create new items that will be replicated to all existing instances across your organization.

More information about the Personal Folder Store and messaging profiles is provided in Chapter 6 and Chapter 7.

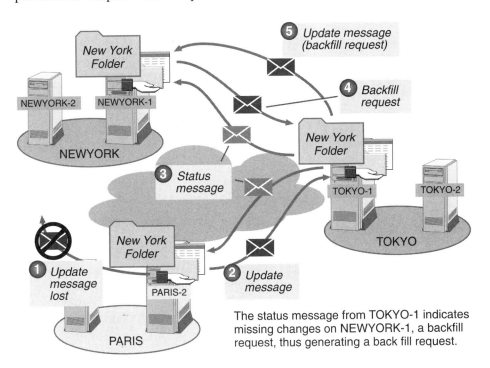

Figure 13-10. Backfilling out-of-sync public folders.

The phases of the backfill process are as follows:

1. The replication message from PARIS-2 to NEWYORK-1 has been deleted and the public folder replication did not take place. So, NEWYORK-1 still has the old change number for the public folder replica.

2. The replication message to TOKYO-1 has been sent successfully and public folder replication was successful. Both PARIS-2 and TOKYO-1 are up to date.

3. The PFRA on TOKYO-1 sends a status message to the PFRA on NEWYORK-1, including its new message state information.

4. NEWYORK-1 determines that the current change number of TOKYO-1 is higher than the number in its predecessor change list, so NEWYORK-1 must be out of date. NEWYORK-1 sends a backfill request to TOKYO-1.

5. TOKYO-1 receives the backfill request and sends the outstanding changes to NEWYORK-1.

6. All three Public Information Stores are synchronized.

Adding and Deleting Replicas

You can create new replicas either by using the **Replicas** property page of a particular public folder object or by using the **Instances** property page of the **Public Information Store** in the Administrator program. Whether you push or pull the new replica to an Exchange Server, you still create an empty replica that must be filled. Conversely, when you delete a particular public folder replica, you must ensure that all other servers stop sending update messages for this replica to your server.

Adding Replicas

The PFRA assigns the current change number, time stamp, and a fresh predecessor change list to each new object. It also does this for new public folder replicas. The change number of the new replica, however, does not yet exist on the predecessor change list of any other instance. Therefore, as soon as the first status message is sent to a remote server maintaining a replica of the same public folder, the new out-of-sync replica is detected. The backfill process is launched in order to bring the new instance to the current state. (See Figure 13-11.)

Deleting Replicas

You can eliminate public folder replicas by using the Administrator program. However, this doesn't mean that you delete the entire public folder from the organization. Only one instance is removed from one server's Public Information Store. Other replicas remain, but they must be informed about the deletion in order to stop sending replication messages to the non-existing instance.

The deletion of a replica eliminates its reference within the DS. Directory replication within the site and between sites distributes the configuration alteration to all other servers in the organization. Therefore, all servers within your organization receive the information about the replica removal. Other servers maintaining an instance of the same public folder stop sending their public folder replication messages to the affected server. The communication between Exchange Server components is covered in Chapter 4.

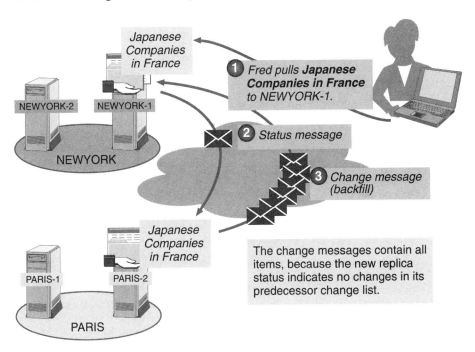

Figure 13-11. Adding a public folder replica.

The steps for adding a replica are as follows:

1. Using the Administrator program, you can create a new replica through the **Public Information Store** or through the public folder object property pages.

2. Backfilling ensures that all replicas are synchronized.

3. The items appear in the new public folder instance.

The steps for deleting a replica are as follows:

1. Using the Administrator program, you can delete a replica through the **Public Information Store** or through the public folder object property pages.

2. The replica is deleted from the Public Information Store.

3. The reference to the replica is removed from the DS.

4. Directory configuration changes are replicated to all other servers.

5. Remote servers stop sending public folder replication messages.

Content Modification and Conflict Resolution

The PFRA replaces older objects with more recent items, replicating modifications between multiple instances of the same folder. But which item does the PFRA replace in a case where two objects are equally the most recent instance? (See Figure 13-12.)

Conflicting Items

As mentioned in the section, "Monitoring Message State Information," earlier in this chapter, a replication conflict is detected if the change number of the local item cannot be found in the predecessor list of the update message. In other words, the incoming update message does not include the current state of the local item. In this case, the IS cannot decide which message to take and which to overwrite.

Recovery

The PFRA is responsible for resolving replication conflicts; but, in this example, it doesn't know which information message to prefer. Therefore, manual intervention is necessary. A *conflict message*, including the conflicting items as attachments, is generated and sent to the users that created the conflict and the public folder owners. This conflict message is also posted into the public folder and replicated to all other instances. You can open this message, analyze the message attachments, and decide which item to keep to resolve the conflict.

As a public folder contact, you can decide whether to keep the local item, the update, or both items. If you accept the local item, the update object is deleted from all public folder instances. On the other hand, if you decide to keep the update message, the local message is replaced. If you decide to keep both items, two messages appear in the public folder because each message represents one item.

Conflicting Design Changes

A replication conflict can also occur when multiple public folder owners have changed the design of a particular public folder in two different instances at the same time. When this occurs, the public folder owners are notified about the design conflict, but no conflict message is posted into the public folder.

The conflict message is only a notification that the last design change has been saved. It overwrites all previous changes automatically. For this reason, it's a good idea to double check which configuration is in effect and to readjust the design.

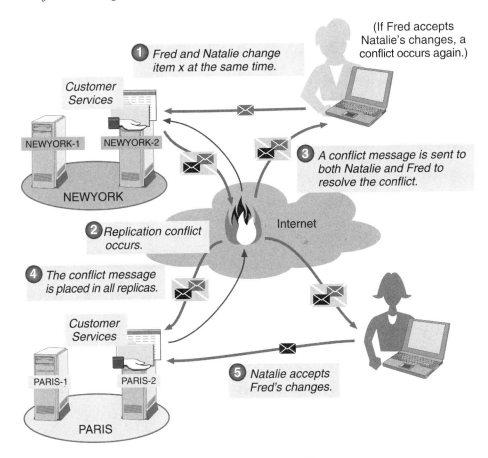

Figure 13-12. Resolving public folder replication conflicts.

The steps involved in creating replication conflicts are as follows:

1. Two replicas of a public folder exist on different servers.
2. Both replicas are synchronized.
3. Two users open the different public folder replicas.
4. Both users modify the same object.
5. Both users save their changes at the same time.

The choices for resolving a replication conflict are as follows:

- Accept both messages; a second object is created for the update message and two similar messages exist in the public folder
- Accept the local message; the update message is ignored and deleted from all other replicas
- Accept the updates; the local message is replaced

Exercise 45: Testing Public Folder Conflict Resolution

If two replicated items exist that do not contain each other's changes, a replication conflict has been created because both represent in someways a most recent item. Content replication conflicts must be resolved manually because the IS cannot decide which modification to accept.

Estimated time to complete this exercise: 25 minutes

Description

In this exercise, you will modify the same item in two different replicas, such as the replicated public folders of Exercise 44, at the same time. Then you will resolve the replication conflict by means of the conflict message.

- Task 45 describes the steps for demonstrating public folder conflict resolution.

Prerequisites

- Completion of Exercise 44

Task 45: Testing Public Folder Conflict Resolution

1. Log on to LONDON-1 as Admin-L1 and as Admin-NY1 on NEWYORK-1.
2. On LONDON-1, start the **Microsoft Exchange Administrator** program and ensure that you are connected to LONDON-1.

3. Select the **Admin-L1 Folder** under the **Recipients** container.

4. On the **File** menu, click **Properties**.

5. Click the **Client Permissions** button.

6. Click **Add** and then select **Fred Pumpkin**.

7. Click **Add** and then click **OK**.

8. In the **Name** field of the **Client Permissions** dialog box, select **Fred Pumpkin**, and then select **Owner** under **Role**.

9. Click **OK** twice and then close the **Microsoft Exchange Administrator** program.

10. Start **Microsoft Outlook** on LONDON-1 and NEWYORK-1. Ensure that you connect to the mailbox **Admin-L1** on LONDON-1 and to the mailbox **Fred Pumpkin** on NEWYORK-1.

11. In both clients simultaneously, expand **Public Folders**, expand **All Public Folders** in the left pane, and then click the folder **Admin-L1 Folder**.

12. In the right pane, double-click the message with the subject **Testing Public Folder Replication.**

13. Modify the content of the message. For example, type *This is a modified message from <server name>*.

14. On the **File** menu, click **Close**. A **Microsoft Outlook** dialog box appears, asking if you want to save the changes.

15. Click **Yes** in both clients at the same time.

16. On the Outlook bar, click **Inbox**. Remain here until you receive a message in your Inbox with the subject **Conflict Message**.

17. Open the conflict message.

18. In the **Conflict Message** dialog box, click **Open Message In Conflict**. Notice that you have a choice to keep both modified messages or to specify one of the messages as the master message.

19. On LONDON-1 only, under **Last Edited By**, select **Admin-L1** and then click **Keep This Item**.

20. On LONDON-1 only, on the **File** menu, click **Close**.

21. On the **File** menu, click **Close**.

22. After a few minutes, notice that the message, which you have elected to keep, now appears in the right pane on both NEWYORK-1 and LONDON-1.

23. Exit and log off Outlook.

24. Log off Windows NT.

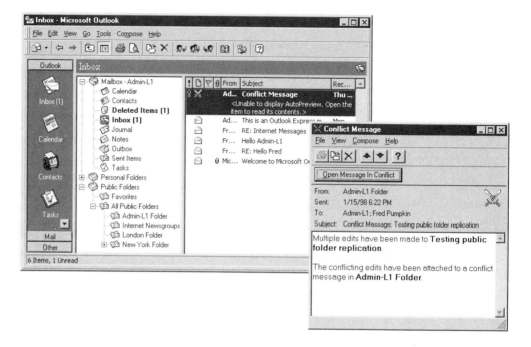

Review

Users have a choice among three options to resolve a content replication conflict. They can take the updated message, they can take the local message, or they can accept both modifications. If both modifications are accepted, a separate object is created for each item. Both are then placed in the public folder and replicated across the organization to all other replicas.

Public Folder Rehoming

In the past and under rare circumstances a critical problem sometimes arose caused by a mechanism known as public folder *rehoming*. Rehoming is a mechanism that assigns a "lost" public folder replica a new home server. Local public folder instances lose their previous home server if they were replicated to the local site before the directory replication connector to the original remote site was removed. The rehoming problem can be described simply; the conditions that lead to it, however, are more complex.

Rehoming Accidents

As shown in Figure 13-13, a folder called **New York Folder** exists on NEWYORK-1 and PARIS-2. The administrative access to **New York Folder** is not limited. The directory replication is configured between NEWYORK and PARIS, and public folder replication synchronizes the instances of **New York Folder** in both sites. The directory replication link between PARIS and NEWYORK is the prerequisite for public folder replication, and this dependency is the weak point of the following scenario.

Let's say Jacques deletes the Directory Replication Connector to NEWYORK. The site NEWYORK is now *unknown,* but it still exists in the directory. To remove its reference from the local directory, Jacques runs the Consistency Adjuster with all options activated. This approach "cleans" the local directory. Orphaned public folder objects (for example, **New York Folder**) are detected and rehomed to PARIS-2. In other words, the home server attribute of the public folder instance **New York Folder** on PARIS-2 changes to **PARIS-2**. Furthermore, unknown user accounts (those of NEWYORK) that once had permissions on **New York Folder** are removed from the permissions list.

So far, no problems. NEWYORK and PARIS exist quite independently of each other and users in each site can work with their local instances of **New York Folder**. But when Jacques reestablishes the directory replication link, public folder replication between both instances of **New York Folder** is reactivated automatically. The server PARIS-2 has the most current information. Consequently, PARIS-2 replicates the contents and the "cleaned" permissions list and other modifications to NEWYORK-1. As a result, effective permissions for users in NEWYORK change unexpectedly. The contents might also change drastically if users in PARIS have deleted messages in the meantime.

Preventing Rehoming

Exchange Server 5.5 is the first version of Exchange Server that provides several features to prevent rehoming accidents. The **Limit Administrative Access To Home Site** option that every public folder object provides is one of them. The corresponding check box can be found on the **General** property page. When enabled—and this is the default setting—rehoming a folder to another site is impossible. Instead, the Consistency Adjuster deletes those public folders completely. In the above example, the contents, definition, and folder container of **New York Folder** no longer exist on PARIS-2 once Jacques adjusts the consistency.

A second feature has been implemented in Exchange Server 5.5 in the form of additional options in the **DS/IS Consistency Adjustment** dialog box. This dialog box launches in the Administrator program when you click the **Consistency Adjuster** button on the **Advanced** property page of a server object (for example, PARIS-2 or NEWYORK-1). Under **Public Information Store**, select the adjustments you want to perform. The option **Synchronize With The Directory And Reset The Home Server Value For Public Folders Homed In**

Unknown Sites rehomes orphaned folders. The option **Remove Unknown User Accounts From Public Folder Permissions** cleans the permission list. Before Exchange Server 5.5, both options were always activated. With version 5.5 you are responsible for such adjustments yourself. If you ever plan to reconnect two sites that once were replicated, do not select these options to prevent unexpected problems once the directory replication is reestablished.

Rehoming Manually

Sometimes you want to rehome public folders. In other words, you want to change their home server attribute. In general, every server that maintains a replica of a public folder can become that folder's home server. By default, the home server is this server where the folder is created. The name of the home server can be found in the public folder's Distinguished Name (DN). For example, the DN /o=STOCKSDATA/ou=NEWYORK/cn=Recipients /cn=NEW YORK FOLDERC539A274C539A274C539A274D93AE2D F005618 might indicate a folder called **New York Folder**. Although users can modify the configuration of public folders and their content on any replica, messages sent to public folders are delivered to their home servers first. In contrast, posted messages first appear in the public folder instance where the user is currently working. Public folder replication always distributes new messages to all instances.

To modify the home server attribute, you must display the property pages of the desired folder in the Administrator program. The **Home Server** list box is located on the **Advanced** tab. When you open this box, all servers that currently maintain a replica are listed. Servers from remote sites are indicated by their site names (<site>\<server>). When you select a different server and click the **OK** button, the folder is rehomed. However, if you select a server in a remote site without deactivating **Limit Administrative Access To Home Site** for the current folder beforehand, you receive only the following notification: *Microsoft Exchange Server is unable to rehome the selected public folder. Ensure that the Limit administrative access to home site option is not set for this folder, and that the server you are currently connected to supports RPC network connections to the new home server.*

Note You can rehome multiple public folders simultaneously by propagating public folder configuration information to subfolders using the **Propagate These Properties To All Subfolders** on a public folders **General** property page.

The steps and conditions that cause rehoming accidents are as follows:

1. You must deactivate the **Limit Administrative Access To Home Site** option for a particular public folder.

2. Replicas must exist in separate sites.

3. The Directory Replication Connector between those sites must be removed.

4. Administrators in both sites must run the Consistency Adjuster with the following options enabled: **Synchronize With The Directory And Reset The Home Server Value For Public Folders Homed In Unknown Sites** and **Remove Unknown User Accounts From Public Folder Permissions**.

5. Directory replication between sites must be reconfigured. Public folder replication replicates the most current information over all other existing instances, changing the access permissions, and so on.

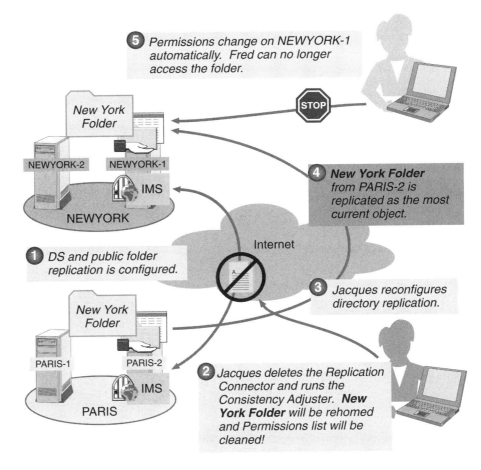

Figure 13-13. Access problems due to rehoming.

Review

1. What are the general advantages of public folder content replication?

   _____

   _____

   _____

   _____

   _____

2. You need to provide a storage location for collaborative information, so you decide to implement a public folder. Each of the items is approximately 5 MB – 10 MB in size and changes occur often. Which public folder strategy would you recommend?

   _____

   _____

   _____

3. Your company has implemented two sites because a WAN connection exists that does not support RPC communication. What needs to be configured in order to provide all public folders within the organization to all users?

   _____

   _____

   _____

4. The replication of the public folder hierarchy happens automatically every 60 seconds. How can you expand the replication interval to two minutes?

   _____

   _____

5. You want to create a public folder that is available in all locations even if RPC communication is not supported. How can you accomplish the configuration by using one Administrator program?

   _____

   _____

   _____

   _____

6. You need to create a local replica for a desired public folder that exists in another site, but you don't want to bother the remote administrator. However, RPC communication is impossible. How can you achieve the desired configuration?

_____

_____

_____

_____

_____

_____

7. What are the components of the message state information and what are the functions of each part?

_____

_____

_____

8. You use the **This Replica (Days)** option on the **Age Limits** property page of the Public Information Store object to specify an age limit for a particular public folder. How does this expiration setting affect other public folder instances in your organization?

_____

_____

_____

_____

9. How does the receiving PFRA determine whether a replication conflict has occurred?

_____

_____

_____

10. What is the backfill process?

_____

_____

_____

_____

11. A user in your organization has deleted important information from a replicated public folder. Why can't you restore the public folder directly onto the existing public server? How can you recover the information?

_____

_____

_____

_____

_____

12. You create a new public folder replica on an Exchange Server computer. What must be performed manually to bring the replica to the current state?

_____

_____

_____

_____

13. What happens if you delete a public folder replica in the Exchange Administrator program?

_____

_____

_____

_____

14. As a public folder contact, you receive a conflict message. What choices do you have for resolving the public folder replication conflict?

_____

_____

15. Two public folder owners have modified the design of a public folder on two different instances at the same time and generate a design conflict. How do you resolve the conflict?

_____

_____

_____

_____

C H A P T E R   1 4

Implementing Advanced Security

This chapter covers message encryption in Microsoft Exchange Server 5.5. The Key Management Server, also known as the KM Server, is the essential Advanced Security component.

Overview

Exchange Server relies on Microsoft Windows NT Server security to prevent unauthorized access to mailboxes. However, e-mail messages are not bound to a company's computer network. When a message leaves your messaging network—for example, through the IMS—you lose control over it. You cannot be sure that the e-mail is not copied or read during its journey over the Internet. But although you cannot prevent unauthorized access to messages in all circumstances, by using Advanced Security you can ensure that the information is in a format that is not understandable to unauthorized readers.

Lesson 1 of this chapter provides a brief overview of the Advanced Security features in Exchange Server 5.5 and lists the various types of security keys used for message signing and sealing.

Lesson 2 covers the architecture of the KM Server, its components, and their interaction. It also discusses KM Server installation and administration and the use of KM Server encryption keys and passwords.

Lesson 3 explains the two stages of enabling Advanced Security. It discusses the tasks required of the KM administrator and the user, along with the storage locations of security objects. The lesson also introduces the person-to-person key exchange feature and provides a detailed explanation of the message signing and sealing processes.

Lesson 4 covers the implementation of Advanced Security in multiple-site environments. Here you can read about key and certificate management as well as maintenance of the KM Server database. The lesson also explains how to move a KM Server and how to use the Bulk Encryption Key utility.

At the end of this chapter is an exercise that guides you through the installation of a KM Server in a multi-site organization. You will also learn an easy way to enable Advanced Security for all existing users.

In the following lessons, you will be introduced to:

- The concept of Advanced Security
- The installation of the KM server
- The steps required for beginning the process of enabling Advanced Security for a user
- The steps required for completing the process of enabling Advanced Security
- The installation of a KM Server in an organization with multiple sites

Lesson 1: Advanced Security Features

Theoretically, all one needs to "steal" e-mail messages is a Network Monitor Agent. As messages are sent through computer networks, a Network Monitor Agent can analyze the communication of remote computers on its local network segment. Reading "stolen" messages is easy, especially when SMTP systems (Internet connections) are involved, because those messages might be kept in clear text, which allows anybody to read them, even with the simplest text editor. Therefore companies such as STOCKSDATA should seriously consider implementing Advanced Security features.

This lesson provides a brief overview of Advanced Security features and lists supported client platforms. It also covers the versions types of security keys and explains the purpose of public, private, and secret keys in Exchange Server 5.5.

At the end of this lesson, you will be able to:

- List the client platforms that support Advanced Security
- Describe the general technique for signing and sealing messages

Estimated time to complete this lesson: 40 minutes

Advanced Security Overview

Advanced Security is the generic term for the features that allow you to sign and seal messages. These features allow you to ensure message confidentiality, origin, and authenticity even if unauthorized persons get access to your e-mail messages.

Client Platforms

Advanced Security is primarily a client feature, as the client is used to create and read encrypted messages. But encryption keys are also managed through the KM Server and the DS. Consequently, your client must communicate with both components through the Microsoft Exchange Server transport service. Every MAPI-based client (such as Microsoft Outlook) can therefore provide Advanced Security features. The configuration of the Exchange Server transport service is covered in Chapter 7.

The following are the supported client platforms for Advanced Security. (See Figure 14-1.)

- Exchange Client or Outlook for Windows 3.x and Windows for Workgroups 3.11

- Exchange Client for Windows 95

- Exchange Client for Windows NT

- Exchange Client for Apple Macintosh

- Outlook for Windows 95 and Windows NT

- Outlook for Apple Macintosh

Signing and Sealing Features of Advanced Security

Using Advanced Security, you can sign messages, seal them, or both. A sealed message does not necessarily carry a digital signature, and a signed message is not automatically sealed. A signed message conveys the actual information plus a digital signature, which proves that the originator sent the message. The digital signature also allows you to determine whether the message was tampered with on its way across the messaging network. Sealing encrypts the message content and any attachment so that only the actual recipient can decrypt and read the information.

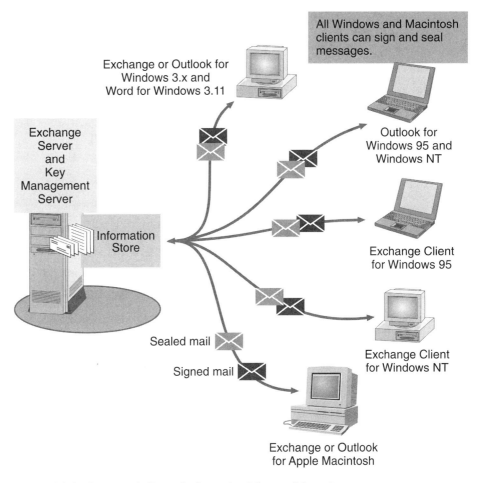

Figure 14-1. Supported client platforms for Advanced Security.

These are the primary Advanced Security features:

- Sealing; the sender encrypts a message and its attachments
- Signing; the sender adds a digital signature to the message to allow verification of its origin and authenticity

Key Technology

Keys are security strings of a certain length used for data encryption. Depending on the Exchange Server version, 40-bit, 56-bit, and 64-bit keys are supported. The longer the key, the higher the security.

Public/Private Key Pair

The X.509 CCITT (ITU) standard describes the handling of public/private key pairs within a messaging system. Advanced Security—and therefore all MAPI-based clients (Exchange Client 4.0 and 5.0 and Outlook 8.03)—relies on two public/private keys, according to X.509 standard version 1. One key pair is used for verifying and signing and the other for sealing and unsealing messages.

Private Key

Private keys are available only to the users to whom they belong. They are stored in local security EPF files, which are created when Advanced Security is enabled.

Because Exchange uses two key pairs, two private keys must exist: the private signing key and the private sealing key. Your e-mail client uses the private signing key for signing messages (see Figure 14-2); you use your private sealing key for unsealing (decrypting) encrypted messages that you have received.

Each private key has its dedicated purpose, and keys are not interchangeable.

- The private sealing key is used to unseal the content of a message so that the actual recipient can read the information.

- The private signing key is used to sign a message to secure integrity and authenticity.

Public Key

Because two different private keys exist, there must also be two corresponding public keys. Public keys are available to the entire organization. Generally, all users except the actual key owner use them.

For example, a recipient can use the sender's public signing key to verify the digital signature of a received message. Your client can also retrieve the public sealing keys of all recipients during the process of message sending in order to seal (encrypt) the message for each of them. (See Figure 14-2.) The process of signing and sealing messages is described in detail later in this chapter in in Lesson 3, "Enabling Advanced Security."

- Each public key has its dedicated purpose, and keys are not interchangeable.

- The public sealing key is used by other users to seal messages sent to this user.

- The public signing key is used by other users to verify the digital signature of this user.

Secret Key

A secret key is a security string (password) that is used for both encryption and decryption of information. Outlook, for instance, uses a secret key to encrypt and decrypt your security EPF file, which stores your security information locally. (See Figure 14-2). The secret key cryptography algorithm is also used in conjunction with the recipients' public sealing keys to seal messages. This provides several advantages, as outlined in detail in Lesson 3 later in this chapter.

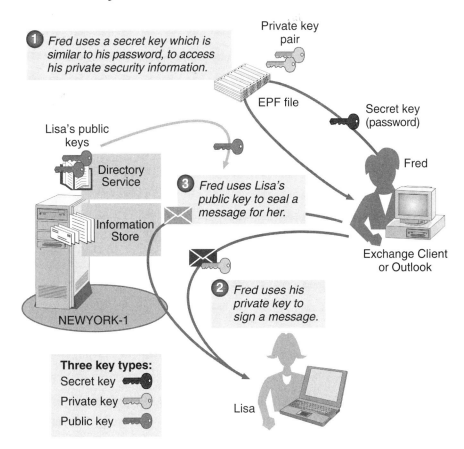

Figure 14-2. Different key types.

The Exchange Server encryption keys and their functions are as follows:

- Private keys; to unseal and to sign messages
- Public keys; to seal messages for other users and to verify digital signatures
- Secret key; to encrypt and to decrypt security files and message contents

Lesson 2: The Key Management Server

As mentioned in Chapter 3, the Key Management Server is not installed by default. You must install this component explicitly to enable Advanced Security in your organization.

This lesson describes the architecture of the KM Server along with its components, important files, and database. It also explains the role of the KM administrator and covers the KM Server installation. It then explains the purpose of an important KM Server encryption key and additional security passwords and discusses international considerations.

At the end of this lesson, you will be able to:

- Identify the components of a KM Server

- Install the KM Server

- Describe the purpose of KM Server–specific keys and security passwords

Estimated time to complete this lesson: 35 minutes

KM Server Architecture

The KM Server is a X.509 Certification Authority (CA), which is responsible for creating and managing security keys and certificates. Only one CA can exist in a single site. However, you can install KM Servers in multiple sites.

KM Server Components

Three main components form a functioning KM Server. They are a Windows NT service called Microsoft Exchange Key Management Server (also known as the KM Server service), a storage database, and a security file called Seckm.dll. Several other components, including the Secadmin.dll on the Administrator program side and Etexch32.dll on the client side, are also required to manage and use Advanced Security features. (See Figure 14-3 on page 897.)

Exchange KM Server Service

The Microsoft Exchange Key Management Server service, which runs on the KM Server computer, is the active component that processes all incoming Advanced Security requests. The Administrator program and the SA are its direct communication partners. (See Figure 14-3.)

Note The KM Server service cannot be installed on more than one server in a site.

KM Database

The KM Server service maintains the KM database, which stores Advanced Security information for users of a particular site, multiple sites, or an entire organization. Only one KM database can exist in a site. For example, a user's public and private sealing keys are temporarily placed in this database during the process of enabling Advanced Security. Even more important, the KM database permanently contains the public signing and private sealing keys for all users that belong to this KM Server. A KM Server must maintain these keys to keep a security key history for all users that have been enabled with Advanced Security.

Note It is important to include the KM database in regular server backups to save the security key history of all users who have been enabled with Advanced Security.

KM Security DLL and the SA

The KM Security DLL (Seckm.dll) supports communication between the SA and the KM Server service. The SA receives KM Server request messages as they are sent during stage 2 of enabling Advanced Security. It sends them to the KM Server service using the functions of the Seckm.dll library. Stage 2 is explained in more detail in Lesson 3, later in this chapter.

Administrator Program Components

Two directory objects are important for managing Advanced Security: the **CA** object and the **Site Encryption Configuration** object, both of which are under the **Configuration** container. The **Site Encryption Configuration** object does always exist. The **CA** configuration object is created only during the KM Server setup. While both objects are used to accomplish Advanced Security management tasks, the **CA** object also identifies the Certification Authority within the site and the organization.

You can use the **Security** tab of each mailbox object to maintain security keys and certificates on a per-mailbox basis, as covered in Lesson 4, "KM Server in Multiple-Site Organizations," later in this chapter.

Security Administration DLL

When you manage Advanced Security using the **Security** tab of a mailbox object or the **Site Encryption Configuration** and **CA** objects, your Administrator program must communicate with the KM Server directly using RPCs. For this purpose, the security administration DLL called Secadmin.dll is accessed. (See Figure 14-3.) It is installed along with the Administrator program and is in the \Exchsrvr\Bin directory.

Note RPC communication must work between the KM Server and the Administrator program if you want to manage Advanced Security. In other words, you cannot act as a KM administrator if the connection to your KM Server does not permit direct communication via RPCs.

KM Administrator

The KM administrator is a privileged Exchange Server administrator who can enable, revoke, and recover Advanced Security features on a per-mailbox basis. By default, only the person who installs the KM Server can be a KM administrator. But you can designate additional KM administrators using the **Administrators** property page of the **CA** object. Click the **Add Administrator** button to add additional accounts. You can also revoke KM administrators by clicking the **Revoke Administrator** button. Use the **Administrators** tab to change your own KM administrator password.

Client Components

Users use Exchange Client and Outlook to send signed and sealed messages, but their mailboxes must be enabled with Advanced Security before they can begin. In general, MAPI-based clients communicate with the KM Server through e-mail messages when they are completing the process of enabling Advanced Security.

Security DLL

The security DLL that provides all kinds of Advanced Security features to the Exchange Client and Outlook is called Etexch.dll on Windows 3.x and Windows for Workgroups platforms and Etexch32.dll for Windows 95 and Windows NT. This DLL provides all the required features for signing and sealing messages.

Although the actual KM Server–Client communication relies on e-mail messages, the security DLL uses RPCs to communicate with the IS and the Directory. The IS must be contacted in order for e-mail-based requests to be transmitted to the KM Server. The Directory is the communication partner when the sealing certificate is stored as an attribute of a mailbox within the directory database. (See Figure 14-3.) Later in the process of sealing messages, the DLL contacts the DS again to obtain a copy of the sealing certificate (public sealing key) of each recipient. The process of sealing messages is explained in detail later in this chapter under the section, "Exchanging Sealed Messages."

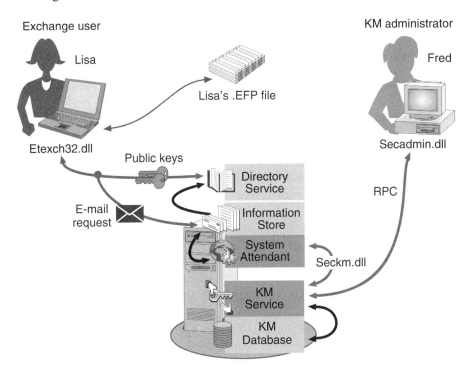

Figure 14-3. The KM Server architecture.

The Advanced Security components and their functions are as follows:

- Etexch.dll and Etexch32.dll; to request security information from the KM Server based on e-mail messages to permit clients to sign and seal messages, and to request public keys from the directory

- Key Manager Service; to process incoming requests from the Administrator program and clients

- KM database to store the security keys (and especially the security key history) for each user that belongs to the corresponding KM Server

- Secadmin.dll; to provide RPC-based communication between the Administrator program and the KM Server

- Seckm.dll; to respond to any request from users indirectly through the SA

- SA; to retrieve requests from users and to manage and store user key pairs using the KM Server service

Installing the KM Server

Theoretically, any Exchange Server can be the designated KM Server of a site or an organization, but because RPC is used for the communication between the KM Server and the Administrator program, the KM Server can be installed only on a computer that uses a LAN-like connection. (See Figure 14-4.)

For maximum security, you should install the KM Server as a dedicated server in a separate site. Powerful hardware is not required for this server because it will be used infrequently for generating security keys during the process of enabling Advanced Security. The hard disks of the KM Server computer should be formatted with NTFS, and the \Kmsdata directory should be backed up regularly.

Setup Program

In Exchange Server 5.5, installation of the KM Server is part of the Exchange Server Setup program. (Earlier Exchange Server versions provided a separate Setup executable file in the \Setup\i386\Exchkm directory on the installation CD.)

To install KM Server, choose the **Complete/Custom** setup option. The KM Server will not be installed by default, so you must select it from the list of optional components. You can display this list by clicking the **Change Option** button in the **Microsoft Exchange Server Setup – Complete/Custom** dialog box.

Because you will create the **CA** object under the local site's **Configuration** container during setup, you must be a Permissions Admin of the local site in order to complete the installation. Administrative Windows NT permissions are also required because the KM Server service must be registered in the Registry during installation.

Note You can install the KM Server at any time by choosing **Add/Remove** option in maintenance mode of the Exchange Server Setup program.

One KM Server per Site

The Setup program first contacts the local server's DS to check for an existing KM Server. If it finds the **CA** object in the local site, it sends a message telling you that you must remove the existing KM Server before you can install a new one. There is no exception to the rule that you can only install one KM Server in a site. However, with Exchange Server 5.5 you can install one KM Server in each site, which might be desirable for distributed administration.

Setup also checks to see whether a KM database already exists in the \Exchsrvr\Kmsdata directory (Kmsmdb.edb). This is usually the case if you removed a previous KM Server installation without deleting the contents of the \Kmsdata directory. If a KM database already exists, you will be told to back up the existing database and then delete all existing files manually. You can restore a backup once the installation is complete. You can read more about the management of the KM Server database under "Managing the KM Server Database," later in this chapter.

Creating the KM Server

The Setup program copies the binary files of the KM Server in the \Exchsrvr\bin directory and creates the KM database in the directory \Exchsrvr\Kmsdata. It also writes the configuration settings of the KM Server service to the Windows NT Registry. To initialize the KM Server service properly, you must supply the correct Site Services Account password during installation. Later, Setup creates the **CA** object within the **Configuration** container of the local site, which is then replicated across the site and the organization.

KM Server Password

During the installation, Setup generates the KM Server password. The administrator can either copy this password to floppy disks or display it on the screen. Floppy disks are more convenient because you don't have to write down the KM Server password—it is written to a file called Kmserver.pwd. You must provide two disks because Setup will back up the KM Server password file on the second disk. If you have only one disk on hand, you can store the backup copy on the computer's hard disk, but you should ensure that unauthorized access to the Kmserver.pwd file is impossible. You cannot save both the original and the backup password files on a nonremovable disk.

Note Both the original and the backup floppy disks must be stored in a secure place to prevent unauthorized access to the KM Server.

You must insert the floppy disk that contains Kmserver.pwd into the A: drive before you can start the KM Server service via the **Services** applet of the Control Panel. (For example, you must start the service explicitly once the installation is complete.) If you did not save the password to a floppy disk, you must enter the password in the **Startup Parameters** box of the **Services** applet of the Control Panel. The password is case sensitive. The KM Server service clears the **Startup Parameters** box during startup, so you must supply the password on every startup.

The KM Server service must obtain the password during startup because it uses the password to decrypt the master encryption key for the KM database. Once the service starts, you can manage Advanced Security using the Administrator program.

Note Unlike other Exchange Server services, the startup type of the KM Server service is Manual because of the KM Server password dependency.

Service Startup Problems

At times you might receive an error message that says *Error 2140: An internal Windows NT error occurred* when you start the KM Server service. To get more detailed information, you can check the Application Event Log. If the Application Event Log contains the error notification *Error ID 5057: The supplied password is not valid*, you should check to see if the floppy disk in the A: drive contains a valid Kmserver.pwd file. If this file is corrupted, you must use the backup copy or specify the password manually using the service's startup parameters.

The following are the steps accomplished by the Setup program:

1. It contacts the DS to check whether a KM Server exists in the site.

2. It checks the local **Configuration** container to see whether a **CA** object exists. If a KM Server has already been installed in the site, it displays a notification that only one KM Server can exist in one site, and then terminates.

3. It checks to see whether the existing \Exchsrvr\Kmsdata directory contains a KM Server database. If it does, Setup suggests backing up and deleting the files before continuing.

4. It creates a password for the KM Server and optionally writes the password to floppy disks.

5. It copies the KM Server files from the CD to the \Exchsrvr\Bin directory.

6. It generates the KM Server database in the \Exchsrvr\Kmsdata directory.

7. It initializes the KM Server service.

8. It creates the **CA** object within the **Configuration** container of the local site.

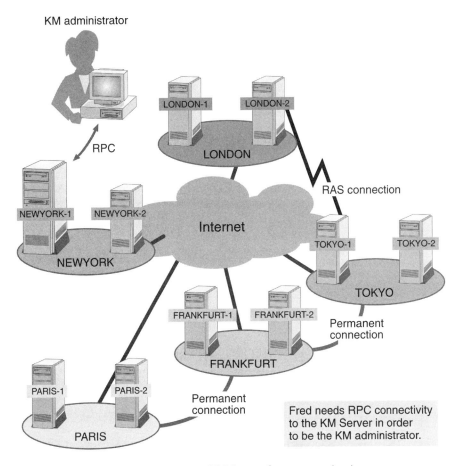

KM administrator

RPC

LONDON-1 LONDON-2

LONDON

RAS connection

NEWYORK-1 NEWYORK-2

Internet

TOKYO-1 TOKYO-2

NEWYORK

TOKYO

FRANKFURT-1 FRANKFURT-2

Permanent
connection

FRANKFURT

PARIS-1 PARIS-2

Permanent
connection

Fred needs RPC connectivity
to the KM Server in order
to be the KM administrator.

PARIS

Figure 14-4. Installing the primary KM Server for an organization.

Function of KM Server Keys and Passwords

Since you will use private and public security keys to encrypt sensitive
messages, those keys must be protected from unauthorized access. Several
security keys and passwords are used for this purpose.

KM Database Master Encryption Key

The KM Database Master Encryption Key is used to encrypt and decrypt the
KM database. The KM Server service and every designated KM administrator
maintaining Advanced Security must have access to this key. However, the
KM Database Master Encryption Key itself is also encrypted to prevent
unauthorized access.

The number of designated KM administrators determines the number of times (+1 for the KM Server service itself) that the KM Database Master Encryption Key is encrypted. The system uses each of the KM n administrator passwords plus the KM Server password for this purpose, creating X+1 lockboxes. Every KM administrator and the KM Server service use a password to open the corresponding lockbox to retrieve the KM Database Master Encryption Key. (See Figure 14-5.)

The KM Database Master Encryption Key is accessed in the following situations:

- When the KM Server service has to maintain the KM database
- When KM administrators need to manage Advanced Security

KM Server Password

As mentioned, the KM Server password is generated and then typically written to floppy disk during the KM Server installation. You must enter this password each time you start the KM Server service by inserting the floppy disk into drive A: or typing it on the **Startup Parameters** line in the **Control Panel**. Otherwise, the service cannot decrypt its lockbox to obtain the KM Database Master Encryption Key, which is required for decrypting the KM database. Without a valid KM Server password, the KM Server service will not start.

KM Administrator Password

Every KM administrator has an individual security password for opening the corresponding KM Database Master Encryption Key lockbox. The default password is *password*; it is wise to change it using the Administrator program. Double-click the **CA** object under the **Configuration** container. On the **Administrators** tab of the **CA Properties** dialog box, click the **Change My KM Server Password** button to change the password.

Note The KM administrator password is case sensitive and must contain at least six characters.

Multiple KM Administrator Passwords

If you designate additional administrators, you can enforce the use of multiple passwords for Advanced Security management. Multiple password policies prevent administrators from making changes to the KM Server without the authorization of another one or more administrators. To set a multiple password policy, switch to the **Passwords** property page of the **CA** object. Under **Add Administrators, Delete Administrators, Or Edit These Multiple Password**

Policies, specify how many administrators must supply their passwords before administrators can be added or deleted. You can also increase the number of passwords for recovering and revoking Advanced Security for users.

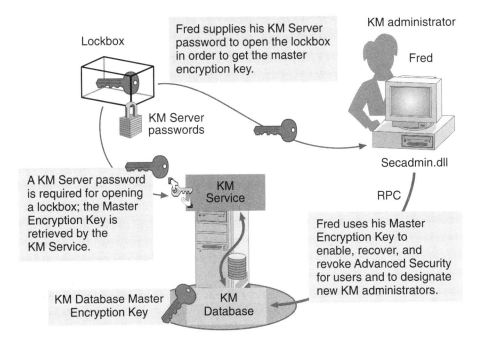

Figure 14-5. The KM Database master encryption key.

The features of encrypted security information and the corresponding password are as follows:

- Communication between the KM Server and the Administrator program is encrypted using the KM administrator's security password.

- Communication between the KM Server and the client is encrypted using a 12-character security token (explained in Lesson 3, "Enabling Advanced Security," later in this chapter).

- KM Database Master Encryption Key is encrypted using the KM administrator passwords and the KM Server password.

- KM database is encrypted using the KM Database Master Encryption Key.

- Your local security (.EPF) file is encrypted using your security password (explained in Lesson 3 later in this chapter).

Different Encryption Types in One Organization

Many countries have specific policies regarding the use and export of encryption technology. The differences in policy and laws in each country make it difficult for international companies working in several countries to use the same encryption technology worldwide.

In 1977, Ron Rivest, Adi Shamir, and Leonard Adleman developed a public key encryption system (RSA) that could be used for both encryption and certification. Their public and private key pairs have been used since then, and are used in Exchange Server.

The North American version of Exchange Server supports DES (Data Encryption Standard), a standard developed by the National Bureau of Standards. DES describes an algorithm that uses 56-bit security key pairs to encrypt sensitive information. It prevents access to data without the appropriate decryption key.

Northern Telecom has developed a proprietary encryption method called CAST (developed by Carlisle Adams and Stafford Tavares) that replaces DES. It provides more flexible encryption methods by allowing an input key that can be between 40 and 128 bits long. The longer the input keys, the more secure the encryption type. Depending on the language of the Exchange Server version, either CAST-40 or CAST-64 is supported.

Country-to-Country Encryption Algorithm

On the **Algorithms** property page of the **Site Encryption Configuration** object, the **Preferred Microsoft Exchange 4.0 and 5.0 Encryption Algorithms** parameters are different for **North America** and for **Others**. While you can select the **DES** 56-bit or **CAST-64** encryption method for **North America**, you can select only **CAST-40** for all countries outside North America. This is because Exchange Server must follow U.S. export restrictions, which prevent exporting the powerful DES and CAST-64 encryption technology. Because of import restrictions, the French Exchange Server version cannot include any encryption technology at all.

Different Versions in One Organization

As a result of the restrictions described above, three different versions of Advanced Security exist, and all can be used in a single organization. As shown in Figure 14-6, STOCKSDATA will use the North American (Very Safe) version in NEWYORK, the French (No Advanced Security) version in PARIS, and the International (Safe) version in FRANKFURT, LONDON, and TOKYO.

It is not desirable to send an encrypted message to a user who cannot decrypt the message—for example, a French user. Messaging clients must check the common Advanced Security level supported by all recipients of a message to find the best encryption method to use. Messages cannot be encrypted for each recipient separately.

Obtaining the Advanced Security Level

Only users who have been enabled with Advanced Security have public sealing keys. The public sealing key is placed in X.509 certificates, which provide information about the supported encryption methods, and is stored in the Directory.

If a message must be encrypted, the Exchange Client and Outlook will contact the DS to retrieve the sealing certificates of all recipients. The client detects the maximum Advanced Security level that the recipients have in common and uses this level to encrypt the message. For example, if Lisa addresses a message to recipients in NEWYORK (DES and CAST-64), FRANKFURT (CAST-40), and PARIS (None), she cannot encrypt the message because the maximum common Advanced Security level is None. (See Figure 14-6.) In this case, the client displays a warning message asking her whether she wants to cancel the send process to remove those recipients from you messages that cannot handle encrypted messages, to send the message to all recipients unsealed.

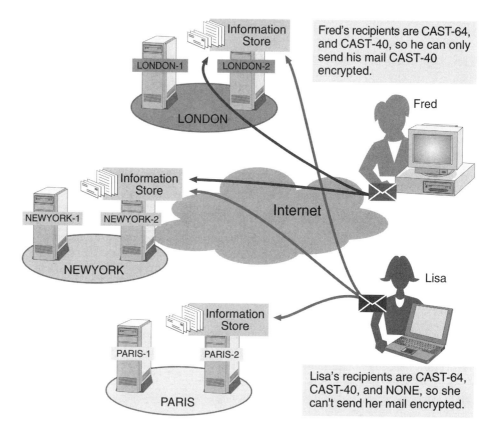

Figure 14-6. Message encryption in international organizations.

Advanced Security features depend on export and import law restrictions:

- No Advanced Security; used for the French Exchange Server version

- Secure 40-bit encryption keys; used for all other international Exchange Server versions

- Very powerful 56-bit and 64-bit encryption keys; used for the North American version only

Lesson 3: Enabling Advanced Security

Enabling Advanced Security is more complex than installing a KM Server in an organization because both the administrator and the user are involved. Users must perform a series of manual configuration steps, so they might need administrative assistance.

In this lesson, you will learn about the tasks that the administrator and users must perform in order to enable Advanced Security features. The lesson also provides an overview of storage locations for security objects and describes the person-to-person security feature for exchanging signed and sealed messages with users in other organizations. Finally, the lesson provides a detailed example of sending and sealing messages.

At the end of this lesson, you will be able to:

- Describe the steps that the KM administrator must perform to enable Advanced Security for a user
- Describe the tasks for completing the process of enabling Advanced Security for a user
- Identify the storage locations for security information
- Use Advanced Security between organizations
- Send and receive secured messages

Estimated time to complete this lesson: 40 minutes

Stage 1: The Administrator's Side

Installation of a KM Server in an organization does not mean that every user has been enabled with Advanced Security. In fact, no user can sign and seal messages by default. The KM administrator completes stage 1 by first enabling Advanced Security on a per-mailbox basis using the Administrator program. Stage 2 is completed by each end user who is enabled with Advanced Security.

Generated Security Information

The most important information generated during stage 1 is a 12-character security key. The sealing key pair is also created. The security token is displayed to the Administrator in a message box, and the sealing key pair is stored temporarily in the KM database until the user downloads this information during stage 2. You must pass the 12-character security token to the user in a secure manner so that he or she can complete the process of enabling

Advanced Security. (See Figure 14-7.) Stage 2 is covered later in this lesson under "The Client's Side."

Security information generated during stage 1 includes:

- Public and private sealing keys
- 12-character security token

Steps in the KM Server Administrator's Process

As shown in Figure 14-7, Fred wants to enable Advanced Security for Lisa. He starts the Administrator program, opens the **Recipients** container of the site NEWYORK, and double-clicks the mailbox of **Lisa Strawberry**. He clicks the **Security** tab, and a **Key Management Server Password** dialog box appears. He enters his KM administrator password, clicks **OK**, and reaches the **Security** property page. Under **Current Status**, Lisa's Advanced Security state is **Undefined**. Fred clicks the **Enable Advanced Security** button and again provides his KM administrator password to enable communication with the KM Server. A dialog box appears, displaying a security token that Fred must give Lisa so that she can enable Advanced Security during stage 2. Fred notices that Lisa's **Current Status** has switched to **New** in the **Lisa Strawberry Properties** dialog box. The status will switch to **Active** as soon as Lisa enables Advanced Security for herself.

Locating the KM Server

During stage 1, the location of the KM Server must be determined in order to establish the RPC connection between the Administrator program and the KM Server. This information can be obtained from the **Site Encryption Configuration** object under the **Configuration** container. Important information can be found under **Primary KM Server Location** on the **General** property page, which points to the site location of the KM Server. If this property page does not display a site name, a KM Server reference has not yet been configured. Once a KM Server is installed in the local site, the local site name is displayed in read-only mode and the **Choose Site** button is unavailable. For more information on KM Server locations, see Lesson 4 later in this chapter.

You can examine the reference to the KM Server in detail when you display the Administrator program in Raw mode (**Admin /R**). You must select the **Site Encryption Configuration** object, open the **File** menu, and then click the **Raw Properties** command. The **Site Encryption Configuration Properties** dialog box will appear. In the **Object Attributes** list, you can find the **KM Server** attribute. If you select this attribute, you will see the complete X.500 reference to the KM Server under **Edit Value**. The Raw mode of the Administrator program is covered in Chapter 8.

Communicating with the KM Server

The Administrator program contacts the KM Server through the Security Administration DLL (Secadmin.dll). It passes the user's distinguished name (DN) (in Lisa's case, */o=STOCKSDATA/ou=NEWYORK/cn=Recipients/ cn=LisaS*) plus the encrypted KM Server password (Fred's KM administrator password) to the KM Server service.

The KM Server service creates Lisa's public and private sealing keys and deposits them in the KM database. The KM Server service also generates a 12-character security token that will be required during stage 2 to encrypt the communication between the client and the KM Server. Using Fred's KM administrator password, the KM Server encrypts the 12-character security token and returns it to the Administrator program. The Security Administration DLL decrypts the security token again before it displays this token in a message box on the screen. (See Figure 14-7.)

Fred must pass the security token to Lisa in a secured manner. E-mail is not advisable in this situation because e-mail communication is not secure. An unauthorized person who gets access to the security token can decrypt the communication between the KM Server and the client during stage 2. The snoop can decrypt this information and steal the public signing key and the private sealing key. The public signing key is less important, but the private sealing key allows the snoop to decrypt Lisa's sealed messages. If you want to use Advanced Security seriously, you must be careful when handling security information.

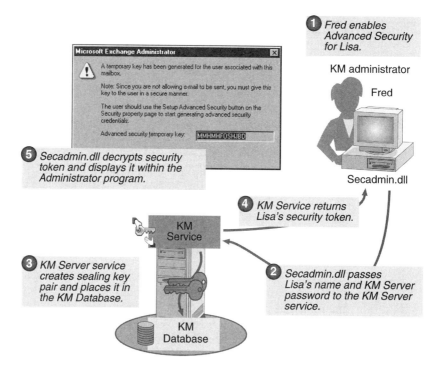

Figure 14-7. The administrator enables Advanced Security.

The following happens during stage 1 of enabling Advanced Security. (See Figure 14-7.)

1. You click the **Enable Advanced Security** button on the **Security** property page of each mailbox object to begin the process of enabling Advanced Security. You must supply the KM Server password of the KM administrator.

2. Secadmin.dll receives the location of the KM Server from the **KM Server** attribute of the **Site Encryption Configuration** object and passes the user's DN and the KM administrator password to the KM Server service.

3. The KM Server service creates the user's sealing key pair and stores it in the KM database.

4. The KM Server service generates a random 12-character security token, encrypts it using the KM administrator password, and returns it to the Administrator program.

5. Secadmin.dll decrypts and displays the security token in a dialog box of the KM administrator's console. The administrator must provide the security token to the user.

Stage 2: The Client's Side

In stage 2, the user sends an e-mail request to the KM Server, the KM Server processes the request, and a response is sent back to the user. The user enables Advanced Security by opening the response, which means that he or she can sign and seal messages. That's it!

Generated Security Information

In stage 1, Lisa's public and private sealing keys were created and placed in the KM database. This information must be received from the KM Server during stage 2. The public and private signing keys and several X.509 certificates are also created during stage 2. (Storage locations and X.509 certificates are discussed under "Security Object Storage," later in this lesson.)

Security information generated during stage 2 is as follows:

- Public and private signing keys
- Signing and sealing X.509 certificates
- User's .EPF file and its password

Initial Steps on the Client Side

Lisa cannot continue the process of enabling Advanced Security until she has received her 12-character security token from Fred (as shown in Figure 14-7). As shown in Figure 14-8, she enters this security token in the **Token** box of the **Set Up Advanced Security** dialog box. (You open this dialog box by opening the client's **Tools** menu, clicking the **Options** command, switching to the **Security** property page, and clicking the **Set Up Advanced Security** button.)

In the **Set Up Advanced Security** dialog box, Lisa must also specify the **Security File** location and a corresponding **Password**. (To provide effective protection for the .EPF file, the password must be six or more characters long.) The security file will be used later to store Lisa's security information locally.

Sending an Advanced Security Request Message

Lisa clicks the **OK** button to close the **Setup Advanced Security** dialog box. The public and private signing keys are generated, encrypted, and stored in the specified .EPF file. The client accesses the security DLL to generate these keys. The public signing key is then encrypted using the 12-character security token and is sent in an e-mail message to the KM Server. A message box informs Lisa that the message has been sent successfully.

The KM Server Recipient

In order for Exchange Client or Outlook to send an Advanced Security request to the KM Server, a recipient for the request message must exist. This recipient is the KM Server's System Attendant service, which maintains a hidden mailbox.

The SA receives Lisa's e-mail request and passes the information to the KM Server service through the Seckm.dll. The KM Server service extracts the public signing key from the message and stores it in the KM database. The KM Server service then generates the signing and sealing certificates and creates an e-mail message (called the KM Server response message) that is used to send the outstanding security information back to Lisa. Again, the message is encrypted using Lisa's 12-character security token. The KM Server service then contacts the IS to send the message on behalf of the SA.

The following information is placed in the KM Server response message:

- CA certificate of the KM Server
- Private sealing key
- Signing and sealing certificates

Receiving the KM Server Response

The KM Server response message makes its way through the messaging network to Lisa's mailbox. Like any other e-mail message, it appears in the Inbox, but the icon shows an envelope locked by a padlock. The originator is the SA, and the subject is *Reply From Security Authority*. When Lisa double-clicks this message, she is asked for her security password. She enters the password and clicks **OK** to complete the process of enabling Advanced Security. A message box informs her that she can now send and receive signed and sealed messages. The KM Server response message is deleted automatically from her Inbox.

Transferring the Security Information into the Security File

The client's security DLL places the private sealing key, the CA certificate, the signing certificate, and the sealing certificate into Lisa's .EPF file. It also contacts the DS to store Lisa's sealing certificate in the Directory. The sealing certificate must be replicated across the entire organization before other users can use Lisa's public sealing key to send her sealed messages. The process of sending sealed messages is explained in detail later in this lesson under "Exchanging Sealed Messages."

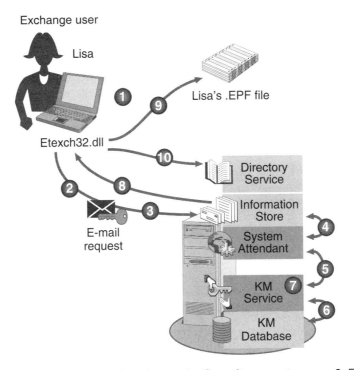

Exchange user

Lisa

Lisa's .EPF file

Etexch32.dll

Directory Service

Information Store

E-mail request

System Attendant

KM Service

KM Database

1. Lisa enters security token on the **Security** property page. *2.* Etexch*.dll generates signing keys. *3.* Client sends public signing key to the SA. *4.* SA receives message. *5.* SA passes request to KM. *6.* KM extracts key and stores it. *7.* KM generates certificates. *8.* IS delivers key and certificates to Lisa. *9.* Etexch*.dll extracts and stores certificates and private keys. *10.* Etexch32.dll stores X.509 certificate in the DS.

Figure 14-8. User-enabled Advanced Security.

The following happens during stage 2 of enabling Advanced Security. (See Figure 14-8.)

1. The KM administrator provides the security token to the user using a secure method.

2. The user clicks the **Set Up Advanced Security** button on the client's **Security** property page and enters the security token in the **Set Up Advanced Security** dialog box.

3. Etexch32.dll generates and encrypts the user's signing key pair using the 12-character security token and sends the public signing key to the SA on the KM Server.

4. The SA passes information to the KM Server service using the KM security DLL (Seckm.dll).

5. The KM Server service decrypts the information, retrieves the public signing key, and saves it in the KM database.

6. The KM Server service generates the sealing and signing certificates. It places these certificates, the CA certificate, and the private sealing key in a KM Server response message. It then encrypts the security information using the security token and sends the message on behalf of the SA to the user.

7. The IS delivers the message to the user's mailbox. The user opens the message and supplies the security password.

8. Etexch32.dll extracts the private sealing key, the CA certificate, and the sealing and signing certificates and places them in the user's .EPF file.

9. Etexch32.dll submits the user's sealing certificate to the local DS for storage and replication.

Security Object Storage

Advanced Security involves private and public signing keys and sealing keys in addition to X.509 certificates that provide detailed information about the user's encryption capabilities. But security information is not always kept in a single place. (See Figure 14-9.)

X.509 Certificates

The KM Server generates two X.509 certificates for each user. Besides other important information, the signing certificate stores the public signing key and the sealing certificate provides access to the public sealing key.

To conform to X.509, Advanced Security certificates must contain:

- Unique serial number generated by the KM Server to identify each user's certificate

- Expiration date for the certificate (Advanced Security expires after a year and a half)

- CA's DN

- CA's signature (an encrypted KM Server password)

- Public keys for signing and sealing

- User's DN

Certification Authority Certificates

The KM Server itself must also prove its authenticity because it represents the CA. For this reason, it maintains a special document known as the CA certificate. It is sent to each user in the organization and is stored in the user's .EPF file to identify the CA that the user belongs to.

Security Object Locations

The private signing and sealing keys, the signing and sealing certificates, and the CA certificate are stored in the user's local .EPF file. They provide all the required security information a user needs for signing and sealing.

In addition, the sealing certificate is stored in the DS to provide public access to the public sealing key. As mentioned in the section, "Key Technology," the public sealing key is required for sealing messages. The various keys are covered further under "Exchanging Signed Messages" and "Exchanging Sealed Messages," later in this lesson.

The third important location is the KM database, although it is not involved directly in the process of signing and sealing messages. This database is used to store the signing key pair temporarily during the process of enabling Advanced Security. It is also the permanent location of the public signing key and the private sealing key so that a backup (or history) exists of important encryption keys. You can read more about maintaining a key history in Lesson 4 later in this chapter.

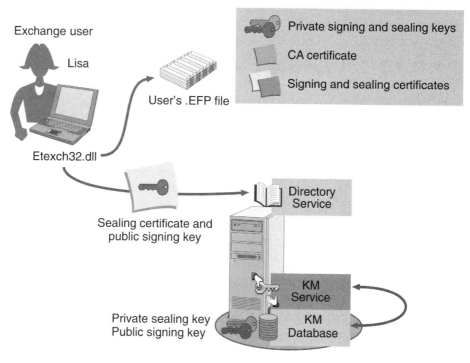

Figure 14-9. Storage locations for security objects.

The storage locations for security objects are as follows. (See Figure 14-9.)

- Directory; stores the user's sealing certificate
- KM database; stores the private signing key and the public signing key
- Security (.EPF) file; stores the CA certificate, private sealing key, private signing key, and the signing and sealing certificates

Person-to-Person Key Exchange

When you want to send a sealed message to a particular user, you must use that person's public sealing key. This key is usually stored in the sealing certificate maintained in the Directory Service. Directory replication guarantees that sealing certificates are available to all users of the organization.

Sending signed or sealed messages to users in another organization might seem impossible because the security information of other organizations is typically not accessible. Directory replication does not work between different organizations. To address this problem, Exchange Client 5.0 and Outlook provide the **Security Key Exchange Message** form, which you can use to exchange signing and sealing certificates with users in other organizations.

The Security Key Form

The **Security Key Exchange Message** form is installed in a hidden organization forms library. You launch it using the **Send Security Keys** button on the **Security** property page of the **Options** dialog box. (Electronic forms and the organization forms library are covered in Chapter 16, "The Microsoft Exchange Server Forms Environment.")

The form has two views, the Send view and the Read view. You use the Send view to send your own security information to other users, and you use the Read view to verify and store received public security keys.

When you open a received security key exchange message, you see the Read view, which provides the **Add To Personal Address Book** button. You click this button to add an entry to your Personal Address Book for the user who sent you his or her public keys. The client also automatically saves the received public security keys in your local .EPF file. At this point, you can send encrypted messages to that user. (See Figure 14-10.)

Key Integrity and Expiration

As messages travel through the messaging network (especially across foreign systems) they might be converted, modified, and permanently changed. This can affect and destroy the security keys attached to a security key exchange message. You should therefore verify that the received keys are in good shape before you add them to your .EPF file.

Verifying Key Integrity

The integrity check requires actions on both the sender side and the receiver side. The Send view provides a **Verify Key Integrity** button, which displays a series of numbers and characters as a checksum. This checksum must exactly match the string that is displayed when the recipient clicks the **Verify Key Integrity** button in the Read view. The sender and the recipient can communicate using a regular interpersonal message, a telephone call, or another communication medium to make sure the checksum is the same.

Key Expiration

You cannot implement an expiration mechanism for public security keys from users in remote organizations. Those public keys are kept only in your local security file. Certificates and keys maintained by the KM Server are valid for a year and a half before they expire. Unfortunately, you cannot modify the expiration deadline. After 18 months, you must use expired encryption keys when sending sealed messages to users in remote organizations. Fortunately, you can encrypt messages using expired public sealing keys because they are kept in your local security file. Receiving users can read your messages because the old security keys remain available for decryption.

Resetting Security Files

There is no convenient way to refresh the person-to-person security keys maintained in an .EPF file. To clean the local security file, you must recover Advanced Security keys completely for the user. A new security file is created, which means you lose all person-to-person security keys. Consequently, you must reset the Personal Address Book to wipe out references to nonexistent .EPF file entries. The process of recovering Advanced Security is explained in Lesson 4 later in this chapter.

Once the Personal Address Book and the local security file have been reset, you can exchange the required person-to-person security information or import the security information using the old security key exchange messages (which might still reside in your message folders).

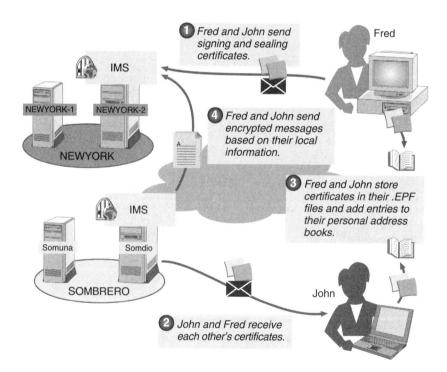

Figure 14-10. Advanced security between organizations.

The following happens when you exchange encryption keys with another user:

1. Click the **Options** command on Exchange Client's **Tools** menu.

2. Switch to the **Security** property page.

3. Click the **Send Security Keys** button.

4. Provide your security password.

5. Send the **Security Keys**.

6. The other user waits until the security key exchange message arrives in his or her Inbox.

7. The user opens the message and verifies the key integrity.

8. The user can click the **Add to Personal Address Book** button.

9. The user must provide the security password to place security information in his or her .EPF file.

Exchanging Signed Messages

With message signing, a message checksum is built, encrypted, and attached to the message. The message content itself is not encrypted. The receiving user builds a checksum and compares it to the decrypted original. If the checksums are identical, the message has not been modified during transmission.

Signing a Message

The client uses a complex mathematical function to derive a unique 128-bit value from the message that you want to sign. This value is called a *hash* or *message digest*; the process of building this value is known as *hashing*. To protect the original digest from unauthorized access, it is encrypted using the sender's private signing key. The encrypted message digest is known as the *digital signature*, and a message is considered *signed* if the digital signature has been attached to it.

Since Exchange Client and Outlook use the same hashing method, the message digest for a particular message will always be the same (on the sender side and the recipient side)—long as the message has not been altered during transmission or elsewhere.

Sending a Signed Message

As shown in Figure 14-11, Lisa wants to send a signed message to Fred, so she composes the message and selects **Add Digital Signature To Message** on the **Security** property page of the message (launched using the **Properties** command on the **File** menu). She clicks the **Send** button, enters her password, and clicks **OK.** Her private signing key is retrieved from the .EPF file, and the original message is hashed. The hash is then encrypted using the private signing key. The client adds the hash and Lisa's signing certificate to the original message before it transfers the message to the IS for delivery.

Verifying a Signed Message

Fred receives Lisa's signed message in his Inbox and can immediately read the information because it has only been signed, not encrypted. To verify Lisa's digital signature, he selects the **Properties** command on the message's **File** menu. He switches to the **Security** property page, where the status **Digitally Signed – Yes** indicates that a digital signature has been attached to the message. He clicks the **Verify Digital Signature** button to check the authenticity. He enters his security password and clicks **OK** one more time.

Lisa's digital signature is decrypted using her public signing key. This key is obtained from Lisa's signing certificate, which is attached to the message. The result of the decryption is the original message digest. Fred's client recalculates the message digest to retrieve a second digest. If Lisa's message digest and the second message digest are the same, the message is OK. (See Figure 14-11.)

When a signed message is sent:

1. The original message is hashed, and a unique message digest is obtained.

2. The user provides a security password to decrypt the .EPF file and to extract the private signing key.

3. To create the digital signature, the message digest is encrypted with the sender's private signing key.

4. The sender's signing certificate and the digital signature are added to the message, which is then sent to the IS for delivery.

When a signed message is verified:

1. The recipient opens a signed message and checks the signature.

2. The client prompts for the user's security password.

3. The sender's public signing key is extracted from the certificate enclosed in the message, and then the digital signature is decrypted to retrieve the original message digest.

4. The client performs hashing on the original message to retrieve the recipient's message digest.

5. The digests are compared.

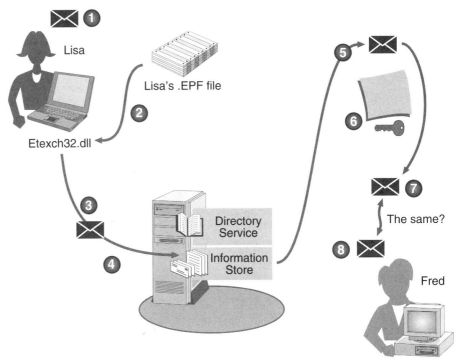

1. *Message is hashed.* 2. *Private signing key is retrieved.* 3. *Client encrypts digest.*
4. *Message, encrypted digest, signing certificate and transmitted to IS.* 5. *Fred checks signature.* 6. *Public signing key is retrieved from certificate.* 7. *Digest is decrypted.*
8. *Client performs hashing on the message.*

Figure 14-11. Sending and verifying signed messages.

Exchanging Sealed Messages

During the sealing process, the contents of a message and all attachments are encrypted. The sealing process is initiated by clicking the **Send** button if you have elected to encrypt the message.

Sending a Sealed Message

Lisa wants to send Fred a sealed message. She composes the message as usual, but this time she selects the **Encrypt Message Contents And Attachments** option on the **Security** property page (launched using the message's **Properties** command on the **File** menu). She clicks the **Send** button, and in the **Microsoft Exchange Security Logon** dialog box she enters her security password and clicks **OK**. Outlook encrypts and sends the message.

Determining the Encryption Method

During the message sealing process, the client contacts the DS to obtain a copy of the sealing certificate for each recipient. Besides the public sealing key, the sealing certificate contains information about the supported encryption method. The maximum common encryption method for all recipients is determined and is used to encrypt the message. If a certificate for a particular user cannot be found, the message cannot be sealed. In this case, the client displays a message box offering the user the choice to remove the recipients for whom the message cannot be encrypted, send the information unsealed, or cancel the send process. If no recipients are available for encryption, you can either send the message unsealed or cancel the message send. More information about the interoperability of encryption methods is provided in Lesson 2 earlier in this chapter.

Bulk Encryption Key

Using the strongest common encryption method (None, CAST-40, DES, or CAST-64), the client generates a bulk encryption key for sealing (and later unsealing) the message. Before the bulk encryption key can be attached to the message, it must be encrypted using each recipient's public sealing key. The public sealing keys are retrieved from the recipients' sealing certificates. The encrypted bulk encryption key must be attached to the message before the client can transfer the message to the IS for delivery. (See Figure 14-12.)

In other words, the client creates a bulk encryption lock box for each recipient. Each lock box is added to the encrypted message to provide the bulk encryption key (in its encrypted form) to all recipients. The client adds the sender's sealing certificate to the message so the originator can read the sealed message as it is stored in his or her **Sent Items** folder.

Unsealing a Sealed Message

Fred receives the message and opens it. At this point, the message must be unsealed. He enters his security password in the **Microsoft Exchange Security Logon** dialog box. Fred's private sealing key is retrieved from the .EPF file and the client uses this key to decrypt (open) the corresponding bulk encryption lock box. This decryption returns the bulk encryption key, which can then the used decrypt the message.

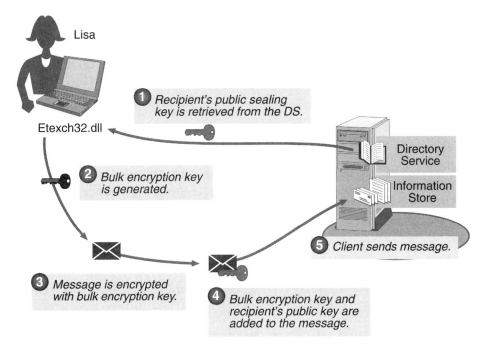

Figure 14-12. Sending a sealed message.

When a message is sealed:

1. The recipient's sealing certificate (public sealing key) is retrieved from the Directory.

2. The bulk encryption key is generated to encrypt the message content.

3. A lock box for each recipient is created (using his or her public sealing key) to encrypt the bulk encryption key.

4. The encrypted message, the lock box for each recipient, and the originator's sealing certificate are sent to the IS for delivery.

Lesson 4: KM Server in Multiple-Site Organizations

You can control the Exchange Server organization in manageable units using multiple sites, but Advanced Security typically demands a centralized CA. Because of this disharmony, you should be careful when you install the KM Server in a multiple-site organization. A carefully planned topology will avoid bottlenecks and problems later on.

This lesson covers the installation of the KM Server in multiple-site organizations. It discusses Advanced Security management tasks and Advanced Security recovery (which might be required when users forget their security passwords). Other topics in this lesson include how to move the KM database to another server and how to enable Advanced Security for multiple users in a convenient way. This lesson ends with an exercise that concludes the chapter.

At the end of this lesson, you will be able to:

- Implement Advanced Security in multiple-site organizations
- Update and revoke keys and certificates for users in an organization
- Manage the KM database
- Move the KM Server within a site
- Enable Advanced Security for multiple users in one step

Estimated time to complete this lesson: 25 minutes

KM Server and Multiple Sites

Only one KM Server can exist in a site, but KM Servers can be installed in multiple sites. However, Advanced Security requires that all existing sites must have knowledge about the location of all KM Server instances.

In fact, providing information about the desired KM Server location is the most important consideration when you implement Advanced Security in a multiple-site organization. The Administrator program must know the location of the KM Server that you want to manage. Once it does that, it establishes an RPC connection using Secadmin.dll. The Exchange Client and Outlook must send their request messages to the correct KM Server in order to complete the process of enabling Advanced Security.

KM Server in a Single Site

Everything is easy in a single-site organization because directory replication distributes configuration changes among all servers automatically, RPC communication is supported, and the KM administrator can connect to the KM Server from any server.

As soon as you install the KM Server, the **CA** object is added to the **Configuration** container. To allow all servers to identify the location of the KM Server, the **KM Server** attribute of the **Site Encryption Configuration** object is modified during the KM Server installation. The modifications are replicated and therefore known to all servers in the site. As mentioned in Lesson 3, you can examine the **KM Server** attribute using the Administrator program in Raw mode.

KM Server and Multiple Sites

When multiple sites exist, information about the location of the KM Server must be provided to all sites, but only the KM Server's local site receives this information automatically. You must therefore manually configure the **Site Encryption Configuration** object in all sites that do not contain a KM Server. (See Figure 14-13.) The important parameter labeled **Primary KM Server Location** on the **General** property page represents a reference to the KM Server in the local directory. This reference allows all servers in the remote site to forward Advanced Security request messages from clients to the actual KM Server.

Starting the Setup Program

It is important to note that you cannot start to configure the **Site Encryption Configuration** object of a remote site if the **CA** object of the desired KM Server has not been replicated to the remote site. If the **CA** object is missing, you cannot select the reference to the KM Server from the list of available sites, which is displayed when you click the **Choose Site** button on the **General** property page.

Multiple KM Servers in One Organization

Before Exchange Server 5.5, only one primary KM Server could be installed in an organization. Version 5.5 allows you to install as many KM Servers as you have sites. Multiple KM Servers are desirable if RPC communication to one central server is not always supported or if you want to diversify KM administration generally.

Nevertheless, only one KM Server is typically required to enable all users of an organization with Advanced Security. The KM administrator can select mailboxes from the Global Address List regardless of the actual site in which they reside. The administrator displays the mailbox properties and switches to the **Security** tab to maintain Advanced Security just as he or she would for any user in the local site.

Note Because clients communicate with the KM Server through e-mail, users do not have to be in the same site as the KM Server.

Let's say you want to install an additional KM Server in LONDON. All users in LONDON have been enabled with Advanced Security, and their KM Server is NEWYORK-1. When you complete the setup process for the second KM Server, the **Site Encryption Configuration** object references the new KM Server in the local site. This means that the security key history for all users in LONDON is lost because the old security key history is still stored in NEWYORK. The administrator in LONDON must once again enable Advanced Security for all users, and the users must complete the process of enabling Advanced Security as described earlier in this chapter. As a result, all users receive new security keys and certificates. Those keys and certificates, however, are not suitable for decrypting old messages because the keys don't match the former ones. In other words, encrypted messages might be unreadable. To prevent this, affected users should use the Bulk Advanced Security tool to decrypt all messages permanently before moving them. This tool is described under "Advanced Security Tools," later in this lesson.

Note It is generally not possible to move users from one KM Server to a KM Server in a different site without losing the security keys.

Here are the steps for configuring KM Server references in remote sites:

1. Start the Administrator program and connect to a server in the remote site.

2. Expand the site container of the KM Server site and then expand the **Configuration** container. Verify that the **CA** object (which identifies the KM Server) exists.

3. Open the **Configuration** container of the remote site.

4. Display the properties of the **Site Encryption Configuration** object.

5. On the **General** property page, click the **Choose Site** button.

6. A **Key Management Server** dialog box appears, listing references to all installed KM Servers and their sites. Select the desired site and click **OK**.

7. Verify that the correct site is displayed under **Primary KM Server Location**. Click **OK**.

8. Close the Administrator program.

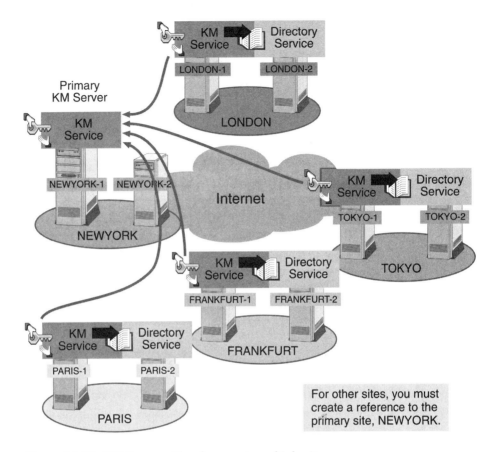

Figure 14-13. KM Server with references in multiple sites.

Key and Certificate Management

Every user who wants to benefit from Advanced Security features must have valid signing and sealing key pairs, X.509 certificates, and a valid CA certificate. You can manage this security information using each mailbox object's **Security** property page in the Administrator program.

General Tasks

The general tasks of a KM administrator are easy to discover by looking at a mailbox object's **Security** tab. You'll see three important buttons: **Enable Advanced Security**, **Recover Security Key**, and **Revoke Advanced Security**.

The general tasks of a KM administrator are as follows:

- Enables Advanced Security
- Recovers security information for users
- Revokes Advanced Security

Key and Certificate Recovery

The recovery of security information is necessary if a user's .EPF file is corrupted or accidentally deleted or if the user has forgotten his or her security password. In all these cases, a new security file must be created.

The User's Perspective

From the user's perspective, the process of recovering Advanced Security is the same as the process of enabling Advanced Security. He or she must send a new Advanced Security request to the KM Server to re-create a valid .EPF file. This time, a 12-character security token is required to create and encrypt the request message. This security token must be obtained from the KM administrator.

The KM Administrator's Perspective

The steps the KM administrator has to take to recover security information for a user differ slightly from the steps for enabling Advanced Security. Using the Administrator program, you can select the affected mailbox object, display its properties, and switch to the **Security** property page. You must provide the KM Server password to display the **Security** tab. Click the **Recover Security Key** button to launch the recovery routines.

During recovery, the KM Server does not create a new sealing key pair. Instead, it restores the original key pair in the KM database. Again, a 12-character security token is returned; you must supply this to the user, as usual.

Key and Certificate Update

X.509 certificates are valid for 18 months, and the validation period cannot be modified. This does not mean that the KM administrator has to update each user's security information every 18 months. The client performs the update automatically. When certificates are nearing expiration, the client sends a request to the KM Server asking to update the certificates for an additional period, and the user receives new signing and sealing key pairs.

The old public signing and private sealing key are not deleted. They are stored in the KM database and also in the user's .EPF file because they are needed to decrypt old (and still encrypted) messages.

Key and Certificate Revocation

Just as you can enable Advanced Security for a user, you can also disable it. Click the **Revoke Advanced Security** button on the mailbox object's **Security** property page to add the user's public signing and private sealing key to an internal revocation list in the KM database. The user's sealing certificate in the Directory as invalid. When the DS adds the unique serial number of the user's sealing certificate to the revocation list of the **CA** directory object, Advanced Security is revoked. Directory replication ensures that the configuration changes are distributed to all servers in the organization. This prevents users from sending sealed messages to the revoked mailbox. (See Figure 14-14.)

Revoked Security Keys

The KM Server service does not delete the revoked security keys. The user's security file also remains. Otherwise, the public signing and the private sealing key would become unavailable and existing sealed messages would not be readable. Also, if you ever re-enable Advanced Security, users will need the old security keys along with the new security information.

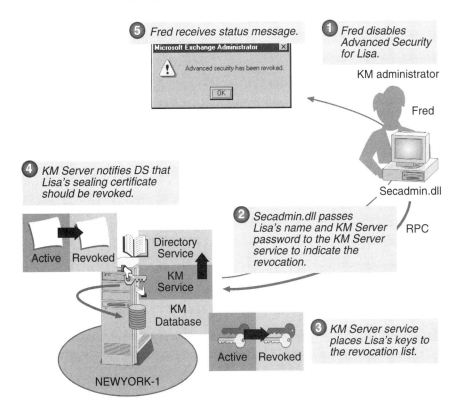

Figure 14-14. The Administrator revokes advanced security.

The steps for revoking Advanced Security for a user are as follows:

1. The KM administrator selects the **Security** property page for the user's mailbox and enters his or her own KM Server password and the clicks **Revoke Advanced Security**.

2. The Security administration DLL (Secadmin.dll) determines the location of the KM Server and passes the DN of the user and the administrator's KM Server password to the KM Server using RPCs.

3. The KM Server adds the user's signing and sealing keys to its internal revocation list.

4. The KM Server service tells the Directory to revoke the user's sealing certificate. The certificate's serial number is added to the revocation list of the **CA** directory object.

5. A message box is displayed in the Administrator program informing the administrator about the success of the revocation.

Managing the KM Server Database

The KM database can be found in form of the Kmsmdb.edb file under \Exchsrvr\Kmsdata. It maintains a history of all security keys and provides them when users need to recover their local .EPF files. This way, older and still encrypted messages remain readable. Therefore, it is advisable to back up the KM database on a regular basis. The **Microsoft Exchange Key Management Server** service should be stopped while the backup is in process.

Note The Exchange Server Backup program does not include the KM database in its online backup operation. You must back up the \Exchsrvr\Kmsdata directory separately by stopping the **Microsoft Exchange Key Management Server** service; otherwise, important database files are left open and may not be backed up successfully.

Restoring the KM Server Database

If you suspect that the KM database is damaged, you should stop the KM Server service and replace the \Exchsrvr\Kmsdata directory with the most recent backup. Then you can start the KM Server service again.

If you restore a KM database that does not reflect current security information (for example, if Advanced Security has been enabled or revoked in the meantime), users might lose messages as they recover local security files because some required public encryption keys might be missing.

Moving the KM Server

You can move a KM Server from server to server within a site. The relocation of a KM Server to another computer in the same site is basically a backup and restore operation. As mentioned before, you cannot move a KM Server between sites.

Removing the Old KM Server

First you must stop the old KM Server service and back up the \Exchsrvr\Kmsdata directory. Then you can remove the KM Server by running the Exchange Server Setup in maintenance mode. During removal, you can opt to delete all files from the \Exchsrvr\Kmsdata directory automatically.

Installing the New KM Server

Directory replication ensures that configuration changes will be replicated across the local site and the organization. When the directory replication has been completed (when the **CA** object has disappeared), you can install the new KM Server on the desired server computer. This re-creates the **CA** object within the **Configuration** container, and directory replication replicates the modification again. But before you can start the new KM Server, you must restore the most recent KM database backup. (See Figure 14-15.)

To start the KM Server service on the new server, you must provide the old server's original Kmserver.pwd file on a floppy disk. The new password generated during the last installation is useless because the KM database has been restored. However, the restored database is encrypted using the old KM server's password.

To complete the move of the KM Server, you must reconfigure the **Primary KM Server Location** reference in all existing remote sites using each corresponding **Site Encryption Configuration** object.

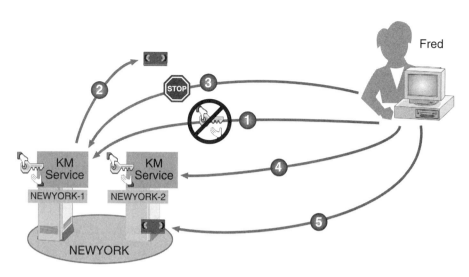

1. Fred backs up KM Database (Kmsmdb.edb). *2. He deletes KM Service and database files via Exchange Server Setup.* *3. He stops the KM Server service.* *4. He installs new KM Server service.* *5. He restores KM Database to NEWYORK-2 and starts the new KM Server using the original KM Server password.*

Figure 14-15. Moving a KM Server.

To move a KM Server:

1. Stop the KM Server service.

2. Back up the KM database on the old KM Server.

3. Run the Exchange Server Setup program in maintenance mode to remove the KM Server service.

4. Specify deletion of the KM database files.

5. Wait for directory replication to complete. (The **CA** object must disappear from the **Configuration** container.)

6. Run the Setup program on the desired server in the same site to install the new KM Server.

7. Restore the KM database to the new KM Server.

8. Start the KM Server service by providing the original KM Server password.

9. Reconfigure references in remote sites.

Advanced Security Tools

So far, you have used the Administrator program to enable Advanced Security features on a per-mailbox basis. This is sufficient if the number of users is small, but if the number is large it might be an awkward method. In this situation, the **Enrollment** property page of the **CA** object is very useful. (See Figure 14-16.)

The Bulk Advanced Security Tool allows you to decrypt sealed messages permanently. This can be useful if you plan to remove a KM Server from an organization completely.

Enabling Advanced Security in Bulk

For your convenience, the **CA** object provides the **Enrollment** property page, which you can use to enable Advanced Security for all mailboxes of a given **Recipients** container in one step. When you click the **Bulk Enrollment** button, a **Bulk Enroll Users In Advanced Security** dialog box appears. Here you can select the desired **Recipients** container on a per-site basis. You must also specify whether you want to save the resulting security tokens for all users in a file or whether you want to send those users their security token in an e-mail message. In the latter case, you can edit the text of the system message; click the **Edit Welcome Message** button on the **Enrollment** tab. To send security tokens to affected users in an e-mail message, you must also select the **Mail Temporary Keys To All Newly Enrolled Users** option in the **Bulk Enroll Users in Advanced Security** dialog box.

At this point, e-mail messages are still nonsecured. A cautious administrator will not allow security information to be sent using a nonsecured path. You can save the resulting security token to a file instead of sending e-mail messages automatically to all users. Once a bulk enrollment cycle has been completed, the specified file contains the distinguished names of all users who have been enabled with Advanced Security, as well as their 12-character security token. It is now your responsibility to distribute the security tokens to the users so that they can complete the process of enabling Advanced Security.

Bulk Advanced Security Tool

The Bulk Advanced Security Tool (Sectool.exe), which comes with the Microsoft Exchange Server Resource Kit, lets you encrypt and decrypt all messages within message folders and subfolders.

Decrypting Messages

To decrypt all messages in a particular message folder, click the **Unsecure Folder** command on the **Exchange Security** menu. Enter your security password and click **OK**. The messages in the selected folder will be decrypted permanently.

Encrypting Messages

The **Secure Folder** command on the **Exchange Security** menu lets you encrypt all messages within a message folder. You can resecure previously encrypted messages or you can specify other options, such as securing all messages. You must supply the security password prior to the operation.

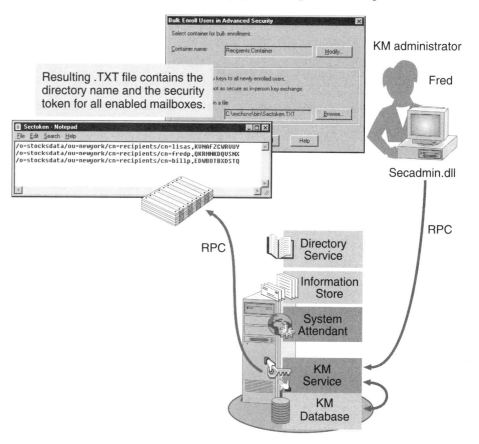

Figure 14-16. Enabling Advanced Security for multiple mailboxes.

The options for enabling Advanced Security for multiple mailboxes are as follows:

- **Container Name**; to specify the mailboxes of users you want to enable; subcontainers are not included

- **Mail Temporary Keys To All Newly Enrolled Users**; to send security tokens to users via e-mail messages; users being enabled for the first time receive this message

- **Save Results In A File**; to specify a file used to retrieve the security tokens for all enabled users (including users that are already enabled)

Exercise 46: Installing and Configuring Advanced Security

Exactly one KM Server must be installed in a site to provide Advanced Security. This server becomes the CA, which means that it is responsible for creating, recovering, and revoking security keys and certificates. Key and certificate management is possible only if the KM Server service is running.

Estimated time to complete this exercise: 45 minutes

Description

In this exercise, you will install a KM Server using the Exchange Server Setup program from the installation CD. You will need a floppy disk to store the KM Server password.

- Task 46a describes the steps for performing the initial installation of a KM Server.

- Task 46b describes the steps for starting the KM Server service and verifying the creation of the KM Server's **CA** object.

- Task 46c describes the steps for verifying the replication of the KM Server's CA object and configuring the KM Server in the second site. This step is necessary to specify LONDON as the KM Server site.

- Task 46d describes the steps for generating security tokens for all users.

- Task 46e describes the steps for setting up additional Advanced Security administrators and enabling Advanced Security for a single mailbox only.

- Task 46f describes the steps for setting up Advanced Security in Outlook.

- Task 46g describes the steps for demonstrating the process of sending, receiving, and reading encrypted messages.

Prerequisites

- Log on to NEWYORK-1 as Admin-NY1 to complete Tasks 46a, 46b, and 46d.

- Log on to LONDON-1 as Admin-L1 to complete Task 46c.

- All other tasks are done on both computers.

- You need a floppy disk to store the KM Server password.

- You must know the password of the Site Services Account.

Task 46a: Performing the Initial Installation

1. Log on to NEWYORK-1 as Admin-NY1.

2. Insert the Microsoft Exchange Server Installation CD into your CD-ROM drive and close the application that will be launched automatically.

3. Click the **Start** button and then click **Run**.

4. In the **Open** box, type *<CD ROM>:\\Server\Setup\i386\Setup*, and then click **OK**.

5. In the **Microsoft Exchange Server Setup** dialog box, click **Add/Remove**.

6. In the **Microsoft Exchange Server Setup - Complete/Custom** dialog box, click **Change Option**.

7. In the **Microsoft Exchange Server Setup – Microsoft Exchange Server** dialog box, select **Key Management Server** and then click **OK**.

8. Click **Continue**.

9. The **Site Services Account** dialog box appears. Under **Account Password**, type *password*.

10. Click **OK**.

11. The **Key Management Server Configuration** dialog box appears. Select **Write The Password To A Removable (Floppy) Disk And Create A Backup Copy. This Option Will Require 2 Blank, Formatted Floppy Disks.**

12. Click **OK**.

13. The **Key Management Server Configuration** dialog box appears. Under **Backup Copy Of Startup Password**, type *C:* and then click **OK**.

14. The **Microsoft Exchange Server Setup** dialog box appears, warning you that you are writing the startup password on a non-removable disk. Click **Yes** to continue.

15. The **Microsoft Exchange Server Setup** dialog box appears, prompting you to insert a floppy disk in drive A. Insert the disk and then click **OK**.

16. Setup installs the KM Server.

17. The **Microsoft Exchange Server Setup** message box appears, stating that the setup has completed successfully. Click **OK**.

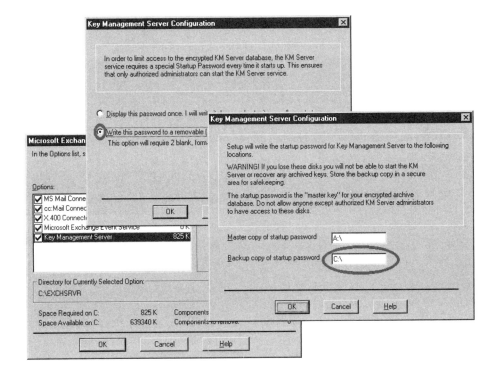

Task 46b: Verifying the KM Server Installation

1. On NEWYORK-1, click the **Start** button, point to **Settings**, and then click **Control Panel**.

2. In the Control Panel, double-click the **Services** icon.

3. In the **Services** dialog box, click **Microsoft Exchange Key Management Server**, and then click **Start**.

4. Close the **Services** dialog box and then close the Control Panel.

5. Click the **Start** button, point to **Programs**, point to **Microsoft Exchange** and then click **Microsoft Exchange Administrator.** Connect to the server NEWYORK-1.

6. Expand **NEWYORK** and then click **Configuration**.

7. Verify that the directory object **CA** is displayed in the right pane.

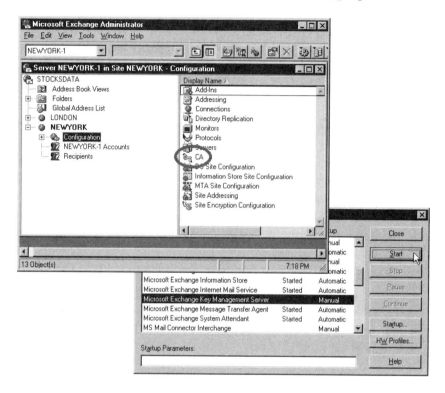

Task 46c: Configuring Advanced Security in an Additional Site

1. Log on to LONDON-1 as Admin-L1.

2. Click the **Start** button, point to **Programs**, point to **Microsoft Exchange**, and then click **Microsoft Exchange Administrator**. Make sure that you are connected to the server LONDON-1.

3. Expand **NEWYORK** and then click **Configuration**.

4. Do not continue until the new directory object **CA** is displayed in the right pane. This will take about five minutes.

5. Expand **LONDON** and then click **Configuration**.

6. In the right pane, double-click the **Site Encryption Configuration** object.

7. The **Site Encryption Configuration Properties** dialog box appears. Click **Choose Site**.

8. A **Key Management Server** dialog box appears. Under **Site Name**, select **NEWYORK** and then click **OK**.

9. Switch to the **Algorithms** tab and notice the default encryption algorithms.

10. Click **OK**.

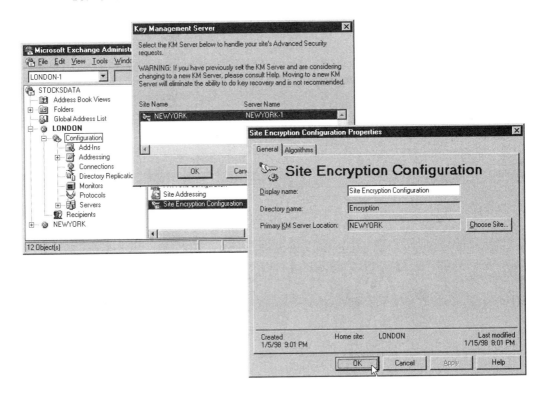

Task 46d: Generating Advanced Security Tokens

1. On NEWYORK-1, make sure that the Administrator program is started and that the **Configuration** container of the site NEWYORK is selected.

2. In the right pane, double-click the **CA** object.

3. A **Key Management Server Password** dialog box appears. Under **KM Server password**, type *password*.

4. Select the **Remember The Password For Up To 5 Minutes** check box and then click **OK**.

5. Switch to the **Enrollment** tab and then click the **Bulk Enrollment** button.

6. A **Bulk Enroll Users In Advanced Security** dialog box appears. Select **Save Results In A File** and then click **Browse**.

7. A **Save Bulk Enrollment Results In** dialog box appears. Under **File Name**, type *Sectoken* and then click **Save**. (The extension .TXT will be appended automatically.)

8. The **Bulk Enroll Users In Advanced Security** dialog box reappears. Click **OK**.

9. If steps 5 through 7 take more than five minutes, a **Key Management Server Password** dialog box will appear. In this case, type *password* in the **KM Server Password** box and then click **OK**.

10. A **Microsoft Exchange Administrator** dialog box appears, informing you that the Bulk Enrollment operation completed successfully. Click **OK**.

11. Click **OK**.

12. Click the **Start** button and then click **Run**.

13. In the **Open** box, type *C:\Exchsrvr\bin\Sectoken.txt*, which opens the bulk enrollment file you created in step 7. (If you chose a different location, you must change the command line accordingly.)

14. Note that the security token can be found in the Sectoken.txt file after **lisas**, **fredp**, and so on.

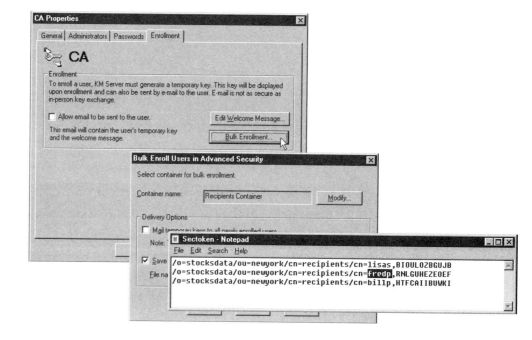

Task 46e: Designating Additional Administrators for Advanced Security

1. On NEWYORK-1, switch to the Administrator program and make sure that the **Configuration** container of the site NEWYORK is selected.

2. In the right pane, double-click the **CA** object.

3. A **Key Management Server Password** dialog box appears. Under **KM Server Password**, type *password*, verify that **Remember This Password For Up To 5 Minutes** is selected, and then click **OK**.

4. The **CA Properties** dialog box appears. Switch to the **Administrators** tab.

5. Click **Add Administrator**.

6. Under **List Names From**, select **ENGLAND**. Under **Names**, select **Admin-L1**.

7. Click **Add** and then click **OK**.

8. Click **OK**.

9. On LONDON-1, make sure that the Administrator program is started.

10. In the **Global Address List**, double-click **Admin-L1**.

11. Switch to the **Security** tab.

12. A **Key Management Server Password** dialog box appears. Under **KM Server Password**, type *password*, select **Remember This Password For Up To 5 Minutes**, and then click **OK**.

13. Click **Enable Advanced Security**.

14. An **Microsoft Exchange Administrator** dialog box appears, displaying the security token for Admin-L1. Write down this token; it is required to enable Advanced Security for this mailbox later on.

15. Click **OK**.

16. Close the Administrator program.

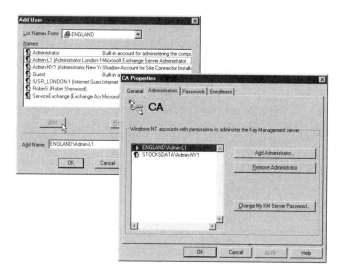

Task 46f: Enabling Advanced Security for the Client Mailbox

1. On the Desktop, double-click the **Microsoft Outlook** shortcut.

2. On the **Tools** menu, click **Options** to display the **Options** dialog box.

3. Click the **Security** tab.

4. Click **Set Up Advanced Security**.

5. The **Set Up Advanced Security** dialog box appears. In the **Token** box, type the security token for the current account as documented in Task 46d.

6. In the **Password** and **Confirm Password** boxes, type *password*. Click **OK**.

7. A **Microsoft Exchange** message box appears, stating that you will be notified by e-mail when your request has been processed. Click **OK**.

8. The **Options** dialog box reappears. Click **OK**, and then wait for the message informing you that you have been enabled for Advanced Security.

9. When you receive the message in your Inbox, open it.

10. A **Microsoft Exchange** dialog box appears, requesting your security password. In the **Password** box, type *password* and then click **OK**.

11. A dialog box appears, indicating that you have been enabled with Advanced Security. Click **OK**.

12. Repeat this task as Admin-L1 on LONDON-1.

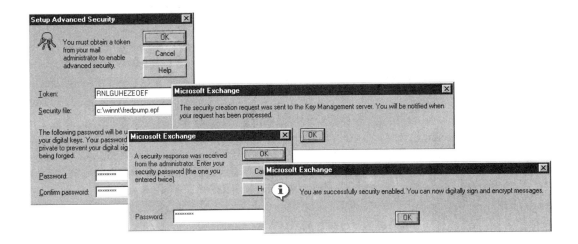

Task 46g: Sending and Receiving Sealed and Signed Messages

1. On the toolbar of the NEWYORK-1 client, click **New Mail Message**.

2. The **Untitled - Message** window appears, displaying a blank message form.

3. Click **To** to display the **Select Names** dialog box

4. Click **Admin-L1**.

5. Click **To**.

6. Click **OK**.

7. In the **Subject** box, type *Testing KM Advanced Security*.

8. Type a short message.

9. On the toolbar, click **Seal Message With Encryption**.

10. On the toolbar, click **Digitally Sign Message**.

11. On the toolbar, click **Send**.

12. The **Microsoft Exchange Security Logon** dialog box appears.

13. In the **Security Password** box, type *password*, and then click **OK**. If a **Non-Secure Recipients** dialog box appears, asking you to send the message unencrypted, click **Cancel Send** and wait for the modified directory information of the mailbox Admin-L1 to be replicated to NEWYORK. Then start over from step 11. As long as the directory replication has not occurred, NEWYORK has not received the information that Admin-L1 is enabled with Advanced Security and the **Non-Secure Recipients** dialog box is displayed. You might need to wait up to five minutes.

14. When the message arrives in the Inbox of Admin-L1, notice the mail message icon associated with this encrypted message.

15. Double-click the message.

16. The **Microsoft Exchange Security Logon** dialog box appears.

17. In the **Security Password** box, type *password* and then click **OK**. If a **Microsoft Exchange** dialog box appears, informing you that a valid certificate revocation list could not be obtained, click **OK**.

18. The message contents appear.

19. On the toolbar, click **Verify Digital Signature**.

20. The **Verify Digital Signature** dialog box appears, displaying the **Verification Results**. Click **OK**.

21. On the **File** menu, click **Close**.

22. On the **File** menu, click **Exit And Log Off**.

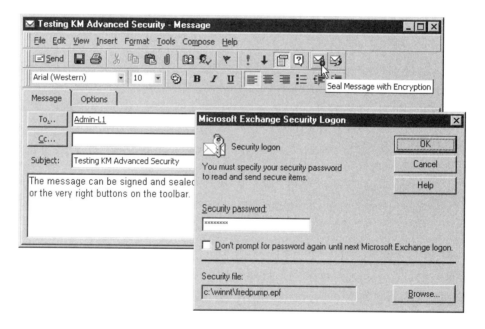

Review

You can install the KM Server using the Exchange Server Setup program. When you select the **Key Management Server** option, it contacts the DS to check whether a KM Server already exists in the organization. If you are installing the first KM Server, the Setup program copies the KM Server files to the computer's local hard disk (\Exchsrvr\bin directory). It writes the configuration settings of the KM Server service to the Windows NT Registry, initializes the KM database, and generates the KM Server password. The password can be displayed on the screen or stored in a file called Kmserver.pwd on a floppy disk. A floppy disk makes starting the KM Server service more convenient.

You can enable users with Advanced Security by using the Administrator program. You can select each single mailbox object, display its property pages, and switch to the **Security** property page to enable Advanced Security. You can also use the **Enrollment** tab of the **CA** object to enable Advanced Security for all users in a particular **Recipients** container. In all cases, a 12-character security token is generated for each user, which you must distribute to the corresponding users.

Users complete the process of enabling Advanced Security using their client program. They open the **Tools** menu, click the **Options** command, switch to the **Security** property page, and then click the **Set Up Advanced Security** button. They enter the security token, create an .EPF file, and define a personal security password. During this process, a request message is sent to the KM Server and the KM Server responds to the message. When a user opens the received response message and supplies the security password again, he or she completes the process of enabling Advanced Security. Messages can then be signed and sealed.

Review

1. What are the features of Advanced Security and when do you use them?

   _____

   _____

   _____

   _____

2. Which client platforms provide support for Advanced Security?

   _____

   _____

   _____

   _____

   _____

3. Exchange Server uses three types of security keys. What are they used for?

_____

_____

_____

_____

4. What are the three main components of a KM Server?

_____

_____

_____

5. What is the name of the DLL that the Administrator program uses to communicate with a KM Server? Which communication mechanism is used?

_____

_____

6. What is the KM Server security password used for, and when do you need it?

_____

_____

_____

_____

7. List the different versions of Advanced Security and the level of security they provide.

_____

_____

_____

8. What does a KM administrator have to do to enable a user with Advanced Security?

_____

_____

_____

_____

9. What does the user have to do to enable Advanced Security?

10. What does a X.509 certificate contain?

11. Each user's CA must be identified in the CA certificate. Where is this certificate stored?

12. You want to send sealed messages to users in remote organizations, so you exchange public secret keys using the person-to-person key exchange feature. Where does the client store the security information for remote users?

13. How can you delete the person-to-person security keys of a particular user?

_____

_____

_____

_____

14. When does Outlook encrypt a message?

_____

15. How does Outlook sign messages?

_____

_____

_____

_____

_____

16. How does Outlook check whether a signed message has been modified?

_____

_____

_____

_____

_____

_____

_____

17. What steps must be taken to send a sealed message?

_____

_____

_____

_____

_____

_____

_____

18. You want to implement Advanced Security in an organization with two sites. How many times do you need to run the KM Server Setup program?

_____

_____

_____

_____

19. When can you begin to configure the reference to a KM Server in a remote site?

_____

_____

_____

20. A user has forgotten the security password for his or her .EPF file. What must the administrator do to allow the user to sign and seal messages again?

_____

_____

_____

_____

_____

21. Advanced Security certificates expire by default after 18 months. How can you adjust the expiration interval to keep certificates valid for only 12 months?

_____

_____

22. Where does the Exchange Server store revoked security information?

_____

_____

23. Which directory must be saved in order to back up the KM Server database?

_____

24. What must be done to move a KM Server to a new computer?

_____

_____

_____

_____

_____

_____

_____

25. You are the administrator of STOCKSDATA, an organization with more than 2000 employees. Recently you installed a KM Server. Now you need to enable all employees with Advanced Security. How do you accomplish this?

_____

_____

_____

C H A P T E R   1 5

Maintaining Servers

This chapter covers the most important server maintenance issues that you will have to manage while ensuring the proper operation of an Exchange Server. Also covered are important troubleshooting utilities and sample situations that illustrate when to use a particular utility.

Overview

No technical system is perfect, so it's recommended that you constantly maintain a messaging network to guarantee its permanent availability. Exchange Server makes it easy to identify and solve most problems and bottlenecks early on without affecting the work of your users. A serious administrator will be prepared for even the worst-case scenarios, such as hardware failure. The more stable the system, the more the users will trust and use the electronic communication media, and the more the enterprise will benefit from efficient information sharing.

The emphasis of Lesson 1 is the maintenance of Exchange Server databases. The lesson starts with a discussion of the database characteristics, including the purpose of transaction log files. This lesson continues with a discussion about available backup strategies and corresponding restore operations. You will also read about all the offline database maintenance tools at the administrator's disposal.

Lesson 2 discusses Server and Link Monitors, their creation, configuration, and usage. You'll find that Server and Link Monitors are valuable tools that can simplify the task of controlling the installed Exchange Server computers.

Lesson 3 lists the most important troubleshooting utilities that come with the Exchange Client, Windows NT Server, and Exchange Server. This lesson discusses the typical situations that may require the use of a particular troubleshooting tool.

Lesson 4 explains the advanced options provided by the Administrator program. It illustrates, for example, how to force the directory replication and how to change the Site Services Account password. This lesson also describes other features of the Administrator program, such as the Message Tracking Center.

Two exercises demonstrate the use of database utilities as well as the creation and usage of Link Monitors.

In the following lessons, you will be introduced to:

- Exchange Server databases, their transaction log files, and the Exchange Server database engine
- Various methods for backing up and restoring an Exchange Server
- The configuration and use of Server and Link Monitors
- Troubleshooting tools, which provide useful support for maintaining Exchange Server computers

Lesson 1: Database Operation and Maintenance

A professional administrator must have a thorough understanding of Exchange Server databases and their maintenance, because it is one of the administrator's primary tasks to keep the messaging system permanently available.

In the sections that follow, you'll be introduced to Exchange Server databases, transaction log files, fault-tolerance mechanisms, and the circular logging setting. Available backup methods and corresponding restore operations are also an important topic. The section about restore operations describes how to move an Exchange Server to a new hardware platform. This lesson will conclude with a listing of database maintenance tools and a discussion about large Exchange Server databases.

At the end of this lesson, you will be able to:

- Identify Exchange Server databases and corresponding files according to their tasks

- Maintain transaction log files

- Backing up the important Exchange Server databases on line

- Restore an Exchange Server from an online backup

- Move an existing Exchange Server to a new computer

Estimated time to complete this lesson: 45 minutes

Defining the Database

Exchange Server databases are repositories of items relevant to messaging, such as e-mail messages and configuration information. Corresponding server services maintain these items privately, which means that if you want to obtain information from a database, you must communicate with the appropriate server component, such as the DS or the IS. Direct access to the databases is always prohibited.

Database Characteristics

Exchange Server databases can be divided into two groups: core databases and optional databases. Core databases maintain all messaging information, while additional databases are required only if the Directory Synchronization with Microsoft Mail has been configured or if a KM Server has been installed on the local computer. (See Figure 15-1.)

Core Databases

Three core databases form the DS, the Private Information Store and the Public Information Store. The DS stores the configuration information of the local server, site, and the organization (such as recipient objects). You can find this database in a file called Dir.edb that resides in the \Exchsrvr\Dsadata directory. The Private Information Store holds mailboxes and gateway folders. Its database has been implemented in a file called Priv.edb, which is located in the \Exchsrvr\Mdbdata directory. The Public Information Store, in turn, maintains the collaborative information of public folders. The corresponding database is called Pub.edb and can also be found in the \Exchsrvr\Mdbdata directory.

Note Databases of the Exchange Server 5.5 Standard Edition can grow to a maximum of 16 GB. Databases of the Enterprise Edition are no longer limited to 16 GB and can grow to the physical capacity of the server's storage media.

Optional Databases

The optional databases that might be found on an Exchange Server computer are the Dirsync database and the KM database. The KM database resides in the \Exchsrvr\Kmsdata directory, provided that you have installed the KM Server on the local computer. This database, which was covered in Chapter 14, preserves the history of the encryption keys for all users who have been enabled with Advanced Security.

The DirSync database, called Xdir.edb, is located in the \Exchsrvr\Dxadata directory. It keeps track of MS Mail DirSync Requestor transactions. The Directory Synchronization Agent uses this database when Directory Synchronization with MS Mail has been configured. You can find more information about Directory Synchronization with MS Mail in Chapter 18, "Connecting to Microsoft Mail and Schedule+."

Note The Exchange Server version of the Backup program does not include the DirSync or KM Server databases in its online backup procedures. Therefore, you can save these database only using an offline backup. Backup operations will be discussed in the section, "Backing Up the Database," later in this lesson.

JET and Log files

All databases rely on Microsoft Joint Engine Technology (JET) 3.0. JET is an advanced 32-bit multithreaded database engine that uses transaction log files. Transaction log files optimize the use of databases (such as DS, Private Information Store, and Public Information Store).

Let's say you send a message to another user on the same home server. The new message is supposed to be written to the Private Information Store database (Priv.edb), but this would require complex database processing, which slows down the send operation. Instead, the IS service buffers the message only in a corresponding transaction log file that allows for faster completion of the send operation. Transaction log files are far less complex than database structures. The IS service then commits the changes to the actual database file at a later time. Users are not aware of this delayed commit. The cooperation of databases and database transaction log files is explained in more detail in the section, "Maintaining Log Files," later in this lesson.

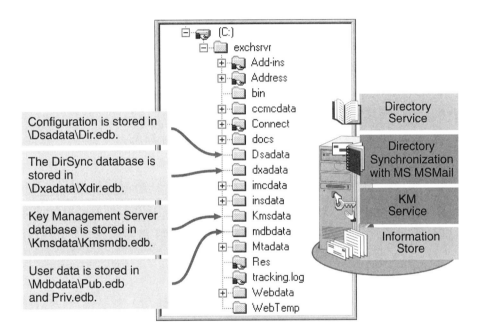

Figure 15-1. Exchange Server and its databases.

The active server components and their corresponding databases are as follows:

- DS uses JET to maintain the configuration information in a directory database called Dir.edb.

- DXA uses JET to keep track of the DirSync Requestor/DirSync Server transactions by means of the Xdir.edb.

- IS service uses JET to maintain the Private Information Store and Public Information Store database in two separate files, called Priv.edb and Pub.edb.

- KM Server service uses JET to maintain private and public keys for users who have Advanced Security enabled in a KM database.

Maintaining Log Files

Let's say you want to create a public folder that will store 500 MB of information. How much disk space must be put aside for this public folder—500 MB, 1 GB, or even more? The answer is, "It depends," but you should make sure that the computer has at least 1 GB of free disk space. Depending on the actual configuration, Exchange Server may twice store each item temporarily before it finally maintains the information within the appropriate database only. As explained in this lesson, Exchange Server maintains the data in transaction log files as well until the log files are purged either automatically or through a full or incremental online backup.

Database Reliance on Log Files

The architecture of the information repository of Exchange Server uses fault-tolerant and transaction-oriented databases. Fault tolerance ensures that data accepted by the server will not be lost. Even in extreme cases (for example, power outages), the data can be reconstructed based on transaction log files that have not yet been written to the database. The reconstruction process is launched at the next system startup.

Transaction Logs

Transaction log files are the primary information repository for new transactions. One transaction log file exists for the DS, and one for the IS. The DS transaction log file, called Edb.log, can be found in the \Exchsrvr\Dsadata directory. The log file for the IS is also called Edb.log, but it resides in the \Exchsrvr\Mdbdata directory. The Edb.log file of the IS is used for both the Priv.edb and the Pub.edb.

JET uses transaction log files to manage the data storage efficiently and with high speed. The data is written to these files sequentially. In other words, JET simply appends new data to the existing data without the need for complex database operations. Database maintenance routines will commit the transactions to the actual databases at a later time in order to bring them up to date.

Note Exchange Server databases and their transaction log files form the most recent state of the IS and the DS. If you want to save an Exchange Server completely, you must back up both the databases and their log files.

Previous Logs

Transaction log files are always exactly 5.242.880 bytes (5 MB) in size. If the files are completely used they are renamed in order to allow the creation of a new, empty file. Renamed transaction log files are called previous log files.

The naming format of previous log files is EDBxxxxx.LOG, where *x* represents a hexadecimal number. The previous log files reside in the same directories as the current transaction log files (\Exchsrvr\Dsadata,\Exchsrvr\Mdbdata, and so forth).

Checkpoint Files

Checkpoint files are used to keep track of transactions that have already been incorporated into the databases from the transaction log files. Checkpoint files guarantee that a particular transaction will not be committed to a database twice. Checkpoint files, called Edb.chk, reside in the \Exchsrvr\Dsadata and \Exchsrvr\Mdbdata directories as well as the directories of optional databases.

The Edb.chk is updated whenever Exchange Server writes a particular transaction into a database. This avoids duplicated or missing database entries, even if a power outage should occur while the DS and IS services are committing transactions. The checkpoint file always points to the last transaction that was transferred successfully. Missing data can be identified and committed at the next system startup. This mechanism prevents inconsistent databases.

Note The Edb.chk files provide the fastest recovery mechanism, although they are not absolutely required to commit transactions to databases. Exchange Server can also process transaction log files directly, determining by itself which transactions have not yet been committed.

Reserved Logs

Reserved logs are the "emergency repository" for transaction logs.They provide enough disk space to write transactions from memory to the hard disk even if a server's hard disk is filled up to a point where no new transaction log file can be created any more. Reserved logs are called Res1.log and Res2.log and can be found in the database directories. They are created automatically during the installation of an Exchange Server because—for obvious reasons—they cannot be created at a later time when they are actually needed. Both the DS and the IS maintain their own set of reserved logs in the corresponding database directories.

JET uses the Res1.log and Res2.log files only to complete a current transaction process. It then sends an error notification to the IS or DS, depending on which database is affected, in order to shut down the service safely to prevent lost user data. You will find an entry that indicates the service shutdown along with a reason for the shutdown in the Application Event Log file. In this situation, you must create additional free hard disk space (for example, add a new hard disk) before you restart the services.

You can immediately restart the IS if it has been automatically shut down due to missing hard disk space. In such a situation, it is recommended that you perform a full backup of the Exchange Server directly once the IS is restarted. The full backup will delete existing transaction logs once their content is written into the .EDB file to free the server's hard disk resources. The mechanism of restarting the affected service and performing a full online backup to purge the transaction log files works for the DS as well. The full backup is explained in the section, "Backing Up the Database," later in this lesson.

Patch Files

Patch files maintain transactions during online backup operations and are deleted automatically once the backup process is completed. Therefore, patch files should not exist in the directories of the databases during regular server operation.

The Exchange Server version of the Backup program allows you to perform backup operations while the server services are running. This means that while you are saving the server databases and transaction log files, users can still send and receive messages. The transaction log files, however, are unavailable in this situation because the Backup program must save these files. Therefore, Exchange Server uses patch files temporarily to catch (possible) current transactions. Patch files are included in the current backup at the end of the online backup procedure. The existing online backup types are covered later in this lesson in the section, "Backing Up the Database."

Note Patch files ensure that the current online backup represents the most recent state.

Preventing Waste of Disk Space

The DS and the IS service incorporate the data of the log files into the databases during their maintenance cycles and during server shutdown, but this doesn't mean that transaction logs or entries in transaction log files are deleted. In fact, when transactions have been committed to a database, items are stored in two locations—the transaction log file and the database.

Manual Deletion

Manually deleting transaction log files is not advisable because you run the risk of deleting messages accidentally. You cannot analyze the checkpoint files to figure out which transactions have already been written to the databases, so you might delete transactions that have not yet been committed. Accidental deletion will lead to an inconsistent database, which cannot be recovered without a recent backup.

Circular Logging

Circular logging is a confusing term that basically means automatically deleting transaction log files and their entries. Circular logging is enabled by default and causes the server to discard transactions as soon as they have been committed to the databases. The checkpoint file indicates which log files and transaction entries can be removed. Any existing previous log files are deleted completely, while transactions within the current transaction log file are marked as obsolete only. New transactions will eventually overwrite the obsolete entries in the current transaction log file before a new transaction log is created as usual.

Database Backups

The Exchange Server version of the Backup program deletes transaction log files when you complete a full backup or an incremental backup. The differential backup type, on the other hand, does not affect the existing previous logs or any entries within the current transaction log file. The online backup types are covered in more detail in the section, "Backing Up the Database," later in this lesson.

Disadvantages of the Circular Logging Feature

Circular logging prevents the waste of disk space, but it also prevents sophisticated fault-tolerant configurations and several online backup types, which rely on the existence of transaction log files. (See Figure 15-2.) You might therefore want to disable this option. The fault-tolerance mechanisms based on transaction log files are covered later in this lesson in the section, "Restoring an Exchange Server."

The **Advanced** property page of each server object in the Administrator program allows you to disable the circular logging feature for the DS and the IS. When you have disabled the circular logging, you must perform online backups to avoid wasting hard disk space. More information about the server-level configuration of Exchange Server is provided in Chapter 8.

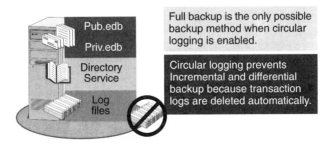

Figure 15-2. Preventing the waste of disk space.

The different types of log files are as follows:

- Transaction logs are the first repository for all transactions because they increase the server performance.

- Previous logs are transaction logs that have been used and filled to capacity.

- Checkpoint files maintain a checkpoint of transactions already written to the databases.

- Reserved logs ensure that there is enough storage space for all transactions, even if room no longer exists on the hard disk for new transaction logs.

- Patch files store transactions during online backup operation.

Backing Up the Database

It is recommended that you use the Exchange Server version of the Backup program to save and restore the data of Exchange Server computers. This version replaces the original Windows NT program and allows you to perform backups of the DS and the IS databases while the server services are running. Of course, you can also run regular file backups if you prefer.

Offline Backups

An offline backup is a regular file-based backup of the \Exchsrvr directory and its subdirectories. It can be performed only when the server services are stopped (off line). Offline backups have an advantage in that they can include the Windows NT Registry, KM database, and MS Mail DirSync database in addition to the core databases. Usually, offline backups incorporate the data of the entire Windows NT Server, including the Registry.

Offline backups have several disadvantages as well, however. The most obvious disadvantage is that the Exchange Server is unavailable during backup operation because the DS and IS services are stopped. Furthermore, you must always perform a complete backup of the entire server, which consumes time and tape space. In addition, the offline backup is not aware of databases and transaction log files, so it does not discard committed transactions nor does it allow the backing up of the DS and databases separately.

Note It is important to include all \Exchsrvr directories into an offline backup to completely save the Exchange Server. If you were previously running the Performance Optimizer, you will most likely find an \Exchsrvr directory on each existing disk drive.

Online Backups

An online backup is a backup that is performed while the server services are running (on line). In fact, the DS and the IS must be running in order to back up their databases. Active server services ensure that users can send and receive messages during the backup operation. Current transactions are included into the backup. Three different types of online backups are available: full backup, incremental backup, and differential backup.

Online backups are aware of the Exchange Server databases and their transaction log files. They guarantee that the entire store of data in the Exchange Server is backed up even if only transaction log files are written to tape. This can save backup time and tape space. A significant disadvantage of online backups is that they do not include the Windows NT Registry, the KM database, or the Dirsync database.

Note Using online backups, you can back up the entire IS and the DS separately, but it is impossible to back up individual mailboxes or public folders.

Full Backup

A full backup covers the data of a particular Exchange Server completely. It saves the DS and the IS databases as well as the transaction log entries that have not yet been committed to the databases. In addition, transaction log files, whose content is already committed to the actual database files, are purged from the system. In other words, a full backup sets the context for the incremental and differential backup types. Remaining or newly created transaction log files contain only new transactions that have occurred since the most recent full backup was carried out. (See Figure 15-3.)

Note A full backup requires more tape space than any other online backup type.

Incremental Backup

An incremental backup saves only new transaction log files, which are purged once they have been backed up. Because transaction log files are purged, the incremental backup sets the context for the next incremental or differential backup. It is important to understand that it does not save any database files, which means that the incremental backup is useless without a previous full backup.

The last full backup and all incremental backups that have been run since the last full back up are necessary for completely restoring an Exchange Server. For example, Fred Pumpkin performs online backups on a regular basis. A full backup is scheduled every Sunday. Incremental backups are run on the other days of the week. On Thursday, the server NEWYORK-1 crashes, so Fred must restore the system. He restores the last full backup and the incremental backups from Monday, Tuesday, and Wednesday. At this point, the databases of last Sunday, plus all the transactions that have been performed since then, are available again. When Fred starts the server services, the transactions are incorporated into the databases again and the server is brought up to date.

The incremental backup has a significant disadvantage. If Fred's backup from Tuesday is destroyed, the backup from Wednesday is also useless. In this case, only the incremental backup from Monday can be restored in addition to the last full backup, so the server has effectively lost the most current information.

Note You should not restart the Exchange Server services until you have restored the last full backup plus all incremental backups.

Differential Backup

A differential backup is a backup that includes only transaction log files, but, unlike an incremental backup, the differential backup does not purge these files, so it does not change the context for the next backup. It is dependent on a previous full backup or incremental backup. (See Figure 15-3.)

If Fred were to perform full backups every Sunday and differential backups on Monday, Tuesday, and Wednesday, he could restore the server NEWYORK-1 by using the last full backup and the differential backup from Wednesday. Other backups are not required in this scenario.

Note Differential backups require more server disk space than incremental backups because transaction log files are not purged between full backup cycles.

Automating the Backup Process

The Windows NT Backup utility provides several command line switches that allow you to specify desired backup operations. The Exchange Server replacement of the original Backup.exe also provides these command line switches. The Exchange Server version provides two additional switches, which allow you to back up the IS and the DS separately. The switches are **\is \\<server name>**, which specifies the IS of the server that is specified by <server name>, and **\ds <\\server name>**, which can be used to indicate the desired server's DS.

The following are standard NTBackup.exe switches that are useful in batch files:

Parameter	Description
path	Specifies one or more paths of the directories to be backed up
/a	Appends backup sets after the last backup set on the tape; when /a is not specified, NTbackup.exe overwrites previous data
/v	Verifies the backup operation
/r	Restricts access to the files on the backup set
/d "text"	Defines a description of the backup set
/b	Indicates that the local Registry should be backed up
/hc:on or /hc:off	Switches hardware compression on or off
/t <option>	Specifies the backup type with the following options: normal, copy, incremental, differential, daily
/l "filename"	Specifies the filename for the backup log
/e	Determines that the backup log includes exceptions only
/tape:<n>	Specifies the tape drive to which the files should be backed up; <n> can range between 0 and 9 according to the number the drive was assigned when the tape drive was installed

Using command line parameters, you can create batch files to perform all desired actions for you. For instance, you can stop all Exchange Server services, perform an offline backup, and then restart all Exchange Server services. Even if you want to perform online backups, a batch file can be configured to initiate the backup of the DS and the IS. The following batch file creates a full backup of the server NEWYORK-1:

```
REM **** Backup of the IS and the DS ****
Ntbackup backup \is \\NEWYORK-1 /t normal
Ntbackup backup \ds \\NEWYORK-1 /t normal
REM **** Batch job finished ****
```

It is a good idea to combine batch files with the Windows NT AT utility (AT.exe). AT.exe provides the functionality for automatically launching an unattended process at a given time. This way you can run your batch jobs at night when nobody is actually working in your department.

The following AT.exe command line switches can be used:

Parameter	Description
\\computername	Specifies a remote computer; if not used, commands are scheduled on the local computer
id	Specifies an identification number assigned to the scheduled command
/delete	Cancels the scheduled command; if an ID is not specified, all scheduled commands on the computer are canceled
/yes	Used with cancel all jobs command when no further confirmation is desired
time	Specifies the time when the command should be executed
/interactive	Allows the job to interact with the desktop of a user logged on at the time the job runs
/every:date[,...]	Runs the command on specified day(s) of the week or month
/next:date[,...]	Runs the specified command on the next occurrence of the date
"command"	Specifies the command or batch to be run

It is important to note that the Schedule service must be running to use the AT command.

The different backup strategies and their functions are as follows:

- Differential backup; saves transaction logs only, but does not purge them; dependent upon a previous full backup

- Full backup; backs up all database and transaction log files; purges transaction logs

- Incremental backup; saves transaction logs only and then purges them dependent upon a previous full backup

- Offline backup; regular file backup that runs while Exchange services are stopped

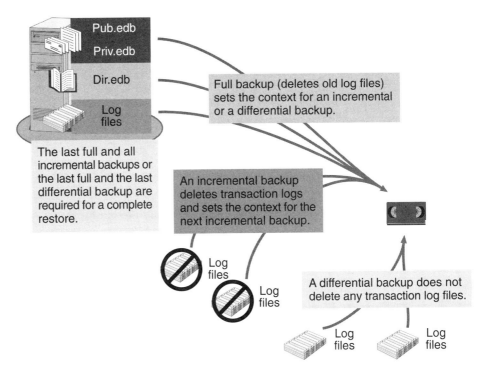

Figure 15-3. Exchange Server backup strategies.

Restoring an Exchange Server

Just as a firefighter prepares constantly for emergencies, so should an administrator prepare and practice frequently for disaster scenarios. It is recommended that you have a test computer permanently at your disposal to run restoration and maintenance routines at least once a month. If you are equipped with detailed theoretical knowledge and solid practical skills, you might one day save your company's bottom line in ranges far beyond the cost of a test computer. The faster you can restore an Exchange Server, the better.

Fault Tolerance of Transaction Logs

Transaction log files can provide fault tolerance because they maintain a copy of the database contents. The idea of fault tolerance is relatively simple: as you place one copy of the data (database files) on one hard disk and a second copy (transaction logs) on another hard disk, the data remains available even if one of the hard disks breaks.

In order to take advantage of the fault tolerance provided by transaction log files, it is necessary that you install at least two hard disks in an Exchange Server computer. In addition, you absolutely must disable the circular logging feature to avoid the automatic deletion of transaction log files. If these requirements are met you can improve the fault tolerance by separating the transaction logs from the database files by placing them on each disk separately. Thus, the disk containing the databases breaks, the current information is still available in the transaction log files. In such a scenario, you would simply install a new hard disk and restore the databases. The most important point to remember is that you must not select the option to delete existing data during the restore operation so that the most current transaction logs remain unaffected on the second disk. When you restart the IS and the DS, the current transaction log information is committed to the databases again, bringing the server back to its most current state.

Note The Performance Optimizer will suggest that the transaction logs be separated from the databases if more than one partition is available. Running this tool offers the most convenient way to achieve a fault-tolerant configuration. However, circular logging must be disabled manually using the Administrator program.

Moving an Exchange Server

If you replace the hardware of an Exchange Server, you might also be in charge of performing backup and restore operations. Briefly, you back up the production server, remove the old computer, install Windows NT Server and Exchange Server on the new computer, and restore the recent backup. (See Figure 15-4.) This process sounds easier than it really is because of several dependencies.

Joining the Existing Windows NT Domain

First you must install the new Windows NT Server computer in the existing Windows NT domain using the old computer name. Otherwise, you cannot restore the directory database successfully.

Exchange Server relies on Windows NT security to provide access to server-based resources. For instance, every mailbox typically maintains a primary Windows NT account. Because these accounts belong to the old Windows NT domain you must join this domain with your new computer. Furthermore, the name of the new Windows NT Server must match the old one because it is part of the directory. As mentioned in Chapter 2, this name cannot be changed without losing the directory database.

Note Using the Windows NT Server Manager, you must first remove the old server reference from the domain before joining the existing domain again with a new Windows NT Server that has the same computer name.

Installing the New Exchange Server Computer in an Existing Site

A newly installed Windows NT Server computer is not sufficient if you want to restore Exchange Server databases. A new Exchange Server must also be installed. Dependencies of the DS and IS databases will require that you specify the former site and organization names during installation. Several Registry settings must match the information in the old DS database that you plan to restore on the computer.

Note Even if the old server actually belonged to an existing site, you will need to install the new server in its own site using the names of the existing organization and site as well as the corresponding Site Services Account. Only a new server installation, as explained in Chapter 2, securely prevents the modification of the existing site. The newly created Directory will later be replaced by the backup version, which integrates the new server in the existing site again. It is not recommended to use **Setup /R** or other setup options to install the new server.

At the end of the installation procedure you have the option to launch the Performance Optimizer. Running this tool allows the new server to use the existing new hardware platform most efficiently. The Performance Optimizer does not affect the planned restore operation.

Restoring and Testing the New Server

Now you can restore the most recent full backup (and, if necessary, the most recent differential and incremental backups) of the old Exchange Server. Once the server services have been restarted successfully, you might want to run the IS/DS consistency adjuster in the Administrator program. This is actually not a required task, but the IS/DS consistency adjuster checks the databases for any inconsistencies, so it is a perfect tool for verifying the restore operation. The IS/DS consistency adjuster can be launched using the **Consistency Adjuster** button on the **Advanced** property page of the corresponding server object. When the IS/DS consistency adjuster finishes, the server will be active and users can access their mailboxes again. The server-level administration using the Administrator program is covered in Chapter 8.

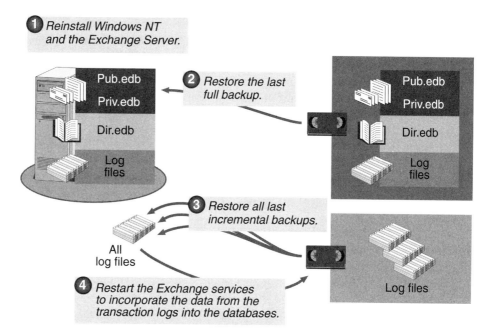

Figure 15-4. Restoring an Exchange Server.

The following are possible methods for restoring an Exchange Server:

- Full backup with differential backup; do not restart the Exchange Server services before the differential backup has been restored

- Full backup with incremental backup; do not restart the Exchange Server services before the last incremental backup has been restored

- Full backup; start the Exchange Server services immediately after the restore operation has been completed

Maintaining the Database

Exchange Server databases are shared between numerous users who create, change, and delete messages, public folders, and the server configuration. As a result, the databases become fragmented over time. This is a normal process that you can't prevent, just as you can't prevent the fragmentation of a computer's hard disk. Database fragmentation slows down the server services, which is not desirable; even worse, significant database fragmentation can lead to database inconsistencies that may cause serious problems. Exchange Server databases must therefore be maintained (defragmented) on a regular basis.

Automatic Online Defragmentation Features

The DS and the IS defragment their databases themselves during their scheduled maintenance cycles. These services also check for database inconsistencies during every startup and shutdown of the server. So while you don't need to worry about database fragmentation too much, you might want to adjust the most important maintenance parameters. The maintenance schedule, for example, can be managed using the **IS Maintenance** property page of the desired server object in the Administrator program. Another important parameter, the **Garbage Collection Interval**, can be controlled through the **General** property page of the **DS Site Configuration** object. This setting determines when the DS will remove deleted items from its database. More information about server-level administration using the Administrator program is provided in Chapter 8.

Offline Defragmentation Tool

The Offline Defragmentation Tool (Eseutil.exe) allows you to perform database consistency checks, defragmentation, and failure correction at the JET level while the DS and the IS services are stopped. If the services have not been stopped before you try to launch the Eseutil.exe tool, the error code -1032 will be returned. Eseutil.exe is a command line utility that is installed along with Exchange Server and can be found in the \Winnt\System32 directory.

Eseutil (formerly known as Edbutil) is a generic JET tool that reorders the items stored in the databases to free unused storage space. In contrast, the online defragmentation does not reduce the size of the databases; rather, it reorders only the deleted objects and marks their space in the database file as available. You must use the Offline Defragmentation Tool if you want to reduce the physical size of the database files (Dir.edb, Priv.edb, and Pub.edb). (See Figure 15-5 on page 973.)

Database Inconsistencies

The Offline Defragmentation Tool provides a **/G** command line parameter, which can be used to verify the integrity of a database. However, recovery operations are not performed with this option. The Integrity mode returns an error only if the databases are not in an accurate state.

Let's say a user reports that unread items are indicated as being in the Inbox, although no visible messages reside in this folder at the moment. To verify whether a problem exists, you can use the Offline Defragmentation Tool to check to see if the Private Information Store is in an inconsistent state. The Offline Defragmentation Tool checks the integrity for the DS, the Private Information Store, and the Public Information Store. You can identify a particular database by using either the path and file name of the database explicitly (for example, **Eseutil /G C:\Exchrvr\Dsadata\Dir.edb**) or by using the predefined switches **/ISPRIV**, **/ISPUB** or **/DS** (for example, **Eseutil /G /DS**). The parameter **/ISPRIV** is a shortcut for the Private Information Store, **/ISPUB** refers to the Public Information Store, and **/DS** identifies the Directory. The location of the corresponding database file is obtained from the Registry.

Database Recovery

If you discover a corrupted database, you can use the Offline Defragmentation Tool to fix the problem. However, it is recommended that you first reboot the Exchange Server because online maintenance routines, which are launched during the server shutdown and startup, might automatically correct the inconsistency. You should also perform a full backup at this point, just to be prepared in case Eseutil acts differently than expected!

If you must launch the Recovery mode, however, you can do so using the **/R** command line parameter. Using this option, Eseutil works the following way: a new database file is created and the Offline Defragmentation Tool then iterates through the old database to find inconsistencies and corruption. Valid items are written immediately to the new database file, while corrupted items are corrected prior to the transfer. Items that cannot be fixed are excluded from the transfer and can therefore no longer be found in the new database.

It is important to note that during the recovery process a second copy of the database is generated, so you should check in advance to see if the server offers enough free disk space to accomplish the recovery operation. If it does not, you can copy the database to another location before you start the Offline Defragmentation Tool. As mentioned previously, the actual location of the old database file can be specified as a command line parameter.

Note You should use the Recovery mode of the Offline Defragmentation Tool only if rebooting the server does not correct the problem and if you do not have a recent backup. Running the Recovery mode may lead to lost user data. Also important is that you check to make sure enough disk space is available to complete the operation.

The Isinteg.exe Utility

Isinteg is short for *Information Store Integrity*. It can find and eliminate inaccuracies of the Private Information Store and Public Information Store databases. Isinteg.exe is a useful utility that offers valuable aids in case of IS problems and can be found in the \Exchsrvr\Bin directory. Isinteg.exe returns the error **JET_errFileAccessDenied** (which corresponds to the JET error 1032 mentioned above) if you start this program while the IS service is running.

Test Mode

The test mode of the Isinteg.exe utility doesn't correct any corruption; it checks the IS only for table errors, incorrect reference counters, and non-referenced items. Isinteg.exe provides the **-pri** and **-pub** command line switches in addition to the actual test parameters. The parameter **-pri** allows you to check the Priv.edb file, while **-pub** allows you to check the Pub.edb file. You must therefore run Isinteg.exe separately for each database file. You can also use the **-verbose** command line parameter to obtain the most detailed information about the integrity check.

Test Name

The Isinteg.exe utility of Exchange Server 5.5 defines a new command line parameter called **test**. This mandatory parameter must be used in conjunction with other parameters to specify which test routines you want to launch. The available tests that you can choose to launch are documented in the Isinteg.rtf file, which is in the \Server\Support\Utils directory of the Exchange Server installation CD-ROM.

Log File

The results of the integrity check are displayed on the screen and written to a log file. The log file can be used for documentation purposes. By default, Isinteg.exe uses a log file called Isinteg.pri for the Private Information Store and Isinteg.pub for the Public Information Store. You can specify an alternative name for the log file by using the **-L** command line parameter.

Correcting the Tables

Without specifying additional parameters, Isinteg.exe simply browses through the IS database tables to find corruption, but it does not correct any corruption it detects. In order to fix existing errors, you must specify the **-fix** option at the command line. As usual, Isinteg.exe writes details about the correction process to the specified log file.

Patch Mode

The patch mode of Isinteg.exe can be launched to adjust the DS and IS databases. However, the DS must be running to allow the utility to obtain the required directory information. This mode might be necessary if the Priv.edb and Pub.edb have been restored from an offline backup.

You must start **Isinteg -patch** if the IS service cannot start and instead reports the error code -1011 in the Application Event Log. Other Errors that can be corrected using **Isinteg –patch** are as follows:

Event log ID	Message Text
1087	IS was restored from an offline backup
1089	IS was not started because the internal reference to <a DN representing the mailbox root> in the mailboxes table could not be found
2083	IS was restored from an offline backup
7202	Database has been copied from the server <server1> to the server <server2>

When the IS has been patched, you can start the service again.

Note Isinteg.exe runs in Patch mode against both Pub.edb and Priv.edb at the same time. A separate treatment of one of the database files is not possible.

Maintaining Large Exchange Server Databases

Under normal circumstances, administrators don't have to care too much about Eseutil.exe and Isinteg.exe at all. In fact, the online maintenance routines of the DS and the IS almost guarantee that you never really need to use them. Furthermore, a perfect backup strategy is a good insurance that makes direct (offline) maintenance of the databases almost obsolete. However, it might happen that you have to rely on Eseutil.exe and Isinteg.exe in order to bring databases to a consistent state.

Offline database maintenance tools are not really optimized for huge databases. The databases of the IS can grow very large, and the Enterprise Edition of Exchange Server 5.5 in particular might encourage you to build huge servers with e-mail repositories of enormous sizes beyond the former limit of 16 GB. Support for clustering might also lead you to implement large messaging nodes. The Exchange Server version of NTBackup.exe is now optimized to back up between 25 GB and 30 GB per hour, so there seem to exist many good reasons for a configuration with fewer and larger servers rather than more and smaller servers.

Nevertheless, it is still a good idea to plan large server installations very carefully, especially considering the fact that Eseutil.exe—depending on the speed of your server—will require up to an hour per GB for defragmentation or recovery. A small calculation illustrates the importance of this topic. Let's assume that the average user stores 20 MB of e-mail messages on a server. Given this, the Private Information Store of a server with 1,000 users might grow larger than 20 GB. Now let's assume that you must run Eseutil.exe because you need to recover the Priv.edb. Because you have a fast and powerful server machine, Eseutil.exe can complete the job in 30 minutes per GB. This means the server is off line for more than 10 hours, which is slightly more than the average workday. Let's assume the average user spends an hour a day for communication using Exchange. In that case, if a server with 1,000 mailboxes becomes unavailable for only one day, you would lose 1,000 hours of work. Because the typical workday has eight hours, you would lose 125 days. That adds up to more than half a year if you consider that a year has approximately 200 workdays.

Therefore, to save your company money, a reliable backup strategy is one essential aspect of implementing huge servers. Whenever possible, you should keep at least the private servers below the 16 GB limit. In almost all respects, two small servers are preferable over one big Exchange Server computer. If these arguments are not sufficient to convince you, you should keep in mind that public servers seem to be more suitable for implementing a huge repository of information than private servers, because public folder replication can provide fault tolerance and load balancing across your organization, as described in Chapter 13.

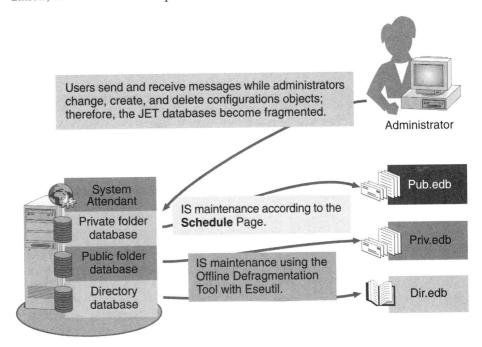

Figure 15-5. Defragmenting the Exchange Server databases.

The Eseutil.exe command line options and their functions are as follows:

- no option; to display the option list only
- **/ds**; to specify the database of the Directory (Dir.edb)
- **/ispriv**; to specify the database of the Private Information Store (Priv.edb)
- **/ispub**; to specify the database of the Public Information Store (Pub.edb)
- **/b path**; to create a backup copy of the original uncompacted database at the specified location (in conjunction with /d only)
- **/d**; to defragment databases
- **/g**; to check the integrity of a database file
- **/o**; to suppress the Exchange Server banner (in conjunction with another command line parameter only)
- **/p**; to retain the old, uncompacted database in its original location and store the new compacted database in the default file called Tempdfrg.edb in the \Exchsrvr\Bin directory
- **/r**; to recover a specified database file
- **/t filename**; to rename the new compacted database (in conjunction with /d only)
- **/u**; to upgrade a database file from a previous version

The Isinteg.exe command line options and their functions are as follows:

- **Isinteg -?**; to display the option list only
- **Isinteg -fix**; to correct table errors, inaccurate cross-reference counts, or unreferenced names
- **Isinteg -l** *filename*; to specify a name for the log file; the defaults are Isinteg.pri for the Private Information Store and Isinteg.pub for the Public Information Store
- **Isinteg -pri**; to test the Private Information Store
- **Isinteg -pub**; to test the Public Information Store
- **Isinteg –test** *testname*; to specify a particular test that will be performed; for better performance it is possible to combine multiple tests such as – **test** *testname1, testname2, testname3*

Exercise 47: Using Eseutil.exe and Isinteg.exe to Check and Fix the Integrity of Exchange Databases

The Offline Defragmentation Tool and the Isinteg.exe utility are the most important offline maintenance tools. The Offline Defragmentation Tool (Eseutil.exe) allows you to defragment all core databases, reorder items, and perform consistency checks at the JET level. This tool can also recover a corrupted database file; however, this mode should be used only if a recent backup is not available and a current backup of the damaged database has been created. The Isinteg.exe utility, in turn, permits you to check the Private Information Store and Public Information Store databases.

Estimated time to complete this exercise: 25 minutes

Description

In this exercise, you will use the Offline Defragmentation Tool to defragment the Exchange Server databases. You can use the Isinteg.exe utility to check the IS databases. The databases of your test computers are more than likely in an accurate state, but you should become familiar with these important tools to be prepared for emergency situations.

- Task 47a describes the steps for using the Eseutil.exe utility to defragment the DS, the Public Information Store, and the Private Information Store in order to make used storage contiguous, to free unused storage, and to compact the databases.

- Task 47b describes the steps for using the Isinteg.exe offline utility to dump the Private Information Store and Public Information Store databases.

- Task 47c describes the steps for restarting all the Exchange Server services.

Prerequisites

- The KM Server floppy disk must be available to restart the KM service (installed in Exercise 46).

- Log on as Admin-NY1 to NEWYORK-1 to complete this exercise.

Task 47a: Running Eseutil.exe Against the Public Information Stores and Private Information Stores and the DS

1. Click the **Start** button, point to **Programs**, and then click **Command Prompt**.

2. Type *Eseutil /?* and then press Enter to display the major parameters for Eseutil.exe.

3. Type *D* to receive the details on the defragmentation parameters.

4. Type *Eseutil /d /ispriv* and then press Enter.

5. Notice the error -1032, which indicates the Exchange Server services are running.

6. Click the **Start** button, point to **Settings**, and then click Control Panel.

7. Double-click the **Services** icon.

8. Select **Microsoft Exchange System Attendant** and then click **Stop**.

9. A **Stopping** dialog box appears, indicating that all other Exchange Server services will be stopped as well. Click **OK**.

10. After the services are stopped, click **Close**.

11. Close the Control Panel and then switch back to the **Command Prompt** window.

12. Type *Eseutil /d /ispriv* and then press Enter.

13. The output for the Eseutil.exe program appears. After the defragmentation has been finished, type *Notepad Dfrginfo*.

14. Review the output from running Eseutil.exe against the Private Information Store.

15. Close Notepad.

16. Type *Eseutil /d /ispub* and then press Enter.

17. The output for the Eseutil.exe program appears.

18. At the command prompt, type *Notepad Dfrginfo*.

19. Review the output from running Eseutil.exe against the Public Information Store. Notice that the information is appended to the log file.

20. Close Notepad.

21. Type *Eseutil /d /ds* and then press Enter.

22. The output for the Eseutil.exe program appears.

23. At the command prompt, type *Notepad Dfrginfo*.

24. Review the output from running Eseutil.exe against the DS database. Notice that the information is always appended to the log file; old entries are not overwritten.

25. Close Notepad.

26. Close the **Command Prompt** window.

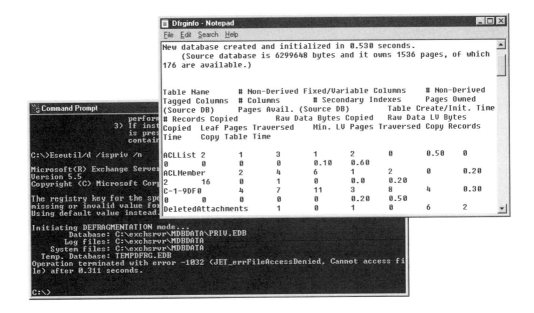

Task 47b: Running Isinteg.exe Against the Information Store

1. Click the **Start** button, point to **Settings**, and then click Control Panel.

2. Double-click the **Services** icon.

3. Verify that all Exchange Server services are stopped. If they are running, stop them by stopping the SA. Don't close the Control Panel.

4. Click the **Start** button, point to **Programs**, and then click **Command Prompt**.

5. In the **Command Prompt** window, change to the **C:\Exchsrvr\Bin** directory.

6. Type *Isinteg /?* and then press Enter to display the parameters for Isinteg.exe.

7. Type *Isinteg -pri -dump -l c:\Isinteg.pri* and then press Enter.

8. The output of the Isinteg.exe program appears.

9. Type *Notepad c:\Isinteg.pri*.

10. Review the output from running Isinteg.exe against the Private Information tion Store.

11. Close Notepad.

12. Type *Isinteg -pub -dump -l c:\Isinteg.pub* and then press Enter.

13. The output for the Isinteg.exe program appears.

14. At the command prompt, type *Notepad Isinteg.pub*.

15. Review the output from running Isinteg.exe against the Public Information Store.

16. Close Notepad, close the **Command Prompt** window, but don't close the Control Panel.

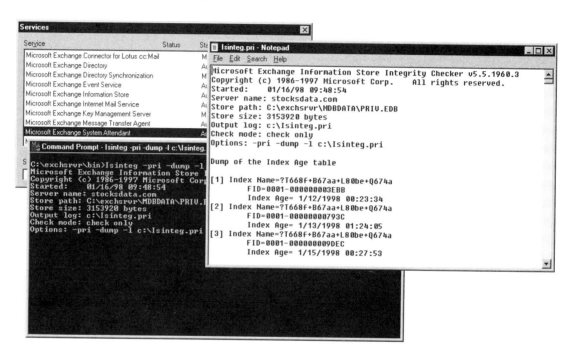

Task 47c: Restarting the Exchange Services

1. Switch to the Control Panel.

2. Double-click the **Services** icon.

3. Start the Exchange services in the following order:
   - Microsoft Exchange System Attendant Service
   - Microsoft Exchange Directory
   - Microsoft Exchange Information Store
   - Microsoft Exchange Message Transfer Agent
   - Microsoft Exchange Event Service

- Microsoft Exchange Key Manager (only when Exercise 46 has been completed and the floppy disk is available)
- Microsoft Exchange Internet Mail Service

4. Close the **Services** dialog box.

5. Close the Control Panel.

6. Log off Windows NT.

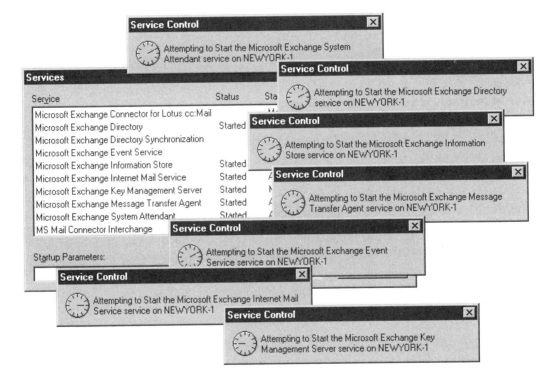

Review

Eseutil.exe and Isinteg.exe are offline utilities that require you to stop the Exchange Server services before you can run them successfully. Both utilities display status information about their operation and write this information to log files for later examination. The Offline Defragmentation Tool displays the time that was required to complete the operation, while Isinteg.exe summarizes the total number of tests, warnings, errors, and fixes.

Lesson 2: Monitors as Maintenance Tools

A reliable backup strategy is good insurance for every Exchange Server administrator, but this insurance only pays if a total disaster occurs. Smaller problems and bottlenecks are not covered by this method. Nevertheless, so-called "small problems" can still make one's life difficult. Unbearable client response times, delays in message delivery, unnecessary NDRs, and frequent unavailability of the messaging system can frustrate your users. Server and Link Monitors cannot prevent these small problems from happening, but they can allow you to discover them as quickly as possible. If you use these valuable tools extensively, you can most likely resolve any problem before the first user becomes aware of it. Even if you cannot solve a problem immediately, it is better to be informed before the first user starts to complain.

This lesson covers both Server and Link Monitors. You will learn about their functions and configuration using the Administrator program. You can also read about the methods for starting and stopping a monitor. A practical exercise concludes this lesson.

Note In addition to the monitoring features built directly into Exchange Server, you can monitor the system using a Simple Network Management Protocol (SNMP) management console. Exchange Server 5.5 supports the Mail and Directory Management-Management Information Base (MADMAN MIB) as defined in 1566, which aloows the packaging of Exchange Server Performance Monitor counters for SNMP-based monitors.

At the end of this lesson, you will be able to:

- Configure and use Server Monitors
- Configure and use Link Monitors

Estimated time to complete this lesson: 25 minutes

Server Monitoring

A Server Monitor is an Administrator program tool that can be used to check the state of Windows NT services to detect critical situations immediately. The Server Monitor can monitor services on both the local and remote server computers.

Monitored Default Services

By default, a Server Monitor takes care of all the Exchange Server core services except the SA, but it is not limited to these core services. In general, you can monitor every Windows NT service that has been configured on an Exchange Server computer. The server needs only to be reached through RPCs. You must specify which services you want monitored through the **Services** property page of the desired server object. (See Figure 15-6 on page 983.) The server-level configuration is covered in more detail in Chapter 8.

Note Server Monitors rely on the SA and cannot function properly if the SA is not started. Hence, Server Monitors cannot monitor the local SA itself, although it is nonetheless appropriate to monitor SAs running on remote servers.

Server Monitor Principle

A Server Monitor periodically checks all specified services. So long as these services are running, the system is considered active, but as soon as one of the monitored services stops for any reason, the system enters a critical state. In this situation, the Server Monitor performs predefined actions such as launching a process, sending a notification message, dispatching a Windows NT alert, restarting the concerned service, or rebooting the entire server computer.

The Server Monitor keeps you up to date at all times. If configured appropriately, it can send a notification message as soon as a critical state has been detected and also if a problem has been resolved.

Configuration

Server Monitors are created and configured using the Administrator program. To create a new monitor object, open the **File** menu, point to **New Other**, and then click the **Server Monitor** command. A **Properties** dialog box appears, asking you for the monitor's **Display Name**, **Directory Name**, **Polling Interval**, monitored servers, the configuration of notifications and predefined actions, and whether the monitor should synchronize the clocks between all servers.

Polling Intervals

The polling interval determines how often the monitor checks the state of Windows NT services. By default, an interval of 15 minutes is assumed as being sufficient, but it will be shortened to 5 minutes if a critical state has been detected.

If you want to adjust the polling interval, display the **General** property page of the Server Monitor object to set the interval separately for **Normal Sites** and **Critical Sites**. A critical site is one where a non-active service has been detected.

Escalation Notification

Switch to the **Notification** property page tab to configure notification messages, which the Server Monitor sends if a critical state has been detected. Three choices are offered in the **New Notification** dialog box when you click the **New** button: you can choose to send a **Mail Message** or a **Windows NT Alert**, or you can **Launch A Process**. The **Launch A Process** option allows you to use a custom application that can, for example, send alerts to your pager.

Monitored Servers

A Server Monitor can check Windows NT services on the local and remote Exchange Server computers regardless of their site, provided a LAN connection exists and RPC communication is supported. Use the **Servers** tab to determine which servers to check. All existing servers of a site are listed when you select the desired site in the **Sites** box and can be easily selected by clicking the **Add** button.

Escalation Actions

Escalation actions are actions that a Server Monitor performs automatically if a critical state has been detected. These actions can be configured on the **Actions** property page. The monitor can be set up to **Take No action**, **Restart The Service**, or **Restart The Server**. These actions can be set independently for three different levels; one escalation level follows the other if a previous action does not solve the critical state. So it is possible to try restarting the critical service two times before the third level is reached that might force restarting the entire server.

It is advisable to allow your users to save their work before a server is automatically restarted; otherwise, they might lose data when working with documents stored on that particular Windows NT server. You can configure a restart notification and a restart delay when specifying the **Restart The Computer** option at any escalation level. The restart notification informs all users connected to the affected server about the scheduled shutdown. The delay determines how much time they have to save their work. The default delay is 60 seconds.

Clock Synchronization and Warning Delays

A Server Monitor can synchronize the clocks between Exchange Server computers if specified on the **Clock** property page. For example, the MTAs of your organization should all be running with a correct clock. Otherwise, if date or time settings (dependent upon the actual time zone) are configured incorrectly, NDRs might be generated unnecessarily due to message expiration. Server clocks that are exactly synchronized can also simplify the comparison of Application Event Log entries regarding time-based events.

Note The Site Service Account needs the Windows NT user right **Change The System Time** in order to change the system time on an Exchange Server computer.

Besides the synchronization of servers, you can modify the warning delays on the **Clock** property page. The **Warning If Off By More Than** and **Alert If Off By More Than** settings determine when nonsynchronized servers are notified through a warning or alert notifications. By default, warnings are written to the Windows NT Event Log if the clock of a monitored server differs from the local clock by more than 15 seconds. An alert is recorded when the clocks are off by more than 60 seconds.

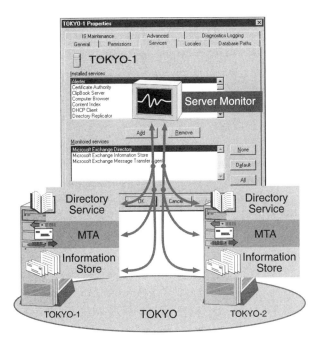

Figure 15-6. Using a Server Monitor.

The actions that a Server Monitor can perform are as follows:

- Launch a process
- Record warnings and alerts in the Application Event Log
- Restart a Windows NT Service
- Restart a Windows NT computer
- Send e-mail messages and Windows NT alerts
- Synchronize clocks between Exchange Server computers

Link Monitors

Active Exchange Server services are a guarantee that your servers are working, but they do not allow you to detect broken messaging connectors. If you want to be sure that messages can reach their destinations in remote sites, remote organizations, and foreign messaging systems, you must configure Link Monitors. A Link Monitor can notify you immediately of broken messaging connectors or if significant delivery delays have been detected.

Function

The principle of a Link Monitor can be explained in brief: it generates a test message, sends the message to a remote recipient, and awaits a reply. The recipient must reply to the test message as soon as the message has been delivered. If this reply can reach the Link Monitor within a given time frame, the message path is considered viable. If the reply is delayed, the administrator are informed about the situation. The SA assists the Link Monitor in generating, receiving and replying test messages. (See Figure 15-7.)

Configuration

As with Server Monitor, you can create a Link Monitor in the Administrator program. But to create a Link Monitor you select the **Link Monitor** command under the **New Other** option on the **File** menu. A **Properties** dialog box appears, asking you for the monitor's **Display Name**, **Directory Name**, and the **Polling Interval**, notification configuration, target servers and recipients, and the time limit for test message replies.

Configuring Time Limits

By default, a link enters the warning state if a reply is outstanding for more than 30 minutes. A link enters the alert state if no reply has been received for more than one hour.

You can modify the time frame for Link Monitor replies through the **Bounce** property page of the Link Monitor object. The desired time frame should express your expectations regarding the messaging connector speed. Take into consideration that you are actually measuring the delivery of two messages; the test message itself and its reply. Therefore, you should set a limit that is sufficient to deliver both; otherwise, you might receive unnecessary warning messages.

Remote Recipients

If the Link Monitor were to have a motto, it would be "All that matters is the reply message." In fact, the Link Monitor can accept replies to test messages from any originator.

The Link Monitor sends test messages to remote SAs if you specify target servers through the **Servers** tab. This is the preferred configuration method because SAs can reply to test messages automatically, requiring no manual interaction. For instance, an administrator in TOKYO can specify LONDON-2, NEWYORK-1, PARIS-1, and FRANKFURT-1 on the **Servers** property page of a Link Monitor running on TOKYO-1 to test the most important Internet connections. (See Figure 15-7.)

You can configure a Link Monitor to send test messages to users and custom recipients using the **Recipients** tab. This is especially useful if you want to test connections to remote Exchange Server organizations or to foreign mail systems. Because the recipient must respond within the specified time frame, he or she might configure an Inbox rule that replies to the test messages always, immediately, and automatically. NDRs generated by a remote messaging system might also represent valid test responses. In this case you must specify a dummy custom recipient, which is considered to be located on the remote system, before you actually configure the Link Monitor. The Link Monitor property pages do not allow you to configure custom recipients. You can read more about the management of recipient objects in Chapter 5.

Polling Intervals

By default, a Link Monitor generates test messages every 15 minutes for normal sites and every 5 minutes for critical sites. A site is considered critical if a test message does not bounce back within the specified time frame. In this situation, it is advisable to poll the affected sites more often than normal in order to determine if the link is functioning basically and whether the delay was a temporary problem. You can adjust the **Polling Interval** on the **General** property page of the Link Monitor object.

Escalation Notification

Like a Server Monitor, a Link Monitor can notify you in case critical sites have been detected through a **Mail Message**, a **Windows NT Alert**, or a custom program via the **Launch A Process** option. You can configure the desired notifications on the **Notification** property page as described earlier for Server Monitors.

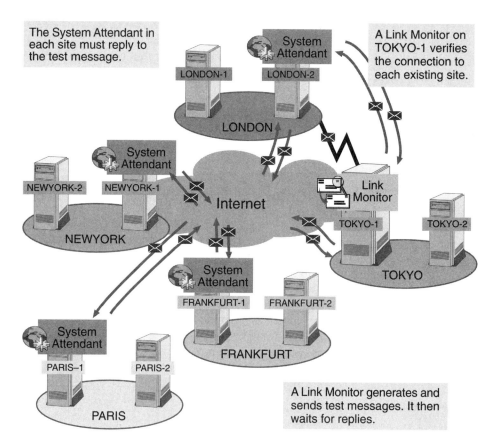

The System Attendant in each site must reply to the test message.

A Link Monitor on TOKYO-1 verifies the connection to each existing site.

A Link Monitor generates and sends test messages. It then waits for replies.

Figure 15-7. Using a Link Monitor.

The following messages are valid Link Monitor replies:

- NDRs generated automatically by remote messaging systems
- Replies generated automatically by SA services
- Replies generated by existing users

Starting and Stopping Monitors

Server and Link Monitor objects are placed in the **Monitors** container under the site's **Configuration** object. Using the Administrator program, you can start the objects either manually or automatically, but they cannot be activated by themselves.

> **Note** It is not possible to run a Server or Link Monitor outside the Exchange Administrator program. As soon as you close the Administrator program, all active monitors stop.

Manual Start

You can start a selected monitor using the **Start Monitor** command on the **Tools** menu. A new child window opens in the Administrator program, displaying the state of each monitored resource. The window displays a green triangle for all functioning systems, an exclamation point if a warning state has been detected, or a red triangle if the alert state has been reached for a particular object.

Automatic Start

You can easily configure the automatic start of a monitor by closing the Administrator program while the Server or Link Monitor is active. The monitor is then restarted the next time you open the Administrator program. The Administrator program keeps track of which monitors are to be started automatically on a per-user basis. The corresponding Registry setting can be found under:

```
HKEY_CURRENT_USER
    \Software
        \Microsoft
            \Exchange
                \MSExchangeAdmin
                    \Desktop
```

The Administrator program also provides a command line parameter that allows you to start a specific monitor. You need to specify the name of the monitor and the site and server where the monitor has been created. You are required to specify the complete path to the executable file if the \Exchsrvr\Bin directory has not been included in the search path. The command format is: **Admin /s** <server_name> **/m**[<site_name>] \<monitor_name>\<target_server_name>.

If you place an appropriate command line in the Windows NT Startup program group, you can ensure that a monitor will always be started when you log on to Windows NT. It is also possible to configure Administrator program shortcuts within the Exchange program group, which makes it easy to start the desired monitors by just clicking the mouse.

Note You can activate the **AutoAdminLogon** feature of the Exchange Server computer to specify that an administrator account logs on automatically at server startup. This allows you to start monitors automatically through references in this administrator's **Startup** group. However, **AutoAdminLogon** is not recommended because of obvious security risks.

Stopping Monitors for Maintenance

By default, an active Server Monitor monitors the DS, IS, and MTA services. But sometimes it's necessary to shut the services down for maintenance, perhaps to perform an offline backup. In this situation, the active Server Monitor should not inform any administrator about critical states or restart the services automatically. In other words, you must suspend the Server Monitor from one computer while it continues to monitor all other servers.

Suspending the Server Monitor from one computer can be accomplished using the **Admin /t nr** command (located in the \Exchsrvr\Bin directory), which must be executed on the computer that you want to maintain. The option **n** suspends any notifications during maintenance mode, while the option **r** suspends any repairs otherwise performed by the monitor (for example, restarting the service). Both options can be used separately or in combination. To reset the server to normal mode, use the **Admin /t** command without further options. Note that you must execute the **Admin /t nr** command before the server goes off line. (See Figure 15-8.)

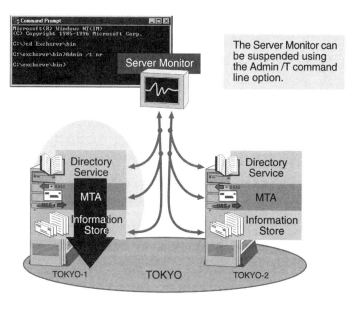

Figure 15-8. Suspending a Server Monitor

The following are command line parameters for the Administrator program:

- Export Mode **/e**; runs the command line export utility

- Help Mode **/h**; displays user help on startup

- Import Mode **/i**; runs the command line import utility

- Monitor Mode **/m**[*<Site_name>*]*<Monitor_name>*
  <Target_server_name>; starts the specified monitor on startup to monitor
  the services on the target server

- Raw Mode **/r**; provides access to all attributes of directory objects

- Server Mode **/s** *<Server name>*; connects to the specified server
  during startup

- Suspend Mode **/t [n][r]**; **n** suspends notifications in cases of problems, **r**
  suspends repairs of problems, no parameter reactivates the monitoring of
  the server that has been shut down for maintenance or backup (for
  example, **Admin /t nr** – backup – **Admin /t**: suspend notifications and
  repair – perform offline backup with services down and then restart the
  services – activate the server monitor again)

Exercise 48: Creating, Configuring, Testing, and Using a Link Monitor

A Link Monitor can examine message paths by sending test messages and measuring the time until those test messages bounce back. A working messaging connector will deliver replies within a configured time limit. If the round trip of a test message exceeds this limit, the path to the remote site will be considered broken. By default, a reply to a test message is considered late after 30 minutes and the link enters the Warning State. Accordingly, the polling interval is set to the value for critical sites and defined actions for the Warning State are triggered. After 60 minutes, the reply is considered very late and, as a consequence, the link enters the Alert State where the actions that you have defined for the Alert State are triggered.

Estimated time to complete this exercise: 35 minutes

Description

In this exercise, you will create a Link Monitor to test the connection between two sites (NEWYORK and LONDON). Both sites have been replicated, which allows you to select a remote server through the **Servers** property page. The SA of the remote server will then reply to the Link Monitor test messages. You will them stop the MTA to simulate a broken message path. You will continue to examine the Link Monitor's behavior as you restart the MTA.

- Task 48a describes the steps for creating and configuring a Link Monitor to monitor the link between two servers.

- Task 48b describes the steps for starting the Link Monitor.

- Task 48c describes the steps for stopping the MTA service to test the Link Monitor.

- Task 48d describes the steps for demonstrating the Link Monitor's ability to detect the failure of a link to another server and for notifying a designated user via e-mail.

- Task 48e describes the steps for restarting the MTA service to complete the testing of the Link Monitor.

- Task 48f describes the steps for demonstrating the Link Monitor's ability to detect the reestablishment of a link to another server after a failure and for notifying a designated user of this reestablishment via e-mail.

Prerequisites

- Log on as Admin-NY1 to NEWYORK-1 to complete Tasks 48a, 48b, 48d, and 48f.

- Log on as Admin-L1 to LONDON-1 to complete Tasks 48c and 48e.

- Make sure that the IMSs are running on NEWYORK-1 and LONDON-1.

- Ensure that the directory replication between NEWYORK and LONDON works and is completed.

Task 48a: Creating and Configuring an Exchange Link Monitor

1. To log on to NEWYORK-1, press CTRL+ALT+DEL.

2. In the **User Name** box, type *Admin-NY1*.

3. In the **Password** box, type *password* and then click **OK**.

4. Click the **Start** button, point to **Programs**, point to **Microsoft Exchange**, click **Microsoft Exchange Administrator**, and then connect to NEWYORK-1.

5. Select the site object **NEWYORK**.

6. On the **File** menu, point to **New Other** and then click **Link Monitor**.

7. A **Microsoft Exchange Administrator** dialog box appears, prompting you to switch to the **Monitors** container. Click **OK** to display the **Properties** dialog box of the new Link Monitor.

8. In the **Directory Name** box, type *Link Monitor to LONDON*.

9. In the **Display Name** box, type *Link Monitor to LONDON*.

10. Under **Polling Interval**, set **Normal** to *2 Minutes* and **Critical Sites** to *30 Seconds*.

11. Click the **Notification** tab.

12. Click **New** to display the **New Notification** dialog box.

13. Click **Mail Message** and then click **OK**.

14. In the **Escalation Editor (Mail Message)** dialog box, set the **Time Delay** to *1 minute*.

15. Clear the **Alert Only** check box.

16. Click **Recipient** to display the **Recipient** dialog box.

17. Click **Fred Pumpkin** and then click **OK**.

18. The **Escalation Editor (Mail Message)** dialog box reappears. Click **OK**.

19. A message box appears, indicating when notification messages will be sent. Click **OK**.

20. Click the **Servers** tab.

21. In the **Site** list, click **LONDON**.

22. In the **Servers** box, click **LONDON-1** and then click **Add**.

23. Click the **Bounce** tab.

24. In the **Enter Warning State After** box, set *2 Minutes*.

25. In the **Enter Alert State After** box, set *3 Minutes*.

26. Click **OK**.

27. **Microsoft Exchange Administrator** appears, displaying the new Link Monitor in the right pane.

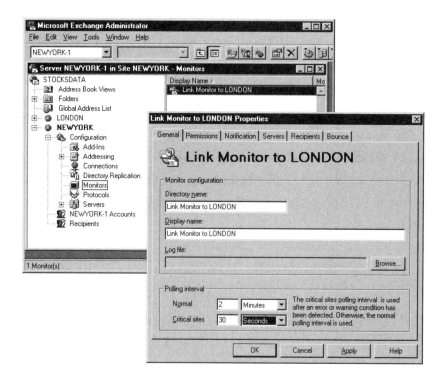

Task 48b: Testing an Exchange Link Monitor

1. Verify that the object **Link Monitor To LONDON** is selected in the **Monitors** container.

2. On the **Tools** menu, click **Start Monitor**.

3. The **Connect To Server** dialog box appears, prompting for a server to connect to.

4. Verify that NEWYORK-1 is selected.

5. Select the **Set As Default** check box and then click **OK**.

6. The **Monitor Link Monitor To LONDON** (or **NEWYORK-1**) dialog box appears.

7. Wait until the Link Monitor to LONDON-1 is working, which is indicated by a green arrow pointing up that appears in the first column.

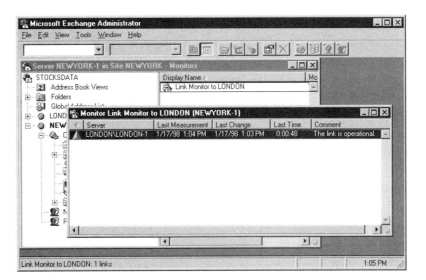

Task 48c: Stopping the Exchange MTA Service

1. To log on to LONDON-1, press CTRL+ALT+DEL.

2. In the **User Name** box, type *Admin-L1*.

3. In the **Password** box, type *password* and then click **OK**.

4. Click the **Start** button, point to **Settings** and then click **Control Panel**.

5. Double-click the **Services** icon.

6. Click **Microsoft Exchange Message Transfer Agent**.

7. Click **Stop**.

8. A **Stopping** dialog box appears, telling you that stopping the MTA will also stop the Microsoft Exchange Internet Mail Service. Click **OK**.

9. Click **Close** to close the **Services** dialog box.

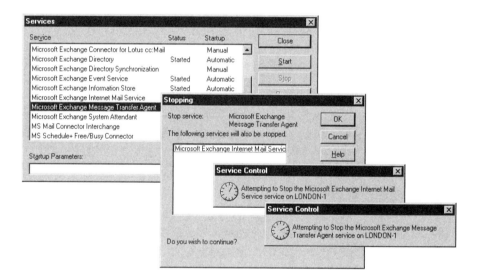

Task 48d: Receiving a Link Monitor Warning Message

1. On the desktop of NEWYORK-1, double-click the Outlook shortcut and verify that you connect to the mailbox of Fred Pumpkin.

2. Wait for a message with a subject of **LONDON-1 Alert Since** to arrive.

3. Open and read the message.

4. Close the message.

5. Switch to the Exchange Administrator program and notice the state of the Link Monitor, which displays a red arrow pointing downward.

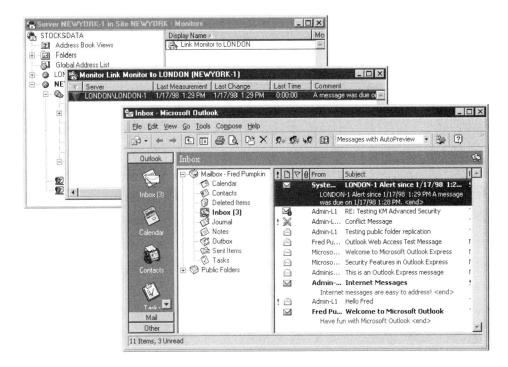

Task 48e: Starting the Exchange MTA Service

1. Switch to the Control Panel on LONDON-1.

2. After the message has been received by Admin-NY1 indicating that the link is down, double-click the **Services** icon in the Control Panel.

3. Click the **Microsoft Exchange Message Transfer Agent** service and then click **Start**.

4. Select the **Microsoft Exchange Internet Mail Service** and then click **Start**.

5. Close the **Services** dialog box and then exit the Control Panel.

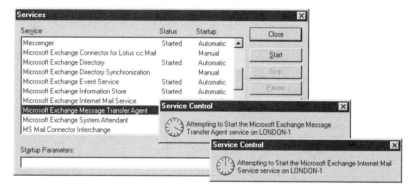

Task 48f: Receiving a Link Monitor Status Message

1. Switch back to Outlook running on NEWYORK-1.

2. Wait for a message with the subject line **LONDON-1 Running Since** to arrive in the Inbox.

3. Open and read the message.

4. Close the message.

5. Exit and log off Outlook.

6. In the Exchange Administrator program, notice the green icon on the Link Monitor and then close the **Monitor Link Monitor To LONDON (NEWYORK-1)** child window.

7. Exit the Exchange Administrator program.

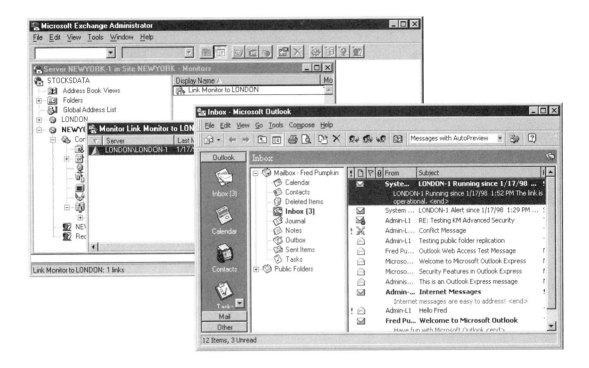

Review

The Link Monitor informs the administrator about a broken messaging path by sending a regular e-mail message or a Windows NT alert. The Link Monitor can also launch a custom application, providing such additional features as pager signals.

The Link Monitor also sends a notification to the administrator if a link becomes active again. In other words, the administrator will be notified that no further action is required if test messages arrive within the configured time limit.

Lesson 3: Troubleshooting Tools and Tasks

The most valuable troubleshooting tool is probably a cup of coffee. Indeed, nothing is more injurious than a confused, frantic, and exhausted administrator who tries to solve an Exchange Server problem quickly. Troubleshooting tools, helpful as they might be, might increase problems if they are used incorrectly or in the wrong way situation. Many tools may have "side effects," so it is always advisable that you back up Exchange Server databases BEFORE you plan to launch them. Fortunately, troubleshooting tools are seldom necessary. Exchange Server 5.5 is a stable and reliable messaging system, but you should never say never.

This lesson describes valuable troubleshooting tools that might help you to resolve client and server problems. You'll read about the reparation of Personal Folder Store files as well as about available tools that allow you to examine client-server connectivity. You'll also read about different methods of fixing MTA startup problems and message queue corruption. This lesson concludes with a brief explanation of the Task Manager.

At the end of this lesson, you will be able to:

- Use the Inbox Repair Tool to fix .PST corruption

- Decide when to use the MTA Check utility

- Verify the possibility of connecting to an Exchange Server via RPCs

- Use the Windows NT Task Manager to control active processes

Estimated time to complete this lesson: 40 minutes

The Inbox Repair Tool

The Inbox Repair Tool (Scanpst.exe) can eliminate corruption of Personal Message Store (.PST) and Offline Message Store (.OST) files. For instance, it might be possible that corrupted folders no longer maintain a normal folder structure. These folders do not appear in the folder hierarchy because they cannot be displayed in the Exchange Client. The Scanpst.exe can reimplement these lost folders back into the folder hierarchy. (See Figure 15-9 on page 1000.)

Installation

The Inbox Repair Tool is installed along with the Exchange Client, and you'll find the corresponding shortcut in the **Programs\Accessories\System Tools** program group. Unfortunately, the Outlook installation procedure does not create a reference to the Inbox Repair Tool in a program group, although it copies the binary file Scanpst.exe to the computers hard disk. In this scenario, you can find the Scanpst.exe in the **C:\Program Files\Windows Messaging** directory. The installation of the Exchange Client and Outlook is covered in Chapter 6.

Blocks, Nodes, B-Trees, and Other Data

The Inbox Repair Tool examines the entire contents of a selected .PST or .OST file. Folder Store files consist of blocks, nodes, B-trees, folders, and message items. A *block* is an array of bytes no larger than 8 KB that stores the actual data. A *node* is a logical group of items that is the foundation for building folders and messages. Personal folders and messages maintain their relationship by means of nodes, and one node can be up to 2 GB in size. A *B-tree* provides a mechanism for organizing the blocks and nodes into a hierarchy.

Eight Steps to a Consistent Folder Store

Before you fix a .PST file or an .OST file, it is highly recommended that you back up the existing information. Folder file corruption can cause the Scanpst.exe to discard numerous messages, which are lost without a current backup.

The Scanpst.exe utility inspects all blocks, nodes, B-trees, folders, and messages in eight steps. The first six steps perform low-level checks of .PST/.OST blocks. The B-tree blocks are examined; corrupt blocks are discarded. If a block has been corrupted, Scanpst.exe searches for other blocks that can help to rebuild the discarded information. Scanpst.exe then verifies the nodes in the B-tree. Again, corrupted nodes are discarded and the Inbox Repair Tool searches for information in the .PST/.OST file that rebuilds the discarded nodes. In the last two steps, the folders and messages inside the folders are counted and checked for corruption. At this point, orphaned messages and folders reappear in the personal folder tree, possibly in a **Lost & Found** folder.

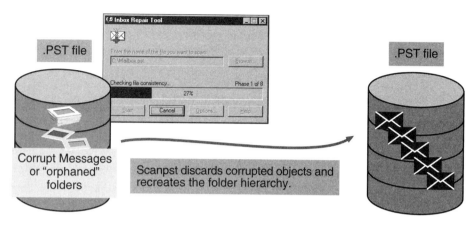

Figure 15-9. Repairing a Personal Folder Store file.

The Inbox Repair Tool performs these steps to repair corrupt Personal Folder Store files:

1. Scanpst.exe checks that the blocks in the B-tree are valid.

2. If the .PST file is corrupt, Scanpst.exe preserves the good blocks of the B-tree and discards the corrupted blocks.

3. Scanpst.exe examines the .PST file for blocks that can be used to rebuild the corrupted blocks.

4. The Inbox Repair Tool inspects the nodes in the B-tree.

5. If the .PST file is corrupt, Scanpst.exe evacuates the good nodes of the B-tree and discards the corrupted nodes.

6. Scanpst.exe attempts to locate node references that can be used to rebuild the corrupted portions of the node's B-tree.

7. Scanpst.exe enumerates and validates all folders and their contents.

8. The .PST file is counterchecked to locate folders and messages that do not exist in the normal folder hierarchy. Scanpst.exe incorporates orphaned folders and messages back into the hierarchy.

The MTA Check Utility

The MTA Check utility (MTACheck.exe) is a powerful troubleshooting tool that allows you to check and fix MTA message queues. This tool is installed along with Exchange Server and can be found in the \Exchsrvr\Bin directory.

Generally you'll launch this utility when you have MTA problems, but it's also a good idea to run this tool on a regular basis to verify the integrity of the message queues. In fact, the MTA Check utility is launched automatically at every MTA service startup following an improper shutdown of the MTA.

Note You must stop the MTA service before you can start the MTA Check utility.

MTA Message Queues

The MTA maintains its message queues in .DAT files, which can be found in the \Exchsrvr\Mtadata directory. (See Figure 15-10.) Several of these .DATs are installed during the Exchange Server setup. These are system .DAT files representing important MTA message queues, for example. Others are added when supplementary components such as messaging connectors are configured. The number of system .DAT files increases because the number of message queues increases. System .DATs might change their contents and size but they won't disappear until the related messaging connector is deleted. System .DAT files have, so to speak, a permanent character.

In addition to the permanent .DAT files, there are also temporary .DAT files, which the MTA creates during distribution list expansion and message conversion. Therefore, the temporary .DAT files might represent the actual contents of a message that is currently located in an MTA message queue. A few moments later, when the MTA has processed the message, the related .DAT file disappears again.

Note Numerous .DAT files can exist within the \Exchsrvr\Mtadata directory, but they must not be deleted manually.

MTA Startup Problems

Unfortunately, .DAT files can become corrupted just like any other file on a computer's hard disk—during an MTA crash, for instance. If this happens, you will experience MTA startup problems later on as well. In other words, if you cannot restart the MTA. It's a good idea to check the Application Event Log for message queue corruption and other MTA-related log entries first. If you do find indications about corrupt files, consider using the MTA Check utility in order to fix the problem.

Fixing Corruption

The MTA Check utility attempts to fix all MTA message queues and the messages and attachments that are currently stored in the queues. The MTA Check utility deletes corrupted objects to bring the message queues back to an accurate state. Items that must be removed are backed up in the Exchsrvr \Mtadata\Mtacheck.out directory. The removed object's identifier, an error code, the queue name, and the Message Transport Identifier (MTS-ID) are written to a log file or displayed on the screen, depending on the specified command line parameter.

The MTS-ID is especially useful if you want to identify the originator of a removed message because it consists of the name of the originating server, the date and time when the message was sent, and a hexadecimal message identifier. The message identifier is unique within your organization and can be used in conjunction with the Message Tracking Center to determine the message originator and the path the message has taken through your messaging network. The Message Tracking Center is covered under Lesson 4, "Other Maintenance Tasks and Troubleshooting Aids," later in this chapter.

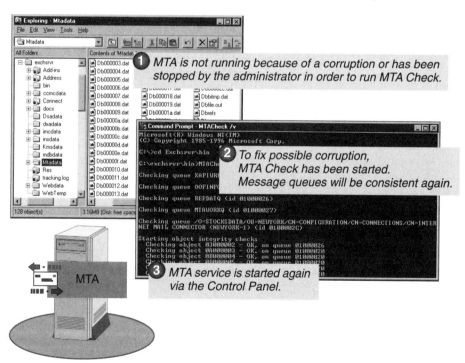

Figure 15-10. Fixing corrupt message queues.

Command Line Parameters

The MTA Check utility is a command line tool that provides several helpful options. Using the **Mtacheck /F**<*file name*> command, for instance, you can specify a log file that will be used to record the MTA Check activities. Furthermore, you can also specify the **/V** parameter to log the most detailed status information.

The Microsoft Exchange Server 5.5 version of the MTA Check utility provides three additional parameters (**/RD**, **/RP**, and **/RL**) that permit you to discard replication messages of the DS (**/RD**), the IS (**/RP**) and test messages of the Link Monitor (**/RL**). You can use the parameters **/RD** and **/RP** if replication messages have filled the MTA's message queues. Replication messages can be deleted without further consequences because the replication mechanisms are fault tolerant. In other words, the DS and the IS can recover from lost replication information. Link Monitor test messages, in turn, are less important than interpersonal messages because the test messages don't represent any user or configuration data at all. Deleting them through the **/RL** parameter won't affect the operation of the organization.

The MTA Check utility command line arguments are as follows:

- **/F <filename>**; to save status information to a text file
- **/RD**; to remove queued directory replication messages
- **/RP**; to remove queued public folder replication messages
- **/RL**; to remove queued Link Monitor test messages
- **/V**; to enable verbose logging

The RPCPing Utility

RPCPing is a program family, rather than a single utility, that allows for the observation of client/server communication. One specific software component must be launched on the server, while the others are executed on the client. The communication between the server-based and the client-based programs is measured to determine the quality of the client/server RPC connectivity. (See Figure 15-11.) All the required software components come with the Exchange Server CD. The programs can be found in the \Server\Support\Rpcping directory.

RPCPing Server

The server component has been implemented in a file called Rpings.exe; it must be started on the server before using any of the client components to measure the quality of the connectivity. Rpings.exe maintains the RPC functions "Echo" and "Stats," which are called later by the client component.

You can run Rpings.exe without any command line options, but additional parameters can be used to restrict the RPC test to specific protocol sequences. You can set any of the following options:

- RPINGS [-p Protocol Sequence]
- -p ipx/spx
- -p namedpipes
- -p netbios
- -p tcpip
- -p vines

To exit the server component, enter the string @*q* at the Rpings.exe command prompt.

RPCPing Client

The operating system on the client machine determines the version of the client component you can use. A separate version exists for MS-DOS, Windows 3.x, and Windows 95/Windows NT. MS-DOS runs Rpingdos.exe, Windows 3.x computers run Rpingc16.exe, and Windows 95 and Windows NT run Rpingc32.exe.

Typically you use Rpingc32.exe to test the RPC connectivity. Rpingc32.exe is a 32-bit Windows program that displays the connection status, available protocol sequences, end points, and the quality of the RPC connection as you attempt to check the RPC connection. Before you can start a particular test, you must set all required communication parameters, such as the destination RPC server and endpoints.

Available endpoints are **Store**, **Admin**, and **Rping**. You can select **Store** within the **Endpoint** field if you want to simulate communication with the IS. Select **Admin** to simulate communication with the DS. **Rping** collects statistics about the RPCPing client-to-server communication itself.

The required RPCPing client parameters are as follows:

- The Exchange Server name (or IP address).
- The protocol sequence, which specifies the RPC mechanism that will be used, such as named pipes.
- The end points specify protocol-specific ports, which will be used by the RPC Ping client to communicate with the server. This end point can be the IS (**Store**), the DS (**Admin**), or the RPCPing server (**Rping**).

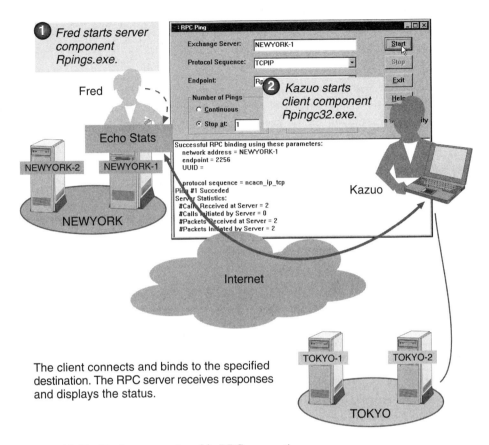

Figure 15-11. Testing a questionable RPC connection.

The Windows NT Task Manager

The Windows NT Task Manager is a powerful tool that allows you to control processes running on a Windows NT computer, including all active Exchange Server services. The Task Manager can be launched by right-clicking the Windows NT Taskbar and clicking the **Task Manager** command within the appearing context menu. Another method of launching the Task Manager is to press CTRL+ALT+DEL and click the **Task Manager** button in the **Windows NT Security** dialog box.

Terminating an Application

The Task Manager lists all running user programs on its **Applications** property page, giving you the option to terminate any of the programs. Let's say you want to terminate Notepad. When you execute Notepad, you'll find an

Untitled - Notepad entry in the task list on the **Applications** property page. You can select this entry and click the **End Task** button. The text editor will disappear immediately.

Note Whenever you terminate a program using the Task Manager, you basically "kill" the process abruptly, leaving no time for cleanup. Therefore, you should not use this feature except when absolutely necessary.

Terminating a Process

Exchange Server services are not listed on the **Applications** property page because they are system services; they can be found on the **Processes** property page instead. If you look closely at this page you'll see that the processes are displayed by their image name. For instance, the Microsoft Exchange Server MTA is listed as **EMSMTA.EXE**. (See Figure 15-12.)

Terminating the MTA Process

You should not terminate the MTA or any other Exchange Server service using the Task Manager without an extremely good reason. Message queues might become corrupted and other unpredictable results might occur. In the worst cases, you can lose messages.

Even if you suspect the MTA is malfunctioning, check twice before you terminate the process. Most likely the MTA is just busy with a distribution list expansion or a similar task. Use the **Processes** property page to examine memory and CPU usage of the **EMSMTA.EXE**. You can use this page to verify the status of other categories, such as page faults and handle counts, as well.

If you find that the MTA is using the CPU at close capacity, you can assume that the MTA service is hanging. However, you should not terminate the MTA process immediately. It's better to use the first troubleshooting tool for a while (which involves getting a cup of coffee). After a reasonable amount of time, check the CPU usage again. If the situation has not changed, it's time to step in.

At this point, select **EMSMTA.EXE** and then click **End Process**. A message box appears, warning you about unpredictable results, and if you confirm this message box with **Yes** you will abruptly erase the MTA process from the server's memory. Once the MTA service has been terminated, it is strongly recommended that you verify the state of the message queues using the MTA Check utility.

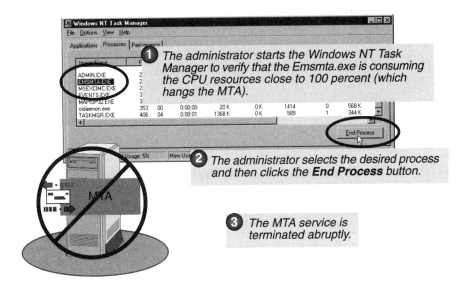

Figure 15-12. Terminating the MTA process.

The Exchange Server services and their binary executables are listed below:

Exchange Server Service	Executable File
Connector for Lotus cc:Mail	Exchsrvr\Connect\CcMail\Bin\Ccmc.exe
DS	Exchsrvr\Bin\Dsamain.exe
Directory Synchronization with MS Mail	Exchsrvr\Bin\Dxa.exe
Event Service	Exchsrvr\bin\events.exe
IS	Exchsrvr\Bin\Store.exe
IMS	Exchsrvr\Connect\Msexcimc\Bin\Msexcimc.exe
INS	Exchsrvr\bin\exchins.exe
KM Server	Security\Bin\Kmserver.exe
MTA	Exchsrvr\bin\emsmta.exe
MS Mail Connector Interchange	Exchsrvr\Connect\Msmcon\Bin\Mt.exe
MS Mail Connector PC MTAs as configured by Admin.	Exchsrvr\Connect\Msmcon\Bin\Async.exe
MS Schedule+ Free/Busy Connector	Exchsrvr\Connect\Msfbconn\Msfbconn.exe
SA	Exchsrvr\bin\mad.exe

Lesson 4: Other Maintenance Tasks and Troubleshooting Aids

The Administrator program has several maintenance features that you can use to manage a particular server or the entire site from a single location. You can force the synchronization of the entire site, which is useful if you identify directory inconsistencies, and you can explore message paths and message queues to check for delivery problems and bottlenecks.

This lesson explains the methods for forcing the directory replication and explains the steps for changing the password of the Site Services Account. The focus of this lesson, however, is the Message Tracking Center, which explores the path a message has taken through your organization. You can also obtain information about the analysis of message queues and their maintenance in case of delivery problems.

At the end of this lesson, you will be able to:

- Force directory replication
- Change the Site Services Account password
- Enable message tracking
- Use the Message Tracking Center to explore the path a message has taken
- Delete items in message queues for troubleshooting purposes

Estimated time to complete this lesson: 45 minutes

Forcing Directory Replication

You can force directory replication in order to distribute configuration changes faster to other servers across the site and organization. To launch a particular process, click the **Update Now** and **Check Now** buttons, which are located on the **General** property page of every server's **Directory Service** object. The Administrator program contains the **Directory Service** object in the local **Server** container.

Regular directory replication within a site is covered in Chapter 4, while directory replication between sites is discussed in Chapter 9.

Pulling Directory Changes

The Update Now button allows you to pull directory changes from other servers within your own site and from replication bridgehead servers. Replication bridgeheads are responsible for intersite directory replication. You can pull changes from remote sites by clicking the **Request Now** button on the **Sites** property page of the corresponding directory replication connector.

Let's say the Japanese administrator, Kazuo, has discovered that the GWART on TOKYO-1 contains additional address spaces, which belong to new messaging connectors somewhere in the organization. TOKYO-1 is the replication bridgehead in TOKYO. In order to provide the new messaging path to all users in TOKYO as quickly as possible, Kazuo decides to force the directory replication on TOKYO-2. To do so, he starts the Administrator program and then opens the server object **TOKYO-2** to double-click the **Directory Service** object in the contents pane. On the **General** property page, he clicks the **Update Now** button to pull the new configuration information from TOKYO-1 to TOKYO-2. (See Figure 15-13.)

Note The **Update Now** button is available only if multiple servers exist in a site. As long as only one server has been installed in your site, this button is deactivated and grayed out. To pull replication information from remote sites, click the **Request Now** button on the **Sites** property page of the corresponding directory replication connector.

Each time you click the **Update Now** button you generate network traffic. For this reason, you should click this button only with great patience to pull directory changes to the local server. Directory replication within the site replicates configuration changes every five minutes. It's a good idea to wait for five minutes to allow the directory replication to distribute the changes, and it doesn't make sense to send an additional replication request over the network during this time. Between sites, directory replication is performed according to the replication schedule as configured through the **Schedule** property page of the corresponding replication connector object. Consequently, you should consider even more time for intersite directory replication before clicking the **Request Now** button on the Sites property page again.

Updating Replication Links

Each server maintains a list of all other servers with which it replicates directory changes. This list must be updated as new servers join the site and replication connectors are created. It is the task of the KCC to examine the directories of the Exchange Servers in a site for configuration changes in order to create and maintain replication links. You can force the KCC to update this list using the **Check Now** button. (See Figure 15-13.)

The responsibility of the KCC becomes obvious when you create a new replication connector. At this point, only an additional directory replication connector object appears in the **Connections** container, but the replication connector itself is not sufficient to begin the intersite replication. The KCC must still create the replication link. If you force this process through the **Check Now** button, you'll notice a new directory object representing the remote site plus an empty **Configuration** container under the directory object once the KCC has finished. This is a clear sign that a new replication link has been created. It is now up to the intersite directory replication to fill these brand new containers.

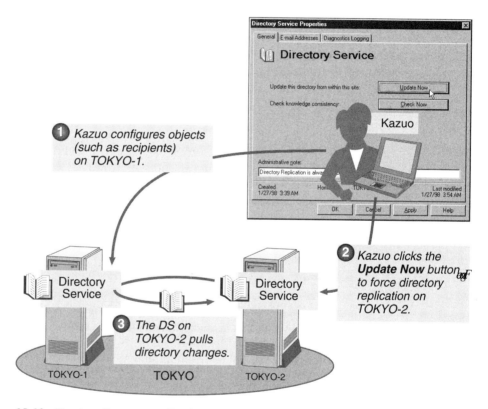

15-13. Forcing directory replication.

The controls for forcing directory replication are as follows:

- **Check Now** button; to check for the existence of new servers and sites with which the DS should replicate

- **Update Now** button; to pull changes from other servers within the site

Changing the Service Account Password

Occasionally you will be prompted for the password of the Site Services Account. This happens, for instance, during the installation of a new server in an existing site. You will also be prompted for the password when installing the IMS, the INS, or the KM Server. Other optional components might also require this information. However, you are so seldom prompted for this password that you might just forget it. If this happens, you don't need to reinstall the entire site nor do you need to worry about the old password. Just change it to a new one. Even if you never forget a password, it is recommended that you change the password of the Site Services Account from time to time to improve security. (See Figure 15-14.)

Changing the Password

Once you have decided to change the password of the Site Services Account you need to do so in two locations: the Administrator program and the User Manager for Domains. The order in which you change the password is not particularly important, but it is advantageous to change the password within the Administrator program first.

Let's say an administrator of your company has changed the password of the Site Services Account in the User Manager, ignoring the suggestion to change it in the Administrator program first. Let's assume further that the administrator forgot to perform this task in the Administrator program. Later you are performing server maintenance on the server. When you try to restart the services, you are confronted with the Windows NT error 1069, *The Service did not start due to a logon failure*. You can't even restart the SA, meaning that you will not be able to configure the Exchange Server through the Administrator program to put the new password into effect if the SA has been stopped for some reason.

To solve this problem, select the **Microsoft Exchange System Attendant** service in the **Services** applet of the Control Panel. Then click the **Startup** button to enter the new password of the Site Services Account under **Password** and **Confirm Password**. You can then start the SA. Now you must repeat the same steps for all the other Exchange Server services.

Note You can avoid taking these additional configuration steps if you always change the password of the Site Services Account in the Administrator program first, and immediately after that in the User Manager for Domains.

Changing the Password in the Administrator Program

As shown in Figure 15-14, Kazuo displays the properties of the **Configuration** object under the site container **TOKYO** within the Administrator program.

Then he switches to the **Service Account Password** property page, which allows him to enter the new password in the **Password** box. The password is not displayed in clear text, so Kazuo must confirm it in order to avoid typos. When he clicks **OK** a message box appears, reminding Kazuo to change the password in the User Manager as well.

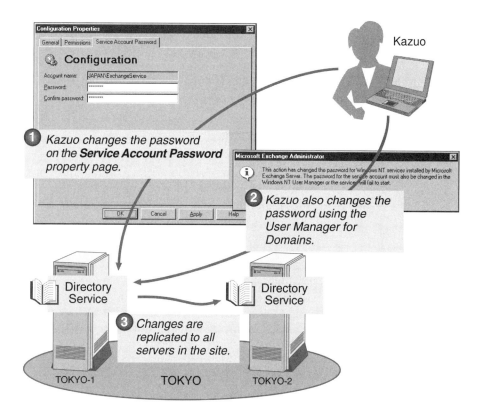

Figure 15-14. Changing the Site Services Account password.

Follow these steps to change the Site Services Account password:

1. Start the Exchange Administrator program.

2. Select the **Configuration** object of the local site and then press ALT+ENTER.

3. The **Configuration Properties** dialog box appears. Switch to the **Service Account Password** property page.

4. Enter the new password in the **Password** box and then confirm it under **Confirm Password**.

5. Click **OK**.

6. Notice the message box indication that the Site Services Account password must be changed in the User Manger also. Click **OK**.

7. Start the User Manager for Domains and then double-click the Site Services Account.

8. In the **Password** box, enter the new password, and then confirm it under **Confirm Password**.

9. Click OK.

Enabling Message Tracking

Message tracking is an Exchange Server feature that allows you to follow the paths of messages as they travel through your organization. The IS, the MTA, and all the optional messaging connectors support this feature. Message tracking is disabled by default.

Reasons for Message Tracking

Message tracking can help you determine where a particular message came from, whether and when it has been delivered to recipients, or where it currently resides while awaiting further routing. In other words, message tracking can provide detailed information about the delivery characteristics of your messaging network.

The features of message tracking are as follows:

- Allows you to find a specific message

- Verifies that a message has been delivered successfully

- Offers to determine delays on each segment of a route for performance tuning

- Permits the detection of slow or stopped message connections

Enabling Message Tracking

You can enable message tracking separately for the IS, MTA, and additional messaging connectors such as the IMS. When you activate this feature, message status information is recorded in daily transaction log files. Their file name follows the scheme <yyyymmdd>.log (for example, 19980524.log). Logs are created in the \Exchsrvr\Tracking.log directory of each Exchange Server computer. (See Figure 15-15 on page 1016.)

> **Note** The SA writes and maintains the tracking log files. The IS, MTA, IMS, Connector for Lotus cc:Mail, and the MS Mail Connector communicate with the SA to deposit their message tracking information.

Message Tracking Within a Server

The IS is usually the active component that delivers messages between users on the same home server. Aside from distribution list expansion, which is an exception to the rule, messages that must be delivered to recipients on the same home server do not leave the IS at all. Consequently, you must enable the message tracking feature only on the **General** property page of the **Information Store Site Configuration** object to track single-server delivery information. You'll find the **Information Store Site Configuration** object in each **Configuration** container. The responsibilities of the IS are covered in Chapter 3.

Message Tracking Between Servers

Just as the IS is responsible for message delivery within a single server, the MTA is the important component for all external communication and the distribution list expansion. Therefore, you must enable the message tracking feature on the **General** property page of the **MTA Site Configuration** object to specify tracking information about the message transfer between servers. Information about distribution list expansions is then recorded as well. You can find the **MTA Site Configuration** object under the **Information Store Site Configuration** object within each **Configuration** container. The role of the MTA is covered in more detail in Chapter 4.

Message Tracking Using a Connector

The MTA manages the Site Connector, the X.400 Connector, and the Dynamic RAS Connector directly. Message tracking is activated implicitly for these connectors through the **MTA Site Configuration** object. The IMS, the Connector for Lotus cc:Mail, the MS Mail Connector, and the other EDK-based connectors are implemented as separate Windows NT services, however. For this reason, they provide their own message tracking information explicitly to the SA.

Internet Mail Service

If you want to maintain tracking information regarding the message queue processing of the IMS, activate the **Enable Message Tracking** option on the **Internet Mail** property page of the desired IMS object within the Administrator program. In order for the changes to take effect, restart the IMS service. More detailed information about the IMS configuration is provided in Chapter 10.

Connector for Lotus cc:Mail

The Connector for Lotus cc:Mail object provides the **Enable Message Tracking** option on its **Post Office** property page. When you enable the option, you can follow messages up to the point when they leave the Exchange Server organization. Message tracking, however, is not supported within the Lotus cc:Mail network. The configuration of the Connector for Lotus cc:Mail is covered in Chapter 19, "Connector for Lotus cc:Mail."

MS Mail Connector

The MS Mail Connector object provides the **Enable Message Tracking** option on its **Interchange** property page. The tracking option allows for the recording of status information about messages for all postoffices that can be reached through this particular connector. The configuration of the MS Mail Connector is covered in Chapter 18. "Connecting to MS Mail and Schedule+."

Disabling Message Tracking on Each Server

When you enable message tracking for the IS or the MTA, you activate this feature for all servers in your site. However, it's possible to suppress message tracking again for specific servers.

You can disable message tracking for a specific IS by setting the X.400 Service Event Log value to 0. If the value doesn't exist, you can add it manually under:

```
HKEY_LOCAL_MACHINE
    \SYSTEM
        \CurrentControlSet
            \Services
                \MSExchangeIS
                    \ParametersPrivate
```

You can disable message tracking for the MTA by setting its X.400 Service Event Log value to 0 as well. If the value does not exist, you can add it manually under:

```
HKEY_LOCAL_MACHINE
    \SYSTEM
        \CurrentControlSet
            \Services
                \MSExchangeMTA
                    \Parameters
```

The value is of the data type REG_DWORD.

This parameter is not required for optional connectors, because they are running on one particular server anyway. Their message tracking information is always bound to one particular server in a site.

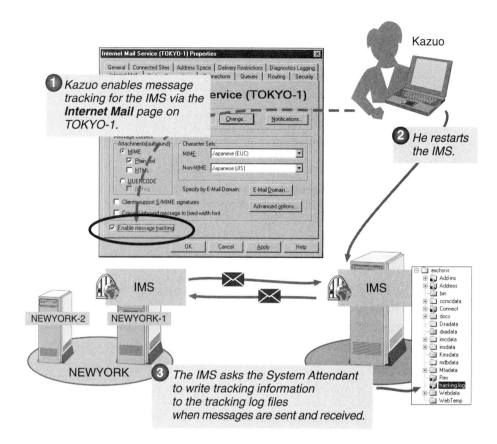

Figure 15-15. Enabling message tracking with the IMS.

The features of message tracking are as follows:

- Can be enabled in the Exchange Administrator Program
- SA creates daily log files
- Message tracking keeps information about those processes that transfer messages
- Message tracking also works between servers in different sites
- Tracking history reflects the delivering process

Using Message Tracking

You can analyze tracking log information by using the Message Tracking Center. The Message Tracking Center is an Administrator program tool that can be launched through the **Track Message** command on the **Tools** menu. This tool reads the tracking information from the \\<Server Name> **\Tracking.log** network share of each server that has been involved in a particular message transfer. You must specify which server to begin with in the **Connect To Server** dialog box that appears right after you have chosen the **Track Message** command.

The Message Tracking Process

Message tracking is a process in two stages. In the first stage you select the message you want to track. In the second stage you examine the tracking logs corresponding to the selected message. The Message Tracking Center automates the tracking process.

Selecting the Message

You can specify a message through the Select Message To Track dialog box, which is displayed automatically when you launch the Message Tracking Center. Fields such as **From, Sent To, Search On Server**, and **Look Back ... Days** allow you to limit the list of displayed messages. The final choice is made by selecting the desired message in the message display area after you have clicked the **Find Now** button.

Displaying the Tracking Information

As you click the **Find Now** button and find messages that meet the specified criteria, select the desired message and click **OK** to switch to the **Message Tracking Center** window. This window contains the **Track** button, which allows you to track the selected message through your organization. A list is displayed containing the active components that have been involved in the message transfer. The list also contains the message ID, send date, and originator information. These fields are read-only and cannot be changed. (See Figure 15-16.)

Advanced Searches

Once you have analyzed the path of a particular message in the Message Tracking Center, you might want to track other messages as well. The **Search** button returns you to the **Select Message To Track** dialog box where you can specify other messages. You can also click the **Advanced Search** button if you want to search for a message by its message ID. Such an ID, for example, can be obtained from the log files of the MTA Check utility that might have wiped out a corrupted message.

By clicking the **Advanced Search** button, you can further select messages that have been sent by the core Exchange Server services. The IS, among other things, is responsible for interpersonal and public folder replication messages. The DS might generate and receive directory replication messages. The SA, as outlined earlier, helps the generation and processing of Link Monitor test messages. The Directory Synchronization with MS Mail, finally, might generate DirSync messages as explained in Chapter 18. In addition, you can specify messages that have been transferred by messaging connectors and gateways installed on the local Exchange Server computer into the Exchange system.

Tracking the Message

Using local tracking logs, the Message Tracking Center determines which component is expected to receive the message next. If this component resides on another server, the tracking center connects to the corresponding \\<Server Name>**Tracking.Log** network share. The tracking center searches the tracking logs on that server to find more information. This process is repeated until the message has been located or until an exit point has been detected, indicating where the message has left the organization.

Note It is important to understand that the <Server Name>, which is used to connect to the desired **Tracking.Log** share, is always derived from the MTA name. You can modify the MTA name through the **Local MTA Name** box on the **General** property page of the **Message Transfer Object** at the server level. However, if the MTA name differs from the computer name, message tracking between servers no longer works.

Message tracking is supported so long as computers are reachable through TCP/IP, SPX/IPX, or NetBEUI and foreign messaging systems are not involved in the message transfer. For instance, **Outbound SMTP Transferred** is displayed as the last tracking entry for outbound SMTP messages in TOKYO if you have enabled message tracking for the IMS on TOKYO-1. (See Figure 15-16.)

Follow these steps to track a message:

1. Select the desired message via the **Select Message To Track** dialog box.
2. Track the message within the **Message Tracking Center** window.

Using Message Queues for Troubleshooting

It is advised that you check the message queues of an Exchange Server frequently to verify that the system is functioning properly. Too many back-logged messages can indicate of a configuration problem. Let's say you just forgot to start the IMS. Outbound messages might fill the IMS message queue, but the IMS would not pick them up. When you glance at the Outbound message queue you'll become aware of this situation, restart the service, and thus fix the "communication problem."

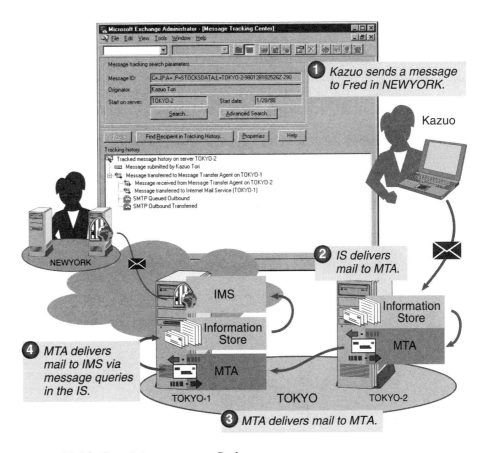

Figure 15-16. Examining a message Path.

Using MTA Message Queues for Troubleshooting

The MTA is the central component that transfers messages to other servers, sites, organizations, and foreign messaging systems. (See Figure 15-17 on page 1022.) You should check its queues first in order to locate delayed messages.

The Queues Property Page

The **Queues** property page of the **Message Transfer Agent** object within the local **Server** container allows you to analyze the queues of the MTA using the Administrator program. You can easily select the message queue through the **Queue name** box by means of a mouse click. All queued messages are then displayed along with their submission time.

Corrupt Messages

In case an MTA message queue has grown unexpectedly large, you should check the very first message, because this message might be corrupt and blocking the entire queue. To determine if a corrupt message is the source of the problem, check the Windows NT Application Log for hints that might indicate message corruption. It is also a good idea to lower the priority of the first message if you are not 100 percent certain about corruption. This way, other messages can bypass the critical message. If you finally figure out that the suspected item is truly corrupted, discard it using the **Delete** button on the **Queues** property page. An NDR informs the originator about the message deletion.

Services Not Operational

While message corruption might be one reason for large message queues, nonactive messaging components are quite likely another reason. To identify communication problems, you should check the state of the local and the remote MTAs. If they are running, you might gather some hints about the cause of the problem from the Application Event Log using the Event Viewer. It might be the case that the Site Services Account between sites is different and not configured correctly on the **Override** property page of the corresponding Site Connector or that configuration parameters of messaging connectors are mismatched. Use the Administrator program to adjust critical settings. The correction of messaging parameters, fortunately, does not affect queued messages.

Using IMS Connector Queues for Troubleshooting

The IMS provides a **Queues** property page that allows you to diagnose the Internet mail transfer. The queue called **Outbound Messages Awaiting Delivery** lists all items that will be sent. When you experience large queues, you can increase the diagnostics logging level for IMS categories such as **SMTP Protocol Log**. You can then examine the Application Event Log and SMTP log files for SMTP communication problems. The **Medium** level should be sufficient for gathering enough status information.

Message Details

Detailed information about queued messages can help to detect delivery problems quickly. The Delivery column displays a status of **Pending** for those messages whose delivery has not yet been attempted. If any submit time is displayed, at least one attempt to deliver the message has failed. In this case, the **Delivery** column displays the scheduled time for the next attempt. You can compare this time to the **Submit Time** to determine delivery delays.

When you analyze all messages that cannot be delivered, you might find some common characteristics. For instance, all these messages might be destined for the same target host. Using the **Details** button, you can check whether the **Recipients** box displays a status of **Host Unreachable**. If it does, you must fix a communication problem in order to free the blocked message queue. A HOSTS entry might be necessary to specify the desired target host if it is not contained in DNS.

Accelerated Delivery

The **Retry Now** button residing on the **Queues** property page allows you to initiate a new delivery attempt manually. Click this button if you have just adjusted the configuration of the IMS and want to test the communication immediately.

Using MS Mail Connector Queues for Troubleshooting

Unlike the other messaging connector objects, the MS Mail Connector does not provide a **Queues** property page. But this doesn't mean that you can't analyze the outgoing message queues for remote MS Mail postoffices within the connector postoffice. To analyze the queue of a postoffice, switch to the **Connections** property page. Select the desired postoffice from the **Connections** list. At this point, you can click the **Queue** button to display the **Messages Queued For** dialog box, which provides the desired information.

The MTA maintains a message queue for the MS Mail Connector as well, which you can analyze just as any MTA queue through the **Queues** property page of the **Message Transfer Agent**. A filled queue might be an indicator that the MS Mail Connector Interchange service has not been started. The architecture of the MS Mail Connector is covered in more detail in Chapter 18.

Using Connector for Lotus cc:Mail Queues for Troubleshooting

The Connector for Lotus cc:Mail provides the **Queues** property page, which can be checked for outbound (MTS-OUT) and inbound (MTS-IN) messages. If you suspect delivery problems, you should also inspect the connector configuration and view the Application Event Log.

A mismatch between the connector configuration and the Import/Export program versions can cause delivery problems because the Import/Export utilities have different version numbers than the related post offices. More information about the Connector for Lotus cc:Mail is provided in Chapter 19.

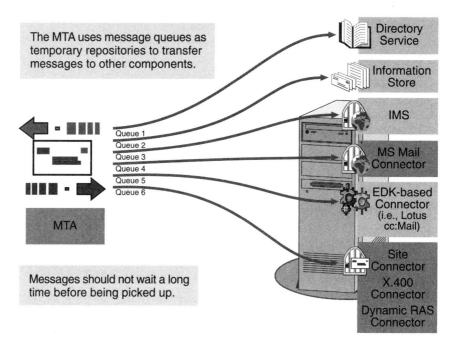

Figure 15-17. A symbolic view of message queues.

Follow these steps to perform troubleshooting based on message queues:

1. Check the **Queues** property page of the MTA and messaging connectors.

2. Verify the submit time and the sent time in order to determine delays.

3. Make sure that the remote system is working.

4. Enable Diagnostics Logging for the MTA and additional messaging connectors to obtain detailed status information.

5. Lower the priority of suspected messages.

6. Delete corrupted messages to free blocked message queues.

Review

1. Which Exchange Server databases rely on JET 3.0 technology?

   _____

   _____

   _____

2. Which files types are maintained by Exchange Server in addition to the actual database files?

   _____

   _____

   _____

3. What does circular logging mean?

   _____

   _____

   _____

4. Which methods can you use to delete previous log files without risking damage to the Exchange Server installation?

   _____

   _____

   _____

5. What is the difference between the incremental backup and the differential backup?

   _____

   _____

   _____

   _____

6. What must be accomplished before moving existing server databases to a new Exchange Server computer?

   _____

   _____

   _____

7. Which tool can you use to defragment the Exchange Server databases manually?

_____

8. You just restored an Exchange Server from an offline backup, but the IS service does not start anymore. How do you fix the problem?

_____

9. Which actions can a Server Monitor perform?

_____

_____

_____

_____

_____

_____

10. Which recipients can be referenced in Link Monitor test messages?

_____

_____

_____

11. How would you suspend a Server Monitor from monitoring a particular server?

_____

_____

12. Which three service states can be signaled by a Server Monitor, and how are they signaled within the Administrator program?

_____

_____

_____

_____

_____

13. When do you launch the Scanpst.exe program?

_____

_____

14. At system startup you are notified that one or more services cannot be started. You check the Windows NT Event log and discover that the MTA service has failed to start. What steps must be taken to fix the MTA startup problem?

    _____

    _____

    _____

15. You fixed an MTA startup problem using the MTA Check utility, but some messages have been deleted from the MTA message queues. Where can you find these deleted objects and further information?

    _____

    _____

    _____

    _____

16. A user complains about connection problems, but Exchange Server runs fine and other users have no problems. How can you inspect the RPC communication?

    _____

    _____

    _____

    _____

17. You notice that the MTA service is consuming 100 percent of the CPU's resources. For this reason you assume that the MTA is hanging. How can you stop the MTA service in this case?

    _____

    _____

    _____

    _____

18. How can you pull directory changes from another Exchange Server computer?

    _____

    _____

19. You have configured a directory replication connector to another site and want to initiate the directory replication immediately. How do you accomplish this task?

_____

_____

_____

_____

20. How can you change the Site Services Account password?

_____

_____

_____

_____

21. When would you use the Message Tracking Center?

_____

_____

_____

_____

22. Which components support message tracking?

_____

_____

23. Users complain that messages have not been delivered for a long time. What should you check first in order to determine the problem?

_____

_____

C H A P T E R   1 6

The Exchange Server Forms Environment

This chapter covers the development, installation, and use of electronic forms and workgroup applications that are supported by Microsoft Exchange Server. Sophisticated design tools such as Electronic Forms Designer and Outlook Forms Designer are at your disposal. You don't need any programming skills to use them.

Overview

A chess game is a good example of a workgroup project. As one player makes a move, the other thinks about an appropriate response. Both players share their responses by means of a chessboard. However, if a chess workgroup application is not a suitable solution for your business needs, you can create bulletin boards for work schedules, a customer tracking tool, and a business travel planner instead.

Lesson 1 of this chapter introduces the electronic forms design environments—Electronic Forms Designer and Outlook Forms Designer.

Lesson 2 covers general management tasks such as the installation of forms using either Exchange Client 5.0 or Microsoft Outlook. It also describes forms libraries where forms are kept.

Lesson 3 lists sample applications that come with Exchange Server, Exchange Client 5.0, and Outlook 97 version 8.03. Sample forms can give you a head start in creating electronic forms and workgroup applications.

This chapter also includes an exercise that guides you through the steps of creating an Organization Forms Library and assigning administrative permissions. You will also derive an electronic form from an existing Outlook sample and install it in the new library.

In the following lessons, you will be introduced to:

- The features of electronic forms designed using Electronic Forms Designer
- The features of electronic forms designed using Outlook Forms Designer
- Management of electronic forms in an Exchange Server organization
- Existing sample applications and how to extend them

Lesson 1: Electronic Forms

Whenever you use Exchange Client 5.0, you are working with electronic forms to send and read messages. The standard forms let you specify recipients, subject line, message text, and a few other options. The appropriate standard form is also displayed if you open a received message item.

In Microsoft Schedule+ 7.x, you use electronic forms to send meeting requests. These are regular e-mail messages, but they are associated with a message request form instead of a standard e-mail form. Consequently, the meeting request form is launched automatically whenever you open a meeting request message.

Outlook 97 takes advantage of electronic forms in many ways. Whether you send messages, create contacts, or manage projects and tasks, you work with electronic forms. Each item is registered with its corresponding form, which lets Outlook display the information in the correct format.

If you want to achieve special results—for example, if you want a special view of a Contacts item—you can create your own customized forms. The Exchange Client family and Outlook both provide forms design tools. The tools are incompatible with each other, so this lesson will briefly discuss interoperability issues.

At the end of this lesson, you will be able to:

- Identify stand-alone and folder applications
- Name types of forms that you can create using Exchange Forms Designer
- List the features of the Outlook application design environment

Estimated time to complete this lesson: 25 minutes

Application Design Environments

Exchange forms applications are not like typical Windows-based applications because they are available only in MAPI-based Exchange clients (such as Outlook). In other words, they are client dependent. Workgroup applications are also backbone dependent because they rely on storage and transport mechanisms provided by an Exchange Server system. (See Figure 16-1.)

Exchange workgroup applications typically consist of three parts: an electronic form, a message folder (usually a public folder), and the folder design (the view, the filters, and the rules). You can also combine workgroup applications with databases such as Microsoft SQL Server. You use the electronic form to create and read special messages. The public folder stores these messages, and the folder design determines how the contents are presented in the messaging client. Folder rules help with workflow automation, and public folder replication can distribute the data items across the organization. You can also publish public folders to the USENET through NNTP and HTTP. Public folders are covered in more detail in Chapter 12.

Types of Exchange Applications

Exchange applications can be divided into two general groups: stand-alone applications and folder applications. Stand-alone applications, also known as Send Forms, are used for direct information exchange between users. In other words, you use a stand-alone form to send another person a specially formatted e-mail message. The meeting request form in Schedule+ 7.x is a good example application. In folder applications, items are posted to a message folder. These applications are therefore known as Post Forms. Because the information is posted to a public folder, the information is shared by multiple users.

Electronic forms are the right choice if you want to:

- Automate workflow processes

- Dedicate public folders to discussion forums in which information is posted in a structured way

- Replace paper forms

Exchange Application Design Environment

The Exchange application design environment consists of the Exchange Forms Designer tool, several templates, sample applications, and a mini (16-bit) version of Visual Basic 4.0. Electronic Forms Designer lets you develop forms without using a programming language. You use the mini Visual Basic version to compile your project to an executable file. Templates provide a starting point for new electronic forms projects.

Note Electronic Forms Designer is a 16-bit development tool that creates 16-bit Visual Basic projects. Therefore, you must use a 16-bit version of Visual Basic 4.0 (or higher) to compile electronic forms.

16-Bit Sample Applications

You can install several sample applications when you install Electronic Forms Designer. They will typically reside in the \Efdforms\Samples directory.

Several other 16-bit examples are provided in Outlook 97 version 8.03. They are on the installation CD-ROM in the \Support\Samples\i386 directory. A Sampapps.pst file is also provided. It contains all compiled and installed sample applications. You can test them by copying the Sampapps.pst file to your hard disk and including the file in your messaging profile. A project file of sample applications is a good starting point for development projects. You can change and modify the applications as desired. They are discussed further in Lesson 3, "Sample Applications," later in this chapter.

Note Exchange Server 4.0 and 5.0 offer to install the 16-bit sample applications during the setup process. If you install them, the applications are placed in the Exchsrvr\Samples\Client directory on the server computer. Exchange Server 5.5 does not provide 16-bit samples.

Outlook Application Design Environment

Outlook integrates all features of Exchange Client, Schedule+, and more in a single application. So you might ask, "Where is the Electronic Forms Designer?" Well, in Outlook it's called Outlook Forms Designer, and it's a 32-bit design tool. As a result, it is incompatible with Electronic Forms Designer.

32-Bit Sample Applications

Outlook provides several sample forms that you can examine to become familiar with the 32-bit design environment. These samples are also starting points for your own development projects. You can use any available form as a template. Examples include the normal Mail Message form and the Expense Reporting, TimeCard, and Helpdesk forms.

Note You cannot modify old Electronic Forms Designer samples using Outlook Forms Designer.

Forms Design

Outlook forms are 32-bit forms that are interpreted at run time. They are smaller and faster than compiled 16-bit forms. Because they are not compiled as executable files, Outlook forms cannot be used in with Exchange Client 4.0 or 5.0. However, Exchange Clients are extended to support 32-bit forms if you install Outlook on the same computer.

Because Outlook forms are not compiled, you cannot extend them using Visual Basic. You can, however, add macros and Visual Basic Script elements to them to create powerful workgroup applications. For example, you can write a macro that appends information contained in a Purchase Order form directly to a Microsoft Access database.

The forms code is stored in .OFT template files. These files are usually less than 10 KB. Since Outlook forms are script based, you can link them to Web pages, text documents, spreadsheets, and other files, as your would any Office 97 document. Because they are script-based, you can create workgroup applications that can be accessed using an Internet browser. See Lesson 4, "Extended Collaboration Features," for more details.

The basic features of Outlook forms are as follows:

- They can be linked to Web pages to provide workgroup computing to the Internet.

- They are small (about 10 KB), fast, and are not compiled.

- All Outlook forms provide built-in extensibility. Users can start with any existing form, such as a build-in module, sample application, or standard message form.

Interoperability Between Clients and Forms Versions

Exchange Client 5.0 and Outlook are MAPI-based applications; they connect to Exchange Server in a similar way. Both can send messages back and forth and both have access to public folders. But while Outlook can handle Exchange Client items without problems, Exchange Client 5.0 does not support Outlook items. Exchange Client 5.0 also does not support several extended Outlook features, so you should be careful when using the two client platforms in a mixed environment.

Forms Support

You can display standard Outlook messages in the Exchange Client, but if you open an extended Outlook form such as a Contacts item, a native Exchange Client will display an error message informing you that a form cannot be started. The contents will be displayed only as normal message text.

The standard Outlook Post Form can also create a small problem. It can post items to public folders using the WordMail option, but Exchange clients cannot support this feature for posted items. Exchange clients convert the message contents to rich text format, which means you'll lose features specific to Word at this point, such as text highlights and Word's spell-checker capabilities.

The old 16-bit forms of Electronic Forms Designer are interchangeable between Exchange Client 5.0 and Outlook, so you should use only 16-bit forms until all users have migrated to Outlook. (See Figure 16-3 on page 1039.)

Note The Exchange Client installation is enhanced if you install Outlook on the same machine. The extended Exchange Client can launch extended Outlook forms.

Public Folder Design

When you design a public folder in Outlook, you must keep in mind that the Exchange Client may not be able to handle all folder views correctly. This is the case whenever you add Outlook-specific fields to views, use Outlook view types, or activate a view for in-cell editing. For example, the Exchange Client cannot display the **TimeLine View** format correctly. However, Outlook users can work with Exchange Client views as usual. When the Exchange Client users format a public folder view, Outlook users see this view as the Exchange 4.0 format.

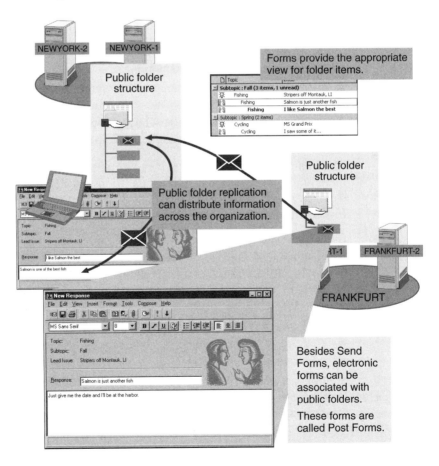

Figure 16-1. Electronic forms and public folders.

The typical components of Exchange applications and their functions are as follows:

- **Folders**; to create the information repository and to share information (public and private folders can be used)

- **Forms**; to compose and read messages

- **Fields**; to store information such as an expiration date, about an object

- **Folder Design**; to determine the information arrangement and to implement workflow automation

Exchange Forms Designer

Exchange Forms Designer is a graphical, nonprogramming design tool that lets you create Exchange applications that are supported by both Exchange Client 5.0 and Outlook.

Installing Exchange Forms Designer

Exchange Forms Designer comes on the Exchange Client CD-ROM. You install it from the \Efdsetup directory using a separate setup program. In addition to the actual Electronic Forms Designer, the Setup program copies a mini version of Visual Basic 4.0 and several sample applications to your hard disk.

Electronic Forms Designer is typically placed in a directory called \Efdforms under the directory of your Exchange Client (by default, \Exchange). Various sample applications are in the Exchange\Efdforms\Samples directory. (See Figure 16-2.)

If you have only the Outlook installation CD-ROM, you can find the Exchange Forms Designer in the \Support\Efdsetup directory. However, you cannot install it without having Exchange Client on your computer. Unfortunately, the Exchange Forms Designer Setup does not recognize Outlook.

Visual Basic 4.0 (16-Bit)

When you design new 16-bit electronic forms, you create full Visual Basic projects (.VBP, .BAS, .FRM, and .FRX files), which are kept in a subdirectory of the current form (the *<FORMNAME>*.VB directory). Electronic Forms Designer uses its own Visual Basic version to compile these projects to executable files. This is sufficient for simple send and post applications in which no programming is required.

To create complex electronic forms, you can extend the basic Visual Basic projects created using Electronic Forms Designer and compile them using a full 16-bit version of Visual Basic 4.0.

Note Once you have made changes to an electronic form using the full 16-bit version of Visual Basic 4.0, you cannot reload the electronic forms project into Electronic Forms Designer or your custom changes will be lost.

Electronic Forms Designer forms projects are saved in .EPF files. These files are actually Access 2.0 databases that contain a list of controls, forms, windows, and fields.

Template Chooser Wizard

A forms template provides predesigned controls (such as the **To**, **From**, **CC**, **BCC**, and **Subject** controls) that must always be added to a new electronic form. A template is generally required if you want to open a new Electronic Forms Designer project.

The Template Chooser Wizard can help you select the appropriate form template. It is launched automatically when you start Electronic Forms Designer. The wizard asks you a series of questions to determine the correct template, which it opens automatically.

Selecting Forms Manually

Forms templates have the extension .EPF. They reside in the \Efdforms Template directory. You can select them manually if you want to skip the Template Chooser Wizard. But before you take this approach, you should be familiar with template naming schemes.

The first three letters of each template name indicate whether the project is a Send Form or a Post Form. Send Form templates begin with *SND*, while Post Form templates start with *PST*. If the fourth character is an *N*, the form is used to create new items. If it is an *R*, the form is used to read messages. If the fifth character is a *1*, the form uses one window to compose and read items; a *2* indicates that the form uses separate compose and read windows.

For example, Sndn2wnd.efp is a template for a Send Form that contains two windows. One window is for composing messages, and the other appears when recipients read the information.

Modifying and Installing Forms

You can start a new project using a form template or you can use a sample application. In fact, modifying a sample application is usually the fastest and most efficient method of creating electronic forms. You can add new labels, text boxes, check boxes, radio buttons, and other controls to the form as needed. (See Figure 16-2.)

Electronic Forms Designer provides the **Open An Existing Form Project** option on startup. If you select this option, you can select an .EFP file using the **Open** box. After you create the application, you can compile and install the form. When you click the **Install** command on the **File** menu, the mini Visual Basic version is launched to compile a 16-bit executable file. Then Electronic Forms Designer connects to your Exchange Server using the current MAPI profile. A dialog box appears, giving you the option to install the new application in one of the Exchange forms libraries. Depending on the selected library, the form might be distributed across the organization automatically. Forms libraries are covered in Lesson 2, "Managing Forms," later in this chapter.

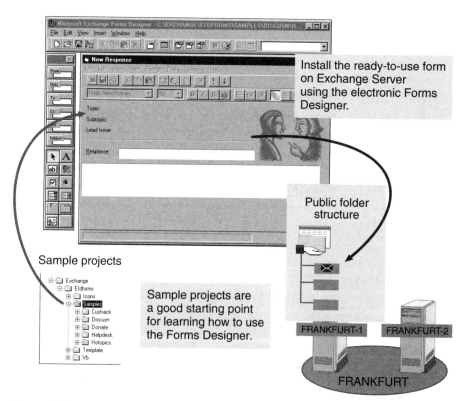

Figure 16-2. Creating new 16-bit forms applications.

Electronic Forms Designer has the following characteristics:

- Creates Send Forms and Post Forms
- Compiles forms using its own mini Visual Basic version
- Creates 16-bit forms only
- Installs forms automatically in a forms library
- Template Chooser Wizard helps you create basic projects
- Allows you to select a form template directly

Outlook Forms Designer

Outlook Forms Designer is a 32-bit design tool that is tightly integrated into Outlook. You can use it to modify all kinds of Outlook forms (including the standard Mail Message form, Contacts form, and Tasks form) without using a programming language.

Starting Outlook Forms Designer

You can launch Outlook Forms Designer using the **Design Outlook Form** command on the **Tools** menu of most Outlook forms. If you open a message in your Inbox, a **Message** window will appear. On the **Tools** menu, click the **Design Outlook Form** command to switch to design mode. The design mode shows **(Design)** on the title bar and offers the **Field Chooser**, which helps you place fields on the form.

Designing Custom Forms

Most Outlook forms can be used as templates for custom applications. You simply launch a template (such as the Mail Message, Contact, Task, or Calendar form) and activate the design mode.

Note Regardless of which 32-bit form you want to modify, you must select the **Design Outlook Form** command on its **Tools** menu.

Send Forms

You can create 32-bit Send Forms using Outlook Forms Designer if you select an appropriate template. The Mail Message form is such a template. You can use any available form that allows addressing mailboxes, distribution lists, public folders, and custom recipients.

Post Forms

You use 32-bit Post Forms to place and view items in a public or personal folder. You can use a Post Form template such as the Contact, Task, or Calendar form to create a customized form. Another good template is the standard Post Form, which you launch using the **New Post In This Folder** command on Outlook's **Compose** menu.

Office 97 Documents

Outlook incorporates messaging features into the Microsoft Office 97 suite, so you can combine Microsoft Word or Microsoft Excel with Outlook. You just wrap a form around Word or Excel documents and send them as e-mail messages or post them to public folders.

Advanced Design Features

You cannot compile or adjust Outlook forms using Visual Basic 4.0. Their design and development must happen within Outlook. You can, however, extend the forms using the Outlook Access Expression Service. You can use this feature to create advanced controls such as validated fields, formulas, and combination fields. A good example is a field that determines an expiration date by adding several days to the current date.

Visual Basic Script (VBScript) can add intelligence to Outlook forms. While users add information in one field, other information can be added to other fields automatically. VBScript also lets you open and close dialog boxes, launch other forms, and perform background calculations while users work with your form in the foreground.

Installing Forms

Like any other electronic forms, Outlook forms can be published using the Exchange Server forms libraries. However, you cannot launch, install, or manage them outside Outlook. (See Figure 16-3.) You must use Outlook Forms Designer to publish customized forms. On the **File** menu of your form in design mode, you select the **Publish Form As** command. Forms libraries and the installation of electronic forms are discussed in Lesson 2 later in this chapter.

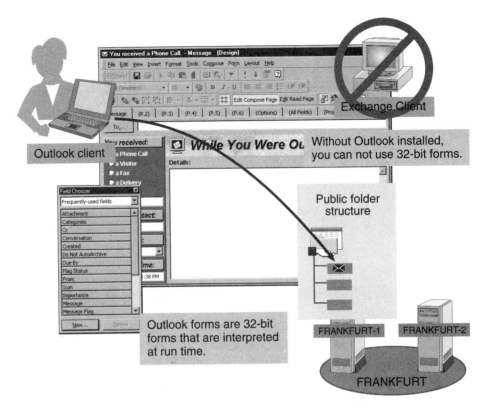

Figure 16-3. Platforms for Outlook forms.

To create a custom form, you must take these steps:

1. Open a form template (for example, the New Mail Message form).

2. Select the **Design Outlook Form** command on the **Tools** menu.

3. Customize the pages by adding, replacing, or deleting controls.

4. Adjust the properties of the form pages.

5. Create custom actions, if desired, using additional program code.

6. Save the form in an Exchange Server forms library using the **Publish Form As** command on the **File** menu in design mode.

Lesson 2: Managing Forms

The most amazing features of electronic forms are their automatic distribution and installation. You simply install the electronic form in a forms library and Exchange Server takes care of the rest. You'll see a new command on the **Compose** menu of your messaging client. You click it to launch the form. If you have not yet used this form, it is copied to the local computer before it is displayed. Even if you have never before installed or used the form, it is installed and displayed as soon as you open an associated forms message. If you install the corresponding form in a public forms library on an Exchange Server, it becomes available to all users in your organization.

This lesson discusses centralized management of Exchange and Outlook forms. It introduces the available forms libraries and the management features of Send Forms and Post Forms. It then covers the management of forms libraries. You'll learn how to create an Organization Forms Library (OFL) and learn about access restrictions. The lesson ends with a discussion about installing electronic forms using Electronic Forms Designer, Exchange Client 5.0, and Outlook 97.

At the end of this lesson, you will be able to:

- Describe the functions of all types of forms libraries and decide which library to use in a given situation

- Manage forms libraries

- Install forms in forms libraries using Exchange Client 5.0

- Install forms using Outlook

Estimated time to complete this lesson: 25 minutes

Forms Libraries

Horst Sauerbier is a brilliant German Visual Basic developer. He has been hired to develop electronic forms for STOCKSDATA worldwide, even though he is not very familiar with Exchange Server 5.5. His first task is to design a survey application. Not a big deal, he thinks. With a few mouse clicks and a bit of extra VBScript code, he creates a gorgeous Send Form using Outlook Forms Designer. He knows that he must publish the form across the Exchange Server organization, but first he must find the appropriate forms library for his form.

Types of Forms Libraries

Exchange Server provides three types of forms libraries: the Folder Forms Library (FFL), the Organization Forms Library (OFL), and the Personal Forms Library (PFL). All three let you maintain Exchange applications centrally on an Exchange Server computer. (See Figure 16-4.)

Folder Forms Library

An FFL associates electronic forms with a message folder. It is the place for folder applications, also known as Post Forms. Whether you install a form in a public folder or a personal folder, the FFL keeps track of the association and provides the form only if the corresponding folder has been opened. For example, let's say that you have installed a Stock Purchase Order form in a public folder called Stocks Order. Because of the association between the form and the folder, the **Stock Purchase Order** command is available on the **Compose** menu only if you have already selected the **Stocks Order** folder.

Public folders let you share information with all users in an organization. These folders are the foundation of Exchange workgroup applications because they share their FFLs and all the electronic forms that they contain. However, you should not publish a workgroup application during the development phase. To test your prototypes, use private and personal folders instead.

Organization Forms Library

An OFL is a system public folder that you can use to maintain Send Forms. Send Forms are not associated with a particular message folder, so they are always available on the **Compose** menu.

OFLs are client language dependent. In other words, you must create a separate OFL for each client language in your organization using the Administrator program. OFLs are replicated across the organization through replication of the public folder hierarchy.

Personal Forms Library

A PFL maintains all the Send Forms that you don't want to share with other users. It resides in your mailbox and is not replicated anywhere. An installed form is available only on the **Compose** menu of your messaging client. Other users cannot launch your private form unless they install it manually in their own PFL.

Note Certain forms, such as Send Forms in the development stage, should be installed in a PFL to prevent their distribution across the entire organization.

Forms Library Administration

All types of forms libraries require administration, but it is mainly an issue with OFLs. By default, OFLs do not exist. FFLs are created implicitly along with their message folders; they inherit the folders' configurations and user permissions. Only a folder owner can install electronic forms. PFLs do not require extensive administration because they are associated with a mailbox. Only the mailbox owner and privileged delegates can install private electronic forms.

Creating an OFL

You can create OFLs using the Forms Administrator tool, which you launch using the **Forms Administrator** command on the **Tools** menu of the Administrator program. You'll see the **Organization Forms Library Administrator** dialog box, which provides the **New**, **Modify**, **Remove**, and **Permissions** buttons. Click the **New** button to create a new OFL. Keep in mind that OFLs are language dependent. You must build one library for each client language in your organization.

Forms and Folder Replication

OFLs are system public folders that are hidden from users and reside under the **EFORMS REGISTRY** object. You can find the **EFORMS REGISTRY** object in the container pane of the Administration window when you open the **Folders** container and then the **System Folders** container.

Exchange Server creates local, nonreplicated instances of OFL folders by default, but you can use the **Replicas** property page of an OFL object to replicate the library contents to other servers. This is required only if direct access to the local OFL instance is not permitted. Public folder replication is covered in detail in Chapter 13.

OFL Security

By default, no one can install electronic forms in an OFL. You must designate privileged OFL owners who can publish Send Forms in your organization. Herr Sauerbier, for instance, must have the permissions of a folder owner for all existing STOCKSDATA OFLs in order to publish his Send Form.

You can use the Forms Administrator and the OFL folder object under the **EFORMS REGISTRY** container to manage user permissions. The Forms Administrator provides the **Permissions** button in the **Organization Forms Library Administrator** dialog box, while the OFL folder object provides a **Client Permissions** button on its **General** property page. You can use either button to specify who is permitted to install forms. Configuration of folder permissions is covered in more detail in Chapter 12.

Note You cannot manage permissions for OFLs using Exchange Client 5.0 or Outlook because OFLs are hidden public folders.

Using Applications Off Line

As shown in Figure 16-4, electronic forms are typically maintained centrally on an Exchange Server computer in OFLs, FFLs, and PFLs. This can be a problem if users want to open forms messages while working off line. The associated form is not available during offline operation.

To work around this problem, you can configure an Offline Folder Store using Exchange Client 5.0 or Outlook. Electronic forms are then downloaded implicitly into the local storage file when private and public folders are synchronized. Once the forms are available locally, users can work on them as if they were on line. The Offline Folder Store is covered in detail in Chapter 7.

Note You can install Post Forms in a personal folder (a .PST file) so that they are available for use off line. However, personal folders cannot be shared with other users in your organization.

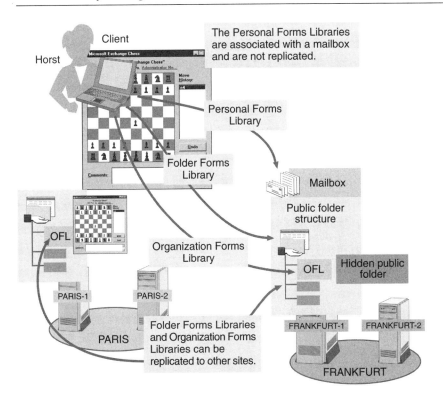

Figure 16-4. Possible repositories for electronic forms.

The forms libraries and their primary functions are as follows:

- **Folder Forms Library**; a public repository associated with a public folder and usually used for Post Forms

- **Organization Forms Library**; a public repository associated with a hidden public folder and usually used for Send Forms

- **Personal Forms Library**; a private repository associated with a mailbox and therefore used for personal Send Forms and Send Form testing

Installing Forms

Forms installation tools can be divided in two groups: the Exchange Forms Installer group and the Outlook Forms Installer group. Members of the Exchange Forms Installer group are Electronic Forms Designer, Exchange Client, and Outlook. The Outlook Forms Installer group is much smaller—Outlook is the only member.

Note You cannot use the Exchange Administrator to install electronic forms in a forms library.

Installing Exchange Forms

The installation of 16-bit forms relies on .CFG configuration files, which provide information about the forms. You must specify the .CFG file during installation to identify the form within Exchange. Electronic Forms Designer builds a .CFG file automatically for every project it creates. The file is in the same directory as the form's Visual Basic project.

Your Exchange Client directory might contain several .CFG files, which you can open using a text editor. A .CFG file contains a description of the form, including MessageClass, DisplayName, Version number, Comment, definitions of icons, and other properties. You can use these properties to define folder views and folder rules.

Note You cannot install a 16-bit Exchange application without a .CFG file.

Electronic Forms Designer

Electronic Forms Designer lets you design, compile, and install 16-bit forms. While you must design the forms yourself, you can accomplish the compilation and installation using the **Install** command on the **File** menu. First the 16-bit Visual Basic 4.0 launches and creates an executable file. Then Electronic Forms Designer connects to your Exchange Server using your current messaging profile to install the form in an available forms library.

Installing Forms from the Exchange Client

When you extend a 16-bit form using the full (16-bit) Visual Basic 4.0, you cannot reload the project into Electronic Forms Designer for installation. You can, however, launch the Forms Manager within the Exchange Client if you have an associated .CFG file. As mentioned before, Electronic Forms Designer creates this file for every generated project.

Let's say that Herr Sauerbier wants to publish his Send Form application. An associated .CFG file exists. Using the Exchange Client, he opens the **Tools** menu and clicks the **Options** command to display the **Options** dialog box. He then switches to the **Exchange Server** property page, where he clicks the **Manage Forms** button to launch the Forms Manager. In the **Forms Manager** window, he selects the desired OFL using the **Set** button in the upper right corner. Then he clicks the **Install** button to open the **Open** dialog box. (The **Install** button is available only if he has permission to install forms in the selected OFL.) Now Horst specifies his .CFG file and clicks the **Open** button. The default settings obtained from the .CFG file are displayed. Horst clicks **OK** to install the Send Form application. (See Figure 16-5.). He clicks the **Close** button and then the **OK** button to close the Forms Manager and the **Options** dialog box.

Installing Forms from Outlook

Outlook can handle compiled 16-bit forms, so the Forms Manager is also available in Outlook. The process of installing a 16-bit form in Outlook is similar to the procedure described above for the Exchange Client. You click the **Options** command on the **Tools** menu to display the **Options** dialog box. You then switch to the **Manage Forms** property page and click the **Manage Forms** button to launch the Forms Manager. You use the Forms Manager as described in the section above.

Installing Outlook Forms

You cannot use the Exchange Client to install 32-bit Outlook forms. You can publish these forms only using Outlook Forms Designer. Select the **Publish Form As** command on the **File** menu of your forms window in design mode. In the dialog box that appears, specify a **Form Name** and click the **Publish In** button to specify a forms library. You can select an OFL, FFL, or PFL. Click the **Publish** button to complete the installation.

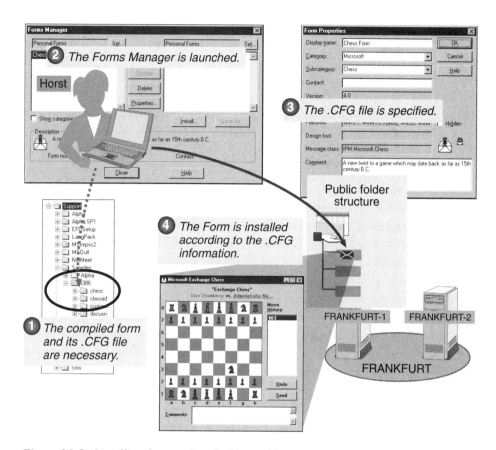

Figure 16-5. Installing forms using the Forms Manager.

The tools for installing forms are as follows:

- **Electronic Forms Designer**; use this for a 16-bit form that has been designed but not compiled

- **The Forms Manager**; use this for a 16-bit form that has been compiled and has an associated .CFG file

- **Outlook Forms Designer**; use this to publish 32-bit forms

Lesson 3: Sample Applications

Sample applications are like small computer games that ship with source code. They demonstrate how products and extensions work, and they can provide a useful starting point for your own development projects. You can explore and modify them as you wish. Sample applications are not copyrighted.

This lesson provides an overview of the sample applications that come with Electronic Forms Designer, Outlook, and the Exchange Server CD. It will also illustrate how to modify sample forms using Outlook.

The lesson ends with an exercise that guides you through five tasks, beginning with the creation of an OFL and ending with a demonstration of a customized Outlook form.

At the end of this lesson, you will be able to:

- Use and extend Outlook sample applications
- List the various Exchange sample applications

Estimated time to complete this lesson: 60 minutes

Sample Application Overview

The first lines of program code are always the hardest to write. Nothing works, you are forced to guess, and sometimes you discover that your beginning was useless. But once a small chunk of code begins to work, you can test it, examine it, and enhance it. The code grows, and programming becomes more exciting and interesting. If you doubt this, start an Outlook forms project from scratch and then create one using the Contacts form, as described in Exercise 49 later in this chapter. You will notice a difference.

Exchange Sample Applications

Electronic Forms Designer samples (\Exchange\Efdforms\Samples) and the Outlook CD (\Support\Samples\i386) provide samples and code that demonstrate the use of 16-bit electronic forms. You can modify, compile, and install these using Electronic Forms Designer. You can install compiled samples without source code, such as the chess application, using Exchange Client 5.0 or Outlook.

To get a quick overview of all the samples, add Sampapps.pst file to your personal messaging profile. Sampapps.pst is a Personal Folder Store that contains numerous 16-bit samples in their compiled and installed form. An introduction to forms development is also included in the **Getting Started Guide** personal folder. Sampapps.pst is located in the \Support\Samples\i386 directory of the Outlook CD-ROM.

The following sample forms applications are in the Sampapps.pst file:

- **Anonymous Submissions**; to support anonymous forums
- **Charity Donation**; to submit charity contributions automatically
- **Chess**; to demonstrate how Visual Basic, OLE messaging, and Exchange can be combined to create form applications
- **Classified Ads**; to post classified ads to a public folder
- **Customer Tracking**; to track contacts using a public folder
- **Discussion & Response**; to group discussions in a public folder by topic, subtopic, and issue
- **Document Filer**; to store files so that all users in the organization have access to the files
- **Getting Started Guide**; contains Exchange tutorial items
- **Help Desk**; to enter help desk problems and their prioritization, assignment, and resolution
- **Hot Topics**; to submit moderator-approved news items
- **Interpersonal Forms**; to store Send Forms in a central location; this application includes Answer, Bug Report, Charity Donation, Purchase Offer, and Vacation/Sick-Day forms
- **Schedule Time Away**; to submit vacation or sick-day notices
- **Survey**; to send custom survey forms

Outlook Sample Applications

The Outlook CD provides a variety of 32-bit form templates that you can use and extend in Outlook. Some basic templates are installed during setup; others can be added later when you run the Setup program for Windows 95 (Outfrms.exe) or for Windows NT (Outfmsnt.exe). Both are in the \Outlook.w32\ValuPack\Template\Outlook directory. Outfrms.exe and Outfmsnt.exe extract a Personal Folder Store called Forms.pst, which you can include in your messaging profile (as described in Chapter 7).

The following sample applications are in the Forms.pst file:

- **Classified Ads**; to provide a bulletin board for buying and selling items or to create announcements

- **Sales Tracking**; to manage sales processes and provide contact management by defining accounts, contacts, contact reports, action items, and so forth

- **Training Management**; to automate the process of enrolling students in a training course

- **Vacation Request**; to request vacations, mark vacation time on calendars, and to approve vacations and sick time

- **While You Were Out**; to take phone messages and other messages for a fellow employee and then to send the information in the form of a message to the employee's Inbox

As mentioned earlier in this chapter, you can use any standard Outlook form to start your own forms project. Exercise 49 uses the Contacts standard form. The following sample forms are usually available when you click the **Choose Template** command on Outlook's **Compose** menu:

- Appointment

- Contact

- Journal Entry

- Message

- Note (cannot be modified)

- Post

- Task

Modifying Forms Using Outlook

After you launch an Outlook form template, you can switch to design mode by clicking the **Design Outlook Form** command on the form's **Tools** menu. Then you can customize the form. You will basically delete existing fields and add new fields to achieve the desired functionality. Later, you can add VBScript elements and macros to implement special effects.

Examples of existing fields are the **To**, **Cc**, and **Sent** lines, which display recipient information and a time stamp. Of course, Outlook provides many other fields as well. They are organized by category, which you can examine using the Field Chooser tool. You launch this utility by selecting the **Field**

Chooser command on Outlook Forms Designer's **View** menu. The Field Chooser allows you to create customized fields if the default versions do not meet your needs. (See Figure 16-6.)

Adding Fields

You can select a field such as the **Message Flag Field** from a category of the Field Chooser and place it on a form using drag and drop. You can opt to have new controls aligned automatically on the left side of other fields if they are placed below them. Other alignment options are available on the **Layout** menu. The **AutoLayout** feature of Outlook Forms Designer, which is enabled by default, automatically aligns the new fields on the form, no matter where you drop them.

Defining New Fields

If you cannot find an appropriate field in the Field Chooser categories, you can create one using the **New** button in the **Field Chooser** window. You specify a name and a field type. (You can select a field type such as **Text**, **Date/Time**, **Number**, or **Currency** in the **Type** combo box in the **New Field** dialog box.) Depending on the field type that you select, you might also have the option to specify a specific data format using the **Format** combo box. After you make your selection, click **OK** to add the custom field to the **User Defined Fields In Folder** category of the Field Chooser. You can place the new item on a form just like any other field, using drag and drop. Your new field can also be included in folder views.

Fields on a Per-Folder Basis

You need read and write permissions for the currently selected folder to create new fields. As you add your own fields to the **User Defined Fields In Folder** category of the Field Chooser, they are associated with a message folder.

Let's say that you have defined a new field called **Introduction** in a folder called **New Customers**. You can add this field to the folder view of **New Customers** without having to open the folder. But you cannot use the **Intro-duction** field to extend a folder view of the Inbox. New fields help to orga-nize items only on a per-folder basis. In other words, you must create the same field for other folders if you want to extend their views using user-defined attributes of forms messages. (See Figure 16-6.)

Field Validation

Field validation is a common programming technique used to ensure that users enter valid information in predefined fields. A check is performed when users close a form during a send or post operation. If a field contains an invalid value, users are informed and are asked for valid input. The form is not closed.

For example, you can create a user-defined field called **Rating Feedback** that indicates acceptance of a suggestion. Users can only enter values from 0 to 5. Other values are not allowed. When you place the field on a form, you can enable the field validation feature. No matter which field you are working with, a right-click on the field displays a context menu that offers the **Properties** command. Selecting this command displays the **Properties** dialog box. On the **Validation** tab, select the **Validate Field Before Closing The Form** option and specify a validation formula and a notification. The validation formula will check whether the user has entered a valid value. You can use predefined formulas or VBScript code. You can enter VBScript code using the **View Code** command on the **Form** menu. A notification will inform users about input errors.

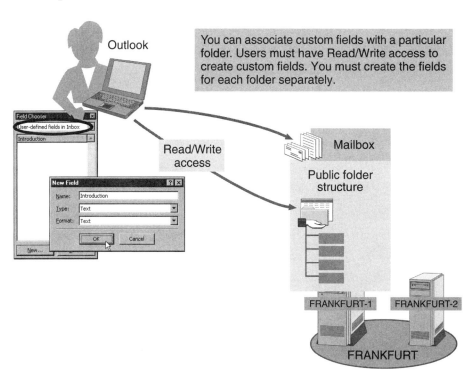

Figure 16-6. Custom fields in Outlook.

The predefined Field Chooser categories are as follows:

Category	Purpose
Address fields	Displays fields that contain address information, such as **To** and **Cc**
All Appointment fields	Helps organize appointments in the **Calendar** folder, such as **Duration** or **End**
All Contact fields	Contains fields that can be used to organize contacts, such as **Business Phone**
All Document fields	Contains all the fields in a document, such as **Creation Time** or **Keywords**
All Journal fields	The same as **Task** and **Appointment** fields, but the fields are associated with **Journals**
All Mail fields	Contains all the fields associated with an e-mail message
All Note fields	Helps organize personal notes in the **Notes** folder, such as **Read** or **Size** fields
All Post fields	Used to specify posted information (such as **Expires** or **Created**) in more detail
All Task fields	Used to order tasks based on fields such as **Conversation** or **Date Completed**
Date/Time fields	Displays time stamps, such as **Sent** or **Modified**
Frequently used fields	Displays the most recently used fields
User-defined fields in Inbox	The place where you can define new custom fields

Exercise 49: Creating and Installing an Outlook Form

Exchange Server 5.5 supports both the old 16-bit forms of Electronic Forms Designer and the new 32-bit Outlook versions. Both let you send special by formatted information to other users (Send Forms) or post the information to a public folder (Post Forms). In either case, the forms must be installed in a forms library before they can be launched.

As mentioned earlier, the three types of forms libraries are the OFL, FFL, and PFL. OFLs require special administrative attention before they can be used. You must create and configure them using the Administrator program.

Estimated time to complete this exercise: 40 minutes

Description

In this exercise, you will use the Administrator program to create an OFL. To allow users to add forms to the OFL, you must modify user permissions appropriately. You will also design a customer tracking form using the Outlook Contacts form as a template and publish it in a public folder to allow posting of customer tracking information.

- Task 49a describes the steps for creating an OFL using the Administrator program.

- Task 49b describes the steps for assigning Owner permissions to selected users so that they can add new forms to the OFL.

- Task 49c describes the steps for creating a custom form from an existing Outlook form and publishing the form in the OFL.

- Task 49d describes the steps for associating a form with a public folder and designating the form as the default and only form that can be used with this public folder.

- Task 49e describes the steps for demonstrating the use of a custom Outlook form.

Prerequisites

- Log on to NEWYORK-1 as Admin-NY1 to complete this exercise.

- Make sure that Outlook and a valid messaging profile are available.

Task 49a: Creating the OFL

1. Click the **Start** button, point to **Programs**, point to **Microsoft Exchange**, click **Microsoft Exchange Administrator**, and then connect to the server NEWYORK-1.

2. On the **Tools** menu, click **Forms Administrator** to display the **Organization Forms Library Administrator** dialog box.

3. Click **New** to display the **Create New Forms Library** dialog box.

4. Verify that the **Library Folder Name** is **Organization Forms** and that the **Language** is **English (USA)**, and then click **OK**.

5. The **Organization Forms Library Administrator** dialog box reappears.

6. Click **Close**.

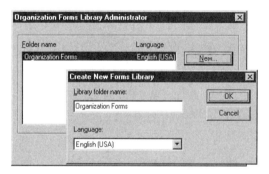

Task 49b: Assigning Permissions to the OFL

1. In the left pane, expand the **Folders** container, expand the **System Folders** container, and then click the **EFORMS REGISTRY** container.

2. The **Organization Forms** folder appears in the right pane.

3. Click **Organization Forms** and then click **Properties** on the **File** menu.

4. Click **Client Permissions** to display the **Client Permissions** dialog box.

5. Click **Add**.

6. Click **Fred Pumpkin** and then click **Add**.

7. Click **OK**.

8. The **Client Permissions** dialog box reappears.

9. Click **Fred Pumpkin**.

10. In the **Roles** list, click **Owner**.

11. Click **OK**.

12. The **Organization Forms Properties** dialog box appears.

13. Click the **Replicas** tab.

14. In the **Site** list, click **LONDON**.

15. In the **Servers** box, click **LONDON-1** and then click **Add**.

16. Click **OK**.

17. On the **File** menu, click **Exit**.

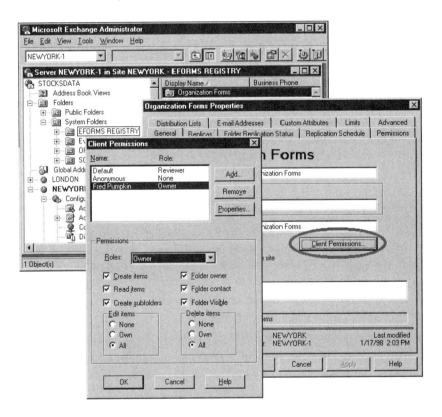

Task 49c: Creating and Installing a Form

1. On the Desktop, double-click the **Microsoft Outlook** shortcut and then log on to **Mailbox - Fred Pumpkin** on the server.

2. On the **File** menu, point to **New** and then click **Contact**.

3. The **Untitled - Contact** dialog box appears. On the **Tools** menu, click **Design Outlook Form**.

4. The **Untitled - Contact (Design)** dialog box appears. Maximize the dialog box.

5. Click the **Properties** tab.

6. In the **Form Caption** box, type *Customer Tracking for NEWYORK*.

7. Click the **(P.2)** tab.

8. On the **Form** menu, click **Rename Page** to display the **Rename Page** dialog box.

9. In the **Page Name** box, type **More Info** and then click **OK**.

10. In the **Field Chooser** dialog box, click **Full Name**, and then drag it to the upper left corner of the Outlook Design form. A blank field is added automatically.

11. The **Field Chooser** list box shows **Frequently-Used Fields** by default. Select **Personal Fields** instead.

12. From the options that appear, drag the **Anniversary**, **Birthday**, **Children**, **Hobbies**, **Referred By**, and **Web Page** fields to an area below the **Full Name** field.

13. At the bottom of the **Field Chooser** dialog box, click **New**.

14. The **New Field** dialog box appears.

15. In the **Name** box, type *Key Customer*.

16. In the **Type** list, click **Yes/No**.

17. Click **OK**.

18. Drag the **Key Customer** field to the area below the **Anniversary**, **Birthday**, **Children**, **Hobbies**, **Referred By**, and **Web Page** fields. Notice that the **Yes/No** option becomes a check box.

19. On the **File** menu, click **Save**.

20. A **Microsoft Outlook** dialog box appears, asking if you want to save this contact with an empty **File As** field. Click **Yes**.

21. On the **File** menu, click **Publish Form As** to display the **Publish Form As** dialog box.

22. Click **Publish In** to display the **Set Library To** dialog box.

23. In the **Forms Library** list, click **Organization Forms** and then click **OK**.

24. Click **Publish**.

25. On the **File** menu, click **Close**.

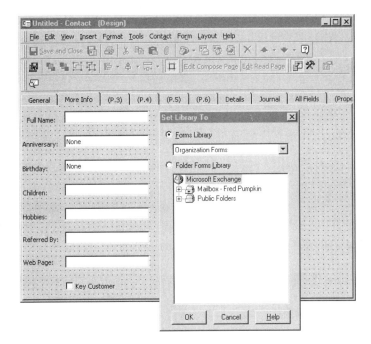

Task 49d: Associating a Form with a Public Folder

1. In the folder pane, expand **Public Folders** and then select **All Public Folders**.

2. On the **File** menu, point to **New** and then click **Folder**.

3. The **Create New Folder** dialog box appears.

4. In the **Name** box, type *Customer List.*

5. In the **Folder Contains** list, click **Contact Items**.

6. Click **OK**.

7. The **Add Shortcut To Outlook Bar?** dialog box appears. Click **No**.

8. Right-click **Customer List** and then click **Properties** to display the **Customer List Properties** dialog box.

9. Click **Forms** and then click **Manage**.

10. In the left pane, click **Customer Tracking For NEWYORK** and then click **Copy**.

11. Click **Close**.

12. In the **Allow These Forms In This Folder** box, click **Only Forms Listed Above**.

13. Click the **General** tab, and then in the **When Posting To This Folder Use** list, click **Forms**.

14. The **New Form** dialog box appears. From the **Organization Forms** list, select **Customer Tracking For NEWYORK** and then click **OK**.

15. Switch to the **Outlook Address Book** tab and select the **Show This Folder As An E-mail Address Book** check box. This action displays the contents of this public folder in the MAPI-based address book through the Outlook Address Book provider.

16. Click **OK**.

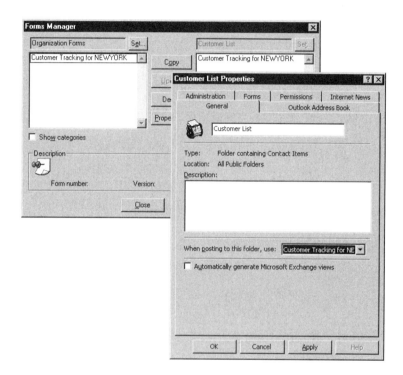

Task 49e: Using the Custom Form

1. Click the **Customer List** public folder and then double-click anywhere in the right pane.

2. In the **Full Name** box, type *Bernd Hopfenmalz*, and then fill in a number of the remaining fields with text of your choosing.

3. Click the **More Info** tab and then fill in each of the fields with information of your choosing.

4. On the toolbar, click **Save And Close**.

5. If **Microsoft Outlook** message boxes appear, asking whether to create events in the personal Calendar, click **No**.

6. If **Microsoft Outlook** message boxes appear, asking if you would like to save a copy of the message in the default folder, click **Yes**.

7. On the **File** menu, click **Exit And Log Off**.

8. Log off Windows NT.

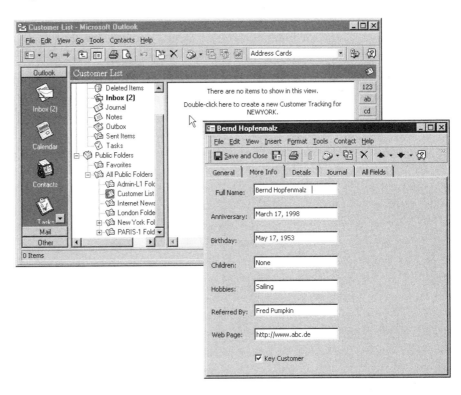

Review

An OFL is the primary repository for standalone applications (Send Forms). It is basically a hidden public folder. Since OFLs do not appear in the Exchange Client or Outlook, you must manage them using the Administrator program. Forms installed in an OFL are always available via the client's **Compose** menu when you are working on line.

An FFL is used to associate folder applications (Post Forms) with message folders. FFLs can be the foundation of Exchange workgroup applications. You can configure a public folder so that users can use Post Forms only to create new items. Post Forms are available only via the client's **Compose** menu if the associated public folder is open.

Outlook, its Contacts folder type, and the Outlook Address Book let you quickly create a companywide phone book. You can add employees and contacts easily. Electronic phone books based on public folders can provide a great variety of information to all users or only to specific users. Users can search public folders using the **Find Items** command on Outlook's **Tools** menu. The contents of a public folder can be displayed in various ways using folder views. Also, the contents of a phone book can be made available using the Outlook Address Book, which makes the information available to all MAPI-aware applications (such as Microsoft Word 97).

Lesson 4: Extended Collaboration Features

The collaboration features of Exchange Server 5.5 are ideal for creating extended workgroup applications. Imagine how many people a discussion forum can reach if you publish a public folder to the Internet. You can create HTML forms to allow reading and posting of information. Depending on how the information is structured, users on the Internet might not even be aware that they are working with an Exchange Server or that event-driven scripts, public folder replication, or replication of articles to the USENET are happening in the background.

This lesson adds to your knowledge of the collaborative features of Exchange Server 5.5—specifically, the use of public folders. The lesson covers script-based folder agents and introduces the HTML sample applications on the Exchange Server 5.5 CD.

At the end of this lesson, you will be able to:

- Create a workgroup application using public folders and Outlook items
- Describe the purpose of the Exchange Event Service
- Configure Public Folder Agents
- Install and test the HTML-based sample applications provided with Exchange Server 5.5

Estimated time to complete this lesson: 45 minutes

Script-Based Folder Agents

Besides offering folder rules, Exchange Server 5.5 offers far-reaching support for folder processing using scripting languages through its Exchange Event Service. You can install this optional component during the Exchange Server setup process. As a matter of fact, the Setup program of Exchange Server 5.5 will suggest the installation of the Exchange Event Service by default, provided that you are not upgrading an existing server to version 5.5. The Event Service works in with the Exchange Server Scripting Agent, which enables server-side scripting. You can write scripts using any text editor, VBScript, or Microsoft JScript. You can also use Microsoft Visual Studio, which includes Microsoft Visual InterDev, in conjunction with Outlook version 8.03 to create scripts.

Folder Events

Folder agents are event-driven scripts that perform defined actions on public folders or folders of a mailbox. Events occur as users create items, modify them, or delete them from a folder. You can also use events triggered automatically by timers in server-side scripts. The term *server-side* indicates that scripts are interpreted at the server, not at the client computer.

Script Installation

Of course, you must the have appropriate permissions to install and enable a server-side script on an Exchange Server. Although this is a minor issue for a private folder, you must have Owner permissions if you want to create a script for a public folder. You must have at least Author permissions for a hidden system folder called **EventConfig_<server name>** (for example, EventConfig_NEWYORK-1). By default, no users have permissions for **EventConfig** folders. One of these folders exists for each server in your site; it binds scripts to the server. You can examine and administer **EventConfig** folders in the Administrator program. They are located under **Events Root** in the **Folders\System Folders** container. More information about configuring public folders is provided in Chapter 12.

In general, you can associate scripts with folders using Outlook 8.03. First you display the properties of the folder. Then you switch to the **Agents** tab (which appears only if you have the required permissions for the **EventConfig** folder of that server). On the **Agents** tab, you can create a script by clicking the **New** button. Every script requires a name and at least one monitored event.

Creating a Server-Side Script

Horst Sauerbier wants to create a folder agent that monitors a public folder. His agent should notify him if the number of messages in that folder exceeds 500. He wants the script to run once a day at 6:00 a.m.

Horst launches his Outlook client, displays the folder list, and navigates to the public folder in the **All Public Folders** tree. (Alternatively, he can select the folder in his **Favorites** folder if a corresponding reference has been created there.) He right-clicks the folder and selects the **Properties** command from the context menu. He then switches to the **Agents** tab and clicks the **New** button. In the **Agent Name** box, he types *More than 500* and then selects **A Scheduled Event Occurs** under **When The Following Event(s) Occur**. To set the schedule to 6:00 a.m., he clicks the **Schedule** button. In the **Scheduled Event** dialog box, he selects **Daily** and specifies **6:00 AM** under **At**. He clicks **OK** to close the dialog box.

To create the script, Horst clicks the **Edit Script** button. This launches Notepad by default. It launches Visual InterDev if it is installed and is associated with .ASP files. A default script containing event stubs opens. Horst edits it as follows:

```
<SCRIPT RunAt=Server Language=VBScript>
'_____
'FILE DESCRIPTION: Exchange Server Event Script
'_____
Option Explicit
'_____
' Global Variables
'_____
      Dim g_CdoPR_CONTENT_COUNT
      g_CdoPR_CONTENT_COUNT = &H36020003
      'Message Count in Folder
      '_____
      ' Event Handlers
      '_____

' DESCRIPTION: This event is fired when
' a new message is added to the folder
Public Sub Folder_OnMessageCreated
End Sub

' DESCRIPTION: This event is fired when
' a message in the folder is changed
Public Sub Message_OnChange
End Sub

' DESCRIPTION: This event is fired when
' a message is deleted from the folder
Public Sub Folder_OnMessageDeleted
End Sub

' DESCRIPTION: This event is fired when
' the timer on the folder expires
Public Sub Folder_OnTimer

      Dim CDOSession       'Session Object
      Dim oMsg             'Message Object
      Dim oFolder          'Current Folder Object
      Dim oFolderOutbox    'Outbox Folder Object
      Dim oRec             'Recipients Object
      Dim iMsgCount

      'Get The Number Of Messages In The Folder
      Set CDOSession = EventDetails.Session
      Set oFolder = CDOSession.GetFolder
      (EventDetails.FolderID, Null )
```

```
iMsgCount = oFolder.Fields(g_CdoPR_CONTENT_COUNT)

If iMsgCount > 500 Then
        'Create Message In Outbox
        Set oFolderOutbox = CDOSession.Outbox
        Set oMsg = oFolderOutbox.
        Messages.Add(cstr("Warning: Too many items in
        folder!"), "There are " & iMsgCount & " mes
        sages in the folder")

        Set oRec = oMsg.Recipients.Add ("Horst
        Sauerbier")oRec.Type = 1 ' Set Recipient in the
        To: line oRec.Resolve = 1' Resolve the Recipi-
        ent Address

        oMsg.Send              'Send The Message

    End If

End Sub


</SCRIPT>
```

Horst closes Notepad (or Visual InterDev), clicks **Yes** when asked whether to save the .ASP file, and clicks **OK** twice to close the dialog box.

Note CDO is an object model that provides the primary interface for accessing and manipulating Exchange items using server-side scripts.

Debugging a Script File

An essential development task is the debugging of code. Even if a programmer is almost perfect, debugging is necessary to ensure that the code actually works.

Let's say that Horst misspelled his mailbox name in the line *Set oRec = oMsg.Recipients.Add ("Horst Sauerbier")*. Because of the error, the script cannot send warning messages to his mailbox. To retrieve information about the problem, he displays the folder's **Agents** property page again and selects the desired agent (**More Than 500**) under **Agents For This Folder**. He clicks the **Edit** button to display the dialog box of the selected agent. He clicks the **Logs** button to display status and debugging information. Horst sees the entry **Run time error at line 41. Source: Active Messaging Error: 4f7. Description: [Active Messaging - [MAPI_E_NOT_FOUND(8004010F)]]**. This is a valuable hint about why his script isn't working properly. He closes the agent log and clicks the **Edit Script** button to correct the mistake.

Note Sophisticated debugging code that provides status information about folder agents using log files is included in all Exchange Server 5.5 sample scripts. The helper function is typically called **DebugAppend**. You can also use the Script Debugger tool in Internet Information Server 4.0 or Internet Explorer 4.0 for debugging server-side scripts. (This debugger is not part of the Exchange Server 5.5 package.)

Sample Script Files

Several sample server-side scripts are provided on the Exchange Server 5.5 CD. They are in the \Server\Support\Collab\Sampler\Scripts directory.

The sample scripts are as follows:

- **Autoaccept**; to automatically accept a meeting request sent to a resource account or to a conference room mailbox

- **Autocategory**; to automatically search the message body for certain keywords and to set the message's keyword field appropriately

- **Bankpost**; to analyze the subject and text of a message and, if it is numeric, to write it to an appropriate bank account

- **Counter**; to automatically count the messages in a folder and to send a status report to the sender of new items (this sample also demonstrates the integration of JScript into VBScript)

Folder Event Processing

The IS notifies the Event Service when a message is posted to a monitored folder. It also sends a notification when messages are changed or deleted. The Event Service converts the notification into an event by calling an *Incremental Change Synchonrization (ICS)* method to request from the IS all changes that have occurred in that folder since the last event occurred. (See Figure 16-7.)

The Event Service maintains all agents that have been registered for a particular folder event type (for example, the Exchange Server Scripting Agent). It initiates agents that have been registered for the appropriate event by calling the *ExecuteEvent* method on the *IExchangeEventHandler* interface of the desired agent. It passes it the identifier of the affected folder, the message identifier of the affected item, and a CDO session object.

The scripting agent obtains the actual script of the folder that is being monitored. It creates a CDO session with the identity of the user who saved the script in the folder. This CDO session object is passed to the script; the script does not have to contain any code to log on to Exchange. Also, because the script runs in a session of the user who saved the script, it can perform any action that the author of the script can. Finally, the scripting agent runs the script and performs the desired folder processing.

Note Because you can make use of VBScript by means of the Event Scripting Agent, you can create a new CDO session through a script. In this case, the session inherits the rights of the Event Service, which might have more rights than the user because the Event Service runs in the context of the Site Services Account. For this reason, it is imperative that security on the Server Scripting Agent be controlled and that you allow only trusted programmers to create scripts on an Exchange Server computer in your organization.

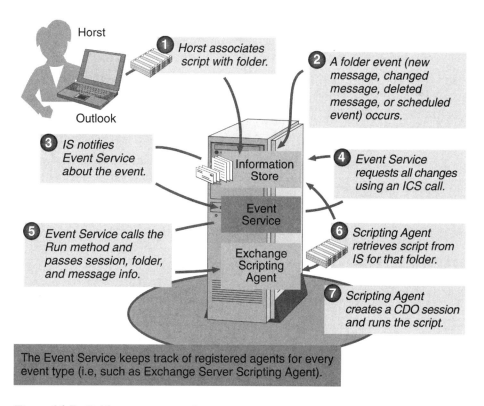

Figure 16-7. Folder event processing.

Server-side scripts can include the following events:

- **Folder_OnTimer**; can run hourly, daily, or weekly in a specified time range (the default for new scheduled events is every hour, all day, from Monday through Friday)

- **Folder_OnMessageCreated**; runs when a new item is created in the associated folder

- **Folder_OnMessageChange**; runs when an item is changed in the associated folder

- **Folder_OnMessageDeleted**; runs when an item is deleted from the associated folder

Exchange HTML Form Design

Publishing Exchange Server resources to the Internet is not a complicated task. In fact, the Exchange Server 5.5 CD provides several sample applications and tools for designing HTML-based forms. If you want to dive deeper into HTTP-based publishing, you might use an HTML and ASP editor such as Microsoft FrontPage. To enhance FrontPage, you can install the Microsoft Exchange Discussion Wizard for FrontPage, which is on the Exchange Server 5.5 CD in the \Server\Support\Collab\Fpwiz directory. You can also use applications such as Visual InterDev to add scripting enhancements to your code.

Prerequisites for HTML Forms

To support HTML forms, you must have HTTP-based access to server-based resources such as public folders and mailboxes. That means you must install Outlook Web Access on IIS 3.0 (or higher) with ASP installed. The primary task involved in creating HTML forms is the conversion of MAPI-based items into HTML-based pages using the CDO library on the Active Server. You can read more about Outlook Web Access and Active Server configurations in Chapter 11.

Exchange Form Design Wizard

The Exchange Form Design Wizard lets you create basic HTML forms quickly. It does not require any additional development tools. The wizard supports both Send Forms and Post Forms.

Installation

To install the Exchange Form Design Wizard, you must run Fdsetup.exe, which is in the \Server\Support\Collab\Sampler\Formwiz directory on the Exchange Server 5.5 CD. This self-extracting file automatically launches the setup routines in a temporary directory. Because Setup replaces several files in your system directory, you should close all applications before installing this utility.

Eight Steps to Success

Click the **Microsoft Form Design Wizard** command on the **Programs** submenu to launch the Exchange Form Design Wizard. The wizard will lead you through the process of creating a basic form. The first page of the wizard informs you about the process. On the second page, you specify whether you want to use an existing HTML forms project or create a new custom form. You must enter the path to the desired Outlook Web Access components under **Enter The Path Where The Exchange Web Server Resides**. When you are working locally on the Web Server, you must enter *C:\Exchsrvr\Webdata* because you installed Exchange Server with default settings. When you use the Outlook Web Access server over the network, you must specify a network share that gives you read and write access to the \Webdata directory. Because \Exchsrvr\Webdata is not shared by default, you must accomplish this task manually.

On the third wizard page, you specify the type of form you want to create. In general, you must specify whether you want to send or post information before you can identify the form type in more detail under **IPM.Post.** (Post Forms) or **IPM.Note.** (Send Forms). This identifier is used later to associate your HTML form with a specific message item. In addition, you can add descriptive text to your form. Compose this text carefully, as it is used to create the hyperlink that users will click to launch the form in their Internet browser.

On the fourth page, you specify the general layout of your form. You can separate the Read Form from the Compose Form, specify a default subject line, determine which visible controls to place on the form, and so forth. Click the **Next** button to specify the caption for form tabs. By default, every form has a **Message** tab and an **Attachments** tab; you can also add additional pages. Send Forms also provide the **Options** tab.

On the sixth page, you specify custom fields for the form. By default, only the message field is available, but you can define additional fields using the **New** button. The **Field Chooser** allows you to select existing fields from the **Frequently-Used Fields** and **Custom** lists.

On the seventh page, you specify the actions you want to allow users to perform on your form. By default, **Reply**, **Reply To All**, **Forward**, and **Reply To Folder** are configured. You can add additional commands and modify or delete existing ones. After you specify all the actions, you reach the final wizard page. No input is required; you simply click the **Finish** button to install the new form. (You can step backward by clicking the **Back** button.)

Note To provide newly-installed forms to Internet users, you must restart the World Wide Web Publishing Service using the **Services** applet of the Control Panel.

File Location

The Exchange Form Design Wizard creates a repository for your form in the \Exchsrvr\Webdata directory so that the form is available via Outlook Web Access. However, the actual location depends on the type of form. For example, a Post Form of the type IPM.Post.Information is placed in the \Exchsrvr\Webdata\usa\forms\ipm\post\information directory. Here you can modify the files of your form project using FrontPage or another tool.

Using a New Custom Form

Let's say that you created a new Post Form by accepting all default options in the Exchange Form Design Wizard. You also specified additional information (such as a form description). Now you should test the form. Launch your Internet browser, connect to the virtual/Exchange directory on the Active Server, and log on to your mailbox (as described in Chapter 11). From the list box next to the **Compose New** hyperlink, select **Custom Form**. Click the **Compose New** hyperlink. A rather plain **Launch Custom Forms** window appears, describing your form. Click the description to launch the form. Enter some text, and then send or post the form to your mailbox. When you update the contents of your Inbox, the newly delivered or posted item will appear. When you open the message, the associated form will be launched again automatically.

Using HTML Forms in Outlook

Besides 16-bit and 32-bit electronic forms, Outlook can launch HTML forms in your default Internet browser. This can be useful for workgroup applications that rely entirely on HTML forms.

First you must configure Outlook to become Outlook Web Access–aware. On the **Manage Forms** tab of the **Options** dialog box, click the **Web Services** button to open the **Web Services** window. Select the **Use Outlook Web Access To Open Messages Not Understood By Outlook Client** check box. Under **Web Services Location,** enter *http://<server name>/Exchange/forms/ openitem.asp* (where *<server name>* is your IIS). You can also specify the server's IP address directly.

Now you can use Outlook to open items associated with HTML forms even if no Outlook form exists. If you enabled the **Prompt User Before Opening Each Form** option in the **Web Services** dialog box, Outlook will inform you that the contents of the current item cannot be displayed and will ask whether you want to view the message using Outlook Web Access. Click **OK**, and your Internet browser will be launched. Log on to your mailbox as usual, and the HTML form and the contents of the item will be displayed automatically.

Sample HTML Forms and Applications

The Exchange Server 5.5 CD provides several HTML forms as sample applications. They demonstrate both simple and complex scenarios and can give you an idea of what you can do. These samples are in the \Server\Support\Collab\Sampler directory.

The following samples are on the CD:

- **Culcorn**; the Culinary Corner Sample, which demonstrates a complex Web application using a public folder for composing and responding to restaurant reviews

- **Orgchart**; the OrgChart Sample, which provides organizational information to the Internet browser from the Exchange Global Address List

- **Survey**; the Survey Sample, which demonstrates a discussion forum for users of an Exchange organization and the Internet

Culinary Corner: A Discussion Forum for Exchange and Internet Users

Culinary Corner is probably the most interesting sample of an Internet forum because it provides 16-bit electronic forms that you can use directly in Exchange Client 5.0 or Outlook, along with HTML forms to support Internet browsers. In fact, you can use this sample to develop a workgroup application that is shared by Internet users and users in your organization.

As shown in Figure 16-8, a heterogeneous discussion forum is fairly simple. On the Exchange Server side, users compose and read items using regular electronic forms provided by Exchange Client 5.0 or Outlook 8.03. Internet users access the same information using an HTML form registered in Outlook Web Access.

General Preparation

To install the Culinary Corner sample on your server, create the C:\InetPub\wwwroot\Culcorn directory and copy to it all files from \Server\Support\Collab\Sampler\Culcorn on the Exchange Server CD. It is also advisable to remove the read-only attribute from all files after you copy them.

Exchange Preparation

To allow Exchange users to participate in the Culinary Corner forum, you must include the Culinary.pst file in your messaging profile. It is in the same directory as the other Culinary Corner files.

Once the **Culinary Corner** folder is in your MAPI profile, you can work with it using the Exchange Client and Outlook. However, to offer this forum to all users in your organization, you must move the folder from the **Culinary** container (.PST) file to the **All Public Folders** container. Associated electronic forms and predefined public folder views are copied to the public folder as well, providing a convenient way to install the entire forum. When you open the **Culinary Corner** folder, the **A Critique Of The Cuisine** and **New Eatery** commands become available on your client's **Compose** menu. Use these commands to work with the discussion forum.

To allow all users, including anonymous users from the Internet, to access the **Culinary Corner** public folder, you must assign the **Anonymous** account at least Author permissions using the folder's **Permissions** property page. The configuration of public folders is covered in detail in Chapter 12.

Finally you should configure the **Culinary Corner** folder as a published folder to allow anonymous Internet users to participate in discussions. Add the folder to the **Folder Shortcuts** of the **HTTP (Web) Site Settings** object in the Administrator program. More information about configuring HTTP-based access to an Exchange Server is provided in Chapter 11.

Active Server Preparation

You must also create a new virtual directory on your IIS. This directory will be used to access the discussion forum via a Web browser. Under IIS 3.0, launch Internet Service Manager from the **Programs\Microsoft Internet Server (Common)** program group. Double-click the **WWW** service running on your server, and then switch to the **Directories** tab of the **WWW Service Properties For <*server name*>** window. Click the **Add** button to display the **Directory Properties** dialog box. Under **Directory**, enter the path to the directory of the Culinary Corner sample. (You can click the **Browse** button to find the directory.) You must also specify an **Alias** for the new **Virtual Directory** (for example, *Culcorn*). You must also select the **Read** and **Write** check boxes under **Access**. Click **OK** twice and close Internet Service Manager.

Outlook Web Access Preparation

Theoretically, Internet users can access the Culinary Corner forum by specifying the new virtual directory in a URL. However, a logical link between the **Culinary Corner** public folder and the HTML pages is missing. To establish the link, you must register the ID of your public folder in the Root.htm file of Culinary Corner.

Obtain the folder ID using an Internet browser logged on anonymously to your Exchange Server. The **Culinary Corner** folder is listed because it has been published to the Internet. Right-click the folder to select **Properties** from the context menu. On the **General** property page, find the *javascript:parent.SetNewFolderPick* reference. Copy the ID under it to the Clipboard. (Use Ctrl+C or use right-click and **Copy**). The following string is an example of a public folder ID:

```
000000001A447390AA6611CD9BC800AA002FC45A03000158289E0C96D1118C760060971
425680000000042870000
```

Paste this string carefully into the Root.htm file of Culinary Corner. To find the correct location, search for the string *<FRAME SRC="discroot.asp?folderID=* and replace the existing identifier. In our example, the result would look like the following. (Note the identifier in bold.)

```
<!-Copyright (c) Microsoft Corporation 1993-1997. All rights
reserved.->
<!- Root.htm ->
<!DOCTYPE HTML PUBLIC "-//IETF//DTD HTML 3.2//EN">
<HTML>
<HEAD>
<TITLE>Cuisines</TITLE>
</HEAD>

<FRAMESET ROWS="43%,56%,1%">
      <FRAME SRC="restrnt.htm" name="existing_fr"
marginheight=0 marginwidth=0>
    <FRAME
SRC="discroot.asp?folderID=000000001A447390AA6611CD9BC800AA002FC45A030
00158289E0C96D1118C7600609714256800000000042870000"
name="ExchangeDiscussion_fr" marginheight=0 marginwidth=0 >-
>
      <Frame SRC="Commands.Asp" scrolling=no>
</FRAMESET>
</HTML>
```

Testing Culinary Corner

Now you can test the results. Switch to your Internet browser and specify the virtual directory of Culinary Corner (for example, *http://FRANKFURT-1/CulCorn*). Root.htm opens, displaying the contents of the **Culinary Corner** public folder in an interesting way. You can browse through existing articles and post new discussion articles into the forum. Outlook users will see your articles as regular message items. In Outlook, the associated 16-bit form will be launched and will present the information in the desired structure, meaning that you'll see the information perfectly positioned in the form just as it was created using the 16-bit form. (See Figure 16-8.)

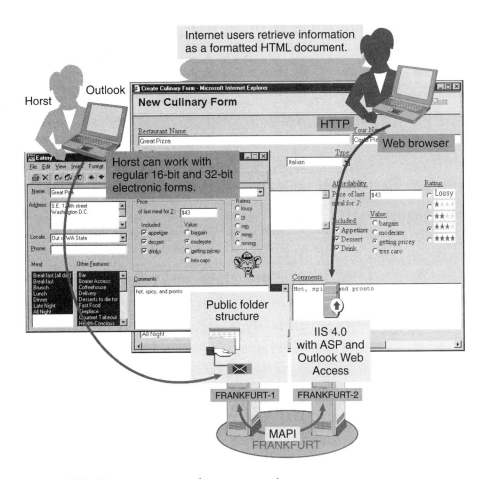

Figure 16-8. Heterogeneous workgroup computing.

The Exchange Form Design Wizard creates the following forms files:

File	Description
frmRoot.asp	The main entry point of the form. (Each custom HTML form has at least a frmRoot.asp form.)
form.ini	Provides a friendly display name that users can use to select this form after it is installed. (You can optionally mark a particular form as hidden so that it cannot be modified but can be used to read existing items.)
cmpTitle.asp /redTitle.asp	Used with Send Forms only; controls the topmost frame users can see on the form that implements the toolbar and tab strip in compose and read mode.

(continued)

(continues)

File	Description
postTitl.asp /redTitle.asp	Used with Post Forms only; controls the topmost frame users can see on the form that implements the toolbar and tab strip in compose and read mode.
cmpMsg.asp /redMsg.asp	Used with Send Forms only; provides contents of the first page in compose and read mode.
postMsg.asp /redMsg.asp	Used with Post Forms only; provides contents of the first page in compose and read mode.
cmpOpt.asp /redOpt.asp	Provides the contents of the Options page in compose and read mode.
cmpAtt.asp	Provides a way to attach files to a send message.
postAtt.asp	Provides a way to attach files to a post message.
page_N.asp /pageR_N.asp	Provides the contents of your custom form pages. (There can be up to five of these files.)
commands.asp	A utility script used for server-side command handling (checking names in the **To:** field against the GAL).
delete.asp	A utility script used to delete an item if you click the **Delete** button on the toolbar.
.gif	Miscellaneous images.
wizard.inc	Contains various constants used by the various form scripts.

Review

1. Which two types of Exchange applications can you create using electronic forms, and what are they used for?

_____

_____

_____

_____

_____

2. Which design environments can you use to develop electronic forms, and what are their key features?

3. Which features of Outlook cannot be used within Exchange Client 5.0?

4. You want to create a new 16-bit electronic form using an existing sample application. Where do you find the sample applications?

5. Which command launches Outlook Forms Designer?

6. Which three types of forms libraries can exist on an Exchange Server computer?

7. You are developing a new forms application and want to test your work. Where do you install the form?

8. Where do you install a Send Form to be used by all users, and what must you do before you can install the form?

9. Which tools are available to install the various types of forms?

    _____

    _____

10. Which file describes the properties of 16-bit forms and is required during installation? Which tool can create them automatically?

    _____

    _____

11. Where can you find preconfigured sample electronic forms, and what must you configure in order to test them?

    _____

    _____

    _____

    _____

    _____

12. How can you modify a 16-bit electronic form?

    _____

    _____

    _____

13. How can you modify Outlook forms?

    _____

    _____

    _____

    _____

14. You are in charge of developing an event-driven folder agent. Which folder events let you perform script-based processing using the Exchange Scripting Agent?

    _____

    _____

    _____

C H A P T E R 1 7

Exchange Clients in the Novell NetWare Environment

This chapter covers the integration of Exchange Server 5.5 into Novell NetWare networks. Native NetWare workstations can access Exchange Server resources without reconfiguration of the network.

Overview

Exchange Server 5.5 is tightly integrated into Windows NT. It is not available on any other platform. When you decide to install Exchange Server, you'll certainly also decide to implement Windows NT server in your network— even if your network does not yet include any Windows NT server computers. If you are a Novell NetWare administrator, you will benefit from knowing about all the tools that let you integrate Windows NT Server 4.0 into your NetWare network even before you implement Exchange Server 5.5.

Lesson 1 of this chapter discusses the components that you must configure on an Exchange Server computer to give native NetWare workstations access to server-based resources. It also covers the main aspects of combining Windows NT server and NetWare and introduces tools that simplify your daily work.

Lesson 2 covers the client-side requirements for establishing RPC connections to an Exchange Server and explains how to troubleshoot client connectivity problems.

In the following lessons, you will be introduced to:

- How to implement Exchange Server into a NetWare environment
- Server requirements for integrating Exchange Server
- NetWare client requirements for accessing Exchange Server resources
- Common troubleshooting issues in an environment with NetWare workstations and Exchange Server

Lesson 1: Exchange Server Requirements

Windows NT server provides all the components necessary for seamless integration into NetWare networks. Exchange Server benefits from those components. As a result, granting native NetWare Workstations access to mailboxes, public folders, and other server-based resources (such as the GAL) is mainly a matter of configuration at the Windows NT level.

This lesson covers the management and configuration issues that you will encounter when you combine Windows NT server and NetWare in a network. You will learn about configuring required components such as the NWLink IPX/SPX-Compatible Transport, Gateway Services for NetWare (GSNW), and the Service Advertising Protocol (SAP) Agent. The lesson also discusses other utilities that can simplify the administration of mixed Windows NT server/NetWare environments.

At the end of this lesson, you will be able to:

- Install the NWLink IPX/SPX–Compatible Transport
- Install and configure GSNW
- Describe the purpose of the SAP Agent
- Identify and use additional utilities for NetWare

Estimated time to complete this lesson: 25 minutes

Installing the NWLink IPX/SPX–Compatible Transport

The IPX/SPX protocol is used most often in NetWare networks. The corresponding Windows NT implementation is known as the NWLink IPX/SPX–Compatible Transport, or IPX/SPX. It is a 32-bit transport stack that supports Novell NetBIOS and RPCs. (See Figure 17-1.)

RPC over SPX

SPX, a part of the IPX/SPX protocol, is similar to TCP in that it provides a transport-level communication mechanism between computer systems. One of its tasks is data package sequencing, which ensures that data move in chronological order.

Exchange clients and Outlook must contact Exchange Server services using RPCs, which means that a communication interface for NetWare workstations that allows use of IPX/SPX for RPC communication must exist. Windows Sockets provides this interface, which is known as SPX Sockets.

Installation

You must install IPX/SPX at the Windows NT server level. You can use the **Network** applet of the Control Panel, or you can right-click the **Network Neighborhood** icon on the Desktop and select **Properties** from the context menu. Either way, you open the **Network** dialog box. On the **Protocols** tab, install IPX/SPX by clicking the **Add** button. Once you install it, you must reboot the server to make the changes take effect.

Frame Types

The frame type corresponds to the format of data packages sent through the network, which is handled by IPX. You must use the same frame type for all computers in the network; otherwise, the communication will fail. The following are the frame types:

Frame type	Network topology
Ethernet II, 802.3, 802.2, SNAP	Ethernet
Token Ring, SNAP	Token Ring
802.2, SNAP	FDDI
ArcNet-frames	ArcNet

The default frame type for NetWare 2.x and 3.11 Ethernet networks is 802.3; the newer versions, 3.12 and 4.x, use 802.2. For Token Ring, as you might expect, the default is Token Ring and for FDDI the default is 802.2.

Typically, you don't have to adjust the frame type manually, because Windows NT detects it automatically. If you experience communication problems, however, you should check the frame type configuration on the **Protocols** property page of the **Network** dialog box. Select **NWLink IPX/SPX Compatible Transport** and click **Properties**. In the **NWLink IPX/SPX Properties** dialog box, click the **Add** button and specify the frame type. **Auto Frame Type Detection** is selected by default.

Note You will also need to specify the corresponding external network number with each frame type added. An external network number is an eight-digit number known as the IPX network ID, which identifies every NetWare network. All resources that belong to a particular NetWare network must use the same external network number. Therefore, frame types and their associated external network number must match the corresponding configuration on the NetWare servers. Windows NT typically detects the external network number automatically, but you must adjust it manually if you use multiple frame types or network adapters. You can check the configuration on the NetWare server by using the **config** command.

Setting the Internal Network Number

The internal network number identifies every NetWare server and possibly every Windows NT server computer. This number must be unique within your NetWare network, and it must not be *0* if the Windows NT server computer is supposed to provide any services to NetWare clients or if it is used to route IPX in the network. In the **NWLink IPX/SPX Properties** dialog box, you will see the **Internal Network Number** box.

NetBIOS over NWLink

As you can see on the **Protocols** property page, NWLink NetBIOS is installed automatically with IPX/SPX. NetBIOS support is especially important if you plan to manage Windows NT server computers remotely. Any router between your workstation and the server must pass the IPX packet type 0x14; otherwise, the NetBIOS communication cannot take place over IPX, and the connection attempt will fail.

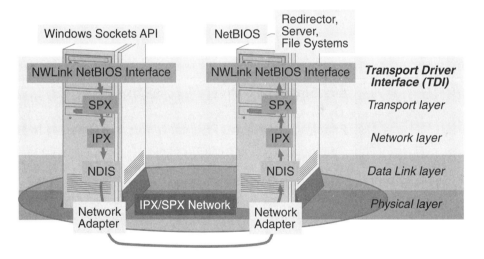

Figure 17-1. The Windows NT NWLink implementation.

The important IPX/SPX configuration parameters are as follows:

- **Frame Type**; must be the same for all computers so that they communicate

- **External Network Number**; must be the same for all computers in a logical network group and must be the same for all servers and workstations in a network

- **Internal Network Number**; must be unique for each particular computer in a logical network group

Installing Gateway Services for NetWare

Gateway Services for NetWare (GSNW) are additional services that enable Windows NT computers to access resources on NetWare servers. Although users on NetWare workstations typically must access your Exchange Server, you can access NetWare servers as an Exchange administrator in several situations as well. Using the **Network** applet of the Control Panel, you can install GSNW from the Windows NT server CD-ROM.

Extracting NetWare Account Information

GSNW lets you configure your Windows NT server as a NetWare client. You might want to do this, for instance, when you want to extract existing NetWare account information from a NetWare 3.12 server using the Exchange Administrator program. NetWare 4.x servers must run bindery emulation to support the Administrator program's account extraction feature.

To obtain account information and to create a mailbox for each NetWare user, open the **Tools** menu and click the **Extract NetWare Account List** command. You must specify a NetWare server, a supervisor account, and an export (.CSV) file before you can launch the extraction process. The .CSV file will be used later with the Administrator program's **Directory Import** feature to create a mailbox for each NetWare user. More information about the **Directory Import** option is provided in Chapter 5.

Enabling Windows NT Server to Act as a Gateway to NetWare Servers

Communication between Windows NT server (configured as a NetWare client by GSNW) and Novell NetWare servers is accomplished through the NetWare Core Protocol (NCP). Communication between Windows NT server and Microsoft-based workstations relies on Server Message Blocks (SMBs). Consequently, if Windows NT server and GSNW could translate NCP into SMBs, Microsoft-based workstations could access NetWare servers through the Windows NT server.

The good news is Windows NT server can act as a gateway to NetWare—translating incoming Windows NT client requests into the correct NetWare format and thus providing NetWare resources to native Windows NT workstations. The Windows NT workstation is not aware of the translation. To the workstation, it appears that the client is working with resources on the Windows NT server computer. (See Figure 17-2.)

Note Windows NT server connects to NetWare servers on behalf of a special NetWare account that must be a member of a special NetWare group called NTGATEWAY. A Novell NetWare administrator must create the account and the group on the NetWare server before GSNW can operate.

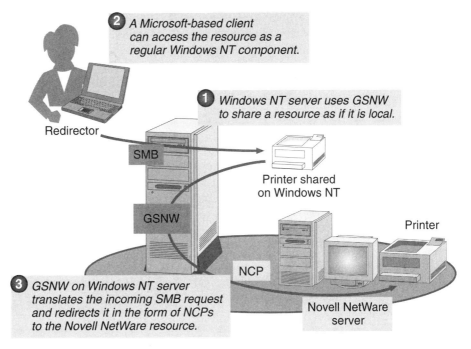

Figure 17-2. Accessing NetWare resources using GSNW.

The characteristics of GSNW are as follows:

- Acts as a nondedicated gateway for Microsoft-based workstations or any other SMB client

- Allows native Microsoft network clients to access files and printers on NetWare servers, which are shared as local Windows NT server resources

- Allows the Exchange Administrator program to extract NetWare account information

Installing the Service Advertising Protocol Agent

To ensure that Exchange Client and Outlook workstations can locate an Exchange Server computer in a NetWare network, you must install the SAP Agent on the Exchange Server in addition to the GSNW. Support for SAP is required because NetWare clients rely on this protocol to perform name resolution. In other words, native NetWare servers, your Exchange Server computer, and all IPX routers must use SAP to periodically broadcast their services, server name, and the IPX internal network address to each other. (See Figure 17-3.)

To install the SAP Agent on a Windows NT Server computer, open the **Network** applet of the Control Panel once again. On the **Services** property page, click the **Add** button to display the **Select Network Service** dialog box. Choose the **SAP Agent** and click **OK**. Insert the Windows NT Server CD into the CD-ROM drive and then click **Continue**. You must reboot the server to complete the installation. You can then start and stop the SAP Agent service using the **Services** applet of the Control Panel.

SAP Broadcast Packet

The SAP Agent itself does not announce an Exchange Server to the NetWare network. This is the task of GSNW. Using both components, the Windows NT server computer advertises itself across the IPX network using a SAP broadcast packet, which contains the server name and the IPX internal network number.

Note Even if you don't plan to contact any NetWare servers from the Windows NT server, you must install GSNW along with the SAP Agent to propagate the existence of the Exchange Server to the NetWare network. Although GSNW is mainly a client component, it is required to complete the server-side configuration.

Logging on to Exchange Server

Clients can establish a connection to an Exchange Server computer if the SAP Agent and GSNW have been installed. Before access to mailboxes is granted, however, users must log on to Windows NT server. To simplify user validation, you should keep account information synchronized between Windows NT and NetWare. If the Windows NT and NetWare account names and passwords are the same, Windows 95 and Windows NT clients can validate users automatically. Otherwise, an extra logon dialog box will appear, asking you for the Windows NT account information.

RPC over SPX is used to:

- Authenticate Exchange Client and Outlook on a Windows NT server for mailbox access (users with clients running Windows 3.x and MS-DOS must provide domain information manually)

- Access resources on the Exchange Server computer such as mailboxes, public folders, and server-based address books

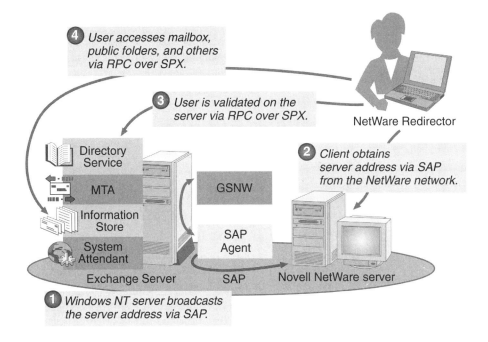

Figure 17-3.   Connecting to an Exchange Server computer from a NetWare workstation.

Additional Utilities for NetWare

Microsoft provides additional components that can simplify the administration and use of Windows NT resources in a NetWare network. However, you must obtain them separately. Together they are known as Microsoft Services for NetWare; separately they are called File and Print Services for NetWare and Directory Service Manager for NetWare. The Migration Tool for NetWare is another useful utility that can help migrate users from NetWare to Windows NT server.

File and Print Services for NetWare

The File and Print Services for NetWare (FPNW) allow users on NetWare workstations to access files, printers, and applications on a Windows NT server computer. The Windows NT server machine acts just like a NetWare 3.x server. (See Figure 17-4.) As a matter of fact, you can use native NetWare utilities to manage—up to a point—Windows NT server if FPNW is installed.

Directory Service Manager for NetWare

The Directory Service Manager for NetWare (DSMN) lets you maintain user accounts for Windows NT and NetWare centrally. It runs on Windows NT 3.51 or later, which supports NetWare 2.x and 3.x servers. As usual, when running NetWare server 4.x, you must enable bindery emulation.

DSMN first copies the NetWare user and group account information to the Windows NT server. Then it propagates any changes applied to accounts in Windows NT back to the NetWare servers. In other words, it keeps the information on the two systems synchronized. Because the accounts are synchronized, only a single logon is required to access resources on NetWare servers and Windows NT server computers simultaneously.

Migration Tool for NetWare

The Migration Tool for NetWare offers you tremendous flexibility in transferring NetWare user account information, group accounts, security information, logon scripts, and administrator accounts from one or more NetWare servers to a Windows NT server computer. You can also move files and directories to Windows NT server while preserving file attributes and file rights, provided that files are moved to an NTFS partition. In other words, the Migration Tool is the right choice if you plan a complete migration of all users from NetWare to Windows NT in a step-by-step process. The NetWare server configuration is not affected during a migration cycle.

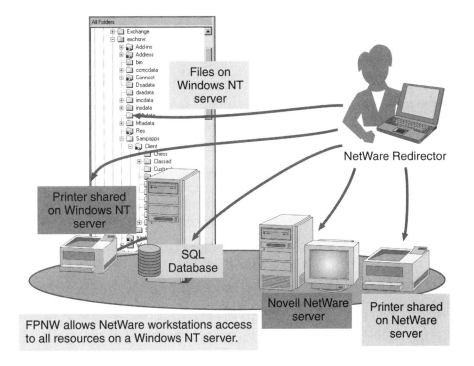

Figure 17-4. File and print services for NetWare.

Additional tools and their uses are as follows:

- **File and Print Services for NetWare**; to provide NetWare workstations with access to printers and shared directories on a Windows NT server without the need for client reconfiguration

- **Directory Service Manager for NetWare**; to let you maintain common user account information for both NetWare servers and Windows NT server computers

- **Migration Tool for NetWare**; to port NetWare user accounts, group accounts, security information, logon scripts, administrator accounts, files, directories, file attributes, and file rights to a Windows NT server computer

Lesson 2: Exchange and NetWare Client Requirements

The integration of Exchange Server into NetWare networks requires only a few configuration steps on the NetWare workstations. Most of the steps achieve client optimization rather than essential configuration.

This lesson discusses the components you must configure on a NetWare workstation to allow access to an Exchange Server. Common troubleshooting tips are also provided.

At the end of this lesson, you will be able to:

- List the NetWare components necessary to access NetWare Server Resources via MS-DOS, Windows 3.x, Windows 95, and Windows NT

- Describe the validation mechanism used by clients to access an Exchange Server

- Troubleshoot client communication problems

Estimated time to complete this lesson: 15 minutes

Network Communication Requirements

One of the most important NetWare communication components is the redirector, which allows the client to communicate with NetWare servers using the NetWare Core Protocol (NCP). On an MS-DOS or Windows 3.x computer, you must load a component called NETX.exe or a VLM redirector. If you are using Windows 95, Client Services for NetWare provide the needed functionality. Windows NT Workstation also uses Client Services for NetWare. However, NetWare redirector components are not directly involved when you contact an Exchange Server.

Communicating with an Exchange Server Computer

As shown in Figure 17-5, NetWare workstations using MS-DOS or Windows 3.x can communicate with an Exchange Server using their real-mode IPX/SPX protocol stack (IPXODI). Windows 95 and Windows NT use the 32-bit IPX/SPX, which provides the best performance.

The actual communication with the Exchange Server computer is accomplished using RPC over SPX. Since NetWare components do not provide any RPC implementations, Exchange Clients and Outlook provide their own RPC libraries, which are installed during the client setup. Client-server RPC communication is explained in Chapter 4.

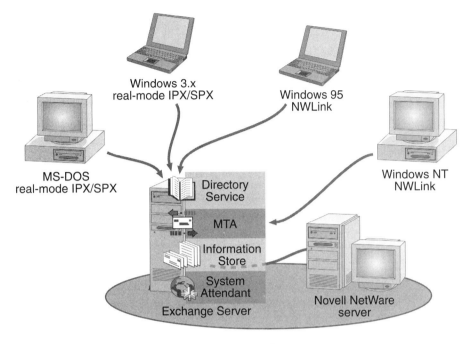

Figure 17-5. Client support in a NetWare network.

Note RPC over SPX uses the Windows Sockets interface, which bypasses any NetWare redirectors. Therefore, you do not have to configure the Exchange Server computer as a NetWare server using FPNW.

Windows NT Domain Validation

Every user who wants to access a mailbox or any other resource on an Exchange Server computer must be validated. While MS-DOS and Windows 3.x ask users for their Windows NT account information, users on Windows 95 and Windows NT usually don't have to log on separately. These clients can automatically send the Exchange Server account information that was used to log on to NetWare. Only when the NetWare account information does not match the Windows NT domain account are you asked for your domain account. You can also force an explicit logon by deselecting the **Use Network Security During Logon** option on the **Advanced** property page of the Microsoft Exchange Server transport. More information about configuring the Exchange Server transport is provided in Chapter 7.

The following are the requirements for accessing NetWare resources in each operating system:

- **MS-DOS and Windows 3.x**; to install NCP-based NETX or VLM redirector
- **Windows 95**; to configure the Client Services for NetWare networks
- **Windows NT**; to add Client Services for NetWare

Troubleshooting Client Connectivity

Implementing an Exchange Server into a NetWare network means that you must manage two different and complex network operating systems.

Routers Must Pass SAP Packets

Complex NetWare networks typically consist of multiple network segments that are switched together using routers. These routers must propagate the SAP server type 0x640 information because this is the SAP type that Exchange Server uses to notify NetWare servers and IPX routers of its presence. If a router does not pass this type of SAP information, Exchange Clients cannot access the server because they cannot resolve the server address.

Verifying That SPX is Loaded

You can unload the SPX stack on workstations running MS-DOS or Windows to save conventional memory. In a standard NetWare configuration, you do this by supplying the **/A** command line switch to the **IPXODI** command of the Startnet.bat file. The switch saves the NetWare client about 9 KB of memory because the client starts without the diagnostic responder and the SPX protocol. Since Exchange Clients use RPC over SPX, however, such a configuration always leads to a communication problem. To correct the problem, you must remove the **/A** switch and reboot the computer to reload SPX. Then you can connect to the Exchange Server.

Improving Client Startup Times

As mentioned in Chapter 7, the Exchange Client tries several RPC communication methods in sequence until it connects. On Windows 95 and Windows NT, the order is determined by the RPC_BINDING_ORDER value in the Registry under the subkey on the following page. (See Figure 17-6.)

```
HKEY_LOCAL_MACHINE
    \SOFTWARE
        \Microsoft
            \Exchange
                \Exchange Provider
```

By default, the value is:

ncalrpc,ncacn_ip_tcp,ncacn_spx,ncacn_np,netbios,ncacn_vns_spp

To optimize the client configuration, you should configure RPC over SPX as the preferred communication mechanism. If ncacn_spx is on top of the binding order (the first position), the client uses RPC over SPX first and avoids superfluous attempts.

The binding order of MS-DOS clients is set in the autoexec.bat file using an environment variable. Windows 3.x clients store the connect order in their Exchange.ini file. You can edit autoexec.bat and Exchange.ini using any text editor to adjust the RPC communication. More information about configuring clients is provided in Chapter 6.

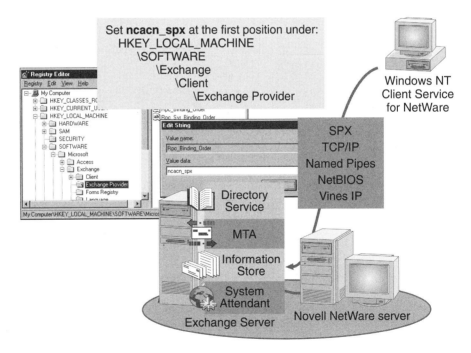

Figure 17-6. Improving client startup time.

Here are some common troubleshooting scenarios:

- **Client startup is slow**: Optimize the RPC binding order and place RPC over SPX in the first position.

- **Clients cannot connect to the server when routers are involved**: Configure the router to pass the SAP server type 0x640 information.

- **MS-DOS and Windows 3.x clients cannot connect to the Exchange Server computer**: Verify that SPX is loaded. Remove the **/A** command line switch from the **IPXODI** command line of the Startnet.bat file.

Review

1. You want to integrate Exchange Server into your NetWare network. You install Windows NT server and IPX/SPX. Which three important configuration parameters of IPX/SPX might have to be configured manually?

2. Why must you install GSNW on a Windows NT server running Exchange Server?

3. Why do you need the SAP Agent and GSNW to allow NetWare workstations to connect to the Exchange Server computer?

4. In addition to Exchange Server resources, you want to provide access to printers connected to the Windows NT Server. Users on NetWare workstations should be able to use them without having to reconfigure their clients. Which additional product must you install on the Windows NT server to achieve the desired functionality?

5. Because Exchange Server validates users based on Windows NT account information, you must create a corresponding Windows NT account for each existing NetWare user. Which tool can you use to maintain the account information for both systems in a centralized place?

6. As an administrator, you must implement Exchange Server in an existing NetWare environment. Windows NT server is already installed in a typical configuration. What else must you install and configure to give NetWare workstations access to mailboxes and other Exchange Server resources?

7. Users on NetWare workstations are complaining about the startup times of their Exchange clients. What should you check first?

C H A P T E R 1 8

Connecting to Microsoft Mail and Schedule+

This chapter covers the Microsoft Mail Connector, Directory Synchronization with MS Mail, and the Microsoft Schedule+ Free/Busy Connector. The MS Mail Connector is the basis for all Exchange Server components that exchange information with an MS Mail network.

Overview

Exchange Server 5.5 can act as an incredibly powerful, multipurpose MS Mail Gateway. It can replace many MS Mail gateways, such as the gateway to X.400, SMTP, or PROFS, as well as connect an MS Mail network to systems such as Lotus cc:Mail and Lotus Notes. If you have several MS-DOS computers running single MS Mail gateway instances, you can replace them all with a single Exchange Server computer. But the integration of Exchange Server into an existing messaging network is risky because if users discover the valuable features of the new messaging system, you might find yourself in charge of replacing the old messaging system completely.

Lesson 1 of this chapter covers the MS Mail Connector in depth. It explains its architecture and configuration, and the flow of messages through its components.

Once you connect your organization to an MS Mail network, you can synchronize the address information between the systems. Lesson 2 explains how to do this. It briefly explains the MS Mail Directory Synchronization process and then explains the possible roles of an Exchange Server computer. It also covers the mapping of Exchange mailbox attributes to MS Mail template information.

Lesson 3 covers the Schedule+ Free/Busy Connector. It explains its architecture, existing dependencies with the MS Mail Connector, and configuration options.

Two exercises round out the chapter. The first and more complex exercise deals with installing the MS Mail Connector. The second exercise guides you through the configuration of a Directory Synchronization server.

In the following lessons, you will be introduced to:

- The MS Mail Connector architecture
- The flow of messages between Exchange Server and MS Mail
- How to install and configure the MS Mail Connector
- How to implement Directory Synchronization between Exchange Server and MS Mail
- How to configure the Schedule+ Free/Busy Connector

Lesson 1: The MS Mail Connector

Exchange Server 4.0 was targeted primarily at the several million clients with MS Mail already installed. A gentle migration to Exchange Server was essential for the success of the new system, particularly for seamless integration into existing MS Mail networks, so Exchange Server 4.0 provided a powerful connecting component to MS Mail. This component has remained basically unchanged in all subsequent Exchange Server versions.

Several components must communicate with each other to form a functioning MS Mail Connector. In this lesson, you'll learn about the architecture of the MS Mail Connector by examining its message handling. The lesson also discusses how to configure the MS Mail Connector.

A complex exercise concludes the lesson. It illustrates the configuration and use of the MS Mail Connector. You will install and configure an MS Mail postoffice and then connect it to an Exchange Server computer.

At the end of this lesson, you will be able to:

- List the required components for exchanging messages between Exchange Server and MS Mail for PC networks
- Identify the components of the MS Mail Connector and their use
- Describe the path a message takes through the MS Mail Connector
- Configure and use the MS Mail Connector

Estimated time to complete this lesson: 60 minutes

Required Components

As shown in Figure 18-1, one MS Mail Connector is sufficient to connect an entire Exchange Server organization to an MS Mail network. Intersite replication can guarantee that associated address spaces are replicated to all servers in the organization. As soon as the GWART is updated on each server, every Exchange user can send messages to MS Mail recipients.

One connector can connect one Exchange Server computer to multiple MS Mail postoffices, and you can theoretically install one MS Mail Connector on each Exchange Server computer in your organization. You cannot, however, connect one site to a particular postoffice multiple times.

MS Mail Connector Installation

You can install the MS Mail Connector using the **Custom/Complete** option of the Exchange Server Setup program. The connector is an additional component that comes only with the Enterprise Edition. To add the connector to an existing Exchange Server, you must launch the Setup program in maintenance mode and click the **Add/Remove** button. You can perform the rest of the installation as usual. The options and the maintenance mode of the Setup program are covered in Chapter 2.

Active Components

As always, the IS and the MTA handle message transfer within the Exchange Server organization. The MTA and the DS handle routing decisions. The MTA can transfer messages for MS Mail recipients to the associated MS Mail Connector using an internal MTA message queue. You can view this queue on the **Queues** property page of the **Message Transfer Agent** object in the Administrator program. Message queues are covered in Chapter 15.

The MS Mail Connector receives messages from the MTA, converts them into MS Mail format, and sends them to their destination postoffices. When inbound messages must be delivered to an Exchange recipient, the MS Mail Connector gathers them from MS Mail postoffices, converts them, and transfers them to the MTA. The MTA routes them to the appropriate IS for delivery. Message routing is explained in Chapter 9.

MS Mail Postoffices

Each Exchange site is seen as a native MS Mail postoffice to the MS Mail network. Using the MS Mail Administrator program, you must register the Exchange sites as External Postoffices on each existing MS Mail postoffice. MS Mail users can then send messages to Exchange recipients.

Native MS Mail Externals

The MS Mail MTA, also known as an *External*, performs the message inter-change between postoffices in a native MS Mail network. Externals can be used even if an Exchange Server machine has been integrated, because they treat that machine as a native MS Mail postoffice. However, the MS Mail Connector is more powerful and should replace Externals if possible.

Gateways

The collaboration between Exchange Server and MS Mail can be advantageous for both sides. MS Mail users can use powerful components such as IMS or X.400 Connectors. Exchange users can benefit from older gateways installed in the MS Mail network, such as an MS Mail Gateway to FAX. However, Exchange Server replaces all existing gateways of an MS Mail network.

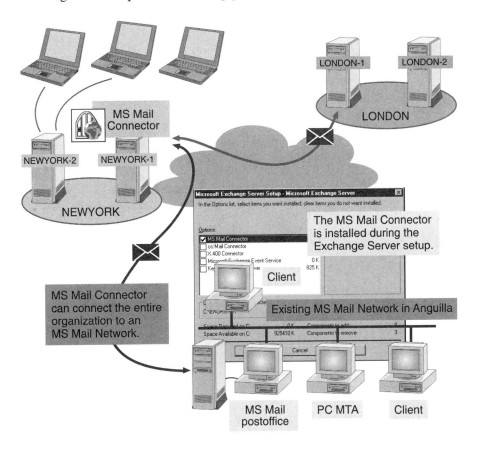

Figure 18-1. Installing the MS Mail Connector.

The features of the MS Mail Connector are as follows:

- Can connect an entire Exchange organization to a MS Mail network
- Can replace MS Mail MTAs, also known as Externals
- Converts and transfers messages between one Exchange Server and multiple postoffices
- Each site can be a postoffice; it must be configured as an External postoffice on each MS Mail postoffice
- One connector can be installed on each server using the Exchange Server Setup program

MS Mail Connector Architecture

The main components of the MS Mail Connector are the MS Mail Connector Interchange service, the Connector postoffice, and one or more MS Mail Connector MTA services. The MS Mail Connector Interchange works between the MTA and the Connector Postoffice. The Connector Postoffice is the MS Mail interface of the Exchange Server. An MS Mail Connector MTA, in turn, transfers messages between the Connector Postoffice and the MS Mail network, just as any MS Mail External does. (See Figure 18-2.)

MS Mail Connector Interchange Service

Once you install the MS Mail Connector, you can find the MS Mail Connector Interchange service in the **Services** applet of the Control Panel. This service is configured to start manually. After you configure an MS Mail Connector on a server, you must install the Enterprise Edition and set it to automatic startup.

As shown in Figure 18-2, the MS Mail Connector Interchange is the component that communicates primarily with the MTA to exchange MS Mail messages. It converts messages from Exchange Server format to MS Mail format and vice versa. It also polls the Connector Postoffice to find inbound messages.

MS Mail Connector Postoffice

The MS Mail Connector Postoffice is the intermediate repository for MS Mail messages. It is a real MS Mail postoffice, and it maintains the messages in MS Mail format. However, it has no user mailboxes. This postoffice is in the \Exchsrvr\Connect\Msmcon\Maildata directory, which is also shared as **Maildat$** for network access. You can use the command **net use m: \\<*server_name*>\Maildat$** to establish a permanent network connection. Every Connector Postoffice has a serial number of 22-28798.

The MS Mail Connector Interchange uses the Connector Postoffice to deposit outbound messages for further delivery. It also polls this repository to obtain inbound messages, which must be converted and transferred to the MTA. The MS Mail Connector MTA accesses this postoffice as a regular MS Mail postoffice to perform message transfer within the MS Mail network. In fact, neither the MS Mail Connector MTA service nor any Externals are aware of the Exchange Server behind the Connector Postoffice. (See Figure 18-2.)

Note Native MS Mail postoffices see an Exchange site as a Connector Postoffice, which you must configure as an External postoffice within MS Mail. All users of the site, regardless of their home servers, are handled as MS Mail users residing on the Connector Postoffice.

MS Mail Connector MTA

The MS Mail Connector MTA is the Exchange Server equivalent of a regular MS Mail External or the Multitasking MTA provided with MS Mail 3.5. The MS Mail Connector MTA is implemented as a Windows NT service, which is created during the MS Mail Connector configuration. Up to 10 MS Mail Connector MTA services can run on one Exchange Server computer. More information about configuring the MS Mail Connector is provided in the section, "Configuring the MS Mail Connector," later in this chapter.

The MS Mail Connector MTA polls all postoffices for which it is responsible. If it detects messages in any outgoing queue, it transfers them to their destinations through the MS Mail network. In other words, the message queues in each postoffice determine the MS Mail routing of the messages.

Note The MS Mail Connector MTA transfers messages only between the Connector postoffice and any MS Mail postoffices. Therefore, regular Externals must be used if the Exchange Server is not included in the message path between two MS Mail postoffices.

Supported Communication Mechanism

The MS Mail Connector MTA supports LAN, X.25, and telephone connections. It can transfer messages directly from postoffice to postoffice if a LAN exists using the NetBEUI, IPX/SPX, or TCP/IP protocol. With X.25 or telephone connections, a remote MTA must be contacted. The remote communication partner (another MTA/External) answers the incoming call, receives the messages, and places them in the appropriate destination postoffice.

Remote Message Transfer

The MS Mail Connector MTA establishes telephone and X.25 connections directly, as a native MS Mail External does, but it is limited to postoffice-to-postoffice communication.

Note Remote MS Mail clients can dial an External machine to send and retrieve their mail; they cannot, however, dial the MS Mail Connector to send or receive messages.

To ensure full compatibility with MS Mail Externals, the MS Mail Connector uses the old-style MS Mail modem scripts to control a modem or X.25 card. In other words, it doesn't use Windows NT RAS Connector for dialing or answering a call. The appropriate modem script must be copied in the GLB directory of the Connector Postoffice. Only the four standard ports COM1-COM4 are supported.

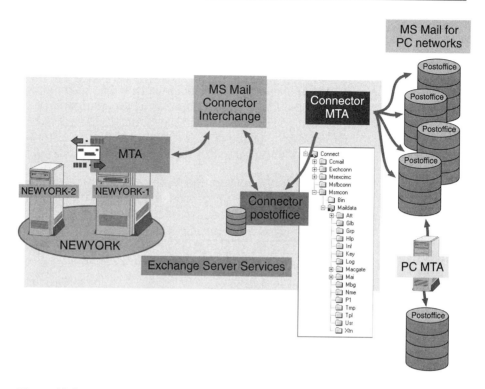

Figure 18-2. Components of the MS Mail postoffice.

The MS Mail Connector components and their functions are as follows:

- **MS Mail Connector Interchange**; accepts messages from the MTA, converts them, and writes them to the Connector Postoffice; MS Mail Connector Interchange also retrieves messages from the Connector Postoffice, converts them, and transfers them to the MTA

- **Connector Postoffice**; the intermediate repository for e-mail messages in MS Mail format; provides the MS Mail interface of Exchange Server

- **MS Mail Connector MTA**; transfers messages within the MS Mail network from the Connector Postoffice to MS Mail postoffices and vice versa; LAN, dial-up, and X.25 connections are supported

Message Flow

You can control the MS Mail Connector services using the **Services** applet of the Control Panel. But where are messages queued if the MS Mail Connector Interchange or a configured MS Mail Connector MTA service stops for any reason?

Outbound Messages from Exchange Server to MS Mail

With outbound message transfer, messages are received from the Exchange Server, converted, stored temporarily in the Connector Postoffice, and then transferred to the target MS Mail postoffice. That's all it takes.

Exchange Server MTA

When the local IS or any remote MTA delivers messages to the local MTA, message routing must be performed. The MTA contacts the DS to accomplish this. Because you have configured an appropriate MS Mail address space for the local MS Mail Connector, messages destined for MS Mail recipients are placed in the connector message queue. This is an internal MTA message queue and is not maintained by the IS. A list of routing issues appears on page 1106.

In the Administrator program, you can examine the internal MTA queue on the **Queues** property page of the local **Message Transfer Agent** object by selecting **MS Mail Connector (*<server_name>*)** from the **Queue Name** box.

Note Messages displayed in the **MS Mail Connector (*<server_name>*)** queue have not yet been received by the MS Mail Connector Interchange. A filled queue might indicate MS Mail Connector Interchange problems.

MS Mail Connector Interchange

The MS Mail Connector Interchange receives messages from the **MS Mail Connector (*<server_name>*)** queue of the local MTA. It converts them from Exchange Server format to MS Mail format in order and deposits them in the Connector Postoffice. Messages are placed in the appropriate outgoing message queues. (See Figure 18-3.)

Note The MTA removes from the **MS Mail Connector (*<server_name>*)** queue all messages already received by the MS Mail Connector Interchange.

Connector Postoffice

The Connector Postoffice has the easiest job. It is simply a passive file structure that maintains outgoing message items until an MS Mail Connector MTA service picks them up. Using the Administrator program, you can examine the Connector Postoffice queues on the **Connections** property page of the local MS Mail Connector. Select a postoffice and click the **Queue** button to verify the current state.

Note If messages remain in the Connector Postoffice, a corresponding MS Mail Connector MTA service might have been configured incorrectly.

MS Mail Connector MTA

The MS Mail Connector MTA transfers messages from the Connector Postoffice to their MS Mail destination. It scans the outgoing queues of the Connector Postoffice periodically to detect messages for which it is responsible. In other words, it polls the Connector Postoffice for outgoing messages using the configuration settings of the MS Mail Connector. It deletes messages from the Connector Postoffice once they have been delivered. (See Figure 18-3.)

Note A particular MS Mail Connector MTA service is not necessarily responsible for all MS Mail postoffices that can be reached through the MS Mail Connector. You can control the list of serviced postoffices using the **Connector MTAs** property page.

Inbound Messages from MS Mail to Exchange Server

The message flow from MS Mail to Exchange Server goes in the opposite direction to that described above, which is no surprise. The same components are involved. Messages are received from MS Mail postoffices, stored temporarily in the Connector Postoffice, converted by the MS Mail Connector Interchange, and then delivered to the MTA of the local Exchange Server.

MS Mail Connector MTA

An MS Mail Connector MTA service periodically scans the outgoing message queues of MS Mail postoffices that it is responsible for. Again, it polls all postoffices using the principle of a shared-file messaging system (MS Mail). In the Administrator program, you can specify postoffices on the **Connector MTAs** property page of the **MS Mail Connector** object with which you want to communicate. If new messages for Exchange recipients are detected there, they are placed in the inbound message queue on the Connector Postoffice. Then the MS Mail Connector MTA service deletes the messages from the MS Mail postoffices.

Connector Postoffice

The Connector Postoffice, as usual, is the temporary repository for MS Mail messages. To examine the inbound queue, you must first stop the MS Mail Connector Interchange service. Then switch to the **Connections** property page of the MS Mail Connector. Select the entry for the Connector Postoffice and then click the **Queue** button. Remember to restart the MS Mail Connector Interchange service afterwards.

Note A filled inbound message queue might indicate a communication problem between the MS Mail Connector Interchange service and the MTA.

MS Mail Connector Interchange

The MS Mail Connector Interchange is the hardest-working component of the MS Mail Connector. It polls the inbound queue of the Connector Postoffice for new messages and receives them once they are detected. It converts inbound messages to Exchange Server format before it transfers them to the local MTA. It then deletes delivered messages from the Connector Postoffice. (See Figure 18-3.)

Exchange Server MTA

As always, the MTA contacts the DS to route incoming messages to their destinations using the GWART. If recipients reside on the local computer, it transfers messages to the local IS for delivery. In all other cases, it places them in an appropriate message queue for further routing. Message routing is explained in Chapter 9. (Address spaces are also covered in more detail in Chapter 9.)

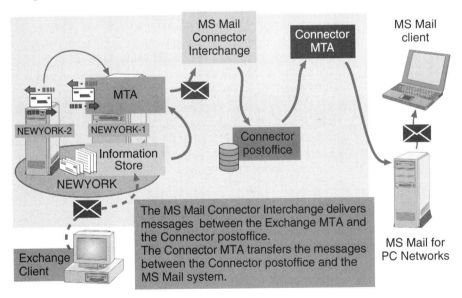

Figure 18-3. Message flow to an MS Mail recipient.

Exchange Server's routing capabilities with MS Mail are as follows:

- Address spaces are used to create routing paths.

- Address spaces are created automatically during the MS Mail Connector configuration.

- Indirect routing information can be extracted automatically from MS Mail postoffices.

- You can use the **MS MS Mail Network Name** and **MS MS Mail Postoffice Name** to define address spaces.

- Wildcard symbols (* and ?) are permitted.

Configuring the MS Mail Connector

To manage a MS Mail Connector, you use the Administrator program and the **Services** applet of the Control Panel. First you must configure the connector through its corresponding **MS Mail Connector** (*<server_name>*) object in the Administrator program. You must specify the postoffices you want to connect to, and you must configure MS Mail Connector MTA services. Then start the MS Mail Connector MTA services using the **Services** applet. You can also use this applet to set the MS Mail Connector Interchange service to start automatically.

Note If you change the configuration of the MS Mail Connector, you must stop and restart the MS Mail Connector Interchange service or the MS Mail Connector MTA service—depending on which service is affected by your changes—before the changes will take effect.

Administrator's Mailbox

When you open your **MS Mail Connector** object in the **Connection** container, the **Interchange** property page is displayed. Here you can set the **Administrator's Mailbox**. In fact, you cannot switch to any other property page until you specify a mailbox. This mailbox receives special connector messages such as messages about undeliverable items.

Local Postoffice Name

The name of an MS Mail postoffice, such as the Connector Postoffice, consists of a network name and a postoffice name, as in *STOCKSDATA/ NEWYORK*. Both names are used for message routing. A complete MS Mail address also includes the name of a mailbox, as in *Network/Postoffice/ Mailbox*. For example, the Exchange Server mailbox of Lisa Strawberry (alias LisaS) shows the proxy MS Mail address *STOCKSDATA/NEWYORK/LISAS* on the **E-Mail Addresses** property page. (The address type is **MS**.)

On the **Site Addressing** property page of the **Site Addressing** object, you can examine the current MS Mail site-addressing format. By default, Exchange Server uses the name of the organization as the network name and the name of the local site as the postoffice name (Organization/Site). However, you cannot use the **Site Addressing** property page to modify the current MS Mail site addressing.

The site-addressing format is determined using the name of the Connector Postoffice displayed on the **Local Postoffice** property page of the **MS Mail Connector** object. For this reason, all Connector Postoffices in a site must have the same name. On the **Local Postoffice** property page, you can change the **Postoffice** or **Network** name. Modifications affect the proxy MS Mail addresses of all users in a site. You can click the **Regenerate** button to apply any changes to the existing proxy MS Mail addresses.

Note If you change the name of a Connector Postoffice, you must restart the MS Mail Connector Interchange and all MS Mail Connector MTA services using the **Services** applet of the Control Panel to update their Network/Postoffice name list.

Specifying MS Mail Postoffices in a LAN

An MS Mail Connector transfers messages only to postoffices specified on the **Connections** property page. To specify a new postoffice, click the **Create** button. This displays the **Create Connection** dialog box, where you click the **Change** button and specify the UNC-path to the postoffice in the **Postoffice Path** box. The **Network** name and **Postoffice** name are obtained automatically from the specified postoffice.

If additional postoffices can be reached indirectly through the specified MS Mail postoffice, you can have them referenced implicitly by clicking the **Upload Routing** button. The Administrator program then gathers information about indirectly accessed postoffices from the specified postoffice, thus creating references automatically. You need only select the desired entries and click **OK**. An associated address space is created for the direct postoffice and all selected indirect postoffices. (See Figure 18-4.)

In contrast, you cannot use the **Upload Routing** feature for connections made through X.25 or asynchronous connections. Furthermore, the required configuration parameters change if you select the **Async** or **X.25** options instead of **LAN**. In any of these cases, you can use the **Indirect** option to specify a postoffice indirectly through another postoffice.

Creating Connector MTAs

An MS Mail Connector without an MS Mail Connector MTA service is like a car without wheels. It is useless to try to deliver messages to the Connector Postoffice using the MS Mail Connector Interchange service if there is no service that obtains them and delivers them. Unlike the MS Mail Connector Interchange, a MS Mail Connector MTA service must be created explicitly. By default, no such service exists.

On the **Connector MTAs** property page of your MS Mail Connector object, you can create one or more MS Mail Connector MTA services. To create a new instance, click the **New** button. In the **New MS Mail Connector (PC) MTA Service** dialog box, specify the **Service Name** and other options such as the **Polling Frequency**. The **Service Name** is particularly important because it identifies the corresponding Windows NT service in the **Services** applet of the Control Panel. Every MS Mail Connector MTA service can be configured to start either automatically or manually.

Once you create an MS Mail Connector MTA service, you must specify the **Postoffices Serviced** by clicking the **List** button on the **Connector MTAs** property page. Select the desired postoffice, click **Add,** and then click **OK**. You must repeat these steps for all direct postoffices. You must start the MS Mail Connector MTA service after you complete the configuration.

The MS Mail Connector property pages and their functions are as follows:

- **Address Space**; to examine address spaces generated automatically during the MS Mail Connector configuration and to define new address spaces

- **Connections**; to create, modify, and delete references to direct and indirect MS Mail postoffices; you can also examine the outgoing and incoming message queues using the **Queue** button

- **Connector MTAs**; to create, modify, and delete MS Mail Connector MTA services or to log their status to the Application Event Log; you must use this property page to specify the postoffices serviced by each created service

- **Diagnostics Logging**; to determine the level of information written to the Application Event Log for the MS Mail Connector Interchange, MS Mail Connector MTA, or MS Mail Connector (AppleTalk) MTA

- **General**; to specify a message size limit for the connector and to add an administrative note

- **Interchange**; to specify the administrator mailbox, specify the primary language for clients, maximize MS Mail 3.x compatibility, and to enable message tracking; you can also configure the connector to connect to MS Mail (AppleTalk)

- **Local Postoffice**; to change the Connector Postoffice name and the sign-on password for asynchronous communication and to regenerate proxy MS Mail addresses

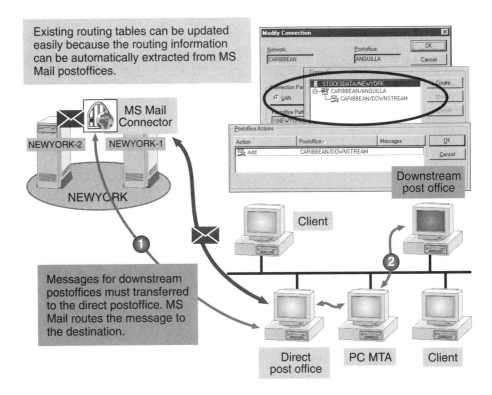

Figure 18-4.   Configuring automatic routing to indirect postoffices.

Exercise 50: Configuring the MS Mail Connector

You can use the MS Mail Connector to connect an Exchange Server organization to an MS Mail network. Using three administrative tools, you must configure four components to establish the connection between the systems. You use the Administrator program to configure the MS Mail Connector Interchange, the Connector postoffice, and one or more MS Mail Connector MTAs. You use the **Services** applet of the Control Panel to control the corresponding Windows NT services. You use the MS Mail Administrator program to configure each existing MS Mail postoffice. Typically, you register each site of your organization as an External postoffice.

Estimated time to complete this exercise: 45 minutes

Description

In this exercise, you will use all three administrative tools to manage the MS Mail Connector and an MS Mail postoffice. Before you begin configuring the connector, check to see whether you can access your MS Mail postoffice. Then you can carry out the remaining tasks and send test messages from an MS Mail Windows-based client to Outlook connected to an Exchange Server computer. You will reply to messages to test the connection in both directions.

- Task 50a describes the steps for installing an MS Mail postoffice and verifying that the connection to your postoffice is functional. You must be able to send a message.

- Task 50b describes the steps for verifying the **Network** and **Postoffice** names, which are required later during the configuration of the MS Mail Connector.

- Task 50c describes the steps for configuring an MS Mail Connector and for creating an MS Mail Connector MTA service between the MS Mail postoffice and the Connector Postoffice.

- Task 50d describes the steps for recalculating and rebuilding the routing table to propagate knowledge of the new MS Mail Connector.

- Task 50e describes the steps for starting the MS Mail Connector MTA service.

- Task 50f describes the steps for defining an External postoffice to which the MS Mail postoffice can then send mail. This External postoffice is the Connector Postoffice of the Exchange Server.

- Task 50g describes the steps for using the MS Mail Windows-based client to send mail to an Outlook client via the MS Mail Connector.

- Task 50h describes the steps for viewing and replying to a message sent by MS Mail 3.x through the MS Mail Connector.
- Task 50i describes the steps for verifying that the MS Mail Windows-based client receives the message.

Prerequisites

- A test MS Mail postoffice is installed during this exercise using a network installation point. If you prefer, you can install the postoffice directly from your floppy disks instead.
- Log on to NEWYORK-1 as Admin-NY1 and log on to LONDON-1 as Admin-L1.

Task 50a: Installing the MS Mail Postoffice

1. Log on to NEWYORK-1 as Admin-NY1.
2. Click the **Start** button, point to **Programs** and then click **Command Prompt**.
3. Switch to the Microsoft Mail network installation or insert disk 1 into the floppy drive and switch to drive A: (mapped to drive F:).
4. Type *Setup* and press **Enter**.
5. A welcome page appears. Press **Enter**.
6. Verify that **Create A New Postoffice** is selected, and then press **Enter**.
7. Press **Enter** to accept **C:\MAILDATA** as the postoffice directory.
8. Type *ANGUILLA* as the name of the postoffice and then press **Enter**.
9. Type *CARIBBEAN* as the network name and then press **Enter**.
10. Accept **Microsoft LAN Manager-Compatible** and then press **Enter**.
11. Select **Server Agents** and press **Enter** to mark the entry with an asterisk.
12. Select **Administration And Utilities** and then press **Enter**
13. Select **DONE** and then press **Enter**.
14. Change the mailexe path to *C:\MAILDATA* and then press **Enter**.
15. Select **Windows And Presentation Manager** and press **Enter** to mark the entry with an asterisk.
16. Select **DONE** and then press **Enter**.
17. Change the mailexe path to *C:\MAILDATA* and then press **Enter**.

18. A summary page is displayed. Verify that **NO CHANGE** is displayed and then press **Enter**.

19. Wait until the postoffice is installed and then press **Enter** to exit Setup.

20. Type *NET SHARE MAILDATA=C:\MAILDATA /UNLIMITED* and then press **Enter**.

21. Type *NET USE M: \\NEWYORK-1\MAILDATA* and then press **Enter**.

22. Switch to drive M, type *MSMAIL* and then press **Enter**.

23. The **Mail Sign In** dialog box appears.

24. In the **Name** box, type *Admin*. In the **Password** box, type *password*.

25. Click **OK**.

26. On the toolbar, click **Compose**.

27. Click **Address** and then double-click **Administrator**.

28. Click **OK**.

29. In **Subject**, type *TEST*.

30. On the toolbar, click **Send**.

31. You should see the message appear in your Inbox.

32. Exit the MS Mail client.

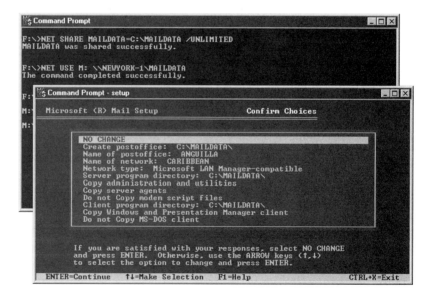

Task 50b: Verifying the Network and
Postoffice Names in the Mail Administrator Program

1. At the command prompt, type *Admin admin –ppassword* and then press **Enter**.

2. This command line syntax logs you on to the Mail Administrator program.

3. Type *C* for **Config**.

4. Type *P* for **Password**.

5. Check that the network name (**CARIBBEAN**) and postoffice name (**ANGUILLA**) are correct.

6. Press **Esc** three times, and then press **Enter** to exit the Mail Administrator program.

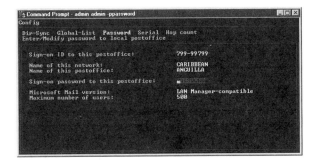

Task 50c: Configuring the MS Mail Connector

1. Click the **Start** button, point to **Programs**, point to **Microsoft Exchange**, and then click **Microsoft Exchange Administrator** to connect to the server NEWYORK-1.

2. Expand **NEWYORK**, expand **Configuration** and then click **Connections**.

3. In the right pane, double-click **MS Mail Connector (NEWYORK-1)** to display the **MS Mail Connector (NEWYORK-1) Properties** dialog box.

4. Click **Change** to display the **Administrator's Mailbox** dialog box.

5. Click **Administrator New York-1** and then click **OK**.

6. Click the **Connections** tab, and then click **Create** to display the **Create Connection** dialog box.

7. In the **Connection Parameters** box, verify that **LAN** is selected, and then click **Change**.

8. In the **Path** box, type *\\NEWYORK-1\MAILDATA* and then click **OK**.

9. The **Create Connection** dialog box reappears. Verify that the **Network** and **Postoffice** names are correct and then click **OK**.

10. The **Apply Changes Now** dialog box appears. Click **OK**.

11. The **MS Mail Connector (NEWYORK-1) Properties** dialog box reappears.

12. Click the **Connector MTAs** tab and then click **New** to display the **New MS Mail Connector (PC) MTA Service** dialog box.

13. Set the **Service Name** to Connector MTA.

14. Set **Update Configuration Every** to 5 minutes.

15. Set **Check For Mail Every** to 1 minute.

16. Click **OK**.

17. In the **MS Mail Connector (NEWYORK-1) Properties** dialog box, click **List**.

18. The **Serviced LAN Postoffices** dialog box appears.

19. In the **Available LAN Postoffices** box, select **CARIBBEAN/ANGUILLA** and then click **Add**.

20. Click **OK**.

21. Click the **Local Postoffice** tab. Verify that **Network** is **STOCKSDATA** and that **Postoffice** is **NEWYORK**.

22. Click the **Diagnostics Logging** tab and then set logging on all options to **Medium**.

23. Click the **Address Space** tab to see the entry. Make no changes.

24. Click **OK** to close the **MS Mail Connector (NEWYORK-1) Properties** dialog box.

Task 50d: Rebuilding Routing Tables

1. Under **NEWYORK**, click **Configuration**.

2. In the right pane, double-click **Site Addressing** to display the **Site Addressing Properties** dialog box.

3. Click the **Routing** tab.

4. Click **Recalculate Routing**.

5. An Exchange Administrator message box appears, stating that it will take several minutes for the new routing information to be replicated across the site. Click **OK**.

6. The **Site Addressing Properties** dialog box reappears. Notice the new routing values with a **Type** of **MS**.

7. Click **OK**.

8. Close Exchange Administrator.

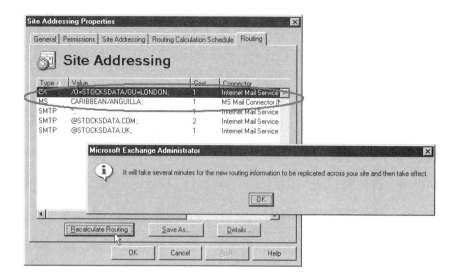

Task 50e: Starting the MS Mail Connector MTA Service

1. Click the **Start** button, point to **Settings** and then click **Control Panel**.

2. Double-click the **Services** icon.

3. In the **Services** dialog box, click **MS Mail Connector Interchange**.

4. Click **Start**.

5. In the **Services** dialog box, click **Connector MTA**. (This is the service you created in Task 50b.)

6. Click **Start**.

7. Close the **Services** dialog box.

8. Exit the Control Panel.

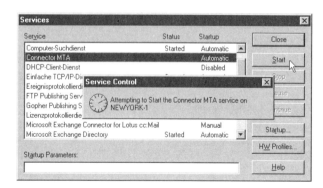

Task 50f: Defining the MS Mail Connector Postoffice in the MS Mail Postoffice

1. Switch to the **Command Prompt** window.

2. Type *Admin admin–password* and then press **Enter**.

3. Type *E* for **External-Admin**.

4. Type *C* for **Create**.

5. In the **Enter Network Name** box, type *STOCKSDATA* and then press **Enter**.

6. In the **Enter Postoffice Name** box, type *NEWYORK* and then press **Enter**.

7. To select **Direct** as the route type, press **Enter**.

8. To select **MS-DOS Drive** as the **Direct Connection Via** type, type *D*.

9. Press **Enter** to create the External postoffice.

10. Press **Esc** twice and then press **Enter** to exit the Mail Administrator program.

Task 50g: Sending Mail from the MS Mail Windows-Based Client to an Outlook Client

1. At the command prompt, type *MSMAIL* and then press **Enter**.

2. The **Mail Sign In** dialog box appears.

3. In the **Name** box, type *Admin*.

4. In the **Password** box, type *Enter*.

5. Click **OK**.

6. On the toolbar, click **Compose** to open the **Send Note** dialog box.

7. On the toolbar, click **Address** to display the address list.

8. On the left, click the single Rolodex card to display the **New** dialog box.

9. Click **Network/Postoffice** and then click **OK**.

10. Set **Alias** to Administrator New York-1.

11. Set **Mailbox** to AdminNY-1.

12. Set **Postoffice** to NEWYORK.

13. Set **Network** to STOCKSDATA.

14. Click **To**.

15. Click **OK**.

16. In the **Subject** box, type *TEST MESSAGE FROM MAIL 3.X TO MICROSOFT OUTLOOK*.

17. Click **Send** to transmit the message.

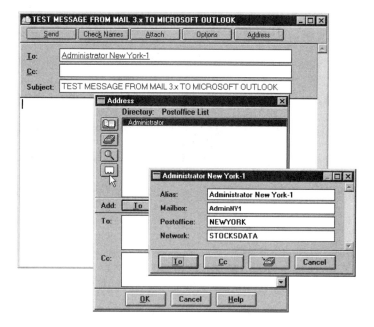

Task 50h: Viewing Messages Using Outlook

1. On the Desktop, double-click the **Microsoft Outlook** shortcut and log on using a profile that connects the client to **Mailbox - Admin-NY1**.

2. Check your Inbox for the message sent from the MS Mail Windows-based client.

Note It might take several minutes for the message to arrive in your Inbox. If you want to track the movement of the message, open the Mail Administrator program and check the queue. If it is in the queue for an extended period, use the **Services** applet of the Control Panel to verify that the MS Mail Connector MTA service has started.

---

3. Read the message.

4. On the toolbar, click **Reply**, and then type *Reply to PC Mail 3.x from Microsoft Outlook.*

5. On the toolbar, click **Send**.

6. On the **File** menu, click **Close**.

7. On the **File** menu, click **Exit And Log Off**.

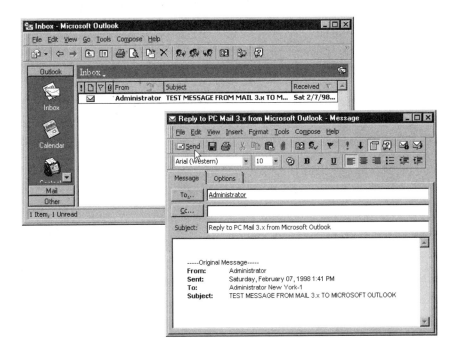

Task 50i: Viewing Messages Using the MS Mail Windows-Based Client

1. Switch to the Mail program.

2. After a few minutes, on the **View** menu, click **New Messages**.

3. The reply message from **Administrator NewYork-1** will appear on the MS Mail Windows-based client.

   > **Note** If, after a few minutes, the message does not appear in your Inbox, do the following in the Exchange Administrator to see where your message resides:
   >
   > - In the **Server** container, check the MTA queue for your server.
   >
   > - In the **Connections** container (in the MS Mail Connector) on the **Connections** tab, check the queue for your postoffice.

4. Open, read, and then close the message.

5. Exit the MS Mail Windows-based client.

6. Log off Windows NT.

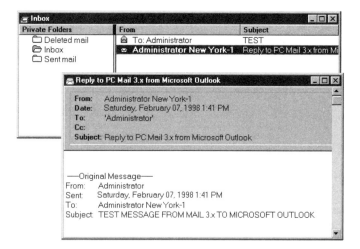

Review

Using the Administrator program, you can configure the MS Mail Connector through the **MS Mail Connector** (*<server_name>*) object in the **Connections** container. One connector can connect the entire site to one or more MS Mail postoffices. You specify direct postoffices using the UNC path to their network share. Indirect postoffices can be configured implicitly. The configured connection is only a logical link, so you must also configure a MS Mail Connector MTA service. Later, this service will transfer messages between the MS Mail network and the Connector Postoffice.

Using the **Services** applet of the Control Panel, you must start all configured services such as the MS Mail Connector Interchange and at least one MS Mail Connector MTA service to activate the connecting component between Exchange Server and MS Mail.

Using the MS Mail Administrator program, you must also configure each MS Mail postoffice. You must configure the Connector Postoffice as a regular external postoffice. MS Mail users can then send messages to Exchange users.

Lesson 2: Configuring Directory Synchronization in Exchange Server

So far, you have configured a connection to an MS Mail network. But, as you might have noticed, addressing e-mail messages to MS Mail users is still rather inconvenient. You must explicitly enter each MS Mail recipient's Network/ Postoffice/Mailbox address (such as CARRIBEAN/ANGUILLA/PHILIPE). You cannot simply select a user-friendly address book entry such as Philipe Coconut. MS Mail users have the same problem if they want to send messages to Exchange users. You therefore must maintain server-based and postoffice-based address lists that let your users address e-mail messages conveniently.

This lesson introduces a way to maintain address information automatically between Exchange Server and MS Mail. It briefly covers MS Mail Directory Synchronization and then explains the roles that an Exchange Server can play in this process. It then explains the configuration of an Exchange Server for each role as well as the mapping of Exchange Server mailbox attributes to MS Mail template information.

An exercise completes the chapter. It guides you through the steps of configuring a DirSync Server and a Remote DirSync Requestor and demonstrates how to force MS Mail Directory Synchronization.

At the end of this lesson, you will be able to:

- Describe the MS Mail Directory Synchronization events
- Identify the Exchange Server components that support the DirSync protocol
- Configure the Exchange Server as a DirSync Server
- Configure the Exchange Server as a DirSync Requestor
- Map the template information of MS Mail recipients to attributes of Exchange Server custom recipients

Estimated time to complete this lesson: 60 minutes

MS Mail Directory Synchronization Events

The MS Mail Directory Synchronization protocol, which updates MS Mail address lists, was introduced with MS Mail 3.0. It has not changed since then. Depending on the DirSync schedule (once a day at most), an active process called Dispatch launches several programs to synchronize the address information of all postoffices in an MS Mail network using e-mail messages.

MS Mail Directory Synchronization relies on a master postoffice known as the DirSync Server, which maintains the GAL on the network. Traditionally, only one DirSync Server is supported. All other postoffices, known as DirSync Requestors, must send their address changes to the DirSync Server to update the GAL. Once the GAL has been updated, it is sent back to all DirSync Requestors. (See Figure 18-5.)

Three Stages, One DirSync Cycle

A complete DirSync cycle consists of three stages called T1, T2, and T3. During T1, the Dispatch program launches the processes to send address list updates to the DirSync Server. During T2, the DirSync Server updates the global master address list and sends any changes to that list back to the Requestors. During T3, Requestors commit the GAL updates to the postoffice address lists.

T1

The Dispatch program launches a process called NSDA -RT, which starts the Reqmain -T process to run a T1 cycle according to the DirSync schedule. Every DirSync Requestor maintains address list changes in a file called Reqtrans.glb in the \Glb subdirectory of the postoffice. During T1, address changes are placed in an e-mail message that is addressed to the DirSync Server. A second message containing the current status information of the Requestor postoffice is also generated.

T1 is the beginning of a complete DirSync cycle. Each configured Requestor postoffice sends its address changes and a status report to the DirSync Server. Between T1 and T2, MS Mail External processes deliver the system messages to the DirSync Server.

T2

Using the DirSync schedule of the DirSync Server, Dispatch launches the NSDA -S process, which starts Srvmain -R and Srvmain -T to perform the necessary processing. Srvmain -R causes the DirSync Server to obtain all changes from its system message queue. It places them in the GAL named Msttrans.glb. This file is in the DirSync Server's \Glb subdirectory. It contains all address transactions of all Requestor postoffices. Srvmain -T then generates an update message for each DirSync Requestor containing the global address changes.

Between T2 and T3, update messages are sent back to the Requestor postoffices using MS Mail External processes. Only Requestor postoffices that have sent at least a status report to the DirSync Server receive an update message. In other words, a Requestor that does not send any system messages to the DirSync Server during T1 does not receive any GAL updates during T2.

T3

At T3, Dispatch launches a process known as NSDA -RT, which starts three independent programs: Reqmain -R, Import, and the optional Rebuild process. Reqmain -R merges received messages in a file called Srvmain.glb, which is in the \Glb subdirectory. Then the Import utility supplies the -Q parameter and commits the DirSync updates to the postoffice address lists. Depending on the configuration, the start of the Rebuild program might complete the T3 cycle. Rebuild creates the GAL, which contains the current state of the postoffice address lists.

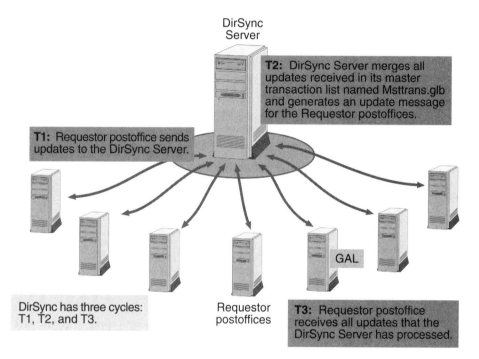

Figure 18-5. MS Mail DirSync events.

The DirSync phases and their descriptions are as follows:

- **T1**; address changes and status reports are placed in the DirSync Server queue in form of e-mail messages

- **T2**; address changes are processed at the DirSync Server and update messages are generated for each Requestor

- **T3**; address updates are incorporated in the postoffice address lists on every DirSync Requestor; the GAL is rebuilt

Directory Synchronization Agent as a Server

An Exchange Server can act as a DirSync Server in an MS Mail network. This has advantages and disadvantages. As a prerequisite, you must have a functioning MS Mail Connector, which transfers the DirSync messages between the Exchange server and the DirSync Requestors.

DXA

A special Exchange Server component, the Directory Synchronization Agent (DXA), performs the DirSync processing. It is a Windows NT service that receives address changes from the Requestor postoffices at T1. The address information is committed to the DS database in form of custom recipients. At T2, the DXA retrieves the necessary address information from the DS to create the update messages. The DXA keeps track of transactions already sent to a particular Requestor using the DirSync database (Xdir.edb), which is in the \Exchsrvr\Dxadata DS. Only transactions that have not yet been received are transferred to a particular Requestor. At T3, the Requestors process the updates.

Note If you find address list inconsistencies between the DXA Server and any Requestor postoffices, you can delete the Xdir.edb to reset MS Mail Directory Synchronization. The complete address list is then sent to all Requestor postoffices during the next DirSync cycle.

Advantages of the DXA Server

The DXA Server can improve the flexibility of MS Mail Directory Synchronization. For instance, the DXA service runs continuously and commits Requestor updates to the DS right when they arrive. There is no delay in the form of a scheduled event.

DirSync Cycles More Than Once a Day

The scheduled T2 time affects only the generation of update messages that are sent back to the Requestor postoffices. As mentioned earlier, only Requestors that have sent a T1 message receive an update message. Using a DXA Server, the DirSync cycle can run more than once a day. In fact, it can theoretically run every 15 minutes if a Requestor message has been received in the meantime. Configuration of the DXA Server is covered under "Configuring the DXA Server," later in this chapter.

Many DXA Servers

As shown in Figure 18-6, you can configure only one DXA Server per site. However, if your organization has multiple sites, you can configure more than one DXA Server to bind independent MS Mail networks together. This mechanism relies on directory replication, which distributes address list updates within the Exchange Server organization. A second Exchange Server in another site can act as a DXA Server for a different MS Mail network. Both MS Mail networks can perform Directory Synchronization as usual, but the organization will synchronize the DXA Servers (in other words, the GALs of both networks) in the background.

Disadvantages of the DXA Server

The advantages of the DXA Server are significant, but it is not always advisable to exploit them. The problem is not the DXA Server itself, but what happens as a result of system reconfiguration.

Let's say that you have integrated Exchange Server into a MS Mail network of 50 postoffices containing 3000 mailboxes in all. The native MS Mail DirSync runs just fine, but you are tempted by the extra features of the DXA, such as having multiple DXA Servers in the network. What would happen if you were to replace the former DXA Server? You would have to reset MS Mail Directory Synchronization on every postoffice to reflect the use of the DXA Server, rather than an MS Mail master postoffice. You would have to carry out a time-consuming and complex task, and all the work would generate a large amount of DirSync messages, because 3000 mailboxes would have to be synchronized again. Also, postoffices would display incomplete address lists until you had reset DirSync on every Requestor and completed the DirSync process.

The DXA Server message flow occurs as follows:

1. At T1, the Requestors send their status message and address changes to the DXA server.

2. When the DXA Server receives the changes, the changes are applied to the Exchange Server directory immediately.

3. At T2, the DXA Server collects address changes from the directory and creates the update message for each Requestor.

4. The update messages are placed in the MTA queue for the MS Mail postoffices. The MS Mail Connector sends the DXA messages to the Requestors.

5. At T3, the Requestor incorporates the changes as usual.

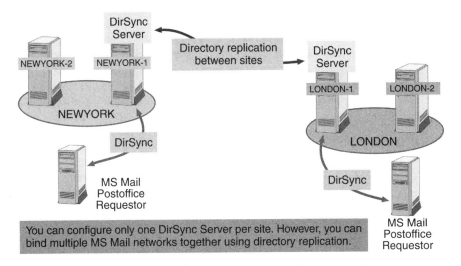

Figure 18-6. Exchange Server as the DXA Server.

DXA as a Requestor

If you decide not configure a DXA Server but you still want to take advantage of MS Mail Directory Synchronization, you must configure a DirSync Requestor. As shown in Figure 18-7, Exchange Server lets you configure one Requestor on each server in a site.

DXA

DXA can act as either a DXA Server or a DXA Requestor, but it cannot do both at the same time. During T1, the DXA Requestor obtains address list updates from the Directory using the Xdir.edb database It places the updates in an e-mail message and sends them to the DXA Server.

The DirSync Server of a DXA Requestor must be a regular MS Mail postoffice that processes the address updates of all Requestors during T2. That is, you cannot configure the DXA as a Requestor that sends address changes to another DXA configured as a DXA Server. Hence, you cannot synchronize addresses of two independent Exchange Server organizations using the MS Mail DirSync protocol. You cannot even carry out Directory Synchronization between multiple organizations using an MS Mail postoffice acting as a relay DXA Server between them.

At T3, the DXA Requestor receives its update message from the DirSync Server through the Mail Connector. When it receives this message, it contacts the DS to commit the address list changes to the DS database. It also updates Xdir.edb to keep track of transactions.

Advantages of the DXA Requestor

The DXA Requestor lets you integrate the Exchange Server organization seamlessly into MS Mail Directory Synchronization. You need only configure a new Requestor entry on the existing DirSync Server, and the DXA can synchronize address updates with the MS Mail network. Major configuration changes are not required.

Many DXA Requestors

Multiple DXA Requestors can synchronize addresses of independent MS Mail networks through the backbone of an Exchange Server organization. The directory replication distributes the address changes committed to the DS by one DXA Requestor to all other servers, including additional DXA Servers and DXA Requestors.

Disadvantages of the DXA Requestor

The DXA Requestor sends address list changes to an MS Mail DirSync Server, which means you cannot run the DirSync cycle more than once a day. As always in MS Mail, the DirSync Server performs the T2 processing of address list changes according to the schedule of the Dispatch program.

The DXA Requestor message flow works as follows:

1. At T1, the DXA Requestor sends address list changes to the MS Mail DirSync Server.

2. The MS Mail DirSync Server performs the T2 processing. The changes are processed along with address changes from other Requestors.

3. The MS Mail DirSync Server sends an update message back to all Requestors, including the DXA Requestor.

4. The DXA Requestor receives the updates and transfers them to the DS immediately. A scheduled T3 time is not necessary.

5. DS replication distributes new changes to all servers in the organization.

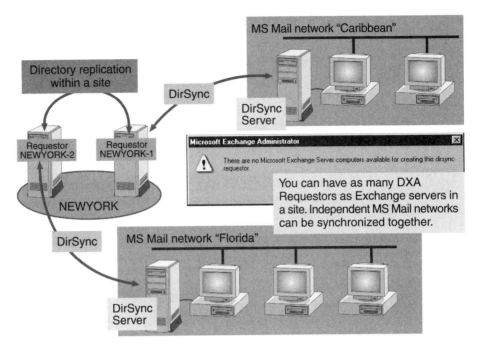

Figure 18-7. Exchange Server as the DXA Requestor.

Configuring the DXA Server

Let's say you want to implement a DXA Server to perform T2 processing, which has so far been accomplished using a MS Mail DirSync Server. Your MS Mail network is small enough to allow a quick reset of the existing postoffices. The MS Mail Connector and all Requestor postoffices have been configured. Now you can begin the DXA configuration. Using the Administrator program, open the **File** menu, point to **New Other**, and click the **DirSync Server** command. This displays the **General** property page of a new **DXA Server** object.

Defining the DXA Configuration Object Name

To distinguish the new DXA Server object from all other objects in the **Connections** container of the directory, you must specify an appropriate DXA Server name in the **Name** box on **General** property page. It is good practice to use a name that identifies the MS Mail network. (See Figure 18-8.)

Tracking Directory Synchronization Messages

The DXA Server incorporates address list changes of remote DirSync Requestors automatically in the DS. MS Mail users are handled as custom recipients. In other words, if custom recipient objects appear for users of your MS Mail network, you know that the Directory Synchronization works. However, in cases of communication problems, you might wait a very long time without success.

To trace Directory Synchronization with MS Mail, you can copy the DirSync messages to an administrative mailbox. Specify the mailbox using the **DirSync Administrator** button, and select the **Forward Incoming DirSync Messages To Administrator** option to receive a copy of the Requestor messages. You can also select the **Copy Administrator On Outgoing Messages** check box if you want to examine your DXA Server's responses.

T2 Schedule

Using its activation schedule, the DXA Server generates update messages for each Requestor that has sent a T1 message. On the **Schedule** property page, you can set when and how often the DXA is active. The shortest possible interval is 15 minutes. This does not, however, mean that the DXA Server sends a particular Mail Requestor an update message every 15 minutes (96 messages per day).

For example, the DXA Server on NEWYORK-1 has been configured to become active every hour. The postoffice CARRIBEAN/ANGUILLA sent its address changes to NEWYORK-1, and they were received at 10:05. The changes were applied immediately in the DS. The update message for this postoffice, however, won't be generated until the next scheduled T2 cycle at 11:00. The delay of 55 minutes allows the DXA Server to include updates of other Requestors received prior to the T2 cycle. Once the T2 replication message is sent to CARRIBEAN/ANGUILLA, the DXA Server will not generate further messages for this postoffice until it receives a new Aguilla-T1-DirSync-message.

The DXA Server property pages and their functions are as follows:

- **General**; to specify the directory object's name, an administrator mailbox, the options for copying DirSync messages to the administrator mailbox, the server where the DirSync processes will be launched, and selecting the Exchange Server that will handle the process
- **Schedule**; to specify T2 times

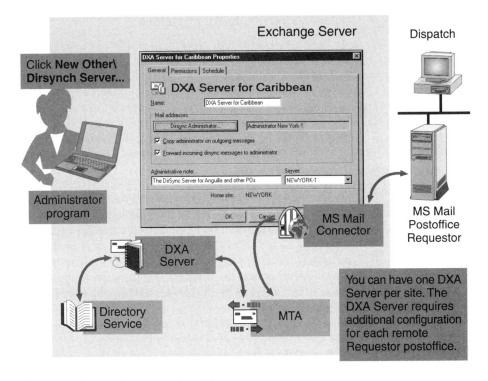

Figure 18-8. Configuring the DXA Server.

Configuring the Remote DirSync Requestor

To complete the configuration, you must designate existing MS Mail
Requestor postoffices as Remote DirSync Requestors by adding a **Remote
Dirsync Requestor**. For this purpose, click the **Remote Dirsync Requestor**
command under **New Other** on the **File** menu. The DXA Server will refuse
DirSync messages from unregistered sources because MS Mail Directory
Synchronization is a secured protocol. You can also define a Requestor
password on the **General** property page of each **Remote DirSync Requestor**
object to increase security. (See Figure 18-9.)

Note In the Administrator program, a DirSync Requestor is an Exchange
Server computer (DXA Requestor). A Remote DirSync Requestor is a MS Mail
postoffice.

Selecting the Requestor Postoffice

As mentioned earlier, in order to designate a Requestor, you must open the **File** menu, point to **New Other**, and click the **Remote DirSync Requestor** command in the Administrator program. In the **New Requestor** dialog box, specify the desired postoffice and click **OK**. In the **Properties** dialog box that appears, supply the required configuration parameters (such as the Import and Export recipient containers). You must also specify a name for the new Requestor object in the **Name** box on the **General** property page.

Importing Addresses

On the **Import Container** property page, you can specify the recipient container that will maintain imported custom recipients for the selected Requestor postoffice. The DXA Server creates custom recipients during the DirSync process. You should use dedicated recipient containers to implement a clear address book structure. You can also select the **Append To Imported Users' Display Name** option on the **General** property page to append the name of the **Remote DirSync Requestor** object to the display name of each custom recipient.

You can also define a trust level between 0 and 100 for all custom recipients in the **Trust Level** box. Only Requestor postoffices that show a trust level higher than the specified value receive the address information of the current Requestor. (See "Exporting Addresses" below.) You can also set the Requestor trust level on the **Export Containers** property page.

Exporting Addresses

On the **Export Containers** property page, you can specify one or more recipient containers that will be exported to the remote Requestor postoffice. To synchronize address information between MS Mail postoffices, you must also select the **Export Custom Recipients** check box. As mentioned earlier, MS Mail users are shown as custom recipients.

To export the address information of the specified recipient containers during the next DirSync cycle, you must select the **Export On Next Cycle** option on the **General** property page of the Requestor object. This causes the DXA Server to send all address information—not only the updates—to the Requestor.

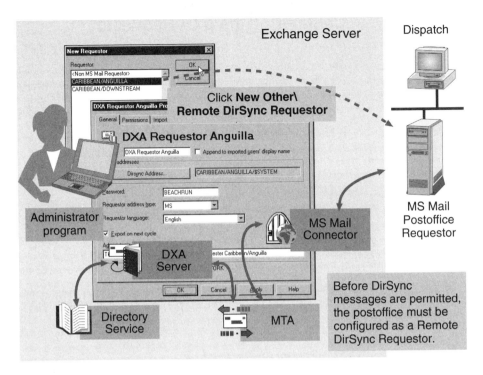

Figure 18-9. Configuring the Remote DirSync Requestor.

The Remote DirSync Requestor property pages and their functions are as follows:

- **Export Containers**; to designate recipients that will be exported to the Requestor chosen from the containers listed in the **Recipient Containers**, to set a trust level, and to determine whether custom recipients should also be exported

- **General**; to set the **Remote DirSync Requestor** object's display name and to define a Requestor password, the postoffice type (PC or MAC), its language, and an administrative note; you can also specify whether to append the Requestor name to imported custom recipients and whether to export all address information during the next cycle

- **Import Container**; to specify the import container where custom recipients for MS Mail users will be created and to set their trust level

Configuring the DXA Requestor

Configuring a DXA Requestor is less complex than configuring a DXA Server. This is not surprising, since the DXA Requestor is responsible only for itself. You can set several configuration parameters just as you do for a Remote DirSync Requestor. For instance, you take the same steps to specify recipient containers using the **Import Container** and **Export Container** property pages.

To create a DXA Requestor, open the **File** menu, point to **New Other**, and click the **DirSync Requestor** command. A **New Requestor** dialog box will appear, asking you for the MS Mail DirSync Server postoffice. Select a postoffice and click **OK** to launch the **Properties** dialog box, which asks for further information. (You must first configure the MS Mail Connector to connect the Exchange Server to the MS Mail postoffice that represents the DirSync Server; otherwise, you cannot select the correct postoffice reference in the **New Requestor** window during the DXA Requestor creation.)

Note You cannot configure both a DXA Server and a DXA Requestor on the same server.

DXA Requestor Parameters

On the **General** property page of the new **DXA Requestor** object, you can set basic configuration parameters such as the **Name** of the **DXA Requestor** object and the **Requestor Language**. Several of the settings have the same effect that they do for a Remote DirSync Requestor (the **Append To Imported User's Display Name** option, for example).

Other parameters pertain only to a DXA Requestor object, so you can specify which address types to accept from the DirSync Server. This is especially important if you want to allow Exchange users to send messages through installed gateways in the MS Mail network. You can select from among the **X.400**, **PROFS**, **MHS**, **FAX**, **SNADS**, and **Microsoft Mail For AppleTalk** check boxes. (See Figure 18-10.)

Note Although you can receive X.400 addresses from the DirSync Server, you should not route X.400 messages to the MS Mail network. Use Exchange Server to configure X.400 messaging connections because its X.400 Connector is much more powerful than the old MS Mail Gateway to X.400.

Directory Synchronization Parameters

Several settings of a DXA Requestor refer directly to the MS Mail Directory Synchronization protocol. For instance, you can secure communication between the DXA Server and the Requestor using a Requestor password. Once you specify a password at the DirSync Server postoffice, the Requestor must provide the password to synchronize addresses. You can enter this password on the **Settings** property page of the **DXA Requestor** object.

On the **Settings** property page, the **Send Updates** and **Receive Updates** options let you specify whether to send and/or receive DirSync updates. Both these options usually are selected, while two other options are usually disabled: **Send Local Template Information** and **Receive Template Information**. Before you select them, you should define appropriate template mapping, as described later under "DirSync Templates."

You can also send all of the address information to the DirSync Server during the next DirSync cycle by selecting the **Export On Next Cycle** check box. The **Import On Next Cycle** option, on the other hand, sends requests the complete address information from the DirSync Server. As a result, the DirSync Server postoffice returns all addresses during the next cycle. Both options are useful if you discover address inconsistencies between postoffices and the Exchange Server.

Directory Synchronization Schedule

Two DirSync times are important for every Requestor: T1 and T3. You have to schedule only the T1 time because updates are committed to the directory database as soon as they reach the DXA. On the **Schedule** property page of the **DXA Requestor** object, you can adjust the T1 time when the DXA sends address updates to the DirSync Server. By default, the DXA Requestor sends its changes at midnight.

Note It is sufficient to send one address update message to the MS Mail DirSync Server each day. The Mail DirSync Server incorporates the changes only once at T2 as scheduled for the Dispatch process.

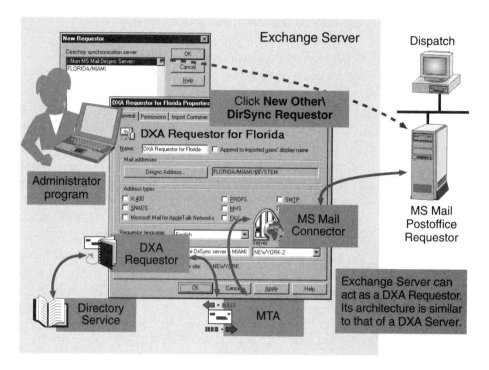

Figure 18-10. Configuring the DXA Requestor.

The DirSync Requestor property pages and their functions are as follows:

- **General**; to define the **Requestor** object's name, to specify whether to append the name to imported users' display name, to enable address types, to specify the Requestor language, and to provide an administrative note

- **Import Container**; to specify which **Recipients** container should contain the custom recipients for MS Mail users and to assign them a trust level

- **Export Containers**; to export the desired address information from specified containers to the MS Mail DirSync Server postoffice and to set the trust level; you can also specify whether custom recipients should be exported

- **Settings**; to enter the DXA Requestor password, to specify whether to send and receive address updates, to supply template information, and to specify whether to initiate the import or export of the entire set of address information during the next DirSync cycle

- **Schedule**; to set the T1 time when address changes are sent to the DirSync Server

DirSync Templates

MS Mail users can display detailed address information for recipients from their postoffice address lists. Exchange users can examine the properties and attributes of mailboxes and custom recipients using their address books as well. So you should map Exchange attributes to MS Mail address information (and vice versa) if MS Mail Directory Synchronization has been configured. This way, Exchange users can examine detailed MS Mail address information, and MS Mail users can display additional information about recipients that seem to reside on the Connector Postoffice address list (which is the MS Mail view of your site).

MS Mail Address Templates

By default, the MS Mail system provides the alias name, display name, address type, postoffice name, network name, and the name of the mailbox. Using address templates, you can define additional information that is displayed if users examine the details of an address entry. For example, one such template, Example.tpl, is in the \Tpl subdirectory of every postoffice installation. It has the following content:

```
Employee Number:~17~6~NP~000001~
Name Title:~17~3~ULP~Mr~
Initials:~17~2~U~MD~
Surname:~17~15~ULP~Davis~
Division:~17~25~A~Electronic Mail~
Department:~17~15~A~Development~
Phone:~17~15~NP~(303) 555-4345~
FAX:~17~15~NP~(303) 555-1378~
Company:~17~25~LUNP~Microsoft Corp.~
Address 1:~17~50~A~1402 Washington Street~
Address 1:~17~50~A~Hollywood, FL~
Postal Code:~17~7~A~33021~
Phone:~17~15~NP~(303) 555-4345~
Group:~17~15~A~Mail Group~
```

These entries are only suggestions, which you can adjust as needed. You'll find documentation in the MS Mail Administrator manual. However, you must rename the Example.tpl file as Admin.tpl in order for it to take additional properties such as **Phone**, **Company**, or **Address**.

Exchange Address Details

Exchange Server does not use template information, as MS Mail does. Detailed information is maintained in the form of recipient object attributes. You'll find more information about recipient objects and their attributes in Chapter 5.

Using Templates to Map Incoming and Outgoing Template Information

To synchronize address details, you must map mailbox attributes to postoffice template labels such as **Phone:**, **Company:**, or **Address:**. (See the template listing above.) You can control the mapping using the Administrator program. The **Directory Synchronization** object under the local **Server** object provides the required property pages. The most important pages are **Incoming Templates** and **Outgoing Templates**. In other words, the **Directory Synchronization** object lets you configure the template transfer in one or both directions.

You can administer the property pages in a similar way. You click the **New** button to define the desired mappings. In the **Incoming Template Mapping** dialog box that appears, you must enter the template string (such as *Phone*) manually. You can select the corresponding mailbox attribute from the **Map The Attribute** box. When you define mappings, you can rename template labels by assigning them different attributes. You can also suppress labels by leaving them unmapped.

Keep in mind that you must include the template information in the Directory Synchronization. You do this by displaying the **Settings** property page of the corresponding DXA Requestor object in the **Connections** container. On this page, you set the options as explained earlier under "Configuring the DXA Requestor." When the next DirSync cycle completes, Exchange Server and MS Mail users can display the information using the address books of their messaging clients. (See Figure 18-11.)

The Directory Synchronization property pages and their functions are as follows:

- **General**; to display information about the DirSync connection and to enter an administrative note

- **E-Mail Addresses**; to display and edit the e-mail addresses of the DXA component

- **Delivery Restrictions**; to specify which users can send messages to the DXA

- **Incoming Templates**; to map MS Mail template information to Exchange Server recipient attributes for incoming address information

- **Outgoing Templates**; to map Exchange Server recipient attributes to MS Mail template information for outgoing address information

- **Diagnostics Logging**; to enable status messages to be written to the Windows NT Event Log

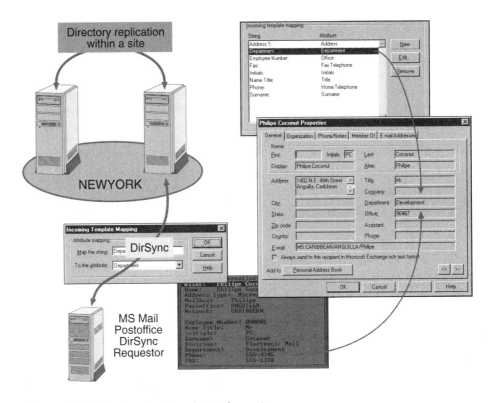

Figure 18-11. Exchanging template information.

Exercise 51: Configuring MS Mail Directory Synchronization

MS Mail Directory Synchronization exchanges address information between postoffices in three phases—T1, T2, and T3. At T1, every Requestor sends its address changes and a status report to the DXA Server. At T2, the DXA Server incorporates all received changes. It creates an update response for each Requestor postoffice, which contains only the changes that the Requestor has not received. The update messages are then sent to each Requestor. At T3, each Requestor incorporates the address updates into the postoffice address lists. (Optionally, the GAL can be generated.)

Estimated time to complete this exercise: 30 minutes

Description

In this exercise, you will configure an Exchange Server to act as the DXA Server for an MS Mail network. You can use the existing postoffice (as configured in Exercise 50). It is configured as a DXA Requestor using the MS Mail Administrator program. To accept the DirSync messages, you must also configure the postoffice as a **Remote DirSync Requestor** in the Exchange Administrator program. Finally, you must run a DirSync cycle manually to verify the MS Mail Directory Synchronization.

- Task 51a describes the steps for configuring the DXA Server in the Exchange Administrator program.

- Task 51b describes the steps for starting the DXA Server service using the **Services** applet of the Control Panel.

- Task 51c describes the steps for registering the Exchange DirSync Server with the MS Mail postoffice. Since the Exchange Server computer is functioning as the DXA Server, you can use a reference to the Connector postoffice to register the Requestor postoffice with the DXA Server.

- Task 51d describes the steps for creating a separate **Recipients** container and for creating Remote DirSync Requestor objects for the MS Mail postoffice, which will be serviced by the DXA Server.

- Task 51e describes the steps for configuring the Remote DirSync Requestor reference of the MS Mail postoffice. Once you configure it, Reqmain can be launched on the postoffice to send address changes to the DXA Server.

- Task 51f describes the steps for running the T1 DirSync cycle at the postoffice manually to transfer the DirSync addresses to the Exchange Server computer. Once the DirSync messages have been received, you must wait for the server to launch the T2 processes.

- Task 51g describes the steps for running the T3 DirSync cycle at the postoffice manually to update address list information on the postoffice and for rebuilding the GAL.

Prerequisites

- Complete Exercise 50.

- Log on to NEWYORK-1 as Admin-NY1.

Task 51a: Configuring the DXA Server

1. Click the **Start** button, point to **Programs**, point to **Microsoft Exchange**, click **Microsoft Exchange Administrator**, and then connect to the server NEWYORK.

2. Expand **NEWYORK**, expand the **Configuration** container and then click the **Connections** container.

3. On the **File** menu, point to **New Other** and then click **DirSync Server**.

4. The **DXA Server Properties** dialog box appears.

5. In the **Name** box, type *DXA Server*.

6. Click **DirSync Administrator**. In the list, click **Administrator NewYork-1**.

7. Click **OK**.

8. Select the **Copy Administrator On Outgoing Messages** check box, and then select the **Forward Incoming DirSync Messages To Administrator** check box.

9. Click the **Schedule** tab, and then select all available times by clicking the blank square above **Sunday** twice.

10. Click **OK**.

11. Minimize Exchange Administrator.

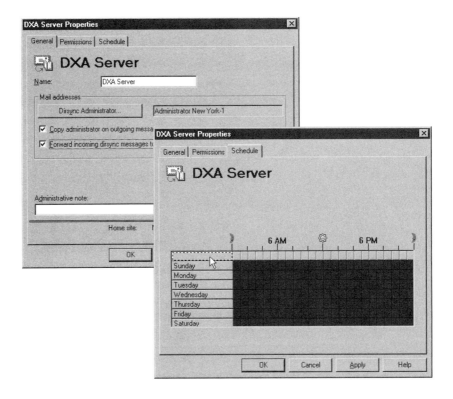

Task 51b: Starting the DXA Server Service

1. Click the **Start** button, point to **Settings**, and then click the Control Panel.

2. Double-click the **Services** icon.

3. Click **Microsoft Exchange Directory Synchronization** and then click **Start**.

4. Click **Startup**. In the **Startup Type** box, click **Automatic**.

5. Click **OK**.

6. Close the **Services** dialog box, and then exit the Control Panel.

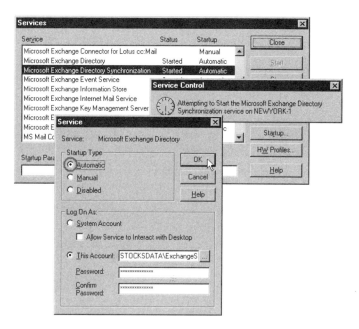

Task 51c: Registering the DXA Server as the MS Mail DirSync Server

1. Open a command prompt window. Type *net use m: \\newyork-1\maildata* and then press **Enter**. (If the drive is already mapped, you will receive the notification *The local device name is already in use.*)

2. Switch to the M: drive.

3. Type *Admin admin -ppassword* and then press **Enter**.

4. Type *C* for **Config**.

5. Type *D* for **DirSync**.

6. Type *R* for **Requestor**.

7. Type *R* for **Registration**.

8. Type *N* for **Name**.

9. Click **STOCKSDATA** and then press **Enter**.

10. Click **NEWYORK** and then press **Enter**.

11. Press **Esc**.

12. Type *E* for *Export*.

13. Press **Enter** to export local users and groups.

14. Press **Esc** four times and then press **Enter** to quit.

15. Minimize the command prompt window.

Task 51d: Creating a Recipients Container

1. Switch to Exchange Administrator.

2. Click **NEWYORK**.

3. On the **File** menu, point to **New Other**, and then click **Recipients Container**.

4. In the **Display name** box, type *DirSync Addresses*.

5. In the **Directory name** box, type *DirSync Addresses*.

6. Click **OK**.

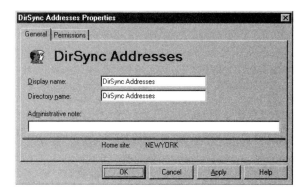

Task 51e: Creating a Remote DirSync Requestor

1. Expand the **Connections** container. In the left pane, double-click the **DXA Server** object.

2. On the **File** menu, point to **New Other** and then click **Remote DirSync Requestor**.

3. The **New Requestor** dialog box appears. In the list, click the **CARRIBEAN/ANGUILLA** postoffice, and then click **OK** to display the **Properties** dialog box.

4. In the **Name** box, type *Anguilla*.

5. Select the **Append To Imported Users' Display Name** check box.

6. Select the **Export On Next Cycle** check box.

7. Select the **Import Container** tab and then click **Container**.

8. In the **Import Container** dialog box, click **DirSync Addresses** and then click **OK**.

9. Click the **Export Containers** tab.

10. Click **Recipients** and then click **Add**.

11. Click **Account On NewYork-1** and then click **Add**.

12. Click **OK**.

13. Minimize the Exchange Administrator window.

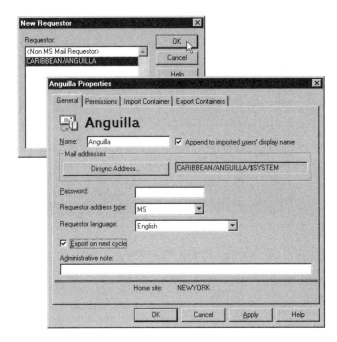

Task 51f: Queuing DirSync Transactions (T1)

1. Switch to the command prompt. Type *reqmain -t* and then press **Enter**. This will initiate DirSync for your postoffice (T1 time). Wait five minutes before continuing with the next procedure.

2. Double-click the **Microsoft Outlook** shortcut on the Desktop and then connect to the mailbox **Administrator NewYork-1**.

3. Verify that a DirSync status message has been received.

4. On the **Tools** menu, click **Address Book**, and then select **DirSync Addresses** from the **Show Names From The** list.

5. Verify that the MS Mail addresses exist in the **Address Book** container as Custom recipients.

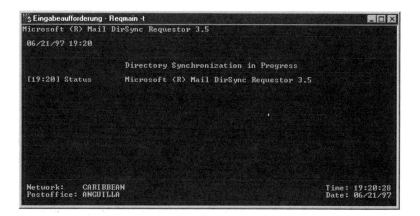

Task 51g: Incorporating Directory Changes from the DXA Server (T3)

1. Wait for the DXA Server to generate the update message for the MS Mail postoffice. This happens on the hour.

2. Verify that the update message has been delivered to the MS Mail postoffice.

3. Switch to the command prompt. Type *reqmain -r* and then press **Enter** to retrieve the DirSync messages from the DXA Server.

4. Type *import admin -ppassword -q -y* and then press **Enter** to import the DirSync changes into the postoffice.

5. Type *rebuild* and press **Enter**. Press **Enter** again to rebuild the GAL on the postoffice.

6. Verify that the addresses for the Exchange organization recipients are available in the GAL of each Windows-based MS Mail client.

```
Eingabeaufforderung - reqmain -r                          _ □ X
Microsoft (R) Mail DirSync Requestor 3.5

06/22/97 00:30


                    Directory Synchronization in Progress

[00:30] Status        Microsoft (R) Mail DirSync Requestor 3.5










Network:    CARIBBEAN                          Time: 00:30:12
Postoffice: ANGUILLA                           Date: 06/22/97
```

Review

DXA, a separate Windows NT service, is responsible for maintaining DirSync updates. It can act as a DirSync Server or as a DirSync Requestor. If a DirSync Server has been configured, existing MS Mail postoffices must send their changes to the Exchange Server at T1. You configure postoffices using the MS Mail Administrator program, and you configure the DirSync Server and Remote DirSync Requestors in the Exchange Administrator program.

You can manually launch the MS Mail DirSync program's Reqmain.exe to force a Directory Synchronization cycle. You start it with the command line **Reqmain -T** to generate an update message. The MS Mail Connector then transfers the message to the DXA Server. You can copy system messages to the Administrator's mailbox if desired. When they are received, the DXA incorporates the updates into the local directory. MS Mail addresses appear as custom recipient objects in the specified **Import** container. Later, at T2, the DXA Server generates the update messages for all Requestors that have sent a system message since the last completed DirSync cycle. The MS Mail Connector transfers the messages to their destinations. They can also be copied to the Administrator's mailbox for a detailed analysis. Once they have been received at the postoffices, you can execute the **Reqmain -R**, **Import -Q**, and **Rebuild -F** commands to commit the changes to the postoffice address lists.

Lesson 3: The Schedule+ Free/Busy Connector

Users in an Exchange Server organization can run Schedule+ 7.0 or Outlook to maintain scheduling and calendar information. Users in an MS Mail network can use Outlook, Schedule+ 7.0, or even Schedule+ 1.0 to work with scheduling information in an MS Mail postoffice. It sounds like six or seven versions of Schedule+ have been released since version 1.0. So what happened to Schedule+ versions 2.0, 3.0, 4.0, 5.0, and 6.0? Well, Schedule+ went from 1.0 to 7.0 to 7.5, and then to Outlook. Using the Schedule+ Free/Busy Connector with the MS Mail Connector, you can synchronize Free/Busy times between Schedule+ and Outlook.

This lesson introduces the Schedule+ Free/Busy Connector and explains its architecture and configuration.

At the end of this lesson, you will be able to:

- Identify the components of the Schedule+ Free/Busy Connector

- Configure the Schedule+ Free/Busy Connector

Estimated time to complete this lesson: 25 minutes

Schedule+ Free/Busy Connector Architecture

Free/Busy times are the free and busy times of users as noted in their schedules, marked by a start date and an end date. This information is shared among all users so that they can plan meetings and appointments efficiently. A user who wants to book a meeting can view the free and busy times of all attendees and determine a time when they are all available.

Free/Busy time distribution was introduced with Schedule+1.0 in conjunction with MS Mail. Users working with different postoffices can share Free/Busy information because active processes in the background distribute that information to all postoffices. This feature is also available in Schedule+ 7.x and Outlook, and is implemented in Exchange Server as well.

MS Mail Free/Busy Time Distribution

Schedule+ 1.0 maintains Free/Busy times on a per-postoffice basis in .POF files, which are in the \Maildata\Cal subdirectory. The file 00000000.POF, for example, contains the Free/Busy times of users who use the local postoffice. However, the postoffice is a passive file structure. A separate process known as Schdist.exe is required to distribute the information across all postoffices in an MS Mail network.

Three components are very important for Free/Busy Time Distribution: Schdist.exe, Adminsch.exe, and a mailbox called ADMINSCH. Schdist.exe distributes the Free/Busy information across the MS Mail network using e-mail messages, which are sent to the ADMINSCH mailbox. Once messages are delivered to this mailbox, Schdist.exe can obtain the information from there to place the Free/Busy information in the corresponding .POF files. Adminsch.exe is the Schedule+ Administrator program. You can use it to manage distribution settings, such as the postoffices that receive Free/Busy information. You should make sure that all target postoffices have an ADMINSCH account that is included in the Directory Synchronization. MS Mail Directory Synchronization propagates the existence of these accounts through the MS Mail network.

Schedule+ Free/Busy Information Public Folder

Exchange users maintain Free/Busy information in a hidden system folder in the Public Information Store called *Schedule+ Free Busy*. You can find a corresponding object under the **Systems Folders** container using the Administrator program. This folder is usually on the first server installed in a site. You can replicate it across the organization or move it to a designated Free/Busy public server. More information about the configuration of public folders is provided in Chapter 12.

The *Schedule+ Free Busy* folder contains a single object for each user. This object stores the user's Free/Busy times. These objects are like regular message items in a visible public folder. If a user stores a Free/Busy item in this folder, all other users can open it there and read the information. Every user in a site has access to the hidden *Schedule+ Free Busy* folder when working with Schedule+ 7.*x* or Outlook.

Let's say you want to book a meeting. Using Schedule+ 7.x or Outlook, you access the *Schedule+ Free Busy* folder to display the Free/Busy information for each person you want to invite. You actually open the *Schedule+ Free Busy* folder implicitly when you click the **Plan A Meeting** command on Outlook's **Calendar** menu. The **Calendar** menu becomes available when you select the **Calendar** folder. However, you can easily find a free time using the **Plan A Meeting** dialog box. You book the meeting, and then a meeting request message is sent to all attendees. When the attendees accept the meeting, their clients immediately synchronize the new appointment with their Free/Busy "messages" in the *Schedule+ Free Busy* folder. Start and end times are written to these messages as regular MAPI properties. All users in your organization can then see that the attendees of your meeting are no longer free during the specified time period, and they won't try to plan another meeting for the same time.

Schedule+ Free/Busy Connector

The Schedule+ Free/Busy Connector uses the Schedule+ 1.0 distribution protocol to exchange Free/Busy information between Exchange users and MS Mail users using e-mail messages. This connector actually accomplishes two tasks. First it creates the Free/Busy messages destined for the MS Mail network. Then it incorporates received information from MS Mail into the *Schedule+ Free Busy* folder. To access the *Schedule+ Free Busy* folder, the connector must communicate with the IS. Once the MS Mail Free/Busy information is stored on the Exchange Server, users can access it just as they can any other Free/Busy information. (See Figure 18-12.)

ADMINSCH User Agent

The Schedule+ Free/Busy Connector uses a user agent called ADMINSCH to send and receive Schedule+ 1.0 Free/Busy information. A user agent is a special Exchange Server account that is associated with an active service instead of a regular user. It is created during the Free/Busy Connector installation and is in the **Recipients** container.

Schdist.exe and ADMINSCH

Schdist.exe sends its local Free/Busy information to all other ADMINSCH mailboxes—in other words, to all other Schdist.exe processes in the MS Mail network. Schdist.exe can include the Exchange Server in its information distribution since the Schedule+ Free/Busy Connector maintains a ADMINSCH user agent. (See Figure 18-12.)

MS Mail Directory Synchronization

As mentioned earlier, the Schedule+ Free/Busy Connector must send Exchange Free/Busy information to MS Mail. For full compatibility, it sends the information in the form of e-mail messages to existing ADMINSCH accounts in the MS Mail network. These ADMINSCH accounts, however, must exist in the GAL of the Exchange Server. Otherwise, Schdist.exe messages cannot be addressed successfully. Therefore, you should enable MS Mail Directory Synchronization to create the required custom recipients automatically.

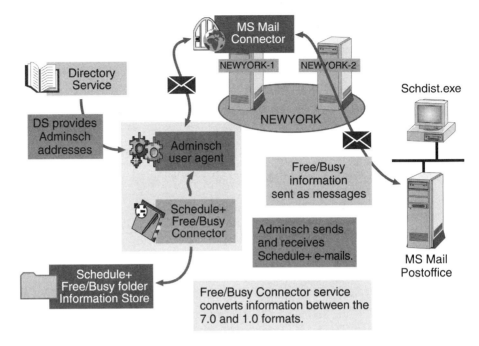

Figure 18-12.   The Schedule+ Free/Busy Connector architecture.

The tasks of the Free/Busy Connector are as follows:

1. Obtains Free/Busy information from the *Schedule+ Free Busy* system folder.

2. Creates and sends Free/Busy messages to the MS Mail Schdist.exe. (Messages are addressed to the ADMINSCH of each involved postoffice.)

3. Processes Free/Busy messages received from the MS Mail Schdist.exe. (Messages are addressed and delivered to the ADMINSCH user agent of the Schedule+ Free/Busy Connector.)

4. Places the received Free/Busy information in the *Schedule+ Free Busy* system folder.

Configuring the Schedule+ Free/Busy Connector

The Schedule+ Free/Busy Connector relies on the MS Mail Connector and on MS Mail Directory Synchronization. The MS Mail Connector must guarantee that Free/Busy Connector messages arrive at the MS Mail postoffice and that Schdist.exe messages reach the Exchange Server. MS Mail Directory Synchronization, in turn, synchronizes the address information—especially the ADMINSCH accounts—of all postoffices and the Exchange Server. The connector can send messages only to accounts that are custom recipients in the directory. (See Figure 18-13.)

Configuration Considerations

You can configure the Schedule+ Free/Busy Connector using the Administrator program. The corresponding configuration object is in the **Recipients** container of your site. It is labeled **Microsoft Schedule+ Free/Busy Connector** and provides two property pages for administration, **General** and **Schedule+ Free/Busy Connector Options**.

Note In order to have a functioning system, you must configure the MS Mail postoffices using the Adminsch.exe program. The Connector postoffice must be included in the list of target postoffices.

Sending Free/Busy Information

On the **Schedule+ Free/Busy Connector Options** property page, you will see the **Schedule+ Distribution List** option, which you can use to specify a distribution list that contains the ADMINSCH accounts of all postoffices you want to include in the Free/Busy synchronization. Using a distribution list simplifies the task of configuring the connector when several postoffices are included. However, you must create this distribution list prior to configuring the connector.

You can select the **Send Updates For This Site Only** option if you want to propagate the Free/Busy information only of users residing in your site to MS Mail.

Information Updates

By default, the Schedule+ Free/Busy Connector sends Free/Busy information updates every 15 minutes to the MS Mail network. This is sufficient for most installations, but you can adjust this using the **Update Frequency (Minutes)** box on the **Schedule+ Free/Busy Connector Options** property page. It is best not to decrease this value to avoid unnecessary message traffic.

If you discover any inconsistencies between Free/Busy information in Mail and in Exchange, click the **Full Export** button to send all of the Free/Busy information to the Mail network.

Monitoring the Schedule+ Free/Busy Connector

You can specify an **Administrative Mailbox** on the **Schedule+ Free/Busy Connector Options** page. The Schedule+ Free/Busy Connector uses this mailbox to store corrupted Free/Busy messages and messages that could not be processed for other reasons. If you discover several Free/Busy Connector messages in this mailbox, you might want to check the connector processing in more detail.

The **Schedule+ Free/Busy Connector Options** property page provides options for monitoring the state of the Free/Busy Connector. Similar to **Diagnostics Logging** property pages of other connector objects such as the MS Mail Connector, it lets you specify the level of detail you want to obtain through the Application Event Log under **Logging Level**. Six levels are available, ranging from **None** for no logging to **Internal** for maximum logging.

To guarantee the permanent availability of recent Free/Busy information, you can monitor the Schedule+ Free/Busy Connector using a Server Monitor. You can configure monitored services using the **Services** property page of the local <server> object (**NEWYORK-1**), which you can reach when you select the <server> object in the Exchange Administrator program and press the ALT+ENTER key combination. The configuration of Server Monitors is covered in Chapter 15.

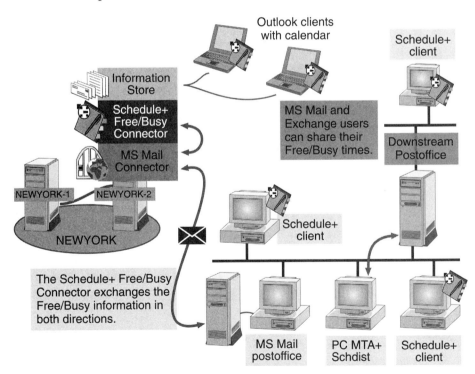

Figure 18-13. Exchanging Free/Busy information with Schedule+ 1.0.

The **Schedule+ Free/Busy Connector** property pages and their functions are as follows:

- **General**; to change the display or the alias name of the Schedule+ Free/Busy Connector and to enter an administrative note for informational purposes
- **Schedule+ Free/Busy Connector Options**; to set the administrator mailbox, the ADMINSCH distribution list, the update frequency, and the logging level, and to specify whether to send updates for this site only; you can click the **Full Export** button to send all of the Free/Busy information to the MS Mail network

Review

1. What are the three components of the MS Mail Connector?

   _____

2. What is the function of the Connector postoffice?

   _____

   _____

3. Some users in a MS Mail network access their postoffices remotely using MS Mail remote clients. You plan to replace all MS Mail Externals with MS Mail Connector MTA services. How can you support the MS Mail remote users once all Externals are replaced?

   _____

   _____

   _____

   _____

4. You plan to connect your organization to an existing MS Mail network. A permanent network connection does not exist. How do you connect both systems?

   _____

   _____

   _____

   _____

5. Which component converts Exchange Server messages to MS Mail messages and vice versa?

_____

6. You have configured the MS Mail Connector, but messages sent to MS Mail users remain in the Connector postoffice. You check the state of the MS Mail Connector services and they have all been started. How can you obtain more information about the source of the problem?

_____

_____

_____

_____

7. You have configured an MS Mail Connector between one MS Mail postoffice and an Exchange Server. Exchange users can send messages, but users on the MS Mail postoffice cannot. How can you correct this problem?

_____

_____

8. What are the three stages of a complete DirSync cycle?

_____

_____

_____

_____

9. You have configured an Exchange Server as a DXA Server. MS Mail Requestor postoffices are sending their address changes to the Exchange Server through the MS Mail Connector. When will address list changes appear in the specified Import container?

_____

_____

_____

10. You have configured an Exchange Server as a DXA Server, and you have configured remote DirSync Requestor postoffices. One of the Requestor postoffices does not show any updates, even though the first DirSync cycle has been completed. Which options should you activate to keep track of whether the Requestor sends its changes to the correct DXA Server and whether the DXA Server sends updates back to the postoffice?

_____

_____

_____

_____

_____

11. You want to configure an Exchange Server computer to act as a DirSync Requestor. How do you schedule the time to incorporate received address updates into the DS (T3)?

_____

_____

12. Which property pages can you use to map MS Mail template information to Exchange mailbox attributes?

_____

_____

_____

13. What is the purpose of the Schedule+ Free/Busy Connector?

_____

_____

14. How does the Schedule+ Free/Busy Connector work?

_____

_____

_____

_____

15. Why must you configure a distribution list before configuring the Schedule+ Free/Busy Connector?

_____

_____

_____

16. You have configured the MS Mail Connector, MS Mail Directory Synchronization, and the Schedule+ Free/Busy Connector. The Free/Busy information is exchanged on a regular basis. You have just discovered that Free/Busy information in one postoffice is displayed incorrectly. What can you do to update the information?

_____

_____

_____

_____

_____

_____

C H A P T E R   1 9

Connector for Lotus cc:Mail

This chapter explains the component that connects Exchange Server to Lotus cc:Mail. E-mail messages and recipient information can be exchanged directly between both systems by using the Connector for Lotus cc:Mail.

Overview

When Exchange Server 4.0 was put on the market, it was released with the goal of replacing the installed Microsoft Mail basis. The MS Mail Connector was provided to support the communication between both systems during the phase of migration. The migration strategy is relatively simple: place an Exchange Server in an existing MS Mail network, establish a messaging path so that users on both systems can send each other messages, and then move your users leisurely to the new platform postoffice by postoffice. If you look at the tremendous success of Exchange Server, you must say that this strategy has worked. However, Lotus cc:Mail administrators who wanted to migrate their systems gently to Exchange Server were ignored.

Today, Exchange Server 5.x is available and the good news is that it provides a Connector for Lotus cc:Mail. This connector allows you to integrate Exchange Server into an existing Lotus cc:Mail network so that it acts as a virtual cc:Mail post office.

Lesson 1 of this chapter covers the Connector for Lotus cc:Mail in detail. It provides an overview about its architecture, components, administration, and Microsoft Windows NT Registry keys. You will learn about critical configuration aspects in addition to other important topics.

Lesson 2 illustrates the message flow between Exchange Server and Lotus cc:Mail. You can read about message conversion phases and interprocess communications within the connector as messages travel from Exchange to Lotus cc:Mail and vice versa.

In the following lessons, you will be introduced to:

- Lotus cc:Mail features that are relevant to the connector
- The architecture of the Connector for Lotus cc:Mail
- Lotus cc:Mail utilities used by the Connector for Lotus cc:Mail
- The customization of Lotus cc:Mail addresses
- The configuration of the Connector for Lotus cc:Mail in the Exchange Administrator program
- The message flow between an Exchange Server and a Lotus cc:Mail post office

Lesson 1: The Connector for Lotus cc:Mail

When it comes out of the box, the Connector for Lotus cc:Mail is an incomplete messaging connector. In fact, you will not be able to use it without installing additional components. The missing pieces are identified in this lesson, but here's one hint right now—Microsoft does not provide the remaining essential components.

This lesson deals with the internal components of the Connector for Lotus cc:Mail, covering its components, installation, and configuration aspects. You can read about special configuration issues regarding the missing parts and learn about the extensions of the Administrator program and the adjustment of the proxy address generation. The end of this lesson describes Directory Synchronization, as well as the configuration of the Lotus cc:Mail post office and advanced connector maintenance tasks.

At the end of this lesson, you will be able to:

- Describe the features of the Connector for Lotus cc:Mail
- Identify its components and architecture
- List issues regarding Lotus cc:Mail utilities
- Adjust the proxy e-mail addresses for Exchange Server recipients
- Configure the Connector for Lotus cc:Mail

Estimated time to complete this lesson: 45 minutes

Introduction to the Connector for Lotus cc:Mail

The Connector for Lotus cc:Mail is an optional Exchange Server component that can be controlled through its own Windows NT service. It has been developed based on the EDK and allows you to connect an Exchange Server to exactly one Lotus cc:Mail post office. Within the Lotus cc:Mail network, e-mail messages can be routed to other post offices further downstream. This connector supports the transfer of e-mail messages as well as Directory Synchronization.

Administrator Programs

If you want to connect two independent messaging systems, you must configure both of them. In order to do this, you must have some knowledge about available administrator utilities. On one hand, you will use the Exchange Administrator program to configure the Connector for Lotus cc:Mail component. On the other hand, you must manage the Lotus cc:Mail post office using the Lotus cc:Mail Administrator program. Lotus cc:Mail post office release 8 includes a Windows-based Administrator utility, while older versions provide only an MS-DOS program (Admin.exe). You will use the Lotus cc:Mail Administrator program primarily to register the Exchange Server as a remote post office. Connector-relevant Lotus cc:Mail administration tasks are covered under "Lotus cc:Mail and Connector Interfaces," later in this lesson.

Connector Installation

The Connector for Lotus cc:Mail can be installed during Exchange Server setup if you select the **Custom/Complete** option. However, the connector is available only in the Enterprise Edition. If you want to add this connector to an existing server, you can install this component by launching the Setup program in maintenance mode. You need to provide the Site Services Account password during installation, as it is required to initialize properly the connector's Windows NT service. The Exchange Server Setup program is covered in Chapter 2.

Multiple Connector Instances

It is not possible to install more than one Connector for Lotus cc:Mail on one Exchange Server. It is also impossible to connect to more than one Lotus cc:Mail post office using one connector instance. (See Figure 19-1.) However, you can install several instances of this connecting component on several Exchange Server computers in your organization. This way, you can provide load balancing between large Exchange and Lotus cc:Mail networks.

Note When connecting a single site to multiple Lotus cc:Mail post offices using multiple connector instances, you must ensure that none of the post offices reside in the same Lotus cc:Mail network. This would lead to routing problems, because a single Exchange Server site will always act as one huge Lotus cc:Mail post office, which can be connected to a particular Lotus cc:Mail network only once.

Message Conversion

The Connector for Lotus cc:Mail is a regular messaging gateway. Therefore, the connector must convert outbound messages destined for a Lotus cc:Mail post office into the Lotus cc:Mail format. Conversely, the connector must convert content and recipient information into the Exchange Server format for inbound messages as well.

Most message attributes are mapped between both systems. The connector can convert e-mail addresses, message submission time, sender and recipient display names, subject lines, message bodies, and any attachments plus their file names. The connector supports special message flags such as *Read Receipt Requested*, and *Last Modified*. In other words, the connector supports Return Receipts in addition to NDRs. However, some special properties are not supported, such as shortcuts to Exchange public folders.

Lotus cc:Mail Import/Export

The Connector for Lotus cc:Mail relies on two Lotus cc:Mail tools: the Import and Export programs. The Import program places converted outbound messages and address information into a Lotus cc:Mail post office. The Export program is responsible for extracting messages and address information from Lotus cc:Mail. Both utilities require a LAN connection to access the post office successfully. Consequently, the Connector for Lotus cc:Mail is supported only in LAN-like environments.

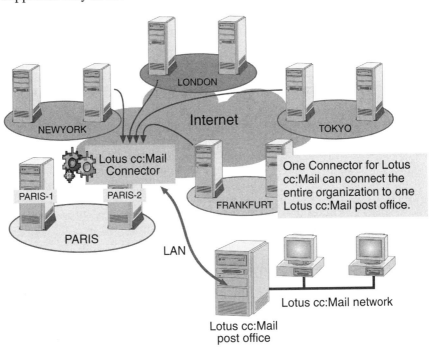

Figure 19-1. Connecting the organization to Lotus cc:Mail.

Note Microsoft does not provide the Import/Export programs, which are required to access a Lotus cc:Mail post office. These programs are included in the Lotus cc:Mail package.

The support for each Post Office Database version is as follows:

- Post Office Database version 6; use cc:Mail Import version 5.15 and Export version 5.14

- Post Office Database version 8; use cc:Mail Import and Export version 6.0

Components of the Connector for Lotus cc:Mail

The Connector for Lotus cc:Mail is less complex than the MS Mail Connector, but it's more complicated than the IMS, even though the IMS provides more configuration options. Like the IMS, the Connector for Lotus cc:Mail maintains message queues at the IS. It is designed as a separate Windows NT service and uses a temporary repository for converted messages, known as the *Connector Store*. The Lotus cc:Mail Import and Export programs, nonetheless, must also be listed as connector components. As mentioned, they are not provided by Microsoft and operate independently of the connector service, which increases the connector's complexity. Several Exchange Administrator program extensions are installed to support the management of this connector.

Connector for Lotus cc:Mail Service

The Connector for Lotus cc:Mail service communicates with the IS to transfer messages from and to Exchange Server. The connector converts inbound and outbound messages as appropriate using the Connector Store as temporary storage for both: while the connector reads inbound mail from the Connector Store it also writes outbound messages into the Connector Store. It also launches the Import and Export programs to place and retrieve messages to and from the connected Lotus cc:Mail post office. (See Figure 19-2.)

Like every EDK gateway, the Connector for Lotus cc:Mail maintains two important gateway folders at the Exchange Server, which are labeled MTS-OUT for outbound messages and MTS-IN for inbound messages. These message queues are not polled. The IS notifies the Connector for Lotus cc:Mail if messages have been placed in the MTS-OUT folder. Conversely, the Connector for Lotus cc:Mail service initiates the communication with the IS if inbound messages are placed in the MTS-IN queue.

Connector Store

The Connector Store is the intermediate storage location for Lotus cc:Mail messages. The Import program reads the messages from this location to write them into the Lotus cc:Mail post office. The Export program, on the other hand, places messages into this repository once they have been extracted from Lotus cc:Mail.

Messages temporarily stored in the Connector Store are also called *scratch files*. Scratch files are plain text files that are structured as required by the Import and Export programs. Take care when setting user access to the Connector Store—every user who can open the \Exchsrvr\Ccmcdata directory potentially can read Lotus cc:Mail messages. It is therefore in your best interest to remove the Windows NT Everyone group from the list of accounts with permissions to the \Ccmcdata directory. Fortunately, the \Ccmcdata directory is not shared for network access, by default.

The following subdirectories temporarily contain messages:

- \Bad; stores messages that could not be converted properly

- \Export and \Export.bak; maintain inbound messages destined for Exchange Server

- \Import and \Import.bak; maintain outbound messages destined for Lotus cc:Mail

- \Submit; temporarily stores outbound messages to Lotus cc:Mail during message conversion

Import and Export of Messages

The Import program checks for scratch files in the \Exchsrvr\Ccmcdata\Import directory, while the Export utility writes scratch files into \Exchsrvr\Ccmcdata\Export. The task of the Connector for Lotus cc:Mail service is to convert outbound messages into scratch files before they are placed in the Connector Store. Likewise, this service must convert scratch files found in the \Export directory into the Exchange Server format before they can be placed in the MTS-IN gateway folder. (See Figure 19-2.)

Note The Connector for Lotus cc:Mail launches the Export program periodically to poll the Lotus cc:Mail post office. A post office is a passive file structure, which means it requires frequent polling for new messages.

Exchange Administrator Program Extensions

The Administrator program is the central management tool for Exchange Server administration; it is extended to support the configuration of the Connector for Lotus cc:Mail. A corresponding directory object is placed in the **Connections** container for each installed Lotus cc:Mail Connector.

Address generator files and address details templates are also installed. The Lotus cc:Mail proxy address generator (Ccmproxy.dll), for instance, can be found in the \Exchsrvr\Address directory and is responsible for the proxy CCMAIL address generation. If the address generator is installed, each Exchange user receives a CCMAIL address, which can be examined and adjusted through the **E-Mail Addresses** property page of the corresponding recipient object. You can also adjust the e-mail address generation format using the **Site Addressing** property page of the **Site Addressing** object, which can be found in the **Configuration** container. You can read more about Lotus cc:Mail proxy addresses under "Lotus cc:Mail Custom Addressing," later in this lesson.

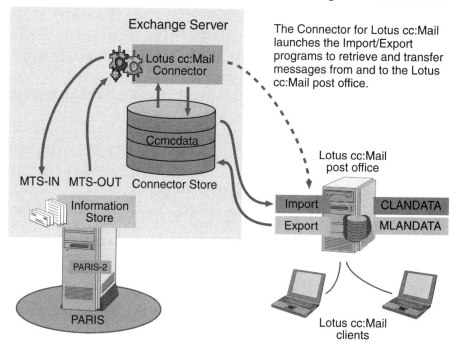

Figure 19-2. Necessary components of the Connector for Lotus cc:Mail.

The Connector for Lotus cc:Mail components are as follows:

- Address Templates
- Connector Store
- MTS-IN and MTS-OUT folders in the IS
- Proxy Address Generator
- Windows NT service executable (Ccmc.exe)
- Import and Export programs that come with Lotus cc:Mail (not installed, but very important)

Lotus cc:Mail Considerations

Lotus cc:Mail provides the utilities for writing information to a Lotus cc:Mail post office (Import.exe) and for retrieving information from the post office (Export.exe). As mentioned earlier, the Connector for Lotus cc:Mail relies on these programs to perform message transfer and Directory Synchronization.

Launching Import and Export

The Connector for Lotus cc:Mail uses the interprocess communication mechanisms of Windows NT to start the Import and Export utilities as appropriate. Both programs are executed in the background. Supplied command line parameters indicate whether to transfer messages or to address information. For example, the /DIRECTORY/L/R/A/P /FORMAT/NOFAN /BATCH command line parameter can be used to initiate a Directory Synchronization export cycle from Lotus cc:Mail to Exchange.

The Import and Export programs and their Ie.ri file must be copied to the Exchange Server computer and they must be located in a directory that is included in the Windows NT system search path, such as the \Winnt\System32 directory. (See Figure 19-3.)

Note The Connector for Lotus cc:Mail will report an error in the Application Event Log if the Import and Export programs cannot be launched. After a number of unsuccessful tries to start the programs, the service terminates automatically.

CLANDATA and MLANDATA

CLANDATA and MLANDATA are the two main files of a Lotus cc:Mail post office, which are accessed through Import and Export. CLANDATA contains most of the configuration information and the message headers. In other words, it contains all data except the message contents and attachments. Contents and attachments are kept in the MLANDATA file.

Recent versions of Lotus cc:Mail, such as Lotus cc:Mail 8, no longer show a direct CLANDATA or MLANDATA implementation. These files have been split into smaller files to avoid corruption problems of large post office files. The post office directory itself (\Ccdata), however, is still the same as in earlier versions.

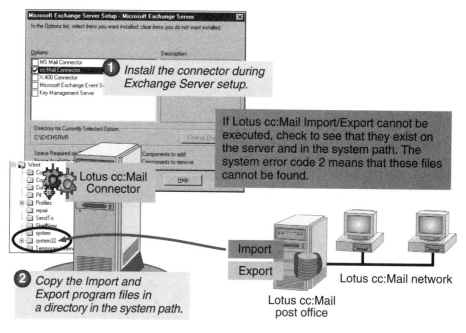

Figure 19-3. Completing the installation of the Connector for Lotus cc:Mail.

Important Lotus cc:Mail programs are as follows:

- Export program; to extract information, such as addresses or mail messages, from a Lotus cc:Mail post office

- Import program; to insert information, such as addresses or mail messages, into a Lotus cc:Mail post office

Lotus cc:Mail Custom Addressing

Lotus cc:Mail uses the address format *<user> at <post office>* (note that *at* is not a synonym for the @ sign, and *<user> @ <post office>* would form an invalid address). In contrast, Exchange Server uses DNs to reference mailboxes.

Let's say you have configured a Connector for Lotus cc:Mail, in which case the address details templates have been installed to allow Exchange users the ease of addressing e-mail messages to Lotus cc:Mail recipients. The corresponding proxy address type CCMAIL identifies addresses of Lotus Notes users. The Exchange Server can handle these addresses correctly.

However, Lotus cc:Mail users cannot simply specify an Exchange address that will reach an Exchange recipient. Rather, Lotus cc:Mail users must handle the entire site as a huge remote Lotus cc:Mail post office. Therefore, it is necessary to assign each Exchange user an appropriate address of the CCMAIL type as well. Lotus cc:Mail users can then use these proxy CCMAIL addresses to reach Exchange users.

Proxy Address Generation

The Exchange Administrator program generates the proxy CCMAIL addresses for each mailbox automatically, using the proxy address generator Ccmproxy.dll to accomplish this task. The default format is *<Last, First> at <site>*, but this format can be modified using the **Site Addressing** property page of the **Site Addressing** object within the **Configuration** container. For example, the proxy CCMAIL address of Jacques Blanc in PARIS would be *Blanc, Jacques at PARIS*.

Custom Address Switches

Using the **Site Addressing** property page, you can change the default format for proxy CCMAIL addresses by clicking the **Edit** button. This displays the **CCMAIL Properties** dialog box, where you can adjust the address generation according to your needs.

Custom address switches allow you to specify exactly how to construct the addresses. For instance, the *%d* switch refers to the display name of a user. If you set *%d at PARIS*, Jacques Blanc will receive the proxy CCMAIL address *Jacques Blanc at PARIS*. (See Figure 19-4.)

It is important to place the custom address switches before the *at* of the CCMAIL address. It is also important to leave a space before and after *at* in order to generate valid proxy addresses. The Exchange Administrator program will warn you if you try to create an invalid addressing scheme before it returns to the **CCMAIL Properties** dialog box. The configuration of the **Site Addressing** object is covered in detail in Chapter 8.

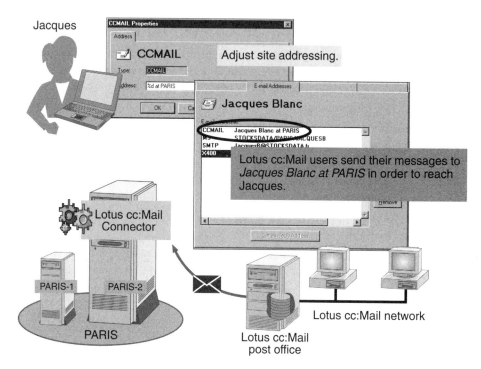

Figure 19-4. Creating custom proxy CCMAIL addresses.

Custom address switches and their related mailbox attributes are as follows:

Custom address switches	Mailbox attributes
%g	First Name
%i	Middle Initials
%s	Last Name
%d	Display Name
%m	Alias

Lotus cc:Mail and Connector Interfaces

The Connector for Lotus cc:Mail is a translator, but the communication partners must first be aware of each other before they begin to "talk." If nobody talks, nothing can be translated, so you must manage both the Lotus cc:Mail post office and the Exchange Server to enable the communication.

Configuring the Lotus cc:Mail Post Office

You can use the Lotus cc:Mail Administrator program to create a reference for your site at the Lotus cc:Mail post office. Multiple references must be created if your organization consists of multiple sites. The following error message is written to the Application Event Log if the Lotus cc:Mail post office has not been configured properly: *Lotus cc:Mail EXPORT to file msg171.ccm returned result code 3. The Microsoft Exchange Connector for Lotus cc:Mail has not been configured correctly or the Post Office it is configured to connect to is not accessible at this time.*

Note Each site within an organization must be referenced through a remote post office entry in the Lotus cc:Mail post office. The site name and the corresponding remote post office name must be the same.

Configuring the Connector for Lotus cc:Mail

Using the Exchange Administrator program, you can complete the configuration through the **Connector for cc:Mail** object that resides in the **Connections** container. A total of nine important property pages allow you to define the remote post office, specify the Import/Export versions in use, and configure Directory Synchronization. Directory Synchronization between Exchange Server and Lotus cc:Mail is covered under "Lotus cc:Mail Directory Synchronization," later in this lesson.

Referencing the Lotus cc:Mail Post Office

The Lotus cc:Mail post office can be specified using the **Post Office** property page of the connector object. Important parameters are the post office name, the post office password, and the network path to the post office. The network path must be specified in Universal Naming Convention (UNC) form (for example, \\NEWYORK-1\Ccdata). The Administrator program will display an error notification if no post office can be found at the specified location.

The Import and Export programs use the post office name and password to access the Lotus cc:Mail post office. Because they operate in the context of the Site Services Account, it is important to ensure that this account has full access rights at the network share of the post office. If this is not the case, the well-known "result code 3," as mentioned above, is issued.

Import/Export Versions

If you examine the **Post Office** property page further, you'll find the **Import/Export Version** option, which must be specified correctly in order to configure a functioning connector.

This option is very confusing and leads often to configuration problems, so let's test it in order to make it clearer. Which version do you select if you want to connect to a Lotus cc:Mail post office release 6.0, **Import 5.15/Export 5.14** or **Import 6.0/Export 6.0**? Don't select **Import 6.0/Export 6.0**, because your connector will not function properly! **Import 5.15/Export 5.14** is the right answer, even though intuitively it seems that you would choose the version 6.0 option to correspond with version 6.0 of the post office. **Import 6.0/Export 6.0** is, in fact, the correct option for Lotus cc:Mail post office release 8. Lotus provides several patches for the Import and Export programs, but be extremely careful with them because you might destroy the post office if you use the wrong program version.

Preserving the Forwarding History

Not all properties of a message can be mapped between the Exchange Server and the Lotus cc:Mail format. The forwarding history of a Lotus cc:Mail message is the type of property that is usually lost. However, you can select the **Preserve Forwarding History On Messages Sent From cc:Mail To Microsoft Exchange** check box on the **Post Office** property page to generate a Forward.txt attachment for all inbound messages from Lotus cc:Mail. This file is attached to the converted Exchange message and contains the desired forwarding information.

Message Tracking

As for every connector, you can enable message tracking to maintain status information about messages that leave and enter your organization through the Connector for Lotus cc:Mail. The corresponding **Enable Message Tracking** option can be found on the **Post Office** property page. The message tracking feature of the Exchange Administrator program is covered in Chapter 15.

Assigning CCMAIL Address Spaces

As for every connector, you must assign address spaces to the Connector for Lotus cc:Mail using the **Address Space** property page. But you won't find a CCMAIL address space button, so use the **Other** button instead in order to specify a CCMAIL address space. Enter *CCMAIL* in the **Type** box, and then enter the corresponding address space, such as the name of the Lotus cc:Mail post office, in the **Address** field. An asterisk will cause the MTA to route all messages destined for Lotus cc:Mail users to the connector. More information about message routing is provided in Chapter 9.

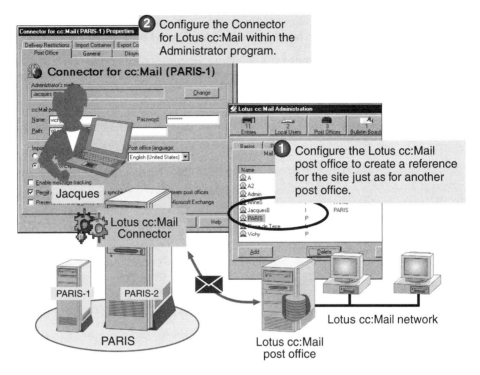

Figure 19-5. Connector for Lotus cc:Mail configuration.

The Connector for Lotus cc:Mail property pages and their functions are as follows:

- **Post Office**; to set information about the Lotus cc:Mail post office, Import/Export version, and the administrator mailbox

- **General**; to enter an administrative note and to set the maximum message size for the connector

- **DirSync Schedule**; to select the Directory Synchronization activation time

- **Address Space**; to define address spaces for routing decisions of the MTA

- **Delivery Restrictions**; to specify which users can send messages through this connector

- **Import Container**; to specify the recipients container to hold the Lotus cc:Mail recipient objects, to specify import filters, and to run a Directory Synchronization cycle manually

- **Export Container**; to set recipients that will be exported to the Lotus cc:Mail post office, and to set their trust level

- **Queues**; to display the contents of the message queues on the server (*MTS-IN* and *MTS-OUT* folders)

- **Diagnostics Logging**; to set the levels of event logging for connector service categories

Advanced Maintenance for the Connector for Lotus cc:Mail

It is recommended that you inspect the Connector for Lotus cc:Mail carefully once it has been configured and launched. The Import/Export versions must be specified correctly and their MS-DOS executables must be located in the Windows NT system search path. The Connector for Lotus cc:Mail reports delivery problems and critical errors through the Application Event Log if the configuration of the Lotus cc:Mail post office does not match the Exchange Server settings.

Windows NT Event Logs

Using the **Diagnostics Logging** property page of the Connector for Lotus cc:Mail object, you can increase and decrease the level of event logging for the categories **General, Outbound, Inbound, NDR, Dir Synch**, and **MAPI**. You can specify a level of **Minimum, Medium**, or **Maximum** logging as appropriate. You can even set the **Diagnostics Logging** for all categories to **None** to trace only critical events. In any case, you can use the Event Viewer to examine the status information of the connector with respect to error notifications. A report of an undeliverable message, for instance, would look like this: *Lotus cc:Mail IMPORT from file *.ccm returned result code 5. Undeliverable message or updates.* Keep in mind that a non-deliverable message does not necessarily indicate a connector problem, because users can specify invalid recipient information.

Generating NDRs

The generation of NDRs is a complex process because both the Lotus cc:Mail Import program and the Exchange connector service are involved in the message transfer. As soon as a message has been converted into a scratch file and placed in the Connector Store, the job of the connector service is basically done. However, the message has not been delivered yet—the Import program still must complete its task.

Let's say that the recipient of a Lotus cc:Mail message is unknown, so an NDR must be generated and sent back to the originator on the Exchange Server. Import cannot generate such an NDR because it is not aware of the Exchange Server system. Instead, it places the undeliverable message as a .UND file (for example, *Ndr904.und*) in the Import directory of the Connector Store. The Connector for Lotus cc:Mail polls this directory, and if it finds any .UND files it generates the non-delivery notifications using the information it can extract from the .UND file. (See Figure 19-6.)

Windows NT Registry Settings

Several connector settings can be specified using the Windows NT Registry Editor. These settings allow you to inspect the operation of the connector in more detail. The important parameters are stored under:

```
HKEY_LOCAL_MACHINE
    \SYSTEM
        \CurrentControlSet
            \Services
                \MSExchangeCCMC
                    \Parameters
```

Modifying Registry Settings

Let's say you want to decrease the limit of unsuccessful attempts to start the Import/Export utilities. By default, the connector service shuts down automatically when it exceeds the limit of 25 attempts (which is 0x19 hexadecimal). This is a valuable feature since it can prevent possible damage and unnecessary resource consumption. Furthermore, a stopped service is easy to find if you are running a Server Monitor. Server Monitors are discussed in Chapter 15.

Using the Registry Editor, set the **Use Registry Settings** value to one (1) to activate the Registry parameters. Then adjust the **Maximum Number Of Exceptions Before Shutdown** value as appropriate. Restart the Connector for Lotus cc:Mail service for the changes to take effect.

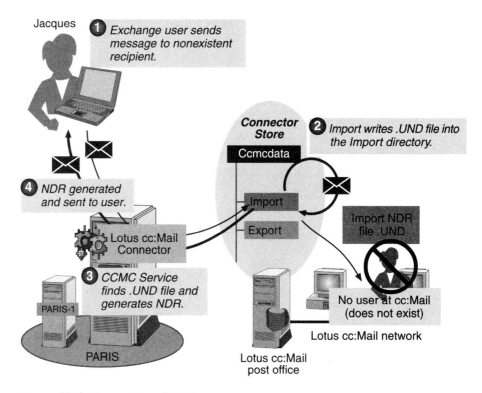

Figure 19-6. Generation of NDRs.

The important Connector for Lotus cc:Mail Registry parameters and their default values are as follows:

Registry parameter	Default value
Always delete Import/Export output	0x1
cc:Mail to Exchange queue size	0x40
CommonName	cc:Mail Connector (<server name>)
Connector Store Path	C:\exchsrvr\CCMCData (the Performance Optimizer might have changed this setting)
Dir Sync alias name rule	%F%1L
Dir Sync display name rule	%F %L
Dir Sync export BB command line	/BBOARD /LIST /BATCH

Registry parameter	Default value
Dir Synch export command line FORMAT/NOFAN /BATCH	/DIRECTORY/L/R/A/P /
Dir Synch export ML command line	/LIST /BATCH
Dir Synch import command line	/DIRECTORY/PROP /BATCH
Exchange to cc:Mail queue size	0x40
Export command line	/ITEMSIZE /FORMAT/FAN / BATCH /FILES/MACBIN2
Export.exe	Export.exe
Import command line	/ITEMSIZE /PARTIAL / BATCH /FILES/MACBIN2
Import.exe	Import.exe
Maximum number of exceptions before shutdown	0x19
Maximum number of messages to Export	0x10
Maximum number of messages to Import	0x5
Mutually Exclude Import and Export	0x1
Outbound Conversion threads	0x2
Save a copy of the exported files	0
Save a copy of the imported files	0
Seconds to wait before Export	0xf
Seconds to wait before Import	0xf
Use Registry settings	0

Lotus cc:Mail Directory Synchronization

Unlike MS Mail Directory Synchronization, Lotus cc:Mail Directory Synchronization does not implement a complex protocol and is therefore easy to configure. On the other hand, Lotus cc:Mail Directory Synchronization always exchanges full address information, which is a disadvantage because redundant information is transferred. As expected, Directory Synchronization must be configured at the Lotus cc:Mail post office and at the Exchange Server.

Configurating the Lotus cc:Mail Post Office

Using the Lotus cc:Mail Administrator program, you must enable the **Directory Propagation** and **Automatic Directory Exchange** (ADE) options at the Lotus cc:Mail post office. Otherwise, you will find one of the following error notifications in the Application Event Log when you activate Directory Synchronization:

Lotus cc:Mail IMPORT from file CCMDEL.IMP returned result code 3. The Microsoft Exchange Connector for Lotus cc:Mail has not been configured correctly or the Post Office it is configured to connect to is not accessible at this time.

or

Lotus cc:Mail IMPORT from file CCMDEL.IMP returned result code 3. The Exchange Connector for Lotus cc:Mail has not been configured correctly or the Post Office it is configured to connect to is not accessible at this time. ADE is not installed; run ADMIN with /DIRPROP/Y.

Configuring the Connector for Lotus cc:Mail

Once ADE has been enabled at the Lotus cc:Mail post office, you can configure Directory Synchronization using the Exchange Administrator program. The Connector for Lotus cc:Mail provides several property pages for this purpose: **General**, **Dirsync Schedule**, **Import Container**, and **Export Container**.

Specifying Imported Addresses

As mentioned earlier, Directory Synchronization with Lotus cc:Mail is a full synchronization of full address information. But you can select which addresses to accept. Generally, three options are at your disposal: **Import All Directory Entries**, **Only Import Directory Entries Of These Formats**, and **Do Not Import Directory Entries Of These Formats**. The default **Import All Directory Entries** option causes the connector to import all addresses in the specified Import container. The remaining two options allow you to restrict the address information. In this case, you can define corresponding import filters using the **New** button. For example, you can specify "* *at Vichy*" under **Directory Entry Format** in the **Import Filter** dialog box to import only the addresses of a post office named *Vichy*.

Specifying Exported Addresses

As Exchange Server organizes recipient addresses into **Recipients** containers, you can specify the appropriate containers that will be exported to the Lotus cc:Mail post office using the **Export Container** property page. More than one container can be selected. Furthermore, you can associate a trust level with the Connector for Lotus cc:Mail. Only those recipients that have a trust level less or equal to the specified value will be synchronized. You can also elect to export custom recipients through the **Export Custom Recipients** check box.

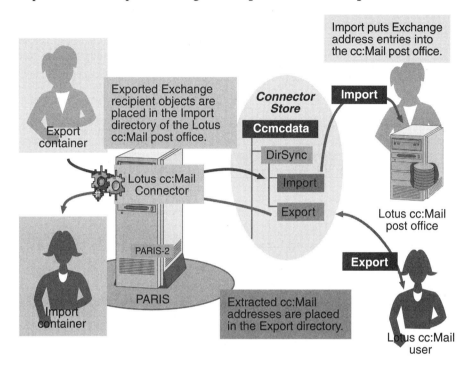

Figure 19-7. Lotus cc:Mail Directory Synchronization.

Important Directory Synchronization property pages and their functions are as follows:

- **Dirsync Schedule**; to specify times for Directory Synchronization activation

- **Export Containers**; to specify which recipient objects to export to the Lotus cc:Mail post office based on recipient containers and trust levels

- **Post Office**; to allow Exchange address information to propagate to downstream Lotus cc:Mail post offices

- **Import Container**; to specify the Import container, set Import filters, and to run Directory Synchronization manually

Lesson 2: Lotus cc:Mail Message Flow

It's easy to configure and run the Connector for Lotus cc:Mail, but it requires instinct and empathy to troubleshoot its components in a critical situation. Just imagine that you call either Microsoft or IBM (Lotus) for support and a support engineer explains that your problem is not their fault. So you call the other company, where another engineer explains the same. Whom will you call now?

This lesson explains in depth the flow of messages from Exchange Server to Lotus cc:Mail and vice versa. When you are equipped with this sort of detailed knowledge about the various processes, you can determine the root of a communication problem when you need support.

At the end of this lesson, you will be able to:

- Describe the flow of messages to the Lotus cc:Mail post office
- Describe the flow of messages to the Exchange Server

Estimated time to complete this lesson: 25 minutes

Exchange to Lotus cc:Mail Message Flow

As shown in Figure 19-8, Jacques sends a message to one or more Lotus cc:Mail recipients. This message is passed, as usual, from his messaging client to the IS on his Exchange Server. Because CCMAIL recipients have been specified, the IS is not responsible for the message delivery, so it must transfer the message to the MTA for further routing. The MTA communicates with the local DS to obtain information about those recipient addresses that are referenced through custom recipient objects. In contrast, communication with the DS is not required if Jacques has typed the CCMAIL addresses directly in the **To** line of his message, thereby creating one-off addresses. In any case, the MTA checks the GWART to find an appropriate address space that has been assigned to one or more messaging connectors.

Because Jacques has specified a CCMAIL recipient and because the CCMAIL address type has been associated with a Connector for Lotus cc:Mail, the MTA transfers the message back to the IS to place it in the outbound message queue (MTS-OUT) of the Lotus cc:Mail Connector. The IS service notifies the corresponding connector service immediately about the message that is now awaiting delivery in the MTS-OUT gateway folder. It is the connector's responsibility to gather the message from the IS. Exchange Server message flow is explained in Chapter 3.

Once the Connector for Lotus cc:Mail has received the outbound message, it contacts the DS to check and replace the address information with proxy CCMAIL addresses. For example, the DN of the sender Jacques is substituted by his proxy address *Jacques Blanc at PARIS*. Furthermore, the message contents and attachments must be converted to plain text. A temporary scratch file, created in the \Submit subdirectory of the Connector Store, is used to store the converted information at this stage. You can identify this file by its .TMP file extension. Later, this extension changes into .CCM to indicate that the connector has completed the conversion. If further outbound messages are still waiting for delivery, they are retrieved and converted to scratch files as well.

Once the conversion cycle has been completed, the messages can be moved to the \Import subdirectory of the Connector Store. The Connector for Lotus cc:Mail service then uses the interprocess communication mechanisms of Windows NT to launch the Lotus cc:Mail Import program. Messages are specified as command line parameters. As soon as Import completes success-fully, the specified messages have been delivered to the Lotus cc:Mail post office. It is up to Lotus cc:Mail to route the messages further to the actual recipients. (See Figure 19-8.)

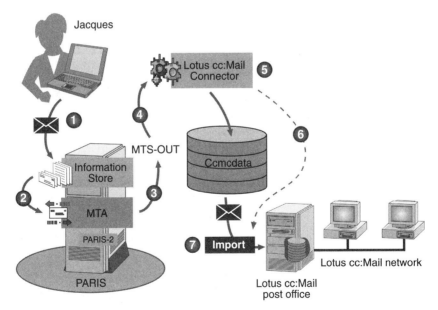

1) User sends mail to Lotus cc:Mail recipient. 2) IS transfers message to MTA. 3) MTA places mail in MTS-OUT. 4) IS notifies Connector. 5) Connector substitutes e-mail addresses and converts message to scratch file. The scratch file is placed in the Connector Store. 6) Connector launches Import. 7) Import writes message to Lotus cc:Mail post office.

Figure 19-8. Sending messages to Lotus cc:Mail users.

The message flow from Exchange Server to Lotus cc:Mail is as follows:

1. The user sends a message to a Lotus cc:Mail recipient and the client transfers the message to the IS.

2. The IS checks whether it is responsible for message delivery and, since it is not, transfers the message to the MTA.

3. The MTA performs routing based on the Lotus cc:Mail address and the GWART. The MTA locates the Connector for Lotus cc:Mail and places the message in the connector's MTS-OUT folder.

4. The MTS-OUT folder is maintained by the IS, so the IS notifies the connector immediately about the new message.

5. The Connector for Lotus cc:Mail receives the message and replaces addresses with a corresponding proxy CCMAIL address if required. The connector converts the interpersonal message and its attachments into plain text and places the scratch file in the Connector Store.

6. The connector launches the Lotus cc:Mail Import program using Windows NT interprocess communication mechanisms.

7. The Import program receives the scratch file from the Connector Store and writes it into the Lotus cc:Mail post office. It then deletes the scratch file. Lotus cc:Mail routes the message to the recipient.

Lotus cc:Mail to Exchange Message Flow

Let's say that a Lotus cc:Mail user wants to reply to Jacques' original message. This user specifies Jacques' proxy CCMAIL address accordingly. The Lotus cc:Mail post office maintains a reference to Jacques' site in the form of a remote post office. Thus, the message can be routed to the correct outgoing queue. It will remain in this queue until the Export program polls the post office. (See Figure 19-9.)

The Export program is launched frequently to poll the post office and the new message is discovered. Export retrieves all waiting messages and places them as a single scratch file in the Connector Store. If multiple messages are awaiting delivery, they are written together into one scratch file.

The Connector for Lotus cc:Mail, again, polls the Connector Store frequently and opens the new scratch file from the \Export directory to convert its contents to interpersonal messages. Once messages have been converted into the Exchange Server format, they can be placed in the incoming message queue (MTS-IN). The connector service must communicate with the IS to accomplish the message transfer.

The IS notifies the MTA about the new messages. At this point, the MTA can gather the messages from the inbound gateway folder (MTS-IN). The MTA contacts the DS to check the recipient addresses for routing decisions based on GWART entries. During this process, the MTA substitutes the CCMAIL addresses with corresponding DNs for all recipients that can be found in the Directory.

Messages destined for users on other servers are routed further while the local IS receives messages for all recipients for whom it is responsible. The local IS must deliver the message to the appropriate mailbox. The IS then notifies the clients that new mail has arrived. If a client is currently disconnected, the notification is postponed until the user (such as Jacques) logs on again.

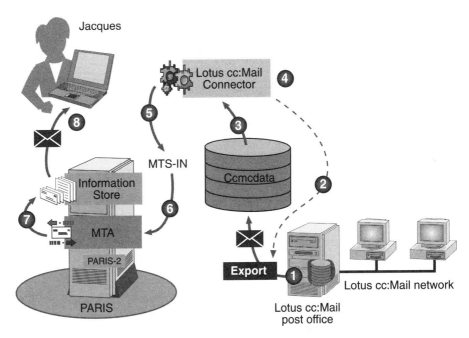

1) Message waits in post office. 2) Connector launches Export regularly. 3) Export writes scratch file into Connector Store. 4) Connector receives scratch file and converts it to an interpersonal message. 5) Connector writes the interpersonal message to MTS-IN. 6) MTA receives the interpersonal message and performs routing. 7) MTA transfers message to IS. 8) User receives mail from Lotus cc:Mail sender.

Figure 19-9. Sending messages to Exchange Server recipients.

Messages flow from Lotus cc:Mail to Exchange Server as follows:

1. A message addressed to one or more Exchange Server recipients waits for delivery in the Lotus cc:Mail post office.

2. The Connector for Lotus cc:Mail service launches the Export.exe program. Export extracts waiting messages from the Lotus cc:Mail post office and places them as a scratch file in the \Export subdirectory of the Connector Store.

3. The Lotus cc:Mail Connector service opens the scratch file and converts the text structures into one or more interpersonal messages as required.

4. The Connector for Lotus cc:Mail places the messages in the MTS-IN folder.

5. The MTA receives the messages and examines and replaces any Lotus cc:Mail address information with Exchange DNs.

6. The MTA performs the necessary message routing. If the MTA discovers that the recipient resides on the local server it puts the message back into the local IS. Otherwise the message is routed according to the rules of message routing in Exchange Server 5.5.

7. The IS places the message in the mailbox and then notifies the client about the arrival of new mail. If the client is currently off line, the notification is postponed until the client logs on again.

Review

1. How many Lotus cc:Mail post offices can a Connector for Lotus cc:Mail communicate with directly?

   _____

2. Which Import and Export program versions are supported by the Connector for Lotus cc:Mail and which post office version can be accessed through each of them?

   _____

   _____

   _____

   _____

3. What are the main components of the Connector for Lotus cc:Mail?

   _____

   _____

   _____

   _____

   _____

   _____

   _____

   _____

   _____

   _____

   _____

4. You have installed and configured the Connector for Lotus cc:Mail and now you want to start the Exchange Connector for Lotus cc:Mail server using the **Services** applet of the Control Panel. The service terminates after a short delay, reporting the error number 2 in the Application Event Log. What is the most likely source of the startup problem?

_____

_____

_____

_____

_____

_____

5. You need to adjust the proxy CCMAIL address format. The convention of your company forces you to use the given name immediately followed by the surname. Where and how can you adjust the proxy address format?

_____

_____

_____

_____

6. Which program is launched by the Connector for Lotus cc:Mail to write messages into the Lotus cc:Mail post office?

_____

7. Which program is used to poll the Lotus cc:Mail post office for Exchange Server–bound messages?

_____

C H A P T E R   2 0

The Connector for Lotus Notes

This chapter introduces the Connector for Lotus Notes, which—as its name implies—lets you connect Exchange Server to Lotus Notes networks. Besides regular e-mail transfer, the connector also supports Directory Synchronization between the systems.

Overview

Lotus Notes is a workgroup computing platform with features similar to those of Exchange Server. In fact, the systems are basically competitors. Either you use Lotus Notes or you use Exchange Server to enable your users to share information. This chapter does not compare the two. It simply explains how to connect the systems to provide users with a powerful Exchange Server–to–Lotus Notes messaging path.

Lesson 1 introduces the architecture and components of the Connector for Lotus Notes, including components that are not part of the connector itself.

Lesson 2 explains in more detail how the components interact to transfer messages and synchronize directory information. You'll learn about the six connector processes that are responsible for data conversion and message transfer, as well as the system folders and databases that serve as inbound and outbound message queues.

Lesson 3 explains how to install, configure, and test the connector.

In the following lessons, you will be introduced to:

- The Connector for Lotus Notes architecture
- The Lotus Notes programs used by the Connector for Lotus Notes
- Preparing the Lotus Notes server for the connection to an Exchange Server organization
- Configuring the Connector for Lotus Notes on the Exchange Server side
- Message flow between Exchange Server and Lotus Notes
- Directory Synchronization between Exchange Server and Lotus Notes

Lesson 1: Introduction to the Connector for Lotus Notes

The Connector for Lotus Notes is a gateway connector that comes with Exchange Server 5.5. The connector itself is not new, but it is new to the Exchange Server package. The connector was a third-party component from LinkAge Software Inc. of Toronto until Microsoft acquired LinkAge, whose products extend Exchange Server to support basically all important IBM and Lotus messaging systems.

This lesson outlines the basic features of the Connector for Lotus Notes as well as its dependencies. It lists its components and explains the conversion of message attributes between Lotus Notes and Exchange Server.

At the end of this lesson, you will be able to:

- Describe the features of the Connector for Lotus Notes

- Identify its main components

- Identify extensions of the Administrator program for the Lotus Notes Connector

Estimated time to complete this lesson: 15 minutes

Connector for Lotus Notes Considerations

The Connector for Lotus Notes is a true gateway connector, which means that it is designed explicitly to establish a messaging path to a foreign system, in this case Lotus Notes. The connector's main purpose is to map message attributes and address information between the two formats to establish a functioning message path. For instance, OLE objects embedded in Exchange messages will end up as Lotus Notes Doclinks. A complete listing of attribute mappings is provided below Figure 20-1.

One-to-One Relationship

Generally, you can use one or many Lotus Notes Connectors to connect your organization to a Lotus Notes network. As a matter of fact, each Exchange Server can run exactly one connector instance that directly services one Lotus Notes server. (See Figure 20-1.)

Note You cannot establish more than one messaging path from one site to a particular Notes server.

The Connector for Lotus Notes can also provide a messaging path from downstream sites to Lotus Notes domains. To accomplish this, you must install only the Address Generator DLL in the downstream sites so that Lotus Notes proxy e-mail addresses are generated for all users. You can also use the connector to reach downstream Lotus Notes domains. In this case, you need only identify downstream Notes domains in Exchange. You'll read more about configuring the Connector for Lotus Notes in Lesson 3.

Application Programming Interfaces

The Connector for Lotus Notes must be able to retrieve and convert messages from Exchange Server as well as from Lotus Notes. On the Exchange Server side, the connector relies on the EDK, much as the Connector for Lotus cc:Mail and the IMS do. On the Lotus Notes side, however, a direct server API cannot be used. Instead, the connector uses the Notes client API. The disadvantage of this approach is that the connector requires that a Lotus Notes client be installed on the Exchange Server that will run the connector. Lotus Notes version 4.0 clients as well as clients for Lotus Notes/Domino Server version 4.5 (or higher) are supported.

Note Before you install the Connector for Lotus Notes, you must configure the Lotus Notes client on the connector server.

Lotus Notes Preparations

Installation of a Lotus Notes client is not sufficient for successful operation of the connector because the connector cannot immediately access a Lotus Notes server. You must first configure a special Lotus Notes ID (also called *Connector ID*) that has permission to access Notes server databases. Lotus Notes maintains databases for all kinds of information, including the address book and repositories for e-mail messages.

To configure a Lotus Notes server for connector access, you must create the Connector ID and two additional databases. (See Figure 20-1.) The Exchange.box database is used to queue inbound messages to Exchange Server, while the Exchange.bad database stores messages that cannot be delivered (corrupt messages).

Note The Connector for Lotus Notes provides a configuration utility for creating the Exchange.box and Exchange.bad databases and assigning permissions to the Connector ID.

Directory Synchronization

The Connector for Lotus Notes also supports the synchronization of address book information between Exchange Server and Lotus Notes. Relevant information is obtained from the Exchange Server side using export recipients containers. You can also specify Source Name and Address Books that you want to retrieve from the Lotus Notes server.

To maintain inbound information, you must specify an import recipients container in Exchange that will hold the references to Lotus Notes users in the form of custom recipients. Lotus Notes servers maintain addresses for Exchange users in a Name and Address Book such as the Public Address Book (Names.nsf).

Note Exchange Server maintains Lotus Notes address information in the form of custom recipients with an underlying address of the type Notes. Lotus Notes receives Exchange address information in the form of Lotus Notes proxy addresses.

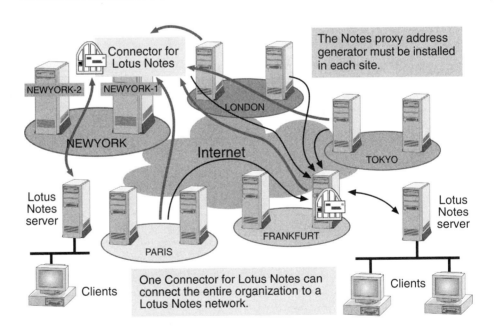

Figure 20-1. Connecting Exchange Server to Lotus Notes.

These are the characteristics of message conversion from Exchange Server to Lotus Notes:

Object in Exchange message	Object in Lotus Notes message
Regular Attachment, position identified by icon	An icon positioned as in an Exchange message.
OLE Lotus Notes Links	Translated back to Lotus Notes Doclinks if the connector has Reader access to the document associated with the Doclink.
Exchange embedded messages	Converted to regular attachment in rich text format, identified by an icon. Embedded messages in embedded messages (multi-layered messages) are not supported.
Exchange message links	Converted to OLE attachments and identified by an icon.
OLE object	OLE attachment identified by an icon, as in the original message.

These are the characteristics of message conversion from Lotus Notes to Exchange Server:

Object in Lotus Notes message	Object in Exchange message
Regular Attachment, position identified by icon	An icon positioned as in an Exchange message.
Lotus Notes Doclinks	Depending on connector configuration: • Converted to Rich Text Format attachment, identified by an icon. • Converted to OLE Lotus Notes link. The recipient must have Reader permission to the associated document.
OLE object with icon	An OLE object identified by icon, as in the original message.

Components of the Connector for Lotus Notes

The components of the Connector for Lotus Notes fall into two groups. The first group is administrative utilities and Administrator program extensions, and the second group is the components actually involved in information handling.

Administrative Utilities

One of the important administrative tools is the Connectivity Administrator. It lets you monitor the Notes connector services and provides features for tracing connector activities. You can install and configure this utility on any Windows NT Server or Workstation for remote administration.

Other members of the administrative utilities group extend the Exchange Administrator program. The connector configuration object (such as **Connector For Lotus Notes (NEWYORK-1)**) is one example. It is under the **Connections** container after the connector is installed. Another extension is the proxy address generator for Lotus Notes addresses. It automatically creates the required proxy addresses for all recipients in a site. Lotus Notes users use these proxy addresses to address messages to Exchange users. As mentioned earlier, you must install the proxy address generator in each site separately if you want the entire organization to be able to communicate with Lotus Notes users.

Connector Components

The group of connector components involved in the actual information handling includes six active processes, several important message folders on the Exchange Server, and three important Lotus Notes databases. As mentioned, the Lotus Notes databases that are related directly to the Connector for Lotus Notes are Exchange.box and Exchange.bad. The third Lotus Notes database is Mail.box, which is the message queue of the Lotus Notes mail router. (See Figure 20-2.)

The Connector for Lotus Notes uses message queues, just as any EDK-based gateway connector does. You can analyze these queues in the Exchange Administrator program on the **Queues** property page of the connector configuration object. The most important message queues maintained on the Exchange Server are MTS-IN (**Inbound To Exchange** message queue) and MTS-OUT (**Outbound From Exchange** message queue). The connector uses two additional queues during message conversion: the folders labeled *Readyout* (**Outbound To Notes** message queue) and *Readyin* (**Inbound From Notes** message queue).

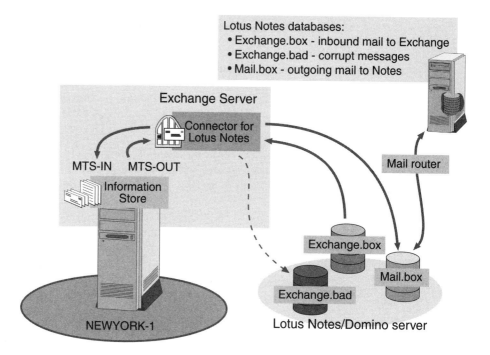

Figure 20-2. The Connector for Lotus Notes architecture.

The remaining six connector components are listed below. Their interaction is covered in detail in Lesson 2.

- MEXIN (Lsmexin.exe); takes converted messages and delivers them to the *MTS-IN* folder of Exchange Server

- MEXOUT (Lsmexout.exe); retrieves messages from the *MTS-OUT* folder and writes them to the *Readyout* folder

- MEXNTS (Lsmexnts.exe); processes messages from the *Readyout* folder and converts them from Exchange Server to Lotus Notes format; writes messages to the Mail.box database on the Lotus Notes server

- NTSMEX (Lsntsmex.exe); reads messages from the Exchange.box database on the Lotus Notes server, converts them to Exchange Server format, and delivers them to the *Readyin* folder

- DXANOTES (Lsdxants.exe); Directory Synchronization agent on the Lotus Notes server; retrieves updates from the Names.nsf database

- DXAMEX (Lsdxamex.exe); Directory Synchronization agent on the Exchange Server; checks the Exchange Server directory for updates

Lesson 2: Message Flow and Directory Synchronization

As mentioned earlier, the Connector for Lotus Notes relies on six components to perform message conversion, message transfer, and Directory Synchronization. You can determine the purpose of a particular component by analyzing its name. MEXOUT, for instance, stands for "Microsoft Exchange Outbound," and MEXNTS means "Microsoft Exchange to Notes" transfer. MEXIN is "Microsoft Exchange Inbound," while NTSMEX is responsible for message transfer from "Notes to Microsoft Exchange." The Directory Synchronization processes follow a similar naming convention. DXANOTES is the Directory Synchronization Agent on the Lotus Notes server, and DXAMEX fulfills the same task on the Exchange Server side.

This lesson covers the transfer of messages from Exchange Server to Lotus Notes and vice versa, as well as Directory Synchronization with Lotus Notes.

At the end of this lesson, you will be able to:

- Describe the flow of messages from Exchange Server to Lotus Notes
- Describe the flow of messages from Lotus Notes to Exchange Server
- Describe Directory Synchronization with Lotus Notes

Estimated time to complete this lesson: 25 minutes

Exchange Server to Lotus Notes Message Flow

The outbound message flow from Exchange Server is handled mainly by two components: MEXOUT, which retrieves messages from the connector's *MTS-OUT* folder, and MEXNTS, which places the converted messages into Lotus Notes. (See Figure 20-3.)

Routing Within Exchange Server

Let's say that Fred Pumpkin has recently connected STOCKSDATA to a Lotus Notes network somewhere in New York. Fred addresses the first test message to a Lotus Notes recipient. When he clicks the Send button, the IS of his home server receives the message, discovers that it is not responsible for the Notes recipient, and transfers the message to the MTA. The MTA checks the recipient address and performs message routing based on the GWART. It discovers the Connector for Lotus Notes and transfers the message back to the IS, which places the message in the connector's outbound message queue (MTS-OUT). If the Connector for Lotus Notes has been installed on another server, the message is first routed to that server (as explained in Chapter 9.)

Message Conversion

When the message arrives in the *MTS-OUT* folder, the IS informs the Connector for Lotus Notes that a message is awaiting delivery. The connector service launches the MEXOUT process to retrieve the message. At this point, sender and recipient addresses are converted to Lotus Notes addresses. Then the message is placed in the connector's *Readyout* folder, which is also in the Private Information Store.

Note The Connector for Lotus Notes does not poll for outbound messages. It is notified by the IS when messages are awaiting delivery in the *MTS-OUT* folder.

Message Transfer

Once the message is in the *Readyout* folder, the connector service launches the MEXNTS process to pick it up and transfer it to Lotus Notes. First MEXNTS converts the message contents. The attributes of the message that still exists in MDBEF are mapped to attributes that are compatible with the Lotus Notes format. Then the message is transferred to the Mail.box database on the Lotus Notes server.

The Lotus Notes mail router obtains the message from the Mail.box database to transfer it to the recipients. The mail router either delivers the message to a local mailbox or routes it to the Notes server where the recipient's mailbox resides.

Note MEXNTS writes bad or corrupted messages to the Exchange.bad database instead of to Mail.box.

Outbound message flow works as follows:

1. The IS receives the message for Lotus Notes recipients.

2. The IS checks recipient information and delivers the message to the MTA.

3. The MTA performs message routing based on the GWART and selects Connector for Lotus Notes.

4. The MTA transfers the message to the IS to place it in the connector's outbound message queue (MTS-OUT).

5. The IS informs the Connector for Lotus Notes, which launches MEXOUT to retrieve the message from MTS-OUT.

6. MEXOUT converts the address information to the Lotus Notes format and places the message in the *Readyout* folder of the IS.

7. MEXNTS obtains the message from the *Readyout* folder and converts the message contents into Lotus Notes format.

8. MEXNTS places the message in Mail.box on the Lotus Notes server. (Corrupted messages are written to Exchange.bad instead.)

9. The Lotus Notes mail router retrieves the message from Mail.box and delivers it to the recipient.

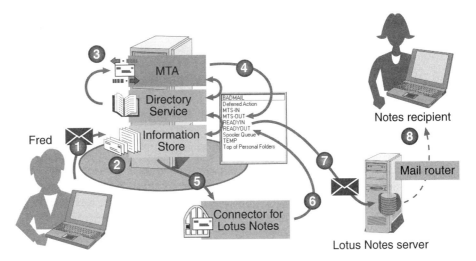

1) Fred sends mail. *2)* IS checks the recipient address. *3)* Message transmitted to MTA. *4)* MTA performs routing and transfers message in MTS-OUT folder. *5)* IS notifies Notes Connector. *6)* Connector's MEXOUT process converts addresses and places message in Readyout folder. *7)* MEXNTS retrieves and converts message before placing it into Mail.box. *8)* Mail router delivers message to recipient's mail database.

Figure 20-3. Exchange-to-Notes message transfer.

Lotus Notes to Exchange Server Message Flow

While MEXOUT and MEXNTS perform outbound message transfer from Exchange Server to Lotus Notes, a different pair of processes handles inbound messages: MEXIN and NTSMEX. (See Figure 20-4.)

Retrieving Messages from Lotus Notes

Let's say that a Lotus Notes administrator has received Fred's test message. This indicates that the Notes Connector is working in one direction. To make sure that the messaging link is fully functional, however, a reply to the test message must end up in Fred's mailbox as well. The Notes administrator replies to the test message, and the mail router delivers the message to the Exchange.box database of the connector's Lotus Notes server. NTSMEX retrieves the message from there.

Note NTSMEX must poll the Exchange.box database frequently to look for any inbound messages awaiting delivery to Exchange Server.

Message Conversion

The Lotus Notes message format is not compatible with the Exchange Server format, so NTSMEX must convert the message contents. NTSMEX also checks the message header information and writes the converted message to the *Readyin* folder of the connector's Private Information Store.

Note Bad or corrupted messages detected by NTSMEX are written to the *Badmail* folder instead of to *Readyin*.

Address Translation and Message Delivery

The MEXIN process is responsible for further processing of inbound messages. It picks up the message from the *Readyin* folder and converts the sender and recipient addresses to Exchange Server format. For this purpose, MEXIN contacts the DS. The connector generates an NDR for all recipients that cannot be found in the local server's GAL.

If valid recipient information is available, the inbound message is placed in the *MTS-IN* folder of the local IS. At this point, the IS can determine whether it is responsible for the recipient because the recipient address has been converted. If custom recipients, distribution lists, or recipients residing on remote servers somewhere in the organization are specified, the IS informs the MTA and the MTA retrieves the message from *MTS-IN* to perform distribution list expansion and message routing. The message is delivered to the destination mailbox as described in Chapter 4.

In our example, the destination IS immediately notifies Fred's client that a reply to his test message has arrived. This proves that the message link between the Exchange Server organization and the Lotus Notes domain is working in both directions. (See Figure 20-4.)

Inbound message flow works as follows:

1. A Lotus Notes user sends a message to an Exchange user. The mail router delivers the message to the Exchange.box database on the connector's server.

2. NTSMEX polls the Exchange.box database and retrieves the inbound message from Exchange Server.

3. NTSMEX converts the message contents and verifies the message header. Correct messages are written to the connector's *Readyin* folder; corrupt messages end up in the *Badmail* folder.

4. MEXIN picks up the message from the *Readyin* folder and converts the address information to valid Exchange addresses. An NDR is generated for all recipients that cannot be found in the DS.

5. MEXIN places the message in the *MTS-IN* folder of the local IS.

6. The IS checks the recipient addresses and delivers the message directly to the local recipients.

7. The IS notifies the MTA about new inbound messages for remote recipients as well as distribution lists and custom recipients. The MTA then retrieves the message from *MTS-IN*.

8. The MTA performs distribution list expansion and message routing.

9. The destination IS is determined, and the message is delivered to it.

10. The IS on the destination server places the message in the recipient's Inbox and informs the client about the new message.

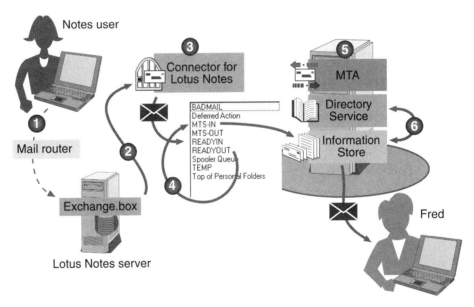

1) After a Notes user sends a message to Fred, the Mail router places it in the Exchange.box database. 2) NTSMEX polls Exchange.box and retrieves message. 3) NTSMEX converts message and places it into Readyin. 4) MEXIN retrieves message, converts addresses, and places message in MTS-IN. 5) IS checks whether it is responsible for recipient; if it is not, it notifies the MTA. 6) IS delivers message directly to local recipients.

Figure 20-4. Notes-to-Exchange message flow.

Directory Synchronization

It is advantageous to configure Directory Synchronization with Lotus Notes because it allows users of both systems to address their messages by selecting references from server-based address books. A properly functioning Directory Synchronization process can guarantee that messages are addressed correctly and are therefore deliverable.

Two Processes of Directory Synchronization

The Connector for Lotus Notes uses two processes to synchronize address information between Exchange Server and Lotus Notes. The DXAMEX process extracts and imports the information on the Exchange Server, and the DXANOTES process accomplishes the same task on the Lotus Notes side. (See Figure 20-5.)

Directory Synchronization Directories

Directory Synchronization with Lotus Notes uses two directories, Dxanotes.in and Dxamex.in, which act as the intermediate storage locations for address information. They are in \Exchsrvr\Connect\Exchconn\Q. During Directory Synchronization, both directories contain Message Interchange Format (MIF) files. (See Figure 20-5.)

The Dxanotes.in directory is the queue for MIF files written by DXAMEX. DXAMEX extracts the address information using export recipients containers from the Exchange Server. This process formats the information in MIF and then writes it to Dxanotes.in. DXANOTES retrieves the MIF file from the Dxanotes.in queue, processes the addresses, and places them in the target Name and Address Books of the Lotus Notes server.

DXANOTES uses the Dxamex.in directory when it retrieves address information from the Lotus Notes Source Name and Address Books. The information is placed in Dxamex.in in the form of an MIF file. The DXAMEX process can retrieve the information from there to place the Lotus Notes addresses as custom recipients in the desired import recipients container. The configuration of the Notes Connector is covered in Lesson 3.

Multiple Lotus Notes Servers

While Exchange address information is specified in **Import** and **Export** containers, Lotus Notes addresses are determined using address books. If your Lotus Notes network consists of several servers and multiple domains, you should configure the Public Address Book (Names.nsf) of the connector's Lotus Notes server as the source and target Name and Address Book. This can simplify the configuration of Directory Synchronization, because it allows automatic replication of the Exchange address information across the Lotus Notes network. However, if you decide to use a different target Name and Address Book, you must create and include this repository of Exchange address information in a Master Address Book in your Lotus Notes domain.

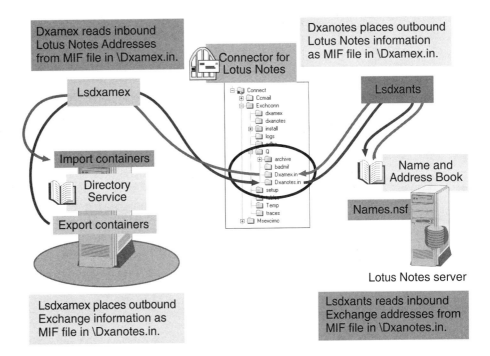

Figure 20-5. Directory Synchronization with Lotus Notes.

Directory Synchronization with Lotus Notes works like this:

- DXAMEX extracts Exchange addresses and writes them as an MIF file in the \Dxanotes.in directory.

- DXANOTES retrieves Exchange addresses from the MIF file in the Dxanotes.in queue and writes them to the target Name and Address Book of the Lotus Notes server.

- DXANOTES extracts Lotus Notes addresses from the source Name and Address Books and writes them as an MIF file in the \Dxamex.in directory.

- DXAMEX retrieves Lotus Notes addresses from the MIF file in the Dxamex.in queue and writes them to the specified import recipient container as custom recipients.

Lesson 3: Installing and Configuring the Connector for Lotus Notes

The Connector for Lotus Notes is not installed by default, and you must meet several hardware and software requirements before you can set it up. You must also prepare the connector's Lotus Notes environment before installation. The configuration process has three main parts: configuring the Lotus Notes server, configuring the connector itself, and configuring Directory Synchronization.

This lesson covers the hardware and software requirements and how to prepare the connector's Lotus Notes server. You will also learn how to configure the connector's Exchange Server components. Directory Synchronization with Lotus Notes is also covered, as is the configuration of downstream Exchange Server sites and Lotus Notes domains.

At the end of this lesson, you will be able to:

- Install the Connector for Lotus Notes

- List hardware and software requirements

- Address Lotus Notes configuration issues relating to the Connector for Lotus Notes

- Configure the Exchange Server components of the Lotus Notes Connector

- Configure Directory Synchronization with Lotus Notes

- Describe how to allow downstream Exchange Server sites and Lotus Notes domains to use the Connector for Lotus Notes for message transfer

Estimated time to complete this lesson: 40 minutes

Lotus Notes Preparations

The Connector for Lotus Notes requires access to one Lotus Notes server to transfer messages and to perform Directory Synchronization. Access is accomplished through the Lotus Notes client API. You must therefore install the Lotus Notes client on the Exchange Server before installing the connector. Other preparations include creating a required Connector ID, generating several database files, and assigning appropriate permissions at the connector's Lotus Notes server.

Creating a Lotus Notes ID for the Connector

In order to access a Lotus Notes server, the Connector for Lotus Notes requires a certified Lotus Notes ID file. You must also create a Person document for the connector in the Public Address Book of Lotus Notes. Do not specify a password for the Connector ID file. This enables unattended operation of the connector when it accesses its Lotus Notes databases. Of course, this introduces a security risk on the Lotus Notes side and you should take appropriate steps to secure the Connector ID file to prevent unauthorized access to the connector's private security keys. In any case, you cannot save the Connector ID in the Public Address Book because this would require you to specify a password.

Note To create a Connector ID, you must be a Lotus Notes administrator with the UserCreator role or Editor access in the Public Address Book.

To create the Connector ID file, launch the Lotus Notes Administration program (using the **Domino Server Administration** shortcut in the **Lotus Applications** program group—Lotus Domino Server version 4.6). Make sure that the **Administration** child window is displayed; if it isn't, open the **File** menu, point to **Tools**, and then click **Server Administration**. In the **Administration** window, click the **People** button to display a context menu, and then select the **Register Person** command. A **Lotus Notes Administration** window will appear, reminding you that each user ID requires a software license. If you have this license, click **Yes**. Now enter the password of the Lotus Notes certifier, which was created during the initial configuration of the Lotus Notes organization, and click **OK**.

In the **Register Person** dialog box that appears, click the **Registration Server** button and select the connector's Lotus Notes server. (This is necessary only if the local server is not the one you want.) If needed, you can select a different certifier by clicking the **Certifier ID** button. The **Security Type** can be **North American** (for highest security) or **International** (for medium security). A Connector ID file created with the **North American** security type cannot be used on a computer with international settings. In the **Certificate Expiration Date** box, you can change the expiration date of the Connector ID. Click **Continue**.

Note When you run the Lotus Notes Administration program on a Windows NT server, you can create a new Windows NT account for each new user ID. This is not required during the configuration of the ID for the Connector for Lotus Notes.

In the **Register Person** dialog box that appears, make sure that the **Password** field is empty (because the connector requires unattended access to its databases) and set the **Minimum Password Length** field to 0. Then specify a name for the connector in the **Last Name** box (for example, *ExchangeConnector*), and set the **License Type** to **Lotus Notes Desktop**. (See Figure 20-6 on page 1210.) Then click the **Mail** button.

Set the **Mail Type** option of the Connector ID to **None** to prevent the automatic creation of any mail files. The **Home Server** attribute must point to the connector's local Lotus Notes server. If it doesn't, select the correct reference from the **Home Server** list box before you click the **Other** button.

To configure the Connector for Lotus Notes, you must prevent the storage of the Connector ID in the Public Address Book by clearing the **In Address Book** option, which is selected by default. You must also select the **In File** option to save the Connector ID file to disk (for example, A:\Exchange.id). Although it is possible to save the Connector ID to the hard disk, you should save it to a floppy disk because the file must be accessible to the server that will run the Lotus Notes Connector. If you want to specify a different location or filename, click the **Set ID File** button under the **In File** option.

Click the **Save** button first and then click the **Register** button to complete the process of creating a Connector ID. You will be asked whether you want to register another person. Click **No**, and then close the Lotus Notes Administration program.

Installing the Lotus Notes Client

Now that you have prepared the connector's Lotus Notes server, you can install the Lotus Notes client on the server that will run the Connector for Lotus Notes. Depending on the Lotus Notes version and installation media, the location of the client's Install program might vary. On the Lotus Domino server version 4.6 installation CD, the client's Install.exe is in the \Client\W32intel\Install directory. The installation program presents a license agreement first, which you must accept if you want to install the client program. After that, you are led through the installation process, where you can accept the default settings. You can select the **Standard Install** option in the **Install Options** dialog box to set up the client with all required components. (See Figure 20-6.)

Note It is a good idea to start the client after installation to check whether you can log on using the Connector ID file.

Completing the Configuration of the Lotus Notes Server

The Connector for Lotus Notes provides a valuable tool that helps you complete the configuration of the Lotus Notes server: the Notes Configuration Utility. It is installed along with the connector. However, you can complete the configuration manually as outlined in this lesson for illustrative purposes. The Notes Configuration Utility is discussed later in the chapter and usually you'll use it to avoid manual configuration.

Note To configure the Lotus Notes server manually, complete the steps given in the following paragraphs in chronological order.

Updating the Connector's Person Document

The Person document identifies the Connector for Lotus Notes as a valid Lotus Notes user. It lets the connector access Lotus Notes databases to perform message transfer and Directory Synchronization. However, the connector's Person document must not be replicated to downstream Lotus Notes domains or synchronized with the Exchange Server directory because the connector is not an actual user.

Note Only a user with Manager permissions can exclude the connector's Person document from Directory Synchronization.

You can use the Lotus Notes Administration program or client program to update the connector's Person document. First open the Public Address Book, where the connector's Person document is listed. Double-click the document to open the **ExchangeConnector/STOCKSDATA** dialog box. (The title of this dialog box might be different if you have used different names.) Select the **Edit Person** command from the **Actions** menu. In the Person document, click the **Administration** reference, and then set the **Foreign Directory Sync Allowed** option to **No**. To complete the configuration, click the **Save** command on the **File** menu. Then close the address book again.

Configuring the Router Mailbox for Connector Access

The router mailbox is a database called Mail.box. As mentioned earlier, Mail.box is used to place outgoing messages from Exchange Server into the connector's Lotus Notes server. Consequently, the Connector for Lotus Notes requires permissions to place items in this database.

Note Even though the default access for router mailboxes is **Depositor**, the Connector for Lotus Notes requires that the **Depositor** access is granted explicitly to its Lotus Notes ID.

You must have **Manager** access to manage the access control list of the Mail.box database in the Lotus Notes Administration program. To assign the connector **Depositor** access, select the **Open** command under the **Database** option on the **File** menu. Then select the connector's server under **Server** and type *Mail.box* in the **Filename** box. Click **Open** to display the *< Server FQDN>* **Mailbox – Mail** dialog box. Open the **File** menu one more time, point to the **Database** option, and then click **Access Control**. Using the **Add** button and subsequent dialog boxes, you can add the Connector ID (for example, *ExchangeConnector*) to the Mail.box database's access control list and set its **Access** level to **Depositor**. Click **OK** to close the *< Server FQDN>* **Mailbox – Mail** window.

Creating Connector Databases

It is now time to create the databases of the connector called Exchange.box and Exchange.bad using the Lotus Notes Administration program. The functions of the databases were covered in Lesson 2.

Note Although you can use different names for the connector mail files, it is best to name them Exchange.box and Exchange.bad. If you use different names, you'll have to supply them at various later stages of the connector configuration.

You can create the databases for the connector using the **New** command under **Databases** on the Administration program's **File** menu. Select the connector's Lotus Notes server under **Server** and then type a name (such as *Outgoing Mail to Exchange*) for the database in the **Title** box. Most important, you must change the name of the database file to Exchange.box under **File Name**. Select the **Mail Router Mailbox** entry (Mailbox.ntf) in the list of available templates under the **Template Server** button, and then click **OK**.

In the **Outgoing Mail to Exchange – Mail** dialog box that appears, grant **Delete Documents** permissions to the Connector ID **Manager**. The connector needs all available permissions. You can manage access control lists in a way similar to that described for the Mail.box database.

Note In addition to Exchange.box, you should create and configure the Exchange.bad database.

Granting Access to the Public Address Book

Because of the Directory Synchronization features, the Connector for Lotus Notes requires special access to the Public Address Book of Lotus Notes. In the Lotus Notes Administration program, click **People**, select **People View**, and then click **Access Control** under the **Databases** option on the **File** menu. The connector requires the Access level of an **Editor** with the right to **Delete Documents**.

Granting Access to Lotus Notes Databases

As mentioned in Lesson 1, the Connector for Lotus Notes can convert Lotus Notes Doclinks to attachments in rich text format or to OLE documents. However, if you want the connector to be able to convert Doclinks to RTF attachments, you must grant the connector Reader access to databases that contain documents associated with Doclinks as well as access to the documents themselves. Otherwise, the attachment appended to the message will contain only an error message. It is a good idea to add the Connector ID to all relevant databases and assign it **Reader** access—if the security policy of your organization allows you to do so. The steps required to grant the Connector ID Reader access are the same as the steps for granting it **Depositor** permissions for the Mail.box database, as described earlier.

Registering Exchange Server as a Foreign Domain

Within Lotus Notes, an Exchange Server organization is treated as a foreign domain. This means you must maintain a foreign domain document in the Public Address Book. You can create this document when you open the Public Address Book in the Lotus Notes client or Administration program.

After you open the Public Address Book, select the **Domains** entry under **Server** in the right pane of the address book window. Then click the **Add Domain** button to open the **New Domain** document. You can type a name for the Exchange Server organization in the **Foreign Domain Name** box, but it is best to use the default name, Exchange. Alternatively, you can supply a **Domain Description** to detail the nature of this foreign domain.

The **Gateway Server Name** parameter must correspond to the fully distinguished name of your Lotus Notes server (for example, *NotesServer/ NotesOrganization*). For the **Gateway Mail File Name** parameter, you must specify the name of the connector's mail file. This is typically **Exchange.box**.

You can set additional parameters under **Administration** and **Restrictions**. Those settings might be important for your Lotus Notes organization, but they are not essential for the operation of the Connector for Lotus Notes. Click the **Save And Close** button to create the foreign domain document.

Performing Routine Maintenance

The Connector for Lotus Notes must compact database files frequently because they become fragmented as messages are created and deleted in the Exchange.box database. To allow the connector to run the compaction utility automatically, you must add the Connector ID to the list of **Administrators** in the server document. You can do this when you open the Public Address Book. Click the **Other** command under the **Server** option on the **View** menu. This displays the **Other** dialog box, where you can select **Server/Servers**. Click **OK** to switch to the list of Lotus Notes servers in your network. Double-click the name of the connector's server to launch the server's associated document. Select the **Edit Server** command from the **Actions** menu to switch the document of the connector's server to edit mode. Now you can add the Connector ID to the list of **Administrators** by clicking the small button in the **Administrators** field, which displays the **Names** dialog box. Here you can add the Connector ID. Click **OK**, and then click the **Save And Close** button to save the changes. The Lotus Notes environment is now ready for the Connector for Lotus Notes.

Notes Configuration Utility

Manual configuration of the connector's Lotus Notes server is a complex task. The good news is that the Notes Configuration Utility automates the preparation of Lotus Notes by creating the required databases and assigning the Connector ID the required permissions for all Notes resources—including those required to convert Doclinks into RTF attachments. It also lets you identify the Exchange Server organization as a foreign Lotus Notes domain. This utility is installed with the Connector for Lotus Notes.

You need administrative permissions (**Manager** access to the Public Address Book) to run the utility. If necessary, first switch your Lotus Notes client to an appropriate administrator account by clicking the Lotus Notes client's **Switch ID** command under the **Tools** option on the **File** menu.

When you are connected to the Lotus Notes server with administrative access, you can start the utility by selecting the **Notes Configuration Utility** command from the **Microsoft Exchange Connectivity** program group. An **About This Database** window will appear, informing you about the configuration utility. A **Cross Certify** window might also appear, telling you that your local Name and Address Book does not contain a cross-certificate for Microsoft. In this case, click **Yes** to create the cross-certificate.

To continue the configuration, close the **About This Database** document and switch to the **Notes Configuration Utility – Main** window. Then click the **New Configuration Document** button. You must fill in the fields as shown in the following table. (See also Figure 20-6.)

Option	Description
Notes Bridgehead Server Name	The name of the Lotus Notes server.
Connector's Notes User Name	The name of the Connector ID.
Allow Connector to be Administrator	Whether the connector should have Administrator permissions.
Path for the notes.ini file	The location of the connector's Notes.ini file. This file is required for the configuration of the Connector for Lotus Notes as well.
Foreign Domain Name of Exchange	The foreign domain name of the Exchange Server organization.
Connector Mail File Name	The name of the Lotus Notes database that will be used for messages inbound to Exchange Server.
Source Name & Address Books	The list of Name and Address Books on the Lotus Notes server that are to be propagated to the Exchange Server organization. It is best to use Names.nsf, which is the Lotus Notes Name and Address Book.
Target Name & Address Book	The Lotus Notes Name and Address Book that is to be updated with entries from the Exchange Server organization. To simplify Directory Synchronization, use Names.nsf here as well.

After you specify the information, click the **Configure** button, and then click **Yes** to create the foreign domain document. Close the Lotus Notes client and the Notes Configuration Utility.

These are the steps for configuring the connector on the Lotus Notes server (after creating the Connector ID):

1. Update the Person document to exclude the Connector ID from Directory Synchronization.

2. Grant the connector **Depositor** access to the router mailbox of the Lotus Notes server (Mail.box).

3. Create the mail databases for the connector.

4. Grant the connector **Editor** access with **Delete Documents** rights to the Name and Address Book of Lotus Notes.

5. Grant the connector **Reader** access to databases that users can use to create Doclinks.

6. Identify the Exchange Server organization as a foreign domain.

7. Grant the Connector ID permission to perform routine database maintenance.

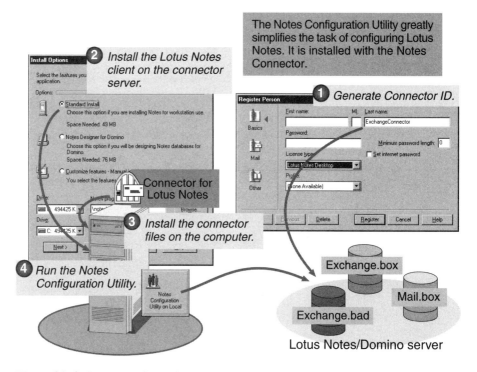

Figure 20-6. Preparing Lotus Notes.

Installing the Connector for Lotus Notes

The actual installation of the Connector for Lotus Notes is done in several phases. However, you must first fulfill the hardware and software requirements.

Hardware Requirements

The hardware requirements for Intel-based computers are the same as for Exchange Server 5.5. (See Chapter 2.) However, for optimal performance, an Intel Pentium Pro processor with 64 MB of RAM is recommended. You should also reserve sufficient hard disk space for the connector's operation (1 GB at a minimum) and the computer should not maintain Exchange user mailboxes. This space will be used for connector files and for temporary files that are created during the conversion and transfer of messages and address information.

Note You cannot install the Connector for Lotus Notes on Digital Alpha computers. Only the proxy address generator is provided for this computer platform, which means that Exchange users on an Alpha machine can communicate with Lotus Notes users if at least one Exchange Server with an Intel processor is available in the Exchange organization running the Connector for Lotus Notes.

Software Requirements

In addition to Windows NT Server 4.0 with Service Pack 3, the Connector for Lotus Notes requires a functioning network connection to the connector's Lotus Notes server. As mentioned earlier, you must first install a client for Lotus Notes version 4.52 (or higher) before setting up the connector.

Several items should *not* be running on the connector computer—including messaging client software (such as Exchange Client 5.0 or Outlook) and OLE-enabled software (such as Microsoft Word). Those applications can interfere with the connector when it converts OLE-based items between the Exchange Server and Lotus Notes formats.

Administrator Account Permissions

To install and manage the Connector for Lotus Notes, you must be a member of the local Windows NT **Administrators** group of the server that will serve as the connector computer. You must also have read and write access to the \Exchsrvr directory. The \Add-ins and \Address directories, in particular, will contain several Exchange Administrator program extensions (the connector configuration object, proxy address generator, and address details templates). You must also have read and write permission for the Connect$ share to configure the connector. The Connect$ share is the \Exchsrvr\Connect directory, which is the root for all directories of gateway connectors. (For example, the Connector for Lotus Notes files are copied under \Exchconn.)

Of course, you must also have administrative permissions within the Exchange Server DS. Theoretically, the installing user needs only administrative access to the **Add-ins**, **Addressing**, and **Connections** containers of the local site and **View Only Admin** permissions at the site level. In practice, however, it is best to be a **Permissions Admin** for the entire site and all its servers. This lets you manage the connector and the site addressing scheme without restrictions.

Remote Administration

When you run the Setup program to install the Connector for Lotus Notes, you have two choices in the **Select Installation Option** dialog box. The first choice lets you install the **Microsoft Exchange Connectivity Administrator**, and the second sets up the actual **Microsoft Exchange Connectivity Services**.

The Connectivity Administrator can run on the same computer as the connector or on a Windows NT Server or Workstation that provides a LAN-like network connection to the connector's Exchange Server. During setup, a shortcut to this program called **Microsoft Exchange Connectivity Administrator** is created in the **Microsoft Exchange Connectivity** program group. You can configure a workstation to run the Exchange Administrator program in addition to the Connectivity Administrator so that you can manage Exchange Server entirely from your office.

Installing the Connector Files and Administrative Extensions

The Connector for Lotus Notes provides its own Setup executable in the \Server\Exchconn\Setup\Ent directory of the Exchange Server 5.5 installation CD. After you launch this program and bypass the **Welcome** message by clicking the **Next** button, select **Microsoft Exchange Connectivity Services** in the **Select Installation Option** dialog box. Then click the **Next** button to display the **Software Selection** window. You will have several choices, such as **Microsoft Exchange Connector for Lotus Notes**, **Microsoft Exchange Connector for SNADS**, and **Microsoft Exchange Connector for OV/VM**. Clear the check boxes for all components except the Notes Connector, and then click **Next** to specify the user name and password that the connector will use to access Exchange Server resources.

Although it is best to use the Site Services Account for the Connector for Lotus Notes, you don't have to. If you select a different account, make sure that the account has the permissions to log on as a service and that its password will never expire. The service account of the connector must have **Administrator** permissions for the **Addressing** object under the connector site's **Configuration** container and must be a **Service Account Administrator** at the server level in the Exchange Directory.

After you specify the account information, click the **Next** button one more time. A warning message will appear, telling you to close all applications that use ODBC before you continue the installation. Click **Yes**. Connector files will be copied to the hard disk, and you will see the **Install Notes E-Mail Addressing** dialog box. Under **Lotus Notes Domain Name**, make sure that the name—by default, **Exchange**—corresponds to the foreign domain name of the Exchange Server organization as configured in Lotus Notes. You can also generate proxy e-mail addresses for all existing users of your site. It is best to leave this option activated (**Yes**). Click **Next**, and Setup will add the connector files and Exchange Administrator program extensions to the server. Finally, a message box will inform you that the software has been installed and that you can configure the Lotus Notes server using the Notes Configuration Utility.

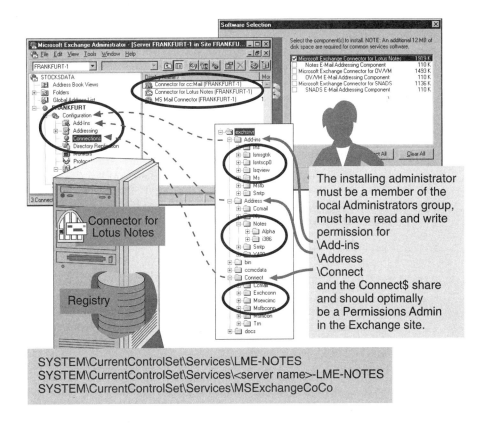

Figure 20-7. Resources accessed during connector installation.

The minimum Administrator account permissions requirements are as follows:

- Membership in the local Windows NT **Administrators** group

- Read and write permissions for the \Exchsrvr\Add-ins, \Exchsrvr\Address, and \Exchsrvr\Connect directories

- **View Only Admin** permissions for the local site of the connector

- **Administrator** permissions for the **Add-ins**, **Address**, and **Connections** containers under the connector-site's **Configuration** container

- **Permissions Account Admin** permissions for the server-level object that references the server running the connector services

Configuring the Connector for Lotus Notes

The services of the Exchange Server must be running when you configure the Connector for Lotus Notes. You must also make sure that the Lotus Notes client uses the correct Connector ID when connecting to the Lotus Notes server. You can verify the ID by using the **User ID** command on the **Tools** menu of the Lotus Notes client's **File** menu. If you are currently working with another ID, you must click the **Switch ID** command to select the correct Connector ID file.

Configuring Important Connector Parameters

To configure administrative extensions such as the **Connector for Lotus Notes (<server name>)** configuration object in the **Connections** container, you must run the Setup program once more, this time from the **Microsoft Exchange Connectivity** program group. This can be considered phase two of the connector installation. After bypassing the **Welcome** message by clicking the **Next** button, you will reach the **Select Installation Option** dialog box, where you must accept the default option **Configure Microsoft Exchange Connector For Lotus Notes**.

Installation Without the Notes Configuration Utility

After you click the **Next** button twice, a warning message might appear, informing you that configuration information for Lotus Notes is missing. This is usually the case if you have configured the Lotus Notes server manually without running the Notes Configuration Utility. At this point, you can either click **Yes** to continue and accept default values or click **No** to exit Setup and run the utility. If you click **Yes**, Setup continues installing administrative extensions with default configuration settings until it notifies you that the installation/configuration is complete. You must then adjust the configuration of the Connector for Lotus Notes using the connector's property pages in the Exchange Administrator program.

Installation with the Notes Configuration Utility

If you execute the Notes Configuration Utility in conjunction with the connector's Lotus Notes client (which is highly recommended), you implicitly update the Notes.ini and Exchconn.ini files. Notes.ini must point to the Connector ID file being used (the **KeyFilename** parameter). This file is typically in the \Winnt directory. Exchconn.ini contains Registry initialization settings for the connector's Windows NT services. Exchconn.ini is in the \Exchsrvr\Connect\Exchconn directory.

Using both .INI files, the connector can be configured automatically. No input is required by Setup, which displays a message box when the installation/configuration is complete. When you click **OK**, you return to the **Select Installation Option** window. Select the **Exit Setup** option and then click **Next**. After installation, you can start the **Microsoft Exchange Connector for Lotus Notes** service through the Control Panel, but it is a good idea to launch the Exchange Administrator program first to verify the accuracy of the connector parameters.

Note   The Notes Configuration Utility is highly recommended. You should use it on the server that will run the connector. The utility modifies Exchconn.ini, which greatly simplifies the task of configuring the connector.

Verifying Configuration Parameters

To check the configuration parameters of the Connector for Lotus Notes in the Exchange Administrator program, open its corresponding configuration object in the **Connections** container. The most important property pages for message transfer are **Options**, **Routing**, and **Advanced**. Less essential is the **General** property page, because it only allows you to specify a maximum message size for the connector and an administrative note. Other property pages (for example, **Address Space**, **Message Tracking**, and **Queues**) also refer to important aspects of message transmission. But their purposes are analogous to the features of other connectors and have been explained throughout this book already, for example in Chapter 9 and in Chapter 15.

You can switch to the **Options** property page to verify that correct information has been used to configure the **Notes Connection**. You can specify the **Notes Server** that the connector will access to transfer messages. You can also check the **Exchange Domain Name In Notes** and adjust the interval—in seconds—at which the connector will poll the Exchange.box database for inbound messages to Exchange Server.

If you specified a name other than *Exchange.box*, you can check the **Routing** property page to see whether the connector polls the correct database. Check the **Advanced** property page to specify settings for converting Lotus Notes Doclinks to Exchange attachments or to determine the location of the Notes.ini file.

Configuring Directory Synchronization

Although the Notes Configuration Utility configures several settings for Directory Synchronization automatically, you must complete the configuration manually using the property pages of the Notes connector object. You must specify Directory Synchronization settings on the **Import Container**, **Export Containers**, **Notes Address Books**, and **Dirsync Schedule** property pages.

Specifying Recipient Containers

Switch to the **Import Container** to identify the recipients container that will receive custom recipient objects during Directory Synchronization. It is a good idea to create a dedicated **Recipients** container for Notes address information. The **Export Containers** property page lets you to specify the collection of recipients containers that will be exported to Lotus Notes. By default, only the **Recipients** container of the local site is exported, but you can add containers of other sites to the **Export These Recipients** list. You can also opt to export custom recipient objects to Lotus Notes by selecting the **Export Custom Recipients** check box. You can specify a **Trust Level** that determines which recipients to export. Only those with a trust level less than or equal to the specified limit are exported. The configuration of trust levels and other recipient properties is covered in Chapter 5.

Identifying Lotus Notes Address Books

Just as you need to specify recipients containers on the Exchange Server side to receive and export address information, you must select the desired Name and Address Books on the Lotus Notes side as well. However, when you switch to the **Notes Address Book** property page, you'll see that the **Default Name And Address Book** and the **Source Name And Address Books** have been configured automatically by the Notes Configuration Utility. The **Source Name And Address Books** will be read to retrieve Notes addresses, while the **Default Name And Address Book** will receive the Exchange address information.

In addition to the Default Name And Address Book, you can configure domain-specific address books. In other words, you can split the Exchange address information across multiple Lotus Notes Name and Address Books depending on the Lotus Notes domain to which the Exchange address belongs. Users with domain names that are not explicitly specified in the list are still placed in the default Name And Address Book.

Let's say that Fred Pumpkin has connected the site NEWYORK to a Lotus Notes network. He used the default settings, which means that the domain name of all users in the site NEWYORK is Exchange. His address is thus *Fred Pumpkin/NEWYORK/STOCKSDATA@Exchange*. Let's assume that users in LONDON want to use the Connector for Lotus Notes in NEWYORK as well. Robin Sherwood installs the proxy address generator in the site LONDON, but he decides to use the NOTES domain name England. His address is thus *Robin Sherwood/LONDON/STOCKSDATA@England*. In this situation, it is possible to map the domain England to a different Name and Address Book by first creating the foreign domain document along with the new address book in Lotus Notes and then assigning the Connector ID explicit permissions (as explained under "Lotus Notes Preparations" earlier in this lesson). Fred Pumpkin clicks the **Add** button under **Domain-Specific Target**

Name And Address Books, types *England* in the **Domain** box, and specifies the name of the address book under **Name And Address Book**. After he clicks **OK**, he can see the association between the domain England and its .NSF file in the **Domain-Specific Target Name And Address Books** list.

Note Splitting Exchange address information across several Name and Address Books other than the Public Address Book provides flexibility in determining who has access to foreign addresses in Lotus Notes.

Scheduling Directory Synchronization

Directory Synchronization with Lotus Notes is disabled by default. You must enable it by selecting the **Enable Scheduled Directory Synchronization** check box on the **Dirsync Schedule** property page. You can also specify the Directory Synchronization schedule on a **Periodic**, **Daily**, **Weekly**, or **Monthly** basis. The **Dirsync Schedule** property page is also important when you test Directory Synchronization, as outlined in the following section.

Testing the Connector for Lotus Notes

It is a golden rule of successful server administration that you should test every connector immediately after installing and configuring it. The Connector for Lotus Notes is no exception. Nevertheless, checking the connector requires a specific strategy because it is unfortunately not very aware of the Windows NT Application Event Log.

Note Only in rare cases does the Connector for Lotus Notes write to the Application Event Log to record critical service states.

Controlling Connector Processes

To analyze the Notes connector, you use the Exchange Connectivity Administrator. You can start this utility by opening the **Microsoft Exchange Connectivity Administrator** shortcut from the **Microsoft Exchange Connectivity** program group or by clicking the **Run Connectivity Administrator** button on the **Advanced** property page of the connector object.

The most important menu in the Exchange Connectivity Administrator is the **Process Manager** menu. It becomes available when you switch to the **Process Manager** window by double-clicking the **Process Manager** reference in the **Overview** window. You can start and stop the individual connector processes using the commands on the **Process Manager** menu while their current state is displayed on line in the **Process Manager** window.

If problems occur, open the **Browse Log** window by double-clicking on the **Log Browser** icon in the **Overview** window. You'll see detailed information on all aspects of the connector.

Testing the Message Path

To test the message path between Exchange Server and Lotus Notes, you can simply send one test message back and forth. First, start all connector processes and verify that they are shown to be in the **Idle** state in the Exchange Connectivity Administrator.

To send a test message from Lotus Notes to Exchange Server, use your new NOTES proxy e-mail address to specify an Exchange recipient in Lotus Notes. After you send the message, check to see if the message has been delivered to the Exchange.box database by selecting the **Open** command under the **Database** option on the Lotus Notes client's **File** menu. Once the message is received in Outlook, reply to the sender directly. When the reply is received in the Lotus Notes client, you know that the message path is working.

Testing Directory Synchronization

Since the Directory Synchronization processes are separate from those that handle message transfer, you must test Directory Synchronization explicitly. The required controls are on the connector's **Dirsync Schedule** property page. The most important ones are the **Immediate Full Reload** buttons under **Exchange To Notes Directory Synchronization** and **Notes To Exchange Directory Synchronization**. Click them to force the immediate synchronization of address information. All available address information will be synchronized, and if the connector is working properly, you will find associated addresses in the import recipients container and the target Name and Address Books once the DirSync cycle completes. If you want to synchronize updates only, click the **Immediate Update** buttons, which are to the right of their **Immediate Full Reload** counterparts.

Note It is good practice to examine the processing phases of the **DX Agents** in the Exchange Connectivity Administrator right after you click the **Immediate Full Reload** button.

Configuring Downstream Sites and Domains

Just as an Exchange Server organization can have multiple sites, a Lotus Notes network can have multiple domains. Sites or domains that need to transfer messages indirectly to the remote system through another site or domain in which the connector has been installed are called *downstream* sites or domains. A particular connector will allow all users in all sites and domains to communicate with each other, but additional configuration is required to support the message transfer.

To ensure that each Exchange user in every site can send messages to Lotus Notes and is accessible to Lotus Notes users, you must install the Lotus e-mail address generator in each downstream site. This will ensure that proper NOTES proxy addresses are generated for all mailboxes. Likewise, you must identify downstream Lotus Notes domains on the **Routing** property page of the connector object. You type the names of foreign domains, separated by a comma, under **Routable Domains**. You can identify Lotus Notes domains in the following documents:

- Foreign domain documents (excluding the Exchange Server domain)
- Connection documents
- Nonadjacent domain documents

The Lotus Notes environment must also be configured properly, which means that you might have to create additional foreign domain documents. Generally, you configure one foreign domain name for the entire Exchange organization in Lotus Notes. Later, the connector's Setup program prompts you for this name during phase one of the installation. By default, the name is Exchange. You will also be asked for this domain name when you install the proxy e-mail address generator in downstream sites.

Note To simplify the configuration of Lotus Notes, you can specify the same domain name for downstream sites that was used for the connector site. Remember to let Setup update the Lotus Notes address format during the installation of the proxy e-mail address generator.

Depending on your actual configuration, you might have to configure multiple domain names. In this case, you must register each domain name in Lotus Notes using a separate foreign domain document. It is particularly important that you specify the Exchange.box database as the **Gateway Mail File Name** for all Exchange domains because the Notes mail router must route all inbound messages destined for Exchange Server to this message queue. You can also split the Exchange address information across multiple Name and Address Books using the domain name, as described under "Configuring Directory Synchronization," earlier in this lesson.

Common Installation and Configuration Problems

Fortunately, the list of common installation problems is not very long. However, a few issues can frustrate the administrator. For instance, the Setup program of the Connector for Lotus Notes does not verify the validity of the

Site Services Account password. In other words, it is possible to specify invalid password information during setup. Obviously, the Exchange Connector for Lotus Notes service will then be unable to start. To correct this problem, you must adjust the password via the **Services** applet of the Control Panel.

A more complex problem can occur if you install the Lotus Notes client and the Connector for Lotus Notes with default options. Let's say that you have configured the Connector ID, installed the Lotus Notes client, and executed the Notes Configuration Utility. You configured the Notes Connector easily, and you carefully checked all parameters afterwards. Nevertheless, when you try to start the Exchange Connector for Lotus Notes service through the **Services** applet of the Control Panel, you get the error message shown in Figure 20-8.

This error message appeared because Nnotes.dll is not in one of the directories included in the system search path—it is in the directory of the Lotus Notes client. Therefore, you must include this directory in the search path. You can do this using the **System** applet of the Control Panel by switching to the **Environment** property page. Nevertheless, the connector still cannot start because it is not aware of the search path modification.

The fastest solution might seem to be copying Nnotes.dll from the \Notes directory to \Winnt\System32. The connector service will then start. However, the connector will not function properly. A glance at the state of the connector processes in the Exchange Connectivity Administrator will indicate that the **LME-NOTES-DXANOTES, LME-NOTES-MEXNTS**, and **LME-NOTES-NTSMEX** processes have problems initializing the Notes interface. Without these processes, there can be no message transfer or Directory Synchronization!

To solve this problem, you must stop the Connector for Lotus Notes one more time, delete Nnotes.dll from the \Winnt\System32 directory, and reboot the computer. This will guarantee that the connector service is aware of the search path modification. Once Nnotes.dll can be found in the \Notes directory, the connector processes can initialize the Notes interface properly, messages can be transferred between Exchange Server and Lotus Notes and Directory Synchronization can be performed.

The **Connector for Lotus Notes** property pages and their functions are as follows:

- **Address Space**; to define address spaces for this connector

- **Advanced**; to set the interval for automatic maintenance of Lotus Notes databases

- **Dirsync Schedule**; to set the frequency of Directory Synchronization

- **Export Containers**; to set the trust level and to specify the recipients containers that are exported to the Lotus Notes target Name and Address Book

- **General**; to set the maximum message size

- **Import Container**; to manage the recipients container, which receives the Lotus Notes custom recipients after Directory Synchronization

- **Message Tracking**; to enable tracking of messages or messages and reports

- **Notes Address Books**; to propagate Lotus Notes address lists to the Exchange Server organization

- **Options**; to set the polling interval

- **Queues**; to display the contents of message queues in the IS

- **Routing**; to specify downstream Lotus Notes servers that can be reached through this connector

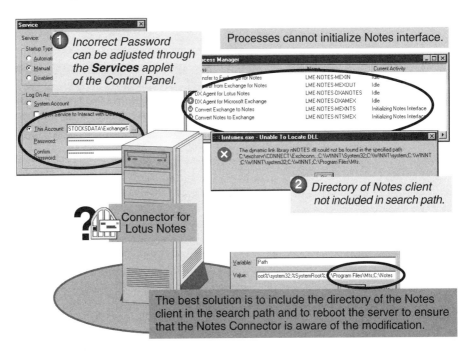

Figure 20-8. Common installation and configuration problems.

Review

1. What type of general information can be transferred between Exchange Server and Lotus Notes through the Connector for Lotus Notes?

   _____

2. You want to install the Connector for Lotus Notes. What non-Microsoft software must you install on the connector server before you begin the installation?

   _____

3. Which two databases must you configure on the Lotus Notes server to allow the Connector for Lotus Notes to function properly? What is the purpose of these databases?

   _____

   _____

   _____

   _____

4. When you send a message containing an embedded message to a Lotus Notes user, how does the recipient receive the embedded message?

   _____

   _____

   _____

5. Which two important system folders does the Connector for Lotus Notes use on the Exchange Server?

   _____

   _____

6. What are the extensions of the Administrator program?

   _____

   _____

   _____

   _____

7. What must you do to allow downstream sites to send messages to Lotus
    Notes users?

    _____

    _____

    _____

8. Which connector component retrieves messages from the MTS-OUT
    queue?

    _____

9. Which connector component converts messages from Exchange Server
    format into Lotus Notes format and places the converted message in the
    Lotus Notes server?

    _____

    _____

10. Which component polls the Lotus Notes Exchange.box directory for
    inbound messages to Exchange Server?

    _____

11. Which component converts address information for inbound messages
    from Lotus Notes into the X.400 address format?

    _____

12. Which processes perform Directory Synchronization with Lotus Notes?

    _____

13. Which utility simplifies configuration of the connector's Lotus Notes
    server?

    _____

14. On which property page can you change the name of the Notes server
    that the Connector for Lotus Notes contacts for message transfer?

    _____

15. What must you do on the Lotus Notes server before installing the connector?

    _____

Questions and Answers

Chapter 1

1. A company is planning to implement Exchange Server. As an administrator, you need to determine the possible client platforms. What platforms
   are supported?
   **Exchange Server supports clients on MS-DOS, Windows 3.1, Win-
   dows for Workgroups 3.11, Windows 95, Windows NT, OS/2, and
   Apple Macintosh version 7.x. UNIX-based clients are supported via
   HTTP, LDAP, POP3, IMAP4, SMTP, and NNTP.**

2. What are the disadvantages of a shared-file messaging system?
   **Shared-file messaging systems provide limited security because every
   user needs read/write access to the post office. They generate high
   network traffic because of client polling for new messages, and they
   provide a reduced scalability because many clients might access
   common files at the post office at the same time. In addition, the post
   office is a passive component, so the clients need to perform all the
   processing of e-mail messages on the local computer.**

3. Why would you prefer a client/server over a shared-file
   messaging system?
   **Client/server messaging systems such as Exchange Server provide
   higher security for server-based resources because clients don't need
   direct read/write permission for them. The active server informs the
   clients about the arrival of new messages; this mechanism makes
   polling obsolete. Therefore, network traffic is reduced. A client/
   server system is scalable, suitable for the needs of small and large
   organizations.**

4. What are the most important levels of the Exchange Server hierarchy?
   **Every Exchange Server system consists of *organization*, *site*, and
   server units. The organization provides the common context for all
   servers. The site simplifies the administration and allows the specification of site level default settings. The server provides properties for
   a configuration of specific server tasks independently of existing site-
   level settings and actually hosts the mailboxes and the user data.**

5. Exchange Server has been implemented tightly into the Windows NT domain security. What are the advantages?
This security model provides secure single logon, individual access control, and auditing capabilities based on Windows NT Event Logs.

6. An organization has installed Exchange Server 5.5. Now it's time to send and receive messages, but the users also want to be able to manage scheduling information. Furthermore, users want to create and design electronic forms, and discussion forums based on public folders and they don't use Office 97. What clients would you suggest?
The Exchange Client family allows you to access messages and other objects stored in mailboxes and public folders. Scheduling information can be organized using Schedule+ 7.5. The Exchange Forms Designer is the design environment used to create 16-bit electronic forms.

7. You want to migrate from Exchange Client to Outlook. What has to be reconfigured?
Nothing. Outlook is able to use the former messaging profile to access the user's mailbox on the Exchange Server.

8. The Exchange Server supports a variety of Internet protocols. What clients can be used to access information on the server?
Clients can access the Exchange Server through POP3, IMAP4, NNTP, HTTP, and LDAP. Therefore, all existing POP3 or IMAP4 clients and newsreader applications are supported. To access the server-based resources via HTTP, an Internet browser with Frames and Java script support such as Internet Explorer 3.x or 4.0 or Netscape Navigator 2.0 (or higher) can be used.

9. What are the most important Exchange Server services that need to be running on every server? What tasks must they be able to handle?
The Directory Service, Message Transfer Agent, Information Store, and System Attendant need to run on every Exchange Server. The DS maintains all information about the organization, including users, distribution lists, servers, and more. The MTA provides routing functions to deliver messages between servers and sites. It is also responsible for distribution list expansion. The IS maintains user messages in mailboxes and collaborative data in public folders. The SA, in turn, provides diagnostic and logging capabilities for connectors and services as well as maintains Exchange Server routing tables.

10. What additional connector components come with Exchange Server 5.5?
The Internet Mail Service (IMS) allows you to connect the organization to the Internet based on SMTP and ESMTP. The Microsoft Mail Connector can connect the Exchange Server to existing Microsoft Mail environments, and the Connector for Lotus cc:Mail can transfer messages to and from one Lotus cc:Mail post office. Furthermore, you can use the Connector for Lotus Notes to connect the Exchange organization to a Lotus Notes network. The latter three connectors can be the basis to perform Directory Synchronization with these foreign mail systems. Likewise, Exchange Server 5.5 includes the PROFS connector for connectivity to messaging systems on IBM mainframes, and the SNADS connector, which can be used to connect to IBM OfficeVision/VM, IBM OfficeVision/400, and other systems.

11. You plan to connect the Exchange organization to the Internet. Users need to be able to send and receive messages to and from SMTP-based systems. Also, relevant newsgroups must be distributed within the organization. Which additional components would you install?
The Internet Mail Service (IMS) provides SMTP connectivity to the Internet, while you need to install the Internet News Service (INS) for NNTP-based distribution of public folder contents to the USENET. The INS can be used to retrieve or send information from or to newsgroups. Regular public folder replication, on the other hand, can distribute the information further across your organization.

12. You are planning to implement a dedicated Exchange Server that will maintain newsgroup information for your organization on a very large scale. What is the largest size your information store databases can grow to?
Exchange Server 5.5 eliminates any limits on information store databases. Thus, the capacity of the dedicated newsgroup server would be limited solely by the capacity of the server's hard disks.

13. What components would you configure to automatically check the status of important services and connections to other sites?
The Server Monitor allows you to check the state of Windows NT Server and Exchange Server services on the local and remote computers. A Link Monitor can be configured to verify whether a messaging connector is functioning reliably.

Chapter 2

1. You're the administrator of a company and you plan to install Exchange Server 5.5 as your messaging system. Users want to send and receive e-mail messages via the Internet. In addition, you want to allow some users access from the Internet to messages stored in mailboxes and public folders. Which Exchange Server components would you need to install to satisfy the users' needs? Which software requirements must be met to run all the necessary components?
   The IMS is required to send and receive messages to and from the Internet. It can be installed through the Exchange Administrator program. Internet browsers can provide users with access to public folders and mailboxes. To allow access via Internet browsers, IIS 3.0 or higher with Active Server Pages needs to be configured prior to the Exchange Server installation. To run IIS 3.0 or higher in conjunction with Exchange Server 5.5, Windows NT Server version 4.0 with SP3 or higher must be installed. If these prerequisites are met, you can launch the setup process by selecting the Complete/Custom option to install the Outlook Web Access components. These components allow HTTP-based access to mailboxes, public folders, and the global address book.

2. Exchange Server 5.5 requires powerful hardware, but you decide to test this system on a smaller machine prior to the actual implementation. What is the minimum hardware equipment you should use for a test computer? What are the recommended hardware requirements?
   An Exchange Server computer requires at the minimum a Pentium 60 with at least 150-MB of available disk space. The computer needs at least 24 MB RAM. To provide an acceptable platform for testing, an Intel Pentium 133 MHz or faster should be considered. This computer needs at least 32 MB RAM and sufficient disk space for users' e-mail and public folder information (250 MB or more). The Windows NT Server pagefile should be 100 MB plus the amount of physical RAM.

3. What are the required Windows NT permissions for the Site Services Account?
   The Site Services Account needs the rights Logon As A Service, Restore Files And Directories, and Act As A Part Of The Operating System so that Windows NT can start the Exchange services under the security context of this account. It does not need to be a member of the Domain Admins group; membership in the Domain Users group is sufficient.

4. To save disk space, you have used the **Minimum** installation option during setup of the first server. Now you want to create mailboxes. Why can't you manage the Exchange Server? What type of installation could you use to install all required components? How can you add the components to the server that was installed with **Minimum** installation type? **The Exchange Administrator program will not be installed during a Minimum installation. To copy the program to the local hard disk of the first Exchange Server computer in a site, select either the Typical or Complete/Custom installation. To add the components to a server that was originally installed using the Minimum installation type, launch Setup in maintenance mode choosing the Add/Remove option.**

5. You want to designate additional administrators in a site. The additional accounts will be responsible for mailbox creation and extended configuration tasks. What are the three security levels you need to configure for new administrators? What minimum permission is required to display the site's configuration information? **The main administrator can run the Exchange Administrator program to assign administrative permissions to other Windows NT accounts. You must assign the role of a Permissions Admin of the Organization, Site, and Configuration container objects to the new administrators. To grant users read-only access to the configuration information of a site, the right of a View Only Admin at the site level is required.**

6. As an administrator, you need to install an Exchange Server in a new site. While Setup is completing successfully, you realize that you have misspelled the organization name. What do you need to do to correct the organization name? **The organization name is case sensitive, must match exactly for all sites, and is read-only. If an administrator has to correct the organization name, the Exchange Server computer needs to be reinstalled.**

7. What important names are required to initialize the directory of a new Exchange Server installation during setup? **The Organization and Site names, which can be up to 64 characters long and are case sensitive. They can be defined by the installing administrator. The Server name, which can be up to 15 characters long and follows the Windows NT naming conventions. The server name cannot be defined by the administrator because it will always be identical with the name of the Windows NT Server on which the Exchange Server is installed.**

8. What are the names of the hard disk directories that Setup creates during the server installation?

When you install Exchange Server with default settings, the server files are placed in various directories under C:\Exchsrvr. Setup creates the directories named Add-ins, Address, Bin, Ccmcdata, Connect, Docs, Dsadata, Dxadata, Imcdata, Insdata, Kmsdata, Mdbdata, Mtadata, Res, Tracking.log, Webdata, and Webtemp. The Exchange Performance Optimizer might create an Exchsrvr directory on every other hard disk drive on the computer. The Optimizer places the files across all drives to increase the Exchange Server performance and reliability.

9. The number of users wanting to send e-mail messages has increased, so you have decided to install an additional Exchange Server computer. You will add the new server to the existing site. What are the advantages of a single site organization?

Single site organizations simplify the administration of multiple Exchange Server computers. All servers automatically replicate all configuration changes with each other. This allows specifying site-level default configurations that affect all servers in a site. Furthermore, the MTAs do not need to use additional messaging connectors to transfer e-mail messages between the servers.

10. You start the installation of a new Exchange Server. This server should join an existing site. During setup, you are informed that you don't have the required permissions to install the server, so the setup process terminates. What are the required Windows NT permissions you must have on the local computer? What permissions must your account possess at the Exchange level to join an existing site?

Your account needs to be a member of the local Windows NT Administrator group. In order to join an existing site, the administrator needs further administrative Windows NT rights at the remote computer and must be a Permissions Admin on the site (Organization, Site, and Configuration level) that will be joined.

11. You are planning to install a new Exchange Server that will be added to an existing site. The server maintains user home directories and will be responsible for messaging tasks in the future. The Windows NT home directories already exist. Users access their directories using NetBEUI, and the network operates without problems. Why do you need to change the server configuration anyway?

NetBEUI is not a supported network protocol for server-to-server communication based on RPC within a site. During the process of joining an existing site, directory replication happens. This is a server-to-server communication that cannot be accomplished if NetBEUI is the only protocol configured. TCP/IP or the NWLink

IPX/SPX-compatible Transport protocol has to be used instead. If you plan to remove NetBEUI from the server completely, however, you need to consider reconfiguring client computers with respect to TCP/IP or the NWLink IPX/SPX-compatible Transport as well.

12. You are using Exchange Server version 4.0 in a complex environment. Because of the extended Internet features implemented in version 5.5, you decide to upgrade the messaging network. What upgrade strategy should you use?

    It is recommended that you upgrade the messaging and directory replication bridgehead servers in each site first. The remaining servers can be upgraded later in any order.

13. Another administrator has previously installed an Exchange Client on a server computer, which is an unsupported configuration. To clean up the unsupported configuration, you have decided to remove the client with all its components. You then find that the IMS no longer works properly because the MAPI32.dll is missing. How can you fix this problem?

    You must start Exchange Server setup. Setup launches the maintenance mode because the server has already been installed. At this point, you can click the Reinstall button. The reinstallation of an Exchange server is useful when Windows NT Registry entries are corrupted or files are missing. The missing files will be reinstalled this way. Note that neither database files nor template information will be overwritten.

14. You plan to install 10 Exchange Server computers. All of them should be added to an existing site. The server installation should be performed unattended in order to run setup simultaneously on more than one computer. Where do you specify setup information? Why shouldn't you add all 10 new servers at the same time to the existing site?

    To install multiple servers simultaneously, a Setup.ini can be created to run the Exchange server in unattended mode. This file will provide all necessary installation options for the setup process. To avoid network problems, however, not all servers should be installed at the same time if they are supposed to join the same existing site. Directory replication will happen at the end of each installation, and this might overload the network. It's better to install only a few servers in one cycle. The others might follow if the replication process on the first servers has been finished.

15. Why should you start the Performance Optimizer at the end of a new Exchange Server installation?

    The Performance Optimizer can configure and optimize the installation of the new Exchange Server. The optimization allows the server to work with the available hardware in the most efficient way.

16. You have doubled the amount of RAM on a server computer. You have also added a disk array for better input/output performance. How can you configure the Exchange Server to access the new hardware resources efficiently?

The Performance Optimizer can be used to optimize the Exchange Server configuration according to the available hardware resources.

17. Some Exchange Server directories such as Add-ins or Tracking.log will be shared for network access during the installation. You don't want regular users to access the existing network shares. How can you secure the Exchange Server installation?

To restrict access to the shared directories, you need to remove the Everyone group from the list of accounts with permissions. You can then grant the appropriate rights to specific accounts. You shouldn't change the permissions for the Site Services Account and the local administrators group, however, because this can lead to a server that is not working as expected.

18. The messaging network of your company consists of one single site. Five server computers exist within this site. You want to administer all these computers from a Windows NT Workstation in your office. What needs to be installed on the Windows NT Workstation? How do you install the additional components?

Only the Exchange Administrator program is required. It can be installed on Windows NT Workstation using Exchange Server setup.

19. During the join of an existing site, setup prompts for the password of the Site Services Account, but none of the available administrators can remember the valid password. What has to be done to successfully add the new server to the site?

You need to use the Exchange Administrator program. The password of the Site Services Account can be changed to a known value at the site's Configuration container object through the Service Account Password property page. To match the password at the Windows NT level, you need to change the account password within the User Manager for Domains as well. You can then switch back to Exchange Server setup, where you can continue the installation by entering the new service account password.

20. Which network protocols are supported for server-to-server communication? Which protocol should not be used if a server is joining an existing site?

TCP/IP and IPX/SPX are supported protocols, but NetBEUI must not be used.

21. The Windows NT Server can't start the Workstation service because another computer with the same name has been detected in the network. How does this problem affect the Exchange Server?
   The System Attendant services (and all Exchange Server services) depend on a running Workstation service. Because of this dependency, the whole Exchange Server cannot be started.

22. Which Exchange Server 5.5 components can be installed in a clustered environment?
   DS, IS, MTA, SA, IMS, and Event Service.

23. During the installation of an additional computer in an existing site you receive the following error message: "Failed to connect to server <Server Name> with the following error. Try a different server or correct the error. You do not have the permissions required to complete the operation." What is most likely the cause of that error?
   Your account does not have the rights of a Permissions Admin at the site's Organization, Site, and Configuration containers.

Chapter 3

1. What are the Exchange Server core components?
    The Directory Service (DS), the Message Transfer Agent (MTA), the Information Store (IS), and the System Attendant (SA).

2. In order to perform an offline backup, you want to shut down the Exchange Server without rebooting the Windows NT Server computer. Which of the core components must be stopped directly in order to stop all other server components as well?
    The System Attendant.

3. As an administrator of your organization, you want to allow users to work with MAPI-based and POP3-based messaging clients. You need to configure POP3 support to allow POP3 clients to send and receive messages. Which additional components must be configured?
    The Internet Mail Service (IMS).

4. In order to provide HTTP-based access to public folders, mailboxes, and the Global Address List, you want to install the Outlook Web Access components. How do you add this component to your Exchange Server? What is required to install Outlook Web Access?
    Outlook Web Access can be installed through the Exchange Server Setup. IIS 3.0 (or IIS 4.0) and Active Server Pages must be configured before you can install the Outlook Web Access components.

5. In order to improve the security in your organization you have decided to implement Advanced Security features. What two relevant features does the Key Management Server (KM Server) provide?
    Signing and sealing e-mail messages.

6. You have stopped the MTA service. How does this affect the behavior of connected Exchange Clients?
    The MTA is responsible for message transfer to other servers in the same site, as well as to remote sites and foreign mail systems. The MTA is also responsible for the expansion of distribution lists and for routing decisions. Therefore, e-mail messages addressed to recipients on a remote server and to distribution lists will remain in the client's Outbox if the MTA service has been stopped.

7. As an administrator you have stopped the IS service. How does this affect Exchange Clients?
    The IS maintains the mailboxes and public folders. Clients communicate primarily with this service and users can't work with the server if the IS service has been stopped.

8. In order to satisfy growing messaging demand, you decide to install a second Exchange Server computer. You will add this server to the existing site to make administration easier. Which two components communicate directly with each other between both servers?
The MTA transfers e-mail messages through RPC. The DS replicates directory changes through RPC.

9. List the core components with which the IS communicates.
DS, MTA, and SA.

10. As a user you can send messages successfully to other users who reside on the same home server. However, messages destined to recipients on other servers within the same site remain in your Outbox. What is the likely source of the problem?
The MTA service has been stopped at the Exchange Server computer.

11. As a user you can send messages successfully to other users who reside in the same site. Messages destined to recipients in other sites cannot be delivered and result in Non-Delivery Reports (NDRs). What is the likely source of the problem?
The Gateway Address Routing Table (GWART) does not contain a valid messaging path to the remote sites.

Chapter 4

1. Which server component is responsible for the exchange of information between Exchange Server computers in different sites?
   The MTA is the only component responsible for transferring all information between sites in the form of e-mail messages.

2. What communication method is used between DSs within a single site?
   The directory replication within a single site is accomplished through RPCs.

3. Which message types are transferred by the MTA?
   Interpersonal messages; directory replication messages, public folder content replication messages, public folder hierarchy replication messages; Link Monitor test messages

4. What is the advantage of the multimaster replication model?
   Configuration changes at the site level can be applied to every existing directory in the site. This means that the site can be administered through any of its Exchange Server computers.

5. You have changed the configuration of a site, but the directory replication has not started immediately. How long will the DS wait before it notifies the other DSs in the site? What is the advantage of this delay?
   By default, the DS will wait five minutes before it notifies other DSs in the site about new changes. This delay allows for replication of these changes in batches.

6. What is the purpose of Universal Sequence Numbers (USNs)?
   USNs allow the DSs to verify which changes have not been received yet. A DS will request only the changes not yet incorporated into its own directory.

7. What is the advantage of a common Site Services Account?
   The validation of security information is simplified because all services run under the same security context. Consequently, the same security information is available to all servers within the site.

8. You are creating new mailboxes on a specific server. You want to send test messages to the new users, but your own mailbox resides on another server within the same site. How long will you have to wait until the new mailboxes appear in the address lists of your server?
   The directory replication is responsible for the distribution of the information about the new mailboxes. By default, a delay of five minutes has been implemented to allow for replicating changes in batches. Therefore, the new information should appear after five minutes, allowing you to send messages to the new recipients by selecting them from the Global Address List.

9. Why do you need to use the same Site Services Account for all servers within a site?

   Because the DS and the MTA communicate directly with their corresponding components on other servers using RPCs. A common Site Services account allows the Exchange Server services to efficiently validate remote services that want to establish a communication link.

10. Which Exchange Server components rely on the MTA to exchange information within a single site?

    The IS and the SA. The IS uses the features of the MTA to replicate the public folder hierarchy and contents based on e-mail messages, and the SA handles Link Monitor test messages.

11. You send an e-mail to a user on another server within your site. How does the MTA locate the final destination of the message?

    The MTA checks the site name segment of the user's DN. Since the DN matches the local site, the MTA asks the DS for the home server attribute of the address. By then the MTA has received the required information about the destination server, and the message will be delivered directly with a maximum hop count of one.

12. What are the parts of a recipient's DN within an Exchange Server organization?

    The organization name, the site name, the Recipients container, and the mailbox name.

Chapter 5

1. What is a custom recipient?

   A custom recipient is a recipient object that does not have a mailbox on an Exchange Server. Instead, custom recipients are wrappers around an underlying e-mail address, which points to the actual recipient somewhere outside the Exchange organization.

2. What is an Exchange Server mailbox?

   A mailbox is a private repository of e-mail–related items on an Exchange Server. Mailboxes are used to deliver new messages to recipients, even if the recipient's client is not running. The client works primarily with the mailbox to send and receive messages. Mailbox information appears in address books so users can easily address messages to others.

3. What is a distribution list?

   A distribution list represents a group of recipient objects. It can contain mailbox addresses, custom recipients, public folders, and additional distribution lists. The distribution list allows users to address messages to many recipients at one time. The Exchange Server is responsible for the expansion of distribution lists into their address elements to send messages to all distribution list members.

4. What must be configured in order to handle public folders as you would any other recipient?

   Public folders are recipient objects, and can therefore be handled like mailboxes, custom recipients and distribution lists. By default, public folders are hidden from the address book; to display them, the Hide From Address Book check box must be deselected on the Advanced property page of the desired public folder object. The public folder will then appear in the Global Address List just like any other recipient object.

5. Which set of permissions is required to create a Windows NT account and the associated mailbox within the User Manager for Domains?

   Windows NT Domain Admins membership is used to create and delete Windows NT domain accounts.

   The rights of a Permissions Admin at the Exchange Organization, Site and Configuration level are used to create and delete mailboxes.

6. You are the administrator of an existing Novell NetWare 4.x network and have installed an Exchange Server to provide extended messaging capabilities. The Windows NT Server, Gateway Services for NetWare, and the Exchange Server are operating perfectly. Now you want to configure mailboxes for all existing users. What steps must be performed to create the mailboxes as efficiently as possible?
The bindery emulation must be enabled at the Novell NetWare 4.x servers. To retrieve the needed account database information successfully, the administrator must log on to Novell NetWare as a supervisor. If these requirements are met, the Exchange Administrator program can be used to extract the NetWare account list into a .CSV file. This file can then be used to create the mailboxes in one step via the Directory Import command from the Tools menu.

7. The export and import features of the Exchange Administrator program can be used to assign additional proxy addresses to mailboxes. These features allow all existing mailboxes to be exported into a file. Additional addresses can then be assigned by editing the file using Excel or any word processing program. The changes need to be reimported into the Exchange Server for the new proxy addresses to take effect. What are the particular steps you need to perform in order to accomplish this task?
First an import header file must be created that includes the Secondary Proxy Addresses field. The file must be saved with a .CSV extension. This file can either be created manually or with the help of the Import Header Tool from the Microsoft Exchange Resource Kit (BackOffice Resource Kit 2.0). Once this .CSV file has been created, you can use the Exchange Administrator program to export all mailboxes into it. The file can be edited using Excel or any text editor, and the secondary proxy addresses can be specified in the row below the Secondary Proxy Addresses field. Once the file is reimported, all mailboxes that were changed in the .CSV file receive a secondary proxy address.

8. How do you hide a particular mailbox from the address book?
Select the Advanced property page of the desired mailbox and select the Hide From Address Book option.

9. How do you move a single mailbox to another server in the same site?
The Home server attribute displayed on the Advanced property page must be changed to point to the new server. The mailbox will be moved automatically.

10. Recipient containers can be used to group recipients to organize the server-based address books. How can you move a particular recipient from one container to another?
It is not possible to move a mailbox to another recipient container.

11. The company STOCKSDATA has 157 employees, and every employee has a mailbox. A distribution list called All Stockers contains all the mailboxes. Recently William Pear sent a 12-MB message to this distribution list to distribute scanned pictures. Fred Pumpkin, one of the administrators, assumes that this will probably happen again and wants to prevent it. What would you recommend?
To avoid having large messages sent to the distribution list, a message size limit should be defined using the Advanced property page of the All Stockers distribution list. Public folders can be used instead to provide large message items to multiple users.

12. You have created a temporary distribution list for a specific and confidential project. You don't want to allow users to explore the list membership. What do you need to configure?
You can activate the Hide Membership option for a selected list on the Advanced property page. Once this option is activated, users will not be able to examine the distribution list membership using their client's address books.

13. How can you accomplish the transfer of distribution list management responsibilities to a regular user?
Designate the user as the distribution list owner.

14. How do you configure a distribution list to send Out-of-Office notifications to originators of messages that have been sent to the distribution list?
Select the Allow Out Of Office Messages To Originator option on the Advanced property page.

15. Your Exchange Server is a very busy server. Another server in another site has fewer tasks to perform so you decide to designate this computer as an expansion server. How do you accomplish the configuration?
You cannot configure a server outside the local site as an expansion server. Servers within the site, however, can be designated separately for each distribution list using the Expansion Server setting on the General property page.

16. You recently connected your Exchange Server organization to an MS Mail network and a Lotus cc:Mail post office. Now you want to exchange address information between all three systems. How do you accomplish this task?

    Directory Synchronization is supported between all three systems through the Exchange Server computer. MS Mail addresses and addresses of the Lotus cc:Mail post office will be handled as custom recipients on the Exchange Server. Because custom recipients are handled in a similar way as regular mailboxes, they can be included in the address information sent from the Exchange Server to the other messaging systems. This allows the MS Mail postoffices to receive Lotus cc:Mail addresses and vice versa. The post offices are not aware of the manipulation.

17. What types of custom recipients can exist?

    There exist five predefined types of custom recipients: MS Mail, MacMail, Lotus cc:Mail, SMTP and X.400. There is also the Other Address option, which allows the administrator to define additional custom recipients' address types.

18. You want to configure an Exchange Server to act as a backbone for an MS Mail system. The MS Mail system should be connected to the Internet through the Exchange Server. MS Mail recipients must be able to send and receive messages to and from the Internet. What do you need to configure on the Exchange Server in order to accomplish this task?

    The IMS must be configured, and custom recipients representing the MS Mail users must be created. Just like any other recipient object, these custom recipients provide the E-Mail Addresses property page. On this page you can examine and, if required, change the proxy SMTP address generated for each custom recipient. If a large number of custom recipients are to be generated automatically on the Exchange Server, it might be a good idea to let Directory Synchronization do this work.

19. You are planning to create multiple mailboxes by using the Directory Import feature of the Administrator program. However, many properties, such as distribution list memberships, are exactly the same for all mailboxes. How would you preconfigure common mailbox properties most efficiently?

    One mailbox must be created and configured with all desired common properties first. To use this mailbox as a template for other mailboxes, select the Directory Import command under the Tools menu. Within the Directory Import dialog box, click the Recipient Template button and specify the template mailbox. All common settings of the template mailbox will be copied into the new mailboxes that have been created using the import .CSV file.

Chapter 6

1. Which programs are parts of the Microsoft Exchange Client family?
The Microsoft Exchange Client family consists of three applications: the Exchange Client itself, Schedule+ and the Electronic Forms Designer.

2. Because of the integrated messaging, calendar, and scheduling capabilities of Outlook, you want to migrate to the new program from your Exchange Client. What needs to be reconfigured once the installation has been completed?
Outlook is a MAPI-based application that uses the same messaging profile as the Exchange Client. Therefore, additional profile configuration is not required. The Outlook Address Book will be added automatically to the existing profile.
Existing Schedule+ appointments and other items must be imported into Outlook before you can work with them. To do this, select the Import and Export command on the File menu. When all information is incorporated into Outlook, the Exchange Client and Schedule+ can be removed from the computer.

3. A user has continued using Schedule+ as the primary calendar application, although Outlook is currently used as the messaging client. Now the user wants to remove the Exchange Client and Schedule+ from the computer. How can you switch to Outlook as the primary calendar application?
If the user wants Outlook as the primary scheduling application, the Use Microsoft Schedule+ 95 As My Primary Calendar option must be deselected. This option is under the Options command on the Tools menu and can be found in the Calendar dialog box.

4. Some users in your organization work on Macintosh computers, so you've installed Outlook for Macintosh. Which features of the Windows-based clients are not available to Macintosh users?
Macintosh clients do not support MAPI transport drivers; therefore, additional messaging systems cannot be connected. Also, Remote Mail functionality does not exist. Electronic forms are unavailable since they rely on MAPI. The Person-to-Person key security feature also has not been implemented into the Macintosh client.

5. What types of messaging applications exist and what are their characteristics?

   Messaging-aware programs use e-mail capabilities as an add-on to their actual features. They can be started regardless of whether an underlying messaging system exists. Messaging-enabled applications rely on the underlying messaging system—they cannot be used without one. Their functionality can be as simple as sending e-mail only, or as complex as the features of the Exchange Web client. Messaging-based applications use the underlying messaging system extensively. Like the messaging-enabled applications, they cannot operate without the existence of a messaging network. The Exchange Client, Schedule+, and Outlook are good examples of this type of application.

6. Which information services can be installed using the Exchange Client Setup?

   The Exchange Client provides the Exchange Server transport and message store, MS Mail transport, Personal Address Book, and Personal Folder Store service.

7. Which information services can be installed using the Outlook Setup?

   Outlook provides the Exchange Server transport and message store, MS Mail transport, Personal Address Book, Outlook Address Book, Personal Folder Store service, and the Internet E-mail transport.

8. What is a messaging profile?

   A messaging profile contains the configuration information about information services, which will be used by the Exchange Client to establish a session with the underlying messaging backbone. The client cannot start without an existing profile.

9. Where in Windows 95 are the messaging profiles of the currently logged-on user stored?

   The profile of the currently logged on user can be found under: HKEY_CURRENT_USER\Software\Microsoft\Windows Messaging Subsystem\Profiles.
   Subkeys exist corresponding to each configured profile.

10. Which two message stores can be configured to keep messages available off line?

    To work off line with messages, they must be copied to the computer's hard disk. To do this, you can configure an Offline and/or a Personal Folder Store. While the Offline Store is a replica of the actual server-based content, the Personal Folder Store normally is used to download and remove messages from the server.

11. How many entries can a .PST file contain and what is its size limit?
A .PST file can contain up to 64,000 entries and can grow up to a maximum size of 2 GB.

12. What are the requirements for installing the Exchange Client on Windows 95?
The Exchange Client for Windows 95 needs between 12 MB and 22 MB of disk space (depending on the selected installation type) and at least 8 MB of RAM to operate properly. The client also requires TCP/IP, IPX/SPX, or NetBEUI to communicate with the Exchange Server.

13. What are the installation requirements of the Exchange Client for Windows NT?
The Exchange Client for Windows NT needs between 12 MB and 22 MB of disk space (depending on the selected installation option) and 16 MB of RAM to operate properly. TCP/IP, IPX/SPX, or NetBEUI is required.

14. What are the installation requirements to install the Windows 95 and Windows NT versions of Outlook 97?
These versions need 8 MB of RAM on Windows 95 (16 MB of RAM are highly recommended), 16 MB of RAM on Windows NT, and between 26 MB and 46 MB of disk space. TCP/IP, SPX/IPX, or NetBEUI are required.

15. You want to install the Exchange Client on your portable computer, which has limited hard disk capacity. Which installation option would you select to save the greatest amount of disk space?
You would select the Laptop installation because it copies only the application files for Exchange Client and Schedule+. No additional files will be installed. The Workstation option cannot be used since it would require that the portable computer always be connected with the network.

16. What process must be completed before installing Outlook using the **Run From Network Server** mode?
First start the Setup program with the /A parameter to create the shared network installation point. Then start Setup from this location to select the Run From Network Server mode.

17. Some users in your company need to install the Exchange Client, and you want to assist them with a preconfigured client configuration. (For example, you want to provide the name of the Exchange Server computer.) What process must be completed before automatically creating a default profile during the client installation?
Run the Exchange Client Setup with /A parameter to install a shared network installation point. This installation point is the location where client settings can be preconfigured. Basic settings can be specified using the Setup Editor. Further editing of the Default.prf is possible using any text editor. Once the desired settings such as HomeServer= are specified, the users can start the setup process from the shared installation point. The predefined settings will automatically take effect.

18. You want to specify messaging profile settings for Outlook so that the client environment is configured automatically. How can you achieve this?
Profile settings can be specified in a file called Outlook.prf. First, create a shared installation point, and then replace the original Outlook.prf with a customized version. The Office 97 Resource Kit provides sample .PRF files that can be used. To adjust advanced settings, which cannot be defined interactively with the Setup Editor, you can edit the Outlook.prf directly using a text editor.

19. You want to install the Outlook for Macintosh client on a Macintosh computer with 64 MB RAM. How should you configure the virtual memory?
The virtual memory must be activated and set to 65 MB (RAM+1 MB).

Chapter 7

1. What are messaging profiles?

   Messaging profiles are sets of information services and their configuration parameters that describe the working environment of a user. Using a MAPI-based messaging client such as the Exchange Client or Outlook, each user uses a profile containing the required information services for accessing the desired messaging systems.

2. Where are messaging profiles stored?

   Windows 95 and Windows NT store profiles in the user-specific sections of the Registry. Windows 3.x clients store profiles in the Exchange.ini file. MS-DOS clients rely on a file called Exchange.pro.

3. Which tool assists you with creating messaging profiles?

   The Outlook Setup Wizard (formerly known as the Exchange Setup Wizard).

4. How do you launch the Setup Wizard?

   You can launch the Setup Wizard using the Mail or Mail And Fax applet of the Control Panel. The wizard can also be started through the Choose Profile dialog box that can be displayed during the client startup. The wizard is started automatically if no profile exists when you launch the client.

5. How do you create a profile automatically without the assistance of the Setup Wizard?

   Using the Exchange Client, you can create a file called Default.prf that is used to create a default messaging profile automatically the first time the client starts.

   Using Outlook, you can create a file called Outlook.prf and place it in the Windows directory of your local computer.

6. What are the MAPI services that come with Outlook?

   Internet E-Mail
   Exchange Server transport
   MS Mail transport
   Outlook Address Book
   Personal Folder Store
   Personal Address Book

7. What is the purpose of a Personal Folder Store?

   Personal Folder Stores maintain e-mail messages locally apart from an Exchange Server. This might be necessary if you want to work while disconnected from the server, or if you want to download messages in order to reduce the size of the server-based mailbox. Another use of Personal Folder Stores is to archive messages.

8. How do you change the path to a .PST file?
   First, move the .PST file to the new location and then you adjust the path through the Personal Folder Store properties within the messaging profile. You can also adjust the path by opening the corresponding root folder within the Exchange Client or Outlook, which displays the Create/Open Personal Folders File dialog box— provided that you haven't canceled this dialog previously.

9. You have configured a Personal Folder Store and the Exchange Server transport. How do you define the Personal Folder Store as the location for incoming messages?
   You can configure the message delivery through the Delivery property tab of the Services dialog box, which can be displayed using the Services command on the client's Tools menu. On this property page, the primary Inbox can be specified under the Deliver New Mail To The Following Location option.

10. What elements must be configured in order to enable local replication?
    The Offline Folder Store must be configured through the Exchange Server transport service.

11. Which folders are automatically configured to be available off line and on line when using the native Exchange Client?
    Deleted Items, Inbox, Outbox, and Sent Items.

12. Which folders are automatically configured to be available off line and on line when using Outlook?
    Deleted Items, Inbox, Outbox, Sent Items, Calendar, Contacts, Journal, Notes, and Tasks.

13. What is the disadvantage of the Offline Folder Store?
    You cannot download or upload messages selectively. The entire server-based and client-based replica is always synchronized. Therefore, it is not advisable to use Offline Folders over slow connections if many changes have occurred since the last synchronization.

14. What is the most significant advantage of Offline Folder Store?
    The Offline Folder Store provides the advantage of being able to synchronize public folders, so you can work with public folders while disconnected from the server.

15. Which Exchange executable command line option must you use to specify the location and name of the messaging profile for MS-DOS–based clients?
    You must use the -P option, as in Exchange -PM:\Exchange.pro.

16. Where can you specify the location of messaging profiles for Windows 3.x–based clients?
Profiles for the Windows 3.x–based client are stored in the Exchange.ini file. The location of this file can be referenced through the [MAPI] section of the Win.ini. The parameter ProfileDirectory16 points to the user's Exchange.ini file.

17. How do you assign centralized messaging profiles to roving users who work on Windows 95 and Windows NT computers?
The profiles for Windows 95–based and Windows NT–based Exchange Clients are stored in the user-specific Registry keys (HKEY_CURRENT_USER). These settings can be included in server-based profiles, which are then activated as soon as the roving users logs on to the Windows NT domain.

18. Which e-mail repository must be configured to use the Remote Mail features of the Exchange Client or Outlook?
A Personal Folder Store.

19. Which e-mail repository must not be configured if you want to use the Synchronize features of the Exchange Client or Outlook?
An Offline Folder Store.

20. Where can you configure scheduled remote connections?
On the Remote Mail property page of the Exchange Server transport.

21. What are the advantages of the Remote Mail features?
You can selectively download messages from an Exchange Server using header files or filters. It is also possible to delete messages directly at the server without downloading them beforehand.

22. Which component must be installed to support Remote Mail connections for Windows 3.1–based clients?
ShivaRemote.

23. Several users in your company work on Macintosh computers running the Macintosh–based Microsoft clients. How can you support remote connections for these users?
You cannot support remote connections for Macintosh users because Remote Mail is supported only for clients based on MS-DOS, Windows 3.x, Windows 95, and Windows NT. However, if you have additional dial-up software at your disposal, you can connect to the server manually and turn the remote connection into a slow LAN-like connection, which the Exchange Client for Macintosh is able to use.

24. What are two extensions of Outlook?
The Inbox Assistant and Out of Office Assistant.

25. You want to display a message box providing the option to read new messages immediately when they arrive in your Inbox. How do you configure Outlook to achieve the desired behavior?
   Activate the Display A Notification Message option on the E-Mail property page within the Options dialog box. This dialog box is displayed when you select the Options command on the Tools menu.

26. During the Setup of Outlook you have selected Schedule+ as your primary calendar application. Now you want to switch entirely to Outlook calendar. How do you configure Outlook to act as your primary calendar application?
   First, display the Options dialog box through the Options command on the Tools menu. Then, switch to the Calendar property page, and clear the option to use Schedule+ as the primary calendar application.

27. As an administrator, you want to designate an assistant for your Inbox. Where can you grant the desired permission?
   On the Delegates property page of the Options dialog box.

28. Where can you optimize the RPC connection order for Windows 95–based and Windows NT–based clients?
   HKEY_LOCAL_MACHINE\SOFTWARE\Microsoft\Exchange \Exchange Provider.

29. What is the default order to connect to a server using Windows 95–based and Windows NT–based clients?
   Local Procedure Call, followed by TCP/IP (Sockets), SPX, Named Pipes, NetBIOS, and Banyan Vines IP.

30. How do you adjust the binding order prior to the installation of the Windows 95–based and Windows NT–based Exchange Client?
   You can use the Exchange Setup Editor in conjunction with a share network installation point to adjust the binding order prior to the installation. The modification will be written to the Exchange.stf within the installation point, which affects the configuration of all clients that will be installed from this location.

31. You want to migrate MS Mail 3.x users from a postoffice into Exchange Server. All .MMF files reside in the postoffice. Which tool can you use to import the existing e-mail messages?
   Use the Migration Wizard to move the mailboxes to the Exchange Server. The e-mail messages that reside in the postoffice can be imported directly into the newly-created mailboxes.

32. You want to migrate MS Mail 3.x users from a postoffice into Exchange Server. All .MMF files reside outside the postoffice. Which tool can you use to import the existing e-mail messages?
The Exchange Client and Outlook provide the required import features, which can be found under the File menu. Existing .MMF files can be imported directly into the server-based mailbox or in any .PST file.

33. You have configured several .PAB files that contain different personal contact information. Now you want to create a .PAB file that contains all of them. How can you accomplish this task?
You can import the existing .PAB files into one .PAB file using the import capabilities of the Exchange Client and Outlook.

34. Which permissions must be granted to an assistant to allow them to answer your incoming correspondence?
The assistant needs the read permission for your mailbox and Inbox, plus the right to send messages on your behalf.

35. A delegate is sending messages on your behalf, but you don't want the delegate's name to appear on the **From** line of the message header. What kind of permission must be granted to the assistant to achieve the desired result?
Using the Exchange Administrator program, an administrator grants the assistant the Send As permission via the Permissions property page of your mailbox.

Chapter 8

1. Some users are complaining that they cannot connect to their home server. As their administrator, you want to verify that all servers are functioning. What tool can you use to check the status of the services on the servers from your Windows NT Workstation?

   The Server Manager provides the features required to check the status of Windows NT services, including those of Exchange Server 5.5, that are running on remote Windows NT computers. Similar to the Services applet of the Control Panel, the Server Manager can stop and restart the services and can check the configuration of the Site Services Account.

2. You want to configure an entire Exchange Server organization using the Administrator program on your Windows NT Workstation computer. How do you install this program and which of the existing servers in your organization can be configured?

   The Administrator program is installed using the Exchange Server Setup. As soon as the Setup program detects that it has been started on a Windows NT Workstation computer, it allows you to install only the Administrator program. Once you have installed this application on your computer, you can administer all Exchange Server computers that can be reached through RPCs if you have the necessary permissions.

3. You add more RAM to an Exchange Server computer. The server performance has been increased but you want to use the new hardware in the most efficient way. What tool should you use to optimize the server configuration?

   The Performance Optimizer should be started whenever the hardware or Exchange Server configuration changes.

4. To connect two sites you must first configure a messaging connector. What is the name of the container object that holds the corresponding leaf objects, and where can it be found within the DIT?

   Messaging connector objects are located in the Connections container, which is a sub-level container of the Configuration object.

5. How do you distinguish between container objects and leaf objects?

   Container objects appear in the container and in the content pane, while leaf objects are displayed only in the content pane of the Administration window.

6. You configure a dedicated workstation that will be used for the administration of a site. Other administrators will also use this workstation to perform their site management tasks. While you are working with the Administrator program, you adjust the order of columns within the Administration window. Will the modifications affect the work of other administrators?
No; view options are maintained on a per-administrator basis.

7. To provide an easy way to generate alias names for new mailboxes, you have changed the **Auto Naming** scheme using the Administrator program. How does this setting affect the work of other administrators who use the same workstation?
The new naming scheme is applied to all administrators. It takes effect regardless of which administrator creates the new mailboxes.

8. The company has hired a new Exchange Server administrator. You, as the main administrator, must assign the new administrator the appropriate role of a **Permissions Admin.** At which three levels must you assign the permissions explicitly?
You must assign the Permission Admin role to the Windows NT account of the new administrator at the organization, site, and Configuration level separately because the Permission Admin role is not inherited between them.

9. You want to adjust the MTA checkpoint size for all servers within a site. To do this you decide to change the corresponding site-level settings. What object provides the necessary properties for configuration? What object is its parent container?
The MTA Site Configuration object provides the required property page to adjust the site-level configuration parameters. Its parent container is the Configuration container.

10. You decide to create a customized Offline Address Book, which should not contain address information of remote sites. Where do you configure the relevant Offline Address Book settings?
To configure the content of the Offline Address Book based on recipient containers, display the property pages of the DS Site Configuration object. On the Offline Address Book property page, you have the option to specify whichever recipient container you want to use as a source for the Offline Address Book. When you click the Generate All button, the address book will be rebuilt.

11. You have added the IMS to an existing site. Now you want to send messages to recipients over the Internet. A message is returned as a non-delivery notification that indicates that the recipient was unknown, although you assigned the correct SMTP address space to the IMS. How do you resolve the routing problem?

    The routing table is probably not yet updated. To check the routing entries, use the Site Addressing object within the Configuration container. You can also click the Routing Recalculation button on the Routing property page. This will update the routing table immediately. Once the SMTP address space is incorporated, you can send messages through the IMS.

12. You want to change the look of the mailbox details dialog box within Outlook. Where do you configure this dialog?

    To modify a details dialog box of the client's Address Book, you must configure the corresponding Details template under the Addressing container. Because templates are language dependent, you will find sub-level containers for each installed language, from which you can select the desired object.

13. You discover that one server within a site does not reflect the current site information. What would you do to force a directory replication cycle? Where can you find detailed information about possible replication problems?

    The Directory Service object at the server level has the Update Now button, which can be used to force a directory replication cycle within the site. To verify that no problems exist regarding the directory replication, you can temporarily increase the diagnostics level for each service category (namely the Replication category) on the corresponding property page.

14. You want to manage the available disk space on the server, so you define storage limits. Lisa Strawberry's mailbox is larger than the **Storage Warning** setting. Bert Melon's mailbox size exceeds the **Prohibit Send** limit. Fred Pumpkin's mailbox size exceeds the **Prohibit Send And Receive** limit. How do the storage limits affect the work of Lisa, Bert, and Fred?

    Lisa will receive warning messages indicating that her mailbox is too large. Bert will receive warning messages and will be unable to send any messages since the Prohibit Send limit has been reached. However, Bert can still receive messages, which means that his mailbox may still be growing. Fred cannot send or receive any messages until he downloads or deletes messages from his mailbox in order to reduce its size.

15. A supervisor of one of the departments calls and wants to know whether Fred Pumpkin is working online. You need to view information about currently logged-on users in order to find out. Which object provides the fastest access to the desired information?
The Logon object under the Private Information Store object provides the fastest access to the desired information. When you select this object, status information regarding all logged on users will be displayed in the content pane of the Administration window.

16. Your company's backup strategy relies on offline backups. You want to check the database locations to ensure that all database files are included in a backup configuration. Which property page provides information about existing database paths within the Administrator program?
The Database Paths property page of the server object (for example, NEWYORK-1).

Chapter 9

1. Your company wants to implement Exchange Server 5.5. The company does not have any subsidiaries, and all of its computers are connected using a LAN. It has two Windows NT domains, one for the human resources department and one for all other employees. Due to security considerations, no trust relationship can exist between the domains. How many sites must be created?
   You must create two independent service accounts and two sites.

2. A fictitious company named Sombrero has two locations, one in New York and one in Mexico City, with a permanent 1 MB X.25 connection between them. The X.25 data transfer generates transmission costs. Should the administrator implement a single site to make administration easier?
   No. The implementation of a single site across WAN connections leads to intensive WAN communication based on RPCs, and intrasite communication cannot be controlled. It is better to implement two sites and connect them using a messaging connector, which can transfer the information using the WAN connection. Using the connector properties, you can optimize the communication on the WAN link and reduce transmission costs.

3. What kind of information is wrapped in e-mail messages for intersite communication?
   Besides interpersonal information that is always handled in form of e-mail messages, intersite connections transfer public folder hierarchy and content replication messages. Intersite directory replication is also performed using e-mail messages. Moreover, Link Monitor test messages can be used to check whether a messaging path is working.

4. What advantages does intersite communication provide?
   The administrator can control the intrasite communication by adjusting the parameters of messaging connectors. This communication method is basically independent of network topology since a variety of messaging connectors can be used for data transfer. Also, directory information sent through a connector is compressed by an average ratio of 5:1. To optimize the communication further, the MTA can include multiple recipients in a single message instance.

5. You need to connect two sites, and you want to enable directory replication. No permanent network connection exists between the sites, but dial-up connections are available, which can also be used to connect to the Internet. Which two messaging connectors can you use to connect the sites together?
   The Dynamic RAS Connector and the IMS.

6. Which three messaging connectors can you use to connect NEW YORK and FRANKFURT? (See Figure 9-3 on page 494.)
The Internet connection requires a messaging connector that supports the communication over TCP/IP. You can use the Site Connector, X.400 Connector, and the IMS.

7. To connect your organization to the Internet, you installed the IMS. Which address space type should you associate with this connector?
SMTP.

8. To exchange messages with users on a DEC ALL-IN-ONE system, you created an X.400 connection to their DEC MailBus400 MTA. The X.400 system uses the address c=*US;a= ;p=StocksData;o=Mailbus.* Routing information about this particular X.400 connection cannot be replicated to other sites in the organization, but you want the users to be able to send messages through the connection. How should you assign the address space to the X.400 Connector?
To avoid replication of the routing information to other sites, you should define local address spaces. Display the property pages of the X.400 Connector and switch to the Address Space property page. Click the New button to display the New Address Space dialog box. Select X.400 and then click OK to enter the address space information *c=US,a= , p=StocksData,o= Mailbus* **on the General property page of the X.400 Properties dialog box. Switch to the Restrictions tab and select the This Site option. To create the new address space, click OK. This site will prevent replication of this address space to other sites.**

9. The workload of the servers within your local site is high, so you implemented local messaging bridgehead computers to offload the intersite message transfer from other servers. Now you need to connect to a new site that contains only one server. You have decided to implement a Site Connector, but you want to keep the messaging bridgehead concept in local site. How do you configure the Site Connector?
On the Site Connector's General property page, use the Messaging Bridgehead In The Local Site box to specify the local bridgehead computer. The target server configuration is not necessary because the remote site contains only one computer, which by itself forms a messaging bridgehead.

10. You need to configure a Site Connector, but the Site Services Accounts in the two sites are different. When you began installing the connector, you received notification that access to the remote server's directory was denied due to missing access rights. You want to configure both sites in a common Windows NT domain. What do you do to configure the Site Connector?

   Ask an administrator to grant your Windows NT user account the rights of a Admin in the remote site. Then you can create and configure the connector. To complete the configuration, you must specify each remote service account using the Override property page.

11. You want to balance the messaging load between three servers in you site. Server A should receive approximately double the amount of messages as server B. Server C should be accessed only if server A and B are not available. Which cost values should you assign to servers A, B, and C?

   Cost value "Server A" = 5
   Cost value "Server B" = 50
   Cost value "Server C" = 100

12. You want to create a Site Connector between sites in non-trusted domains. What steps should you take in Windows NT and Exchange Server to install the connector?

   First, create an identical user account in both domains. Then, grant both user accounts Admin rights for the local site (Organization, Site, and Configuration level). Using this account, install and configure the Site Connector. Since the identical accounts allow you to configure the connector in both sites, you can complete the installation in one procedure. However, you must specify each remote Site Services Account using the connector's Override property page within the Administrator program.

13. Your company is using a worldwide X.400 messaging network using various protocols such as TCP/IP and X.25. As an administrator, you have the task of implementing Exchange Server. How can you benefit from the existing messaging network?

   You can tightly implement the Exchange Server organization into the existing X.400 backbone because you can use the X.400 Connector to connect to any foreign X.400 system using the TCP/IP, TP4, or X.25 protocol. Using Exchange Server only, you can replace the existing X.400 components. A heterogeneous environment will become homogenous, and administration will become easier.

14. You connected two sites using a X.400 Connector that uses a X.25 connection. The communication between both sites worked without any problems, but the demand on messaging has increased and the X.400 Connector has become a bottleneck in one site. Intersite messages are queued back on this server and delivery is delayed. What should you do to remove the bottleneck?

The X.400 Connector uses the messaging bridgehead concept, which means you cannot connect to multiple servers using the same connector. But you can configure multiple connector instances. That is, you can connect two sites several times. You can configure an additional X.400 Connector on a second Exchange Server, thus removing the bottleneck from the site.

15. A company has three sites, which are connected using X.400 Connectors. You want to connect the organization to a public X.400 provider. The provider has sent you the required configuration parameters for the X.400 connection, and the required MTA name and password differ from the local MTA name and password. How should you configure the X.400 Connector?

Use the Override property page of the particular connector object to overwrite the local information with the required MTA name and password from the public carrier.

16. To connect your organization to the Internet, you need to install the IMS. What should you install on the server before I begin, and which tool should you use to begin the IMS installation?

Before you can install the IMS, you must install and configure the TCP/IP protocol under Windows NT. Then you can use the Internet Mail Setup Wizard within the Exchange Administrator program to install the IMS.

17. What are the disadvantages of directory replication over dynamic RAS connections?

The Dynamic RAS Connector uses dial-up connections that are basically not designed to handle large data transfer. Intersite directory replication, on the other hand, typically generates many replication messages that transfer many megabytes of directory information. This can backlog your connector. Also, you cannot specify message size limits to optimize connector usage.

18. You have configured two messaging connectors between NEWYORK and LONDON. One connector, the Site Connector, uses TCP/IP for communication, while the X.400 Connector uses the TP4 protocol. What do you do to provide load balancing between the Site Connector and the X.400 Connector?
You must assign the same cost values to the address spaces of both connectors.

19. A member of your administration team has changed address spaces. Messages are incorrectly routed because of the new entries. Now, you are in charge of correcting the routing problem. Where do you find information about correct routing table entries?
Whenever the GWART changes, the routing table is dumped to a new text file that is always called Gwart0.mta. The old dump file is called Gwart1.mta.

20. Your company is planning to connect two sites. Directory replication must be performed. Which connector do you use to connect the sites? Which connector makes intersite replication configuration easiest?
You can enable intersite directory replication using any main messaging connector, including the Site Connector, X.400 Connector, Dynamic RAS Connector, and the IMS. The Site Connector makes configuration easy because it configures the Connected Sites information automatically.

21. Your company has three sites that are connected via X.400 Connectors. You are planning to enable intersite replication to share all directory information within the organization. You configured the Connected Sites information and began creating Directory Replication Connectors. Within site A, you created a replication link to site B and site C. You also wanted to configure the replication link between site B and site C, but it didn't work. Why?
Site A already maintains links to site B and site C, so both sites are transient to each other. Therefore, you cannot create an additional Directory Replication Connector between them.

22. You want to configure directory replication connectors between three sites. Sites A and B are connected through a Site Connector while sites A and C use a X.400 Connector to transfer messages. What will be different when you configure the replication connector between sites A and B and between sites A and C?
You can create the Directory Replication Connector between sites A and B immediately because the Site Connector maintains the Connected Sites information automatically. But you must configure the X.400 connector manually to provide the Connected Sites information before you begin installing the Directory Replication Connector between sites A and C. You can define the remote site using the X.400 Connector's Connected Sites property page.

23. Which topology is an optimal directory replication configuration?
The star configuration is the best because it implements a maximum hop count of two hops regardless of the number of sites in an organization.

24. You created a directory connector between two sites, and to speed up the replication process you clicked the Check Now button to force replication. The KCC created the replication link, and the new container objects appeared in the Directory Information Tree. But now, after a long time, the container objects are still empty. What should you do to see if a replication problem exists?
You should check the MTA message queues because intersite directory replication is performed based on regular e-mail messages.

Chapter 10

1. As an administrator of an organization, you need to connect two sites. Both locations have permanent network connections to the Internet. Which three messaging connectors can you use? Which one should you prefer? Why?
The Internet generally relies on the TCP/IP protocol. Since the Site Connector, X.400 Connector, and the IMS can use TCP/IP, they can all connect the sites. But the IMS is the best choice because it also allows you to connect the sites to foreign SMTP systems across the Internet.

2. Which TCP/IP port is used to connect to a remote SMTP system?
The SMTP protocol defines TCP/IP port 25 for incoming connections.

3. What are the names of the outbound and inbound system folders of the IMS?
The IMS uses the IS to maintain its message queues on an Exchange Server. The MTS-OUT folder is the outbound message queue. MTS-IN places inbound messages on the server.

4. How does the IMS retrieve the IP address of the destination host?
First it queries the DNS database to resolve the domain name. If no MX record exists for the desired e-mail domain, it uses the HOSTS file next. If a NetBIOS name has been specified instead of a domain name, the usual NetBIOS name resolution will be used, which includes a query to LMHOSTS and WINS.

5. Which utility can you use to test name resolution and TCP/IP connectivity?
To test TCP/IP connectivity and the remote SMTP system, you can use Ping or Telnet. To check the DNS database for MX records, use NSLookup or Restest.

6. Your organization has been connected to various foreign mail systems, including MS Mail, and now you are connected to the Internet. A remote administrator calls you because a strange-looking e-mail address has been received from your SMTP domain. The format of the address is *IMCEAMS-cz_prague_pavel@STOCKSDATA.UK*. What kind of address is this and which recipient does it reference?
The address indicates an IMS encapsulated address. The encapsulated address type is MS:, which indicates a user residing in an MS Mail network. The MS Mail user address is CZ/PRAGUE/Pavel.

7. You want to increase the security of a messaging network, so you decide to implement a relay host. The host will forward SMTP messages to and from an Exchange Server organization and the Internet. Can you use an Exchange Server to achieve a relay host configuration?
Yes.

8. Which command should you select within the Administrator program to start the IMS installation? Which Windows NT and Exchange Server configuration information is required?

Select the Internet Mail Service command under New Other on the File menu. To install the IMS information about site addressing, the local computer, an administrative mailbox, and the DNS configuration are required. Also, you must assign an address space for the new connector. To allow the IMS to work within the context of the Site Services Account, you must enter the service account password during installation. Because the IMS uses the TCP/IP transport protocol, you must specify a valid IP address, subnet mask, default gateway, host name, domain name, and DNS server at the Windows NT level.

9. Two Exchange Server computers exist in one site. One server was installed using the Typical installation option and the other using the Minimum installation option. Now you want to install and configure the IMS on the server that was installed with the Minimum installation. What do you have to do to install the IMS?

The Internet Mail Wizard was not installed with the Minimum installation because it is part of the Administrator program. You can specify that the IMS be installed on a remote server within the local site, so you can start the Administrator program on the Typical server and then launch the wizard. Select the Minimum server in the wizard.

10. Since you implemented an IMS, your company has become the target of attacks from the Internet. Large messages have been sent to the company's SMTP entry point to block the IMS. What can you do to reduce the effects of those attacks?

You should specify a default message size limit for messages handled by the IMS using the General property page. This limit will affect both outgoing and incoming messages. If an incoming message exceeds the limit, the IMS will stop writing the data to disk. Remaining portions of large messages are discarded, so the IMS can no longer be blocked.

11. You want to provide fault tolerance for incoming Internet messages. Messages should arrive at their destinations even when one IMS is down for maintenance. Which topology is best for an organization with two sites?

You can implement multiple instances of the IMS in an Exchange organization—one per server. At least one IMS should be installed in each site to handle local inbound and outbound SMTP traffic. Both sites should have different e-mail domain names because it is up to the DNS configuration to provide fault tolerance. The two most important MX records should associate each IMS with the domain name of its local site. A less important MX record should also point to the IMS of each remote site. If the local IMS is unavailable, the IMS in the other site is contacted instead. An additional messaging connector between both sites can then transfer the message to the recipient.

12. Which commands can the IMS use to request queued messages from a remote SMTP host?

The IMS supports the TURN command, ETRN command, and custom commands notify remote SMTP hosts that it can receive messages.

13. Which command requests queued SMTP messages from an Exchange Server computer?

Exchange Server 5.5 supports the ETRN command completely. Other hosts can use ETRN to request messages on a per-domain basis.

Chapter 11

1. As an administrator of STOCKSDATA, you have connected the organization to the Internet through the IMS. Now you want to support common Internet clients as well. Which Internet protocols does Exchange Server 5.5 support?
   In addition to supporting SMTP, Exchange Server 5.5 supports IMAP4, POP3, NNTP, HTTP, and LDAP.

2. Name six client types that you can use to connect to resources located on an Exchange Server.
   You can use MAPI-based, POP3-based, IMAP4-compliant, and LDAP-based clients as well as newsreader programs to connect to an Exchange server. Outlook Web Access also supports Internet browsers.

3. Fred's mailbox resides on NEWYORK-1. He is the assistant for Lisa and Paul, both of whom have granted delegate permission to Fred. Lisa's mailbox resides on NEWYORK-1 while Paul's home server is NEWYORK-2. Lisa must not access her mailbox using POP3. How do you configure the site to allow Fred access to all three mailboxes using a POP3 client?
   The POP3 protocol must be enabled for the entire site, or separately for NEWYORK-1 and NEWYORK-2, and POP3 must be disabled for Lisa's mailbox because Lisa must not be able to access her mailbox. This means also that Fred will not be able to access her mailbox. Access to Fred's and Paul's mailboxes is enabled. Because delegate access to other mailboxes is not possible when using POP3 clients, Fred must log on as Paul in order to work with Paul's messages.

4. You want to increase the access security for Exchange Server resources. How do you limit the group of workstations that can access existing servers in your site through Internet protocols?
   Using the Administrator program, activate the Accept/Reject Specified Connections option on the Connections property page of the Protocols container to specify workstations based on their IP addresses that will be accepted or rejected.

5. What are the features of a POP3 client?
   A POP3 client uses POP3 to download, read, and delete messages from a POP3 host. Send commands are not defined. To send messages, an SMTP system, such as a computer running the IMS, must be available.

6. What are the three possible states of a POP3 session?
   The three states are AUTHORIZATION, TRANSACTION, and UPDATE.

7. What are the states an IMAP4 client will enter during an entire session?
   When the client connects to the IMAP4 host, it enters the Non-Authenticated State. At this point, the LOGIN command can be used to enter the Authenticated State. The Selected State follows when the client opens a mailbox or message folder through the SELECT command. Finally, the Logout State is reached when the user quits his or her IMAP4 client. To initiate the release of the connection, the client sends the LOGOUT command to the host.

8. Using a POP3 client, you delete messages out of your Inbox and then you switch to Outlook. You discover that the messages have not been deleted. Why not?
   Messages will be processed and deleted during the UPDATE phase but the POP3 client has not disconnected from the server yet. The UPDATE phase is launched when the client sends the QUIT command to release the connection.

9. Which authentication methods can you use to support all possible POP3/IMAP4 clients?
   Exchange Server supports these authentication methods: Basic (Clear Text), Basic (Clear Text) Using SSL, Windows NT Challenge/Response, and Windows NT Challenge/Response Using SSL. These four methods are enabled by default. Clients can be authenticated using the methods of the MCIS Membership System and MCIS Membership System Using SSL.

10. Paul complains that his IMAP4 client program is unable to send messages, but he can download new messages from the Exchange Server. What is the most likely cause of the send problem?
    Either the IMS is not running on the user's home server, or the user specified a wrong SMTP server name during IMAP4 client configuration.

11. A particular IMAP4 client has problems connecting to an Exchange Server. You test the connection using Telnet and are able to log on. How can you determine the source of the connection problem?
    The IMAP4 (Mail) Settings object at the server level provides Diagnostics logging categories, which can be enabled to receive detailed information about the IS operation through the Application Even Log. In addition, the IMAP4 communication between the server and the client can be written to a trace file, which can help to identify the source of the communication problem. Using the Windows NT Registry Editor, configure the values IMAP4 Protocol LogPath and IMAP4 Protocol Logging Level under HKEY_LOCAL_MACHINE \System\CurrentControlSet\Services\MSExchangeIS\ParametersSystem.

12. You recently connected your organization to the Internet and now you want to provide access to server-based directory information using LDAP clients. What must you do to the Exchange Server to allow LDAP clients access to the Directory?
Nothing; LDAP access is enabled by default.

13. Which directory attributes are returned to validated users by default?
Validated users can look up every available directory attribute.

14. The STOCKSDATA company has five sites called NEWYORK, LONDON, PARIS, FRANKFURT, and TOKYO. In this organization, Fred Pumpkin wants to configure server referrals so that LDAP clients can be redirected to LONDON-1 in case a search on NEWYORK-1 cannot be fulfilled. What does he have to accomplish to achieve the desired configuration?
Nothing; the desired configuration cannot be achieved because he can specify only the LDAP servers outside his organization through server referrals.

15. What is a USENET hub node?
A hub node is an architectural USENET unit that maintains newsgroups and newsfeeds. A USENET hub node replicates its own information and the information it receives from other instances to remote hubs. The communication between two hubs is bidirectional.

16. What is a USENET leaf node?
A leaf node is the second architectural USENET unit. Leaf nodes receive news from an ISP and distribute this information locally.

17. What is a push feed?
A push feed is a newsfeed where the connection is initiated by the ISP. A push feed is typically used when the replicated amount of information is very large.

18. What is a pull feed?
A pull feed initiates the connection to a remote USENET host and pulls the information from existing newsgroups. A pull feed is flexible; you can use it to specify which newsgroups you would like to receive.

19. What is an active file?
An active file describes the list of all available newsgroups an ISP has to offer. Using the active file, you can subscribe to newsgroups to maintain a replica in your organization. This file can be downloaded using NNTP during the newsfeed installation.

20. What must you configure in order to provide a public folder as an outbound newsgroup to the USENET?
First, create a public folder under a newsgroup hierarchy parent using Exchange Client or Outlook. Then, configure an outbound newsfeed using the Administrator program. On the newsfeed's Outbound property page, include the public folder into the replication with the remote USENET host.

21. Because of a disk crash, an Exchange Server needs to be restored. This server is responsible for maintaining newsgroups and the most recent backup is several days old. What should you do in order to avoid having old articles transferred back to the server once the backup has been restored?
Click the Mark All As Delivered button on the newsfeed's Advanced property page. The newsfeed will not retrieve or send any articles that have been placed in the newsgroups thus far.

22. A public folder named *Ticker And More* exists in the Internet newsgroups folder. Several subfolders have been created and they all are published to the USENET. You want to stop newsreader access to the *Ticker And More* public folder. How can you do this without affecting the subfolders?
Display the desired folder's properties using the Exchange Client or Outlook and switch to the Internet News property page. Clear the Publish This Folder To Users Of Newsreader Software option to stop newsreader access to this public folder. Subfolders will not be affected and will retain their newsgroup properties.

23. Which NNTP setting of a public folder can be modified within the Administrator program?
You can specify the character set for MIME and non-MIME messages through the NNTP property page.

24. Can you allow anonymous access to newsgroups?
Anonymous access is not enabled by default, but the Anonymous property page of the NNTP (News) Site Defaults and NNTP (News) Settings objects allow you to enable the anonymous access either at the site level or server level. Anonymous accounts must be granted access to public folders through the folder's Permissions property page.

25. How can you test the NNTP service?
Connect to the server's port 119 using Telnet. Enter the command AUTHINFO USER *<Domain/Account/Mailbox>*, followed by AUTHINFO PASS *<password>* to log on. To release the connection again, use the QUIT command.

26. What is an Active Server?
IIS 3.0 with ASPs is called an Active Server. It is the server-side and script-based programming model that allows developers to create Web server applications.

27. List the three core components of the Active Server platform.
ActiveX, Active Desktop, and Active Server.

28. Which features must a browser support to get access to an Exchange Server computer over the Web?
The browser must support Java script and Frames. Internet Explorer 4.01 or Netscape Navigator are examples of Internet browsers that support these features.

29. You want to create your own Web client to achieve special functionality. Which scripting language do you need to use?
You can use scripting languages such as VBScript or JavaScript.

30. What are the main parts of Outlook Web Access?
Outlook Web Access is divided into two parts, the CDO (messaging) library and the CDO rendering library. The first library is necessary for accessing the resources on an Exchange Server computer. The second library is essential for representing MAPI items as HTML documents.

31. What is the default directory of the .ASP files for Exchange Server?
By default, Setup copies all files to the Exchsrvr\Webdata directory.

32. How do you access an Exchange Server using a browser?
By default, the Active Server components are published as the virtual directory /Exchange. Internet browsers that need access the Exchange Server over the Web specify this directory to reach the Welcome page (such as *//www.stocksdata.com/Exchange*).

Chapter 12

1. What is a public server?

   It is a server that maintains public folders in its Public Information Store.

2. What is a dedicated public server?

   It is an Exchange Server that maintains only the Public Information Store. The Private Information Store has been deleted.

3. Which communication method is used to access the public folder content of a public server?

   The Exchange Client and Outlook use RPC in every case, whether or not the content is stored on the user's home server or on another public server within the site or organization.

4. You have configured a dedicated public server in your site. All public folders are placed there, but you did not create any other special server configuration. A user working with Outlook creates a new top-level folder. Where will the new public folder be stored?

   It will be stored on the user's home server because it is the default public folder server for the user.

5. You have configured a dedicated public server in your site. All public folders are placed there, but you did not create any other special server configuration. A user working with the Exchange Client creates a new subfolder. Where will it be stored?

   All subfolders are created on the server that maintains the parent folder; therefore, they are created on the dedicated public server.

6. You want to allow users to send e-mail messages conveniently to a particular public folder by selecting it from the Global Address List (GAL). What must you do to accomplish this?

   Using the Administrator program, you can include a specific public folder in the GAL by deselecting the Hide From Address Book check box on the Advanced property page of the public folder object. Users can then select the public folder as a recipient, just like they would select a regular mailbox. However, a user who wants to send messages to a particular public folder must have permission to create messages in the folder or the message will be rejected.

7. Lisa complains that some users can't see her new public folder in their public folder trees, but users on the local server can work with the new folder. What is most likely the cause of the problem?

   The public folder hierarchy replication probably has not been completed. The public folder will eventually appear in the public folder hierarchy.

8. You have configured a **Recipients** container for all public folders. However, older public folders remain in the **Recipients** container of your site. Can you move these public folder references to the new container? **No. Public folders cannot be moved between recipient containers.**

9. Users of your site must work with a public folder called Sales Tracking. This folder is not kept in the local site, and you don't want to create a local replica of it. RPC communication works between your site and the site where the folder exists. What should you do in Exchange to allow your users access to the public folder content? **You can assign an affinity value to the remote site using the Public Folder Affinity property page of the Information Store Site Configuration object. Using this value, the client can access the public folder directly.**

10. Clients access the content of a public folder through RPC. As the administrator of a large site, you want to focus this RPC communication within local network segments to offload bandwidth consumption from the backbone. How can you configure the site so that clients will try to locate a public folder's content on servers in their local segment first? **You must define server locations using the General property pages of the servers' configuration objects. Servers in a local network segment will be grouped together in one location.**

11. You want to ensure that items older than five days are deleted from all public folder replicas in your organization. How can you do this? **You can configure an age limit for each public folder instance. On the Age Limits property page of the Public Information Store object, click the Modify button to display the Modify Age Limits dialog box. Type 5 in the All Replicas box. Any items older than five days will be deleted automatically.**

12. Can you use the Administrator program to create public folders? If not, which programs can you use? **You cannot create public folders directly using the Administrator program. You must use Outlook, the Exchange Client, or Outlook Web Access.**

13. You want to create a new public folder within Outlook. Which command should you choose? **Point to the Folder option on the File menu, and then click the Create Subfolder command. Or you can point to New on the File menu and then click the Folder command. The Create New Folder dialog box appears and prompts you for the folder name and folder type.**

14. You want to prevent a user from viewing the contents of a public folder. Which permission should you revoke?
    The Read Items permission.

15. Which predefined roles can you use to assign public folder permissions?
    The predefined roles are Owner, Publishing Author, Publishing Editor, Editor, Author, Nonediting Author, Reviewer, Contributor, and None.

16. You have configured permissions on a public folder. You also want to include all subfolders. What must you do to change the permissions for all subfolders through the parent folder?
    First display the properties of the parent folder within the Administrator program and change the parent folder permissions using the Client Permissions button on the General property page. Then select the Propagate These Properties To All Subfolders check box. Existing permissions of the parent folder will be propagated to all subfolders.

17. What are the disadvantages of single public folder instances within an organization?
    Fault tolerance cannot be implemented.
    A single public folder server must handle all incoming open requests.
    Load balancing cannot be provided.
    The network topology must support RPC.
    Multiple Windows NT domains typically must trust each other.

18. What are the advantages of multiple replicas of a particular public folder?
    Fault tolerance can be implemented based on multiple public folder servers.
    Load balancing can also be provided between multiple public folder servers.
    Data transfer between replicas is performed through e-mail messages and is therefore independent of RPCs and the network topology.
    You can control the replication through the replication schedule and messaging connector parameters.

19. What are the advantages of a dedicated public server configuration?
    You can design the topology of sites in a structured way.
    You can configure hardware resources explicitly.
    A dedicated public server removes workload from other servers, thereby increasing the response time of private server.

Chapter 13

1. What are the general advantages of public folder content replication?
   Public folder content replication permits you to maintain multiple synchronized copies of a particular public folder. You can use multiple replicas to distribute the workload load between multiple public servers. This improves the response time for all users in the organization. Also, multiple replicas provide fault tolerance. Public folder replication relies on e-mail messages, which means the replication is basically independent of network topology.

2. You need to provide a storage location for collaborative information, so you decide to implement a public folder. Each of the items is about 5 MB–10 MB in size and changes occur often. Which public folder strategy would you recommend?
   The granularity of public folder replication is at the message level. If modifications occur, and they occur often, at least 5 MB must be replicated whenever the content changes. Therefore, public folder replication should not be configured. One single instance must be sufficient for all users.

3. Your company has implemented two sites because a WAN connection exists that does not support RPC. What needs to be configured in order to provide all public folders within the organization to all users?
   If a WAN connection that prevents the RPC communication between sites exists, clients of one site cannot access public folder resources in the other site. Therefore, all public folders must be kept locally in all sites. The contents of each public folder must be replicated to at least one server in each remote site to ensure that the content is accessible.

4. The replication of the public folder hierarchy happens automatically every 60 seconds. How can you expand the replication interval to two minutes?
   Set the Replication Send Folder Tree value to 120 under: HKEY_LOCAL_MACHINE\SYSTEM\CurrentControlSet\Services \MSExchangeIS\ParametersPublic.

5. You want to create a public folder that is available in all locations even if RPC is not supported. How can you accomplish the configuration by using one Administrator program?
   Display the properties of the desired public folder, then switch to the Replicas property page, where you can select one public server from each site. This pushes a replica of the public folder onto the servers, which makes its items available in all sites.

6. You need to create a local replica for a desired public folder that exists in another site, but you don't want to bother the remote administrator. However, RPC communication is impossible. How can you achieve the desired configuration?

   You can use the Administrator program to pull the public folder replica onto the desired server in the local site. Connect to the target public server and display the properties of its Public Information Store object. Then, switch to the Instances property page to add a replica of the public folder to the list of "Folders On This Information Store." When you click OK, the replica is created and filled. However, administrative access to the public folder must be possible from outside the folder's local site.

7. What are the components of the message state information and what are the functions of each part?

   The message state information contains a change number, a time stamp, and the predecessor change list. The change number reflects the sequential changes for all items of a particular IS. The time stamp identifies less recent and more recent changes. The predecessor change list allows public folder replication conflicts to be detected.

8. You use the **This Replica (Days)** option on the **Age Limits** property page of the Public Information Store object to specify an age limit for a particular public folder. How does this expiration setting affect other public folder instances in your organization?

   The option specifies an age limit on a per-folder basis. When messages expire, they are deleted only from the local IS. A replication message is not generated and the items may remain in all other public folder instances.

9. How does the receiving PFRA determine whether a replication conflict has occurred?

   The receiving PRFA checks whether the change number of the local message is included in the predecessor list of the updated message. If it is, the information can be replaced. If the local message change number is not included, a replication conflict is detected.

10. What is the backfill process?

    The backfill process is the mechanism that discovers out-of-sync replicas by using message status information. The status information is included in every replication message. If no changes are to be replicated, status information is exchanged automatically, one time per day. If a PFRA discovers missing changes, it requests them from any IS that maintains a more recent replica.

11. A user in your organization has deleted important information from a replicated public folder. Why can't you restore the public folder directly onto the existing public server? How can you recover the information?
The backfill process ensures that the items are deleted again if you restore a backup on the original server. Therefore, a test machine is necessary. The server must be installed with exactly the same computer, site, and organization name, but not in the same computer network. The administrator restores the server and logs by using an Exchange Client. Now the content of the public folder can be downloaded into a Personal Folder Store file. The Personal Folder Store file can be included into the actual messaging profile and the items can be uploaded into the desired public folder again.

12. You create a new public folder replica on an Exchange Server computer. What must be performed manually to bring the replica to the current state?
Nothing; the IS exchanges status information with all other servers that maintain a replica also. The backfill process is launched once the out-of-date replica has been detected, which fills the new instance automatically.

13. What happens if you delete a public folder replica in the Exchange Administrator program?
The replica is deleted from the Public Information Store and its reference is removed from the DS. The DS replicates the configuration change to all other servers in the organization. Therefore, all servers within the organization know that the replica no longer exists. Public servers which maintain a replica of the affected public folder stop sending replication messages to the server where the replica has been eliminated.

14. As a public folder contact, you receive a conflict message. What choices do you have for resolving the public folder replication conflict?
You can accept the local item, the updated item, or both replicated items.

15. Two public folder owners have modified the design of a public folder on two different instances at the same time and generate a design conflict. How do you resolve the conflict?
A design conflict doesn't need to be resolved explicitly because the most recent changes overwrite all others. In the case of a design conflict, only the public folder contacts or public folder owners are notified. The public folder contact can then check if the desired design is still in effect.

Chapter 14

1. What are the features of Advanced Security and when do you use them?
Advanced Security supports the signing and sealing of messages. Signing permits a sender to add a digital signature to a message, which proves the message's origin and authenticity. Sealing is another term for message encryption. Both features can be used individually or simultaneously.

2. Which client platforms provide support for Advanced Security?
Exchange Client and Outlook for Apple Macintosh
Exchange Client for Windows 95
Exchange Client for Windows NT
Exchange Client and Outlook for Windows 3.x and Windows for Workgroups 3.11
Outlook for Windows 95 and for Windows NT
S/MIME-compatible clients such as Outlook Express

3. Exchange Server uses three types of security keys. What are they used for?
Private keys are used to unseal messages and to encrypt digital signatures.
Public keys are used for sealing messages and verifying digital signatures.
The secret key is used to encrypt and decrypt security files and messages.

4. What are the three main components of a KM Server?
The KM Server service, the KM database, and the security DLL (Seckm.dll).

5. What is the name of the DLL that the Administrator program uses to communicate with a KM Server? Which communication mechanism is used?
The Administrator program uses the Secadmin.dll to contact the KM Server service. RPC is the communication method.

6. What is the KM Server security password used for, and when do you need it?
The KM Server security password is used to decrypt the KM Database Master Encryption Key in order to gain access to the KM database. You must enter it during the KM Server service startup. Every KM administrator also needs a KM Server security password.

7. List the different versions of Advanced Security and the level of security they provide.
North American: DES and CAST-64 are supported
Others: CAST-40 is supported
French: No Advanced Security is provided

8. What does a KM administrator have to do to enable a user with Advanced Security?

The KM administrator displays the user's mailbox properties in the Administrator program. On the Security property page, the administrator clicks the Enable Advanced Security button to launch the process of enabling Advanced Security. Once this process is completed, a 12-character security token is returned and displayed in a dialog box. This security token must be provided to the user.

9. What does the user have to do to enable Advanced Security?

First the user must receive the security token from the KM administrator. Then he or she clicks the Options command on the client's Tools menu, switches to the Security property page, and clicks the Set Up Advanced Security button. In the Setup Advanced Security dialog box, the user enters the security token, sets the location and name of the .EPF file, and specifies a security password for this file. He, or she, clicks OK to send the request message to the KM Server. Finally, the user receives a response from the KM Server and opens it. The user enters the security password in the Microsoft Exchange Security Logon dialog box to complete the process of enabling Advanced Security. Once the security information has been written to the .EFP file and the Directory, the user can sign and seal messages.

10. What does a X.509 certificate contain?

A X.509 certificate must contain:
A unique serial number generated by the KM Server to identify each user's certificate
The CA's DN
The CA's signature (an encrypted KM Server password)
The public keys for signing and sealing
The user's DN
An expiration date for the certificate

11. Each user's CA must be identified in the CA certificate. Where is this certificate stored?

In each user's .EPF file.

12. You want to send sealed messages to users in remote organizations, so you exchange public secret keys using the person-to-person key exchange feature. Where does the client store the security information for remote users?

An entry for the remote user is stored in the Personal Address Book, but the certificates for signing and sealing are stored in the .EPF file.

13. How can you delete the person-to-person security keys of a particular user?

There is no convenient way to delete person-to-person security keys from the .EPF file. Once a user is considered trusted, this status does not change. You can recover the entire .EFP file, but this erases all person-to-person security information.

14. When does Outlook encrypt a message?
When the user clicks the Send button.

15. How does Outlook sign messages?
The original message is hashed and the user's private signing key is retrieved from the .EPF file. The hash is then encrypted using the private signing key. The encrypted hash is added to the message along with the user's signing certificate, which contains the public signing key. The client then transfers the message to the IS for delivery.

16. How does Outlook check whether a signed message has been modified?
When a user verifies the signature of a signed message, the sender's digital signature is decrypted using the sender's public signing key. This key is enclosed in the signing certificate attached to the message. Exchange Client then hashes the message again to generate a second message digest. The original digest and the second digest are compared. If they are the same, the message has not been modified.

17. What steps must be taken to send a sealed message?
First the client contacts the Directory to receive each recipient's sealing certificate, which contains the public sealing key and the supported encryption method. Using this information, the encryption method for the message is determined. The client then generates a bulk encryption key and encrypts the message content. The bulk encryption key is then encrypted using each recipient's public sealing key, creating a bulk encryption lockbox for each recipient. The lockbox is attached to the encrypted message. The sender's sealing certificate is also added to the message before it is transferred to the IS for delivery.

18. You want to implement Advanced Security in an organization with two sites. How many times do you need to run the KM Server setup program?
You must run it once to install the KM Server in the first site. The Site Encryption Configuration object of the second site must be configured manually to point to the correct KM Server site.

19. When can you begin to configure the reference to a KM Server in a remote site?
The directory replication must replicate the first site's configuration changes (CA object) before you can begin to configure the Primary KM Server Location on the General property page of the Site Encryption Configuration object.

20. A user has forgotten the security password for his or her .EPF file. What must the administrator do to allow the user to sign and seal messages again?
The KM administrator must recover Advanced Security for the user. The KM Server will generate a new 12-character security token, which the administrator must provide to the user. The user completes the recovery process by repeating the steps for enabling Advanced Security (using the new security token). A new .EPF file is created for the user's security information.

21. By default, Advanced Security certificates expire after 18 months. How can you adjust the expiration interval to keep certificates valid for only 12 months?
You cannot adjust the expiration interval.

22. Where does the Exchange Server store revoked security information?
In the revocation list of the KM database and in the revocation list of the CA's directory object.

23. Which directory must be saved in order to back up the KM Server database?
The \Exchsrvr\Kmsdata directory.

24. What must be done to move a KM Server to a new computer?
First, you must stop the KM Server service and save the original KM database. Then, you run the Exchange Server setup progam to remove the KM Server and its KM database from the old computer. On the new computer, you can install the KM Server once the directory replication has removed the old CA object from the Configuration container. The KM database must also be restored. Once these steps have been accomplished, the KM Service service can be started with the original KM Server password. References in remote sites might be reconfigured to point to the correct KM Server.

25. You are the administrator of STOCKSDATA, an organization with more than 2000 employees. Recently you installed a KM Server. Now you need to enable all employees with Advanced Security. How do you accomplish this?
You use the Bulk Enrollment button on the CA object's Enrollment property page to enable Advanced Security for multiple users. You can either send the generated security keys to all newly enabled users in an e-mail message or write the results to a file to provide the security tokens manually and more securely.

Chapter 15

1. Which Exchange Server databases rely on JET 3.0 technology?
   Private and Public Information Store databases. (Priv.edb and Pub.edb)
   Directory database. (Dir.edb)
   Dirsync database. (Xdir.edb)
   KM Server database. (Kmsmdb.edb)

2. Which files types are maintained by Exchange Server in addition to the actual database files?
   Transaction logs, previous logs, reserved logs, checkpoint files and patch files.

3. What does circular logging mean?
   Circular logging is the automatic deletion of transaction logs once their contents have been written to the databases. Previous log files and old transactions in the current log file are discarded according to the state of the corresponding checkpoint file. Circular logging is enabled by default.

4. Which methods can you use to delete previous log files without risking damage to the Exchange Server installation?
   Circular logging deletes previous log files automatically.
   Previous log files are also deleted when you perform a full or incremental online backup.

5. What is the difference between the incremental and the differential backup?
   The incremental backup purges transaction log files and sets the context for the next incremental backup in this manner. The differential backup, on the other hand, does not discard any transactions. It does not set the context for any subsequent backup.

6. What must be accomplished before moving existing server databases to a new Exchange Server computer?
   First create a recent backup of the databases using a full online backup. Then shut down the old server. The reference of the old computer must be removed from the Windows NT domain using the Server Manager for Domains. Now install the new Windows NT Server in the same domain and with the same computer name. When this has been accomplished, the new Exchange Server can be installed using the Setup program. In order to suppress directory replication, install the new server in a new site but use the organization name and the site name of the old site. Once the new Exchange Server has been installed the full backup can be restored. It is advisable that you check the DS/IS consistency before you allow users to log on again.

7. Which tool can you use to defragment the Exchange Server databases manually?
ESEUTIL.EXE.

8. You just restored an Exchange Server from an offline backup, but the IS service does not start anymore. How do you fix the problem?
Run ISINTEG -PATCH from the Windows NT command prompt.

9. Which actions can a Server Monitor perform?
Alert the administrator through e-mail messages and Windows NT alerts.
Launch custom applications.
Track events in the Application Event Log.
Restart Services.
Reboot the server.
Synchronize clocks between computers.

10. Which recipients can be referenced in Link Monitor test messages?
SA services.
Regular Exchange users.
Custom recipients.

11. How would you suspend a Server Monitor from monitoring a particular server?
You can execute the ADMIN /T command with a combination of the options 'N' and 'R' on the server before it goes off line.

12. Which three service states can be signaled by a Server Monitor, and how are they signaled within the Administrator program?
An active service rests in the normal state, which is indicated by a green triangle.
A stopped service enters the warning state first, which is indicated by an exclamation point.
After 60 seconds (default setting) the service enters the alert state, which is indicated by a red triangle.

13. When do you launch the Scanpst.exe program?
If .PST files are corrupted, folder counters are off, or if there are noticeable anomalies in your Personal Folder Store.

14. At system startup you are notified that one or more services cannot be started. You check the Windows NT Event log and discover that the MTA service has failed to start. What steps must be taken to fix the MTA startup problem?
In most cases, the MTA does not start because of message queue corruption. Such a corruption can be fixed using the MTA Check utility, which can be launched at the Windows NT command prompt.

15. You fixed an MTA startup problem using the MTA Check utility, but some messages have been deleted from the MTA message queues. Where can you find these deleted objects and further information?
Removed objects are placed in the \Exchsrvr\Mtadata\Mtacheck.out directory. The object's identifier, an error type, the queue name, and the Message Transport Identifier (MTS-ID) are displayed on the screen or written to a log file, depending on the specified command line parameter.

16. A user complains about connection problems, but Exchange Server runs fine and other users have no problems. How can you inspect the RPC communication?
You can use the RPC Ping utilities to verify whether RPC works. Rpings must be started on the server. After that, the user can test the connection using the client component (for example, Rpingc32). The Rpingc program displays the status of the connection.

17. You notice that the MTA service is consuming 100 percent of the CPU's resources. For this reason you assume that the MTA is hanging. How can you stop the MTA service in this case?
If you cannot use the Windows NT Control Panel to stop the MTA service, use the Task Manager. The process that must be terminated is called Emsmta.exe. To check for message queue corruption afterwards, run the MTA Check utility before restarting the MTA service.

18. How can you pull directory changes from another Exchange Server computer?
Click the Update Now button on the General property page of the Directory Service object.

19. You have configured a directory replication connector to another site and want to initiate the directory replication immediately. How do you accomplish this task?
Click the Check Now button on the General property page of the Directory Service object. The Check Now button launches the KCC that creates the replication link to the new site. Once the replication link has been established, intersite replication can take place.

20. How can you change the Site Services Account password?
The Service Account Password property page of the Configuration container allows you to change the service account password within the Exchange Server Directory. You then must change the password in the User Manager for Domains.

21. When would you use the Message Tracking Center?
To locate stopped message connections.
To find a specific message in the organization.
To determine slow segments of a route for performance tuning.
To verify that a message has been delivered to a recipient.

22. Which components support message tracking?
The IS, the MTA, and optional messaging connectors such as the IMS, Connector for Lotus cc:Mail, or the MS Mail Connector.

23. Users complain that messages have not been delivered for a long time. What should you check first in order to determine the problem?
The MTA message queues and the message queues of each existing messaging connector.

Chapter 16

1. Which two types of Exchange applications can you create using electronic forms, and what are they used for?
You can create stand-alone applications (Send Forms) and folder applications (Post Forms). You use stand-alone applications to send formatted information to directly other users. Folder applications let you share information with other users indirectly using public folders.

2. Which design environments can you use to develop electronic forms, and what are their key features?
You can use Electronic Forms Designer and Outlook Forms Designer. Electronic Forms Designer is a separate application that generates compiled 16-bit Visual Basic forms. Outlook Forms Designer is part of Outlook. It generates 32-bit forms that are not compiled but are interpreted at run time.

3. Which features of Outlook cannot be used within Exchange Client 5.0?
Extended Outlook forms cannot be displayed in Exchange Client. Users see an error notification before the information is displayed as normal message text. Also, Exchange Client 5.0 converts posted WordMail items to rich text because the WordMail option is not supported for Exchange Post Forms. In addition, special Outlook folder views are not supported in Exchange Client 5.0. If a public folder must be shared between Outlook and Exchange Client, the Exchange 4.0 type must be used.

4. You want to create a new 16-bit electronic form using an existing sample application. Where do you find the sample applications?
The 16-bit sample applications come with Exchange Forms Designer. If you installed them during setup, they are in the \Exchange\Efdforms\Samples directory on the client computer. Outlook also provides 16-bit sample forms in the \Support\Samples\i386 directory on the installation CD.

5. Which command launches Outlook Forms Designer?
The Design Outlook Form command on the Tools menu of an Outlook form launches Outlook Forms Designer.

6. Which three types of forms libraries can exist on an Exchange Server computer?
Organization Forms Libraries, Folder Forms Libraries, and Personal Forms Libraries.

7. You are developing a new forms application and want to test your work. Where do you install the form?
In a Personal Forms Library.

8. Where do you install a Send Form to be used by all users, and what must you do before you can install the form?
You must install the Send Form in an Organization Forms Library, which you create using the Administrator program.

9. Which tools are available to install the various types of forms?
You can use Electronic Forms Designer, Exchange Client, and Outlook to install 16-bit forms. You can install 32-bit forms only using Outlook Forms Designer.

10. Which file describes the properties of 16-bit forms and is required during installation? Which tool can create them automatically?
The .CFG configuration file describes the electronic form. You can generate it using Electronic Forms Designer.

11. Where can you find preconfigured sample electronic forms, and what must you configure in order to test them?
Preconfigured 16-bit sample applications are in the Sampapps.pst file. You must add the file to the current messaging profile to test them. The Outlook ValuePack also provides a file called Forms.pst, which you can add to a messaging profile. You can use it to demonstrate various 32-bit forms.

12. How can you modify a 16-bit electronic form?
Exchange Forms Designer offers the Open An Existing Form Project option on startup. Select the option and then specify the .EFP file in the Open box. The form opens, and you can make the desired modifications.

13. How can you modify Outlook forms?
You must use Outlook Forms Designer to modify an Outlook form. To load an Outlook form into Outlook Forms Designer, open the form and click the Design Outlook Form command on the Tools menu. The form switches to design mode, where you can make modifications and add custom functionality. You can also publish the form in design mode.

14. You are in charge of developing an event-driven folder agent. Which folder events let you perform script-based processing using the Exchange Scripting Agent?
You can perform folder processing in the event of message creation, modification, and deletion. You can also fire a folder event on a scheduled basis (hourly, daily, or weekly).

Chapter 17

1. You want to integrate Exchange Server into your NetWare network. You install Windows NT server and IPX/SPX. Which three important configuration parameters of IPX/SPX might have to be configured manually?
The Frame Type, the External Network Number, and the Internal Network Number.

2. Why must you install GSNW on a Windows NT server running Exchange Server?
GSNW is required to announce the Exchange Server services to NetWare networks via SAP. In addition, GSNW permits extraction of existing NetWare accounts within the Exchange Administrator program to create corresponding mailboxes.

3. Why do you need the SAP Agent and GSNW to allow NetWare workstations to connect to the Exchange Server computer?
Both components are required for making the Exchange Server computer visible in a NetWare network. Without support for SAP, clients cannot obtain the server address, which is required to establish a connection to the server.

4. In addition to Exchange Server resources, you want to provide access to printers connected to the Windows NT server. Users on NetWare workstations should be able to use them without having to reconfigure their clients. Which additional product must you install on the Windows NT server to achieve the desired functionality?
File and Print Services for NetWare.

5. Because Exchange Server validates users based on Windows NT account information, you must create a corresponding Windows NT account for each existing NetWare user. Which tool can you use to maintain the account information for both systems in a centralized place?
The Directory Service Manager for NetWare.

6. As an administrator, you must implement Exchange Server in an existing NetWare environment. Windows NT server is already installed in a typical configuration. What else must you install and configure to give NetWare workstations access to mailboxes and other Exchange Server resources?

First, you must configure the Windows NT server for the NWLink IPX/SPX-Compatible transport. GSNW and the SAP Agent are also required because they make the Exchange Server computer visible in the NetWare network. If the connectivity between Windows NT server and the NetWare network works, you install Exchange Client on the NetWare workstations. Exchange Client provides the RPC libraries, which are necessary to communicate with the Exchange Server using RPC over SPX. Finally, you must configure the mailboxes and corresponding Windows NT accounts for each NetWare user who will use the messaging system.

7. Users on NetWare workstations are complaining about the startup times of their Exchange clients. What should you check first?

First check the RPC_Binding_Order value in the Registry under HKEY_LOCAL_MACHINE\SOFTWARE\Microsoft\Exchange\Exchange Provider. The RPC over SPX communication method (ncacn_spx) should be on top.

Chapter 18

1. What are the three components of the MS Mail Connector?
   They are the MS Mail Connector Interchange, the Connector postoffice, and the MS Mail Connector MTA.

2. What is the function of the Connector postoffice?
   It is the intermediate repository for MS Mail messages sent between an Exchange Server and an MS Mail postoffice.

3. Some users in a MS Mail network access their postoffices remotely using MS Mail remote clients. You plan to replace all MS Mail Externals with MS Mail Connector MTA services. How can you support the MS Mail remote users once all Externals are replaced?
   The MS Mail Connector MTA doesn't support MS Mail Remote clients, meaning you cannot support MS Mail remote users in a network that doesn't run MS Mail External processes. One solution to this problem could be to leave at least one External running at the postoffice for remote access. Another solution could be the migration of remote users to Exchange Server. They can then use Exchange Clients or Outlook with built-in remote functionality.

4. You plan to connect your organization to an existing MS Mail network. A permanent network connection does not exist. How do you connect both systems?
   The MS Mail Connector MTA supports dial-up connections, so you need a modem and an appropriate modem script to configure a connection to the destination MS Mail network. The modem script must be copied in the GLB directory of the Connector postoffice so that the MS Mail Connector MTA can communicate with a remote MS Mail External over a telephone line to transfer messages between the Connector postoffice and the MS Mail postoffice.

5. Which component converts Exchange Server messages to MS Mail messages and vice versa?
   The MS Mail Connector Interchange.

6. You have configured the MS Mail Connector, but messages sent to MS Mail users remain in the Connector postoffice. You check the state of the MS Mail Connector services and they have all been started. How can you obtain more information about the source of the problem?
   The MS Mail Connector MTA service is responsible for message transfer within the MS Mail network. Therefore, you can enable the Diagnostics Logging feature for the MSExchangePCMTA category. You can use Event View to examine the Application Event Log for details.

7. You have configured an MS Mail Connector between one MS Mail postoffice and an Exchange Server. Exchange users can send messages, but users on the MS Mail postoffice cannot. How can you correct this problem?

   This is an MS Mail problem. Use the MS Mail Administrator program to check that the Connector postoffice was registered as an External postoffice.

8. What are the three stages of a complete DirSync cycle?

   They are T1, T2, and T3. At T1, the Requestor address updates are generated. They are sent to the DXA Server. At T2, address updates are incorporated into the master address list. The update messages for the Requestor postoffices are generated and sent back to the Requestors. At T3, address changes are committed to the postoffice address lists and the GAL can be rebuilt.

9. You have configured a Exchange Server as an DXA Server. MS Mail Requestor postoffices are sending their address changes to the Exchange Server through the MS Mail Connector. When will address list changes appear in the specified Import container?

   The DXA is a Windows NT service that is permanently active. It commits the changes to the directory as soon as they are received. MS Mail addresses are maintained as custom recipients.

10. You have configured an Exchange Server as a DXA Server, and you have configured remote DirSync Requestor postoffices. One of the Requestor postoffices does not show any updates, even though the first DirSync cycle has been completed. Which options should you activate to keep track of whether the Requestor sends its changes to the correct DXA Server and whether the DXA Server sends updates back to the postoffice?

    To verify that DirSync messages have been received and sent, you enable the Forward Incoming Dirsync Messages To Administrator option and the Copy Administrator On Outgoing Messages option. The first option causes the DXA to forward all received Requestor update and status messages to the Administrator's mailbox. The second option copies the T2 messages generated by the DXA Server.

11. You want to configure an Exchange Server computer to act as a DirSync Requestor. How do you schedule the time to incorporate received address updates into the DS (T3)?

    The DXA Requestor applies the changes as soon as they are received. Therefore you do not have to configure a scheduled T3 time separately.

12. Which property pages can you use to map MS Mail template information to Exchange mailbox attributes?
You can map the MS Mail template labels to mailbox attributes using the Directory Synchronization property pages. You can define mapping for both incoming and outgoing information on the Incoming Templates and Outgoing Templates property pages.

13. What is the purpose of the Schedule+ Free/Busy Connector?
It shares Free/Busy information among Schedule+ 7.x users in an Exchange Server organization and Schedule+ 1.0 users with MS Mail postoffices.

14. How does the Schedule+ Free/Busy Connector work?
It reads the Free/Busy information from the *Schedule+ Free Busy* system folder and places the information in e-mail messages addressed to the ADMINSCH accounts of the postoffices with which it exchanges the information. It also incorporates the information received from the MS Mail network in the *Schedule+ Free Busy* system folder to give Schedule+ 7.x users access to the Free/Busy times of Schedule+ 1.0 users.

15. Why must you configure a distribution list before configuring the Schedule+ Free/Busy Connector?
The distribution list must contain the ADMINSCH accounts of the MS Mail postoffices. The Schedule+ Free/Busy Connector uses this distribution list to address the Free/Busy update messages.

16. You have configured the MS Mail Connector, MS Mail Directory Synchronization, and the Schedule+ Free/Busy Connector. The Free/Busy information is exchanged on a regular basis. You have just discovered that Free/Busy information in one postoffice is displayed incorrectly. What can you do to update the information?
You should start the Exchange Administrator program and display the properties of the Schedule+ Free/Busy Connector object. This object is in the Recipients container. On the Schedule+ Free/Busy Connector Options property page, click the Full Export button. During the next synchronization cycle, the complete Free/Busy information will be sent to all postoffices, including the postoffice that is out-of-date.

Chapter 19

1. How many Lotus cc:Mail post offices can a Connector for Lotus cc:Mail communicate with directly?
The Connector for Lotus cc:Mail supports only one Lotus cc:Mail post office.

2. Which Import and Export program versions are supported by the Connector for Lotus cc:Mail and which post office version can be accessed through each of them?
The Connector for Lotus cc:Mail the Post Office Database version 6 by means of Lotus cc:Mail Import version 5.15 and Export version 5.14
The Connector for Lotus cc:Mail the Post Office Database version 8 by means of Lotus cc:Mail Import/Export version 6.0

3. What are the main components of the Connector for Lotus cc:Mail?
A gateway folder structure in the IS maintains the message queues (MTS-OUT and MTS-IN).
The actual Connector for Lotus cc:Mail service performs the transfer and conversion of messages and addresses.
The Connector Store acts as the intermediate repository of scratch files.
The Lotus cc:Mail Import and Export programs access the Lotus cc:Mail post office.
Address and Details Templates allow for the specification of Lotus cc:Mail recipients using the Exchange Client and Microsoft Outlook.
The Proxy Address Generation DLL generates proxy CCMAIL addresses for all mailboxes on the Exchange Server.

4. You have installed and configured the Connector for Lotus cc:Mail and now you want to start the Exchange Connector for Lotus cc:Mail server using the **Services** applet of the Control Panel. The service terminates after a short delay, reporting the error number 2 in the Application Event Log. What is the most likely source of the startup problem?
The Lotus cc:Mail Import and Export programs cannot be found on the Exchange Server computer. They must be copied into a directory that is included in the Windows NT system path. The Connector for Lotus cc:Mail service terminates automatically if these programs cannot be launched successfully.

5. You need to adjust the proxy CCMAIL address format. The convention of your company forces you to use the given name immediately followed by the surname. Where and how can you adjust the proxy address format? **Use the Site Addressing object in the Configuration container of the local site to select the existing CCMAIL address on the Site Addressing property page. Then you can click Edit to enter the following formula: *%g%1s at site*.**

6. Which program is launched by the Connector for Lotus cc:Mail to write messages into the Lotus cc:Mail post office? **Import.exe.**

7. Which program is used to poll the Lotus cc:Mail post office for Exchange Server–bound messages? **Export.exe.**

Chapter 20

1. What type of general information can be transferred between Exchange Server and Lotus Notes through the Connector for Lotus Notes?
   Interpersonal messages and address information.

2. You want to install the Connector for Lotus Notes. What non-Microsoft software must you install on the connector server before you begin the installation?
   The Lotus Notes client program.

3. Which two databases must you configure on the Lotus Notes server to allow the Connector for Lotus Notes to function properly? What is the purpose of these databases?
   You must configure the Exchange.box and the Exchange.bad data-bases. The Exchange.box database is the message queue for messages destined for Exchange Server. The Exchange.bad database stores all messages that are corrupted or cannot be delivered for any other reason.

4. When you send a message containing an embedded message to a Lotus Notes user, how does the recipient receive the embedded message?
   The embedded message is converted to an attachment in Rich-Text Format. An icon represents the attachment at the same position as in the original message.

5. Which two important system folders does the Connector for Lotus Notes use on the Exchange Server?
   The folders are MTS-IN, the inbound message queue, and MTS-OUT, the outbound message queue.

6. What are the extensions of the Administrator program?
   The connector configuration object under the Connections container, the Lotus Notes proxy address generator DLL and various address details templates placed under the Addressing container.

7. What must you do to allow downstream sites to send messages to Lotus Notes users?
   You must install the proxy address generator DLL in all downstream sites to provide all Exchange users with a Lotus Notes proxy address.

8. Which connector component retrieves messages from the MTS-OUT queue?
   The MEXOUT process.

9. Which connector component converts messages from Exchange Server format into Lotus Notes format and places the converted message in the Lotus Notes server?
The MEXNTS process performs the message conversion and writes the message to the Mail.box database on the Lotus Notes server.

10. Which component polls the Lotus Notes Exchange.box directory for inbound messages to Exchange Server?
The NTSMEX process.

11. Which component converts address information for inbound messages from Lotus Notes into the X.400 address format?
The MEXIN process.

12. Which processes perform Directory Synchronization with Lotus Notes?
DXANOTES and DXAMEX.

13. Which utility simplifies configuration of the connector's Lotus Notes server?
The Notes Configuration Utility.

14. On which property page can you change the name of the Notes server that the Connector for Lotus Notes contacts for message transfer?
The Options property page.

15. What must you do on the Lotus Notes server before installing the connector?
You must create a Connector ID.

Index

as smart host, 636, 646
S/MIME support, 628
SMTP and, 153, 495, 597, 598,
    625–29
stopping and restarting, 652–53
TCP/IP and, 600–601
testing features, 620–21
UUENCODE support, 628
X.400 and X.500 standards, 597
IMS Queues.pmw, 418
IMS Statistics.pmw, 418
IMS Traffic.pmw, 418
Inbox, assigning for incoming e-mail,
    357–58
Inbox Assistant, 276, 380. *See also*
    e-mail
Inbox folder
    read access permissions, 397
    replication including, 361
    send-on-behalf-of permissions, 402
    synchronized when offline folder files
        are configured, 301
Inbox Repair Tool (Scanpst.exe), 287,
    998–1000
Inbox rules, 276–77
Inbox Setup Wizard. *See* Microsoft
    Outlook Setup Wizard
incremental backups, 479, 961–62
Incremental Change Synchronization
    (ICS), 1065
individual access control, 22–23
Inetab32.dll, 348
information repositories, 214
information services, 346
    configuring for Microsoft Outlook,
        516–17

default, 350
registered in Mapisvc.inf, 346
storing messages in message folders,
    300
Information Store Integrity utility
    (Isinteg.exe), 970–72, 974, 975–79
Information Store (IS), 11, 37. *See also*
    IMAIL; Private Information Store;
    Public Information Store
accessing, 149
backing up, 420
buffers, 117
communication
    with Connector for Lotus cc:Mail,
        175, 1164
    with DS, 167
    with EDK gateways, 176
    with IMS, 598
    with Microsoft Schedule+ Free/
        Busy Connector, 175
    with MTA, 168, 1183
    with other components, 160–61,
        162, 163–64, 170–71, 173, 490
    with SA, 165
configuration, 792–95
as core component, 4, 11, 149–50
creating mailboxes while down, 214
databases, 970–72, 974, 975–79
dependencies, 136
IMAIL features and IMS, 607
installation, 76
KM Server and, 896–97
location, 122
log files, 956
maintenance, 478–79
message flow, 179–80, 181

L

Lotus Notes Administration, 1203–4
Lotus Notes ID, 1203–4, 1205
LPCs (Local Procedure Calls), 160
Lsdxamex.exe, 1194, 1195
Lsdxants.exe, 1194, 1195
Lsmexin.exe, 1194, 1195
Lsmexnts.exe, 1194, 1195
Lsmexout.exe, 1194, 1195
Lsntsmex.exe, 1194

M

Macintosh. *See* Apple Macintosh
MacMail address format, 253
macros, 1031
MacTCP, 306
Mail.box, 1193, 1196, 1205–6
mailboxes, 4. *See also* e-mail
  accessing, 24, 173, 400–402, 689, 749–50, 765–68
  for administrators, 1106
  Advanced Security, 925–26, 933–35, 942–43
  Alias name, 219
  arranging (grouping), 118, 237–38
  assigning locations for incoming e-mail, 357–58
  associated with Microsoft Windows NT accounts, 219
  automatic naming scheme, 428
  cleaning, 262–63
  configuration, 127, 147, 228–29, 679, 696
  creating
    Administrator program, 228–33
    Directory Import, 238–41

  permissions necessary for, 220–25
  for several Microsoft Windows NT users, 513–14
  User Manager for Domains, 71, 218–20, 226–27
  while IS is down, 214
  custom recipients referencing, 215
  dedicated servers for, 92
  Display name, 219
  in distribution lists, 215
  DS replicating, 214
  Exchsrvr directory, 60, 954
  hiding, 242–43
  IMAP4 configuration, 696
  load simulation, 54
  local site routing, 206
  maintenance, 22, 60, 242–45
  on Microsoft Windows NT Servers, 22
  moving, 92, 263–64, 301
  names, 389, 428
  opening with delegate access, 403–4
  Primary Windows NT Account attribute, 219
  in Private Information Store (Priv.edb), 35, 60, 214, 954
  properties, 234–35, 473–74
  quota setting, 243–44
  RAM needed for, 60
  recipient objects and, 214–15, 295
  recipients, finding, 262
  server-based, 214, 301
  size, 263, 264, 301, 474
  templates for creating, 262
mailbox folders, 29
mailbox level settings, 678–79, 741–42